$22⁹⁵

4th EDITION

1900-1965
American Premium

RECORD GUIDE

78's, 45's and LP's

IDENTIFICATION AND VALUES

By L.R. DOCKS

ISBN 0-89689-088-0

BOOKS AMERICANA
INC.

ACKNOWLEDGEMENTS

Special thanks must be given to my wife, Pam, for her encouragement and indispensable assistance in compiling and revising this reference work, for the many hours she spent putting together and revising the index, and for her tolerant understanding during those periods when I was holed up in the "shellac shack," virtually incommunicado, compensating for earlier procrastination, getting everything ready to send to the publisher.

I am indebted also to the following for furnishing records for photography and for contribution of data: Werner Benecke (whose contribution to a more accurate second and third edition is especially appreciated), George Blacker, Dan Campbell, Fred Chambers, Rex Clark, Scott Cleveland, F. Curran, Lou Curtiss, Rick Dembinsky, Ron Evry, Don Gray, Doug Gregory, Steve Gronda, E.J. Henke, The John Edwards Memorial Foundation (and Linda Painter, then Editor of its J.E.M.F. Quarterly), Glenn Keck, Bob Mays, William C. (Bill) Menor, Jerry Nieporte, Charlie O'Haver, Robert R. Olson, Dan Stevens, Keith Titterington, Pete Whelan.

There are a few contributors to whom I am also indebted, perhaps as much as to any of the foregoing, but to whom thanks must be given privately, it being their wish to remain anonymous.

My appreciation must also be expressed to Elaine Cary for her able typing services furnished on short notice, and to Dan Alexander, President of Books Americana, Inc., for his patience each time this book and its revisions took shape.

INTRODUCTION

There is nothing "official" about this or any other price guide. It, like other books on collectibles reflects the opinions of the author, based upon lengthy experience buying selling and trading records, consulting countless auction lists, sales lists, record publications, discographies, record company promotional literature, and collectors' want lists. Also important are the contributions of those who have supplied information, opinions on pricing, and photographs. Undoubtedly, many errors and omissions will be noted by knowledgeable collectors; it is hoped that these will be brought to my attention by writing to: L.R. DOCKS, P.O. Box 691035, San Antonio, Texas 78269.

Here, in a single volume, are listed thousands of desirable records in the most widely collected categories: Jazz, Dance Bands, Celebrity, Blues, Rhythm and Blues, Country and Western, Hillbilly, Rockabilly, and Rock and Roll. Included are 78s, 45s, EPs, and LPs. Emphasis is given to categories heretofore neglected and/or inadequately treated, such as early jazz, blues and country 78s.

As in previous editions, the majority of records listed are unfamiliar to non-collectors. Indeed, many are so obscure as to be unfamiliar even to sophisticated collectors. Quick now: Who were Dubin's Dandies? Very few of the records listed are top-selling hits. This book is intended to be a guide to scarce, sought-after, and otherwise desirable discs that *ought to be* recognized as collectible. It is not meant to afford readers a "nostalgia trip," by listing thousands of familiar old favorites, complete with titles. (Those seeking documentation and information about hit, or "charted" records should consult other references, such as those by Joel Whitburn, listed in the Bibliography.) Those treasured (when was the first time they were dug out of the cellar and played?) records by Bing Crosby, Al Jolson, Glenn Miller, et al., even if they are indeed "originals" are probably not discs that are saleable to a knowledgeable collector, and certainly not at more than a nominal sum. Common sense ought to suggest that records which sold in the largest quantities remain relatively common and inexpensive today. But common sense sometimes seems uncommon: "I have an original "White Christmas" by Bing Crosby; what will you give me for it?" Oh, well! I don't really expect to get many calls offering me a store stock of 8000 series Okeh records.

Readers of previous editions will note, however, the inclusion this time of many more relatively common and inexpensive records, i.e. records valued at two to five dollars, by the more familiar artists, and on commonly found labels such as red Columbia. They may well ask, "Has Docks sold out?" The answer is a resounding "no." Well, maybe not so resounding. This seeming concession is only slightly in response to popular (and publisher, to whom Kay Kyser fans owe their gratitude) demand. The real purpose is to create a sense of relative scarcity and desirability between very common and scarcer records, and to avoid having to answer numerous inquiries about why certain common records aren't listed and whether the correspondent has unearthed a heretofore unknown rarity. I know that I can't foreclose all such inquiries, even from those who do read this introduction. But at least I shouldn't get any more letters from owners of Gene Autry red label *Columbia* records who think that they are unlisted rarities.

What kinds of records are regarded as desirable by knowledgeable collectors? Records in the categories mentioned above, regarded as excellent examples of their idiom; or records which are historically important, as for example records featuring the early work of a future star; or records issued on rare or interesting labels. There are certainly other factors; sometimes there's no accounting for taste. Many of the records listed herein were issued in special series or on labels aimed at limited markets. "Race" series and labels, aimed at the Negro, and hillbilly series (styled "Songs From Dixie" series or the like) aimed at the white, rural folk never attained the levels, of distribution of the more popular, acceptable, and civilized music of polite society. So, the music that was denigrated, isolated and segregated in its own time is today the music that is most appreciated and prized.

DEFINITIONS, SYMBOLS and TERMS

Following are brief explanations of some of the terms and symbols used by record collectors and dealers. Some of them are forthright and succinct. Others, attempting to define the various styles and idioms of music, are somewhat amorphous, if not downright evasive. Music appeals to the emotions and senses, and does not invite verbal analysis. Most people know jazz (or blues, or country/western music) when they hear it. "It Don't Mean A Thing If It Ain't Got That Swing" is better than any dictionary definition. If you have a record you're not familiar with—for example, "Four Or Five Times" by McKinney's Cotton Pickers, play it. You'll probably know what category it falls into without reading any definition. Or, just consult the Complete Artist Index at the end of this book, starting at page 408.

BLUES: Webster's New Collegiate Dictionary defines blues as "a song of lamentation characterized by 12-bar phrases, 3-line stanzas in which the words of the second stanza repeat those of the first, and continual occurance of blue notes in melody and harmony." A bit of overdubbing: The songs relate to the troubles, hardships and common experiences of blacks (and poor whites). Some blues are country style will accompaniments usually consisting of stringed or even makeshift instruments; some blues are urbanized, closer to jazz, with wind instruments often accompanying the vocalist. If all this seems meaningless, play a blues record; it-even just 12 bars of it- will be worth a thousand words.

BOOTLEG: An unauthorized issue of a previously unreleased performance in derogation of the rights of the real owner of the tape or master and the artist. The term also is used in reference to an unauthorized copy or reissue of a previously issued record. Where the unauthorized copy closely resembles the original record in label design, the more correct term is "REPRODUCTION," or "COUNTERFEIT." Since the practice of bootlegging or reproducing rare and valuable 45rpm records of the 1950's has become widespread, collectors are advised to exercise caution when expending large sums on records of that period. There is no substitute for personal familiarity with the subtle characteristics of the original records: such things as the distinctness of the lettering, the texture of the paper used for the label, the appearance of the grooves, master numbers in the wax, the thickness of the pressing, etc.

CONTEMPORANEOUS ISSUES: Contemporaneous issue of the same performance on two or more labels was common in the 1920s and 1930s. This was the result of contractual arrangement, corporate affiliation, or the ownership of several labels by the same company. The most frequently encountered grouping comprises Banner, Conqueror, Melotone, Oriole, Perfect, Romeo, and sometimes Vocalion. Many recordings of the 1930s for the American Record Company were issued at the same time on several if not all of the labels mentioned. The song titles, the artists' names, the typography, and even the catalog number of the record on many, would be identical on each label. Other examples from the 1930s are Champion and Decca; Bluebird, Electradisk, Montgomery Ward, and Timely Tunes (all RCA Victor products). In the 1920s, the following label affiliations commonly occurred: Cameo, Lincoln, Romeo; Harmony, Diva, Velvet-Tone (and later, about 1930, Clarion); Perfect and Pathe-Actuelle; Gennett Champion, Challenge, Claxtonola, Herschel Gold Seal, Silvertone, Superior, Supertone; Harmograph, Paramount, Black Swan; Arto, Bell, Cleartone, Globe, Grey Gull, Radiex; Brunswick, Vocalion; Banner, Cameo, Jewel, Oriole, Regal, Romeo. The practice also existed in the 1950s; for example Sun and Flip labels. It should be noted that the affiliated labels may not have been issued at exactly the same time; technically, one might be regarded as the original issue. Collectors of 1950s records are far more particular in this regard than are collectors of vintage 78s. It should also be noted that the real name of the artist was not always used on all of the affiliated labels; the use of pseudonyms was extensive. The purpose was often to evade exclusive recording artist contractual restrictions, or to avoid making royalty payments to artists. Several examples: Performances by Irving Mills' groups were variously credited as by Jimmy Bracken's Toe Ticklers, Dixie Jazz Band; Kentucky Grasshoppers, The Lumberjacks and The Whoopee Makers on Banner, Jewel, Oriole, Regal and Romeo. The Wolverine Orchestra on Gennett became the Jazz Harmonizers on Claxtonola. Bradley Kincaid on Gennett became Dan Hughey on Champion. If this isn't confusing enough, one pseudonym, such as Dixie Jazz Band on Oriole, might conceal the true identity of a dozen or more bands, whose performances appeared on other labels perhaps under different pseudonyms! Records listed in this volume are listed according to the label credits, without regard to pseudonyms. The real name behind pseudonyms should be sought in the various discographies listed in the Bibliography. Those wishing to delve further into the complexities of label affiliation and the corporate evolution of record companies should consult "From Tin Foil to Stereo," by Read and Welch, and "The American Record Label Book", by Brian Rust, both listed in the Bibliography.

COUNTRY/WESTERN/HILLBILLY MUSIC: Webster's New Collegiate Dictionary defines this music as "derived from or imitating the folk style of the southern U.S. or of the Western cowboy." At least this definition seems to exclude much of the watered-down Nashville product. Is it broad enough to include Jimmie Rodgers, Bob Wills, Ernest Stoneman, Fiddlin' John Carson, et al?

DISCOGRAPHY: A compilation of data concerning the recorded work of an artist including recordings issued and unissued, recording dates, personnels, locations, master numbers. Of course, discographies can vary as to completeness and accuracy. Discographies of a single artist usually are found in record collectors' publications. The term many also refer to books such as the outstanding works by Brian Rust in the areas of Jazz, Dance Bands, and Entertainment. These attempt to list all records by all artists, to the extent that their recordings fall within the subject field. Label discographies are numerical listings of particular labels, according to catalog number. Some offer only record numbers and song titles. See, for example, Roger Kinkle's four-volume work, listed in the Bibliography. Kinkle offers numerical listings of nine major labels of the 1920s, 1930s, and 1940s, which listings are often useful, even though abbreviation of titles and artists' names is often cause for puzzlement. Ken Clee's four-volume collection consists of 45 rpm labels of the 1950s and later; it is also listed in the Bibliography. Other label discographies are more thorough, offering, in addition to song titles and record numbers, master numbers, release dates, production figures, and more. See, for example, Dan Mahoney's "The Columbia 13000/14000-D Series," also listed in the Bibliography. Label discographies are often found in record collectors' publications.

"D.J. COPY" refers to Disc Jockey, or Promotional records, which are issued to radio stations. The label color often differs from that of the regular issue, and usually bears the statement "Promotional Copy-Not For Sale" or words of similar import. The pressing quality of some D.J. copies is higher than that of the regular issue. Some are pressed from translucent colored vinyl rather than black.

"E.P." refers to extended Play records. These are usually 45rpm records containing four or more songs, issued in a stiff cardboard jacket similar to those for LPs. Some EPs were issued in series of two and three, together containing the contents of an LP issued concurrently. Records issued in the early 1930s having extended playing time, such as some Clarion and Hit of the Week records, are not distinguished herein by the abbreviation "E.P."

JAZZ: Webster's New Collegiate Dictionary defines jazz as "American music developed...from ragtime and blues and characterized by syncopated rhythms, contrapuntal ensemble playing, and...improvisation often with special melodic features (as blue notes) peculiar to the individual interpretation of the player," or "popular dance music influenced by jazz and played in a loud rhythmic manner." You'll know it when you hear it. The second part of the definition is particularly noteworthy. Many records of jazz interest are ordinary fox trots having one or more "hot" solos by a jazz musician or some unknown stepping out of character and assuming that role. There are jazz records by the orchestras of Jan Garber and Guy Lombardo, believe it or not. Conversely, not every record whose label suggests the presence of hot music should be believed. The Missouri Jazz Band (often encountered on Banner and Regal discs of the 1920s) rarely produced anything sounding like jazz, and probably weren't from Missouri, either. Take a few weeks off and study Rust's "Jazz Records, 1897-1942."

"JUNKING" The practice of record collector of visiting fleas markets, garage sales, and second hand stores in quest of records.

"L.P." The abbreviation of "Long Play, " which refers to a record utilizing a finer groove, and therefore containing more playing time, than a single 45 or 78 rpm record of equivalent diameter. Most LPs have several or more songs on each side, but may instead have a single extended performace. Most modern LPs are 12-inches in diameter; issues from the early 1950s are 10-inches in diameter. Playing speed is 33⅓ rpm. Some early LPs issued by Edison in the 1920s contained as much as 20 minutes playing time on each side—at 36 rpm! These were failures, technically and commercially, and the records are quite scarce today. Musically, they contain little of interest to most collectors. In the early 1930s, RCA Victor issued 10-inch 33⅓ rpm records called "Program Transcriptions." These too were technically inadequate and failed to sell well. Some of these scarce discs do have interesting musical content, and are listed herein. See photo in label section under RCA Victor.

PICTURE RECORD This is a record displaying a picture over its entire surface, including the portion normally occupied by a label. The picture, which may be of the artist or a fanciful device (See Vogue picture record, in label listing), are printed on paper which is laminated between the clear plastic or vinyl which constitutes the playing surface. The current mania for picture records may be unprecedented, but the basic idea is not new. Vogue picture records attained respectable sales levels briefly in the late 1940s. Picture records were commercially issued in the early 1930s, most successfully by RCA Victor; but even these are quite scarce. (See Fig.1).

Figure 1

PICTURE SLEEVE A record sleeve of a 45rpm record having no center hole exposing the record, but rather having a picture usually of the artist or group. Some picture sleeves are more highly valued than the subject record.

PROMOTIONAL COPY (See D.J. COPY)

"RACE" RECORDS Records of the 1920s and 1930s produced for the Negro market, utilizing primarily Negro talent. Musical content is usually blues, jazz, or gospel. Certain labels were almost entirely 'race' oriented (Black Swan and Black Patti) and were even owned and managed by blacks. Usually, however, race records were issued by the larger labels in special series bearing a special numerical sequence or even a variation in label design to distinguish the race records from the popular white-oriented series. (Hillbilly records were similarly distinguished.) Examples are the Victor V-38000 series, the Vocalion 1000 series, the Brunswick 7000 series (employing the distinctive "lightning" label design in addition to the special number series), the Columbia 13000-D and 14000-D series, and the Okeh 8000 series. While this musical segregation persisted well into the 1950s, the labels which were then the strongholds of black talent (Federal, DeLuxe, Vee Jay, Jubilee, to name just a few) became "rhythm and blues" labels rather than race labels. Few white radio stations would play them.

"R & B" (Abbreviation for "rhythm and blues") The music of the 1950s by the essentially for the Negro market, which evolved from blues, jazz, and jump blues. This music was a major force in the emergence of rock and roll and rockabilly.

"RED PLASTIC" (or other colored plastic) "RED WAX," etc. Records which are made of other than the usual black material. The most frequent variation from black is translucent red vinyl. Many 45 rpm records from the 1950s issued in this form are highly prized. Other records were made of translucent green, blue or orange vinyl. Still others were made of opaque colored plastic, in the style of children's records. Where a record occurs in both black and colored form, the colored version usually commands a substantial premium over the black. In the 1920s, some 78s were made of other than black material. Perfect and early Vocalion records were a brownish-orange; Pathe-Actuelle was mottled. In the early 1930s, Columbia attempted to spur lagging sales with its "Royal Blue" issues, which today are a favorite of collectors.

REISSUE: A re-release of a previously issued record by the owner of the performance or under license from such owner. A reissue may be on the original label, with the same catalog number, or with a different catalog number.

Figure 2   **Figure 3**

The label design may also have changed between the time of the original or the reissue may be on an entirely different label than the original issue. (See Figs. 2 & 3) (Veteran collectors may note that some of the "reissues" are "alternate takes" issued for the first time, years after recording.)

RHYTHM & BLUES (SEE "R & B")

ROCKABILLY: Rock and roll sung by a hillbilly-sounding singer; up-tempo country music. Other elements are a "slappin' bass," "hot" guitar and/or piano, and echo effects. Back-up voices or horns detract from desirability, according to rockabilly purists. The style is defined by early Elvis Presley records, as well as by such artists as Jerry Lee Lewis, Carl Perkins, and more obscure rockers such as Sonny Fisher and Pat Cupp.

ROCK AND ROLL: Popular, usually up-tempo, hard-driving music with solid rhythm, often having frantic vocals, wailing saxophones, hot piano, and elements of hillbilly boogie and jump blues and rhythm and blues from which it evolved. Although rock and roll is identified with the 1950s, and such artists as Chuck Berry, Elvis Presley, and Bill Haley, rock and roll was actually being performed several years earlier by rhythm and blues artists such as Jackie Brenston and The Dominoes.

78 RPM; 78s: The playing speed of most pre-1950 single records. Actually, many early 78 rpm records were intended to be played at 80 rpm, or some other speed, but these are treated herein as 78s without distinction.

TEST PRESSING: A record pressed to give the artist and/or record company executive a chance to hear and judge the merits of a recording and its suitability for issue commercially. The record may be pressed on one side or on both sides. The label is usually plain white with the information handwritten, often cryptically, or printed (See Fig. 4 and 4a). (Test pressings should not be confused with the ubiquitous home recordings, with "labels" such as Wilcox-Gay and Audio Disc.)

Figure 4   **Figure 4a**

The edge of the disc may be somewhat jagged and irregular, rather than smooth. Not pressed for sale to the public, any test pressing is scarce. But not every test pressing is valuable or highly collectible. Let the next one you find be a previously unissued jazz, blues, or rockabilly performance, or an "alternate take" of an issued performance; and let me know about it!

ORGANIZATION OF THIS BOOK
The main listing of this book is divided into four sections:

1. Jazz, Dance Bands, Big Bands, Swing, Personality; primarily 78 rpm records, 1900 to about 1950

2. Blues; primarily 78s, 1920s—early 1950s

3. Country/Western, hillbilly, old-time singing, string bands, fiddling; primarily 78 rpm, 1920s—early 1950s

4. Rhythm & Blues, Blues, Rock & Roll, Rockabilly, etc.; primarily 45 rpm, EPs and LPs, with selected 78s; 1950s and early 1960s.

The inclusion of a given artist in a particular section is often a matter of arbitrary choice. For example, many records by blues artists are found in the Jazz, etc., section due to the fact that their accompaniment is of jazz interest. Some artists are found more than one section. Where recordings were made in the 1930s and also in the 1950s, that artist might appear in both sections; for example, Lonnie Johnson. An index of all artists listed in this book, following the listings, on page 408 will enable readers to find all listed records by an artist even when that artist appears in more than one section.

Within each category, the listings are alphabetical by artist. The listings for each artist are presented alphabetically by label, and by catalog number, from lowest to highest, within each label. This may not reflect the chronological order of issue. For example Bluebirds are listed before Victors; but the Victors are almost always earlier issues than the Bluebirds. And the Gennett 3000 numbers are later than the 5000 numbers. The true order of recording and issue is left to the discographies. The intention here is to provide ease of usage.

Some listings embrace a number of issues on the same label:

    Bluebird, most other issues 2.00-4.00

Such a listing, while consisting of records of minimal scarcity and value, may well include some discs so common that they are virtually unsaleable to any real record collector.

Catalog number prefixes and suffixes (numbers or letters) common to all or most issues on a label or series are usually omitted. Thus, RCA Victor 47-6604 is listed as RCA Victor 6604. The prefix "47-" (or "20-" in the case of 78s) appears on the majority of RCA Victor 45rpm records. Also omitted are the ubiquitous suffixes "-A" and "-B" (and variants such as "-L" and "-R" on Edison). Prefixes and suffixes do serve to distinguish between seemingly overlapping numerical series on Columbia records, and are therefore included.

All listings reflect the names as credited on the actual records, without regard to whether such names are actual or pseudonyms. Cross-references are kept to a minimum, it being assumed that interested collectors will seek any further information about pseudonyms (and any other matters beyond the scope of this reference, such as personnels, recording dates, additional recordings, reissues) from the discographies and other sources listed in the Bibliography.

WHERE TO BUY, SELL OR TRADE RECORDS
Every record collector, whether novice or veteran, obtains at least some of his discs by "junking." (See definition on page v.) The more avid the collector, the more time, effort and expense he devotes to junking; and this is often true even though the resultant finds aren't worth the trouble—either for their musical enjoyment or their value. But there's always the possibility of that great find: King Oliver on Gennett; Charlie Spand on Paramount; Hank Williams on Sterling; Elvis Presley on Sun; or maybe a whole box of "goodies." And getting up before daybreak to get first pick at the flea market or an estate sale, certainly increases your chances!

Most collectors are not content to leave the acquisition of their wants to the fortuities of junking. The best source of collectible records is other collectors and dealers (in many instances the same persons). Often, a knowledgeable collector is easier to deal with than a casual or one-time vendor of records. I've seen common, middle-of-the-road records at flea markets priced at $5.00 each, accompanied by a warning against handling the treasures! To get in contact with other collectors and/or dealers, begin in any case with record collectors publications (See Publications listing, page 405).

Some leading record publications are largely market-places for selling, buying and trading records. It is advisable to utilize those most appropriate to your interests. If you specialize in Rockabilly, you'll find little of interest in *Vintage Jazz Mart; Goldmine* contains little for the collector of Edison discs. Once you've gotten familiar with the appropriate publications, and the terms and conditions of transacting business with advertisers, you might consider advertising your wants, as well as contacting other advertisers, particularly those who invite "want lists."

Record collectors' conventions have become almost common in larger metropolitan areas. The publications usually contain a number of advertisements and notices about forthcoming conventions. The crowds often present at these conventions attest to the high level of enthusiasm record collectors have for their hobby. Nowhere was this more evident than at the record flea-market (termed as "brizarre ritual" in *Goldmine,* November, 1980) which until several years ago was held in the parking lot of Capitol Records in Hollywood, California; it began in the middle of the night, and would actually break up by late morning! The scope of interests represented at most of these conventions appeals increasingly to collectors of more modern records and peripheral memorambilia, i.e. albums, picture discs, and CDs of the 1960s and later. Usually, there will be little of interest to the collector of vintage 78s.

In a number of cities, there are stores specializing in collectors' records. Unfortunately, the majority of these shops do not advertise in record collector publications. I have visited such shops in Bloomington, Indiana, Chicago, Detroit, Fort Worth, Glendale, California, Salt Lake City, San Diego and Santa Monica, California, and elsewhere. It might be helpful to consult Record Finder's NATIONAL DIRECTORY OF COLLECTIBLE RECORD DEALERS (see Sources, page 406).

VALUATION OF RECORDS

The prices herein are estimations of what records might reasonably be expected to bring in transactions between knowledgeable buyers and sellers. Most estimations are stated as a range, e.g. $10.00 to $15.00, rather than a specific figure. This method of pricing recognizes the partial validity of the widely held contention that it is impossible at this time, given the fluid and formative state of the market, to assign definite values to records.

Although most of the really desirable records are bought and sold by mail, often at auction, the prices herein are not intended to reflect the highest sale prices or winning bids. A given record might bring $10.00 in one auction and $4.00 in the next. Indeed, in the same auction, the array of bids often demonstrates a wide disparity in bidders' estimations of value; and auction bidders are generally fairly knowledgeable. Widely differing prices on the same record are also found when comparing set sale lists or minimum bid figures in auction lists. Certainly these dealers in records must also be regarded as fairly knowledgeable. So, what is any record really worth? The only sure answer is, whatever you can get for it.

The casual seller of records, such as the flea market or garbage sale vendor, who has no real knowledge of appreciation of records, who does not intelligently and selectively acquire records, who does not properly organize and preserve them, and who does not seek, by appropriate advertising, knowledgeable collectors as customers, will have difficulty realizing even a small fraction of the prices quoted herein for the better records. There is nothing unfair about this situation. One not disposed to invest the time, effort and expense (beyond the cost of a price guide) necessary to deal with some expertise should perhaps be in another business. I have seen several such record vendors, compelled by economic realities, make just that decision.

One factor contributing to the difficulty in valuing records with more certainty is the reluctance of many collectors and dealers to divulge prices they have paid or received for records. Several prominent collectors and dealers I have contacted in the dozen years since this book was conceived, have expressly refused to furnish pricing information; a few others were very helpful, but only on condition of anonymity. The appearance of this book engendered hostile and unjustly critical letters, and even personal attacks. I can only conclude that some of these critics feel that they have a vested interest in being able to buy rare records for token sums, and that my dissemination of pricing information constitutes an infringement!

On the other hand, there is one area in which many dealers have no reluctance about publicizing record prices: in their own auctions. Anyone who peruses the ads in record publications will find that many of the offerings have "minimum bids" for some or all of the records listed. In some cases, these minimums are reasonable reserves, which will foreclose submission of bids that would only waste the time of both bidder and seller. But, in most cases, minimums are more like maximums, set at levels higher than the offeror or thinks the subject records would bring without his bidding floors. I have seen "minimum bids" several times the amount comparable records have sold for in my own auctions and elsewhere. Whether sellers employing these maximum minimums are motivated by greed, uncertainty as to their own pricing knowledge, or actual belief that their records are worth (at the very least!) the exhorbitant sums stated, no one can say. Perhaps if more bidders and would-be bidders would question the purpose and validity of the practice, sellers would be more likely to run sales that are sales, or auctions that are auctions.

Finally, I will address the criticism of those who have said that my prices are too low: that is, the criticisms of knowledgeable dealers and collectors. Those seeking to increase the value or marketability of certain records or categories of records in which they have an interest will find no accomdation here. First, I repeat, the intention is not to reflect the highest prices realized for records, i.e. winning bids at auction. Second, information about pricing should be submitted with specificity in a timely manner, as to be useful in revising this book, not as vague criticism after the fact. Third, and last, it will become obvious from perusal of this book, that some drastic price changes have been made in response to information received since the publication of the third edition. While most of the new information was supplied to me by others, some was the result of my own auctions and sales. When a record received a number of bids far above, indeed, multiples of, prices stated in this book, I just had to suppress my embarrassment, accept the exhorbitant sums, and resolve to do better next edition.

GRADING OF RECORDS

The condition of a record is of paramount importance. A new, apparently (who can be certain?) unplayed copy might be worth many times the price of a worn "junk-shop" copy. Indeed, a very worn copy may not be saleable at all.

The prices quoted herein are for records in excellent condition. "Excellent" is more or less a term or art, being part of the standard grading code following, which has been in use for many years:

"NEW" or "N": apparently unplayed and of course showing no signs of wear.

"EXCELLENT" or "E": Showing only slight wear; playing surfaces still retain much of thier original shine. Surface noise is minimal.

"VERY GOOD" or "V": Somewhat more worn than an "excellent" record, slight grayness appearing in the grooves, especially in louder passages. Still a fairly clean and acceptable copy. Surface and extraneous noise is noticeable, but does not overwhelm the music.

"GOOD" or "G": A misnomer, a "good" record is really not so good. It shows considerable wear and usage, grayness in the grooves, random mars and light abrasions from an undoubted sleeveless existance. Surface noise is prominent enough to impair enjoyment of music.

"FAIR ("F") and "POOR" ("P") indicate the lowest grades of the condition code. Since only the rarest records would be saleable in these grades, they appear infrequently.

Plus and minus signs are often suffixed to above grades to indicate a somewhat better or worse grade, when appropriate.

Another grading code is often employed by persons and publications concerned with the music of the 1950s and later, which are primarily 45s, EPs, and LPs: "Mint" or "M" is used in place of "New" or "N"; "Very Good" or "VG" corresponds more closely to "Excellent" ("E") than to the older system's "Very Good" ("V"); "Good" or "G" is roughly equivalent to the older system's "Very Good" ("V").

In addition to the wear factor, defects and impairments can drastically affect the value and saleability of a record. Some of these, affecting the playing surface, are cracks, digs, and warps. A crack usually renders a record practically worthless; even the value of a rarity is generally reduced to a nominal sum by the presence of a crack. This is true even if the crack is "tight" and negotiable by a needle. There are exceptions, such as "lamination cracks" which affect only one side of a laminated record (having a cardboard core between the playing surfaces) such as Columbia or Okeh: these cracks severely affect, but do not necessarily destroy, the record's value. With most defects, how much the value of the record is reduced is a matter of degree. Is that scratch inaudible, or does it make the tone-arm jump half an inch? Does that dig allow the needle to negotiate the groove, or does the affected passage repeat? Other defects, such as the label or stickers on the label, do not affect play, but only appearance; but this can be very important. In short, the acknowledgement of defects is an essential part of the grading process.

Most auction lists and price lists will contain and explanation of the grading system and symbols used. But it is important that the system, whichever is used, be applied fairly and objectively. Often it is not; overgrading has become commonplace in the collectors' record market. A reputable dealer will make adjustments or refunds if a record proves to be erroneously graded.

TRENDS AND FADS IN RECORD COLLECTING

Record collecting has undergone great change over the decades. Prior to 1935, most record collectors favored classical and operatic records. In the 1930s and 1940s, jazz and blues records (particularly blues records with jazz accompaniments) became the primary area of interest. Prior to the era of the LP as a vehicle for reissuing, some original 78s commanded prices higher than they do now (particularly if the decline in the value of the dollar is taken into account.) The extensive reissuing of jazz has undoubtedly affected the market for the original 78s, although there are many collectors who insist upon owning the original discs. Furthermore, many of the old-time collectors lose interest or relinquish their 78s in favor of LP reissues. Additional comments about the effects of advances in recording technology will follow.

Interest in jazz records has shifted somewhat in recent years. Demand for original 78 rpm jazz classics by big names has peaked, or even waned. The most intense demand, and the largest price increases, are for some of the more obscure bands, such as regional or "territory" bands. A record by EDDIE & SUGAR LOU'S HOTEL TYLER ORCHESTRA will draw more bids than most DUKE ELLINGTON records of the same era. Also, there is increased interest in the semi-hot dance bands of the 1920s and 1930s.

Perhaps the most intense demand for early 78s is for obscure, country blues by such artists as William Harris and Robert Johnson. The records are scarce to rare, and are infrequently offered (most auctions contain few or none), and even more infrequently found. Pursued by a relatively small number of hard-core, knowledgeable collectors, the records, when offered, command some of the highest prices in the world of collectible records. Yet, if the scarcity of the records (some are estimated to exist in quantities fewer than ten) is considered, one can only imagine what would happen if demand were to increase, and records were to gain the recognition of certain other collectibles.

Interest in early country and western records developed considerably later than did the mania for jazz. The reissuing of this music has also lagged far behind, and still has a long way to go to reach the point, which might be said of jazz, where most significant performances have been reissued. Contrary to the situation with jazz 78s, the demand for these records (and consequently their values) has yet to peak, much less decline. The expected appearance of a country-western discography is certain to heighten interest in this field of collecting.

Seemingly the most active category of record collecting is the music of the 1950s and 1960s, including Rock and Roll, Rhythm and Blues, Rockabilly, and Blues. In the early 1960s, Rhythm and Blues records, particularly vocal groups, were already being collected seriously, with obscure discs of only a few years earlier commanding respectable premiums. Interest spread to single-artist Rhythm and Blues, Blues, Rockabilly, and Rock and Roll obscurities. Certain artists such as Elvis Presley, The Beatles, The Beach Boys, and The Four Seasons, have a following bordering on fanaticism, with some collectors seeking any tangible object relating to the artist, recorded or otherwise (see comment preceding Elvis Presley listing). Notable among many of the newer crop of collectors is their penchant for acquiring, displaying and preserving visual, graphic art souvenirs of recording artists, relegating the audio aspect to secondary importance. Thus, many albums remain sealed, and Elvis' Sun records find homes on collectors' walls. The jacket of an album is more important than the record in some cases (see The Beatles and Frank Ifield, in listings); picture sleeves can be worth more than the subject record; picture records find a market at exhorbitant prices. Not too long ago, there were only the colored wax freaks to wonder at!

Advances in technology do not necessarily affect the market for vintage records. According to some, as CDs supplant LPs, there is a mad scramble underway to buy up LPs. But, even if this is the case, in the long-term, the situation will be about the same as that surrounding old 78s. Each record will be regarded as collectible according to its recorded content, not the obsolescence of its technology. There are plenty of the thick Edison discs, discontinued in 1929, that can be bought for as little as two or three dollars, when lacking the musical content that makes a record collectible. There are millions of "junk" 78s around, and there will be millions of junk LPs for many years to come.

This is a good place to insert my axiom: The quality of the music recorded varies inversely with the technology used to record it. I will not engage in any correspondence seeking to dispute the matter, or seeking my explanation. Suffice it to say, that the coverage of this book, ending as it does with the mid-1960s, avoids documenting the transition from music to decibel laden, electronic anarchy.

The following information is presented in answer to some frequently asked questions. Answers to other questions might be pursued by reviewing the Bibliography, and the Publications and Sources listings, at pages 405-407 of this book, and writing to the publication, publisher, or source most likely to be helpful. As a last resort, write to me.

PLAYING 78 R.P.M. RECORDS

Of course, an old wind-up player, such as those on which early 78s were originally played (and destroyed!), will play your records. If you don't care about the fact that your records will be damaged somewhat each time the nail-like needle negotiates the grooves, you'll be satisfied with the result, particularly when playing early acoustically recorded discs (pre-1925). When playing later, electrically recorded records, the reproduction afforded by mechanical means will be rather tinny, and most of the richer sound provided by electrical recording will be lost. Also, playing records from the "swing era" and later on the old wind-ups seems incongruous. But, if you want to play Perry Como records on a **Victrola,** that's your privilege. You'll save money on electricity, and get some exercise. See your local antiques dealer or flea marketeer.

For the person wanting better sound, and longer life for his records, I recommend getting an older children's record player, many of which have 78 rpm speed, or better yet, an older schoolroom record player. The schoolroom record players are more durable, and offer better reproduction than the usual children's player. Sometimes these can be found at flea markets. But, an inquiry of your local school board, or whatever division thereof deals with school property and/or surplus property, would be more fruitful.

Playing 78s on more sophisticated equipment, such as older stereo players (which often have 78 rpm speed), is usually **less** satisfactory, without special modifications and adaptations. Avid collectors of 78s, particularly those who want to do clean taping, obtain specially modified cartridges, needles (styli), and equalizers, from sources such as those mentioned in the Sources listing, page 406 of this book.

PLAYING EDISON RECORDS

Edison records (the quarter-inch thick ones) were recorded by a different process than ordinary 78s ("vertically," rather than "laterally"). They cannot, indeed, must not be played on an ordinary wind-up record player. No sound will be reproduced, and irreparable damage to the record will result from just a single attempt at playing. Playing on high-fidelity or stereo players will not damage the record (at least, not noticeably), but will not give satisfactory results. Proper playing on high-fidelity or stereo players is accomplished with the use of special needles (styli), and specially "strapped" cartridges. See Sources listing, page 406, for suppliers of this special equipment. If you don't have this modified equipment, or an Edison phonograph (or other make, with reproducer designed for "vertical" recordings), you will not be able to obtain satisfactory results from Edison records.

CARE AND RESTORATION OF RECORDS

CLEANING RECORDS:

Dusty and/or dirty records can be improved by washing in lukewarm (never hot!) water with a mild liquid soap (such as Ivory Liquid). Rubbing with as soft cloth or paper towel in a circular motion (to follow the direction of the grooves) might help eliminate dirt deposited within the grooves. In more difficult cases, a soft-bristled brush might be more effective. Note that 78 RPM records will withstand a more vigorous scrubbing without the possibility of adding new scuffs and scratches than is the case with modern LPs, EPs, and 45 RPM records (vinyl "microgroove" records). Records should be cleaned and dried as quickly as possible, avoiding prolonged soaking (which could result in label damage or even removal of the label—a common occurance in the case of the thick **Edison** discs). Rinse, dry (with paper or other towel) sufficiently to take up most of the water, and set in a dish drying rack to complete drying process.

Commerical record cleaning preparations, sprays, "anti-static" applications, and the like vary in effectiveness. In the case of records with apparent dirty and/or surfaces, commercial preparations are largely ineffective, but should be used only **after** the above washing procedure.

There is **no** cleaning or restoration method that will completely remove all dirt from the grooves of records. Perhaps someone will adapt ultrasonic cleaning (such as the process used by jewelers to clean rings, etc.) to record cleaning. I'd be interested in the results, if anyone should actually do it. Records that have been subjected to moisture (floods, etc.) are particularly difficult to improve. Microgroove records are more difficult, as a rule, to improve to a satisfactory level than are 78s.

SCRATCHED AND CRACKED RECORDS:

There is no effective method of removing or minimizing the effects of scrathes, scuffs, digs, and other defects resulting from the extensive use (or abuse, often from not replacing records in their sleeves/jackets) of records. The application of waxes, shoe polish, or the like might make a record look better to an unwary buyer. But it will not result in any net gain in playing enjoyment, because the music will be dampened along with the extraneous noise. Also, the needle used to play records so treated will quickly become disabled by waxy buildup.

Cracks cannot be removed or mended in any way that will truly restore a record. If a crack is "tight," and the record is still playable, some protection against further damage might be afforded by application of an appropriate glue to the edge of the record (never within the playing surface). But a cracked record has little, if any, value, and no efforts at repair or restoration can change that fact.

WARPED RECORDS:

78 RPM records can be straightened by at least two methods:

(1) "THE RECIPE": Basically, this is baking the record in an oven. The amount of time, as well as the temperature, are variable, depending upon

the oven used, how many records are being baked, etc. Therefore, before trying this method on any prized disc, would-be shellac chefs are strongly advised to experiment with valueless records. The success of this method depends upon the fact that after a certain time at a certain temperature, most 78 RPM rcords (of the old "shellac" type) "relax" (become completely pliable, like a pancake) and while in this state, can be "poured" onto a perfectly smooth, flat surface and there be allowed to again become rigid.

The following procedure is suggested (again, experimentation with regard to time and temperature is advised):

A) Preheat oven to 200 degrees.

B) Place record to be straightened on a flat, smooth-surfaced utensil (the back of a cookie sheet, etc.) and place it in the oven.

C) In about two and one-half minutes, look in the oven. If the record has "relaxed," and appears flat (no vestiges of the warpage, even at the very edge remain), quickly remove from the oven.

D) "Pour" (allow to slide) the now-soft, pliable record onto a perfectly smooth, cool surface (a cutting board, a piece of glass or marble), making sure that no part overhangs the edge.

E) Allow the record to cool somewhat in its (now flat) position. Do not try to lift it or move it about. It will soon lose its pliability and become rigid (and flat, if you've done it right).

NOTE: If, when you "pour" the record onto the flat surface, some warping remains, you probably didn't allow the record to become hot enough to really "relax." Try again. On the other hand, if you found that the record wouldn't "pour," but rather remained stuck to the utensil, you've overcooked it, and have damaged the record (irreparably).

(2) "SUNBATHING": This method is slower, but involves basically the same principle. There is less risk of "overcooking" and ruining the record. Requirement: Bright sunshine.

A) Place the warped record on a piece of marble or thick glass.

B) Place another piece of glass over the record.

C) Put this "sandwich" in a place where it will remain undisturbed and will receive the sunshine.

D) Depending upon the temperature, brightness of the sun, etc., the record will be straightened.

E) When record is sufficiently straightened, leave it on the marble or glass and allow to cool in a shady place.

NOTE: This method might also be tried on vinyl (45s, EPs, LPs) records, but degree of success is less promising than on 78s.

"Microgroove" records (45s, LPs, EPs) are more difficult to straighten. The application of weight for long periods (weeks, perhaps) while maintaining record in completely flat state has been known to work. Daring and skillful record restorers have used electric hair dryers, deftly applied, with varying degrees of success (and failure).

MAILING RECORDS

Many correspondents express apprehension about mailing records, particularly 78s. (Even postal clerks have told me that records can't be mailed; can be mailed, but not insured; that there is no special postal rate applicable to records; and other nonsense.) Records may be mailed, without undue risk of damage, if properly packed, and there is a "Special Fourth Class Rate," which is lower than regular parcel post, in most cases, applicable to sound recordings. Packing is largely a matter of common sense. A sturdy carton large enough to hold the records, with packing material about all sides (edge, top, and bottom), should be used. The records should not be able to shift about within the box. To get the "Special Fourth Class Rate," clearly mark the parcel: "Contents: Phonograph Records," and "Special Fourth Class Rate," and make sure that you are given this special, lower rate. Overcharges, even though the parcel is clearly labeled, indicating contents and election to use the special rate, are common. It shouldn't be necessary to say the following, but my experience dictates that it is: No records should be sent to anyone, without prior authorization and approval. Unsolicited shipments of records, which usually prove to be unwanted junk, create no obligation on the part of the recipient, who need not acknowledge or pay for same.

Figure 5

Figure 6

Figure 7

Figure 8

Figure 9

RECORD LABELS

What's on a record label? Referring to figure 5, you'll find the name of the label (Columbia) and logo; the song title in English and Spanish ("Mi Muchacha Linda"); composer/lyricist credits (Fulcher); the name of the artist/group/orchestra (Fletcher Henderson & His Orchestra); the record catalog number (2586-D) the master number 151276); the type of music and whether vocal or instrumental (Fox Trot, Vocal Refrain"); copyright, patent or trademark registration numbers of dates; the name and address of the manufacturer. Labels may also contain a picture of the artist (see fig. 7); the suggested retail price; and occasionally a release date (see Gennett fig. 8); "11-25" at 3 o'clock position indicates November, 1925); or a designation "Race Record"); (see fig. 9). A common feature is a slogan referring to the use of electrical recording processes: "Electrically Recorded," "Electrical Process," "Super Electrical Recorded," "Viva-Tonal Recording," "Electrobeam," "Orthophonic Recording," "Truetone,"

and others. Starting in the early 1930s, an admonition against use for radio braodcast was commonly used (see fig.6).

Information usually not found on record labels includes the date of recording, or release of the record. There are exceptions, such as Gennett (see fig.8), Champion, and Mercury, and there are other instances where the date of release appears cryptically, such as the mid-1930s Banner Melotone, Oriole, Perfect and Romeo issues. A knowledge of when various record labels were issued, and their rate of usage of master numbers and catalog numbers, will make possible a reasonable close estimation of recording and issue dates. Referring to a discography or to Steven Barr's THE (ALMOST) COMPLETE 78 RPM RECORD DATING GUIDE, listed in the Bibliography, will provide the best information. Normally, dates appering on the label relate to copyright, patient and trademark registration, and have little relation to the recording or issue date. For example, the 1921 copyright date on Regal records might appear on a record recorded and issued several (or more) years later.

Personnels usually don't appear on record labels until the late 1930s when they began to be used on some original jazz and swing issues, principally by Columbia and Victor (which even had a special "Swing Classic" series).

Reissues for collectors are likely to have personnels, recording dates, the name and number of the original issue label, and many even credit the name of the artist differently than did the original issues. These reissues often were sold in album sets; Brunswick, Columbia and RCA Victor engaged in considerable such reissuing in the late 1930s and 1940s. Few collectors' reissues will be found listed in this reference because of their minimal value; but they do contain many great, classic performances of vintage jazz which are practically unobtainable as original issues.

The record labels themselves are often colorful and interesting, as a perusal of pages 1 through 58 will (or perhaps already has) confirmed. The song titles are amusing relics of other times and cultures. Perhaps it isn't such a bad idea to decorate your wall with interesting labels and titles.

Certain labels have a more than usual attraction, or even a mystique which leads some collectors to collect by label, rather then by artist or type of music. Most collectors are guilty (is this the correct word?) of this tendency perhaps only to the extent of having favorite labels. But some collectors seek to obtain every issue on a certain label, regardless of artist or musical content. The label most commonly collected in this manner is the "SUN" label which in the 1950s assumed a major role in producing first-class rockabilly and rock and roll with such artists as Elvis Presley, Carl Perkins and Jerry Lee Lewis. Of course, not everything issued on that label was great and worthy of collecting, but sometimes it seems that way. In any event, substantial sums have been paid on occasion for scarce but musically mediocre Sun records in order to fill a numerical gap. Other labels of the 1950s collected in this manner include Atlantic, Federal, and Vee Jay; and probably any of the Rhythm and Blues Labels you can think of has its specialists. Among the 78rpm labels, some of the most popular among label collectors are the Vogue picture record, Columbia 14000-D (Race) series, Victor 23000 and V-38000 series, Gennett, Paramount, and Okeh 8000 series. Few collectors of the early 78s really are in earnest, however, about obtaining a complete numerical run as are "Sun" collectors. Incidentally, for the enlightenment, amusement and perhaps frustration of "Sun" collectors. I offer the following photo of a "Sun" record from the early 1900s (having no relationship, of course, to the 1950s-1960s Memphis product):

There are a relatively small number of collectors who strive to obtain as many different labels as they can, often without regard to musical content. Auction lists of vintage 78s occasionally offer a "rare and unusual label" section. A scarce label such as Autograph may bring several dollars even though the pipe-organ solo it offers is of no musical interest to the bidders. Other scarce labels (early 78s) include Bu-Disc, Black Patti, Black Swan, Buddy, Connorized, Claxtonola, Edison (thin), Electradisk, everybody's, Gennett (Electrobeam), Harmograph, Herschel Gold Seal, Herwin, Hudson, Hy-Tone, Meritt, Mitchell, national (Iowa City label), New Flexo, Nordskog, Odeaon (U.S. issue), Parlophone (U.S. issue), Q.R.S., Rich-Tone, Stark, Superior, Sunshine, Timely Tunes, Up-To-Date. Some of these are so scarce that photographs for this book have only recently come to hand; two or three are lacking yet! Some scarce 1950s labels include After Hours, Blue Lake, Chance, Club-51, Drexel, Great Lakes, Jax, J-V-B, Luna, Meteor, Parrot, Recorded in Hollywood, Red Robin, S.R.C., Sabre, States, Tin Pan Alley, United. These are by no means all of the scarce labels. Particularly in the 1950s, a local or regional label might have been in existence for only one or two issues; the labels preceding are better known or of longer duration, but still scarce.

Knowledge of record labels is helpful in the intelligent acquisition of records, whether such acquisition consists

of bidding in auctions by mail or just "junking" in local second-hand stores. If you know your labels, you're not likely to bid $50.00 on BIX & HIS RHYTHM JUGGLERS on English Brunswick only to find out later that original issue is on Gennett. And you won't buy Chess (LP) 1433 by The Flamingos with an orange label if you require originals only (see Chess photos). Errors in "junking" purchases usually involve no great financial loss if it turns out that the supposed $20.00 record you've gotten for .25 proves to be third pressing. But label knowledge can be handy when time is of the essence, for example, when on your weekly visit to the Salvation Army Thrift Store you find that a local radio station has just donated its record library, but another record sharpshooter is also there, shuffling vinyl. Of course, it's always a relief to find that he has beaten you to a choice copy of "The Chipmunk Song," leaving you to settle for all that unheard-of junk on labels such as Chess, Parrot and Red Robin. Or maybe *you'd* prefer "The Chipmunk Song."

PRESENTATION OF LABELS (PHOTOGRAPHS)

Labels are presented in the photo section following in alphabetical order, without regard to vintage. 78s, 45s, EPs, and LPs are illustrated in the following section. For a given label, more than one speed or type of record may be shown first, followed by 45s. EPs, and finally LPs. It is intended that the reader use this section to identify most of the important, interesting and rare labels and significant variations thereof. Photos of a number of worthwhile labels could not be obtained in time for publication, and it is hoped that a fifth edition of this book will contain additional photographs. Of course, it is not intended that every record label mentioned in the listings, much less every known record label, be represented.

In the 1950s, records were often issued in both 78 and 45 rpm form. Where the label design and/or logo is similar on the two speeds, only one is usually illustrated.

In the case of major, long-lived labels such as Okeh or Victor, significant changes in label design are shown in chronological order. Also, special "race" and hillbilly series, distinguishable by number series and/or label variation, are often illustrated and identified. See, for example, the Brunswick 7000-7233 series and the Brunswick 100 series, both having the "lightning" label.

Accompanying the photos are approximate issue dates, e.g. "late 1920s." Where a label is primarily a "race" or rhythm and blues label, this is indicated.

For further information on pre-1943 labels, see Rust's "American Record Label Book," listed in the Bibliography. I have just received word of the publication a work dealing with post-war labels, "The American Record Label Directory & dating Guide," by Galen Gart, which reference I have not yet seen. Ken Clee's "The Directory of American 45 R.P.M. Records" (also listed in the Bibliography) is a discography. Also, illustrated essays on post-war labels may be found in current and back issues of the various record collectors' publications.

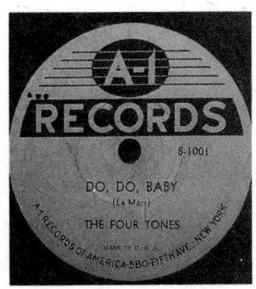

A-1 RECORDS
Ca. 1950 (78)

A-J
Ca. 1960 (45)

AARDELL
Late 1950s (45)

ABBEY
Ca. 1950 (78)

ABBEY
D.J. Copy Ca. 1950 (78)

ABBOTT
Early 1950s (78)

ABCO
Rhythm & Blues (78)
Mid 1950s

ABNER
Late 1950s (78)

ABC PARAMOUNT
Late 1950s (78)

ABC PARAMOUNT
Late 1950s (78)

ABC PARAMOUNT
Late 1950s Early 1960s (45)

ACE
Ca. 1950 (78)

ACE
Ca. 1950 (78)

ACE
Ca. 1950 (78)

ACE
Mid-Late 1950s (45)

ACE
Mid to Late 1950s

ACT IV
Ca. 1960 (45)

ACTUELLE
Ca. 1925 (78)

ADMIRAL
Late 1950s (45)

AEOLIAN-VOCALION
Ca. 1918 (78)

AEOLIAN-VOCALION
Ca. 1920 (Lateral) (78)

AFTER HOURS
Early 1950s (45)

AJAX
(Canadian) "Race" (78)
Early-Mid 1920s

ALADDIN
Rhythm & Blues, Jazz
Late 1940s

ALADDIN
Rhythm & Blues (78)
Early 1950s

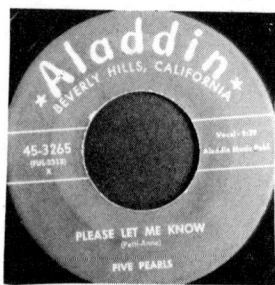

ALADDIN
Rhythm & Blues (78)
Mid 1950s

ALBEN
Ca. 1950 (78)

ALERT
Late 1940s (78)

AL-JACK'S
Late 1950s (45)

ALLEN
Rhythm & Blues (45)
Mid 1950s

ALL STAR
Rhythm & Blues (45)
Late 1950s

ALL STAR
Rhythm & Blues (45)
Late 1950s

ALLSTAR
Late 1950s (45)

AL'S
Ca. 1960 (45)

ALTAIR
Ca. 1959 (45)

ALVERA
Early 1960s (45)

ALVIN
Ca. 1950 (78)

AMCO
Grey Gull Ca. 1925 (78)
Grey Gull affiliate

AMERICAN MUSIC
1940s (78)

AMERICA RECORD COMPANY
Ca. 1916 (78)

AMERICAN RECORD CORP.
Ca. 1930 (78)

AMMOR
Ca. 1940 (78)

AMMOR
Ca. 1940 (78)

ANDEX
Ca. 1960 (45)

ANDIE
Early 1960s (45)

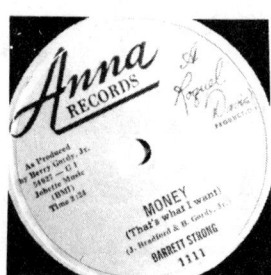

ANNA
Rhythm & Blues (78)
Late 1959-60

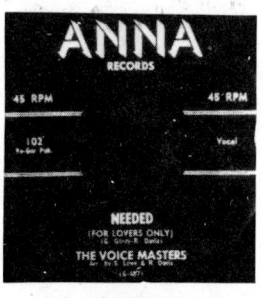

ANNA
Rhythm & Blues (45)
Late 1959-60s

ANTHEM
Ca. 1960 (45)

ANTLER
Ca. 1960 (45)

THE ANTONES
Country & Western (78)
Late 1940s

APEX
Mid 1920s (78)
Canadian

APEX
Late 1950s (45)

APOLLO
Perfect Affiliate
Ca. 1927 (78)

APOLLO
Late 1940s (78)

APOLLO
Rhythm & Blues (78)
Ca. 1950

APOLLO
Rhythm & Blues (45)
Mid 1950s

APOLLO
Mid 1950s (45)

APPLAUSE
Ca. 1960 (45)

ARA
Ca. 1947 (78)

ARC
Late 1950s (45)

ARC
Late 1950s (45)

ARCADE
Late 1950s (45)

ARCADIA
Ca. 1950 (78)

ARCADIA
Ca. 1956 (78)

ARCTIC
Late 1950s (45)

ARGO
Late 1950s (78)

ARGO
Late 1950s (78)

ARGO
Late 1950s (45)

ARISTA
Ca. 1950 (78)

ARISTOCRAT
Rhythm & Blues (78)
Late 1940s

ARISTOCRAT
Rhythm & Blues (78)
Late 1940s

ARTISTIC
Late 1950s (78)

ARTO
Early 1920s (78)

ARVEE
Ca. 1960 (45)

ARWIN
Late 1950s (78)

ASCH
1940s (78)

ATCO
Late 1950s (78)

ATCO
Rhythm & Blues (78)
Late 1950s

ATHENS
Late 1950s (45)

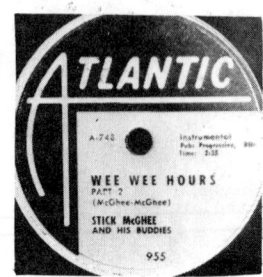

ATLANTIC
Rhythm & Blues
Early 1950s

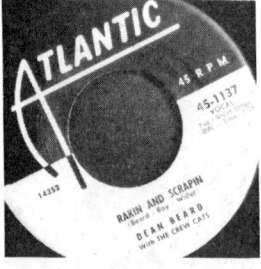

ATLANTIC
Rhythm & Blues (45)
1950s

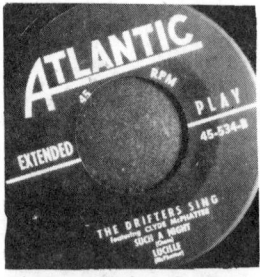

ATLANTIC
Rhythm & Blues (E.P.)
Mid 1950s

ATLANTIC
Rhythm & Blues (LP)
Mid 1950s

ATLANTIC
Rhythm & Blues (LP)
Later Pressing

ATLAS
Late 1940s (78)

ATOMIC
Late 1940s (78)

ATOMIC
Mid 1950s (45)

ATOMIC-H
Mid 1950s (45)

AUTOGRAPH
Ca. 1924 (78)

AUTOGRAPH
Electrically Recorded
Ca. 1925 (78)

AUTOGRAPH
Ca. 1925 (78)

AUTOGRAPH
Ca. 1925 (78)

AYO
Late 1940s (78)

AZALEA
Late 1950s (45)

B & S
Ca. 1950 (78)

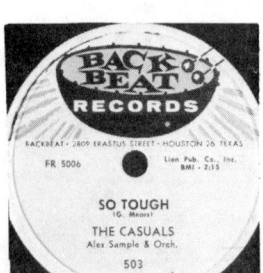

BACK BEAT
Mid 1950s (78)

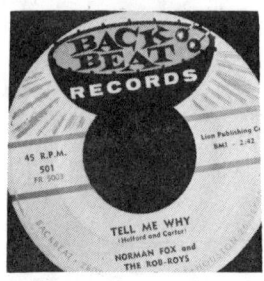

BACK BEAT
Mid 1950s (45)

BAMA
Early 1950s (78)

BAND BOX
Ca. 1960

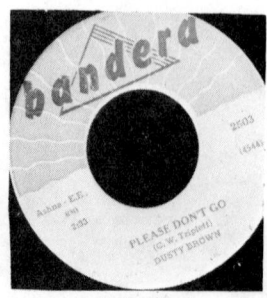

BANDERA
Rhythm & Blues (45)
Late 1950s

BANNER
Ca. 1930 (78)

BATON
Late 1950s (45)

BAYOU
Rhythm & Blues (45)
Mid 1950s

BAY-TONE
Late 1950s (45)

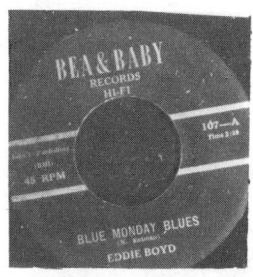

BEA & BABY
Rhythm & Blues (45)
Ca. 1960

BEACON
Late 1940s (78)

BELL
Early 1920s (78)

BELL
Mid 1920s (78)

BELL
Early 1920s (78)

BELL
Late 1940s (78)

BELL
Early 1950s (78)
7-inch record

BEL-TONE
Late 1940s (78)

BENNETT
Ca. 1950 (78)

**BERLINER'S
GRAMOPHONE**
Late 1890s (78)

BERNARDO
Ca. 1929 (78)

BIG
Early 1960s (45)

BIG HOWDY
Late 1950s (45)

BIG TOWN
Rhythm & Blues (78)
Mid 1950s

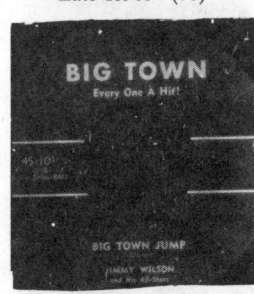

BIG TOWN
Mid 1950s (45)

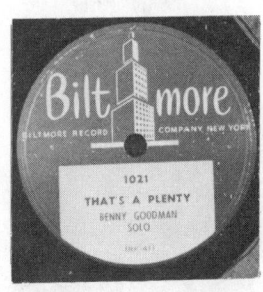

BILTMORE
1940s (78)
(A reissue label for jazz
collectors)

BINGO
Ca. 1960s (45)

BLACK AND WHITE
Blues and Jazz (78)
Late 1940s

BLACK AND WHITE
Late 1940s (78)

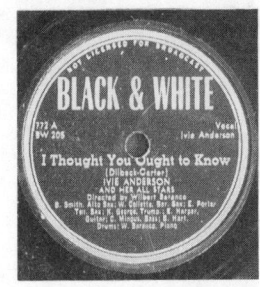

BLACK AND WHITE
Late 1940s (78)

BLACK AND WHITE
Late 1940s (45)

BLACK PATTI
Ca. 1927 (78)
"Race" label

BLACK SWAN
"Race" (78)
Early 1920s

BLACK SWAN
"Race" (78)
Early 1920s

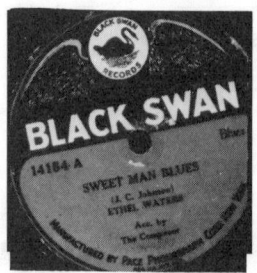

BLACK SWAN
"Race" (78)
Early 1920s

BLAZE
Early 1960s (45)

BLAZON
Late 1940s (78)

BLUE BIRD
Early 1920s (78)
(Unrelated to more familiar
RCA Victor product)

BLUE BIRD
Ca. 1933 (78)

BLUE BIRD
Mid 1930s (78)

BLUEBIRD
Late 1930s (78)

BLUEBIRD
Late 1930s-41 (78)

BLUE BONNET
Country & Western (78)
Late 1940s

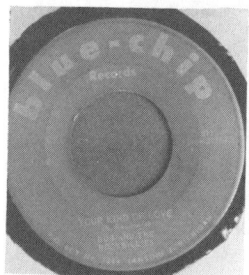

BLUE CHIP
Late 1950s (45)

BLUE CHIP
Ca. 1960 (45)

BLUE RIVER
Late 1950s (45)

BLUES & RHYTHM
Ca. 1950 (78)

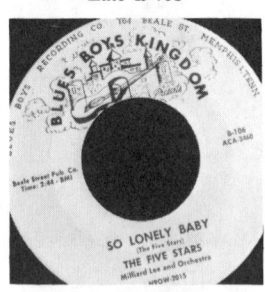

**BLUES BOYS
KINGDOM**
Rhythm & Blues (45)

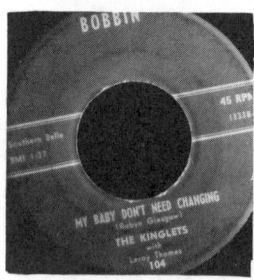

BOBBIN
Rhythm & Blues (45)
Late 1950s

BO-KAY
Late 1950s (45)

BONNIE BLUE
Ca. 1950 (78)

BOULEVARD
Mid 1950s (45)

BRAX
Ca. 1960 (45)

BRENT
Rhythm & Blues (45)
Mid 1960s

BROADWAY
Mid 1920s (78)

BROADWAY
Late 1920s (78)

7

BROADWAY
Popular Series (78)
Late 1920s

BROADWAY
"Race" (78)
5000 series

BROADWAY
8000 series (78)
Country & Western
Late 1920s

BROKEN
Ca. 1950 (78)

BRONZE
Ca. 1940 (78)

BRUCE
Late 1950s (45)

BRUNSWICK
Mid 1920s (78)

BRUNSWICK
100 series-Hillbilly (78)
Late 1920s

BRUNSWICK
7000 series-"Race" (78)
Late 1920s

BRUNSWICK
Ca. 1931 (78)

BRUNSWICK
Mid 1930s (78)

BRUNSWICK
Early 1930s (78)

BRUNSWICK
Late 1930s (78)

BRUNSWICK
1940s-Early 1950s (78)
(collector's reissue series)

BRUNSWICK
Late 1940s (78)
Early 1950s

BRUNSWICK
Late 1950s (78)

BRUNSWICK
Late 1950s (45)

BRYAN
Ca. 1950 (78)

BRYTE
Late 1950s (45)

BUDDY
Ca. 1925 (78)

BULLET
Blues Late 1940s (78)

BULL DOG
Late 1950s (45)

BULLSEYE
Late 1950s (45)

BUSY BEE
Ca. 1910 (78)

CMI
Late 1950s (45)

CADDY
Late 1950s (45)

CADENCE
Late 1950s (78)

CADENCE
Late 1950s (45)

CALVERT
Early 1960s (45)

CAMEO
Ca. 1924 (78)

CAMEO
Late 1920s (78)

CAMEO
Late 1950s (78)

CAMEO
Late 1950s (45)

CAMEO
Early 1960s (45)

CANDIX
Early 1960s (45)

**CANDLELIGHT
RECORDS**
Ca. 1960 (45)

CAPITOL
1950s (78)

CAPITOL
Late 1950s (78)

CAPITOL
Ca. 1969 (78)
special commemorative
record

CAPITOL
Late 1950s (45)

CAPITOL
Mid 1960s (45)

CAPITOL
Late 1950s (L.P.)

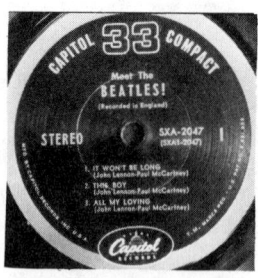

CAPITOL
7-inch (L.P.)
Mid 1960s

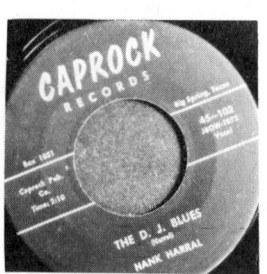

CAPROCK
Country & Western (45)
Late 1950s

CARDINAL
Early 1920s (78)

CARDINAL
Early 1920s (78)

CARDINAL
Ca. 1950 (78)

CARLTON
Late 1950s (L.P.)

CASA GRANDE
Late 1950s (45)

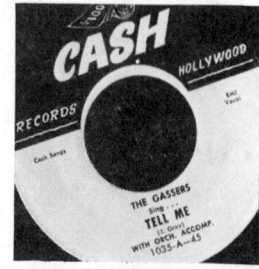

CASH
Rhythm & Blues (45)
Mid 1950s

CASINO
Late 1950s (45)

CASTLE RECORDS
Ca. 1949 (78)

CAT
Late 1950s (78)

CAT
Late 1950s (45)

CAVA-TONE
Ca. 1950 (78)

CELEBRITY
Late 1940s (78)

CENTRAL
Late 1950s (45)

CENTRAL
Late 1950s (45)

CHALLENGE
Late 1920s (78)

CHALLENGE
Late 1950s (78)

CHALLENGE
Late 1950s (45)

CHAMPION
Mid 1920s (78)
Early 1930s

CHAMPION
Mid 1930s (78)

CHAMPION
Ca. 1960 (45)

CHANCE
Rhythm & Blues (78)
Early 1950s

CHANCE
Rhythm & Blues (78)
Mid 1950s

CHANCE
Rhythm & Blues (45)
Mid 1950s

CHANCELLOR
Late 1950s (78)

CHANT
Early 1960s (45)

CHAPPELLE AND STINNETTE
Ca. 1921 (78)

CHART
Late 1950s (45)

CHARTBUSTER
Ca. 1960 (45)

CHAUTAUQUA
Ca. 1922 (78)

CHECKER
Rhythm & Blues (78)
Early 1950s

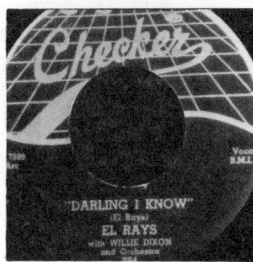

CHECKER
Rhythm & Blues (45)
Mid 1950s

CHECKER
Rhythm & Blues   (78)
Late 1950s

CHECKER
Bhythm & Blues (L.P.)
Late 1950s

CHECK-MATE
Early 1960s   (45)

CHERRY
Ca. 1960   (45)

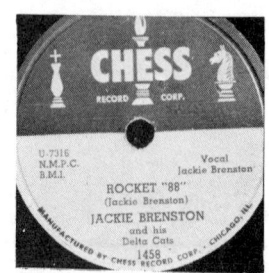

CHESS
Rhythm & Blues   (78)
Early 1950s

CHESS
Rhythm & Blues   (78)
Late 1950s

CHESS
Rhythm & Blues   (78)
Late 1950s

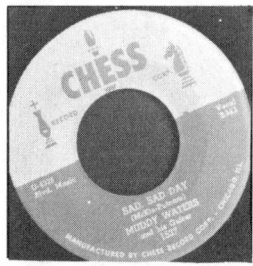

CHESS
Rhythm & Blues   (45)
Mid 1950s

CHESS
Late 1950s   (45)

CHESS
Rhythm & Blues   (78)
Late 1950s

CHESS
Rhythm & Blues (L.P.)
Later Pressing

CHIEF
Mid 1950s   (45)

CHIEF
Late 1950s   (45)

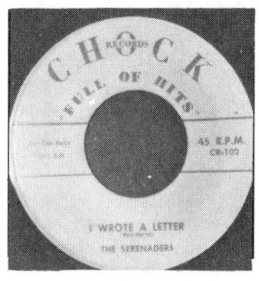

**CHOCK FULL
OF HITS**
Late 1950s   (45)

CHOICE
Ca. 1960   (45)

CIMARRON
Early 1960s   (45)

CINDY
Ca. 1960   (45)

CIRECO
Ca. 1948   (78)

CLARION
Ca. 1910   (78)

CLARION
Ca. 1921   (78)

CLARION
Early 1930s   (78)

CLARION
Early 1930s   (78)
"Double Track" record

CLASS
Late 1950s   (78)

CLAXTONOLA
Mid 1920s   (78)

CLEARTONE
Early 1920s   (78)

CLEARTONE
Early 1920s (78)

CLEAR TONE
Late 1940s (78)

CLIF
Mid 1950s (45)

CLIMAX RECORD
Ca. 1910 (78)

CLIMAX
Ca. 1910 (78)

CLOVER
Ca. 1926 (78)

CLUB 51
Mid 1950s (45)

CLUB
Late 1950s (45)

COBRA
Late 1950s (78)

COBRA
Rhythm & Blues (45)
Late 1950s

COBRA
Early 1960s (45)

COIN
Ca. 1960 (45)

COLONIAL
Ca. 1950 (78)

COLONIAL
Late 1950s (78)

COLONIAL
Late 1950s (45)

COLONIAL
Late 1950s (45)

COLONY
Ca. 1950 (78)

COLPIX
Ca. 1960 (45)

COLUMBIA
Ca. 1904 (78)

**COLUMBIA DISC
RECORD**
Ca. 1905 (78)

COLUMBIA
Ca. 1905 (78)

COLUMBIA
Ca. 1905 (78)

COLUMBIA
Ca. 1905 (78)

COLUMBIA
Ca. 1907 (78)

COLUMBIA
Ca. 1907 (78)

COLUMBIA
Ca. 1907 (78)

COLUMBIA
Ca. 1910 (78)

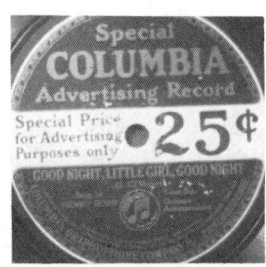

COLUMBIA
Advertising Record (obverse)
Ca. 1915 (78)

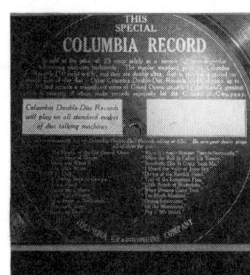

COLUMBIA
Advertising Record (reverse)
Ca. 1910

COLUMBIA
Personal
Ca. 1915 (78)

COLUMBIA
Ca. 1915 (78)
Panama-Pacific Exposition
Souvenir Record

COLUMBIA
Early 1920s (78)

COLUMBIA
Mid 1920s (78)

COLUMBIA
14000-D Series is "Race"
15000-D Series is Country
& Western Late 20s (78)

COLUMBIA
Picture Label (78)
Late 1920s
(Ted Lewis)

COLUMBIA
Spanish Series
Ca. 1930 (78)

COLUMBIA
Folk Series
Ca. 1933 (78)

COLUMBIA
Ted Lewis Logo
Ca. 1933 (78)

COLUMBIA
Rudy Vallee Logo
Ca. 1933 (78)

COLUMBIA
Mid 1930s (78)

COLUMBIA
Mid 1930s (78)

COLUMBIA
1939-1950s (78)

COLUMBIA
Sacred Series
Ca. 1950 (78)

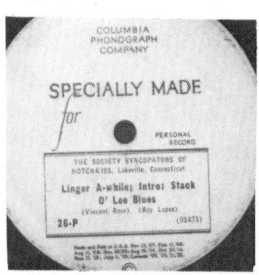

COLUMBIA
Personal
Ca. 1924 (78)

COLUMBIA
Early 1950s (45)

COLUMBIA
Late 1950s (78)

COLUMBIA
Late 1950s (78)

COLUMBIA
Early 1960s (45)

COMBO
Mid 1950s (78)

COMBO
Mid 1950s (45)

COMBO
Mid 1950s (45)

COMMODORE
Jazz (78)
Late 1930s Early 1940s

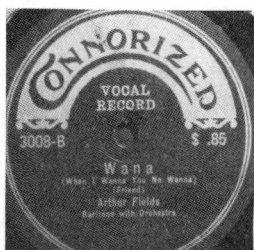

CONNORIZED
Ca. 1922 (78)
(Vocal Series)

CONNORIZED
Dance Series
Ca. 1923 (78)

CONQUEROR
Late 1920s (78)

CONQUEROR
Early 1930s (78)

CONQUEROR
Late 1930s-1940 (78)

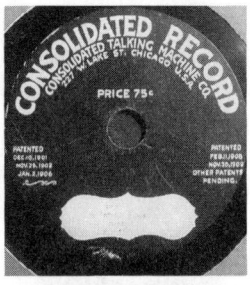

**CONSOLIDATED
RECORD**
Ca. 1912 (78)

CONTINENTAL
1940s (78)

CONTINENTAL
Ca. 1947 (78)

THE COOK
Ca. 1922 (78)

CORAL
Late 1950s (78)

CORAL
Late 1950s (45)

CORAL
Late 1950s (L.P.)

CORMAC
Ca. 1950 (78)

CORMAC
Ca. 1950 (78)

CORT
Ca. 1915 (78)

CORT RECORD
Ca. 1915 (78)

COSMO
Ca. 1950 (78)

COSMO
Ca. 1950 (78)
Jazz Series

COURTNEY
Ca. 1950 (78)

COURTNEY
Ca. 1950 (78)

COVER
Late 1950s (45)

COWTOWN
Ca. 1950 (78)

COWTOWN
Late 1950s (45)

CREST
Early 1950s (78)
7-inch record

CREST
Late 1950s (45)

CREST
Early 1960s (45)

CROSS COUNTRY
Mid-1950s (45)

CROWN
Early 1930s (78)

CROWN
Canadian
Ca. 1928 (78)

CRYSTAL
Ca. 1950 (78)

CRYSTALETTE
Early 1950s (78)

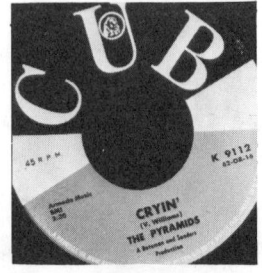

CUB
Late 1950s (45)
Early 1960s

CULLMAN
Ca. 1960 (45)

D
Late 1950s (45)

D
Ca. 1960 (45)

D & R
Ca. 1910 (78)

DALE
Late 1950s (45)

DAMON
Mid 1950s (45)

DANDY
Ca. 1924 (78)

DARL
Mid 1950s (45)

DARSA
Late 1950s (45)

DART
Early 1960s (45)

DAVEGA
Ca. 1924 (78)

DAVIS
Late 1940s (78)

DAVIS
Late 1950s (45)

DAWN
Late 1950s (45)

DAWN
Ca. 1960 (45)

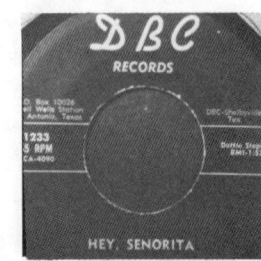

D B C
Ca. 1960 (45)

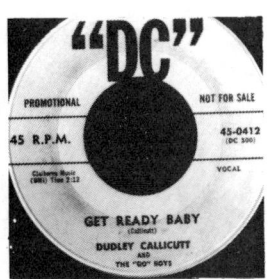
DC
Rhythm & Blues (45)
Late 1950s

DECCA
7000 series "Race" (78)
Mid 1930s

DECCA
"Race" series
Ca. 1938 (78)

DECCA
Ca. 1941 (78)

DECCA
Late 1940s (78)

DECCA
Mid 1950s (45)

DECCA
Late 1950s (78)

DECCA
Late 1950s (45)

DEL-CO
Late 1950s (45)

DEL-FI
Late 1950s (45)

DELTA
Mid 1950s (45)

DELTA
Ca. 1960 (45)

DELTONE
Early 1960s (45)

DE-LUXE
Late 1940s (78)

DE LUXE
Late 1940s (78)

DeLUXE
Rhythm & Blues (78)
Mid 1950s

DeLUXE
Mid 1950s (45)

DEMON
Late 1950s (78)

DERBY
Mid 1950s (45)

DIADON
Ca. 1960 (45)

DIAL
Late 1940s (78)

DIAL
Ca. 1960 (45)

DIAMOND RECORD
Ca. 1912 (78)

DIAMOND
Ca. 1950 (78)

DIG
Late 1950s (45)

DIR
Late 1950s (45)

DISC-COVERY
Ca. 1950 (78)

DISCOVERY
Ca. 1950 (78)

DITTO
Late 1950s (45)

DIVA
Late 1920s (78)

DIX
Early 1950s (78)

DIXIE
Late 1950s (45)

DOKE
Late 1950s (45)

DOMINO
Mid 1920s (78)

DOMINO
Late 1920s (78)

DOMINO
Ca. 1928 (78)
Canadian

DOMINO
Late 1950s (45)

DONA
Late 1950s (45)

DON TAN
Ca. 1960 (45)

DOOTONE
Late 1950s (78)

DOOTONE
Late 1950s (45)

DOT
Early 1950s (78)

DOT
Mid 1950s (78)

DOT
Mid 1950s (45)

DOT
Late 1950s (78)

DOVE
Late 1950s (45)

DOWN BEAT
Rhythm & Blues (78)
Late 1940s

DOWN TOWN
Late 1940s (78)

DRAG RACE
Mid 1950s (78)

DREW-BLAN
Early 1960s (45)

DRUMFIRE
Ca. 1960 (45)

DRUMMOND
Mid 1950s (45)

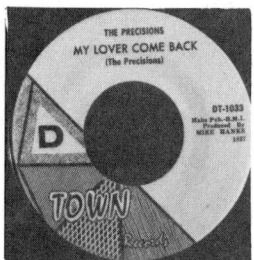

D TOWN
Ca. 1960 (45)

DUB
Late 1950s (45)

DUCHESS
Early 1960s (45)

DUKE
Mid 1950-Early 1960s (45)

DUNCAN
Ca. 1959 (45)

DUOPHONE
(English) Ca. 1929 (78)

DUPLEX
Late 1950s (78)

DURIUM JUNIOR
Early 1930s (78)
paper record, 4″ diam

DYNAMIC
Ca. 1964 (45)

E & M
Early 1960s (45)

EAGLE
Ca. 1908 (78)

EAGLE
Early 1960s (45)

EAST-WEST
Late 1950s (45)

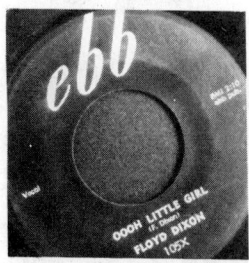

EBB
Rhythm & Blues (45)
Mid-late 1950s

ECHO
Ca. 1950 (78)

ECHO
Late 1950s (45)

EDDIE'S
Late 1940s (78)

EDISON
Late 'Teens (78)
Embossed, not paper, label

EDISON
Late 'Teens (78)
Embossed, not paper, label

EDISON
1920s thick (78)

EDISON
Special Pressing (thick)
Ca. 1924 (78)

EDISON
Ca. 1929 (thin) (78)

EDISON
Ca. 1926 (36) Long Play

**EDISON
INTERNATIONAL**
Late 1950s (45)

ELECTRA
Ca. 1925 (78)
Autograph/Marsh
Laboraties Affiliate

ELECTRADISK
Early 1930s (78)

EMBER
Late 1950s (78)

EMBER
Ca. 1960 (45)

EMBER
Late 1950s (78)

EMBER
Late 1950s (45)

EMERSON
Late 'Teens (78)
7-inch record

EMERSON
Late 'Teens (78)
7-inch record

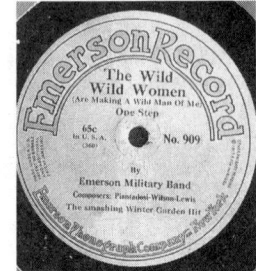

EMERSON
Late 'Teens (78)
9-inch record

EMERSON
Ca. 1918 (78)

EMERSON
Ca. 1922 (78)

EMERSON
Mid 1920s (78)

EMPIRE
Ca. 1919 (78)

EMPIRE
Ca. 1920 (78)

EMPIRE
Late 1950s (45)

EMPRESS
Ca. 1960 (45)

ENCINO
Mid 1950s (45)

END
Late 1950s (78)

END
Late 1950s (45)

ENSIGN
Ca. 1960 (45)

ENTERPRISE
Ca. 1950 (78)

ERA
Late 1950s (45)

ESSEX
Mid 1950s (78)

ESSEX
Mid 1950s (45)

EVEREST
Ca. 1960 (45)

EVERLAST
Late 1950s (45)

EVERYBODY'S
Mid 1920s (78)

EVERSTATE
Ca. 1948 (78)

EXCEL
Late 1950s (45)

EXCELLO
Mid 1950s (78)

EXCELSIOR
Ca. 1910 (78)

EXCELSIOR
Late 1940s (78)

EXCELSIOR
Late 1940s (78)

EXCLUSIVE
Late 1940s (78)

EXCLUSIVE
Ca. 1947 (78)

FABLE
Ca. 1957 (45)

FABOR
Late 1950s (45)

FALCON
Late 1950s (45)

FAMOUS
Early 1920s (78)

FAN
Late 1950s (45)

FARGO
Ca. 1950 (78)

FASCINATION
Mid 1950s (45)

FASCINATION
Late 1950s (45)

FASCINATION
Late 1950s (45)

**FAULTLESS
CONCERT RECORD**
Ca. 1910 (78)

FEATURE
Mid 1950s (45)

FEATURE
Late 1950s (45)

FEDERAL
Ca. 1923 (78)

FEDERAL
Mid 1950s (78)

FEDERAL
Mid 1950s (45)

FEDERAL
Mid 1950s (L.P.)

FEDERAL
Late 1950s (78)

FEDERAL
Late 1950s (45)

FEE BEE
Ca. 1956 (45)

FELSTED
Late 1950s (45)

FERNWOOD
Late 1950s (45)

FIDELITY
Early 1950s (78)

FIRE
Ca. 1960 (78)

FIRE
Early 1960s (45)

FLAIR
Rhythm & Blues (78)
Mid 1950s

FLAIR
Mid 1950s (45)

FLAIR-X
Late 1950s (45)

FLASH
Ca. 1950 (78)

FLASH
Late 1950s (78)

FLASH
Late 1950s (45)

FLIP
Mid 1950s (78)

FLIP
Mid 1950s (78)

FLIP
Mid 1950s (45)

FLIP
Late 1950s (78)

FLIP
Late 1950s (45)

FLICK
Late 1950s (45)

F M
Early 1950s (78)

FONSCA
Ca. 1960 (45)

FORD
Mid 1950s (78)

FORTUNE
Early 1950s (78)

FORTUNE
Mid 1950s (45)

4 STAR
Ca. 1950 (78)

FOX
Late 1950s (45)

FOX MOVIETONE
Mid 1930s (78)

FRANSIL
Mid 1950s (45)

FRATERNITY
Late 1950s (78)

FRATERNITY
Late 1950s (45)

FREEDOM
Ca. 1950 (78)

FREEDOM
Ca. 1950 (78)

FREEDOM
Late 1950s (45)

FURY
Late 1950s (45)

FURY
Late 1950s (45)

FURY
Ca. 1960 (45)

G & G
Late 1940s (78)

GAMETIME
Late 1950s (45)

GARY
Late 1950s (45)

GATEWAY
Late 1950s (45)

GEE
Mid 1950s (45)

GEE
Late 1950s (78)

GEE
Late 1950s (78)

GEE
Ca. 1960 (45)

GEM
Ca. 1950 (78)

GEM
Mid 1950s (45)

GENERAL
Ca. 1940 (78)

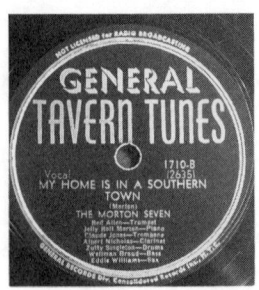

GENERAL TAVERN TUNES
Early 1940s (78)

GENNETT
Mid 1920s (78)

GENNETT
Personal Early 1920s (78)

GENNETT
Late 1920s (78)

GENNETT
Ca. 1930 (78)
Transcription

GENNETT SOUND EFFECTS
Early 1930s (78)

GENNETT
1940s (78)

GILBERT
Mid 1950s (45)

GILT-EDGE
Late 1940s (78)

GILT-EDGE
DJ issue Early 1950s (45)

GINA
Ca. 1960 (45)

GLOBAL
Early 1960s (45)

GLOBE
Ca. 1922 (78)

GLOBE
Mid 1920s (78)

GLOBE
Late 1940s (78)

GLOBE
Mid 1950s (45)

GOLDBAND
Late 1950s (45)

GOLDBAND
Late 1950s (45)

GOLDEN
Mid 1920s (78)

GOLDEN CREST
Early 1960s (45)

GOLD MEDAL RECORD
Ca. 1950 (78)

GOLD STAR
Late 1940s (78)

GONE
Late 1950s (78)

GONE
Mid 1950s (45)

GONE
Late 1950s (45)

GOOD
Late 1950s (45)

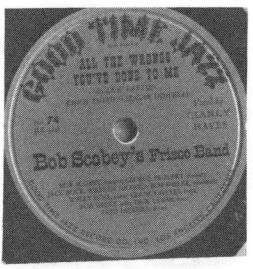

GOOD TIME JAZZ
Mid 1950s (78)

GOSPEL TRUMPET CO.
Mid 1920s (78)

GOTHAM
Late 1940s to Early 1950s (78)

GOTHAM
Early 1950s (45)

GRAND
Ca. 1947 (78)

GRAND
Mid 1950s (45)

GRANITE
Late 1950s (45)

GREYCLIFF
Ca. 1960 (45)

GREY GULL
Ca. 1922 (78)

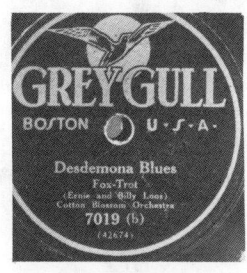

GREY GULL
Mid 1920s (78)

GREY GULL
1920s (78)

GREY GULL
Ca. 1929 (78)

GROOVE
Late 1950s (45)

GROOVE
Mid 1950s (45)

GROOVE
Late 1950s (45)

GROOVY
Late 1940s (78)

GUARDSMAN
(English) Ca. 1917 (78)

GULF
Late 1940s (78)

GUYDEN
Late 1950s (78)

GUYDEN
Late 1950s (45)

H.R.S.
Late 1940s (78)

HALL-WAY
Ca. 1960 (45)

HAMILTON
Late 1950s (45)

HANOVER
Ca. 1960 (45)

HARLEM
Late 1940s (78)

HARLEM
Late 1950s (78)

HARLEM
Ca. 1960 (45)

HARMOGRAPH
Early 1920s (78)

HARMOGRAPH
Early 1920s (78)

HARMONY RECORD
Ca. 1912 (78)

HARMONY
1925 to Early 1930s (78)

**HARMONY DISC
RECORD**
Ca. 1908 (78)

HARMONY
Ca. 1958 (LP)

HART
Late 1950s (45)

**HARVARD DISC
RECORD**
Ca. 1908 (78)

**HARVARD DISC
RECORD**
Ca. 1908 (78)

HARVEY
Early 1960s (45)

HEART RECORDS
Ca. 1950 (78)

HEP
Ca. 1960 (45)

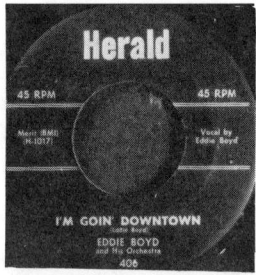

HERALD
Rhythm & Blues
Mid 1950s (45)

HERALD
Mid 1950s (45)

HERALD
Mid 1950s (45)

HERALD
Mid 1950s (78)

HERALD
Late 1950s (45)

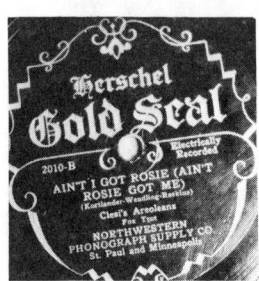

**HERSCHEL GOLD
SEAL**
Late 1920s (78)

HERMITAGE
Ca. 1960 (45)

HERWIN
Ca. 1926 (78)

HERWIN
Late 1920s (78)
Electrically Recorded

HI
Late 1950s (45)

HICKORY
Late 1950s (45)

HIS MASTER'S VOICE
(Canadian) Ca. 1924 (78)

THE HIT
Ca. 1940 (78)

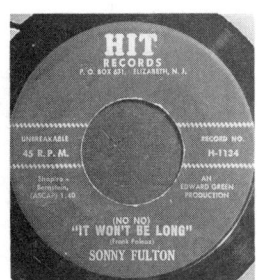

HIT RECORDS
Late 1950s (45)

HIT MAKER
Late 1950s (45)

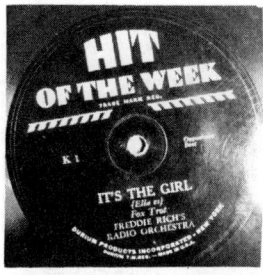

HIT OF THE WEEK
Paper Record (78)
Early 1930s

HOB (HOUSE OF BEAUTY)
Early 1960s (45)

HOLIDAY
Late 1950s (45)

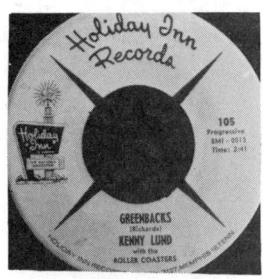

HOLIDAY INN
Early 1960s (45)

HOLLYWOOD
Mid 1920s (78)

HOLLYWOOD
Mid 1950s (45)

HOLLYWOOD HOT SHOTS
Ca. 1940 (78)

HOMESTEAD
Ca. 1930 (78)

HOT JAZZ CLUB OF AMERICA
1940s (78)
(Collectors reissue series)

HOT RECORD SOCIETY
Ca. 1939 (78)
(Collectors Series)

HOT WAX
Ca. 1948 (78)

HUB
Late 1940s

HUDSON
Ca. 1925 (78)

HULL
Late 1950s (78)

HULL
Late 1950s (45)

HULL
Late 1950s (45)

HUMMING BIRD
Ca. 1950 (78)

HUMMING BIRD
Early 1950s (45)

HUNTER
Late 1960s (45)

HYTONE
Early 1920s (78)

HY-TONE
Late 1940s (78)

HY-TONE
Late 1950s (45)

IMPERIAL
Late 'Teens (78)

IMPERIAL
Ca. 1950 (78)
(Country series)

IMPERIAL
Early 1950s (78)

IMPERIAL
Mid 1950s (45)

IMPERIAL
Late 1950s (78)

IMPERIAL
Late 1950s (45)

IMPERIAL
Late 1950s (45)

IMPERIAL
Late 1950s (L.P.)

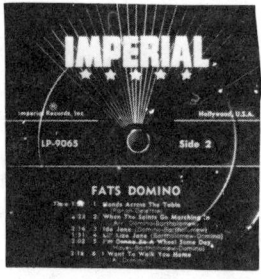

IMPERIAL (LP)
Late 1950s to Early 1960s

IMPRA
Late 1950s (45)

IMPROVED RECORD
Ca. 1901 (78)
Victor-affiliated

INCO
Ca 1940 (78)

INTRO
Early 1950s (78)

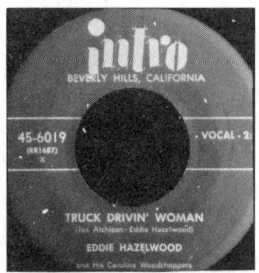

INTRO
Country & Western
Late 1950s (45)

IRAGEN
1930s (78)

IRMA
Late 1950s (78)

IVORY
Ca. 1961 (45)

J & S
Ca. 1956 (45)

J—B
Ca. 1950 (78)

JACKPOT
Ca. 1960 (45)

JACKSON
Mid 1950s (45)

JAGUAR
Mid 1950s (45)

JALO
Late 1950s (45)

JALYNNE
Early 1950s (45)

JAMIE
Late 1950s (78)

JAMIE
Late 1950s (45)

JAMIE
Late 1950s (45)

JAN
Late 1950s (45)

JAN
Late 1950s (45)

JAX
Ca. 1950 (78)

JAX
Early 1950s (45)

JAX
Early 1950s (45)

JAY
Ca. 1950 (78)
Collectors' Reissue

JAY-DEE
Mid 1950s (78)

JAY-DEE
Mid 1950s (45)

JAY WING
Late 1950s (45)

JAZZ DISC
Late 1940s (78)

JAZZ MAN
Late 1940s (78)

JAZZ MAN
Late 1940s (78)

JAZZ RECORD
1940s (78)

J-B
Mid 1950s (45)

JEWEL
Early 1920s (78)
(Grey Gull affiliated)

JEWEL
Ca. 1930 (78)

JEWEL
Late 1940s (78)

JEWEL
Late 1940s (78)

JEWEL
Early 1960s (45)

JIFFY
Mid 1950s (45)

JIFFY
Mid 1950s (45)

JIN
Late 1950s (45)

JIN
Late 1950s (45)

JIN
Ca. 1960 (45)

J.O.B.
Early 1950s (78)

J.O.B.
Late 1950s (45)

JOE DAVIS
Late 1940s (78)

JOHNSON
Ca. 1960 (45)

JOZ (JOSIE)
Late 1950s (78)

JOZ (JOSIE)
Late 1950s (45)

JOSIE
Ca. 1960 (45)

JUBILEE
Rhythm & Blues (78)
Early 1950s

JUBILEE
Early 1950s (45)

JUBILEE
Mid 1950s (78)

JUBILEE
Mid 1950s (45)

JUDD
Ca. 1960 (45)

JUMP
Ca. 1950 (78)

JUKE BOX
Late 1940s (78)

JVB
Ca. 1950 (78)

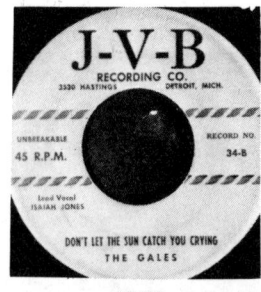

JVB
Rhythm & Blues
Late 1950s (45)

JVB
Late 1950s (45)

JVB
Rhythm & Blues
Late 1950s (78)

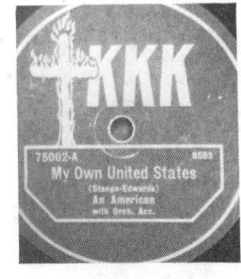

K K K
Mid 1920s (78)

KRC
Late 1950s (45)

K-ARK
Late 1950s (45)

KAYO
Late 1950s (45)

KEEN
Late 1950s (78)

KEEN
Late 1950s (78)

KENT
Ca. 1960 (45)

KENTUCKY
Early 1950s (78)

**KEYBOARD
RECORDS**
Ca. 1950 (78)

KHOURY'S
1950s (78)

KHOURY'S
Mid 1950s (45)

KHOURY'S
Late 1950s (45)

KICK
Late 1950s (45)

KICKS
Late 1950s (45)

KING
Late 1940s (78)

KING
Late 1950s (78)

KING
Late 1950s (45)

KING
Late 1950s (LP-33rpm)

KLIFF
Late 1950s (45)

KLIK
Mid 1950s (45)

KOOL
Early 1960s (45)

KUDO
Late 1950s (45)

LA BELLE
Ca. 1911 (78)

LAKESIDE
Ca. 1910 (78)

LAMP
Mid 1950s (45)

LASSO
Early 1950s (78)

LAURIE
Late 1950s (45)

LAURIE
Early 1960s (45)

LE CAM
Early 1960s (45)

LEE
Early 1950s (78)

LEE
Late 1950s (45)

LEEDS
Ca. 1910 (78)

LEGRAND
Ca. 1960 (45)

LESLEY
Late 1950s (45)

LIBERTY
Late 1950s (78)

LIBERTY
Late 1950s (45)

LIDO
Late 1950s (45)

LIGHTNING
Mid 1950s (45)

LIN
Late 1950s (78)

LIN
Late 1950s (45)

LIN
Ca. 1960 (45)

LITTLE WONDER
Ca. 1915 (78)
5½" record

LITTLE WONDER
Late 'Teens (78)
5½" record

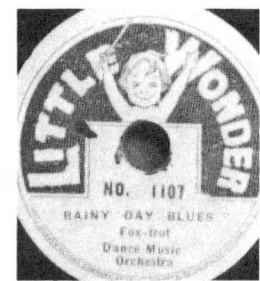

LITTLE WONDER
Ca. 1918 (78)
5½" record

LLOYDS
Late 1950s (45)

LODE
Late 1950s (45)

LODE
Late 1950s (45)

LONDON
Early 1950s (78)

LONGHORN
Early 1960s (45)

LOST-NITE
Mid 1960s (45)
Reissue Label

LUCKY
Mid 1950s (45)

LUCKY
Ca. 1960 (45)

LUCKY FOUR
Ca. 1960 (45)

LUCKY SEVEN
Ca. 1950 (45)

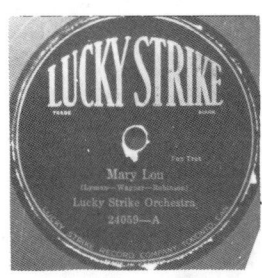

LUCKY STRIKE
Mid 1920s (78)
Canadian

LUDWIG
Late 1950s (45)

LUNA
Mid 1950s (45)

LUNIVERSE
Late 1950s (78)

LUNIVERSE
Late 1950s (45)

LUNIVERSE
Late 1950s (78)

LUNIVERSE
Late 1950s (45)

LYNN
Early 1960s (45)

LYRIC RECORD
Ca. 1919 (78)

LYRIC
Ca. 1919 (78)

LYRIC
Ca. 1920 (78)

LYRIC
Early 1950s (78)

LYRIC
Ca. 1960 (45)

MGM
Late 1950s (78)

MGM
Late 1950s (45)

MGM
Mid 1950s (L.P.)

MacGREGOR
Mid 1930s (78)
(transcription)

MacGREGOR
Mid 1930s (78)
(transcription)

MACY'S
Ca. 1950 (78)

MADISON
Late 1920s (78)

MAGNOLIA
Ca. 1950 (78)

MAH'S
Early 1960s (45)

MAIL CALL
Early 1960s (45)

MAJESTIC
Late 1940s (78)

MAJOR
Late 1930s (78)

MAJOR
Late 1950s (45)

MANCO
Ca. 1960 (45)

**MANHATTAN
RECORD**
Ca. 1910 (78)

MANOR
Late 1940s (78)

MARATHON
Ca. 1950 (78)

MARCONI
Ca. 1910 (78)

MARCONI
Reverse

MARTIN
Ca. 1950 (78)

MAR-VEL
Late 1950s (45)

MASTER
Late 1930s (78)

MASTER
Late 1940s (78)

MASTER
Ca. 1960 (45)

MASTERTONE
Early 1920s (78)

MAXSA
Mid 1920s (78)

MELADEE
Late 1950s (45)

MEDALLION
Ca. 1919 (78)

MEDALLION
Ca. 1920 (78)

MEDIA
Mid 1950s (78)

MELBA
Late 1950s (45)

MELLOW
Ca. 1950 (78)

MELODISC
Early 1920s (78)

MELODISC
Late 1940s (78)

MELODY
Ca. 1923 (78)

MELODY
Ca. 1950 (78)

MELOTONE
Early 1930s (78)

MELOTONE
Ca. 1937 (78)

MEMO
Early 1950s (78)

MEMO
Ca. 1950 (78)

MERCER
Ca. 1950 (78)

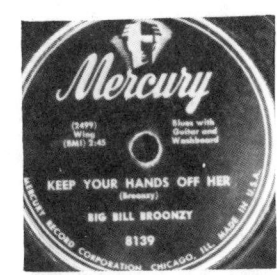

MERCURY
800 Series (78)
Rhythm & Blues
Early 1950s

MERCURY
Mid 1950s (45)

MERCURY
Late 1950s (78)

MERCURY
Late 1950s (45)

MERCURY
Late 1950s (45)

MERCURY
Late 1950s (L.P.)

MERIDIAN
Ca. 1960 (45)

MERITT
Ca. 1927 (78)

METEOR
Mid 'Teens (78)

METEOR
Mid 1950s (78)

METEOR
Mid 1950s (45)

METEOR
Late 1950s (45)

METRO
Late 1950s (45)

**METRO-
GOLDWYNMAYER**
Ca. 1929 (78)

METROTONE
Ca. 1950 (78)

MICROPHONE
Mid 1920s (78)
(Canadian)

**MIDNIGHT
RECORDS**
Late 1940s (78)

MILTONE
(Label Design Varies)
Late 1940s (78)

MILTONE
Late 1940s (78)

MILTONE
Late 1940s (78)

MINIT
Ca. 1960 (45)

MINOR
Late 1950s (45)

MIRACLE
Late 1940s (78)

MIRWOOD
Ca. 1960 (45)

MITCHELL
Mid 1920s (78)

MODE
Late 1950s (45)

**MODERN
(HOLLYWOOD)**
1950s (78)

MODERN
Mid 1950s (45)

MODERN (MUSIC)
Late 1940s (78)

MODERN (MUSIC)
Late 1940s (78)

MOHAWK
Ca. 1960 (45)

**MONARCH
RECORD**
Ca. 1906 (78)

MONEY
Late 1950s (45)

MONTEL
Ca. 1960 (45)

**MONTGOMERY
WARD**
Mid 1930s (78)

**MONTGOMERY
WARD**
Late 1930s (78)

MONUMENT
Early 1960s (45)

MOOD
Mid 1950s (78)

MOTOWN
Ca. 1960 (45)

MOVIN'
Ca. 1960 (45)

MOULDIE FYGGE
Late 1940s (78)
(Collectors series)

MUSE
Early 1920s (78)

MUSIC CITY
Late 1950s (45)

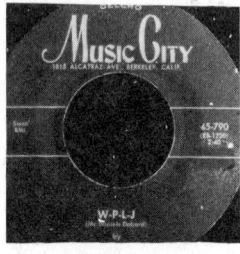

MUSIC CITY
Late 1950s (45)

MUSIC CITY
Ca. 1960 (45)

MUSICNOTE
Ca. 1960 (45)

35

MUSICRAFT
Late 1940s (78)

NRC
Ca. 1958 (45)

NRC
1960 (45)

NADSCO
Early 1920s (78)

NASCO
Late 1950s (78)

NATIONAL
Mid 1920s (78)

NATIONAL
Late 1940s (78)

NATIONAL MUSIC LOVERS
Mid 1920s (45)

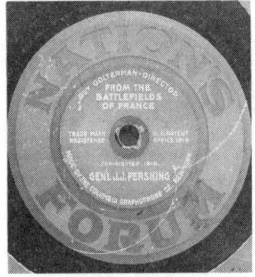
NATION'S FORUM
Ca. 1918 (78)

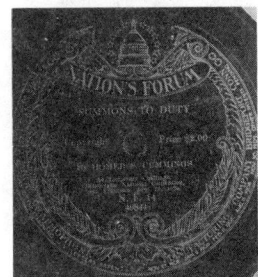
NATION'S FORUM
Early 1920s (78)

NATURAL
Ca. 1950 (78)

NEW COMFORT
Mid 1920s (78)

NEW FLEXO
Ca. 1925 (78)

NEW PHONIC
Ca. 1928 (78)

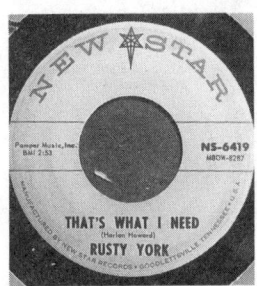
NEW STAR
Ca. 1960 (45)

NIKE
Late 1950s (45)

NOCTURNE
Ca. 1940 (78)

NORDSKOG
Ca. 1922 (78)

NORDSKOG
Early 1920s (78)

NORDSKOG
Ca. 1951 (78)

NORMAN
Late 1950s (45)

NORTHERN
Late 1950s (45)

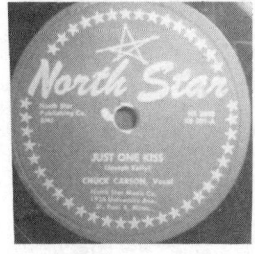
NORTH STAR
Mid 1950s (78)

NOR-VA-JAK
Late 1950s (45)

NOTE
Mid 1950s (45)

NUCRAFT
Ca. 1950   (78)

OT
Ca. 1950   (78)

ODEON
Early 1920s   (78)

ODEON
(American) Ca. 1930 (78)

OKEH
Late 'Teens   (78)

OKEH
Ca. 1920   (78)
Lateral

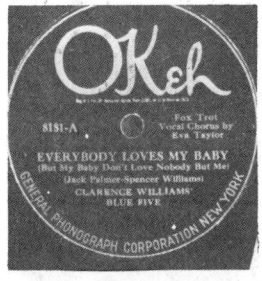

OKEH
Early 1920s   (78)
Race Series

OKEH
Mid 1920s   (78)

OKEH
Ca. 1926   (78)

OKEH
Mid 1920s   (78)
Race Series

OKEH
Ca. 1927   (78)

OKEH
Ca. 1930   (78)

OKEH
Note: 8000 Series is "race"
45000 Series is Hillbilly
Early 1930s   (78)

OKEH
Ca. 1931   (78)
Seger Ellis Logo

OKEH
1940-1942   (78)

OKEH
Late 1950s   (45)

OKLAHOMA
Late 1950s   (45)

**OLD SWING
MASTER**
Late 1940s   (78)

OLD TOWN
Mid 1950s   (45)

OLD TOWN
Late 1950s   (78)

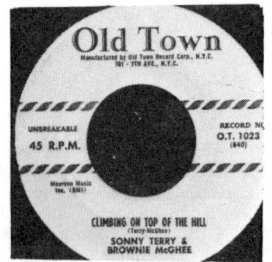

OLD TOWN
Late 1950s   (45)

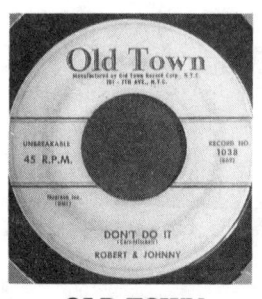

OLD TOWN
Late 1950s   (45)

OLIMPIC
Ca. 1960   (45)

OLYMPIC
Early 1920s   (78)

ONYX
Late 1950s   (45)

ONYX
Late 1950s (45)

OPAL
Ca. 1950 (78)

OPERA
Ca. 1950 (78)

OPERAPHONE
Ca. 1919 (78)

ORBIT
Mid 1950s (45)

ORBIT
Ca. 1959 (45)

ORIOLE
Early-Mid 1920s (78)

ORIOLE
Late 1920s (78)
Early 1930s

ORIOLE
Ca. 1960 (45)

**OXFORD DISC
RECORD**
Ca. 1905 (78)

**OXFORD DISC
RECORD**
Ca. 1909 (78)

PACEMAKER
Ca. 1950 (78)

PACIFIC
Late 1940s (78)

PAM-NOR
Ca. 1950 (78)

PARADISE
Late 1940s (78)

PARAGON
Ca. 1950 (78)

PARAMOUNT
BLACK SWAN
Ca. 1926 (78)

PARAMOUNT
Early 1920s (78)

PARAMOUNT
Race Series (78)
12-13000 Series
Late 1920s

PARAMOUNT
Hillbilly 3000 series (78)
Late 1920s

PARIS
Late 1950s (45)

PARK
Late 1950s (45)

PARKWAY
Ca. 1960 (45)

PARLOPHONE
Late 1920s (78)

PARLOPHONE
Late 1920s (78) (English)

PARROT
Mid 1950s (45)

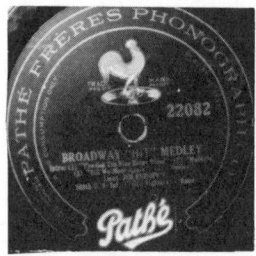

PATHE
Late Teens-Early 1920s (78)

PATHE
Ca. 1921 (78)

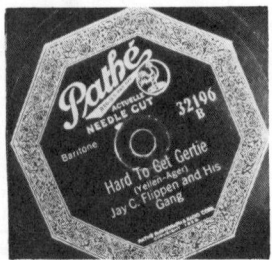

PATHE ACTUELLE
Mid-Late 1920s (78)

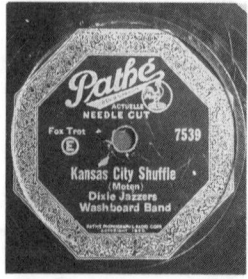

PATHE-ACTUELLE
Race Series Late 1920s (78)

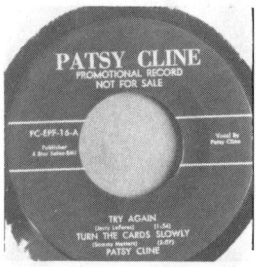

PATSY CLINE
Late 1950s (EP)

PEACOCK
Mid 1950s (78)

PEACOCK
Late 1950s (45)

PEAK
Ca. 1950 (78)

PEARL
Late 1950s (45)

PEN JOY
Late 1950s (45)

PENNINGTON
Ca. 1924 (78)

PENTHOUSE
Late 1950s (45)

PEPPER
Early 1960s (45)

PERFECT
Ca. 1922 (78)

**PERFECT
(STAR SERIES)**
Mid-Late 1920s (78)

PERFECT
Mid-Late 1920s (78)

PERFECT
Late 1920s (78)

PERFECT
Early 1930s (78)

PERFECT
Early 1930s (78)

PERFECT
Ca. 1937 (78)

PERFECT
Late 1950s (45)

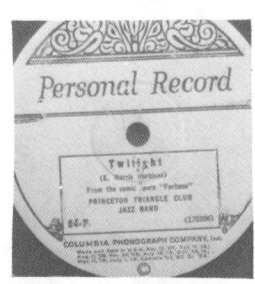

PERSONAL RECORD
Ca. 1927 (78)

PERSONAL
Late 1920s (78)

**PERSONAL
RECORDING**
Ca. 1928 (78)

PERSONALITY
Late 1940s (78)

PERSONALITY
Late 1950s (45)

PETAL
Early 1960s (45)

PETITE
Late 1950s (45)

PHAMOUS
Ca. 1950 (78)

PHANTASIE
Early 1920s (78)

PHILCO
"Hip Pocket"
Ca. 1968 (45)
3⅞" diam.

PHILHARMONIC
Ca. 1940 (78)

PHILLES
Early 1960s (45)

PHILLIPS
Late 1950s (78)

PHILLIPS
Late 1950s (78)

PHILO
Late 1940s (78)

**PHONO-CUT
RECORD**
Ca. 1919 (78)

PIC 1
Ca. 1960 (45)

PICTURE
Late 1950s (45)

PIKE
Ca. 1960 (45)

PILGRIM
Late 1950s (45)

PILGRIM
Late 1950s (78)

PILGRIM
Mid 1950s (78)

PINK
Late 1950s (45)

PLA-BAC
Mid 1950s (78)

PLUS
Late 1950s (45)

POLK
Ca. 1930 (78)

PONTIAC
Ca. 1960 (45)

POPLAR
Ca. 1960 (45)

PREMIUM
Late 1940s (78)

PREMIUM
Late 1950s (45)

PRESTIGE
Mid 1950s (45)

PRINCESS
Early 1960s (45)

PROCESS
Ca. 1950 (78)

PROFILE
Late 1950s (45)

PUBLIX
Ca. 1930 (78)

PURETONE
Mid 1920s (78)

PURITAN
Ca. 1920 (78)

PURITAN
Early 1920s (78)

PURITAN
Early 1920s (78)

PURITAN
Mid 1920s (78)

PURITAN
Ca. 1927 (78)

PURITONE
Ca. 1920 (78)

PURITONE
Late 1920s (78)

Q.R.S.
7000 "Race Series"
9000 Series is
Hillbilly (78)

Q.R.S.
Ca. 1930 (78)

QUE
Late 1950s (45)

QUEEN
Late 1940s (78)

R n B
Late 1950s (45)

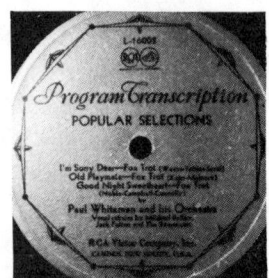

RCA VICTOR
Program Transcription
Early 1930s (L.P.)

RCA VICTOR
Ca. 1933 (78)
(obverse)

RCA VICTOR
Jimmie Rodgers (78)
(reverse)

RCA VICTOR
Mid 1950s (78)

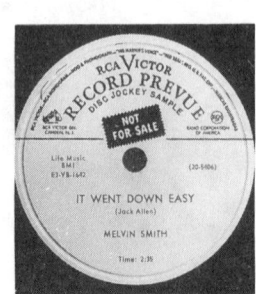

RCA VICTOR
Ca. 1952 (78) D.J. Copy

RCA VICTOR
Early 1950s (45)

RCA VICTOR
Early 1950s (45)

RCA VICTOR
Late 1950s (78)

RCA VICTOR
Mid 1950s (45)

RCA VICTOR
Ca. 1956-59 (L.P.)

RCA VICTOR
Ca. 1960-1963 (L.P.)

RCA VICTOR
Late 1950s (33⅓)
(7-inch record)

RPM
Early 1950s (45)

RPM
Early 1950s (78)

RPM
Late 1950s (45)

RADIEX
Ca. 1924 (78)

RADIEX
Late 1920s (78)

RADIO
Ca. 1960 (45)

RADIO ARTIST
Ca. 1950 (78)

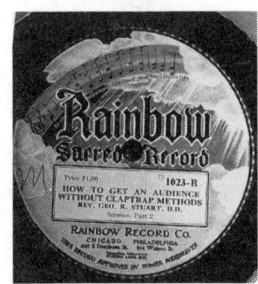

RAINBOW
Early 1920s (78)
Sacred Record

RAINBOW
Mid 1920s (78)

RAINBOW
Mid 1950s (78)

RAINBOW
Early 1950s (45)

RAM RECORDS
Late 1950s (45)

RAMA
Mid 1950s (78)

RAMA
Mid 1950s (45)

RAMA
Rhythm & Blues
Late 1950s (45)

RAVEN
Ca. 1950 (78)

RAYMOND
Ca. 1950 (78)

RAYS
Mid 1950s (45)

RECORTE
Late 1950s (45)

RED BARN RECORD
Early 1950s (78)

RED BIRD
Ca. 1950 (78)

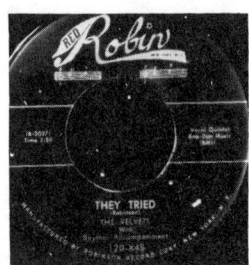

RED ROBIN
Rhythm & Blues
Mid 1950s (45)

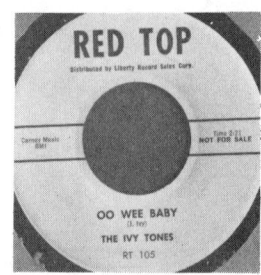

RED TOP
Late 1950s (45)

RED TOP
Late 1950s (45)

REELFOOT
Late 1950s (45)

REGAL
Late 1920s (78)

REGAL
Early 1920s to Early 1930s

REGAL
Late 1940s (78)

REGENT
Late 1940s (78)

REINA
Ca. 1950 (78)

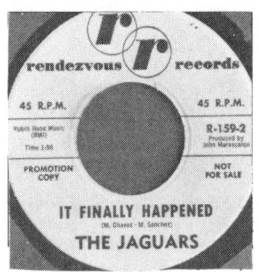

**RENDEZVOUS
RECORDS**
Ca. 1960 (45)

RENNER
Early 1960 (45)

REO
Ca. 1959 (78)
(Canadian)

REPUBLIC
Ca. 1950 (78)

REPUBLIC
Mid 1950s (45)

REPUBLIC
Ca. 1960 (45)

RESERVE
Late 1950s (45)

RESONA
Early 1920s (78)

RESONA
Ca. 1924 (78)

REV
Late 1950s (45)

REX RECORD
Late 'Teens (78)

REX
Ca. 1918 (78)

REX
Ca. 1960 (45)

RHUMBOOGIE
Late 1940s (78)

RHYTHM
Early 1950s (78)

RHYTHM
Mid 1950s (45)

RIALTO
Early 1920s (78)

RIC
Rhythm & Blues
Ca. 1960 (45)

RIC
Early 1960s (45)

RICH-R'-TONE
Ca. 1950 (78)

RICH-TONE
Ca. 1922 (78)

RIVERMONT
Late 1950s (45)

ROCKET
Ca. 1950 (78)

ROCKIN'
Mid 1950s (45)

ROME
Ca. 1960 (45)

ROMEO
Late 1920s (78)

ROMEO
Ca. 1930s (78)

ROMEO
Ca. 1932 (78)

ROMEO
Early 1930s (78)

ROMEO
Ca. 1937 (78)

RON
Late 1950s (78)

RON
Late 1950s (45)

ROOST
Ca. 1950 (78)

ROULETTE
Late 1950s (78)

ROULETTE
Late 1950s (78)

ROULETTE
Late 1950s (45)

ROULETTE
Late 1950s (78)

ROULETTE
Late 1950s (45)

ROULETTE
Ca. 1960 (L.P.)

ROYAL
Ca. 1922 (78)

ROYAL ROOST
Mid 1950s (45)

ROYAL ROOST
Mid 1950s (78)

ROYALE
Ca. 1940 (78)

ROYALTY
Late 1940s (78)

RUDDER RECORDS
Ca. 1950 (78)

RUST
Ca. 1960 (45)

S D
Late 1940s (78)

S D
Late 1940s (78)

S & G
Mid 1950s (45)

S M R
Ca. 1950 (78)

S.R.C.
Late 1950s (45)

SABINA
Ca. 1960 (45)

SABRA
Ca. 1960 (45)

SABRE
Early 1950s (78)

SABRE
Mid 1950s (45)

SABRINA
Late 1950s (45)

SAGE
Late 1950s (78)

SAGE
Late 1950s (45)

SANDY
Late 1950s (45)

SAPPHIRE
Mid 1950s (45)

SARG
Late 1950s (45)

SATIN
Ca. 1960 (45)

SAVOY
Ca. 1930 (78)

SAVOY
Ca. 1950 (78)
Reissue

SAVOY
Rhythm & Blues
Ca. 1950 (78)

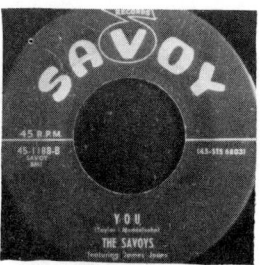

SAVOY
Rhythm & Blues
Late 1950s

SCARLET
Ca. 1960 (45)

SCEPTER
Early 1960s (45)

SCOOP
Ca. 1950 (78)

SCORE
Late 1940s (78)

SCOTTIE
Ca. 1960 (45)

SCOTTY'S
Late 1940s (78)

SEE BEE
Early 1920s (78)

SELECTIVE
Ca. 1950 (78)

SELMA
Late 1950s (45)

SENSATION
Late 1940s (78)

SESSION
Jazz 1940s (78)

SEVEN ELEVEN
Mid 1950s (78)

SEVEN ELEVEN
Mid 1950s (45)

SHADE
Late 1950s (45)

SHAN-TODD
Ca. 1960 (45)

SHARP
Early 1960s (45)

SHELL
Ca. 1960 (45)

SHO-BIZ
Ca. 1959 (45)

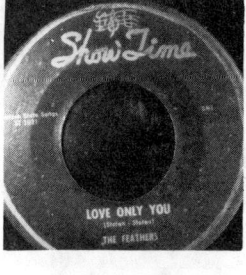

SHOW TIME
Mid 1950s (78)

SHOWTIME
Mid 1950s (45)

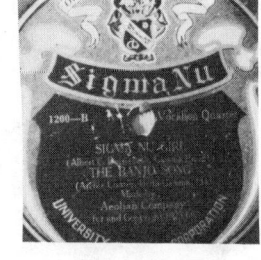

SIGMA NU
Ca. 1924 (78)

SIGNATURE
Late 1940s (78)

SIGNATURE
Late 1940s (78)

SILHOUETTE
Late 1950s (45)

SILVERTONE
Ca. 1916 (78)

SILVERTONE
Ca. 1916 (78)

SILVERTONE
Ca. 1920 (78)

SILVERTONE
Mid 1920s (78)

SIMS
Late 1950s (45)

SINGULAR
Late 1950s (45)

SIR
Late 1950s (45)

SITTIN' IN WITH
Ca. 1950 (78)

SITTIN' IN WITH
Early 1950s (45)

SKYLA
Ca. 1960 (45)

SKYLARK
Mid 1950s (78)

SKYSTREAK
Ca. 1949 (78)

SKYWAY
Ca. 1950 (78)

SLIM WILLET
Ca. 1956 (78)

SMASH
Ca. 1960 (45)

SMOKE
Late 1950s (45)

SOLO
Ca. 1950 (78)

SONORA
Late 1940s (78)

SOUND
Late 1950 (45)

SOUND TEX
Early 1960s (45)

SPANGLE
Late 1950s (45)

SPAR
Ca. 1960 (45)

SPARK
Mid 1950s (78)

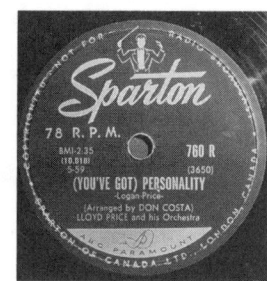

SPARK
Mid 1950s (45)

SPARK
Rhythm & Blues
Mid 1950s (45)

SPARKELL
Late 1950s (45)

SPARTAN
Early 1960s (45)

SPARTON
Ca. 1959 (78)
Canadian

SPECIAL
Ca. 1923 (78)

SPECIAL EDITIONS
1940s (78)

SPECIAL RECORD
Ca. 1927 (78)

SPECIALTY
Ca. 1950 (78)

SPECIALTY
1950s (78)

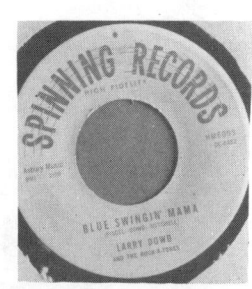

SPECIALTY
1950s (45)

SPEED
Early 1950s (78)

SPEED
Late 1950s (45)

SPINNA
Late 1940s (78)

SPINNING
Late 1950s (45)

SPIRE
Late 1950s (78)

SPOTLIGHT
Late 1950s (45)

STACY
Ca. 1960 (45)

STAFF
Ca. 1947 (78)

STAFF
Mid 1950s (45)

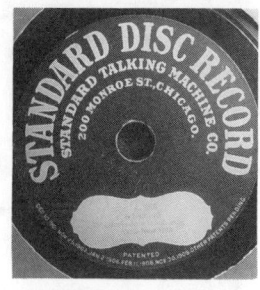

**STANDARD DISC
RECORD**
Ca. 1912 (78)

**STANDARD DISC
RECORD**
Ca. 1914 (78)

**STANDARD DISC
RECORD**
Ca. 1915 (78)

**STANDARD DISC
RECORD**
Ca. 1915 (78)

**STANDARD DISC
RECORD**
Ca. 1915 (78)

STAR RECORD
Ca. 1912 (78)

STAR RECORD
Ca. 1914 (78)

STAR X
Late 1950s (45)

STARCK
Mid 1920s (78)

STARDAY
Mid 1950s (78)

STARDAY
Late 1950s (45)

STARDAY
Late 1950s (45)

STARDAY
Early 1960s (45)

STARLIGHT
Ca. 1950 (78)

STARR
Ca. 1921 (78)

STAR GENNETT
Early 1920s (78)

STARRETT
Ca. 1960 (45)

STARTIME
Ca. 1959 (45)

STATES
Mid 1950s (78)

STATES
Mid 1950s (45)

STATUE
Early 1960s (45)

STERLING
Ca. 1930 (78)

STERLING
Late 1940s (78)

STERLING
Late 1950s (45)

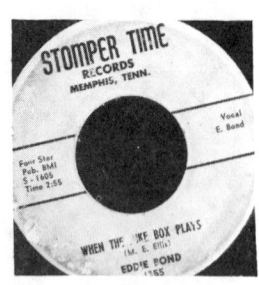

STOMPER TIME
Late 1950s (45)

STORM
Ca. 1960 (45)

SUAVE
Late 1950s (45)

SUE
Late 1950s (45)

SUEDE
Late 1950s (45)

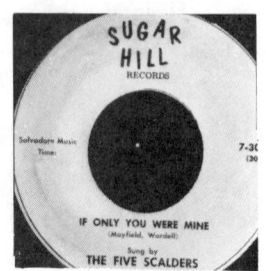

SUGAR HILL
Mid 1950s (45)

SULLIVAN
Late 1950s (45)

SUMMIT
Late 1950s (45)

SUN RECORD
Ca. 1914 (78)

SUN
Mid 1950s (78)

SUN
Mid 1950s (45)

SUN
Late 1950s (33)

SUN (DJ COPY)
Mid 1960s (45)

SUNBEAM
Late 1950s (45)

SUNBIRD RECORDS
Mid 1950s (45)

SUNDOWN
Late 1950s (45)

SUNRISE
Ca. 1929 (78)

SUNRISE
Ca. 1933 (78)

SUNRISE
Late 1940s (78)

SUNRISE
Late 1940s (78)

SUNSET
Mid 1920s (78)

SUNSET
1940s (78)

SUNSHINE
Early 1920s (78)

SUNSHINE
Late 1940s (78)

SUPER DISC
Late 1940s (78)

SUPERIOR
Ca. 1928 (78)

SUPERIOR
Ca. 1930 (78)

SUPERIOR
Ca. 1950 (78)

SUPERTONE
Ca. 1925 (78)

SUPERTONE
Late 1920s (78)

SUPERTONE
Ca. 1927 (78)

SUPREME
Ca. 1926 (78)

SUPREME
Ca. 1950s (78)

SUPREME
Early 1960s (45)

SURE
Late 1950s (45)

SURF
Late 1950s (45)

SWAN
Late 1950s (45)

SWAN
Early 1960s (45)

SWING
Late 1940s (78)

SWING BEAT
Late 1940s (78)

SWINGIN'
Early 1960s (45)

SWING TIME
Early 1950s (78)

SWING TIME
Early 1950s (45)

SYMPHONOLA
Ca. 1919 (78)

TNT
Early 1950s (78)

TNT
Late 1950s (78)

TNT
Mid 1950s (45)

TNT
Late 1950s (45)

TNT
Late 1950s (45)

TNT
Late 1950s (45)

TALENT
Ca. 1950 (78)

TALENT
Early 1960s (45)

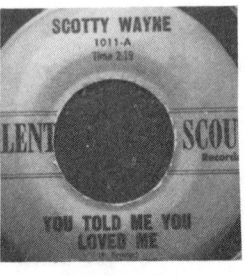

TALENT SCOUT
Ca. 1959 (45)

TALLY
Ca. 1960 (45)

TAMLA
1959-60 (45)

TAMLA
Ca. 1960 (45)

TAMPA
Late 1950s (78)

TAMPA
Late 1950s (45)

TARA
Ca. 1959 (45)

TEE GEE
Late 1950s (45)

TEEN
Mid 1950s (78)

TEENAGE
Mid 1950s (45)

TEEN LIFE
Late 1950s

TELL
Late 1940s (78)

TEMPO
Early 1950s (78)

TENDER
Late 1950s (45)

TENNESSEE
Early 1950s (78)

TENNESSEE
Mid 1950s (78)

TENNESSEE
Mid 1950s (45)

TERP
Mid 1950s (45)

TERRACE
Late 1950s (45)

TETRA
Late 1950s (78)

TETRA
Late 1950s (45)

TEXADISC
Ca. 1951 (78)

TEX-TALENT
Early 1950s (78)

THANKS!
Ca. 1960 (45)

THELMA
Early 1960s (45)

THEME
Ca. 1950 (78)

**THE THOMAS
RECORD**
Ca. 1915 (78)

TIFFANY
Early 1950s (78)

TILT
Early 1960s (45)

TIME
Late 1950s (45)

TIMELY
Mid 1950s (45)

TIMELY TUNES
Early 1930s (78)

TIN PAN ALLEY
Late 1950s (45)

TIP TOP
Late 1950s (45)

TIP TOP
Late 1950s (45)

TITAN
Late 1950s (45)

TONE
Late 1950s (45)

TOP HAT
Late 1940s (78)

TOP HAT
Ca. 1950 (78)

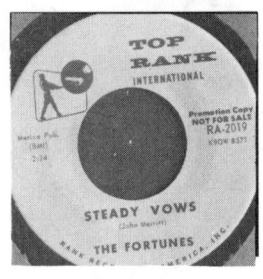

TOP RANK
Ca. 1960 (45)

TOP TEN
Ca. 1947 (78)

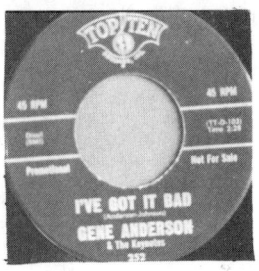

TOP TEN
Early 1960s (45)

TOP TUNE
Ca. 1950 (78)

TOPS
Ca. 1950 (78)

TORCH
Ca. 1950 (78)

TOWN & COUNTRY
Late 1940s (78)

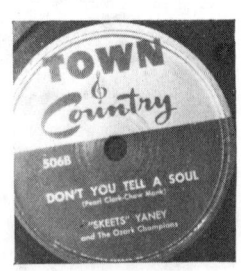

TOWN & COUNTRY
Late 1940s (78)

TREAT
Mid 1950s (78)

TREL
Ca. 1960 (45)

TREMONT
Mid 1920s (78)

TREND
Ca. 1960 (45)

TRESS
Late 1950s (45)

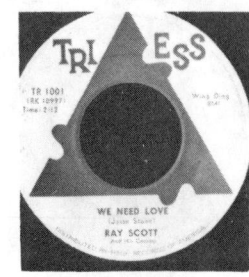

TRI ESS
Early 1960s (45)

TRIANGLE
Early 1920s (78)

TRIDELT
Early 1960s (45)

TRILON
Late 1940s (78)

TRIUMPH
Ca. 1960 (45)

TROPHY
Late 1950s (45)

TRUMPET
Mid 1950s (78)

TRUMPET
Mid 1950s (45)

TURF
Late 1950s (45)

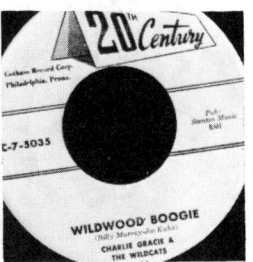

20th CENTURY
Mid 1950s (45)

**TWENTIETH
CENTURY**
Late 1950s (45)

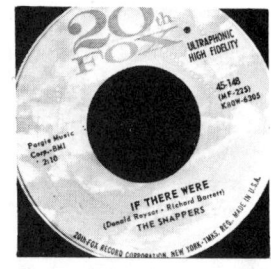

20th FOX
Late 1950s (45)

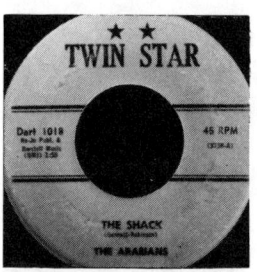

TWIN STAR
Late 1950s (45)

TWIRL
Ca. 1960 (45)

U.H.C.A.
Late 1930s (78)
Collectors Series

U.S.A.
Early 1960s (45)

ULTRA
Late 1950s (45)

UNITED
Ca. 1950 (78)

UNITED
Ca. 1950 (78)

UNITED
Ca. 1951 (78)

UNITED
Mid 1950s (78)

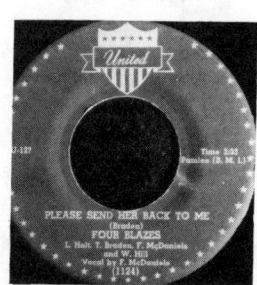

UNITED
Rhythm & Blues
Mid 1950s (45)

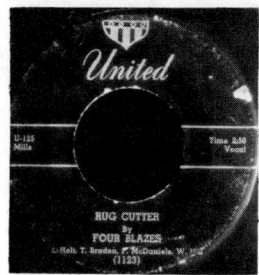

UNITED
Rhythm & Blues
Early 1950s (45)

UNITY
Ca. 1925 (78)

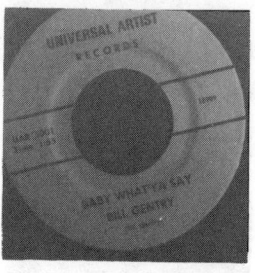

UNIVERSAL ARTIST
Ca. 1960 (45)

UNIVERSAL-FOX
Ca. 1950 (78)

UNIVERSITY
Late 1940s (78)

UP-TO-DATE
Ca. 1924 (78)

UPTOWN
Ca. 1950 (78)

**URBAN RECORD
COMPANY**
Ca. 1949 (78)

VADEN
Late 1950s (45)

VADEN
Late 1950s (45)

VALLEY
Late 1950s (45)

**VALLEY'S
MEADOWLARK**
Late 1950s (45)

VALOR
Ca. 1960 (45)

VAN
Late 1950s (45)

VANDAN
Late 1950s (45)

VAN DYKE
Ca. 1930 (78)

VAN-ES
Ca. 1950 (78)

VARIETY
Mid 1920s (78)

VARIETY
Late 1930s (78)

VARSITY
Ca. 1940 (78)

V-DISC
Ca. 1947 (78) 12 inch
Issued for armed forces.

VEE
Late 1950s (45)

VEE-JAY
Mid 1950s (78)

VEE-JAY
Late 1950s (L.P.)

VEE-JAY
Early 1960s (45)

VEGA
Early 1960s (45)

VEL-TONE
Late 1950s (45)

VELTONE
Mid 1950s (45)

VELVET TONE
Late 1920s (78)

VELVET TONE
Ca. 1932 (78)

VENUS
Late 1950s (45)

VESTA
Late 1950s (45)

VICEROY
Late 1950s (45)

VICTOR
Ca. 1902 (78)
See also: "IMPROVED"

**VICTOR MONARCH
RECORD**
Ca. 1902 (78) 7-inch

**VICTOR MONARCH
RECORD**
Ca. 1902-1903 (78)

**VICTOR MONARCH
RECORD**
Ca. 1902 (78)

VICTOR RECORD
Ca. 1907 (78)

VICTOR RECORD
1910-1916 (78)

VICTOR
Ca. 1915 (78)

VICTOR
1917-Early 1920s (78)

VICTOR
Ca. 1925 (78)

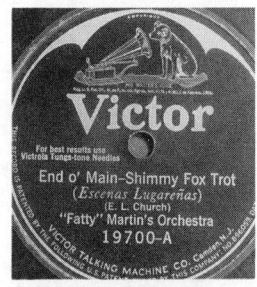

**VICTOR SPECIAL
RECORD**
Ca. 1923 (78)

VICTOR
Mid 1920s (78)

VICTOR
Special Record Late 1920s

VICTOR
"Hot Dance" V-38000
Series 1929-1930 (78)

VICTOR
V-38500 series
Ca. 1929 (78)

**VICTOR
"PICT-UR-MUSIC"**
Ca. 1930 (78)

VICTOR
Ca. 1932 (78)
Canadian

**VICTOR
"SWING CLASSIC"**
Mid 1930s (78)

VICTOR
Late 1930s (78)

VICTOR
1940s (78)
Collectors' reissue series

VIK
Late 1950s (78)

VIK
Mid 1950s (45)

VIN
Ca. 1960 (78)

VIN
Ca. 1960 (45)

VITA
Rhythm & Blues
Late 1950s (78)

VITA
Late 1950s (45)

VOCALION
Mid 1920s (78)

VOCALION
1000 Series "Race"
(78)

VOCALION
Early 1930s (78)

VOCALION
Ca. 1934 (78)

VOCALION
Mid 1930s (78)

VOCALION
Ca. 1937 (78)

VOCALION
Late 1930s (78)

VOGUE
Ca. 1950 (78)

VOGUE Picture Disc
Late 1940s (78)
Pictures vary

VOGUE Picture Disc
Another issue

VOGUE Picture Disc
Ca. 1947 Another issue
Representative of the series

VOGUE Picture Disc

**VOGUE PICTURE
RECORD**

**VOGUE PICTURE
RECORD**

**VOGUE PICTURE
RECORD**

**VOGUE PICTURE
RECORD**

**VOGUE PICTURE
RECORD**

**VOGUE PICTURE
RECORD**

**VOGUE PICTURE
RECORD**

**VOGUE PICTURE
RECORD**

**VOGUE PICTURE
RECORD**

**VOGUE PICTURE
RECORD**

VOGUE PICTURE RECORD

VOGUE PICTURE RECORD

VOGUE PICTURE RECORD

VOGUE PICTURE RECORD

VOGUE PICTURE RECORD

NOTE: The story of **Vogue Picture Records** including a discography, appeared in *Record Research*, numbers 148 (July, 1977) and 151/152 (January, 1978).

V-TONE
Late 1950s (45)

VULCAN
1920s (78)

VULCAN
Late 1950s (45)

WALDORF
Late 1950s (EP)

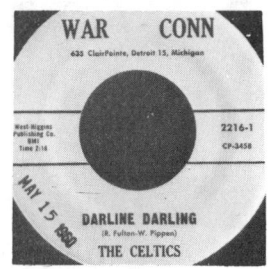

WAR CONN
Early 1960s (45)

WARNER BROS.
Early 1960s (45)

WARRIOR
1959-1960 (45)

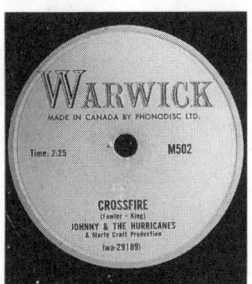

WARWICK
Ca. 1959 (78) Canadian

WASCO
Early 1950s (78)

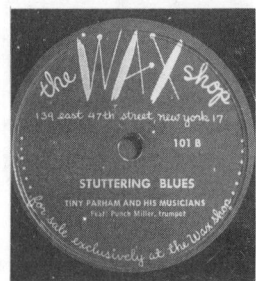

THE WAX SHOP
Ca. 1950 (78)

WAYSIDE
Late 1950s (45)

WELLS
Late 1950s (45)

WESTENAIR
Ca. 1950 (78)

WESTPORT
Late 1950s (45)

WHIPPET
Late 1950s (78)

WHIRLIN DISC
Late 1950s (45)

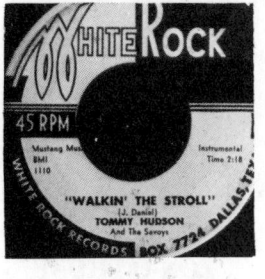

WHITE ROCK
Late 1950s (45)

WIGGS, INC.
Ca. 1950 (78)

WILDCAT
Early 1960s (45)

WINDSOR
Ca. 1950 (78)

WING
Late 1950s (78)

WING
Late 1950s (45)

WINLEY
Late 1950s (45)

WIZARD
Early 1960s (45)

WONDER
Late 1950s (45)

WOR FEATURE
Ca. 1940 (78)

WORLD RECORD
Ca. 1920 (78)

WORLD RECORD
Ca. 1918 (78)

WORLD RECORDS
Ca. 1950 (78)

"X"
Mid 1950s (78)

X-TRA
Late 1950s (45)

XYZ
Late 1950s (45)

"Y"
Late 1950s (45)

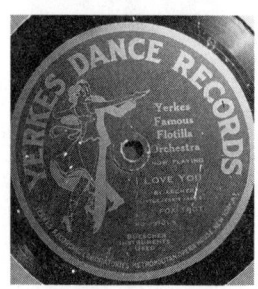

**YERKES DANCE
RECORDS**
Ca. 1921 (78)

YORK
Ca. 1950 (78)

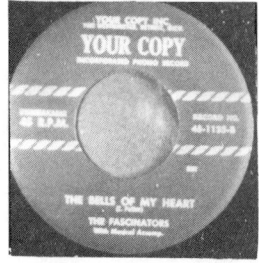

YOUR COPY
Late 1950s (45)

YUCCA
Late 1950s (45)

ZERO
Ca. 1961 (45)

**ZON-O-PHONE
RECORD**
Ca. 1901 (78)
Embossed Label

**ZON-O-PHONE
RECORD**
Ca. 1901 (78)
Embossed Label

**ZON-O-PHONE
RECORD**
1905-1910 (78)

**ZON-O-PHONE
RECORD**
1905-1910 (78)

ZON-O-PHONE
1907-1910 (78)

**ZON-O-PHONE
RECORD**
1910-1915 (78)

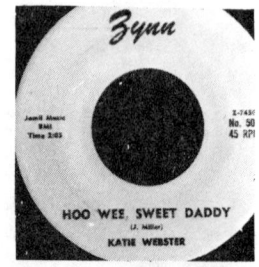

ZYNN
Early 1960s (45)

JAZZ, BIG BANDS, DANCE BANDS, PERSONALITY, "POP," RAGTIME
1900 to 1950 (approximately)
All records in this section are ten-inch 78 rpm unless otherwise indicated.

IRVING AARONSON & HIS COMMANDERS:
Columbia 2946-D *Pardon My Southern Accent* .. 10.00 - 15.00
Columbia 2980-D *Flirtation Walk* .... 10.00 - 15.00
Columbia 2981-D *Let's Be Thankful* .... 10.00 - 15.00
Columbia 3037-D *An Evening In June* .... 10.00 - 15.00
Columbia 3043-D *Commanderism* .... 15.00 - 20.00
Edison 51685 *Don't Wake Me Up* .... 5.00 - 8.00
Victor 20002, 20034, 20059, 20063, 20083,
 20094, 20095, 20100, 20117, 20473, 21451,
 21778, 21834, 21867 .... 4.00 - 7.00
Victor 20385 *Everything's Peaches* .... 5.00 - 8.00
Victor 21260 *Let's Misbehave* .... 5.00 - 8.00
Victor 21745 *Let's Do It* .... 5.00 - 8.00
Victor 21888 *Outside* .... 5.00 - 8.00
Vocalion 2535 *That's How Rhythm Was Born* ... 10.00 - 15.00
Vocalion 2536 *The Day You Came Along* ...... 7.00 - 10.00
Vocalion 2570, 2571 .... 5.00 - 8.00
Vocalion 25004 *Shadows on the Swanee* .... 10.00 - 15.00
Vocalion 25005 *I've Gotta Get Up And Go
To Work*........................... 10.00 - 15.00

LARRY ABBOTT & HIS ORCHESTRA:
Okeh 41044 *I'm More Than Satisfied* .... 25.00 - 40.00

**IRWIN ABRAMS & HIS (HOTEL
 MANAGER/KNICKERBOCKER GRILL)
 ORCHESTRA:**
Banner, *most titles* .... 3.00 - 5.00
Domino, *most titles* .... 3.00 - 5.00
Edison 51633 *The Co-Ed* .... 8.00 - 12.00
Edison 51625, 52106, 52107, 52114 .... 5.00 - 10.00
Edison 52148 *Dream Kisses* .... 15.00 - 20.00
Edison 52168 *Moon of Japan* .... 10.00 - 15.00
Okeh 40783, 40864, 40869, 40918, 40948 ...... 4.00 - 7.00
Okeh 40798 *Shanghai Dream Man* .... 7.00 - 10.00
Okeh 40846 *Magnolia*.................... 8.00 - 12.00

BERNARD ADDISON & HIS RHYTHM:
Bluebird 6144 *Lovely Liza Lee* .... 8.00 - 12.00
 6174 *Toledo Shuffle*................ 8.00 - 12.00

**ADRIAN & HIS ORCHESTRA/TAP ROOM
 GANG; ADRIAN'S RAMBLERS:**
Brunswick 6786 *Get Goin'* .... 8.00 - 12.00
 6877 *Why Don't You Practice What
 You Preach?* .... 8.00 - 12.00
 6889 *I Wish I Were Twins* .... 8.00 - 12.00
Columbia 2785-D *Happy As The Day Is Long* ... 15.00 - 20.00
Victor 25072 *Weather Man* .... 7.00 - 10.00
Victor 25085 *Nagasaki* .... 7.00 - 10.00
Victor 25208 *Honeysuckle Rose* .... 7.00 - 10.00

ANDREW AIONA'S NOVELTY FOUR:
Columbia 1728-D *Hula Girl* .... 10.00 - 15.00
 1788-D *That Lovin' Hula* .... 10.00 - 15.00

ALABAMA CREOLE BAND:
Claxtonola 40397 *Choo Choo* .... 10.00 - 15.00

ALABAMA FUZZY WUZZIES:
Champion 15366 *Fuzzy Wuzzy*............. 150.00 - 250.00
 15415 *Congo Stomp* .... 150.00 - 250.00

ALABAMA HARMONY BOYS:
Champion 15398 *Chicken Supper Strut* .... 150.00 - 250.00
Silvertone 5139 *Sweet Patootie* .... 150.00 - 200.00

ALABAMA JAZZ PIRATES:
Bell 1182 *Canned Heat Blues* .... 150.00 - 250.00

ALABAMA JUG BAND:
Decca 7000 *My Gal Sal* .... 10.00 - 15.00
Decca 7001 *Gulf Coast Blues* .... 10.00 - 15.00
Decca 7041 *Somebody Stole My Gal* .... 10.00 - 15.00
Decca 7042 *Crazy Blues* .... 10.00 - 15.00

ALABAMA RASCALS:
Titles, issued contemporaneously on Banner,

Melotone, Oriole, Perfect, Romeo: *Dirty
Dozen's Cousins, Endurance Stomp; Georgia
Grind; Jockey Stomp; Rukus Juice Shuffle;
Stomp That Thing*..................... 30.00 - 40.00

ALABAMA RED JACKETS:
Champion 15228 *You Can't Cry Over My
Shoulder* .... 8.00 - 12.00
Champion 15229 *I'm Gonna Meet My
Sweetie Now* .... 8.00 - 12.00

ALABAMA RED PEPPERS:
Titles, issued contemporaneously on Cameo,
Lincoln, Romeo: *The Drag; Eccentric; The
New Twister; Red Head Blues; Riverboat
Shuffle; San* .... 6.00 - 12.00
A Good Man Is Hard To Find .... 10.00 - 15.00

ALABAMA SERENADERS:
Champion 15140 *Alabama Stomp* .... 20.00 - 30.00
Champion 15213 *There Ain't No Maybe In My
Baby's Eyes* .... 10.00 - 15.00
Champion 15238 *Underneath the Weeping
Willow* .... 10.00 - 15.00
Champion 15239 *What Do I Care What
Somebody Said?* .... 10.00 - 15.00
Champion 15271 *South Wind* .... 10.00 - 15.00
Champion 15292 *I'm In Love Again* .... 10.00 - 15.00
Herwin 92044 *Congo Stomp* .... 200.00 - 300.00

ALABAMA WASHBOARD STOMPERS:
Vocalion 1546 *I Want A Little Girl* .... 20.00 - 30.00
Vocalion 1587 *Who Stole The Lock?* .... 20.00 - 30.00
Vocalion 1626 *I Surrender, Dear* .... 20.00 - 30.00
Vocalion 1630 *Corinne Corinna* .... 20.00 - 30.00
Vocalion 1635 *I Need Lovin'* .... 20.00 - 30.00
Vocalion 1684 *Can't We Talk It Over?* .... 20.00 - 30.00
Vocalion 1689 *If All The World Was Made
Of Glass* .... 20.00 - 30.00
Vocalion 1697 *Pepper Steak* .... 30.00 - 50.00

ALAMEDA WONDER PLAYERS/ORCH.:
Cardinal 501 *Black Eyed Blues* .... 15.00 - 25.00
 517 *Virginia Blues* .... 15.00 - 25.00
 527 *Lonesome Mammy Blues* .... 15.00 - 25.00
 540 *Stop Your Kidding* .... 15.00 - 25.00
 552 *Yankee Doodle Blues* .... 15.00 - 25.00
 559 *Sugar Blues* .... 15.00 - 25.00

DON ALBERT & HIS ORCHESTRA:
Vocalion 3401 *True Blue Lou* .... 10.00 - 15.00
Vocalion 3411 *The Sheik of Araby* .... 10.00 - 15.00
Vocalion 3423 *On The Sunny Side Of The Street* . 10.00 - 15.00
Vocalion 3491 *Liza* .... 10.00 - 15.00

AL ALBERTS & HIS ORCH.:
Cameo 8280 *You're My Sweetheart* .... 3.00 - 5.00
 8315 *The Jazz Patrol* .... 4.00 - 7.00
 8322 *In a Little Two-By-Four For Two* ... 5.00 - 8.00
 9142 *Building a Nest for Mary* .... 10.00 - 15.00
 9157 *That's My Idea of Heaven* .... 3.00 - 5.00
 9167 *My Rock-A-Bye Baby* .... 7.00 - 10.00

9194 *With Some One Like You*	7.00 -	10.00
9213 *Who Ya Gonna Fool*	5.00 -	8.00
9299 *Where the Sweet Forget-Me-Nots Remember*	5.00 -	8.00
Romeo 959 *That's My Idea Of Heaven*	3.00 -	5.00

JACK ALBIN'S ORCHESTRA; JACK ALBIN & HIS HOTEL PENNSYLVANIA MUSIC:

Crown 3002, 3006, 3012, 3013, 3029, 3047, 3069, 3089, 3091, 3098	5.00 -	10.00
Edison 51811 *Wasn't It Nice?*	10.00 -	15.00
Edison 51829 *Hugs And Kisses*	15.00 -	20.00
Edison 51831 *The Two Of Us*	10.00 -	15.00
Edison 51851 *Cover Me Up With Sunshine*	15.00 -	20.00
Edison 51852 *I Found A Million Dollar Baby*	15.00 -	20.00

VAN ALEXANDER & HIS ORCHESTRA:

Bluebird, various titles	3.00 -	6.00
Varsity, various titles	3.00 -	6.00

HENRY ALLEN (JR.) HIS (NEW YORK) ORCHESTRA; HENRY ALLEN-COLEMAN HAWKINS & THEIR ORCHESTRA:

Titles, issued contemporaneously on Banner, Melotone, Oriole, Perfect, Romeo: *"Aintcha Got Music?"*, *"Believe I, Beloved,"* *"Dark Clouds,"* *"Don't Let Your Love Go Wrong,"* *"How's About Tomorrow Night?"*, *"I Never Slept A Wink Last Night,"* *"It's Written All Over Your Face,"* *"I Wish I Were Twins,"* *"My Galveston Gal,"* *"Pardon My Southern Accent,"* *"The River's Takin' Care Of Me,"* *"Rug Cutter Swing,"* *"Shadows On The Swanee,"* *"Smooth Sailing,"* *"Stringin' Alone On A Shoe String,"* *"There's A House In Harlem For Sale,"* *"Whose Honey Are You?,"* *"Why Don't You Practice What You Preach?",* *"You're Gonna Lose Your Gal"*	7.00 -	12.00
Victor 23006 *Patrol Wagon Blues*	40.00 -	60.00
Victor 23338 *Singing Pretty Songs*	100.00 -	150.00
Victor 38073 *It Should Be You*	35.00 -	50.00
Victor 38080 *Feeling Drowsy*	35.00 -	50.00
Victor 38121 *Dancing Dave*	40.00 -	60.00
Victor 38140 *Sugar Hill Function*	50.00 -	75.00
Vocalion 2956 *Get Rhythm In Your Feet*	10.00 -	15.00
Vocalion 2965 *Rosetta*	8.00 -	12.00
Vocalion 2997 *I Wished On The Moon*	8.00 -	12.00
Vocalion 2998 *Dinah Lou*	8.00 -	12.00
Vocalion 3097 *Red Sails In The Sunset*	7.00 -	10.00
Vocalion 3098 *On Treasure Island*	7.00 -	10.00
Vocalion 3214 *I'll Bet You Tell That To All The Girls*	7.00 -	10.00
Vocalion 3215 *Every Minute Of The Hour*	7.00 -	10.00
Vocalion 3244 *Would You?*	7.00 -	10.00
Vocalion 3245 *Nothing's Blue But The Sky*	8.00 -	12.00
Vocalion 3261 *Take My Heart*	7.00 -	10.00
Vocalion 3262 *You're Not The King*	7.00 -	10.00
Vocalion 3292 *Am I Asking Too Much?*	7.00 -	10.00
Vocalion 3302 *Algiers Stomp*	7.00 -	10.00
Vocalion 3305 *Out Where The Blues Begin*	7.00 -	10.00
Vocalion 3306 *Picture Me Without You*	7.00 -	10.00
Vocalion 3339 *Whatcha Gonna Do When There Ain't No Swing?*	7.00 -	10.00
Vocalion 3340 *Lost In My Dreams*	7.00 -	10.00
Vocalion 3377 *Did You Mean It?*	7.00 -	10.00
Vocalion 3389 *Here's Love In Your Eye*	7.00 -	10.00
Vocalion 3422 *Let's Put Our Heads Together*	7.00 -	10.00
Vocalion 3432 *He Ain't Got Rhythm*	8.00 -	12.00
Vocalion 3490 *There's A Kitchen Up In Heaven*	7.00 -	10.00
Vocalion 3524 *I Was Born To Swing*	7.00 -	10.00
Vocalion 3564 *Sticks And Stones*	7.00 -	10.00
Vocalion 3574 *Meet Me In The Moonlight*	7.00 -	10.00
Vocalion 3594 *The Merry-Go-Round Broke Down*	7.00 -	10.00
Vocalion 3607 *Till The Clock Strikes Three*	7.00 -	10.00
Vocalion 3690 *Can I Forget You?*	7.00 -	10.00

Vocalion 3704 *Have You Ever Been In Love*	7.00 -	10.00

ALL STAR BAND:

Victor 26144 *The Blues*	2.00 -	3.00

ALL STAR CALIFORNIANS:

Melotone 12000 *Cheerful Little Earful*	15.00 -	25.00
Melotone 12002 *Never Swat A Fly*	5.00 -	8.00

ALL STAR COLLEGIANS:

Titles, on Oriole, Perfect: *Now's The Time To Fall In Love; She's So Nice*	7.00 -	10.00
Other titles on Oriole, Perfect	3.00 -	5.00

ALL STAR ORCHESTRA:

Victor 21149 *Chloe*	5.00 -	8.00
21212 *My Melancholy Baby*	5.00 -	8.00
21326 *I Must Be Dreaming*	8.00 -	12.00
21423 *Oh, Baby!*	7.00 -	10.00
21605 *I'm More Than Satisfied*	7.00 -	10.00
21667 *There's a Rainbow 'Round My Shoulder*	5.00 -	8.00
22054 *My Dream Memory*	5.00 -	8.00
22073 *Waiting at the end of the Road*	5.00 -	8.00
22104 *Too Wonderful For Words*	7.00 -	10.00
22197 *Deep in the Arms of Love*	5.00 -	8.00

ALL-STAR RHYTHM BOYS:

Titles issued contemporaneously on Clarion, Diva, Velvet Tone: *Pardon Me, Pretty Baby; Sensation*	10.00 -	15.00

ALOMO GARDEN BAND/JAZZERS:

Buddy 8052 *Spanish Mamma*	50.00 -	75.00
Champion 15132 *St. Louis Hop*	8.00 -	12.00

OVIE ALSTON & HIS ORCHESTRA:

Vocalion 4448 *Junk Man's Serenade*	7.00 -	10.00
Vocalion 4462 *How Much Do You Mean To Me?*	7.00 -	10.00
Vocalion 4500 *Home Cookin' Mama*	7.00 -	10.00
Vocalion 4577 *Spare-Ribs and Spaghetti*	7.00 -	10.00

DANNY ALTIER & HIS ORCHESTRA:

Vocalion 15740 *My Gal Sal*	150.00 -	200.00

THE AMBASSADORS:

Vocalion 14620, 14668, 14686, 14810, 14823, 14851, 14907, 14916, 14928, 15131	4.00 -	7.00
Vocalion 14933 *The 'Throw-Down' Blues*	8.00 -	12.00
Vocalion 15156 *Military Mike*	8.00 -	12.00
Vocalion 15752 *Me and the Man in the Moon*	7.00 -	10.00
Vocalion 15793 *You've Never Been Blue*	7.00 -	10.00

AMERICAN MARIMBAPHONE BAND:

Columbia A2634 *Tishomingo Blues*	7.00 -	10.00

ALBERT AMMONS (AND HIS RHYTHM KINGS):

Blue Note 2 *Boogie Woogie Stomp*	10.00 -	15.00
Blue Note 4 *Chicago In Mind*	10.00 -	15.00
Blue Note 21 *Suitcase Blues*	10.00 -	15.00
Decca 749 *Boogie Woogie Stomp*	10.00 -	15.00
Decca 975 *Early Mornin' Blues*	10.00 -	15.00
Solo Art 12000 *Monday Struggle*	10.00 -	15.00
Solo Art 12001 *Boogie Woogie*	10.00 -	15.00
Solo Art 12003 *St. Louis Blues*	10.00 -	15.00
Vocalion 4608 *Shout For Joy*	7.00 -	10.00

AMOS 'N' ANDY (See CORRELL and GOSDEN)

EDDIE "ROCHESTER" ANDERSON:

Columbia 35442, 36185	5.00 -	8.00

IVIE ANDERSON & HER BOYS FROM DIXIE:

Variety 591 *All God's Chillun Got Rhythm*	10.00 -	15.00

WALT/WALTER ANDERSON & HIS GOLDEN PHEASANT HOODLUMS:

Titles, issued contemporaneously on Bell, Challenge, Gennett: *After I've Called You Sweetheart; Alabama Stomp; Melancholy; Mokus; Rain; Sugar Foot Stomp; What'll We Do For Dough?*	40.00 -	75.00

THE ANDREWS SISTERS:

Decca 1496 *Just a Simple Melody*	8.00 -	12.00
Decca 1562 *Bei Mir Bist du Schoen*	8.00 -	12.00

Decca 1691, 1703, 1744, 1859, 1875, 1912, 1974,
　2016, 2082, 2214, 2290, 2414 . . . . 4.00 - 8.00
Decca, most other titles . . . . 3.00 - 5.00

ANONYMOUS (Records on which no artist credit, actual or pseudonymous, is given. Descriptions such as "Band." "Orchestra," "Fox Trot with Vocal Chorus," "Baritone," "Banjo Solo with Orchestra," are typical. In most cases, the identity of the artist is known. The following have been recognized as collectible. No effort has been made to list "test pressings.")

Brunswick "Mood Accompaniment Library"
　(most dance band selections) . . . . 5.00 - 10.00
Climax K346 *Ramshackle Rag* ("Band") . . . . . . 8.00 - 12.00
Grey Gull 1522 *Loveless Love Blues* . . . . 5.00 - 8.00
　1591 *And Then* . . . . 7.00 - 10.00
Grey Gull 1701 *Battleship Kate* . . . . 5.00 - 10.00
Grey Gull 1702 *Jimtown Blues* . . . . 5.00 - 10.00
Grey Gull 1706 *Lead Pipe Blues* . . . . 5.00 - 10.00
Grey Gull 1710 *Coal Black Blues* . . . . 20.00 - 30.00
Grey Gull 1718 *Close Fit Blues* . . . . 20.00 - 30.00
Grey Gull 1724 *Baby, Won't You Please*
　Come Home? . . . . 20.00 - 30.00
Grey Gull 7028 *Sure Enough Blues* . . . . 8.00 - 12.00
Grey Gull 7029 *Mississippi Mud Blues* . . . . 8.00 - 12.00
Grey Gull 7037 *Jimtown Blues* . . . . 8.00 - 12.00
La Belle 5077 *Smoky Mokes* . . . . 8.00 - 12.00
Little Wonder 9 *20th Century*
　Rag ("Band") . . . . — - —
Little Wonder 20 *Back To The Carolina You Love* . . 15.00 - 20.00
　(Note: The unidentified baritone on the above is
　　Al Jolson.)
Little Wonder 568 *That Broadway Chicken*
　Walk ("Banjo solo") . . . . 7.00 - 10.00
　569 *The Smiler* (Banjo solo") . . . . 7.00 - 10.00
Okeh 1028 *The Tickle Toe* ("Band") . . . . 7.00 - 10.00
Oxford 406 *At A Georgia Camp Meeting* . . . . . . 8.00 - 12.00
　686 *Mr. Black Man* . . . . 8.00 - 12.00
　1038 *Cotton (Southern Breakdown)* . . . . 8.00 - 12.00
　4117 *Black And White-Ragtime Two-Step* . . . . . 8.00 - 12.00
　5534 *Just Noise* . . . . 8.00 - 12.00
　(Note: Above Oxford records are one-sided discs)
Radiex 1594 *I'm Lost Without You* . . . . 5.00 - 8.00
　1701 *Battleship Kate* . . . . 5.00 - 10.00
　1706 *Sweat Blues* . . . . 5.00 - 10.00
　1721 *Oh Gee, There Ain't No Justice* . . . . 5.00 - 8.00
　7037 *Jimtown Blues* . . . . 5.00 - 12.00
Silvertone 38644 *Too Much Mustard* . . . . 8.00 - 12.00
　46909 *Pretty Baby* . . . . 7.00 - 10.00
　(Note: Above Silvertone records are one-sided)
Victor 4445 *Mr. Black Man* . . . . 10.00 - 20.00
　(Note: Above Victor is one-sided disc)

ARCADIAN SERENADERS:
Okeh 40272 *Fidgety Feet* . . . . 30.00 - 40.00
Okeh 40378 *San Sue Strut* . . . . 30.00 - 40.00
Okeh 40440 *Who Can Your Regular*
　Be Blues . . . . 30.00 - 40.00
Okeh 40503 *The Co-Ed* . . . . 30.00 - 40.00
Okeh 40517 *Angry* . . . . 30.00 - 40.00
Okeh 40538 *Carry It On Down* . . . . 40.00 - 60.00
Okeh 40562 *Yes Sir, Boss* . . . . 40.00 - 60.00

ARCADIA PEACOCK ORCHESTRA OF ST. LOUIS:
Okeh 40044 *Dream Boat* . . . . 8.00 - 12.00
Okeh 40052 *Ain't You Ashamed?* . . . . 15.00 - 20.00
Okeh 40254 *Where's My Sweetie Hiding?* . . . . . . 8.00 - 12.00
Okeh 40264 *Ah! Ah! Archie* . . . . 15.00 - 20.00
Okeh 40272 *Dog On The Piano* . . . . 30.00 - 40.00
Okeh 40372 *Waiting For The Moon* . . . . 15.00 - 20.00

HARRY ARCHER & HIS ORCHESTRA:
Brunswick (*most issues*) . . . . 3.00 - 5.00

ARDEN-OHMAN & THEIR ORCHESTRA:
Brunswick (*most issues*) . . . . 3.00 - 5.00
Victor (*most issues*) . . . . 3.00 - 5.00

ARKANSAS/ARKANSAW TRAVELERS:
Titles, issued contemporaneously on Diva,
　Harmony, Velvet Tone: *Birmingham*
　Breakdown; Boneyard Shuffle; I Ain't Got
　Nobody; Ja Da; Sensation; Stompin' Fool:
　Washboard Blues . . . . 8.00 - 12.00
　　Red Head Blues; That's No Bargain . . . . . . 12.00 - 20.00
Okeh 40124 *Georgia Blues* . . . . 7.00 - 10.00
Okeh 40183 *Any Way The Wind Blows* . . . . 7.00 - 10.00
Okeh 40236 *Copenhagen* . . . . 10.00 - 15.00
Okeh 40267 *Homebound* . . . . 8.00 - 12.00
Okeh 40277 *I'll See You In My Dreams* . . . . . . 5.00 - 8.00
Okeh 40426 *Row, Row, Rosie* . . . . 8.00 - 12.00
Okeh 40438 *Indian Nights* . . . . 8.00 - 12.00
Okeh 40640 *Breezin' Along With The Breeze* . . . . 8.00 - 12.00
Okeh 40641 *I'm Walkng Around In Circles* . . . . . 8.00 - 12.00
Okeh 40674 *Ting-a-ling, The Bells'll Ring* . . . . . . 8.00 - 12.00
Okeh 40700 *Give Me A Ukelele* . . . . 8.00 - 12.00
Okeh 40724 *Take In The Sun, Hang Out*
　The Moon . . . . , ... 8.00 - 12.00
Okeh 40727 *Brown Sugar* . . . . 8.00 - 12.00

ARKANSAS TRIO:
Edison 51373 *Boll Weevil Blues* . . . . 7.00 - 10.00

FRED ARMSTRONG & HIS SYNCOPATORS:
Timely Tunes C-1578 *When I Can't Be With You* 50.00 - 80.00
Timely Tunes C-1587 *Sugar Blues* . . . . 20.00 - 30.00

LIL ARMSTRONG & HER SWING BAND/ORCHESTRA:
Decca 1059, 1092, 1182, 1272, 1299, 1388, 1502 . 5.00 - 10.00

LOUIS ARMSTRONG & HIS HOT FIVE/SAVOY BALLROOM FIVE/ORCHESTRA/ SEBASTIAN NEW COTTON CLUB ORCHESTRA:
Bluebird 5086 *Mahogany Hall Stomp* . . . . 4.00 - 6.00
Bluebird 5173 *Hustlin' and Bustlin' For Baby* . . . 4.00 - 6.00
Bluebird 5280 *St. Louis Blues* . . . . 4.00 - 6.00
Bluebird 5363 *Laughin' Louie* . . . . 7.00 - 10.00
Bluebird 5408 *Dusky Stevedore* . . . . 4.00 - 6.00
Bluebird 5409 *Mighty River* . . . . 4.00 - 6.00
Bluebird 6501 *Mississippi Basin* . . . . 4.00 - 6.00
Bluebird 6590 *Some Sweet day* . . . . 4.00 - 6.00
Bluebird 6644 *That's My Home* . . . . 4.00 - 6.00
Bluebird 6771 *High Society* . . . . 4.00 - 6.00
Bluebird 6910 *I've Got The World On A String* . . 4.00 - 6.00
Bluebird 7506 *Sittin' in the Dark* . . . . 4.00 - 6.00
Bluebird 7787 *Honey, Do!* . . . . 5.00 - 8.00
Bluebird 10225 *Swing, You Cats* . . . . 4.00 - 7.00
Bluebird 10236 *That's My Home* . . . . 4.00 - 6.00
Columbia 2754-D *Star Dust* . . . . 8.00 - 12.00
Columbia 2606-D *All Of Me* . . . . 8.00 - 12.00
Columbia 2631-D *The New Tiger Rag* . . . . 8.00 - 12.00
Columbia 2646-D *Keepin' Out Of Mischief Now* . 8.00 - 12.00
Columbia 2688-D *Rockin' Chair* . . . . 8.00 - 12.00
Columbia 2709-D *Body And Soul* . . . . 8.00 - 12.00
Columbia 2727-D *After You've Gone* . . . . 8.00 - 12.00
Decca 579 *Got A Bran' New Suit* . . . . 5.00 - 10.00
Decca 580 *You Are My Lucky Star* . . . . 5.00 - 10.00
Decca 622 *Old Man Mose* . . . . 5.00 - 10.00
Decca 623 *I'm Shooting High* . . . . 5.00 - 10.00
Decca 648 *Red Sails In The Sunset* . . . . 5.00 - 10.00
Decca 666 *Thanks A Million* . . . . 5.00 - 10.00
Decca 672 *Shoe Shine Boy* . . . . 5.00 - 10.00
Decca 685 *Rhythm Saved The World* . . . . 5.00 - 10.00
Decca 698 *I'm Putting All My Eggs In*
　One Basket . . . . 8.00 - 12.00
Decca 797 *Somebody Stole My Break* . . . . 5.00 - 10.00
Decca 824 *Mahogany Hall Stomp* . . . . 5.00 - 8.00
Decca 835 *Lyin' To Myself* . . . . 5.00 - 8.00
Decca 866 *Swing That Music* . . . . 5.00 - 8.00
Decca 906 *Dipper Mouth Blues* . . . . 5.00 - 8.00

Decca 914 *On A Cocoanut Island*	4.00 -	6.00
Decca 949 *Hurdy-Gurdy Man*	5.00 -	8.00
Decca 1049 *When Ruben Swings The Cuban*	5.00 -	10.00
Decca 1245 *Carry Me Back To Old Virginny*	7.00 -	10.00
Decca 1347 *Public Melody Number One*	5.00 -	10.00
Decca 1353 *Cuban Pete*	5.00 -	8.00
Decca 1360 *The Old Folks At Home*	7.00 -	10.00
Decca 1369 *Yours And Mine*	5.00 -	8.00
Decca 1408 *Alexander's Ragtime Band*	5.00 -	8.00
Decca 1495 *In The Shade Of The Old Apple Tree*	7.00 -	10.00
Decca 1560 *On The Sunny Side Of The Street*	5.00 -	8.00
Decca 1635 *Jubilee*	5.00 -	8.00
Decca 1636 *Satchel Mouth Swing*	5.00 -	8.00
Decca 1653 *The Trumpet Player's Lament*	5.00 -	8.00
Decca 1661 *Struttin' With Some Barbecue*	5.00 -	8.00
(Original issues of early Deccas have shaded letters in logo)		
Decca *(most late numbers)*	3.00 -	6.00
Decca 3011 *Bye and Bye*	5.00 -	8.00
Decca 3151 W.P.A. *(with THE MILLS BROTHERS)*	20.00 -	30.00
Okeh 8261 *Gut Bucket Blues*	100.00 -	150.00
Okeh 8299 *Oriental Strut*	80.00 -	120.00
Okeh 8300 *Heebie Jeebies*	40.00 -	60.00
Okeh 8318 *Georgia Grind*	50.00 -	75.00
Okeh 8320 *Cornet Chop Suey*	50.00 -	75.00
(Note: Original issues of early Okeh records have the large, maroon label, product of General Phonograph Corporation. Later issues, and reissues of early issues, are products of Okeh Phonograph Corporation or Columbia Phonograph Corporation, with the "Truetone" or "Electric" emblem above the center hole, and are laminated pressings.)		
Okeh 8343 *I'm Gonna Gitcha*	50.00 -	75.00
Okeh 8357 *Dropping Shucks*	50.00 -	75.00
Okeh 8379 *Sweet Little Papa*	60.00 -	90.00
Okeh 8396 *The King Of The Zulus*	60.00 -	90.00
Okeh 8423 *Big Butter And Egg Man*	50.00 -	75.00
Okeh 8436 *Jazz Lips*	50.00 -	75.00
Okeh 8447 *Irish Black Bottom*	50.00 -	75.00
Okeh 8474 *Wild Man Blues*	50.00 -	75.00
Okeh 8482 *Willie The Weeper*	50.00 -	75.00
Okeh 8496 *Keyhole Blues*	50.00 -	75.00
Okeh 8503 *Potatoe Head Blues*	30.00 -	50.00
Okeh 8519 *Weary Blues*	30.00 -	50.00
Okeh 8535 *Savoy Blues*	30.00 -	50.00
Okeh 8551 *Got No Blues*	30.00 -	50.00
Okeh 8566 *Struttin' With Some Barbecue*	30.00 -	50.00
Okeh 8597 *West End Blues*	20.00 -	40.00
Okeh 8609 *Sugar Foot Strut*	20.00 -	40.00
Okeh 8631 *Knee Drops*	20.00 -	40.00
Okeh 8641 *Squeeze Me*	20.00 -	40.00
Okeh 8649 *Tight Like This*	20.00 -	40.00
Okeh 8657 *Save It, Pretty Mama*	20.00 -	40.00
Okeh 8669 *No-One Else But You*	20.00 -	40.00
Okeh 8680 *Beau-Koo Jack*	20.00 -	40.00
Okeh 8690 *Basin Street Blues*	20.00 -	40.00
Okeh 8703 *Knockin' A Jug*	30.00 -	50.00
Okeh 8714 *Ain't Misbehavin'*	15.00 -	25.00
Okeh 8729 *Some Of These Days*	15.00 -	25.00
Okeh 8756 *Rockin' Chair*	15.00 -	25.00
Okeh 8774 *Bessie Couldn't Help It*	15.00 -	25.00
Okeh 8800 *Dinah*	15.00 -	25.00
Okeh 41078 *Fireworks*	15.00 -	25.00
Okeh 41157 *Knee Drops*	8.00 -	12.00
Okeh 41180 *Save It, Pretty Mama*	8.00 -	12.00
Okeh 41204 *No-One Else But You*	12.00 -	15.00
Okeh 41241 *Basin Street Blues*	12.00 -	15.00
Okeh 41276 *Black And Blue*	12.00 -	15.00
Okeh 41281 *Sweet Savannah Sue*	15.00 -	20.00
Okeh 41298 *Some Of These Days*	15.00 -	20.00
Okeh 41350 *After You've Gone*	15.00 -	20.00
Okeh 41375 *Song Of The Islands*	10.00 -	15.00
Okeh 41415 *My Sweet*	15.00 -	20.00
Okeh 41423 *Exactly Like You*	15.00 -	20.00
Okeh 41442 *I'm A Ding Dong Daddy*	15.00 -	20.00
Okeh 41448 *Confessin'*	15.00 -	20.00
Okeh 41454 *Weather Bird*	20.00 -	25.00
Okeh 41463 *You're Lucky To Me*	12.00 -	16.00
Okeh 41468 *Body And Soul*	12.00 -	16.00
Okeh 41478 *You're Drivin' Me Crazy*	12.00 -	16.00
Okeh 41486 *Shine*	12.00 -	16.00
Okeh 41497 *Walkin' My Baby Back Home*	12.00 -	16.00
Okeh 41498 *Blue Again*	12.00 -	16.00
Okeh 41501 *Them There Eyes*	12.00 -	16.00
Okeh 41504 *When It's Sleepy Time Down South*	12.00 -	16.00
Okeh 41530 *Star Dust*	12.00 -	16.00
Okeh 41534 *Chinatown, My Chinatown*	12.00 -	16.00
Okeh 41538 *The Lonesome Road*	12.00 -	16.00
Okeh 41541 *Lazy River*	12.00 -	16.00
Okeh 41550 *Kickin' The Gong Around*	12.00 -	16.00
Okeh 41552 *All Of Me*	12.00 -	16.00
Okeh 41557 *The New Tiger Rag*	12.00 -	16.00
Okeh 41560 *Keepin' Out Of Mischief Now*	12.00 -	16.00
Victor 24200 *That's My Home*	8.00 -	12.00
Victor 24202 *I Hate To Leave You Now*	8.00 -	12.00
Victor 24232 *High Society*	8.00 -	12.00
Victor 24233 *I Gotta Right to Sing The Blues*	8.00 -	12.00
Victor 24245 *Sittin' In The Dark*	8.00 -	12.00
Victor 24257 *Some Sweet Day*	8.00 -	12.00
Victor 24320 *St. Louis Blues*	8.00 -	12.00
Victor 24321 *Mississippi Basin*	8.00 -	12.00
Victor 24334 *There's A Cabin In The Pines*	8.00 -	12.00
Victor 24351 *Basin Street Blues*	8.00 -	12.00
Victor 24369 *Snowball*	8.00 -	12.00
Victor 24425 *Don't Play Me Cheap*	8.00 -	12.00
Victor 36084 (12 inch) *Medley of Armstrong Hits*	7.00 -	10.00
Vocalion 3008 *Basin Street Blues*	4.00 -	7.00
Vocalion 3009 *Tiger Rag*	4.00 -	7.00
Vocalion 3025 *Dallas Blues*	5.00 -	8.00
Vocalion 3026 *The Lonesome Road*	5.00 -	8.00
Vocalion 3039 *Chinatown, My Chinatown*	5.00 -	8.00
Vocalion 3040 *Exactly Like You*	4.00 -	7.00
Vocalion 3055 *Mahogany Hall Stomp*	4.00 -	7.00
Vocalion 3059 *Confessin'*	4.00 -	7.00
Vocalion 3072 *Body And Soul*	5.00 -	8.00
Vocalion 3073 *Georgia On My Mind*	5.00 -	8.00
Vocalion 3085 *Beau Koo Jack*	5.00 -	8.00
Vocalion 3102 *I Ain't Got Nobody*	5.00 -	8.00
Vocalion 3114 *Lazy River*	5.00 -	8.00
Vocalion 3115 *Black And Blue*	5.00 -	8.00
Vocalion 3124 *The New Tiger Rag*	5.00 -	8.00
Vocalion 3125 *Home*	5.00 -	8.00
Vocalion 3135 *All Of Me*	5.00 -	8.00
Vocalion 3136 *Sweet Savannah Sue*	5.00 -	8.00
Vocalion 3137 *Keyhole Blues*	5.00 -	8.00
Vocalion 3148 *Sugar Foot Strut*	5.00 -	8.00
Vocalion 3172 *Wrap Your Troubles In Dreams*	5.00 -	8.00
Vocalion 3180 *You're Lucky To Me*	10.00 -	15.00
Vocalion 3181 *Keepin' Out Of Mischief Now*	5.00 -	8.00
Vocalion 3193 *Gully Low Blues*	5.00 -	8.00
Vocalion 3194 *The Peanut Vendor*	4.00 -	7.00
Vocalion 3202 *When You're Smiling*	5.00 -	8.00
Vocalion 3203 *When It's Sleepy Time Down South*	5.00 -	8.00
Vocalion 3204 *West End Blues*	4.00 -	7.00
Vocalion 3205 *That Rhythm Man*	5.00 -	8.00
Vocalion 3216 *You're Driving Me Crazy*	5.00 -	8.00
Vocalion 3217 *Savoy Blues*	4.00 -	7.00
Vocalion 3237 *Hotter Than That*	4.00 -	7.00
Vocalion 3301 *I'm In The Market For You*	5.00 -	8.00
Vocalion 3303 *Tight Like This*	4.00 -	7.00
Vocalion 3337 *Them There Eyes*	4.00 -	7.00

Vocalion 3370 *Indian Cradle Song* . . . . 4.00 - 7.00
Vocalion 3381 *Save It Pretty Mama* . . . . 4.00 - 7.00
Vocalion 3643 *After You've Gone* . . . . 4.00 - 7.00

FELIX ARNDT:
Victor 17558 *From Soup To Nuts* . . . . 8.00 - 12.00
17608 *Desecration Rag (A Classic Nightmare)* . . 8.00 - 12.00

GUS ARNHEIM & HIS (AMBASSADOR HOTEL/COCOANUT GROVE) ORCHESTRA:
Brunswick 6683, 6693, 6729, 6734, 6751, 6765 . 5.00 - 8.00
Brunswick 7900 *The Image Of You* . . . . 10.00 - 15.00
Brunswick 7904 *Exactly Like You* . . . . 10.00 - 15.00
Brunswick 7919 *So Rare* . . . . 10.00 - 15.00
Brunswick 7922 *High, Wide and Handsome* . . . . 10.00 - 15.00
Brunswick 7933 *All You Want To Do Is Dance* . . . 10.00 - 15.00
Brunswick 7937 *On With The Dance* . . . . 10.00 - 15.00
Okeh 41037 *If I Can't Have You* . . . . 8.00 - 12.00
Okeh 41057 *Feelin' Good* . . . . 8.00 - 12.00
Okeh 41208 *Glad Rag Doll* . . . . 8.00 - 12.00
Victor L-16011 *Medley of Popular Selections* . . . . 30.00 - 50.00
(Preceding is long-playing "Program
Transcription")
Victor 22054 *Lovable and Sweet* . . . . 5.00 - 8.00
Victor 22384 *Dancing to Save Your Sole* . . . . 7.00 - 10.00
Victor 22470 *I've Gotta Yen For You* . . . . 8.00 - 12.00
Victor 22561 *Fool Me Some More* . . . . 5.00 - 8.00
Victor 22580 *Them There Eyes* . . . . 5.00 - 8.00
Victor 22618 *I Surrender, Dear* . . . . 5.00 - 8.00
Victor 22691 *I'm Gonna Get You* . . . . 8.00 - 12.00
Victor 22700 *One More Time* . . . . 7.00 - 10.00
Victor 22851 *There's Nothing Too Good For
My Baby* . . . . 8.00 - 12.00
Victor 24061 *Evening* . . . . 5.00 - 8.00
Victor 24234 *Love Is a Dream* . . . . 5.00 - 8.00
Victor 24235 *Love in the Moonlight* . . . . 5.00 - 8.00

BILLY "PETE" ARTZ & HIS HENRY AND GEORGE ORCHESTRA:
Titles, issued contemporaneously on Banner,
Conqueror, Oriole, Perfect, and Romeo: *I'm
All Dressed Up with a Broken Heart; Never;
Parkin' in the Moonlight; There's a Time and
Place for Everything* . . . . 7.00 - 10.00

PAUL ASH & HIS MERRY MAD MUSICAL GANG/ORCHESTRA:
Brunswick 2482 *Pesticatin' Mama* . . . . 5.00 - 8.00
Brunswick *(most other issues)* . . . . 3.00 - 6.00
Clarion 5104-C *I Got Rhythm* . . . . 10.00 - 15.00
Columbia 707-D *Oh! If I Only Had You* . . . . 5.00 - 8.00
828-D *Take In The Sun, Hang Out The Moon* . 5.00 - 8.00
1066-D *Ain't That a Grand And Glorious
Feeling* . . . . 5.00 - 8.00
1349-D *My Pet* . . . . 5.00 - 8.00
1531-D *Out Of The Dawn* . . . . 7.00 - 10.00
1616-D *Salty* . . . . 8.00 - 12.00
2796-D *Shadows On The Swanee* . . . . 10.00 - 15.00
2798-D *Louisville Lady* . . . . 10.00 - 15.00
Columbia *(most other issues)* . . . . 4.00 - 7.00
Harmony 1234-H *I Got Rhythm* . . . . 10.00 - 15.00
Variety 649 *Raggin' The Scale* . . . . 7.00 - 10.00

FRED ASTAIRE:
Brunswick 7486 *Cheek To Cheek* . . . . 7.00 - 10.00
Brunswick 7608 *Let's Face the Music and Dance* . 7.00 - 10.00
Brunswick 7609 *I'm Putting All My eggs In
One Basket* . . . . 7.00 - 10.00
Brunswick 7610 *I'd Rather Lead a Band* . . . . 7.00 - 10.00
Brunswick 7716 *A Fine Romance* . . . . 7.00 - 10.00
Brunswick 7717 *Pick Yourself up* . . . . 7.00 - 10.00
Brunswick 7718 *Never Gonna Dance* . . . . 7.00 - 10.00
Brunswick 7855 *Beginner's Luck* . . . . 7.00 - 10.00
Brunswick 7856 *Slap That Bass* . . . . 7.00 - 10.00
Brunswick 7857 *Let's Call the Whole Thing Off* . 7.00 - 10.00
Brunswick 7982 *A Foggy Day* . . . . 7.00 - 10.00
Brunswick 7983 *Nice Work If You Can Get It* . . . . 7.00 - 10.00

Brunswick 8189 *Change Partners* . . . . 7.00 - 10.00
Brunswick 8190 *The Yam Step Explained* . . . . . . 7.00 - 10.00
Columbia 3164-D *They Can't Take That Away
From Me* . . . . 10.00 - 15.00
Columbia 3165-D *They All Laughed* . . . . 10.00 - 15.00
Columbia 3166-D *Shall We Dance?* . . . . 10.00 - 15.00
Columbia 35517, 35815, 35852 . . . . 3.00 - 5.00

THE ASTORITES:
Harmony 201-H *Who Wouldn't* . . . . 5.00 - 8.00
228-H *Up and Down The Eight Mile Road* . . . . 7.00 - 10.00
251-H *Black Bottom* . . . . 5.00 - 8.00
266-H *Gone Again Gal* . . . . 5.00 - 8.00
273-H *Just A Little Longer* . . . . 4.00 - 7.00
303-H *It Made You Happy When You Made
Me Cry* . . . . 5.00 - 8.00
305-H *I'd Love To Call You My Sweetheart* . . . 5.00 - 8.00
438-H *One O'Clock Baby* . . . . 5.00 - 8.00
528-H *Among My Souvenirs* . . . . 5.00 - 8.00
709-H *Nagasaki* . . . . 5.00 - 8.00

ATLANTA MERRYMAKERS:
Madison 1935 *Black Stomp* . . . . 10.00 - 15.00
Madison 50015 *Sweet Little Sis* . . . . 7.00 - 10.00
Madison 50024 *Sweet Little Sis* . . . . 7.00 - 10.00

ATLANTA SYNCOPATORS:
Grey Gull 1888 *That Wicked Stomp* . . . . 20.00 - 30.00
Madison 50008 *That Wicked Stomp* . . . . 20.00 - 30.00
Madison 50009 *Step On It* . . . . 10.00 - 15.00
Madison 50015 *Lead Pipe Blues* . . . . 8.00 - 12.00
Radiex 5008 *That Wicked Stomp* . . . . 20.00 - 30.00
Radiex 5015 *Beale Street Blues* . . . . 8.00 - 12.00
Van Dyke 508 *That Wicked Stomp* . . . . 20.00 - 30.00

FRANK AUBURN & HIS ORCHESTRA:
Clarion 5179-C *I'm Tickled Pink With a
Blue-Eyed Baby* . . . . 8.00 - 12.00
Clarion 5180-C *A Peach of a Pair* . . . . 8.00 - 12.00
Clarion 5212-C *Would You Like To Take a Walk?* . 7.00 - 10.00
Clarion 5273-C *Rockin' Chair* . . . . 8.00 - 12.00
Clarion 5277-C *When I Take My Sugar To Tea* . . . 8.00 - 12.00
Clarion 5283-C *I'm Crazy 'Bout My Baby* . . . . . . 8.00 - 12.00
Clarion 5286-C *You'll Be Mine in Apple
Blossom Time* . . . . 8.00 - 12.00
Clarion 5335-C *Faithfully Yours* . . . . 5.00 - 8.00
Clarion 5340-C *I Found a Million Dollar Baby* . . 8.00 - 12.00
Clarion 5356-C *Hikin' Down the Highway* . . . . . . 8.00 - 12.00
Clarion 5369-C *Me!* . . . . 8.00 - 12.00
Clarion 5450-C *Goodnight, Moon* . . . . 5.00 - 8.00
Clarion 5451-C *One Little Quarrel* . . . . 7.00 - 10.00
Clarion 5455-C *Between the Devil and the Deep
Blue Sea* . . . . 10.00 - 15.00
Clarion 11001-C *Little Girl* . . . . 15.00 - 20.00
(Above is a "double track" record)
Harmony 1138-H *Kickin' a Hole in the Sky* . . . . . 8.00 - 12.00
Harmony 1200-H *Why Am I So Romantic?* . . . . . . 7.00 - 10.00
Harmony 1202-H *Good Evenin'* . . . . 7.00 - 10.00
Harmony 1234-H *It's a Great Life* . . . . 8.00 - 12.00
Harmony 1240-H *My Ideal* . . . . 8.00 - 12.00
Harmony 1249-H *Cheerful Little Earful* . . . . 8.00 - 12.00
Harmony 1269-H *I'm So Afraid of You* . . . . 8.00 - 12.00
Harmony 1306-H *Rockin' Chair* . . . . 8.00 - 12.00
Harmony 1327-H *My Cradle Sweetheart* . . . . 5.00 - 8.00
Harmony 1331-H *In the Merry Month of Maybe* . 8.00 - 12.00
Harmony 1344-H *Hikin' Down the Highway* . . . . . 8.00 - 12.00
Harmony 1357-H *Give Me Your Affection, Honey* . 8.00 - 12.00
Harmony 1412-H *Between the Devil and the
Deep Blue Sea* . . . . 10.00 - 15.00
Harmony 6001-H *Sunny Skies* . . . . 15.00 - 20.00
(Above is a "double track" record)
Velvet Tone 2333-V *Got the Bench-Got the Park* . 7.00 - 10.00
Velvet Tone 2339-V *Rockin' Chair* . . . . 8.00 - 12.00
Velvet Tone 2343-V *When I Take My Sugar
To Tea* . . . . 8.00 - 12.00
Velvet Tone 2349-V *I'm Crazy 'Bout My Baby* . . . 8.00 - 12.00

Velvet Tone 2352-V *You'll Be Mine in Apple
Blossom Time* .... 8.00 - 12.00
Velvet Tone 2404-V *In the Merry Month
of Maybe* .... 8.00 - 12.00
Velvet Tone 2420-V *The Hour of Parting* .... 7.00 - 10.00
Velvet Tone 2433-V *Give Me Your Affection,
Honey* .... 7.00 - 10.00
Velvet Tone 2510-V *Goodnight, Moon* .... 5.00 - 8.00
Velvet Tone 2511-V *One Little Quarrel* .... 7.00 - 10.00
Velvet Tone 2515-V *Between the Devil and the
Deep Blue Sea* .... 10.00 - 15.00
Velvet Tone 10001-V *Sunny Skies* .... 15.00 - 20.00
(Above is a "double track" record.)

GEORGE AULD & HIS ORCHESTRA:
Varsity 8152, 8159, 8163, 8199, 8212 .... 4.00 - 8.00

AUSTIN & HIS MUSICAL AMBASSADORS:
Paramount 12359 *Don't Forget to
Mess Around* .... 20.00 - 30.00

GENE AUSTIN:
Titles, issued contemporaneously on Banner,
Conqueror, Melotone, Oriole, Perfect, Romeo:
*Blue Kentucky Moon; Easter Parade;
Everything I Have Is Yours; A Faded Summer
Love; A Ghost of a Chance; Goodnight,
Sweetheart; Guilty; If I Didn't Have You; In a
Dream; Just a Little Home for the Old Folks; A
Little Street Where Old Friends Meet; The
Lonesome Road; When I Was a Boy From the
Mountains* .... 5.00 - 10.00
Titles, issued contemporaneously on Banner,
Conqueror, Melotone, Oriole, Perfect, Romeo:
*Build a Little Home; Did You Ever See a
Dream Walking?* .... 8.00 - 12.00
Titles, issued contemporaneously on Banner,
Conqueror, Melotone, Oriole, Perfect, Romeo;
*Dear Old Southland; I'm Sorry, Dear; Jail
House Blues; Lies* .... 10.00 - 15.00
Decca 904 *When I'm With You* .... 7.00 - 10.00
Decca 926 *I Cried For You* .... 7.00 - 10.00
Decca 1578 *Marie* .... 7.00 - 10.00
Decca 1656 *Dear Old Southland* .... 10.00 - 15.00
Decca 1832, 3102, 3939, 4175, 4333, 4354 ..... 4.00 - 8.00
Hit-of-the-Week L-3 *Now That You're Gone* .... 5.00 - 8.00
Victor 19585, 19599, 19625, 19637, 19677, 19656,
19857, 19864, 19899, 19928, 19950, 19968,
20030, 20044, 20084, 20143, 20371, 20397,
20411, 20561, 20568, 20569, 20730,, 20964,
20977, 21015, 21098, 21329, 21334, 21374,
21454, 21545, 21564, 21714, 21779, 21798,
21833, 21856, 21893, 21915, 21916, 21952,
22033, 22068 .... 3.00 - 8.00
Victor 22128, 22223 .... 4.00 - 7.00
Victor 22299 *After You've Gone* .... 8.00 - 12.00
Victor 22341, 22416, 22451, 22490, 22518, 22527,
22539, 22601, 22635, 22687 .... 5.00 - 10.00
Victor 22739 *Without That Gal!* .... 8.00 - 12.00
Victor 22806 *Love Letters in the Sand* .... 7.00 - 10.00
Victor 24663 *All I Do Is Dream of You* ..... 15.00 - 20.00
Victor 24725 *Blue Sky Avenue* .... 10.00 - 15.00

**LOVIE AUSTIN & HER (BLUES)
SERENADERS:**
Paramount 12255 *Steppin' On The Blues* .... 100.00 - 150.00
Paramount 12277 *Peepin' Blues* .... 100.00 - 150.00
Paramount 12278 *Charleston Mad* .... 100.00 - 150.00
Paramount 12283 *Heebie Jeebies* .... 100.00 - 150.00
Paramount 12300 *Rampart Street Blues* ...... 100.00 - 150.00
Paramount 12313 *Too Sweet For Words* ...... 100.00 - 150.00
Paramount 12361 *Frog Tongue Stop* .... 100.00 - 150.00
Paramount 12380 *Chicago Mess Around* ...... 150.00 - 200.00
Paramount 12391 *In The Alley Blues* .... 150.00 - 200.00

AUSTIN'S SERENADERS:
Broadway 1018 *Jackass Blues* .... 80.00 - 120.00

THE AVALONIAMNS:
Vocalion 15577 *Zulu Wall* .... 8.00 - 12.00
CHARLES AVERY:
Paramount 12896 *Dearborn Street Breakdown* ...150.00 - 200.00
JOHN AYRES' ORCHESTRA:
Parlophone PNY-34084 *What's The Use Of
Cryin' Baby?* .... 25.00 - 35.00
PNY-34085 *When You're Feelin' Blue* .... 25.00 - 35.00
BABS & HER BROTHERS:
Decca 505 *Let's Swing It* .... 7.00 - 10.00
Decca 518 *Double Trouble* .... 7.00 - 10.00
Decca 634 *A Little Bit Independent* .... 7.00 - 10.00
Decca 635 *Yankee Doodle Never Went To Town* .. 7.00 - 10.00
BABY ARISTOCRATS BAND:
Gennett 6198 *Darktown Shuffle* .... 75.00 - 100.00
BABY ROSE MARIE:
Brunswick 6570 *My Bluebird's Singing
The Blues* .... 7.00 - 10.00
Victor 22960 *Take A Picture Of The Moon* ..... 20.00 - 30.00
Victor 24196 *In the Dim, Dim Dawning* .... 15.00 - 20.00
THE BADGERS:
Broadway 1055 *I Gotta Get Myself Somebody
to Love* .... 7.00 - 10.00
Broadway 1058 *It All Depends On You* .... 7.00 - 10.00
Broadway 1087 *You Don't Like It—Not Much* .... 5.00 - 8.00
Broadway 1150 *Back In Your Own back Yard* .... 5.00 - 8.00
Broadway 1180 *Just A Little Way From Home* .... 5.00 - 8.00
Broadway 1261 *He, She and Me* .... 5.00 - 8.00
Broadway 1263 *My Castle in Spain Is a Shack in
the Lane* .... 5.00 - 8.00
Broadway 1272 *There's a Four Leaf Clover In My
Pocker* .... 5.00 - 8.00
Broadway 1274 *Do Something* .... 5.00 - 8.00
Broadway 1278 *I'm Just a Vagabond Lover* ..... 4.00 - 7.00
Broadway 1297 *Miss You* .... 5.00 - 8.00
Broadway 1312 *Orange Blossom Time* .... 5.00 - 8.00
Broadway 1334 *Great Day* .... 5.00 - 8.00
Broadway 1339 *Singin' in the Bathtub* .... 5.00 - 8.00
Broadway 1378 *Just Like In A Story Book* ..... 5.00 - 8.00
Broadway 1379 *Exactly Like You* .... 5.00 - 8.00
Broadway 1409 *If I Could Be With You One Hour
Tonight* .... 7.00 - 10.00
Paramount 20820 *Exactly Like You* .... 7.00 - 10.00
Silvetone 3580 *It All Depends On You* .... 7.00 - 10.00
Silvetone 3583 *I Gotta Get Myself Somebody
To Love* .... 7.00 - 10.00
**MOE BAER & HIS WARDMAN PARK
ORCHESTRA:**
Vocalion 15760 *Susianna* .... 20.00 - 30.00
BAILEY'S DIXIE DUDES:
Gennett 5562 *I Want to See My Tennessee* ...... 7.00 - 10.00
Gennett 5577 *I'm Satisfied* .... 7.00 - 10.00
Gennett 5606 *Go' Long Mule* .... 7.00 - 10.00
BAILEY'S LUCKY SEVEN:
Gennett 3008 *Isn't She The Sweetest Thing?* .... 7.00 - 10.00
3009 *Susie* .... 7.00 - 10.00
3011 *Flag That Train* .... 10.00 - 15.00
3015 *No Wonder* .... 4.00 - 8.00
3086 *Row Row Rosie* .... 7.00 - 10.00
3088 *Collegiate* .... 7.00 - 10.00
3093 *If I Had A Girl Like You* .... 10.00 - 15.00
3094 *Marguerite* .... 7.00 - 10.00
3114 *Cecilia* .... 7.00 - 10.00
3125 *On A Night Like This* .... 5.00 - 8.00
3135 *Desdemona* .... 7.00 - 10.00
Gennett 3140 *The Baby Looks Like Me* .... 5.00 - 8.00
3154 *Who Loved You Best?* .... 5.00 - 8.00
3155 *Dream Pal* .... 5.00 - 8.00
3156 *Don't Wake Me Up, Let Me Dream* ...... 5.00 - 8.00
3163 *Tomorrow Morning* .... 7.00 - 10.00
3175 *Five Foot Two, Eyes Of Blue* .... 7.00 - 10.00
3191 *Don't Wait Too Long* .... 7.00 - 10.00

3192 *Mother Me, Tennessee*	7.00 -	10.00
3198 *Bamboola*	8.00 -	12.00
3204 *I Love My Baby*	8.00 -	12.00
3216 *Tie Me To Your Apron Strings Again*	7.00 -	10.00
3220 *When You're In The Arms Of The One You Love*	7.00 -	10.00
3224 *I Wish't I Was In Peoria*	7.00 -	10.00
3225 *Kentucky's Way Of Saying "Good Morning"*	7.00 -	10.00
3233 *Sweet Child (I'm Wild About You)*	8.00 -	12.00
3236 *I Want Somebody To Cheer Me Up*	8.00 -	12.00
3241 *Behind The Clouds*	7.00 -	10.00
3243 *Dinah*	7.00 -	10.00
3249 *Static*	7.00 -	10.00
5532 *Go, Emmaline*	8.00 -	12.00
5540 *Cold Mamas Burn Me Up*	10.00 -	15.00
5625 *Oh! Mabel*	10.00 -	15.00
5629 *I'll See You In My Dreams*	10.00 -	15.00
5637 *Dear One*	7.00 -	10.00
5645 *Why Couldn't It Be Poor Little Me*	10.00 -	15.00
5676 *When I Think Of You*	10.00 -	15.00
5710 *Flag That Train*	10.00 -	15.00
Gennett 4795, 4815, 4831, 4855, 4857, 4868, 4872, 4874, 4887, 4903, 4908, 4909, 4910, 4922, 4929, 4933, 4934, 4935, 4969, 4975, 4979, 4980, 5001, 5004, 5005, 5013, 5016, 5017, 5022, 5030, 5049, 5057, 5076, 5078, 5110, 5145, 5153, 5154, 5183, 5186, 5197, 5232, 5241, 5243, 5249, 5258, 5264, 5290, 5300, 5301, 5308, 5324, 5325, 5344, 5349, 5350, 5357, 5363	4.00 -	7.00
Gennett 5364, 5407, 5424, 5432, 5433, 5452, 5463, 5471	5.00 -	8.00

THE BAILEY SWING GROUP

Juke Box 506 *Eccentric Rag*	3.00 -	6.00

BUSTER BAILEY & HIS RHYTHM BUSTERS/SEVEN CHOCOLATE DANDIES

Variety 668 *Dizzy Debutante*	10.00 -	15.00
Varsity 8333 *The Blue Room*	7.00 -	10.00
Varsity 8337 *April in Paris*	8.00 -	12.00
Varsity 8358 *Fable of a Rose*	8.00 -	12.00
Varsity 8365 *Eccentric Rag*	7.00 -	10.00
Vocalion 2887 *Call of the Delta*	15.00 -	20.00
Vocalion 3846 *Afternoon in Africa*	10.00 -	15.00
Vocalion 4089 *Sloe Jam Fizz*	5.00 -	8.00
Vocalion 4564 *Man With a Horn Goes Berserk*	8.00 -	12.00
Vocalion 5510 *Chained to a Dream*	7.00 -	10.00

JENE BAILEY'S ORCHESTRA

Gennett 5681 *All Aboard for Heaven*	10.00 -	15.00

MILDRED BAILEY

Brunswick 6558, 6587, 6655, 6680	7.00 -	12.00
6184 *Wrap Your Troubles In Dreams*	10.00 -	15.00
6190 *Blues In My Heart*	10.00 -	15.00
Victor 22874, 22880, 22891, 22942, 24117, 24137	8.00 -	12.00
Vocalion 3056, 3057, 3367, 3378, 3449, 3456, 3508, 3553, 3615, 3626, 3931, 3932	6.00 -	10.00
Vocalion (most others)	4.00 -	7.00

WILLIAM BAILEY

Banner 1563 *Squeeze Me*	15.00 -	25.00

MAYNARD BAIRD & HIS ORCHESTRA/ SOUTHERN SERENADERS

Vocalion 1615 *Postage Stomp*	100.00 -	150.00
Vocalion 15834 *Sorry*	150.00 -	250.00

BELLE BAKER:

Brunswick 4843 *Cheer Up*	5.00 -	8.00
Brunswick (most other issues)	3.00 -	6.00

FRANK BAKER'S GROUP:

Tremont 436 *Sweet Papa Joe*	8.00 -	12.00
471 *Hootin' De Hoot*	8.00 -	12.00

SMITH BALLEW & HIS ORCHESTRA

Columbia 2320-D *You're Simply Delish*	7.00 -	10.00

Columbia 2350-D *Nine Little Miles From Ten-Ten-Tennessee*	7.00 -	10.00
Columbia 2406-D *I Hate Myself (For Falling In Love With You)*	7.00 -	10.00
Okeh 41254 *Hittin' The Ceiling*	7.00 -	10.00
Okeh 41282 *Blondy*	7.00 -	10.00
Okeh 41304 *Can't We Be Friends?*	7.00 -	10.00
Okeh 41329 *Lady Luck*	7.00 -	10.00
Okeh 41365 *Funny, Dear, What Love Can Do*	7.00 -	10.00
Okeh 41384 *Sing, You Sinners*	7.00 -	10.00
Okeh 41385 *We'll Build a Little World of Our Own*	7.00 -	10.00
Okeh 41394 *Where the Golden Daffodils Grow*	7.00 -	10.00
Okeh 41429 *You Brought a New Kind Of Love To Me*	8.00 -	12.00
Victor 22147 *Same Old Moon*	8.00 -	12.00

THE BALTIMORE BELLHOPS

Columbia 2449-D *Hot And Anxious*	15.00 -	20.00

BALTIMORE SOCIETY ORCHESTRA:

Oriole 446 *Oh Say! Can I See You Tonight*	5.00 -	8.00
569 *Up And At 'Em*	7.00 -	10.00

BANJO BUDDY:

Brunswick 3637 *Oh Doris! Where Do You Live?*	7.00 -	10.00
3865 *Let's Misbehave*	7.00 -	10.00

BANJO IKE & IVORY CHITISON (See: IVORY CHITTISON & BANJO JOE)

BILLY BANKS & HIS ORCHESTRA

Titles, issued contemporaneously on Banner, Oriole, Perfect, Romeo: *Bald-Headed Mama; Bugle Call Rag; Margie; Oh Peter, Spider Crawl; Who's Sorry Now?*	20.00 -	30.00
Victor 23399 *Mighty Sweet*	75.00 -	125.00
Victor 24027 *The Scat Song*	10.00 -	15.00
Victor 24148 *It Don't Mean A Thing*	10.00 -	15.00

BANNER DANCE ORCHESTRA:

Banner 1229 *Bugle Call rag*	7.00 -	10.00

FRANK BANTA:

Gennett 4735 *Wild Cherry rag*	15.00 -	20.00
Victor 19705 *My Sugar*	5.00 -	8.00
20667 *An Operatic Nightmare*	8.00 -	12.00

BARBARY COAST ORCHESTRA

Personal Record 72-P *Washboard Blues*	50.00 -	75.00
Personal Record 94-P *Weary Blues*	50.00 -	75.00

BARBECUE JOE & HIS HOT DOGS

Champion 16127 *Up The Country Blues*	150.00 -	200.00
Champion 16153 *Tin Roof Blues*	150.00 -	200.00
Champion 16192 *Shake That Thing*	150.00 -	250.00
Champion 40005, 40055	15.00 -	20.00
Gennett 7320 *Weary Blues*	250.00 -	400.00

BARBECUE PETE:

Champion 15904 *Avenue Strut*	35.00 -	50.00

EDDIE BAREFIELD & HIS QUINTETTE:

Sonora 104 *After Hours*	5.00 -	8.00

ROY BARGY:

Victor 19320 *Rufenreddy*	10.00 -	15.00
19537 *Jim-Jams*	10.00 -	15.00

BAR HARBOR (SOCIETY) ORCHESTRA:

Banner 1477 *Fascinating Rhythm*	5.00 -	8.00
Harmony x6505-H *Delishious*	8.00 -	12.00
Pathe-Actuelle 036138 *My Best Girl*	5.00 -	8.00
Perfect 14319 *My Best Girl*	5.00 -	8.00
Perfect 14628 *When The Red, Red, Robin Comes Bob, Bob, Bobbin Along*	5.00 -	8.00
Perfect 14754 *It Made You Happy When You Made Me Cry*	5.00 -	8.00
Puritan 11390 *Insufficient Sweetie*	4.00 -	7.00
Puritan 11403 *Yes Sir, That's My Baby*	5.00 -	8.00
Puritan 11417 *Breezin' Along (To Georgia)*	5.00 -	8.00
Silvertone 2498 *If You Knew Susie*	10.00 -	15.00

TOM BARKER & HIS ORCHESTRA:

Parlophone PNY-34084 *Happy Feet*	20.00 -	30.00

Parlophone PNY-34085 *I Like To Do Things For You* .... 20.00 - 30.00
Parlophone PNY-34119 *What's The Use?* .... 20.00 - 30.00
Parlophone PNY-34120 *Hittin' The Bottle* ...... 20.00 - 30.00

BILLIE BARNES:
Broadway 5063 *Dearborn Street Breakdown* ....100.00 - 150.00

FAYE BARNES:
Paramount 12209 *The Gouge Of Armour Avenue* . 20.00 - 30.00

WALTER BARNES & HIS ROYAL CREOLIANS:
Brunswick 4187 *How Long How Long Blues* .... 30.00 - 50.00
Brunswick 4244 *It's Tight Like That* .... 75.00 - 100.00
Brunswick 4480 *Birmingham Bertha* .... 30.00 - 50.00
Brunswick 7072 *Third Rail* .... 50.00 - 80.00

CHARLIE BARNET & HIS (GLEN ISLAND CASINO) ORCHESTRA:
Titles, issued contemporaneously on Banner, Conqueror, Melotone, Oriole, Perfect, Romeo; *Baby, Take a Bow; Buckin' The Wind; Butterfingers; Cross Patch ; Emaline; I Lost Another Sweetheart; I'm No Angel; Infatuation; I Want You, I Need You; My First Thrill; The Swing Waltz; This Is Our Last Night Together; Too Good To Be True; What Is Sweeter?* .... 5.00 - 10.00
Bluebird 5814 *I'm Keeping Those Keepsakes* .... 5.00 - 8.00
Bluebird 5815 *Nagasaki* .... 5.00 - 8.00
Bluebird 5816 *Growlin'* .... 5.00 - 8.00
Bluebird 6432 *Long Ago And Far Away* .... 5.00 - 8.00
Bluebird 6433 *But Definitely* .... 5.00 - 8.00
Bluebird 6448 *Empty Saddles* .... 5.00 - 8.00
Bluebird 6487 *Always* .... 5.00 - 8.00
Bluebird 6488 *A Star Fell Out of Heaven* .... 5.00 - 8.00
Bluebird 6504 *Make-Believe Ballroom* .... 5.00 - 8.00
Bluebird 6593 *The Milkman's Matinee* .... 4.00 - 6.00
Bluebird 6594 *It's Love I'm After* .... 5.00 - 8.00
Bluebird 6605 *Did You Mean It?* .... 5.00 - 8.00
Bluebird 6619 *Rainbow on the River* .... 5.00 - 8.00
Bluebird 6967 *A Sailboat in the Moonlight* ..... 4.00 - 7.00
Bluebird 6973 *The First Time I Saw You* .... 4.00 - 7.00
Bluebird 6975 *In Your Own Little Way* .... 5.00 - 8.00
Bluebird, most higher numbers .... 2.00 - 4.00
Capitol 843 *All The Things You Are* .... -
Variety 627 *Shame on You* .... 7.00 - 10.00
Variety 633 *Surrealism* .... 7.00 - 10.00
Vocalion 3835 *Overheard in a Cocktail Lounge* .. 7.00 - 10.00

BARREL HOUSE FIVE (ORCHESTRA):
Paramount 12851 *Hot Lovin'* .... 100.00 - 150.00
Paramount 12875 *Endurance Stomp* ....100.00 - 150.00
Paramount 12942 *Scufflin' Blues* ....100.00 - 150.00
QRS 7019 *Endurance Stomp* ....100.00 - 150.00
QRS 7057 *Nobody's Business* ....100.00 - 150.00
QRS 7059 *Hot Lovin'* ....100.00 - 150.00

DICK BARRIE & HIS ORCHESTRA:
Vocalion 4193, 4209, 4271, 4285, 4334, 4348, 4366, 4397, 4409, 4421 .... 3.00 - 5.00

BLUE BARRON & HIS ORCHESTRA:
Bluebird 7419, 7429, 7456, 7540, 7542, 7554, 7605, 7608, 7620, 7709, 7711, 7736, 7856, 7872, 7886 .... 3.00 - 5.00
Bluebird, higher numbers .... 2.00 - 3.00
MGM, most issues .... 2.00 - 3.00
Vocalion 3772 *Yours and Mine* .... 7.00 - 10.00

RAYMOND BARROW:
Paramount 12803 *Walking Blues* .... 75.00 - 125.00

TED BARTELL & HIS ORCHESTRA:
Harmony 912-H *With a Song In My Heart* ...... 5.00 - 8.00
913-H *I Get the Blues When It Rains* .... 5.00 - 8.00
965-H *Now I'm In Love* .... 7.00 - 10.00
973-H *True Blue Lou* .... 7.00 - 10.00
(Note: Above titles on Diva, Velvet Tone are similarly valued)

ALEX BARTHA & HIS HOTEL

TRAYMORE ORCHESTRA:
Victor 24056 *On The Merry-Go-Round* .... 8.00 - 12.00
24059 *Hot Biscuits* .... 15.00 - 20.00

SLIM BARLETT & HIS ORCHESTRA:
Superior 2692 *Asphalt Walk* ....250.00 - up

COUNT BASIE & HIS ORCHESTRA: COUNT BASIE'S KANSAS CITY SEVEN:
Columbia 35231 *Riff Interlude* .... 4.00 - 7.00
Columbia 35338 *Hollywood Jump* .... 4.00 - 7.00
Columbia 35357 *Ham 'n' Eggs* .... 3.00 - 5.00
Columbia 35448 *Louisiana* .... 4.00 - 7.00
Columbia 35500 *Somebody Stole My Gal* ...... 4.00 - 6.00
Columbia 36601, 36647, 36675, 36685, 36709, 36710, 36711, 36712, 36766, 36795, 36831, 36845, 36889, 36946, 36990, 37070, 37093 ... 2.00 - 4.00
Decca 1121 *Pennies From Heaven* .... 7.00 - 10.00
Decca 1141 *Honeysuckle Rose* .... 7.00 - 10.00
Decca 1228 *The Glory Of Love* .... 7.00 - 10.00
Decca 1252 *Exactly Like You* .... 7.00 - 10.00
Decca 1363 *One O' Clock Jump* .... 7.00 - 10.00
Decca 1379 *Smarty (You Know It All)* .... 7.00 - 10.00
Decca 1446 *Good Morning Blues* .... 7.00 - 10.00
Decca 1538 *Let Me Dream* .... 7.00 - 10.00
Decca 1581 *I Keep Remembering* .... 7.00 - 10.00
Decca 1682 *Blues In The Dark* .... 5.00 - 8.00
Decca 1728 *Every Tub* .... 5.00 - 8.00
Decca 1770 *Don't You Miss Your Baby?* ...... 5.00 - 8.00
Decca 1880 *Swinging The Blues* .... 4.00 - 7.00
Decca 1965 *Doggin' Around* .... 4.00 - 7.00
Decca 2004 *London Bridge Is Falling Down* ... 5.00 - 8.00
Decca 2030 *Texas Shuffle* .... 4.00 - 7.00
Decca 2249 *Sing For Your Supper* .... 5.00 - 8.00
Decca 2284 *The Blues I Like To Hear* .... 5.00 - 8.00
Decca (other) .... 3.00 - 6.00
Okeh 5623, 5629, 5732, 5773, 5862, 5884, 5897, 5922, 5963, 6010, 6047 .... 3.00 - 6.00
Okeh (other) .... 3.00 - 5.00
Vocalion 4734, 4747, 4748, 4784, 4860, 4886, 4967, 5036, 5085, 5118, 5169 .... 4.00 - 7.00

PHIL BAXTER & HIS ORCHESTRA:
Okeh 40522 *Something Tells Me* .... 50.00 - 80.00
Okeh 40637 *If I Had You And You Had Me* ..... 50.00 - 80.00
Victor V-40160 *I Ain't Got No Gal Now* .... 40.00 - 60.00
Victor V-40204 *Honey Child* .... 30.00 - 50.00

JOHNNY BAYERSDORFFER & HIS JAZZOLA NOVELTY ORCHESTRA:
Okeh 40133 *The Waffle Man's Call* .... 50.00 - 75.00

BERLYN BAYLOR'S ORCHESTRA:
Champion 16422 *Clarinet Marmalade* .... 50.00 - 75.00
Champion 40000 *Riverboat Shuffle* .... 15.00 - 25.00
Genett 6457 *Clarinet Marmalade* .... 60.00 - 90.00

BEALE STREET FIVE:
Cameo 553 *Who Is The Meanest Gal In Town? Josephine* .... 5.00 - 8.00
Lincoln 2219 *Waitin' Around* .... 5.00 - 8.00

BEALE STREET SEVEN:
Lincoln 2190 *Sweet Papa Joe* .... 8.00 - 12.00

BEALE STREET WASHBOARD BAND:
Vocalion 1403 *Forty And Tight* ....150.00 - 250.00

IRENE BEASLEY:
Victor 21467 *Choo Choo Train* .... 7.00 - 10.00
Victor 21639 *Missin' My Pal* .... 7.00 - 10.00
Victor V40092 *Baby's Back Today* .... 7.00 - 10.00
Victor V40125 *Sometimes I Wonder* .... 7.00 - 10.00
Victor V40173 *You'll Come Back To Me Someday* 15.00 - 20.00

JOSEPHINE BEATTY, ACCOMPANIED BY THE RED ONION JAZZ BABIES:
Buddy 8024 *Early Every Morn* ....150.00 - 200.00
Buddy 8025 *Everybody Loves My Baby* ....150.00 - 200.00
Gennett 3049 *Everybody Loves My Baby* ......100.00 - 150.00
Gennett 3044 *Early Every Morn* ....100.00 - 150.00
Gennett 5594 *Texas Moaner Blues* ....100.00 - 150.00
Silvertone 4030 *Early Every Morn* ....100.00 - 150.00

Silvertone 4033 *Texas Moaner Blues* . . . . 100.00 - 150.00

SIDNEY BECHET & HIS NEW ORLEANS FEETWARMERS/ORCHESTRA: SIDNEY BECHET'S BLUE NOTE QUARTET/ QUINTET:

Bluebird 8509 *Sidney's Blues*	5.00 -	8.00
Bluebird 10623 *Indian Summer*	5.00 -	8.00
Blue Note 6 *Summertime*	5.00 -	8.00
Blue Note 13 *Lonesome Blues*	5.00 -	8.00
Blue Note 502 *Bechet's Steady Rider*	5.00 -	8.00
Victor 26640, 26663, 26746, 27204, 27240, 27337, 27386, 27485, 27447, 27574, 27600, 27663, 27707, 27904	3.00 -	5.00
Vocalion 4537 *Jungle Drums*	5.00 -	8.00
Vocalion 4575 *What A Dream*	5.00 -	8.00

NOAH BEERY:

Brunswick 4828 *One Little Drink* . . . . 5.00 - 10.00

DICK BEESON & HIS ORCHESTRA:

Champion 15054 *Roll 'Em, Girls*	8.00 -	12.00
15055 *That Certain Party*	8.00 -	12.00

BIX BEIDERBECKE (& HIS GANG/ ORCHESTRA):
(See also: BIX & HIS RHYTHM JUGGLERS)

Okeh 40916 *In A Mist*	30.00 -	50.00
Okeh 40923 *At The Jazz Band Ball*	25.00 -	35.00
Okeh 41001 *Sorry*	20.00 -	30.00
Okeh 41030 *Somebody Stole My Gal*	20.00 -	30.00
Okeh 41088 *Ol' Man river*	20.00 -	30.00
Okeh 41173 *Rhythm King*	20.00 -	30.00
Special Edition 5013-S *Margie*	7.00 -	10.00
Vicotr 23008 *I Don't Mind Walking In The Rain*	25.00 -	40.00
Victor 23018 *Deep Down South*	25.00 -	40.00
Victor 25370 *Deep Down South*	5.00 -	8.00
Vocalion (most issues)	4.00 -	7.00

LEON BELASCO & HIS ORCHESTRA:

Vocalion 7863 *Jammin'*	20.00 -	30.00
Vocalion 7872 *Wake Up and Live*	20.00 -	30.00

BELL RECORD BOYS:

Bell 533 *Oh Constantine* . . . . 5.00 - 8.00

ANNA BELL:

QRS 7007 *Hopeless Blues*	100.00 -	150.00
QRS 7008 *Kitchen Woman Blues*	100.00 -	150.00
QRS 7009 *Shake It, Black Bottom*	100.00 -	150.00

GEORGE BELSHAW & HIS KFAB ORCHESTRA:

Brunswick 4365 *Sweet Liza* . . . . 25.00 - 40.00

BENNETT'S SWAMPLANDERS:

Columbia 14557-D *Big Ben*	80.00 -	120.00
Columbia 14662-D *Jet Black Blues*	50.00 -	75.00

PHIL BENNETT & HIS ORCHESTRA:

Broadway 1391 *Rollin' Down The River* . . . . 8.00 - 12.00

BEN'S BAD BOYS:

Victor 21971 *Wang Wang Blues* . . . . 10.00 - 15.00

BENSON ORCHESTRA OF CHICAGO:

Victor 18850 *Railroad Blues*	7.00 -	10.00
19130 *Sobbin' Blues*	5.00 -	8.00
19138 *Mean, Mean, Mamma*	5.00 -	8.00
19140 *Wolverine Blues*	5.00 -	8.00
19235 *Forgetful Blues*	5.00 -	8.00
19257 *Oklahoma Indian Jazz*	5.00 -	8.00
19361 *Lonely Little Wallflower*	5.00 -	8.00
19386 *The Doddle-Um Blues*	7.00 -	10.00
19470 *Copenhagen*	5.00 -	8.00
19484 *Go Emmaline*	5.00 -	8.00
19568 *Heart-Broken Strain*	5.00 -	8.00
19688 *Riverboat Shuffle*	5.00 -	8.00
19693 *Because Of You The World Is Mine*	7.00 -	10.00

BENNY BENSON'S ORCHESTRA:

Champion 15886 *"Tain't No Sin*	20.00 -	30.00
Champion 15932 *Honeysuckle Rose*	20.00 -	30.00

BUNNY BERIGAN & HIS BOYS/ORCHESTRA:

Brunswick 7784 *That Foolish Feeling* . . . . 8.00 - 12.00

Brunswick 7823 *Who's Afraid Of Love?*	7.00 -	10.00
Brunswick 7832 *The Gonna Goo*	8.00 -	12.00
Brunswick 7847 *Big Boy Blue*	8.00 -	12.00
Brunswick 7858 *Dixieland Shuffle*	8.00 -	12.00
Elite 5005, 5006, 5019, 5020	4.00 -	7.00
Victor (most issues)	4.00 -	8.00
Vocalion 3178 *I'd Rather Lead A Bard*	10.00 -	15.00
Vocalion 3179 *Swing, Mister Charlie*	10.00 -	15.00
Vocalion 3224 *A Melody From The Sky*	8.00 -	12.00
Vocalion 3225 *I Can't Get Started*	8.00 -	12.00
Vocalion 3254 *If I Had My Way*	8.00 -	12.00
Vocalion 15875, 15884, 15887, 15891	5.00 -	10.00

AL BERNARD:

Banner 1211 *St. Louis Blues*	5.00 -	8.00
Brunswick 2084 *Strut Miss Lizzie*	5.00 -	8.00
2107 *Memphis Blues*	5.00 -	8.00
2448 *Stavin' Change*	5.00 -	8.00
Okeh 1235 *Shake, Rattle And Roll*	— -	—
Okeh 40962 *St. Louis Blues*	7.00 -	10.00
Regal 9426 *Whoa Tillie*	5.00 -	8.00

MIKE BERNARD:

Columbia A1266 *Everybody Two-Step*	8.00 -	12.00
A1313 *That Peculiar Rag*	15.00 -	20.00
A1386 *Tantalizing Tingles*	15.00 -	20.00
A1427 *1915 Rag*	15.00 -	20.00
A2577 *Blaze Away*	10.00 -	15.00

BEN BERNIE & HIS (HOTEL ROOSEVELT) ORCHESTRA:

Brunswick 3042 *Fallen Arches*	7.00 -	10.00
3082 *Bell-Hoppin' Blues*	7.00 -	10.00
3126 *Jig walk*	7.00 -	10.00
3145 *Up And At 'Em*	7.00 -	10.00
3887 *Borneo*	7.00 -	10.00
Brunswick 4020 *When Polly Walks Through The Hollyhocks*	7.00 -	10.00
Brunswick 4042 *Cannon Ball Rag*	10.00 -	15.00
Brunswick 4767 *You Brought a New Kind of Love To Me*	8.00 -	12.00
Brunswick 6165 *This Is The Missus*	8.00 -	12.00
20064 (12") *Ol' Man River*	10.00 -	20.00
Brunswick, most other issues	4.00 -	7.00
Columbia 2804-D *Marching Along Together*	8.00 -	12.00
Columbia 2809-D *The Duke Is On A Bat Again*	8.00 -	12.00
Columbia 2820-D *This Is Romance*	8.00 -	12.00
Columbia 2824-D *Shanghai Lil*	8.00 -	12.00
Columbia 2836-D *So This Is Susie?*	8.00 -	12.00
Decca 874 *Long Ago and Far Away*	5.00 -	8.00
Decca 877 *Am I Asking Too Much?*	5.00 -	8.00
Decca 878 *When Did You Leave Heaven?*	3.00 -	5.00
Vocalion, most issues	4.00 -	7.00

CHU BERRY & HIS STOMPY STEVEDORES

Commodore 516, 541, 1502, 1508	3.00 -	5.00
Variety 532 *Too Marvelous For Words*	8.00 -	12.00
Variety 587 *Limehouse Blues*	7.00 -	10.00
Variety 657 *My Secret Love Affair*	7.00 -	10.00

VIC BERTON & HIS ORCHESTRA:

Columbia 3074-D *Devil's Kitchen*	15.00 -	25.00
Columbia 3092-D *Imitations of You*	15.00 -	25.00
Vocalion 2915 *Dardanella*	15.00 -	20.00
Vocalion 2944 *Lonesome and Sorry*	15.00 -	20.00
Vocalion 2964 *A Smile Will Go A Long, Long Way*	15.00 -	20.00
Vocalion 2974 *Blue*	15.00 -	20.00

JIMMY BERTRAND'S WASHBOARD WIZARDS:

Vocalion 1035 *Little Bits*	30.00 -	50.00
Vocalion 1060 *47th Street Stomp*	75.00 -	100.00
Vocalion 1099 *I'm Goin' Huntin'*	80.00 -	120.00
Vocalion 1100 *The Blues Stampede*	80.00 -	120.00
Vocalion 1280 *I Won't Give You Some*	100.00 -	150.00

DON BESTOR & HIS ORCHESTRA:

Victor 19988 *Say Mister! Have You Met*		
Rosie's Sister?	7.00 -	10.00
21080 *Baby Your Mother*	5.00 -	8.00
24253 *Forty-Second Street*	8.00 -	12.00
24505 *Armful Of Trouble*	15.00 -	20.00
Victor 24556, 24596, 24658	5.00 -	8.00
Victor (most other issues)	3.00 -	6.00

HENRY BIAGINI & HIS ORCHESTRA:

Titles, on Banner, Melotone, Oriole, Perfect,		
Romeo: *Go Into Your Dance: The Little Things*		
You Used To Do	5.00 -	8.00

PAUL BIESE & HIS ORCHESTRA:

Columbia (most issues)	3.00 -	5.00
Brunswick (most issues)	3.00 -	5.00
Victor 19314 *Cinderella Blues*	5.00 -	8.00
19474 *Bye Bye Baby*	7.00 -	10.00

THE BIG ACES:

Okeh 41136 *Cherry*	15.00 -	20.00

BARNEY BIGARD & HIS ORCHESTRA/ JAZZOPATORS:

Bluebird 10981, 11098, 11581	3.00 -	5.00
Variety 515, 525, 564, 596, 626, 655	6.00 -	10.00
Vocalion 03809, 03813, 03820, 03828, 03834,		
03842, 03985	6.00 -	10.00

JACK BINNEY & HIS ORCHESTRA:

Parlophone PNY-34096 *Freshman Hop*	25.00 -	40.00

BIRMINGHAM BLUETETTE:

Herwin 92019 *Old Man Blues*	200.00 -	300.00

BIRMINGHAM FIVE:

Champion 15008 *Red Hot Henry Brown*	10.00 -	15.00
Champion 15015 *Sweet Georgia Brown*	10.00 -	15.00
Champion 15018 *Oh Boy! What A Girl*	10.00 -	15.00
Champion 15028 *Siberia*	10.00 -	15.00
Champion 15046 *I'm Gonna Hang Around*		
My Sugar	10.00 -	15.00
Champion 15047 *No Man's Mama*	10.00 -	15.00
Champion 15049 *Melancholy Lou*	10.00 -	15.00
Champion 15050 *Everybody's Doin' The*		
Charleston Now	10.00 -	15.00

BIRMINGHAM JUG BAND:

Okeh 8856 *German Blues*	75.00 -	100.00
Okeh 8866 *Kickin' Mules Blues*	75.00 -	100.00
Okeh 8895 *Birmingham Blues*	75.00 -	100.00
Okeh 8908 *Wild Cat Squall*	75.00 -	100.00

BIRMINGHAM SERENADERS:

Decca 7052 *Black Gal Blues*	20.00 -	30.00
Decca 7060 *Milk Cow Blues*	20.00 -	30.00

BIX & HIS RHYTHM JUGGLERS:

Gennett 5654 *Davenport Blues*	75.00 -	100.00

BLACKBIRDS OF PARADISE:

Black Patti 8053 *Razor Edge*	300.00 -	500.00
Gennett 6210 *Tishomingo Blues*	150.00 -	300.00
Gennett 6211 *Muddy Water*	150.00 -	300.00

BLACK DIAMOND ORCHESTRA:

Gennett 6442 *I've Got Somebody Now*	20.00 -	30.00

BLACK DIAMOND SERENADERS:

Pathe 36503 *Toe-To-Toe*	8.00 -	12.00
Pathe 36511 *Ace In The Hole*	8.00 -	12.00
Perfect 14684 *Sally's Not The Same Old Sally*	8.00 -	12.00
Perfect 14692 *Ace In The Hole*	8.00 -	12.00

THE BLACK DOMINOES:

Gennett 5263, 5347	7.00 -	10.00

BLACK KIDS OF HARMONY:

Silvertone 3831 *So's Your Old Man*	10.00 -	20.00

THE BLACK PIRATES:

Broadway 1230 *My Old Girl's My New Girl Now*	5.00 -	8.00
1374 *Some Of These Days*	10.00 -	15.00

BLACK SWAN DANCE ORCHESTRA:

Black Swan 2014 *Pretty Ways*	10.00 -	15.00

FRANK BLACK & HIS ORCHESTRA:

Brunswick (most issues)	3.00 -	6.00

BLAKE'S JAZZONE ORCHESTRA:

Pathe 20430 *The Jazz Dance*	10.00 -	15.00

EUBIE BLAKE (& HIS ORCHESTRA); EUBIE BLAKE TRIO:

Crown 3086 *When Your Lover Has Gone*	15.00 -	20.00
Crown 3090 *I'm No Account Any More*	15.00 -	20.00
Crown 3105 *It Looks Like Love*	15.00 -	20.00
Crown 3111 *One More Time*	15.00 -	20.00
Crown 3130 *Nobody's Sweetheart*	15.00 -	20.00
Crown 3193 *River Stay 'Way From My Door*	15.00 -	20.00
Crown 3197 *Sweet Georgia Brown*	15.00 -	20.00
Emerson 10450, 10519	4.00 -	8.00
Emerson 10434 *Baltimore Buzz*	20.00 -	30.00
Pathe 20326 *American Jubilee*	8.00 -	12.00
Pathe 20358 *Sarah From Sahara*	8.00 -	12.00
Victor 22735 *My Blue Days Blew Over*	15.00 -	20.00
Victor 22737 *Thumpin And Bumpin*	15.00 -	20.00

JACK BLAND & HIS RHYTHMAKERS

Titles, issued contemporaneously on Banner,		
Melotone, Oriole, Perfect, Romeo: *It's Gonna*		
Be You: A Shine On Your Shoes; Someone		
Stole Gabriel's Horn; Who Stole The Lock	15.00 -	25.00

RUBE BLOOM (& HIS BAYOU BOYS):

Brunswick 3366 *Back Beats*	50.00 -	75.00
Cameo 1153 *Spring Fever*	7.00 -	10.00
Columbia 2103-D *The Man From The South*	10.00 -	15.00
Columbia 2186-D *Bessie Couldn't Help it*	10.00 -	15.00
Columbia 2218-D *On Revival Day*	10.00 -	15.00
Harmony 164-H *Soliloquy*	5.00 -	8.00
Victor 25060 *On The Green*	5.00 -	8.00
Victor 25227 *One Finger Joe*	5.00 -	8.00

THE BLU-DISC ORCH.:

Blu-Disc 1005 *I Want To Be Happy*	30.00 -	50.00
Blu-Disc 1006 *It Had To Be You*	30.00 -	50.00

THE BLUEBIRDS:

Vocalion 15652 *Let's Misbehave*	8.00 -	12.00

BLUE GRASS FOOT WARMERS:

Harmony 206-H *Senorita Mine*	10.00 -	15.00
Harmony 248-H *Old Folks Shuffle*	10.00 -	15.00
(Same titles also appear on Diva, Velvet Tone.)		

BLUE JAY BOYS:

Decca 7224 *Endurance Stomp*	10.00 -	15.00
Decca 7225 *Some Do And Some Don't*	10.00 -	15.00
Decca 7240 *My Baby*	10.00 -	15.00

BLUE MOON MELODY BOYS:

Champion 15429 *Louisiana*	15.00 -	20.00

BLUE RHYTHM BAND/BOYS:

Brunswick 6143 *Blue Flame*	30.00 -	40.00
Brunswick 6199 *Snake Hips*	30.00 -	40.00

BLUE RHYTHM ORCHESTRA:

Pathe-Actuelle 36350 *Santa Claus Blues*	50.00 -	75.00
Pathe-Actuelle 36364 *Keep Your Temper*	50.00 -	75.00
Perfect 14531 *Santa Claus Blues*	50.00 -	75.00
Perfect 14545 *Keep Your Temper*	50.00 -	75.00

BLUE RIBBON BOYS:

Titles, issued contemporaneously on Banner,		
Conqueror, Regal, Romeo: *Black And Tan*		
Fantasy; Futuristic Jungleism; Low Down On		
The Bayou; Poor Minnie The Moocher; Star		
Dust; Sugar Blues	8.00 -	15.00

BLUE RIBBON SYNCOPATORS:

Columbia 14215-D *Memphis Sprawler* ....100.00 - 150.00
Columbia 14235-D *Whale Dip* ....100.00 - 150.00

BLUE ROOM ORCHESTRA:
Broadway 1244 *Glad Rag Doll* ....　5.00 -　8.00
　1245 *My Man* . . . .　4.00 -　7.00
　1246 *Guess Who!* . . . .　4.00 -　7.00
　1268 *Pretty Little Thing* . . . .　5.00 -　8.00
　1270 *A Garden in the Rain* . . . .　4.00 -　6.00
　1306 *Waiting at the End of the Road* . . . .　5.00 -　8.00

BOB BLUE:
Okeh 41464 *I'll Be Blue, Just Thinking Of You* . . .　8.00 - 12.00

BUDDY BLUE & HIS TEXANS:
Banner 0695 *Any Old Place With You* . . . .　5.00 -　8.00
Banner 6411 *Ol' Man River* . . . .　5.00 -　8.00
Banner 6515 *Ev'ry Day Away From You* . . . .　5.00 -　8.00
Banner 6547 *By The Way (I'm Still In Love With
　You)* . . . .　5.00 -　8.00
Cameo　0295 *Any Old Place With You* . . . .　5.00 -　8.00
Cameo　0332 *Got a Great Big Date (With
　Someone Nice)* . . . .　5.00 -　8.00

THE BLUES CHASERS:
Perfect 14428 *Sweet Georgia Brown* . . . .　7.00 - 10.00
Perfect 14432 *Charleston* . . . .　7.00 - 10.00

BLUMENBERG'S ORCHESTRA:
Broadway 1490 *Love Letters In The Sand* . . . . . .　7.00 - 10.00

BLYTHE'S BLUE BOYS:
Champion 15344 *There'll Come A Day* . . . . .150.00 - 200.00
Champion 15399 *Cootie Stomp* . . . . .150.00 - 200.00
Champion 15528 *My Baby* . . . . .150.00 - 200.00
Champion 15551 *Pleasure Mad* . . . . .150.00 - 200.00
Champion 15570 *Tell Me, Cutie* . . . . .150.00 - 200.00
Champion 15615 *Endurance Stomp* . . . . .150.00 - 200.00
Champion 15676 *Oriental Man* . . . . .150.00 - 200.00
Champion 40023 *Oriental Man* . . . . 30.00 - 50.00
Champion 40025 *Endurance Stomp* . . . . 30.00 - 50.00
Champion 40062 *Tack It Down* . . . . 30.00 - 50.00
Champion 40115 *Tell Me, Cutie* . . . . 30.00 - 50.00

BLYTHE'S SINFUL FIVE;
Paramount 12346 *Pump Tillie Pump* . . . . .100.00 - 150.00

**BLYTHE'S WASHBOARD BAND/
RAGAMUFFINS:**
Paramount 12368 *Bohunkus Blues* . . . . .150.00 - 250.00
Paramount 12428 *Ape Man* . . . . .150.00 - 200.00

**JAMES/JIMMIE/JIMMY BLYTHE (& BURTON/
& HIS RAGAMUFFINS); JIMMIE BLYTHE'S
OWLS/WASHBOARD WIZARDS:**
Champion 16451 *Bow To Your Papa* . . . . 80.00 - 120.00
Gennett 6502 *Dustin' The Keys* . . . . .100.00 - 150.00
Paramount 12207 *Chicago Stomp* . . . . .100.00 - 150.00
Paramount 12304 *Jimmie Blues* . . . . .100.00 - 150.00
Paramount 12370 *Mr. Freddie Blues* . . . . .100.00 - 150.00
Paramount 12376 *Messin Around* . . . . .100.00 - 150.00
Vocalion 1135 *Weary Way Blues* . . . . .100.00 - 150.00
Vocalion 1136 *Have Mercy!* . . . . .100.00 - 150.00
Vocalion 1180 *Oriental Man* . . . . .100.00 - 150.00
Vocalion 1181 *Alley Rat* . . . . 75.00 - 100.00

BOBBY'S REVELERS:
Silvertone 3551 *Heebie Jeebies* . . . . 50.00 - 75.00
Silvertone 3552 *Mojo Blues* . . . . 50.00 - 75.00

BOGAN'S BIRMINGHAM BUSTERS:
Titles, issued contemporaneously on Banner,
　Melotone, Oriole, Perfect, Romeo: *Everything
　Is Rhythm Now; She Caught The Boat* . . . . . . 20.00 - 30.00
Vocalion 03540 *She Caught the Boat* . . . . 20.00 - 30.00
Vocalion 03570 *The Sheik of Araby* . . . . 20.00 - 30.00

TOMMY BOHN PENN-SIRENS ORCHESTRA:
Odeon ONY-36047 *You've Got That Thing* . . . . . 25.00 - 40.00
Okeh 41372 *Amos 'n' Andy* . . . . 25.00 - 35.00
Okeh 41374 *You've Got That Thing* . . . . 25.00 - 35.00

PAUL BOLOGNESE & HIS ORCHESTRA:
Globe 8109 *Charleston Choo Choo* . . . . 7.00 - 10.00
Grey Gull 1439 *At Sundown* . . . . 5.00 - 8.00

**BOLTON AND CIPRIANI'S WESTCHESTER
　BILTMORE ORCHESTRA:**
Columbia Personal 93-P *You'll Do It Someday* . . 20.00 - 30.00

**PETE BONTSEMA & HIS HOTEL TULLER
　ORCHESTRA OF DETROIT:**
Gennett 20016 *Salt Your Sugar* . . . . 15.00 - 20.00

BOOKER ORCHESTRA:
Gennett 6375 *Salty Dog* . . . . 75.00 - 100.00

BOOTS AND HIS BUDDIES:
Bluebird 6063 *Rose Room* . . . .　7.00 - 10.00
Bluebird 6081 *Riffs* . . . .　7.00 - 10.00
Bluebird 6132 *Anytime* . . . .　5.00 -　8.00
Bluebird 6301 *Georgia* . . . .　8.00 - 12.00
Bluebird 6307 *Coquette* . . . .　6.00 - 10.00
Bluebird 6333 *The Vamp* . . . .　7.00 - 10.00
Bluebird 6357 *Sweet Girl* . . . .　6.00 - 10.00
Bluebird 6862 *Jealous* . . . .　8.00 - 12.00
Bluebird 6880 *Haunting Memories* . . . .　8.00 - 12.00
Bluebird 6921 *Swanee River Blues* . . . . 10.00 - 15.00
Bluebird 6968 *Sleepy Gal* . . . .　8.00 - 12.00
Bluebird 7005 *San Antonio Tamales* . . . . 10.00 - 15.00
Bluebird 7187 *Blues of Avalon* . . . .　7.00 - 10.00
Bluebird 7217 *The Goo* . . . .　7.00 - 10.00
Bluebird 7236 *The Sad* . . . . 10.00 - 15.00
Bluebird 7241 *Ain't Misbehavin'* . . . .　7.00 - 10.00
Bluebird 7245 *The Happy* . . . .　7.00 - 10.00
Bluebird 7269 *The Somebody* . . . . 10.00 - 15.00
Bluebird 7556 *Deep South* . . . .　8.00 - 12.00
Bluebird 7596 *True Blue Lou* . . . .　7.00 - 10.00
Bluebird 7669 *Lonely Moments* . . . .　7.00 - 10.00
Bluebird 7944 *A Salute To Harlem* . . . . 10.00 - 15.00
Bluebird 10036 *East Commerce Stomp* . . . .　7.00 - 10.00
Bluebird 10043 *Sweet Girl* . . . .　5.00 -　8.00
Bluebird 10044 *San Antonio Tamales* . . . .　5.00 -　8.00
Bluebird 10106 *Boots Stomp* . . . .　7.00 - 10.00
Bluebird 10113 *Lonesome Road Stomp* . . . .　7.00 - 10.00

BORBEE'S JASS ORCHESTRA:
Columbia A2363 *The Ragtime Volunteers Are Off
　To War* . . . .　7.00 - 10.00

BOSTON SOCIETY ORCHESTRA:
Oriole 1454 *Glad Rag Doll* . . . .　5.00 -　8.00

THE BOSTONIANS:
Banner 7246 *My Blackbirds Are Bluebirds Now* .　5.00 -　8.00
Domino 4216 *My Blackbirds Are Bluebirds Now* .　5.00 -　8.00
Regal 8654 *My Blackbirds Are Bluebirds Now* . . .　5.00 -　8.00
Vocalion 15275 *So Does Your Old Mandarin* . . . .　5.00 -　8.00
Vocalion 15298 *I've Found a New Baby* . . . .　7.00 - 10.00

THE BOSWELL SISTERS:
Brunswick 6083, 6109, 6151, 6170, 6173, 6218,
　6231, 6257, 6271, 6291, 6302, 6335, 6360,
　6395, 6418, 6442, 6470, 6483, 6545, 6596,
　6625, 6650, 6733, 6798　　　　　　　　　 　7.00 - 12.00
Brunswick 6847, 6929, 6951, 7302, 7348, 7412,
　7454, 7467　　　　　　　　　　　　　　　　　5.00 - 10.00
Decca 574, 671, 709 . . . .　5.00 -　8.00
Victor 19639 *Nights When I'm Lonely* . . . . 20.00 - 30.00

CONNIE BOSWELL:
Brunswick 6162, 6210, 6223, 6267, 6297, 6405,
　6483　　　　　　　　　　　　　　　　　　　　6.00 - 10.00
Brunswick 6552, 6592, 6603, 6632, 6640, 6754,
　6862, 6871, 6921, 6962, 7303, 7354, 7363,
　7445, 7457 . . . .　4.00 -　7.00
Victor 19639 *I'm Gonna Cry* . . . . 20.00 - 30.00

JIMMY BRACKEN'S TOE TICKLERS:
Titles, issued contemporaneously on Banner,
　Conqueror, Domino, Regal: *After You've
　Gone; Icky Blues; It's So Good; It's Tight Like
　That; Making Friends; Four Or Five Times;
　Shirt Tail Stomp; Tiger Rag; Twelfth Street Rag* 8.00 - 15.00

**PERRY BRADFORD & HIS GANG: PERRY
　BRADFORD'S JAZZ PHOOLS:**
Titles, issued contemporaneously on Claxtonola,

Harmograph, Paramount, Puritan: *Day Break*		
Blues; Fade Away Blues	75.00 -	125.00
Additional titles: *Charleston, South Carolina;*		
Hoola Boola Dance	75.00 -	100.00
Columbia 14142-D *So's Your Old Man*	35.00 -	50.00
Okeh 8324 *So's Your Old Man*	75.00 -	100.00
Okeh 8416 *Kansas City Blues*	75.00 -	100.00
Okeh 8450 *Lucy Long*	75.00 -	100.00
Vocalion 15165 *Lucy Long*	75.00 -	100.00

WILL BRADLEY AND HIS ORCHESTRA:

Columbia 35333, 35354, 35399, 35414, 35464,		
35470, 35485, 35530, 35542, 35543, 35545,		
35566, 35597, 35607, 35645	3.00 -	6.00
Columbia, most others	2.00 -	4.00
Signature 15048, 15049, 15111, 15134	2.00 -	4.00
Vocalion 5130, 5182, 5210, 5237, 5262	3.00 -	6.00

TINY BRADSHAW & HIS ORCHESTRA:

Decca 194, 236, 317, 456	6.00 -	10.00

ARDELL/ARDELLA/ARDELLE ("SHELLEY")
BRAGG (& HER TEXAS BLUE BLOWERS):

Paramount 12398 *Pig Meat Blues*	75.00 -	100.00
Paramount 12410 *Bird Nest Blues*	75.00 -	100.00
Paramount 12429 *That's Alright*	75.00 -	100.00
Paramount 12458 *Wolf Man*	75.00 -	100.00

J.H. BRAGG AND HIS RHYTHM FIVE:

Vocalion 03060 *Ethiopian Stomp*	15.00 -	25.00
Vocalion 03174 *Frisky Honey*	15.00 -	25.00

BRASHEAR'S CALIFORNIA ORCHESTRA:

Black Swan 2078 *Stuttering*	15.00 -	20.00
Black Swan 10074 *Stuttering*	15.00 -	20.00
Black Swan 10079 *Carolina Shout*	15.00 -	20.00

BRUCE BRAY'S ORCHESTRA:

Bell 569 *Sweetheart Of Sigma Chi*	20.00 -	30.00
Challenge 759 *Sweetheart Of Sigma Chi*	20.00 -	30.00

LEW BRAY Accompanied by SUNNY CLAPP
& HIS BAND O'SUNSHINE:

Okeh 41261 *We Can't Use Each Other Any More*	25.00 -	35.00

PERLEY BREED'S (SHEPARD COLONIAL)
ORCHESTRA:

Gennett 3059 *Honey, I'm In Love With You*	15.00 -	20.00
5608 *Tell Me, Dreamy Eyes*	15.00 -	20.00

ACE BRIGODE & HIS TEN/FOURTEEN
VIRGINIANS:

Cameo (most issues)	3.00 -	5.00
Columbia 398-D *Yes, Sir! That's My Baby*	5.00 -	8.00
Columbia (most other issues)	4.00 -	7.00
Edison 51511 *Tokio Blues*	5.00 -	8.00
51533 *Fooling*	5.00 -	8.00
Okeh (most issues)	3.00 -	6.00

(A.) BRILLHARDT'S ORCHESTRA:

Pathe-Actuelle 36430 *The Girl Friend*	8.00 -	12.00
Pathe-Actuelle 36438 *Hello, Aloha! How*		
Are You?	8.00 -	12.00
Pathe-Actuelle 36450 *State Street Shuffle*	10.00 -	15.00
Perfect 14611 *The Girlfriend*	8.00 -	12.00
14619 *Hello, Aloha! How Are You*	8.00 -	12.00
14631 *State Street Shuffle*	10.00 -	15.00

MATT BRITT & HIS ORCHESTRA:

Victor 21760 *Goose Creek-Stomp*	15.00 -	20.00
Victor 22933 *Learning*	8.00 -	12.00
Victor 22956 *Down The Old Back Road*	8.00 -	12.00
Victor V-40012 *Sadness Will Be Gladness*	30.00 -	40.00

BROADWAY BELL-HOPS:

Harmony 120-H *But I Do—You Know I Do*	7.00 -	10.00
Harmony 121-H *Wimmin—Aaah!*	10.00 -	15.00
Harmony 147-H *Here Comes Malinda*	5.00 -	8.00
Harmony 159-H *Show That Fellow the Door*	5.00 -	8.00
Harmony 163-H *Honey Bunch*	5.00 -	8.00
Harmony 210-H *I'm Walking Around in Circles*	4.00 -	7.00
Harmony 223-H *Someone Is Losin' Susan*	5.00 -	8.00
Harmony 225-H *In A Little Garden*	4.00 -	7.00
Harmony 241-H *She Knows Her Onions*	5.00 -	8.00

Harmony 243-H *Mary Lou*	5.00 -	8.00
Harmony 253-H *Don't Be Angry With Me*	4.00 -	7.00
Harmony 258-H *I Never Knew What the*		
Moonlight Could Do	4.00 -	7.00
Harmony 272-H *Hello Bluebird*	4.00 -	7.00
Harmony 279-H *Here Comes Fatima*	5.00 -	8.00
Harmony 288-H *Don't Take That Black Bottom*		
Away	5.00 -	8.00
Harmony 298-H *I Love the Moonlight*	5.00 -	8.00
Harmony 327-H *He's The Last Word*	7.00 -	10.00
Harmony 338-H *Collette*	4.00 -	7.00
Harmony 355-H *I Wonder How I Look When*		
I'm Asleep	5.00 -	8.00
Harmony 365-H *That's My Hap-Hap-Happiness*	5.00 -	8.00
Harmony 390-H *Don't Somebody Want*		
Somebody To Love	4.00 -	7.00
Harmony 429-H *Under the Moon*	4.00 -	7.00
Harmony 450-H *I'm In Love Again*	5.00 -	8.00
Harmony 479-H *Someday You'll Say "O.K."*	5.00 -	8.00
Harmony 504-H *There Ain't No Land Like*		
Dixieland To Me	40.00 -	60.00
Harmony 536-H *Where the Cot-Cot-Cotton*		
Grows	5.00 -	8.00
Harmony 564-H *Let a Smile Be Your Umbrella*	5.00 -	8.00
Harmony 630-H *Happy-Go-Lucky Lane*	5.00 -	8.00
Harmony 644-H *Get Out and Get Under the*		
Moon	5.00 -	8.00
Harmony 661-H *Old Man Sunshine*	5.00 -	8.00
(Note: Above titles, on *Diva* and *Velvet Tone*, are		
similarly valued)		

BROADWAY BROADCASTERS:

Brunswick 4119 *I Must Have That Man*	5.00 -	8.00
Brunswick 4124 *Pompanola*	5.00 -	8.00
Cameo 498 *Sobbin' Blues*	5.00 -	8.00
Cameo 522 *Somebody Stole My Gal*	3.00 -	5.00
Cameo 632 *I Want To See My Tennessee*	5.00 -	8.00
Cameo 713 *All Aboard For Heaven*	5.00 -	8.00
Cameo 738 *Oh, How I Miss You Tonight*	4.00 -	7.00
Cameo 815 *If I Had a Girl Like You*	5.00 -	8.00
Cameo 836 *No Man's Mamma*	5.00 -	8.00
Cameo 839 *Spanish Shawl*	5.00 -	8.00
Cameo 850 *I Love My Baby (My Baby Loves Me)*	5.00 -	8.00
Cameo 883 *Wimmin—Aaah!*	5.00 -	8.00
Cameo 896 *Rhythm Rag*	7.00 -	10.00
Cameo 912 *Talkin' to the Moon*	4.00 -	7.00
Cameo 938 *I've Found a Round-A-Bout Way To*		
Heaven	4.00 -	7.00
Cameo 985 *The Birth of the Blues*	4.00 -	7.00
Cameo 996 *High Fever*	5.00 -	8.00
Cameo 1088 *Here or There As Long As I'm With*		
You	5.00 -	8.00
Cameo 1149 *St. Louis Blues*	7.00 -	10.00
Cameo 1218 *Some Day You'll Say "O.K."*	3.00 -	5.00
Cameo 1239 *Marvelous*	3.00 -	5.00
Cameo 8143 *Beautiful*	5.00 -	8.00
Cameo 8163 *She's a Great, Great Girl*	5.00 -	8.00
Cameo 8179 *Lila*	7.00 -	10.00
Cameo 8195 *Wob-A-Ly Walk*	7.00 -	10.00
Cameo 8227 *South Bound*	5.00 -	8.00
Cameo 8228 *Lots O' Mama*	5.00 -	8.00
Cameo 8245 *Ready for the River*	5.00 -	8.00
Cameo 9008 *Adorable Dora*	7.00 -	10.00
Cameo 9036 *Gypsy*	15.00 -	20.00
Cameo 9056 *Dream Train*	4.00 -	7.00
Cameo 9057 *If I Had You*	5.00 -	8.00
Cameo 9084 *I Want To Be Bad*	5.00 -	8.00
Cameo 9088 *He, She and Me*	5.00 -	8.00
Cameo 9130 *Honey*	5.00 -	8.00
Cameo 9158 *Do Something*	5.00 -	8.00
Cameo 9209 *Maybe! Who Knows?*	7.00 -	10.00
Cameo 9213 *With A Song In My Heart*	5.00 -	8.00
Romeo 625 *Wob-A-Ly Walk*	7.00 -	10.00

Romeo 668 *Ready for the River* . . . . 5.00 - 8.00
Romeo 775 *Come On, Baby!* . . . . 7.00 - 10.00
Romeo 861 *If I Had You* . . . . 5.00 - 8.00
Romeo 900 *What A Girl! What A Night!* . . . . 8.00 - 12.00
Romeo 932 *Honey* . . . . 5.00 - 8.00
Romeo 942 *Down Among The Sugar Cane* . . . . . 4.00 - 7.00

BROADWAY DANCE ORCHESTRA:
Broadway 1002, 1003, 1015 . . . . 4.00 - 7.00
Edison 51302 *An Orange Grove In California* . . . . 8.00 - 12.00
Edison 51303 *Old Fashioned Love* . . . . 8.00 - 12.00
Edison 51412 *Sally Lou* . . . . 10.00 - 15.00
Edison 51420 *Eliza* . . . . 8.00 - 12.00
Edison 51421 *Doodle-Doo-Doo* . . . . 5.00 - 8.00

BROADWAY MELODY MAKERS:
Broadway 11284 *Wild Papa* . . . . 10.00 - 15.00
Puretone 11373 *Sooke Hey Hey* . . . . 15.00 - 20.00
Triangle 11200 *Bees Knees* . . . . 10.00 - 15.00
Triangle 11284 *Two Time Dan* . . . . 10.00 - 15.00

BROADWAY PICKERS:
Broadway 5069 *Salty Dog* . . . . 200.00 - 300.00

BROADWAY PLAYERS:
Q.R.S. 1008 *All Day Long* . . . . 8.00 - 12.00
1021 *Should I Be Sorry* . . . . 10.00 - 15.00
1022 *With You* . . . . 10.00 - 15.00

BROADWAY RASTUS:
Paramount 12764 *Rock My Soul* . . . . 75.00 - 100.00

BROADWAY SEVEN:
Grey Gull 1190 *St. Louis Gal* . . . . 8.00 - 12.00
1192 *Back O' Town Blues* . . . . 8.00 - 12.00

BROADWAY SYNCOPATERS:
Vocalion 14586 *Louisville Lou* . . . . 5.00 - 8.00
14598 *Two-Time Dan* . . . . 5.00 - 8.00
14670 *House Of David Blues* . . . . 7.00 - 10.00
14675 *Sittin' In A Corner* . . . . 5.00 - 8.00
Vocalion (other issues) . . . . 4.00 - 7.00

IRVING BRODSKY & HIS ORCHESTRA:
Harmony 1021-H *If You Believed In Me* . . . . 8.00 - 12.00
Harmony 1041-H *The End of the Lonesome Trail* . 8.00 - 12.00

HARVEY BROOKS' QUALITY FOUR:
Hollywood 1008 *Mistreating Daddy* . . . . 150.00 - 200.00
Hollywood 1021 *Nobody's Sweetheart* . . . . 200.00 - 300.00
Hollywood 1022 *Down On The Farm* . . . . 200.00 - 300.00

BROWN-MORRIS ORCHESTRA:
Harmony 521-H *Headin' For Harlem* . . . . 7.00 - 10.00
528-H *Rose Of Monterey* . . . . 5.00 - 8.00
(Note: Above titles, on *Diva* and *Velvet Tone*, are similarly valued)

BROWN AND TERRY'S JAZZOLA BOYS:
Okeh 8006 *Hesitating Blues* . . . . 10.00 - 15.00
Okeh 8014 *All By Myself* . . . . 10.00 - 15.00
Okeh 8017 *Saxophone Blues* . . . . 10.00 - 15.00
Okeh 8018 *Aunt Hagar's Blues* . . . . 10.00 - 15.00
Okeh 8021 *Jump Steady Blues* . . . . 15.00 - 20.00

BILL BROWN & HIS BROWNIES:
Brunswick 7003 *Bill Brown Blues* . . . . 15.00 - 20.00
Brunswick 7142 *Zonky* . . . . 35.00 - 50.00
Vocalion 1128 *Bill Brown Blues* . . . . 30.00 - 40.00

CLEO BROWN:
Hollywood Hot Shots L-0349 *Who'll Chop Your Suey* . . . . 10.00 - 20.00

FRANK BROWN & HIS TOOTERS:
Parlophone PNY-34154 *Ring Dem Bells* . . . . 20.00 - 30.00
Parlophone PNY-34156 *Three Little Words* . . . . . 20.00 - 30.00

HENRY BROWN:
Brunswick 7086 *Stomp 'Em Down To The Bricks* 100.00 - 150.00
Paramount 12825 *Twenty-First Street Stomp* . . . . 150.00 - 200.00
Paramount 12934 *Blues Stomp* . . . . 150.00 - 200.00
Paramount 12988 *Eastern Chimes Blues* . . . . . . 150.00 - 200.00

IDA G. BROWN & HER BOYS:
Banner 1343 *Jail House Blues* . . . . 20.00 - 30.00
Regal 9639 *Kiss Me Sweet* . . . . 20.00 - 30.00

KID BROWN & HIS BLUE BAND:

Black Patti 8049 *Bo-Lita* . . . . 250.00 - Up

LES BROWN & HIS (DUKE UNIVERSITY) BLUE DEVILS/ORCHESTRA:
Bluebird 7796, 7812, 7858, 7869 . . . . 4.00 - 6.00
Bluebird, most others . . . . 3.00 - 5.00
Decca 991 *Swing For Sale* . . . . 7.00 - 10.00
Decca 1231 *Swamp Fire* . . . . 4.00 - 7.00
Decca 1238 *Rigamorole* . . . . 5.00 - 8.00
Decca 1296 *Ramona* . . . . 5.00 - 8.00
Decca 1323 *Lazy River* . . . . 5.00 - 8.00
Decca 2045, 3155, 3167 . . . . 3.00 - 5.00
Okeh, most issues . . . . 3.00 - 5.00

RUSSELL BROWN & HIS ORCHESTRA:
Parlophone PNY-34088 *Washin' The Blues From My Soul* . . . . 25.00 - 40.00
PNY-34089 *Washin' The Blues From My Soul* . . . 25.00 - 40.00
PNY-34090 *Absence Makes The Heart Grow Fonder* . . . . 15.00 - 20.00
PNY-34091 *I Remember You From Somewhere* . . 15.00 - 20.00
PNY-34130 *Little Sunshine* . . . . 15.00 - 20.00
PNY-34133 *When The Organ Played At Twilight* . 15.00 - 20.00

TED BROWNAGLE AND HIS ORCHESTRA:
Victor 20262 *Arcadia Shuffle* . . . . 50.00 - 80.00

SAM BROWNE & HIS ORCHESTRA:
Superior 2693 *Hard Times Stomp* . . . . 75.00 - 100.00

BROWNLEE'S ORCHESTRA OF NEW ORLEANS:
Okeh 40337 *Dirty Rag* . . . . 75.00 - 100.00

BROX SISTERS:
Brunswick (most issues) . . . . 3.00 - 6.00
Victor (most issues) . . . . 3.00 - 6.00

ALBERT BRUNIES & HIS HALFWAY HOUSE ORCHESTRA:
Columbia 1959-D *Just Pretending* . . . . 12.00 - 16.00

MERRITT BRUNIES & HIS FRIARS INN ORCHESTRA:
Autograph (unnumbered) *Up Jumped The Devil* . 75.00 - 100.00
Autograph 610 *Angry* . . . . 75.00 - 100.00
Autograph 624 *Clarinet Marmalade* . . . . 75.00 - 100.00
Okeh 40526 *Sugar Foot Stomp* . . . . 50.00 - 75.00
Okeh 40576 *I'm As Blue As The Blue Grass of Kentucky* . . . . 35.00 - 50.00
Okeh 40579 *Flamin' Mamie* . . . . 35.00 - 50.00
Okeh 40593 *Someone's Stolen My Sweet Baby* . . 35.00 - 50.00
Okeh 40618 *Up Jumped The Devil* . . . . 35.00 - 50.00

LAURA BRYANT:
Paramount 12870 *Saturday Night Jag* . . . . 100.00 - 150.00
QRS 7055 *Dentist Chair Blues* . . . . 75.00 - 100.00

WILLIE BRYANT & HIS ORCHESTRA:
Bluebird 6361, 6362, 6374, 6435, 6436 . . . . . . 5.00 - 10.00
Decca 1772, 1881 . . . . 5.00 - 8.00
Victor 24847, 24858, 25038, 25045, 25129, 25160 . . . . 6.00 - 10.00

TIM BRYMN & HIS BLACK DEVIL ORCH.:
Okeh 4310 *Wang Wang Blues* . . . . 8.00 - 12.00
4339 *Camp Meeting Blues* . . . . 8.00 - 12.00
8002 *Arkansas Blues* . . . . 8.00 - 12.00
8003 *Don't Tell Your Monkey Man* . . . . . . 8.00 - 12.00
8005 *The Jazz Me Blues* . . . . 8.00 - 12.00

THE BUBBLING-OVER FIVE:
Okeh 8737 *Get Up Off That Jazzophone* . . . . . . 50.00 - 80.00

BUCK AND BUBBLES:
Columbia 2873-D *Rhythm For Sale* . . . . 20.00 - 30.00

THE BUCKTOWN FIVE:
Gennett 5405 *Mobile Blues* . . . . 75.00 - 100.00
Gennett 5418 *Buddy's Habits* . . . . 75.00 - 100.00
Gennett 5419 *Steady Roll Blues* . . . . 75.00 - 100.00
Gennett 5518 *Hot Mittens* . . . . 75.00 - 100.00

THE BUFFALODIANS:
Banner 1776 *Baby Face* . . . . 5.00 - 8.00
Banner 1778 *How Many Times?* . . . . 5.00 - 8.00
Columbia 665-D *Deep Henderson* . . . . 8.00 - 12.00

Columbia 723-D *Wouldja?*	8.00 -	12.00
Domino 3747 *How Many Times?*	5.00 -	8.00

CHUCK BULLOCK (& HIS LEVEE LOUNGERS):

Titles, selected from this artist's large output, contemporaneously issued on Banner, Conqueror, Melotone, Oriole, Perfect, Romeo: *And Still No Luck With You; Any Time, Any Day, Any Where; Chasing Shadows; Extra! (All About That Gal of Mine); I Can't Get Mississippi Off My Mind; I Know You're Lying, But I Love It; I'm Hummin', I'm Whistlin', I'm Singin', Keepin' Out Of Mischief Now; I'm Gonna Sit Right Down And Write Myself A Letter; My Melancholy Baby; Sing A New Song; Stop The Sun, Stop The Moon; What's Good For The Goose; With Plenty Of Money And You; You Oughta Be In Pictures; You*

Rascal, You	5.00 -	8.00

Additional Titles: *Frankie and Johnnie; I Can't Dance (I Got Ants In My Pants); Swingy Little*

Thingy	10.00 -	15.00

Vocalion 15882 *Low Down Upon The Harlem*

River	15.00 -	20.00

BILLY BUNCH & HIS SMOKY RHYTHM:

Bluebird 10305 *Three Little Maids*	6.00 -	10.00

FRANK BUNCH & HIS FUZZY WUZZIES:

Gennett 6278 *Fuzzy Wuzzy*	200.00 -	300.00
Gennett 6293 *Fourth Avenue Stomp*	200.00 -	300.00

SONNY BURKE AND HIS ORCHESTRA:

Okeh 5139, 5813, 5873, 5955, 5989	4.00 -	7.00
Vocalion 5356, 5397, 5459	4.00 -	7.00

JOHNNY BURRIS AND HIS ORCHESTRA:

Gennett 6850 *So Comfy*	20.00 -	30.00

SAMMY BURRIS AND HIS NIGHT OWLS:

Vocalion 03917 *Blue Baby*	15.00 -	25.00
Vocalion 03980 *Reefer Man's Dream*	15.00 -	25.00

CHARLIE BURSE (See: MEMPHIS JUG BAND)

DICK BURTON'S ORCHESTRA:

Bell 572 *Sweet Violets*	20.00 -	30.00

BUSSE'S BUZZARDS; HENRY BUSSE & HIS ORCHESTRA:

Columbia 2932-D *Fool That I Am*	8.00 -	12.00
2937-D *Hot Lips*	8.00 -	12.00
Decca (most issues)	3.00 -	6.00
Victor 19727 *Deep Elm*	5.00 -	8.00
19782 *Red Hot Henry Brown*	5.00 -	8.00
19934 *The Monkey Doodle-Doo*	5.00 -	8.00
Victor (most other issues)	4.00 -	7.00

(EZRA) BUZZINGTON'S RUBE BAND/ RUSTIC REVELERS:

Gennett 6575 *Bass Blues*	75.00 -	100.00
6894 *Alfalfa*	— -	—
21024 *Brown Jug Blues*	50.00 -	80.00
Iragen 18-29-01 *Brown Jug Blues*	20.00 -	30.00

HALE BYERS & HIS ORCHESTRA:

Brunswick 3092 *Sea Legs*	8.00 -	12.00
3108 *So Does Your Old Mandarin*	8.00 -	12.00
Vocalion 15370 *Roses*	10.00 -	15.00

EMILIO CACERES TRIO:

Victor 25710, 25719, 26109	7.00 -	10.00

CAHN-CHAPLIN ORCHESTRA:

Champion 40113 *Christopher Columbus*	15.00 -	20.00

LOU CALABRESE & HIS HOT SHOTS:

Gennett 64211 *Lip-Stick*	50.00 -	80.00

CALIFORNIA COLLEGIANS:

Conqueror 7189 *Louder And Funnier*	5.00 -	8.00

CALIFORNIA MELODY MEN:

Bell 433 *That's Annabelle*	5.00 -	8.00

CALIFORNIA POPPIES:

Sunset 506/507 *What A Wonderful Time*	250.00 -	500.00

CALIFORNIA RAMBLERS:

This orchestra appeared on a very large number of records during the 1920s and 1930s, under its own name and pseudonyms (principally THE GOLDEN GATE ORCHESTRA). The records, even those of general interest to collectors, do not generally command sizable premiums. Following is a selected listing only:

Bluebird 6076, 6077, 6078, 6082, 6083, 6145, 6146, 6156, 6173, 6189, 6190, 6238, 6239, 6240	5.00 -	10.00
Broadway 1081 *Magnolia*	7.00 -	10.00
Columbia 9-D, 15-D, 39-D, 43-D, 49-D, 67-D, 91-D, 92-D, 103-D, 105-D, 127-D, 153-D, 171-D, 179-D, 199-D, 218-D, 223-D	4.00 -	8.00
Columbia 236-D, 268-D, 278-D, 293-D, 340-D, 380-D, 419-D, 449-D, 522-D, 527-D, 610-D, 638-D, 647-D, 669-D, 704-D, 758-D, 800-D, 834-D, 883-D, 992-D, 1038-D, 1148-D, 1227-D, 1275-D, 1314-D, 1411-D, 1504-D, 1574-D, 1642-D, 2208-D	5.00 -	10.00
Columbia A3554, A3635, A3956, A3970, A3979, A3986, A3994	4.00 -	8.00
Edison (thin) 11000 and 14000 series	20.00 -	30.00
Edison (thick) 52602 *Wedding Of The Painted Doll*	15.00 -	20.00
Edited 52610 *I Get The Blues When It Rains*	15.00 -	20.00
Edison 52622 *Painting The Clouds With Sunshine*	15.00 -	20.00
Edison 52629 *Tip-Toe Through The Tulips With Me*	15.00 -	20.00
Edison 52638 *Song Of The Blues*	15.00 -	20.00

(Note; Most of the considerable output of THE CALIFORNIA RAMBLERS on *Edison* was issued as by THE GOLDEN GATE ORCHESTRA, q.v.)

Puritan 11103, 11116, 11117, 11174, 11222	4.00 -	10.00

CALIFORNIA VAGABONDS:

Gennett 6140 *I'm Back In Love Again*	10.00 -	20.00
Gennett 6170 *S-L-U-E Foot*	10.00 -	20.00
Gennett 6172 *Yes She Do—No She Don't*	10.00 -	20.00
Gennett 6426 *Waitin' For Katy*	10.00 -	20.00

BOB CALL:

Brunswick 7137 *Thirty-One Blues*	75.00 -	100.00

BLANCHE CALLOWAY (& HER JOY BOYS/BAND)

Titles, issued contemporaneously on Banner, Melotone, Perfect, Oriole, Romeo: *Catch On; Growlin' Dan; I Need Lovin'; What's A Poor Girl Gonna Do?*

	10.00 -	15.00
Okeh 8279 *Lazy Woman's Blues*	100.00 -	200.00
Victor 22640 *Casey Jones Blues*	20.00 -	30.00
Victor 22641 *I Need Lovin'*	8.00 -	12.00
Victor 22659 *Loveless Love*	10.00 -	15.00
Victor 22661 *Sugar Blues*	8.00 -	12.00
Victor 22717 *It's Right Here For You*	8.00 -	12.00
Victor 22738 *It Looks Like Susie*	8.00 -	12.00
Victor 22736 *Make Me Know It*	15.00 -	20.00
Victor 22862 *Last Dollar*	8.00 -	12.00
Victor 22866 *I Got What It Takes*	8.00 -	12.00
Victor 22896 *Blue Memories*	8.00 -	12.00
Vocalion 3112 *Louisiana Liza*	10.00 -	15.00
Vocalion 3113 *Line-A-Jive*	10.00 -	15.00

CAB CALLOWAY & HIS ORCHESTRA:

Titles, issued contemporaneously on Banner, Cameo, Conqueror, Domino, Jewel, Melotone, Oriole, Perfect, and Romeo: *Ain't Got No Gal In This Town; Angeline; Beale Street Mama; Between The Devil And The Deep Blue Sea; Black Rhythm; Bugle Call Rag; Dinah; Dixie Doorway; Doin' The Rumba; Eadie Was A Lady; Harlem Holiday; Hot Water; How Come You Do Me Like You Do? I'm Now Prepared To Tell The World It's You; Is That Religion?;*

Kickin' The Gong Around; The Man From Harlem; Minnie The Moocher; Nobody's Sweetheart; The Old Man Of The Mountain; Reefer Man; Six Or Seven Times; Some Of These Days; St. James Infirmary; Strange As It Seems; Swanee Lullaby; This Time It's Love; Trickeration; Wah-Dee-Dah; You Gotta Ho-De-Ho (To Get Along With Me); You Rascal, You . . . . 7.00 - 10.00

Additional Titles:

Basin Street Blues; Blues In My Heart; Corinne Corinna; Creole Love Song; Down-Hearted Blues; Farewell Blues; I'm Crazy 'Bout My Baby; It Looks Like Susie; The Levee Low-Down; Mood Indigo; Somebody Stole My Gal; Stack O'Lee Blues; Stardust; Sweet Georgia Brown; Sweet Jennie Lee; The Viper's Drag; Without Rhythm; Yaller; You Can't Stop Me From Lovin' You; You Dog . . . . 8.00 - 12.00

A few more titles:

Dixie Vagabond; Happy Feet; My Honey's Lovin' Arms; The Nightmare . . . . 10.00 - 15.00
Brunswick 6020 *Some Of These Days* . . . . 8.00 - 12.00
Brunswick 6074 *Minnie The Moocher* . . . . 8.00 - 12.00
Brunswick 6105 *Nobody's Sweetheart* . . . . 8.00 - 12.00
Brunswick 6141 *Black Rhythm* . . . . 8.00 - 12.00
Brunswick 6196 *You Rascal, You* . . . . 8.00 - 12.00
Brunswick 6209 *Kickin' The Going Around* . . . . 8.00 - 12.00
Brunswick 6214 *Trickeration* . . . . 8.00 - 12.00
Brunswick 6272 *The Scat Song* . . . . 8.00 - 12.00
Brunswick 6292 *Strictly Cullud Affair* . . . . 10.00 - 15.00
Brunswick 6321 *Minnie The Moocher's Wedding Day* . . . . 8.00 - 12.00
Brunswick 6340 *Reefer Man* . . . . 7.00 - 10.00
Brunswick 6400 *Old Yazoo* . . . . 8.00 - 12.00
Brunswick 6424 *I've Got The World On A String* 8.00 - 12.00
Brunswick 6435 *Dixie Doorway* . . . . 8.00 - 12.00
Brunswick 6450 *My Sunday Gal* . . . . 8.00 - 12.00
Brunswick 6460 *I Gotta Right To Sing The Blues* . . . . 8.00 - 12.00
Brunswick 6473 *Gotta Go Places and Do Things* . . . . 8.00 - 12.00
Brunswick 6511 *Minnie The Moocher* . . . . 5.00 - 8.00
Brunswick 6992 *Chinese Rhythm* . . . . 8.00 - 12.00
Brunswick 7386 *Good Sauce From the Gravy Bowl* . . . . 8.00 - 12.00
Brunswick 7411 *Moonlight Rhapsody* . . . . 8.00 - 12.00
Brunswick 7504 *Nagasaki* . . . . 8.00 - 12.00
Brunswick 7530 *I Ain't Got Nobody* . . . . 7.00 - 10.00
Brunswick 7638 *Save Me, Sister* . . . . 7.00 - 10.00
Brunswick 7639 *You're The Cure For What Ails Me* . . . . 8.00 - 12.00
Brunswick 7677 *Love Is The Reason* . . . . 7.00 - 10.00
Brunswick 7685 *When You're Smiling* . . . . 7.00 - 10.00
Brunswick 7748 *The Wedding of Mr. and Mrs. Swing* . . . . 8.00 - 12.00
Brunswick 7756 *The Hi-De-Ho Miracle Man* . . . 8.00 - 12.00
Columbia (red label, most issues) . . . . 4.00 - 7.00
Conqueror (most 9000 series) . . . . 4.00 - 7.00
Okeh (most issues) . . . . 4.00 - 10.00
Variety 501 *That Man Is Here Again* . . . . 7.00 - 10.00
Variety 535 *Don't Know If I'm Comin' Or Goin'*. 8.00 - 12.00
Variety 593 *My Gal Mezzanine* . . . . 8.00 - 12.00
Variety 612 *Manhattan Jam* . . . . 5.00 - 8.00
Variety 643 *She's Tall, She's Tan, She's Terrific*. . 7.00 - 10.00
Variety 644 *Mama, I Wanna Make Rhythm* . . . 7.00 - 10.00
Variety 651 *Hi-De-Ho Romeo* . . . . 7.00 - 10.00
Variety 662 *Savage Rhythm* . . . . 5.00 - 8.00
Victor 24414 *Harlem Hospitality* . . . . 8.00 - 12.00
Victor 24451 *The Lady With The Fan* . . . . 8.00 - 12.00
Victor 24494 *Little Town Gal* . . . . 8.00 - 12.00
Victor 24511 *The Scat Song* . . . . 8.00 - 12.00

Victor 24557 *Zaz Zuh Zaz* . . . . 8.00 - 12.00
Victor 24592 *Jitter Bug* . . . . 8.00 - 12.00
Victor 24659 *Margie* . . . . 8.00 - 12.00
Victor 24690 *Moon Glow* . . . . 8.00 - 12.00
Vocalion 3787 *I'm Always in the Mood for You* . . 7.00 - 10.00
Vocalion 3788 *Go South, Young Man* . . . . 7.00 - 10.00
Vocalion 3789 *Moon At Sea* . . . . 7.00 - 10.00
Vocalion 3796 *Queen Isabella* . . . . 5.00 - 8.00
Vocalion 3807 *Swing, Swing, Swing* . . . . 7.00 - 10.00
Vocalion 3825 *Congo* . . . . 7.00 - 10.00
Vocalion 3830 *Peckin'* . . . . 5.00 - 8.00
Vocalion 3896 *Every Day's a Holiday* . . . . 7.00 - 10.00
Vocalion 3970 *Doing The Reactionary* . . . . 7.00 - 10.00
Vocalion 3995 *Three Swings And Out* . . . . 7.00 - 10.00
Vocalion 4019 *Bugle Blues* . . . . 7.00 - 10.00
Vocalion 4045 *Skrontch* . . . . 7.00 - 10.00
Vocalion 4100 *Azure* . . . . 7.00 - 10.00
Vocalion 4144 *Rustle of Swing* . . . . 7.00 - 10.00
Vocalion 4400 *The Boogie-Woogie* . . . . 7.00 - 10.00
Vocalion most other issues . . . . 4.00 - 7.00

ERMINE CALLOWAY:
Edison (thin) 14024 *Do Something* . . . . 20.00 - 30.00
Edison 14071 *S Nice, Like This* . . . . 20.00 - 30.00
Edison (thick) 52519 *Good Little, Bad Little You* . 15.00 - 20.00
Edison 52567 *I Want To Be Bad* . . . . 15.00 - 20.00
Edison 52570 *Do Something* . . . . 15.00 - 20.00
Edison 52617 *When We Get Together In The Moonlight* . . . . 15.00 - 20.00

JEAN CALLOWAY'S ORCHESTRA:
Victor 22959 *Sadie, The Shaker* . . . . 7.00 - 10.00

BUDDY CAMPBELL & HIS ORCHESTRA:
Okeh 41503 *Let's Get Friendly* . . . . 8.00 - 15.00
Okeh 41507 *When Yuba Plays The Rumba On The Tuba* . . . . 8.00 - 15.00
Okeh 41511 *My Sweet Tooth Says 'I Wanna'* . . . 8.00 - 15.00
Okeh 41524 *Little Mary Brown* . . . . 8.00 - 15.00
Okeh 41527 *Charlie Cadet* . . . . 8.00 - 15.00
Okeh 41532 *Last Dollar* . . . . 8.00 - 12.00
Okeh 41540 *I Wonder Who's Under The Moon* . . . 8.00 - 12.00
Okeh 41543 *Bend Down, Sister* . . . . 8.00 - 15.00
41563 *What A Life* . . . . 8.00 - 12.00
41564 *Sing A New Song* . . . . 8.00 - 12.00

JOHNNIE CAMPBELL'S ORCHESTRA:
New Flexo 301 *Jimtown Blues* . . . . 75.00 - 100.00
New Flexo 302 *Somebody Loves Me* . . . . 50.00 - 75.00
New Flexo 303 *The Only, Only One* . . . . 50.00 - 75.00
New Flexo 304 *Tin Roof Blues* . . . . 75.00 - 100.00
New Flexo 305 *Where's My Sweetie Hiding?* . . . 50.00 - 75.00
New Flexo 307 *Charleston Cabin* . . . . 50.00 - 75.00
New Flexo 308 *No Wonder* . . . . 50.00 - 75.00

THE CAMPUS BOYS:
Banner 6124 *Is She My Girl Friend?* . . . . 5.00 - 8.00
Banner 6127 *Make My Cot Where The Cot-Cot-Cotton Grows* . . . . 5.00 - 8.00
Banner 6263 *My Supressed Desire* . . . . 5.00 - 8.00
Banner 6264 *I'm Wild About Horns on Automobiles* . . . . 7.00 - 10.00
Banner 6300 *When I'm Walking With My Sweetness* . . . . 5.00 - 8.00
Banner 6357 *I Used To Love Her In The Moonlight* . . . . 5.00 - 8.00
Banner 6425 *Rainbow Man* . . . . 7.00 - 10.00
Banner 6439 *Singing In The Rain* . . . . 5.00 - 8.00
Banner 6449 *Ain't Misbehavin'* . . . . 5.00 - 8.00
Banner 6453 *Where the Sweet Forget-Me-Nots Remember* . . . . 5.00 - 8.00
Banner 6483 *Lovable And Sweet* . . . . 8.00 - 12.00
Banner 7051 *Hello! Montreal* . . . . 5.00 - 8.00
Banner 7137 *Sweet Lorraine* . . . . 8.00 - 12.00
Banner 7220 *Here's That Party Now In Person* . . 7.00 - 10.00

THE CAMPUS CUT-UPS:
Edison 11049 *Farewell Blues* . . . . 20.00 - 30.00

Edison 11050 *Ballin' The Jack* . . . . 20.00 - 30.00
Edison 14044 *Campus Rush* . . . . 20.00 - 30.00
Edison (thick) 52591 *Wabash Blues* . . . . . . 8.00 - 12.00
Edison 52616 *Ballin' The Jack* . . . . 8.00 - 12.00
Edison 52649 *Campus Rush* . . . . 8.00 - 12.00

CANADIAN CLUB ORCHESTRA:
Pathe-Actuelle 36367 *Keep Your Skirts Down,*
Mary Ann . . . . 7.00 - 10.00
Perfect 14548 *Keep Your Skirts Down, Mary*
Ann . . . . 7.00 - 10.00

JOE CANDULLO & HIS (EVERGLADES)
ORCHESTRA:
Banner 1780 *Hard-To-Get Gertie* . . . . 5.00 - 8.00
Banner 1784 *Deep Henderson* . . . . 5.00 - 8.00
Banner 1796 *Black Bottom* . . . . 5.00 - 8.00
Banner 1800 *Nervous Charlie Stomp* . . . . 7.00 - 10.00
Banner 1814 *I Wonder What's Become of Joe?* . . . 7.00 - 10.00
Banner 1815 *Blowin' Off Steam* . . . . 7.00 - 10.00
Banner 1836 *Tuck In Kentucky And Smile* . . . . 7.00 - 10.00
Banner 1839 *St. Louis Blues* . . . . 7.00 - 10.00
Banner 1986 *St. Louis Blues* . . . . 8.00 - 12.00
Banner 7169 *A Jazz Holiday* . . . . 8.00 - 12.00
Banner 7192 *Deep Hollow* . . . . 8.00 - 12.00
Banner 7217 *What-Cha-Call 'Em Blues* . . . . . . 8.00 - 12.00
Banner 7218 *When Sweet Susie Goes Stepping By* 7.00 - 10.00
Banner 7220 *Dusky Stevedore* . . . . 7.00 - 10.00
Broadway 1203 *Dusky Stevedore* . . . . 7.00 - 10.00
Buddy 8069 *Black Bottom* . . . . 50.00 - 100.00
Buddy 8070 *Messin' Around* . . . . 50.00 - 100.00
Cameo 1074 *Everything's Made For Love* . . . . . 5.00 - 8.00
Cameo 1105 *Song of the Wanderer* . . . . 7.00 - 10.00
Cameo 1048 *Brown Sugar* . . . . 7.00 - 10.00
Cameo 1049 *I Still Believe In You* . . . . 7.00 - 10.00
Cameo 1077 *Delilah* . . . . 5.00 - 8.00
Challenge 130 *Cry Baby* . . . . 7.00 - 10.00
Challenge 137 *That's Why I Love You* . . . . 7.00 - 10.00
Domino 3751 *Jackass Blues* . . . . 5.00 - 8.00
Domino 3768 *Nervous Charlie Stomp* . . . . 7.00 - 10.00
Domino 3772 *Messin' Around* . . . . 5.00 - 8.00
Domino 3808 *St. Louis Blues* . . . . 7.00 - 10.00
Domino 3809 *Tuck In Kentucky and Smile* . . . . 7.00 - 10.00
Domino 3956 *St. Louis Blues* . . . . 7.00 - 10.00
Domino 4167 *A Jazz Holiday* . . . . 8.00 - 12.00
Domino 4201 *When Sweet Susie Goes*
Stepping By . . . . 7.00 - 10.00
Edison 51826 *Bass Ale Blues* . . . . 15.00 - 20.00
Edison 51836 *Scatter Your Smiles* . . . . 12.00 - 16.00
Edison 51848 *The Birth of the Blues* . . . . 15.00 - 20.00
Edison 51852 *Brown Sugar* . . . . 15.00 - 20.00
Edison 51912 *Windy City Stomp* . . . . 15.00 - 20.00
Gennett 3316 *The Nightmare* . . . . 8.00 - 12.00
Gennett 3331 *That's Why I Love You* . . . . 7.00 - 10.00
Gennett 3351 *Only You and Lonely Me* . . . . . . 5.00 - 8.00
Gennett 3352 *Cry Baby* . . . . 7.00 - 10.00
Gennett 3358 *St. Louis Hop* . . . . 8.00 - 12.00
Gennett 3359 *Messin' Around* . . . . 8.00 - 12.00
Gennett 3385 *She's Still My Baby* . . . . 8.00 - 12.00
Gennett 3392 *Don't Be Angry With Me* . . . . . . 7.00 - 10.00
Gennett 3402 *Bobadilla* . . . . 7.00 - 10.00
Gennett 3405 *Tomboy Sue* . . . . 10.00 - 15.00
Gennett 3406 *Lonely Eyes* . . . . 7.00 - 10.00
Gennett 6009 *Lonely Eyes* . . . . 10.00 - 15.00
Harmony 150-H *Bass Ale Blues* . . . . 10.00 - 15.00
Harmony 208-H *18th Street Strut* . . . . 8.00 - 12.00
Harmony 211-H *She Belongs To Me* . . . . 8.00 - 12.00
Harmony 235-H *Sadie Green* . . . . 7.00 - 10.00
Harmony 260-H *Susie's "Feller"* . . . . 7.00 - 10.00
Harmony 286-H *Blowin' Off Steam* . . . . 8.00 - 12.00
Harmony 361-H *Yes Flo! (The Gal Who Never*
Says "No") . . . . 8.00 - 12.00
Harmony 397-H *Go Wash an Elephant (If You*
Wanna Do Something?) . . . . 7.00 - 10.00

Harmony 700-H *Out of the Dawn* . . . . 5.00 - 8.00
Harmony 703-H *Imagination* . . . . 5.00 - 8.00
Harmony 710-H *Remember Me To Mary* . . . . . 5.00 - 8.00
Harmony 888-H *Till We Meet* . . . . 5.00 - 8.00
Harmony 890-H *You Wanted Someone To*
Play With . . . . 5.00 - 8.00
(Note: The above titles, on *Diva* and *Velvet Tone*,
are similarly valued.)
Herwin 55004 *Messin' Around* . . . . 20.00 - 30.00
Pathe-Actuelle 36436 *Reaching for the Moon* . . . 5.00 - 8.00
Pathe-Actuelle 36444 *Betty* . . . . 5.00 - 8.00
Pathe-Actuelle 36461 *Mary Lou* . . . . 5.00 - 8.00
Pathe-Actuelle 36462 *Jackass Blues* . . . . 7.00 - 10.00
Pathe-Actuelle 36469 *As Long As I Have You* . . . 5.00 - 8.00
Pathe-Actuelle 36486 *Baby Face* . . . . 5.00 - 8.00
Pathe-Actuelle 36487 *Turkish Towel* . . . . 8.00 - 12.00
Pathe-Actuelle 36539 *All Alone Monday* . . . . . 5.00 - 8.00
Pathe-Actuelle 36540 *Stampede* . . . . 7.00 - 10.00
Pathe-Actuelle 36541 *Oh! How I Love Bulgarians* 5.00 - 8.00
Pathe-Actuelle 36660 *It's a Million To One*
You're In Love . . . . 5.00 - 8.00
Pathe-Actuelle 36663 *Sweet Yvette* . . . . 5.00 - 8.00
Pathe-Actuelle 36693 *Phantom Blues* . . . . 7.00 - 10.00
Perfect 14617 *Reaching for the Moon* . . . . 5.00 - 8.00
Perfect 14625 *Betty* . . . . 5.00 - 8.00
Perfect 14642 *I Wish You Were Jealous of Me* . . . 5.00 - 8.00
Perfect 14643 *Jackass Blues* . . . . 7.00 - 10.00
Perfect 14650 *As Long As I Have You* . . . . 5.00 - 8.00
Perfect 14667 *Down By The Old Sea Shore* . . . . 5.00 - 8.00
Perfect 14668 *Crazy Quilt* . . . . 8.00 - 12.00
Perfect 14720 *All Alone Monday* . . . . 5.00 - 8.00
Perfect 14721 *Stampede* . . . . 7.00 - 10.00
Perfect 14722 *Oh! How I Love Bulgarians* . . . . 5.00 - 8.00
Perfect 14750 *To Love You* . . . . 5.00 - 8.00
Perfect 14752 *Everything's Made For Love* . . . . 5.00 - 8.00
Perfect 14841 *It's A Million To One You're*
In Love . . . . 5.00 - 8.00
Perfect 14844 *Sweet Yvette* . . . . 5.00 - 8.00
Perfect 14874 *Phantom Blues* . . . . 7.00 - 10.00
Regal 8089 *Jackass Blues* . . . . 7.00 - 10.00
Regal 8109 *Nervous Charlie Stomp* . . . . 7.00 - 10.00
Regal 8120 *I Wonder What's Become of Joe* . . . 7.00 - 10.00
Regal 8126 *Blowin' Off Steam* . . . . 7.00 - 10.00
Regal 8146 *Tuck In Kentucky and Smile* . . . . . 7.00 - 10.00
Regal 8150 *St. Louis Blues* . . . . 7.00 - 10.00
Regal 8310 *St. Louis Blues* . . . . 8.00 - 12.00
Regal 8595 *A Jazz Holiday* . . . . 7.00 - 10.00

CANDY AND COCO:
Vocalion 2833 *Kingfish Blues* . . . . 20.00 - 30.00
Vocalion 2849 *China Boy* . . . . 20.00 - 30.00

CANNON'S JUG STOMPERS:
Bluebird 5030 *Minglewood Blues* . . . . 50.00 - 75.00
Bluebird 5287 *Big Railroad Blues* . . . . 50.00 - 75.00
Bluebird 5389 *Bugle Call Rag* . . . . 75.00 - 100.00
Bluebird 5413 *Goin' To Germany* . . . . 75.00 - 100.00
Sunrise 3117 *Minglewood Blues* . . . . — - —
3368 *Big Railroad Blues* . . . . — - —
Victor 21267 *Minglewood Blues* . . . . 100.00 - 150.00
Victor 21351 *Springdale Blues* . . . . 150.00 - 200.00
Victor 23262 *Money Never Runs Out* . . . . 150.00 - 250.00
Victor 23272 *Wolf River Blues* . . . . 150.00 - 250.00
Victor V38006 *Pig Ankle Strut* . . . . 100.00 - 150.00
Victor V38515 *Feather Bed* . . . . 100.00 - 150.00
Victor V38523 *Viola Lee Blues* . . . . 100.00 - 150.00
Victor V38539 *Ripley Blues* . . . . 100.00 - 150.00
Victor V38566 *Hollywood Rag* . . . . 150.00 - 200.00
Victor V38585 *Goin To Germany* . . . . 150.00 - 200.00
Victor V38593 *Last Chance Blues* . . . . 150.00 - 200.00
Victor V38611 *Walk Right In* . . . . 150.00 - 200.00
Victor V38629 *Jonestown Blues* . . . . 150.00 - 200.00

EDDIE CANTOR:
Aeolian Vocalion 1220 *The Modern Maiden's Prayer* 15.00 - 20.00

1228 *Down In Borneo Isle*	15.00 -	20.00
1233 *Dixie Volunteers*	15.00 -	20.00
Columbia 56-D *If You Do What You Do*	10.00 -	15.00
Columbia 120-D, 140-D, 182-D, 196-D, 213-D, 234-D, 256-D, 277-D, 283-D	5.00 -	10.00
Columbia 364-D, 397-D, 415-D, 457-D	5.00 -	10.00
Columbia 2723-D *What a Perfect Combination*	15.00 -	20.00
Columbia A-3624, A-3682, A-3754, A-3784, A-3906, A-3934, A-3964	5.00 -	10.00
Columbia 35325, 35428	3.00 -	6.00
Durium De Luxe K-6 *Ballyhoo*	8.00 -	12.00
Emerson 1071, 1094, 10102, 10105, 10119, 10134, 10200, 10212, 10263, 10292, 10301, 10327, 10349, 10352, 10397	5.00 -	8.00
Melotone 13183, 13184	7.00 -	10.00
Pathe 22163, 22201, 22260, 22318	5.00 -	10.00
Victor 18342, 21831, 21982, 22189, 24330	5.00 -	10.00

THE CAPTIVATORS (DIRECTION OF RED NICHOLS):

Brunswick 4308 *I Used To Love Her In The Moonlight*	7.00 -	10.00
4321 *Building A Nest For Mary*	5.00 -	8.00
4591 *Get Happy*	10.00 -	15.00
Melotone 12005 *Sweet Jennie Lee*	10.00 -	15.00
12049 *We're Friends Again*	10.00 -	15.00

CARDINAL DANCE ORCHESTRA:

Cardinal 503 *I've Got The Wonder Where He Went Blues*	10.00 -	20.00
504 *My Mammy Knows*	10.00 -	20.00
523 *On the Gin-Gin-Ginny Shore*	10.00 -	20.00
527 *Those Longing For You Blues*	15.00 -	30.00
529 *Mary Dear*	10.00 -	20.00
556 *Apple Sauce*	10.00 -	20.00
558 *Carolina Mammay*	10.00 -	20.00
560 *Everything Is K.O. in K.Y.*	10.00 -	20.00
563 *Down Among the Sleepy Hills of Tennessee*	10.00 -	20.00
565 *Snakes Hips*	10.00 -	20.00
566 *My Old Ramshackle Shack*	10.00 -	20.00

ERNEST CARL'S (DANCE) ORCHESTRA:

Cameo 9055 *You Should Know The Girl Friend*	5.00 -	8.00
Cameo 9057 *The Way I'm Feeling Today*	5.00 -	8.00
Romeo 861 *The Way I'm Feeling Today*	5.00 -	8.00
Romeo 934 *Redskin*	3.00 -	5.00
Romeo 968 *We Can't Live On Love*	5.00 -	8.00
Romeo 1085 *For I'm In Love*	3.00 -	5.00

CARLETON TERRACE ORCHESTRA:

Harmony 78-H *Pretty Little Baby*	5.00 -	8.00
86-H *A Cup Of Coffee, A Sandwich, And You*	5.00 -	8.00
97-H *Drifting Apart*	5.00 -	8.00
100-H *Mysterious Eyes*	5.00 -	8.00

EDDIE CARLEW'S BABY ARISTOCRATS:

Gennett 6184 *Indiana Mud*	75.00 -	100.00

BILL CARLSEN & HIS ORCHESTRA:

Broadway 1359 *Milenburg Joys*	30.00 -	50.00
1365 *Baby, Won't You Please Come Home?*	30.00 -	50.00
Paramount 20797 *Clarinet Marmalade*	30.00 -	50.00

ROY CARLSON'S DANCE ORCHESTRA:

Banner 0504 *Hummin' With Love*	5.00 -	8.00
Banner 0516 *I'm Kissing the Ground You Walk On*	5.00 -	8.00
Banner 0542 *Oh, Molly, My Molly-O*	5.00 -	8.00
Banner 0559 *Yearning*	5.00 -	8.00
Banner 0563 *I Can't Blame The Boys for Loving You*	7.00 -	10.00
Banner 0567 *We'll Be Married in June*	5.00 -	8.00
Banner 0573 *Whenever I Think Of You*	5.00 -	8.00
Banner 0595 *Rainy Weather Rose*	7.00 -	10.00
Banner 0625 *Dearest Adorable*	5.00 -	8.00
Banner 0655 *My Little Dixie Home*	5.00 -	8.00
Banner 0694 *I'll Keep On Loving You*	5.00 -	8.00
Banner 0729 *Smile The Blues Away*	7.00 -	10.00
Banner 0752 *Fascinating You*	10.00 -	15.00

Banner 0779 *The Princeton Prance*	7.00 -	10.00
Banner 0780 *Making Believe*	5.00 -	8.00
Banner 0801 *I Can't Believe It's True*	7.00 -	10.00
Banner 6417 *After All*	5.00 -	8.00
Banner 6419 *In Springtime*	5.00 -	8.00
Banner 6423 *Mama Be Nice*	5.00 -	8.00
Banner 6437 *Beautiful*	5.00 -	8.00
Banner 6443 *Tomorrow Means To Love, To Me*	5.00 -	8.00
Banner 6444 *Any Old Night Is a Peach of a Night*	5.00 -	8.00
Banner 6468 *Loving You*	5.00 -	8.00
Banner 6471 *Dimples*	5.00 -	8.00
Banner 6478 *My Baby's Sweet, But Oh How Cross-Eyed*	5.00 -	8.00
Banner 6497 *That's My Idea*	5.00 -	8.00
Banner 6503 *Evening Brings Memories of You*	5.00 -	8.00
Banner 6504 *Send Love Through The Breeze*	7.00 -	10.00
Banner 6505 *You're Just an Armful of Love*	5.00 -	8.00
Banner 6512 *If I Only Loved You a Little Bit Less*	5.00 -	8.00
Banner 6513 *When I Found You*	5.00 -	8.00
Banner 6539 *Now That You Are Mine*	5.00 -	8.00
Banner 6542 *Sweet Kentucky Sue*	5.00 -	8.00
6552 *Would You Believe Me?*	5.00 -	8.00
Cameo 0104 *Hummin' With Love*	5.00 -	8.00
0116 *I'm Kissing The Ground You Walk On*	5.00 -	8.00
0173 *Whenever I Think Of You*	5.00 -	8.00
0294 *I'll Keep On Loving You*	5.00 -	8.00
Oriole 1829 *Whenever I Think Of You*	5.00 -	8.00
Regal 10113 *Syncopated Jamboree*	8.00 -	12.00
Romeo 1189 *We'll Be Married In June*	5.00 -	8.00
1203 *Just A Lone Hill Billy*	5.00 -	8.00
1244 *Dearest Adorable*	5.00 -	8.00

RUSS CARLSON & HIS ORCHESTRA:

Banner 6410 *Sure Enough Blues*	5.00 -	8.00
Banner 6411 *Just Tellin' My Troubles to the Moon*	5.00 -	8.00
Crown 3136 *Love Is Like That*	5.00 -	8.00
Crown 3137 *Under Your Window Tonight*	7.00 -	10.00
Crown 3147 *Minnie The Moocher*	8.00 -	12.00
Crown 3163 *It's The Girl!*	8.00 -	12.00
Crown 3177 *Me!*	5.00 -	8.00
Crown 3198 *Now That You're Gone*	5.00 -	8.00
Crown 3246 *Goodnight, Moon*	5.00 -	8.00
Crown 3259 *I Thank You, Mr. Moon*	5.00 -	8.00
Crown 3301 *I Know You're Lying, But I Love It*	8.00 -	12.00
Crown 3311 *Hello, Gorgeous!*	7.00 -	10.00
Crown 3315 *Got a Date With An Angel*	5.00 -	8.00
Crown 3330 *Hummin' To Myself*	5.00 -	8.00
Crown 3334 *A Great Big Bunch of You*	5.00 -	8.00
Crown 3338 *The Clouds Will Soon Roll By*	5.00 -	8.00
Crown 3347 *You're Blase*	5.00 -	8.00
Crown 3351 *My Heart's At Ease*	5.00 -	8.00
Crown 3353 *Banking On The Weather*	5.00 -	8.00
Crown 3360 *I Can't Believe It's True*	7.00 -	10.00
Crown 3367 *Thou Shalt Not*	7.00 -	10.00
Crown 3373 *Everyone Says "I Love You"*	7.00 -	10.00

BUD CARLTON'S ORCHESTRA:

Crown (Canadian) 81234 *A Little Kiss Each Morning*	5.00 -	8.00
81308 *Rainy Weather Rose*	7.00 -	10.00
81469 *Syncopated Jamboree*	10.00 -	15.00

HOAGY CARMICHAEL & HIS ORCHESTRA/ PALS: CARMICHAEL'S COLLEGIANS:

Gennett 6311 *Stardust*	75.00 -	100.00
6474 *Walkin' The Dog*	75.00 -	100.00
Victor L-16009 (*long-playing "Program Transcription"*) Dance Medley of Hoagy Carmichael Compositions	35.00 -	50.00
Victor 22864 *Bessie Couldn't Help It*	20.00 -	30.00

23013 *One Night In Havana*	20.00 -	30.00
23034 *Lazy River*	20.00 -	30.00
24119 *After Twelve O'Clock*	8.00 -	12.00
24123 *Mighty River*	8.00 -	12.00
24182 *Sing It Way Down Low*	8.00 -	12.00
24402 *Lazy Bones*	8.00 -	12.00
24484 *Stardust*	10.00 -	15.00
24505 *One Morning In May*	15.00 -	20.00
24627 *Moon Country*	10.00 -	15.00
V-38139 *Barnacle Bill The Sailor*	25.00 -	40.00

CAROLINA CLUB ORCHESTRA:

Harmony 639-H *Waitin' For Katy*	8.00 -	12.00
Harmony 844-H *Dream Train*	7.00 -	10.00
Harmony 852-H *I'm Marching Home To You*	7.00 -	10.00
Harmony 853-H *Guess Who?*	7.00 -	10.00
Harmony 872-H *My Sugar and Me*	7.00 -	10.00

(Note: Above titles on *Diva* and *Velvet Tone* are similarly valued.)

Melotone 12110 *Smile, Darn Ya, Smile*	8.00 -	12.00
12177 *Sing A Little Jingle*	5.00 -	10.00
12365 *Business in "Q"*	10.00 -	15.00
Okeh 41199 *The Eyes Of Texas*	5.00 -	8.00
41226 *Honey*	7.00 -	10.00
41237 *That's You, Baby*	7.00 -	10.00
41277 *Do Something*	7.00 -	10.00
41309 *Miss Wonderful*	8.00 -	12.00
41326 *He's So Unusual*	15.00 -	20.00
41332 *The World's Greatest Sweetheart Is You*	8.00 -	12.00
41337 *How I'll Miss You*	7.00 -	10.00
41356 *Nobody But You*	8.00 -	12.00
41358 *Hangin' On The Garden Gate*	8.00 -	12.00
41360 *Under A Texas Moon*	10.00 -	15.00
41366 *D'Ya Love Me?*	7.00 -	10.00
41408 *Can't Yo' Heah Me Callin', Caroline?*	10.00 -	15.00
41409 *Allah's Holiday*	10.00 -	15.00
Pathe-Actuelle 036181 *Bye-Bye Baby*	7.00 -	10.00
36370 *Sweet Child*	5.00 -	8.00
36371 *Pretty Little Baby*	5.00 -	8.00
36381 *I Never Knew How Wonderful You Were*	5.00 -	8.00
Perfect 14362 *Everybody Loves My Baby*	7.00 -	10.00
Perfect 14378 *Who Takes Care Of The Caretaker's Daughter*	7.00 -	10.00
Perfect 14426 *Hurry Back, Old Sweetheart Of Mine*	7.00 -	10.00
Perfect 14551 *Sweet Child*	5.00 -	8.00
Perfect 14552 *Pretty Little Baby*	5.00 -	8.00
Perfect 14562 *I Never Knew How Wonderful You Were*	5.00 -	8.00

CAROLINA COLLEGIANS:

Banner 6316 *Wedding Bells*	7.00 -	10.00
6319 *Before The Rain*	7.00 -	10.00

CAROLINA COTTON PICKERS:

Vocalion 03527 *Let's Get Together*	20.00 -	30.00
03539 *Western Swing*	20.00 -	30.00
03580 *Off And On Blues*	20.00 -	30.00

CAROLINA DANDIES:

Victor 22776 *Come Easy, Go Easy Love*	30.00 -	50.00

THE CAROLINERS:

Banner 0847 *I'm happy*	8.00 -	12.00
Cameo 799 *Bam Bam Bamy Shore*	5.00 -	8.00
Cameo 800 *Melancholy Lou*	5.00 -	8.00
Cameo 850 *She Was Just a Sailor's Sweetheart*	5.00 -	8.00
Cameo 1063 *There Ain't No "Maybe" in My Baby's Eyes*	5.00 -	8.00
Cameo 1103 *Lolling Around With Lolly*	4.00 -	7.00
Cameo 8322 *Ev'rything We Like We Like Alike*	5.00 -	8.00
Cameo 8325 *Got The Blue Blues*	5.00 -	8.00
Cameo 8336 *It Goes Like This*	4.00 -	7.00
Cameo 8348 *I Don't Care*	4.00 -	7.00
Cameo 8373 *Blue Shadows*	4.00 -	7.00
Cameo 9030 *Where The Sky Little Violets Grow*	8.00 -	12.00

Cameo 9086 *I Can't Keep You Out Of My Dreams*	4.00 -	7.00
Cameo 9099 *Lover, Come Back To Me!*	4.00 -	7.00
Cameo 9158 *Your Disposition Is Mine*	5.00 -	8.00
Cameo 9299 *That's What Love Did To Me*	5.00 -	8.00
Domino 4656 *Sweet Jennie Lee*	8.00 -	12.00
Lincoln 2117 *The House Of David Blues*	4.00 -	7.00
Lincoln 2196 *Sobbin' Blues*	3.00 -	5.00
Lincoln 2242 *Go 'Long Mule*	5.00 -	8.00
Lincoln 2388 *I'm Knee Deep In Daisies*	3.00 -	5.00
Romeo 457 *I'm Coming, Virginia*	3.00 -	5.00
Romeo 858 *I'm Rolling Around In Sunshine*	7.00 -	10.00

ROY CARROLL & HIS SANDS POINT ORCHESTRA:

Clarion 5252-C, 5253-C, 5255-C, 5262-C, 5263-C	5.00 -	8.00
Clarion 5321-C *Moonlight Savings Time*	10.00 -	15.00
5337-C *Two Little, Blue Little Eyes*	7.00 -	10.00
5338-C *Let's Get Friendly*	10.00 -	15.00
5343-C *High and Low*	10.00 -	15.00
5351-C *On The Beach With You*	10.00 -	15.00
5357-C *I Can't Write The Words*	7.00 -	10.00
5393-C *Waitin' For A Call From You*	7.00 -	10.00
Clarion 5406-C, 5407-C, 5455-C	5.00 -	8.00
Clarion 5420-C *Bend Down, Sister*	10.00 -	15.00
5442-C *Chances Are*	15.00 -	20.00
Harmony 1253-H *Overnight*	8.00 -	12.00
1261-H *Little Did I Know*	8.00 -	12.00
1271-H *Royal Garden Blues*	10.00 -	15.00
Harmony 1289-H, 1297-H	7.00 -	10.00
Harmony 1322-H *Roll On, Mississippi, Roll On*	10.00 -	15.00
1328-H *Love Is Like That*	7.00 -	10.00
1329-H *One More Time*	10.00 -	15.00
1334-H *Dancing in the Dark*	10.00 -	15.00
1340-H *Without That Gal!*	10.00 -	15.00
1345-H *I Can't Write The Words*	7.00 -	10.00
1379-H *Waiting For A Call From You*	7.00 -	10.00
1397-H *Bend Down, Sister*	10.00 -	15.00
Harmony 1403-H *Chances Are*	15.00 -	20.00
Harmony 1406-H, 1407-H, 1412-H	5.00 -	8.00
Velvet Tone 2328-V, 2329-V, 2506-V, 2507-V, 2515-V	5.00 -	8.00
Velvet Tone 2387-V *Moonlight Savings Time*	10.00 -	15.00
2401-V *Love Is Like That*	7.00 -	10.00
2402-V *One More Time*	10.00 -	15.00
2407-V *High And Low*	10.00 -	15.00
2415-V *On the Beach With You*	10.00 -	15.00
2421-V *I Can't Write the Words*	7.00 -	10.00
2457-V *Waitin' for a call from you*	7.00 -	10.00
2480-V *Bend Down, Sister*	10.00 -	15.00
2502-V *Chances Are*	15.00 -	20.00

ROB CARSON & HIS ORCHESTRA:

Broadway 1295 *Whoopee' In Up*	7.00 -	10.00

CARTER'S ORCHESTRA:

Brunswick (most issues)	3.00 -	6.00

BENNY CARTER & HIS ORCHESTRA:

Columbia 2898-D *Devil's Holiday*	20.00 -	30.00
Crown 3321 *Tell All Your Day Dreams To Me*	30.00 -	40.00
Okeh 41567 *Blue Lou*	20.00 -	30.00
Vocalion 2870 *Everybody Shuffle*	20.00 -	30.00
2898 *Shoot The Works*	20.00 -	30.00
4984, 5112, 5224, 4294, 5399	7.00 -	10.00

KING CARTER & HIS ROYAL ORCHESTRA:

Columbia 2439-D *Minnie The Moocher*	20.00 -	30.00
2504-D *Blue Rhythm*	20.00 -	30.00
2638-D *Low Down On The Bayou*	20.00 -	30.00

MARGARET CARTER:

Pathe-Actuelle 7511 *I Want Plenty Grease In My Frying Pan*	15.00 -	20.00
Perfect 111 *I Want Plenty Grease In My Frying Pan*	15.00 -	20.00

CASA LOMA ORCHESTRA:

Brunswick 6085 *When I Take My Sugar To Tea* ..	7.00 -	10.00
6092 *White Jazz*	7.00 -	10.00
6100 *Alexander's Ragtime Band*	5.00 -	10.00
6124 *I Wanna Sing About You*	7.00 -	10.00
6150 *Do The New York*	7.00 -	10.00
6153 *It's The Girl*	7.00 -	10.00
6187 *Blue Kentucky Moon*	7.00 -	10.00
6201 *Time On My Hands*	7.00 -	10.00
6242 *Maniac's Ball*	7.00 -	10.00
6252 *Rain On The Roof*	7.00 -	10.00
6256 *One Of Us Was Wrong*	7.00 -	10.00
6263 *You're Still In My Heart*	7.00 -	10.00
6289 *Smoke Rings*	5.00 -	8.00
6311 *Lazy Day*	7.00 -	10.00
6318 *All Of A Sudden*	7.00 -	10.00
6337 *Indiana*	7.00 -	10.00
6397 *After Tonight*	7.00 -	10.00
6402 *Mighty River*	7.00 -	10.00
6463 *Rhythm Man*	7.00 -	10.00
6486 *New Orleans*	7.00 -	10.00
6494 *Why Can't This Go On Forever*	7.00 -	10.00
6513 *Blue Parade*	7.00 -	10.00
6584 *Love Is The Thing*	7.00 -	10.00
6588 *Wild Goose Chase*	7.00 -	10.00
6602 *For You*	7.00 -	10.00
6681 *Mississippi Basin*	7.00 -	10.00
6626 *That's How Rhythm Was Born*	7.00 -	10.00
6628 *Music From Across The Sea*	7.00 -	10.00
6642 *This Is Romance*	7.00 -	10.00
6647 *Savage Sereade*	7.00 -	10.00
6660 *Sweet Madness*	7.00 -	10.00
6666 *And So, Goodbye*	7.00 -	10.00
6679 *Heat Wave*	7.00 -	10.00
6708 *You're Gonna Lose Your Gal*	7.00 -	10.00
6726 *Dixie Lee*	7.00 -	10.00
6738 *Shadows Of Love*	7.00 -	10.00
6764 *That's Love*	7.00 -	10.00
6775 *A Hundred Years From Today*	7.00 -	10.00
6791 *Infatuation*	7.00 -	10.00
6800 *Ol' Man River*	7.00 -	10.00
6858 *This House Is Haunted*	7.00 -	10.00
6870 *Ridin' Around In The Rain*	7.00 -	10.00
6886 *Limehouse Blues*	7.00 -	10.00
6910 *Spellbound*	7.00 -	10.00
6922 *Milenberg Joys*	7.00 -	10.00
6927 *Long May We Love*	7.00 -	10.00
6932 *Jungle Fever*	7.00 -	10.00
6937 *You Ain't Been Living Right*	7.00 -	10.00
6945 *Pardon My Southern Accent*	7.00 -	10.00
6954 *Two Cigarettes In The Dark*	7.00 -	10.00
6964 *Out In The Cold Again*	7.00 -	10.00
6983 *How Can You Face Me?*	7.00 -	10.00
7321 *Nocturne*	7.00 -	10.00
7325 *Linger Awhile*	7.00 -	10.00
7427 *Corrine Corrina*	7.00 -	10.00
7532 *Avalon*	7.00 -	10.00

(Some of above Brunswicks are as Glen Gray &
   The Casa Loma Orchestra)

Brunswick 20108 *(12-inch) Washboard Blues*	30.00 -	50.00
Brunswick paper advertising record,		
unnumbered: *Limehouse Blues*	50.00 -	75.00
Columbia 2884-D *San Sue Strut*	10.00 -	15.00
Okeh 41339 *Happy Days Are Here Again*	10.00 -	15.00
41373 *Sweeping The Clouds Away*	10.00 -	15.00
41403 *Alexander's Ragtime Band*	10.00 -	15.00
41477 *Overnight*	10.00 -	15.00
41492 *Casa Loma Stomp*	10.00 -	15.00

**CASTLE FARMS SERENADERS/
ENTERTAINERS:**
Titles, issued contemporously on Broadway,
  Paramount: *Chili Blues; High On A Hilltop;*
  Ol' Man River; Silver Moon; 'Taint So, Honey,

'Taint So; Tennessee Lazy	8.00 -	15.00

**SID CATLETT QUARTETTE/
SEXTETTE/TRIO:**

Delta, Session	3.00 -	6.00

BOB CAUSER & HIS CORNELLIANS:

Melotone 12848 *Puddin' Head Jones*	10.00 -	15.00
Perfect 15858 *Puddin' Head Jones*	10.00 -	15.00

**CELESTIN'S ORIGINAL TUXEDO JAZZ
ORCHESTRA:**

Columbia 636-D *Station Calls*	20.00 -	30.00
14200-D *I'm Satisfied You Love Me*	20.00 -	30.00
14220-D *Papa's Got The Jim-Jams*	20.00 -	30.00
14259-D *As You Like It*	25.00 -	40.00
14323-D *It's Jam Up*	25.00 -	40.00
14396-D *The Sweetheart of T.K.O.*	25.00 -	40.00

THE CELLAR BOYS:

Vocalion 1503 *Barrel House Stomp*	150.00 -	200.00

RON CHADWICK & HIS ORCHESTRA:

Broadway 1312 *I'm The Medicine Man For*		
The Blues	5.00 -	8.00
1331 *The Things We Want Most Are Hard To*		
Get	5.00 -	8.00

CHALLENGE DANCE ORCHESTRA:

Challenge 210 *Don't Sing Aloha When I Go*	10.00 -	20.00
809 *Sweetheart*	—	—

CHAMPION RHYTHM KINGS:

Champion 16387 *Sweet Georgia Brown*	75.00 -	100.00

**CHARLIE CHAPLIN CONDUCTING ABE
LYMAN'S AMBASSADOR ORCHESTRA:**

Brunswick 2912 *Sing a Song*	7.00 -	10.00

**JACK CHAPMAN & HIS (DRAKE HOTEL)
ORCHESTRA:**

Victor 19775 *Carolina Blues*	—	—
Victor (most other issues)	3.00 -	6.00

JUANITA STINNETTE CHAPPELLE:

Chappelle & Stinnette 5003, 5004, 5005, 5006 .	10.00 -	20.00
Victor 21062 *Florence*	15.00 -	20.00

THE CHARLESTON CHASERS:

Columbia 446-D *Red Hot Henry Brown*	10.00 -	15.00
Columbia 861-D *After You've Gone*	8.00 -	12.00
909-D *Davenport Blues*	8.00 -	12.00
911-D *One Sweet Letter From You*	8.00 -	12.00
1076-D *Delirium*	15.00 -	20.00
1229-D *Five Pennies*	7.00 -	10.00
1335-D *My Melancholy Baby*	7.00 -	10.00
1539-D *Farewell Blues*	8.00 -	12.00
1891-D *Ain't Misbehavin'*	8.00 -	12.00
1925-D *Lovable And Sweet*	8.00 -	12.00
1989-D *Turn On The Heat*	12.00 -	16.00
2133-D *Sing, You Sinners*	8.00 -	12.00
2219-D *Here Comes Emily Brown*	15.00 -	20.00
2309-D *You're Lucky To Me*	15.00 -	20.00
2415-D *Basin Street Blues*	15.00 -	25.00

CHARLESTON MELODY SYNCOPATORS:

Dandy 5073 *Always Got The Blues*	15.00 -	30.00

The CHARLESTON SEVEN:

Edison 51446 *Nashville Nightingale*	20.00 -	30.00

CHECKER BOX BOYS:

Broadway 1179 *Is It Gonna Be Long*	5.00 -	8.00
Broadway 1209 *It Goes Like This*	5.00 -	8.00
Broadway 1231 *You're the Cream in My Coffee*	4.00 -	7.00
Broadway 1242 *Don't Be Like That*	4.00 -	7.00
Broadway 1244 *I's Rather Be Blue Over You*	5.00 -	8.00
Broadway 1251 *Cradle of Love*	4.00 -	7.00
Broadway 1259 *My Mother's Eyes*	4.00 -	7.00
Broadway 1262 *Outside*	5.00 -	8.00
Broadway 1266 *My Kinda Love*	4.00 -	7.00
Broadway 1272 *Louise*	5.00 -	8.00
Broadway 1276 *Breakaway*	5.00 -	8.00
Broadway 1287 *Am I Blue?*	5.00 -	8.00
Broadway 1301 *One Sweet Kiss*	4.00 -	7.00

Broadway 1328 *If I Had a Talking Picture of You* .	5.00 -	8.00
Broadway 1382 *Dream Avenue*	4.00 -	7.00
Broadway 1391 *Bye Bye Blues*	8.00 -	12.00
Broadway 1406 *My Baby Just Cares For Me*	7.00 -	10.00

DICK CHERWIN & HIS ORCHESTRA:

Banner 6497 *Birmingham Bertha*	5.00 -	8.00
Banner 6511 *I'm The Medicine Man for the Blues*	5.00 -	8.00
Banner 6537 *He's a Good Man To Have Around* .	5.00 -	8.00
Banner 6547 *Georgia Pines*	5.00 -	8.00
Cameo x8179 *Real Estate Papa*	7.00 -	10.00
Cameo x9184 *Hittin' The Ceiling*	5.00 -	8.00
Cameo x9208 *I'm Doing What I'm Doing For Love*	10.00 -	15.00
Cameo x9227 *True Blue Lou*	5.00 -	8.00
Conqueror 7716 *Got the Bench, Got the Park* . . .	5.00 -	8.00
Romeo 607 *Little Log Cabin of Dreams*	3.00 -	5.00
Romeo 934 *Swanee Cradle of Mine*	3.00 -	5.00

FRED CHESS & THE MERRYMAKERS:

Supertone 9381 *My Sugar And Me*	8.00 -	12.00

CHICAGO BLACK SWANS:

Titles, issued contemporaneously on Banner, Melotone, Oriole, Perfect, Romeo, Vocalion; *Don't Tear My Clothes No 2; You Drink Too Much*	7.00 -	10.00

CHICAGO BLUES DANCE ORCHESTRA:

Columbia A-3923 *Blue Grass Blues*	15.00 -	20.00

CHICAGO DE LUX ORCHESTRA:

Autograph 585 *Sad-Hearted Blues*		-
Paramount 20341 *St. Louis Blues*	15.00 -	20.00
Puritan 11341 *St. Louis Blues*	15.00 -	20.00

THE CHICAGO FOOTWARMERS:

Okeh 8533 *Ballin' The Jack*	50.00 -	75.00
8548 *Oriental Man*	50.00 -	75.00
8599 *Get 'Em Again Blues*	50.00 -	75.00
8613 *Brown Bottom Bess*	50.00 -	75.00
8675 *Goin' To Town*	35.00 -	50.00
8792 *Sweep 'Em Clean*	75.00 -	100.00

CHICAGO HOT FIVE:

Victor 23285 *Star Dust*	25.00 -	35.00
23300 *Wake 'Em Up*	25.00 -	35.00
23326 *Oh! What A Thrill*	25.00 -	40.00

CHICAGO HOTTENTOTS:

Vocalion 1008 *All Nights Shags*	80.00 -	120.00

THE CHICAGO LOOPERS:

Pathe-Actuelle 36729 *Three Blind Mice*	100.00 -	150.00
Perfect 14910 *Clorinda*	100.00 -	150.00

CHICAGO RHYTHM KINGS:

Bluebird 6371 *Little Sandwich Wagon*	10.00 -	15.00
6412 *Stompin' At The Savoy*	5.00 -	8.00
Brunswick 4001 *I've Found A New Baby*	15.00 -	20.00
Vocalion 03208 *You Battle Head Beetle Head* . . .	50.00 -	75.00

THE CHICAGO STOMPERS:

Champion 16297 *Wild man Stomp*	100.00 -	150.00

THE CHICKASAW SYNCOPATORS:

Columbia 14301-D *Memphis Rag*	50.00 -	80.00

IVORY CHITTISON AND BANJO JOE:

Vocalion 25011 *Unlucky Blues*	75.00 -	100.00

THE CHOCOLATE DANDIES:

Columbia 2543-D *Bugle Call Rag*	15.00 -	25.00
2875-D *I Never Knew*	20.00 -	30.00
Okeh 8668 *Birmingham Break-Down*	20.00 -	30.00
41568 *One upon A Time*	20.00 -	30.00
Vocalion 1610 *Loveless Love*	100.00 -	150.00
1617 *That's My Stuff*	100.00 -	150.00
1646 *Levee Low Down*	30.00 -	50.00

CHOO CHOO JAZZERS:

Ajax 17038 *Snuggle Up A Bit*	10.00 -	20.00

BUDDY CHRISTIAN'S CREOLE FIVE/JAZZ RIPPERS:

Okeh 8311 *Sunset Blues*	150.00 -	200.00
8342 *Sugar House Stomp*	100.00 -	150.00
Pathe-Actuelle 8518 *South Rampart Street Blues*	150.00 -	200.00

Perfect 118 *South Rampart Street Blues*	150.00 -	200.00

LILLIE DELK CHRISTIAN:

Okeh 8317 *Sweet Georgia Brown*	10.00 -	15.00
8356 *Baby O'Mine*	50.00 -	75.00
8475 *Ain't She Sweet?*	20.00 -	30.00
8536 *My Blue Heaven*	30.00 -	40.00
8596 *Too Busy*	30.00 -	50.00
8607 *You're A Real Sweetheart*	30.00 -	50.00
8650 *I Can't Give You Anything But Love*	30.00 -	50.00
8660 *I Must Have That Man*	30.00 -	50.00

TOMMY CHRISTIAN & HIS ORCHESTRA:

Harmony 264-H *How Could Red Riding Hood?* .	5.00 -	8.00
Harmony 330-H *Sam, The Old Accordion Man* . .	5.00 -	8.00
Harmony 348-H *'Deed I Do*	5.00 -	8.00
Harmony 358-H *Proud*	5.00 -	8.00
Harmony 394-H *Beedle Um Bo*	5.00 -	8.00
Harmony 427-H *Swamp Blues*	7.00 -	10.00
(Note: Above titles, on *Diva* and *Velvet Tone*, are similarly valued.)		

CHUBB-STEINBERG ORCHESTRA (OF CINCINNATI):

Gennett 3058 *Mandy, Make Up Your Mind*	20.00 -	30.00
5663 *Because They All Love You*	20.00 -	30.00
Okeh 40106 *From One Till Two*	20.00 -	30.00
40107 *Blue Evening Blues*	20.00 -	30.00

CINCINNATI JUG BAND:

Paramount 12743 *Newport Blues*	200.00 -	300.00

SUNNY CLAPP & HIS BAND O' SUNSHINE:

Harmony 899-H *Remember I Love You*	8.00 -	12.00
Okeh 41283 *A Bundle of Southern Sunshine* . . .	30.00 -	40.00
Victor 22682 *Treat Me Like A Baby*	10.00 -	15.00
22684 *When My Baby Smiles At Me*	10.00 -	15.00
22777 *Reflections of You*	10.00 -	15.00
V-40152 *Down On Biscayne Bay*	35.00 -	50.00

CLARINET JOE & HIS HOT FOOTERS:

Harmony 8-H *Rabbit Foot Blues*	7.00 -	10.00

DON CLARK & HIS LOS ANGELES BILTMORE HOTEL ORCHESTRA:

Columbia 824-D *I've Got The Girl!*	20.00 -	30.00
Victor 19622, 19736	5.00 -	10.00

JIM CLARKE:

Vocalion 1536 *Fat Funny Stomp*	80.00 -	120.00

SONNY CLAY'S PLANTATION/HARTFORD BALLROOM ORCHESTRA; SONNY CLAY & HIS ORCHESTRA:

Sonny Clay 22/23 *When It's Sleepy Time Down South*	— -	—
Vocalion 1000 *Plantation Blues*	75.00 -	100.00
1050 *California Stomp*	100.00 -	150.00
15078 *Jambled Blues*	75.00 -	100.00
15641 *Devil's Serenade*	100.00 -	150.00

CLAYTON, JACKSON AND DURANTE:

Columbia 1860-D *So I Ups To Him*	8.00 -	12.00

JOHNNY CLESI'S AREOLIANS:

Gennett 3380 *Ain't I Got Rosie?*	30.00 -	50.00
6033 *Brotherly Love*	50.00 -	75.00
Herschel Gold Seal 2010 *Ain't I Got Rosie?*	50.00 -	100.00

THE CLEVELANDERS:

Banner 0784 *I Still Get A Thrill*	5.00 -	8.00
Brunswick 3047 *Rhythm Of The Day*	5.00 -	8.00
Brunswick 3279 *She Belongs To Me*	5.00 -	8.00

Brunswick (Most other issues) . . . . 4.00 - 7.00
Cameo 0144 *Sunny Side Up* . . . . 3.00 - 5.00
Cameo 0223 *With You* . . . . 5.00 - 8.00
Cameo 0294 *You Brought a New Kind of Love
to Me* . . . . 5.00 - 8.00
Cameo 0405 *I Don't Mind Walkin' in the Rain* . . 4.00 - 7.00
Challenge 764 *I Don't Mind Walkin' in the Rain* . 4.00 - 7.00
Perfect 15258 *A Year From Today* . . . . 5.00 - 8.00
Romeo 1159 *Sunny Side Up* . . . . 3.00 - 5.00
Romeo 1243 *With You* . . . . 5.00 - 8.00

CLICQUOT CLUB ESKIMOS:
Banner 0700 *'Leven Thirty Saturday Night* . . . . . . 5.00 - 8.00
Banner 0721 *Ro-Ro-Rolling Along* . . . . 5.00 - 8.00
Banner 0779 *Hittin' The Bottle* . . . . 7.00 - 10.00
Cameo 0172 *You've Got That Thing* . . . . 5.00 - 8.00
Cameo 0358 *Out Of Breath (And Scared To
Death Of You)* . . . . 7.00 - 10.00
Columbia 795-D *Some Day* . . . . 5.00 - 8.00
Columbia 921-D *My Sunday Girl* . . . . 5.00 - 8.00
Columbia 1060-D *I Wonder Who's With You
When I'm Not There* . . . . 5.00 - 8.00
Columbia 1213-D *My One And Only* . . . . 5.00 - 8.00
Columbia 1281-D *Henry's Made a Lady Out of
Lizzie* . . . . 7.00 - 10.00
1592-D *Come On, Baby!* . . . . 7.00 - 10.00
Columbia 1625-D *Watching The Clouds Roll By* . 7.00 - 10.00
Columbia 1718-D *In a Little Town Called Home
Sweet Home* . . . . 7.00 - 10.00
Romeo 1189 *I Want To Be Happy* . . . . 5.00 - 8.00
Romeo 1203 *Hallelujah* . . . . 5.00 - 8.00
Romeo 1374 *Little White Lies* . . . . 3.00 - 5.00

CLIFFORD'S LOUISVILLE JUG BAND:
Okeh 8221 *Dancing Blues* . . . . 75.00 - 100.00
8238 *Struttin' The Blues* . . . . 75.00 - 100.00
8248 *Mammy O'Mine Blues* . . . . 75.00 - 100.00
8269 *Get It Fixed Blues* . . . . 75.00 - 100.00

CLINE'S COLLEGIANS:
DAL-571/572 *Chicadore Stomp* . . . . . 75.00 - 100.00
(Note: Above is a test pressing.)
Brunswick 4162 *Peruna* . . . . 15.00 - 20.00

TOM CLINES & HIS MUSIC:
Brunswick (most issues) . . . . 4.00 - 8.00
Diva 2928-G *Sing A Little Love Song* . . . . 8.00 - 12.00
Diva (most other issues) . . . . 4.00 - 8.00
Harmony 928-H *Sing A Little Love Song* . . . . . . 8.00 - 12.00
Harmony (most other issues) . . . . 4.00 - 8.00
Velvet Tone 1928-V *Sing A Little Love Song* . . . 8.00 - 12.00
Velvet Tone (most other issues) . . . . 4.00 - 8.00

LARRY CLINTON AND HIS ORCHESTRA:
LARRY CLINTON'S BLUEBIRD
ORCHESTRA:
Bluebird, most issues . . . . 3.00 - 6.00
Decca, most issues . . . . 3.00 - 6.00
Victor, most issues . . . . 4.00 - 7.00

CLOVERDALE COUNTRY CLUB
ORCHESTRA:
Okeh 41519, 41520, 41523, 41528, 41531, 41535,
41539, 41542, 41544, 41555, 41564 . . . . . . 5.00 - 10.00
41551 *Chances Are* . . . . 15.00 - 20.00

CLUB ALABAM' ORCHESTRA:
Domino 354, 355, 356, 366, 368, 369, 370, 371 . 6.00 - 10.00

415 *How Come you Do Me Like You Do?* . . . . . 8.00 - 12.00
426 *One Of These Days* . . . . 8.00 - 12.00
430 *My Dream Man* . . . . 8.00 - 12.00

CLUB AMBASSADORS ORCHESTRA:
Brunswick 7096 *Apex Blues* . . . . 50.00 - 75.00

CLUB WIGWAM ORCHESTRA:
Domino 3458 *Alabamy Bound* . . . . 10.00 - 15.00

JACK COAKLEY'S (FLEXO RECORDING)
ORCHESTRA:
Flexo 103 *It Seems To Be Spring* . . . . 30.00 - 50.00
117 *Wabash Blues* . . . . 50.00 - 80.00
130 *Walkin' My Baby Back Home* . . . . 30.00 - 50.00
131 *Reaching For The Moon* . . . . 30.00 - 50.00

TOM COAKLEY & HIS (PALACE HOTEL)
ORCHESTRA:
Brunswick 6577, 6702 . . . . 4.00 - 8.00
Victor (most issues) . . . . 4.00 - 8.00

E.C. COBB & HIS CORN EATERS:
Victor 38023 *Transatlantic Stomp* . . . . 25.00 - 40.00

J.C. JUNIE COBB & HIS GRAINS OF CORN:
JUNIE COBB'S HOMETOWN BAND:
Paramount 12382 *East Coast Trot* . . . . 150.00 - 300.00
Vocalion 1204 *Endurance Stomp* . . . . 50.00 - 75.00
1263 *Shake That Jelly Roll* . . . . 75.00 - 100.00
1269 *Smoke Shop Drag* . . . . 75.00 - 100.00
1449 *Once Or Twice* . . . . 50.00 - 75.00
(Note: Repressings, on black and gold, or blue
and gold label are valued much lower.)

OLIVER COBB (& HIS RHYTHM KINGS):
Brunswick 7107 *Hot Stuff* . . . . 80.00 - 120.00
Paramount 13002 *Cornet Pleading Blues* . . . . . . 200.00 - 300.00

GEORGE M. COHAN:
Victor 60042, 60043, 60044, 60045, 60049,
60052, 70039 . . . . 5.00 - 10.00

EDDIE COLE'S SOLID SWINGERS:
Decca 7210 *Thunder* . . . . 15.00 - 20.00
7215 *Stomping At The Panama* . . . . 15.00 - 20.00

KING COLE QUARTET/TRIO; KING COLE'S
SWINGSTERS:
Ammor 108 *On The Sunny Side Of The Street* . . . -
109 *Black Spider* . . . . -
Davis & Schwegler 108 *Land of Make-Believe* . . . -
Davis & Schwegler 110 *Ta-De-Ah* . . . . -
111 *Riffin' At The Barbeque* . . . . -
113 *I Lost Control Of Myself* . . . . -
115 *That Please Be Mineable feeling* . . . . -
119 *Let's Get Happy* . . . . -
Decca 8520 *This Side Up* . . . . 10.00 - 15.00
8535 *Honeysuckle Rose* . . . . 10.00 - 15.00
8541 *Early Morning Blues* . . . . 10.00 - 15.00
8556 *Slow Down* . . . . 10.00 - 15.00
8571 *Hit The Ramp* . . . . 10.00 - 15.00
8592 *I Like To Riff* . . . . 10.00 - 15.00
8604 *Call The Police* . . . . 10.00 - 15.00
8630 *That Ain't Right* . . . . 10.00 - 15.00
Excelsior 104/105 *Pitchin' Up A Boogie* . . . . . . -
Premier 100 *F.S.T.* . . . . 15.00 - 20.00
Varsity 8340 *I Like To Riff* . . . . -

E.L. COLEMAN:
Okeh 8216 *Steel String Blues* . . . . 35.00 - 50.00

EMIL COLEMAN & HIS ORCHESTRA:
Brunswick 6006 *I'm Getting Myself Ready For
You* . . . . 7.00 - 10.00
Brunswick (other issues) . . . . 4.00 - 8.00
Columbia 2831-D, 2846-D, 2847-D, 2859-D,
2869-D, 2877-D, 2882-D, 2893-D, 2894-D,
2930-D, 2933-D, 2960-D, 2961-D . . . . 5.00 - 10.00
Vocalion (most issues) . . . . 3.00 - 6.00

COLLEGE SERENADERS:
Champion 15227 *A Tree In The Park* . . . . 100.00 - 150.00

THE COLLEGIANS:
Broadway 1349 *Crying For The Carolines* . . . . . 5.00 - 8.00

Pathe-Actuelle 36924 *He Ain't Never Been In College* .... 7.00 - 10.00
Perfect 15105 *He Ain't Never Been In College* ... 7.00 - 10.00
Victor 19049 *That Red-Head Gal* .... 5.00 - 8.00

ARTIE COLLINS & HIS ORCHESTRA:
Broadway 1371 *It Happened in Monterey* .... 5.00 - 8.00
Broadway 1375 *Red Hot and Blue Rhythm* ...... 8.00 - 12.00
Broadway 1376 *I Never Dreamt You'd Fall In Love With Me* .... 7.00 - 10.00

ROY COLLINS' DANCE ORCHESTRA:
Banner 1181 *Maxie Jones (King of the Saxophones)* .... 7.00 - 10.00
Banner 1239 *Steamboat Sal* .... 5.00 - 8.00
Banner 1270 *Sittin' in a Corner* .... 5.00 - 8.00
Challenge 914 *I Love To Ride A Camel* .... 5.00 - 8.00
Challenge 933 *Papa's Mama's Blue* .... 7.00 - 10.00
Jewell 5145 *Homing Bird (Headin' For Home)* ... 8.00 - 12.00
Oriole 652 *Waffles* .... 5.00 - 8.00
Oriole 706 *Blowin' Off Steam* .... 5.00 - 8.00
Oriole 724 *The Birth of the Blues* .... 5.00 - 8.00
Oriole 1044 *There's Always Somebody Lookin' For Somebody* .... 5.00 - 8.00
Oriole 1389 *Just Today* .... 5.00 - 8.00
Oriole 1459 *"Hoo" Ray, I Want To Play* ...... 5.00 - 8.00
Oriole 1460 *I'd Love To Go Around With You* ... 5.00 - 8.00
   1488 *Shake Off The Blues* .... 7.00 - 10.00
   1541 *Papa's Mama's Blue* .... 7.00 - 10.00
   1549 *Why Didn't You Tell Me?* .... 5.00 - 8.00
   1627 *My Rosalie* .... 5.00 - 8.00
   1723 *Any Old Time Is Loving Time For Me* .... 5.00 - 8.00

COLONIAL CLUB ORCHESTRA:
Brunswick 3244 *My Pal Jerry* .... 7.00 - 10.00
   4058 *Where The Shy Little Violets Grow* ..... 5.00 - 8.00
Brunswick (most other issues) .... 4.00 - 8.00

COLUMBIA NOVELTY ORCHESTRA:
Columbia 131-D *Oh, Baby!* .... 5.00 - 8.00

COLUMBIA PHOTO PLAYERS:
Columbia 2105-D *Mona* .... 8.00 - 12.00
   2131-D *Sweepin' The Clouds Away* ...... 8.00 - 12.00
   2149-D *The "Free And Easy"* .... 8.00 - 12.00
   2177-D *Leave It That way* .... 8.00 - 12.00
   2187-D *I'm In The Market For You* ...... 8.00 - 12.00
   2196-D *Dust* .... 8.00 - 12.00

RUSS COLUMBO:
Bluebird 6503 *Time On My hands* .... 5.00 - 8.00
Brunswick 6972 *Too Beautiful For Words* .... 10.00 - 15.00
Victor 22801 *I Don't Know Why (I Just Do)* .... 8.00 - 12.00
   22802 *Sweet And Lovely* .... 8.00 - 12.00
   22826 *Time On My Hands* .... 8.00 - 12.00
   22861 *You Try Somebody Else* .... 8.00 - 12.00
   22867 *Prisoner Of Love* .... 8.00 - 12.00
   22903 *All Of Me* .... 10.00 - 15.00
   22909 *Just Friends* .... 10.00 - 15.00
   22976 *Auf Widersehen, My Dear* .... 10.00 - 15.00
   24045 *Just Another Dream Of You* .... 10.00 - 15.00
   24076 *As You Desire Me* .... 10.00 - 15.00
   24077 *My Love* .... 10.00 - 15.00
   24194 *Street Of Dreams* .... 10.00 - 15.00
   24195 *Make Love The Thing* .... 10.00 - 15.00

EDDIE CONDON & HIS FOOTWARMERS/ ORCHESTRA:
Brunswick 6743 *Home Cooking* .... 10.00 - 15.00
Okeh 41142 *I'm Sorry I Made You Cry* .... 15.00 - 20.00

CONNIE'S INN ORCHESTRA:
Crown 3180 *You Rascal, You* .... 15.00 - 25.00
   3194 *Sugar Foot Stomp* .... 15.00 - 25.00
   3212 *Milenberg Joys* .... 15.00 - 25.00
Melotone 12145 *I'm Crazy 'Bout My baby* ..... 15.00 - 20.00
   12216 *The House Of David Blues* .... 15.00 - 20.00
   12239 *Sugar Foot Stomp* .... 15.00 - 20.00
   12340 *Goodbye Blues* .... 15.00 - 20.00
Victor 22698 *Moan, You Moaners* .... 10.00 - 15.00

   22721 *Singing The Blues* .... 10.00 - 15.00

LOU CONNOR & HIS COLLEGIANS/ COLLEGIATES/ORCHESTRA:
Jewel 5000 *I'm Looking Over A Four Leaf Clover* 5.00 - 8.00
   5189 *Keep Sweeping The Cobwebs Off The Moon* .... 5.00 - 8.00
Oriole 670 *How Many Times?* .... 5.00 - 8.00
   1124 *My Ohio Home* .... 5.00 - 8.00
   1126 *Keep Sweeping The Cobwebs Off The Moon* .... 5.00 - 8.00
   1156 *My Melancholy Baby* .... 7.00 - 10.00
   1171 *Where Will I Be?* .... 8.00 - 12.00
   1172 *Moten Stomp* .... 8.00 - 12.00
   1483 *Four Or Five Times* .... 8.00 - 12.00

JEROME CONRAD & HIS ORCHESTRA:
Harmony 693-H *When Eliza Rolls Her Eyes* .... 5.00 - 8.00
Harmony 694-H *Mississippi Mud* .... 5.00 - 8.00
Harmony 698-H *Mr. Hoover and Mr. Smith* .... 5.00 - 8.00
Harmony 738-H *Etiquette Blues* .... 5.00 - 8.00
Harmony 824-H *Susianna* .... 5.00 - 8.00
Harmony 842-H *I Faw Down An' Go Boom!* .... 5.00 - 8.00
Harmony 844-H *Wedding Bells (Are Breaking Up That Old Gang of Mine)* .... 7.00 - 10.00
Harmony 964-H *Mississippi Mud* .... 5.00 - 8.00
(Note: Above titles, on *Diva* and *Velvet Tone*, are similarly valued.)

CONSOLIDATED CLUB ORCHESTRA:
Pathe-Actuelle 36392 *Static Strut* .... 7.00 - 10.00
Perfect 14573 *Static Strut* .... 7.00 - 10.00

CONWAY'S BAND:
Okeh 4208 *Ragtime In A Toy Shop* .... 5.00 - 8.00
Victor 17628 *Sweetie Dear* .... 7.00 - 10.00
Victor 17850 *Ragging The Scale* .... 7.00 - 10.00
Victor 17851 *Bon Ton One-Step* .... 7.00 - 10.00
Victor 18109 *American Jubilee (A Patriotic Rag)* . 7.00 - 10.00
Victor 35600 *The Evolution of Dixie (12-inch)* ... 7.00 - 10.00

COOK & HIS DREAMLAND ORCHESTRA:
COOK'S DREAMLAND ORCHESTRA:
"DOC" COOK & HIS 14 DOCTORS OF SYNCOPATION:
Columbia 727-D *Spanish Mama* .... 30.00 - 50.00
   813-D *High Fever* .... 30.00 - 50.00
   862-D *Sidewalk Blues* .... 25.00 - 35.00
   1070-D *Willie The Weeper* .... 25.00 - 35.00
   1298-D *Alligator Crawl* .... 25.00 - 35.00
   1430-D *Hum And Strum* .... 25.00 - 35.00
Gennett 5360 *So This Is Venice* .... 35.00 - 50.00
   5373 *Moanful Man* .... 50.00 - 75.00
   5374 *Scissor Grinder Joe* .... 50.00 - 75.00
Silvertone 4044 *Scissor Grinder Joe* .... 50.00 - 75.00
   4045 *Moanful Man* .... 50.00 - 75.00

COOKIE'S GINGERSNAPS:
Okeh 8369 *High Fever* .... 150.00 - 200.00
   8390 *Messin' Around* .... 125.00 - 175.00
   40675 *Love Found You For Me* .... 125.00 - 175.00

PRESIDENT CALVIN COOLIDGE:
Victor 35835 (12") *Pres. Coolidge Welcomes Colonel Lindbergh* .... 8.00 - 12.00

COON-SANDERS (ORIGINAL NIGHTHAWK) ORCHESTRA:
Victor 19316 *Night Hawk Blues* .... 5.00 - 8.00

Victor 19325	*Oriental Love Dreams*	5.00 -	8.00
Victor 19357	*There's No-One Just Like You*	5.00 -	8.00
Victor 19522	*Lazy Waters*	5.00 -	8.00
Victor 19525	*Moonlight And You*	5.00 -	8.00
Victor 19600	*Some Of These Days*	5.00 -	8.00
Victor 19727	*I'm Gonna Charleston Back To Charleston*	5.00 -	8.00
Victor 19728	*Alone At Last*	5.00 -	8.00
Victor 19745	*Yes Sir! That's My Baby*	5.00 -	8.00
Victor 19750	*That's All There Is—There Ain't No More*	5.00 -	8.00
Victor 19754	*Who Wouldn't Love You?*	5.00 -	8.00
Victor 19804	*Dreaming Of To-morrow*	5.00 -	8.00
Victor 19852	*I Can't Realize*	7.00 -	10.00
Victor 19922	*Flamin' Mamie*	5.00 -	8.00
Victor 19958	*Louise, You Tease*	5.00 -	8.00
Victor 19979	*Moon Deer*	5.00 -	8.00
Victor 20003	*Everything's Gonna Be All Right*	5.00 -	8.00
Victor 20015	*Sittin' Around*	7.00 -	10.00
Victor 20081	*Deep Henderson*	5.00 -	8.00
Victor 20390	*Brainstorm*	7.00 -	10.00
Victor 20408	*I Need Lovin'*	8.00 -	12.00
Victor 20461	*High Fever*	25.00 -	35.00
Victor 20785	*I Ain't Go Nobody*	5.00 -	8.00
Victor 21148	*Is She My Girl Friend?*	5.00 -	8.00
Victor 21258	*Stay Out Of The South*	5.00 -	8.00
Victor 21305	*The Wail*	7.00 -	10.00
Victor 21397	*Hallucinations*	10.00 -	15.00
Victor 21501	*Oh! You Have No Idea*	5.00 -	8.00
Victor 21546	*Too Busy!*	7.00 -	10.00
Victor 21562	*Indian Cradle Song*	5.00 -	8.00
Victor 21680	*Blazin'*	7.00 -	10.00
Victor 21803	*What a Girl! What a Night!*	7.00 -	10.00
Victor 21812	*Here Comes My Ball And Chain*	8.00 -	12.00
Victor 21891	*Rhythm King*	7.00 -	10.00
Victor 21895	*Little Orphan Annie*	7.00 -	10.00
Victor 21939	*Kansas City Kitty*	7.00 -	10.00
Victor 22077	*And Especially You!*	7.00 -	10.00
Victor 22089	*The Flippety Flop*	7.00 -	10.00
Victor 22123	*Gotta Great Big Date With A Little Bitta Girl*	5.00 -	8.00
Victor 22262	*Alone In The Rain*	5.00 -	8.00
Victor 22278	*Moanin' For You*	7.00 -	10.00
Victor 22300	*Harlem Madness*	7.00 -	10.00
Victor 22304	*We Love Us*	5.00 -	8.00
Victor 22342	*After You've Gone*	7.00 -	10.00
Victor 22346	*Sweepin' The Clouds Away*	7.00 -	10.00
Victor 22950	*Let That Be a Lesson To You*	7.00 -	10.00
Victor 22951	*Sing A New Song*	8.00 -	12.00
Victor 22969	*Keepin' Out of Mischief Now*	10.00 -	15.00
Victor 22972	*I Want To Go Home*	7.00 -	10.00
Victor 22979	*On Revival Day*	10.00 -	15.00
Victor V38083	*Louder And Funnier*	15.00 -	20.00

AL COOPER & HIS (ORIGINAL) SAVOY SULTANS:

Decca 2526	*Jumpin' At The Savoy*	7.00 -	10.00
2608	*Stitches*	7.00 -	10.00
2819	*Love Gave Me You*	7.00 -	10.00
2930	*Jumpin' The Blues*	7.00 -	10.00
3142	*Frenzy*	7.00 -	10.00
3274	*Sophisticated Jump*	7.00 -	10.00
7499	*Rhythm Doctor Man*	7.00 -	10.00
7525	*Gettin' In The Groove*	7.00 -	10.00
7549	*Looney*	7.00 -	10.00
8540	*Norfolk Ferry*	7.00 -	10.00
8545	*Second Balcony Jump*	7.00 -	10.00
8598	*Fis For Your Supper*	7.00 -	10.00
8615	*'At's In There*	7.00 -	10.00

ROBERT COOPER:

Bluebird 5459	*West Dallas Drag*	15.00 -	20.00
5947	*West Dallas Drag—No.2*	15.00 -	25.00

ANDREW COPELAND:

Black Swan 14124	*Buzz Mirandy*	20.00 -	30.00

PAUL CORNELIUS & HIS ORCHESTRA:

Champion 16282	*Ho Hum!*	15.00 -	30.00
16523	*Say It Isn't So*	30.00 -	50.00
16534	*Sentimental Gentleman From Georgia*	50.00 -	75.00
16572	*The Scat Song*	75.00 -	100.00
16593	*Bubbling Over With Love*	30.00 -	50.00
16727	*Smoke Gets In Your Eyes*	30.00 -	50.00
16734	*I'm Still Dreaming Of You*	100.00 -	150.00
16746	*Cinderella's Fella*	50.00 -	75.00
16749	*Rhymes*	50.00 -	75.00
40084	*I've Found A New Baby*	20.00 -	30.00

CORNELL & HIS ORCHESTRA:

Okeh 41386	*Accordion Joe*	20.00 -	30.00
41395	*I Was Made To Love You*	20.00 -	30.00

FRANK CORNWELL & HIS ORCHESTRA:

Cameo 1056	*Have You Forgotten*	5.00 -	8.00
Edison 52166	*Dawn*	7.00 -	10.00
Harmony 320-H	*Here Or There*	5.00 -	8.00
333-H	*Schultz Is Back Again*	5.00 -	8.00
341-H	*Voom Voom*	5.00 -	8.00
378-H	*Roses For Remembrance*	5.00 -	8.00
Silvertone 3302	*Crazy Words-Crazy Tune*	5.00 -	8.00

(Note: Above titles, on *Velvet Tone*, are similarly valued)

(CHARLES) CORRELL AND (FREEMAN) GOSDEN (AS SAM 'N' HENRY; AMOS 'N' ANDY)

Victor 20032, 20093, 20375, 20788		4.00 -	7.00
Victor 21608	*Presidential Election*	7.00 -	10.00
22119	*Is Everybody In Your Family Dumb As You Is?*	7.00 -	10.00
22234	*At The Bullfight*	7.00 -	10.00
22393	*Check And Double Check*	8.00 -	12.00

COTTON CLUB ORCHESTRA:

Columbia 287-D	*Down And Out Blues*	30.00 -	40.00
374-D	*Riverboat Shuffle*	30.00 -	50.00
14113-D	*Everybody Stomp*	50.00 -	75.00

THE COTTON PICKERS:

Brunswick 2292	*Hot Lips*	5.00 -	8.00
Brunswick 2338	*Got To Cool My Doggies Now*	5.00 -	8.00
Brunswick 2380	*Great White Way Blues*	5.00 -	8.00
Brunswick 2382	*Loose Feet*	5.00 -	8.00
Brunswick 2404	*You Tell Her, I Stutter*	5.00 -	8.00
Brunswick 2418	*Snakes' Hips*	5.00 -	8.00
Brunsiwck 2436	*Down By The River*	5.00 -	8.00
Brunswick 2461	*Duck's Quack*	5.00 -	8.00
Brunswick 2486	*Back O'Town Blues*	5.00 -	8.00
Brunswick 2490	*Walk, Jenny, Walk*	5.00 -	8.00
Brunswick 2507	*Just Hot*	7.00 -	10.00
Brunswick 2532	*Do Yo' Dooty, Daddy*	7.00 -	10.00
Brunswick 2766	*Jimtown Blues*	8.00 -	12.00
Brunswick 2818	*Mishawaka Blues*	8.00 -	12.00
Brunswick 2879	*Down And Out Blues*	8.00 -	12.00
Brunswick 2937	*Milenberg Joys*	8.00 -	12.00
Brunswick 2981	*Stomp Off—Let's Go*	8.00 -	12.00
Brunswick 3001	*Fallin' Down*	8.00 -	12.00
4325	*Rampart Street Blues*	10.00 -	15.00
4404	*Sweet Ida Joy*	10.00 -	15.00
4440	*St. Louis Gal*	10.00 -	15.00
4446	*Moanin' Low*	10.00 -	15.00
4447	*Shoo Shoo Boogie Boo*	10.00 -	15.00
Cameo 9207	*Hot Heels*	10.00 -	15.00
Cameo 9048	*Railroad Man*	10.00 -	15.00
Gennett 6380	*What'll You Do?*	50.00 -	75.00
6396	*After Awhile*	50.00 -	75.00
Lincoln 3077	*Railroad Man*	10.00 -	15.00
Romeo 852	*Railroad Man*	10.00 -	15.00

WALLIE COULTER & HIS BAND:

Gennett 6369	*Hollywood Shuffle*	200.00 -	300.00

DEL COURTNEY AND HIS ORCHESTRA:

Vocalion 4850, 4864, 4985, 4992, 5046, 5061,

5088, 5127, 5212, 5279, 5291, 5306, 5332,
5354, 5608, 5616 . . . . 3.00 - 6.00

IDA COX (Accompanied by Lovie Austin's Blues Serenaders; Her Five Blue Spells, et al.):

Paramount 12022 Come Right In	20.00 -	30.00
12044 Weary Way Blues	75.00 -	100.00
12045 Bama Bound Blues	20.00 -	30.00
12053 Blue Monday Blues	20.00 -	30.00
12056 Chicago Bound Blues	20.00 -	30.00
12063 I've Got The Blues For Rampart Street . .	75.00 -	100.00
12064 Moanin' Groanin' Blues	75.00 -	100.00
12085 Worried Mama Blues	75.00 -	100.00
12086 Confidential Blues	75.00 -	100.00
12087 Mail Man Blues	75.00 -	100.00
12094 Down The Road Bound Blues	20.00 -	30.00
12097 Mean Papa, Turn Your Key	75.00 -	100.00
12202 Chicago Monkey Man Blues	75.00 -	100.00
12212 Last Time Blues	75.00 -	100.00
12220 Kentucky Man Blues	75.00 -	100.00
12228 Cherry Picking Blues	75.00 -	100.00
12237 Worried In Mind Blues	75.00 -	100.00
12251 Mississippi River Blues	50.00 -	80.00
12258 Misery Blues	50.00 -	80.00
12263 Georgia Hound Blues	50.00 -	80.00
12275 Mister Man	50.00 -	80.00
12282 Someday Blues	75.00 -	100.00
12291 Black Crepe Blues	75.00 -	100.00
12298 Southern Woman's Blues	75.00 -	100.00
12307 Lonesome Blues	75.00 -	100.00
12318 Coffin Blues	75.00 -	125.00
12325 One Time Woman Blues	75.00 -	100.00
12334 I Ain't Got Nobody	75.00 -	100.00
12344 Trouble Trouble Blues	100.00 -	150.00
12353 Night And Day Blues	100.00 -	150.00
12381 Don't Blame Me	100.00 -	150.00
12488 'Fore Day Creep	50.00 -	75.00
12502 Mercy Blues	50.00 -	75.00
12513 Pleading Blues	75.00 -	100.00
12540 Mojo Hand Blues	75.00 -	100.00
12556 Seven Day Blues	50.00 -	75.00
12582 Midnight Hour Blues	50.00 -	75.00
12664 Bone Orchard Blues	75.00 -	100.00
12667 Broadcasting Blues	75.00 -	100.00
12690 Fogyism	75.00 -	100.00
12727 Separated Blues	100.00 -	150.00
12965 Jail House Blues	150.00 -	200.00
Vocalion 05298, 05336	7.00 -	10.00

DICK COY & HIS RACKETEERS:

Gennett 7175 Barnacle Bill The Sailor	— -	—

FRANCIS CRAIG & HIS ORCHESTRA:

Columbia 567-D Steady Roll Blues	10.00 -	15.00
709-D Hard-To-Get Gertie	7.00 -	10.00
1266-D That Florida Low Down	8.00 -	12.00
1544-D Coon-Tail	8.00 -	12.00

JACK CRAWFORD & HIS BOYS/ ORCHESTRA:

Champion 15383 Down South	25.00 -	40.00
15384 The Best Things In Life Are Free	25.00 -	40.00
15400 Together We Two	20.00 -	30.00
15404 For My Baby	20.00 -	30.00
15418 One More Night	15.00 -	20.00
15422 Beautiful	25.00 -	35.00
15439 Dear On A Night Like This	15.00 -	20.00
Victor 20847 Who's That Pretty Baby?	5.00 -	8.00
Victor 20901 I'd Walk a Million Miles	5.00 -	8.00
Victor 20994 Baltimore	5.00 -	8.00
Victor 21173 Kiss And Make Up	5.00 -	8.00
Victor 21217 Beautiful	5.00 -	8.00

WILTON CRAWLEY (& HIS ORCHESTRA/ THE WASHBOARD RHYTHM KINGS):

Bluebird 5827 She's Got What I Need	15.00 -	20.00
Okeh 8479 Crawley Blues	30.00 -	50.00

8492 Geechie River Blues	30.00 -	50.00
8539 Love Will Drive Me Crazy	20.00 -	30.00
8555 She's Nothing But Nice	20.00 -	30.00
8589 I'm Forever Changing Sweetheart	30.00 -	50.00
8619 Shadow Of The Blues	30.00 -	50.00
8718 My Perfect Thrill	30.00 -	50.00
Victor 23292 Big Time Woman	150.00 -	250.00
23344 New Crawley Blues	150.00 -	250.00
V-38094 Snake Hip Dance	75.00 -	100.00
V-38116 She's Got What I Need	80.00 -	120.00
V-38136 You Oughta See My Gal	80.00 -	120.00

WILLIE CREAGER & HIS ORCHESTRA/ ENTERTAINERS/RHYTHM ACES:

Banner 6263 Wide Open Gate	5.00 -	8.00
Banner 6285 Pepper Pot	5.00 -	8.00
Banner 6484 Sweet Tootsies	5.00 -	8.00
Banner 6501 Contrary Mary	5.00 -	8.00
Banner (most other issues)	3.00 -	6.00
Gennett (most issues)	4.00 -	8.00
Pathe-Actuelle (most issues)	4.00 -	7.00
Perfect (most issues)	4.00 -	7.00
Regal (most issues)	3.00 -	6.00
Romeo (most issues)	3.00 -	6.00

CHAS. CREATH'S JAZZ-O-MANIACS:

Okeh 8201 Pleasure Mad	50.00 -	75.00
8210 King Porter Stomp	75.00 -	100.00
8217 My Daddy Rocks Me	50.00 -	80.00
8257 Grandpa's Spell	75.00 -	100.00
8280 Market Street Stomp	75.00 -	100.00
8477 Crazy Quilt	150.00 -	200.00

BING CROSBY:

Bluebird 7102, 7118	4.00 -	7.00
Brunswick 6090 Out Of Nowhere	8.00 -	12.00
6120 Were You Sincere?	8.00 -	12.00
6140 At Your Command	8.00 -	12.00
6169 Star Dust	8.00 -	12.00
6179 I Apologize	8.00 -	12.00
6200 Now That You're Gone	8.00 -	12.00
6203 Goodnight Sweetheart	8.00 -	12.00
6226 Where The Blue Of The Night	8.00 -	12.00
6240 Can't We Talk It Over?	8.00 -	12.00
6248 I Found You	8.00 -	12.00
6259 How Long Will It Last?	8.00 -	12.00
6268 Love, You Funny Thing	8.00 -	12.00
6276 Shadows On The Window	8.00 -	12.00
6285 Paradise	8.00 -	12.00
6306 Lazy Day	8.00 -	12.00
6320 Sweet Georgia Brown	8.00 -	12.00
6329 Cabin In The Cotton	8.00 -	12.00
6351 Some Of These Days	8.00 -	12.00
6394 Please	8.00 -	12.00
6406 Here Lies Love	8.00 -	12.00
6414 Brother, Can You Spare A Dime?	8.00 -	12.00
6427 I'll Follow You	8.00 -	12.00
6454 Just An Echo In The Valley	8.00 -	12.00
6464 Street Of Dreams	8.00 -	12.00
6472 Young And Healthy	8.00 -	12.00
6477 You're Beautiful Tonight, My Dear	8.00 -	12.00
6480 Try A Little Tenderness	8.00 -	12.00
6485 Shine	8.00 -	12.00
6491 You've Got Me Crying Again	7.00 -	10.00

6525 *Someone Stold Gabriel's Horn*	7.00 -	10.00
6594 *Learn To Croon*	7.00 -	10.00
6599 *I've Got To Sing A Torch Song*	7.00 -	10.00
6601 *Down The Old Ox Road*	7.00 -	10.00
6610 *There's A Cabin In The Pines*	7.00 -	10.00
6623 *I Would If I Could But I Can't*	7.00 -	10.00
6643 *Black Moonlight*	7.00 -	10.00
6644 *The Day You Came Along*	5.00 -	8.00
6663 *Home On The Range*	5.00 -	8.00
6694 *Beautiful Girl*	5.00 -	8.00
6695 *Temptation*	5.00 -	8.00
6696 *Our Big Love Scene*	5.00 -	8.00
6724 *Did You Ever See A Dream Walking?*	5.00 -	8.00
6594 *Little Dutch Mill*	5.00 -	8.00
6852 *Love Thy Neighbor*	5.00 -	8.00
6853 *She Reminds Me Of You*	5.00 -	8.00
6854 *One In A Blue Moon*	5.00 -	8.00
6936 *Straight From The Shoulder*	5.00 -	8.00
6953 *Give Me A Heart To Sing To*	5.00 -	8.00

(Note: Many of the foregoing titles were issued contemporaneously and/or reissued within several years of initial release on Banner, Brunswick, Conqueror, Melotone, Oriole, Perfect and Romeo.)

Brunswick 20105 (12 inch) *St. Louis Blues*	15.00 -	20.00
20109 (12-inch) *Lawd, You Made The Night Too Long*	20.00 -	30.00
Columbia 1773-D *My Kinda Love*	8.00 -	12.00
1851-D *I Kiss Your Hand, Madame*	8.00 -	12.00
2001-D *Can't We Be Friends?*	8.00 -	12.00
Decca 100 *I Love You Truly*	5.00 -	8.00
101 *Let Me Call You Sweetheart*	5.00 -	8.00
179 *The Very Thought Of You*	5.00 -	8.00
245 *Two Cigarettes In The Dark*	5.00 -	8.00
309 *With Every Breath I Take*	5.00 -	8.00
310 *June In January*	5.00 -	8.00
391 *It's Easy To Remember*	5.00 -	8.00
392 *Down By The River*	5.00 -	8.00
543 *I Wished On The Moon*	5.00 -	8.00
547 *From The Top Of Your Head*	5.00 -	8.00
548 *Takes Two To Make A Bargain*	5.00 -	8.00
616 *Red Sails In The Sunset*	5.00 -	8.00
617 *On Treasure Island*	5.00 -	8.00
621 *Adeste Fidelis*	5.00 -	8.00
631 *Sailor, Beware*	5.00 -	8.00
756 *Lovely Lady*	5.00 -	8.00
757 *The Touch Of Your Lips*	5.00 -	8.00
791 *Robins And Roses*	5.00 -	8.00
806 *I Got Plenty O'Nuttin'*	5.00 -	8.00
870 *Empty Saddles*	5.00 -	8.00
871 *I Can't Seem To Escape From You*	5.00 -	8.00
905 *The House Jack Built For Jill*	5.00 -	8.00
Decca, most other issues on Blue label Decca	2.00 -	3.00
Victor 22701 *Wrap Your Troubles In Dreams*	5.00 -	8.00

Note: recordings on which Bing makes mistakes and curses, such as "Blue Serenade" and "Wrap Your Troubles In Dreams" were widely, although illegally, distributed, and are not valuable rarities as some would assume.

BOB CROSBY (& HIS BOB CATS/ ORCHESTRA):

Decca 112 *It's My Night to Howl*	5.00 -	8.00
478 *The Dixieland Band*	5.00 -	8.00
502 *And Then Some*	5.00 -	8.00
508 *I'm In The Mood For Love*	5.00 -	8.00
544 *Tender Is The Night*	5.00 -	8.00
614 *On Treasure Island*	5.00 -	8.00
615 *I Found A Dream*	5.00 -	8.00
629 *A Little Bit Independent*	5.00 -	8.00
633 *Eeny Meeny Miney Mo*	5.00 -	8.00
727 *What's The Name Of That Song?*	5.00 -	8.00
728 *I Don't Want To Make History*	5.00 -	8.00

753 *Christopher Columbus*	5.00 -	8.00
759 *You're Toots To Me*	5.00 -	8.00
Decca 836, 841, 896, 903, 930, 1094, 1170, 1196, 1346, 1370, 1539, 1552, 1555, 1556, 1566, 1576, 1580, 1593	4.00 -	6.00

CROSSTOWN RAMBLERS:

Champion 15030 *River Bottom Glide*	40.00 -	60.00
15039 *Nellie, Where You Goin'?*	35.00 -	50.00

FRANK CRUM & HIS ORCHESTRA:

Edison 51474 *Lonely And Blue*	8.00 -	12.00

CUBAN DANCE PLAYERS:

Challenge 210 *I'll Fly To Hawaii*	40.00 -	60.00

BERNIE CUMMINS & HIS ORCHESTRA:

Brunswick 3722 *Where The Cot-Cot-Cotton Grows*	5.00 -	8.00
Brunswick 3916 *Sugar Babe, I'm Leavin'!*	5.00 -	8.00
Brunswick 3952 *Out-O'-Town Gal*	5.00 -	8.00
Brunswick 3980 *Old Man Sunshine*	5.00 -	8.00
Brunswick (most other issues)	4.00 -	7.00
Columbia 2827-D *You've Got Everything*	8.00 -	12.00
2828-D *I'm Dancin' On A Rainbow*	8.00 -	12.00
2830 *That Co-Ed Party*	8.00 -	12.00
2838-D *In A One-Room Flat*	8.00 -	12.00
2844-D *I Guess It Had To Be That Way*	8.00 -	12.00
2848-D *Our Big Love Scene*	8.00 -	12.00
2874-D *Alice From Dallas*	8.00 -	12.00
Gennett 3395 *Home Folks Blues*	15.00 -	20.00
5466 *St. Louis Blues*	15.00 -	20.00
5468 *Jiminy Gee*	10.00 -	15.00
5546 *Keep On Dancing*	10.00 -	15.00
5555 *That's Georgia*	10.00 -	15.00
5641 *Poplar Street Blues*	15.00 -	20.00
Victor 22088 *Little By Little*	7.00 -	10.00
22110 *Don't Hang Your Dreams On A Rainbow*	5.00 -	8.00
Victor 22295 *Cooking Breakfast for the One I Love*	5.00 -	8.00
Victor 22331 *Lucky Little Devil*	5.00 -	8.00
Victor 22355 *Minnie The Mermaid*	5.00 -	8.00
Victor 22408 *Tellin' It To The Daisies*	5.00 -	8.00
Victor 22409 *Livin' in the Sunlight—Lovin' in the Moonlight*	5.00 -	8.00
Victor 22525 *In My Heart It's You*	5.00 -	8.00
Victor 24053 *Deep Sea Low Down*	8.00 -	12.00

JOE CURRAN & HIS ORCHESTRA:

Parlophone PNY-34012 *Thank Your Father*	25.00 -	40.00
PNY-41231 *Louise*	25.00 -	40.00
PNY-41232 *That's A Plenty*	25.00 -	40.00
PNY-41254 *Hittin' The Ceilin'*	25.00 -	40.00
PNY-41282 *Just You—Just Me*	25.00 -	40.00
PNY-41301 *Love Ain't Nothin' But The Blues*	25.00 -	40.00
PNY-41310 *Sophomore Prom*	25.00 -	40.00
PNY-41313 *Turn On The Heat*	25.00 -	40.00

(FORD) DABNEY'S BAND/(SYNCOPATED) (NOVELTY) ORCHESTRA:

Aeolian-Vocalion 1204 *The Darktown Strutters' Ball*	15.00 -	20.00
1218 *That's It*	15.00 -	20.00
1243 *Sally Trombone*	10.00 -	15.00
12017 *Slidin' Sid*	15.00 -	20.00
12066 *Swinging Along*	10.00 -	15.00
12068 *Just Blue*	10.00 -	15.00
12097 *Indigo Blues*	15.00 -	20.00
12101 *Johnny's In Town*	10.00 -	15.00
12105 *Rainy Day Blues*	15.00 -	20.00
12119 *Lassus Trombone*	10.00 -	15.00
12126 *Missouri Blues*	15.00 -	20.00
12179 *Squealing Pig Blues*	15.00 -	20.00
12195 *Slow Drag Blues*	10.00 -	15.00
12211 *Florida Blues*	10.00 -	15.00
12217 *The Dancing Deacon*	10.00 -	15.00
12229 *I Ain't Gonna Give Nobody None Of This Jelly-Roll*	10.00 -	15.00

12245 *Blues My Naughty Sweetie Gives To Me* .	10.00 -	15.00
12246 *Camp Meeting Blues*	10.00 -	15.00
36202 *I'm Sorry I Made You Cry*	15.00 -	20.00
36205 *Mr. Sousa's Yankee Band*	15.00 -	20.00
Banner 1061 *Sweet Man O'Mine*	15.00 -	20.00
Paramount 20120 *Doo Dah Blues*	15.00 -	20.00
Paramount 20125 *Bugle Call Blues*	15.00 -	20.00
Puritan 11125 *Bugle Call Blues*	15.00 -	20.00
Triangle 11124 *Bugle Call Blues*	15.00 -	20.00

FRANK DAILEY'S MEADOWBROOKS/
ORCHESTRA/MEADOWBROOK
ORCHESTRA:

Bell 345 *Suite Sixteen*	5.00 -	10.00
349 *Save Your Sorrow*	5.00 -	10.00
485 *Blue Skies*	7.00 -	10.00
497 *My Regular Gal*	10.00 -	15.00
Bell (most other issues)	4.00 -	7.00
Bluebird (most issues)	3.00 -	5.00
Emerson 3117 *Blue Skies*	7.00 -	10.00
3127 *My Regular Gal*	10.00 -	15.00
Emerson (most other issues)	4.00 -	7.00
Okeh 40774 *There's Everything Nice About You* . .	5.00 -	8.00
Variety (most issues)	5.00 -	10.00
Vocalion (most issues)	5.00 -	10.00

FLORA DALE:

Domino 360 *Jail House Blues*	20.00 -	30.00

DALLAS JAMBOREE JUG BAND: (See also:
CARL DAVIS)

Vocalion 03092 *Dusting the Frets*	100.00 -	150.00

JACK DALTON & THE 7 BLUE BABIES:

Edison 52508 *I Love To Bumpity Bump On A*		
Bumpity	15.00 -	20.00
52516 *Where Did You Get That Name*	15.00 -	20.00
52528 *Outside*	15.00 -	20.00
52556 *If I Give Up The Saxophone*	15.00 -	20.00
52583 *She's A Good Girl*	15.00 -	20.00
52621 *I Don't Work For A Living*	15.00 -	20.00
Edison (thin), last three titles above	20.00 -	30.00

THE DANCING CHAMPIONS:

Champion 15183 *Don't Take That Black Bottom*		
Away	8.00 -	12.00
15184 *I Still Believe In You*	7.00 -	10.00
15185 *A Little Music In The Moonlight*	7.00 -	10.00

THE DANCING STEVEDORES:

Silvertone 3054 *Panama*	15.00 -	20.00
3056 *Stretch It, Boy*	15.00 -	20.00

PUTNEY DANDRIDGE & HIS ORCHESTRA:

Vocalion 2935 *You're A Heavenly Thing*	7.00 -	10.00
2982 *Chasing Shadows*	7.00 -	10.00
3006 *Isn't This A Lovely Day?*	7.00 -	10.00
3007 *I'm In The Mood For Love*	7.00 -	10.00
3024 *Nagasaki*	7.00 -	10.00
3082 *Double Trouble*	7.00 -	10.00
3083 *Eeny Meeny Miney Mo*	7.00 -	10.00
3122 *A Little Bit Independent*	7.00 -	10.00
3123 *You Took My Breath Away*	7.00 -	10.00
3189 *Dinner For One, Please James*	7.00 -	10.00
3190 *Honeysuckle Rose*	7.00 -	10.00
3252 *It's A Sin To Tell A Lie*	7.00 -	10.00
3269 *Ol' Man River*	7.00 -	10.00
3277 *Cross Patch*	7.00 -	10.00
3287 *Mary Had A Little Lamb*	7.00 -	10.00
3291 *Here Comes Your Pappy*	7.00 -	10.00
3304 *You Turned The Tables On Me*	7.00 -	10.00
3315 *It's The Gypsy In Me*	7.00 -	10.00
3351 *You Do The Darndest Things, Baby*	7.00 -	10.00
3352 *The Skeleton In The Closet*	7.00 -	10.00
3399 *I'm In A Dancing Mood*	7.00 -	10.00
3409 *Gee! But You're Swell*	7.00 -	10.00

JACK DANFORD AND HIS BEN FRANKLIN
HOTEL ORCHESTRA:

Phonograph Recording Co. of San Francisco

(un-numbered) *Alabama Stomp*	100.00 -	up

DOT DARE: (See also: ANNETTE HANSHAW,
GAY ELLIS)

Harmony 792-H *I Wanna Be Loved By You*	10.00 -	15.00
829-H *I Faw Down An' Go Boom!*	7.00 -	10.00

(Note: DOT DARE and GAY ELLIS are
pseudonyms for ANNETTE HANSHAW.
These titles, and others which may be found in
the other listings referred to, were issued on
Harmony, Diva, and Velvet Tone under one or
more of these names.)

DOC DAUGHERTY & HIS ORCHESTRA:

Victor 23040 *She's A Gorgeous Thing!*	8.00 -	12.00
Victor V-40111 *Ninety In The Shade*	25.00 -	40.00
V-40119 *Baby Girl*	15.00 -	25.00

DAVE'S HARLEM HIGHLIGHTS:

Timely Tunes 1576 *Rockin' Chair*	75.00 -	100.00
1577 *Loveless Love*	75.00 -	100.00
1587 *Somebody Stole My Gal*	75.00 -	100.00
1588 *St. Louis Blues*	75.00 -	100.00

CHARLES (COW COW) DAVENPORT:
CHARLIE DAVENPORT:

Broadway 5046 *Chimes Blues*	125.00 -	175.00
Gennett 6829 *Givin' It Away*	150.00 -	200.00
6838 *Chimes Blues*	150.00 -	200.00
6869 *Atlanta Rag*	150.00 -	200.00
Paramount 12439 *Jim Crow Blues*	75.00 -	125.00
12452 *Stealin' Blues*	75.00 -	125.00
Supertone 9517 *Atlanta Rag*	125.00 -	175.00
Vocalion 1198 *Cow Cow Blues*	50.00 -	80.00
1227 *Alabama Mistreater*	75.00 -	100.00
1282 *Back In The Alley*	75.00 -	100.00
1291 *Texas Shout*	75.00 -	100.00
1434 *Mama Don't Allow No Easy Riders*	75.00 -	100.00

(COW COW) DAVENPORT AND (IVA/IVY)
SMITH:

Gennett 7231 *Alabammy Mistreated*	150.00 -	200.00
Superior 2763 *Alabammy Mistreated*	150.00 -	200.00
Vocalion 1253 *Alabama Strut*	75.00 -	100.00

COW COW DAVENPORT AND SAM THEARD:

Vocalion 1408 *That'll Get It*	75.00 -	100.00

JED DAVENPORT:

Vocalion 1440 *How Long How Long Blues*	50.00 -	80.00

JED DAVENPORT & HIS BEALE STREET
JUG BAND:

Vocalion 1478 *The Dirty Dozen*	100.00 -	150.00
1504 *Jug Blues*	100.00 -	150.00
1513 *Save Me Some*	100.00 -	150.00

JACK DAVIES' KENTUCKIANS:

Champion 16607 *Sick O'Licks*	100.00 -	200.00

CARL DAVIS WITH THE DALLAS
JAMBOREE JUG BAND:

Vocalion 03132 *Flying Crow Blues*	100.00 -	150.00

CHARLIE DAVIS AND HIS ORCHESTRA:

Vocalion 15701 *The Drag*	50.00 -	75.00
15702 *Just Like A Melody Out Of The Sky*	20.00 -	30.00

GENEVIEVE DAVIS:

Victor 20648 *I've Got Something*	75.00 -	100.00

JASPER DAVIS & HIS ORCHESTRA:

Harmony 944-H *Georgia Gigolo*	40.00 -	60.00

JOHNNIE DAVIS & HIS ORCHESTRA:
Decca 256, 257, 271, 272 .... 7.00 - 10.00
JULIA DAVIS:
Paramount 12248 *Black Hand Blues* .... 75.00 - 100.00
MADLYN DAVIS (& HER HOT SHOTS):
Paramount 12498 *Climbing Mountain Blues* ..... 75.00 - 100.00
    12528 *Hurry Sundown Blues* .... 75.00 - 100.00
    12615 *Winter Blues* .... 75.00 - 100.00
    12755 *Death Bell Blues* .... 75.00 - 100.00
PAUL DAVIS & HIS ORCHESTRA:
Champion 16524 *Underneath The Harlem Moon* . 100.00 - 150.00
RED HOT SHAKIN' DAVIS:
Paramount 12703 *It's Red Hot* .... 75.00 - 100.00
WILMER DAVIS:
Vocalion 1034 *Gut Struggle* .... 75.00 - 100.00
THE DEAN & HIS KIDS:
Vocalion 3342 *Spreadin' Knowledge Around* .... 8.00 - 12.00
EDDIE DEAS AND HIS BOSTON BROWNIES:
Victor 22841 *Jes' Shufflin'* .... 20.00 - 30.00
    22844 *Little Mary Brown* .... 20.00 - 30.00
DEAUVILLE DOZEN:
Pathe-Actuelle 36338 *Pep* .... 10.00 - 15.00
Perfect 14519 *Pep* .... 10.00 - 15.00
DEAUVILLE SYNCOPATORS:
Parlophone PNY-34144 *Satan's Holiday* .... 24.00 - 40.00
PNY-34149 *I Got Rhythm* .... 20.00 - 30.00
PNY-34155 *I'm Tickled Pink With A Blue-Eyed*
    Baby .... 20.00 - 30.00
PNY-34157 *Cheerful Little Earful* .... 20.00 - 30.00
PNY-34172 *Would You Like To Take A Walk?* .... 20.00 - 30.00
PNY-34186 *The Last One Left On The Corner* ... 20.00 - 30.00
PNY-34199 *Just A Crazy Song* .... 20.00 - 30.00
JOHNNY DE DROIT & HIS NEW ORLEANS
  JAZZ ORCHESTRA:
Okeh 40090 *The Swing* .... 25.00 - 40.00
    40150 *Number Two Blues* .... 25.00 - 40.00
    40192 *Brown Eyes* .... 20.00 - 30.00
    40240 *Panama* .... 35.00 - 50.00
    40285 *Lucky Kentucky* .... 35.00 - 50.00
DEEP RIVER ORCHESTRA:
Pathe-Actuelle 36574, 36575, 36635, 36679,
    36690 .... 5.00 - 8.00
Perfect 14755, 14756, 14816, 14871 .... 5.00 - 8.00
VOLTAIRE DE FAUT:
Autograph 623 *Wolverine Blues* .... 150.00 - 300.00
MAUD DE FORREST:
Black Swan 14143 *Roamin' Blues* .... 20.00 - 30.00
Paramount 12147 *Roamin' Blues* .... 20.00 - 30.00
    12148 *Cruel Papa Blues* .... 20.00 - 30.00
BOB DEIKMAN & HIS ORCHESTRA:
Gennett 3087 *Ah-Ha!* .... 10.00 - 15.00
    3161 *The Camel Walk* .... 20.00 - 30.00
    3196 *Spanish Shawl* .... 20.00 - 30.00
    3236 *Shanghai Honeymoon* .... 20.00 - 30.00
    6235 *Dew-Dew-Dewy Day* .... 10.00 - 15.00
    6248 *Here I Am—Broken Hearted* .... 10.00 - 15.00
    6325 *Cobble-Stones* .... 10.00 - 15.00
    6339 *Roll Up The Carpets* .... 30.00 - 50.00
    6356 *When The Moon Comes Peeping Through* 50.00 - 75.00
EDDIE DE LANGE AND HIS ORCHESTRA:
Bluebird, most issues .... 3.00 - 5.00
DEL DELBRIDGE AND HIS CAPITOL
  THEATRE ORCHESTRA:
Brunswick 4393 *Do Something* .... 5.00 - 8.00
VAUGHN DE LEATH: (& HER BUDDIES):
Edison (most issues) .... 5.00 - 10.00
Okeh 40844 *Dew-Dew-Dewy Day* .... 7.00 - 10.00
HAL DENMAN AND HIS CAROLINA
  COTTON PICKERS:
Champion 16221 *She Loves Me Just The Same* .. 10.00 - 20.00
    16266 *I Can't Get Enough Of You* .... 10.00 - 20.00
    16274 *When I Take My Sugar To Tea* .... 10.00 - 20.00

    Champion 16355 *How's Your Uncle?* .... 30.00 - 50.00
    16397 *Was That The Human Thing To Do* .... 30.00 - 50.00
    16533 *Bugle Call Rag* .... 30.00 - 50.00
    16655 *Sweet And Lovely* .... 30.00 - 50.00
JACK DENNY & HIS ORCHESTRA:
Brunswick (most issues) .... 4.00 - 7.00
Cameo 646 *Easy Goin' Mama* .... 5.00 - 8.00
DEPPE'S SERENADERS:
Gennett 20012 *Falling* .... 50.00 - 100.00
LOUIS DEPPE:
Gennett 20021 *Southland* .... 20.00 - 30.00
    20022 *Isabel* .... 20.00 - 30.00
THE DETROITERS:
Cameo 8137 *Nothin' To Do (But Worry 'Bout You)* 4.00 - 7.00
Cameo 8149 *Maybe Yes—Maybe No* .... 4.00 - 7.00
Cameo 8195 *Spanish Mamma* .... 7.00 - 10.00
Cameo 8371 *I'm Choosin' Black Eyed Susan* .... 4.00 - 7.00
Cameo 9204 *Am I Blue?* .... 5.00 - 8.00
Cameo 9309 *Any Old Time (Is Loving Time For*
    Me) .... 5.00 - 8.00
Romeo 500 *Dream Dream Dream* .... 3.00 - 5.00
Romeo 572 *Maybe Yes—Maybe No* .... 3.00 - 5.00
Romeo 625 *Spanish Mamma* .... 7.00 - 10.00
Romeo 706 *Sally of My Dreams* .... 4.00 - 7.00
Romeo 995 *It's a Funny Feeling* .... 3.00 - 5.00
Romeo 1006 *Am I Blue?* .... 5.00 - 8.00
Romeo 1100 *Any Old Time (Is Loving Time For*
    Me) .... 5.00 - 8.00
DEVINE'S WISCONSIN ROOF ORCHESTRA:
Broadway 1123 *Black Maria* .... 15.00 - 25.00
    1140 *Tiger Rag* .... 10.00 - 20.00
    1141 *Riverboat Blues* .... 15.00 - 25.00
Paramount 20582 *Tiger Rag* .... 10.00 - 20.00
    20583 *Singapore Sorrows* .... 15.00 - 25.00
    20651 *Farewell Blues* .... 15.00 - 25.00
FRED DEXTER'S PENNSYLVANIANS:
Gennett 7256 *What's The Use?* .... 30.00 - 50.00
HARRY DIAL'S BLUSICIANS:
Queen 4164 *I Like What I Like Like I Like It* .... 20.00 - 30.00
Vocalion 1515 *Don't Give It Away* .... 150.00 - 200.00
    1567 *I Like What I Like Like I Like It* .... 100.00 - 150.00
    1594 *Poison* .... 150.00 - 200.00
CARROLL DICKERSON'S SAVOY
  ORCHESTRA:
Brunswick 3990 *Missouri Squabble* .... 20.00 - 30.00
CHARLES DICKSON:
Jewel 5043 *Vo-Do-Do-De-O Blues* .... 7.00 - 10.00
Oriole 940 *Vo-Do-Do-De-O Blues* .... 7.00 - 10.00
DUKE DIGGS & HIS ORCHESTRA:
Supertone 9487 *Nightmare* .... 150.00 - 200.00
    9653 *After You've Gone* .... 150.00 - 200.00
THE DIXIE BOYS:
Autograph (unnumbered) *Popular Street Blues* .. 100.00 - 150.00
Champion 15227 *I've Found A New Baby* .... 100.00 - 150.00
DIXIE DAISIES:
Titles, issued contemporaneously on Cameo,
    Lincoln, Romeo: *Baby; Bugle Call Rag; Eyes*
    Of Blues, You're My Waterloo; I'm Just
    Wondering Who; Japanese Dream .... 10.00 - 15.00
Banner 0839 *St. Louis Blues* .... 8.00 - 12.00
Cameo 291 *Lovin' Sam* .... 3.00 - 5.00
Cameo 333 *Farewell Blues* .... 5.00 - 8.00
Cameo 348 *Papa Blues* .... 5.00 - 8.00
Cameo 357 *Long Lost Mama* .... 5.00 - 8.00
Cameo 392 *Salt Your Sugar* .... 5.00 - 8.00
Cameo 414 *I've Got a Song For Sale* .... 5.00 - 8.00
Cameo 418 *Oh! Sister Ain't That Hot* .... 5.00 - 8.00
Cameo 428 *The House of David Blues* .... 5.00 - 8.00
Cameo 476 *Dancin' Dan* .... 5.00 - 8.00
Cameo 781 *Headin' For Baltimore* .... 5.00 - 8.00
Cameo 834 *Paddlin' Madelin' Home* .... 5.00 - 8.00
Cameo 835 *Clap Hands! Here Comes Charlie* .. 5.00 - 8.00

Cameo 986 *Where'd You Get Those Eyes?*	5.00 -	8.00
Cameo 1044 *Yiddisha Charleston*	4.00 -	7.00
Cameo 1168 *Stompin' Fool*	10.00 -	15.00
Cameo 8105 *Changes*	5.00 -	8.00
Cameo 8111 *Stay Out of The South*	5.00 -	8.00
Cameo 8229 *Brotherly Love*	7.00 -	10.00
Cameo 8245 *Got Everything (Don't Want*		
Anything But You)	5.00 -	8.00
Cameo 8316 *Imagination*	5.00 -	8.00
Cameo 8317 *There's a Rainbow 'Round My*		
Shoulder	5.00 -	8.00
Cameo 8325 *Somebody Sweet Is Sweet On Me* . .	5.00 -	8.00
Cameo 8339 *Doin' The Racoon*	5.00 -	8.00
Cameo 8353 *She's Wonderful*	5.00 -	8.00
Cameo 8373 *There's a Rainbow 'Round My*		
Shoulder	5.00 -	8.00
Cameo 9004 *Digga Digga Do*	10.00 -	15.00
Cameo 9035 *Bugle Call Rag*	10.00 -	15.00
Cameo 9127 *Somebody Misses Somebody's*		
Kisses	5.00 -	8.00
Cameo 9142 *Eyes of Blue, You're My Waterloo* . .	10.00 -	15.00
Cameo 9204 *It Took A Lot Of Blue*	5.00 -	8.00
Lincoln 3033 *'Cause I'm In Love*	10.00 -	15.00
Romeo 264 *High Fever*	5.00 -	8.00
Romeo 491 *Sorry*	5.00 -	8.00
Romeo 659 *Peek-A-Boo Eyes*	5.00 -	8.00
Romeo 668 *Got Everything (Don't Want Anything*		
But You)	5.00 -	8.00
Romeo 700 *Ya Gonna Be Home Tonight?*	5.00 -	8.00
Romeo 776 *She's Wonderful*	5.00 -	8.00
Romeo 887 *There's Something New 'Bout The*		
Old Moon Tonight	7.00 -	10.00
Romeo 1006 *It Took A Lot Of Blue*	5.00 -	8.00

DIXIE DANCE DEMONS:

Cameo 8162 *Birmingham Break Down*	8.00 -	12.00

THE DIXIE DEVILS:

Van Dyke 71804 *In Harlem's Araby*	15.00 -	20.00
71805 *Miss Golden Brown*	15.00 -	20.00

DIXIE FOUR:

Paramount 12661 *St. Louis Man*	150.00 -	200.00
12674 *Five O'Clock Stamp*	150.00 -	200.00

DIXIE JAZZ BAND:

Challenge 628 *The Crawl*	8.00 -	12.00
929 *Dusky Stevedore*	8.00 -	12.00
952 *Missouri Squabble*	8.00 -	12.00
958 *Icky Blues*	8.00 -	12.00
995 *Long Lost Daddy*	7.00 -	10.00
999 *Makin' Friends*	8.00 -	12.00
Conqueror 7189 *Missouri Squabble*	8.00 -	12.00
Jewel 5002 *The Crawl*	8.00 -	12.00
5048 *Black Bottom*	7.00 -	10.00
5067 *Struttin' Jerry*	8.00 -	12.00
5145 *There's A Rickety Rackety Shack*	8.00 -	12.00
5171 *Sorry*	8.00 -	12.00
5199 *Steppin' It Off*	7.00 -	10.00
5263 *Moten Stomp*	8.00 -	12.00
5291 *Know Nothin' Blues*	8.00 -	12.00
5335 *Deep Hollow*	8.00 -	12.00
5392 *What-Cha-Call-Em-Blues*	8.00 -	12.00
5405 *Baby's Coming Back*	10.00 -	15.00
5412 *West End Blues*	10.00 -	15.00
5446 *Dixie Drag*	10.00 -	15.00
5488 *Cat's Kittens*	5.00 -	8.00
5521 *Some Of These Days*	7.00 -	10.00
5547 *Icky Blues*	8.00 -	12.00
5565 *Long Lost Daddy*	7.00 -	10.00
5569 *Makin' Friends*	8.00 -	12.00
5575 *Sweet Liza*	8.00 -	12.00
5576 *Pa's Old Hat*	7.00 -	10.00
5677 *My Sweetie Turned Sour On Me*	5.00 -	8.00
5748 *Twelfth Street Rag*	8.00 -	12.00
5685 *It's So Good*	8;00 -	12.00

5729 *The Way He Loves Is Just Too Bad*	10.00 -	15.00
5730 *Broadway Rhythm*	15.00 -	25.00
Oriole 269 *My Lovie Lee*	10.00 -	15.00
271 *How Could You Leave Me Now?*	10.00 -	15.00
291 *Copenhagen*	10.00 -	15.00
315 *Hot Sax*	15.00 -	20.00
347 *West Texas Blues*	15.00 -	20.00
Oriole 364 *When My Sugar Walks Down The*		
Street	5.00 -	8.00
Oriole 413 *Some Of These Days*	10.00 -	15.00
424 *Flag That Train*	5.00 -	8.00
445 *Right Or Wrong*	10.00 -	15.00
464 *Red Hot Henry Brown*	10.00 -	15.00
475 *Angry*	7.00 -	10.00
517 *Hot Aire*	7.00 -	10.00
521 *I'm Sitting On Top Of The World*	5.00 -	8.00
530 *Has Been Blues*	7.00 -	10.00
531 *My Charleston Dancing Man*	5.00 -	8.00
565 *Wait Till You See My Baby Do The*		
Charleston	15.00 -	20.00
590 *Say Mister! Have You Met Rosie's Sister?* .	5.00 -	8.00
598 *For No Reason*	5.00 -	8.00
601 *I've Got Those Charleston Blues*	5.00 -	8.00
605 *On The Puppy's Tail*	7.00 -	10.00
619 *I'm Gonna Tear Your Playhouse Down* . . .	7.00 -	10.00
625 *Junk Bucket Blues*	7.00 -	10.00
674 *Deep Henderson*	15.00 -	20.00
682 *Jackass Blues*	7.00 -	10.00
685 *Hard-To-Get Gertie*	7.00 -	10.00
688 *Black Bottom*	7.00 -	10.00
691 *Nervous Charlie Stomp*	7.00 -	10.00
705 *I Wonder What's Become of Joe?*	7.00 -	10.00
717 *Old Folks' Shuffle*	30.00 -	40.00
723 *St. Louis Blues*	7.00 -	10.00
748 *Brown Sugar*	7.00 -	10.00
762 *Stampede*	8.00 -	12.00
776 *Any Day*	8.00 -	12.00
778 *Serenadin' Sarah*	7.00 -	10.00
784 *That Sweet Patootie Of Mine*	5.00 -	8.00
799 *St. Louis Shuffle*	10.00 -	15.00
804 *Stockholm Stomp*	10.00 -	15.00
819 *Indiana Shuffle*	8.00 -	12.00
828 *Coffee Pot Blues*	8.00 -	12.00
829 *The Crawl*	8.00 -	12.00
846 *Ain't She Sweet?*	8.00 -	12.00
880 *I'm In Love Again*	8.00 -	12.00
883 *Rosy Cheeks*	8.00 -	12.00
896 *South Wind*	5.00 -	8.00
909 *Slow River*	5.00 -	8.00
926 *Sugar*	8.00 -	12.00
927 *Some Of These Days*	8.00 -	12.00
952 *Memphis Blues*	8.00 -	12.00
956 *Lighthouse Blues*	8.00 -	12.00
960 *Rarin' To Go*	8.00 -	12.00
963 *My Melancholy Baby*	8.00 -	12.00
977 *Struttin' Jerry*	8.00 -	12.00
984 *Tiger Rag*	8.00 -	12.00
1022 *Jelly Roll Blues*	8.00 -	12.00
1033 *Hello Miss Liberty!*	5.00 -	8.00
1046 *Washington And Lee Swing*	5.00 -	8.00
1071 *There's A Rickety Rackety Shack*	8.00 -	12.00
1100 *Sorry*	8.00 -	12.00
1122 *Chloe*	5.00 -	8.00
1123 *Steppin' It Off*	7.00 -	10.00
1127 *Once Over Lightly*	5.00 -	8.00
1131 *Candied Sweets*	5.00 -	8.00
1163 *You're Gonna Regret*	4.00 -	7.00
Oriole 1171 *Where Will I Be?*	8.00 -	12.00
1172 *Moten Stomp*	8.00 -	12.00
1178 *Lila*	7.00 -	10.00
1181 *She's A Great, Great Girl*	7.00 -	10.00
1226 *Collegiana*	5.00 -	8.00

1253 *Persian Rug*	5.00	-	8.00
1256 *Try To Smile*	5.00	-	8.00
1275 *Somebody's Making A Fuss Over*			
Somebody	8.00	-	12.00
1278 *Puttin' On The Dog*	10.00	-	15.00
1282 *If I Can Ba-Ba-Baby You*	5.00	-	8.00
1287 *A Jazz Holiday*	8.00	-	12.00
1308 *Bring Back My Lovin' Man*	7.00	-	10.00
1313 *Deep Hollow*	8.00	-	12.00
1339 *When Sweet Susie Goes Steppin' By*	8.00	-	12.00
1343 *What-Cha-Call-'Em Blues*	8.00	-	12.00
1348 *Dusky Stevedore*	8.00	-	12.00
1360 *Baby's Coming Back*	10.00	-	15.00
1363 *High Hattin' Hattie*	10.00	-	15.00
1368 *Easy*	10.00	-	15.00
1371 *Cool Papa*	10.00	-	15.00
1387 *Sunday Afternoon*	10.00	-	15.00
1396 *Dixie Drag*	10.00	-	15.00
1403 *Fraternity Prom*	7.00	-	10.00
1416 *Missouri Squabble*	8.00	-	12.00
1417 *Talkin' To Myself*	5.00	-	8.00
1423 *Happy In The Rain*	5.00	-	8.00
1426 *I Love My Best Girl Best*	5.00	-	8.00
1447 *Wide Open Gate*	5.00	-	8.00
1450 *Mystic Bengal Bay*	5.00	-	8.00
1454 *Cat's Kittens*	5.00	-	8.00
1457 *You Please Me*	5.00	-	8.00
1474 *Pepper Pot*	7.00	-	10.00
1475 *Susianna*	7.00	-	10.00
1476 *She's My Sweet Patootie*	5.00	-	8.00
1481 *Some Of These days*	7.00	-	10.00
1504 *Geraldine*	5.00	-	8.00
1505 *What Do You Think Of My Baby?*	5.00	-	8.00
1507 *Let's Get Together*	5.00	-	8.00
1515 *Icky Blues*	8.00	-	12.00
1536 *Pa's Old Hat*	7.00	-	10.00
1537 *Makin' Friends*	8.00	-	12.00
1540 *Sweet Liza*	8.00	-	12.00
1576 *Where Has Mammy Gone?*	5.00	-	8.00
1582 *I've Got The San Francisco Blues*	7.00	-	10.00
1612 *Some Of These Days*	7.00	-	10.00
1624 *After You've Gone*	8.00	-	12.00
1638 *Whoopeein' Up*	8.00	-	12.00
1663 *You're Gonna Regret*	5.00	-	8.00
1668 *It's So Good*	8.00	-	12.00
1690 *St. Louis Blues*	7.00	-	10.00
1726 *The Way He Loves Is Just Too Bad*	10.00	-	15.00
1728 *Broadway Rhythm*	15.00	-	25.00
1730 *Saturday Night Function*	15.00	-	20.00
1768 *Sweet Baby, Tell Me You're My*			
Pretty Baby	5.00	-	8.00
Regal 8874 *Flaming Youth*	15.00	-	20.00

DIXIE JAZZERS WASHBOARD BAND:

Pathe-Actuelle 7536 *Memphis Shake*	50.00	-	75.00
7539 *Kansas City Shuffle*	50.00	-	75.00
Perfect 136 *Memphis Shake*	50.00	-	75.00
139 *Kansas City Shuffle*	50.00	-	75.00

DIXIE JAZZ HOUNDS:

Domino 306 *Hula Lou*	10.00	-	15.00
308 *Lots O'Mamma*	10.00	-	15.00
328 *31st Street Blues*	15.00	-	20.00
329 *Waitin' Around*	15.00	-	20.00

DIXIELAND JUG BLOWERS:

Victor 20403 *Florida Blues*	35.00	-	50.00
20415 *Memphis Shake*	15.00	-	20.00
20420 *Don't Give All The Lard Away*	35.00	-	50.00
20480 *Carpet Alley*	40.00	-	60.00
20649 *Hen Party Blues*	40.00	-	60.00
20770 *When I Stopped Runnin' I Was At Home*	50.00	-	75.00
20854 *I Never Did Want You*	50.00	-	75.00
20954 *Southern Shout*	50.00	-	75.00
21126 *Garden Of Joy Blues*	75.00	-	100.00

21472 *Banjoreno*	75.00	-	100.00

DIXIELAND THUMPERS:

Paramount 12525 *Weary Way Blues*	200.00	-	300.00
12595 *Oriental Man*	200.00	-	300.00

DIXIE MUSIC MAKERS:

Romeo 307 *Messin' Around*	7.00	-	10.00

DIXIE RHYTHM KINGS:

Brunswick 7115 *Congo Love Song*	80.00	-	120.00
7127 *Easy Rider*	80.00	-	120.00

DIXIE SERENADERS:

Champion 16341 *When It's Sleepy-Time Down*			
South	150.00	-	200.00
16365 *St. Louis Blues*	150.00	-	200.00
40003 *St. Louis Blues*	30.00	-	50.00

THE DIXIE STOMPERS:

Harmony 70-H *Spanish Shawl*	10.00	-	15.00
Harmony 88-H *Get It Fixed*	10.00	-	15.00
Harmony 92-H *Chinese Blues*	10.00	-	15.00
Harmony 121-H *I Found a New Baby*	10.00	-	15.00
Harmony 153-H *Nervous Charlie Stomp*	10.00	-	15.00
Harmony 166-H *Jackass Blues*	10.00	-	15.00
Harmony 179-H *Hi-Diddle-Diddle*	8.00	-	12.00
Harmony 197-H *Static Strut*	10.00	-	15.00
Harmony 209-H *Dynamite*	10.00	-	15.00
Harmony 283-H *Alabama Stomp*	8.00	-	12.00
Harmony 299-H *Off To Buffalo*	10.00	-	15.00
Harmony 353-H *Ain't She Sweet?*	7.00	-	10.00
Harmony 407-H *The Wang Wang Blues*	8.00	-	12.00
Harmony 451-H *The St. Louis Blues*	8.00	-	12.00
Harmony 467-H *St. Louis Shuffle*	8.00	-	12.00
Harmony 526-H *Black Maria*	8.00	-	12.00
Harmony 545-H *Goose Pimples*	10.00	-	15.00
Harmony 636-H *Feelin' Good*	10.00	-	15.00
Harmony 974-H *I'm Feeling Devilish*	15.00	-	20.00
(Note: Above titles, on Diva and Velvet Tone,			
are similarly valued.)			

DIXIE WASHBOARD BAND:

Banner 1696 *Shake That Thing*	20.00	-	30.00
1781 *I've Found A New Baby*	15.00	-	20.00
Columbia 14128-D *Livin' High*	30.00	-	40.00
14141-D *My Own Blues*	30.00	-	40.00
14172-D *King Of The Zulus*	35.00	-	50.00
14188-D *Gimmie Blues*	35.00	-	50.00
14239-D *Cushion Foot Stomp*	35.00	-	50.00
Regal 8093 *Boodle Am*	15.00	-	20.00

DIXON'S CHICAGO SERENADERS:

Black Patti 8010 *Monte Carlo Joys*	150.00	-	300.00

DIXON'S JAZZ DUO/MANIACS:

Paramount 12385 *Headache Blues*	50.00	-	75.00
12405 *Tiger Rag*	50.00	-	75.00
12446 *Crazy Quilt*	50.00	-	75.00

VANCE DIXON & HIS PENCILS:

Columbia 14608-D *Hot Peanuts*	30.00	-	50.00
14673-D *Who Stole The Lock?*	30.00	-	50.00
Okeh 8891 *Who Stole The Lock?*	30.00	-	50.00

DIXON AND CHANNEY:

Paramount 12471 *Sweet Patunia*	80.00	-	120.00

JOHNNY DODDS: JOHNNY DODDS' BLACK BOTTOM STOMPERS/ORCHESTRA/TRIO/WASHBOARD BAND; JOHNNY DODDS & HIS CHICAGO BOYS:

Brunswick 3567 *Wild Man Blues*	15.00	-	20.00
3568 *After You've Gone*	15.00	-	25.00
3574 *Clarinet Wobble*	15.00	-	25.00
3565 *The New St. Louis Blues*	15.00	-	25.00
3997 *Joe Turner Blues*	15.00	-	25.00
7015 *The New St. Louis Blues*	30.00	-	50.00
7016 *San*	30.00	-	50.00
Decca 1676, 2111, 7413	6.00	-	10.00
Victor 21552 *Bull Fiddle Blues*	20.00	-	30.00
21554 *Blue Clarinet Stomp*	20.00	-	30.00
23396 *Goober Dance*	150.00	-	200.00

V-38004 *Bucktown Stomp*	75.00 -	100.00
V-38038 *Pencil Papa*	60.00 -	90.00
V-38541 *My Little Isabel*	60.00 -	90.00
Vocalion 1128 *Melancholy*	75.00 -	100.00
1148 *After You've Gone*	50.00 -	80.00
15632 *Weary Blues*	100.00 -	150.00

DODDS AND PARHAM:

Paramount 12471 *Oh Daddy*	100.00 -	150.00
12483 *19th Street Blues*	100.00 -	150.00

CLYDE DOERR AND HIS ORCHESTRA:

Edison 51988 *Ain't She Sweet?*	7.00 -	10.00
52065 *Dew-Dew-Dewy Day*	5.00 -	8.00

PAT DOLLOHAN AND HIS ORCHESTRA:

Gennett 6711 *My Supressed Desire*	20.00 -	30.00
6784 *True Blue*	25.00 -	40.00

AL DONOHUE AND HIS ORCHESTRA:

Decca 559, 604, 608, 626, 630, 665, 673, 981, 989	3.00 -	6.00
Okeh, most issues	4.00 -	7.00
Vocalion, most issues	4.00 -	8.00

CHARLES DORNBERGER & HIS ORCHESTRA:

Victor 19138 *Oh, Sister! Ain't That Hot*	5.00 -	8.00
19346 *Nobody's Sweetheart*	5.00 -	8.00
19580 *I Can't Stop Babying You*	5.00 -	8.00
19633 *Oh! That Sweet In Suite 16*	10.00 -	15.00
20647 *Tiger Rag*	5.00 -	8.00
22031 *Maybe! Who Knows?*	5.00 -	8.00
22215 *Campus Capers*	7.00 -	10.00
24198 *Jingle Bells*	7.00 -	10.00
24199 *Old MacDonald Had A Farm*	7.00 -	10.00
Victor (most other issues)	4.00 -	8.00

D'ORSAY DANCE ORCHESTRA:

Clarion 5394-C *Little Mary Brown*	8.00 -	12.00
Clarion 5440-C, 5450-C, 5466-C	5.00 -	10.00
Harmony 1380-H, *Little Mary Brown*	8.00 -	12.00
Harmony 1409-H, 1419-H	5.00 -	10.00
Velvet Tone 2458-V, *Little Mary Brown*	8.00 -	12.00
Velvet Tone 2510-V, 2526-V	5.00 -	10.00

THE DORSEY BROTHERS' ORCHESTRA: THE DORSEY BROTHERS AND THEIR ORCHESTRA:

Banner 0566 *Congratulations*	7.00 -	10.00
Banner 0571 *Have a Little Faith in Me*	7.00 -	10.00
Banner 0589 *Beside an Open Fireplace*	7.00 -	10.00
Brunswick 6409, 6537, 6624, 6722, 6938	8.00 -	12.00
Columbia 2581-D *Ooh! That Kiss*	10.00 -	15.00
2589-D *Why Did It Have To Be Me?*	10.00 -	15.00
Decca 115, 116, 117, 118, 195, 196, 206, 207, 208, 258, 259, 260, 283, 291, 296, 297, 311, 314, 318, 319, 320, 321, 335, 340, 348, 357, 358, 367, 368, 370, 371, 469, 476, 482, 515, 516, 519, 520, 559, 560, 561, 1503 (12-inch)	3.00 -	7.00
Okeh 40995 *Mary Ann*	15.00 -	20.00
41007 *The Yale Blues*	15.00 -	20.00
41032 *My Melancholy Baby*	15.00 -	20.00
41050 *Dixie Dawn*	15.00 -	20.00
41065 *Evening Star*	10.00 -	15.00
41124 *Out Of The Dawn*	10.00 -	15.00
41151 *Cross Roads*	10.00 -	15.00
41158 *She's Funny That Way*	15.00 -	20.00
41181 *The Spell Of The Blues*	30.00 -	50.00
41188 *My Kinda Love*	30.00 -	50.00
41210 *Mean To Me*	15.00 -	20.00
41220 *I'll Never Ask For More*	10.00 -	15.00
41272 *Singin' In The Rain*	15.00 -	20.00
41279 *Maybe—Who Knows?*	15.00 -	20.00
Oriole 1827 *Have a Little Faith in Me*	7.00 -	10.00
Oriole 1828 *Congratulations*	7.00 -	10.00

JIM/JIMMY DORSEY (AND HIS ORCHESTRA):

Brunswick 6352 *Oodles of Noodles*	7.00 -	10.00
Decca 570, 571, 602, 607, 655	4.00 -	7.00
Decca 762, 764, 768, 776, 782, 808, 873, 901	4.00 -	7.00
Decca 939 *Rap Tap On Wood*	5.00 -	8.00
940 *Swingin' The Jinx Away*	5.00 -	8.00
Decca 941, 950, 951, 1040, 1086, 1187, 1200, 1203, 1204, 1256, 1301, 1377, 1378, 1508, 1651, 1652, 1660, 1671, 1723, 1724, 1745, 1746, 1784, 1799, 1809, 1834, 1860, 1921, 1939	3.00 -	6.00
Decca most other issues	3.00 -	5.00
MGM, most issues	2.00 -	3.00

TOM DORSEY (& HIS NOVELTY ORCHESTRA); TOMMY DORSEY & HIS CLAMBAKE SEVEN/ORCHESTRA:

Okeh 41178 *It's Right Here For You*	15.00 -	20.00
41422 *You Can't Cheat A Cheater*	20.00 -	30.00
Victor 25144, 25145, 25158, 25159, 25172, 25173, 25183, 25191, 25201, 25206, 25216, 25217, 25214, 25220, 25246, 25256, 25284, 25291, 25292, 25335, 25341, 35349, 25352, 25476, 25482	4.00 -	8.00
Victor 25314, 25320 25363, 25446, 25447, 25467, 25484, 25496, 25508, 25509, 25513, 25516, 25519, 25523, 25532, 25534, 25539, 25544, 25549, 25553, 25556, 25557, 25568, 25570, 25573, 25577, 25581, 25591, 25596, 25600, 25603, 25605, 25607, 25610, 25620, 25623, 25625, 25630, 25635, 25647, 25648, 25649, 25652, 25657, 25663, 25673, 25676, 25686, 25692, 25693, 25694, 25695	3.00 -	6.00
(Note: Foregoing issues, if first pressings, have the "scroll" label.)		
Victor 25703, 25741, 25750, 25763, 25768, 25774, 25780, 25795, 25799, 25803, 25813, 25815, 25821, 25824, 25828, 25832, 25848, 25856, 25862, 25866, 25899, 26005, 26016, 26030	3.00 -	6.00
Victor, most other issues	2.00 -	4.00

MIKE DOTY AND HIS ORCHESTRA:

Bluebird 5251 *Puddin' Head Jones*	8.00 -	12.00
5252 *Lenox Avenue*	8.00 -	12.00
5253 *My Galveston Gal*	8.00 -	12.00
5277 *You're My Thrill*	8.00 -	12.00
(Note: The above titles, on Electradisk, bring somewhat more; on Sunrise, substantially more.)		

DOWN HOME SERENADERS:

Champion 15399 *Cootie Crawl*	150.00 -	200.00

GEORGE DREW & HIS ORCHESTRA:

Superior 2829 *Hard Luck*	50.00 -	100.00

LEO DREYER AND HIS ORCHESTRA:

Crown 3404 *Fit As A Fiddle*	10.00 -	15.00
Edison 52466 *Pompanola*	10.00 -	15.00

EDDIE DROESCH AND HIS ORCHESTRA:

Clarion 5407-C *Last Dollar*	10.00 -	15.00
Harmony 1388-H *Last Dollar*	10.00 -	15.00
Velvet Tone 2467-V *Last Dollar*	10.00 -	15.00

GEORGE DRUCK'S SWEETS BALLROOM ORCHESTRA:

Flexo (unnumbered) *Tiger Rag*	75.00 -	100.00

DUBIN'S DANDIES:

Banner 0505 *Gettin' Along*	7.00 -	10.00

Banner 0510 *What Do You Care?* . . . .   5.00 -   8.00
Banner 0513 *I Wouldn't Care (If You Cared*
For Me . . . .   5.00 -   8.00
Banner 0515 *Will You Think of Me As I Think*
of You? . . . .   5.00 -   8.00
Banner 0533 *Can You Fry An Egg?* . . . .   5.00 -   8.00
Banner 0537 *Can't Stop Caring For You* . . . . . .   5.00 -   8.00
Banner 0557 *Stay in the Sunshine and Smile* . . . .   7.00 - 10.00
Banner 0564 *You Know Better Than That* . . . . . .   5.00 -   8.00
Banner 0569 *In Harlem's Araby* . . . .   8.00 - 12.00
Banner 0570 *When the Moon Shines Down on*
Sunshine and Me . . . .   7.00 - 10.00
Banner 0572 *Angel Eyes* . . . .   5.00 -   8.00
Banner 0584 *Just a Lone Hillbilly* . . . .   5.00 -   8.00
Banner 0590 *Lonely Lady* . . . .   8.00 - 12.00
Banner 0619 *One Hour of Happiness* . . . .   5.00 -   8.00
Banner 0623 *She Stole My Heart* . . . .   7.00 - 10.00
Banner 0659 *Are You Blue?* . . . .   5.00 -   8.00
Banner 0691 *Ain't Life a Load of Happiness?* . . .   7.00 - 10.00
Banner 0693 *Every Highway, Every By Way*
(Points My Way Home) . . . .   5.00 -   8.00
Banner 0748 *Just a Song About You* . . . .   5.00 -   8.00
Banner 0750 *Myrtle (My Little Turtle Dove)* . . . . . 10.00 - 15.00
Banner 0756 *I've Got My Mind On You* . . . .   5.00 -   8.00
Banner 0757 *The Harvard Hop* . . . .   7.00 - 10.00
Banner 0784 *Let's Be Sweethearts Now* . . . .   5.00 -   8.00
Banner 0802 *The Recipe Song* . . . .   5.00 -   8.00
Banner 6425 *Hoodoo Voodoo Man* . . . .   5.00 -   8.00
Banner 6426 *Along About Now* . . . .   5.00 -   8.00
Banner 6439 *Sweet Baby* . . . .   5.00 -   8.00
Banner 6440 *My Rosalie* . . . .   5.00 -   8.00
Banner 6445 *Doesn't That Mean Anything*
To You? . . . .   5.00 -   8.00
Banner 6447 *Queen of the Caravan* . . . .   5.00 -   8.00
Banner 6449 *Adorable You* . . . .   5.00 -   8.00
Banner 6451 *What Will I Do Without You,*
Sweetheart . . . .   5.00 -   8.00
Banner 6452 *Whoopeein' Up* . . . .   7.00 - 10.00
Banner 6468 *Loving You* . . . .   5.00 -   8.00
Banner 6470 *Who's Making You Forget Me* . . . . .   5.00 -   8.00
Banner 6472 *My Sweetie Turned Sour On Me* . . .   5.00 -   8.00
Banner 6473 *Someone Thinks There's No One*
Like Me . . . .   5.00 -   8.00
Banner 6477 *You're Gonna Regret* . . . .   5.00 -   8.00
Banner 6502 *What Am I Now?* . . . .   5.00 -   8.00
Banner 6506 *Happy Highways* . . . .   5.00 -   8.00
Banner 6507 *In My Wedding Gown* . . . .   5.00 -   8.00
Banner 6511 *Whisper Why You Feel Blue* . . . . . .   5.00 -   8.00
Banner 6516 *That's What Love Did To Me* . . . . . .   5.00 -   8.00
Banner 6537 *Any Old Time Is Loving Time*
For Me . . . .   5.00 -   8.00
Cameo 0105 *Gettin' Along* . . . .   5.00 -   8.00
Cameo 0137 *Can't Stop Caring For You* . . . .   3.00 -   5.00
Cameo 0157 *Stay In The Sunshine and Smile* . . . .   5.00 -   8.00
Cameo 0172 *Angel Eyes* . . . .   5.00 -   8.00
Cameo 0223 *She Stole My Heart* . . . .   5.00 -   8.00
Jewel 6056 *The Recipe Song* . . . .   5.00 -   8.00
Oriole 1786 *Can't Stop Caring For You* . . . .   5.00 -   8.00
Romeo 1133 *Will You Think of Me As I Think*
of You . . . .   3.00 -   5.00
Romeo 1151 *Can't Stop Caring For You* . . . .   3.00 -   5.00
1398 *Let's Be Sweethearts Now* . . . .   7.00 - 10.00

EDDIE DUCHIN AND HIS (CENTRAL PARK
CASINO) ORCHESTRA:
Brunswick 6425, 6431, 6439, 6445, 6458, 6476,
6481, 6488 . . . .   4.00 -   8.00
Brunswick 8155 *Between the Devil and the Deep*
Blue Sea . . . .   7.00 - 10.00
Brunswick, most other issues . . . .   3.00 -   5.00
Columbia 2625-D *Can't We Talk It Over?* . . . . .   7.00 - 10.00
2626-D *By The Fireside* . . . .   7.00 - 10.00
2677-D *You're Blase* . . . .   7.00 - 10.00

2680-D *The Clouds Will Soon Roll By* . . . .   7.00 - 10.00
Columbia, most other issues . . . .   2.00 -   4.00
Victor 24274, 24275, 24280, 24325, 24326,
24327, 24376, 34277, 24380, 24441, 24447,
24461, 24477, 24479, 24492, 24510, 24512,
14518, 24576 . . . .   4.00 -   8.00
Victor 24579 *As Long As I Live* . . . .   7.00 - 10.00
Victor, most other issues . . . .   3.00 -   6.00
ROBERTA DUDLEY:
Nordskog 3007 *Krooked Blues* . . . . .150.00 - 300.00
Sunshine 3001 *Krooked Blues* . . . . .150.00 - 300.00
(Sunshine label is pasted over Nordskog label.)
HERVE DUERSON:
Gennett 7009 *Avenue Strut* . . . . .150.00 - 200.00
7191 *Easy Drag* . . . . .150.00 - 200.00
LOUIS DUMAINE'S JAZZOLA EIGHT:
Victor 20580 *Red Onion Drag* . . . . 80.00 - 120.00
20723 *Pretty Audrey* . . . . 80.00 - 120.00
SONNY DUNHAM AND HIS ORCHESTRA:
Bluebird 11124, 11148, 11200, 11214, 11239, 11253,
11305, 11337, 11504, 11514 . . . .   5.00 -   8.00
Varsity 8205, 8227, 8234 . . . .   5.00 -   8.00
Vogue R-774 *Save Me A Dream* . . . . 20.00 - 30.00
R-775 *Clementine* . . . . 20.00 - 30.00
BLIND WILLIE DUNN: BLIND WILLIE
DUNN'S GIN BOTTLE FOUR:
Okey 8633 *Church Street Sobbin' Blues* . . . . 25.00 - 40.00
8689 *Jet Black Blues* . . . . 75.00 - 100.00
JOHNNY DUNN (& HIS BAND/JAZZ BAND):
DUNN'S ORIGINAL JAZZ HOUNDS:
Columbia 124-D *Dunn's Cornet Blues* . . . . 10.00 - 15.00
Columbia A-3541, A-3579, A-3729, A-3839,
A-3878, A-3893 . . . .   5.00 - 10.00
13004-D *Jazzin' Babies Blues* . . . . 15.00 - 25.00
14306-D *Buffalo Blues* . . . . .100.00 - 150.00
14358-D *Ham and Eggs* . . . . .100.00 - 150.00
Vocalion 1176 *Original Bugle Blues* . . . . .150.00 - 200.00
JIMMY DURANTE: JIMMY DURANTE'S
JAZZ BAND:
Brunswick 6774 *Inka Dinka Doo* . . . .   5.00 -   8.00
Gennett 9045 *Why Cry Blues* . . . .   7.00 - 10.00
(See also: CLAYTON, JACKSON AND
DURANTE)
BURT EARLE with ANGLO-AMERICAN
ORCHESTRA:
Pathe 30124 *King Chanticleer* . . . . 15.00 - 20.00
CHARLIE EATON:
Herwin 93017 *Bucket of Blood* . . . . .100.00 - 150.00
GEORGE ECKHARDT, JR., & HIS (CAFE
LAFAYETTE) ORCHESTRA:
Vocalion 15738 *Roses Of Yesterday* . . . .   8.00 - 12.00
15796 *Broadway Melody* . . . .   8.00 - 12.00
15803 *My Sin* . . . .   8.00 - 12.00
15806 *You Were Meant For Me* . . . .   8.00 - 12.00
WILLIE ECKSTEIN:
Okeh 40018 *Maple Leaf Rag* . . . .   8.00 - 12.00
40121 *Puttin' On The Dog* . . . .   8.00 - 12.00
EDDIE'S HOT SHOTS:
Victor V-38046 *That's A Serious Thing* . . . . 35.00 - 50.00
EDDIE AND SUGAR LOU'S HOTEL TYLER
ORCHESTRA:
Vocalion 1445 *K.W.K.H. Blues* . . . . .150.00 - 200.00
1455 *There'll Be Some Changes Made* . . . . . .150.00 - 200.00
1514 *Eddie And Sugar Lou Stomp* . . . . .150.00 - 200.00
1714 *Sympathetic Blues* . . . . .200.00 - 300.00
1723 *Cruel Mama Blues* . . . . .200.00 - 300.00
EDGEWATER CROWS:
Titles, issued contemporaneously on Banner,
Melotone, Oriole, Perfect Romeo: *No Bonus*
Blues; Swinging Rhythm Around . . . . 50.00 - 80.00
EDDIE EDINBOROUGH & HIS NEW
ORLEANS WILDCATS/WASHBOARD BAND:

Columbia 14613-D *Wild Cat's Ball* . . . . 75.00 - 100.00
14629-D *Brown Baby* . . . . 75.00 - 100.00
Vocalion 1701 *Dream Sweetheart* . . . . 50.00 - 75.00
1702 *Nobody's Sweetheart* . . . . 50.00 - 75.00

THOMAS A. EDISON: (See also: "Holiday Greetings From The Bunch At Orange")
Edison (master number) 6540 *"Let Us Not Forget"* . . . . 50.00 - 75.00

CLIFF EDWARDS:
Pathe-Actuelle 025159, 025160, 025163, 025164, 025167, 025169, 025173, 25198, 25199, 25200, 25203, 25204, 25206, 25208 . . . . 5.00 - 10.00
Perfect 11593, 11594, 11597, 11598, 11601, 11603, 11607, 11632, 11633, 11634, 11637, 11638, 11640, 11642 . . . . 5.00 - 10.00

DAVID EDWARDS & HIS BOYS:
Okeh 41492 *Just A Crazy Song* . . . . 10.00 - 15.00

GUS C. EDWARDS & HIS ORCHESTRA:
Victor 20167 *Crying For The Moon* . . . . 5.00 - 8.00
20207 *Monte Carlo Joys* . . . . 7.00 - 10.00
20230 *Alabama Stomp* . . . . 5.00 - 8.00

JOAN EDWARDS WITH THE VOGUE RECORDING ORCHESTRA:
Vogue R-761 *More Than You Know* . . . . 20.00 - 30.00
R-767 *This Is Always* . . . . 20.00 - 30.00
R-782 *Maybe You'll Be There* . . . . 25.00 - 35.00

BOB EFFROS:
Brunswick 4620 *Tin Ear* . . . . 20.00 - 30.00

EL COTA:
Columbia A1118 *Black And White-Ragtime Two-Step* . . . . 8.00 - 12.00
A1149 *Red Pepper-A Spicy Rag* . . . . 8.00 - 12.00

ROY ELDRIDGE & HIS ORCHESTRA:
Vocalion 3458, 3479, 3577 . . . . 5.00 - 10.00

ELGAR'S CREOLE ORCHESTRA:
Brunswick 3404 *Nightmare* . . . . 20.00 - 30.00
Vocalion 15477 *Cafe Capers* . . . . 75.00 - 100.00
15478 *Brotherly Love* . . . . 75.00 - 100.00

FRED ELIZALDE'S CINDERELLA ROOF ORCHESTRA:
Hollywood 1012 *Boneyard Shuffle* . . . . 150.00 - 200.00
1013 *Melancholy Weeps* . . . . 150.00 - 200.00
1014 *Tonight's My Night With Baby* . . . . 150.00 - 200.00
1015 *Tickling Julie* . . . . 150.00 - 200.00

DUKE ELLINGTON (& HIS ORCHESTRA/ COTTON CLUB ORCHESTRA/KENTUCKY CLUB ORCHESTRA/WASHINGTONIANS):
Blu-Disc 1004 *Rose Marie* . . . . 40.00 - 60.00
Bluebird 6269, 6280, 6305, 6306, 6335, 6396, 6415, 6430 . . . . 5.00 - 8.00
6450 *Old Man Blues* . . . . 10.00 - 15.00
6531, 6565, 6614, 6727, 6728, 7182 . . . . 5.00 - 8.00
10242, 10243, 10245 . . . . 4.00 - 7.00
Brunswick 3480 *Birmingham Breakdown* . . . . 10.00 - 15.00
3987 *Tishomingo Blues* . . . . 10.00 - 15.00
4110 *Louisiana* . . . . 10.00 - 15.00
4122 *The Mooche* . . . . 10.00 - 15.00
6093 *Creole Rhapsody* . . . . 10.00 - 15.00
6265, 6288, 6317, 6355, 6374, 6404, 6432, 6516, 6527, 6571, 6600, 6607, 6638, 6646 . . 6.00 - 10.00
Brunswick 6987, 7310, 7440, 7461, 7514, 7526, 7546, 7547, 7625, 7627, 7650, 7667, 7710, 7734, 7752, 7989, 7990, 7994, 8004, 8029, 8044, 8063, 8083, 8093, 8099, 8108, 8131, 8168, 8169, 8174, 8186, 8200, 8204, 8221, 8231, 8256, 8293, 8297, 8306, 8344, 8365, 8380, 8405, 8411 . . . . 5.00 - 10.00
Buddy 8010 *If You Can't Hold The Man You Love* 150.00 - 200.00
8063 *Animal Crackers* . . . . 150.00 - 200.00
Champion 15105 *(You've Got Those) Wanna Go Back Again Blues* . . . . 100.00 - 150.00
15118 *I'm Just Wild About Animal Crackers* . . . 50.00 - 75.00

15120 *Li'l Farina* . . . . 50.00 - 75.00
Columbia 953-D *Hop Head* . . . . 15.00 - 20.00
1076-D *Down In Our Alley Blues* . . . . 15.00 - 20.00
Gennett 3291 *Wanna Go Back Again Blues* . . . . . 50.00 - 75.00
3342 *Animal Crackers* . . . . 50.00 - 75.00
Okeh 8521 *Black And Tan Fantasy* . . . . 15.00 - 20.00
8602 *Diga Diga Doo* . . . . 15.00 - 20.00
8636 *Black Beauty* . . . . 15.00 - 20.00
8662 *Misty Mornin'* . . . . 15.00 - 20.00
40955 *Black And Tan Fantasy* . . . . 15.00 - 20.00
41013 *Jubilee Stomp* . . . . 15.00 - 20.00
Pathe-Actuelle 7504 *Georgia Grind* . . . . 75.00 - 100.00
36333 *Trombone Blues* . . . . 50.00 - 80.00
Perfect 104 *Georgia Grind* . . . . 75.00 - 100.00
14514 *Trombone Blues* . . . . 50.00 - 80.00
Victor L-16006* *Mood Indigo Plus 2* . . . . 75.00 - 100.00
L-16007* *East St. Louis Toodle-Oo Plus 2* . . . . . . 75.00 - 100.00
(*These are long-playing "Program Transcriptions")

Victor 21137 *Creole Love Call* . . . . 15.00 - 20.00
21284 *Washington Wobble* . . . . 15.00 - 20.00
21490 *The Blues I Love To Sing* . . . . 20.00 - 30.00
21580 *Black Beauty* . . . . 15.00 - 20.00
21703 *Got Everything But You* . . . . 20.00 - 30.00
22528 *Three Little Words* . . . . 5.00 - 8.00
22586 *What Good Am I Without You* . . . . 10.00 - 15.00
22587 *Mood Indigo* . . . . 8.00 - 12.00
22603 *Blue Again* . . . . 8.00 - 12.00
22614 *Keep A Song In Your Soul* . . . . 10.00 - 15.00
22743 *Limehouse Blues* . . . . 10.00 - 15.00
22791 *It's Glory* . . . . 10.00 - 15.00
22800 *The Mystery Song* . . . . 10.00 - 15.00
22938 *Bugle Call Rag* . . . . 15.00 - 20.00
23016 *Hittin' The Bottle* . . . . 20.00 - 30.00
23017 *You're Lucky To Me* . . . . 20.00 - 30.00
23022 *Jungle Nights In Harlem* . . . . 20.00 - 30.00
23036 *Sam And Delilah* . . . . 15.00 - 20.00
23041 *Shout 'Em, Aunt Tillie* . . . . 20.00 - 30.00
24431 *Rude Interlude* . . . . 10.00 - 15.00
24501 *Daybreak Express* . . . . 8.00 - 12.00
24617 *Cocktails For Two* . . . . 8.00 - 12.00
24622 *Ebony Rhapsody* . . . . 10.00 - 15.00
24651 *My Old Flame* . . . . 10.00 - 15.00
24755 *Delta Serenade* . . . . 8.00 - 12.00
V 38007 *Bandanna Babies* . . . . 20.00 - 30.00
V 38008 *Diga Diga Doo* . . . . 20.00 - 30.00
V 38034 *The Mooche* . . . . 30.00 - 40.00
V 38025 *Flaming Youth* . . . . 20.00 - 30.00
V 38036 *Saturday Night Function* . . . . 20.00 - 30.00
V 38045 *Japanese Dream* . . . . 15.00 - 25.00
V 38053 *Stevedore Stomp* . . . . 15.00 - 25.00
V 38058 *Saratoga Swing* . . . . 15.00 - 25.00
V 38065 *Hot Feet* . . . . 20.00 - 30.00
V 38079 *Cotton Club Stomp* . . . . 20.00 - 30.00
V 38089 *Swanee Shuffle* . . . . 20.00 - 30.00
V 38092 *The Duke Steps Out* . . . . 20.00 - 30.00
V 38115 *Breakfast Dance* . . . . 20.00 - 30.00
V 38129 *Jazz Lips* . . . . 20.00 - 30.00
V 38143 *Sweet Jazz O'Mine* . . . . 25.00 - 40.00
Vocalion 1064 *Birmingham Breakdown* . . . . 50.00 - 80.00
1077 *Immigration Blues* . . . . 75.00 - 100.00

1086 *New Orleans Low-Down*	75.00 -	100.00
1153 *Red Hot Band*	75.00 -	100.00

FAY ELLIOTT'S NEW YORKERS:

Flexo 1640 *Come Easy Go Easy Love*	75.00 -	100.00

**GAY ELLIS: (See also: DOT DARE and
ANNETTE HANSHAW**, the latter being the real
name of this artist, whose recordings for *Diva,
Harmony,* and *Velvet Tone* were issued under all
three names.)

Diva 2706-G *I Must Have That Man*	7.00 -	10.00
Harmony 766-H *My Blackbirds Are Bluebirds Now*	7.00 -	10.00
785-H *You're The Cream In My Coffee*	8.00 -	12.00
832-H *When The World Is At Rest*	8.00 -	12.00
859-H *Mean To Me*	7.00 -	10.00
981-H *True Blue Lou*	7.00 -	10.00

**SEGER ELLIS; SEGER ELLIS & HIS
(CHOIRS OF BRASS) ORCHESTRA:**

Ammor 118 *Way Down*	8.00 -	12.00
Brunswick 6022 *It's a Lonesome Old Town*	10.00 -	15.00
Brunswick 6050 *Tie a Little String Around Your Finger*	8.00 -	12.00
Brunswick 6076 *One Little Raindrop*	5.00 -	8.00
Brunswick 6078 *I've Found What I Wanted In You*	5.00 -	8.00
Brunswick 6135 *Nevertheless*	5.00 -	8.00
Columbia 2362-D *Cheerful Little Earful*	7.00 -	10.00
Decca 1275 *Shivery Stomp*	7.00 -	10.00
1322 *I Know That You Know*	7.00 -	10.00
1350 *Bees Knees*	7.00 -	10.00
Okeh 5966 *No Jug, No Jazz*	7.00 -	10.00
6051 *Mellow Stuff*	7.00 -	10.00
Okeh 40970 *Among My Souvenirs*	7.00 -	10.00
Okeh 41024 *I Must Be Dreaming*	7.00 -	10.00
Okeh 41047 *If I Can't Have You*	8.00 -	12.00
Okeh 41061 *Sweet Sue—Just You*	5.00 -	8.00
Okeh 41077 *I Can't Give You Anything But Love*	5.00 -	8.00
Okeh 41103 *Out Of The Dawn*	5.00 -	8.00
Okeh 41127 *Dream House*	4.00 -	7.00
Okeh 41160 *Don't Be Like That*	8.00 -	12.00
Okeh 41165 *Where the Shy Little Violets Grow*	5.00 -	8.00
Okeh 41190 *My Inspiration Is You*	5.00 -	8.00
Okeh 41221 *Louise*	5.00 -	8.00
Okeh 41222 *Mean To Me*	7.00 -	10.00
Okeh 41224 *You, Just You*	7.00 -	10.00
Okeh 41225 *Only For You*	7.00 -	10.00
Okeh 41255 *To Be In Love (Espesh'ly With You)*	20.00 -	30.00
Okeh 41289 *Nobody But You*	7.00 -	10.00
Okeh 41290 *True Blue Lou*	15.00 -	20.00
Okeh 41291 *Ain't Misbehavin'*	15.00 -	20.00
Okeh 41321 *If I Had a Talking Picture of You*	8.00 -	12.00
Okeh 41349 *Have a Little Faith In Me*	7.00 -	10.00
Okeh 41396 *Should I?*	8.00 -	12.00
Okeh 41405 *What Is This Thing Called Love?*	7.00 -	10.00
Okeh 41413 *The Moon Is Low*	8.00 -	12.00
Okeh 41417 *Sentimental Blues*	15.00 -	20.00
Okeh 41424 *Exactly Like You*	8.00 -	12.00
Okeh 41436 *Swinging in a Hammock*	10.00 -	15.00
Okeh 41441 *Confessin'*	8.00 -	12.00
Okeh 41443 *Little White Lies*	8.00 -	12.00
Okeh 41447 *Shivery Stomp*	15.00 -	20.00
Okeh 41452 *If I Could Be With You One Hour Tonight*	10.00 -	15.00
Okeh 41467 *Sweet Jennie Lee*	10.00 -	15.00
Okeh 41473 *You're Driving Me Crazy*	10.00 -	15.00
Okeh 41479 *You're the One I Care For*	10.00 -	15.00
Victor 19755 *Prairie Blues*	15.00 -	20.00
Victor 19952 *Ash Can Blues*	15.00 -	20.00
Vocalion 5534 *Bye Bye Blues*	7.00 -	10.00
5966 *When It's Sleepy Time Down South*	7.00 -	10.00
5721 *Happy Travelin'*	7.00 -	10.00

ZIGGY ELMAN & HIS ORCHESTRA:

Bluebird (most issues)	3.00 -	6.00

M-G-M (most issues)	2.00 -	5.00

**EMERSON DANCE/SYMPHONY
ORCHESTRA; EMERSON MILITARY
BAND:**

Emerson 7122 *Honky-Tonk Rag*	10.00 -	15.00
7145 *Razzazza Mazzazza*	10.00 -	15.00
7161 *Chicken Walk*	8.00 -	12.00
7162 *Rooster Rag*	10.00 -	15.00
7163 *Saxophone Sobs*	10.00 -	15.00
7211 *Shim-Me-Sha-Wabble*	10.00 -	15.00
7212 *The Darktown Strutters' Ball*	8.00 -	12.00
7224 *Indiana*	8.00 -	12.00
7225 *Zamp-A-Zamp Rag*	10.00 -	15.00
7265 *Spooky Spooks*	10.00 -	15.00
7295 *Yah-De-Dah*	8.00 -	12.00
7319 *Indianola*	8.00 -	12.00
7322 *The Wild, Wild Women Are Making A Wild Man Of Me*	8.00 -	12.00

(Note: Above are 7-inch records)

THE EMPERORS:

Harmony 362-H *Clarinet Marmalade*	10.00 -	15.00
383-H *Go, Joe, Go*	10.00 -	15.00

PEGGY ENGLISH:

Vocalion 15093 *Charleston Baby O'Mine*	7.00 -	10.00
15118 *You Can't Shush Katy*	7.00 -	10.00
15132 *Sweet Man*	7.00 -	10.00
15381 *How Many Times?*	7.00 -	10.00
15504 *High-High-High Up In The Hills*	10.00 -	15.00

SHARLIE ENGLISH:

Paramount 12610 *Transom Blues*	75.00 -	100.00
12644 *Broke Woman Blues*	75.00 -	100.00

**EQUINOX ORCHESTRA OF PRINCETON,
NEW JERSEY:**

Personal Record 115-P *China Boy*	75.00 -	100.00

**WALLY ERICKSON'S COLISEUM
ORCHESTRA:**

Gennett 3068 *The Meanest Kind of Blues*	20.00 -	30.00
3069 *The Call Of The South*	20.00 -	30.00
Vocalion 15778 *Hard Luck*	50.00 -	100.00

ERWING BROTHERS' ORCHESTRA:

Vocalion 2564 *The Erwing Blues*	50.00 -	75.00

ESSEX CLUB ORCHESTRA:

Vocalion 15170 *A Little Bit Bad*	5.00 -	8.00
Vocalion 15221, 15224, 15230	3.00 -	5.00
Vocalion 15423, 15424	4.00 -	7.00

RUTH ETTING:

Titles, issued contemporaneously on Banner,
Conqueror, Melotone, Oriole, Perfect, Romeo:
*All Of Me; Can't We Talk It Over; Happy-Go-
Lucky You; Have You Forgotten?; Hey! Young
Fella; How Can I Go On Without You; If I
Didn't Have You; I'll Follow You; I'll Never Be
The Same; I'll Never Have To Dream Again; It
Was So Beautiful; Just One More Chance; Lazy
Day; Let Me Call You Sweetheart; Linger A
little While Longer in the Twilight; Love Letters
In the Sand; Nevertheless; Some Day We'll
Meet Again; Take Me In Your Arms Again;
That's What Heaven Means To Me; Try a Little
Tenderness; Without That Gal; With Summer
Coming On; You've Got Me Crying Again*

	8.00 -	12.00
Brunswick 6657 *Close Your Eyes*	8.00 -	12.00
6671 *What Is Sweeter*	8.00 -	12.00
6697 *Build A Little Home*	8.00 -	12.00
6719 *Everything I Have Is Yours*	8.00 -	12.00
6761 *Keep Romance Alive*	8.00 -	12.00
6769 *Smoke Gets In Your Eyes*	8.00 -	12.00
6892 *Easy Come, Easy Go*	8.00 -	12.00
6914 *Were Your Ears Burning?*	8.00 -	12.00
7646 *It's Been So Long*	8.00 -	12.00
Columbia 580-D *Let's Talk About My Sweetie*	8.00 -	12.00
Columbia 633-D, 644-D, 692-D	5.00 -	10.00

675-D *What A Man!*	7.00	-	10.00
722-D *Her Beaus Are Only Rainbows*	7.00	-	10.00
764-D *Stars*	7.00	-	10.00
Columbia 827-D, 865-D, 908-D, 924-D, 979-D	5.00	-	10.00
Columbia 995-D, 1288-D, 1312-D	5.00	-	8.00
Columbia 1052-D, 1075-D, 1104-D	5.00	-	10.00
Columbia 1113-D *Shaking the Blues Away*	7.00	-	10.00
Columbia 1196-D, 1208-D, 1352-D	5.00	-	10.00
Columbia 1237-D *The Varsity Drag*	7.00	-	10.00
Columbia 1393-D, 1420-D, 1454-D, 1563-D, 1595-D	5.00	-	10.00
Columbia 1680-D, 1707-D, 1733-D, 1801-D	5.00	-	10.00
Columbia 1762-D *Button Up Your Overcoat*	8.00	-	12.00
Columbia 1830-D, 1883-D	5.00	-	10.00
Columbia 1958-D *Ain't Misbehavin'*	8.00	-	12.00
1998-D *The Right Kind Of Man*	8.00	-	12.00
2038-D *A Place To Call Home*	8.00	-	12.00
2073-D *Crying For The Carolines*	8.00	-	12.00
2146-D *Ten Cents A Dance*	5.00	-	8.00
2172-D *Let Me Sing And I'm Happy*	7.00	-	10.00
2199-D *Exactly Like You*	7.00	-	10.00
2216-D *Dancing With Tears In My Eyes*	5.00	-	8.00
2280-D *The Kiss Waltz*	5.00	-	8.00
2300-D *If I Could Be With You*	8.00	-	12.00
2307-D *Just A Little Closer*	8.00	-	12.00
2318-D *Laughing At Life*	8.00	-	12.00
2377-D *Reaching For The Moon*	8.00	-	12.00
2398-D *You're The One I Care For*	8.00	-	12.00
2445-D *Were You Sincere?*	8.00	-	12.00
2454-D *Out Of Nowhere*	10.00	-	15.00
2470-D *Moonlight Saving Time*	10.00	-	15.00
2505-D *I'm Falling In Love*	10.00	-	15.00
2529-D *Guilty*	10.00	-	15.00
2557-D *Goodnight, Sweetheart*	8.00	-	12.00
2580-D *Cuban Love Song*	10.00	-	15.00
2630-D *When We're Alone*	10.00	-	15.00
2660-D *The Voice in the Old Village Choir*	10.00	-	15.00
2681-D *Holding My Honey's Hand*	10.00	-	15.00
2954-D *Talkin' To Myself*	10.00	-	15.00
2955-D *Out In The Cold Again*	10.00	-	15.00
2979-D *A Needle In A Haystack*	10.00	-	15.00
2985-D *Am I To Blame?*	10.00	-	15.00
3014-D *March Winds and April Showers*	10.00	-	15.00
3031-D *It's Easy To Remember*	10.00	-	15.00
3070-D *I Wished on the Moon*	10.00	-	15.00
3085-D *Ten Cents A Dance*	7.00	-	10.00
Decca 1084 *There's Something in the Air*	5.00	-	8.00
1107 *Goodnight, My Love*	5.00	-	8.00
1212 *It's Swell Of You*	5.00	-	8.00
1259 *On A Little Dream Ranch*	5.00	-	8.00

EUROPE'S SOCIETY ORCHESTRA; LT. JIM EUROPE'S 369th INFANTRY (HELL FIGHTERS) BAND:

Pathe 22081 *Darktown Strutters' Ball*	8.00	-	12.00
Pathe 22082 *Ja Da*	8.00	-	12.00
Pathe 22085 *Memphis Blues*	10.00	-	15.00
Pathe 22086 *Hesitating Blues*	10.00	-	15.00
Pathe 22087 *St. Louis Blues*	10.00	-	15.00
Pathe 22103 *Jazz Baby*	8.00	-	12.00
Pathe 22167 *Clarinet Marmalade*	10.00	-	15.00
Pathe (most other issues, including those by singing groups)	5.00	-	10.00
Victor 17533 *Castle Walk*	7.00	-	10.00
Victor 35359 *Down Home Rag (12-inch)*	8.00	-	12.00
Victor 35372 *Castle House Rag (12-inch)*	8.00	-	12.00

EDITH EVANS:

Brunswick 4291 *My Kinda Love*	7.00	-	10.00

ROY EVANS:

Columbia 1559-D, 1934-D, 2198-D, 2257-D, 2338-D, 2469-D	3.00	-	7.00
Crown 3154 *One More Time*	7.00	-	10.00

EVERETT'S SERENADERS:

Dandy 5118 *I Wonder Where My Baby Is Tonight*	7.00	-	10.00

ELIOT EVERETT AND HIS ORCHESTRA:

Victor 22921 *Blue Danube Blues*	7.00	-	10.00
24080 *In a Little Blue Canoe With You*	7.00	-	10.00
24085 *Little Nell*	7.00	-	10.00

WILL EZELL:

Paramount 12549 *Barrel House Man*	100.00	-	150.00
12688 *Mixed Up Rag*	100.00	-	150.00
12729 *Crawlin' Spider Blues*	100.00	-	150.00
12753 *Barrel House Woman*	100.00	-	150.00
12773 *Bucket of Blood*	100.00	-	150.00
12855 *Pitchin' Boogie*	100.00	-	150.00
12914 *Freakish Mistreater Blues*	150.00	-	200.00

SAMMY FAIN:

Harmony 904-H *The Things That Were Made For Love*	7.00	-	10.00
943-H *What A Day!*	10.00	-	15.00
961-H *Why Can't You*	10.00	-	15.00
Harmony 993-H, 1014-H, 1163-H, 1179-H	7.00	-	10.00
Velvet Tone 1943-V *To Be In Love*	10.00	-	15.00

OWEN FALLON AND HIS CALIFORNIANS:

Melotone 12199 *Under Your Window Tonight*	10.00	-	15.00
12212 *Take It From Me (I'm Takin' To You)*	8.00	-	12.00
12337 *I Know You're Lying, But I Love It*	8.00	-	12.00
12409 *Sleep (Come On And Take Me)*	8.00	-	12.00
Sunset 1135 *Darktown Shuffle*	30.00	-	50.00
1152 *I Love My Baby*	20.00	-	30.00

WILLIE FARMER AND HIS ORCHESTRA:

Bluebird 7024, 7026, 7036, 7170, 7171, 7181, 7183, 7519, 7527, 7685, 7687, 7698, 7722, 7724, 7735, 7795, 7799, 7813	5.00	-	10.00

FRANK FARRELL & HIS (GREENWICH VILLAGE INN) ORCHESTRA:

Cameo 1195 *Zulu Wail*	7.00	-	10.00
Cameo (most other issues)	3.00	-	6.00
Harmony 371-H *South Wind*	5.00	-	8.00
Harmony 402-H *I'm Back In Love Again*	5.00	-	8.00
Harmony 434-H *Gorgeous*	5.00	-	8.00
Harmony 462-H *Miss Annabelle Lee*	5.00	-	8.00
Harmony 471-H *Are You Happy?*	4.00	-	7.00
Harmony 483-H *Shaking the Blues Away*	7.00	-	10.00
Harmony 488-H *The Varsity Drag*	7.00	-	10.00
Harmony 584-H *Back In Your Own Back Yard*	5.00	-	8.00
Harmony 590-H *Singapore Sorrows*	5.00	-	8.00
(Note: Above titles, on *Diva* and *Velvet Tone*, are similarly valued.)			
Lincoln 2658 *Zulu Wail*	7.00	-	10.00
2674 *It's A Million To One You're In Love*	8.00	-	12.00
Lincoln (most other issues)	3.00	-	6.00
Romeo 423 *Zulu Wail*	7.00	-	10.00
437 *It's A Million To One You're In Love*	8.00	-	12.00
Romeo (most other issues)	3.00	-	6.00

ALICE FAYE:

Titles, issued contemporaneously on Banner, Brunswick, Melotone, Oriole, Perfect, Romeo: *According To The Moonlight; I Love To Ride The Horses; I'm Shootin' High; I've Got My Fingers Crossed; My Future Star; Oh, I Didn't Know; Spreadin' Rhythm Around; Yes To You*	7.00	-	12.00
Brunswick 7821, 7825, 7860, 7876	5.00	-	10.00

CARL FENTON & HIS ORCHESTRA:

Brunswick 3519 *Delirium*	5.00	-	8.00
4421 *What A Day!*	15.00	-	20.00
Brunswick (most other issues)	3.00	-	5.00
Q.R.S. 1004 *Night Time Is Love Time*	10.00	-	15.00
1005 *Bless Her Little Heart*	15.00	-	25.00
1018 *Hello Little Sweetheart*	10.00	-	15.00
1023 *Shake It Down*	50.00	-	100.00
1026 *Won'tcha*	10.00	-	15.00
Q.R.S. 1038 *The Moon Is Low*	10.00	-	15.00
1039 *Sing You Sinners*	15.00	-	25.00
1046 *The Stein Song*	10.00	-	15.00

1049 *Exactly Like You*	10.00 -	15.00
1051 *Whippoorwill*	10.00 -	15.00
1060 *Without You, Emaline*	10.00 -	15.00
Supertone 9360 *Mississippi, Here I Am*	7.00 -	10.00
9378 *That's What I Call Heaven*	7.00 -	10.00
9480 *I've Made A Habit Of You*	7.00 -	10.00

JERRY FENWYCK AND HIS ORCHESTRA:

Clarion 5282-C *Little Joe*	5.00 -	8.00
5305-C *That Little Boy Of Mine*	5.00 -	8.00
5352-C *How The Time Can Fly*	7.00 -	10.00
5360-C *Take It From Me*	10.00 -	15.00
5364-C *Do The New York*	10.00 -	15.00
5398-C *A Faded Summer Love*	7.00 -	10.00
5408-C *You Didn't Know The Music*	7.00 -	10.00
5415-C *Now's The Time To Fall in Love*	10.00 -	15.00
5420-C *By The Sycamore Tree*	10.00 -	15.00
5421-C *I Wouldn't Change You For The World*	7.00 -	10.00
5442-C *All Of Me*	10.00 -	15.00
11500-C *You Call It Madness*	10.00 -	15.00
11503-C *Who's Your Little Who-Zis!*	20.00 -	30.00

(Note: 11503-C is a five-minute record having
two cuts of the tune—one instrumental, the
other vocal.)

Harmony 1301-H *Little Joe*	5.00 -	8.00
1314-H *That Little Boy Of Mine*	5.00 -	8.00
1341-H *How The Time Can Fly*	7.00 -	10.00
1348-H *Take It From Me*	10.00 -	15.00
1352-H *Do The New York*	10.00 -	15.00
1384-H *A Faded Summer Love*	7.00 -	10.00
1389-H *You Didn't Know The Music*	7.00 -	10.00
1394-H *Now's The Time To Fall In Love*	10.00 -	15.00
1397-H *By The Sycamore Tree*	10.00 -	15.00
1398-H *I Wouldn't Change You For The World*	7.00 -	10.00
1403-H *All Of Me*	10.00 -	15.00
6500-H *You Call It Madness*	10.00 -	15.00
Velvet Tone 2348-V *Little Joe*	5.00 -	8.00
2371-V *Out Of Nowhere*	7.00 -	10.00
2373-V *That Little Boy Of Mine*	5.00 -	8.00
2416-V *How The Time Can Fly*	7.00 -	10.00
2424-V *Take It From Me*	10.00 -	15.00
2461-V *Lies*	7.00 -	10.00
2462-V *A Faded Summer Love*	7.00 -	10.00
2468-V *You Didn't Know The Music*	7.00 -	10.00
2475-V *Now's The Time To Fall In Love*	10.00 -	15.00
2480-V *By The Sycamore Tree*	10.00 -	15.00
2481-V *I Wouldn't Change You For the World*	7.00 -	10.00
2502-V *All Of Me*	10.00 -	15.00
10500-V *When The Rest of the Crowd Goes Home*	10.00 -	15.00

**ARTHUR FIELDS AND HIS ASSASSINATORS/
NOODLERS/WINDJAMMERS:**

Banner 6314 *Let's Get Together*	5.00 -	8.00
6315 *Geraldine*	5.00 -	8.00
6317 *What Do You Think Of My Baby*	5.00 -	8.00
Edison (thin) *Sophomore Prom*	20.00 -	30.00
14075 *Piccolo Pete*	20.00 -	30.00
Edison (thick) 52123 *Is It Possible?*	15.00 -	20.00
52180 *Look In The Mirror*	15.00 -	20.00
52264 *She's A Great, Great Girl*	20.00 -	30.00
52535 *She Only Laughs At Me*	15.00 -	20.00
52553 *I Faw Down An' Go 'Boom*	15.00 -	20.00
Grey Gull 1753 *Humpty Dumpty Baby*	5.00 -	8.00
1781 *Bluer Than You*	5.00 -	8.00
1833 *So Do I*	5.00 -	8.00

(Note: Other titles by ARTHUR FIELDS & HIS
WINDJAMMERS on Grey Gull, Radiex, Van
Dyke, and possibly other related labels not yet
documented, are similarly valued.)

BUDDY FIELDS AND HIS ORCHESTRA:

Romeo 1052, 1053, 1069, 1070, 1084	4.00 -	8.00
Romeo 1068 *Lovable and Sweet*	7.00 -	10.00

ERNIE FIELDS & HIS ORCHESTRA:

Vocalion 5073 *Lard Stomp*	8.00 -	12.00
5157 *High Jivin'*	8.00 -	12.00
5240 *I'm Living In A Great Big Way*	8.00 -	12.00
5344 *Blues At Midnight*	8.00 -	12.00

**SHEP FIELDS AND HIS ORCHESTRA/
RIPPLING RHYTHM:**

Bluebird, most issues	2.00 -	5.00
Musicraft, most issues	2.00 -	3.00
Victor, most issues	2.00 -	3.00
Vogue R-712 *Atlanta, Ga*	20.00 -	30.00
R-715 *I Can't Begin To Tell You*	75.00 -	100.00
R-764 *Whattaya Gonna Do*	20.00 -	30.00
R-765 *What Is Love*	75.00 -	100.00

LLOYD FINLAY AND HIS ORCHESTRA:

Victor 19643 *You'll Want Me Back Someday*	25.00 -	40.00
19644 *Fido Blues*	35.00 -	50.00
19696 *Ride 'Em, Cowboy*	35.00 -	50.00

BOB FINLEY AND HIS ORCHESTRA:

Cameo 9101 *Doin' The Campus Crawl*	7.00 -	10.00
9103 *Nobody's Baby But Mine*	7.00 -	10.00
9105 *Audition Blues*	10.00 -	15.00
Romeo 903 *Doin' The Campus Crawl*	7.00 -	10.00
905 *Nobody's Baby But Mine*	7.00 -	10.00
907 *Audition Blues*	10.00 -	15.00

**DOUGLAS FINNELL AND HIS ROYAL
STOMPERS:**

Brunswick 7123 *Sweet Sweet Mama*	100.00 -	150.00

ETHEL FINNIE:

Ajax 17015 *Don't You Quit Me, Daddy*	20.00 -	30.00
17027 *Hula Blues*	20.00 -	30.00
Emerson 10846 *Heart-Breakin' Joe*	35.00 -	50.00

**FINZEL'S ARCADIA ORCHESTRA
OF DETROIT:**

Okeh 4735 *Stop Your Kiddin'*	7.00 -	10.00
4743 *I Gave You Up Just Before You Threw Me Down*	7.00 -	10.00
4758 *Falling*	7.00 -	10.00
4759 *Teddy Bear Blues*	7.00 -	10.00
4847 *Farewell Blues*	10.00 -	15.00
4858 *Morning Will Come*	5.00 -	8.00
4859 *Who's Sorry Now?*	7.00 -	10.00
4861 *Barney Google*	7.00 -	10.00
4985 *Stealing To Virginia*	7.00 -	10.00
4999 *Mama Loves Papa, Papa Loves Mama*	8.00 -	12.00
40043 *Keep A-Goin'*	7.00 -	10.00
40053 *Mom-Ma*	5.00 -	8.00
40069 *The Animal Fair*	5.00 -	8.00
40148 *Lots O' Mama*	10.00 -	15.00
40161 *Dicty Blues*	15.00 -	20.00
40298 *Laff It Off*	8.00 -	12.00
40301 *Weepin' The Blues*	15.00 -	20.00
40304 *I Can't Stop Babying You*	8.00 -	12.00

**TED FIORITO AND HIS (EDGEWATER
BEACH HOTEL) ORCHESTRA:**

Brunswick 6422, 6478, 6479, 6493, 6503, 6505, 6526, 6555, 6556, 5686, 6598, 6627, 6670, 6705, 6706, 6736, 6746, 6859, 6860, 6863, 6902, 6919, 6924, 6928, 7311, 7315, 7327, 7364, 7379, 7380, 7392, 7399, 7446, 7451, 7452, 7478, 7489	4.00 -	7.00
Columbia 1967-D *Then You've Never Been Blue*	5.00 -	8.00
Decca 677, 678, 679, 694, 697, 746, 771, 777, 784, 793, 894, 909, 910, 925, 935, 936, 954, 1176, 1193, 1257, 1258, 1450, 1452, 1453, 1561, 1567, 1591	4.00 -	7.00
Decca, most other issues	2.00 -	4.00

**MARK FISHER AND HIS EDGEWATER
BEACH HOTEL ORCHESTRA:**

Columbia 2749-D *Black-Eyed Susan Brown*	8.00 -	12.00

ELLA FITZGERALD & HER SAVOY EIGHT:

Decca 1061, 1062, 1148, 1302, 1339, 1596, 1669	5.00 -	10.00

FIVE BIRMINGHAM BABIES:

Pathe-Actuelle 036129 *Tessie! Stop Teasing Me* ..   5.00 -   8.00
036130 *Hard-Hearted Hannah* ....   5.00 -   8.00
036142 *Arkansas* ....   5.00 -   8.00
036168 *Go, Emmaline* ....   5.00 -   8.00
036169 *Copenhagen* ....   5.00 -   8.00
36218 *Pickin' On Your Baby* ....   7.00 - 10.00
36228 *Down and Out Blues* ....   7.00 - 10.00
36235 *You're In Wrong With The Right Baby* ..   7.00 - 10.00
36236 *Mamie* ....   7.00 - 10.00
36274 *I'm Grieving For You* ....   7.00 - 10.00
36296 *I Know What It Means* ....   7.00 - 10.00
36340 *Dixie Stomp* ....   8.00 - 12.00
36349 *Indigo Blues* ....   7.00 - 10.00
36350 *One Week From Now* .... 50.00 - 75.00
36352 *Go Back Where You Stayed Last Night* ..   8.00 - 12.00
36379 *What! No Women?* .... 10.00 - 15.00
36432 *What A Man!* .... 10.00 - 15.00
36451 *She's Not Too Hot, Not Too Cold* ...... 10.00 - 15.00
36454 *Remember The Night* ....   5.00 -   8.00
36467 *Some Baby, My Gal* ....   7.00 - 10.00
Perfect 14310 *Tessie! Stop Teasing Me* ....   5.00 -   8.00
Perfect 14311 *Hard-Hearted Hannah* ....   5.00 -   8.00
Perfect 14323 *Arkansas* ....   7.00 - 10.00
Perfect 14349 *Go, Emmaline* .... 10.00 - 15.00
Perfect 14350 *Copenhagen* ....   5.00 -   8.00
Perfect 14399 *You Better Keep The Home Fires
Burning* ....   7.00 - 10.00
Perfect 14409 *Not Now—Not Yet—But Soon* .....   7.00 - 10.00
Perfect 14416 *You're In Wrong With The Right
Baby* ....   7.00 - 10.00
Perfect 14417 *What Do We Get From Boston?* ....   7.00 - 10.00
Perfect 14447 *Tiger Rag* ....   8.00 - 12.00
Perfect 14455 *Love Me Daddy Blues* ....   7.00 - 10.00
Perfect 14477 *As Far As I'm Concerned* ....   7.00 - 10.00
Perfect 14521 *Dixie Stomp* ....   8.00 - 12.00
Perfect 14530 *Indigo Blues* ....   7.00 - 10.00
Perfect 14531 *One Week From Now* .... 50.00 - 75.00
Perfect 14533 *Go Back Where You Stayed Last
Night* ....   8.00 - 12.00
Perfect 14560 *What! No Women?* .... 10.00 - 15.00
Perfect 14613 *What A Man!* .... 10.00 - 15.00
Perfect 14632 *She's Not Too Hot, Not Too Cold* .. 10.00 - 15.00
Perfect 14635 *Remember The Night* ....   5.00 -   8.00
Perfect 14648 *Some Baby, My Gal* ....   7.00 - 10.00

FIVE HARMANIACS: FIVE HARMONIACS:
Brunswick 3664 *Carolina Bound* .... 15.00 - 20.00
7002 *Sleepy Blues* .... 25.00 - 40.00
Edison 51902 *Rippin' In Off* .... 30.00 - 50.00
Gennett 6033 *What Did Romie-O-Juliet* .... 50.00 - 75.00
Victor 20293 *Coney Island Washboard* ....   8.00 - 12.00
20507 *What Makes My Baby Cry?* .... 15.00 - 20.00

FIVE HOT CHOCOLATES:
Radiex 952 *Baby Knows How* .... 20.00 - 30.00
Van Dyke 71767 *Baby Knows How* .... 20.00 - 30.00
71775 *Alabama Shuffle* .... 30.00 - 50.00
71786 *Memphis Stomp* .... 30.00 - 50.00

FIVE LITTLE CHOCOLATE DANDIES:
Okeh 8627 *Paducah* .... 15.00 - 25.00

FIVE MUSICAL BLACKBIRDS:
Pathe-Actulle 7508 *18th Street Strut* .... 50.00 - 75.00
36404 *Hot Coffee* .... 50.00 - 75.00
Perfect 108 *18th Street Strut* .... 50.00 - 75.00
14585 *Hot Coffee* .... 50.00 - 75.00

FIVE RHYTHM KINGS:
Victor 23269 *Minnie The Moocher* .... 40.00 - 60.00

FLEETWOOD ORCHESTRA:
Vocalion 15152, 15422, 15462, 15466, 15470,
15516 ....   5.00 - 10.00

**JAY C. FLIPPEN (& HIS HOT
COMBINATION):**
Pathe-Actuelle 32218 *She Knows Her Onions* ....   7.00 - 10.00
32223 *Short And Sweet* .... 10.00 - 15.00

32229 *If I Didn't Know Your Husband* ....   7.00 - 10.00
32260 *South Wind* ....   7.00 - 10.00
32288 *You Don't Like It-Not Much* ....   7.00 - 10.00
32294 *I Ain't Got Nobody* ....   7.00 - 10.00
32313 *Oh! My Operation* ....   7.00 - 10.00
32321 *I Told Them All About You* ....   7.00 - 10.00
32329 *Let a Smile Be Your Umbrella* ....   7.00 - 10.00
Perfect 12297 *How Could Red Riding Hood?* ....   7.00 - 10.00
Perfect 12302 *For My Sweetheart* .... 10.00 - 15.00
Perfect 12308 *Hello Bluebird* ....   7.00 - 10.00
Perfect 12339 *Sixty Seconds Every Minute* .....   7.00 - 10.00
Perfect 12367 *Clementine (From New Orleans)* ..   7.00 - 10.00
Perfect 12373 *An' Furthermore* ....   7.00 - 10.00
Perfect 12392 *Did You Mean It?* ....   7.00 - 10.00
Perfect 12400 *Is She My Girl Friend?* ....   7.00 - 10.00
Perfect 12406 *Away Down South in Heaven* .....   7.00 - 10.00

**TROY FLOYD & HIS PLAZA HOTEL/
SHADOWLAND ORCHESTRA:**
Okeh 8571 *Shadowland Blues* .... 50.00 - 75.00
8719 *Dreamland Blues* .... 50.00 - 75.00

BILL FOLEY'S KEYSTONE SERENADERS:
Vocalion 15122 *Everything Is Hotsy Totsy Now* ...   7.00 - 10.00
Vocalion 15123, 15124 ....   5.00 - 10.00

**FOOR-ROBINSON CAROLINA CLUB
ORCHESTRA:**
Okeh 40466 *Collegiate* .... 20.00 - 30.00

LOUIS FORBSTEIN'S ROYAL SYNCOPATORS:
Okeh 40379 *Deep Elm* .... 25.00 - 40.00
40392 *Someday We'll Meet Again* .... 25.00 - 40.00
41417 *Down And Out Blues* .... 25.00 - 40.00

FORD AND FORD:
Paramount 12244 *I'm Three Times Seven* .... 100.00 - 125.00

**REGINALD FORESYTHE, THE NEW
MUSIC OF:**
Columbia 3012-D *Dodging A Divorcee* .... 15.00 - 20.00
3060-D *Melancholy Clown* .... 15.00 - 20.00

GENE FOSDICK'S HOOSIERS:
Vocalion 14496 *'Way Down Yonder In New
Orleans* ....   8.00 - 12.00
14503 *Apple Sauce* ....   5.00 - 10.00
14535 *Farewell Blues* ....   8.00 - 12.00
14585 *Railroad Man* ....   8.00 - 12.00

DEACON FOSTER & HIS BOYS:
Champion 15656 *Black And Blue Rhapsody* ..... 150.00 - 200.00

ISA FOSTER & HER MELODEARS:
Broadway 1499 *The Cute Little Things You Do* ..   8.00 - 12.00

**FOUR ACES AND THE JOKER (See
JABBO SMITH)**

**FOUR HAWAIIAN GUITARS: (See also:
Q.R.S. BOYS)**
Q.R.S. 1015 *Singin' In The Bathtub* .... 50.00 - 75.00

THE FOUR SPADES:
Columbia 14028-D *Squabblin' Blues* .... 20.00 - 30.00

**LEMUEL FOWLER; FOWLER'S FAVORITES/
WASHBOARD WONDERS:**
Columbia A-3959 *Blues Mixture* ....   8.00 - 12.00
14084-D *Chitterlin' Strut* .... 20.00 - 30.00
14096-D *Pig Foot Shuffle* .... 20.00 - 30.00
14101-D *Express Train Blues* .... 20.00 - 30.00
14111-D *Salty Dog* .... 20.00 - 30.00
14155-D *Jelly Roll Blues* .... 25.00 - 40.00
14230-D *Percolatin' Blues* .... 30.00 - 50.00

**WILLIAM FRANCIS AND RICHARD
SOWELL:**
Vocalion 1090 *John Henry Blues* .... 40.00 - 60.00

FRANCISCO ORCHESTRA:
Emerson 10587 *Dreary Weary Blues* ....   7.00 - 10.00

**ARNOLD FRANK & HIS (ROGERS CAFE)
ORCHESTRA:**
Okeh 40896 *Black Maria* ....   8.00 - 12.00
41086 *You're A Real Sweetheart* ....   8.00 - 12.00

FRANKIE & HER JAZZ DEVILS:

Pathe-Actuelle 7507 *Those Creeping Sneaking Blues*	40.00 -	60.00
Perfect 107 *Those Creeping Sneaking Blues*	40.00 -	60.00

FRANKIE AND JOHNNIE ORCHESTRA:

Bluebird 6470 *Swing Fever*	15.00 -	20.00
6499 *Stompin'*	15.00 -	20.00
6564 *I'm Looking For Someone To Love*	15.00 -	20.00
6760 *Frankie And Johnnie Swing*	15.00 -	20.00

FRANKIE FRANKO & HIS LOUISIANIANS:

Melotone 12009 *Somebody Stole My Gal*	80.00 -	120.00

EDDIE FRAZIER AND HIS PLANTATION ORCHESTRA:

Sunset 1100 *Cheatin' On Me*	20.00 -	30.00

JAKE FRAZIER:

Ajax 17117 *Jake's Weary Blues*	30.00 -	40.00

BUD FREEMAN & HIS ORCHESTRA:

Okeh 41168 *Craze-O-Logy*	20.00 -	30.00

JAY/JERRY FREEMAN AND HIS ORCHESTRA:

Titles, issued contemporaneously on Banner, Melotone, Oriole, Perfect, Romeo: *Alabama Barbecue; Copper-Colored Gal; Getting Away With Murder; I'm At The Mercy Of Love; Mr. Ghost Goes To Town; A Moment In The Dark; My Newest Excitement; That's What You Mean To Me*	5.00 -	10.00
Additional titles issued on Banner, Melotone, Oriole, Perfect, Romeo: *Sugar Foot Stomp; Night Ride*	7.00 -	12.00
Bluebird 5231, 5232, 5233	5.00 -	8.00
Variety 511 *Poor Robinson Crusoe*	8.00 -	12.00

FRENCHY'S STRING BAND:

Columbia 14387-D *Sunshine Special*	80.00 -	120.00

FRIARS SOCIETY ORCHESTRA:

Gennett 4966 *Farewell Blues*	15.00 -	25.00
4967 *Bugle Call Blues*	15.00 -	25.00
4968 *Panama*	15.00 -	20.00
5009 *Eccentric*	15.00 -	20.00

AL FRIEDMAN & HIS ORCHESTRA:

Cameo 1149 *Somebody Else*	7.00 -	10.00
Edison 52128 *My Blue Heaven*	5.00 -	8.00
52244 *Speedy Boy*	15.00 -	20.00
52342 *After I've Called You Sweetheart*	10.00 -	15.00
52352 *Flora*	7.00 -	10.00
52529 *Guess Who's In Town*	7.00 -	10.00
52560 *Broadway Melody*	20.00 -	30.00

BEN FRIEDMAN'S PARAMOUNT HOTEL ORCHESTRA:

Timely Tunes 1580 *The One-Man Band*	20.00 -	30.00
1583 *Some Of These Days*	20.00 -	30.00
1584 *Swamp Ghosts*	20.00 -	30.00
1588 *Roll On Mississippi, Roll On*	75.00 -	100.00

FRISCO "JASS" BAND; FRISCO JAZZ BAND:

Edison 50470 *Johnson "Jass" Blues*	7.00 -	12.00
(Note: Record number on above may be found on record's edge)		
Edison 50950 *That's It*	7.00 -	10.00
51081 *Yah-De-Dah*	7.00 -	10.00

FRISCO SYNCOPATORS:

Claxtonola 40244 *Buddy's Habits*	25.00 -	50.00
40264 *Arkansas Mule*	25.00 -	50.00
40291 *Forgetful Blues*	25.00 -	50.00
Puritan 11244 *Buddy's Habits*	25.00 -	50.00
11271 *Sweet Henry*	25.00 -	50.00
11291 *Forgetful Blues*	25.00 -	50.00
11330 *Back O' Town Blues*	10.00 -	15.00
Resona 11359 *Sioux City Sue*	10.00 -	15.00
Triangle 11270 *Sittin' In A Corner*	8.00 -	12.00
11384 *I Can't Get The One I Want*	10.00 -	15.00
11431 *Choo Choo*	7.00 -	10.00

FRANK FROEBA & HIS SWING BAND:

Columbia 3110-D *The Music Goes 'Round and Around*	10.00 -	15.00
3131-D *Just To Be In Caroline*	15.00 -	20.00
3151-D *Organ Grinder's Swing*	15.00 -	20.00
3152-D *It All Begins And Ends With You*	15.00 -	20.00

(CHARLIE) FRY & HIS MILLION DOLLAR PIER ORCHESTRA; FRY'S MILLION DOLLAR PIER ORCHESTRA:

Edison 51406 *Copenhagen*	5.00 -	8.00
Edison 51416 *Shanghai Shuffle*	5.00 -	8.00
Edison 51435 *Tessie (Stop Teasing Me)*	5.00 -	8.00
Edison 51469 *Gotta Getta Girl*	5.00 -	8.00
Edison 51471 *Dixie Dreams*	7.00 -	10.00
Edison 51474 *I Can't Stop Babying You*	8.00 -	12.00
Edison 51503 *No Wonder (That I Love You)*	5.00 -	8.00
Edison 51574 *Deep Elm*	7.00 -	10.00
Pathe-Actuelle 036122 *Where The Dreamy Wabash Flows*	7.00 -	10.00
Pathe-Actuelle (most other issues)	3.00 -	5.00
Perfect 14303 *Where The Dreamy Wabash Flows*	7.00 -	10.00
Perfect (most other issues)	3.00 -	5.00
Victor 20726, 21496, 21610	4.00 -	8.00

CHARLES FULCHER & HIS ORCHESTRA; FULCHER'S DANCE TRIO:

Columbia 316-D *The Georgia Stomp*	15.00 -	20.00
551-D *My Pretty Girl*	15.00 -	20.00
726-D *Blue Georgia Moon*	10.00 -	15.00
1267-D *After That*	10.00 -	15.00
1706-D *Hey! Hey!*	10.00 -	15.00
1734-D *Atlanta Gal*	10.00 -	15.00
Okeh 4889 *The Eskimo Song*	15.00 -	25.00

BOB FULLER:

Ajax 17088 *Crossword Puzzle Blues*	15.00 -	25.00
17091 *Spread Yo' Stuff*	15.00 -	25.00
17117 *Growin' Old Blues*	25.00 -	40.00
Banner 7151 *Alligator Crawl*	10.00 -	15.00
Brunswick 7006 *I Ain't Got Nobody*	20.00 -	30.00
Columbia 14068-D *Black Cat Blues*	10.00 -	15.00
14120-D *Grand Opera Blues*	15.00 -	25.00
Domino 0249 *Here 'Tis*	10.00 -	15.00
Harmony 580-H *Too Bad Jim*	7.00 -	10.00
688-H *Ridiculous Blues*	7.00 -	10.00
(Note: Above titles, on *Diva* and *Velvet Tone*, are similarly valued.)		
Regal 8589 *Fireworks*	10.00 -	15.00

EARL FULLER'S FAMOUS JAZZ BAND/ RECTOR NOVELTY ORCHESTRA:

Columbia A2298 *Twelfth Street Rag*	5.00 -	8.00
Columbia A2523 *Graveyard Blues*	5.00 -	8.00
Columbia (most other issues)	3.00 -	5.00
Edison 50505 *Jazzbo Jazz One Step*	7.00 -	10.00
Edison 50521 *I'm Sorry I Made You Cry*	7.00 -	10.00
Edison 50541 *Jazz de Luxe*	7.00 -	10.00
Emerson 952 *Jazz De Luxe*	10.00 -	15.00
Victor 18321 *Slippery Hank*	5.00 -	8.00
Victor 18369 *Beale Street Blues*	5.00 -	8.00
Victor 18394 *A Coon Band Contest*	5.00 -	8.00
Victor 18456 *Fuzzy Wuzzy Rag*	50.00 -	75.00

SLIM GAILLARD AND HIS FLAT FOOT FLOOGIE BOYS:

Okeh, most issues	4.00 -	8.00
Vocalion, most issues	4.00 -	8.00

ALBERT GALE AND HIS ORCHESTRA:

Vocalion 03514 *Horses and Numbers*	20.00 -	30.00

GALVESTON SERENADERS:

Champion 15266 *Twin Blues*	150.00 -	200.00
15285 *Monte Carlo Joys*	150.00 -	200.00

JAN GARBER & HIS (GREATER COLUMBIA RECORDING) ORCHESTRA:

Brunswick, most issues	3.00 -	6.00
Columbia 1306-D *Since My Best Gal Turned Me Down*	7.00 -	10.00

1334-D *Back In Your Own Back Yard*	7.00	-	10.00
1372-D *She's a Great, Great Girl*	7.00	-	10.00
1615-D *Louisiana*	7.00	-	10.00
1642-D *Tin Ear*	7.00	-	10.00
1823-D *'Way Down Yonder in New Orleans*	7.00	-	10.00
2115-D *Puttin' On The Ritz*	10.00	-	15.00
Columbia, most other issues	2.00	-	5.00
Decca, most issues	2.00	-	4.00
Okeh, most issues	2.00	-	3.00
Victor 19496 *If You Don't Want Me (Stop Doggin' Me 'Round*	5.00	-	8.00
Victor 20322 *How Could Red Riding Hood?*	15.00	-	20.00
24885 *Love and a Dime*	7.00	-	10.00
Victor, most other issues	4.00	-	7.00
Vocalion, most issues	3.00	-	6.00

LOUIS "KING" GARCIA AND HIS SWING BAND:

Bluebird 6302 *Love Is Like A Cigarette*	5.00	-	8.00
6303 *Christopher Columbus*	5.00	-	8.00
6357 *Swing, Mr. Charlie*	7.00	-	10.00

FRED GARDNER'S TEXAS UNIVERSITY TROUBADOURS:

Okeh 41440 *Papa's Gone*	25.00	-	40.00
41458 *No Trumps*	25.00	-	40.00

JACK GARDNER'S ORCHESTRA:

Okeh 40245 *Ponjola*	15.00	-	20.00
40465 *Too Late Now*	15.00	-	20.00
40339 *Who'd A Thunk It?*	25.00	-	35.00
40495 *Hitch Up The Horses*	30.00	-	40.00
40501 *Ida, I Do*	30.00	-	40.00
40518 *Hot Aire*	35.00	-	50.00
40555 *Japp-A-Jazz*	30.00	-	40.00
40572 *You'll Never Know The Difference*	30.00	-	40.00

JUDY GARLAND:

Decca 848 *Stompin' At The Savoy*	7.00	-	10.00
1432 *All God's Chillun Got Rhythm*	7.00	-	10.00
1463 *You Can't Have Everything*	7.00	-	10.00
1796 *Sleep, My Baby, Sleep*	5.00	-	8.00
Decca (blue label), most others	3.00	-	7.00

BLIND LEROY GARNETT:

Paramount 12879 *Louisiana Glide*	100.00	-	150.00

SID GARRY:

Melotone 12069 *At Last I'm Happy*	15.00	-	20.00

TOM GATES & HIS ORCHESTRA/TOM GATES ORCHESTRA:

Champion 15305 *The Bucket's Got A Hole In It*	60.00	-	90.00
15307 *Wabash Blues*	60.00	-	90.00
Gennett 6184 *The Bucket's Got A Hole In It*	75.00	-	100.00
6198 *Wabash Blues*	75.00	-	100.00

CARL GAY & HIS ORCHESTRA:

Tremont 436 *Limehouse Blues*	8.00	-	12.00

GLORIA GEER:

Banner 1530 *When My Sugar Walks Down The Street*	5.00	-	8.00
Cameo 761 *Yes Sir, That's My Baby*	4.00	-	7.00
Cameo 804 *Alone At Last*	4.00	-	7.00
Cameo 845 *Clap Hands! Here Comes Charlie!*	4.00	-	7.00
Cameo 963 *Bye Bye Blackbird*	4.00	-	7.00
Regal 8901 *He's So Unusual*	5.00	-	8.00

HENRI GENDRON & HIS STRAND ROOF ORCHESTRA:

Banner 1490 *Prince Of Wails*	15.00	-	20.00
Edison 51494 *Me Neenyah (My Little One)*	7.00	-	10.00

GENE & HIS GLORIANS:

Timely Tunes 1575 *Lazy River*	15.00	-	20.00
1579 *Left My Gal In The Mountains*	15.00	-	20.00
1581 *Georgia On My Mind*	15.00	-	20.00
1582 *Jig Time*	15.00	-	20.00

AL GENTILE & HIS ORCHESTRA:

Gennett 3379 *Blowin' The Blues Away*	20.00	-	30.00
Gennett 6055 *A Tree In The Park*	20.00	-	30.00

GEORGIA COTTON PICKERS:

Diva 6064-G *Cotton Pickers' Shuffle*	15.00	-	20.00
Harmony 1090-H *Cotton Pickers' Shuffle*	15.00	-	20.00
1127-H *Louisiana Bo Bo*	15.00	-	20.00

GEORGIA JUMPERS:

Columbia 14603-D *California Blues*	50.00	-	75.00
14620-D *The Big Feet Rag*	50.00	-	75.00

GEORGIA MELODIANS:

Edison 51336 *Wop Blues*	10.00	-	15.00
51338 *Wait'll You See My Gal*	8.00	-	12.00
51346 *Savannah*	10.00	-	15.00
51347 *Tea Pot Dome Blues*	10.00	-	15.00
51359 *How You Gonna Keep Kool?*	10.00	-	15.00
51378 *Why Did You Do It?*	7.00	-	12.00
51394 *Red Hot Mama*	10.00	-	15.00
51412 *San*	10.00	-	15.00
51419 *Everybody Loves My Baby*	10.00	-	15.00
51420 *Do Wacka Doo*	8.00	-	12.00
51425 *I'm Satisfied Beside That Sweetie O'Mine*	7.00	-	12.00
51437 *I'm Bound For Tennessee*	10.00	-	15.00
51438 *My Mammy's Blues*	20.00	-	30.00
51588 *Give Us The Charleston*	10.00	-	20.00
51598 *She's Drivin' Me Wild*	15.00	-	25.00
51678 *Charleston Ball*	15.00	-	20.00
51730 *Rhythm Of The Day*	15.00	-	20.00

THE GEORGIANS:

Cameo 8111 *Without You Sweetheart*	5.00	-	8.00
Columbia 11-D *Learn To Do The Strut*	7.00	-	10.00
Columbia 23-D *Home Town Blues*	7.00	-	10.00
Columbia 30-D *Shake Your Feet*	7.00	-	10.00
Columbia 40-D *I've Got a Cross-Eyes Papa*	7.00	-	10.00
Columbia 62-D *Dancin' Dan*	7.00	-	10.00
Columbia 70-D *Hula Lou*	7.00	-	10.00
Columbia 142-D *Savannah*	7.00	-	10.00
Columbia 252-D *Everybody Loves My Baby*	7.00	-	10.00
Columbia 407-D *Charleston Baby O'Mine*	10.00	-	15.00
Columbia 523-D *Spanish Shawl*	8.00	-	12.00
Columbia 634-D *Spring Is Here*	8.00	-	12.00
Columbia 923-D *'Frisco Bay*	8.00	-	12.00
Columbia A3775 *Chicago (That Toddlin' Town)*	5.00	-	8.00
Columbia A3804 *'Way Down Yonder in New Orleans*	7.00	-	10.00
Columbia A3825 *Aggravatin' Papa*	7.00	-	10.00
Columbia A3857 *You Tell Her—I Stutter*	5.00	-	8.00
Columbia A3864 *Farewell Blues*	5.00	-	8.00
Columbia A3902 *Barney Google*	7.00	-	10.00
Columbia A3907 *Henpecked Blues*	5.00	-	8.00
Columbia A3987 *Land of Cotton Blues*	7.00	-	10.00
Columbia A3996 *Mama Goes Where Papa Goes*	7.00	-	10.00
Harmony 776-H *Glorianna*	8.00	-	12.00
Harmony 1005-H *You Want Lovin' (But I Want Love)*	7.00	-	10.00
Harmony 1008-H *When You're Counting the Stars Alone*	5.00	-	8.00
Harmony 1010-H *A Year From Today*	5.00	-	8.00
Harmony 1023-H *Georgia Pines*	5.00	-	8.00
Harmony 1034-H *If I Had a Talking Picture of You*	5.00	-	8.00
Harmony 1062-H *Can't We Be Friends?*	7.00	-	10.00
Harmony 1063-H *Singin' in the Bathtub*	8.00	-	12.00

(Note: Above titles on Harmony were also issued on *Diva* and *Velvet Tone*; these are similarly valued.)

GEORGIA STRUTTERS:

Harmony 231-H *Georgia Grind*	15.00	-	20.00
311-H *Original Black Bottom Dance*	15.00	-	20.00
468-H *It's Right Here For You*	30.00	-	50.00

GEORGIA WASHBOARD STOMPERS:

Bluebird 5027 *Wake 'Em Up*	10.00	-	15.00
5088 *Happy As The Day Is Long*	10.00	-	15.00
5089 *My Pretty Girl*	10.00	-	15.00
5092 *Bug A-Boo*	10.00	-	15.00

5127 *Dinah*	10.00 -	15.00
Decca 7002 *Everybody Loves My Baby*	10.00 -	15.00
7004 *I Can't Dance (I Got Ants In My Pants)*	10.00 -	15.00
7005 *Limehouse Blues*	10.00 -	15.00
7006 *After You've Gone*	10.00 -	15.00
7094 *You're An Angel*	10.00 -	15.00
7095 *Lulu's Back In Town*	10.00 -	15.00
7096 *Every Little Moment*	10.00 -	15.00
7097 *The Lady In Red*	10.00 -	15.00

GEORGE GERSHWIN:

Columbia 809-D, 812-D	5.00 -	8.00
Victor 35833 *Rhapsody In Blue (12-inch)*	5.00 -	10.00

TOM GERUN/GERUNOVITCH & HIS (ROOF GARDEN) ORCHESTRA:

Brunswick 4050 *My Gal Sal*	10.00 -	15.00
4115 *I Gotta Tell Someone*	5.00 -	8.00
4430 *The Boogie Man Is Here*	5.00 -	8.00
4727 *Sing, You Sinners*	7.00 -	10.00
4755 *Atta Boy*	7.00 -	10.00
Brunswick (most other issues)	4.00 -	8.00

THE GET-HAPPY BAND:

Columbia 14091-D *Harlem's Araby*	75.00 -	100.00
14099-D *Puddin' Pappa*	75.00 -	100.00

IRENE GIBBONS (& JAZZ BAND); IRENE GIBBONS & CLARENCE WILLIAMS' JAZZ BAND:

Columbia A-3834, A-3922	5.00 -	10.00
14296-D *Longing*	20.00 -	30.00
14362-D *I'm Busy And You Can't Come In*	50.00 -	75.00

ARTHUR GIBBS & HIS GANG:

Victor 19070 *Beale Street Mama*	5.00 -	8.00
19165 *Charleston*	5.00 -	8.00

CLEO GIBSON:

Okeh 8700 *Nothing But Blues*	30.00 -	50.00

GENE GIFFORD & HIS ORCHESTRA:

Victor 25041, 25065	6.00 -	10.00

EMERSON GILL & HIS (BAMBOO GARDEN/ CASTLE OF PARIS) ORCHESTRA:

Columbia 1355-D, 1396-D, 1408-D	5.00 -	10.00
2416-D *I've Got Five Dollars*	7.00 -	10.00
Okeh 40065 *On Saturday Night*	10.00 -	15.00
40066 *Days Of Yesterday*	10.00 -	15.00
40313 *My Name Will Always Be Chickie*	15.00 -	25.00
40315 *That's My Gal*	15.00 -	25.00
40369 *Birmingham Bound*	20.00 -	30.00
40577 *It Must Be Love*	15.00 -	20.00
40590 *Say It Again*	15.00 -	20.00
40594 *The Rhythm Rag*	25.00 -	40.00
40615 *Lo-Nah*	15.00 -	20.00

ART GILLHAM:

Columbia 2265-D, 2291-D, 2331-D	5.00 -	10.00

MAX GILMORE AND HIS BOYS:

Superior 2565 *I'll Sing A Love Song*	10.00 -	20.00

JOSEPH GISH AND HIS ORCHESTRA:

New Flexo 311 *Milenberg Joys*	100.00 -	Up

PERCY GLASCOE:

Columbia 14088-D *Stomp 'Em Down*	20.00 -	30.00

JACK GLASSNER AND HIS COLONIAL INN ORCHESTRA:

Okeh 40559 *Hot Coffee*	7.00 -	10.00
40644 *Tonight's My Night With Baby*	7.00 -	10.00

AL GOERING'S COLLEGIANS:

Banner 1693 *Up And At 'Em*	7.00 -	10.00
Banner 7001 *Once Over Lightly*	5.00 -	8.00
Banner 7004 *Candied Sweets*	5.00 -	8.00
Banner 7005 *Steppin' It Off*	5.00 -	8.00
Domino 3666 *Up And At 'Em*	7.00 -	10.00
Vocalion 15337 *What Was I To Do?*	5.00 -	8.00
15374 *Hard-To-Get Gertie*	7.00 -	10.00
15409 *Baby Face*	5.00 -	8.00
15495 *Hello! Swanee, Hello!*	5.00 -	8.00

LOU GOLD & HIS ORCHESTRA:

Banner 1544 *Everything Is Hotsy Totsy Now*	10.00 -	15.00
Banner 1636 *Roll 'Em, Girls*	5.00 -	8.00
Banner 1640 *No Man's Mama*	5.00 -	8.00
Banner 6209 *When Polly Walks Through the Hollyhocks*	5.00 -	8.00
Cameo 713 *Love Light Lane*	5.00 -	8.00
Cameo 759 *Say Arabella*	5.00 -	8.00
Cameo 799 *When You See That Aunt Of Mine*	5.00 -	8.00
Cameo 800 *Let's Wander Away*	5.00 -	8.00
Cameo 815 *Better Get Acquainted*	5.00 -	8.00
Cameo 847 *Nobody's Business*	5.00 -	8.00
Cameo 860 *Keep Your Skirts Down, Mary Ann*	5.00 -	8.00
Cameo 883 *I'd Rather Be Alone*	5.00 -	8.00
Cameo 898 *Say Mister! Have You Met Rosie's Sister?*	5.00 -	8.00
Cameo 1260 *Go Home and Tell Your Mother*	10.00 -	15.00
Cameo (most other issues)	3.00 -	6.00
Domino 3634 *What Did I Tell Ya*	5.00 -	8.00
Domino 4229 *When Polly Walks Through the Hollyhocks*	5.00 -	8.00
Harmony 95-H *Let Me Introduce You To My Rosie*	5.00 -	8.00
Harmony 98-H *Sweet and Low-Down*	5.00 -	8.00
Harmony 616-H *Luscious*	5.00 -	8.00
Harmony 635-H *That's My Mammy*	5.00 -	8.00
Harmony 659-H *Is It Gonna Be Long? (Till You Belong To Me)*	5.00 -	8.00
Harmony 660-H *I Can't Give You Anything But Love*	5.00 -	8.00
Harmony 669-H *I Must Be Dreaming*	7.00 -	10.00
Harmony 698-H *Skadatin-Dee*	5.00 -	8.00
Harmony 702-H *If You Want the Rainbow*	5.00 -	8.00
Harmony 732-H *Come On, Baby!*	5.00 -	8.00
Harmony 745-H *My Blackbirds Are Bluebirds Now*	5.00 -	8.00
Harmony 770-H *You're the Cream In My Coffee*	5.00 -	8.00
Harmony 851-H *It's Tight Like That*	7.00 -	10.00
Harmony 891-H *In Old Tia Juana*	5.00 -	8.00
Harmony 920-H *Walking With Susie*	7.00 -	10.00
Harmony 950-H *He's a Good Man To Have Around*	5.00 -	8.00
Harmony 976-H *Lovable and Sweet*	5.00 -	8.00
Harmony 977-H *Moanin' Low*	5.00 -	8.00
Harmony 1000-H *Hang On To Me*	5.00 -	8.00
Harmony 1001-H *Lonesome Little Doll*	5.00 -	8.00
1052-H *Piccolo Pete*	5.00 -	8.00
(Note: Above titles on Harmony are also found on *Diva* and *Velvet Tone*, similarly valued.)		
Lincoln 2352 *Who's Loving My Sweetie Now?*	5.00 -	8.00
Oriole 2007 *Nobody Cares If I'm Blue*	7.00 -	10.00
Pathe-Actuelle 36349 *Roll 'Em, Girls*	7.00 -	10.00
36353 *Who*	7.00 -	10.00
Perfect 14414 *If You Knew Suzie (sic)*	5.00 -	8.00
Perfect 14468 *Speech*	7.00 -	10.00
Perfect 14469 *Let's Wander Away*	7.00 -	10.00
Perfect 14476 *I'm Gonna Charleston Back To Charleston*	5.00 -	8.00
Perfect 14503 *I Wonder Where My Baby Is Tonight?*	5.00 -	8.00
14530 *Roll 'Em, Girls*	7.00 -	10.00
Perfect 14534 *Who*	7.00 -	10.00
Perfect 14542 *Someone's Stolen My Sweet, Sweet Baby*	5.00 -	8.00
Perfect 14550 *I Want Someone To Cheer Me Up*	5.00 -	8.00
Perfect 14584 *I've Found A New Baby*	7.00 -	10.00
Perfect 14797 *South Wind*	5.00 -	8.00
Perfect 14906 *Mary (What Are You Waiting For?)*	8.00 -	12.00
Perfect 14907 *What'll You Do?*	8.00 -	12.00
Perfect 14914 *Who Gives You All Your Kisses?*	8.00 -	12.00
Perfect 14932 *You Gotta Be Good To Me*	8.00 -	12.00
Perfect 14933 *In the Sing Song Sycamore Tree*	8.00 -	12.00
Perfect 14940 *After My Laughter Came Tears*	8.00 -	12.00

Perfect 14942 *Losin' You*	8.00	12.00
Regal 10118 *Am I To Blame?*	5.00	8.00
Regal 10153 *Loving You the Way I Do*	5.00	8.00
Regal (most other issues)	3.00	6.00
Romeo (most issues)	3.00	6.00

ERNIE GOLDEN & HIS (HOTEL McALPIN) ORCHESTRA:

Banner 0758 *Dirty Hot*	8.00	12.00
6226 *Doin' The Raccoon*	5.00	8.00
6227 *Come On, Baby*	5.00	8.00
7244 *My Blackbirds Are Bluebirds Now*	5.00	8.00
Brunswick 2999, 3302, 3359	4.00	8.00
Cameo 0358 *Dirty Hot*	8.00	12.00
Champion 16661 *Dirty Hot*	100.00	150.00
Edison 51658 *Sleepy Time Gal*	8.00	12.00
51944 *Oriental Moonlight*	15.00	20.00
52109 *The Varsity Drag*	20.00	30.00

GOLDEN GATE (DANCE) ORCHESTRA:
(See comments on CALIFORNIA RAMBLERS)

Banner 0663 *She's Nobody's Fool*	5.00	8.00
Banner 0664 *If You Were All My Own*	5.00	8.00
Banner 0666 *Wouldn't It Be Wonderful, Baby?*	5.00	8.00
Banner 1409 *I'm Satisfied Beside That Sweetie of Mine*	5.00	8.00
Banner 1413 *Look-a What I Got Now*	5.00	8.00
Banner 1459 *Nobody Knows What a Red Head Mama Can Do*	5.00	8.00
Banner 1472 *Oh! Mabel*	5.00	8.00
Banner 1474 *Blue Eyed Sally*	5.00	8.00
Banner 1500 *I Ain't Got Nobody To Love*	5.00	8.00
Banner 1502 *My Gal Don't Love Me Anymore*	5.00	8.00
Banner 1566 *Oh Say! Can I See You Tonight*	5.00	8.00
Banner 1568 *Say Arabella*	5.00	8.00
Banner 1569 *I Miss My Swiss*	5.00	8.00
Banner 1623 *She Was Just a Sailor's Sweetheart*	5.00	8.00
Banner 1999 *Magnolia*	7.00	10.00
6007 *Zulu Wail*	7.00	10.00
6048 *Beale Street Blues*	10.00	15.00
6049 *Delirium*	10.00	15.00
6050 *Someday, Sweetheart*	10.00	15.00
6082 *Jelly Roll Blues*	10.00	15.00
Broadway 11404 *Manda*	30.00	40.00
Cameo 0266 *Wouldn't It Be Wonderful, Baby*	5.00	8.00
Cameo 0269 *She's Nobody's Fool*	5.00	8.00
Domino 3535 *I Miss My Swiss*	5.00	8.00
Domino 3973 *Zulu Wail*	7.00	10.00
3990 *Vo-Do-Do-Deo-O Blues*	8.00	12.00
4011 *Beale Street Blues*	10.00	15.00
4014 *Delirium*	10.00	15.00
4027 *I Ain't Got Nobody*	10.00	15.00
4039 *Jelly Roll Blues*	10.00	15.00
Edison 51387 *Sing A Little Song*	10.00	15.00
51388 *Lucille*	10.00	15.00
51443 *Southern Rose*	10.00	15.00
51491 *Oh! Mabel*	15.00	20.00
51538 *On The Oregon Trail*	15.00	20.00
51542 *Charleston*	15.00	20.00
51551 *Everything Is Hosty-Totsy Now*	15.00	20.00
51562 *Cheatin' On Me*	15.00	20.00
51580 *Collegiate*	10.00	15.00
51590 *Manhattan*	15.00	20.00
51591 *Look Who's Here*	15.00	20.00
51622 *Sweet Man*	15.00	20.00
51633 *Freshie*	10.00	15.00
51661 *Five Foot Two, Eyes Of Blue*	15.00	20.00
51725 *Here Comes Malinda*	20.00	30.00
51737 *Shake*	20.00	30.00
51746 *Static Strut*	20.00	30.00
51762 *Hard-To-Get Gertie*	20.00	30.00
51768 *I Wonder What's Become Of Joe?*	20.00	30.00
51797 *To Be With You*	15.00	20.00
51799 *When The Red Red Robin Comes Bob,*		

Bob Bobbin' Along	15.00	20.00
51814 *Looking At The World Thru Rose Colored Glasses*	15.00	20.00
51820 *Up And At 'Em*	20.00	30.00
51822 *How Many Times?*	15.00	20.00
51824 *You Need Someone To Love*	15.00	20.00
51851 *Lay Me Down To Sleep In Carolina*	15.00	20.00
51860 *Pretty Cinderella*	15.00	20.00
51862 *All Alone Monday*	15.00	20.00
51897 *Stockholm Stomp*	25.00	40.00
51960 *Lonely Eyes*	15.00	20.00
51970 *Look At The World And Smile*	15.00	20.00
51975 *Crazy Words—Crazy Tune*	15.00	20.00
52014 *Yes She Do—No She Don't*	20.00	30.00
52043 *Beedle-Um Bo*	20.00	30.00
52075 *Miss Annabelle Lee*	20.00	30.00
52097 *You Don't Like It—Not Much*	20.00	30.00
52101 *Dawning*	20.00	30.00
51205 *Blue River*	20.00	30.00
52109 *Clementine*	20.00	30.00
52162 *Tell Me, Little Daisy*	15.00	20.00
Edison 52164 *Make My Cot Where The Cot-Cot-Cotton Grows*	20.00	30.00
52181 *The Pay Off*	20.00	30.00
52206 *Third Rail*	25.00	40.00
52366 *Dream House*	7.00	10.00
52390 *Vaniteaser*	25.00	40.00
52399 *'Cause I Feel Low Down*	30.00	40.00
52416 *Get Out And Get Under The Moon*	25.00	40.00
52437 *There's A Rainbow 'Round My Shoulder*	25.00	35.00
52444 *You're The Cream In My Coffee*	30.00	40.00
52477 *Along Came Sweetness*	25.00	35.00
52480 *To Know You Is To Love You*	10.00	15.00
52486 *Glad Rag Doll*	15.00	20.00
52506 *Sweethearts On Parade*	25.00	35.00
52513 *Button Up Your Overcoat*	30.00	40.00
52515 *I Loved You Then*	10.00	15.00
52535 *Guess Who?*	15.00	20.00
52542 *When I'm Walking With My Sweetness*	25.00	40.00
52547 *A Precious Little Thing Called Love*	25.00	40.00
52550 *My Suppressed Desire*	25.00	35.00
52553 *The One I Love Loves Me*	10.00	15.00
52561 *Avalon Town*	20.00	30.00
52562 *Lover Come Back*	20.00	30.00
52568 *That's Living*	25.00	35.00
52580 *Honey*	25.00	35.00
52590 *Huggable, Kissable You*	25.00	35.00
Harmony 719-H *Vaniteaser*	7.00	10.00
Harmony 760-H *My Old Girl's My New Girl Now*	7.00	10.00
Harmony 778-H *Me And The Man in the Moon*	7.00	10.00
Harmony 816-H *My Troubles Are Over*	7.00	10.00
Harmony 839-H *Weary River*	5.00	8.00
Harmony 840-H *I'd Rather Be Blue Over You*	7.00	10.00
Harmony 923-H *Croonin' a Tune About June*	7.00	10.00
Harmony 938-H *Am I Blue?*	5.00	8.00
Harmony 947-H *Painting the Clouds With Sunshine*	5.00	8.00
Harmony 958-H *Song of the Blues*	7.00	10.00
Harmoony 962-H *Why Can't You*	7.00	10.00
Harmony 973-H *The Flippity Flop*	7.00	10.00
Harmony 984-H *Just You, Just Me*	5.00	8.00
Harmony 1015-H *Love Ain't Nothin' But the Blues*	5.00	8.00
Harmony 1041-H *Blondy*	8.00	12.00

(Note: Above titles on Harmony also occur on *Diva* and *Velvet Tone*, and are similarly valued.)

Paramount 20349, 20352, 20353, 20380, 20389, 20394, 20395, 20405	5.00	10.00
Pathe-Actuelle 036095, 036121, 036128, 036130, 036167, 036260, 036266, 036283, 36304,		

36307, 36315, 36318, 36319, 36361, 36441,
36497, 36509, 36540, 36543, 36554, 36590,
36613, 36650, 36656, 36693, 36711, 36716,
36719 .... 5.00 - 10.00
36707 *Goin' Home Again Blues* .... 15.00 - 20.00
Pathe-Actuelle 36724 *For My Baby* .... 75.00 - 100.00
Perfect 14275, 14302, 14309, 14311, 14348, 14386,
14412, 14416, 14441, 14457, 14464, 14485,
14488, 14496, 14499, 14500, 14542, 14622,
14678, 14690, 14691, 14721, 14724, ,14735,
14771, 14773, 14794, 14831, 14834, 14874,
14897 .... 5.00 - 10.00
Perfect 14888 *Goin' Home Again Blues* .... 15.00 - 20.00
14905 *For My Baby* .... 75.00 - 100.00
Regal 8334 *Zulu Wail* .... 7.00 - 10.00
8377 *Someday, Sweetheart* .... 10.00 - 15.00
8413 *Jelly Roll Blues* .... 10.00 - 15.00
9970 *She Was Just A Sailor's Sweetheart* ..... 7.00 - 10.00
Puritan 11285, 11352, 11353, 11380, 11389, 11394,
11395, 11405 .... 5.00 - 10.00
Triangle 11421 *Tessie, Stop Teasing Me* .... 7.00 - 10.00
11462 *The Only, Only One* .... 7.00 - 10.00
Velvet Tone 2394-V *I'd Be Lying* .... 7.00 - 10.00

GOLDEN GATE SERENADERS:
Gennett 6487 *On! Baby* .... 10.00 - 15.00
6488 *He's Worth His Weight In Gold* .... 8.00 - 12.00

JEAN GOLDKETTE & HIS (BOOK-CADILLAC) ORCHESTRA:
Victor 19308 *Where The Lazy Daisies Grow* .... 5.00 - 8.00
Victor 19313 *My Sweetheart* .... 5.00 - 8.00
Victor 19317 *Cover Me Up With the Sunshine of
Virginia* .... 5.00 - 8.00
Victor 19327 *Eileen* .... 5.00 - 8.00
Victor 19345 *Fox Trot Classique* .... 5.00 - 8.00
Victor 19548 *I Want To See My Tennessee* ...... 5.00 - 8.00
Victor 19600 *It's The Blues (No. 14 Blues)* ...... 5.00 - 8.00
Victor 19664 *Play Me Slow* .... 5.00 - 8.00
Victor 19947 *After I Say I'm Sorry* .... 5.00 - 8.00
Victor 19965 *Behind The Clouds* .... 5.00 - 8.00
Victor 19975 *Drifting Apart* .... 5.00 - 8.00
Victor 20033 *Roses* .... 5.00 - 8.00
Victor 20031, 20256, 20257, 20268, 21527, 21689,
21871 .... 3.00 - 6.00
Victor 20270 *Idolizing* .... 5.00 - 8.00
20273 *Sunday* .... 5.00 - 8.00
20300 *Just One More Kiss* .... 7.00 - 10.00
20466 *I'm Looking Over a Four Leaf Clover* .. 7.00 - 10.00
20469 *Proud of a Baby Like You* .... 35.00 - 50.00
20471 *Hoosier Sweetheart* .... 5.00 - 8.00
20472 *Look At The World and Smile* .... 5.00 - 8.00
20491 *A Lane in Spain* .... 5.00 - 8.00
20493 *Sunny Disposish* .... 8.00 - 12.00
20588 *My Pretty Girl* .... 7.00 - 10.00
20675 *I'm Gonna Meet My Sweetie Now* .... 5.00 - 8.00
20926 *Slow River* .... 5.00 - 8.00
20961 *Blue River* .... 5.00 - 8.00
20994 *Clementine* .... 5.00 - 8.00
Victor 21150 *Just a Little Kiss From a Little Miss* .. 7.00 - 10.00
Victor 21166 *My Ohio Home* .... 5.00 - 8.00
Victor 21565 *Just Imagine* .... 5.00 - 8.00
Victor 21590 *That's Just My Way of Forgetting
You* .... 5.00 - 8.00
Victor 21800 *That's What Puts the "Sweet" in
Home, Sweet Home* .... 5.00 - 8.00
Victor 21804 *Withered Roses* .... 5.00 - 8.00
Victor 21805 *My Blackbirds Are Bluebirds Now* . 7.00 - 10.00
Victor 21853 *She's Funny That Way* .... 5.00 - 8.00
Victor 21889 *Take a Good Look At Mine* ...... 7.00 - 10.00
Victor 22027 *Painting the Clouds with Sunshine* . 5.00 - 8.00
Victor 22077 *Birmingham Bertha* .... 7.00 - 10.00
Victor 22123 *An Old Italian Love Song* .... 5.00 - 8.00
Victor 25354 *Slow River* .... 7.00 - 10.00

Victor (unnumbered) *In My Merry Oldsmobile* .. 100.00 - Up
(Note: Above is a special pressing, designated
"SPECIAL RECORD for private use only,"
having the tune rendered as a fox-trot on one
side, as a waltz on the flip side.)

BENNY GOODMAN: BENNY (BENNIE) GOODMAN'S BOYS (WITH JIM AND GLENN); BENNY GOODMAN AND HIS (MUSIC HALL) ORCHESTRA:
Brunswick 3975 *Shirt Tail Stomp* .... 10.00 - 15.00
4013 *Jungle Blues* .... 10.00 - 15.00
4968 *After A While* .... 15.00 - 20.00
7644 *Bugle Call Rag* .... 4.00 - 6.00
Capitol, most issues .... 2.00 - 4.00
Columbia 2542-D *Not That I Care* .... 15.00 - 25.00
2835-D *Ain'tcha Glad?* .... 15.00 - 25.00
2845-D *Dr. Heckle and Mr. Jibe* .... 15.00 - 25.00
2856-D *Your Mother's Son-in-Law* .... 15.00 - 25.00
2687-D *Riffin' The Scotch* .... 15.00 - 25.00
2871-D *Love Me Or Leave Me* .... 15.00 - 25.00
2892-D *Junk man* .... 15.00 - 25.00
2927-D *Breakfast Ball* .... 15.00 - 25.00
2947-D *Take My Word* .... 15.00 - 25.00
2958-D *Bugle Call Rag* .... 15.00 - 20.00
2988-D *Like A Bolt From The Blue* .... 15.00 - 20.00
3003-D *Blue Moon* .... 15.00 - 20.00
3011-D *Music Hall Rag* .... 15.00 - 20.00
3015-D *Night Wind* .... 15.00 - 20.00
3018-D *Singing A Happy Song* .... 15.00 - 20.00
3022-D *Down Home Rag* .... 15.00 - 20.00
Columbia 35201, 35210, 35211, 35230, 35241,
35254, 35289, 35308, 35313, 35331, 35374,
35391, 35396, 35420, 35461, 35472, 35487 ... 4.00 - 7.00
Columbia, most others on red label .... 3.00 - 5.00
Melotone 12023 *He's Not Worth Your Tears* ..... 15.00 - 20.00
12024 *Overnight* .... 15.00 - 20.00
12079 *Falling In Love Again* .... 15.00 - 20.00
12100 *99 Out Of A Hundred Wanna Be Loved* .. 15.00 - 20.00
12120 *We Can Live On Love* .... 15.00 - 20.00
12138 *I Wanna Be Around My Baby All The
Time* .... 15.00 - 20.00
12149 *It Looks Like Love* .... 15.00 - 20.00
12205 *Slow But Sure* .... 15.00 - 20.00
12208 *Pardon Me, Pretty Baby* .... 15.00 - 20.00
Victor 25009 *Hunkadola* .... 8.00 - 12.00
25011 *Hooray For Love* .... 8.00 - 12.00
25021 *Restless* .... 8.00 - 12.00
25024 *Japanese Sandman* .... 7.00 - 10.00
25081 *Ballad In Blue* .... 7.00 - 10.00
25090 *King Porter* .... 5.00 - 8.00
Victor 25115, 25136, 25145 .... 4.00 - 8.00
Victor 25193 *No Other One* .... 7.00 - 10.00
25195 *Eeeny Meeny Miney Mo* .... 7.00 - 10.00
Victor 25215, 25245, 25247, 25258 .... 4.00 - 8.00
Victor 25263 *Madhouse* .... 7.00 - 10.00
Victor 25279, 25290, 25316, 25320, 25329,
25333, ... 4.00 - 8.00
Victor 25340 *Sing Me A Swing Song* .... 5.00 - 8.00
25345, *Nobody's Sweetheart* .... 4.00 - 8.00
25350 *House Hop* .... 7.00 - 10.00
Victor 25351, 25355, 25363, 25387, 25391,
25398, 25406, 25411, 25434, 25445 .... 4.00 - 8.00
25461 *Goodnight My Love (vocal Ella
Fitzgerald)/Take Another Guess (vocal, Ella
Fitzgerald)* .... 15.00 - 20.00
25461 *Goodnight My Love (vocal, Frances
Hunt)/Tain't No Use* .... 10.00 - 15.00
25469 *Did You Mean It?/Tain't No Use* .... 15.00 - 20.00
Victor 25467, 25473, 25481, 25497 .... 3.00 - 6.00
Victor 25486 *Smoke Dreams* .... 7.00 - 10.00
25492 *Swing Low, Sweet Chariot* .... 7.00 - 10.00
Victor 25500, 25505, 25510, 25521, 25529,

25531,	3.00 -	6.00
Victor 25621, 25627, 25634	4.00 -	7.00
Victor 25644, 26660, 25678, 25683, 25705,		
25708, 25711, 25717, 25720, 25720, 25725,		
25726, 25727, 25751	3.00 -	6.00

(Note: The foregoing, up to number 25683, if original pressings, are of the "scroll" label or scroll label "Swing Classic" label.)

Victor 25808 *Pop-Corn Man/BOOM-BOOM*	250.00 -	Up

(Note: The rare coupling above should be distinguished from the common issue, below, which does not have the song "Pop-Corn Man".)

Victor 25808 *Always and Always/oooOO-Oh-Boom!*	4.00 -	6.00
Victor 25814, 25822, 25827	3.00 -	5.00
Victor 25840 *Feelin' High and Happy*	5.00 -	8.00
25846 *It's The Dreamer In Me*	5.00 -	8.00
25867 *Don't Wake Up My Heart*	5.00 -	8.00
Victor 25871, 25880	3.00 -	6.00
Victor 25878 *What Goes On Here In My Heart*	5.00 -	8.00
26000 *I've Got a Date With A Dream*	5.00 -	8.00
26021 *When I Go A Dreamin'*	5.00 -	8.00
Victor 26044, 26060	3.00 -	5.00
Victor 26053 *You're Lovely, Madame*	5.00 -	8.00
26071 *I Have Eyes*	5.00 -	8.00
26082 *I Had To Do It*	5.00 -	8.00
Victor 26087, 26090, 26095	3.00 -	5.00
Victor 26099 *Sing For Your Supper*	5.00 -	8.00
26107 *Smoke House Rhythm*	4.00 -	7.00
26110 *I Must See Annie Tonight*	4.00 -	7.00
Victor 26125, 25130, 26134, 26139, 26166,		
26170, 26230, 26240, 26263	3.00 -	5.00
Victor 26159 *Good For Nothin' But Love*	5.00 -	8.00
26175 *Cuckoo in the Clock*	5.00 -	8.00
26187 *Estrellita*	4.00 -	7.00
26211 *The Lady's In Love With You*	4.00 -	7.00
Vocalion 15656 *A Jazz Holiday*	150.00 -	200.00
Vocalion 15795 *That's A Plenty*	150.00 -	200.00

LILLIAN GOODNER:

Ajax 17018 *Ramblin' Blues*	20.00 -	30.00
17020 *Chicago Blues*	20.00 -	30.00
17028 *Four-Flushin' Papa*	20.00 -	30.00

GOODY'S GOOD TIMERS:

Pathe-Actuelle 36902 *Diga Diga Doo*	10.00 -	15.00
36924 *'Cause I'm In Love*	10.00 -	15.00
Perfect 15083 *Diga Diga Doo*	10.00 -	15.00
15105 *'Cause I'm In Love*	10.00 -	15.00

THE GOOFUS FIVE (AND THEIR ORCHESTRA):

Okeh 40179 *Them Ramblin' Blues*	7.00 -	10.00
40208 *Go, Emmaline*	7.00 -	10.00
40233 *Go ' Long, Mule*	7.00 -	10.00
40244 *Everybody Loves My Baby*	8.00 -	12.00
40261 *Oh! Mabel*	7.00 -	10.00
40292 *Alabamy Bound*	8.00 -	12.00
40314 *Hot Tamale Molly*	10.00 -	15.00
40340 *I Had Someone Else Before I Had You*	8.00 -	12.00
40423 *Yes, Sir! That's My Baby*	10.00 -	15.00
40442 *I'm Gonna Charleston Back To Charleston*	15.00 -	20.00
40464 *Loud Speakin' Papa*	10.00 -	15.00
40500 *Clap Hands! Here Comes Charlie*	8.00 -	12.00
40534 *That Certain Party*	8.00 -	12.00
40624 *I Wonder What's Become of Joe?*	10.00 -	15.00
40644 *You Gotta Know How To Love*	10.00 -	15.00
40649 *Where'd You Get Those Eyes*	10.00 -	15.00
40661 *Mary Lou*	10.00 -	15.00
46087 *Crazy Quilt*	10.00 -	15.00
40690 *Heebie Jeebies*	10.00 -	15.00
40739 *I've Got The Girl*	10.00 -	15.00
40767 *Farewell Blues*	10.00 -	15.00

40809 *Muddy Water*	10.00 -	15.00
40817 *Arkansas Blues*	10.00 -	15.00
40821 *The Whisper Song*	10.00 -	15.00
40841 *Vo-Do-Do-De-O Blues*	10.00 -	15.00
40886 *Clementine*	10.00 -	15.00
40997 *Nothin' Does-Does Like To Used To Do-Do-Do*	10.00 -	15.00
41069 *Ready For The River*	8.00 -	12.00
41110 *Right Or Wrong*	8.00 -	12.00
41113 *Vaniteaser*	8.00 -	12.00
41138 *My Blackbirds Are Bluebirds Now*	8.00 -	12.00
41169 *Sweetheart of All My Dreams*	7.00 -	10.00
41177 *Rambling Wreck From Georgia Tech*	7.00 -	10.00
41220 *Deep Night*	8.00 -	12.00

EDDIE GORDON'S BAND:

Odeon ONY-36008 *March Of The Hoodlums*	25.00 -	40.00
ONY-41153 *Wild Oat Joe*	25.00 -	40.00
ONY-41204 *No One Else But You*	25.00 -	40.00
ONY-41273 *Birmingham Bertha*	25.00 -	40.00
Parlophone PNY-41320 *Chant Of The Jungle*	25.00 -	40.00

GRAY GORDON & HIS TIC-TOC RHYTHM:

Bluebird (most issues)	3.00 -	6.00
Victor (most issues)	3.00 -	5.00

HERB(ERT) GORDON & HIS (HOTEL ADELPHIA/TEN EYCK) (WHISPERING) ORCHESTRA:

Brunswick 4064 *Jo-Anne*	5.00 -	8.00
4372 *Then We Canoe-dle-oodle Along*	7.00 -	10.00
Brunswick (most other issues)	4.00 -	8.00

JIMMIE GORDON (AND HIS VIP VOP BAND):

Decca 7322, 7334, 7373, 7409, 7474, 7490, 7519,		
7536, 7555, 7592, 7611, 7624, 7661, 7702,		
7764, 7794	4.00 -	8.00

RALPH GORDON & HIS ORCHESTRA:

Victor 26033, 26041	5.00 -	10.00

REX GORDON AND HIS ACES:

Champion 15701 *She's Got Great Ideas*	25.00 -	35.00

ROSS GORMAN & HIS (EARL CARROLL) ORCHESTRA/FIRE EATERS/VIRGINIANS:

Columbia 435-D, 460-D, 495-D	5.00 -	8.00
Columbia 498-D *Rhythm of the Day*	8.00 -	12.00
516-D *Sleepy Time Gal*	8.00 -	12.00
Columbia 563-D, 576-D, 615-D, 631-D	4.00 -	8.00
Edison 51876 *Idolizing*	15.00 -	20.00
51896 *You're Burning Me Up*	15.00 -	20.00
51905 *Come Day, Go Day*	15.00 -	20.00
51944 *High, High, High Up In The Hills*	15.00 -	20.00
Gennett 6057 *She Looks Like Helen Brown*	20.00 -	30.00
6118 *Phantom Blues*	30.00 -	50.00
6132 *Pardon The Glove*	30.00 -	50.00
Harmony 322-H *Sidewalk Blues*	8.00 -	12.00
Harmony 350-H *You're the One For Me*	5.00 -	8.00
Harmony 372-H *She Looks Like Helen Brown*	8.00 -	12.00
Harmony 379-H *Ev'ry Little Whitle*	5.00 -	8.00
Harmony 403-H *My Wife's in Europe Today*	7.00 -	10.00
Harmony 427-H *Phantom Blues*	7.00 -	10.00

(Note: Above titles on *Harmony* also are found on *Diva* and *Velvet Tone*, similarly valued.)

THE GOTHAM NIGHTINGALES:

Okeh 40291 *Keep Smiling at Trouble*	8.00 -	12.00
40679 *Bobadilla*	8.00 -	12.00
40686 *She Belongs To Me*	8.00 -	12.00

THE GOTHAM STOMPERS:

Variety 541 *Did Anyone Ever Tell You*	8.00 -	12.00
629 *My Honey's Lovin' Arms*	8.00 -	12.00

GOWAN'S RHAPSODY MAKERS:

Gennett 3408 *I'll Fly To Hawaii*	75.00 -	100.00
6039 *Sunny Hawaii*	80.00 -	120.00

PORTER GRAINGER:

Ajax 17039 *In Harlem's Araby*	40.00 -	60.00

GRANDVIEW INN ORCHESTRA:

Challenge 362 *Here I Am Broken Hearted*	10.00 -	15.00
Champion 15342 *Dew-Dew-Dewy Day*	10.00 -	15.00

Champion 15343 *No Wonder I'm Happy*	15.00 -	20.00
Champion 15345 *(Here I Am) Broken Hearted* . .	10.00 -	15.00
Champion 15401 *Roll Up The Carpets*	15.00 -	20.00

GLEN GRAY & HIS CASA LOMA
ORCHESTRA: (See also THE CASA LOMA
ORCH.)

Decca 192 *I'm In Love*	7.00 -	10.00
193 *You're A Builder-Upper*	7.00 -	10.00
199 *Chinatown, My Chinatown*	7.00 -	10.00
200 *Nagasaki*	7.00 -	10.00
286 *Stompin' Around*	7.00 -	10.00
287 *Maybe I'm Wrong Again*	7.00 -	10.00
298 *Two In A Dream*	7.00 -	10.00
312 *Blue Moon*	6.00 -	10.00
334 *You Took Advantage Of Me*	6.00 -	10.00
339 *In My Country That Means Love*	6.00 -	10.00
349 *The Night Is Young*	6.00 -	10.00
352 *Fare Thee Well, Annabelle*	6.00 -	10.00
375 *Ain't It Just Too Bad?*	6.00 -	10.00
379 *Who's Sorry Now?*	6.00 -	10.00
386 *My Heart Is An Open Book*	6.00 -	10.00
387 *My Dance*	6.00 -	10.00
405 *You're Walking In My Sleep*	6.00 -	10.00
430 *Once Upon A Midnight*	6.00 -	10.00
463 *Chant Of The Jungle*	6.00 -	10.00
552 *Without A Word Of Warning*	6.00 -	10.00
553 *The Devil Is Afraid Of Music*	6.00 -	10.00
603 *Yankee Doodle Never Went To Town* . . .	6.00 -	10.00
652 *With All My Heart*	6.00 -	10.00
688 *Moonburn*	6.00 -	10.00
696 *I'd Rather Lead A Band*	6.00 -	10.00
869 *Bugle Call Rag*	5.00 -	8.00
986 *Shades Of Hades*	5.00 -	8.00
1048 *Jungle Jitters*	5.00 -	8.00
1126 *You're Laughing At Me*	5.00 -	8.00
1129 *Swing High, Swing Low*	5.00 -	8.00
1158 *Too Marvelous For Words*	5.00 -	8.00
1159 *A Study In Brown*	5.00 -	8.00
1179 *I'd Be A Fool Again*	5.00 -	8.00
1180 *Was It Rain?*	5.00 -	8.00
1211 *Never In A Million Years*	5.00 -	8.00
1246 *One, Two Three Little Hours*	5.00 -	8.00
1312 *Zig-Zag*	5.00 -	8.00
1368 *Yours And Mine*	5.00 -	8.00
1396 *Swing Low, Sweet Chariot*	5.00 -	8.00
1412 *Casa Loma Stomp*	5.00 -	8.00
1473 *Smoke Rings*	5.00 -	8.00
Decca 1519, 1520, 1530, 1540, 1541, 1575, 1596, 1607, 1608, 1634, 1650, 1672, 1679, 1725, 1755, 1783, 1864	4.00 -	7.00
Decca (higher numbers)	3.00 -	6.00
Victor L-16023 *Dardanella and 2 other tunes* . . .	40.00 -	60.00
(above is long-playing "Program Transcription")		
Victor 24222 *Hey! Young Fella*	8.00 -	12.00
24224 *Sittin' By The Fire With You*	8.00 -	12.00
24254 *Black-Eyed Susan Brown*	8.00 -	12.00
24256 *Casa Loma Stomp*	8.00 -	12.00

JANE GRAY:

Harmony 300-H, 395-H, 485-H, 513-H, 646-H .	4.00 -	8.00
Harmony 464-H *Miss Annabelle Lee*	7.00 -	10.00
(Note: titles also appear on *Diva* and *Velvet Tone*.)		

KITTY GRAY & HER WAMPUS CATS:

Vocalion 03869 *Swingology*	10.00 -	20.00
03992 *I Can't Dance (I Got Ants In My Pants)* .	10.00 -	20.00
04014 *Weeping Willow Swing*	10.00 -	20.00
04121 *My Baby's Ways*	10.00 -	20.00
04629 *I'm Yours To Command*	10.00 -	20.00

RUSSELL GRAY & HIS ORCHESTRA:

Okeh 40486 *Ain't That A Grand And Glorious Feeling*	8.00 -	12.00
40938 *Sugar*	40.00 -	60.00

GREEN BROTHERS' NOVELTY BAND:

Aeolian-Vocalion 12098 *Ring-Tail Blues*	10.00 -	15.00
Edison 51321 *New Orleans Wiggle*	8.00 -	12.00
51425 *Some Other Day*	7.00 -	12.00
51437 *Back Where the Daffodils Grow*	10.00 -	15.00
51493 *Those Panama Mamas*	10.00 -	15.00
51497 *Fascinating Rhythm*	8.00 -	12.00
51876 *That's What God Made Mothers For*	15.00 -	20.00
52072 *Say It With a Red, Red Rose*	15.00 -	20.00
52410 *I Wanna Be Loved By You*	10.00 -	15.00
Odeon 20074 *I've Got The Joys*	7.00 -	10.00
Okeh 4180 *The Blacksmith Rag*	7.00 -	10.00
Pathe 22067 *Tackin' 'Em Down*	7.00 -	10.00

GREEN PARROT INN ORCHESTRA:

Champion 15322 *At Sundown*	30.00 -	50.00
15326 *One O'Clock Baby*	50.00 -	75.00
15345 *Is It Possible That She Loves Me*	50.00 -	75.00

BOB GREEN'S DANCE ORCHESTRA:

Oriole 722 *Tuck In Kentucky And Smile*	7.00 -	10.00
1126 *A Little West Of West Virginia*	5.00 -	8.00
1134 *Stay Out Of The South*	5.00 -	8.00
1313 *Ready For The River*	8.00 -	12.00
1338 *They Don't Come Better Than Betty*	5.00 -	8.00
1477 *I Must Be Falling In Love*	5.00 -	8.00
1580 *Why Can't It Be Me?*	5.00 -	8.00
1598 *Sure Enough Blues*	7.00 -	10.00
1613 *Momma Be Nice (Papa Will Be Nice To You)*	5.00 -	8.00
1692 *If I Only Loved You A Little Bit Less*	5.00 -	8.00
1700 *When I Found You*	5.00 -	8.00

JOHNNY GREEN AND HIS ORCHESTRA:

Brunswick 6797 *Live and Love Tonight*	15.00 -	20.00
6855 *Easy Come, Easy Go*	15.00 -	20.00
Brunswick 7441, 7455, 7521, 7522, 7661, 7662, 7716	5.00 -	10.00
Brunswick 7487 *Isn't This a Lovely Day?*	7.00 -	10.00
7497 *Fruitas*	7.00 -	10.00
Columbia 2940-D, 2943-D, 2959-D, 2999-D, 3002-D, 3022-D, 3024-D, 3028-D, 3029-D . . .	5.00 -	10.00

GREENWICH VILLAGE ORCHESTRA:

Titles, issued comtemporaneously on Broadway, Claxtonola, Harmograph, Paramount, Pennington, Puritan, Triangle: *House of David Blues; Ringside Blues*	15.00 -	25.00

SONNY GREER & THE D'C'ns/HIS
MEMPHIS MEN:

Blu-Disc 1003 *Oh! How I Love My Darling*	150.00 -	300.00
Columbia 1868-D *Saturday Night Function*	10.00 -	15.00
2833-D *Saturday Night Function*	7.00 -	10.00

EARL GRESH AND HIS GANGPLANT
ORCHESTRA; EARL GRESH'S
ORCHESTRA:

Columbia 424-D, 469-D	5.00 -	10.00
672-D *Ace In The Hole*	8.00 -	12.00
Columbia 693-D, 841-D, 1031-D	5.00 -	10.00
Pathe-Actuelle 36636 *White Ghost Shivers*	10.00 -	15.00
Perfect 14818 *White Ghost Shivers*	10.00 -	15.00

JIMMIE GRIER & HIS (COCOANUT GROVE)
ORCHESTRA:

Brunswick 6597, 7306, 7307, 7308, 7355, 7381, 7383, 7505, 7519	5.00 -	8.00

Brunswick 7528 *Bugle Call Rag* . . . . 7.00 - 10.00
Brunswick 7619, 7622, 7679, 7683, 7733, 7760,
  7790, 7802, 7887, 7901, 7908 . . . . 4.00 - 8.00
Decca 1474, 1475, 1486, 1497 . . . . 4.00 - 8.00
Decca 1797, 1812, 1813 . . . . 4.00 - 8.00
Victor 22970, 22971 . . . . 5.00 - 10.00
Victor 24174 *Here Lies Love* . . . . 7.00 - 10.00
  24175 *Second-Hand Heart* . . . . 7.00 - 10.00

GORDON GRIMES & HIS ORCHESTRA:
Champion 15290 *Yes She Do—No She Don't* . . . . 10.00 - 20.00
  15293 *I'm Back In Love Again* . . . . 10.00 - 20.00
  15322 *S-L-U-E Foot* . . . . 30.00 - 50.00
  15456 *In The Sing-Song Sycamore Tree* . . . . . . 15.00 - 25.00
  15495 *Oh! Baby* . . . . 15.00 - 20.00
  15496 *Delores* . . . . 15.00 - 20.00

TOM GRISELLE AND HIS ORCHESTRA:
Gennett 3081 *Stop, You're Tickling Me* . . . . 10.00 - 15.00

FERDIE GROFE AND HIS ORCHESTRA:
Columbia 2851-D *Cinderella's Fella* . . . . 10.00 - 15.00
  2858-D *Inka Dinka Doo* . . . . 10.00 - 15.00

WALTER GROSS:
Bluebird 10795, 10937 . . . . 5.00 - 10.00

ELMER GROSSO AND HIS ORCHESTRA:
Champion 16154 *You're Driving Me Crazy* . . . . . . 10.00 - 15.00
  16176 *Cheerful Little Earful* . . . . 10.00 - 15.00
Gennett 7184 *Sing, You Sinners* . . . . 10.00 - 20.00

FRANK GUARENTE AND HIS ORCHESTRA:
Harmony 787-H *Sweethearts On Parade* . . . . . . 7.00 - 10.00
  788-H *My Mother's Eyes* . . . . 7.00 - 10.00
  830-H *When Polly Walks Through The*
   Hollyhocks . . . . 7.00 - 10.00
(Note: Above titles, on *Diva* and *Velvet Tone*, are
  similarly valued.)

VERA GUILAROFF:
Pathe-Actuelle 21178 *Calico Rag* . . . . 8.00 - 12.00
Perfect 11251 *Calico Rag* . . . . 8.00 - 12.00

THE GULF COAST SEVEN:
Columbia A-3916 *Daybreak Blues* . . . . 20.00 - 30.00
  A-3978 *Memphis, Tennessee* . . . . 25.00 - 40.00
  14107-D *Santa Claus Blues* . . . . 50.00 - 75.00
  14373-D *Daylight Savin' Blues* . . . . 35.00 - 50.00

GULF COAST TRIO:
Buddy 8041 *Grand Opera Blues* . . . . 50.00 - 100.00

JOE GUMIN AND HIS ORCHESTRA:
Broadway 1430 *Tie a Little String Around Your*
  Finger . . . . 10.00 - 15.00
Columbia 2571-D *I'll Think Of You* . . . . 10.00 - 15.00

JIMMIE GUNN AND HIS ORCHESTRA:
Bluebird 6469 *My Blue Heaven* . . . . 10.00 - 15.00
  6500 *I've Found a New Baby* . . . . 10.00 - 15.00
  6508 *Slats Shuffle* . . . . 10.00 - 15.00
  6578 *The Operator Special* . . . . 10.00 - 15.00

MICKEY GUY AND HIS ROSE-TREE CAFE
ORCHESTRA; MICKEY GUY'S
HOTTENTOTS:
Okeh 40462 *Rose-Tree Strut* . . . . 30.00 - 50.00
  40588 *In Your Green Hat* . . . . 30.00 - 40.00
Pathe-Actuelle 36433 *Rhythm Rag* . . . . 10.00 - 15.00
  36478 *Two-Ton Tessie* . . . . 10.00 - 15.00
Perfect 14614 *Philadelphia* . . . . 10.00 - 15.00
  14659 *Two-Ton Tessie* . . . . 10.00 - 15.00

GUYON'S PARADISE ORCHESTRA:
Okeh 4732, 4737, 4742 . . . . 4.00 - 7.00
Okeh 4862 *Louisville Lou* . . . . 7.00 - 10.00
  4866 *I've Got The Ain't Got Nothin' Never*
   Had Nothin' Blues . . . . 7.00 - 10.00
  4999 *Land Of Cotton Blues* . . . . 8.00 - 12.00

BOBBY HACKETT AND HIS ORCHESTRA:
Okeh 4047, 4142, 4499, 4565, 4806, 4877, 5198,
  5375, 5493, 5620 . . . . 5.00 - 10.00
Vocalion 4047, 4152, 4499, 4565, 4806, 4877,
  5198, 5375, 5493, 5620 . . . . 5.00 - 10.00

(W.G.) HAENSCHEN'S (BANJO) ORCHESTRA
SAINT LOUIS:
Personal Record 60781 *Country Club Melody* . . . 35.00 - 50.00
  M61068 *Honky Tonky* . . . . 35.00 - 50.00
  M61070 *Maple Leaf Rag* . . . . 35.00 - 50.00
  M61071 *Admiration* . . . . 35.00 - 50.00
(Note: Other records by this band if they exist,
  would probably be of equal interest to
  collectors.)

CASS HAGAN AND HIS (HOTEL MANAGER/
PARK CENTRAL HOTEL) ORCHESTRA:
Columbia 966-D *Sometimes I'm Happy* . . . . 5.00 - 8.00
  1033-D *Melancholy Charlie* . . . . 7.00 - 10.00
  1089-D *Havana* . . . . 7.00 - 10.00
  1114-D *The Varsity Drag* . . . . 7.00 - 10.00
  1138-D *Manhattan Mary* . . . . 5.00 - 8.00
  1176-D *My Lady* . . . . 4.00 - 6.00
  1222-D *Dear, On a Night Like This* . . . . 4.00 - 6.00
  1301-D *My Ohio Home* . . . . 7.00 - 10.00
  1334-D *Golden Gate* . . . . 7.00 - 10.00
Edison 51959 *It All Depends On You* . . . . 15.00 - 20.00
  52012 *Lily* . . . . 15.00 - 20.00

HAGER'S BAND/(DANCE) ORCHESTRA:
Okeh 4406 *Broncho Trot* . . . . 7.00 - 10.00
Rex 5271 *Rigo(letto) Rag* . . . . 30.00 - 50.00
Zonophone 160 *Dixie Belles* . . . . 10.00 - 20.00

BILL HAID & HIS CUBS/THIEVES OF SLEEP:
Broadway 1187 *Slue Foot* . . . . 10.00 - 15.00
Broadway 1188 *I'm Walking Between the*
  Raindrops . . . . 10.00 - 15.00
Broadway 1200 *Blue Grass* . . . . 10.00 - 15.00
Broadway 1201 *If You Don't Love Me* . . . . 8.00 - 12.00
Broadway 1205 *Pickin' Cotton* . . . . 8.00 - 12.00
Broadway 1206 *I Can't Give You Anything But*
  Love . . . . 7.00 - 10.00
Broadway 1207 *That's My Way of Forgetting You* . 7.00 - 10.00
Broadway 1211 *Good Girl* . . . . 7.00 - 10.00
Broadway 1217 *A Good Man Is Hard To Find* . . . 8.00 - 12.00
Broadway 1220 *Shake It Down* . . . . 10.00 - 15.00
Broadway 1229 *Marie* . . . . 4.00 - 7.00
Broadway 1235 *Me and The Man in the Moon* . . . 5.00 - 8.00
Broadway 1237 *Lonesome* . . . . 5.00 - 8.00
Paramount 20628 *Slue Foot* . . . . 10.00 - 15.00
paramount 20630 *I'm Walking Between the*
  Raindrops . . . . 10.00 - 15.00
Paramount 20643 *Jeannine, I Dream of Lilac*
  Time . . . . 8.00 - 12.00
Paramount 20644 *Hold Everything, Here Comes*
  My Girl . . . . 10.00 - 15.00
Paramount 20646 *Etiquette* . . . . 8.00 - 12.00
Paramount 20647 *Crazy Rhythm* . . . . 7.00 - 10.00
Paramount 20648 *Blue Shadows* . . . . 7.00 - 10.00
Paramount 20652 *Good Girl* . . . . 7.00 - 10.00
Paramount 20658 *I Ain't Got Nobody* . . . . 8.00 - 12.00
Paramount 20660 *That Old Sweetheart of Mine* . . 4.00 - 7.00
Paramount 20661 *Weary Weasel* . . . . 10.00 - 15.00
Paramount 20676 *Doin' The Raccoon* . . . . 5.00 - 8.00
Paramount 20678 *Lonesome* . . . . 5.00 - 8.00

HAITIAN ORCHESTRA:
Varsity 8360, 8363, 8364, 8399, 8405 . . . . 5.00 - 10.00

HALFWAY HOUSE (DANCE) ORCHESTRA:
Columbia 476-D *Maple Leaf Rag* . . . . 15.00 - 25.00
  541-D *New Orleans Shuffle* . . . . 15.00 - 20.00
  681-D *Since You're Gone* . . . . 15.00 - 20.00
  1041-D *Snookum* . . . . 15.00 - 20.00
  1263-D *When I'm Blue* . . . . 15.00 - 20.00
  1542-D *Tell Me Who* . . . . 15.00 - 20.00
Okeh 40318 *Pussy Cat Rag* . . . . 40.00 - 60.00

ADELAIDE HALL:
Brunswick 4031, 6362, 6376, 6518 . . . . 7.00 - 10.00

FRED "SUGAR" HALL AND HIS (ROSELAND)
ORCHESTRA/SUGAR BABIES; FRED

HALL'S JAZZ BAND:

Banner 6264 *Missouri Squabble*	7.00 -	10.00
6269 *Louder and Funnier*	7.00 -	10.00
7248 *West End Blues*	10.00 -	15.00
Emerson 3007 *Say It Again*	7.00 -	10.00
3021 *After I Say I'm Sorry*	7.00 -	10.00
3082 *Here Comes Fatima*	7.00 -	10.00
3089 *The Sphinx*	7.00 -	10.00
3094 *Tell Me Tonight*	7.00 -	10.00
3112 *The Birth of the Blues*	7.00 -	10.00
Harmony 13-H *Say Arabella*	5.00 -	8.00
Marathon 210 *Hello Montreal!*	20.00 -	Up
229 *I'm Trying So Hard To Be Happy*	20.00 -	Up
230 *I Can't Give You Anything But Love*	20.00 -	Up
231 *Tonight's The Night*	20.00 -	Up
232 *You're The Only Girl For Me*	20.00 -	Up
234 *On A Moonlight Night*	20.00 -	Up
235 *Tell Me When*	20.00 -	Up

(Note: Above are seven-inch records. Other issues on this scarce label are similarly valued.)

National Music Lovers 1138 *Charleston With Me*	7.00 -	10.00
1147 *Nice And Pretty*	7.00 -	10.00
1159 *Forever With You*	5.00 -	8.00
1171 *Take It From Me*	5.00 -	8.00
1184 *I'll See You In Kentucky*	5.00 -	8.00
Okeh 40410 *Look Who's Here!*	15.00 -	20.00
40437 *Dallas Blues*	15.00 -	20.00
40442 *She's Driving Me Wild*	15.00 -	20.00
40482 *Melancholy Lou*	15.00 -	20.00
40496 *I Ain't Got Nobody*	15.00 -	20.00
40891 *Is It Possible?*	8.00 -	12.00
40986 *Plenty Of Sunshine*	8.00 -	12.00
41008 *It's Balogney*	8.00 -	12.00
41026 *Waitin' For Katy*	8.00 -	12.00
41055 *Chilly Pom-Pom-Pee*	8.00 -	12.00
41112 *Butternut*	8.00 -	12.00
41123 *It Goes Like This*	8.00 -	12.00
41152 *Come On, Baby*	8.00 -	12.00
41183 *She Only Laughs At Me*	8.00 -	12.00
41239 *Here's That Party Now In Person*	10.00 -	15.00
41269 *It Ain't No Fault Of Mine*	10.00 -	15.00
41310 *Sophomore Prom*	10.00 -	15.00
41317 *Piccolo Pete*	10.00 -	15.00
41369 *Harmonica Harry*	10.00 -	15.00
41425 *When I Look To The West*	8.00 -	12.00
Regal 8648 *Louder And Funnier*	7.00 -	10.00
8655 *West End Blues*	8.00 -	12.00

GEORGE HALL AND HIS (HOTEL TAFT) ORCHESTRA:

Bluebird, most issues	3.00 -	6.00
Cameo 8300 *Ten Little Miles From Town*	7.00 -	10.00
Cameo (most other issues)	3.00 -	5.00
Okeh, most issues	3.00 -	5.00
Vocalion, most issues	4.00 -	10.00

WENDELL HALL:

Brunswick (most issues)	3.00 -	6.00
Columbia 1028-D *Headin' Home*	5.00 -	8.00
Edison (most issues)	5.00 -	10.00
Victor (most issues)	3.00 -	6.00

MAL HALLETT AND HIS ORCHESTRA:

Titles, issued contemporaneoulsy on Banner, Conqueror, Melotone, Oriole, Perfect: *An Earful Of music; Okay, Toots; When My Ship Comes In; Your Head On My Shoulder*	5.00 -	10.00
Columbia 917-D *Oh, Lizzie*	7.00 -	10.00
967-D *(Does She Love Me) Positively-Absolutely*	7.00 -	10.00
996-D *Ya Gonna Be Home Tonight? (Oh Yeh? Then I'll Be Over)*	7.00 -	10.00
1287-D *My New York*	7.00 -	10.00
1341-D *The Sunrise*	5.00 -	8.00

Decca 1163 *Big Boy Blue*	7.00 -	10.00
Decca 1167, 1281, 1282, 1384	5.00 -	8.00
Edison (thin) 14080 *Boomerang*	50.00 -	75.00
Okeh 40573 *Whose Who Are You*	7.00 -	10.00
Pathe-Actuelle 36435 *Lonesome And Sorry*	5.00 -	8.00
36437 *She's A Corn-fed Indiana Girl*	8.00 -	12.00
Perfect 14616 *What Good Is "Good Morning"?*	5.00 -	8.00
14618 *She's A Corn-fed Indiana Girl*	8.00 -	12.00
Vocalion 3235 *The Glory Of Love*	8.00 -	12.00
3236 *Swing Fever*	8.00 -	12.00
Vocalion 3268 *I'm An Old Cowhand*	7.00 -	10.00
3278 *The Boston Tea-Party*	7.00 -	10.00

WILL HALLEY:

Victor 17728 *Ruff Johnson's Harmony Band*	10.00 -	15.00

HENRY HALSTEAD & HIS ORCHESTRA:

Victor 19406 *Sweet Little You*	5.00 -	8.00
Victor 19474 *Tessie (Stop Teasing Me)*	7.00 -	10.00
Victor 19482 *That's My Girl*	7.00 -	10.00
Victor 19498 *China Girl*	7.00 -	10.00
Victor 19511 *Bull Frog Serenade*	7.00 -	10.00
Victor 19513 *Frantic*	15.00 -	25.00
Victor 19514 *Panama*	15.00 -	25.00
Victor 19575 *Playmates*	7.00 -	10.00
Victor 19579 *Moonlight and Roses*	5.00 -	8.00
Victor 20061 *Give Me Today*	10.00 -	15.00
Victor 20062 *Dream Of Love And You*	5.00 -	8.00
Victor 20688 *Pal of My Lonesome Hours*	5.00 -	8.00
Victor 20689 *My Idea of Heaven (Is To Be In Love With You)*	5.00 -	8.00
Victor 20691 *Ain't That Too Bad?*	8.00 -	12.00
Victor 22000 *One More Moment With You*	7.00 -	10.00

PAUL HAMILTON AND HIS ORCHESTRA:

Vocalion 2662 *She Reminds Me Of You*	15.00 -	20.00
2708 *I've Had My Moments*	15.00 -	20.00
2721 *Easy Come, Easy Go*	15.00 -	20.00

FRED HAMM AND HIS ORCHESTRA:

Victor 19672 *Stomp Off, Let's Go*	7.00 -	10.00
Victor 19737, 19915, 20023	5.00 -	8.00

CHARLES W. HAMP:

Columbia 1816-D *Pretty Little Thing*	7.00 -	10.00
Okeh 41266 *I'm In Seventh Heaven*	8.00 -	12.00
41308 *Sweethearts' Holiday*	8.00 -	12.00

JOHNNY HAMP'S KENTUCKY SERENADERS; JOHNNY HAMP AND HIS ORCHESTRA:

Bluebird, 6745, 6746, 6748	4.00 -	8.00
Victor 20101, 20105, 20207, 20241, 20290, 20644, 20759, 20819, 20823, 20829, 20900, 20923	5.00 -	10.00
Victor 21323 *Oh Look At That Baby*	8.00 -	12.00
Victor 21511, 21547, 21804, 21829, 22219, 22650, 22722, 22727, 22730, 22795, 22796	5.00 -	10.00
Victor 22636 *All On Account Of Your Kisses*	8.00 -	12.00
22999 *Cabin In The Cotton*	8.00 -	12.00
24000 *Whistle And Blow Your Blues Away*	8.00 -	12.00
Victor (most other issues)	4.00 -	6.00

LIONEL HAMPTON & HIS ORCHESTRA:

Victor 25527, 25535, 25575, 25586, 25592, 25601, 25658, 25666, 25674, 25682, 25699	5.00 -	10.00
Victor, most other issues	4.00 -	8.00

EPH HANAFORD'S BAND:

Banner 1295 *I'm Goin' South*	7.00 -	10.00

HOGAN HANCOCK & HIS ORCHESTRA:

Gennett 6354 *Lady Of Havana*	15.00 -	20.00
6368 *Keep Sweeping The Cobwebs Off The Moon*	20.00 -	30.00
6413 *So Long*	30.00 -	50.00

AL HANDLER AND HIS (ALAMO CAFE) ORCHESTRA:

Columbia 713-D *Crying For The Moon*	10.00 -	15.00
Columbia 833-D, 866-D, 1047-D, 1126-D	5.00 -	10.00

KATHERINE HANDY:

Paramount 12011 *Loveless Love*	40.00 -	60.00

(W.C.) HANDY'S MEMPHIS BLUES BAND:
HANDY'S ORCHESTRA (OF MEMPHIS):

Banner 1036 *St. Louis Blues*	20.00 -	30.00
1053 *She's A Mean Job*	15.00 -	20.00
Black Swan 2053 *Yellow Dog Blues*	20.00 -	30.00
2054 *Muscle Shoals Blues*	15.00 -	20.00
Columbia A-2417, A-2481, A-2419, A-2420, A-2421	5.00 -	10.00
Lyratone 4211 *Beale Street Blues*	50.00 -	80.00
4212 *Yellow Dog Blues*	50.00 -	80.00
Okeh 4789 *Aunt Hagar's Blues*	25.00 -	40.00
4880 *Gulf Coast Blues*	25.00 -	40.00
4886 *Florida Blues*	25.00 -	40.00
4896 *Memphis Blues*	25.00 -	40.00
8046 *Louisville Blues*	25.00 -	40.00
8059 *Down-Hearted Blues*	30.00 -	50.00
8066 *Mama's Got The Blues*	30.00 -	50.00
8110 *Darktown Revelle*	30.00 -	50.00
Paramount 20098 *St. Louis Blues*	20.00 -	30.00
20012 *She's A Mean Job*	15.00 -	20.00
Puritan 11098 *St. Louis Blues*	20.00 -	30.00
Puritan 11112 *Muscle Shoals Blues*	15.00 -	20.00
Varsity 8261, 8163	5.00 -	10.00

(MISS) ANNETTE HANSHAW (AND HER SIZZLIN' SYNCOPATORS):

Titles, issued contemporaneously on Banner, Conqueror, Melotone, Oriole, Perfect, Romeo, include: *Don't Blame Me; Give Me Liberty Or Give Me Love; Fit As A Fiddle; I Cover The Waterfront; Love Me Tonight; Moon Song; Say It Isn't So*	10.00 -	15.00
Clarion 5017-C *I Want A Good Man*	10.00 -	15.00
5037-C *The Way I Feel Today*	10.00 -	15.00
5093-C *Yes Indeedy*	10.00 -	15.00
5101-C *Now I Know*	10.00 -	15.00
5216-C *Crying To The Moon*	10.00 -	15.00
5217-C *I'll Lock You In My Arms*	10.00 -	15.00
5248-C *Walkin' My Baby Back Home*	10.00 -	15.00
5249-C *Would You Like To Take A Walk?*	10.00 -	15.00
5327-C *Moonlight Saving Time*	10.00 -	15.00
5390-C *I Don't Know Why*	10.00 -	15.00
Columbia 1769-D *Lover, Come Back To Me*	10.00 -	15.00
1812-D *Big City Blues*	10.00 -	15.00
Diva 2915-G *The One in the World*	7.00 -	10.00
2940-G *Am I Blue?*	7.00 -	10.00
2981-G *True Blue Lou*	7.00 -	10.00
3012-G *Tip-Toe Thru The Tulips With Me*	7.00 -	10.00
3066-G *Aren't We All?*	8.00 -	12.00
3106-G *I'm Following You*	7.00 -	10.00
3196-G *Nobody Cares If I'm Blue*	8.00 -	12.00
Harmony 706-H *I Must Have That Man*	7.00 -	10.00
Harmony 734-H *High Up on a Hill Top*	7.00 -	10.00
Harmony 1196-H *Nobody Cares If I'm Blue*	7.00 -	10.00
Harmony 1224-H *Body And Soul*	8.00 -	12.00
Harmony 1273-H *You're the One I Care For*	10.00 -	15.00
Harmony 1288-H *Walkin' My Baby Back Home*	10.00 -	15.00
Harmony 1324-H *Ho Hum!*	10.00 -	15.00
1376-H *Guilty*	10.00 -	15.00
Okeh 41292 *Moanin' Low*	15.00 -	20.00
41327 *If I Can't Have You*	15.00 -	20.00
41351 *I Have To Have You*	15.00 -	20.00
41370 *When A Woman Loves A Man*	15.00 -	20.00
41397 *With You*	15.00 -	20.00
Pathe-Actuelle 32207 *Black Bottom*	10.00 -	15.00
32211 *Six Feet Of Papa*	10.00 -	15.00
32213 *Don't Take That Black Bottom Away*	10.00 -	15.00
Pathe-Actuelle 32217, 32222, 32226, 32230, 32240, 32244, 32250, 32255, 32259, 32267, 32283	7.00 -	12.00
Pathe-Actuelle 32235 *Here Or There*	10.00 -	15.00
32275 *Under The Moon*	10.00 -	15.00
Pathe-Actuelle 32309, 32314, 32320, 32332	8.00 -	12.00

Pathe-Actuelle 32293 *It Was Only A Sun Shower*	10.00 -	15.00
32340 *I Just Roll Along*	10.00 -	15.00
32348 *Lila*	10.00 -	15.00
32358 *Ready For The River*	10.00 -	15.00
32365 *Get Out And Get Under The Moon*	10.00 -	15.00
36664 *I'm Somebody's Somebody Now*	10.00 -	15.00
Perfect 12286 *Black Bottom*	10.00 -	15.00
12290 *Falling In Love With You*	10.00 -	15.00
12292 *Cherie, I Love You*	10.00 -	15.00
Perfect 12296, 12301, 12305, 12309, 12319, 12323, 12329, 12334, 12338, 12346, 12362	8.00 -	12.00
Perfect 12314 *Here Or There*	10.00 -	15.00
12354 *Ain't That A Grand And Glorious Feeling*	10.00 -	15.00
12372 *Who's That Knocking At My Door?*	10.00 -	15.00
12419 *I Just Roll Along*	10.00 -	15.00
12427 *'Cause I Feel Low Down*	10.00 -	15.00
12437 *Ready For The River*	10.00 -	15.00
12444 *We Love It*	10.00 -	15.00
14845 *I Like What You Like*	10.00 -	15.00
Velvet Rone 1706-V *I Must Have That Man!*	7.00 -	10.00
1734-V *That's Just My Way Of Forgetting You*	7.00 -	10.00
1766-V *My Blackbirds Are Bluebirds Now*	7.00 -	10.00
1785-V *My Inspiration Is You*	8.00 -	12.00
1792-V *I Wanna Be Loved By You*	10.00 -	15.00
1832-V *In a Great Big Way*	8.00 -	12.00
1859-V *Mean To Me*	7.00 -	10.00
1910-V *My Sin*	7.00 -	10.00
1915-V *The One In The World*	7.00 -	10.00
1940-V *Daddy Won't You Please Come Home*	7.00 -	10.00
1981-V *Here We Are*	7.00 -	10.00
2012-V *What Wouldn't I Do For That Man*	7.00 -	10.00
2066-V *If I Had a Talking Picture of You*	8.00 -	12.00
2106-V *Happy Days Are Here Again*	7.00 -	10.00
2155-V *I've Got "It"*	10.00 -	15.00
2178-V *My Future Just Passed*	8.00 -	12.00
2196-V *Nobody Cares If I'm Blue*	8.00 -	12.00
2274-V *Crying To The Moon*	10.00 -	15.00
2289-V *Wasting My Love On You*	10.00 -	15.00
2314-V *Ever Since Time Began*	10.00 -	15.00
2315-V *Would You Like To Take a Walk*	10.00 -	15.00
2393-V *Ho Hum!*	10.00 -	15.00
2454-V *Guilty*	10.00 -	15.00
Vocalion 2735 *Let's Fall In Love*	10.00 -	15.00

THE HAPPINESS BOYS:

The large recorded legacy of Billy Jones and Ernest Hare, consisting of mostly humorous and novelty songs, and issued on most labels of the 1920s, is beyond the scope of this book. Most of their records are of minimal value. Following are a few examples:

Banner 1772 *My Cutie's Due At Two To Two Today*	5.00 -	8.00
Banner 1875 *If My Baby Cooks As Good As She Looks*	5.00 -	8.00
Banner 1953 *I've Never Seen A Straight Banana*	5.00 -	8.00
Banner 7116 *She's The Sweetheart of Six Other Guys*	5.00 -	8.00
Broadway 1063 *I've Never Seen a Straight Banana*	5.00 -	8.00
Brunswick 2654 *The Big Butter and Egg Man*	5.00 -	8.00
Brunswick 2888 *If You Knew Susie*	5.00 -	8.00
Cameo 504 *Does the Spearmint Lose Its Flavor On The Bedpost Over Night?*	5.00 -	8.00
707 *In Sweet Onion Time*	5.00 -	8.00
Columbia 378-D *As A Porcupine Pines For Its Pork*	5.00 -	8.00
534-D *I Wish't I Was In Peoria*	5.00 -	8.00
Edison 51555 *Don't Bring Lulu*	5.00 -	10.00
51660 *Show Me The Way To Go Home*	5.00 -	10.00
51704 *Wimmin-Aaah!*	5.00 -	10.00
52149 *Get 'Em In A Rumble Seat*	8.00 -	12.00

52236 *It's In The Bag*	8.00	-	12.00
52333 *Must You Wear A Moustache?*	8.00	-	12.00
Harmony 9-H *I Miss My Swiss*	5.00	-	8.00
Harmony 665-H *Gotta Big Date With A Little Girl*	5.00	-	8.00
Puritan 11236 *Barney Google*	5.00	-	8.00
Regal 8014 *Tie Me To Your Apron Strings Again*	5.00	-	8.00
9954 *That Certain Party*	5.00	-	8.00
Romeo 1169 *Singin' In The Bathtub*	5.00	-	8.00
Victor 21797 *Etiquette Blues*	5.00	-	8.00
Victor 35953 (12-inch) *Twisting The Dials*	10.00	-	15.00

THE HAPPY HARMONISTS:

Gennett 5286 *Home Brew Blues*	50.00	-	100.00
5402 *Ethiopian Nightmare*	50.00	-	100.00
5518 *Steady Steppin' Papa*	50.00	-	100.00

THE HAPPY SIX:

Columbia A2929 *Shake Your Little Shoulder*	5.00	-	8.00
Columbia A2949 *Dance-O-Mania*	5.00	-	8.00
Columbia A2971 *Goodbye Sunshine, Hello Moon*	5.00	-	8.00
Columbia A3379 *Siam Soo*	10.00	-	15.00
Columbia A3645 *Nobody Lied*	5.00	-	8.00
Columbia (most other issues)	3.00	-	6.00

LIL HARDAWAY'S ORCHESTRA; DIAMOND LIL HARDAWAY & HER GEMS OF RHYTHM:

Vocalion 1252 *Milenberg Joys*	150.00	-	200.00
Decca 7293, 7241, 7247, 7276	8.00	-	12.00

(LATE PRESIDENT) WARREN G. HARDING:

Victor 35718 *Address at Washington/Hoboken*	5.00	-	8.00

GLENN HARDMAN & HIS HAMMOND FIVE:

Columbia 35263, 25341	5.00	-	10.00
Vocalion 4971 *Exactly Like You*	7.00	-	10.00

MARLOW HARDY & HIS ALABAMIANS:

Columbia 2034-D *Song of The Bayou*	15.00	-	20.00

ERNEST HARE (See: THE HAPPINESS BOYS)

BOB HARING AND HIS ORCHESTRA:

Banner 32162 *Ho Hum!*	7.00	-	10.00
Brunswick 4545 *Revolutionary Rhythm*	5.00	-	8.00
4608 *Georgia Pines*	7.00	-	10.00
4672 *Do Ya Love Me?*	5.00	-	8.00
Brunswick (most other issues)	4.00	-	7.00
Cameo 797 *Angry*	7.00	-	10.00
824 *Roll 'Em, Girls (Roll Your Own)*	7.00	-	10.00
9025 *Me And The Man In The Moon*	10.00	-	15.00
9033 *All By Yourself In The Moonlight*	10.00	-	15.00
9041 *I Faw Down An' Go Boom*	7.00	-	10.00
Cameo (most other issues)	3.00	-	7.00
Oriole 2222 *When I Take My Sugar To Tea*	7.00	-	10.00
Romeo 555 *I Just Roll Along Havin' My Ups And Downs*	7.00	-	10.00
810 *How About Me?*	7.00	-	10.00
907 *Four Or Five Times*	10.00	-	15.00
Romeo (most other issues)	4.00	-	7.00

EARL HARLAN AND HIS ORCHESTRA:

Banner 32806, 32924	7.00	-	12.00
Melotone 12417, 12739, 12840, 12848, 12867	7.00	-	12.00
Oriole 2798, 2812	7.00	-	12.00
Perfect 15789, 15852, 15862	7.00	-	12.00
Romeo 2095, 2171, 2185	7.00	-	12.00

THE HARLEM FOOTWARMERS:

Columbia 14670-D *Sweet Chariot*	50.00	-	80.00
Okeh 8720 *Jungle Jamboree*	35.00	-	50.00
8746 *Syncopated Shuffle*	35.00	-	50.00
8760 *Lazy Duke*	35.00	-	50.00
8836 *Big House Blues*	35.00	-	50.00
8840 *Mood Indigo*	35.00	-	50.00
8869 *Old Man Blues*	35.00	-	50.00

HARLEM HAMFATS:

Decca 7182, 7196, 7205, 7206, 7218, 7229, 7245, 7251, 7266, 7274, 7310, 7362, 7283, 7299, 7312, 7326, 7339, 7351, 7367, 7382, 7395, 7406, 7439, 7484	5.00	-	10.00

7454, 7466, 7530, 7761	5.00	-	10.00
Vocalion 04813, 04828, 04870, 04925, 05136, 05179, 05233, 05287	7.00	-	12.00

HARLEM HARLEY & HIS WASHBOARD BAND:

Decca 7492, 7505	7.00	-	12.00

HARLEM HOT CHOCOLATES:

Hit of the Week 1045 *Sing, You Sinners*	10.00	-	15.00
1046 *St. James Infirmary*	10.00	-	15.00

HARLEM HOT SHOTS:

Titles, issued contemporaneously on Banner, Melotone, Oriole, Perfect, Romeo: *Dust Off That Old Pianna; Love Is Just Around The Corner; House Rent Party Day; March Winds And April Showers*	10.00	-	15.00
Bluebird 5481 *Somebody Stole My Gal*	7.00	-	10.00
Electradisk 1931 *St. Louis Blues*	75.00	-	100.00
Oriole 2284 *Black and Tan Fantasy*	10.00	-	15.00

HARLEM HOUSE RENT STOMPERS:

Brunswick 7120 *Gravel Pit Stomp*	80.00	-	120.00

HARLEM STOMPERS:

Decca 7600 *The Monkey Swing*	7.00	-	10.00
7616 *Jammin' In Georgia*	7.00	-	10.00

HARLEM TRIO:

Herwin 93012 *Fuzzy Wuzzy*	150.00	-	200.00
Okeh 8072 *Clarinet Laughing Blues*	40.00	-	60.00
8158 *The Poor Man's Blues*	40.00	-	60.00
8189 *Bass Clarinet Blues*	40.00	-	60.00
40220 *Muddy Water Blues*	40.00	-	60.00

DAVE HARMAN & HIS ORCHESTRA:

Bluebird 5436, 5437, 5438	5.00	-	10.00
Edison 51458 *Prince Of Wails*	8.00	-	12.00
51479 *Hot-Hot-Hottentot*	10.00	-	15.00
51510 *Sob Sister Sadie*	10.00	-	15.00

HARMANIAC FIVE:

Paramount 20476 *Harmaniac Blues*	35.00	-	50.00
Puritan 11476 *Harmaniac Blues*	35.00	-	50.00

HARMOGRAPH DANCE ORCHESTRA:

Harmograph 888 *My Sweetie's Sweeter Than That*	15.00	-	20.00
889 *Forgetful Blues*	30.00	-	50.00

THE HARMONIANS:

Harmony 127-H *Say It Again*	5.00	-	8.00
Harmony 170-H *Lonesome and Sorry*	5.00	-	8.00
Harmony 185-H *I Wonder What's Become of Joe?*	5.00	-	8.00
Harmony 321-H *There Ain't No Maybe in My Baby's Eyes*	5.00	-	8.00
Harmony 350-H *I'm Looking Over a Four Leaf Clover*	5.00	-	8.00
Harmony 393-H *Positively—Absolutely*	5.00	-	8.00
Harmony 447-H *You Don't Like It-Not Much*	5.00	-	8.00
Harmony 503-H *Everybody Loves My Girl*	5.00	-	8.00
Harmony 560-H *Keep Sweeping the Cobwebs Off The Moon*	5.00	-	8.00
Harmony 596-H *I Just Roll Along*	5.00	-	8.00
Harmony 638-H *Hello Montreal!*	5.00	-	8.00
Harmony 667-H *That's My Weakness Now*	5.00	-	8.00
Harmony 679-H *If You Don't Love Me*	5.00	-	8.00
Harmony 693-H *I'm Walking Between the Raindrops*	5.00	-	8.00
Harmony 701-H *Ten Little Miles From Town*	5.00	-	8.00
Harmony 702-H *Half Way To Heaven*	5.00	-	8.00
Harmony 716-H *What a Night For Spooning*	7.00	-	10.00
Harmony 735-H *I'm Sorry Sally*	5.00	-	8.00
Harmony 749-H *There's a Rainbow 'Round My Shoulder*	5.00	-	8.00
Harmony 762-H *I Wanna Be Loved By You*	5.00	-	8.00
Harmony 763-H *Here's That Party Now In Person*	8.00	-	12.00
Harmony 801-H *Sunny Skies*	5.00	-	8.00
Harmony 802-H *Along Came Sweetness*	5.00	-	8.00
Harmony 863-H *Some Sweet Day*	7.00	-	10.00

Harmony 962-H *I'm In Seventh Heaven*	7.00 -	10.00
Harmony 964-H *Sweet Ella May*	5.00 -	8.00
Harmony 1308-H *If You Should Ever Need Me*	5.00 -	8.00
Harmony 1310-H *I'm Crazy 'Bout My Baby*	7.00 -	10.00
Harmony 1311-H *You'll Be Mine in Apple Blossom Time*	5.00 -	8.00

HARMONICA TIM:

Clarion 5194-C *Harmonica Blues*	20.00 -	30.00
5195-C *Mean Low Blues*	20.00 -	30.00
Velvet Tone 7123-V *Mean Low Blues*	20.00 -	30.00

HARMONY DANCE ORCHESTRA:

Harmony 10-H *Yes, Sir, That's My Baby*	5.00 -	8.00
60-H *Tweedle-Dee Tweedle-Doo*	5.00 -	8.00

HAMTREE HARRINGTON:

Brunswick 2465 *I'm Gone, Dat's All*	7.00 -	10.00
2588 *C.O.D.*	7.00 -	10.00

ACE HARRIS & HIS SUNSET ROYAL ORCHESTRA:

Vocalion 3864 *Hurly Burly*	10.00 -	15.00
3935 *Rhythm 'Bout Town*	10.00 -	15.00

HELEN HARRIS ACCOMPANIED BY SKILLET DICK & HIS FRYING PANS:

Champion 15881 *Don't Say Goodbye*	125.00 -	175.00

LILLIAN HARRIS:

Banner 1173 *Four O'Clock Blues*	20.00 -	30.00
1212 *Mama's Got The Blues*	20.00 -	30.00
1224 *Down-Hearted Blues*	20.00 -	30.00
Regal 9445 *Sugar Blues*	20.00 -	30.00
9497 *Baby, Won't You Please Come Home*	20.00 -	30.00
9510 *Gulf Coast Blues*	20.00 -	30.00

MARION HARRIS:

Brunswick 2395 *St. Louis Blues*	5.00 -	8.00
Brunswick 2552 *St. Louis Gal*	5.00 -	8.00
Brunswick 2622 *Hey Hey and Hee Hee*	5.00 -	8.00
Brunswick 2651 *There'll Be Some Changes Made*	5.00 -	8.00
Brunswick 2672 *Go, Emmaline*	5.00 -	8.00
Brunswick 2735 *Charleston Charlie*	5.00 -	8.00
Brunswick 2784 *Why Couldn't It Be Poor Little Me?*	5.00 -	8.00
Brunswick 2807 *Does My Sweetie Do-And How!*	5.00 -	8.00
Brunswick (most other issues)	3.00 -	7.00
Victor 18398 *When I Hear That Jazz Band Play*	7.00 -	10.00
Victor 18593 *Take Me To The Land Of Jazz*	5.00 -	8.00

PHIL HARRIS & HIS (COCOANUT GROVE) ORCHESTRA:

Columbia 2761-D *You've Got Me Crying Again*	10.00 -	20.00
2766-D *How's About It?*	10.00 -	20.00
Vocalion 3447 *Swing High, Swing Low*	8.00 -	12.00
3466 *Swingin' For The King*	8.00 -	12.00
3488 *Too Marvelous For Words*	8.00 -	12.00
3533 *Jammin'*	8.00 -	12.00
3565 *The Darktown Strutters' Ball*	8.00 -	12.00
3583 *That's What I Like About The South*	8.00 -	12.00

HARRIS BROTHERS TEXANS:

Brunswick 4644 *Gut Bucket Shuffle*	50.00 -	100.00
6047 *The South's Been A Mother To Me*	40.00 -	70.00
Vocalion 15747 *The Pay-Off*	75.00 -	125.00

HARRY'S HAPPY FOUR:

Okeh 8229 *Swinging The Swing*	40.00 -	60.00
8266 *Western Melody*	40.00 -	60.00

HARRY'S MELODY MEN:

Broadway 1051 *I Never See Maggie Alone*	5.00 -	8.00
Broadway 1204 *Someone Left Me Mighty Lonesome*	5.00 -	8.00
Broadway 1208 *My Wonderful You*	5.00 -	8.00
Broadway 1209 *Tennessee Mammy*	5.00 -	8.00
Broadway 1234 *My Arms Are Open For You*	5.00 -	8.00
Broadway 1240 *Happy in the Rain*	5.00 -	8.00

HARRY'S RECKLESS FIVE:

Broadway 1355 *Wailing Blues*	150.00 -	200.00

BOB HARTMAN & HIS ORCHESTRA:

Broadway 1501 *Charley Cadet*	10.00 -	15.00

GEORGIA HARVEY:

Black Swan 14119 *Castaway*	20.00 -	30.00
14135 *That Sweet Something, Dear*	20.00 -	30.00

COLEMAN HAWKINS AND HIS ALL-STAR OCTET/ORCHESTRA/RHYTHM:

Apollo 751, 752, 753	4.00 -	7.00
Bluebird 10253, 10477, 10523, 10693, 10770	4.00 -	7.00
Capitol, most issues	3.00 -	5.00
Mercury, most issues	3.00 -	5.00
Okeh 6284, 6347	5.00 -	8.00

ERSKINE HAWKINS AND HIS 'BAMA STATE COLLEGIANS:

Bluebird, most issues	4.00 -	6.00
Victor, most issues	3.00 -	5.00
Vocalion 3280 *I Can't Escape From You*	10.00 -	15.00
3289 *It Was A Sad Night in Harlem*	10.00 -	15.00
3318 *Big John's Special*	10.00 -	15.00
3336 *A Swingy Little Rhythm*	10.00 -	15.00
3545 *Uproar Shout*	10.00 -	15.00
3567 *Dear Old Southland*	10.00 -	15.00
3668 *Red Cap*	10.00 -	15.00
3689 *I'll See You In My Dreams*	10.00 -	15.00
4007 *Lost in the Shuffle*	10.00 -	15.00
4072 *Who's Sorry Now?*	10.00 -	15.00

BILL HAWLEY:

Victor 21383 *Delores*	10.00 -	15.00

CLIFFORD HAYES' LOUISVILLE STOMPERS:

Victor 20955 *Blue Guitar Stomp*	10.00 -	15.00
21489 *Bare-Foot Stomp*	100.00 -	150.00
21583 *Blue Harmony*	20.00 -	30.00
21584 *The Petter's Stomp*	20.00 -	30.00
23346 *Tenor Guitar Fiend*	150.00 -	200.00
23407 *Automobile Blues*	150.00 -	250.00
V 38011 *Clef Club Stomp*	50.00 -	100.00
V 38022 *Old Chord's Stomp*	100.00 -	150.00
V 38529 *You're Ticklin' Me*	100.00 -	150.00
V 38557 *Hey! Am I Blue*	100.00 -	150.00

EDGAR HAYES AND HIS ORCHESTRA:
EDGAR HAYES QUINTET:

Decca 1338 *Caravan*	5.00 -	8.00
1382 *Satan Takes a Holiday*	5.00 -	8.00
1416 *Stomping at the Renny*	5.00 -	8.00
1444 *So Rare*	5.00 -	8.00
1509 *I Know Now*	5.00 -	8.00
1527 *Queen Isabella*	5.00 -	8.00
Decca 1665 *Swingin' in the Promised Land*	5.00 -	8.00
1684 *Blue Skies*	5.00 -	8.00
1748 *Fugitive from a Harem*	5.00 -	8.00
1882 *Star Dust*	3.00 -	5.00
1940 *Meet The Band*	5.00 -	8.00
2048 *Shindig*	5.00 -	8.00
2193 *Help Me*	5.00 -	8.00

NAP HAYES:

Okeh 45231 *Somethin' Doin'*	75.00 -	100.00

JOE HAYMES & HIS ORCHESTRA:

Banner, Bluebird, Conqueror, Melotone, Oriole, Perfect, Romeo	5.00 -	10.00
Columbia 2704-D, 2716-D, 2739-D, 2781-D, 2784-D	10.00 -	15.00
Victor 24007, 24038, 24040, 24055, 24123, 24152, 25353	8.00 -	12.00
Vocalion 3307, 3335, 3369	8.00 -	12.00

LENNIE HAYTON'S BLUE FOUR:

Vocalion 15750 *Old-Fashioned Girl*	60.00 -	100.00

MONK HAZEL & HIS BIENVILLE ROOF ORCHESTRA:

Brunswick 4181 *High Society*	20.00 -	30.00
4182 *Git-Wit-It*	20.00 -	30.00

LUCILLE HEGAMIN (AND HER BLUE FLAME SYNCOPATORS/JAZZ ARTISTS):

Arto 9045, 9053, 9058, 9063, 9068, 9069, 9074, 9105, 9119, 9129, 9169	5.00 -	10.00

Banner 1014, 1048, 1072, 1093; *Bell*	5.00 -	10.00
Black Swan 2032, *Arkansas Blues*	15.00 -	20.00
2049 *He May Be Your Man*	15.00 -	20.00
Cameo, most issues	4.00 -	8.00
Columbia 14164-D *Senorita Mine*	20.00 -	30.00
Globe 7045, 7053, 7058, 7063, 7068, 7074, 7105,		
7119, 7129, 7169	5.00 -	10.00
Claxtonola, Harmograph, Paramount	8.00 -	15.00
Famous, Muse, Puritan, Regal	5.00 -	8.00

HORACE HEIDT AND HIS MUSICAL KNIGHTS/ORCHESTRA:

Brunswick, most issues	3.00 -	5.00
Columbia, most issues	2.00 -	3.00
Victor 20608 *Hello Cutie!*	7.00 -	10.00
21310 *Golden Gate*	8.00 -	12.00
21311 *Get 'Em in a Rumble Seat*	8.00 -	12.00
21312 *Every Evening*	7.00 -	10.00
Victor 21335, 21568, 21956, 21957, 22195, 22222 .	5.00 -	10.00

SIG HELLER & HIS ORCHESTRA:

Broadway 1509 *Snuggled On Your Shoulder*	7.00 -	10.00
1513 *Somebody Loves You*	7.00 -	10.00

BUD HELMS & HIS BAND:

Champion 15285 *Pee Wee Blues*	100.00 -	150.00
15364 *Hot Lips*	50.00 -	75.00

BERTHA HENDERSON:

Paramount 12511 *Six Thirty Blues*	100.00 -	150.00
Okeh 8265 *Jamboree Blues*	50.00 -	75.00

CATHERINE HENDERSON:

Diva 6040-G *Keep It To Yourself*	20.00 -	30.00
6050-G *What If We Do?*	20.00 -	30.00
Okeh 8240 *Four Thirty Blues*	25.00 -	40.00
Velvet Tone 7066-V *What If We Do?*	20.00 -	30.00
7076-V *Keep It To Yourself*	20.00 -	30.00

EDMONIA HENDERSON:

Paramount 12084 *Black Man Blues*	75.00 -	100.00
12095 *Brownskin Man*	75.00 -	100.00
12097 *If You Sheik On Your Mama*	75.00 -	100.00
12203 *Hateful Blues*	75.00 -	100.00
12239 *Jelly Roll Blues*	100.00 -	150.00
Vocalion 1015 *Nobody Else Will Do*	100.00 -	150.00
1043 *Dead Man Blues*	150.00 -	250.00

FLETCHER HENDERSON & HIS (CONNIE INN) ORCHESTRA/SAWIN'SIX; F.H. HENDERSON (JR.); HENDERSON'S (CLUB ALABAM'/DANCE) ORCHESTRA/HOT SIX/SIX WONDER BOYS:

Titles, issued contemporaneously on Broadway,		
Claxtonola, Famous, Harmograph, Puritan,		
Triangle: *Beale Street Mama; Down Hearted*		
Blues, My Sweetie Went Away; When You		
Walked Out	10.00 -	15.00
Ajax 17016 *Bull Blues*	20.00 -	30.00
17017 *Chattanooga*	20.00 -	30.00
17022 *Mistreatin' Daddy*	20.00 -	30.00
17023 *House Rent Ball*	20.00 -	30.00
17029 *Just Blues*	20.00 -	30.00
17030 *I'm Crazy Over You*	20.00 -	30.00
17109 *Everybody Loves My Baby*	35.00 -	50.00
17113 *Alabama Bound*	20.00 -	25.00
17114 *I'll See You In My Dreams*	20.00 -	25.00
17123 *Why Couldn't It Be Poor Little Me?*	20.00 -	25.00
Apex 8194, 8205, 8218, 8230, 8233, 8280	7.00 -	10.00
8300 *Everybody Loves My Baby*	35.00 -	50.00
8309 *Alabamy Bound*	10.00 -	15.00
8311 *I'll See You In My Dreams*	10.00 -	15.00
8316 *Why Couldn't It Be Poor Little Me?*	10.00 -	15.00
8419 *Sleepy Time Gal*	10.00 -	15.00
Banner 1361 *Jiminy Gee*	7.00 -	10.00
Banner 1364 *Red Hot Mama*	8.00 -	12.00
Banner 1372 *You Know Me Alabam'*	8.00 -	12.00
Banner 1373 *Wait'll You See My Gal*	8.00 -	12.00
Banner 1375 *Oh Eva!*	10.00 -	15.00

Banner 1383 *Hard Hearted Hannah*	5.00 -	8.00
Banner 1384 *I Can't Get the One I Want*	7.00 -	10.00
Banner 1388 *Where the Dreamy Wabash Flows* . .	7.00 -	10.00
Banner 1445 *How Come You Do Me Like You Do*	10.00 -	15.00
Banner 1457 *One Of These Days*	10.00 -	15.00
Banner 1470 *I'll See You In My Dreams*	10.00 -	15.00
Banner 1471 *Everybody Loves My Baby*	15.00 -	20.00
Banner 1475 *My Dream Man*	10.00 -	15.00
Banner 1476 *Why Couldn't It Be Poor Little Me?* .	15.00 -	20.00
Banner 1488 *Alabamy Bound*	10.00 -	15.00
Banner 1490 *Prince of Wails*	15.00 -	20.00
Banner 1508 *Swanee Butterfly*	7.00 -	10.00
Banner 1639 *Sleepy Time Gal*	7.00 -	10.00
Banner 1654 *Then I'll Be Happy*	7.00 -	10.00
Black Swan 2022 *My Oriental Rose*	20.00 -	30.00
2026 *The Unknown Blues*	30.00 -	40.00
2076 *Love Days*	20.00 -	30.00
2079 *Blue*	20.00 -	30.00
2116 *Chime Blues*	40.00 -	60.00
10072 *Love Days*	20.00 -	30.00
10075 *Blue*	20.00 -	30.00
10083 *Dumbell*	15.00 -	20.00
Bluebird 5682 *Hocus Pocus*	10.00 -	15.00
6515, 10246	5.00 -	10.00
Brunswick 2592 *War Horse Mama*	8.00 -	12.00
Brunswick 3026 *Let me Introduce You To*		
My Rosie	10.00 -	15.00
3406 *Clarinet Marmalade*	10.00 -	15.00
3460 *Stockholm Stomp*	10.00 -	15.00
3521 *Sensation*	10.00 -	15.00
4119 *Hop Off*	15.00 -	20.00
Cameo 9033 *Old Black Jack Joe's Blues*	15.00 -	20.00
9174 *Freeze and Melt*	15.00 -	20.00
9175 *Raisin' The Roof*	15.00 -	20.00
Columbia 126-D *Somebody Stole My Gal*	10.00 -	15.00
164-D *Muscle Shoals Blues*	10.00 -	15.00
202-D *That's Georgia*	10.00 -	15.00
209-D *He's The Hottest Man In Town*	10.00 -	15.00
228-D *Manda*	15.00 -	20.00
249-D *The Meanest Kind Of Blues*	15.00 -	20.00
292-D *Play Me Slow*	15.00 -	20.00
383-D *Money Blues*	15.00 -	20.00
395-D *Sugar Foot Stomp*	15.00 -	20.00
509-D *Carolina Stomp*	15.00 -	20.00
532-D *Pensacola*	15.00 -	20.00
654-D *The Stampede*	15.00 -	20.00
817-D *The Chant*	15.00 -	20.00
854-D *Sweet Thing*	15.00 -	20.00
970-D *Rocky Mountain Blues*	15.00 -	20.00
1002-D *P.D.Q. Blues*	15.00 -	20.00
1059-D *Whiteman Stomp*	15.00 -	20.00
1543-D *King Porter Stomp*	15.00 -	20.00
1913-D *Blazin'*	15.00 -	20.00
2329-D *Somebody Loves Me*	15.00 -	20.00
2352-D *Keep A Song In Your Soul*	15.00 -	20.00
2414-D *Sweet And Hot*	15.00 -	20.00
2513-D *Clarinet Marmalade*	15.00 -	20.00
2559-D *Sugar*	15.00 -	20.00
2565-D *Singin' The Blues*	15.00 -	20.00
2586-D *My Gal Sal*	15.00 -	20.00
2615-D *Business in F*	15.00 -	20.00
2732-D *Honeysuckle Rose*	15.00 -	20.00
2825-D *Nagasaki*	15.00 -	20.00
A-3951 *Gulf Coast Blues*	10.00 -	15.00
A-3995 *Dicty Blues*	10.00 -	15.00
14392-D *Easy Money*	30.00 -	50.00
Crown 3093 *After You've Gone*	15.00 -	20.00
3107 *Tiger Rag*	15.00 -	20.00
Decca 157 *Limehouse Blues*	8.00 -	12.00
158 *Shanghai Shuffle*	8.00 -	12.00
213 *Tidal Wave*	8.00 -	12.00
214 *Big John's Special*	8.00 -	12.00

342 *Rug Cutter's Swing*	8.00	-	12.00
555 *Hotter Than 'Ell*	8.00	-	12.00
Edison 51276 *Shake Your Feet*	15.00	-	25.00
51277 *Linger Awhile*	15.00	-	20.00
Emerson 10713 *Mamma's Gonna Slow You Down*	20.00	-	30.00
10714 *Steppin' Out*	20.00	-	30.00
10744 *Ghost Of The Blues*	20.00	-	30.00
Gennett 3285 *When Spring Comes Peeping Through*	35.00	-	50.00
3286 *Honeybunch*	35.00	-	50.00
Lincoln 3062 *Old Black Joe's Blues*	10.00	-	15.00
3201 *Freeze and Melt*	15.00	-	20.00
3202 *Raisin' The Roof*	15.00	-	20.00
Paramount 12143 *Chimes Blues*	20.00	-	30.00
12486 *Off To Buffalo*	75.00	-	100.00
20367 *Prince of Wails*	30.00	-	40.00
Pathe-Actuelle 036027, 036042, 036069, 036083, 036084, 036090, 036213, 036214	8.00	-	12.00
036156, 036266	10.00	-	15.00
036157 *Shanghai Shuffle*	20.00	-	30.00
Perfect 14208, 14223, 14250, 14264, 14265, 14271,	8.00	-	12.00
14337, 14447	10.00	-	15.00
14338 *Shanghai Shuffle*	20.00	-	30.00
Puritan 11226 *Don't Think You'll Be Missed*	10.00	-	15.00
Puritan 11251 *My Sweetie Went Away*	80.00	-	120.00
Regal 8441, 8442, 9658, 9673, 9682, 9668, 9680, 9681, 9683, 9684, 9739, 9767, 9789, 9803, 9961	7.00	-	12.00
8455, 9753, 9770, 9775	10.00	-	15.00
Romeo 837 *Old Black Joe's Blues*	10.00	-	15.00
976 *Freeze and Melt*	15.00	-	20.00
977 *Raisin' the Roof*	15.00	-	20.00
Victor 20944 *St. Louis Shuffle*	20.00	-	30.00
22775 *Malinda's Wedding Day*	15.00	-	20.00
22786 *Oh, It Looks Like Rain*	15.00	-	20.00
22955 *Strangers*	15.00	-	20.00
24008 *Poor Old Joe*	15.00	-	20.00
24699 *Harlem Madness*	10.00	-	15.00
25298, 25317, 25334, 25339, 25373, 25375, 25379	7.00	-	10.00
Vocalion 1065 *Clarinet Marmalade*	50.00	-	80.00
1079 *Some Of These Days*	75.00	-	100.00
1092 *Fidgety Feet*	50.00	-	75.00
2527 *Yeah Man!*	15.00	-	25.00
2583 *Queer Notions*	15.00	-	25.00
3211 *Christopher Columbus*	7.00	-	10.00
3213 *Stealin' Apples*	7.00	-	10.00
3485 *Slumming On Park Avenue*	7.00	-	10.00
3487 *It's Wearin' Me Down*	7.00	-	10.00

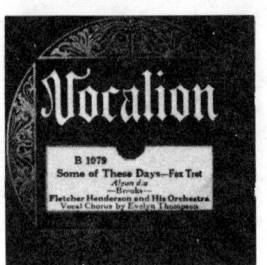

3511 *Back In Your Own Backyard*	7.00	-	10.00
3534 *Stampede*	7.00	-	10.00
3627 *If You Should Ever Leave*	7.00	-	10.00
3641 *All God's Children Got Rhythm*	7.00	-	10.00
3713 *Worried Over You*	7.00	-	10.00
3760 *What's Your Story*	7.00	-	10.00
3850 *If It's The Last Thing I Do*	7.00	-	10.00
4125 *Sing You Sinners*	7.00	-	10.00
4154 *Saving Myself For You*	7.00	-	10.00
4167 *There's Rain In My Eyes*	7.00	-	10.00
4180 *Moten Stomp*	7.00	-	10.00

14636 *Gulf Coast Blues*	8.00	-	12.00
14654 *Dicty Blues*	8.00	-	12.00
14726 *Charleston Crazy*	8.00	-	12.00
14740 *Potomac River Blues*	8.00	-	12.00
14759 *Lots O'Mama*	8.00	-	12.00
14788 *Chicago Blues*	8.00	-	12.00
14800 *Tea Pot Dome Blues*	8.00	-	12.00
14828 *Strutter's Drag*	8.00	-	12.00
14838 *Do That Thing*	8.00	-	12.00
14880 *A New Kind Of Man*	8.00	-	12.00
14892 *Forsaken Blues*	8.00	-	12.00
14926 *Copenhagen*	20.00	-	30.00
14935 *Shanghai Shuffle*	20.00	-	30.00
15030 *Memphis Bound*	50.00	-	75.00
15174 *Hay Foot, Straw Foot*	50.00	-	75.00
15204 *Dinah*	30.00	-	50.00
15205 *Let Me Introduce You To My Rosie*	30.00	-	50.00
15497 *Clarinet Marmalade*	30.00	-	50.00
15532 *Stockholm Stomp*	30.00	-	50.00

FRANK HENDERSON & HIS ORCHESTRA:

15323 *Brain Storm*	40.00	-	60.00

HORACE HENDERSON & HIS ORCHESTRA:

Okeh 5433, 5518, 5579, 5606, 5632, 5748, 5841, 5900, 5953, 5978, 6026	5.00	-	10.00
Vocalion 5433, 5518, 5579, 5606	5.00	-	10.00

HENNY HENDRICKSON'S LOUISVILLE SERENADERS:

Victor 22749 *On The Beach With You*	15.00	-	20.00
22750 *Without That Gal!*	15.00	-	20.00

TAL HENRY AND HIS NORTH CAROLINIANS/ORCHESTRA:

Bluebird 5364, 5365, 5366	5.00	-	8.00
Victor 21404 *Some Little Someone*	7.00	-	10.00
21471 *Lonesome*	7.00	-	10.00
21573 *Louise, I Love You*	7.00	-	10.00
V-40034 *When Shadows Fall*	15.00	-	20.00
V-40035 *Found My Gal*	35.00	-	50.00
V-40133 *Shame On You*	15.00	-	20.00

RAY HERBECK AND HIS MUSIC WITH ROMANCE:

Okeh, most issues	3.00	-	5.00
Vocalion, most issues	3.00	-	6.00

JULES HERBUVEAUX AND HIS PALMER HOUSE VICTORIANS:

Vocalion 15380 *Where'd You Get Those Eyes?*	5.00	-	8.00
15402 *Mandy*	5.00	-	8.00
15403 *Someone Is Losin' Susan*	5.00	-	8.00
15426 *Havin' Lots Of Fun*	5.00	-	8.00

JOE HERLIHY & HIS ORCHESTRA:

Edison 52059 *Cornfed*	20.00	-	30.00
52076 *State and Madison*	20.00	-	30.00
52098 *Bye-Bye, Pretty Baby*	15.00	-	20.00
52100 *Rolling Around In Roses*	15.00	-	20.00

WOODY HERMAN & HIS ORCHESTRA:

Columbia, most issues	2.00	-	5.00
Decca 1056 *The Goose Hangs High*	8.00	-	12.00
1057 *I Can't Pretend*	7.00	-	10.00
1064 *Old Fashioned Swing*	7.00	-	10.00
1079 *Mr. Ghost Goes To Town*	7.00	-	10.00
1288 *Dupree Blues*	7.00	-	10.00
1307 *Trouble In Mind*	7.00	-	10.00
1385 *Stardust On The Moon*	7.00	-	10.00
1397 *Double Or Nothing*	7.00	-	10.00
1523, 1535, 1570, 1583	5.00	-	8.00
1801, 1839, 1879, 1900	4.00	-	7.00
Decca, blue label, most other issues	3.00	-	5.00

MILT HERTH (TRIO):

Decca, blue label, most issues	4.00	-	7.00

HERWIN HOT SHOTS:

Herwin 93015 *Salty Dog*	200.00	-	300.00

EDDIE HEYWOOD/AND HIS JAZZ SIX ORCHESTRA:

Decca, most issues . . . . 3.00 - 6.00
Okeh 8094 *The Mixed Up Blues* . . . . 75.00 - 100.00
    8402 *Trombone Moanin' Blues* . . . . . . .100.00 - 150.00

BILLY HICKS & HIS SIZZLIN' SIX
Variety 601 *Fade Out* . . . . 10.00 - 15.00

RAMONA HICKS:
Bluebird 8173, 8200, 8233 . . . . 8.00 - 12.00

J.C. HIGGINBOTHAM & HIS SIX HICKS; J. C. HIGGINBOTHAM QUINTET:
Okeh 8772 *Higginbotham Blues* . . . . 40.00 - 60.00
Session 10013, 12016 . . . . 7.00 - 10.00

SI HIGGINS & HIS SODBUSTERS:
Harmony 739-H *The Prune Song* . . . . 7.00 - 10.00
(Note: Also issued on *Diva* and *Velvet Tone*,
    similarly valued.)

THE HIGH HATTERS:
Victor 21682 *Some Sweet Someone* . . . . 7.00 - 10.00
Victor 21835 *Wipin' The Pan* . . . . 5.00 - 8.00
Victor 22041 *Low Down Rhythm* . . . . 7.00 - 10.00
Victor 22046 *Daddy, Won't You Please*
    Come Home . . . . 5.00 - 8.00
Victor 22219 *Singin' in the Bathtub* . . . . . . 5.00 - 8.00
Victor 22409 *You Brought a New Kind of Love*
    To Me . . . . 5.00 - 8.00

THE HIGH STEPPERS:
Crown 3184 *You Can't Stop Me From Loving You* 10.00 - 15.00
    3298 *Lawd, You Made The Night Too Long* . . . 10.00 - 15.00
    3300 *Keepin' Out of Mischief Now* . . . . 10.00 - 15.00
    3394 *Please* . . . . 10.00 - 15.00

HIGHTOWER'S NIGHT HAWKS:
Black Patti 8045 *Boar Hog Blues* . . . . .300.00 - 600.00

ALEX HILL/AND HIS HOLLYWOOD SEPIANS/ORCHESTRA:
Vocalion 1270 *Tack Head Blues* . . . . .100.00 - 150.00
    1465 *Southbound* . . . . .150.00 - 200.00
    1493 *Dyin' With The Blues* . . . . .150.00 - 200.00
    2826 *Ain't It Nice?* . . . . 50.00 - 80.00
    2848 *Song of the Plow* . . . . 50.00 - 80.00

JUD HILL'S BLUE DEVILS/CLUB MOROCCO ORCHESTRA:
Gennett 3180, 3186, 3200, 3211, 3218, 3230 . . . . . 5.00 - 10.00

SAM HILL & HIS ORCHESTRA:
Oriole 245 *One Of These Days* . . . . 10.00 - 15.00
    290 *My Dream Man* . . . . 10.00 - 15.00
    303 *Everybody Loves My Baby* . . . . 20.00 - 30.00
    304 *How Come You Do Me Like You Do* . . . . . 10.00 - 15.00
    341 *I'll See You In My Dreams* . . . . 10.00 - 15.00
    347 *Alabamy Bound* . . . . 15.00 - 20.00
    348 *Why Couldn't It Be Poor Little Me?* . . . . . 15.00 - 20.00
    365 *Swannee Butterfly* . . . . 10.00 - 15.00
    437 *Naughty Man* . . . . 20.00 - 30.00

TEDDY HILL & HIS (NBC) ORCHESTRA:
Titles, issued contemporaneously on Banner,
    Conqueror, Melotone, Oriole, Perfect, Romeo:
    Got Me Doin' Things; Here Comes Cookie;
    When The Robin Sings His Song Again . . . . . 10.00 - 15.00
Bluebird 6897 *The Love Bug Will Bite You* . . . . . . 8.00 - 12.00
    6898 *My Marie* . . . . 8.00 - 12.00
    6908 *Big Boy Blue* . . . . 8.00 - 12.00
    6941 *China Boy* . . . . 8.00 - 12.00
    6943 *A Study In Brown* . . . . 7.00 - 10.00
    6954 *I Know Now* . . . . 7.00 - 10.00
    6988 *King Porter Stomp* . . . . 10.00 - 15.00
    6989 *Blue Rhythm Fantasy* . . . . 10.00 - 15.00
    7013 *Yours And Mine* . . . . 10.00 - 15.00
Vocalion 3247 *Blue Rhythm Fantasy* . . . . 10.00 - 15.00
    3294 *Uptown Rhapsody* . . . . 10.00 - 15.00

TINY HILL AND HIS ORCHESTRA:
Mercury, most issues . . . . 2.00 - 3.00
Okeh, most issues . . . . 2.00 - 4.00
Vocalion, most issues . . . . 2.00 - 4.00

HILL TOP INN ORCHESTRA:

Champion 15031 *Choose Your Pal* . . . . 15.00 - 20.00
    15203 *Brotherly Love* . . . . 50.00 - 75.00

RICHARD HIMBER & HIS ESSEX HOUSE/ RHYTHMIC PYRAMIDS RITZ-CARLTON) ORCHESTRA; RICHARD HIMBER'S SEVEN STYLISTS:
Bluebird 5418, 5419, 5421 . . . . 5.00 - 10.00
Victor 24661, 24662, 24670, 24672, 24680,
    24745, 24750, 24756, 24757, 24764, 24811,
    24823, 24824, 24829, 24868, 24869, 24886,
    25036, 25037, 25042, 25049, 25073, 25074,
    25077, 25119, 25122, 25124, 25128, 25132,
    25161, 25179, 25189, 26101, 26148 . . . . 5.00 - 10.00
    25235, 25239, 25243, 25293, 25298, 25299,
      25365, 25392, 25443, 25457, 25738, 25754 . 5.00 - 8.00
Vocalion 2526, 2537, 2538, 2551, 2560, 2572,
    2588, 2589, 25008 . . . . 7.00 - 12.00

EARL HINES & HIS ORCHESTRA:
Bluebird 6744 *Blue Nights* . . . . 7.00 - 10.00
Bluebird 7040 *Beau-Koo Jack* . . . . 7.00 - 10.00
    7768 *Good Little, Bad Little You* . . . . 7.00 - 10.00
    10555 *Glad Rag Doll* . . . . 7.00 - 10.00
Brunswick 6345 *Blue Drag* . . . . 8.00 - 12.00
    6379 *Sensational Mood* . . . . 8.00 - 12.00
    6403 *Love Me Tonight* . . . . 8.00 - 12.00
    6541 *Rosetta* . . . . 8.00 - 12.00
    6710 *Bubbling Over* . . . . 8.00 - 12.00
    6771 *Harlem Lament* . . . . 8.00 - 12.00
    6872 *Blue* . . . . 8.00 - 12.00
    6960 *Just To Be In Caroline* . . . . 8.00 - 12.00
Columbia 2800-D *Fifty-Seven Varieties* . . . . 10.00 - 15.00
Decca 182 *That's A Plenty* . . . . 7.00 - 10.00
    183 *Cavernism* . . . . 7.00 - 10.00
    218 *Maple Leaf Rag* . . . . 7.00 - 10.00
    337 *Copenhagen* . . . . 7.00 - 10.00
    389 *Rhythm Lullaby* . . . . 7.00 - 10.00
    577 *Wolverine Blues* . . . . 7.00 - 10.00
    654 *Japanese Sandman* . . . . 7.00 - 10.00
    714 *Bubbling Over* . . . . 7.00 - 10.00
Okeh 8832 *A Monday Date* . . . . 50.00 - 75.00
    8653 *Fifty-Seven Varieties* . . . . 50.00 - 75.00
    41175 *Fifty-Seven Varieties* . . . . 50.00 - 75.00
Q.R.S. 7036 *Off Time Blues* . . . . .150.00 - 200.00
    7037 *A Monday Date* . . . . .150.00 - 200.00
    7038 *Chimes In Blues* . . . . .150.00 - 200.00
    7039 *Panther Rag* . . . . .150.00 - 200.00

Victor 22683 *Sister Kate* . . . . 20.00 - 30.00
    22842 *Sweet Ella May* . . . . 30.00 - 50.00
    V 38042 *Chicago Rhythm* . . . . 30.00 - 40.00
    V 38043 *Beau-Koo Jack* . . . . 30.00 - 40.00
    V 38048 *Have You Ever Felt That Way?* . . . . 30.00 - 40.00
    V 38096 *Grand Piano Blues* . . . . 35.00 - 50.00
Vocalion 3379 *Madhouse* . . . . 7.00 - 10.00
    3392 *Swingin' Down* . . . . 7.00 - 10.00
    3467 *Rhythm Sundae* . . . . 7.00 - 10.00
    3501 *Flany Doodle Swing* . . . . 7.00 - 10.00
    3586 *Honeysuckle Rose* . . . . 7.00 - 10.00
    4008 *Please Be Kind* . . . . 7.00 - 10.00
    4032 *Dominick Swing* . . . . 7.00 - 10.00
    4143 *Tippin' At The Terrace* . . . . 7.00 - 10.00
    4272 *Jack Climbed A Beanstalk* . . . . 7.00 - 10.00

HITCH'S HAPPY HARMONISTS:

Gennett 3066 *Boneyard Shuffle*	40.00 -	70.00
5633 *Cataract Rag Blues*	50.00 -	100.00

LES HITE & HIS ORCHESTRA:

Bluebird 11109, 11210,; Hit 7001, 7002	5.00 -	10.00
Varsity 8373, 8391, 8396	7.00 -	10.00

RICHARD HITTER'S BLUE KNIGHTS/ CABINEERS:

Everbody's 1062 *Eccentric*	100.00 -	150.00
1063 *Riverboat Shuffle*	100.00 -	150.00
Gennett 3149 *Stomp Off, Let's Go*	50.00 -	75.00

ART HODES' ART HODES' COLUMBIA QUINTET:

Jazz Records 1001, 1002, 1003, 1004, 1005, 1009	7.00 -	12.00
Solo Art 12005	10.00 -	15.00

JOHNNY HODGES & HIS ORCHESTRA:

Variety 546, 586	7.00 -	12.00
Vocalion 3948, 4046, 4115, 4213, 4242, 4309, 4335, 4351, 4386, 4573, 4622, 4710, 4849, 4917, 4941, 5100, 5170, 5330, 5353, 5533, 5940	5.00 -	10.00

HARVEY HOFFMAN & HIS ORCHESTRA:

Champion 15263 *Original Black Bottom Dance*	150.00 -	200.00
15266 *All That I Has Is Gone*	150.00 -	200.00

HOKUM TRIO:

Titles, issued comtemporaneously on Clarion, Diva, Velvet Tone: *He Wouldn't Stop Doing It; I'm Havin' My Fun; You're Bound to Look Like a Monkey; You've Had Your Way*	30.00 -	50.00

BILLIE HOLIDAY & HER ORCHESTRA:

Conqueror 9097, 9457, 9458	4.00 -	8.00
Harmony 1075 *Wherever You Are*	5.00 -	8.00
Okeh 3276, 3288, 3333, 3334, 3431, 3440, 3520, 3543, 3593, 3605, 3701, 3748, 3947, 4029, 4126, 4151, 4208, 4238, 4396, 4457, 4631, 4786, 4834, 5021, 5129, 5302, 5377, 5481, 5609, 5719	4.00 -	8.00
5806 *Practice Makes Perfect*	5.00 -	10.00
5831 *I'm All For You*	7.00 -	10.00
5991 *Time On My Hands*	7.00 -	10.00
6064 *St. Louis Blues*	5.00 -	8.00
6134 *Let's Do It*	5.00 -	8.00
6214 *All Of Me*	5.00 -	8.00
6270 *Solitude*	7.00 -	10.00
6369 *Love Me Or Leave Me*	5.00 -	8.00
6451 *Gloomy Sunday*	5.00 -	8.00
Vocalion 3276 *Did I Remember?*	8.00 -	12.00
3288 *Billie's Blues*	8.00 -	12.00
3333 *A Fine Romance*	8.00 -	12.00
3334 *Let's Call A Heart A Heart*	8.00 -	12.00
3431 *One Never Knows, Does One?*	8.00 -	12.00
3440 *If My Heart Could Only Talk*	8.00 -	12.00
3520 *Let's Call The Whole Thing Off*	8.00 -	12.00
3543 *Where Is The Sun?*	8.00 -	12.00
3593 *Without Your Love*	8.00 -	12.00
3605 *A Sailboat In The Moonlight*	8.00 -	12.00
3701 *Getting Some Fun Out Of Life*	8.00 -	12.00
3748 *He's Funny That Way*	8.00 -	12.00
3947 *Now They Call It Swing*	8.00 -	12.00
4029 *When A Woman Loves A Man*	8.00 -	12.00
4126 *You Go To My Hear*	8.00 -	12.00
4156 *If I Were You*	8.00 -	12.00
4208 *Having Myself A Time*	8.00 -	12.00
4238 *I Wish I Had You!*	5.00 -	8.00
4396 *I've Got A Date With A Dream*	7.00 -	10.00
4457 *The Very Thought Of You*	5.00 -	8.00
4631 *Dream Of Life*	7.00 -	10.00
4786 *Under A Blue Jungle Moon*	7.00 -	10.00
4834 *You're Too Lovely To Last*	7.00 -	10.00
5021 *Them There Eyes*	7.00 -	10.00
5129 *Swing, Brother Swing*	7.00 -	10.00
5302 *You're Just A No-Account*	7.00 -	10.00
5377 *Night And Day*	5.00 -	8.00
5481 *Body And Soul*	5.00 -	8.00
5609 *Falling In Love Again*	5.00 -	8.00
5719 *Tell Me More*	5.00 -	8.00

"HOLIDAY GREETINGS FROM THE BUNCH AT ORANGE":

Edison (master number) 10068 "jazzed" by various various Edison officers, including "Thomas A. Edison Himself." (Red and green label, issued to Edison dealers)	75.00 -	100.00

HOLLYWOOD DANCE ORCHESTRA:

Banner 0503 *Gonna Be a Moon Out Tonight*	5.00 -	8.00
Banner 0506 *Find A Sweetheart (Who'll Kiss Your Troubles Goodbye)*	5.00 -	8.00
Banner 0509 *Walk on the Sunny Side*	5.00 -	8.00
Banner 0517 *Let Me Drown in an Ocean of Love*	5.00 -	8.00
Banner 0539 *I'm Following You*	5.00 -	8.00
Banner 0563 *Hello Baby*	7.00 -	10.00
Banner 0564 *I Have To Have You*	5.00 -	8.00
Banner 0573 *I've Got To Have You*	5.00 -	8.00
Banner 0596 *What Do I Care?*	7.00 -	10.00
Banner 0598 *Nobody's Sweetheart*	10.00 -	15.00
Banner 0632 *Sweetheart*	5.00 -	8.00
Banner 0730 *I Love You So Much*	5.00 -	8.00
Banner 0786 *Go Home and Tell Your Mother*	5.00 -	8.00
Banner 1429 *Everything You Do*	5.00 -	8.00
Banner 1727 *What Good Is "Good Morning"?*	5.00 -	8.00
Banner 1762 *June, The Moon and You*	5.00 -	8.00
Banner 6052 *Oh! Constantine*	5.00 -	8.00
Banner 6106 *Let's Make Love in the Moonlight*	5.00 -	8.00
Banner 6131 *Lonely Melody*	5.00 -	8.00
Banner 6210 *That's What's Good For Me*	5.00 -	8.00
Banner 6232 *What's The Answer*	5.00 -	8.00
Banner 6257 *Cat's Kittens*	5.00 -	8.00
Banner 6259 *Just a Little Cuter Than The Rest*	5.00 -	8.00
Banner 6268 *I'd Love To Go Around With You*	5.00 -	8.00
Banner 6292 *Shake Off The Blues*	5.00 -	8.00
Banner 6326 *My Castle In Spain Is a Shack in the Lane*	5.00 -	8.00
Banner 6348 *Papa's Mama's Blue ('Cause Mama's Papa's Through)*	5.00 -	8.00
Banner 6388 *Ditto*	5.00 -	8.00
Banner 6417 *I'm Doing What I'm Doing For Love*	5.00 -	8.00
Banner 6453 *That's What I Call Love*	5.00 -	8.00
Banner 6455 *Me and That Gal O'Mine*	5.00 -	8.00
Banner 6515 *Bashful*	5.00 -	8.00
Banner 6544 *Every Once In a While*	5.00 -	8.00
Banner 6552 *Same Old Moon*	5.00 -	8.00
Banner 7049 *What Good Is The Moon Above?*	5.00 -	8.00
Banner 7076 *Though You Threw Me Down*	5.00 -	8.00
Banner 7136 *A Pretty Girl, A Pretty Tune*	5.00 -	8.00
Banner 7158 *Bring Back My Lovin' Man*	5.00 -	8.00
Banner 7162 *I'm Sorry And You're Sorry (We're Both Sorry Now)*	5.00 -	8.00
Banner 7213 *Nobody Knows*	5.00 -	8.00
Banner 7241 *They Don't Come Better Than Betty*	5.00 -	8.00
Cameo 0109 *Walk On The Sunny Side*	5.00 -	8.00
Cameo 0117 *Let Me Drown In An Ocean Of Love*	5.00 -	8.00
Cameo 0173 *I've Got To Have You*	5.00 -	8.00
Cameo 0330 *I Love You So Much*	5.00 -	8.00
Oriole 1770 *Let Me Drown in an Ocean of Love*	5.00 -	8.00
Regal 8475 *Chloe*	5.00 -	8.00
Romeo 1402 *Dixianna*	7.00 -	10.00
Silvertone 21512 *Who's That Pretty Baby?*	5.00 -	8.00

HOLLYWOOD SHUFFLERS:

Vocalion 15837 *Low Down Rhythm*	100.00 -	150.00
15841 *Bigger and Better Than Ever*	100.00 -	150.00

HOLLYWOOD SYNCOPATORS:

Nordskog 3013 *Pacific Coast Blues*	30.00 -	50.00

THE HOME TOWNERS:

Banner 0532 *College Days*	5.00 -	8.00
Banner 0541 *Yes Indeedy*	5.00 -	8.00
Banner 0558 *There's a Czechoslavak Waiting for Me*	5.00 -	8.00

Banner 0631 *Headin' South* .... 7.00 - 10.00
Banner 0657 *There's No Good Reason Why* ..... 7.00 - 10.00
Banner 0658 *Why Don't You Marry The Girl?* ... 7.00 - 10.00
Banner 0668 *Coming Thru The Sky* .... 7.00 - 10.00
Cameo 0224 *What's The Use?* .... 7.00 - 10.00
    0226 *What A Funny World This Would Be* ..... 4.00 - 7.00
    9130 *Let's Get Together* .... 5.00 - 8.00
    9131 *What D'Ya Think Of My Baby?* .... 5.00 - 8.00
Jewel 5883 *Headin' South* .... 7.00 - 10.00
Jewel 5921 *Coming Thru The Sky* .... 7.00 - 10.00
Oriole 1883 *Headin' South* .... 7.00 - 10.00
Romeo 932 *Let's Get Together* .... 5.00 - 8.00
    1246 *Headin' South* .... 7.00 - 10.00

HONEY SWAMP STOMPERS:
Harmony 856-H *Wipin' The Pan* .... 8.00 - 12.00

CLAUDE HOPKINS AND HIS ORCHESTRA:
Ammor 114, 115, 116 .... 8.00 - 12.00
Brunswick 6750 *Washington Squabble* ...... 10.00 - 15.00
    6864 *My Gal Sal* .... 10.00 - 15.00
    6981 *I Can't Dance* .... 10.00 - 15.00
    6916 *Everybody Shuffle* .... 10.00 - 15.00
Columbia 2665-D *Mad Moments* .... 15.00 - 20.00
    2674-D *Mush Mouth* .... 15.00 - 20.00
    2741-D *California, Here I Come* ...... 15.00 - 20.00
    2747-D *He's A Son of the South* ...... 15.00 - 20.00
    2880-D *Ain't Misbehavin* .... 15.00 - 20.00
    2904-D *Marie* .... 15.00 - 20.00
Decca 184 *King Porter Stomp* .... 10.00 - 15.00
    185 *Just You, Just Me* .... 10.00 - 15.00
    270 *Walkin' The Dog* .... 10.00 - 15.00
    353 *Do You Ever Think Of Me?* ...... 10.00 - 15.00
    374 *Love In Bloom* .... 10.00 - 15.00
    441 *Chasing All The Blues Away* ..... 10.00 - 15.00
    674 *Monkey Business* .... 7.00 - 10.00
    1153 *Sunday* .... 7.00 - 10.00
    1286 *Church Street Sobbin' Blues* .... 7.00 - 10.00
    1316 *My Kinda Love* .... 7.00 - 10.00

DE WOLF HOPPER:
Victor 35290 (12-inch) *Casey At The Bat* ...... 8.00 - 12.00

HOTEL PENNSYLVANIA MUSIC:
Harmony 1082-H *Lucky Little Devil* .... 5.00 - 8.00
    1086-H *Nobody's Sweetheart* .... 5.00 - 8.00
    1092-H *Tiger Rag* .... 7.00 - 10.00
(Note: Titles also occur on *Diva* and *Velvet Tone*,
    similarly valued. Numerous other titles on
    these labels, and *Clarion*, are of lesser value.)

HORSEY'S HOT FIVE:
Gennett 6722 *Weeping Blues* .... 200.00 - 400.00

THE HOT AIR MEN:
Columbia 2092-D *Navy Blues* .... 10.00 - 15.00
    2175-D *Red Hot Chicago* .... 10.00 - 15.00

HOT AND HEAVY:
Pathe-Actuelle 7510 *Memphis Rag* .... 75.00 - 100.00
Perfect 110 *Memphis Rag* .... 75.00 - 100.00

THE HOT DOGS:
Silvertone 3560 *Hot Mustard* .... 150.00 - up
    3567 *Mojo Blues* .... 80.00 - 120.00
    3572 *Carolina Shuffle* .... 80.00 - 120.00
    3574 *Steady Roll* .... 100.00 - 150.00

THE HOSTY TOTSY GANG: (See also:
    IRVING MILLS)
Brunswick 4014, *Doin' The New Low Down* .... 10.00 - 15.00
    4044 *Don't Mess Around With Me* ...... 15.00 - 20.00
    4112 *I Couldn't If I Wanted To* ...... 8.00 - 12.00
    4122 *Since You Went Away* .... 10.00 - 15.00
    4200 *Futuristic Rhythm* .... 15.00 - 20.00

THE HOTTENTOTS:
Paramount 12539 *Lots O'Mama* .... 20.00 - 30.00
Supertone 9447 *Chicago Rhythm* .... 50.00 - 80.00
Vocalion 15161 *Down And Out Blues* ...... 30.00 - 50.00
    15209 *Pensacola* .... 30.00 - 50.00

THE HOUR OF CHARM ALL GIRL

ORCHESTRA:
Vogue R-725 *Alice Blue Gown* .... 20.00 - 30.00
Vogue R-726 *Blue Skies* .... 20.00 - 30.00
(Note: The above two records comprise Vogue
    album no. V100, "A Study In Blue".)
Vogue R-733 *Seville* .... 20.00 - 30.00

BOB HOWARD & HIS ORCHESTRA:
Decca 343 *Throwin' Stones At The Sun* .... 8.00 - 12.00
    347 *It's Unbelievable* .... 8.00 - 12.00
    400 *Pardon My Love* .... 8.00 - 12.00
    407 *Breakin' The Ice* .... 8.00 - 12.00
    439 *I'll Never Change* .... 8.00 - 12.00
    460 *A Porter's Love Song* .... 7.00 - 10.00
    484 *Corrine Corrina* .... 7.00 - 10.00
    504 *If The Moon Turns Green* .... 7.00 - 10.00
    513 *In A Little Gypsy Tea Room* ..... 7.00 - 10.00
    524 *I'm Painting The Town Red* ...... 7.00 - 10.00
    598 *It's Written In The Stars* ...... 5.00 - 8.00
    627 *Give Me A Break, Baby* .... 5.00 - 8.00
    689 *You Hit The Spot* .... 7.00 - 10.00
    720 *Spreadin' Rhythm Around* .... 7.00 - 10.00
    722 *Much Too Much* .... 7.00 - 10.00
    839 *Let's Not Fall In Love* .... 7.00 - 10.00
    862 *Public Weakness No. 1* .... 7.00 - 10.00
Decca 917, 927, 983, 1195, 1205, 1293, 1306 . 4.00 - 8.00

GORDON HOWARD & HIS MULTNOMAH
    CHIEFTAINS:
Gennett 6381 *Wob-A-Ly Walk* .... 20.00 - 30.00
    6395 *Golden-Gate* .... 20.00 - 30.00

PAUL HOWARD'S QUALITY SERENADERS:
Bluebird 5804 *Stuff* .... 15.00 - 20.00
Victor 22660 *New Kinda Blues* .... 50.00 - 80.00
    23354 *California Swing* .... 200.00 - 300.00
    23420 *Gettin' Ready Blues* .... 200.00 - 300.00
V 38068 *The Ramble* .... 50.00 - 80.00
V 38070 *Charlie's Idea* .... 50.00 - 80.00
V 38122 *Quality Shout* .... 75.00 - 100.00

BERT HOWELL:
Paramount 13063 *You're Driving Me Crazy* ..... 30.00 - 50.00
Victor 21062 *Bve Bve Florence* .... 20.00 - 30.00

HUDSON TRIO:
Famous 3024 *Twelfth Street Rag* .... 7.00 - 10.00

HUDSON-DE LANGE ORCHESTRA; WILL
    HUDSON & HIS ORCHESTRA/SEVEN
    SWINGSTERS:
Brunswick 7598, 7618, 7656, 7667, 7700, 7708,
    7715, 7727, 7743, 7785, 7795, 7809, 7828, 7991,
    7996, 7998, 8002, 8007, 8016, 8023, 8040,
    8049, 8071, 8077, 8081, 8090, 8113, 8147, 8156,
    8164, 8177, 8191, 8195, 8213, 8222 .... 5.00 - 10.00
Master 103, 112, 125, 132, 138 .... 5.00 - 12.00

CLAIRE HULL & HIS WANDERERS:
Gennett 6356 *Nobody's Sweetheart* .... 50.00 - 75.00

PHIL HUGHES AND HIS HIGH HATTERS:
Clarion 5304-C *Just A Crazy Song* .... 10.00 - 15.00
    5342-C *Treat Me Like A Baby* .... 7.00 - 10.00
    5365-C *It's A Long Time Between Kisses* ..... 7.00 - 10.00
Harmony 1313-H *Just A Crazy Song* .... 10.00 - 15.00
    1333-H *Look in the Looking Glass* ...... 7.00 - 10.00
    1353-H *It's a Long Time Between Kisses* ..... 7.00 - 10.00
Velvet Tone 2370-V *Just a Crazy Song* .... 10.00 - 15.00
    2406-V *Treat Me Like a Baby* .... 7.00 - 10.00
    2429-V *It's a Long Time Between Kisses* ..... 7.00 - 10.00

HUNTER'S SERENADERS:
Vocalion 1621 *Sensational Mood* .... 150.00 - 200.00

CHARLEY HUNTER'S ORCHESTRA:
Broadway 5023 *Bottomland* .... 75.00 - 100.00

INA RAY HUTTON & HER MELODEARS:
Victor 24692 *How's About Tomorrow Night?* .... 10.00 - 15.00
Vocalion 2801 *Georgia's Gorgeous Gal* .... 10.00 - 15.00
    2816 *Wild Party* .... 10.00 - 15.00

JOHN HYMAN'S BAYOU STOMPERS:

Victor 20593 *Alligator Blues*	75.00 -	100.00

BERTHA IDAHO:

Columbia 14437-D *Move It On Out Of Here*	30.00 -	50.00

IDEAL SERENADERS:

Columbia 1131-D *Dawning*	7.00 -	10.00

IMPERIAL DANCE ORCHESTRA:

Banner 0505 *Can't We Be Friends*	7.00 -	10.00
Banner 0514 *It's Not a Secret Any More*	5.00 -	8.00
Banner 0532 *Lady Luck*	5.00 -	8.00
Banner 0589 *Ring Around the Moon*	7.00 -	10.00
Banner 0631 *Sing You Sinners*	8.00 -	12.00
0747 *Because I'm Lonesome*	8.00 -	12.00
0759 *Hear Dem Bells*	7.00 -	10.00
Banner 1943 *The Dixie Vagabond*	5.00 -	8.00
Banner 6070 *Strolling In The Sunshine*	5.00 -	8.00
Banner 6245 *Let's Do It*	5.00 -	8.00
Banner 6379 *Time Will Tell*	5.00 -	8.00
Banner 6444 *I Want To Meander in the Meadow*	5.00 -	8.00
Banner 6500 *Where Do Holes Go In Doughnuts?*	5.00 -	8.00
Banner 7131 *Boo-Hoo-Hoo (What Am I Gonna Do?)*	5.00 -	8.00
Banner 7165 *I Wanna Go Back To Indiana*	5.00 -	8.00
7192 *Ready For The River*	8.00 -	12.00
Cameo 0105 *Can't We Be Friends?*	7.00 -	10.00
Cameo 0226 *The Stein Song*	4.00 -	7.00
Domino 4449 *Miss Wonderful*	7.00 -	10.00
4469 *I'm Following You*	5.00 -	8.00
Domino 4479, 4485	4.00 -	8.00
Domino 4646 *Just A Little Dance, Mamselle*	15.00 -	20.00
Jewel 5883 *Sing You Sinners*	8.00 -	12.00
Oriole 1766 *It's Not A Secret Any More*	5.00 -	8.00
1883 *Sing You Sinners*	8.00 -	12.00
1998 *Because I'm Lonesome*	8.00 -	12.00
Perfect 15258 *I'm Following You!*	5.00 -	8.00
15264 *Hello Baby*	5.00 -	8.00
15274 *What Do I Care?*	7.00 -	10.00
Regal 8041 *Show That Fellow The Door*	5.00 -	8.00
8893 *Miss Wonderful*	7.00 -	10.00
8914 *I'm Following You*	5.00 -	8.00
8943 *What Do I Care?*	7.00 -	10.00
Romeo 1246 *Sing You Sinners*	8.00 -	12.00

IMPERIAL ORCHESTRA:

Bell 534 *Sing Me A Baby Song*	7.00 -	10.00

INDIANA FIVE: (See ORIGINAL INDIANA FIVE)

INDIANA HOTEL BROADCASTERS:

Champion 15110 *Spanish Mamma*	10.00 -	15.00
15111 *The Nightmare*	8.00 -	12.00
15119 *That's Why I Love You*	7.00 -	10.00

INDIANA SYNCOPATERS:

LaBelle 1418 *Bees Knees*	10.00 -	20.00

THE INK SPOTS:

Decca 817, 883, 1036, 1154, 1236, 1251	5.00 -	10.00
Victor 24851 *Your Feet's Too Big*	30.00 -	50.00
24876 *Swing Gate, Swing*	30.00 -	50.00

INTERNATIONAL DANCE ORCHESTRA:

Globe 1333 *Lady Lou*	8.00 -	12.00

INTERSTATE BLUE JACKETS:

Champion 15037 *The Camel Walk*	15.00 -	25.00
15040 *Mama, Let Rosie Alone*	15.00 -	25.00
Champion 15053 *Spanish Shawl*	15.00 -	25.00
15064 *Shanghai Honeymoon*	15.00 -	25.00
15304 *Indiana Mud*	50.00 -	75.00

IPANA TROUBADOURS:

Columbia 503-D *Paddlin' Madeline Home*	5.00 -	8.00
528-D *Jig Walk*	5.00 -	8.00
1009-D *Side By Side*	5.00 -	8.00
1463-D *Nagasaki*	8.00 -	12.00
1638-D *Glorianna*	15.00 -	20.00
1694-D *Rose Of Mandalay*	20.00 -	30.00
1717-D *Mississippi*	5.00 -	8.00
1881-D *There Was Nothing Else To Do*	5.00 -	8.00

1920-D *Hang On To Me*	5.00 -	8.00
1982-D *True Blue Lou*	5.00 -	8.00
2006-D *My Sweeter Than Sweet*	5.00 -	8.00
2117-D *Kickin' A Hole in the Sky*	7.00 -	10.00
2174-D *Whippoorwill*	5.00 -	8.00
2220-D *Sing*	5.00 -	8.00
2317-D *Three Little Words*	5.00 -	8.00
2368-D *I'm So Afraid of You*	5.00 -	8.00
2486-D *On The Beach With You*	5.00 -	8.00
Columbia 3585-X *Just a Little Glimpse of Paradise*	10.00 -	15.00

(Note: Above is part of a Spanish series, lacking the vocal present in the performance issued for U.S. market and issued as by "Trovadores Ipana." Other similar issues probably exist, and would possibly be of interest to collectors.)

KITTY IRVIN:

Gennett 5592 *Copenhagen*	80.00 -	120.00

VIC/VICTOR IRWIN & HIS ORCHESTRA:

Titles, issued contemporaneously on Banner, Oriole, Perfect, Romeo: *I Don't Blame You; Now's The Time To Fall In Love; She's So Nice; Who's Your Little Who-Zis?*

	5.00 -	10.00
Harmony 422-H *Rhapsody In Blue*	5.00 -	8.00
487-H *I Can't Believe That You're In Love With Me*	5.00 -	8.00
571-H *Lady Of Havana*	5.00 -	8.00
610-H *Danger! Look Out For That Gal*	5.00 -	8.00

(Note: Above titles, on *Diva* and *Velvet Tone*, are similarly valued.)

JACK'S FAST-STEPPIN' BELLHOPS:

Champion 15088 *Honey Bunch*	30.00 -	50.00

JACKSON & HIS SOUTHERN STOMPERS:

Marathon (7-inch record) 227 *Dusky Stevedore*	150.00 -	200.00

ALEX JACKSON'S PLANTATION ORCHESTRA:

Gennett 6249 *Jackass Blues*	150.00 -	200.00
6296 *Missouri Squabble*	150.00 -	200.00

DEWEY JACKSON'S PEACOCK ORCHESTRA:

Vocalion 1039 *Go 'Won To Town*	125.00 -	175.00
1040 *She's Cryin' For Me*	150.00 -	200.00

DUKE JACKSON'S SERENADERS:

Gennett 6124 *Now Cut Loose*	150.00 -	200.00

EARL JACKSON'S MUSICAL CHAMPIONS:

Melotone 12080 *Is That Religion?*	15.00 -	20.00
12093 *Rockin' Chair*	8.00 -	12.00
12164 *Red Devil*	8.00 -	12.00
Perfect 15468 *Star Dust*	8.00 -	12.00
15481 *Black and Tan Fantasy*	8.00 -	12.00

FRISKY FOOT JACKSON & HIS THUMPERS:

Champion 15696 *Good Time Mama*	200.00 -	300.00
15929 *Mississippi Stomp*	200.00 -	300.00
40043 *Good Time Mama*	50.00 -	75.00

LITTLE JOE JACKSON & HIS BOYS:

Bell 1174 *Fourth Avenue Stomp*	200.00 -	300.00

MARY JACKSON:

Pathe-Actuelle 032013, Perfect 12097 *All The Time*	8.00 -	10.00

MIKE JACKSON:

Victor 20181 *Just Too Bad*	10.00 -	15.00
20482 *Alabama Mama*	8.00 -	12.00

PRESTON JACKSON & HIS UPTOWN BAND:

Paramount 12400 *Harmony Blues*	125.00 -	175.00
12411 *Trombone Man*	125.00 -	175.00

SLIM JACKSON TRIO:

Cameo 705 *Freakish Blues*	8.00 -	12.00

SMOKE JACKSON & HIS RED ONIONS:

Champion 15714 *It's Tight Like That*	90.00 -	130.00
15905 *Wailin' Blues*	150.00 -	200.00

JACKSONVILLE HARMONY TRIO:

Victor 20960 *Jacksonville Blues*	15.00 -	20.00

21204 *I Wonder*	20.00 -	30.00

BUD JACOBSON'S JUNGLE KINGS:
Signature 103, 106, 903, 904	3.00 -	6.00

JAFFE'S COLLEGIANS:
Okeh 40561 *Sweet and Low Down*	7.00 -	10.00

JAMAICA JAZZERS:
Okeh 40117 *West Indies Blues*	50.00 -	75.00

BILLY JAMES' DANCE ORCHESTRA:
Banner 6356 *Pa's Old Hat*	7.00 -	10.00
Challenge 964 *Dixieanna (The Pride of the South)*	5.00 -	8.00
Jewel 5028 *Do a Little of Everything*	5.00 -	8.00
Jewel 5073 *I'm Her Beau*	5.00 -	8.00
Jewel 5146 *Lonely Melody*	5.00 -	8.00
Oriole 271 *Hard Hearted Hannah*	10.00 -	15.00
547 *I Wish't I Was In Peoria*	5.00 -	8.00
565 *Sweet Child*	15.00 -	20.00
599 *Indiana's Calling Me*	5.00 -	8.00
829 *Muddy Water*	8.00 -	12.00
850 *Annabelle*	5.00 -	8.00
984 *Blame It On The Black Bottom Craze*	8.00 -	12.00
1008 *Swanee's Calling Me*	8.00 -	12.00
1250 *Straight Back Home*	5.00 -	8.00
1284 *I Wanna Go Back To Indiana*	5.00 -	8.00
1319 *Nobody Knows*	5.00 -	8.00
Oriole 1480 *Copper Colored Sam*	5.00 -	8.00
Oriole 1489 *And Then*	5.00 -	8.00
Oriole 1512 *What Have We Lost? We Found Each Other*	5.00 -	8.00
Oriole 1536 *Mean To Me*	7.00 -	10.00
Oriole 1543 *Get Yourself a Sweetie and Kiss Your Troubles*	5.00 -	8.00
Oriole 1548 *While I Am Here and You Are There*	5.00 -	8.00
Oriole 1570 *Why Are the Days So Long?*	5.00 -	8.00
Oriole 1634 *What Will I Do Without You, Sweetheart?*	5.00 -	8.00
Oriole 1637 *Adorable You*	5.00 -	8.00
Oriole 1721 *Now That You Are Mine*	5.00 -	8.00

CORKY JAMES & HIS BLACKBIRDS:
Bell 1182 *Bugahoma Blues*	150.00 -	250.00

HARRY JAMES & HIS ORCHESTRA: HARRY JAMES & THE BOOGIE WOOGIE TRIO:
Brunswick 8035 *When We're Alone*	7.00 -	10.00
8038 *(I Can Dream) Can't I?)*	7.00 -	10.00
8055 *One O'Clock Jump*	7.00 -	10.00
8067 *Texas Chatter*	7.00 -	10.00
8136 *Out Of Nowhere*	5.00 -	8.00
8178 *Wrap Your Troubles In Dreams*	5.00 -	8.00
8318 *Boo-Woo*	7.00 -	10.00
8326 *Blame It On My Last Affair*	5.00 -	8.00
8327 *Ciribiribin*	5.00 -	8.00
8337 *Two O'Clock Jump*	5.00 -	8.00
8350 *Home James*	7.00 -	10.00
8355 *Got No Time*	5.00 -	8.00
8366 *King Porter Stomp*	5.00 -	8.00
8395 *I Can't Afford To Dream*	5.00 -	8.00
8406 *I Found A New Baby*	7.00 -	10.00
8443 *From The Bottom Of My Heart*	50.00 -	100.00
Columbia 35209 *It's Funny To Everyone But Me*	7.00 -	10.00
35227 *Here Comes The Night*	7.00 -	10.00
35242 *My Buddy*	7.00 -	10.00
35261 *Who Told You I Cared?*	7.00 -	10.00
Columbia, most other issues	2.00 -	5.00
Varsity (most issues)	4.00 -	7.00

JEANETTE JAMES:
Paramount 12451 *What's That Thing?*	150.00 -	200.00
12470 *Midnight Stomp*	150.00 -	200.00

JELLY JAMES & HIS FEWSICIANS:
Gennett 6045 *Georgia Bo Bo*	100.00 -	150.00

MADELYN JAMES:
Brunswick 7155 *Long Time Blues*	150.00 -	250.00

ART JARRETT:

Columbia 2672-D *Goodbye Blues*	10.00 -	15.00
2691-D *Music, Music Everywhere*	10.00 -	15.00

HOTSY JARVIS (& HER GANG):
Banner 1848 *The Birth Of The Blues*	5.00 -	8.00
Domino 3821 *Lucky Day*	5.00 -	8.00
Oriole 807 *Sunday*	8.00 -	12.00
Regal 8132 *Breezin' Along With The Breeze*	5.00 -	8.00
8159 *Lucky Day*	5.00 -	8.00

JAUDAS' SOCIETY ORCHESTRA:
Edison 50469 *The Darktown Strutters' Ball*	5.00 -	10.00
(Note: record number may be found only on record's edge)		

FRANKIE "HALF-PINT" JAXON (& HIS HOT SHOTS):
Black Patti 8040 *Can't You Wait Till You Get Home*	100.00 -	150.00
8048 *Willie the Weeper*	150.00 -	250.00
Decca 7286, 7304, 7345, 7360, 7482, 7523, 7548, 7619, 7638, 7733, 7742, 7786, 7795, 7806	7.00 -	12.00
Gennett 6214 *Can't You Wait Till You Get Home?*	50.00 -	100.00
6244 *She's Got "It"*	50.00 -	80.00
Vocalion 1226 *Down at Jasper's Bar-Be-Que*	75.00 -	125.00
1257 *Fan It*	30.00 -	50.00
1285 *Let's Knock a Jug*	75.00 -	100.00
1424 *Take It Easy*	100.00 -	150.00
1472 *Down Home in Kentucky*	100.00 -	150.00
1539 *Jive Man Blues*	40.00 -	60.00
1583 *Scuddlin*	40.00 -	60.00
2553 *My Baby's Hot*	20.00 -	30.00
2603 *Fifteen Cents*	20.00 -	30.00

JAZZ-BO'S CAROLINA SERENADERS:
Cameo 218 *My Honey's Lovin' Arms*	5.00 -	8.00
232 *Hopeless Blues*	5.00 -	8.00
257 *Hot Lips*	5.00 -	8.00
258 *Yankee Doodle Blues*	5.00 -	8.00
269 *Achin' Hearted Blues*	5.00 -	8.00

THE JAZZ HARMONISTS/HARMONIZERS:
Claxtonola 40336 *Copenhagen*	100.00 -	150.00
40339 *Riverboat Shuffle*	100.00 -	150.00
40375 *Sensation*	100.00 -	150.00
Rich-Tone 7014 *How Many Times?*	7.00 -	10.00
7022 *In My Heart, On My Mind, All Day Long*	7.00 -	10.00
7037 *Carolina Rolling Stone*	7.00 -	10.00

THE JAZZ MASTERS:
Black Swan 2109 *Bees Knees*	10.00 -	20.00

THE JAZZ-O-HARMONISTS:
Edison 51157 *Snakes Hips*	10.00 -	15.00
51161 *Funny Feet*	10.00 -	15.00
51165 *Long-Lost Mama*	10.00 -	15.00
51168 *The Cat's Whiskers*	10.00 -	15.00
51171 *I Ain't Never Had Nobody Crazy Over Me*	10.00 -	15.00
51172 *Henpecked Blues*	10.00 -	15.00
51229 *I've Got the 'Yes We Have No Bananas Blues'*	8.00 -	12.00
51247 *Darktown Reveille*	15.00 -	25.00
51302 *I'm Goin' South*	10.00 -	15.00
51303 *If I Stay Away Too Long From Carolina*	10.00 -	15.00

THE JAZZOPATORS:
Grey Gull 1797 *Don't Know and Don't Care*	10.00 -	15.00
1816 *Everybody Dance*	10.00 -	15.00
1819 *Blue Ridge Blues*	10.00 -	15.00
Van Dyke *Sweet Little Sis*	7.00 -	10.00

SPEED JEFFRIES & HIS NIGHT OWLS:
Superior 2648 *Georgia Grind*	150.00 -	300.00
2670 *Kentucky Blues*	150.00 -	300.00
2728 *Stomp Your Stuff*	150.00 -	300.00
2738 *Sic 'Em, Tige*	150.00 -	300.00
2755 *Tiger Moon*	150.00 -	300.00
2797 *Richmond Stomp*	150.00 -	300.00

THE JELLY WHIPPERS:
Herwin 92018 *S.O.B. Blues*	150.00 -	200.00

FREDDY JENKINS & HIS HARLEM SEVEN:
Bluebird 6129 *Old Fashioned Love* . . . . 8.00 - 12.00
   6193 *Swingin' 'Em Down* . . . . 8.00 - 12.00
JACK JENNEY & HIS ORCHESTRA:
Vocalion 3972, 4130, 4803, 5304, 5407, 5494,
   5535, 5545 . . . . 5.00 - 10.00
**JETER-PILLARS CLUB PLANTATION
ORCHESTRA:**
Vocalion 3715 *Lazy Rhythm* . . . . 20.00 - 30.00
   3973 *Make Believe* . . . . 20.00 - 30.00
THE JIM-DANDIES:
Harmony 55-H *Shake That Thing* . . . . 10.00 - 15.00
JIMMIE'S BLUE MELODY BOYS:
Vocalion 1439 *Love Me* . . . . 75.00 - 125.00
JIMMIE'S JOYS:
Golden 1858 *No No Nora* . . . . 100.00 - 200.00
   1865 *Bugle Call Rag* . . . . 150.00 - 200.00
JOE'S HOT BABIES:
Paramount 12783 *Beans and Greens* . . . . 150.00 - 200.00
JOE & HIS RHYTHM ORCHESTRA:
Bluebird 6447 *Confessin'* . . . . 8.00 - 12.00
THE JOHNSON BOYS:
Okeh 8708 *Violin Blues* . . . . 75.00 - 100.00
JOHNSON'S JAZZERS
Columbia 14247-D *Can I Get It Now?* . . . . 50.00 - 75.00
JOHNSON'S PLANTATION SERENADERS:
Silvertone 5024 *A Blues Serenade* . . . . 50.00 - 75.00
ARNOLD JOHNSON & HIS ORCHESTRA:
Brunswick 2355 *China Boy* . . . . 5.00 - 8.00
   3914 *What's The Reason?* . . . . 5.00 - 8.00
   3980 *Georgie Porgie* . . . . 5.00 - 8.00
   4037 *Pickin' Cotton* . . . . 5.00 - 8.00
   4080 *That's How I Feel About You* . . . . 5.00 - 8.00
   4125 *Me And The Man In The Moon* . . . . . . 7.00 - 10.00
Brunswick (most other issues) . . . . 3.00 - 6.00
BERT JOHNSON:
Brunswick 7136 *Nasty But Nice* . . . . 150.00 - 200.00
BILL JOHNSON'S LOUISIANA JUG BAND:
Brunswick 7067 *Don't Drink It In Here* . . . . . . 100.00 - 150.00
BLANCHE JOHNSON:
Herwin 92016 *Galveston Blues* . . . . 150.00 - 200.00
BUNK JOHNSON & HIS BAND:
American Music 101 . . . . 5.00 - 10.00
American Music (12-inch) 251, 253, 255 . . . . 5.00 - 10.00
Jazz Information 12, 14 . . . . 5.00 - 10.00
Jazz Man 8, 9, 10 . . . . 5.00 - 10.00
V-Disc (12-inch) 630, 658 . . . . 5.00 - 10.00
CAROLINE JOHNSON:
Buddy 8033 *Mama's Losin' a Mighty Good
   Chance* . . . . 100.00 - 150.00
   8034 *Ain't Got Nobody To Grind My Coffee* . . . 100.00 - 150.00
Gennett 3307 *Mama's Losin' a Might Good
   Chance* . . . . 75.00 - 100.00
Pathe-Actuelle 7503 *Georgia Grind* . . . . 75.00 - 100.00
Perfect 103 *Georgia Grind* . . . . 75.00 - 100.00
**CHARLIE JOHNSON'S (ORIGINAL)
(PARADISE) ORCHESTRA/TEN: CHARLIE
JOHNSON & HIS (PARADISE) BAND/
ORCHESTRA:**
Bluebird 10248 *Walk That Thing* . . . . 8.00 - 12.00
Emerson 10854 *Don't Forget You'll Regret Day
   By Day* . . . . 50.00 - 100.00
   10856 *Meddlin' With The Blues* . . . . 50.00 - 100.00
Victor 20551 *Paradise Wobble* . . . . 75.00 - 100.00
   20653 *Don't You Leave Me Here* . . . . 75.00 - 100.00
   21247 *You Ain't The One* . . . . 75.00 - 100.00
   21491 *Charleston is the Best Dance After All* . . 75.00 - 100.00
   21712 *Walk That Thing* . . . . 75.00 - 100.00
   38059 *Hot Bones and Rice* . . . . 75.00 - 100.00
EDDIE JOHNSON'S CRACKERJACKS:
Victor 23329 *The Duck's Yas Yas Yas* . . . . 150.00 - 200.00
FLO JOHNSON & BEALE STREET FIVE:

Cameo 318 *Four O'Clock Blues* . . . . 5.00 - 8.00
   319 *Sugar Blues* . . . . 5.00 - 8.00
GRAVEYARD JOHNSON & HIS GANG:
Supertone 9369 *Good Times Mama* . . . . 200.00 - 300.00
   9431 *Original Stomp* . . . . 200.00 - 300.00
   9432 *Shake Your Shimmy* . . . . 200.00 - 300.00
HAVEN JOHNSON & HIS ORCHESTRA:
Vocalion 3457 *There Is No Moon* . . . . 15.00 - 20.00
HENRY JOHNSON'S BOYS:
Gennett 6156 *Blue Hawaii* . . . . 150.00 - 250.00
   6168 *Ash Can Stomp* . . . . 150.00 - 250.00
Herwin 92024 *Hawaiian Harmony Blues* . . . . . . 200.00 - 300.00
J.C. JOHNSON & HIS FIVE HOT SPARKS:
QRS 7064 *Red Hot Hottentot* . . . . 200.00 - 300.00
**JAMES P. JOHNSON; JAMES P. JOHNSON'S
HARMONY EIGHT: JIMMIE JOHNSON'S
JAZZ BOYS; JIMMIE/JIMMY JOHNSON &
HIS BAND/ORCHESTRA:**
Black Swan 2026 *The Harlem Strut* . . . . 50.00 - 75.00
Brunswick 4712 *Crying for the Carolines* . . . . . 20.00 - 30.00
   4762 *You've Got To Be Modernistic* . . . . . . 20.00 - 30.00
Cleartone P-96 *Carolina Shout* . . . . 50.00 - 75.00
Columbia A-3950 *Weeping Blues* . . . . 15.00 - 20.00
   2248-D *Go Harlem* . . . . 20.00 - 30.00
   14204-D *Snowy Morning Blues* . . . . 50.00 - 75.00
   14334-D *Chicago Blues* . . . . 75.00 - 100.00
   14417-D *Fare Thee Honey Blues* . . . . 75.00 - 100.00
   14502-D *I've Found a New Baby* . . . . 50.00 - 80.00
   14668-D *A Porter's Love Song* . . . . 75.00 - 100.00
Okeh 4495 *Carolina Shout* . . . . 30.00 - 50.00
   4504 *Dear Old Southland* . . . . 40.00 - 60.00
   4937 *Toddlin'* . . . . 40.00 - 60.00
   8770 *Riffs* . . . . 50.00 - 75.00
Paramount 12144 *The Harlem Strut* . . . . 40.00 - 60.00
Victor 19123 *Bleeding Hearted Blues* . . . . 10.00 - 15.00
   38099 *You Don't Understand* . . . . 50.00 - 75.00
Vocalion 4768 *Harlem Woogie* . . . . 10.00 - 15.00
   4903 *Back Water Blues* . . . . 10.00 - 15.00
**JOHNNY JOHNSON & HIS (POST LODGE)
ORCHESTRA/STATLER
PENNSYLVANIANS:**
Cameo 476 *Climbing Up The Scale* . . . . 5.00 - 8.00
   477 *WOP Blues* . . . . 5.00 - 8.00
   553 *My Papa Doesn't Two-Time No Time* . . . . 5.00 - 8.00
Lincoln 2158 *WOP Blues* . . . . 5.00 - 8.00
Victor 21113 *Thou Swell* . . . . 7.00 - 10.00
   21275 *The Grass Grows Greener* . . . . 5.00 - 8.00
   22468 *On Revival Day* . . . . 8.00 - 12.00
   22493 *What's The Use* . . . . 7.00 - 10.00
   22525 *Sittin' On A Rainbow* . . . . 5.00 - 8.00
   22564 *I'm A Ding Dong Daddy* . . . . 5.00 - 8.00
Victor (most other issues) . . . . 4.00 - 7.00
Vocalion 2811 *Rock And Roll* . . . . 5.00 - 8.00
   2847 *Ding Dong Daddy* . . . . 5.00 - 8.00
**LEM JOHNSON (& HIS WASHBOARD
BAND):**
Decca 7820 *Louise Louise* . . . . 10.00 - 15.00
   7895 *Goin' Down Slow* . . . . 8.00 - 12.00
LEROY JOHNSON:
Bluebird 8075 *Syncopated Swing* . . . . — - —
**PETE JOHNSON (AND HIS BOOGIE
WOOGIE BOYS):**
Solo Art 12004 *How Long How Long* . . . . 7.00 - 10.00
   12005 *Pete's Blues* . . . . 7.00 - 10.00
   12006 *B & O Blues* . . . . 7.00 - 10.00
   12010 *Shuffle Boogie* . . . . 7.00 - 10.00
Vocalion 4997 *Cherry Red* . . . . 5.00 - 8.00
ROY JOHNSON'S HAPPY PALS:
Okeh 8723 *Savoy Rhythm* . . . . 75.00 - 125.00
GRACE JOHNSTON:
Melotone 12010 *Sweet Jennie Lee!* . . . . 8.00 - 12.00
   12032 *Them There Eyes* . . . . 8.00 - 12.00

12065 *Walkin' My Baby Back Home*	10.00 -	15.00
12095 *Keep A Song In Your Soul*	10.00 -	15.00
12104 *By A Lazy Country Lane*	10.00 -	15.00
12151 *I'm Crazy 'Bout My Baby*	8.00 -	12.00
12168 *One More Time*	8.00 -	12.00

MERLE JOHNSTON & HIS CECO COURIERS:

Columbia 1968-D *Where The Sweet Forget-Me-Nots Remember*	10.00 -	15.00
2114-D *Watching My Dreams Go By*	8.00 -	12.00

THE JOLLY THREE:

Vocalion 03955 *Ain't Got a Dime Blues*	20.00 -	30.00

AL JOLSON:

Brunswick 2567, 2569, 2582, 2595, 2611, 2650, 2671, 2743, 2763, 3013, 3014, 3183, 3196, 3222, 3719, 3775, 3867, 3912, 4033	5.00 -	10.00
Brunswick 4400, 4401, 4402, 4721, 4722	7.00 -	12.00
Brunswick 6500 *You Are Too Beautiful*	15.00 -	20.00
6502 *April Showers*	20.00 -	30.00
Columbia A-1356 *That Little German Band*	25.00 -	40.00
A-1374 *Pullman Porter's Parade*	25.00 -	40.00
A-1621 *Back To The Carolina You Love*	10.00 -	15.00
A-1671 *Sister Susie's Sewing Shirts For Soldiers*	10.00 -	15.00
Columbia A-1956, A-1976, A-2007, A-2021	7.00 -	10.00
Columbia, most other issues	5.00 -	10.00
Victor 17037 *That Haunting Melody*	15.00 -	25.00
17068 *Brass Band Ephram Jones*	15.00 -	25.00
17075 *Snap Your Fingers*	15.00 -	20.00
17081 *Ragging The Baby To Sleep*	15.00 -	20.00
17119 *That Lovin' Traumerei*	15.00 -	20.00
17915 *Asleep In The Deep*	7.00 -	10.00

(Note: See ANONYMOUS listing, Little Wonder 20.)

BILLY JONES & ERNEST HARE (See THE HAPPINESS BOYS)

BOBBY JONES & HIS NEW YORKERS/ ORCHESTRA:

Buddy 8001 *Leaky Roof Blues*	50.00 -	100.00
Champion 15177 *Blowin' The Blues Away*	20.00 -	30.00
Champion 15203 *A Blues Serenade*	50.00 -	75.00
15294 *St. Louis Blues*	40.00 -	60.00

CLARENCE M. JONES

Titles, on Autograph (unnumbered) are: *Modulation; Trot Along; Hula Lou; Maybe*	50.00 -	100.00
Okeh 8404 *The Arm Breaker*	75.00 -	100.00
Paramount 12716 *'Mid the Pyramids*	75.00 -	100.00
12747 *Hold It Boy Blues*	75.00 -	100.00

HANK JONES & HIS GINGER:

Champion 15338 *Neck Bones And Beans*	150.00 -	200.00
15437 *Ash Can Stomp*	150.00 -	200.00
15509 *Down Home Special*	150.00 -	200.00

ISHAM JONES & HIS ORCHESTRA: ISHAM JONES' JUNIORS:

Brunswick 2854 *River Boat Shuffle*	5.00 -	8.00
2877 *Poplar Street Blues*	5.00 -	8.00
3027 *It's The Blues*	5.00 -	8.00
3204 *Three-Thirty Blues*	5.00 -	8.00
4868 *Miss Hannah*	8.00 -	12.00
4914 *I'll Be Blue, Just Thinking Of You*	7.00 -	10.00
4985 *Travelin' All Alone*	7.00 -	10.00
6277 *Keepin' Out Of Mischief Now*	8.00 -	12.00
Brunswick (most other issues, 6000 series)	5.00 -	10.00
Brunswick (most other 2000, 3000, and 4000 series)	4.00 -	7.00
Decca 170 *Out Of Space*	8.00 -	12.00
220 *You're O.K.*	8.00 -	12.00
262 *I've Found A New Baby*	8.00 -	12.00
300 *Jimtown Blues*	8.00 -	12.00
Decca 443 *China Boy*	8.00 -	12.00
493 *Blue Room*	8.00 -	12.00
569 *Dallas Blues*	8.00 -	12.00
662 *Rock Your Blues Away*	8.00 -	12.00

754 *Stompin' At The Savoy*	8.00 -	12.00
Decca 168, 169, 171, 219, 261, 327, 338, 605, 610, 695, 704, 713, 770, 834, 1022	5.00 -	10.00
Melotone (most issues)	5.00 -	8.00
Perfect (most issues)	5.00 -	8.00
Victor 24098 *Music, Music Everywhere*	8.00 -	12.00
24099 *Sentimental Gentleman From Georgia*	8.00 -	12.00
24209 *Darkness On The Delta*	8.00 -	12.00
24298 *Blue Prelude*	8.00 -	12.00
24394 *Ain't Cha Glad?*	8.00 -	12.00
24409 *Doin' The Uptown Lowdown*	8.00 -	12.00
24421 *That Dallas Man*	10.00 -	15.00
24496 *Got The Jitters*	10.00 -	15.00
24500 *Roll Out Of Bed With A Smile*	8.00 -	12.00
24519 *Junk Man*	10.00 -	15.00
24606 *I Ain't Lazy, I'm Just Dreaming*	10.00 -	15.00
24628 *Don't Let Your Love Go Wrong*	10.00 -	15.00
24649 *China Boy*	15.00 -	20.00
24695 *Out Of Space*	10.00 -	15.00
24701 *The Blue Room*	15.00 -	20.00
Victor (most other issues)	5.00 -	10.00
Vocalion (most issues)	5.00 -	8.00

PIGGY JONES & HIS ORCHESTRA:

Gennett 3104 *Does My Sweetie Do-And How!*	8.00 -	12.00
3109 *Mighty Blue*	8.00 -	12.00

RICHARD M. JONES: RICHARD M. JONES' (THREE) JAZZ MEN/WIZARDS; JONES' CHICAGO COSMOPOLITANS; RICHARD M. JONES & HIS JAZZ WIZARDS:

Bluebird 6569 *Trouble In Mind*	15.00 -	20.00
Decca 7051 *Blue Reefer Blues*	15.00 -	20.00
7064 *Muggin' The Blues*	15.00 -	20.00
7115 *Joe Louis Chant*	20.00 -	30.00
Gennett 5174 *Jazzin' Babies' Blues*	75.00 -	100.00
Okeh 8260 *29th and Dearborn*	100.00 -	150.00
8290 *New Orleans Shags*	100.00 -	150.00
8349 *Mushmouth Blues*	150.00 -	200.00
8390 *Baby O'Mine*	125.00 -	175.00
8431 *Dusty Bottom Blues*	100.00 -	150.00
Paramount 12705 *Hot and Ready*	150.00 -	200.00
Session 12-006, 12-007	8.00 -	12.00
Victor 20812 *Hollywood Shuffle*	30.00 -	40.00
20859 *Smoked Meat Blues*	40.00 -	60.00
21203 *Boar Hog Blues*	40.00 -	60.00
21345 *African Hunch*	75.00 -	100.00
V38040 *Tickle Britches Blues*	30.00 -	50.00

WILLIE JONES & HIS ORCHESTRA:

Gennett 6326 *Michigan Stomp*	150.00 -	200.00
6370 *Ragamuffin Stomp*	150.00 -	200.00

JONES AND COLLINS ASTORIA HOT EIGHT:

Bluebird 10952 *Damp Weather*	10.00 -	15.00
Victor V38576 *Astoria Strut*	100.00 -	150.00

JONES' PARAMOUNT CHARLESTON FOUR:

Paramount 12279 *Old Steady Roll*	75.00 -	125.00

JONES-SMITH INCORPORATED:

Vocalion 3441 *Shoe-Shine Boy*	10.00 -	15.00
3459 *Lady Be Good*	10.00 -	15.00

JOE JORDAN'S TEN SHARPS AND FLATS:

Banner 1821 *Morocco Blues*	30.00 -	40.00
Columbia 14144-D *Senegalese Stomp*	75.00 -	100.00
Domino 3791 *Morocco Blues*	30.00 -	40.00
Regal 8129 *Old Folks Shuffle*	30.00 -	40.00

TAFT JORDAN AND THE MOB:

Titles, issued contemporaneously on Banner, Conqueror, Melotone, Oriole, Perfect, Romeo: *Devil In The Moon; If The Moon Turns Green; Louisiana Fairy Tale; Night Wind*	7.00 -	10.00

JIMMIE/JIMMY JOY'S (BAKER ST. ANTHONY HOTEL) ORCHESTRA:

Brunswick 3905 *From Monday On*	8.00 -	12.00
3959 *I Got Worry*	8.00 -	12.00
3960 *Today Is Today*	8.00 -	12.00

4640 *Harmonica Harry*	15.00 -	20.00
Okeh 40251 *Milenberg Joys*	50.00 -	75.00
40329 *Clarinet Marmalade Blues*	50.00 -	75.00
40381 *China Girl*	30.00 -	50.00
40388 *Riverboat Shuffle*	75.00 -	100.00
40420 *Wild Jazz*	50.00 -	80.00
40484 *Springtime Is Love Time*	15.00 -	20.00
40494 *Fallin' Down*	50.00 -	75.00
40504 *Everybody Stomp*	75.00 -	100.00
40539 *St. Louis Blues*	50.00 -	75.00
40627 *Stomp It, Mr. Kelly*	75.00 -	100.00

TEDDY JOYCE & HIS PENN STAGE RECORDERS:

Harmony 1009-H *Collegiate Sam*	7.00 -	10.00

(Note: Also issued on *Diva, Velvet Tone*)

THE JUNGLE BAND:

Brunswick 3956 *Tiger Rag*	10.00 -	15.00
4238 *Tiger Rag*	15.00 -	20.00
4309 *Paducah*	15.00 -	20.00
4345 *Doin' The Voom Voom*	15.00 -	20.00
4450 *Dog Bottom*	15.00 -	20.00
4492 *Jungle Jamboree*	15.00 -	20.00
4760 *Sweet Mama*	15.00 -	20.00
4776 *Maori*	15.00 -	20.00
4783 *Double Check Stomp*	15.00 -	20.00
4889 *Wall Street Wail*	15.00 -	20.00
4936 *St. Louis Blues*	15.00 -	20.00
4952 *Runnin' Wild*	15.00 -	20.00
6003 *Wang Wang Blues*	10.00 -	15.00
6038 *Rockin' In Rhythm*	10.00 -	15.00
6732 *Rockin' Chair*	8.00 -	12.00

JUNGLE KINGS:

Paramount 12654 *Friars Point Shuffle*	200.00 -	300.00

JUNGLE TOWN STOMPERS:

Okeh 8686 *Slow As Molasses*	75.00 -	100.00

ART KAHN & HIS ORCHESTRA:

Titles, issued contemporaneously on Banner, Melotone, Oriole, Perfect Romeo: *The Gold-diggers' Song; Pettin' in the Park*	7.00 -	10.00
Columbia 16-D *Sobbin' Blues*	10.00 -	15.00
45-D *Bahama*	10.00 -	15.00
104-D *Blue Evening Blues*	8.00 -	12.00
221-D *Off And Gone*	8.00 -	12.00
310-D *Lucky Kentucky*	8.00 -	12.00
624-D *Hobo's Prayer*	10.00 -	15.00
Columbia 769-D *Hoodle Dee Doo Doodoo*	8.00 -	12.00
Columbia (other issues)	4.00 -	8.00
Conqueror 8279 *I'll Be Faithful*	7.00 -	10.00
Melotone 12090 *I'm Happy When You're Happy*	15.00 -	20.00
Melotone 12415, 12568, 12660, 12692	7.00 -	10.00
Okeh 40857 *When Day Is Done*	15.00 -	20.00
Supertone 9334 *Blue Night*	10.00 -	20.00

ROGER WOLFE KAHN & HIS ORCHESTRA:

Brunswick 4374 *Pretty Little Thing*	8.00 -	12.00
Brunswick 4479 *Do What You Do*	7.00 -	10.00
Brunswick 4571 *Then You've Never Been Blue*	7.00 -	10.00
Brunswick 4699 *Cooking Breakfast for the One I Love*	7.00 -	10.00
Brunswick 4742 *Exactly Like You*	5.00 -	8.00
Brunswick 4811 *Into My Heart*	5.00 -	8.00
Brunswick 4826 *Cheer Up (Good Times Are Comin')*	7.00 -	10.00
Brunswick 4583, 4600, 4614, 4750	3.00 -	6.00
Columbia 2653-D *Lazy Day*	8.00 -	12.00
Columbia 2662-D *There I Go Dreaming Again*	8.00 -	12.00
Columbia 2695-D *You've Got Me In The Palm Of Your Hand*	8.00 -	12.00
Columbia 2697-D *Another Night Alone*	8.00 -	12.00
Columbia 2722-D *It Don't Mean a Thing (If It Ain't Got That Swing)*	10.00 -	15.00
Columbia 2726-D *Fit As A Fiddle*	10.00 -	15.00
Victor 19616 *Hot-Hot-Hottentot*	5.00 -	8.00

Victor 19808 *Look Who's Here!*	5.00 -	8.00
Victor 19845 *I Never Knew*	5.00 -	8.00
Victor 19851 *You Told Me To Go*	5.00 -	8.00
Victor 19860 *Lucky Boy*	5.00 -	8.00
Victor 19866 *Down And Out Blues*	5.00 -	8.00
Victor 19935 *A Cup of Coffee, A Sandwich and You*	5.00 -	8.00
Victor 19939 *Looking For a Boy*	5.00 -	8.00
Victor 19942 *Baby*	5.00 -	8.00
Victor 20379 *Wouldn't You?*	5.00 -	8.00
Victor 20466 *Yankee Rose*	7.00 -	10.00
Victor 20493 *A Little Birdie Told Me So*	8.00 -	12.00
Victor 20634 *Just The Same*	5.00 -	8.00
Victor 21326 *She's a Great, Great Girl*	8.00 -	12.00
Victor 21398 *Crazy Rhythm*	5.00 -	8.00
Victor 21425 *Give Me The Sunshine*	5.00 -	8.00
Victor 21507 *Say "Yes" Today*	5.00 -	8.00
Victor 21801 *A Room With A View*	5.00 -	8.00
Victor Most other issues	3.00 -	6.00

ELMER KAISER & HIS BALLROOM ORCHESTRA:

Autograph (unnumbered) *Monkey Business*	50.00 -	75.00

CHARLES KALEY:

Columbia 910-D *Alabama Stomp*	8.00 -	12.00
Columbia 1541-D *I'm Waiting For Ships That Never Come In*	5.00 -	8.00

HELEN KANE:

Victor 21557, 21684, 21830, 21863, 21917, 22080	5.00 -	10.00
Victor 22192 *Ain't cha?*	8.00 -	12.00
22397 *Thank Your Father*	8.00 -	12.00
22407 *Dangerous Nan McGrew*	8.00 -	12.00
22475 *My Man Is On The Make*	8.00 -	12.00
22520 *Readin' Ritin' Rhythm*	8.00 -	12.00

KANSAS CITY FIVE/FOUR:

Ajax 17072 *Louisville Blues*	50.00 -	75.00
17078 *Believe Me, Hot Mama*	50.00 -	75.00
17128 *Dark Gal Blues*	50.00 -	75.00
Pathe-Actuelle 036175 *Get Yourself A Monkey Man*	40.00 -	60.00
36355 *Get It Fixed*	40.00 -	60.00
36366 *Growin' Old Blues*	40.00 -	60.00
Perfect 14356 *Get Yourself A Monkey Man*	40.00 -	60.00
14377 *Lousiville Blues*	40.00 -	60.00
14516 *Dark Gal Blues*	40.00 -	60.00
14547 *Jake's Weary Blues*	40.00 -	60.00

KANSAS CITY FRANK (AND HIS FOOTWARMERS):

Brunswick 7062 *Jelly Roll Stomp*	100.00 -	150.00
Paramount 12898 *Wailing Blues*	200.00 -	300.00
14026 *Blue Slug*	5.00 -	10.00

KANSAS CITY (TIN ROOF) STOMPERS:

Brunswick 7066 *Aunt Jemima Stomp*	150.00 -	200.00
7091 *Shanghai Honeymoon*	150.00 -	200.00

DAVE KAPLAN & HIS ORCHESTRA; KAPLAN'S MELODISTS:

Edison 52058 *Sweet Marie*	7.00 -	10.00
Edison 52091 *It's A Million To One You're In Love*	5.00 -	8.00
Edison 52106 *Good News*	5.00 -	8.00
Edison 52108 *Barbara*	20.00 -	30.00
Edison 52147 *My New York*	20.00 -	30.00
Edison 52170 *Lady Of Havana*	5.00 -	8.00
Edison 52234 *Golden Gate*	7.00 -	10.00
Edison 52304 *You May Be Right—You May Be Wrong*	7.00 -	10.00
Edison 52595 *Am I A Passing Fancy?*	7.00 -	10.00
Edison (most other issues)	4.00 -	8.00

GENE KARDOS & HIS ORCHESTRA:

Titles, issues contemporaneously on Banner, Conqueror, Melotone, Oriole, Perfect, Romeo: *Did You Ever See a Dream Walking?; Good Morning, Glory; Many Moons Ago; You're*

Such a Comfort To Me	7.00 -	10.00
Victor 22790 *China Boy*	10.00 -	15.00
22792 *Waiting For The Moon*	10.00 -	15.00
22840 *A Hot Dog, A Blanket, And You*	7.00 -	10.00
22843 *You've Got To Sell It*	7.00 -	10.00
22863 *Sweet Violets*	7.00 -	10.00
22865 *Now's The Time To Fall In Love*	7.00 -	10.00
22897 *Tell Tales*	7.00 -	10.00
22899 *Business in "F"*	10.00 -	15.00
Victor 22918 *Fate Introduced Me To You*	7.00 -	10.00
22920 *Alexander's Ragtime Band*	8.00 -	12.00
22957 *Sailin' On The Robert E. Lee*	8.00 -	12.00
22986 *My Extraordinary Gal*	8.00 -	12.00
24006 *I Can't Believe That It's You*	7.00 -	10.00
24081 *Sing*	8.00 -	12.00

ART KARLE & HIS BOYS:

Vocalion 3146 *Moon Over Miami*	15.00 -	20.00
3147 *Lights Out*	15.00 -	20.00

BETTY KASHMAN:

Okey 8942 *Hoochee Miss Lou*	20.00 -	30.00

ART KASSEL'S IN THE AIR: ART KASSEL & HIS ORCHESTRA:

Bluebird, most issues	3.00 -	5.00
Columbia 2636-D, 2643-D	7.00 -	10.00
Columbia 2682-D *Hell's Bells*	10.00 -	15.00
2687-D *Rain, Rain, Go Away*	10.00 -	15.00
Columbia 2742-D, 2743-D, 2745-D	7.00 -	10.00
Columbia 2765-D *Chant of the Swamp*	10.00 -	15.00
Victor 21884, 21885	5.00 -	8.00
Vogue R-714 *Doodle Doo Doo*	20.00 -	30.00
R-723 *Wave To Me My Lady*	25.00 -	40.00
R-734 *A Little Consideration*	25.00 -	40.00
R-770 *The Wiffenpoof Song*	20.00 -	30.00
R-771 *Jeannine*	20.00 -	30.00
R-780 *Touch Me Not*	25.00 -	35.00
R-781 *Sooner Or Later*	25.00 -	35.00
R-785 *The Echo Said No*	25.00 -	40.00

AL KATZ AND HIS KITTENS:

Victor 20081 *Ace in the Hole*	5.00 -	8.00

IRVING KAUFMAN:

Banner 1756 *Tonight's My Night With Baby*	5.00 -	8.00
Banner 6015 *Oh! Constaine*	5.00 -	8.00
Banner 6323 *St. Louis Blues*	8.00 -	12.00
Banner 6508 *St. Louis Blues*	5.00 -	8.00
Challenge 554 *Henry's Made a Lady out of Lizzie*	5.00 -	8.00
Harmony 424-H *Vo-Do-Do-De-O Blues*	5.00 -	8.00
Harmony 440-H *Who-oo? You-oo, That's Who!* . .	5.00 -	8.00
Okeh 41230 *You Were Meant For Me*	8.00 -	12.00
Okeh 41412 *Let Me Sing And I'm Happy*	10.00 -	15.00
Perfect 12432 *Every Evening*	5.00 -	8.00
Q.R.S. 1012 *Blowin' Off Steam*	10.00 -	15.00
Q.R.S. 1031 *Blue Turning Grey Over You*	10.00 -	15.00
Vocalion 14950 *Nobody Knows What a Red Head Mama Can Do*	7.00 -	10.00
Vocalion 15024 *Red Hot Henry Brown*	7.00 -	10.00

JACK KAUFMAN (& THE 7 BLUE BABIES):

Banner 6492 *My Wife Is On a Diet*	5.00 -	8.00
Cameo 8115 *I Scream—You Scream—We All Scream For Ice-Cream*	5.00 -	8.00
Cameo 8145 *I've Got Nothin'—You've Got Nothin'—We Ain't Got Nothin'*	5.00 -	8.00
Cameo 8204 *When a Blonde Makes Up Her Mind*	5.00 -	8.00
Cameo 8272 *Oh! You Have No Idea*	5.00 -	8.00
Cameo 8311 *I Should Shay Sho!*	5.00 -	8.00
Cameo 9013 *Oh, Boy! It's A Pleasure*	5.00 -	8.00
Cameo 9089 *What Good Is a Sandwich (If It Hasn't Any Bread)*	7.00 -	10.00
Cameo 9210 *He Always Goes Farther Than Father*	5.00 -	8.00
Edison 52209 *The Grass Grows Greener*	15.00 -	20.00
52298 *What's The Color Of A Yellow Horse?* . .	15.00 -	20.00

52323 *Since She Learned To Ride A Horse*	15.00 -	20.00
52364 *That's My Weakness Now*	20.00 -	30.00
52405 *Nagasaki*	20.00 -	30.00
Romeo 695 *Oh! You Have No Idea*	5.00 -	8.00
Romeo 704 *He's Our Al*	5.00 -	8.00
Romeo 734 *I Should Shay Sho!*	7.00 -	10.00
Romeo 891 *What Good Is a Sandwich (If It Hasn't Any Bread)*	7.00 -	10.00

WHITEY KAUFMAN'S ORIGINAL PENNSYLVANIA SERENADERS; WHITEY KAUFMAN & HIS ORCHESTRA:

Victor 19127 *Henpecked Blues*	5.00 -	8.00
19304 *Charleston Cabin*	5.00 -	8.00
19384 *Come On, Red*	5.00 -	8.00
19638 *Who Takes Care Of The Caretakers Daughter?*	5.00 -	8.00
19673 *My Girl*	5.00 -	8.00
19834 *Paddlin' Madelin' Home*	5.00 -	8.00
19996 *Tamiami Trail*	5.00 -	8.00
20125 *Deep River Blues*	8.00 -	12.00

DOLLY KAY:

Columbia 102-D *Mindin' My Bus'ness*	8.00 -	12.00
Columbia 117-D *Someday, Sweetheart*	8.00 -	12.00
Columbia 151-D *Hard Hearted Hannah*	5.00 -	8.00
Columbia A3534 *Got To Have My Daddy Blues* .	5.00 -	8.00
Columbia A3644 *Buzz Mirandy*	5.00 -	8.00
Columbia A3664 *Lonesome Longin' Blues*	5.00 -	8.00
Columbia A3692 *I'm Nobody's Gal*	5.00 -	8.00
Columbia A3758 *Hot Lips*	7.00 -	10.00
Columbia A3808 *You've Got To See Mama Ev'ry Night*	7.00 -	10.00
Columbia A3828 *Seven Or Eleven*	7.00 -	10.00
Columbia A3882 *Don't Think You'll Be Missed* . .	7.00 -	10.00
Columbia A3955 *Oh! Sister, Ain't That Hot!* . . .	7.00 -	10.00
Columbia A3980 *The Gold-Digger*	7.00 -	10.00
Harmony 268-H *How Could Red Riding Hood?* .	5.00 -	8.00
Vocalion 15664 *A Good Man Is Hard To Find* . .	30.00 -	40.00

SWING AND SWAY WITH SAMMY KAYE; SAMMY KAYE AND HIS ORCHESTRA:

Titles, issued contemporaneously on Banner, Conqueror, Melotone, Oriole, Perfect, Romeo: *After you, Alibi Baby; Avalon; Cry, Baby, Cry; The Dipsy Doodle; Dreamy Eyes; Good Mornin'; Have You Met Miss Jones?; If I Can Count On You; If You Were Someone Else; Indiana; It Looks Like Rain In Cherry Blossom Lane' Josephine; Moonlight On The Highway; My Buddy, Night and Day; Rosalie; Somebody Loves Me; So You Won't Sing; A Strange Loneliness; Swing Is Here To Stay; True Confession; We'll Ride The Tide Together; What Makes You So Sweet?*	4.00 -	7.00
Victor, most issues	2.00 -	3.00
Vocalion, most issues	3.00 -	6.00

JOE KAYSER AND HIS NOVELTY ORCHESTRA:

Gennett Personal (unnumbered) *Everybody Step* .	— -	—

LLOYD KEATING AND HIS MUSIC/ ORCHESTRA:

Clarion 5045-C *I Love You So Much*	5.00 -	8.00
5103-C *I'll Be Blue*	7.00 -	10.00
5186-C *You're Driving Me Crazy*	8.00 -	12.00
5322-C *Wrap Your Troubles in Dreams*	8.00 -	12.00
5328-C *Sweet and Hot*	8.00 -	12.00
5334-C *Under Your Window Tonight*	8.00 -	12.00
5339-C *Sing A Little Jingle*	8.00 -	12.00
5350-C *I'm Keepin' Company*	8.00 -	12.00
5355-C *Let's Drink a Drink to the Future*	8.00 -	12.00
5362-C *My Sweet Tooth Says I Wanna*	8.00 -	12.00
5368-C *There's No Depression In Love*	8.00 -	12.00
5379-C *I Apologize*	7.00 -	10.00
5386-C *Can't You See*	7.00 -	10.00

5407-C *You Try Somebody Else*	8.00 -	12.00
11002-C *Love Letters in the Sand*	15.00 -	20.00

(Note: 11002-C is a "double track" record, with instrumental and vocal versions of the same title occupying the same playing surface.)

Diva 3052-G *Low Down Rhythm*	7.00 -	10.00
Diva 3118-G *Sing You Sinners*	7.00 -	10.00
Harmony 1053-H *Turn On The Heat*	8.00 -	12.00
Harmony 1143-H *Strike Up The Band!*	8.00 -	12.00
1145-H *Looking At You Across The Breakfast Table*	8.00 -	12.00
1181-H *I Love You So Much*	7.00 -	10.00
1233-H *I'll Be Blue*	7.00 -	10.00
1246-H *I'm Tickled Pink With A Blue-Eyed Baby*	8.00 -	12.00
Harmony 1251-H *You're Driving Me Crazy!*	8.00 -	12.00
1252-H *I Hate Myself*	7.00 -	10.00
1274-H *Keep A Song In Your Soul*	8.00 -	12.00
1290-H *Sweet And Hot*	8.00 -	12.00
1323-H *Wrap Your Troubles In Dreams*	8.00 -	12.00
1326-H *Under Your Window Tonight*	8.00 -	12.00
1339-H *I'm Keepin' Company*	8.00 -	12.00
1343-H *Let's Drink a Drink To The Future*	8.00 -	12.00
1350-H *My Sweet Tooth Says I Wanna*	8.00 -	12.00
1356-H *There's A Time And Place For Everything*	8.00 -	12.00
1366-H *I Apologize*	7.00 -	10.00
Harmony 1367-H *As Time Goes By*	8.00 -	12.00
1372-H *Can't You See*	7.00 -	10.00
1388-H *You Try Somebody Else*	8.00 -	12.00
6501-H *An Evening In Caroline*	8.00 -	12.00
6502-H *Ooh! That Kiss*	8.00 -	12.00
Velvet Tone 2394-V *Sweet And Hot*	8.00 -	12.00
2388-V *Wrap Your Troubles In Dreams*	8.00 -	12.00
2398-V *Under Your Window Tonight*	8.00 -	12.00
2414-V *I'm Keepin' Company*	8.00 -	12.00
2419-V *Let's Drink a Drink to the Future*	8.00 -	12.00
2426-V *My Sweet Tooth Says I Wanna*	8.00 -	12.00
Velvet Tone 2432-V *There's No Depression In Love*	8.00 -	12.00
2442-V *I Apologize*	7.00 -	10.00
2450-V *Can't You See*	8.00 -	12.00
2467-V *You Try Somebody Else*	8.00 -	12.00
10501-V *An Evening In Caroline*	8.00 -	12.00
10502-V *Ooooh! That Kiss*	8.00 -	12.00

EDDIE KELLY'S WASHBOARD BAND:

Bluebird 7127 *Come On 'Round To My House*	20.00 -	30.00
7134 *Corina, I'm Goin' Away*	20.00 -	30.00
7148 *Shim Shaming*	10.00 -	15.00
7204 *Blues in the Rain*	20.00 -	30.00
7277 *Goin' Back To Alabama*	20.00 -	30.00

GEORGE KELLY (See: THE ORIGINAL SIX)

HAL KEMP AND HIS ORCHESTRA (from THE UNIVERSITY OF NORTH CAROLINA):

Brunswick 3486 *Brown Sugar*	7.00 -	10.00
3536 *Go, Joe, Go*	7.00 -	10.00
Brunswick 3792 *If I Can't Have You*	5.00 -	8.00
Brunswick 3841 *Who's Blue Now?*	5.00 -	8.00
Brunswick 3863 *She's a Great, Great Girl*	7.00 -	10.00
Brunswick 3937 *I Don't Care*	7.00 -	10.00
3954 *Oh, Baby!*	7.00 -	10.00
4078 *High Up On A Hill Top*	5.00 -	8.00
4151 *My Troubles Are Over*	5.00 -	8.00
4212 *My Lucky Star*	5.00 -	8.00
4307 *That's What I Call Heaven*	5.00 -	8.00
4327 *That's You, Baby*	5.00 -	8.00
4388 *To Be In Love*	5.00 -	8.00
4424 *In The Hush Of The Night*	5.00 -	8.00
4580 *I Gotta Have You*	8.00 -	12.00
4612 *A Little Kiss Each Morning*	8.00 -	12.00
4676 *Navy Blues*	8.00 -	12.00
4805 *Washin' The Blues From My Soul*	8.00 -	12.00

4807 *If I Had A Girl Like You*	8.00 -	12.00
4988 *Fraternity Blues*	10.00 -	15.00
4992 *Them There Eyes*	8.00 -	12.00
Brunswick 6055 *Would You Like To Take A Walk?*	7.00 -	10.00
6056 *I Want You For Myself*	7.00 -	10.00
6071 *Little Joe*	7.00 -	10.00
6108 *Moonlight Saving Time*	8.00 -	12.00
6110 *Whistles*	8.00 -	12.00
6130 *I'm Keepin' Company*	8.00 -	12.00
Brunswick 6416, 6419, 6436, 6437, 6452, 6471, 6487, 6492, 6528, 6532, 6568, 6574, 6582, 6583, 6598, 6605, 6609, 6613, 6616, 6636, 6648, 6656, 6703, 6707, 6790	5.00 -	10.00
Brunswick 6587 *Hold My Hand*	7.00 -	10.00
Brunswick 6925, 6943, 6947, 6974, 6985, 7315, 7317, 7319, 7322, 7334, 7343, 7351, 7357, 7360, 7369, 7370, 7385, 7388, 7404, 7413, 7429, 7434, 7437, 7458, 7493, 7503, 7509, 7517, 7552, 7553, 7565, 7566, 7578, 7587, 7589, 7600, 7601, 7626, 7630, 7634, 7636, 7668, 7681, 7707, 7711, 7720, 7730, 7745, 7749, 7766, 7769, 7775, 7783, 7812, 7830, 7854, 7865, 7883	4.00 -	7.00
Victor, most issues	3.00 -	5.00

HERMAN KENIN & HIS AMBASSADOR/ MULTNOMAH HOTEL ORCHESTRA:

Victor 20725 *Pretty Little Thing*	8.00 -	12.00
Victor 20782 *Some Other Day*	7.00 -	10.00
Victor 21313 *Persian Rug*	5.00 -	8.00
Victor 21314 *Rose of Monterey*	7.00 -	10.00
Victor 21336 *When Love Comes Stealing*	5.00 -	8.00
Victor 21568 *There's Somebody New*	5.00 -	8.00
Victor 21980 *After Thinking It Over*	5.00 -	8.00
Victor 21991 *Building a Nest For Mary*	5.00 -	8.00
Victor 22005 *He's a Good Man To Have Around*	5.00 -	8.00
Victor 22006 *There's a Place in the Sun For You*	5.00 -	8.00
Victor 22016 *I'm Doin' What I'm Doin' For Love*	5.00 -	8.00

JOE KENNEDY & HIS RHYTHM ORCHESTRA:

Bluebird 6062 *Double Trouble*	10.00 -	15.00
6080 *Rosetta*	10.00 -	15.00
6102 *I Never Knew*	10.00 -	15.00
6233 *Rhythm Is Our Business*	10.00 -	15.00
6245 *You Can Depend On Me*	10.00 -	15.00

KEN KENNY & HIS ORCHESTRA:

Champion 40100 *Let Yourself Go*	8.00 -	12.00
40101 *Misty Islands Of The Highlands*	8.00 -	12.00
40107 *What's The Name Of That Song?*	8.00 -	12.00

THE KENTUCKY BLOWERS:

Gennett 5517 *Rambling Blues*	8.00 -	12.00
5602 *Choo Choo*	8.00 -	12.00

THE KENTUCKY COLONELS:

Vocalion 14697 *Mama Loves Papa (Papa Loves Mama)*	7.00 -	10.00
Vocalion 14714 *Learn To Do The Strut*	7.00 -	10.00
Vocalion 14738 *I'm Goin' South*	7.00 -	10.00
Vocalion 14748 *If You'll Come Back*	7.00 -	10.00

KENTUCKY GRASSHOPPERS:

Banner 6295 *Four Or Five Times*	8.00 -	12.00
6323 *Icky Blues*	8.00 -	12.00
6355 *Tiger Rag*	8.00 -	12.00
6358 *Sweet Liza*	8.00 -	12.00
6360 *Makin' Friends*	8.00 -	12.00
Conqueror 7303 *Icky Blues*	8.00 -	12.00

KENTUCKY HOT HOPPERS:

Pathe-Actuelle 36841 *Red Head Blues*	8.00 -	12.00
Perfect 15022 *Red Head Blues*	8.00 -	12.00

KENTUCKY JAZZ BABIES:

Victor V38616 *Old Folks Shake*	150.00 -	200.00

KENTUCKY JUG BAND:

Vocalion 1564 *Walkin' Cane Stomp*	100.00 -	150.00

KENTUCKY SERENADERS:

Regal 9134 *Shake It And Break It*	7.00 -	10.00

9139 *My Sunny Tennessee*	5.00 -	8.00
9143 *Gypsy Blues*	5.00 -	8.00

FREDDIE KEPPARD'S JAZZ CARDINALS:

Paramount 12399 *Stock Yards Strut*	200.00 -	300.00

CHARLIE KERR'S ORCHESTRA; KERR'S FAMOUS PLAYERS:

Edison 51147, 51164, 51167, 51194	5.00 -	10.00
Gennett 3219, *What Did I Tell Ya?*	10.00 -	20.00

FRANK KEYES & HIS ORCHESTRA:

Perfect 15358 *Just A Little Dance, Mam'selle*	15.00 -	20.00

KING BRADY'S CLARINET BAND:

Champion 15455 *Lazybone Blues*	125.00 -	175.00
15491 *Embarrasment Blues*	200.00 -	300.00
Gennett 6393 *Embarrassment Blues*	200.00 -	300.00

KING DAVID'S JUG BAND:

Okeh 8861 *Georgia Bo Bo*	100.00 -	150.00
8901 *Sweet Potato Blues*	100.00 -	150.00
8913 *Rising Sun Blues*	100.00 -	150.00

KING GEORGE (AND QUEEN MARY) OF ENGLAND:

Victor 19072 *Empire Day Messages*	5.00 -	8.00
22338 At the opening of the five-power naval conference	5.00 -	8.00

KING MUTT AND HIS TENNESSEE THUMPERS:

Gennett 6796 *Nut House Stomp*	250.00 -	400.00
6844 *Good Time Mama*	250.00 -	400.00

CHUCK KING & HIS KENTUCKIANS:

Champion 15456 *Isabella (Tell Your Fella)*	20.00 -	30.00
Champion 15458 *Caroline*	25.00 -	50.00
15459 *Green River Blues*	20.00 -	30.00

FRANCES KING:

Okeh 40854 *She's Got It*	10.00 -	15.00

HENRY KING AND HIS ORCHESTRA:

Columbia 2941-D, 2945-D, 2949-D, 2950-D, 2991-D, 2992-D, 2998-D, 3005-D, 3010-D, 3036-D, 3042-D, 3049-D	5.00 -	10.00
Decca, most issues	3.00 -	6.00
Victor, most issues	3.00 -	7.00
Vocalion 2550, 2561, 2562, 2573, 2579, 2580	5.00 -	10.00

REX KING & HIS SOVEREIGNS:

Clarion (most issues)	4.00 -	7.00
Odeon ONY-36204 *African Lament*	20.00 -	40.00
Velvet Tone (most issues)	4.00 -	7.00

ROY KING & HIS ORCHESTRA:

Romeo 369 *Pardon The Glove*	10.00 -	15.00

TEMPO KING AND HIS KINGS OF TEMPO:

Titles, issued contemporaneously on Banner, Conqueror, Melotone, Oriole, Perfect, Romeo: *Alligator Crawl; All Over Nothing At All; Am I Dreaming?; Don't You Know Or Don't You Care?; The Folks Who Live On The Hill; High, Wide and Handsome; I Can Always Dream; I'm Gonna Put You In Your Place; On With The Dance; The One Rose; Riding On The Old Ferris Wheel; You've Got Me Under Your Thumb*	7.00 -	10.00
Bluebird 6553, 6534, 6335, 6560, 6563, 6575, 6637, 6642, 6643, 6684, 6687, 6688, 6721, 6725, 6758, 6768, 6770, 6880	5.00 -	10.00

WAYNE KING & HIS ORCHESTRA:

Brunswick (most issues, 6000 series)	4.00 -	8.00
Victor 22240 *Sally*	5.00 -	8.00
Victor 22256 *Put A Little Salt On The Bluebird's Tail*	5.00 -	8.00
Victor 22642 *Hello, Beautiful!*	5.00 -	8.00
Victor 22643 *Dream a Little Dream of Me*	5.00 -	8.00
Victor 22656 *Star Dust*	7.00 -	10.00
Victor 22979 *Way Down Between Dem Rows (A-Pickin' Dat Cotton)*	10.00 -	15.00
Victor (most other 22000 series issues)	4.00 -	7.00

THE KING'S JESTERS (AND LOUISE):

Bluebird 5149 *After You've Gone*	8.00 -	12.00
5184 *China Boy*	8.00 -	12.00
(Note: Above titles, on *Electradisk*, are valued somewhat higher; on *Sunrise*, substantially higher.)		
Bluebird 6517 *Some Of These Days*	8.00 -	12.00
Vogue R-708 *I Surrender, Dear*	25.00 -	35.00
R-716 *Mean To Me*	75.00 -	100.00
R-750 *Who's Got A Tent For Rent*	25.00 -	35.00
R-751 *Humphrey, The Sweet Singing Pig*	25.00 -	35.00
R-766 *Sepulveda*	25.00 -	35.00

KIRBY'S KINGS OF JAZZ:

Bell 589 *Oh! Daisy*	20.00 -	30.00
591 *Green River Blues*	20.00 -	30.00
592 *Isabella (Tell Your Fella)*	20.00 -	30.00
598 *Caroline*	20.00 -	30.00

JOHN KIRBY & HIS ONYX CLUB BOYS/ ORCHESTRA:

Decca 2216 *Undecided*	7.00 -	10.00
2367 *Pastel Blue*	7.00 -	10.00
Okeh 4624, 4653, 4890, 5048, 5187, 5520, 5542, 5570, 5605, 5632, 5661, 5705, 5761, 5805	5.00 -	10.00
Vocalion 4624, 4653, 4890, 5048, 5187, 5520, 5542, 5570	5.00 -	10.00

ANDY KIRK & HIS TWELVE CLOUDS OF JOY:

Brunswick 4653 *Casey Jones Special*	30.00 -	40.00
4694 *Blue Clarinet Stomp*	30.00 -	40.00
4803 *I Lost My Gal From Memphis*	30.00 -	40.00
4863 *Once Or Twice*	20.00 -	30.00
4878 *Snag It*	30.00 -	40.00
4893 *Froggy Bottom*	20.00 -	30.00
4981 *Honey, Just For You*	30.00 -	40.00
6027 *Saturday*	30.00 -	40.00
6129 *Dallas Blues*	25.00 -	40.00
Decca 729 *Froggy Bottom*	7.00 -	10.00
744 *All The Jive Is Gone*	8.00 -	12.00
772 *Blue Illusion*	8.00 -	12.00
809 *Walkin' And Swingin'*	8.00 -	12.00
853 *Moten Swing*	8.00 -	12.00
931 *Steppin' Pretty*	8.00 -	12.00
1046 *Bearcat Shuffle*	8.00 -	12.00
1085 *The Lady Who Swings The Band*	8.00 -	12.00
1146 *Fifty-Second Street*	7.00 -	10.00
1208 *Puddin' Head Serenade*	7.00 -	10.00
1261 *In The Groove*	7.00 -	10.00
1303 *Wednesday Night Hop*	7.00 -	10.00
1349 *Skies Are Blue*	7.00 -	10.00
1422 *Better Luck Next Time*	7.00 -	10.00
1477 *With Love In My Heart*	7.00 -	10.00
1531 *Downstream*	7.00 -	10.00
1579 *A Mellow Bit Of Rhythm*	7.00 -	10.00
1606 *The Big Dipper*	7.00 -	10.00
1663 *Poor Butterfly*	7.00 -	10.00
Decca (higher numbers)	5.00 -	8.00

MANNIE KLEIN/KLINE & HIS ORCHESTRA:

Brunswick 7605 *Ringside Table For Two*	10.00 -	15.00
7606 *Hot Spell*	10.00 -	15.00

THE KNICKERBOCKERS:

Columbia 450-D *Breezin' Along (To Georgia)*	5.00 -	8.00
549-D *Sweet And Low Down*	5.00 -	8.00

1940-D *Song Of The Blues* . . . . 7.00 - 10.00
2003-D *From Now On* . . . . 7.00 - 10.00
2067-D *My Man Is On The Make* . . . . 8.00 - 12.00
2129-D *Good For You, Bad For Me* . . . . 10.00 - 15.00
2502-D *Me!* . . . . 7.00 - 10.00
Columbia (most other issues) . . . . 3.00 - 8.00

KOLSTER DANCE ORCHESTRA:
Columbia 2072-D *When I Am Housekeeping*
  For You . . . . 8.00 - 12.00

HOWARD KOPP:
Columbia A2241 *Calico Rag* . . . . 15.00 - 20.00
Columbia A2282 *Night Time In Little Italy* . . . . 7.00 - 10.00
Columbia A2321 *Oh, Johnny! Oh, Johnny!* . . . . 7.00 - 10.00
Columbia A2376 *One Step More* . . . . 7.00 - 10.00

ART KRUEGER & HIS ORCHESTRA:
Broadway 1523 *Sing A New Song* . . . . 8.00 - 12.00

BENNIE KRUEGER & HIS ORCHESTRA:
Brunswick 2105 *Satanic Blues* . . . . 5.00 - 8.00
Brunswick 2109 *Dangerous Blues* . . . . 5.00 - 8.00
Brunswick 2419 *Wild Papa* . . . . 5.00 - 8.00
Brunswick 2445 *Long Lost Mamma* . . . . 5.00 - 8.00
Brunswick 2563 *Steppin' Out* . . . . 5.00 - 8.00
Brunswick 2667 *Pleasure Mad* . . . . 5.00 - 8.00
Brunswick 3060 *Forever And Ever With You* . . . . 5.00 - 8.00
Brunswick (most others, 2000 and 3000 series) . 3.00 - 6.00
Brunswick 6280 *Sing A New Song* . . . . 7.00 - 10.00
Brunswick (most others, 6000 series) . . . . . . 4.00 - 7.00
Columbia 2918-D *Once In A Blue Moon* . . . . . . 7.00 - 10.00
  2919-D *A Thousand Goodnights* . . . . 7.00 - 10.00
Victor 21903 *That's The Good Old Sunny South* . 5.00 - 8.00

JERRY KRUGER (AND HER ORCHESTRA):
Variety 666 *The Bed Song* . . . . 10.00 - 15.00
Vocalion 3799 *So You Won't Sing* . . . . 10.00 - 15.00
  4927 *Rain, Rain, Go Away* . . . . 10.00 - 15.00

**GENE KRUPA AND HIS ORCHESTRA/GENE
KRUPA'S SWING BAND:**
Brunswick 8123, 8124, 8139, 8161, 8166, 8188,
  8198, 8205, 8211, 8246, 8249, 8253, 8274,
  8280, 8282, 8289, 8296, 8335, 8340, 8346,
  8361, 8387, 8400, 8412, 8448, 8451 . . . . 5.00 - 10.00
Columbia 32505, 35218, 35237, 35262, 35304,
  35324, 35336, 35361, 35366, 35387, 35408,
  35415, 35423, 35429, 35444 . . . . 5.00 - 10.00
Columbia, most higher numbers . . . . 3.00 - 5.00
Okeh, most issues . . . . 3.00 - 5.00
Victor 25263, 25276 . . . . 5.00 - 8.00

KXYZ NOVELTY BAND:
Bluebird 5831 *The Sheik Of Araby* . . . . 10.00 - 15.00
  5832 *I Never Knew* . . . . 10.00 - 15.00
  5852 *Bugle Call Rag* . . . . 10.00 - 15.00
  5868 *Indiana* . . . . 10.00 - 15.00

BILLY KYLE & HIS SWING CLUB BAND:
Variety 531 *Big Boy Blue* . . . . 10.00 - 15.00
  574 *Havin' A Ball* . . . . 10.00 - 15.00
  617 *Can I Forget You?* . . . . 10.00 - 15.00
  659 *Girl Of My Dreams* . . . . 10.00 - 15.00
Vocalion 3778 *All You Want To Do Is Dance* . . . 10.00 - 15.00
  3815 *Margie* . . . . 10.00 - 15.00
  3843 *Handle My Heart With Care* . . . . 10.00 - 15.00

KAY KYSER AND HIS ORCHESTRA:
Brunswick 7449, 7453, 7465, 7470, 7541, 7555,
  7647, 7648, 7682, 7701, 7755, 7759, 7793,
  7805, 7819, 7826, 7836, 7846 . . . . 4.00 - 8.00
Brunswick 7881, 7891, 8114, 8120, 8126, 8143,
  8149, 8165, 8170, 8181, 8185, 8193, 8197, 8201,
  8209, 8210, 8215, 8222, 8225, 8228, 8234,
  8244, 8258, 8263, 8267, 8279, 8295, 8301,
  8308, 8312, 8317, 8320, 8324, 8328, 8338,
  8353, 8368, 8377, 8381, 8385, 8392, 8415,
  8439, 8440, 8446, 8456 . . . . 4.00 - 7.00
Columbia, most issues . . . . 2.00 - 5.00
Victor V-40028 *Broken Dreams of Yesterday* . . . 10.00 - 20.00

V-40222 *Rainy Weather* . . . . 15.00 - 20.00
V-40258 *Collegiate Fanny* . . . . 30.00 - 50.00

LADA'S LOUISIANA LADS/ORCHESTRA:
Emerson 10567 *Early In The Morning Blues* . . . 7.00 - 10.00
Emerson 10570 *Jimbo Jambo* . . . . 5.00 - 8.00
Emerson 10587 *Nothing But* . . . . 7.00 - 10.00
Emerson 10598 *Farewell Blues* . . . . 7.00 - 10.00
Sunset 1149 *Everybody Stomp* . . . . 75.00 - 100.00
  1151 *Everything's Gonna Be All Right* . . . . . 30.00 - 50.00

LADD'S BLACK ACES:
Gennett 4762 *Shake It And Break It* . . . . 8.00 - 12.00
Gennett 4794 *Gypsy Blues* . . . . 8.00 - 12.00
Gennett 4806 *Brother Low Down* . . . . 8.00 - 12.00
Gennett 4809 *She's A Mean Job* . . . . 8.00 - 12.00
Gennett 4843 *Virginia Blues* . . . . 8.00 - 12.00
Gennett 4856 *My Honey's Lovin' Arms* . . . . . . 10.00 - 15.00
Gennett 4869 *Muscle Shoals Blues* . . . . 10.00 - 15.00
Gennett 4896 *Hopeless Blues* . . . . 10.00 - 15.00
Gennett 4938 *You Can Have Him, I Don't*
  Want Him . . . . 7.00 - 10.00
Gennett 4995 *Yankee Doodle Blues* . . . . 8.00 - 12.00
Gennett 5018 *Great White Way Blues* . . . . . . 8.00 - 12.00
Gennett 5023 *Aggravatin' Papa* . . . . 8.00 - 12.00
Gennett 5035 *Runnin' Wild* . . . . 7.00 - 10.00
Gennett 5060 *Aggravatin' Papa* . . . . 8.00 - 12.00
Gennett 5075 *Beale Street Mama* . . . . 8.00 - 12.00
Gennett 5125 *I'm A Harmony Baby* . . . . 8.00 - 12.00
Gennett 5127 *Papa Blues* . . . . 8.00 - 12.00
Gennett 5142 *Papa, Better Watch Your Step* . . . 7.00 - 10.00
Gennett 5150 *Two-Time Dan* . . . . 7.00 - 10.00
Gennett 5164 *I Ain't Never Had Nobody Crazy*
  Over Me . . . . 7.00 - 10.00
Gennett 5187 *Bad News Blues* . . . . 8.00 - 12.00
Gennett 5272 *I've Got A Song For Sale* . . . . . 7.00 - 10.00
Gennett 5366 *Lots O'Mama* . . . . 7.00 - 10.00
Gennett 5422 *Unfortunate Blues* . . . . 7.00 - 10.00
Gennett 5521 *Any Way The Wind Blows* . . . . . 7.00 - 10.00
Superior 2748 *When It's Sleepy Time Down South* . 150.00 - 200.00
  2771 *St. Louis Blues* . . . . 150.00 - 200.00

TOMMY LADNIER & HIS ORCHESTRA:
Bluebird 10086, 10089 . . . . 5.00 - 10.00

**SLIM LAMAR & HIS SOUTHERNERS; SLIM
LAMAR'S ORCHESTRA:**
Victor 21710 *Happy* . . . . 20.00 - 30.00
  V-40005 *I'm Crazy Over Daisy* . . . . 35.00 - 50.00
  V-40049 *I'm Glad It Was Somebody Else* . . . . 25.00 - 40.00
  V-40093 *Nancy* . . . . 40.00 - 60.00
  V-40130 *You Never Did That Before* . . . . . . 40.00 - 60.00
  V-40146 *Memphis Kick-Up* . . . . 50.00 - 75.00

DOROTHY LAMOUR:
Brunswick 7829, 7838, 7017, 8132, 8154, 8291,
  8304 . . . . 7.00 - 10.00

**LAMPE'S ORCHESTRA FROM THE
TRIANON BALLROOM; DELL LAMPE &
HIS ORCHESTRA:**
Autograph (unnumbered) *Trianon (A New Dance)* 50.00 - 100.00
  604 *Prince Of Wails* . . . . 75.00 - 100.00
  628 *Lady Of The Nile* . . . . 30.00 - 50.00
  629 *Candied Sweets* . . . . 50.00 - 100.00
Crown 3409 *Street Of Dreams* . . . . 10.00 - 15.00
  3426 *My River Home* . . . . 10.00 - 15.00
  3441 *Darkness on the Delta* . . . . 10.00 - 15.00
Victor 24005 *Spring is Here Again* . . . . 10.00 - 15.00
  24020 *Scattin' The Skeeter Scott* . . . . 15.00 - 20.00

**MIKE LANDAU & HIS OAKLAND TERRACE
ORCHESTRA:**
Edison 52538 *Sugar Is Back In Town* . . . . 10.00 - 20.00

**ART LANDRY'S CALL OF THE NORTH
ORCHESTRA/SYNCOPATIN' SIX; ART
LANDRY AND HIS ORCHESTRA:**
Gennett 5053, 5170, 5220, 5255 . . . . 5.00 - 10.00
Gennett 5171 *Rip Saw Blues* . . . . 8.00 - 12.00

5184 *Choo Choo Blues*	15.00 -	20.00
5189 *Some Of These Days*	10.00 -	15.00
Victor 19398 *Rip Saw Blues*	5.00 -	8.00
19488 *Lazy Blues*	5.00 -	8.00
19514 *I'm A Lonesome Little Mama*	15.00 -	25.00
19843 *Sleepy-Time Gal*	5.00 -	8.00
19850 *Don't Wait Too Long*	5.00 -	8.00
19858 *Everybody Stomp*	7.00 -	10.00
19866 *Swamp Blues*	5.00 -	8.00
Victor (most other issues)	4.00 -	7.00

**EDDIE LANG; ED LANG & HIS
ORCHESTRA:**

Brunswick 6254 *Pickin' My Way*	10.00 -	15.00
Okeh 8696 *Freeze An' Melt*	20.00 -	30.00
40807 *Eddie's Twister*	15.00 -	20.00
40936 *Melody Man's Dream*	15.00 -	20.00
40989 *A Little Love, A Little Kiss*	15.00 -	20.00
41134 *Add a Little Wiggle*	15.00 -	20.00
41253 *Freeze An' Melt*	20.00 -	30.00
41344 *Walkin' The Dog*	20.00 -	30.00
41410 *Bugle Call Rag*	25.00 -	40.00

**LANGE-McKAY ORCHESTRA AT CASTLE
FARMS:**

Gennett 5584 *Leaky Roof Blues*	25.00 -	40.00

ART/ARTHUR LANGE & HIS ORCHESTRA:

Cameo 321, 391, 545, 557, 898	4.00 -	8.00
Cameo (most other issues)	3.00 -	5.00

**HENRY LANE: HENRY LANGE & HIS
(BAKER HOTEL) ORCHESTRA:**

Brunswick 2344 *Rufenreddy*	7.00 -	10.00
Brunswick 4161 *I Want You More*	10.00 -	15.00
4478 *China Boy*	50.00 -	75.00
Champion 16294 *Moonlight Saving Time*	35.00 -	50.00
16332 *Mood Indigo*	75.00 -	100.00
Gennett 6263 *Hot Lips*	75.00 -	100.00
20389 *Sweet*	40.00 -	60.00

FRANCES LANGFORD:

Nasty Man, issued contemporaneously on Banner, Melotone, Oriole, Perfect, Romeo:	10.00 -	15.00
Bluebird 5016 *Moon Song*	8.00 -	12.00
Columbia 2696-D *I Can't Believe It's True*	15.00 -	20.00
Victor 24191 *When Mother Played The Organ*	10.00 -	15.00

**LANIN'S RED HEADS; LANIN'S
SOUTHERN SERENADERS (See SAM
LANIN) HOWARD LANIN AND HIS
BENJAMIN FRANKLIN HOTEL
ORCHESTRA:**

Victor 19711 *On A Night Like This*	5.00 -	8.00
19797 *Melancholy Lou*	5.00 -	8.00

**SAM LANIN & HIS ORCHESTRA/FAMOUS
PLAYERS (AND SINGERS); LANIN'S RED
HEADS; SAM LANIN'S DANCE
ORCHESTRA/TROUBADOURS; LANIN'S
SOUTHERN SERENADERS:**

Arto 9097 *Memphis Blues*	10.00 -	15.00
Banner 0503 *Great Day*	5.00 -	8.00
Banner 0601 *Mona*	5.00 -	8.00
Banner 0688 *Exactly Like You*	5.00 -	8.00
Banner 1015 *Shake It And Break It*	8.00 -	12.00
Banner 1182 *Aunt Hagar's Children Blues*	8.00 -	12.00
Banner 1500 *When My Sugar Walks Down The Street*	5.00 -	8.00
Banner 1517, 1518, 1521, 1524, 1542, 1543	3.00 -	6.00
Banner 1538 *Smile All The While*	5.00 -	8.00
Banner 1541 *Flag That Train*	5.00 -	8.00
Banner 1567 *Marguerite*	5.00 -	8.00
Banner 1570 *If I Had A Girl Like You*	5.00 -	8.00
Banner 1617 *I Wonder Where My Baby Is Tonight*	5.00 -	8.00
Banner 1619 *Hugo, I Go Where You Go*	5.00 -	8.00
Banner 1620 *Fond Of You*	5.00 -	8.00
Banner 1622 *Five Foot Two, Eyes Of Blue*	5.00 -	8.00
Banner 1644 *I'm Sitting On Top Of The World*	5.00 -	8.00

Banner 1655 *Good Mornin'*	5.00 -	8.00
Banner 1659 *I Love My Baby, My Baby Loves Me*	5.00 -	8.00
Banner 1663 *Smile A Little Bit*	5.00 -	8.00
Banner 1674 *I Wish't I Was In Peoria*	5.00 -	8.00
Banner 1676 *Sweet Child*	5.00 -	8.00
Banner 1711 *Could I? I Certainly Could*	5.00 -	8.00
Banner 1747 *I'm In Love With You, That's Why*	5.00 -	8.00
Banner 1862 *I'm On My Way Home*	5.00 -	8.00
Banner 1883 *Angel Eyes*	5.00 -	8.00
Banner 6261 *Happy Days And Lonely Nights*	5.00 -	8.00
Banner 6325 *There's a Four Leaf Clover In My Pocket*	5.00 -	8.00
Banner 6328 *He, She and Me*	5.00 -	8.00
Banner 6388 *Do Something*	5.00 -	8.00
6445 *Wishing And Waiting For Love*	5.00 -	8.00
Banner 6452 *What A Day!*	5.00 -	8.00
Banner 7031 *Back In Your Own Back Yard*	5.00 -	8.00
Banner 7161 *Two Lips (To Kiss My Cares Away)*	5.00 -	8.00
32219 *Little Girl*	7.00 -	10.00
Cameo 0104 *Without a Song*	5.00 -	8.00
Cameo 874 *After I Say I'm Sorry?*	5.00 -	8.00
Cameo 987 *Baby Face*	5.00 -	8.00
Cameo 993 *How Many Times*	5.00 -	8.00
Cameo 997 *Crazy Quilt*	7.00 -	10.00
Cameo 1012 *Just a Bird's Eye View (Of My Old Kentucky Home)*	5.00 -	8.00
Cameo 1044 *Sunday*	5.00 -	8.00
Cameo 1090 *High-High-High Up In The Hills*	5.00 -	8.00
Cameo 1103 *There's Everything Nice About You*	5.00 -	8.00
Cameo 1106 *I Wonder How I Look When I'm Asleep*	5.00 -	8.00
Cameo 1164 *At Sundown*	5.00 -	8.00
Cameo 1268 *What'll You Do?*	5.00 -	8.00
Cameo 8103 *Let a Smile Be Your Umbrella*	5.00 -	8.00
Cameo 8109 *My Ohio Home*	7.00 -	10.00
Cameo 8225 *My Pet*	7.00 -	10.00
8227 *Sweet Sue—Just You*	7.00 -	10.00
8228 *Who Wouldn't Be Blue?*	7.00 -	10.00
Cameo 8234 *I Can't Give You Anything But Love*	5.00 -	8.00
8245 *Ready For The River*	7.00 -	10.00
Cameo 8247 *That's My Weakness Now*	5.00 -	8.00
Cameo 8248 *That's Just My Way Of Forgetting You*	5.00 -	8.00
Cameo 8251 *Old Man Sunshine*	5.00 -	8.00
Cameo 8258 *Just Like a Melody Out Of The Sky*	5.00 -	8.00
Cameo 8290 *You Took Advantage Of Me*	5.00 -	8.00
Cameo 8348 *Don't Be Like That*	5.00 -	8.00
Cameo 9003 *You're The Cream In My Coffee*	5.00 -	8.00
Cameo 9103 *Mean To Me*	7.00 -	10.00
Cameo 9157 *Louise*	5.00 -	8.00
Cameo 9167 *I Wanna Go Places And Do Things*	7.00 -	10.00
Challenge 543 *Down Where the Sun Goes Down*	5.00 -	8.00
Champion 16039 *Hullabaloo*	15.00 -	20.00
Columbia 279-D, 285-D, 324-D, 360-D	4.00 -	8.00
Columbia 327-D *King Porter Stomp*	15.00 -	20.00
Columbia 376-D *Flag That Train*	10.00 -	15.00
Columbia 396-D *Who Loved You Best?*	7.00 -	10.00
Columbia 414-D *If I Had a Girl Like You*	7.00 -	10.00
Columbia 438-D *Cecilia*	5.00 -	8.00
Columbia 447-D *Desdemona*	7.00 -	10.00
483-D *Five Foot Two, Eyes Of Blue*	10.00 -	15.00
Conqueror 7810 *Little Girl*	7.00 -	10.00
Diva 3083-G *Crying For The Carolines*	8.00 -	12.00
Domino 3536 *If I Had a Girl Like You*	5.00 -	8.00
Domino 3626 *I Love My Baby, My Baby Loves Me*	5.00 -	8.00
Domino 3628 *Good Mornin'*	5.00 -	8.00
Domino 3644 *Sweet Child*	5.00 -	8.00
Domino 3647 *I Wish't I Was In Peoria*	5.00 -	8.00
Domino 3682 *Let's Talk About My Sweetie*	5.00 -	8.00
Emerson 10439 *Aunt Hagar's Children Blues*	8.00 -	12.00
Emerson 10496 *Arkansas Blues*	8.00 -	12.00

Harmony 968-H *Don't Hang Your Dreams on a Rainbow*	5.00 -	8.00
Harmony 984-H *Marianne*	5.00 -	8.00
Harmony 1001-H *Little By Little*	5.00 -	8.00
Harmony 1018-H *Melancholy*	5.00 -	8.00
Harmony 1029-H *Campus Capers*	7.00 -	10.00
Harmony 1036-H *Sophomore Prom*	7.00 -	10.00
Harmony 1049-H *That Wonderful Something Is Love*	5.00 -	8.00
Harmony 1065-H *Hoosier Hop*	7.00 -	10.00
Harmony 1083-H *Crying for the Carolines*	8.00 -	12.00
1084-H *When I'm Housekeeping For You*	15.00 -	20.00
1107-H *Hangin' On The Garden Gate*	7.00 -	10.00
1109-H *Keepin' Myself For You*	7.00 -	10.00
1139-H *The Free And Easy*	7.00 -	10.00
1165-H *Be Careful With Those Eyes*	7.00 -	10.00
1265-H *You're Simply Delish*	8.00 -	12.00
Odeon ONY-36112 *Seems To Me*	25.00 -	35.00
ONY-36113 *Rollin' Down The River*	25.00 -	35.00
ONY-36189 *Please Don't Talk About Me When I'm Gone*	25.00 -	35.00
ONY-36190 *I Surrender, Dear*	25.00 -	35.00
ONY-36195 *The One-Man Band*	25.00 -	35.00
Okeh 40111 *Big Boy*	7.00 -	10.00
40170 *Somebody Loves Me*	5.00 -	8.00
40208 *My Best Girl*	5.00 -	8.00
40219 *I Want to See My Tennessee*	5.00 -	8.00
40738 *I Gotta Get Myself Somebody To Love*	8.00 -	12.00
40766 *I'm Looking Over A Four Leaf Clover*	8.00 -	12.00
40810 *Side By Side*	7.00 -	10.00
40833 *She's Got "It"*	8.00 -	12.00
40855 *Sing Me A Baby Song*	8.00 -	12.00
40863 *Just Once Again*	7.00 -	10.00
40914 *Everybody Loves My Girl*	8.00 -	12.00
40933 *There Must Be Somebody Else*	7.00 -	10.00
40937 *My New York*	7.00 -	10.00
40977 *Let A Smile Be Your Umbrella*	7.00 -	10.00
41031 *Sweet Sue—Just You*	7.00 -	10.00
41038 *Get Out And Get Under The Moon*	8.00 -	12.00
41063 *Sorry For Me*	7.00 -	10.00
41097 *Ten Little Miles From Town*	10.00 -	15.00
41121 *Roses Of Yesterday*	7.00 -	10.00
41159 *Sweethearts On Parade*	7.00 -	10.00
Okeh 41188 *If I Had You*	30.00 -	50.00
41228 *If I'm Crazy Over You*	30.00 -	50.00
Okeh 41383 *Cooking Breakfast For The One I Love*	15.00 -	25.00
41385 *Mona*	10.00 -	15.00
Pathe-Actuelle 036075 *Unfortunate Blues*	7.00 -	10.00
036184 *Forsaken Blues*	7.00 -	10.00
036202 *Lucky Kentucky*	5.00 -	8.00
036203 *Alabamy Bound*	7.00 -	10.00
036219 *All Aboard For Heaven*	5.00 -	8.00
36342 *I'm Sitting On Top Of The World*	5.00 -	8.00
36343 *Five Foot Two, Eyes Of Blue*	5.00 -	8.00
36344 *Say, Who Is That Baby Doll?*	5.00 -	8.00
Pathe-Actuelle 36357 *Spanish Shawl*	7.00 -	10.00
36363 *No Man's Mama*	8.00 -	12.00
Pathe-Actuelle 36512, 36545, 36547,	5.00 -	8.00
Pathe-Actuelle 36797 *My Pet*	7.00 -	10.00
36798 *Get Out And Get Under The Moon*	7.00 -	10.00
36802 *Sweet Sue, Just You*	7.00 -	10.00
36804 *Who Wouldn't Be Blue?*	7.00 -	10.00
Perfect 14256 *Nobody's Sweetheart Now*	7.00 -	10.00
14330 *I Want To See My Tennessee*	5.00 -	8.00
14365 *Forsaken Blues*	7.00 -	10.00
14383 *Lucky Kentucky*	5.00 -	8.00
14384 *Alabamy Bound*	7.00 -	10.00
14400 *All Aboard For Heaven*	5.00 -	8.00
14415 *Don't Bring Lulu*	5.00 -	8.00
14440 *Yes Sir, That's My Baby*	5.00 -	8.00
14486 *Sweet Man*	5.00 -	8.00
14497 *Paddlin' Madelin' Home*	5.00 -	8.00
14523 *I'm Sitting On Top Of The World*	5.00 -	8.00
14524 *Five Foot Two, Eyes Of Blue*	5.00 -	8.00
14525 *Say, Who Is That Baby Doll?*	5.00 -	8.00
14538 *Spanish Shawl*	7.00 -	10.00
14544 *No Man's Mama*	8.00 -	12.00
14555 *After I Say I'm Sorry*	5.00 -	8.00
Perfect 14693 *Any Ice Today, Lady?*	5.00 -	8.00
14726 *Sunday*	5.00 -	8.00
14728 *My Baby Knows How*	5.00 -	8.00
Perfect 14978 *My Pet*	7.00 -	10.00
14979 *Get out And Get Under The Moon*	7.00 -	10.00
14983 *Sweet Sue—Just You*	7.00 -	10.00
14985 *Who Wouldn't Be Blue?*	7.00 -	10.00
15486 *Little Girl*	7.00 -	10.00
Perfect (most other issues)	4.00 -	7.00
Puritan 11222 *Aunt Hagar's Blues*	8.00 -	12.00
Regal 8059 *I'm In Love With You, That's Why*	5.00 -	8.00
Regal 8120 *She's Still My Baby*	7.00 -	10.00
8413 *The Varsity Drag*	8.00 -	12.00
8557 *Rag Doll*	5.00 -	8.00
8598 *You're A Real Sweetheart*	5.00 -	8.00
8600 *Two Lips*	5.00 -	8.00
8610 *Down Where The Sun Goes Down*	5.00 -	8.00
8671 *Me And The Man In The Moon*	5.00 -	8.00
8701 *Happy Days And Lonely Nights*	5.00 -	8.00
8745 *He, She And Me*	5.00 -	8.00
8817 *Wishing And Waiting For Love*	5.00 -	8.00
8818 *What A Day!*	5.00 -	8.00
8945 *I'm On A Diet Of Love*	8.00 -	12.00
Regal 9200 *Doo Dah Blues*	8.00 -	12.00
Regal 9486 *Blue Hoosier Blues*	5.00 -	8.00
Regal 9704 *Tessie, Stop Teasing Me*	5.00 -	8.00
Regal 9866 *Marguerite*	5.00 -	8.00
Regal 9900 *Let's Wander Away*	5.00 -	8.00
Regal 9919 *Bam Bam Bamy Shore*	5.00 -	8.00
Regal 9967 *Smile A Little Bit*	5.00 -	8.00
Regal 9970 *I Love My Baby, My Baby Loves Me*	5.00 -	8.00
Regal 9981 *Sweet Child (I'm Wild About You)*	5.00 -	8.00
Romeo 700 *Because My Baby Don't Mean "Maybe" Now*	5.00 -	8.00
Romeo 887 *Wedding Bells (Are Breaking Up That Old Gang Of Mine)*	7.00 -	10.00
Romeo 948 *That's Her Now!*	5.00 -	8.00
Romeo 959 *Louise*	5.00 -	8.00
Romeo 1306 *Just Like in a Story Book*	5.00 -	8.00
Romeo 1580 *Walkin' My Baby Back Home*	5.00 -	8.00
Silvertone 2498 *My Sweet Louise*	10.00 -	15.00
Supertone 9458 *I'm In Seventh Heaven*	10.00 -	15.00
9480 *Or What Have You*	10.00 -	15.00
9550 *Hang On To Me*	10.00 -	15.00
9576 *Miss Wonderful*	10.00 -	15.00
9580 *Lady Luck*	10.00 -	15.00
9744 *Hullabaloo*	15.00 -	20.00

LA PALINA BROADCASTERS:

Conqueror 7412 *Little By Little*	7.00 -	10.00
Domino 4405 *Little By Little*	7.00 -	10.00
4408 *Sweetheart, We Need Each Other*	7.00 -	10.00
Pathe-Actuelle 37022 *Sweetness*	7.00 -	10.00
37024 *Piccolo Pete*	7.00 -	10.00
37037 *Little By Little*	7.00 -	10.00
37043 *Sweetheart, We Need Each Other*	7.00 -	10.00
Perfect 15203 *Sweetness*	7.00 -	10.00
15205 *Piccolo Pete*	7.00 -	10.00
15218 *Little By Little*	7.00 -	10.00
15224 *Sweetheart, We Need Each Other*	7.00 -	10.00

HAL LASKA AND HIS ORCHESTRA:

Parlophone PNY-34034 *Romance*	20.00 -	30.00
PNY-34038 *Sweeping The Clouds Away (instrumental)*	50.00 -	75.00
PNY-34039 *Any Time's The Time To Fall in Love (instrumental)*	50.00 -	75.00

PNY-34040 *Sweeping The Clouds Away*	30.00 -	50.00
PNY-34041 *Any Time's The Time To Fall In*		
Love	30.00 -	50.00
PNY-34064 *When The Little Red Roses Get*		
The Blues	30.00 -	50.00
PNY-34070 *Exactly Like You*	25.00 -	40.00
PNY-34072 *Dust*	25.00 -	40.00
PNY-34073 *Leave It That Way*	25.00 -	35.00
PNY-34074 *On The Sunny Side of the Street*	25.00 -	35.00
PNY-34161 *Put On Your Old Grey Bonnet*	20.00 -	30.00
PNY-34162 *Alexander's Ragtime Band*	20.00 -	30.00
PNY-34164 *Overnight*	20.00 -	30.00
PNY-34165 *Little Did I Know*	20.00 -	30.00

HARLAN LATTIMORE & HIS CONNIE'S INN ORCHESTRA:

Columbia 2675-D *Chant of the Weed*	20.00 -	30.00
2678-D *Reefer Man*	20.00 -	30.00

LA VEEDA DANCE ORCHESTRA:

Columbia 1549-D *Strut Yo' Stuff*	20.00 -	30.00

THELMA LA VIZZO:

Paramount 12206 *Trouble In Mind Blues*	50.00 -	75.00
12250 *The Stomps*	100.00 -	150.00

GERTRUDE LAWRENCE:

Columbia 512-D, 513-D, 514-D	5.00 -	10.00
Victor 20331	5.00 -	8.00

SARA LAWRENCE:

Oriole 894 *Don't Love Me*	30.00 -	50.00

DAVE LAWSON'S ORCHESTRA:

Challenge 365 *Me and My Shadow*	15.00 -	20.00
Champion 15326 *Me and My Shadow*	50.00 -	75.00

YANK LAWSON'S JAZZ BAND:

Signature	4.00 -	7.00

LAZY LEVEE LOUNGERS:

Columbia 2243-D *Shout, Sister, Shout*	30.00 -	40.00

LEE'S BLACK DIAMONDS:

Broadway 1294 *Piggly Wiggly Blues*	150.00 -	300.00

BARON LEE & THE BLUE RHYTHM BAND:

Titles, issued contemporaneously on Banner, Melotone, Oriole, Perfect, Romeo: *Cabin In The Cotton; The Crawl; Doin' The Shake; Heatwaves; Jazz Cocktail; Mighty Sweet; Minnie The Moocher's Wedding Day; Old Yazoo; Reefer Man; Rhythm Spasm; The Scat Song; Sentimental Gentleman From Georgia; Smoke Rings; White Lightning; Wild Waves; You Gave Me Everything But Love*	10.00 -	20.00

CHAUNCEY C. LEE:

Okeh 40321 *Banjo Rag*	75.00 -	100.00

GEORGE E. LEE & HIS (NOVELTY SINGING) ORCHESTRA:

Brunswick 4684 *Ruff Scuffin'*	75.00 -	100.00
7132 *Paseo Strut*	80.00 -	120.00
Merrit 2206 *Down Home Syncopated Blues*	300.00 -	600.00

JULIA LEE:

Brunswick 4761 *He's Tall and Dark and Handsome*	75.00 -	100.00

MANDY LEE:

Titles, issued contemporaneously on Banner, Conqueror, Domino, Regal: *Crap Shootin' Poppa, Mama Done Caught Your Dice; I Needs Plenty Of Grease In My Frying Pan*	10.00 -	15.00
Additional titles: *Harlem Blues: Someone's Been Lovin' My Baby*	15.00 -	20.00
Pathe-Actuelle 7509 *Rounders Blues*	50.00 -	75.00
Perfect 109 *Wandering Papa Blues*	50.00 -	75.00

MARGUERITE LEE:

Vocalion 1150 *You Will Always Live in Our Memory*	100.00 -	150.00

RUTH LEE:

Nordskog 3008 *Maybe Someday*	150.00 -	300.00
Sunshine 3002 *Maybe Someday*	150.00 -	300.00
(Sunshine 3002 label is passed over Nordskog label)		

WINTHROP LEE & HIS ORCHESTRA:

Parlophone PNY-34124 *Loveless Love*	40.00 -	60.00
PNY-34148 *Daniel's Blues*	40.00 -	60.00

BOBBIE LEECAN: BOBBIE LEECAN'S NEEDMORE BAND:

Victor 20251 *Black Cat Bone Blues*	35.00 -	50.00
20660 *Midnight Susie*	75.00 -	100.00
20768 *Blue Harmonica*	75.00 -	100.00
20853 *Apaloosa Blues*	75.00 -	100.00
20958 *Royal Palm Blues*	75.00 -	100.00

CHESTER LEIGHTON AND HIS SOPHOMORES:

Clarion 5125-C *Cheerful Little Earful*	8.00 -	12.00
5177-C *Someone Sang a Sweeter Song To Mary*	7.00 -	10.00
5180-C *A Peach of a Pair*	7.00 -	10.00
5186-C *The Little Things in Life*	7.00 -	10.00
5276-C *If You Should Ever Need Me*	7.00 -	10.00
5277-C *When I Take My Sugar To Tea*	8.00 -	12.00
5319-C *Star Dust*	8.00 -	12.00
5337-C *Love Is Like That*	7.00 -	10.00
5351-C *On The Beach With You*	8.00 -	12.00
5353-C *Just One More Chance*	8.00 -	12.00
5363-C *The Kiss That You've Forgotten*	7.00 -	10.00
Harmony 1233-H *A Peach of a Pair*	7.00 -	10.00
1242-H *My Love For You*	7.00 -	10.00
1248-H *Satan's Holiday*	10.00 -	15.00
1251-H *Someone Sang a Sweeter Song To Mary*	7.00 -	10.00
1307-H *When I Take My Sugar To Tea*	8.00 -	12.00
1328-H *Love Is Like That*	7.00 -	10.00
1340-H *Without That Gal!*	8.00 -	12.00
1342-H *Makin' Faces at the Man in the Moon*	8.00 -	12.00
1351-H *The Kiss That You've Forgotten*	7.00 -	10.00
Velvet Tone 2343-V *When I Take My Sugar To Tea*	8.00 -	12.00
2342-V *If You Should Ever Need Me*	7.00 -	10.00
2401-V *Love Is Like That*	7.00 -	10.00
2415-V *On The Beach With You*	8.00 -	12.00
2417-V *Just One More Chance*	8.00 -	12.00
2427-V *The Kiss That You've Forgotten*	7.00 -	10.00

FRANK LEITHNER & HIS ORCHESTRA:

Banner 6418 *I'm Feathering a Nest*	5.00 -	8.00
Banner 6422 *With a Song In My Heart*	5.00 -	8.00
Banner 6468 *I'm In Seventh Heaven*	5.00 -	8.00
Conqueror 7366 *With a Song In My Heart*	5.00 -	8.00

HAROLD LEM & HIS ORCHESTRA:

Okeh 41465 *I Got Rhythm*	10.00 -	15.00

LENOX DANCE ORCHESTRA:

Perfect 14394 *Me Neenyah*	10.00 -	15.00

JAMES I. LENT WITH ARTHUR PRYOR'S BAND:

Victor 17092 *The Ragtime Drummer*	10.00 -	15.00

AL LENTZ & HIS (DANCE) ORCHESTRA:

Banner 1812 *Sweet Thing*	7.00 -	10.00
Banner 1818 *No One But You Knows How To Love*	5.00 -	8.00
Domino 3793 *Sweet Thing*	7.00 -	10.00
Regal 8130 *Sweet Thing*	7.00 -	10.00
Regal 8146 *Just a Bird's Eye View of My Old Kentucky Home*	7.00 -	10.00
Regal 8177 *How Could Red Riding Hood?*	5.00 -	8.00

HARLAN LEONARD & HIS ROCKETS:

Bluebird	5.00 -	8.00

HAROLD LEONARD & HIS RED JACKETS:

Gennett 5137 *China Boy*	7.00 -	10.00
Gennett 5138 *The Cat's Whiskers*	7.00 -	10.00
Okeh 40030 *Forgetful Blues*	7.00 -	10.00
Okeh 40042 *WOP Blues*	7.00 -	10.00
Okeh 40083 *Limehouse Blues*	7.00 -	10.00
Okeh 40091 *Unfortunate Blues*	7.00 -	10.00

LEROY'S DALLAS BAND:

Columbia 14402-D *Tampa Shout*	100.00 -	150.00

LEW LESLIE'S BLACKBIRD'S ORCHESTRA:

Brunswick 4030 *Bandanna Babies*	10.00 -	15.00

NATE LESLIE & HIS ORCHESTRA:
Vocalion 3584 *Shake Yo' Bones* . . . . 15.00 - 20.00

LEVEE LOUNGERS:
Pathe-Actuelle 36637 *The Devil Is Afraid Of*
   Music . . . . 10.00 - 15.00
   36679 *Frankie And Johnnie* . . . . 10.00 - 15.00
   36745 *My Melancholy Baby* . . . . 7.00 - 10.00
   36857 *'Tain't So, Honey, 'Tain't So* . . . . 7.00 - 10.00
   36883 *Easy Goin'* . . . . 8.00 - 12.00
   Perfect 14818 *The Devil Is Afraid Of Music* . . . . . 10.00 - 15.00
   14860 *Frankie And Johnnie* . . . . 10.00 - 15.00
   14926 *My Melancholy Baby* . . . . 7.00 - 10.00
   15064 *Easy Goin'* . . . . 8.00 - 12.00
   (Note: Most other issues on Pathe-Actuelle and
   Perfect . . . . 4.00 - 7.00

LEVEE SERENADERS:
Vocalion 1154 *Midnight Mama* . . . . 150.00 - 200.00

LEVEE SYNCOPATORS:
Titles, issued contemporaneously on Gray Gull,
   Radiex, Van Dyke: *The Rackett: The Harlem*
   Stomp Down . . . . 20.00 - 30.00

ALFRED LEWIS:
Vocalion 1498 *Friday Moan Blues* . . . . 50.00 - 75.00

MEADE LUX LEWIS:
Blue Note . . . . 5.00 - 10.00
Decca 819 *Yancey Special* . . . . 8.00 - 12.00
Paramount 12896 *Honky Train Blues* . . . . 150.00 - 200.00
Solo Art 12002, 12003, 12004 . . . . 7.00 - 10.00
Victor 25541 *Honky Tonk Train Blues* . . . . 8.00 - 12.00
Vocalion 4606 *Boogie Woogie Prayer* . . . . 7.00 - 10.00
   4608 *Bear Cat Crawl* . . . . 7.00 - 10.00

NOAH LEWIS; NOAH LEWIS'S JUG BAND:
Bluebird 5675 *Ticket Agent Blues* . . . . 100.00 - 150.00
Victor 23266 *New Minglewood Blues* . . . . 150.00 - 200.00
   23336 *Like I Want To Be* . . . . 150.00 - 200.00
   V38681 *Chickasaw Special* . . . . 100.00 - 150.00

SAMMY LEWIS (AND HIS BAMVILLE SYNCOPATORS):
Okeh 8285 *Just Too Late* . . . . 50.00 - 75.00
Vocalion 1029 *Hateful Papa Blues* . . . . 75.00 - 100.00
   1030 *Arkansas Shout* . . . . 75.00 - 100.00

TED LEWIS & HIS BAND:
Columbia 1-S *Popular Favorites (medley)* . . . . 4.00 - 7.00
Columbia 48-D *Unfortunate Blues* . . . . 7.00 - 10.00
   122-D *San* . . . . 7.00 - 10.00
   170-D *Barnyard Blues* . . . . 10.00 - 15.00
   195-D *Eccentric* . . . . 7.00 - 10.00
   439-D *Tin Roof Blues* . . . . 8.00 - 12.00
   478-D *The Camel Walk* . . . . 7.00 - 10.00
   600-D *I've Found A New Baby* . . . . 7.00 - 10.00
Columbia 52-D, 82-D, 157-D, 227-D, 241-D,
   255-D, 274-D, 295-D, 311-D, 406-D, 416-D,
   504-D, 543-D, 565-D, 585-D, 620-D, ... 4.00 - 8.00
Columbia 667-D *Where'd You Get Those Eyes?* . . 7.00 - 10.00
   670-D *Hi-Diddle-Diddle* . . . . 7.00 - 10.00
   697-D *The New St. Louis Blues* . . . . 7.00 - 10.00
   770-D *Tiger Rag* . . . . 7.00 - 10.00
   826-D *Bugle Call Rag* . . . . 7.00 - 10.00
   922-D *When My Baby Smiles At Me* . . . . 7.00 - 10.00
   1017-D *Frankie And Johnny* . . . . 7.00 - 10.00
   1050-D *The Memphis Blues* . . . . 7.00 - 10.00
   1084-D *The Darktown Strutters' Ball* . . . . 7.00 - 10.00
   1207-D *Is Everybody Happy Now?* . . . . 7.00 - 10.00
Columbia 844-D, 895-D, 988-D, 1296-D . . . . . . 5.00 - 8.00
Columbia 1242-D *Away Down South In Heaven* . 7.00 - 10.00
   1313-D *Cobble-Stones* . . . . 7.00 - 10.00
   1346-D *Hello, Montreal!* . . . . 7.00 - 10.00
   1391-D *Oh Baby!* . . . . 7.00 - 10.00
   1428-D *A Good Man Is Hard To Find* . . . . . . 8.00 - 12.00
   1485-D *Moonlight Madness* . . . . 7.00 - 10.00
Columbia 1525-D *A Jazz Holiday* . . . . 10.00 - 15.00
   1573-D *Clarinet Marmalade* . . . . 10.00 - 15.00

   1656-D *She's Funny That Way* . . . . 8.00 - 12.00
   1709-D *Glad Rag Doll* . . . . 8.00 - 12.00
   1789-D *Limehouse Blues* . . . . 8.00 - 12.00
   1854-D *Maybe Who Knows?* . . . . 7.00 - 10.00
   1882-D *I'm The Medicine Man For The Blues* . 7.00 - 10.00
   1916-D *Lewisada Blues* . . . . 8.00 - 12.00
   1957-D *Lonely Troubadour* . . . . 7.00 - 10.00
   1999-D *Lady Luck* . . . . 7.00 - 10.00
   2029-D *Farewell Blues* . . . . 10.00 - 15.00
   2088-D *Harmonica Harry* . . . . 10.00 - 15.00
   2113-D *Aunt Hagar's Blues* . . . . 10.00 - 15.00
   2144-D *Singing a Vagabond Song* . . . . 10.00 - 15.00
   2181-D *Dinah* . . . . 10.00 - 15.00
   2217-D *Sobbin' Blues* . . . . 10.00 - 15.00
   2246-D *The World Is Waiting For The Sunrise* . 8.00 - 12.00
   2311-D *Laughing At Life* . . . . 15.00 - 20.00
   2336-D *Somebody Stole My Gal* . . . . 15.00 - 20.00
   2378-D *Headin' For Better Times* . . . . 15.00 - 20.00
   2408-D *At Last I'm Happy* . . . . 15.00 - 20.00
   2428-D *Egyptian Ella* . . . . 15.00 - 20.00
   2452-D *Ho Hum!* . . . . 15.00 - 20.00
   2467-D *Dip Your Brush in the Sunshine* . . . . . 15.00 - 25.00
   2492-D *I'm All Dressed Up with a Broken*
      Heart . . . . 15.00 - 20.00
   2527-D *Royal Garden Blues* . . . . 15.00 - 20.00
   2560-D *An Evening In Caroline* . . . . 15.00 - 20.00
   2635-D *Somebody Loves You* . . . . 15.00 - 20.00
   2652-D *A Shanty in Old Shanty Town* . . . . . . 15.00 - 20.00
   2728-D *Play, Fiddle, Play* . . . . 10.00 - 15.00
   2748-D *Buy American!* . . . . 15.00 - 20.00
   2753-D *There's A New Day Coming* . . . . 15.00 - 20.00
   2758-D *All Aboard For Dreamland, Baby* . . . . 15.00 - 20.00
   2774-D *Stormy Weather* . . . . 20.00 - 30.00
   2775-D *The Gold-Diggers' Song* . . . . 20.00 - 30.00
   2777-D *In a Garden In Old Kalua* . . . . 10.00 - 15.00
   2786-D *Rhythm* . . . . 20.00 - 30.00
   2799-D *Here You Come With Love* . . . . 20.00 - 30.00
   2807-D *Ten Thousand Years Ago* . . . . 20.00 - 30.00
(Note: Most of the foregoing, after number
   1656-D, were issued with the special Ted Lewis
   picture label, and some earlier numbers were
   repressed with that special label.)
Columbia A2798, A-2844, A-2895 . . . . 3.00 - 6.00
Columbia A-2908, A-2927, A-2945, A-2998,
   A-3306, A-3329, A-3351, A-3400, A-3411,
   A-3421, A-3434, A-3453 . . . . 4.00 - 7.00
Columbia A-3464, A-3473, A-3499, a-3538,
   A-3590, A-3647, A-3662, A-3676, A-3709,
   A-3730, A-3738 . . . . 4.00 - 7.00
Columbia A-3790, A-3813 . . . . 5.00 - 8.00
Columbia A-3814, A-3957 . . . . 4.00 - 7.00
Columbia A-3879, A-3892, A-3972 . . . . 5.00 - 8.00
Decca 106, 107, 239, 240, 241, 242 . . . . 7.00 - 10.00
Decca, most other issues . . . . 3.00 - 6.00

JOIE LICHTER'S STRAND SYMPHONISTS:
Gennett 5409 *I'm In A Fool's Paradise* . . . . — - —
   5423 *Patricia Mine* . . . . — - —
   5427 *Orange Blossom Time* . . . . — - —
Harmograph 887 *I'm All Broke Out With The*
   Blues . . . . 25.00 - 40.00
Paramount 20289 *Linger Awhile* . . . . 25.00 - 35.00
   20428 *Spanish Shawl* . . . . 25.00 - 35.00
   20439 *Slippery Elm* . . . . 25.00 - 35.00
Puritan 11428 *Sandy* . . . . 25.00 - 35.00
   11439 *After I Said I'm Sorry* . . . . 25.00 - 35.00
Silvertone 3502 *Spanish Shawl* . . . . 25.00 - 35.00
   3507 *Slippery Elm* . . . . 25.00 - 35.00

(GLEN) LIETZKE'S MIDNIGHT/MIDNITE SERENADERS:
Broadway 1399 *So Beats My Heart For You* . . . . . 8.00 - 12.00
   1425 *You're The One I Care For* . . . . 8.00 - 12.00

LOUIS LILIENFELD & HIS HOTEL

BILTMORE ORCHESTRA:

Edison 52128 *The Calinda*	5.00 -	8.00
Edison 52176 *Normandy*	5.00 -	8.00
Edison 52216 *My Ohio Home*	7.00 -	10.00
Edison 52237 *Mary Ann*	10.00 -	15.00
Edison 52241 *Let a Smile Be Your Umbrella*	20.00 -	30.00
Edison 52272 *Forever And Ever*	15.00 -	20.00
Edison 52289 *Ma Belle*	7.00 -	10.00

LILL'S HOT SHOTS:

Vocalion 1037 *Drop That Sack*	80.00 -	120.00

DONALD LINDLEY (& HIS BOYS):

Columbia 546-D, 1443-D	8.00 -	12.00
Edison 51771 *Hot As A Summer's Day*	20.00 -	30.00

JACK LINX & HIS (BIRMINGHAM) SOCIETY SERENADERS:

Okeh 40188 *Doodle Doo Doo*	10.00 -	15.00
40192 *How Come You Do Me Like You Do?*	20.00 -	30.00
40365 *Sweet Georgia Brown*	15.00 -	20.00
40429 *She's My Sheba, I'm Her Sheik*	15.00 -	20.00
40439 *When Eyes Of Blue Are Fooling You*	15.00 -	20.00
40458 *Don't You Try To High-Hat Me*	15.00 -	20.00
40587 *Nobody's Rose*	15.00 -	20.00
40602 *Fallen Arches*	30.00 -	50.00
40619 *Tiger Rag*	30.00 -	50.00
40803 *Beale Street Blues*	25.00 -	40.00
41014 *Pardon The Glove*	25.00 -	40.00

THE LITTLE ACES:

Okeh 41136 *Four Or Five Times*	15.00 -	25.00

THE LITTLE CHOCOLATE DANDIES:

Okeh 8728 *Six or Seven Times*	20.00 -	30.00

LITTLE'S COLLEGIANS:

Superior 2817 *Clarinet Marmalade*	75.00 -	100.00

THE LITTLE RAMBLERS:

Bluebird 6043, 6045, 6077, 6130, 6131, 6144, 6189, 6191, 6192, 6193, 6220, 6232, 6237	5.00 -	10.00
Columbia 175-D, 203-D, 217-D, 248-D, 346-D, 403-D, 423-D, 524-D, 535-D, 628-D, 679-D, 719-D, 1103-D	7.00 -	12.00

LITTLE JACK LITTLE & HIS ORCHESTRA:

Bluebird 5056, 5065	5.00 -	10.00
Columbia 2895-D, 2900-D, 2969-D, 2978-D, 2984-D, 2993-D, 3006-D, 3009-D, 3068-D, 3069-D, 3095-D, 3107-D, 3108-D	8.00 -	12.00

ED LLOYD AND HIS ORCHESTRA (SEE ED LOYD)

PAUL LOCH & HIS ORCHESTRA:

Parlophone PNY-34059 *I Was Made To Love You*	25.00 -	40.00
PNY-34063 *Accordion Joe*	25.00 -	40.00
PNY-34065 *Collegiate Love*	25.00 -	40.00

LOCKE BROTHERS' RHYTHM ORCHESTRA:

Bluebird 6287 *Don't You Tear My Clothes*	20.00 -	30.00
6288 *Sills Stomp*	20.00 -	30.00
6297 *Elephant Stomp*	20.00 -	30.00
6216 *Some Of These Days*	20.00 -	30.00
6332 *China Boy*	20.00 -	30.00

LOFNER-HARRIS ST. FRANCIS HOTEL ORCHESTRA:

Victor 22830 *I Got The Ritz From The One I Love*	10.00 -	15.00
22831 *River, Stay 'Way From My Door*	10.00 -	15.00

GUY LOMBARDO & HIS ROYAL CANADIANS:

Brunswick (most issues, 6000 series)	4.00 -	8.00
Columbia 1395-D *Waitin' For Katy*	7.00 -	10.00
1451-D *The Cannon Ball*	8.00 -	12.00
1721-D *Baby*	7.00 -	10.00
2457-D *Moonlight Saving Time*	7.00 -	10.00
2578-D *River, Stay 'Way From My Door*	8.00 -	12.00
Columbia (most other issues)	4.00 -	7.00
Decca (most issues numbers 102 through 585)	4.00 -	7.00
Decca (most issues, higher numbers)	2.00 -	5.00

Gennett 5416 *So This Is Venice*	35.00 -	50.00
5417 *Cotton Picker's Ball*	50.00 -	75.00
Melotone (most issues)	4.00 -	8.00
Oriole (most issues)	4.00 -	8.00
Perfect (most issues)	4.00 -	8.00
Personal Record 140-P *She'll Come Along*	15.00 -	20.00
Romeo (most issues)	4.00 -	8.00
Victor (25000 series, most issues)	4.00 -	8.00

FRED LONGSHAW:

Columbia 14080-D	20.00 -	30.00

ERNEST LOOMIS' ORCHESTRA:

Victor 20755 *Sweet Someone*	30.00 -	50.00

VINCENT LOPEZ & HIS (CASA LOPEZ/ HOTEL PENNSYLVANIA) ORCHESTRA:

Banner 0557 *Look For The Silver Lining*	7.00 -	10.00
0569 *'Tain't No Sin*	8.00 -	12.00
Banner (most other issues)	4.00 -	8.00
Bluebird (most issues)	3.00 -	6.00
Brunswick 20065 (12-inch) *St. Louis Blues*	10.00 -	20.00
20066 (12-inch) *Alexander's Ragtime Band*	10.00 -	20.00
Brunswick (most other issues)	4.00 -	7.00
Cameo (most issues)	4.00 -	8.00
Domino (most issues)	4.00 -	8.00
Hit-of-the-Week (most issues)	3.00 -	6.00
(Note: Above are one-sided, paper records)		
Okeh 4783 *Aggravatin' Papa*	5.00 -	8.00
Okeh 4819 *You've Got To See Mama Ev'ry Night*	5.00 -	8.00
Okeh 4869 *Blue Hoosier Blues*	7.00 -	10.00
Okeh 40009 *Raggedy Anny*	5.00 -	8.00
Okeh 40024 *Steppin' Out*	5.00 -	8.00
Okeh 40199 *Me and The Boy Friend*	5.00 -	8.00
Okeh 40478 *Stomp Off, Let's Go*	8.00 -	12.00
Okeh 40552 *Black Horse Stomp*	8.00 -	12.00
Okeh 40586 *Rhythm of the Day*	8.00 -	12.00
Oriole (most issues)	4.00 -	8.00
Perfect 15262 *Look For The Silver Lining*	7.00 -	10.00
Pefect 7-02-12 *Love And Learn*	7.00 -	10.00
7-04-12 *Music On The Mall*	7.00 -	10.00
8-01-09 *Ham On Rye*	7.00 -	10.00
Perfect (most other issues)	4.00 -	7.00
Regal (most issues)	4.00 -	8.00
Romeo (most issues)	4.00 -	8.00
Vocalion 4129 *Day Dreaming (All Night Long)*	7.00 -	10.00
4141 *There's Honey On The Moon Tonight*	7.00 -	10.00

LOS ANGELES BILTMORE HOTEL TRIO:

Okeh 41064 *Clowin' The Frets*	7.00 -	10.00

LOU & HIS GINGER SNAPS:

Banner 6536 *Broadway Rhythm*	15.00 -	25.00
6540 *The Way He Loves Is Just Too Bad*	10.00 -	15.00
Cameo 9319 *Broadway Rhythm*	15.00 -	25.00
9320 *The Way He Loves Is Just To Bad*	10.00 -	15.00

LOUIS' HARLEM STOMPERS:

Columbia 2615-D *Casa Loma Stomp*	15.00 -	20.00

LOUISIANA FIVE (JAZZ ORCHESTRA):

Columbia A2742 *Yelping Hound Blues*	5.00 -	8.00
Columbia A2949 *Slow And Easy*	5.00 -	8.00
Columbia　most other issues	4.00 -	7.00
Edison 50609 *Clarinet Squawk*	5.00 -	8.00
Edison 50622 *Yelping Hound Blues*	5.00 -	8.00
Emerson 10116 *Weary Blues*	7.00 -	10.00
Emerson 10172 *Big Fat Ma*	7.00 -	10.00
Emerson 10229 *Be Happ-E*	5.00 -	8.00
Emerson 10241 *Town Topic Rag*	7.00 -	10.00
Emerson 1026 *Dixie Blues*	8.00 -	12.00
Emerson 1076 *Virginia Blues*	8.00 -	12.00
Emerson 1083 *Ringtail Blues*	8.00 -	12.00
Emerson 501 *High Brown Babies' Ball* (12-inch)	15.00 -	20.00
Emerson 7481 *Heart Sickness Blues* (7-inch)	8.00 -	12.00
Emerson 7517 *Church Street Sobbin' Blues* (7-inch)	10.00 -	15.00
Emerson 7519 *Yama Yama Blues* (7-inch)	7.00 -	10.00
Emerson 7549 *Thunderbolt* (7-inch)	7.00 -	10.00

Emerson 9150 *Heart-Sickness Blues*	8.00 -	12.00
Emerson 9158 *A Good Man Is Hard To Find*	8.00 -	12.00
Emerson 9178 *Rainy Day Blues*	7.00 -	10.00
Emerson 9179 *Yama Yama Blues*	8.00 -	12.00
Medallion (some of above titles are found on Medallion, similarly valued)	—	—
Okeh 1200 *After All*	7.00 -	10.00
Okeh 1249 *Laughing Blues*	7.00 -	10.00

LOUISIANA JOE AND SLIM:

Champion 50063 *Crossin' Beale Street*	30.00 -	40.00

LOUISIANA RHYTHM KINGS:

Brunswick 4706 *Oh, Lady Be Good*	15.00 -	20.00
4845 *Swanee*	15.00 -	20.00
4908 *Karavan*	15.00 -	20.00
4923 *Lazy Daddy*	15.00 -	20.00
4938 *Pretty Baby*	15.00 -	20.00
4953 *Squeeze Me*	15.00 -	20.00
Vocalion 15657 *Nobody's Sweetheart*	20.00 -	30.00
15710 *I Can't Give You Anything But Love*	50.00 -	75.00
15716 *Dusky Stevedore*	35.00 -	50.00
15729 *Skinner's Sock*	35.00 -	50.00
15779 *Futuristic Rhythm*	100.00 -	150.00
15784 *That's A Plenty*	100.00 -	150.00
15810 *I'm Walking Through Clover*	100.00 -	150.00
15815 *Last Cent*	100.00 -	150.00
15828 *Ballin' The Jack*	100.00 -	150.00
15833 *Waiting at the End of the Road*	100.00 -	150.00
15841 *Little By Little*	100.00 -	150.00

LOUISIANA RHYTHMAKERS:

Titles, issued contemporaneously on Banner, Melotone, Oriole, Perfect, Romeo; *Casa Loma Stomp; Clarinet Marmalade; Runnin' Wild; Twelfth Street Rag*	10.00 -	15.00

LOUISIANA STOMPERS:

Paramount 12550 *Hop Off*	75.00 -	100.00

LOUISIANA SUGAR BABES:

Bluebird 10260 *Thou Swell*	7.00 -	10.00
Victor 21346 *Persian Rug*	7.00 -	10.00
21348 *Willow Tree*	7.00 -	10.00

LOUISIANA WASHBOARD BAND:

Domino 3671 *Shake That Thing*	50.00 -	75.00

LOUISIANA RHYTHM KINGS:

Okeh 41189 *Let's Sit and Talk About You*	20.00 -	30.00

LOUISIANA WASHBOARD BAND:

Domino 3755 *I've Found a New Baby*	15.00 -	20.00
Oriole 650 *Boodle Am*	15.00 -	20.00
674 *I've Found a New Baby*	15.00 -	20.00

BERT LOWN & HIS LOUNGERS/ ORCHESTRA/HOTEL BILTMORE ORCHESTRA:

Titles, issued contemporaneously on Banner, Cameo, Conqueror, Perfect, Oriole, Regal, Romeo: *Blue Is The Night; I Love You, Believe Me; I Never Dream; Keepin' Myself For You; The One I Love Just Can't Be Bothered With Me; The Perfect Song; Strike Up The Band*	7.00 -	12.00
Bluebird 5067 *Isn't It Heavenly?*	7.00 -	10.00
5068 *I Cover The Waterfront*	7.00 -	10.00
5087 *My Heart's Desire*	7.00 -	10.00
5088 *We'll Have A Honeymoon Some Day*	10.00 -	15.00
5099 *Here You Come With Love*	10.00 -	15.00
5100 *Black Panther*	10.00 -	15.00
(Note: Above titles, on *Electradisk*, are valued similarly, or slightly higher; on *Sunrise*, substantially higher.)		
Columbia 2258-D *Bye Bye Bues*	8.00 -	12.00
2292-D *Maybe It's Love*	8.00 -	12.00
Harmony 852-H *Redskin*	7.00 -	10.00
Harmony 853-H *My Castle in Spain Is a Shack in the Lane*	7.00 -	10.00
Harmony 863-H *Tomorrow's Violets*	7.00 -	10.00

Harmony 892-H *Here Comes My Ball and Chain*	10.00 -	15.00
Harmony 920-H *Big City Blues*	7.00 -	10.00
Harmony 974-H *The Jazz Me Blues*	15.00 -	20.00
Harmony 1088-H *Under a Texas Moon*	8.00 -	12.00
Harmony 1111-H *Only A Rose*	7.00 -	10.00
(Note: Above titles, on *Diva* and *Velvet Tone*, are similarly valued.)		
Victor 22603 *To Whom It May Concern*	10.00 -	15.00
Victor 22541, 22568, 22582, 22583, 22602, 22612, 22623, 22563, 22654, 22689, 22696, 22715, 22738, 22740, 22744, 22787, 22795, 22804, 22805, 22810, 22908, 22927, 24086, 24087, 24116	5.00 -	10.00

ED LOYD AND HIS ORCHESTRA:

Banner 6413 *Walking With Susie*	5.00 -	8.00
Banner 6421 *To Be In Love*	5.00 -	8.00
Odeon ONY-36060 *The Free And Easy (instrumental)*	30.00 -	50.00
ONY-36061 *The Free And Easy*	25.00 -	40.00
ONY-36065 *You Brought a New Kind of Love To Me*	20.00 -	30.00
ONY-36080 *Reminiscing*	20.00 -	30.00
ONY-36081 *Nobody Cares If I'm Blue*	20.00 -	30.00
ONY-36089 *You For Me*	20.00 -	30.00
ONY-36090 *Ro-Ro Rolling Along*	20.00 -	30.00
ONY-36113 *Just a Little Closer*	20.00 -	30.00
ONY-36123 *Hullabaloo*	20.00 -	30.00
ONY-36124 *My One Ambition Is You*	20.00 -	30.00
ONY-36132 *I'm Doin' That Thing*	20.00 -	30.00
ONY-36133 *Don't Tell Her*	20.00 -	30.00
ONY-36147 *I'll Still Belong To You*	20.00 -	30.00
ONY-36150 *Sweet Jennie Lee*	20.00 -	30.00
ONY-36161 *Morning, Noon and Night*	20.00 -	30.00
Odeon ONY-36172 *Fall In Love with Me*	20.00 -	30.00
ONY-36176 *Where Have You Been?*	20.00 -	30.00
ONY-36177 *He's My Secret Passion*	20.00 -	30.00
ONY-36182 *It Must Be True*	20.00 -	30.00
ONY-36185 *Sing Song Girl*	20.00 -	30.00
ONY-36186 *Hello! Beautiful*	20.00 -	30.00
ONY-36193 *All On Account Of Your Kisses*	20.00 -	30.00
Okeh 41250 *I Get The Blues When It Rains*	8.00 -	12.00
41259 *The One In The World*	8.00 -	12.00
41294 *Lovable and Sweet*	8.00 -	12.00
41295 *I'm Doing What I'm Doing For Love*	8.00 -	12.00
41312 *Wouldn't It Be Wonderful?*	8.00 -	12.00
41319 *Lonely Troubadour*	8.00 -	12.00
41338 *A Little Kiss Each Morning*	8.00 -	12.00
41348 *If You Were The Only Girl In The World*	8.00 -	12.00
41353 *What Do I Care?*	8.00 -	12.00
41354 *Put A Little Salt On The Bluebird's Tail*	8.00 -	12.00
41367 *Singing a Vagabond Song*	8.00 -	12.00
41368 *Beside an Open Fireplace*	7.00 -	10.00
41392 *The Free and Easy*	10.00 -	15.00
41407 *You Brought A New Kind of Love To Me*	10.00 -	15.00
41428 *I'm Needin' You*	10.00 -	15.00
41435 *I've Got My Eye On You*	10.00 -	15.00

LUCKY TEN ENTERTAINERS:

Domino 3992 *Dew Dew Dewy Day*	5.00 -	8.00
3996 *Sing Me a Baby Song*	7.00 -	10.00
Regal 8352 *Dew Dew Dewy Day*	5.00 -	8.00
8355 *Sing Me a Baby Song*	7.00 -	10.00

THE LUMBERJACKS:

Cameo 8352 *Black Beauty*	5.00 -	8.00
8356 *Spanish Dream*	7.00 -	10.00
9007 *Oh, Boy! It's A Pleasure*	5.00 -	8.00
9020 *I Found My Sunshine in the Rain*	5.00 -	8.00
9030 *Whoopee Stomp*	7.00 -	10.00
9041 *Blue Little You*	7.00 -	10.00
9045 *Let Me Be Alone With You*	5.00 -	8.00
9084 *I've Never Been Loved By Anyone Like You*	5.00 -	8.00
9147 *Would You Be Happy?*	5.00 -	8.00

Cameo 9183 *Crazy Baby*	7.00 -	10.00
Cameo 9209 *Somebody Loves You*	7.00 -	10.00
Lincoln 3000 *Spanish Dream*	7.00 -	10.00
3036 *Oh, Boy! It's a Pleasure*	5.00 -	8.00
3049 *I Found My Sunshine in the Rain*	5.00 -	8.00
3059 *Whoopee Stomp*	7.00 -	10.00
3070 *Blue Little You*	7.00 -	10.00
3074 *Let Me Be Alone With You*	5.00 -	8.00
3111 *I've Never Been Loved By Anyone Like You*	5.00 -	8.00
3174 *Would You Be Happy?*	5.00 -	8.00
Romeo 775 *Black Beauty*	7.00 -	10.00
779 *Spanish Dream*	7.00 -	10.00
811 *Oh, Boy! It's a Pleasure*	5.00 -	8.00
824 *I Found My Sunshine in the Rain*	5.00 -	8.00
834 *Whoopee Stomp*	10.00 -	15.00
845 *Blue Little You*	7.00 -	10.00
849 *Let Me Be Alone With You*	7.00 -	10.00
886 *I've Never Been Loved By Anyone Like You*	5.00 -	8.00
949 *Would You Be Happy?*	5.00 -	8.00

GUY LUMPKIN:

QRS 7078 *Decatur Street Rag*	150.00 -	200.00

JIMMIE LUNCEFORD & HIS CHICKASAW SYNCOPATORS/ORCHESTRA:

Bluebird 5330 *Sweet Rhythm*	10.00 -	15.00
5713 *White Heat*	5.00 -	8.00
6133 *Breakfast Ball*	5.00 -	8.00
Decca 129 *Sophisticated Lady*	5.00 -	8.00
130 *Nana*	7.00 -	10.00
131 *Mood Indigo*	7.00 -	10.00
299 *Solitude*	7.00 -	10.00
369 *Stardust*	5.00 -	8.00
415 *Because You're You*	7.00 -	10.00
453 *Since My Best Gal Turned Me Down*	7.00 -	10.00
503 *Four Or Five Times*	5.00 -	8.00
572 *Rhythm In My Nursery Rhymes*	5.00 -	8.00
576 *Thunder*	5.00 -	8.00
628 *Charmaine*	5.00 -	8.00
639 *Bird Of Paradise*	5.00 -	8.00
668 *Swanee River*	5.00 -	8.00
682 *I'm Nuts About Screwy Music*	5.00 -	8.00
712 *My Blue Heaven*	5.00 -	8.00
765 *Hittin' The Bottle*	5.00 -	8.00
788 *The Best Things In Life Are Free*	5.00 -	8.00
805 *The Melody Man*	5.00 -	8.00
908 *Organ Grinder's Song*	5.00 -	8.00
915 *Me And The Moon*	5.00 -	8.00
960 *Living From Day To Day*	5.00 -	8.00
980 *Harlem Shout*	5.00 -	8.00
1035 *Running A Temperature*	5.00 -	8.00
1128 *He Ain't Got Rhythm*	5.00 -	8.00
1219 *Honest And Truly*	5.00 -	8.00
1229 *Linger Awhile*	5.00 -	8.00
1318 *I'll See You In My Dreams*	5.00 -	8.00
1340 *For Dancer's Only*	5.00 -	8.00
1355 *Honey, Keep Your Mind On Me*	5.00 -	8.00
1364 *Ragging The Scale*	5.00 -	8.00
1506 *Hell's Bells*	5.00 -	8.00
1569 *Annie Laurie*	5.00 -	8.00
1617 *Margie*	5.00 -	8.00
1659 *Pigeon Walk*	5.00 -	8.00
1734 *Teasin' Tessie Brown*	5.00 -	8.00
1808 *My Melancholy Baby*	5.00 -	8.00
1927 *Down By The Old Mill Stream*	5.00 -	8.00
Victor 24522 *Jazznocracy*	10.00 -	15.00
24586 *White Heat*	15.00 -	20.00
24601 *Breakfast Ball*	15.00 -	20.00
24669 *Swingin' Uptown*	15.00 -	20.00
38141 *In Dat Mornin'*	75.00 -	100.00
Vocalion 4582, 4595, 4667, 4712, 4754, 4831, 4875, 4979, 5033, 5116, 5156, 5276	5.00 -	10.00

HUNK LUNSFORD & HIS CLARINET:

Champion 15263 *Mississippi Valley Blues*	150.00 -	200.00

JIMMY LUVERTE & HIS SOCIETY TROUBADOURS:

Vocalion 03559 *You Think She Ain't*	20.00 -	30.00
03602 *Music Box Blues*	20.00 -	30.00

ABE LYMAN & HIS CALIFORNIA ORCHESTRA: ABE LYMAN'S SHARPS & FLATS: ABE LYMAN'S CALIFORNIA (AMBASSADOR HOTEL) ORCHESTRA:

Bluebird, most issues	3.00 -	6.00
Brunswick 2481 *Bugle Call Rag*	5.00 -	8.00
Brunswick 2504 *Weary Weazel*	5.00 -	8.00
Brunswick 2563 *Honey Babe*	5.00 -	8.00
Brunswick 2780 *Sally's Got The Blues*	5.00 -	8.00
Brunswick 2980 *Everybody Stomp*	5.00 -	8.00
Brunswick 3069 *Shake That Thing*	7.00 -	10.00
Brunswick 3084 *Too Bad*	5.00 -	8.00
Brunswick 3241 *Ace In The Hole*	5.00 -	8.00
Brunswick 3286 *Havin' Lots Of Fun*	5.00 -	8.00
Brunswick 3316 *New St. Louis Blues*	5.00 -	8.00
Brunswick 3317 *Wistful And Blue*	5.00 -	8.00
3964 *Weary Weasel*	7.00 -	10.00
4155 *A Jazz Holiday*	8.00 -	12.00
4912 *Hullabaloo*	10.00 -	15.00
4924 *Never Swat a Fly*	8.00 -	12.00
6314 *Farewell Blues*	8.00 -	12.00
6325 *Milenberg Joys*	8.00 -	12.00
6380 *Riddle Me This*	7.00 -	10.00
6637 *Weary Blues*	8.00 -	12.00
Brunswick 6637, 6674, 6756	5.00 -	8.00
Brunswick (12-inch) 20063 *"Good News"* medley	15.00 -	20.00
20103 (12") *"The Laugh Parade"* medley	20.00 -	30.00
20122 (12") *"Stormy Weather"*	25.00 -	35.00
Brunswick, most others	4.00 -	7.00
Columbia, most others	3.00 -	5.00
Decca 1098, 1104, 1105, 1119, 1120, 1127, 1130, 1225, 1226, 1235	4.00 -	8.00

LYNCH'S RHYTHM ACES:

Challenge 742 *She's My Baby Now*	7.00 -	10.00

AL LYNCH & HIS ORCHESTRA:

Banner 6149 *I'm Gonna March With April In May*	5.00 -	8.00
Banner 6151 *Sweet Mandy*	5.00 -	8.00
Banner 6155 *I'm Just Wondering*	5.00 -	8.00
Banner 7032 *I've Got The Blue Grass Blues*	7.00 -	10.00
Banner 7033 *For My Gal And Me*	7.00 -	10.00
Banner 7038 *Oh, How I Love To Look At You*	5.00 -	8.00
Banner 7077 *Who Says They Don't Care*	5.00 -	8.00
Banner 7107 *Light The Way To Somebody's Heart*	8.00 -	12.00
Banner 7109 *Put Your Loving Arms Around Me*	8.00 -	12.00
Banner 7112 *They Can't Take You Away From Me Now*	5.00 -	8.00
Banner 7130 *What Do I Care*	5.00 -	8.00
Broadway 1105 *Washington & Lee Swing*	5.00 -	8.00
Broadway 1106 *Sweetheart of Sigma Chi*	5.00 -	8.00
Broadway 1107 *Baltimore*	5.00 -	8.00
Challenge 615 *Light The Way To Somebody's Heart*	8.00 -	12.00
Challenge 616 *Put Your Loving Arms Around Me*	8.00 -	12.00

AL LYNN'S MUSIC MASTERS:

Edison 51952 *Indian Butterfly*	8.00 -	12.00
Edison 52004 *There Ain't No Maybe In My Baby's Eyes*	15.00 -	20.00
Edison 52041 *Sometimes I'm Happy*	15.00 -	20.00
Edison 52086 *Me And My Shadow*	15.00 -	20.00
Edison 52099 *Marvelous*	15.00 -	20.00
Edison 52101 *Who Gives You All Your Kisses*	20.00 -	30.00
Edison 52148 *I'm Telling The World (That I Love You)*	15.00 -	20.00
Edison 52226 *Anything To Make You Happy*	15.00 -	20.00
Edison 52227 *Symphonic Raps*	20.00 -	30.00
Edison 52270 *Whisper Sweet And Whisper Low*	50.00 -	100.00

Edison 52399 *Lonely Little Bluebird* . . . . 30.00 - 40.00
Oriole 874 *I'm Crazy For Her* . . . . 7.00 - 10.00
Oriole 883 *Take a Little Walk* . . . . 8.00 - 12.00

GLEN LYTE & HIS ORCHESTRA:
Broadway 1459 *When I Take My Sugar To Tea* . . . 8.00 - 12.00
  1475 *Pardon Me, Pretty Baby* . . . . 8.00 - 12.00

JIMMY LYTELL:
Pathe-Actuelle 36568 *Old Folks Shuffle* . . . . 10.00 - 15.00
  36584 *Messin' Around* . . . . 10.00 - 20.00
  36607 *Pardon The Glove* . . . . 10.00 - 20.00
  36665 *Zulu Wail* . . . . 10.00 - 20.00
  36717 *Headin' For Harlem* . . . . 10.00 - 20.00
  36741 *Stockholm Stomp* . . . . 10.00 - 20.00
  36775 *Missouri Squabble* . . . . 10.00 - 20.00
  36824 *Yellow Dog Blues* . . . . 10.00 - 20.00
Perfect 14749 *Old Folks Shuffle* . . . . 10.00 - 15.00
  14765 *Messin' Around* . . . . 10.00 - 20.00
  14788 *Pardon The Glove* . . . . 10.00 - 20.00
  14846 *Zulu Wail* . . . . 10.00 - 20.00
  14898 *Headin' For Harlem* . . . . 10.00 - 20.00
  14922 *Stockholm Stomp* . . . . 10.00 - 20.00
  14956 *Missouri Squabble* . . . . 10.00 - 20.00
  15005 *Yellow Dog Blues* . . . . 10.00 - 20.00

BABY MACK:
Okeh 8313 *What Kind Of Man Is You?* . . . . 80.00 - 120.00

CHARLES E. MACK:
Columbia 50061-D (12-inch record) *Our Child* . . 10.00 - 15.00

ENRIC MADRIGUERA AND HIS
ORCHESTRA:
Vogue R-760 *So It Goes* . . . . 25.00 - 40.00
  R-776 *Mujercita* . . . . 25.00 - 40.00
  R-777 *La Rumbita Tropical* . . . . 25.00 - 40.00
  R-778 *Guilty Of Love* . . . . 40.00 - 60.00
  R-779 *A Man, A Moon, and a Maid* . . . . 35.00 - 50.00

SHERRY MAGEE & HIS DIXIELANDERS:
Okeh 5436 *Satanic Blues* . . . . 5.00 - 8.00
Vocalion 5281 *Shake It and Break It* . . . . 7.00 - 10.00
  5436 *Bluin' The Blues* . . . . 7.00 - 10.00

MAJESTIC DANCE ORCHESTRA:
Banner 0537 *Love Me In My Dreams* . . . . 5.00 - 8.00
Banner 0561 *My Way Right Back To Arkansas* . . . 5.00 - 8.00
Banner 0590 *The Man From The South* . . . . 8.00 - 12.00
Banner 0596 *I've Seen My Baby* . . . . 5.00 - 8.00
Banner 0692 *My Love Parade* . . . . 5.00 - 8.00
Banner 0851 *You're Simply Delish* . . . . 7.00 - 10.00
Cameo 0139 *I'm Following You* . . . . 5.00 - 8.00
  0196 *I've Seen My Baby* . . . . 5.00 - 8.00
  0451 *You're Simply Delish* . . . . 7.00 - 10.00
Challenge 892 *Sweetheart* . . . . 5.00 - 8.00
Conqueror 7623 *I'll Be Blue (Just Thinking of*
  You) . . . . 5.00 - 8.00
Domino 4449 *Somebody Mightly Like You* . . . . . 5.00 - 8.00
Oriole 928 *Magnolia* . . . . 7.00 - 10.00
  933 *Zulu Wail* . . . . 8.00 - 12.00
Oriole 961 *Dew Dew Dewy Day* . . . . 5.00 - 8.00
Oriole 977 *Sing Me a Baby Song* . . . . 7.00 - 10.00
  980 *Delirium* . . . . 10.00 - 15.00
  990 *Farewell Blues* . . . . 8.00 - 12.00
Oriole 2379 *An Ev'ning in Caroline* . . . . 5.00 - 8.00
Pathe-Actuelle 37004 *Am I Blue?* . . . . 7.00 - 10.00
Perfect 15034 *If You Don't Love Me* . . . . 5.00 - 8.00
  15185 *Am I Blue?* . . . . 7.00 - 10.00
  15244 *Somebody Mighty Like You* . . . . 5.00 - 8.00
Regal 8893 *Somebody Mighty Like You* . . . . 5.00 - 8.00
  8960 *My Love Parade* . . . . 5.00 - 8.00
Regal 10118 *Always In All Ways* . . . . 5.00 - 8.00
Romeo 1129 *Somebody Mighty Like You* . . . . . . 5.00 - 8.00
  1426 *Always In All Ways* . . . . 5.00 - 8.00
  1605 *Out Of Nowhere* . . . . 5.00 - 8.00

MAJOR & HIS ORCHESTRA:
Hollywood 1028 *Blue Evening Blues* . . . . 150.00 - 250.00

THOMAS MALIN:

Pathe 20376 *Romping Bessie* . . . . 7.00 - 10.00

TERRY MANDEL & HIS ORCHESTRA:
Broadway 1498 *Black And Tan Fantasy* . . . . 20.00 - 30.00

MANHATTAN DANCE MAKERS:
Harmony 458-H *Dew-Dew-Dewy Day* . . . . 5.00 - 8.00
  462-H *Is It Possible? (That She Loves Me)* . . . . 5.00 - 8.00
  486-H *Dawning* . . . . 7.00 - 10.00
  604-H *Down South* . . . . 5.00 - 8.00
(Note: Above titles, on *Diva* and *Velvet Tone*, are
similarly valued.)

MANHATTAN DANCE ORCHESTRA:
National Music Lovers 1099 *I Can't Get The*
One I Want . . . . 10.00 - 15.00

MANHATTAN IMPERIAL ORCHESTRA:
Broadway 11312 *Bathing Beauty Blues* . . . . 25.00 - 40.00
Puritan 11229 *Farewell Blues* . . . . 10.00 - 15.00
  11264 *Bathing Beauty Blues* . . . . 25.00 - 40.00
Triangle 11268 *Louisville Lou* . . . . 10.00 - 20.00

MANHATTAN MUSICIANS:
National Music Lovers 1163 *I'll Make You*
Answer Yes . . . . 7.00 - 10.00
National Music Lovers 1187 *Can You Picture*
That . . . . 10.00 - 15.00
National Music Lovers (most other issues) . . . . . . 3.00 - 6.00
New Phonic 1243 *Somebody's Making A Fuss* . . . 8.00 - 12.00
  1247 *If I Can Ba-Ba-Baby You* . . . . 7.00 - 10.00

MARION MANN WITH BOB HAGGART'S
ORCHESTRA:
Vogue R-731 *You Took Advantage of Me* . . . . . . 25.00 - 40.00
  R-758 *Long, Strong and Consecutive* . . . . 25.00 - 40.00

SAM MANNING & HIS COLE JAZZ
ORCHESTRA/BLUE HOT SYNCOPATORS:
Columbia 14110-D *Bingo* . . . . 30.00 - 50.00
Okeh 8302 *Keep Your Hand Off That* . . . . 50.00 - 75.00

JOE MANNONE'S HARMONY KINGS; JOE
"WINGY" MANNONE & HIS CLUB
ROYALE ORCHESTRA; WINGY
MANNONE & HIS ORCHESTRA:
Bluebird 6359, 6360, 6375, 6393, 6411, 6472,
  6473, 6483, 6536, 6537, 6549, 6605, 6606,
  6616, 6618, 6804, 6806, 6816, 7002, 7003, 7014,
  7197, 7198, 7214, 7389, 7391, 7395 . . . . 5.00 - 10.00
Bluebird (others) . . . . 4.00 - 8.00
Brunswick 6911 *No Calling Card* . . . . 10.00 - 15.00
  6940 *Send Me* . . . . 10.00 - 15.00
Columbia 1044-D *Up The Country Blues* . . . . . . 75.00 - 100.00
  14282-D *Cat's Head* . . . . 75.00 - 100.00
Okeh 41569 *She's Crying For Me* . . . . 10.00 - 15.00
  41570 *Royal Garden Blues* . . . . 10.00 - 15.00
  41573 *Nickel In The Slot* . . . . 10.00 - 15.00
Special Edition 5011-S *Never Had No Lovin* . . . . 10.00 - 15.00
Vocalion 15728 *Fare Thee Well* . . . . 100.00 - 150.00
  15797 *Isn't There a Little Love?* . . . . 150.00 - 250.00
Vocalion 2913 *I Believe In Miracles* . . . . 8.00 - 12.00
  2914 *Fare Thee Well, Annabelle* . . . . 8.00 - 12.00
  2933 *You're An Angel* . . . . 8.00 - 12.00
  2934 *Let's Spill The Beans* . . . . 8.00 - 12.00
  2963 *Black Coffee* . . . . 8.00 - 12.00
  2972 *Lulu's Back In Town* . . . . 8.00 - 12.00
  2989 *Love And Kisses* . . . . 8.00 - 12.00
  2990 *Let's Swing It* . . . . 8.00 - 12.00
  3023 *From The Top Of Your Head* . . . . 8.00 - 12.00
  3058 *I'm Gonna Sit Right Down And Write*
  Myself A Letter . . . . 8.00 - 12.00
  3070 *You Are My Lucky Star* . . . . 10.00 - 15.00
  3071 *I've Got A Note* . . . . 10.00 - 15.00
  3134 *The Music Goes 'Round And 'Round* . . . 8.00 - 12.00
  3135 *I've Got My Fingers Crossed* . . . . 8.00 - 12.00
  3158 *The Broken Record* . . . . 8.00 - 12.00
  3159 *Old Man Mose* . . . . 8.00 - 12.00
  3171 *Nickel In The Slot* . . . . 8.00 - 12.00
  3191 *Is It True What They Say About Dixie?* . . . 8.00 - 12.00

3192 *Shoe-Shine Boy*	8.00 -	12.00

EDDIE MAPP:

QRS 7078 *Riding The Blues*	150.00 -	200.00

PAUL MARES & HIS FRIARS SOCIETY ORCHESTRA:

Okeh 41574 *Nagasaki*	15.00 -	20.00
41575 *Reincarnation*	15.00 -	20.00

THE MARIGOLD ENTERTAINERS:

Vocalion 15800 *Jealous*	15.00 -	20.00

THE MARINERS:

Okeh 41433 *Happy Feet*	7.00 -	10.00
41449 *I Don't Mind Walkin' in the Rain*	7.00 -	10.00

MIKE MARKEL & HIS ORCHESTRA; MARKEL'S ORCHESTRA; MARKELS' ORCHESTRA; MARKEL'S SOCIETY ORCHESTRA:

Brunswick 3091 *Flamin' Mamie*	7.00 -	10.00
3189 *Lulu Belle*	7.00 -	10.00
3263 *Precious*	7.00 -	10.00
Brunswick (most other issues)	4.00 -	7.00
Columbia 617-D *Black Horse Stomp*	10.00 -	15.00
Edison 51752 *Tonight's My Night With Baby*	15.00 -	20.00
51800 *Baby Face*	15.00 -	20.00
Edison (most other issues)	5.00 -	8.00
Okeh 4580 *Lonesome Mama Blues*	8.00 -	12.00
4610 *Black Eyed Blues*	8.00 -	12.00
4656 *Blued Eyed Blues*	7.00 -	10.00
4902 *Waitin' For The Evenin' Mail*	5.00 -	8.00
4967 *Stavin' Change*	8.00 -	12.00
40045 *31st Street Blues*	8.00 -	12.00
40161 *Africa*	15.00 -	20.00
40625 *Deep Henderson*	10.00 -	15.00
40686 *For My Sweetheart*	10.00 -	15.00

GERALD MARKS AND HIS ORCHESTRA:

Columbia 1432-D *If I Can't Have You*	7.00 -	10.00

EARL MARLOW AND HIS ORCHESTRA:

Parlophone PNY-34018 *Wrapped in a Red, Red Rose*	20.00 -	30.00
PNY-34019 *Put a Little Salt on the Bluebird's Tail*	20.00 -	30.00
PNY-34022 *What Do I Care?*	20.00 -	30.00
PNY-34025 *There's Danger in Your Eyes, Cherie*	20.00 -	30.00
PNY-34026 *Singing a Vagabond Song*	20.00 -	30.00
PNY-34058 *Living in the Sunlight, Loving in the Moonlight*	25.00 -	35.00
PNY-34059 *You Brought a New Kind Of Love To Me*	25.00 -	35.00
PNY-34074 *Nobody Cares If I'm Blue*	25.00 -	35.00
PNY-34075 *Mysterious Mose*	25.00 -	35.00
PNY-34082 *I'm Needin' You*	25.00 -	35.00
PNY-34083 *Ro-Ro-Rolling Along*	25.00 -	35.00
PNY-34105 *This Love*	15.00 -	25.00
PNY-34106 *I've Got My Eye On You*	20.00 -	30.00
PNY-34115 *Dixiana*	20.00 -	30.00
PNY-34116 *My One Ambition Is You*	20.00 -	30.00
PNY-34124 *I'm Doing That Thing*	20.00 -	30.00
PNY-34125 *A Big Bouquet For You*	15.00 -	25.00
PNY-34126 *Don't Tell Her*	15.00 -	25.00
PNY-34139 *I Am The Words*	15.00 -	25.00
PNY-34140 *I Still Belong To You*	15.00 -	25.00
PNY-34142 *Sweet Jennie Lee*	20.00 -	30.00
PNY-34143 *Roamin' Thru' The Roses*	20.00 -	30.00
PNY-34167 *Reaching For The Moon*	15.00 -	25.00
PNY-34168 *Fall In Love With Me*	15.00 -	25.00
PNY-34169 *He's My Secret Passion*	15.00 -	25.00
PNY-34170 *Lady, Play Your Mandolin*	15.00 -	25.00
PNY-34174 *It Must Be True*	15.00 -	25.00
PNY-34176 *Hello! Beautiful*	25.00 -	35.00
PNY-34177 *Walkin' My Baby Back Home*	25.00 -	35.00
PNY-34178 *Sing Song Girl*	25.00 -	35.00
PNY-34179 *Wabash Moon*	15.00 -	25.00

PNY-34184 *All On Account Of Your Kisses*	30.00 -	40.00

RUDY MARLOW AND HIS ORCHESTRA:

Harmony 988-H *How Am I To Know?*	5.00 -	8.00
Harmony 1062-H *Dixie Jamboree*	7.00 -	10.00
1063-H *He's So Unusual*	8.00 -	12.00
1088-H *Do Ya Love Me?*	8.00 -	12.00
1119-H *Thank Your Father*	5.00 -	8.00
1137-H *Get Happy*	5.00 -	8.00
1162-H *Dark Night*	5.00 -	8.00
1232-H *Three Little Words*	5.00 -	8.00
(Note: Some of above also issued on *Diva* and *Velvet Tone*, similarly valued.)		

JOE MARSALA & HIS DELTA FOUR; JOE MARSALA'S CHICAGOANS:

General 1717, 3001	5.00 -	10.00
Variety 565 *Wolverine Blues*	10.00 -	15.00

GILBERT MARSH & HIS ORCHESTRA:

Parlophone PNY-34038 *Navy Blues*	35.00 -	50.00
PNY-34039 *Lucky Little Devil*	35.00 -	50.00
PNY-34040 *Navy Blues*	25.00 -	35.00
PNY-34041 *Lucky Little Devil*	25.00 -	35.00

FATTY MARTIN'S ORCHESTRA:

Victor 19700 *Jimtown Blues*	25.00 -	40.00

FREDDIE MARTIN & HIS ORCHESTRA:

Brunswick 6407, 6408	5.00 -	10.00
Columbia 2703-D, 2708-D, 3770-D	7.00 -	12.00

MARY MARTIN:

Brunswick 8282	5.00 -	10.00
V-Disc (12-inch) 542	5.00 -	10.00

SARA MARTIN'S JUG BAND:

Okeh 8188 *Blue Devil Blues*	75.00 -	125.00

JELLY ROLL MARTON & HIS ORCHESTRA:

Muddy Water Blues issued contemporaneously on Famous 3245, Harmograph 834, National 12251, Paramount 12050 and 20251, Puritan 11251	80.00 -	120.00

FRANK MARVIN: (See also country-western listing)

Brunswick 400, 4949	5.00 -	10.00

JOHNNY MARVIN:

Columbia 2655-D, 15750-D	5.00 -	10.00
Edison 51709 *The Memphis Blues*	10.00 -	15.00
Melotone 12610	5.00 -	7.00
Victor 20386, 20714, 20731, 20832, 21650	4.00 -	8.00
21376 *Angel*	10.00 -	15.00
21435 *My Pet*	10.00 -	15.00
23691, 23708, 23728	5.00 -	10.00

ALBERT MASON'S ORCHESTRA:

Parlophone PNY-34069 *Girl Trouble*	20.00 -	30.00
PNY-34104 *Rollin' Down The River*	20.00 -	30.00
PNY-34105 *Seems To Me*	20.00 -	30.00
PNY-34114 *I Wonder How It Feels*	20.00 -	30.00
PNY-34174 *Keep a Song In Your Soul*	20.00 -	30.00
PNY-34185 *The One Man Band*	20.00 -	30.00
PNY-34187 *Got the Bench-Got the Park*	20.00 -	30.00

JERRY MASON'S CALIFORNIANS:

Harmony 795-H *Don't Hold Everything*	15.00 -	20.00
Harmony 965-H *Ain't Misbehavin'*	7.00 -	10.00
Harmony 1242-H *Can This Be Love?*	7.00 -	10.00

MASON—DIXON ORCHESTRA:

Columbia 1861-D *What A Day!*	15.00 -	20.00

MASTER MELODY MAKERS:

National Music Lovers 1133 *Then I'll Be Happy*	7.00 -	10.00
1161 *Keep Your Kisses*	5.00 -	8.00
1164 *This Is My Lucky Day*	5.00 -	8.00
1169 *Bird's Eye View Of My Old Kentucky Home*	5.00 -	8.00
1178 *Baby Face*	7.00 -	10.00
New Phonic 1245 *Get Out And Get Under The Moon*	7.00 -	10.00
1249 *My Pet*	7.00 -	10.00

FRANKIE MASTERS & HIS ORCHESTRA:

Victor 21102 *I'm Walkin' On Air*	5.00	-	8.00
21217 *Everywhere You Go*	5.00	-	8.00
21565 *My Darling*	5.00	-	8.00
21602 *Is It Gonna Be Long (Till You Belong To Me?)*	5.00	-	8.00
Vocalion, most issues	3.00	-	5.00
Vogue R-724 *Everybody Knew But Me*	25.00	-	40.00
R-735 *Welcome To My Dreams*	25.00	-	40.00
R-772 *All By Myself*	25.00	-	40.00

FRANK MATER:

Diva 2759-G *Doin' The Raccoon*	7.00	-	10.00
Harmony 759-H *Doin' The Raccoon*	7.00	-	10.00
Harmony 808-H *Let's Do It*	8.00	-	12.00
825-H *Makin' Whoopee*	8.00	-	12.00

CHARLES A MATSON'S CREOLE SERENADERS: MATSON'S LUCKY SEVEN:

Edison 51222 *Tain't Nobody's Business If I Do*	15.00	-	25.00
51224 *I Just Want A Daddy*	20.00	-	30.00
Lawdy, Lawdy Blues issued contemporaneously on Claxtonola, Paramount, Puritan	40.00	-	60.00

LIEUTENANT MATT & HIS ORCHESTRA/ RHAPSODISTS:

Gennett 6064 *You're The One For Me*	8.00	-	12.00
Perfect 14649 *Hoodle Dee Doo Dee Doodoo*	5.00	-	8.00

EMMETT MATTHEWS & HIS ORCHESTRA:

Vocalion 3226 *I'll Stand By*	10.00	-	15.00
3228 *Take A Good Look At Mine*	10.00	-	15.00
3371 *Bojangles of Harlem*	10.00	-	15.00
3332 *You Came To My Rescue*	10.00	-	15.00

GEORGE MATTHEWS & THE CAROLINA NIGHT HAWKS:

Gennett 6183 *Oh Miss Hannah!*	50.00	-	75.00

NORRIDGE MAYHAMS & HIS BARBECUE BOYS:

Sloppy Drunk Woman; Wrap Your Troubles In Dreams; issued contemporaneously on Banner, Melotone, Oriole, Perfect, Romeo	15.00	-	20.00
Vocalion 03429 *Ash Haulin' Blues*	15.00	-	20.00
03465 *If I Had My Way*	15.00	-	20.00
03498 *Sloppy Drunk Woman*	15.00	-	20.00

TED MAYS AND HIS BAND:

Bluebird 7193, *Gee, It Must Be Love*	8.00	-	12.00
7206 *Take It One Home To Grandma*	8.00	-	12.00
7237 *Married Man Blues*	8.00	-	12.00

THE McALPINEERS:

Edison 52237 *One More Night*	10.00	-	15.00
52239 *Persian Rug*	10.00	-	15.00
52266 *Rhapsody In Rhythm*	20.00	-	30.00
52371 *I'm On the Crest Of A Wave*	20.00	-	30.00
52385 *Memories Of France*	5.00	-	8.00
52411 *High Up On A Hill-Top*	20.00	-	30.00

GEORGE McCLENNON; GEORGE McCLENNON'S JAZZ BAND/DEVILS:

Okeh 8143 *Dark Alley Blues*	80.00	-	120.00
8150 *New Orleans Wiggle*	100.00	-	150.00
8236 *Home Alone Blues*	75.00	-	100.00
8314 *Cut Throat Blues*	75.00	-	100.00
Okeh 8329 *While You're Sneakin' Out*	75.00	-	100.00
8337 *Everybody But Me*	75.00	-	100.00
8397 *Pig Foot Blues*	100.00	-	150.00
8406 *Disaster*	100.00	-	150.00

CLYDE McCOY & HIS (DRAKE HOTEL) ORCHESTRA:

Columbia 2389-D *Sugar Blues*	7.00	-	10.00
2453-D *It Looks Like Love*	7.00	-	10.00
2466-D *Black And Tan Fantasy*	10.00	-	15.00
2531-D *I Found A New Baby*	15.00	-	20.00
2597-D *Creole Love Call*	10.00	-	15.00
2794-D *Smoke Rings*	10.00	-	15.00
2801-D *Some Of These Days*	10.00	-	15.00
2808-D *Nobody's Sweetheart*	15.00	-	20.00

2865-D *Palooka*	10.00	-	15.00
2866-D *Little Women*	10.00	-	15.00
2874-D *Business on the Q.T.*	8.00	-	12.00
Decca 381 *Sugar Blues*	3.00	-	6.00
Decca 382 *Japanese Sandman*	7.00	-	10.00
Decca 422 *China Boy*	7.00	-	10.00
Decca 461 *There'll Be Some Changes Made*	7.00	-	10.00
Decca 509 *Twelfth Street Rag*	7.00	-	10.00
Decca 566 *Dry Ice*	7.00	-	10.00
Decca 620 *Basin Street Blues*	7.00	-	10.00
Decca 681 *Maple Leaf Rag*	7.00	-	10.00
Decca 758 *Ridin' To Glory On A Trumpet*	7.00	-	10.00
Decca 833 *Roseland Stomp*	7.00	-	10.00
Decca 1109 *The "Gonna Goo"*	7.00	-	10.00
Decca 1152 *Black And Tan Fantasy*	7.00	-	10.00
Decca 1230 *Doodle Doo Doo*	5.00	-	8.00
Decca 1297 *Doo Wacka Doo*	5.00	-	8.00
Decca (most other issues)	3.00	-	5.00
Vogue R-707 *Sugar Blues*	15.00	-	25.00
R-722 *Tear It Down*	20.00	-	30.00
R-752 *There's Good Blues Tonight*	15.00	-	30.00
R-753 *Way Down Yonder In New Orleans*	15.00	-	30.00

RANDOLPH McCURTAIN'S COLLEGE RAMBLERS:

Okeh Ramblers' 1 *Low Down Brown*	50.00	-	75.00

EARL McDONALD'S ORIGINAL LOUISVILLE JUG BAND:

Columbia 14206-D *Under the Chicken Tree*	100.00	-	150.00
14226-D *Rocking Chair Blues*	100.00	-	150.00
14255-D *She's In The Graveyard Now*	100.00	-	150.00
14371-D *Casey Bill*	100.00	-	150.00

DICK McDONOUGH & HIS ORCHESTRA:

Titles, issued contemporaneously on Banner, Melotone, Oriole, Perfect, Romeo: *Afterglow; All God's Chillun Got Rhythm; The Big Apple; Dardanella; Dear Old Southland; The Gonna Goo; He Ain't Got Rhythm; I'm in a Dancing Mood; It Ain't Right; Love, What Are You Doing To My Heart; The Mood That I'm In; Now Or Never; When The Moon Hangs High; With Thee I Swing; You and I Know*	7.00	-	10.00

ABE McDOW & HIS BAND SOUTHERN/ ORCHESTRA:

Broadway 1481 *I Idolize My Baby's Eyes*	10.00	-	15.00
1482 *Minnie The Moocher*	10.00	-	15.00

COLE McELROY'S SPANISH BALLROOM ORCHESTRA:

Columbia 1677-D *Ida! Sweet As Apple Cider*	8.00	-	12.00
Columbia (most other issues)	3.00	-	7.00
Victor 22837, 22850	4.00	-	8.00

EDWIN J. McENELLY'S ORCHESTRA:

Victor 19851 *Spanish Shawl*	5.00	-	8.00
20589 *My Sunday Girl*	7.00	-	10.00
21154 *What Are We Waiting For?*	5.00	-	8.00
21773 *Take Your Tomorrow (And Give Me Today)*	7.00	-	10.00
Victor (most other issues)	4.00	-	7.00

HOWARD McGHEE:

Dial 1005, 1007, 1010, 1011, 1027	5.00	-	10.00

BOB McGOWAN & HIS ORCHESTRA:

Gennett 6709 *Me and the Man In The Moon*	15.00	-	30.00
6754 *As Long As We're In Love*	10.00	-	20.00

JIMMY McHUGH'S BOSTONIANS:

Harmony 763-H *I Don't Care*	8.00	-	12.00
Harmony 795-H *Baby*	15.00	-	20.00
823-H *Let's Sit and Talk About You*	15.00	-	25.00
836-H *The Whoopee Stomp*	15.00	-	25.00
(Note: Above titles, *Diva* and *Velvet Tone*, are similarly valued.)			

MARION McKAY & HIS ORCHESTRA:

Gennett 5615 *Doo Wacka Doo*	8.00	-	12.00
6294 *My Blue Heaven*	8.00	-	12.00

RED McKENZIE; McKENZIE'S CANDY KIDS; RED McKENZIE & HIS MUSIC BOX/RHYTHM KINGS; RED McKENZIE WITH THE SPIRITS OF RHYTHM:
Titles, issued contemporaneously on Banner, Melotone, Oriole, Perfect, Romeo:

Georgianna; Farewell My Love	8.00 -	12.00
Columbia 2556-D Just Friends	8.00 -	12.00
2587-D I'm Sorry, Dear	8.00 -	12.00
2620-D Can't We Talk It Over?	8.00 -	12.00
2645-D Dream Sweetheart	8.00 -	12.00
Decca 186 From Monday On	10.00 -	15.00
243 It's All Forgotten Now	7.00 -	10.00
302 As Long As I Live	7.00 -	10.00
507 Let's Swing It	7.00 -	10.00
521 Double Trouble	7.00 -	10.00
587 Every Now And Then	7.00 -	10.00
609 Georgia Rockin' Chair	7.00 -	10.00
667 I'm Building Up To An Awful Letdown	8.00 -	12.00
721 Don't Count Your Kisses (Before You're Kissed)	8.00 -	12.00
734 When Love Has Gone	8.00 -	12.00
790 I Can't Get Started With You	8.00 -	12.00
Okeh 40893 There'll Be Some Changes Made	30.00 -	50.00
41071 From Monday On	30.00 -	50.00
Variety 520 Sweet Lorraine	8.00 -	12.00
589 I Cried For You	10.00 -	15.00
Vocalion 2534 It's The Talk Of The Town	10.00 -	15.00
3875 Farewell, My Love	7.00 -	10.00
3898 You're Out Of This World	7.00 -	10.00
14977 Panama	10.00 -	20.00
14978 Stretch It, Boy	10.00 -	20.00
15088 The Morning After Blues	10.00 -	20.00
15166 Hot Honey	10.00 -	20.00
15539 Nervous Puppies	10.00 -	20.00

McKENZIE & CONDON'S CHICAGOANS:

Okeh 40971 Nobody's Sweetheart	20.00 -	30.00
41011 China Boy	20.00 -	30.00

RAY McKINLEY'S JAZZ BAND:

Decca 1019, 1020	8.00 -	12.00

McKINNEY'S COTTON PICKERS:

Victor 21583 Four Or Five Times	15.00 -	20.00
21611 Milenberg Joys	15.00 -	20.00
21730 Cherry	20.00 -	30.00
22511 Hullabaloo	15.00 -	20.00
22628 She's My Secret Passion	10.00 -	15.00
22640 Talk To Me	20.00 -	30.00
22683 I Want Your Love	20.00 -	30.00
22736 Wherever There's a Will, Baby	15.00 -	20.00
22811 Wrap Your Troubles In Dreams	15.00 -	20.00
22932 Rocky Road	30.00 -	50.00
23000 Okay, Baby	15.00 -	20.00
23012 Just a Shade Corn	25.00 -	40.00
23020 Never Swat a Fly	20.00 -	30.00
23024 I Miss a Little Miss	20.00 -	30.00
23031 Hello!	25.00 -	35.00
23035 To Whom It May Concern	20.00 -	30.00
V 38000 Nobody's Sweetheart	15.00 -	20.00
V 38013 It's Tight Like That	15.00 -	20.00
V 38025 Put It There	15.00 -	20.00
V 38051 Do Sometime	15.00 -	20.00
V 38052 Sellin' That Stuff	15.00 -	20.00
V 38061 I've Found a New Baby	15.00 -	20.00
V 38097 Plain Dirt	30.00 -	40.00
V 38102 Miss Hannah	30.00 -	40.00
V 38112 Travelin' All Alone	30.00 -	40.00
V 38118 Zonky	15.00 -	20.00
V 38133 I'd Love It	30.00 -	40.00
V 38142 I'll Make Fun For You	30.00 -	40.00

McLAUGHLIN'S MELODIANS:

Pathe-Actuelle 36515 Play, Gypsies	5.00 -	8.00
36517 I Never Knew What The Moonlight		

Could Do	7.00 -	10.00
36518 Someone Is Losin' Susan	10.00 -	15.00
36524 Broken-Hearted Sue	7.00 -	10.00
Perfect 14696 Play, Gypsies, Dance, Gypsies	5.00 -	8.00
14698 I Never Knew What The Moonlight Could Do	7.00 -	10.00
14699 Someone Is Losin' Susan	10.00 -	15.00
14705 Broken-Hearted Sue	7.00 -	10.00

CONNIE McLEAN & HIS RHYTHM ORCHESTRA; CONNIE McLEANS RHYTHM BOYS:

Bluebird 6474, 6482, 6485	5.00 -	10.00
Decca 7175, 7176, 7189	5.00 -	10.00

McMURRAY'S CALIFORNIA THUMPERS:

Gennett 4904 Haunting Blues	8.00 -	12.00
4943 Oogie Oogie Wa Wa	10.00 -	15.00

JIMMY McPARTLAND'S SQUIRRELS:

Hot Record Society 1003, 1004	5.00 -	10.00

JAY McSHANN (AND HIS ORCHESTRA/ QUARTET):

Decca 4387, 4418, 8559, 8570, 8583, 8595, 8607, 8623, 8635	5.00 -	10.00
Supreme 1540 McShann's Bounce	5.00 -	8.00

THE MELODY FOUR:

Victor 23289 I'm Crazy 'Bout My Baby	30.00 -	50.00

MELODY KINGS DANCE ORCHESTRA:

His Master's Voice (Canadian) 216450 Limehouse Blues	7.00 -	10.00

THE MELODY SHEIKS:

Okeh 40279 Tokio Blues	8.00 -	12.00
40303 Why Couldn't It Be Poor Little Me	8.00 -	12.00
40326 Sob Sister Sadie	8.00 -	12.00
40341 All Aboard For Heaven	7.00 -	10.00
40357 If You Knew Susie	7.00 -	10.00
40358 Isn't She The Sweetest Thing?	7.00 -	10.00
40369 Let Me Linger Longer In Your Arms	10.00 -	15.00
40387 Steppin' In Society	7.00 -	10.00
40412 Ukelele Lady	5.00 -	8.00
40438 Indian Nights	5.00 -	8.00
40451 Marguerite	7.00 -	10.00
40472 Brown Eyes, Why Are You Blue?	7.00 -	10.00
40484 Mighty Blue	15.00 -	20.00
40529 Tomorrow Morning	7.00 -	10.00
40550 Pretty Little Baby	7.00 -	10.00
40560 Behind The Clouds	5.00 -	8.00
40580 So Does Your Ole Mandarin	7.00 -	10.00
40590 Let's Talk About My Sweetie	10.00 -	15.00
40603 The Blue Room	7.00 -	10.00
40632 Roses Remind Me Of You	5.00 -	8.00
Okeh 40649 Baby Face	8.00 -	12.00
40651 Barcelona	5.00 -	8.00

JAMES MELTON:

Brunswick 20115 (12-inch)	8.00 -	12.00
Columbia 2065-D, 2084-D	7.00 -	10.00

MEMPHIS BELL-HOPS:

Challenge 134 Li'l Farina	40.00 -	70.00
135 Animal Crackers	40.00 -	70.00

MEMPHIS DADDY & HIS BOYS:

Silvertone 5023 Georgia Bo Bo	90.00 -	130.00

MEMPHIS FIVE (See ORIGINAL MEMPHIS FIVE)

MEMPHIS HOT SHOTS:

I'm So In Love With You; issued contemporaneously on Clarion 5391-C, Harmony 1377-H, Velvet Tone 2455-V	20.00 -	30.00
Shout, Sister, Shout; issued contemporaneously on Clarion 5381-C, Harmony 1368-H, Velvet Tone 2455-V	40.00 -	60.00

MEMPHIS JAZZERS:

Miss Golden Brown; In Harlem's Araby; issued contemporaneously on Gray Gull, Radiex, Supreme	10.00 -	15.00

MEMPHIS JUG BAND:

Bluebird 5040 *Oh Ambulance Man*	30.00 -	50.00
5430 *Kansas City Blues*	20.00 -	30.00
5675 *Stonewall Blues*	100.00 -	150.00
Okeh 8955 *Jazzbo Stomp*	80.00 -	120.00
8956 *Boodle Bum Bum*	80.00 -	120.00

8958 *Gator Wobble*	80.00 -	120.00
8960 *Mary Anna Cut Off*	80.00 -	120.00
8963 *My Love Is Cold*	80.00 -	120.00
8966 *Jug Band Quartette*	80.00 -	120.00
Victor 20552 *Sun Brimmers*	75.00 -	100.00
20576 *Newport News*	75.00 -	100.00
20781 *Sunshine Blues*	100.00 -	150.00
20809 *Memphis Boy*	100.00 -	150.00
21066 *Beale Street Mess Around*	100.00 -	150.00
21185 *State of Tennessee Blues*	75.00 -	100.00
21278 *Coal Oil Blues*	100.00 -	150.00
21412 *Bob Lee Junior Blues*	100.00 -	150.00
21524 *Snitchin' Gambler Blues*	80.00 -	120.00
21657 *Evergreen Money Blues*	100.00 -	150.00
21740 *Sugar Pudding*	100.00 -	150.00
23251 *Fourth Street Mess Around*	150.00 -	250.00
23347 *Taking Your Place*	200.00 -	300.00
23421 *Meningitis Blues*	200.00 -	300.00
V 38015 *On The Road Again*	100.00 -	150.00
V 38540 *Whitewash Station Blues*	100.00 -	150.00
V 38537 *Jug Band Waltz*	100.00 -	150.00
V 38551 *I Can't Stand It*	125.00 -	175.00
V 38558 *K.C. Moan*	125.00 -	175.00
V 38578 *Feed You Friend With a Long-Handled Spoon*	125.00 -	175.00
V 38586 *Tired Of Your Driving Me*	125.00 -	175.00
V 38599 *Bumble Bee Blues*	150.00 -	200.00
V 38605 *Cave Man Blues*	150.00 -	200.00
V 38620 *Cocaine Habit Blues*	150.00 -	200.00
Vocalion 03175 *Take Your Fingers Off It*	80.00 -	120.00
03050 *Little Green Slippers*	75.00 -	100.00
03081 *My Love Is Cold*	75.00 -	100.00
03182 *Boodle Bum Bum*	75.00 -	100.00

MEMPHIS MELODY BOYS:

Buddy 8005 *Washboard Blues*	80.00 -	120.00

MEMPHIS MELODY MEN:

Superior 2724 *Minnie The Moocher*	100.00 -	150.00
2737 *New Moten Stomp*	100.00 -	150.00

MEMPHIS MELODY PLAYERS:

Challenge 233 *Song Of The Wanderer*	8.00 -	12.00
234 *A Blues Serenade*	40.00 -	70.00
237 *Indian Butterfly*	8.00 -	12.00

MEMPHIS NIGHT HAWKS:

Vocalion 1736 *Sweet Feet*	75.00 -	100.00
1744 *Biscuit Roller*	75.00 -	100.00
2593 *Shanghai Honeymoon*	75.00 -	100.00

MEMPHIS SHEIKS:

Victor 23256 *He's In The Jailhouse Now*	150.00 -	200.00

MEMPHIS STOMPERS:

Electradisk 1930 *Somebody Stole My Gal*	75.00 -	100.00
Victor 21270 *Kansas City Blues*	20.00 -	30.00
21541 *Memphis Stomp*	20.00 -	30.00
21709 *Yea Alabama*	8.00 -	12.00
23371 *Stompin' Away*	75.00 -	100.00

THE MEMPHIS STRUTTERS:

Champion 15415 *Canned Heat Blues*	150.00 -	200.00

MENDELLO'S DANCE ORCHESTRA:

Banner 6205 *Baby's Coming Back*	10.00 -	15.00
6206 *Cool Papa*	10.00 -	15.00
6213 *High Hattin' Hattie*	10.00 -	15.00
6214 *Dixie Drag*	10.00 -	15.00
7246 *Easy*	10.00 -	15.00
7248 *Sunday Afternoon*	10.00 -	15.00

JOHNNY MERCER:

Decca 142 *The Bathtub Ran Over Again*	10.00 -	15.00

BENNY MEROFF AND HIS ORCHESTRA:

Brunswick 4709 *The Talk Of The Town*	7.00 -	10.00
Columbia 3065-D *Yankee In Havana*	10.00 -	15.00
Okeh 40847, 40967, 41079	7.00 -	10.00
40912 *Just An Hour Of Love*	20.00 -	30.00
41171 *Smiling Skies*	20.00 -	30.00

ROY MERRITT & HIS ORCHESTRA:

Champion 15637 *Me and the Man in the Moon*	15.00 -	25.00

CYRIL MERRIVALE & HIS ORCHESTRA; CYRIL MERRIVALE'S ORCHESTRA:

Parlophone PNY-34016 *I'm Following You*	20.00 -	30.00
PNY 34020 *I'm Following You*	20.00 -	30.00
PNY 34024 *Cryin' For The Carolines*	20.00 -	30.00
PNY 34025 *Have A Little Faith In Me*	20.00 -	30.00
PNY 34045 *Montana Call*	20.00 -	30.00
PNY 34046 *The Moon Is Low*	20.00 -	30.00
PNY 34047 *Montana Call*	20.00 -	30.00
PNY 34048 *The Moon Is Low*	20.00 -	30.00
PNY 34049 *Leven-Thirty Saturday Night*	25.00 -	40.00
PNY 34053 *It Must Be You*	20.00 -	30.00
PNY 34056 *It Must Be You*	20.00 -	30.00
PNY 34086 *Sharing*	20.00 -	30.00
PNY 34087 *Sharing*	20.00 -	30.00
PNY 34088 *The Song Without a Name*	20.00 -	30.00
PNY 34089 *The Song Without a Name*	20.00 -	30.00
PNY 34092 *Lo Lo*	20.00 -	30.00

*Note: Duplication of titles is due to the issuance of vocal and non-vocal takes.

METOMKIN INN ORCHESTRA:

Champion 15458 *So Long*	25.00 -	50.00

METROPOLITAN DANCE PLAYERS:

Harlem's Araby, issued contemporaneously on Globe, Grey Gull, Nadsco, Radiex	8.00 -	12.00

METROPOLITAN ORCHESTRA:

Berliner (titles as below, and others)	35.00 -	Up
Monarch 1023 *Creole Belles*	20.00 -	40.00
Victor 251 *A Bunch O'Blackberries*	20.00 -	40.00
271 *Smoky Mokes*	25.00 -	50.00
289 *Who Dat Say Chicken In Dis Crowd?*	25.00 -	50.00
872 *Rag Time Society*	25.00 -	50.00

(Note: Above turn-of-the-century recordings are single-sided discs. Berliners and Victor 872 are seven-inch discs, or approximately that diameter. Berliners have embossed, crudely executed labels. Some of above recordings have spoken introductions.)

METZGER'S CAMPUS/NIGHT OWLS:

Superior 2629 *When Dreams Come True*	15.00 -	20.00
2646 *It's That Rhythm*	20.00 -	30.00

KEN MEYERS:

Regal 8183 *Stampede*	8.00 -	12.00

VIC MEYERS AND HIS ORCHESTRA: VIC MEYERS' MUSIC:

Brunswick 2501 *Shake It And Break It*	10.00 -	15.00
Brunswick 2630 *Springtime Rag*	10.00 -	15.00
Brunswick 2664 *Weary Blues*	7.00 -	10.00
Brunswick 2685 *Burmalone*	7.00 -	10.00
Brunswick 2733 *Mean Looks*	7.00 -	10.00
Brunswick 2774 *The Only, Only One For Me*	5.00 -	8.00
Brunswick 2800 *Shimmy*	7.00 -	10.00
Columbia 1456-D *Ada*	5.00 -	8.00
Columbia 1516-D *Estrellita*	5.00 -	8.00

Columbia 1530-D *Nobody's Sweetheart*	7.00 -	10.00
Columbia 1678-D *Could I Cry?*	5.00 -	8.00
Columbia 2026-D *Congratulations*	5.00 -	8.00
Columbia 2120-D *Rose Room*	5.00 -	8.00
Volcalion 15056 *Three O'Clock Blues*	20.00 -	30.00

**MEZZ MEZZROW AND HIS ORCHESTRA/
SWING BAND: MEZZROW LADNIER
QUINTET:**

Bluebird 6319 *The Panic Is On*	8.00 -	12.00
6320 *Lost*	8.00 -	12.00
6321 *I'se a-Muggin'*	8.00 -	12.00
10085, 10087, 10090	5.00 -	10.00
Brunswick 6778 *Swingin' With Mezz*	10.00 -	15.00
7551 *Dissonance*	10.00 -	15.00
Victor 25019 *Sendin' The Vipers*	7.00 -	10.00
25202 *Old Fashioned Love*	7.00 -	10.00
25612 *Hot Club Stomp*	7.00 -	10.00
25636 *Blues In Disguise*	7.00 -	10.00

MIAMI GARDEN ORCHESTRA:

Silvertone 5027 *She Looks Like Helen Brown* ...	15.00 -	20.00

MIAMI LUCKY SEVEN:

Challenge 757 *So Tired*	10.00 -	15.00
Gennett 3165 *Fallin' Down*	10.00 -	15.00
3174 *Slippery Elm*	10.00 -	15.00
5473 *Red Hot Mama*	8.00 -	12.00
5585 *Boll Weevil Blues*	8.00 -	12.00

MIAMI ROYAL PALM ORCHESTRA:

Cameo 8136 *There Must Be A Silver Lining*	7.00 -	10.00
Cameo 8137 *Back In Your Own Back Yard*	5.00 -	8.00
8162 *Why Do I Love You?*	8.00 -	12.00
8236 *Get Out And Get Under The Moon*	5.00 -	8.00
Lincoln 2884 *Get Out And Get Under The Moon*	5.00 -	8.00
Romeo 659 *Get Out And Get Under The Moon* ..	5.00 -	8.00

**ERNEST MICHALL (CLARINET BAND);
ERNEST MICHALL & HIS NEW ORLEANS
BOYS:**

Black Patti 8046 *Sidewalk Blues* ....250.00 -	400.00
Challenge 372 *Embarrassment Blues* ....100.00 -	150.00

MICHIGAN MELODY MAKERS:

Pennington 1453 *Indian Love Call*	20.00 -	30.00
1455 *Dixie Dreams*	20.00 -	30.00

**MICKEY MOUSE & THE TURTLE (See also:
WILLIAMS' WASHBOARD BAND)**

Bluebird 5202 *Move Turtle*	15.00 -	20.00

THE MIDNIGHT AIREDALES:

Columbia 1981-D *Swanee Shuffle*	15.00 -	20.00

THE MIDNIGHT RAMBLERS:

Broadway 1114 *Together, We Two*	5.00 -	8.00
Broadway 1121 *Make My Cot Where the Cot-Cot-
Cotton Grows*	5.00 -	8.00
Broadway 1122 *Is She My Girl Friend?*	5.00 -	8.00
Broadway 1175 *Too Busy*	5.00 -	8.00
Broadway 1179 *Just Like a Melody Out of the Sky*	5.00 -	8.00
Broadway 1242 *I Faw Down An' Go Boom*	5.00 -	8.00
Broadway 1259 *That's What I Call Heaven*	5.00 -	8.00
Broadway 1263 *I'm Wild About Horns on
Automobiles*	5.00 -	8.00
Broadway 1264 *Kansas City Kitty*	5.00 -	8.00
Broadway 1271 *Honey*	5.00 -	8.00
Broadway 1275 *When My Dreams Come True* ...	5.00 -	8.00
Broadway 1276 *That's You, Baby*	5.00 -	8.00
Broadway 1281 *My Sin*	5.00 -	8.00
Broadway 1302 *Ain't Misbehavin'*	5.00 -	8.00
Broadway 1310 *Lovable and Sweet*	7.00 -	10.00

THE MIDNIGHT ROUNDERS:

Vocalion 1218 *Shake Your Shimmy* ....150.00 -	200.00
1237 *Bull Fiddle Rag* ....100.00 -	150.00

THE MIDNIGHT SERENADERS:

Broadway 1216 *Tin Roof Blues*	15.00 -	25.00
Paramount 20657 *Tin Roof Blues*	15.00 -	25.00

THE MIDWAY DANCE ORCHESTRA:

Columbia 33-D *The Black Sheep Blues*	15.00 -	25.00

51-D *Cotton Pickers' Ball*	15.00 -	25.00

MIDWAY GARDEN ORCHESTRA:

Claxtonola 40272 *Black Sheep Blues* ....100.00 -	150.00
40273 *Lots O' Mama*	25.00 -	40.00
Harmograph 863 *Black Sheep Blues* ....100.00 -	150.00
864 *Sobbin' Blues*	25.00 -	40.00
Paramount 20272 *Black Sheep Blues* ....100.00 -	150.00
20273 *Sobbin' Blues*	25.00 -	40.00
Puritan 11273 *Lots O' Mama*	25.00 -	40.00
Triangle 11311 *Sobbin' Blues*	25.00 -	40.00

**EDDIE MILES & HIS FLORENTINE
ORCHESTRA:**

Gennett 6200 *One O'Clock Baby*	50.00 -	80.00
6247 *Is It Possible?*	50.00 -	80.00

BUBBER MILEY & HIS MILEAGE MAKERS:

Victor 23010 *The Penalty Of Love*	20.00 -	30.00
V 38138 *I Lost My Gal From Memphis*	20.00 -	30.00
V 38146 *Black Maria*	20.00 -	30.00

**EMMETT MILLER (Acc. by HIS GEORGIA
CRACKERS):**

Bluebird 6550, 6577	5.00 -	8.00
Okeh 40239, 40465, 40545	8.00 -	12.00
Okeh 41062 *I Ain't Got Nobody*	10.00 -	15.00
41095 *Anytime*	10.00 -	15.00
41135 *Take Your Tomorrow*	10.00 -	15.00
41182 *You're The Cream In My Coffee*	10.00 -	15.00
41205 *The Lion Tamers*	10.00 -	15.00
41280 *Right Or Wrong*	10.00 -	15.00
41305 *Lovin' Sam*	10.00 -	15.00
41342 *Sweet Mama*	15.00 -	20.00
41377 *The Pickaninnies' Paradise*	15.00 -	20.00
41438 *God's River Blues*	10.00 -	15.00

GLENN MILLER AND HIS ORCHESTRA:

Bluebird, most issues	3.00 -	5.00
Brunswick, 7915 *I Got Rhythm*	7.00 -	12.00
7923 *Sleepy Time Gal*	7.00 -	12.00
8034 *My Fine Feathered Friend*	7.00 -	12.00
8041 *Sweet Stranger*	7.00 -	12.00
8062 *Doin' The Jive*	7.00 -	12.00
8152 *Don't Wake Up My Heart*	7.00 -	12.00
8173 *Dippermouth Blues*	7.00 -	12.00
Columbia 3052-D *A Blues Serenade*	35.00 -	50.00
3058-D *Solo Hop*	35.00 -	50.00
Decca 1239 *How Am I To Know*	8.00 -	12.00
1284 *Wistful And Blue*	8.00 -	12.00
1342 *I'm Sitting On Top Of The World*	7.00 -	10.00
Decca, most other issues	2.00 -	5.00
Victor, most issues	2.00 -	5.00

**JOHNNIE MILLER'S NEW ORLEANS
FROLICKERS:**

Columbia 1546-D *Dipper Mouth Blues*	30.00 -	50.00

RAY MILLER & HIS ORCHESTRA:

Brunswick 2546 *I'm Goin' South*	5.00 -	8.00
Brunswick 2573 *Nine O'Clock Sal*	5.00 -	8.00
Brunswick 2606 *Come On Red*	5.00 -	8.00
Brunswick 2607 *You Can Take Me Away From
Dixie*	5.00 -	8.00
Brunswick 2613 *Lots O'Mama*	5.00 -	8.00
Brunswick 2632 *Mama's Gone, Good Bye*	5.00 -	8.00
Brunswick 2643 *I Can't Get The One I Want*	5.00 -	8.00
Brunswick 2681 *Red Hot Mama*	5.00 -	8.00
Brunswick 2724 *Doodle-Doo-Doo*	5.00 -	8.00
Brunswick 2753 *Me And The Boy Friend*	5.00 -	8.00
Brunswick 2823 *That's My Girl*	5.00 -	8.00
Brunswick 2830 *Tessie*	5.00 -	8.00
Brunswick 2855 *Red Hot Henry Brown*	5.00 -	8.00
Brunswick 2898 *Phoebe Snow*	5.00 -	8.00
Brunswick 2935 *Ya! Ya! Alma*	5.00 -	8.00
Brunswick 2989 *Spanish Shawl*	5.00 -	8.00
Brunswick 3132 *Stomp Your Stuff*	5.00 -	8.00
Brunswick 3133 *Oh! Oh! Oh! What a Night!*	7.00 -	10.00
Brunswick 3328 *Mercy Percy*	5.00 -	8.00

Brunswick 3676 *Blue Baby* . . . . 5.00 - 8.00
Brunswick 3677 *I Ain't Got Nobody* . . . . 5.00 - 8.00
Brunswick 3828 *My Honey's Lovin' Arms* . . . . . 7.00 - 10.00
Brunswick 3829 *Is She My Girl Friend?* . . . . 5.00 - 8.00
Brunswick 4077 *Anything You Say* . . . . 7.00 - 10.00
Brunswick 4131 *Rose Of Mandalay* . . . . 7.00 - 10.00
Brunswick 4194 *Mississippi, Here I Am* . . . . 7.00 - 10.00
Brunswick 4223 *In A Great Big Way* . . . . 7.00 - 10.00
    4224 *That's A Plenty* . . . . 8.00 - 12.00
    4233 *Cradle Of Love* . . . . 8.00 - 12.00
    4258 *He, She and Me* . . . . 5.00 - 8.00
    4425 *You Want Lovin' (But I Want Love)* . . . . . 7.00 - 10.00
    4669 *Blue Butterfly* . . . . 7.00 - 10.00
    4682 *That's Where You Come In* . . . . 7.00 - 10.00
    4687 *Hoosier Hop* . . . . 8.00 - 12.00
    4692 *Harlem Madness* . . . . 8.00 - 12.00
Brunswick (most other issues) . . . . 3.00 - 6.00
Columbia A3563 *Doo-Dah Blues* . . . . 5.00 - 8.00
Columbia (most other issues) . . . . 3.00 - 6.00

LUCKY MILLINDER WITH MILLS BLUE RHYTHM BAND; MILLS BLUE RHYTHM BAND:
Bluebird 5688 *The Growl* . . . . 15.00 - 25.00
Brunswick 6156 *Moanin'* . . . . 20.00 - 30.00
    6199 *Snake Hips* . . . . 15.00 - 20.00
    6229 *Savage Rhythm* . . . . 15.00 - 20.00
Columbia 2963-D *Let's Have a Jubilee* . . . . 15.00 - 20.00
    2994-D *Keep The Rhythm Going* . . . . 15.00 - 20.00
    3020-D *Back Beats* . . . . 15.00 - 20.00
    3038-D *African Lullaby* . . . . 15.00 - 20.00
    3071-D *Harlem Heat* . . . . 15.00 - 20.00
    3078-D *Truckin'* . . . . 15.00 - 20.00
    3083-D *Dinah Lou* . . . . 15.00 - 20.00
    3087-D *Congo Caravan* . . . . 8.00 - 12.00
    3111-D *Yes! Yes!* . . . . 15.00 - 20.00
    3134-D *Everything Is Still Okay* . . . . 15.00 - 20.00
    3135-D *Red Rhythm* . . . . 15.00 - 20.00
    3147-D *Merry-Go-Round* . . . . 15.00 - 20.00
    3148-D *In a Sentimental Mood* . . . . 15.00 - 20.00
    3156-D *Balloonacy* . . . . 15.00 - 20.00
    3157-D *Showboat Shuffle* . . . . 15.00 - 20.00
    3158-D *Algiers Stomp* . . . . 15.00 - 20.00
    3162-D *Big John's Special* . . . . 15.00 - 20.00
Variety 503 *Jungle Madness* . . . . 10.00 - 15.00
    546 *Rhythm Jam* . . . . 10.00 - 15.00
    604 *The Lucky Swing* . . . . 10.00 - 15.00
    624 *Camp Meeting Jamboree* . . . . 10.00 - 15.00
    634 *Jammin' For The Jack-Pot* . . . . 10.00 - 15.00
Victor 22763 *Heebie Jeebies* . . . . 15.00 - 20.00
    22800 *Moanin'* . . . . 10.00 - 15.00
    24442 *Harlem After Midnight* . . . . 15.00 - 20.00
    24482 *Break It Down* . . . . 15.00 - 20.00
Vocalion 3808 *Blue Rhythm Fantasy* . . . . 10.00 - 15.00
    3817 *Rhythm Jam* . . . . 10.00 - 15.00

THE MILLS BROTHERS
Brunswick 6197, 6225, 6240, 6269, 6276, 6278,
    6305, 6330, 6357, 6430, 6785, 6913 . . . . 5.00 - 10.00
    6517 *Doin' The New Low-Down* . . . . 10.00 - 15.00
    6519 *Diga Diga Doo* . . . . 10.00 - 15.00
    6225 *Smoke Rings* . . . . 7.00 - 10.00
    6894 *Swing It, Sister* . . . . 7.00 - 10.00
Decca 165, 166, 167, 228, 380, 402, 497, 1148 . . . 7.00 - 10.00
Note: In the February, 1979 issue of
GOLDMINE'S RECORD SWAPPER, an
advertiser offers "up to $950.00 for a Mills
Brothers 78 on the Gennett label cut in 1928.
Titles unknown." The author has not verified
the existence of any Gennett issues by The
Mills Brothers.

MILLS CAVALCADE ORCHESTRA:
Columbia 3066-D *Lovely Liza Lee* . . . . 10.00 - 15.00
MILLS' MERRY MAKERS:

Titles, issued contemporaneously on Cameo,
    Lincoln, and Romeo: *Bad Girl; Distortion; I'm
    Rollin' In Love; I'm Talking About My
    Wonderful Gal; Moanin' Low; You Oughta
    Know* . . . . 5.00 - 10.00
Additional titles:
    In A Great Big Way; The Junior-Senior Prom . . 10.00 - 15.00
    Milwaukee Walk . . . . 20.00 - 30.00
Harmony 1099-H *When You're Smiling* . . . . 15.00 - 25.00
    1104-H *St. James Infirmary* . . . . 15.00 - 25.00
(Note: Above two titles, on *Diva* and *Velvet Tone*,
    are similarly valued.)
Pathe-Actuelle 36961 *Honey* . . . . 7.00 - 10.00
    37027 *Moanin' Low* . . . . 7.00 - 10.00
Perfect 15142 *Honey* . . . . 7.00 - 10.00
    15208 *Moanin' Low* . . . . 7.00 - 10.00
Velvet Tone 7121-V *Farewell Blues* . . . . 20.00 - 30.00
MILLS MUSICAL CLOWNS:
Pathe-Actuelle 36930 *Railroad Man* . . . . 10.00 - 20.00
    36944 *Futuristic Rhythm* . . . . 10.00 - 20.00
    36974 *Wipin' The Pan* . . . . 8.00 - 12.00
Perfect 15111 *Railroad Man* . . . . 10.00 - 20.00
    15125 *Futuristic Rhythm* . . . . 10.00 - 20.00
    15155 *Wipin' The Pan* . . . . 8.00 - 12.00
MILLS SWINGPHONIC ORCHESTRA:
Master 119, 126 . . . . 10.00 - 15.00
MILLS' TEN BLACK BERRIES:
Titles, issued contemporaneously on Clarion,
    Diva, Velvet Tone: *Black and Tan Fantasy;
    Double Check Stomp; East St. Louis Toodle-
    oo; Hot and Bothered; The Mooche; Sweet
    Mama* . . . . 15.00 - 20.00
FLOYD MILLS & HIS MARYLANDERS:
Gennett 6909 *Hard Luck* . . . . 75.00 - 100.00
IRVING MILLS & HIS HOTSY TOTSY GANG/ MODERNISTS/ORCHESTRA: (See also: HOTSY TOTSY GANG)
Brunswick 4482 *Sweet Savannah Sue* . . . . 15.00 - 20.00
    4498 *Some Fun* . . . . 15.00 - 20.00
    4559 *Harvey* . . . . 15.00 - 20.00
    4587 *Star Dust* . . . . 15.00 - 20.00
    4641 *Manhattan Rag* . . . . 15.00 - 20.00
    4674 *My Little Honey and Me* . . . . 15.00 - 20.00
    4838 *Railroad Man* . . . . 15.00 - 20.00
    4920 *Barbaric* . . . . 15.00 - 20.00
    4983 *Deep Harlem* . . . . 30.00 - 50.00
    4998 *What A Night!* . . . . 15.00 - 20.00
    5013 *High And Dry* . . . . 15.00 - 20.00
Victor V-38105 *At The Prom* . . . . 30.00 - 50.00
WARREN MILLS & HIS BLUES SERENADERS:
Victor 35962 (12-inch) *St. Louis Blues* . . . . 15.00 - 20.00
MISSISSIPPI MAULERS:
Columbia 1545-D *My Angeline* . . . . 10.00 - 15.00
MISSISSIPPI MUSIC MAKERS:
Issued contemporaneously on Cameo, Lincoln,
    Romeo: *If You Want The Rainbow (You Must
    Have The Rain)* . . . . 7.00 - 10.00
MISSISSIPPI TRIO:
Supertone 9528 *Doin' That Thing* . . . . 75.00 - 100.00
Van Dyke 77039 *Coal Black Blues* . . . . 15.00 - 20.00
THE MISSOURIANS:
Victor V38067 *Market Street Stomp* . . . . 50.00 - 75.00
    V 38071 *Ozark Mountain Blues* . . . . 50.00 - 75.00
    V 38084 *Scotty Blues* . . . . 75.00 - 100.00
    V 38103 *Vine Street Drag* . . . . 75.00 - 100.00
    V 38120 *Stoppin' The Traffic* . . . . 75.00 - 100.00
    V 38145 *Two Hundred Squabble* . . . . 75.00 - 100.00
MISSOURI DANCE ORCHESTRA; MISSOURI JAZZ BAND:
Banner 0518 *I'm Gonna Count My Sheep* . . . . . . 5.00 - 8.00
Banner 1399 *San* . . . . 5.00 - 9.00

Banner 1409 *Any Way The Wind Blows*	5.00 -	8.00
Banner 1456 *How I Love That Girl*	10.00 -	15.00
Banner 1457 *Where's My Sweetie Hiding?*	10.00 -	15.00
Banner 1564 *Save Your Sorrow (For Tomorrow)*	5.00 -	8.00
Banner 1621 *Stomp Off, Let's Go*	10.00 -	15.00
Banner 1624 *Sweet Man*	8.00 -	12.00
Banner 1644 *I'm Gonna Charleston Back To Charleston*	5.00 -	8.00
Banner 1657 *(How She Loves Me Is) Nobody's Business*	5.00 -	8.00
Banner 1662 *Spanish Shawl*	5.00 -	8.00
Banner 1674 *Keep Your Skirts Down, Mary Ann*	5.00 -	8.00
Banner 1728 *I've Got The Charleston Blues*	5.00 -	8.00
Banner 1733 *Show That Fellow The Door*	5.00 -	8.00
Banner 1764 *Waffles*	5.00 -	8.00
Banner 1795 *She Belongs To Me*	5.00 -	8.00
Banner 1797 *Out In The New Mown Hay*	5.00 -	8.00
Banner 1819 *The Captivating Rhythm*	5.00 -	8.00
Banner 1842 *Susie, My Susie, Why Don't You Marry Me*	5.00 -	8.00
Banner 1846 *Sadie Green (The Vamp of New Orleans)*	5.00 -	8.00
Banner 1863 *My Baby Knows How*	5.00 -	8.00
Banner 1864 *I Love Her*	5.00 -	8.00
Banner 1904 *How Could Red Riding Hood?*	5.00 -	8.00
Banner 1999 *How I Hate That Desert Song*	7.00 -	10.00
Banner 6030 *Miss Annabelle Lee*	5.00 -	8.00
Banner 6031 *Twelfth Street Rag*	7.00 -	10.00
Banner 6099 *Who's Got The Blues For You Now*	5.00 -	8.00
Banner 6100 *That's When a Feller Needs a Sweetheart*	5.00 -	8.00
Banner 6129 *Homing Bird (Headin' For Home)*	7.00 -	12.00
Banner 6202 *I Could Stand A Lot Of Lovin' From You*	5.00 -	8.00
Banner 6209 *Don't Send Your Wifey To The Country*	5.00 -	8.00
Banner 6238 *I Love My Best Girl Best*	5.00 -	8.00
Banner 6262 *Mystic Bengal Bay*	5.00 -	8.00
Banner 6267 *Lily Lou*	5.00 -	8.00
Banner 6271 *"Hoo" Ray, I Want To Play*	5.00 -	8.00
Banner 7052 *Do I Get It? (I'll Say I Do)*	5.00 -	8.00
Banner 7054 *My Little Sunshine*	5.00 -	8.00
Banner 7077 *You Can't Blame Me For That*	5.00 -	8.00
Banner 7106 *Know Nothin' Blues*	7.00 -	10.00
Banner 7140 *Straight Back Home*	7.00 -	10.00
7157 *Puttin' On The Dog*	7.00 -	10.00
7160 *If I Can't Ba-Ba-Baby You*	5.00 -	8.00
Banner 7193 *Raggedy Maggie*	5.00 -	8.00
Banner 7199 *Oh! How She Could Shake Her Tambourine*	5.00 -	8.00
Banner 7212 *See My Tennessee*	5.00 -	8.00
Banner 7221 *I Love To Ride a Camel*	5.00 -	8.00
Banner 7239 *Tennessee Mammy*	5.00 -	8.00
Challenge 543 *Oh! How She Could Shake Her Tambourine*	5.00 -	8.00
Challenge 900 *If I Can Ba-Ba-Baby You*	5.00 -	8.00
Conqueror 7110 *Ready For The River*	8.00 -	12.00
7487 *The Man From The South*	8.00 -	12.00
Domino 3507 *Ah-Ha!*	5.00 -	8.00
Domino 3592 *Stomp Off, Let's Go*	10.00 -	15.00
3594 *Sweet Man*	8.00 -	12.00
Domino 3605 *Angry*	5.00 -	8.00
Domino 3696 *I've Got Those Charleston Blues*	5.00 -	8.00
4010 *Tiger Rag*	8.00 -	12.00
4184 *Ready For The River*	8.00 -	12.00
4497 *Nobody's Sweetheart*	10.00 -	15.00
Oriole 518 *Fallin' Down*	5.00 -	8.00
521 *When A Blonde Makes Up Her Mind To Do You Good*	5.00 -	8.00
528 *Then I'll Be Happy*	7.00 -	10.00
536 *Sleepy Time Gal*	7.00 -	10.00
Perfect 15273 *Nobody's Sweetheart*	10.00 -	15.00

15283 *Sing, You Sinners*	8.00 -	12.00
Regal 8361 *Bye-Bye Pretty Baby*	5.00 -	8.00
8478 *My Ohio Home*	5.00 -	8.00
Regal 8480 *Keep Sweeping The Cobwebs Off The Moon*	5.00 -	8.00
8942 *Nobody's Sweetheart*	10.00 -	15.00
8959 *Sing You Sinners*	8.00 -	12.00
9504 *Long Lost Mama*	5.00 -	8.00
9514 *My Sweetie Went Away*	5.00 -	8.00
9925 *Stomp Off, Let's Go*	10.00 -	15.00
9970 *My Charleston Dancing Man*	5.00 -	8.00
9985 *Dinah*	5.00 -	8.00

EDDIE MITCHELL & HIS ORCHESTRA:

Gennett 5612 *Pleasure Mad*	20.00 -	40.00

THE MODERNISTS:

Titles, issued contemporaneously on Banner, Conqueror, Melotone, Oriole, Perfect, Romeo:

Solitude; I'm Getting Sentimental Over You	10.00 -	15.00

MIFF MOLE'S (LITTLE) MOLERS;
MIFF MOLE:

Brunswick 7842 *How Could You?*	10.00 -	15.00
Okeh 40758 *Alexander's Ragtime Band*	15.00 -	20.00
40784 *The Darktown Strutters' Ball*	15.00 -	20.00
40848 *Hurricane*	15.00 -	20.00
40890 *Imagination*	15.00 -	20.00
40932 *My Gal Sal*	15.00 -	20.00
40984 *The New Twister*	15.00 -	20.00
41098 *Crazy Rhythm*	15.00 -	20.00
41153 *Wild Oat Joe*	15.00 -	20.00
41232 *That's A Plenty*	15.00 -	20.00
41273 *Birmingham Bertha*	15.00 -	20.00
41371 *Navy Blues*	15.00 -	20.00
41445 *After You've Gone*	15.00 -	20.00
Parlophone (English) R-647 *You Made Me Love You*	20.00 -	30.00
Premium 852, 853	5.00 -	8.00
Vocalion 3468 *Love and Learn*	10.00 -	15.00

TOOTS MONDELLO; TOOTS MONDELLO & HIS ORCHESTRA:

Brunswick 8031 *Thanks For The Memory*	7.00 -	10.00
8061 *You're In Love With Love*	7.00 -	10.00
8094 *Let Me Day Dream*	7.00 -	10.00
8105 *At Sundown*	5.00 -	10.00
Royal 1817 *Burnin' Sticks*	8.00 -	12.00
1823 *Shades Of Jade*	8.00 -	12.00
Varsity 8110 *Sweet Lorraine*	7.00 -	10.00
8118 *St. Louis Gal*	7.00 -	10.00

J. NEAL MONTGOMERY & HIS ORCHESTRA:

Okeh 8682 *Atlanta Low-Down*	80.00 -	120.00

JACK MONTROSE & HIS ORCHESTRA:

Q.R.S. 1022 *I'm So Tired Of It All*	10.00 -	15.00
1027 *Valparaiso*	15.00 -	20.00

HENRY MOON & GEORGE THOMAS:

Herwin 92025 *Neck Bones And Beans*	150.00 -	200.00

ART MOONEY & HIS ORCHESTRA:

*Vogue R-711 *Seems Like Old Times*	50.00 -	Up
*Vogue R-713 *I've Been Working On The Railroad*	35.00 -	Up
R-730 *Piper's Junction*	30.00 -	40.00
*R-732 *In The Moonmist*	25.00 -	40.00

(*Note: These occur with different record numbers on each side, e.g. 713/732. Some of these combinations are very scarce, and are valued more highly than the foregoing by Vogue record collectors.)

THE MOONLIGHT REVELERS:

Grey Gull 1767 *Baby Knows How*	20.00 -	30.00
1775 *Alabama Shuffle*	30.00 -	50.00
1786 *Memphis Stomp*	30.00 -	50.00

MOONLIGHT SERENADERS:

Bell 383 *Hot Stuff Blues*	5.00 -	8.00

GRANT MOORE & HIS NEW ORLEANS

BLACK DEVILS:
Vocalion 1622 *Original Dixieland One-Step* . . . . . 150.00 - 200.00

SAM MOORE:
Gennett 4747 *Laughing Rag* . . . . 10.00 - 15.00
Okeh 4412 *Chain Gang Blues* . . . . 10.00 - 15.00
    4423 *Wang-Wang Blues* . . . . 10.00 - 15.00
Victor 18849 *Laughing Rag* . . . . 8.00 - 12.00

WEBSTER MOORE & HIS HIGH HATTERS:
Harmony 1197-H *I Wonder How It Feels* . . . . 10.00 - 15.00
Velvet Tone 2197-V *I Wonder How It Feels* . . . . . . 10.00 - 15.00

**FATE MORABLE'S SOCIETY
SYNCOPATORS:**
Okeh 40113 *Frankie and Johnny* . . . . 100.00 - 150.00

MORAN AND MACK:
Columbia 935-D, 1094-D, 1198-D . . . . 4.00 - 8.00
Columbia 1350-D *Two Black Crows, Part 7/8* . . . 7.00 - 10.00
    1560-D *Two Black Crows In Jail* . . . . 7.00 - 10.00
    1652-D *Two Black Crows in Hades* . . . . 7.00 - 10.00
    1929-D *Foolishments* . . . . 8.00 - 12.00
Columbia Personal 170330 *Two Black Crows in
    the AEF* . . . . 30.00 - 50.00
(Note: Above is a one-sided record made for
    Bobbs-Merrill Co.)

**CHAUNCEY MOREHOUSE & HIS SWING
SIX/ORCHESTRA:**
Brunswick 8122 *Plastered In Paris* . . . . 7.00 - 10.00
    8142 *Oriental Nocturne* . . . . 7.00 - 10.00
Variety 608 *Blues In B Flat* . . . . 7.00 - 10.00
    638 *My Gal Sal* . . . . 7.00 - 10.00

BETTY MORGAN:
Pathe Actuelle 32256 *There's Everything Nice About You* 10.00 - 15.00
Perfect 12335 *There's Everything Nice About You* 10.00 - 15.00

**RUSS MORGAN AND HIS ORCHESTRA;
MUSIC IN THE RUSS MORGAN MANNER:**
Brunswick, most issues . . . . 4.00 - 7.00
Columbia 3050-D *Tidal Wave* . . . . 10.00 - 15.00
    3067-D *Sliphorn Sam* . . . . 10.00 - 15.00
Columbia 3063-D, 3064-D . . . . 5.00 - 10.00
Decca, most issues . . . . 2.00 - 4.00
Odeon ONY-36094 *Washin' the Blues From My
    Soul* (instrumental) . . . . 20.00 - 30.00
ONY-36097, ONY-36140 . . . . 15.00 - 25.00

SAM MORGAN'S JAZZ BAND:
Columbia 14213-D *Sing On* . . . . 100.00 - 150.00
    14258-D *Steppin' On The Gas* . . . . 100.00 - 150.00
    14267-D *Down By The Riverside* . . . . 100.00 - 150.00
    14351-D *Short Dress Gal* . . . . 100.00 - 150.00
    14539-D *Over In The Glory Land* . . . . 100.00 - 150.00

**THOMAS MORRIS & HIS ORCHESTRA/
SEVEN HOT BABIES; THOMAS MORRIS
PAST JAZZ MASTERS:**
Okeh 4867 *Lonesome Journey Blues* . . . . 30.00 - 40.00
    4940 *Those Blues* . . . . 30.00 - 40.00
    8055 *Original Charleston Strut* . . . . 30.00 - 40.00
    8075 *Just Blues, That's All* . . . . 30.00 - 40.00
Victor 20179 *Ham Gravy* . . . . 20.00 - 30.00
    20180 *Georgia Grind* . . . . 20.00 - 30.00
    20316 *Who's Dis Heah Stranger?* . . . . 20.00 - 30.00
    20331 *P.D.Q. Blues* . . . . 20.00 - 30.00
    20364 *The Mess* . . . . 20.00 - 30.00
    20483 *The Chinch* . . . . 20.00 - 30.00

**HERB MORRISON & CHARLES NEHLSEN
OF W.L.S.:**
''The Crash of the Hindenberg,'' issued

---

contemporaneously on Melotone, Perfect . . . . . 8.00 - 12.00

MORSE AND FRANK:
Pathe 20430 *Jazzin' Around* . . . . 10.00 - 15.00

**(MISS) LEE MORSE (& HER BLUE GRASS
BOYS):**
Columbia 1922-D *Sweetness* . . . . 7.00 - 10.00
    2136-D *'Tain't No Sin* . . . . 7.00 - 10.00
    2165-D *Sing, You Sinners* . . . . 7.00 - 10.00
    2333-D *Loving You The Way I Do* . . . . 7.00 - 10.00
    2348-D *He's My Secret Passion* . . . . 7.00 - 10.00
    2417-D *I've Got Five Dollars* . . . . 15.00 - 20.00
    2497-D *It's The Girl!* . . . . 15.00 - 20.00
Pathe-Actuelle 25152 *Are You Sorry?* . . . . 5.00 - 8.00
    25156 *Only This Time I'll Be True* . . . . 7.00 - 10.00
    25157 *Sweet Man* . . . . 7.00 - 10.00
    25158 *I Love You So* . . . . 7.00 - 10.00
    25161 *Want a Little Lovin'* . . . . 7.00 - 10.00
    25168 *The Deep Wide Ocean Blues* . . . . 7.00 - 10.00
    25182 *Could I? I Certainly Could* . . . . 7.00 - 10.00
    25187 *Hoodle Dee Doo Dee Doodoo* . . . . 7.00 - 10.00
    25201 *The Little White House (In Honeymoon
    Lane)* . . . . 5.00 - 8.00
    25202 *With All My Heart* . . . . 7.00 - 10.00
    25205 *Ain't That Too Bad?* . . . . 7.00 - 10.00
    36541 *Bolshevik* . . . . 5.00 - 8.00
    36545 *Look Up And Smile* . . . . 5.00 - 8.00
    36546 *Ev'rything's Peaches (For Peaches
    And Me)* . . . . 7.00 - 10.00
    36556 *Tuck In Kentucky (And Smile)* . . . . 7.00 - 10.00
Perfect 11586 *Blue Soldier Blues* . . . . 5.00 - 8.00
Perfect 11590 *What-Cha-Call-'Em Blues* . . . . . . 7.00 - 10.00
Perfect 11591 *Sweet Man* . . . . 7.00 - 10.00
Perfect 11592 *Oh Boy! What a Girl* . . . . 7.00 - 10.00
Perfect 11595 *Want a Little Lovin'* . . . . 7.00 - 10.00
Perfect 11602 *I Love My Baby (My Baby
    Loves Me)* . . . . 7.00 - 10.00
Perfect 11616 *Could I? I Certainly Could* . . . . . . 7.00 - 10.00
Perfect 11621 *Hoodle Dee Doo Dee Doodoo* . . . . 7.00 - 10.00
Perfect 11635 *The Little White Horse (In
    Honeymoon Lane)* . . . . 5.00 - 8.00
Perfect 11636 *The Jersey Walk* . . . . 7.00 - 10.00
Perfect 11639 *Ain't That Too Bad?* . . . . 7.00 - 10.00
Perfect 14722 *Bolshevik* . . . . 5.00 - 8.00
Perfect 14726 *Look Up And Smile* . . . . 5.00 - 8.00
Perfect 14727 *Ev'rything's Peaches (For Peaches
    and Me)* . . . . 7.00 - 10.00
Perfect 14737 *Tuck In Kentucky (And Smile)* . . . . . 7.00 - 10.00

BENNY MORTON & HIS ORCHESTRA:
Columbia 2902-D *Get Goin'* . . . . 30.00 - 40.00
    2924-D *Taylor Made* . . . . 30.00 - 40.00

**FERD (JELLY ROLL) MORTON: FRED
(JELLY ROLL) MORTON; JELLY ROLL
MORTON'S INCOMPARABLES/JAZZ
BAND/JAZZ KIDS/KINGS OF JAZZ/
STEAMBOAT FOUR/STOMPS KINGS/TRIO;
JELLY ROLL MORTON & HIS
ORCHESTRA/RED HOT PEPPERS:**
Autograph 606 *Fish Tail Blues* . . . . 300.00 - 600.00

    607 *Weary Blues* . . . . 300.00 - 600.00
    623 *Wolverine Blues* . . . . 300.00 - 600.00
Broadway 11397 *Mr. Jelly Lord* . . . . 100.00 - 150.00
Buddy 8015 *Bucktown Blues* . . . . 100.00 - 200.00

Carnival 11397 *Mr. Jelly Lord* . . . . .100.00 - 150.00
Champion 15105 *Mr. Jelly Lord* . . . . .100.00 - 150.00
Gennett 3043 *Tia Juana* . . . . 75.00 - 100.00
 3259 *Mr. Jelly Lord* .100.00 - 150.00
 5218 *Grandpa's Spells* . . . . 75.00 - 125.00
 5289 *Wolverine Blues* . . . . 75.00 - 125.00
 5323 *The Pearls* . . . . 75.00 - 125.00
 5486 *New Orleans (Blues) Joys* . . . . 75.00 - 125.00
 5515 *Tom Cat Blues* . . . . 75.00 - 125.00
 5552 *Big Foot Ham* . . . . 75.00 - 125.00
 5590 *Stratford Hunch* . . . . 75.00 - 125.00
 5632 *Tia Juana* . . . . 75.00 - 125.00
Mitchell 11397 *Mr. Jelly Lord* . . . . .100.00 - 150.00
Okeh 8105 *London Blues* . . . . .150.00 - 200.00
Oriole 1007 *The Pearls* . . . . 75.00 - 100.00
Paramount 12216 *Mamanita* . . . . .150.00 - 200.00
 14032 *Froggie Moore* . . . . 7.00 - 10.00

 20332 *Mr. Jelly Lord* . . . . .100.00 - 150.00
Puritan 11332 *Mr. Jelly Lord* . . . . .100.00 - 150.00
 11397 *Mr. Jelly Lord* . . . . .100.00 - 150.00
 12216 *Mamanita* . . . . .150.00 - 250.00
Rialto (unnumbered) *London Blues* . . . . .500.00 - Up
Silvertone 4028 *Mamanita* . . . . 75.00 - 100.00
 4036 *Stratford Hunch* . . . . 75.00 - 100.00
 4040 *Tom Cat Blues* . . . . 75.00 - 100.00
 4041 *Perfect Rag* . . . . 75.00 - 100.00
 4048 *Tia Juana* . . . . 75.00 - 100.00
Triangle 11397 *Mr. Jelly Lord* . . . . .100.00 - 150.00
Victor 20221 *Black Bottom Stomp* . . . . 15.00 - 20.00
 20252 *Sidewalk Blues* . . . . 15.00 - 20.00
 20296 *Steamboat Stomp* . . . . 25.00 - 40.00
 20405 *Someday Sweetheart* . . . . 25.00 - 40.00
 20415 *Doctor Jazz* . . . . 15.00 - 20.00
 20431 *Cannon Ball Blues* . . . . 30.00 - 50.00
 20772 *Hyena Stomp* . . . . 30.00 - 50.00
 20948 *Beale Street Blues* . . . . 25.00 - 40.00
 21064 *Wolverine Blues* . . . . 20.00 - 30.00
 21345 *Jungle Blues* . . . . 75.00 - 100.00
 21658 *Shoe Shiner's Drag* . . . . 15.00 - 20.00
 22681 *Blue Blood Blues* . . . . 25.00 - 40.00
Victor 23004 *Mushmouth Shuffle* . . . . 50.00 - 75.00
 23019 *Fickle Fay Creep* . . . . 75.00 - 100.00
 23307 *Gambling Jack* . . . . .200.00 - 300.00
 23321 *Oil Well* . . . . .200.00 - 300.00
 23334 *Low Gravy* .200.00 - 300.00
 23351 *Strokin' Away* . . . . .150.00 - 250.00
 23424 *Primrose Stomp* . . . . .250.00 - 400.00
 23429 *Load Of Coal* . . . . .250.00 - 400.00
V 38010 *Kansas City Stomps* . . . . 25.00 - 40.00
V 38024 *Georgia Swing* . . . . 25.00 - 40.00
V 38055 *Deep Creek* . . . . 30.00 - 50.00
V 38075 *Burnin' The Iceberg* . . . . 50.00 - 75.00
V 38078 *New Orleans Bump* . . . . 50.00 - 75.00
V 38093 *Courthouse Bump* . . . . 50.00 - 75.00
V 38108 *Turtle Twist* . . . . 50.00 - 75.00
V 38113 *Down My Way* . . . . 60.00 - 90.00
V 38125 *Ponchatrain* . . . . 75.00 - 100.00
V 38135 *Little Lawrence* . . . . 75.00 - 100.00
V 38527 *Freakish* . . . . .100.00 - 150.00
V 38601 *My Little Dixie Home* . . . . .100.00 - 150.00
V 38627 *Pep* . . . . .100.00 - 150.00

Vocalion 1019 *Fat Meat and Greens* . . . . 75.00 - 100.00
 1020 *The Pearls* . . . . 75.00 - 100.00

**TOM MORTON'S ORCHESTRA; TOMMY
MORTON'S GRANGERS:**
Harmony 930-H *Birmingham Bertha* . . . . 7.00 - 10.00
 937-H *Broadway Baby Dolls* . . . . 7.00 - 10.00
(Note: Above titles also issued on *Diva* and
 Velvet Tone.)
Pathe-Actuelle 36544 *How Could Red Riding
 Hood?* . . . . 8.00 - 12.00
 36548 *Baby Mine* . . . . 8.00 - 12.00
 36549 *When I Kissed You I Kissed The Blues
 Goodbye* . . . . 8.00 - 12.00
Perfect 14725 *How Could Red Riding Hood?* . . . . 8.00 - 12.00
 14729 *Baby Mine* . . . . 8.00 - 12.00
 14730 *When I Kissed You I Kissed The Blues
 Goodbye* . . . . 8.00 - 12.00

**CURTIS MOSBY & HIS DIXIELAND BLUE
BLOWERS:**
Columbia 1191-D *Weary Stomp* . . . . 50.00 - 75.00
 1192-D *Tiger Stomp* . . . . 50.00 - 75.00
 1442-D *Blue Blowers Blues* . . . . 50.00 - 75.00
 40001-D *Between You And Me* . . . . 75.00 - 100.00

MIKE MOSIELLO'S RADIO STARS:
Van Dyke 901 *Wow Wow Blues* . . . . 10.00 - 15.00
 909 *Meanest Kind of Blues* . . . . 10.00 - 15.00
 914 *Two Red Lips* . . . . 8.00 - 12.00

JOSEPH MOSKOWITZ:
Victor 17978 *Operatic Rag* . . . . 10.00 - 20.00

SID MOSLEY'S BLUE BOYS:
Supertone 9686 *Asphalt Walk* . . . . .100.00 - 150.00

**SNUB MOSELY AND HIS BAND/
ORCHESTRA:**
Decca 7728, 7768, 8586, 8614, 8626, 8636 . . . . . 5.00 - 10.00
Sonora . . . . 5.00 - 10.00

**BENNIE MOTEN'S KANSAS CITY
ORCHESTRA; BUSTER MOTEN-BENNIE
MOTEN:**
Bluebird 5078 *The Only Girl I Ever Loved* . . . . . . 7.00 - 10.00
 5585 *Milenberg Joys* . . . . 7.00 - 10.00
 6032 *Moten Swing* . . . . 7.00 - 10.00
 6204 *Moten Stomp* . . . . 5.00 - 8.00
 6218 *New Orleans* . . . . 7.00 - 10.00
 6304 *Terrific Stomp* . . . . 7.00 - 10.00
 6431 *It's Hard To Laugh Or Smile* . . . . 8.00 - 12.00
 6638 *Mary Lee* . . . . 7.00 - 10.00
 6709 *New Moten Stomp* . . . . 7.00 - 10.00
 6710 *New Vine Street Blues* . . . . 8.00 - 12.00
 6711 *Now That I Need You* . . . . 15.00 - 20.00
 6719 *The Count* . . . . 10.00 - 15.00
 6851 *Sweetheart Of Yesterday* . . . . 7.00 - 10.00
 7938 *Moten's Blues* . . . . 7.00 - 10.00
Okeh 8100 *Elephant's Wobble* . . . . 50.00 - 75.00
 8184 *Goofy Dust* . . . . 75.00 - 100.00
 8194 *South* . . . . 75.00 - 100.00
 8213 *Baby Dear* . . . . 75.00 - 100.00
 8242 *18th Street Strut* . . . . 75.00 - 100.00
 8255 *South Street Blues* . . . . 75.00 - 100.00
 8277 *Kater Street Rag* . . . . 75.00 - 100.00
Victor 20406 *Thick Lip Stomp* . . . . 30.00 - 50.00
 20422 *Missouri Wobble* . . . . 30.00 - 50.00
 20485 *Kansas City Shuffle* . . . . 20.00 - 30.00
 20811 *White Lightnin' Blues* . . . . 25.00 - 40.00
 20855 *Dear Heart* . . . . 25.00 - 40.00
 20946 *12th Street Rag* . . . . 25.00 - 40.00
 20955 *Moten Stomp* . . . . 10.00 - 15.00
 21199 *Ding Dong Blues* . . . . 25.00 - 40.00
 21584 *The New Tulsa Blues* . . . . 20.00 - 30.00
 21693 *Kansas City Breakdown* . . . . 20.00 - 30.00
 21739 *Justrite* . . . . 20.00 - 30.00
 22660 *As Long As I Love You* . . . . 50.00 - 80.00
 22680 *Ya Got Love* . . . . 25.00 - 40.00

22734 *When I'm Alone*	25.00	-	40.00
22793 *That Too, Do*	30.00	-	40.00
22958 *Oh! Eddie*	40.00	-	60.00
23007 *New Vine Street Blues*	30.00	-	40.00
23023 *Liza Lee*	30.00	-	40.00
23028 *Somebody Stole My Gal*	20.00	-	30.00
23030 *Bouncin' Round*	30.00	-	40.00
23037 *Rumba Negro*	25.00	-	35.00
23342 *Small Black*	150.00	-	200.00
23357 *The Jones Law Blues*	150.00	-	200.00
23378 *The Only Girl I Ever Loved*	150.00	-	200.00
23384 *Moten Swing*	150.00	-	200.00
23391 *The Count*	200.00	-	300.00
23393 *Prince Of Wails*	200.00	-	300.00
23429 *Professor Hot Stuff*	250.00	-	400.00

24216 *Lafayette*	50.00	-	75.00
24381 *Milenberg Joys*	50.00	-	75.00
24893 *South*	5.00	-	10.00
V 38012 *Slow Motion*	25.00	-	40.00
V 38021 *South*	25.00	-	35.00
V 38037 *Tough Breaks*	20.00	-	30.00
V 38048 *Sad Man Blues*	25.00	-	50.00
V 38072 *Moten's Blues*	25.00	-	40.00
V 38081 *Terrific Stomp*	25.00	-	40.00
V 38091 *Kansas City Squabble*	30.00	-	50.00
V 38104 *Rite Tite*	30.00	-	50.00
V 38114 *Mary Lee*	25.00	-	40.00
V 38123 *It Won't Be Long*	30.00	-	50.00
V 38132 *When Life Seems So Blue*	30.00	-	50.00
V 38144 *Boot It*	35.00	-	50.00

MOUND CITY BLUE BLOWERS:

Bluebird 6270 *Hello, Lola*	5.00	-	8.00
6456 *One Hour*	5.00	-	8.00
Brunswick 2581 *Arkansaw Blues*	5.00	-	8.00
Brunswick 2602 *Red Hot!*	5.00	-	8.00
Brunswick 2648 *Bard Wire Blues*	5.00	-	8.00
Brunswick 2804 *Deep Second Street Blues*	7.00	-	10.00
Brunswick 2849 *Gettin' Told*	7.00	-	10.00
Brunswick 2908 *Wigwam Blues*	7.00	-	10.00
Brunswick 3484 *Nervous Puppies*	8.00	-	12.00
Champion 40059 *Thanks A Million*	8.00	-	12.00
40060 *Red Sails In The Sunset*	8.00	-	12.00
40073 *Eeeney Meeney Miney Mo*	8.00	-	12.00
40076 *I'm Shottin' High*	8.00	-	12.00
40081 *The Broken Record*	8.00	-	12.00
40082 *Rhythm In My Nursery Rhymes*	8.00	-	12.00
40091 *Mama Don't Allow It*	8.00	-	12.00
40098 *You Hit The Spot*	8.00	-	12.00
40090 *Wah-Hoo!*	8.00	-	12.00
40103 *High Society*	8.00	-	12.00
Columbia 1946-D *Indiana*	15.00	-	20.00
Okeh 41515 *Georgia On My Mind*	30.00	-	50.00
41526 *You Rascal, You*	30.00	-	50.00
Victor V38087 *Tailspin Blues*	15.00	-	25.00
V38100 *Hello, Lola*	15.00	-	25.00
Vocalion 2957 *What's The Reason*	10.00	-	15.00
2973 *Indiana*	10.00	-	15.00

KEN "GOOF" MOYER; KEN MOYER'S NOVELTY TRIO:

| Banner 1872 *Stampede* | 8.00 | - | 12.00 |
| Banner 1891 *Mellophone Stomp* | 8.00 | - | 12.00 |

Domino 3841, 3861	8.00	-	12.00
Pathe-Actuelle 36511, 36528	8.00	-	12.00
Perfect 14692, 14709	8.00	-	12.00
Regal 8203 *Mellophone Stomp*	8.00	-	12.00

JIMMY MUNDY AND HIS ORCHESTRA/ SWING CLUB SEVEN:

Variety 598 *Ain't Misbehavin'*	10.00	-	15.00
Varsity 8136 *A Lover Is Blue*	7.00	-	10.00
8148 *Sunday Special*	7.00	-	10.00

LARRY MURPHY & HIS ORCHESTRA:

| Cameo 1146 *That's My Hap-Hap-Hapiness* | 7.00 | - | 10.00 |
| 1169 *You Know I Love You* | 5.00 | - | 8.00 |

LYLE "SPUD" MURPHY AND HIS ORCHESTRA:

| Bluebird 10151, 10157, 10539, 10875 | 5.00 | - | 10.00 |
| Decca 1853, 2040, 2109 | 5.00 | - | 10.00 |

BILLY MURRAY (& HIS MERRY MELODY MEN/& THE SEVEN BLUE BABIES):

Edison 52448 *Doin' The Raccoon*	20.00	-	30.00
52454 *Don't Do That To The Poor Puss Cat*	15.00	-	20.00
52518 *Ever Since The Movies Learned To Talk*	15.00	-	20.00
Harmony 784-H *Ever Since the Movies Learned To Talk*	5.00	-	8.00
Victor 16144 *American Ragtime*	7.00	-	10.00
Victor 17584 *This Is The Life*	5.00	-	8.00
Victor 17620 *Fido Is A Hot Dog Now*	5.00	-	8.00
Zon-o-phone 260 *Hiram Green Good Bye*	10.00	-	15.00
Zon-o-phone 392 *Don't Be What You Ain't*	10.00	-	15.00
Zon-o-phone 415 *Keep On The Sunny Side*	10.00	-	15.00
Zon-o-phone 419 *Nothing Like That In Our Family*	10.00	-	15.00

GLADYS MURRAY:

Banner 1464 *Big Bad Bill Is Sweet William Now*	15.00	-	20.00
1479 *Nobody Knows What A Red Head Mama Can Do*	15.00	-	20.00
Regal 9760 *Everybody Loves My Baby*	15.00	-	20.00
9782 *I'm Done Done Done With You*	15.00	-	20.00

MUSICAL COMEDY ORCHESTRA:

| Harmony 686-H *I'm On The Crest Of A Wave* | 5.00 | - | 8.00 |
| 699-H *Watch My Baby Walk* | 5.00 | - | 8.00 |

(Note: Above titles, on *Diva* and *Velvet Tone*, are similarly valued.)

THE MUSICAL COMRADES:

| Tremont 0515, 0526, 0537, 0544 | 7.00 | - | 12.00 |

THE MUSICAL MANIACS:

| Vocalion 3655, 3691 | 7.00 | - | 10.00 |

MUSICAL STEVEDORES:

| Columbia 14406-D *Happy Rhythm* | 50.00 | - | 80.00 |

MUSICAL TRIO:

| Madison 1920 *Beale Street Blues* | 8.00 | - | 12.00 |

THE MUSICAL VOYAGERS:

| Parlophone PNY-34152 *Can This Be Love?* | 20.00 | - | 30.00 |
| PNY-34153 *Fine and Dandy* | 20.00 | - | 30.00 |

THE MUSIC MASTERS:

Broadway 1470 *Wrap Your Troubles In Dreams*	7.00	-	10.00
1471 *Little Girl*	7.00	-	10.00
1476 *Without That Gal*	7.00	-	10.00
Brunswick (most issues)	3.00	-	6.00

MUSTANG BAND OF SOUTHERN METHODIST UNIVERSITY:

| Decca 705 *Peruna* | 8.00 | - | 12.00 |
| 706 *Limehouse Blues* | 8.00 | - | 12.00 |

VICK MEYER'S ATLANTA MELODY ARTISTS:

Okeh 40281 *Blue-Eyed Sally*	25.00	-	40.00
40364 *Flag That Train*	25.00	-	40.00
40386 *Sweet Man Blues*	25.00	-	40.00
40434 *Nantucket Nan*	25.00	-	40.00
40614 *I'd Rather Be Alone*	15.00	-	20.00

VICK MYERS' MELODY ORCHESTRA:

| Cameo 576 *Africa* | 5.00 | - | 8.00 |

PHIL NAPOLEON & HIS EMPERORS OF

RHYTHM/ORCHESTRA/WHISPERING RHYTHM; NAPOLEON'S EMPERORS:

Edison 51908 *Tiger Rag*	20.00 -	30.00
51960 *It Made You Happy When You Made Me Cry*	15.00 -	20.00
51962 *The Cat*	20.00 -	30.00
51996 *Underneath The Weeping Willow*	15.00 -	20.00
51997 *La Lo La*	15.00 -	20.00
52021 *Clarinet Marmalade*	20.00 -	30.00
52147 *Five Pennies*	20.00 -	30.00
Variety 656, 669	7.00 -	10.00
Victor 20605, 20647	5.00 -	8.00
V38057 *Mean To Me*	15.00 -	25.00
V38069 *You Can't Cheat a Cheater*	15.00 -	25.00
Vocalion 3792, 3860	7.00 -	10.00

WILLIAM NAPPI & HIS ORCHESTRA:

Columbia 1042-D *I'll Dream Of You*	10.00 -	15.00
1262-D *If You Just Knew*	10.00 -	15.00

SAM NASH & HIS ORCHESTRA:

Parlophone PNY-34098 *Can I Help It?*	20.00 -	30.00
PNY-34099 *I Love You So Much*	20.00 -	30.00
PNY-34187 *I've Found What I Wanted In You*	30.00 -	40.00
PNY-34197 *I'm Crazy 'Bout My Baby*	30.00 -	40.00

NASHVILLE JAZZERS:

St. Louis Blues, issued contemporaneously on Madison, Van Dyke	15.00 -	20.00

NATIONAL MUSIC LOVERS DANCE ORCHESTRA:

National Music Lovers 1097, 1152, 1156, 1186	5.00 -	12.00

NAYLOR'S SEVEN ACES:

Gennett 5375 *Hugo (I Go Where You Go)*	20.00 -	30.00
5376 *Whe Wouldn't Do (What I Asked Her To)*	20.00 -	30.00
5386 *So I Took The Fifty Thousand Dollars*	20.00 -	30.00
5392 *31st Street Blues*	50.00 -	75.00
5393 *Ringleberg Blues*	50.00 -	75.00
5432 *Twilight Rose*	15.00 -	20.00
5470 *Say, Say, Sadie*	15.00 -	20.00
5638 *Susquehanna Home*	15.00 -	20.00
5643 *Bye Bye Baby*	15.00 -	20.00
Victor 19688 *Sweet Georgia Brown*	5.00 -	8.00

NOBBY NEALE & AL LYONS:

Paramount 12775 *Go To It*	50.00 -	75.00

ARNETT NELSON & HIS HOT FOUR:

Oh! Red issued contemporaneously on Banner, Conqueror, Melotone, Oriole, Perfect, Romeo.	10.00 -	15.00

CHUCK NELSON & HIS BOYS:

Champion 40016 *West End Blues*	20.00 -	30.00

(D.C.) NELSON'S PARAMOUNT SERENADER'S:

Paramount 12494 *Phillip's Street Stomp*	100.00 -	150.00
12543 *New Orleans Breakdown*	100.00 -	150.00

DAVE NELSON & THE KING'S MEN:

Victor 22639 *I Ain't Got Nobody*	40.00 -	60.00
23039 *Some Of These Days*	75.00 -	100.00

JEWELL NELSON:

Columbia 14390-D *Beating Me Blues*	50.00 -	75.00

OZZIE NELSON & HIS ORCHESTRA:

Bluebird 6875, 6965, 6974, 7256, 7502, 7517, 7726, 7814	5.00 -	8.00
Bluebird, most other issues	3.00 -	5.00
Brunswick 4897, 4922, 4979, 6018	5.00 -	10.00
Brunswick 6060 *Dream A Little Dream of Me*	10.00 -	15.00
Brunswick 6131, 6155, 6186, 6228, 6313, 6347, 6372, 6373, 6410, 6413, 6443, 6447, 6547, 6551	4.00 -	7.00
Brunswick 6861 *Dr. Heckle and Mr. Jibe*	7.00 -	10.00
7523 *Tiger Rag*	7.00 -	10.00
7651 *Streamline Strut*	7.00 -	10.00
7659 *Stompin' at the Savoy*	7.00 -	10.00
Brunswick, most other issues	4.00 -	7.00
Vocalion 2547, 2558, 2559, 2581, 2582, 2600, 2601, 2625, 2636, 2642	5.00 -	10.00

RUBY NEWMAN AND HIS ORCHESTRA:

Brunswick 7632, 7633	5.00 -	8.00
Decca, most issues	3.00 -	5.00
Victor 22931, 22934	5.00 -	8.00
Victor 24042, 24043, 24048, 24072, 24073, 24074	4.00 -	8.00
Victor 24894, 25005, 25327, 25328, 25337, 25344	4.00 -	8.00
Victor 25401 *Make-Believe Ballroom*	5.00 -	10.00
Victor 25402, 25405, 25468, 26470, 25543, 25546	4.00 -	7.00

NEW ORLEANS BLACK BIRDS:

Victor V38027 *Playing The Blues*	15.00 -	25.00

NEW ORLEANS BLUE FIVE:

Victor 20316 *The King of the Zulus*	20.00 -	30.00
20364 *My Baby Doesn't Squawk*	20.00 -	30.00
20653 *South Rampart Street Blues*	75.00 -	100.00

NEW ORLEANS BLUES BAND:

Varsity 6029 *Big Blues*	15.00 -	20.00

NEW ORLEANS BOOTBLACKS:

Columbia 14337-D *Flat Foot*	80.00 -	120.00
14465-D *Mixed Salad*	80.00 -	120.00

NEW ORLEANS FEETWARMERS:

Victor 23358 *Lay You Racket*	150.00 -	200.00
23360 *Maple Leaf Rag*	75.00 -	100.00
24150 *I've Found A New Baby*	75.00 -	100.00

NEW ORLEANS FIVE:

Oriole 371 *Memphis Blues*	10.00 -	15.00

NEW ORLEANS JAZZ BAND:

Banner 1318 *Tin Roof Blues*	10.00 -	15.00
1445 *Copenhagen*	10.00 -	15.00
1544 *Some Of These Days*	10.00 -	15.00
1556 *My Sweet Louise*	10.00 -	15.00
1618 *The Camel Walk*	8.00 -	12.00
1624 *Melancholy Lou*	8.00 -	12.00
6049 *Tiger Rag*	7.00 -	10.00
Domino 335 *It Had To Be You*	10.00 -	15.00
338 *Limehouse Blues*	10.00 -	15.00
387 *How Could You Leave Me Now?*	10.00 -	15.00
389 *I'm Gonna Get Acquainted in a Quaint Old Fashioned Town*	10.00 -	15.00
403 *Alabamy Stay At Home*	10.00 -	15.00
3439 *Hot Sax*	15.00 -	20.00
3509 *Some Of These Days*	10.00 -	15.00
3524 *My Sweet Louise*	10.00 -	15.00
3590 *The Camel Walk*	8.00 -	12.00
3594 *Melancholy Lou*	8.00 -	12.00
Okeh 1155 *Ja Da*	7.00 -	10.00
Okeh 1156 *Ole Miss*	7.00 -	10.00
Regal 9615 *Tin Roof Blues*	10.00 -	15.00
9739 *Copenhagen*	10.00 -	15.00
9839 *Some Of These Days*	10.00 -	15.00
9852 *My Sweet Louise*	10.00 -	15.00
9920 *Melancholy Lou*	8.00 -	12.00
9923 *The Camel Walk*	8.00 -	12.00

NEW ORLEANS LUCKY SEVEN:

Okeh 8544 *Goose Pimples*	50.00 -	75.00

NEW ORLEANS OWLS:

Columbia 489-D *Stomp Off, Let's Go*	25.00 -	40.00
605-D *The Owls' Hoot*	15.00 -	25.00
688-D *West End Romp*	20.00 -	30.00
823-D *Blowin' Off Steam*	20.00 -	30.00
862-D *White Ghost Shivers*	25.00 -	35.00
943-D *Eccentric*	20.00 -	30.00
1045-D *Dynamite*	20.00 -	30.00
1158-D *Meat On The Table*	20.00 -	30.00
1261-D *Goose Pimples*	20.00 -	30.00
1547-D *That's A Plenty*	20.00 -	30.00

NEW ORLEANS PEPSTERS:

Van Dyke 77038 *Close Fit Blues*	20.00 -	30.00
81836 *The Harlem Stomp Down*	20.00 -	30.00
81843 *The Rackett*	20.00 -	30.00

NEW ORLEANS RAMBLERS:

Melotone 12133 *No Wonder I'm Blue*	15.00	-	25.00
12230 *That's The Kind Of Man For Me*	15.00	-	25.00

NEW ORLEANS RHYTHM KINGS (FORMERLY FRIARS SOCIETY ORCHESTRA):

Bluebird 10956 *She's Cryin' For Me*	10.00	-	15.00
Buddy 8001 *Tin Roof Blues*	150.00	-	200.00
8002 *Angry*	150.00	-	200.00
8003 *Weary Blues*	150.00	-	200.00
8004 *Clarinet Marmalade*	150.00	-	200.00
Decca 161 *San Antonio Shout*	7.00	-	10.00
162 *Panama*	7.00	-	10.00
229 *Original Dixieland One-Step*	7.00	-	10.00
388 *Dust Off That Old Piano*	7.00	-	10.00
401 *Baby Brown*	7.00	-	10.00
464 *Sensation*	7.00	-	10.00
Gennett 3076 *Milenberg Joys*	80.00	-	100.00
Gennett 5102 *Wolverine Blues*	40.00	-	60.00
5104 *Maple Leaf Rag*	35.00	-	50.00
5105 *That's A Plenty*	30.00	-	40.00
5106 *Da Da Strain*	50.00	-	80.00
5217 *Milenberg Joys*	75.00	-	100.00
5219 *Sobbin' Blues*	75.00	-	100.00
5220 *Mr. Jelly Lord*	80.00	-	120.00
5221 *London Blues*	80.00	-	120.00
Victor 19645 *She's Cryin' For Me*	50.00	-	80.00

NEW ORLEANS STRUTTERS:

Champion 15398 *Fourth Avenue Stomp*	150.00	-	250.00

NEW ORLEANS WANDERERS:

Columbia 698-D *Perdido Street Blues*	50.00	-	80.00
735-D *Papa Dip*	50.00	-	80.00

NEW ORLEANS WILD CATS WITH TAP DANCING JOE:

14662-D *Baby Mine*	75.00	-	100.00
14668-D *Wild Cat Stomp*	75.00	-	100.00

NEWPORT SOCIETY ORCHESTRA:

Banner 1655 *Headin' For Louisville*	5.00	-	8.00
Harmony 659-H *Hiding In The Corner Of Your Smile*	5.00	-	8.00

(Note: Above also issued on *Diva* and *Velvet Tone*, similarly valued.)

NEWPORT SYNCOPATORS:

Van Dyke 81850 *Ring Around The Moon*	20.00	-	30.00
81851 *Because I'm Lonesome*	20.00	-	30.00
81854 *Desert Blues*	20.00	-	30.00
81879 *The Terror*	20.00	-	30.00

NEW SYNCO BAND; NEW SYNCO JAZZ BAND: (See also: SYNCO JAZZ BAND)

Pathe-Actuelle 020920 *Liza*	8.00	-	12.00
021075 *House of David Blues*	5.00	-	8.00
036016 *Land Of Cotton Blues*	5.00	-	8.00
036061 *Red Hot!*	8.00	-	12.00
036134 *West Indies Blues*	7.00	-	10.00
036190 *Big Bad Bill Is Sweet William Now*	5.00	-	8.00
036200 *The Blues Have Got Me*	5.00	-	8.00
36401 *Say Mister! Have You Met Rosie's Sister?*	5.00	-	8.00
36403 *Bell Hoppin' Blues*	7.00	-	10.00
Perfect 14104 *Liza*	8.00	-	12.00
Perfect 14242 *Red Hot!*	8.00	-	12.00
Perfect 14315 *West Indies Blues*	7.00	-	10.00

FRANK NEWTON & HIS (CAFE SOCIETY ORCHESTRA/UPTOWN SERENADERS: FRANK NEWTON QUINTET:

Bluebird 10176 *The World Is Waiting For The Sunrise*	7.00	-	10.00
10186 *Minor Jive*	7.00	-	10.00
10216 *Who?*	7.00	-	10.00
Blue Note 14 *After Hour Blues*	10.00	-	15.00
501 *Daybreak Blues*	10.00	-	15.00
Variety 518 *You Showed Me The Way*	10.00	-	15.00

550 *Cause My Baby Says It's So*	10.00	-	15.00
571 *I Found A New Baby*	10.00	-	15.00
616 *Where Or When*	10.00	-	15.00
647 *Who's Sorry Now?*	10.00	-	15.00
Vocalion 3777 *Easy Living*	10.00	-	15.00
3811 *You Showed Me The Way*	10.00	-	15.00
3839 *The Onyx Hop*	10.00	-	15.00
4821 *Tab's Blues*	7.00	-	10.00
4851 *Jam Fever*	7.00	-	10.00
5410 *Parallel Fifths*	7.00	-	10.00

THE NEWTOWN PIPPINS:

Gennett 6413 *Isabella (Tell Your Fella)*	30.00	-	50.00
6741 *Caroline*	30.00	-	40.00

THE NEW YORKERS:

Brunswick 6164 *Parkin' In The Moonlight*	10.00	-	15.00
Q.R.S. 1002 *Go Get 'Em Caroline*	15.00	-	20.00
1003 *Under A Texas Moon*	10.00	-	15.00
1027 *Kicking A Hole In The Sky*	15.00	-	20.00
1037 *If I Were King*	10.00	-	15.00
1053 *Let Me Sing And I'm Happy*	15.00	-	20.00

NEW YORK MILITARY BAND:

Edison 50514 *Creole Belles; Soldiers In The Park*	5.00	-	8.00
50636 *At A Georgia Campmeeting*	7.00	-	10.00

NEW YORK SYNCOPATORS:

Odeon ONY-36148 *It's A Great Life*	25.00	-	35.00
ONY-36149 *When Kentucky Bids The World "Good Morning"*	25.00	-	35.00
ONY-36152 *Satan's Holiday*	25.00	-	40.00
ONY-36157 *I'll Be Blue, Just Thinking Of You*	25.00	-	35.00
ONY-36158 *I Got Rhythm*	25.00	-	35.00
ONY-36159 *Ukelele Moon*	20.00	-	30.00
ONY-36165 *Cheerful Little Earful*	20.00	-	30.00
ONY-36189 *I'm So In Love With You*	25.00	-	50.00
ONY-36190 *I Can't Realize You Love Me*	25.00	-	50.00
ONY-36194 *The King's Horses*	20.00	-	30.00
ONY-36206 *Dream A Little Dream Of Me*	20.00	-	30.00
ONY-36208 *Just A Crazy Song*	20.00	-	30.00
Okeh 40757 *There Ain't No Maybe In My Baby's Eyes*	10.00	-	15.00
40860 *Bless Her Little Heart*	10.00	-	15.00
40965 *Mary*	10.00	-	15.00
41003 *I've Been Looking For A Girl Like You*	10.00	-	15.00
41202 *Dream Train*	10.00	-	15.00
41264 *The One That I Love Loves Me*	10.00	-	15.00
Parlophone PNY-34155 *I'm Tickled Pink With a Blue-Eyed Baby*	25.00	-	35.00

NICK NICHOLS & HIS ORCHESTRA:

Grey Gull 1820 *Breakin' A Leg*	15.00	-	20.00

RAY NICHOLS & HIS FOUR TOWERS ORCHESTRA:

Bluebird 5902 *Who's Sorry Now?*	8.00	-	12.00
5904 *Restless*	8.00	-	12.00
6013 *Black Coffee*	8.00	-	12.00
Bluebird, other issues	4.00	-	8.00
Harmony 909-H *I've Got A Feeling I'm Falling*	8.00	-	12.00

(Note: Above, on *Diva* and *Velvet Tone*, is similarly valued.)

RED NICHOLS & HIS FIVE PENNIES/ ORCHESTRA/CAPTIVATORS; RED NICHOLS' STOMPERS; LORING NICHOLS & HIS ORCHESTRA; RED NICHOLS & HIS WORLD-FAMOUS PENNIES:

Bluebird 5547 *Rockin' In Rhythm*	7.00	-	10.00
5548 *Rollin' Home*	5.00	-	8.00
5549 *The Prize Waltz*	5.00	-	8.00
5552 *Straight From The Shoulder*	5.00	-	8.00
5553 *Runnin' Wild*	7.00	-	10.00
5583 *Old White's Whiskers*	5.00	-	8.00
Bluebird 10179, 10190, 10200, 10328, 10332, 10360, 10408, 10451, 10522, 10593, 10683	4.00	-	7.00
Brunswick 3407 *Washboard Blues*	10.00	-	15.00
3477 *Buddy's Habits*	10.00	-	15.00

3490 *Back Beats*	10.00 -	15.00
3550 *Alabama Stomp*	10.00 -	15.00
3597 *Mean Dog Blues*	10.00 -	15.00
3626 *Feelin' No Pain*	8.00 -	12.00
3627 *Riverboat Shuffle*	8.00 -	12.00
3850 *Whispering*	10.00 -	15.00
Brunswick 3854 *Avalon*	10.00 -	15.00
3855 *Five Pennies*	10.00 -	15.00
3931 *I Never Knew*	10.00 -	15.00
3955 *There'll Come a Time*	10.00 -	15.00
3961 *Panama*	10.00 -	15.00
3989 *Original Dixieland One-Step*	10.00 -	15.00
3991 *I'm Marching Home To You*	10.00 -	15.00
4243 *Who's Sorry Now?*	10.00 -	15.00
4286 *Roses Of Picardy*	10.00 -	15.00
4363 *Chinatown, My Chinatown*	10.00 -	15.00
4373 *Indiana*	10.00 -	15.00
4701 *Sometimes I'm Happy*	12.00 -	16.00
4724 *I Want To Be Happy*	12.00 -	16.00
4778 *Rose Of Washington Square*	15.00 -	20.00
4790 *Smiles*	15.00 -	20.00
4839 *After You've Gone*	15.00 -	20.00
4844 (Canadian issue) *Five Pennies (plays My Gal Sal*, which was not issued on U.S. Brunswick)	100.00 -	Up
4877 *China Boy*	15.00 -	20.00
4885 *The Sheik Of Araby*	15.00 -	20.00
4925 *Carolina In The Morning*	15.00 -	20.00
4944 *Sweet Georgia Brown*	15.00 -	20.00
4957 *I Got Rhythm*	15.00 -	20.00
4982 *Yours And Mine*	15.00 -	20.00
6014 *Building A Nest For Mary*	8.00 -	12.00
6012 *My Honey's Lovin' Arms*	15.00 -	20.00
6014 *Blue Again*	15.00 -	20.00
6026 *On Revival Day*	15.00 -	20.00
6029 *Sweet and Hot*	15.00 -	20.00
6035 *The Peanut Vendor*	10.00 -	15.00
6058 *Bugaboo*	10.00 -	15.00
6068 *Keep a Song In Your Soul*	15.00 -	20.00
6070 *Were You Sincere?*	10.00 -	15.00
6118 *Love Is Like That*	10.00 -	15.00
6133 *You Rascal, You*	15.00 -	20.00
6138 *Little Girl*	15.00 -	20.00
6149 *Moan, You Moaners*	15.00 -	20.00
6160 *Fan It*	15.00 -	20.00
6164 *How The Time Can Fly*	10.00 -	15.00
6191 *Singin' The Blues*	15.00 -	20.00
6198 *Honolulu Blues*	15.00 -	20.00
6219 *Junk Man Blues*	15.00 -	20.00
6234 *Haunting Blues*	15.00 -	20.00
6241 *Twenty-One Years*	15.00 -	20.00
6266 *Clarinet Marmalade*	15.00 -	20.00
6312 *Goofus*	8.00 -	12.00
6348 *Our Home Town Mountain Band*	15.00 -	20.00
6451 *Love, Nuts and Noodles*	15.00 -	20.00
6461 *Everybody Loves My Baby*	15.00 -	20.00
6534 *Dinah Lou*	15.00 -	20.00
6767 *Slow and Easy*	15.00 -	20.00
Brunswick 6681, 6711, 6718, 6753, 6814, 6815, 6816, 6817, 6818, 6819, 6820, 6821, 6822, 6823, 6827, 6828, 6830, 6831, 6832, 6833, 6834, 6835, 6836, 6839, 6841, 6842, 6843, 6844, 6845	5.00 -	10.00
6824, 6825, 6826, 6829, 6834, 6837, 6838, 6840, 7358, 7460	6.00 -	10.00
20062 (12-inch) *Poor Butterfly*	15.00 -	30.00
20070 (12-inch) *Dear Old Southland*	15.00 -	30.00
20091 (12-inch) *Some Of These Days*	20.00 -	30.00
20092 (12-inch) *It Had To Be You*	20.00 -	30.00
20107 (12-inch) *California Medley*	25.00 -	35.00
20110 (12-inch) *New Orleans Medley*	25.00 -	35.00
Okeh 5648, 5676	4.00 -	7.00

University 507 *Perfidia*	4.00 -	7.00
Variety 502 *They All Laughed*	7.00 -	10.00
524 *Wake Up And Live*	7.00 -	10.00
545 *Troublesome Trumpet*	7.00 -	10.00
595 *Humoresque*	7.00 -	10.00
655 *Twilight In Turkey*	7.00 -	10.00
Victor 21056 *Sugar*	10.00 -	15.00
21560 *Five Pennies*	10.00 -	15.00
Vocalion 3816 *Love's Old Sweet Song*	5.00 -	8.00
3827 *Humoresque*	5.00 -	8.00
3833 *Cream Puff*	5.00 -	8.00
Vocalion 15498 *Washboard Blues*	25.00 -	40.00
15566 *Alabama Stomp*	30.00 -	50.00
15536 *Back Beats*	30.00 -	50.00

NICK NICHOLSON & HIS BAND:

Champion 15699 *True Blue*	25.00 -	35.00

NIGHT CLUB ORCHESTRA:

Harmony 256-H *Hum Your Troubles Away*	5.00 -	8.00
Harmony 302-H *Hello, Swanee, Hello!*	5.00 -	8.00
Harmony 308-H *Where Do You Work-a, John?*	5.00 -	8.00
Harmony 345-H *Cock-A-Doodle, I'm Off My Noodle*	5.00 -	8.00
Harmony 349-H *Pretty Lips*	5.00 -	8.00
Harmony 473-H *I'm Gonna Dance With the Guy Wot Brung Me*	5.00 -	8.00
Harmony 573-H *Is Everybody Happy Now*	5.00 -	8.00
Harmony 610-H *I Found a Horseshoe*	5.00 -	8.00
Harmony 624-H *Hey! Hey! Hazel*	5.00 -	8.00
(Note: Above on *Diva* and *Velvet Tone*, are similarly valued.)		

THE NIGHT OWLS:

Silvertone 3549 ''*Pump Tille*''	75.00 -	125.00

TOM NILES & HIS ORCHESTRA:

Parlophone PNY-34032 *The Perfect Song*	40.00 -	60.00
PNY-34033 *Amos 'n' Andy*	40.00 -	60.00

RAY NOBLE & HIS ORCHESTRA:

Brunswick 8098 *Crazy Rhythm*	7.00 -	10.00
8180 *Alexander's Ragtime Band*	7.00 -	10.00
Brunswick, most other issues	3.00 -	5.00
Columbia, most issues	2.00 -	5.00
Victor 24879 *Down By The River*	10.00 -	15.00
25070 *Let's Swing It*	8.00 -	12.00
Victor 24865, 24891, 25040, 25082, 25094, 25104, 25105, 25187, 25190, 25200, 25209, 25223, 25240, 25241, 25277, 25282, 25336, 25346, 25422, 25428, 25448, 25459, 25504, 25507	5.00 -	10.00

JIMMIE NOONE'S APEX CLUB ORCHESTRA: JIMMIE NOONE & HIS ORCHESTRA: JIMMIE NOONE TRIO:

Bluebird 8609 *They Got My Number Now*	10.00 -	15.00
8649 *Then You're Drunk*	10.00 -	15.00
Brunswick 6174 *I Need Lovin'*	30.00 -	50.00
6192 *River, Stay 'Way From My Door*	30.00 -	50.00
Decca 1584 *I Know That You Know*	7.00 -	10.00
1621 *Four Or Five Times*	7.00 -	10.00
1730 *I'm Walkin' This Town*	8.00 -	12.00
7553 *Sweet Lorraine*	8.00 -	12.00
Vocalion 1184 *I Know That You Know*	30.00 -	50.00
Vocalion 1185 *Four Or Five Times*	30.00 -	50.00
1188 *Ready For The River*	40.00 -	60.00
1207 *Apex Blues*	50.00 -	80.00
1215 *Oh, Sister! Ain't That Hot?*	50.00 -	80.00
1229 *A Monday Date*	50.00 -	80.00
1238 *It's Tight Like That*	50.00 -	80.00
1240 *She's Funny That Way*	75.00 -	100.00
1267 *Chicago Rhythm*	75.00 -	100.00
1272 *Love Me Or Leave Me*	75.00 -	100.00
1296 *Birmingham Bertha*	75.00 -	100.00
1415 *True Blue Lou*	75.00 -	100.00
1416 *Satisfied*	75.00 -	100.00
1436 *He's A Good Man To Have Around*	75.00 -	125.00

1466 *Cryin' For The Carolines*	75.00 -	125.00
1471 *Should I?*	75.00 -	125.00
1490 *Deep Trouble*	75.00 -	125.00
1497 *When You're Smiling*	75.00 -	100.00
1506 *On Revival Day*	75.00 -	100.00
1518 *Virginia Lee*	75.00 -	100.00
1531 *Little White Lies*	75.00 -	100.00
1554 *Three Little Words*	75.00 -	100.00
1580 *Trav'lin' All Alone*	75.00 -	100.00
1584 *You Rascal, You*	75.00 -	100.00
2619 *Inka Dinka Doo*	50.00 -	75.00
2620 *Delta Blues*	50.00 -	75.00
2779 *Apex Blues*	50.00 -	75.00
2862 *Liza*	50.00 -	75.00
2888 *Shine*	50.00 -	75.00
2907 *It's Easy To Remember*	50.00 -	75.00
2908 *Lullaby Of Broadway*	50.00 -	75.00
15819 *Ain't Misbehavin'*	100.00 -	150.00
15823 *Anything You Want*	100.00 -	150.00

NORTHWEST MELODY BOYS:

Champion 15362 *After I've Called You Sweetheart*	30.00 -	40.00
15363 *Sugar Foot Strut*	50.00 -	75.00
15364 *Melancholy*	50.00 -	75.00
15365 *Rain*	25.00 -	40.00
Gennett 6278 *Sugar Foot Strut*	200.00 -	300.00

RED NORVO; RED NORVO & HIS SWING SEXTETTE/SEPTET/OCTET/ORCHESTRA:

Brunswick 6562 *Hole In The Wall*	10.00 -	15.00
6906 *In A Mist*	10.00 -	15.00
7732, 7744, 7761, 7767, 7813, 7815, 7868, 7928, 7932, 7970, 7975, 8068, 8069, 8085, 8088, 8089, 8103, 8135, 8145, 8171, 8182, 8194, 8202, 8227, 8230, 8240, 8288	5.00 -	10.00
Columbia 2927-D *Tomboy*	15.00 -	20.00
3026-D *The Night Is Blue*	15.00 -	20.00
3059-D *Old Fashioned Love*	15.00 -	20.00
3079-D *Bughouse*	15.00 -	20.00
Decca 670, 691, 779	7.00 -	10.00
Vocalion 4083, 4109, 4282, 4345, 4432, 4548, 4632, 4648, 4698, 4738, 4785, 4818, 4833, 4953, 5009	5.00 -	8.00

NOVELTY FIVE:

Aeolian-Vocalion 12117 *Bluin' The Blues*	8.00 -	12.00
12124 *Shake, Rattle And Roll*	8.00 -	12.00
12135 *Lonesome Road Blues*	8.00 -	12.00
12148 *St. Louis Blues*	8.00 -	12.00

SAM NOWLIN:

Champion 16828 *So What*	50.00 -	100.00

JACK OAKIE:

Titles, issued contemporaneously on Banner, Melotone, Oriole, Perfect, Romeo: *Miss Brown To You; Why Dream*	8.00 -	12.00
Melotone 13236 *College Rhythm*	10.00 -	15.00

(JIMMIE/JIMMY O'BRYANT'S (FAMOUS ORIGINAL) WASHBOARD BAND:

Paramount 12246 *Red Hot Mama*	80.00 -	120.00
12260 *Skoodlum Blues*	80.00 -	120.00
12265 *Brand New Charleston*	80.00 -	120.00
12277 *Georgia Breakdown*	100.00 -	150.00
12287 *Clarinet Getaway*	100.00 -	150.00
12288 *Blue Eyed Sally*	100.00 -	150.00
12294 *Steppin' On The Gas*	100.00 -	150.00
12297 *The Joys*	100.00 -	150.00
12308 *Down To The Bricks*	100.00 -	150.00
12312 *Charleston Fever*	100.00 -	150.00
12321 *Milenberg Joys*	100.00 -	150.00
12329 *Thirty-Eight And Two*	100.00 -	150.00
12339 *Chicago Skiffle*	100.00 -	150.00
12346 *Shake That Thing*	100.00 -	150.00
20400 *Alabamy Bound*	100.00 -	150.00

JACK ODIN & HIS ORCHESTRA:

Broadway 1415 *You're Driving Me Crazy*	8.00 -	12.00
1432 *Fall In Love With Me*	7.00 -	10.00

HUSK O'HARE'S SUPER ORCHESTRA OF CHICAGO; HUSK O'HARE'S WOLVERINES:

Cardinal 512 *Tiger Rag*	20.00 -	30.00
Gennett 4850 *Tiger Rag*	15.00 -	25.00
5009 *San*	15.00 -	20.00
Vocalion 15646 *Milenberg Joys*	150.00 -	200.00

OKEH MELODIANS:

Okeh 40876 *The Varsity Drag*	7.00 -	10.00
40898 *There Ain't No Land Like Dixieland To Me*	8.00 -	12.00
40905 *When The Morning Glories Wake Up In The Morning*	8.00 -	12.00
40941 *How Long Has This Been Going On?*	8.00 -	12.00
40960 *I Fell Head Over Heels In Love*	8.00 -	12.00
40978 *Oh, Gee! Oh Joy!*	8.00 -	12.00
41002 *I Just Roll Along (Havin' My Ups And Downs)*	8.00 -	12.00
41017 *Rain Or Shine*	5.00 -	8.00

OKEH MELODY STARS:

Okeh 8382 *Look Out, Mr. Jazz*	— -	—

OKEH SYNCOPATORS:

Okeh 4694 *I Wish I Could Shimmy Like My Sister Kate*	5.00 -	8.00
Okeh 40072 *Nobody's Sweetheart*	5.00 -	8.00
Okeh 40100 *Savannah (The Georgianna Blues)*	5.00 -	8.00
Okeh 40316 *Birmingham Papa*	5.00 -	8.00
Okeh 40493 *Footloose*	7.00 -	10.00
40614 *Jig Walk*	15.00 -	20.00
40641 *Black Bottom*	7.00 -	10.00
40642 *Just A Little Dance*	7.00 -	10.00

OLD SOUTHERN JUG BAND:

Silvertone 3061 *Hatchet Head Blues*	100.00 -	150.00
Vocalion 14958 *Hatchet Head Blues*	100.00 -	150.00

ANNA OLIVER & YOUNG'S CREOLE JAZZ BAND:

Paramount 12060 *What's The Use Of Lovin'*	125.00 -	175.00

EARL OLIVER'S JAZZ BABIES:

Edison 51698, 51724, 51745, 51760, 51776, 51877, 51900, 51929	5.00 -	10.00
51762 *Lulu-Lou*	20.00 -	30.00

JOE "KING" OLIVER; KING OLIVER'S (CREOLE) JAZZ BAND; KING OLIVER & HIS DIXIE SYNCOPATORS:

Autograph 617 *King Porter*	500.00 -	1000.00
Bluebird 5466 *St. James Infirmary*	7.00 -	10.00
6546 *Call Of The Freaks*	10.00 -	15.00
6778 *Boogie Woogie*	10.00 -	15.00
7242 *What You Want Me To Do?*	10.00 -	15.00
10707 *Shake It And Break It*	10.00 -	15.00
Brunswick 3398 *Showboat Shuffle*	15.00 -	20.00
3741 *Farewell Blues*	15.00 -	20.00
4028 *Four Or Five Times*	20.00 -	30.00

4469 *I'm Watching The Clock*	30.00 -	50.00
6053 *Papa De Da Da*	35.00 -	50.00
6065 *I'm Crazy 'Bout My Baby*	35.00 -	50.00
Claxtonola 40292 *Riverside Blues*	150.00 -	250.00
Columbia 13003-D *Chattanooga Stomp*	40.00 -	60.00
14003-D *Camp Meeting Blues*	40.00 -	60.00

Gennett 5132 *Weather Bird Rag*	125.00	200.00
5133 *Canal Street Blues*	125.00	200.00
5134 *Mandy Lee Blues*	125.00	200.00
5135 *Froggie Moore*	125.00	200.00
5184 *Snake Rag*	150.00	250.00
5274 *Krooked Blues*	200.00	400.00
5275 *Zulus Ball*	Extremely Rare	
Harmograph 890 *Mabel's Dream*	150.00	250.00
Okeh 4906 *Sobbin' Blues*	80.00	120.00
4918 *Dipper Mouth Blues*	80.00	120.00
4933 *Snake Rag*	80.00	120.00
4975 *Jazzin' Babies' Blues*	80.00	120.00
8148 *Room Rent Blues*	100.00	150.00
8235 *Mabel's Dream*	100.00	150.00
40000 *Buddy's Habits*	80.00	120.00
40034 *Riverside Blues*	80.00	120.00
Paramount 12088 *The Southern Stomps*	150.00	300.00
20292 *Mabel's Dream*	150.00	250.00
Puritan 11292 *Mabel's Dream*	150.00	250.00
Victor 22298 *When You're Smiling*	8.00	12.00
22681 *Olga*	25.00	40.00
23001 *Struggle Buggy*	35.00	50.00
23009 *Shake It And Break It*	35.00	50.00
23011 *You Were Only Passing Time With Me*	30.00	40.00
23029 *I Can't Stop Loving You*	50.00	75.00
23388 *New Orleans Shout*	200.00	300.00
V 38034 *West End Blues*	30.00	40.00
V 38039 *Call Of The Freaks*	35.00	50.00
V 38049 *My Good Man Sam*	35.00	50.00
V 38090 *Too Late*	40.00	60.00
V 38101 *Sweet Like This*	50.00	75.00
V 38109 *Frankie and Johnny*	35.00	50.00
V 38124 *I Must Have It*	75.00	100.00
V 38134 *Boogie Woogie*	75.00	100.00
V 38137 *Edna*	75.00	100.00
V 38521 *Freakish Light Blues*	100.00	150.00
Vocalion 1007 *Too Bad*	150.00	200.00
1014 *Jackass Blues*	50.00	75.00

Vocalion 1033 *Sugar Foot Stomp*	35.00	50.00
1049 *Tack Annie*	100.00	200.00
1059 *Dead Man Blues*	20.00	30.00
1112 *Willie The Weeper*	80.00	120.00
1113 *Doctor Jazz*	150.00	300.00
1114 *Showboat Shuffle*	100.00	150.00
1152 *Farewell Blues*	75.00	100.00
1189 *West End Blues*	100.00	200.00
1190 *Sweet Emmaline*	150.00	200.00
1225 *Speakeasy Blues*	150.00	200.00
15394 *Deep Henderson*	50.00	80.00
15493 *Dead Man Blues*	30.00	50.00
15503 *Snag It*	50.00	75.00

GEORGE OLSEN & HIS MUSIC:

Columbia 2790-D *Let's Make Up*	8.00	12.00
2791-D *The Last Round-Up*	8.00	12.00
2803-D *Bless Your Heart*	8.00	12.00
2810-D *Savage Serenade*	10.00	15.00
2811-D *It's Only a Paper Moon*	10.00	15.00
2837-D *There's a Home in Wyomin'*	8.00	12.00
2842-D *Everything I Have Is Yours*	8.00	12.00
2843-D *Sing a Low-Down Tune*	8.00	12.00
2848-D *Roll Out of Bed with a Smile*	8.00	12.00

2857-D *Surprise*	8.00	12.00
2860-D *The Colonel From Kentucky*	8.00	12.00
2872-D *I'm Weaving Rainbows*	8.00	12.00
2878-D *This Little Piggie Went To Market*	8.00	12.00
2881-D *Wagon Wheels*	8.00	12.00
2891-D *Old Man Jingle*	8.00	12.00
Decca 1785, 1786, 1824	4.00	6.00
Victor 19374, 19375, 19405, 19419, 19457, 19507	4.00	7.00
Victor 19509 *Sax-O-Phun*	5.00	8.00
Victor 19573 *Why Couldn't It Be Poor Little Me?*	7.00	10.00
Victor 19580 *Nobody Knows What a Red-Head Mama Can Do*	5.00	8.00
Victor 19610 *Everybody Loves My Baby*	5.00	8.00
Victor 19633 *Those Panama Mamas*	10.00	15.00
Victor 19710 *Say Arabella*	5.00	8.00
Victor 19715 *Save Your Sorrow for Tomorrow*	5.00	8.00
Victor 19761 *Hot Aire*	7.00	10.00
Victor 19834 *Just a Little Thing Called Rhythm*	5.00	8.00
Victor 19852 *A Little Bit Bad*	7.00	10.00
Victor 20024, 20029	5.00	8.00
Victor 20101, 20105, 20112, 20116	4.00	8.00
Victor 20322 *I'm Tellin' The Birds Tellin' The Bees*	15.00	25.00
Victor 20327, 20337, 20352, 20359, 20367	4.00	8.00
Victor 20394 *Thinking of You*	5.00	8.00
20425 *Sam, The Old Accordion Man*	7.00	10.00
Victor 22279, 22430, 22935, 22937, 22947, 22967, 22968, 22994, 22998, 24002, 24069, 24070, 24090, 24124, 24125, 24138	5.00	10.00
Victor 24139 *It's Gonna Be You*	7.00	10.00
Victor 24165, 24166, 24179, 24220, 24221, 24229	5.00	10.00

OLE OLSEN AND HIS ORCHESTRA:

Pathe-Actuelle 36488 *Sadie Green*	10.00	15.00
36510 *Take Your Time*	8.00	12.00
Perfect 14669 *Snag It*	10.00	15.00
14691 *Take Your Time*	8.00	12.00

ZELMA O'NEAL:

Brunswick (most issues)	3.00	7.00

D. ONIVAS & HIS ORCHESTRA:

Pathe-Actuelle 036196 *Louisville Blues*	15.00	20.00

ORESTE & HIS QUEENSLAND ORCHESTRA:

Edison 51857 *Ev'rything's Peaches*	15.00	20.00
51885 *Thinking Of You*	10.00	15.00
51886 *Hello! Swanee Hello*	15.00	20.00
51920 *Yankee Rose*	8.00	12.00
51983 *I'm Looking Over a Four-Leaf Clover*	15.00	20.00
51988 *Coronado Nights*	8.00	12.00
52017 *High Hat Harry*	20.00	30.00
52057 *Rosa Lee*	15.00	20.00
52058 *She's Got It*	15.00	20.00
52167 *I'm Walkin' on Air*	20.00	30.00
52169 *When the Morning Glories Wake Up*	20.00	30.00
52214 *Danger! (Look Out For that Gal)*	20.00	30.00
52272 *Borneo*	30.00	50.00
52273 *Lila*	30.00	50.00
52383 *Ten Little Miles From Town*	20.00	30.00
52466 *Cross Roads*	20.00	30.00
52560 *Where The Shy Little Violets Grow*	20.00	30.00
52592 *Me and The Clock (Tick-I-Ty Tock and You*	20.00	30.00

ORIGINAL ATLANTA FOOTWARMERS:

Bell 585 *Hot Licks*	30.00	50.00

ORIGINAL CRESCENT CITY JAZZERS:

Okeh 40101 *Sensation Rag*	100.00	150.00

ORIGINAL DIXIELAND FIVE:

Victor 25502 *Original Dixieland One-Step*	7.00	10.00
25524 *Tiger Rag*	7.00	10.00
25525 *Clarinet Marmalade*	7.00	10.00

ORIGINAL DIXIELAND JAZZ BAND:

Aeolian Vocalion 1205 *Barnyard Blues*	50.00	75.00
1206 *Ostrich Walk*	50.00	75.00

1242 *Reisenweber Rag*	50.00 -	75.00
12097 *Oriental Jazz*	50.00 -	75.00
Bluebird 7442 *Please Be Kind*	5.00 -	8.00
7444 *In My Little Red Book*	5.00 -	8.00
7454 *Drop a Nickel In The Slot*	5.00 -	8.00
Columbia A-2297 *Indiana*	8.00 -	12.00
Okeh 4738 *Toddlin' Blues*	50.00 -	75.00
4841 *Tiger Rag*	50.00 -	75.00
Victor 18255 *Livery Stable Blues*	8.00 -	12.00
18457 *At The Jazz Band Ball*	8.00 -	12.00
18472 *Skeleton Jangle*	8.00 -	12.00
18483 *Sensation Rag*	8.00 -	12.00
18513 *Clarinet Marmalade Blues*	8.00 -	12.00
18564 *Lazy Daddy*	8.00 -	12.00
18717 *Palesteena*	4.00 -	7.00
18722 *Broadway Rose*	5.00 -	8.00
18729 *Home Again Blues*	7.00 -	10.00
18772 *Jazz Me Blues*	7.00 -	10.00
18798 *Royal Garden Blues*	7.00 -	10.00
18850 *Bow Wow Blues*	7.00 -	10.00
Vocalion 3084 *I Live For Love*	7.00 -	10.00
3099 *You Stayed Away Too Long*	7.00 -	10.00

ORIGINAL DIXIE RAG PICKERS:

My Own Blues, issued contemporaneously on Grey Gull, Mitchell, Radiex	10.00 -	15.00

ORIGINAL INDIANA FIVE:

Banner 1931 *Indiana Shuffle*	7.00 -	10.00
6006 *Some Of These Days*	7.00 -	10.00
6008 *Sugar*	8.00 -	12.00
6023 *Struttin' Jerry*	7.00 -	10.00
6028 *The Lighthouse Blues*	8.00 -	12.00
6031 *Rarin' To Go*	7.00 -	10.00
6032 *My Melancholy Baby*	7.00 -	10.00
7027 *My Melancholy Baby*	7.00 -	10.00
7057 *Where Will I Be?*	8.00 -	12.00
7084 *Moten Stomp*	7.00 -	10.00
7137 *Somebody's Making a Fuss Over Somebody*	8.00 -	12.00
Bell 456 *My Baby Knows How*	15.00 -	20.00
Bell 463 *Brown Sugar*	15.00 -	20.00
490 *St. Louis Blues*	15.00 -	20.00
547 *Low-Down Sawed-Off Blues*	15.00 -	20.00
Cameo 924 *Pensacola*	10.00 -	15.00
1138 *Memphis Blues*	10.00 -	15.00
8154 *Nobody's Sweetheart*	10.00 -	15.00
Clover 1755 *Jackass Blues*	15.00 -	20.00
Conqueror 7143 *Moten Stomp*	7.00 -	10.00
Domino 3901 *Indiana Shuffle*	7.00 -	10.00
3971 *Some Of These Days*	7.00 -	10.00
3995 *My Melancholy Baby*	7.00 -	10.00
3997 *Struttin' Jerry*	7.00 -	10.00
3998 *The Lighthouse Blues*	8.00 -	12.00
4165 *Moten Stomp*	7.00 -	10.00
Emerson 3069 *Can You Picture That?*	15.00 -	20.00
3070 *Gettin' The Blues*	15.00 -	20.00
3079 *My Baby Knows How*	15.00 -	20.00
3088 *There Ain't No Maybe In My Baby's Eyes*	15.00 -	20.00
3119 *St. Louis Blues*	15.00 -	20.00
3131 *Memphis Blues*	15.00 -	20.00
Gennett 3059 *Sweet Georgia Brown*	15.00 -	20.00
3060 *Everything Is Hosty Totsy Now*	10.00 -	15.00
3083 *Say, Arabella*	10.00 -	15.00
3093 *Two Tired Eyes*	10.00 -	15.00
3106 *Croonin' A Tune*	10.00 -	15.00
3112 *Red Hot Henry Brown*	10.00 -	15.00
3121 *Oh! Boy, What A Girl*	10.00 -	15.00
3148 *I'm Goin' Out If Lizzie Comes In*	10.00 -	15.00
3150 *Siberia*	10.00 -	15.00
3153 *Pretty Puppy*	10.00 -	15.00
3165 *Melancholy Lou*	10.00 -	15.00
3166 *I'm Gonna Hang Around My Sugar*	10.00 -	15.00
3181 *Everybody Stomp*	10.00 -	15.00

3182 *Everybody's Doin' The Charleston Now*	30.00 -	50.00
3183 *No Man's Mama*	15.00 -	20.00
3218 *Pensacola*	10.00 -	15.00
3230 *Fallen Arches*	10.00 -	15.00
Harmony 47-H *Everybody Stomp*	10.00 -	15.00
58-H *Everybody's Doin' The Charleston Now*	10.00 -	15.00
Harmony 101-H *I'd Rather Be Alone*	8.00 -	12.00
Harmony 106-H *Fallin' Down*	8.00 -	12.00
134-H *Running After You*	8.00 -	12.00
179-H *So Is Your Old Lady*	8.00 -	12.00
217-H *Spanish Mamma*	8.00 -	12.00
245-H *I'd Leave Ten Men Like Yours To Love One Man Like Mine*	8.00 -	12.00
267-H *Florida Low-Down*	8.00 -	12.00
327-H *Delilah*	7.00 -	10.00
387-H *Stockholm Stomp*	8.00 -	12.00
432-H *Play It, Red*	8.00 -	12.00
459-H *Struttin' Jerry*	8.00 -	12.00
501-H *Someday, Sweetheart*	7.00 -	10.00
510-H *Clementine*	7.00 -	10.00
632-H *Junk Man's Dream*	8.00 -	12.00
Lincoln 2499 *Hard-To-Get Gertie*	10.00 -	15.00
2808 *Nobody's Sweetheart*	10.00 -	15.00
National Music Lovers 1191 *Cow Bell Blues*	10.00 -	15.00
Okeh 40456 *Indiana Stomp*	20.00 -	30.00
40599 *Hard-To-Get Gertie*	20.00 -	30.00
Olympic 1443 *Two-Time Dan*	10.00 -	15.00
1444 *Bebe*	10.00 -	15.00
Pathe-Actuelle 021070 *Stavin' Change*	10.00 -	15.00
036019 *Tin Roof Blues*	10.00 -	15.00
036044 *Jubilee Blues*	10.00 -	15.00
36377 *I'd Rather Be Alone*	8.00 -	12.00
36379 *Lo-Nah*	10.00 -	15.00
36420 *Sittin' Around*	10.00 -	15.00
36428 *Hard-To-Get Gertie*	7.00 -	10.00
Perfect 14173 *Mean, Mean Mama*	10.00 -	15.00
14200 *St. Louis Gal*	10.00 -	15.00
14225 *Back O'Town Blues*	10.00 -	15.00
14558 *I'd Rather Be Alone*	8.00 -	12.00
14560 *Lo-Nah*	10.00 -	15.00
14601 *Too Bad*	10.00 -	15.00
14609 *Hard-To-Get Gertie*	7.00 -	10.00
Regal 8248 *Coffee Pot Blues*	7.00 -	10.00
8337 *Some Of These Days*	7.00 -	10.00
8354 *Struttin' Jerry*	7.00 -	10.00
8356 *My Melancholy Baby*	7.00 -	10.00
8368 *The Lighthouse Blues*	8.00 -	12.00
8592 *Moten Stomp*	7.00 -	10.00
Silvertone 4002 *I'm Goin' Out If Lizzie Comes In*	10.00 -	15.00
Velvet Tone 1501-V *I'm Coming, Virginia*	7.00 -	10.00
1510-V *Clementine*	7.00 -	10.00

ORIGINAL INDIANA SYNCOPATORS:

Olympic 1439 *Louisville Lou*	20.00 -	30.00

ORIGINAL JAZZ HOUNDS:

Columbia 14086-D *Fo-Day Blues*	75.00 -	100.00
14094-D *Slow Down*	75.00 -	100.00
14124-D *Cannon Ball Blues*	75.00 -	100.00
14207-D *Lucy Long*	75.00 -	100.00

ORIGINAL LOUISIANA FIVE:

Titles, issued contemporaneously on Puritan, Triangle: *The Hoodoo Man; Louisiana Toddle San; Too Tired*	15.00 -	25.00

ORIGINAL MEMPHIS FIVE:

This band recorded a large number of records, which appeared on almost every label, under its own name and pseudonyms (such as THE COTTON PICKERS on Brunswick, q.v.). The following listing is not exhaustive. Any not listed are probably not of exceptional value.

Arto 9149 *Cuddle Up Blues*	15.00 -	20.00
9153 *Pacific Coast Blues*	20.00 -	30.00
9168 *Chicago*	8.00 -	12.00

9177 *Indigo Blues*	15.00	-	20.00	Mind	15.00	-	20.00

9177 *Indigo Blues*	15.00	-	20.00
9185 *The Wicked Dirty Fives*	15.00	-	20.00
9192 *Railroad Man*	15.00	-	20.00
9199 *Hot 'N' Cold*	15.00	-	20.00
9204 *Papa Blues*	15.00	-	20.00
Banner 1062 *Don't Pan Me*	8.00	-	12.00
Banner 1068 *Lonesome Mama Blues*	7.00	-	10.00
Banner 1082 *Buzz Mirandy*	8.00	-	12.00
Banner 1104 *I Wish I Could Shimmy Like My Sister Kate*	7.00	-	10.00
Banner 1110 *Struttin' at the Strutters' Ball*	7.00	-	10.00
Banner 1132 *Stop Your Kidding*	7.00	-	10.00
Banner 1143 *Runnin' Wild*	7.00	-	10.00
Banner 1178 *Papa Blues*	7.00	-	10.00
Banner 1193 *Shufflin' Mose*	7.00	-	10.00
Banner 1254 *Sad News Blues*	7.00	-	10.00
Banner 1282 *Oh Sister Ain't That Hot*	7.00	-	10.00
Banner 1292 *Dancin' Dan*	7.00	-	10.00
Banner 1296 *Your Mama's Gonna Slow You Down*	7.00	-	10.00
Banner 1309 *That Bran' New Gal O'Mine*	7.00	-	10.00
Banner 1322 *Maybe She'll Write Me, Maybe She'll Phone Me*	7.00	-	10.00
Banner 1336 *31st Street Blues*	8.00	-	12.00
Banner 1346 *Forgetful Blues*	8.00	-	12.00
Banner 1360 *Big Boy!*	8.00	-	12.00
Banner 1373 *Sioux City Sue*	8.00	-	12.00
Banner 1375 *A Man Never Knows When a Woman's Gonna Change Her Mind*	10.00	-	15.00
Bell P-149 *Lonesome Mamma Blues*	15.00	-	20.00
P-153 *Pacific Coast Blues*	20.00	-	30.00
P-168 *Got To Cool My Doggies Now*	8.00	-	12.00
P-177 *That Da Da Strain*	15.00	-	20.00
P-185 *Stop Your Kiddin'*	15.00	-	20.00
P-192 *Great White Way Blues*	15.00	-	20.00
P-199 *Hot 'N' Cold*	15.00	-	20.00
P-204 *Sweet Mama, Please Come Back To Me*	15.00	-	20.00
P-210 *Farewell Blues*	15.00	-	20.00
P-216 *Laughin' Cryin' Blues*	15.00	-	20.00
P-224 *You've Got To See Mama Ev'ry Night*	8.00	-	12.00
P-262 *Steppin' Out*	8.00	-	12.00
Brunswick 3039 *Chinese Blues*	10.00	-	15.00
3630 *Lovely Lee*	8.00	-	12.00
Cameo 478 *Sweet Papa Joe*	8.00	-	12.00
Cameo 481 *Hootin' De Hoot*	8.00	-	12.00
Chautauqua 11138 *Deedle-Deedle-Dum*	50.00	-	Up
Claxtonola 40139 *Buzz Mirandy*	8.00	-	12.00
40161 *Struttin' At The Strutters' Ball*	8.00	-	12.00
40192 *Four O'Clock Blues*	15.00	-	20.00
40281 *St. Louis Gal*	15.00	-	20.00
Clover 1527 *The Meanest Blues*	15.00	-	20.00
Columbia 50-D *St. Louis Gal*	7.00	-	10.00
155-D *Red Hot Mamma*	7.00	-	10.00
186-D *Sioux City Sue*	7.00	-	10.00
Columbia 308-D *Doo Wacka Doo*	7.00	-	10.00
480-D *Indiana Stomp*	10.00	-	15.00
502-D *'Tain't Cold*	10.00	-	15.00
2577-D *St. Louis Gal*	20.00	-	30.00
2588-D *Anything*	20.00	-	30.00
Edison 51204 *Shufflin' Mose*	15.00	-	20.00
51246 *The Jelly-Roll Blues*	15.00	-	25.00
Emerson 10723 *I've Got A Cross-Eyed Papa*	10.00	-	15.00
10725 *Lots O'Mama*	10.00	-	15.00
10740 *Sioux City Sue*	10.00	-	15.00
10741 *31st Street Blues*	20.00	-	30.00
10782 *Red Hot Mama*	10.00	-	15.00
10783 *You Know Me, Alabam'*	10.00	-	15.00
10815 *The Meanest Blues*	10.00	-	15.00
10820 *Take Me*	10.00	-	15.00
Famous 3125 *Lonesome Mama Blues*	8.00	-	12.00
3132 *Buzz Mirandy*	8.00	-	12.00
3136 *I'm Going Away To Wear You Off My*			

Mind	15.00	-	20.00
3186 *Haunting Blues*	15.00	-	20.00
Globe 7013 *Four O'Clock Blues*	15.00	-	20.00
Grey Gull 1200 *Mindin' My Business*	8.00	-	12.00
Harmograph 951 *Superstitious Blues*	15.00	-	25.00
975 *The Meanest Blues*	15.00	-	25.00
992 *Mama's Boy*	15.00	-	25.00
Nordskog 3013 *Pacific Coast Blues*	35.00	-	50.00
Oriole 127 *That Teasin' Squeezin' Man O' Mine*	7.00	-	10.00
Oriole 173 *Mindin' My Business*	7.00	-	10.00
Paramount 20131 *Those Longing For You Blues*	8.00	-	12.00
Paramount 20139 *Buzz Mirandy*	8.00	-	12.00
Paramount 20161 *Struttin' at the Strutters Ball*	8.00	-	12.00
Paramount 20192 *Haunting Blues*	15.00	-	20.00
Pathe-Actuelle 11471 *Nothin'*	25.00	-	35.00
020855 *Stop Your Kidding*	7.00	-	10.00
020888 *Great White Way Blues*	7.00	-	10.00
020920 *Farewell Blues*	8.00	-	12.00
020939 *I Never Miss the Sunshine*	7.00	-	10.00
020977 *Keep It Under Your Hat*	8.00	-	12.00
020995 *Papa Better Watch Your Step*	7.00	-	10.00
036061 *Just Hot!*	8.00	-	12.00
036095 *Shine*	7.00	-	10.00
036096 *I Never Care 'Bout To-Morrow*	8.00	-	12.00
036117 *Africa*	10.00	-	15.00
036134 *I'm Going Back To Those Who Won't Go Back On Me*	10.00	-	15.00
036141 *Somebody Stole My Gal*	8.00	-	12.00
036142 *The Meanest Blues*	8.00	-	12.00
036151 *Choo Choo*	10.00	-	15.00
036168 *Mama's Boy*	10.00	-	15.00
36358 *Jacksonville Gal*	15.00	-	20.00
36384 *Throw Down Blues*	15.00	-	20.00
36413 *Military Mike*	15.00	-	20.00
36422 *Indiana Stomp*	15.00	-	20.00
36565 *The Chant*	15.00	-	20.00
36576 *Go, Joe, Go*	15.00	-	20.00
36623 *Wistful And Blue*	12.00	-	16.00
Perfect 14067 *He May Be Your Man But He Comes To See Me*	7.00	-	10.00
Perfect 14104 *Farewell Blues*	8.00	-	12.00
Perfect 14121 *That Red Head Gal*	7.00	-	10.00
Perfect 14138 *Henpecked Blues*	7.00	-	10.00
Perfect 14242 *Just Hot!*	8.00	-	12.00
Perfect 14275 *Shine*	7.00	-	10.00
Perfect 14276 *Oh Baby*	8.00	-	12.00
Perfect 14298 *Africa*	10.00	-	15.00
14315 *I'm Going Back To Those Who Won't Go Back On Me*	10.00	-	15.00
14322 *Somebody Stole My Gal*	8.00	-	12.00
Perfect 14323 *The Meanest Blues*	8.00	-	12.00
14349 *Mama's Boy*	10.00	-	15.00
14539 *Nobody's Rose*	15.00	-	20.00
14565 *Thrown Down Blues*	15.00	-	20.00
14594 *Bass Ale Blues*	15.00	-	20.00
14603 *Indiana Stomp*	15.00	-	20.00
14746 *One Sweet Letter From You*	15.00	-	20.00
14757 *Go, Joe, Go*	15.00	-	20.00
14804 *What Do I Care What Somebody Said*	12.00	-	16.00
Puritan 11131 *Lonesome Mama Blues*	8.00	-	12.00
Puritan 11139 *Deedle-Deedle-Dum*	8.00	-	12.00
Puritan 11161 *I Wish I Could Shimmy Like My Sister Kate*	8.00	-	12.00
Puritan 11209 *Four O'Clock Blues*	15.00	-	20.00
Regal 9628 *31st Street Blues*	8.00	-	12.00
Regal 9656 *Big Boy*	8.00	-	12.00
Victor 19052 *Who's Sorry Now?*	7.00	-	10.00
Victor 19480 *Meanest Blues*	7.00	-	10.00
19594 *Throw Down Blues*	7.00	-	10.00
19805 *Military Mike*	8.00	-	12.00
20039 *Static Strut*	8.00	-	12.00
Vocalion 14461 *Stop Your Kidding*	8.00	-	12.00

Vocalion 14506 *Four O'Clock Blues*	8.00 -	12.00
14527 *Loose Feet*	8.00 -	12.00
Vocalion 15623 *Lovey Lee*	30.00 -	50.00
15712 *My Angeline*	75.00 -	100.00
15761 *Fireworks*	75.00 -	100.00
15805 *Memphis Blues*	75.00 -	100.00
15810 *Kansas City Kitty*	100.00 -	150.00

ORIGINAL MEMPHIS MELODY BOYS:

Cardinal 562 *Wonderful Dream*	15.00 -	20.00
Champion 15005 *Made A Monkey Out Of Me*	15.00 -	20.00
Gennett 3097 *Made a Monkey Out Of Me*	15.00 -	20.00
5123 *Wonderful Dream*	15.00 -	20.00
5157 *Blue Grass Blues*	20.00 -	30.00

ORIGINAL MIDNIGHT RAMBLERS ORCHESTRA:

Autograph (unnumbered) *Owl Strut*	— -	—

ORIGINAL NEW ORLEANS RHYTHM KINGS:

Okeh 40327 *Golden Leaf Strut*	75.00 -	125.00
40422 *Baby*	75.00 -	125.00

ORIGINAL ST. LOUIS CRACKERJACKS:

Decca 7235 *Swing Jackson*	10.00 -	15.00
7236 *Crackerjack Stomp*	10.00 -	15.00
7248 *Echo In The Dark*	10.00 -	15.00
7265 *Chasing The Blues Away*	10.00 -	15.00

THE ORIGINAL SIX:

Okeh 4546 *She's A Mean Job*	5.00 -	8.00
4655 *Jump Steady Blues*	7.00 -	10.00
4694 *The Broadway Strut*	5.00 -	8.00
4847 *Mad (Cause You Treat Me This Way)*	10.00 -	15.00
Okeh (most other issues)	4.00 -	6.00

ORIGINAL TAMPA FIVE:

Dandy 5154 *My Own Blues*	15.00 -	25.00
5248 *Heebie Jeebies*	15.00 -	25.00

ORIGINAL TUXEDO JAZZ ORCHESTRA:

Okeh 8198 *Black Rag*	150.00 -	200.00
8215 *Original Tuxedo Rag*	150.00 -	200.00

THE ORIGINAL WOLVERINES:

Brunswick 3707 *Shim-Me-Sha-Wabble*	15.00 -	20.00
3708 *Royal Garden Blues*	15.00 -	20.00
4000 *Royal Garden Blues*	10.00 -	15.00
Vocalion 15635 *Royal Garden Blues*	30.00 -	50.00
15708 *Limehouse Blues*	50.00 -	75.00
15732 *There's a Rainbow Round My Shoulder*	35.00 -	50.00
15751 *Sweethearts On Parade*	35.00 -	50.00
15766 *If I Had You*	100.00 -	150.00
15784 *He, She and Me*	100.00 -	150.00
15795 *Some Sweet Day*	30.00 -	50.00

ORIGINAL YELLOW JACKETS:

Vocalion 03504 *Business After Midnight*	20.00 -	30.00
03549 *Swingin' At The Chat 'n' Chew*	20.00 -	30.00
03591 *Cross Street Swing*	20.00 -	30.00

ORIOLE (DANCE) ORCHESTRA; ORIOLE (TERRACE) ORCHESTRA:

Brunswick 2466 *Shim-Me-Sha-Wabble*	5.00 -	8.00
Brunswick 2560 *Sobbin' Blues*	5.00 -	8.00
Brunswick 2616 *Eccentric Rag*	5.00 -	8.00
Brunswick 2633 *You'll Never Get To Heaven With Those Eyes*	5.00 -	8.00
Brunswick 2637 *I Need Some Pettin'*	5.00 -	8.00
Brunswick 2741 *Mandy, Make Up Your Mind*	5.00 -	8.00
Brunswick 2752 *Copenhagen*	5.00 -	8.00
Brunswick 2832 *Off And Gone*	5.00 -	8.00
Brunswick (most other issues)	3.00 -	6.00
Oriole 272 *Alabamy Stay At Home*	10.00 -	15.00
Oriole 777 *Tell 'Em Nothing*	5.00 -	8.00
Oriole 1394 *Me and the Man in the Moon*	5.00 -	8.00
Oriole 1612 *I'm Doing What I'm Doing For Love*	7.00 -	10.00
Oriole (most other issues)	3.00 -	6.00

HAROLD ORTLI & HIS OHIO STATE COLLEGIANS:

Okeh 40332 *My Daddy Rocks Me*	35.00 -	50.00

ORY'S SUNSHINE ORCHESTRA:

Sunshine 3003 *Ory's Creole Trombone*	200.00 -	400.00

GEORGE OSBORN & HIS ORCHESTRA:

Gennett 6215 *Brainstorm*	50.00 -	75.00

WILL OSBORNE & HIS ORCHESTRA:

Banner, most issues	4.00 -	7.00
Columbia 3080-D *That's What You Think*	10.00 -	15.00
3081-D *I Wish I Were Aladdin*	8.00 -	12.00
Columbia, most other issues	2.00 -	5.00
Conqueror, most issues	4.00 -	7.00
Melotone 12099 *Hello! Beautiful*	8.00 -	12.00
12189 *Star Dust*	7.00 -	10.00
Melotone, most other issues	4.00 -	7.00
Oriole, most issues	4.00 -	7.00
Perfect, most issues	4.00 -	7.00
Romeo, most issues	4.00 -	7.00

OSCAR'S CHICAGO SWINGERS:

Decca 7186 *I Wonder Who's Boogiein' My Woogie*	10.00 -	15.00
7201 *Try Some Of That*	10.00 -	15.00

VESS L. OSSMAN; OSSMAN'S BANJO ORCHESTRA; OSSMAN-DUDLEY TRIO:

Columbia A218 *The Buffalo Rag*	7.00 -	10.00
Columbia A220 *Chicken Chowder*	8.00 -	12.00
Columbia A224 *Florida Rag*	7.00 -	10.00
Columbia A228 *Maple Leaf Rag*	7.00 -	10.00
Columbia A787 *Moose March*	7.00 -	10.00
Columbia A937 *St. Louis Tickle*	7.00 -	10.00
Columbia A972 *The Smiler Rag*	8.00 -	12.00
Columbia A2321 *He's Just Like You*	7.00 -	10.00
Columbia 290 *Hunky Dory (one-sided disc)*	10.00 -	15.00
Columbia 461 *A Coon Band Contest (one-sided disc)*	10.00 -	15.00
Columbia 464 *Hot Corn (one-sided disc)*	10.00 -	20.00
Columbia 465 *Creole Belles (one-sided disc)*	10.00 -	20.00
Columbia 469 *Rusty Rags Medley (one-sided disc)*	10.00 -	20.00
Columbia 723 *Whistling Rufus (one-sided disc)*	10.00 -	15.00
Columbia 1540 *Hiawatha (one-sided disc)*	10.00 -	20.00
Columbia 3360 *The Buffalo Rag (one-sided disc)*	10.00 -	15.00
Columbia 3591 *Chicken Chowder (one-sided disc)*	10.00 -	20.00
Silvertone 3626 *Maple Leaf Rag (one-sided disc)*	10.00 -	15.00
Victor 149 *Whistling Rufus (one-sided disc)*	10.00 -	15.00
Victor 150 *An Ethiopian Mardi Gras (one-sided disc)*	10.00 -	15.00
Victor 153 *A Bunch Of Rags (one-sided disc)*	10.00 -	15.00
Victor 154 *A Coon Band Contest (one-sided disc)*	10.00 -	15.00
Victor 1291 *Creole Belles (one-sided disc)*	10.00 -	15.00
Victor 1660 *Harmony Moze (one-sided disc)*	15.00 -	30.00
Victor 1664 *Old Plunk's New Coon Medley (one-sided disc)*	15.00 -	30.00
Victor 2616 *Keep Off The Grass (one-sided disc)*	10.00 -	15.00
Victor 3042 *A Coon Band Contest (one-sided disc)*	10.00 -	15.00
Victor 3043 *An Ethiopian Mardi Gras (one-sided disc)*	10.00 -	15.00
Victor 3050 *A Bunch Of Rags (one-sided disc)*	10.00 -	15.00
Victor 4628 *The Buffalo Rag (one-sided disc)*	10.00 -	15.00
Victor 16092 *St. Louis Tickle*	7.00 -	10.00
Victor 16127 *Persian Lamb Rag*	8.00 -	12.00
Victor 16667 *A Bunch Of Rags*	5.00 -	8.00
Victor 16779 *Buffalo Rag*	7.00 -	10.00

(Note: Foregoing are only representative of the early ragtime recordings of banjoist Vess L. Ossman. Many of the titles were issued on affiliated and antecedent labels, some of which are of far greater interest and value than most of the records above. Most notable are recordings on the primitive *Berliner* discs, and some of the other companies' small-sized-usually, seven-inch-records.

Also, a given tune may have been recorded at several sessions, with the various "takes" being issued with the same catalog number; no attempt to distinguish between these performances is made here. Finally, some recordings were issued anonymously, e.g. Little Wonder 569, in the ANONYMOUS listing.)

GLEN OSWALD'S SERENADERS:
Victor 19733 *Bucktown Blues* . . . . 15.00 - 20.00

RED OWENS & HIS GANG:
Champion 15759 *Chicago Rhythm* . . . . 50.00 - 75.00
16423 *Hard Luck* . . . . 75.00 - 125.00

THE OXFORD RHYTHM MAKERS:
Parlophone PNY-34045 *Puttin' On The Ritz* . . . . 35.00 - 50.00
PNY-34046 *With You* . . . . 35.00 - 50.00

HAROLD OXLEY AND HIS POST LODGE ORCHESTRA:
Okeh 40134 *Step, Henrietta* . . . . 8.00 - 12.00
40180 *I Don't Know Why* . . . . 8.00 - 12.00

PACIFIC COAST PLAYERS:
Radiex 1326 *Jazzing Around* . . . . 8.00 - 12.00

HOT LIPS PAGE & HIS BAND; HOT LIPS PAGE TRIO:
Bluebird 7567, 6568, 7583, 7680, 7682, 7684,
8634, 8660, 8981 . . . . 5.00 - 10.00
Decca 7433, 7451, 7699, 7714, 7757, 8531 . . . . . . 7.00 - 10.00

WALTER PAGE'S BLUE DEVILS:
Vocalion 1463 *Blue Devil Blues* . . . . 150.00 - 250.00

PALACE DANCE ORCHESTRA:
Broadway 1330 *Same Old Moon* . . . . 5.00 - 8.00
1349 *I'm Following You* . . . . 5.00 - 8.00

PALLEDO ORCHESTRA OF ST. LOUIS:
Okeh 40521 *What-Cha-Call-'Em Blues* . . . . 35.00 - 50.00

CHARLIE PALLOY & HIS ORCHESTRA:
Crown 3389 *You're Telling Me* . . . . 10.00 - 15.00
3392 *Brother, Can You Spare A Dime?* . . . . . . 10.00 - 15.00
3410 *What A Perfect Combination* . . . . 10.00 - 15.00
3512 *Pettin' In The Park* . . . . 10.00 - 15.00

GLADYS PALMER:
Decca 7106 *I'm Livin' In A Great Big Way* . . . . . 7.00 - 10.00
7017 *Get Behind Me, Satan* . . . . 7.00 - 10.00

PALMER HOUSE VICTORIANS (See JULES HERBUVEAUX):

PALMETTO NIGHT CLUB ORCHESTRA:
Champion 15308 *Darktown Shuffle* . . . . 50.00 - 75.00

PALOOKA WASHBOARD BAND:
Decca 7378 *We Gonna Move* . . . . 10.00 - 15.00
7398 *You Done Tore Your Pants With Me* . . . . . 10.00 - 15.00

LOUIS PANICO & HIS ORCHESTRA:
Brunswick 4736 *Wabash Blues* . . . . 15.00 - 20.00

PAPALIA & HIS ORCHESTRA:
Okeh 40347 *Cross-Word Mama, You're Puzzling Me* . . . . 75.00 - 100.00

PARADISE CLUB ORCHESTRA:
Conqueror 7189 *It Goes Like This (That Funny Melody)* . . . . 5.00 - 8.00
7209 *Glorianna* . . . . 5.00 - 8.00

THE PARAMOUNTEERS:
Publix 2008-P *I Have To Have You* . . . . 10.00 - 15.00

PARAMOUNT PICKERS:
Paramount 12779 *Salty Dog* . . . . 200.00 - 300.00

TONY PARENTI; ANTHONY PARENTI & HIS FAMOUS MELODY BOYS; (TONY) PARENTI'S LIBERTY SYNCOPATORS/ NEW ORLEANIANS:
Old Man Rhythm, issued contemporaneously on
Banner, Cameo, Jewel, Oriole, Romeo . . . . . . 8.00 - 12.00
Brunswick 4148 *Gumbo* . . . . 30.00 - 40.00
Columbia 545-D *Midnight Papa* . . . . 25.00 - 40.00
836-D *Up Jumped The Devil* . . . . 25.00 - 40.00
1264-D *African Echoes* . . . . 25.00 - 40.00
1548-D *In The Dungeon* . . . . 25.00 - 40.00
Okeh 40308 *That's A Plenty* . . . . 30.00 - 40.00
Victor 19647 *Creole Blues* . . . . 20.00 - 30.00

19697 *Dizzy Lizzy* . . . . 25.00 - 40.00
19698 *Be Yourself* . . . . 30.00 - 40.00

PARHAM'S BLACK PATTI BAND:
Black Patti 8038 *Um-Te-Da-Da-Da* . . . . 300.00 - 500.00

TINY PARHAM & HIS "FORTY" FIVE; TINY PARHAM & HIS MUSICIANS:
Bluebird 5146 *Black Cat Moan* . . . . 8.00 - 12.00
6031 *Subway Sobs* . . . . 8.00 - 12.00
6570 *Washboard Wiggles* . . . . 8.00 - 12.00
7005 *Blue Island Blues* . . . . 10.00 - 15.00
8130 *Stuttering Blues* . . . . 8.00 - 12.00
Paramount 12586 *Jim Jackson's Kansas City Blues* . . . . 200.00 - 300.00
Victor 21553 *Cuckoo Blues* . . . . 50.00 - 75.00
21659 *Snake Eyes* . . . . 50.00 - 75.00
22778 *Sud Buster's Dream* . . . . 50.00 - 75.00
22842 *Rock Bottom* . . . . 30.00 - 50.00
23027 *Blue Moon Blues* . . . . 75.00 - 100.00
23386 *Nervous Tension* . . . . 200.00 - 300.00
23410 *Steel String Blues* . . . . 200.00 - 300.00
23426 *Golden Lily* . . . . 200.00 - 300.00
23432 *My Dreams* . . . . 200.00 - 300.00
V 38009 *Jogo Rhythm* . . . . 50.00 - 75.00
V 38041 *Subway Sobs* . . . . 35.00 - 50.00
V 38047 *Blue Melody Blues* . . . . 35.00 - 50.00
V 38054 *Voodoo* . . . . 50.00 - 75.00
V 38060 *Stompin' On Down* . . . . 50.00 - 75.00
V 38076 *Echo Blues* . . . . 50.00 - 75.00
V 38082 *Jungle Crawl* . . . . 50.00 - 75.00
V 38111 *Dixieland Doin's* . . . . 50.00 - 75.00
V 38126 *Fat Man Blues* . . . . 75.00 - 100.00

CHARLIE PARKER QUINTET (& OTHER COMBINATIONS):
Dial 1002, 1006, 1007, 1012, 1013, 1015, 1058 . . . . 5.00 - 8.00

ED PARKER & HIS ORCHESTRA:
Okeh 41537 *Potatoes Are Cheaper, Tomatoes Are Cheaper* . . . . 8.00 - 12.00

PARK LANE ORCHESTRA:
Brunswick 3513 *You Can't Cry Over My Shoulder* 7.00 - 10.00
Brunswick (most other issues) . . . . 4.00 - 7.00

ART PAYNE & HIS ORCHESTRA:
Gennett 5063 *Some Winter Night* . . . . 10.00 - 15.00
5064 *Jingle Bells* . . . . 10.00 - 15.00
5631 *Oh Maud* . . . . 20.00 - 30.00
6644 *Igloo Stomp* . . . . 30.00 - 50.00
6694 *Jo-Anne* . . . . 20.00 - 30.00

RAY PEARL AND HIS ORCHESTRA:
Vocalion 3408, 3420, 3522, 3536 . . . . 7.00 - 10.00

PELHAM INN SOCIETY ORCHESTRA:
Banner 7082 *I'm Riding To Glory (With a Glorious Girl)* . . . . 5.00 - 8.00
Conqueror 7142 *Get Out And Get Under The Moon* . . . . 5.00 - 8.00
Domino 4134 *I'm Riding To Glory (With A Glorious Girl)* . . . . 5.00 - 8.00

PAUL PENDARVIS AND HIS ORCHESTRA:
Columbia 2973-D, 2974-D, 3025-D, 3032-D,
3082-D, 3091-D . . . . 7.00 - 10.00

ANDY PENDLETON:
Okeh 8625 *Sweet Emmaline* . . . . 20.00 - 30.00
Victor 23389 *Thinking Of You* . . . . 50.00 - 75.00

TWIN-SIX GUITAR JACK PENEWELL:
Autograph 608 *Penewell Blues* . . . . 20.00 - 30.00

THE PENNSYLVANIA SYNCOPATORS:
Emerson 10773 *I Can't Get The One I Want* . . . . 15.00 - 20.00
10868 *My Sweet Louise* . . . . 10.00 - 15.00

ALBERTA PERKINS:
Ajax 17125 *Levee Man* . . . . 20.00 - 30.00
Harmograph 983 *Sweet Mandy* . . . . 20.00 - 30.00

GERTRUDE PERKINS:
Columbia 14313-D *Gold Daddy Blues* . . . . 30.00 - 50.00

RED PERKINS & HIS DIXIE RAMBLERS:

Champion 16288 *Hard Times Stomp* ....100.00 - 150.00
16439 *Old Man Blues*.....................75.00 - 100.00
16661 *My Baby Knows How* ....100.00 - 150.00

SLIM PERKINS:
Banner 1515 *Freakish Blues* ....5.00 - 8.00
1533 *Spread Yo' Stuff* ....5.00 - 8.00

PERRY & HIS STOMP BAND:
Black Patti 8037 *Ash Can Stomp* ....150.00 - 250.00

PERRY'S HOT DOGS:
Banner 1615 *There Ain't No Flies On Auntie* ....5.00 - 8.00
1617 *Tweedle Dee, Tweedle Doo* ....5.00 - 8.00
1618 *Milenberg Joys* ....8.00 - 12.00
1641 *Has Been Blues* ....7.00 - 10.00
1692 *Flamin' Mamie* ....5.00 - 8.00
1714 *Say Mister! Have You Met Rosie's Sister?* .5.00 - 8.00

PERRY'S ORCHESTRA:
Paramount 20431 *Headin' For Louisville* ....10.00 - 15.00
Puritan 11431 *That Certain Party* ....10.00 - 15.00

SAM PERRY'S RUBE BAND:
Supertone 9039 *Bass Blues* ....50.00 - 75.00

TEDDY PETERS:
Vocalion 1006 *Georgia Man* ....150.00 - 200.00

JACK PETTIS AND HIS BAND/PETS:
Banner 1907 *Stockholm Stomp* ....8.00 - 12.00
Banner 1908 *St. Louis Shuffle* ....8.00 - 12.00
Banner 1911 *He's The Last Word* ....7.00 - 10.00
Banner 1927 *It All Depends On You* ....5.00 - 8.00
Banner 1929 *I Gotta Get Myself Somebody To
Love* ....7.00 - 10.00
Banner 1940 *I'm Back In Love Again* ....7.00 - 10.00
Banner 1942 *That's My Hap-Hap-Happiness* ....7.00 - 10.00
Domino 3883 *Stockholm Stomp* ....8.00 - 12.00
3884 *St. Louis Shuffle* ....8.00 - 12.00
Domino 3895, 3897 ....5.00 - 8.00
Domino 3914 *That's My Hap-Hap- Happiness* ..7.00 - 10.00
3916 *I'm Back In Love Again* ....7.00 - 10.00
4080 *Candied Sweets* ....5.00 - 8.00
4094 *Once Over Lightly* ....5.00 - 8.00
Okeh 41410 *Bag O'Blues* ....25.00 - 40.00
41411 *Freshman Hop*.................30.00 - 40.00
Regal 8221 *St. Louis Shuffle* ....8.00 - 12.00
8229 *Stockholm Stomp* ....8.00 - 12.00
Regal 8225, 8243, 8244 ....5.00 - 8.00
Regal 8263 *That's My Hap-Hap-Happiness* ..7.00 - 10.00
8267 *Ain't She Sweet?* ....7.00 - 10.00
Regal 8463 *Candied Sweets* ....5.00 - 8.00
8483 *Steppin' It Off* ....5.00 - 8.00
Victor 21559 *Doin' The New Low Down* ...10.00 - 15.00
21793 *Freshman Hop* ....10.00 - 15.00
V38105 *Bugle Call Blues* ....30.00 - 50.00
Vocalion 15703 *Hot Heels* ....75.00 - 100.00
15761 *Broadway Stomp*................75.00 - 100.00

PHILLIPS' LOUISVILLE JUG BAND:
Brunswick 7187 *Smackin' The Sax* ....100.00 - 150.00
7194 *Tiger Rag* ....100.00 - 150.00
7207 *Soldier Boy Blues* ....100.00 - 150.00

SIDNEY PHILLIPS & HIS ORCHESTRA:
Brunswick 8133, 8187, 8332 ....4.00 - 6.00
Variety 654 ....4.00 - 6.00
Vocalion 3934 ....4.00 - 6.00

**THE PICCADILLY PLAYERS (&
SINGERS/&THE RADIO GIRL):**
Edison (thin) 14023 *Susianna* ....20.00 - 30.00
14032 *The One In The World* ....20.00 - 30.00
14034 *Hittin' The Ceiling* ....20.00 - 30.00
14035 *Someday Soon* ....20.00 - 30.00
14036 *Maybe—Who Knows?* ....20.00 - 30.00
14038 *You Ought To See My New Baby* ..20.00 - 30.00
14056 *Tip Toe Thru The Tulips With Me* ..30.00 - 40.00
Edison (thick) 52167 *Someday, Sweetheart* ..20.00 - 30.00
52169 *She Don't Wanna* ....20.00 - 30.00
52198 *What'll You Do?* ....20.00 - 30.00

52215 *Rose Room* ....20.00 - 30.00
52232 *Feelin' Good* ....20.00 - 30.00
52273 *That's What I Call Keen* ....30.00 - 50.00
52280 *My One And Only* ....20.00 - 30.00
52327 *You're Just A Great Big Baby Doll* .....20.00 - 30.00
52363 *Old Man Sunshine* ....20.00 - 30.00
52391 *Take Your Tomorrow* ....20.00 - 30.00
52442 *I'm Sorry, Sally* ....20.00 - 30.00
52478 *Easy Goin'* ....20.00 - 30.00
52527 *Susianna* ....20.00 - 30.00
52545 *You Were Meant For Me* ....20.00 - 30.00
52562 *My Lucky Star* ....20.00 - 30.00
52565 *I'm Thirsty For Kisses, Hungry For Love* 20.00 - 30.00
52574 *On With The Dance!* ....20.00 - 30.00
52590 *I've Made A Habit Of You* ......20.00 - 30.00
52613 *Walking With Susie* ....20.00 - 30.00
52635 *You Ought To See My New Baby* ......20.00 - 30.00

WALTER PICHON:
Victor V38544 *Yo Yo* ....50.00 - 75.00

THE PICKENS SISTERS:
Victor 22929, 22965, 22975, 24025, 24180, 24190,
24335, 24468, 24471, 24625, 24630, 24751,
24753, 24815 ....5.00 - 12.00

**PICKETT-PARHAM APOLLO
SYNCOPATORS:**
Paramount 12441 *Mojo Strut* ....150.00 - 250.00

CHARLES PIERCE & HIS ORCHESTRA:
Paramount 12619 *China Boy* ....150.00 - 200.00
12640 *Jazz Me Blues* ....150.00 - 200.00
20616 *Nobody's Sweetheart* ....150.00 - 200.00

PIERROT SYNCOPATORS:
Crown (Canadian) 81008 *Somebody's Making A
Fuss Over Somebody* ....8.00 - 12.00
81020 *Dixie Drag* ....10.00 - 15.00
81109 *The Rainbow Man* ....5.00 - 10.00
81161 *Piccolo Pete* ....7.00 - 10.00

PINKIE'S BIRMINGHAM FIVE:
Gennett 3208 *Carolina Stomp* ....25.00 - 40.00

PIRON'S NEW ORLEANS ORCHESTRA:
Columbia 99-D *Ghost Of The Blues* ......15.00 - 25.00
14007-D *Sud Bustin' Blues* ....20.00 - 30.00
Okeh 40021 *Bouncing Around* ....40.00 - 60.00
40189 *Lou'siana Swing* ....50.00 - 75.00
Victor 19233 *New Orleans Wiggle* .....8.00 - 12.00
19255 *West Indies Blues* ....8.00 - 12.00
19646 *Red Man Blues* ....20.00 - 30.00

THE PLANTATION SERENADES:
Champion 15386 *Missouri Squabble* ......100.00 - 150.00
15402 *I Call You Sugar* ....125.00 - 175.00
Silvertone 5138 *Jackass Blues* ....100.00 - 150.00
5502 *I Call You Sugar* ....100.00 - 150.00

PLETCHER'S ELI PROM TROTTERS:
QRS Q-1055 *That's Where You're Wrong* ....40.00 - 60.00

STEW PLETCHER & HIS ORCHESTRA:
Bluebird 6343 *You Never Looked So Beautiful* ...8.00 - 12.00
6344 *I Don't Want To Make History* ....8.00 - 12.00
6345 *I Hope Gabriel Likes My Music* ....8.00 - 12.00

THE PODS OF PEPPER:
Columbia 14590-D *You've Had Your Way* ....80.00 - 120.00
14664-D *I Was A Good Loser Until I Lost You* ...80.00 - 120.00

POLLA'S CLOVER GARDENS ORCHESTRA:
Edison 51456 *Travelling Blues (An Indigo Wail)* ..7.00 - 10.00
51554 *The Time Will come* ....7.00 - 10.00
51575 *Isn't She The Sweetest Thing?* ....7.00 - 10.00
51586 *Save Your Sorrow (For Tomorrow)* .....7.00 - 10.00
51613 *The Promenade Walk* ....7.00 - 10.00
Edison (most other issues) ....3.00 - 6.00

**BEN POLLACK & HIS CALIFORNIANS
(PARK CENTRAL) ORCHESTRA/PICK-A-
RIB BOYS; BEN POLLACK'S ORCHESTRA:**
Titles, issued contemporaneously on Banner,
Cameo, Conqueror, Domino, Jewel, Oriole,

Perfect, Regal, Romeo: *Fall In Love With Me;*
If I Could Be With You (One Hour Tonight);
I'm A Ding Dong Daddy; I've Got Five
Dollars; Rollin' Down The River; Sing-Song
Girl; Sweet and Hot; There's A Wah Wah Girl
In Agua Caliente; You Didn't Have To Tell Me . 8.00 - 15.00
Brunswick 7747, 7751, 7764 . . . . 8.00 - 12.00
Columbia 2870-D *Got The Jitters* . . . . 15.00 - 20.00
2879-D *Deep Jungle* . . . . 15.00 - 20.00
2886-D *Goin' To Heaven On A Mule* . . . . 15.00 - 20.00
2901-D *Dancing In The Moonlight* . . . . 15.00 - 20.00
2905-D *Here Goes* . . . . 15.00 - 20.00
2906-D *The Voodoo* . . . . 15.00 - 20.00
2910-D *Alone On The Range* . . . . 15.00 - 20.00
2929-D *Sleepy Head* . . . . 15.00 - 20.00
2931-D *Freckle Face, You're Beautiful* . . . . . . 15.00 - 20.00
Decca 1424, 1435, 1458, 1465, 1476, 1488, 1517,
1546 . . . . 5.00 - 10.00
Hit-of-the-Week 1026 *I'm Following You* . . . . 10.00 - 15.00
1027 *Cryin' For The Carolines* . . . . 15.00 - 20.00
(Note: Above are single-sided cardboard records)
Variety 504 *Deep Elm* . . . . 10.00 - 15.00
556 *Peckin'* . . . . 10.00 - 15.00
Victor 20394 *When I First Met Mary* . . . . 5.00 - 8.00
20408 *Deed I Do* . . . . 8.00 - 12.00
20425 *He's The Last Word* . . . . 7.00 - 10.00
20461 *You're The One For Me* . . . . 25.00 - 35.00
21184 *Memphis Blues* . . . . 8.00 - 12.00
21437 *Singapore Sorrows* . . . . 8.00 - 12.00
21743 *Buy, Buy For Baby* . . . . 7.00 - 10.00
21827 *Sentimental Baby* . . . . 8.00 - 12.00
21858 *Futuristic Rhythm* . . . . 7.00 - 10.00
21941 *Louise* . . . . 7.00 - 10.00
21944 *On With The Dance!* . . . . 8.00 - 12.00
22071 *In The Hush of the Night* . . . . 7.00 - 10.00
22074 *Bashful Baby* . . . . 10.00 - 15.00
22089 *True Blue Lou* . . . . 7.00 - 10.00
22101 *Sweetheart, We Need Each Other* . . . . . . 8.00 - 12.00
22106 *Where The Sweet Forget-Me-Nots*
Remember . . . . 8.00 - 12.00
22147 *Song of the Blues* . . . . 8.00 - 12.00
22158 *You've Made Me Happy Today* . . . . 8.00 - 12.00
22252 *I'd Like To Be A Gypsy* . . . . 5.00 - 8.00
22267 *Keep Your Undershirt On* . . . . 10.00 - 15.00
24284 *Two Tickets To Georgia* . . . . 15.00 - 20.00
Vocalion 3769 *The Moon Is Grinning At Me* . . 10.00 - 15.00
3819 *In a Sentimental Mood* . . . . 10.00 - 15.00

HARRY POLLOCK'S BLUE DIAMONDS/
CLUB MAURICE DIAMONDS; HARRY
POLLOCK'S ORCHESTRA:
Edison 51933 *How'd Ya Like To Meet Me In The*
Moonlight? . . . . 7.00 - 10.00
51934 *Where's That Rainbow?* . . . . 10.00 - 15.00
Gennett 3377 *Alabama Stomp* . . . . 20.00 - 30.00
6026 *There Ain't No Maybe In My Baby's Eyes* 10.00 - 15.00
6067 *You Can't Cry Over My Shoulder* . . . . . . 10.00 - 15.00
6069 *Underneath The Weeping Willow* . . . . . . 10.00 - 15.00
6083 *What Do I Care What Somebody Said?* . . 10.00 - 15.00
6383 *There Ain't No Sweet Man That's Worth*
The Salt of My Tears . . . . 10.00 - 15.00

BOB POPE AND HIS (HOTEL CHARLOTTE)
ORCHESTRA:
Titles, issued contemporaneously on Banner,
Melotone, Oriole, Perfect, Romeo: *Always;*
Blue Skies; Nero; Rockin' Chair; Whoa Babe! . 10.00 - 15.00
Bluebird 6283 *Early Bird* . . . . 8.00 - 12.00
6284 *Moon Rose* . . . . 8.00 - 12.00
6285 *Breakin' In A Pair of Shoes* . . . . 8.00 - 12.00
6286 *Shoe-Shine Boy* . . . . 8.00 - 12.00
6299 *That Never-To-Be Forgotten Night* . . . . . . 8.00 - 12.00
6300 *Stop That Dog* . . . . 8.00 - 12.00
6452 *Big Chief De Sota* . . . . 8.00 - 12.00

6453 *On Your Toes* . . . . 8.00 - 12.00
6454 *Let's Sing Again* . . . . 8.00 - 12.00
6471 *Swamp Fire* . . . . 8.00 - 12.00
6502 *On The Alamo* . . . . 8.00 - 12.00
6508 *Madhouse* . . . . 8.00 - 12.00

PORTER'S BLUE DEVILS:
Gennett 5210 *Original Charleston Strut* . . . . . . 10.00 - 15.00
5249 *Steamboat Sal* . . . . 10.00 - 15.00
5251 *Somebody's Wrong* . . . . 8.00 - 12.00
5281 *Mama Loves Papa (Papa Loves Mama)* . . 8.00 - 12.00
5282 *Walk, Jenny, Walk* . . . . 8.00 - 12.00
5305 *When It's Night Time In Italy* . . . . 8.00 - 12.00

COLE PORTER:
Victor 24766, 24825, 24843, 24859 . . . . 5.00 - 10.00

DICK PORTER & HIS ORCHESTRA:
Vocalion 3355 *Sweet Thing* . . . . 10.00 - 15.00
3469 *There's No Two Ways About It* . . . . 10.00 - 15.00
3478 *Poor Robinson Crusoe* . . . . 10.00 - 15.00

KING PORTER & HIS ORCHESTRA:
Champion 15305 *Oh Miss Hannah!* . . . . 60.00 - 90.00

PORT OF HARLEM JASSMEN/SEVEN:
Blue Note 3 *Rocking The Blues* . . . . 10.00 - 15.00
6 *Pounding Heart Blues* . . . . 10.00 - 15.00
7 *Blues For Tommy* . . . . 10.00 - 15.00
14 *Port Of Harlem Blues* . . . . 10.00 - 15.00

POWELL'S JAZZ MONARCHS:
Okeh 8333 *Laughing Blues* . . . . 75.00 - 100.00

DICK POWELL:
Brunswick 4884, 7469 . . . . 7.00 - 10.00
Conqueror 8183, 8184 . . . . 5.00 - 10.00
Perfect 12919, 12920 . . . . 5.00 - 10.00
Romeo 2084 . . . . 5.00 - 10.00
Vocalion 15647, 15648, 15674, 15675, 15686,
15699, 15700 . . . . 8.00 - 15.00

MEL POWELL & HIS ORCHESTRA:
Commodore 543, 544 . . . . 5.00 - 10.00

TEDDY POWELL AND HIS ORCHESTRA:
Bluebird, most issues . . . . 4.00 - 7.00
Decca . . . . 4.00 - 8.00

TOMMY POWELL AND HIS HI-DE-HO BOYS:
Decca 7231 *That Cat Is High* . . . . 10.00 - 15.00

WALTER POWELL & HIS ORCHESTRA:
Vocalion 4612 *Devil's Holiday* . . . . 8.00 - 12.00

OLLIE POWERS' HARMONY
SYNCOPATORS/ORCHESTRA:
Claxtonola 40263 *Play That Thing* . . . . 150.00 - 200.00
Harmograph 851 *Play That Thing* . . . . 150.00 - 200.00
Paramount 12059 *Jazzbo Jenkins* . . . . 150.00 - 200.00
Puritan 11263 *Play That Thing* . . . . 150.00 - 200.00

ANDY PREER & THE COTTON CLUB
ORCHESTRA:
Gennett 6056 *I've Found A New Baby* . . . . 150.00 - 200.00

EVELYN PREER:
Banner 1824 *Breezin' Along With The Breeze* . . . 5.00 - 8.00
Banner 1873 *Sadie Green (The Vamp of New*
Orleans) . . . . 5.00 - 8.00
Banner 1895 *Sunday* . . . . 8.00 - 12.00
Banner 1972 *Muddy Water* . . . . 5.00 - 8.00
Banner 6016 *One Sweet Letter From You* . . . . . 5.00 - 8.00
Banner 6036 *Magnolia* . . . . 5.00 - 8.00
Domino 3864 *Cock-A-Doodle, I'm Off My*
Noodle . . . . 8.00 - 12.00
Victor 20306 *Make Me Know It* . . . . 15.00 - 20.00

SAMMY PRICE AND HIS FOUR QUARTERS/
TEXAS BLUSICIANS:
Brunswick 7136 *Blue Rhythm Stomp* . . . . 150.00 - 200.00
Decca 7732, 7781, 7877, 7820, 7836, 7850, 8505,
8515, 8547, 8557, 8566, 8575, 8601, 8624,
8649 . . . . 5.00 - 10.00

VIC PRICE AND HIS ORCHESTRA:
Gennett 6411 *When* . . . . 15.00 - 25.00
6440 *I'm More Than Satisfied* . . . . 15.00 - 20.00

6475 *Back In Your Own Back Yard*	15.00 -	20.00
6612 *Here's That Party Now In Person*	15.00 -	20.00
Herwin 8046 *Everywhere You Go*	20.00 -	30.00
8049 *Back In Your Own Back Yard*	20.00 -	30.00
8052 *Mary Ann*	20.00 -	30.00
Supertone 9003 *Back In Your Own Back Yard* ...	15.00 -	20.00
9006 *Speedy Boy*	15.00 -	20.00
9043 *Here's That Party Now In Person*	15.00 -	20.00

LOUIS PRIMA & HIS NEW ORLEANS
GANG:

Brunswick 7320 *I Still Want You*	8.00 -	12.00
7335 *Star Dust*	8.00 -	12.00
7376 *House Rent Party Day*	8.00 -	12.00
7394 *Sing It 'Way Down Low*	8.00 -	12.00
7419 *I'm Livin' In A Great Big Way*	7.00 -	10.00
7431 *Swing Me With Rhythm*	7.00 -	10.00
7448 *The Lady In Red*	7.00 -	10.00
7456 *Basin Street Blues*	7.00 -	10.00
7471 *It's The Rhythm In Me*	7.00 -	10.00
7479 *Let's Swing It*	7.00 -	10.00
7499 *Plain Old Me*	7.00 -	10.00
7524 *Jamaica Shout*	7.00 -	10.00
7531 *Solitude*	7.00 -	10.00
7586 *I've Got My Fingers Crossed*	7.00 -	10.00
7596 *Sweet Sue*	7.00 -	10.00
7628 *Sing, Sing, Sing*	7.00 -	10.00
7657 *Alice Blue Gown*	7.00 -	10.00
7666 *Lazy River*	7.00 -	10.00
7680 *Swing Me A Lullaby*	7.00 -	10.00
7709 *Confessin'*	7.00 -	10.00
7740 *Let's Get Together And Swing*	7.00 -	10.00
Decca 1618, 1674, 1871, 1953, 2242, 2279, 2660, 2749	4.00 -	8.00
Hit, most issues	3.00 -	6.00
Majestic, most issues	3.00 -	6.00
Varsity 8245, 8247	4.00 -	7.00
Vocalion 3376 *Pennies From Heaven*	7.00 -	10.00
3388 *The Goose Hangs High*	7.00 -	10.00
3509 *Fifty-Second Street*	7.00 -	10.00
3628 *Danger, Love At Work*	7.00 -	10.00
3657 *Tin Roof Blues*	7.00 -	10.00
3921 *Rhythm On The Radio*	7.00 -	10.00

ALBERTA PRIME:

Blu-Disc T-1007 *Parlor Social De Luxe*	200.00 -	300.00

PRINCE'S (MILITARY) BAND/ORCHESTRA:

Columbia A139 *St. Louis Tickle*	8.00 -	12.00
Columbia A711 *Black And White Rag*	8.00 -	12.00
Columbia A854 *Temptation Rag*	8.00 -	12.00
Columbia A901 *Porcupine Rag*	10.00 -	15.00
Columbia A972 *Tickled To Death*	8.00 -	12.00
Columbia A1031 *Red Pepper—A Spicy Rag*	8.00 -	12.00
Columbia A1038 *High Society*	10.00 -	15.00
Columbia A1107 *Ramshackle Rag*	8.00 -	12.00
Columbia A1140 *Black Diamond Rag*	8.00 -	12.00
A1149 *The Gaby Glide*	8.00 -	12.00
Columbia A1164 *Cabaret Rag*	10.00 -	15.00
Columbia A1292 *Another Rag*	8.00 -	12.00
Columbia A1307 *Too Much Mustard*	8.00 -	12.00
Columbia A2327 *Beale Street*	7.00 -	10.00
Columbia A2347 *Everybody's Jazzin' It*	5.00 -	8.00
Columbia A2370 *Mr. Jazz Himself*	5.00 -	8.00
Columbia A2499 *Rigoletto Rag*	5.00 -	8.00
Columbia A2825 *Miss Trombone (A Slippery Rag)*	5.00 -	8.00
Columbia A5582 *That's A Plenty (12-inch)*	8.00 -	12.00
Columbia A5591 *Memphis Blues (12-inch)*	8.00 -	12.00
Columbia A5772 *St. Louis Blues (12-inch)*	8.00 -	12.00
Columbia A5938 *Inner Circle Toddle (12-inch)* ..	8.00 -	12.00
Columbia A5983 *New Orleans Jazz (12-inch)* ...	8.00 -	12.00
Columbia (Most other issues)	3.00 -	5.00

(Note: Many of the above titles appear anonymously
    on affiliated labels, such as Climax and Oxford.)

PRINCETON TRIANGLE CLUB DANCE
ORCHESTRA:

Columbia Personal (170615/170614) *Make Time* ..	50.00 -	75.00

(Note: The vocalist "J.M. Stewart" on the flip
side is actor Jimmy Stewart.)

PRINCETON TRIANGLE CLUB JAZZ BAND:

Personal Record 30-P *Join The Navy*	50.00 -	75.00
31-P *Pirate Gold*	50.00 -	75.00
59-P *I'll Build A Igloo For You*	50.00 -	75.00
63-P *Broke Again*	50.00 -	75.00
84-P *Twilight*	30.00 -	50.00
85-P *Pretty Please*	30.00 -	50.00
100-P *Rhythmic Refrain*	50.00 -	75.00
114-P *You Know Who*	50.00 -	75.00

CLARENCE PROFIT TRIO:

Brunswick 8341 *Tea For Two*	8.00 -	12.00
Columbia 35378 *Body And Soul*	8.00 -	12.00
Decca 8503 *Hot And Bothered*	8.00 -	12.00
8527 *Dark Eyes*	8.00 -	12.00

ALBERTA PRYME (See: ALBERTA PRIME)
ARTHUR PRYOR'S BAND:

*Victor 5607 *A Georgia Sunset—Cakewalk*	20.00 -	30.00
Victor 16021 *Artful Artie*	8.00 -	12.00
Victor 16043 *That Rag*	8.00 -	12.00
Victor 16073 *Southern Beauties Rag*	8.00 -	12.00
Victor 16079 *A Coon Band Contest*	5.00 -	8.00
Victor 16155 *A Southern Belle*	8.00 -	12.00
Victor 16306 *White Wash Man*	8.00 -	12.00
Victor 16444 *The African 400 (An Educated Rag)*	10.00 -	15.00
Victor 16482 *Dill Pickles Rag*	8.00 -	12.00
Victor 16511 *Temptation Rag*	8.00 -	12.00
Victor 16668 *Mr. Black Man*	8.00 -	12.00
Victor 16796 *Georgia Sunset—Cake-Walk*	8.00 -	12.00
Victor 16816 *Razzazza Mazzazza*	8.00 -	12.00
Victor 16818 *Sweetmeats—Ragtime March*	8.00 -	12.00
Victor 16821 *The King Of Rags (a Two-Step Oddity)*	8.00 -	12.00
Victor 16834 *A Rhinewine Rag*	8.00 -	12.00
Victor 16883 *Canhanibalmo Rag*	10.00 -	15.00
Victor 17044 *Surprise*	7.00 -	10.00
Victor 17063 *Oh, You Beautiful Doll-Two-Step* ...	5.00 -	8.00
Victor 17111 *Grizzly Bear Turkey Trot*	8.00 -	12.00
Victor 17138 *Red Rose Rag*	8.00 -	12.00
Victor 17223 *Frozen Bill-Cake-Walk*	8.00 -	12.00
Victor 35040 *Razzazza Mazzazza (12-inch)*	8.00 -	12.00
Victor 35098 *Tobasco—A Rag Waltz (12-inch)* ...	8.00 -	12.00

*(Note: Some of the above titles were issued
    earlier on the single-sided Victor records of
    2000, 4000, 5000 series. Since some of these
    were issued anonymously ("Band, " "Dance
    Orchestra"), and others have not been verified,
    an authoritative listing is not attempted.
    Generally, as "original issues" and examples of
    turn-of-the-century recordings, they are of
    greater interest and value than most of the
    records listed above. This is especially true of
    those issued in seven-inch and eight-inch sizes.)

JACK PURVIS; JACK PURVIS & HIS
ORCHESTRA:

Odeon ONY-36093 *When You're Feelin' Blue* ...	75.00 -	100.00
Okeh 8782 *Down Georgia Way*	40.00 -	60.00
8808 *Dismal Dan*	40.00 -	60.00
41404 *Copyin' Louis*	35.00 -	50.00

FRANKIE QUARTELL & HIS LITTLE CLUB
ORCHESTRA/MELODY BOYS:

Brunswick 4183 *Sweet Baby*	20.00 -	30.00
Okeh 40257 *Heart Broken Strain*	15.00 -	20.00
40258 *Prince Of Wails*	30.00 -	50.00

QUEEN CITY BLOWERS:

Champion 15030 *Stomp Off, Let's Go*	50.00 -	75.00

MAE QUESTAL:

Decca 346, 447, 540, 653, 680, 769, 832, 876 ...	7.00 -	12.00

Victor 24261 *Sweet Betty* .... 20.00 - 30.00
QUINTONES:
Vocalion 4928 *Chew-Chew-Chew (Your Bubble
    Gum)* .... 10.00 - 15.00
    5172 *When My Sugar Walks Down The Street* .. 10.00 - 15.00
    5409 *Midnight Jamboree* .... 10.00 - 15.00
    5509 *Sly Mongoose* .... 10.00 - 15.00
    5596 *Harmony In Harlem* .... 10.00 - 15.00
**Q.R.S. BOYS: (See also: FOUR HAWAIIAN
GUITARS)**
QRS 7062 *Wiggle Yo' Toes* .... 50.00 - 100.00
    7067 *Black Boy Blues* .... 50.00 - 100.00
**HARRY RADERMAN'S (BILTMORE
CASCADE ROOF/JAZZ) ORCHESTRA;
ORCHESTRA; RADERMAN'S RED
HOTTERS/ROYSTERERS:**
Everybody's 1067 *Seminola* .... 7.00 - 10.00
    1068 *Oh Say, Can I See You Tonight?* .... 7.00 - 10.00
Harmony 22-H *Sweet Man* .... 5.00 - 8.00
    25-H *Want A Little Lovin'* .... 5.00 - 8.00
    45-H *Hugo, I Go Where You Go* .... 5.00 - 8.00
    48-H *I Ain't Got Nobody* .... 5.00 - 8.00
Lyric 4218 *Railroad Blues* .... 7.00 - 10.00
Okeh 4477 *Muscle Shoals Blues* .... 5.00 - 8.00
    4885 *Tin Roof Blues* .... 7.00 - 10.00
    4923 *Play Day Blues* .... 5.00 - 8.00
Paramount 20263 *Bleeding Hearted Blues* ...... 7.00 - 10.00
Okeh 40610, 40652, 40663, 40712, 40736, 40773,
    40829 .... 4.00 - 8.00
Paramount 20263 *Bleeding Hearted Blues* ...... 7.00 - 10.00
**LOU RADERMAN & HIS PELHAM HEATH
INN ORCHESTRA:**
Banner 7133 *Georgie Porgie* .... 5.00 - 8.00
Banner 7135 *Get Out and Get Under The Moon* . 5.00 - 8.00
Harmony 607-H *Ol' Man River* .... 8.00 - 12.00
Harmony 611-H *Oh Gee!—Oh Joy!* .... 7.00 - 10.00
(Note: Above two titles, on *Diva* and *Velvet Tone*,
    are similarly valued.)
"Show Boat" Special Record 1086-P *Why Do I
    Love You?* .... 10.00 - 15.00
RADIO ALL STAR NOVELTY ORCHESTRA:
Brunswick 4755 *Mysterious Mose* .... 7.00 - 10.00
THE RADIOLITES:
Columbia 1432-D *Sweet Lorraine* .... 5.00 - 8.00
Columbia 2540-D *I Don't Know Why* .... 7.00 - 10.00
KARL RADLACH & HIS ORCHESTRA:
Titles, issued contemporaneously on Banner,
    Broadway, Cameo, Oriole, Perfect: *Absence
    Makes The Heart Grow Fonder; Around The
    Corner; Be Careful With Those Eyes; Cheer
    Up (Good Times Are Comin'); Dust; Give
    Yourself a Pat On The Back; Hand Me Down
    My Walking Cane; Mysterious Mose; Telling It
    To The Daisies* .... 5.00 - 10.00
IKE RAGON & HIS ORCHESTRA:
Vocalion 03513 *Maple Leaf Rag* .... 20.00 - 30.00
    03547 *Truckin' On The Old Camp Ground* .... 20.00 - 30.00
RAG PICKERS:
Autograph (unnumbered) *Suite 16* .... 100.00 - 150.00
RAINBOW DANCE ORCHESTRA:
Romeo 366 *St. Louis Blues* .... 7.00 - 10.00
MA RAINEY (AND HER GEORGIA BAND):
Paramount 12080 *Last Minute Blues* .... 75.00 - 100.00
    12081 *Bad Luck Blues* .... 75.00 - 100.00
    12082 *Walking Blues* .... 75.00 - 100.00
    12083 *Southern Blues* .... 75.00 - 100.00
    12098 *Dream Blues* .... 50.00 - 75.00
    12200 *Ma Rainey's Mystery Record* .... 75.00 - 125.00
    12215 *Lucky Rock Blues* .... 75.00 - 125.00
    12222 *Farewell Daddy Blues* .... 50.00 - 75.00
    12227 *South Bound Blues* .... 75.00 - 125.00
    12238 *Jelly Bean Blues* ....100.00 - 150.00

    12242 *Toad Frog Blues* .... 75.00 - 125.00
    12252 *See See Rider Blues* ....100.00 - 150.00
    12257 *Cell Bound Blues* .... 75.00 - 125.00
    12284 *Explaining The Blues* .... 75.00 - 125.00
    12290 *Louisiana Hoo Doo Blues* .... 75.00 - 125.00
    12295 *Stormy Sea Blues* .... 75.00 - 125.00
    12303 *Night Time Blues* .... 75.00 - 125.00
    12311 *Rought and Tumble Blues* .... 75.00 - 125.00
    12332 *Slave To The Blues* .... 75.00 - 125.00
    12338 *Chain Gang Blues* .... 75.00 - 125.00
    12352 *Seeking Blues* .... 75.00 - 125.00
    12357 *Stack O'Lee Blues* .... 75.00 - 125.00
    12364 *Broken Hearted Blues* .... 75.00 - 125.00
    12374 *Titanic Man Blues* .... 75.00 - 125.00
    12384 *Sissy Blues* ....100.00 - 150.00
    12395 *Down In The Basement* ....100.00 - 150.00
    12419 *Grievin' Hearted Blues* ....100.00 - 150.00
    12438 *Don't Fish In My Sea* ....100.00 - 150.00
    12455 *Morning Hour Blues* ....100.00 - 150.00
    12508 *Misery Blues* ....150.00 - 200.00
    12526 *Gone Daddy Blues* ....150.00 - 200.00
    12548 *Big Boy Blues* ....150.00 - 200.00
    12566 *Oh Papa Blues* ....150.00 - 200.00
    12590 *Georgia Cake Walk* ....100.00 - 150.00
    12603 *Moonshine Blues* ....100.00 - 150.00
    12612 *Ice Bag Papa* ....150.00 - 200.00
    12647 *Blues The World Forgot* ....100.00 - 150.00
    12668 *Prove It On Me Blues* ....150.00 - 200.00
    12687 *Victim Of The Blues* ....150.00 - 200.00
    12706 *Traveling Blues* ....150.00 - 200.00
    12718 *Big Feeling Blues* ....100.00 - 150.00
    12735 *Tough Luck Blues* ....100.00 - 150.00
    12760 *Sleep Talking Blues* ....100.00 - 150.00
    12804 *Log Camp Blues* ....100.00 - 150.00
    12902 *Runaway Blues* ....100.00 - 150.00
    12926 *Sweet Rough Man* ....100.00 - 150.00
    12963 *Daddy Goodbye Blues* ....100.00 - 150.00
THE RAMBLERS:
Romeo 266 *She Knows Her Onions* .... 5.00 - 8.00
    315 *Lonely Eyes* .... 5.00 - 8.00
RAMONA AND HER GANG/GRAND PIANO:
Victor 24260 *A Penny For Your Thoughts* .... 10.00 - 15.00
    24268 *What Have We Got To Lose?* .... 10.00 - 15.00
    24303 *I've Got To Sing A Torch Song* ...... 10.00 - 15.00
    24310 *Was My Face Red?* .... 10.00 - 15.00
    24316 *Raisin' The Rent* .... 10.00 - 15.00
    24389 *You Excite Me!* .... 10.00 - 15.00
    24408 *Ah! The Moon Is Here* .... 10.00 - 15.00
    24440 *I'm No Angel* .... 10.00 - 15.00
    24445 *Not For All The Rice in China* .... 10.00 - 15.00
    25138 *Every Now And Then* .... 10.00 - 15.00
    25156 *Barrel-House Music* .... 10.00 - 15.00
RAMPART STREET WASHBOARD BAND:
Titles, issued contemporaneously on Banner,
    Conqueror, Oriole, Perfect, Romeo: *Forty and
    Tight; Piggly Wiggly* ....125.00 - 200.00
CLARK RANDALL & HIS ORCHESTRA:
Brunswick 7415 *Troublesome Trumpet* .... 8.00 - 12.00
    7436 *Drifting Tide* .... 8.00 - 12.00
    7466 *Jitter Bug* .... 8.00 - 12.00
DUKE RANDALL & HIS BOYS:
Champion 15491 *Squeeze Me* ....200.00 - 300.00
SLATZ RANDALL & HIS ORCHESTRA:
Brunswick 4331 *Bessie Couldn't Help It* .... 7.00 - 10.00
    4562 *Blame It On The Moon* .... 7.00 - 10.00
Brunswick 4568 *Let's Don't 'n' Say We Did* .... 7.00 - 10.00
    4779 *I'm A Ding Dong Daddy (From Dumas)* . 7.00 - 10.00
    6304 *Hello! Gorgeous* .... 7.00 - 10.00
AMANDA RANDOLPH & HER ORCHESTRA:
Bluebird 6615, 6616, 6617, 6619 .... 5.00 - 10.00
TED/TEDDY RAPH & HIS ORCHESTRA:
Columbia 2440-D *When I Take My Sugar To Tea* . 7.00 - 10.00

2450-D *Dream A Little Dream Of Me*	7.00 -	10.00
2482-D *Wrap Your Troubles In Dreams*	7.00 -	10.00

JIMMY RASCHEL & HIS ORCHESTRA:

Champion 16534 *It Don't Mean A Thing*	100.00 -	150.00

REB'S LEGION CLUB FORTY FIVES:

Hollywood (unnumbered) *My Mammy's Blues* ..	200.00 -	300.00

RECTORS' JAZZ BAND:

Arto 9003 *Bluin' The Blues*	7.00 -	10.00

RED & HIS BIG TEN:

Victor 23026 *That's Where The South Begins* ...	15.00 -	25.00
23033 *At Last I'm Happy*	15.00 -	25.00

RED AND MIFF'S STOMPERS:

Edison 51854 *Alabama Stomp*	75.00 -	100.00
51878 *Black Bottom Stomp*	75.00 -	100.00
Victor 20778 *Delirium*	10.00 -	15.00
21183 *Feelin' No Pain*	15.00 -	20.00
21397 *Slippin' Around*	10.00 -	15.00

THE RED CAPS:

Victor 23382 *Niagara Falls*	100.00 -	150.00

THE RED DEVILS:

Ballin The Jack, issued contemporaneously on

Banner, Oriole, Romeo	50.00 -	75.00
Columbia 14586-D *Tiger Rag*	50.00 -	75.00

THE RED HEADS:

Melotone 12443 *Feelin' No Pain*	7.00 -	10.00
12495 *Bugaboo*	5.00 -	8.00
Oriole 2555 *Nobody's Sweetheart*	7.00 -	10.00
2574 *Bugaboo*	5.00 -	8.00
Pathe-Actuelle 11347 *Get A Load Of This*	30.00 -	50.00
36347 *Nervous Charlie*	15.00 -	20.00
36384 *Fallen Arches*	15.00 -	20.00
36387 *Poor Papa*	10.00 -	15.00
36419 *'Tain't Cold*	15.00 -	20.00
36458 *Dynamite*	15.00 -	20.00
36492 *Wild And Foolish*	20.00 -	30.00
36527 *Alabama Stomp*	15.00 -	20.00
36536 *The Hurricane*	15.00 -	20.00
36557 *Heebie Jeebies*	15.00 -	20.00
36576 *That's No Bargain*	15.00 -	20.00
Pathe-Actuelle 36583 *Tell Me Tonight*	10.00 -	15.00
36593 *You Should See My Tootsie*	10.00 -	15.00
36701 *A Good Man Is Hard To Find*	15.00 -	20.00
36707 *Nothin' Does-Does Like It Used To Do-Do-Do*	15.00 -	20.00
Perfect 14528 *Headin' For Louisville*	15.00 -	20.00
14565 *Fallen Arches*	15.00 -	20.00
14568 *Poor Papa*	10.00 -	15.00
14600 *Hangover*	15.00 -	20.00
14639 *Hi-Diddle-Diddle*	15.00 -	20.00
14673 *Wild And Foolish*	20.00 -	30.00
14708 *Brown Sugar*	15.00 -	20.00
14717 *The Hurricane*	15.00 -	20.00
14738 *Black Bottom Stomp*	15.00 -	20.00
14757 *That's No Bargain*	15.00 -	20.00
14764 *Here Or There*	10.00 -	15.00
14774 *You Should See My Tootsie*	10.00 -	15.00
14882 *Baltimore*	15.00 -	20.00
14888 *Nothin' Does-Does Like It Used To Do-Do-Do*	15.00 -	20.00

RED HOT DOGS:

Banner 6057 *Blame It On The Black Bottom Craze*	7.00 -	10.00
6069 *Swanee's Calling Me*	7.00 -	10.00

RED HOT SYNCOPATORS: (See aslo: ORIGINAL INDIANA FIVE)

Bell 445 *Jackass Blues*	15.00 -	20.00

THE RED HOTTERS:

Silvertone 3526 *St. Louis Blues*	15.00 -	20.00
3527 *Gin Houn' Blues*	15.00 -	20.00
3560 *Third Alley Breakdown*	100.00 -	Up

DON REDMAN & HIS ORCHESTRA:

Titles, issued contemporaneously on Banner,

Conqueror, Melotone, Oriole, Perfect, Romeo;

A Little Bit Later On; Bugle Call Rag' I Gotcha; Lazy Weather; Moonrise On The Lowlands; Too Bad; We Don't Know From Nothin'; Who Wants To Sing My Love Song? ..	10.00 -	15.00
Bluebird 10061 *Down Home Rag*	7.00 -	10.00
10071 *Milenberg Joys*	7.00 -	10.00
10081 *'Deed I Do*	7.00 -	10.00
10095 *Auld Lang Syne*	7.00 -	10.00
10615 *You Ain't Nowhere*	7.00 -	10.00
10765 *Shim-Me-Sha-Wabble*	7.00 -	10.00
Brunswick 6211 *Chant of the Weed*	10.00 -	15.00
6233 *I Heard*	10.00 -	15.00
6273 *How'm I Doin'?*	10.00 -	15.00
6344 *It's A Great World After All*	10.00 -	15.00
6354 *Tea For Two*	10.00 -	15.00
6368 *Hot And Anxious*	10.00 -	15.00
6401 *Ain't I The Lucky One?*	10.00 -	15.00
6412 *Two-Time Man*	10.00 -	15.00
6429 *Nagasaki*	10.00 -	15.00
6517 *Doin' The New Low-Down*	10.00 -	15.00
6520 *Doin' The New Low-Down*	7.00 -	10.00
6523 *How Ya Feelin?*	10.00 -	15.00
6560 *Sophisticated Lady*	10.00 -	15.00
6585 *I Won't Tell*	10.00 -	15.00
6622 *Lazy Bones*	10.00 -	15.00
6684 *I Found A New Way To Go*	10.00 -	15.00
6745 *Got The Jitters*	10.00 -	15.00
6935 *Lonely Cabin*	10.00 -	15.00
Variety 580 *On The Sunny Side Of The Street* ...	10.00 -	15.00
605 *Stormy Weather*	10.00 -	15.00
635 *The Man On The Flying Trapeze*	10.00 -	15.00
Victor 26206 *Jump Session*	5.00 -	8.00
26258 *Igloo*	5.00 -	8.00
26266 *Ain't I Good To You?*	5.00 -	8.00
Vocalion 3354 *Bugle Call Rag*	10.00 -	15.00
3359 *We Don't Know From Nothin'*	10.00 -	15.00
3823 *Exactly Like You*	10.00 -	15.00
3829 *Sweet Sue*	10.00 -	15.00
3836 *The Man On The Flying Trapeze*	10.00 -	15.00

RED ONION JAZZ BABIES:

Gennett 5607 *Terrible Blues*	100.00 -	150.00
5627 *Cake Walking Babies*	100.00 -	150.00
Silvertone 4029 *Cake Walking Babies*	100.00 -	150.00
4032 *Santa Claus Blues*	100.00 -	150.00
5024 *Brotherly Love*	50.00 -	70.00

REUBEN "RIVER" REEVES & HIS RIVER BOYS/TRIBUTARIES:

Vocalion 1292 *River Blues*	150.00 -	200.00
1297 *Bugle Call Blues*	150.00 -	200.00
1407 *Moanin' Low*	150.00 -	200.00
1411 *Texas Special Blues*	150.00 -	200.00
2638 *Screws, Nuts and Bolts*	50.00 -	75.00
2723 *Zuddan*	100.00 -	150.00
15836 *Head Low*	100.00 -	150.00
15839 *Shoo Shoo Boogie Boo*	100.00 -	150.00

REILLY-FARLEY AND THEIR ONYX CLUB BOYS (See Riley-Farley)

LEO REISMAN AND HIS ORCHESTRA:

Columbia 701-D, 776-D, 973-D, 1467-D, 1561-D, .	5.00 -	8.00
Victor L-16005 *Music From The Cat and The Fiddle*	30.00 -	40.00
Victor L-16026, L-16028	30.00 -	40.00
(Above are Long-Playing "Program Transcriptions.")		
Victor 22306 *Puttin' On The Ritz*	7.00 -	10.00
22398 *Happy Feet*	7.00 -	10.00
22433 *Rollin' Down The River*	7.00 -	10.00
Victor 22459, 22537, 22538, 22546, 22605.		
22606, 22647, 22668, 22670, 22696	4.00 -	8.00
Victor 22746 *Without That Gal!*	5.00 -	8.00
22755 *New Sun In The Sky*	5.00 -	8.00

22757 *Without That Gal!* .... 5.00 - 8.00
Victor 22794, 22798 .... 5.00 - 8.00
Victor 22836 *White Heat* .... 7.00 - 10.00
Victor 22839, 22849 .... 4.00 - 8.00
Victor 22851 *Bend Down, Sister* .... 8.00 - 12.00
Victor 22869, 22870, 22904, 22912, 22913,
  22914, 22915, 22927, 22954, 22961 ... 4.00 - 8.00
Victor 24011 *If It Ain't Love* .... 7.00 - 10.00
Victor 24029, 24044, 24047 .... 5.00 - 8.00
Victor 24048 *Got The South In My Soul* .... 7.00 - 10.00
Victor 24126, 24131, 24132, 24156 .... 5.00 - 8.00
Victor 24157 *A Rainy Day* .... 7.00 - 10.00
  24193 *I've Got You On My Mind* .... 8.00 - 12.00
Victor 24192, 24259, 24262, 24269 .... 5.00 - 8.00
Victor 24312 *My Temptation* .... 7.00 - 10.00
  24315 *Happy Is The Day Is Long* .... 8.00 - 12.00
Victor 24358 *Smoke Rings* .... 8.00 - 12.00
Victor 24398, 24399, 24407 .... 5.00 - 8.00
Victor 24418 *Easter Parade* .... 7.00 - 10.00
  24419 *Savage Serenade* .... 7.00 - 10.00
  24428 *Not For All the Rice In China* .... 7.00 - 10.00
Victor 24429, 24448 .... 4.00 - 7.00

HENRY "KID" RENA'S JAZZ BAND:
Delta 800, 801, 802, 803, 804, 805, 806, 807 .... 7.00 - 10.00

JACQUES RENARD AND HIS ORCHESTRA:
Brunswick 4918 *Lucky Seven* .... 5.00 - 8.00
  4919 *Can This Be Love?* .... 5.00 - 8.00
  4939 *Three Little Words* .... 5.00 - 8.00
  4940 *Readin' 'Ritin,' Rhythm* .... 5.00 - 8.00
Brunswick, most other issues .... 3.00 - 5.00
Columbia 3086-D, 3090-D .... 5.00 - 10.00
Victor 20728 *Just Call On Me* .... 5.00 - 8.00

DUNK RENDLEMAN & THE ALABAMIANS;
RENDLEMAN'S DANCE ORCHESTRA:
Gennett 6233 *Hot Heels* ....100.00 - 150.00
  6322 *Mean Dog Blues* ....150.00 - 150.00
Silvertone 5052 *Hot Heels* .... 90.00 - 130.00

HARRY RESER'S JUMPING JACKS/
ROUNDERS/SYNCOPATORS; HARRY
RESER AND HIS ORCHESTRA:
Banner 6052 *I Ain't That Kind Of A Baby* ...... 5.00 - 8.00
Brunswick 2308 *Pickin's* .... 5.00 - 8.00
Columbia 454-D *Sweet Man* .... 5.00 - 8.00
Columbia 510-0 *Fond Of You* .... 5.00 - 8.00
Columbia 594-D *Behind The Clouds* .... 5.00 - 8.00
Columbia 604-D *Love Bound* .... 5.00 - 8.00
Columbia 678-D *Just a Little Dance* .... 5.00 - 8.00
Columbia 708-D *Who Wouldn't?* .... 5.00 - 8.00
Columbia 725-D *Wasn't It Nice?* .... 5.00 - 8.00
Columbia 774-D *Susie's "Feller"* .... 5.00 - 8.00
Columbia 803-D *Fire!* .... 5.00 - 8.00
Columbia 853-D *"Je t'aime"- Means "I Love
  You"* .... 5.00 - 8.00
Columbia 857-D *Where's That Rainbow?* .... 5.00 - 8.00
Columbia 907-D *I Wonder How I Look When
  I'm Asleep* .... 5.00 - 8.00
Columbia 981-D *(What Do I Care What)
  Somebody Said* .... 5.00 - 8.00
Columbia 1087-D *Meet Me in the Moonlight* .... 5.00 - 8.00
Columbia 1109-D *Shaking The Blues Away* ..... 7.00 - 10.00
Columbia 1244-D *I Scream-You Scream- We All
  Scream for Ice Cream* .... 7.00 - 10.00
Columbia 1378-D *Crazy Rhythm* .... 7.00 - 10.00
Columbia 1524-D *What a Night For Spooning* ... 7.00 - 10.00
Columbia 1696-D *Don't Be Like That* .... 7.00 - 10.00
Columbia 1761-D *Kansas City Kitty* .... 7.00 - 10.00
Columbia 1806-D *I Got a "Code" in My
  "Doze"* .... 7.00 - 10.00
Columbia 1835-D *Here Comes The Show Boat* .. 7.00 - 10.00
Columbia 1884-D *The Flippity Flop* .... 7.00 - 10.00
Columbia 1973-D *Piccolo Pete* .... 7.00 - 10.00
Columbia 2818-D *I Want To Ring Bells* .... 7.00 - 10.00

Columbia 2833-D *When You Were the Girl on
  the Scooter* .... 7.00 - 10.00
Columbia 2840-D *My Galveston Gal* .... 7.00 - 10.00
Columbia *(Most other issues)* .... 4.00 - 7.00
Edison 14032 *I'm Still Caring* .... 15.00 - 20.00
Edison 52034 *Hello Cutie* .... 10.00 - 15.00
Edison 52184 *Highways Are Happy Ways* ...... 10.00 - 15.00
  52282 *Hey! Hey! Hazel* .... 10.00 - 15.00
  52525 *That's The Good Old Sunny South* ... 15.00 - 20.00
Okeh 4452 *Everybody Step* .... 7.00 - 10.00
Variety 510 *Top Of The Town* .... 7.00 - 10.00
  588 *Hook And Ladder 31* .... 7.00 - 10.00

FRANKIE REYNOLDS AND HIS
ORCHESTRA:
Bluebird 7137 *Chicken On The Apple* .... 5.00 - 8.00
  7241 *Lady, Be Good* .... 7.00 - 10.00

LEW REYNOLDS FLEXO RECORDING
ORCHESTRA:
Flexo 123 *At Last I'm Happy* .... 20.00 - 40.00
  124 *You're Driving Me Crazy* .... 20.00 - 40.00
  125 *To Whom It May Concern* .... 20.00 - 40.00
  128 *What A Fool I've Been* .... 20.00 - 40.00
  133 *Casey Jones* .... 20.00 - 40.00
  134 *I Surrender Dear* .... 20.00 - 40.00
  138 *Ho Hum!* .... 20.00 - 40.00

LYST REYNOLDS' LOGOLA ORCHESTRA:
Gennett 6235 *What Do We Do On a Dew-Dew
  Dewy Day* .... 30.00 - 50.00
  6263 *Barbara* .... 30.00 - 50.00

ROSS REYNOLDS & HIS PALAIS GARDENS
ORCHESTRA:
Gennett 5611 *Creole* .... 15.00 - 20.00

THE RHYTHM ACES:
Brunswick 4244 *Jazz Battle* .... 75.00 - 100.00
  7120 *I Got The Stinger* .... 80.00 - 120.00

THE RHYTHMAKERS:
Titles, issued contemporaneously on Banner,
  Melotone, Oriole; *I Would Do Anything For
  You; Mean Old Bed Bug Blues; Yellow Dog
  Blues; Yes, Suh!* .... 20.00 - 30.00

THE RHYTHM KINGS:
Victor 23279 *You Rascal, You* .... 40.00 - 60.00
  23283 *Please Tell Me* .... 40.00 - 60.00

THE RHYTHM MAKERS:
Vocalion 15763 *Wabash Blues* .... 75.00 - 100.00

THE RHYTHM WRECKERS:
Vocalion 3341 *Sugar Blues* .... 5.00 - 8.00
  3390 *Wabash Blues* .... 5.00 - 8.00
  3523 *Twelfth Street Rag* .... 5.00 - 8.00
  3566 *St. Louis Blues* .... 5.00 - 8.00
  3608 *September In The Rain* .... 5.00 - 8.00
  3642 *Desert Blues* .... 5.00 - 8.00
  3670 *Blue Yodel No. 3* .... 5.00 - 8.00

RIALTO DANCE ORCHESTRA:
Domino 356 *I Can't Get The One I Want* .... 7.00 - 10.00
  416 *Copenhagen* .... 10.00 - 15.00

FRED/FREDDIE RICH AND HIS (LA
PALINA/RADIO/TIMES SQUARE)
ORCHESTRA:
Banner 0508 *Sweetheart, We Need Each Other* .. 7.00 - 10.00
  0804 *I've Got A Yen For You* .... 10.00 - 15.00
  0806 *Good Evenin'* .... 5.00 - 8.00
  0835 *Sing Something Simple* .... 5.00 - 8.00
  6360 *I Get The Blues When It Rains* .... 8.00 - 12.00
  6477 *Sweetness* .... 5.00 - 8.00
  6503 *Little By Little* .... 5.00 - 8.00
  6508 *Piccolo Pete* .... 5.00 - 8.00
  6512 *Wouldn't It Be Wonderful?* .... 5.00 - 8.00
Cameo 0108 *Sweetheart, We Need Each Other* ... 7.00 - 10.00
  0435 *Sing Something Simple* .... 5.00 - 8.00
  872 *Shake That Thing* .... 7.00 - 10.00
  938 *Betty* .... 5.00 - 8.00

1019 *I Can't Get Over A Girl Like You*	5.00	-	8.00
9183 *To Be In Love*	7.00	-	10.00
9194 *Kids Again*	7.00	-	10.00
9203 *Now I'm In Love*	20.00	-	30.00
9229 *Sweetness*	5.00	-	8.00
9233 *Piccolo Pete*	5.00	-	8.00
9265 *Little By Little*	5.00	-	8.00
9300 *Singin' In The Rain*	5.00	-	8.00
9320 *How Am I To Know*	10.00	-	15.00
Columbia 1838-D *Singin' In The Rain*	7.00	-	10.00
1893-D *Don't Hang Your Dreams on a Rainbow*	7.00	-	10.00
1924-D *Wishing And Waiting For Love*	7.00	-	10.00
1965-D *Revolutionary Rhythm*	8.00	-	12.00
1979-D *I Don't Want Your Kisses*	7.00	-	10.00
2043-D *Dixie Jamboree*	10.00	-	15.00
2132-D *Strike Up The Band!*	8.00	-	12.00
2299-D *Sing Something Simple*	8.00	-	12.00
2328-D *I Got Rhythm*	10.00	-	15.00
2387-D *Tie A Little String Around Your Finger*	10.00	-	15.00
2484-D *Pardon Me Pretty Baby*	10.00	-	15.00
2536-D *As Time Goes By*	8.00	-	12.00
Columbia 2534-D, 2751-D, 2752-D, 2868-D, 2872-D	5.00	-	10.00
Columbia 3613-X *Don't Hang Your Dreams on a Rainbow*	10.00	-	20.00

(Note: No. 3613-X is part of a Spanish series having green labels and utilizing instrumental versions of songs which, for U.S. market, have vocal choruses. See Columbia 1893-D.)

Gennett 6001 *Don't Take That Black Bottom Away*	10.00	-	15.00
6015 *I Love To Baby You*	8.00	-	12.00
6016 *Sweeter Than You*	8.00	-	12.00
6133 *I'm On My Merry Way*	8.00	-	12.00
6151 *Ask Me Another*	8.00	-	12.00
6159 *I Adore you*	8.00	-	12.00
Harmony 37-H *You Told Me To Go*	7.00	-	10.00
38-H *Feelin' Kind O'Blue*	5.00	-	8.00
57-H *I Would Be Where I Am If You Hadn't Gone Away*	7.00	-	10.00
64-H *I'm Sitting On Top Of The World*	7.00	-	10.00
90-H *Someone's Stolen My Sweet, Sweet Baby*	5.00	-	8.00
119-H *Bell Hoppin' Blues*	8.00	-	12.00
136-H *Could I? I Certainly Could*	7.00	-	10.00
Hit of-the-Week J-4 *Little Girl*	7.00	-	10.00
K-1 *It's The Girl*	7.00	-	10.00
Okeh 41489 *When I Take My Sugar To Tea*	10.00	-	15.00
Pathe Actuelle 36389, 36394, 36401	5.00	-	8.00
36452 *Up And At 'Em*	7.00	-	10.00
Perfect 14570, 14575, 14582	5.00	-	8.00
14633 *Up And At 'Em*	7.00	-	10.00
Regal 8761 *I Get The Blues When It Rains*	5.00	-	8.00
10113 *I've Got A Yen For You*	10.00	-	15.00
Romeo 968 *When My Dreams Come True*	5.00	-	8.00
1109 *Singin' In the Rain*	5.00	-	8.00
Vocalion 5420 *How High The Moon*	7.00	-	10.00
5507 *I'm Forever Blowing Bubbles*	7.00	-	10.00

CHUCK RICHARDS:

Vocalion 2877 *Blue Interlude*	10.00	-	15.00

PETE RICHARDS & HIS ORCHESTRA:

Champion 15402 *Bugs*	125.00	-	175.00
15455 *Michigan Stomp*	125.00	-	175.00

VINCENT RICHARDS & HIS ORCHESTRA:

Cameo 9024 *That's When I'll Stop Loving You*	5.00	-	8.00
Cameo 9072 *Weary River*	5.00	-	8.00
Cameo 9086 *Broadway Melody*	5.00	-	8.00
Cameo 9101 *You Were Meant For Me*	7.00	-	10.00
Cameo 9184 *My Different Kind Of Baby*	5.00	-	8.00
Cameo 9199 *Tell Me You're My Pretty Baby*	5.00	-	8.00
Romeo 849 *I'd Rather Be Blue Over You*	7.00	-	10.00

DICK RICHARDSON & HIS BAND/ ORCHESTRA:

Parlophone PNY-34091 *Dancing With Tears In My Eyes*	25.00	-	35.00
PNY-34092 *Promises*	25.00	-	35.00
PNY-34129 *Out Of Breath*	25.00	-	35.00
PNY-34130 *I Am Only Human After All*	25.00	-	35.00

INEZ RICHARDSON:

Black Swan 2023 *My June Love*	30.00	-	40.00

BUD RICHIE & HIS BOYS:

Champion 16109 *Slappin' The Bass*	50.00	-	75.00
Champion 40010 *Rockin' Chair*	15.00	-	20.00

HARRY RICHMAN:

Banner 1510 *No Hot Water*	7.00	-	10.00
Brunswick 4677 *Puttin' On The Ritz*	7.00	-	10.00
Brunswick (most other issues)	4.00	-	7.00
Columbia 2701-D *I Love A Parade*	8.00	-	12.00
Columbia 2965-D *When Love Comes Swinging Along*	8.00	-	12.00
Columbia 2995-D *June In January*	8.00	-	12.00
Columbia 3017-D *According To The Moonlight*	8.00	-	12.00
Decca 700 *Let's Go*	10.00	-	15.00
Decca 701 *There'll Be No South*	10.00	-	15.00
Vocalion 15457 *Susie's "Feller"*	5.00	-	8.00
Vocalion 15511 *Blue Skies*	5.00	-	8.00
Vocalion 15540 *Moonbeam, Kiss Her For Me*	5.00	-	8.00
Vocalion 15560 *Rosy Cheeks*	5.00	-	8.00
Vocalion 15725 *Out Of The Dawn*	10.00	-	15.00

BOB RICKETTS' BAND:

Gennett 5156 *Mean Mean Mama*	8.00	-	12.00

THE RIFFERS:

Columbia 14677-D *Rhapsody In Love*	30.00	-	40.00

MIKE RILEY, EDDIE FARLEY & THEIR ONYX CLUB BOYS:

Decca 578 *The Music Goes 'Round and 'Round*	5.00	-	8.00
619 *I Never Knew*	7.00	-	10.00
641 *Blue Clarinet Stomp*	7.00	-	10.00
683 *I'm Gonna Clap My Hands*	7.00	-	10.00
684 *I Wish I Were Aladdin*	7.00	-	10.00
994 *Trouble Don't Like Music*	7.00	-	10.00
1031 *Jingle Bells*	5.00	-	8.00
1041 *With Thee I Swing*	7.00	-	10.00
1263 *I'm Hatin' This Waitin' Around*	7.00	-	10.00
1271 *That's Southern Hospitality*	7.00	-	10.00
655, 1662	5.00	-	8.00

JUSTIN RING & HIS OKEH ORCHESTRA:

Okeh 40869, 40904, 40972	5.00	-	10.00
41295 *True Blue Lou*	10.00	-	15.00

JOHNNY RINGER'S ROSEMONT ORCHESTRA:

Gennett 6183 *Buffalo Rhythm*	50.00	-	75.00
6199 *Swamp Blues*	50.00	-	75.00
6264 *Moonlit Waters*	30.00	-	40.00
6280 *The Varsity Drag*	30.00	-	40.00

VINCENT RIZZO AND HIS HOTEL SYLVANIA ORCHESTRA OF PHILA.:

Okeh 40130, 40135	5.00	-	8.00
Okeh 40725 *Clap Yo' Hands*	7.00	-	10.00

ROANE'S PENNSYLVANIANS:

Victor 22919 *Chinatown, My Chinatown*	8.00	-	12.00
22922 *Between The Devil and The Deep Blue Sea*	8.00	-	12.00
24036 *Goodbye Blues*	10.00	-	15.00

EVERETT ROBBINS & HIS SYNCOPATING ROBBINS:

Autograph (unnumbered) *You Didn't Want Me*	-		

JOESPH ROBECHAUX & HIS NEW ORLEANS RHYTHM BOYS:

Vocalion 2539 *King Kong Stomp*	15.00	-	25.00
2540 *Lazy Bones*	15.00	-	25.00
2545 *Jig Music*	15.00	-	25.00
2575 *Ring Dem Bells*	15.00	-	25.00
2592 *Shake It And Break It*	15.00	-	25.00
2610 *Why Should I Cry For You?*	15.00	-	25.00

2646 *Zola*	15.00	-	25.00
2796 *Foot Scuffle*	15.00	-	25.00
2827 *Every Tub*	15.00	-	25.00
2881 *Just Like A Falling Star*	15.00	-	25.00

ORLANDO ROBERSON:

Variety 513 *Just A Quiet Evening*	8.00	-	12.00

CLIFF ROBERTS' (DANCE) ORCHESTRA:

Cameo 9020 *That's How I Feel About You, Sweetheart*	5.00	-	8.00
Cameo 9032 *The Sun Is At My Window*	10.00	-	15.00
Cameo 9127 *My Sin*	5.00	-	8.00
Cameo 9165 *I've Got A Feeling I'm Falling*	5.00	-	8.00
Cameo 9201 *Big City Blues*	5.00	-	8.00
Regal 10117 *Rough House Rosie*	7.00	-	10.00
Romeo 1003 *Big City Blues*	5.00	-	8.00

DICK ROBERTSON (& HIS ORCHESTRA):

Brunswick 4367 *Some Sweet Day*	10.00	-	15.00
Champion 40077 *Moon Over Miami*	8.00	-	12.00
40078 *With All My Heart*	8.00	-	12.00
40087 *Lights Out*	8.00	-	12.00
40088 *Alone*	8.00	-	12.00
40092 *But Where Are You?*	8.00	-	12.00
40093 *I'd Rather Lead A Band*	8.00	-	12.00
40104 *Welcome Stranger*	8.00	-	12.00
40105 *Is It True What They Say About Dixie?*	8.00	-	12.00
40106 *The Touch Of Your Lips*	8.00	-	12.00
40111 *Robins and Roses*	8.00	-	12.00
40116 *The Glory Of Love*	8.00	-	12.00
40117 *She Shall Have Music*	8.00	-	12.00
40118 *On The Beach At Bali Bali*	8.00	-	12.00
Crown 3306 *Minnie The Moocher*	10.00	-	15.00
Crown 3427, 3428, 3438, 3440, 3491	5.00	-	10.00
Decca 1125, 1131, 1169, 1181, 1209, 1215, 1260, 1283, 1334, 1335, 1367, 1374, 1407, 1415, 1436, 1487, 1498, 1511, 1512, 1536, 1585, 1599, 1601, 1619, 1620	4.00	-	6.00
Decca, most other issues (blue label)	4.00	-	6.00
Edison 52194, 52379, 52473, 52551	10.00	-	15.00
Melotone 12082 *Would You Like To Take A Walk?*	8.00	-	12.00
12162 *Moonlight Saving Time*	8.00	-	12.00
12163 *I Wanna Sing About You*	8.00	-	12.00
12408 *Holding My Honey's Hand*	8.00	-	12.00
12417 *West Bound Freight*	10.00	-	15.00
12418 *Bull Fiddle Blues*	10.00	-	15.00

ROBINSON'S KNIGHTS OF REST:

Champion 16607 *Mean Baby Blues*	150.00	-	200.00

BILL ROBINSON:

Brunswick 4535, 6134, 6520	5.00	-	10.00

BOB ROBINSON & HIS BOB CATS; BOB ROBINSON TRIO:

Bluebird 6929, 7898	10.00	-	15.00
Crying For Love, issued contemporaneously on Banner, Melotone, Oriole, Perfect, Romeo, Vocalion	10.00	-	15.00

ELZADIE ROBINSON:

Paramount 12417 *Barrel House Man*	80.00	-	120.00
12420 *Houston Bound*	100.00	-	150.00
12469 *Baltimore Blues*	80.00	-	120.00
12509 *Whiskey Blues*	80.00	-	120.00
12544 *Tick-Tock Blues*	80.00	-	120.00
12573 *St. Louis Cyclone Blues*	80.00	-	120.00
12627 *Love Crazy Blues*	80.00	-	120.00
12635 *Elzadie's Policy Blues*	150.00	-	200.00
12676 *Mad Blues*	100.00	-	150.00
12689 *Wicked Daddy*	80.00	-	120.00
12701 *Arkansas Mill Blues*	100.00	-	150.00
12724 *Rowdy Man Blues*	100.00	-	150.00
Paramount 12745 *Unsatisfied Blues*	80.00	-	120.00
12768 *Cheatin' Daddy*	80.00	-	120.00
12795 *My Pullman Porter Man*	80.00	-	120.00
12900 *Driving Me South*	80.00	-	120.00

("BANJO") IKEY ROBINSON & HIS (BULL

FIDDLE) BAND/WINDY CITY FIVE:

Brunswick 4963 *Got Butter On It*	75.00	-	125.00
4964 *Rock Me Mama*	75.00	-	125.00
7052 *Rock Pile Blues*	75.00	-	125.00
7057 *Got Butter On It*	75.00	-	125.00
7059 *Rock Me Mama*	75.00	-	125.00
7068 *Without A Dime*	75.00	-	125.00
Champion 40011 *Swing It*	20.00	-	30.00
50073 *Sunshine*	20.00	-	30.00
Decca 7430 *Scrunch-Lo*	15.00	-	20.00
7650 *Sunshine*	15.00	-	20.00

ROB ROBINSON (AND MEADE LUX LEWIS):

Paramount 13028 *I Got Some Of That*	150.00	-	200.00
13030 *Don't Put That Thing*	150.00	-	200.00
13064 *I Don't Want It Now*	150.00	-	200.00

CARSON ROBISON'S KANSAS CITY JACKRABBITS/MADCAPS; THE CARSON ROBISON ORCHESTRA:

Edison (thin) 14085 *Nonsense*	20.00	-	30.00
Okeh 41389 *Nothin'*	10.00	-	15.00
Victor V38074 *Nonsense*	35.00	-	50.00

WILLARD ROBISON & HIS ORCHESTRA; WILLARD ROBISON'S DEEP RIVER FOUR:

Autograph 600 *The Rhythm Rag*	75.00	-	100.00
Pathe-Actuelle 36723, 36744, 36757, 36766, 36783, 36785, 36796	8.00	-	12.00
36724 *I'm More Than Satisfied*	75.00	-	100.00
Perfect 14904, 14925, 14938, 14942, 14963, 14966, 14977	8.00	-	12.00
14905 *I'm More Than Satisfied*	75.00	-	100.00

TOM ROCK & HIS ORCHESTRA:

Odeon ONY-36157 *I'll Be Blue, Just Thinking Of You*	20.00	-	30.00
ONY-36158 *A Peach Of A Pair*	20.00	-	30.00
ONY-36159 *My Love For You*	20.00	-	30.00
ONY-36164 *The Little Things In Life*	20.00	-	30.00
ONY-36179 *Would You Like To Take A Walk?*	20.00	-	30.00

ROCKY MOUNTAIN TRIO:

Gennett 3002 *Freakish Blues*	10.00	-	15.00
Gennett 3184 *Grand Opera Blues*	10.00	-	15.00
3288 *Blowin' Off Steam*	10.00	-	15.00

GENE RODEMICH & HIS ORCHESTRA:

Brunswick 2474 *Wicki Wacki Woo*	5.00	-	8.00
Brunswick 2480 *St. Louis Tickle*	5.00	-	8.00
Brunswick 2527 *Blue Grass Blues*	5.00	-	8.00
Brunswick 2558 *St. Louis Gal*	5.00	-	8.00
Brunswick 2599 *Tenth Interval Rag*	7.00	-	10.00
Brunswick 2616 *Eileen*	5.00	-	8.00
Brunswick 2731 *Worryin' Blues*	5.00	-	8.00
Brunswick 2760 *Shanghai Shuffle*	5.00	-	8.00
Brunswick 2843 *Everybody Loves My Baby*	5.00	-	8.00
Brunswick 2892 *Isn't She The Sweetest Thing?*	5.00	-	8.00
Brunswick 3073 *Hot Notes*	5.00	-	8.00
Brunswick (most other issues)	2.00	-	5.00

IKE RODGERS (& HIS BIDDLE STREET BOYS):

Broadway 5081 *It Hurts So Good*	150.00	-	200.00
7086 *Malt Can Blues*	150.00	-	200.00
Paramount 12816 *It Hurts So Good*	150.00	-	200.00

GIL RODIN & HIS ORCHESTRA; GIL RODIN'S BOYS:

Titles, issued contemporaneously on Banner,
Conqueror, Melotone, Oriole, Perfect, Romeo;
*Love's Serenade; Restless; Right About Face;
What's The Reason* .... 7.00 - 10.00
It's So Good, on Banner, Conqueror, Domino,
Regal .... 8.00 - 12.00
Crown 3016 *If I Could Be With You One Hour
Tonight* .... 30.00 - 50.00
    3017 *Beale Street Blues* .... 30.00 - 50.00
    3045 *Ninety-Nine Out Of a Hundred Wanna
Be Loved* .... 15.00 - 20.00
    3046 *Hello, Beautiful*.................. 25.00 - 40.00

BUDDY ROGERS (AND HIS CALIFORNIA CAVLIERS); CHARLES "BUDDY" ROGERS:
Columbia 2143-D *Sweepin' The Clouds Away* ... 8.00 - 12.00
    2183-D *My Future Just Passed*............. 8.00 - 12.00
Victor 24001, 24015, 24031, 24049 .... 7.00 - 10.00

GINGER ROGERS:
Bluebird 7981 *I Used To Be Color Blind*........ 10.00 - 15.00
Decca 638 *Eeny, Meeny, Miney Mo* .... 7.00 - 10.00

MACK ROGERS & HIS GUNTER HOTEL ORCHESTRA:
Bluebird 5603 *Casa Loma Stomp* .... 10.00 - 15.00
    5635 *Here Comes The Show Boat* .... 10.00 - 15.00
Bluebird (other issues) .... 4.00 - 8.00

RODNEY ROGERS RED PEPPERS:
Brunswick 3744 *Milenberg Joys* .... 7.00 - 10.00

WILL ROGERS:
Victor 45347, 45369, 45374 .... 5.00 - 10.00

B.A. ROLFE & HIS LUCKY STRIKE DANCE/ PALAIS D'OR ORCHESTRA:
Edison 14003 *Fioretta* .... 15.00 - 20.00
Edison 14006 *Mean To Me* .... 15.00 - 20.00
Edison 14012 *Am I Blue?* .... 15.00 - 20.00
Edison 14020 *Spanish Doll* .... 15.00 - 20.00
Edison 14033 *The Flippity Flop* .... 15.00 - 20.00
Edison 14048 *Why Can't You?* .... 15.00 - 20.00
Edison 14049 *Do What You Do!* .... 15.00 - 20.00
Edison 14050 *Little Pal* .... 15.00 - 20.00
Edison 14059 *Wouldn't It Be Wonderful?* ...... 15.00 - 25.00
Edison 14068 *Won't You Give In?* .... 15.00 - 25.00
(Note: Foregoing are the "thin," "Needle Type
Electric" Edison records.)
Edison 51750 *What Good Is Good Morning?* .... 7.00 - 10.00
Edison 51757 *Bye Bye Blackbird* .... 7.00 - 10.00
Edison 51761 *Blue Bonnet—You Make Me Feel
Blue* .... 7.00 - 10.00
Edison 51772 *Roses Remind Me Of You* .... 7.00 - 10.00
Edison 51782 *Only You And Lonely Me* .... 7.00 - 10.00
Edison 51790 *Crazy Quilt* .... 8.00 - 12.00
Edison 51797 *Wondering Why* .... 15.00 - 20.00
Edison 51799 *Barcelona* .... 15.00 - 20.00
Edison 51810 *And Then I Forget* .... 7.00 - 10.00
Edison 51814 *Ain't We Carryin' On?* .... 15.00 - 20.00
Edison 51817 *The One I'm Looking For* .... 7.00 - 10.00
Edison 51821 *Oo-gle Oo-gle—Ee* .... 7.00 - 10.00
Edison 51828 *Trudy* .... 7.00 - 10.00
Edison 51829 *Who Are You Vamping Tonight?* ... 15.00 - 20.00
Edison 51840 *Zoubeeda*.................. 7.00 - 10.00
Edison 51848 *Why Do Ya Roll Those Eyes?* ..... 15.00 - 20.00
Edison 51866 *Chinese Moon* .... 7.00 - 10.00
Edison 51872 *Stars (Are The Windows of Heaven)* 7.00 - 10.00
Edison 51888 *No One But You Knows How To
Love* .... 10.00 - 15.00
Edison 51890 *My Baby's Back* .... 15.00 - 20.00
Edison 51925 *One Alone* .... 7.00 - 10.00
Edison 51954 *It's O.K., Katy, With Me* .... 7.00 - 10.00
Edison 51972 *You're The One For Me* .... 7.00 - 10.00
Edison 52002 *There's Everything Nice About You* 7.00 - 10.00
Edison 52013 *Some Other Day* .... 7.00 - 10.00
Edison 52015 *Oh! Isabella* .... 7.00 - 10.00
Edison 52037 *Buffalo Rhythm* .... 15.00 - 20.00

Edison 52047 *Sax Appeal* .... 10.00 - 15.00
Edison 52049 *Magnolia* .... 10.00 - 15.00
Edison 52057 *Gonna Get A Girl* .... 15.00 - 20.00
Edison 52059 *S-L-U-E-F-O-O-T* .... 20.00 - 30.00
Edison 52094 *It Was Only a Sun Shower* ...... 7.00 - 10.00
Edison 52105 *A Siren Dream* .... 20.00 - 30.00
Edison 52107 *Just A Memory* .... 7.00 - 10.00
Edison 52124 *Wherever You Are* .... 7.00 - 10.00
Edison 52130 *Playground In The Sky* .... 7.00 - 10.00
Edison 52132 *Down South* .... 7.00 - 10.00
Edison 52155 *Among My Souvenirs* .... 7.00 - 10.00
    52166 *Singapore Sorrows* .... 10.00 - 15.00
    52168 *When The Robert E. Lee Comes To Town* 10.00 - 15.00
    52202 *Maybe I'll Baby You* .... 8.00 - 12.00
    52210 *My Heart Stood Still* .... 10.00 - 15.00
    52223 *Can't Help Lovin' Dat Man* ...... 10.00 - 15.00
Edison 52239 *My Blue Ridge Mountain Home*... 10.00 - 15.00
Edison 52244 *Louisiana Bo Bo* .... 15.00 - 20.00
Edison 52261 *What'll I Do If The Mississippi
Goes Dry?* .... 10.00 - 15.00
Edison 52268 *Hiding in the Corner of Your Smile* 10.00 - 15.00
Edison 52295 *St. Louis Blues* .... 15.00 - 20.00
Edison 52300 *She Didn't Say "Yes," She Didn't
Say "No,"* .... 10.00 - 15.00
Edison 52319 *Deep Hollow* .... 15.00 - 20.00
Edison 52321 *Tomorrow* .... 20.00 - 30.00
Edison 52326 *When Sweet Susie Goes Steppin'
By* .... 10.00 - 15.00
Edison 52342 *Georgie Porgie* .... 10.00 - 15.00
Edison 52343 *That's My Weakness Now* ...... 10.00 - 15.00
Edison 52353 *No Parking* .... 15.00 - 20.00
Edison 52366 *Pell Street Bells* .... 7.00 - 10.00
Edison 52402 *It Must Be Love* .... 10.00 - 15.00
Edison 52424 *Where Were You— Where Was I?* .. 10.00 - 15.00
Edison 52455 *Blue Night* .... 10.00 - 15.00
Edison 52462 *A Room With A View* .... 10.00 - 15.00
Edison 52474 *Makin' Whoopee* .... 15.00 - 20.00
Edison 52480 *A Love Tale of Alsace-Lorraine* ... 10.00 - 15.00
Edison 52505 *Let's Do It* .... 10.00 - 15.00
Edison 52515 *I'll Get By* .... 10.00 - 15.00
Edison 52531 *If I Had You* .... 10.00 - 15.00
Edison 52548 *Hello Sweetie* .... 10.00 - 15.00
Edison 52584 *Mean To Me* .... 10.00 - 15.00
Edison 52597 *Spanish Doll* .... 10.00 - 15.00
Edison 52604 *Birmingham Bertha* .... 10.00 - 15.00
Edison 52626 *Singin' In The Rain* .... 10.00 - 15.00
Edison 52640 *Liza (All The Clouds'll Roll Away)* 10.00 - 15.00
Edison 52645 *Why Can't You?* .... 10.00 - 15.00

THE ROLLICKERS:
Edison 52600 *Lonely Little Cinderella* .... 15.00 - 20.00

ADRIAN ROLLINI & HIS ORCHESTRA:
Titles, issued contemporaneously on Banner,
Conqueror, Melotone, Oriole, Perfect, Romeo;
*Ah! But Is It Love?; And So, Goodbye; Beloved;
By A Waterfall; Coffee In The Morning and
Kisses In The Night; Dream On; Got The
Jitters; Have You Ever Been Lonely?; Hustlin'
And Bustlin' For Baby; If I Had Somebody To
Love; I Gotta Get Up and Go To Work; I'll Be
Faithful; I Raised My Hat; Ol' Pappy; On The
Wrong Side Of The Fence; Savage Serenade;
Sittin' On A Backyard Fence; Sittin' On A Log;
Song of Surrender; Sweet Madness; Who Walks
In When I Walk Out?; You Must Believe Me;
You've Got Everything; You've Got Me Cryin'
Again* .... 8.00 - 15.00
Decca 265 *Sugar* .... 8.00 - 12.00
    359 *Davenport Blues* .... 8.00 - 12.00
Master 114 *Slap That Bass* .... 10.00 - 15.00
Vocalion 2672 *Butterfingers* .... 10.00 - 15.00
    2673 *Waitin' At The Gate For Katy* .... 10.00 - 15.00
    2675 *A Hundred Years From Today* .... 10.00 - 15.00

TODD ROLLINS AND HIS ORCHESTRA:
Titles, issued contemporaneously on Banner, Melotone, Oriole, Perfect, Romeo; *The Boogie Man; Christmas Night In Harlem; Fare Thee Well To Harlem; Get Goin'; Jimmy Had A Nickel; Jungle Fever; Junk Man; Moon Country; Take A Lesson From The Lark* ...... 7.00 - 12.00
Romeo 2222 *Let's Go Places and Do Things* .... 15.00 - 20.00

ROMANCE OF HARMONY ORCHESTRA:
Gennett 20068 *Blue Evening Blues* .... 15.00 - 20.00

PHIL ROMANO AND HIS ORCHESTRA:
Victor 19803 *I'm Goin' Out If Lizzie Comes In* .. 7.00 - 10.00

THEODORE ROOSEVELT:
Victor 31872 *The Liberty of the People* (12-inch, one-sided) .... 8.00 - 12.00
35249 (12-inch) *Abyssinian Treatment* .... 5.00 - 10.00
Victor 35250 (12-inch) *The Farmer And The Business Man* .... 5.00 - 10.00

DAVID ROSE & HIS ORCHESTRA:
Bluebird 5708 *Jig-Saw Rhythm* .... 10.00 - 15.00

VINCENT ROSE & HIS ORCHESTRA:
Titles, issued contemporaneously on Banner, Conqueror, Melotone, Oriole, Perfect, Romeo: *Learning; Stars Fell On Alabama* .... 10.00 - 15.00
Additional titles; *My Dog Loves Your Dog; Nasty Man' Without That Gal* .... 8.00 - 12.00
Victor 19379 *String Beans* .... 5.00 - 8.00
19398 *Helen Gone* .... 5.00 - 8.00
19511 *Sadie (You Are The Lady For Me)* ...... 7.00 - 10.00
19513 *Montmartre* .... 15.00 - 25.00
19515 *Since You've Been Gone* .... 5.00 - 8.00

ROSELAND DANCE ORCHESTRA:
Ajax 17119 *Where's My Sweetie Hiding?* .... 10.00 - 15.00
Banner 6129 *There's A Rickety Rackety Shack* ... 8.00 - 12.00
6154 *Sorry* .... 8.00 - 12.00
Domino 3441 *Araby* .... 8.00 - 12.00
3445 *I'll See You In My Dreams* .... 10.00 - 15.00

TIMME ROSENKRANTZ & HIS BARRELHOUSE BARONS:
Victor 25876, 25883 .... 5.00 - 10.00

HARRY ROSENTHAL & HIS ORCHESTRA:
Columbia 2982-D *Say When* .... 15.00 - 20.00
2986-D *You're The Top* .... 15.00 - 20.00
3016-D *The Hunkadola* .... 8.00 - 12.00
3019-D *My Heart Is An Open Book* .... 8.00 - 12.00

ROSE ROOM ORCHESTRA:
Banner 6202 *How About Me?* .... 5.00 - 8.00
6205 *Glorianna* .... 10.00 - 15.00
6206 *It Must Be Love* .... 10.00 - 15.00
6268 *Glad Rag Doll* .... 5.00 - 8.00
Banner 6317 *I Want To Be Bad* .... 5.00 - 8.00
Banner 6354 *Get Yourself a Sweetie and Kiss Your Troubles* .... 5.00 - 8.00
Banner 6381 *I've Got a Feeling I'm Falling* ..... 5.00 - 8.00
Banner 6390 *She's Got Great Ideas* .... 7.00 - 10.00
Banner 6473 *Waiting at the End of the Road* .... 5.00 - 8.00
Banner 6507 *Sweetheart's Holiday* .... 5.00 - 8.00
Domino 4340 *I've Got A Feeling I'm Falling* .... 5.00 - 8.00
Domino 4386 *Waiting At The End Of The Road* .. 5.00 - 8.00
Regal 8664 *How About Me?* .... 5.00 - 8.00
Regal 8831 *Waiting At The End Of The Road* .... 5.00 - 8.00

ARTHUR ROSS AND HIS WESTERNERS:
Harmony 701-H *Moonlight Madness* .... 5.00 - 8.00
Harmony 709-H *Jo-Anne* .... 5.00 - 8.00
Harmony 723-H *Take Your To-morrow* .... 8.00 - 12.00
748-H *Where The Shy Little Violets Grow* .... 7.00 - 10.00
793-H *A Room With a View* .... 5.00 - 8.00
874-H *The One That I Love Loves Me* .... 7.00 - 10.00
Harmony 891-H *My Sin* .... 5.00 - 8.00
892-H *She's My Girl (Oh! What a Diff'rence That Makes)* .... 10.00 - 15.00
Harmony 913-H *Do Something* .... 5.00 - 8.00

Harmony 926-H *Alabamy Snow* .... 5.00 - 8.00
(Note: Above titles also issued on *Diva* and *Velvet Tone*.)

ROSS DE LUXE SYNCOPATORS:
Victor 20952 *Mary Bell* .... 50.00 - 80.00
20961 *Skad-O-Lee* .... 50.00 - 80.00
21077 *Monia* .... 50.00 - 80.00
21537 *Believe Me, Dear* .... 50.00 - 80.00

THE ROUNDERS:
Domino 4386 *Lovable and Sweet* .... 5.00 - 8.00
Regal 8617 *I'm On the Crest of a Wave* .... 5.00 - 8.00
Regal 8688 *Where The Shy Little Violets Grow* .. 5.00 - 8.00
Regal 8727 *Down Among the Sugar-Cane* ...... 5.00 - 8.00
Regal 8744 *Broadway Melody* .... 5.00 - 8.00
Regal 8781 *When My Dreams Come True* ...... 5.00 - 8.00
Regal 8818 *Ain't Misbehavin'* .... 5.00 - 8.00
Regal 8831 *Lovable and Sweet* .... 5.00 - 8.00

THE ROVING ROMEOS:
Romeo 291 *If My Baby Cooks (As Good As She Looks)* .... 5.00 - 8.00

ROYAL DANCE ORCHESTRA:
Broadway 1297 *I Want To Meander In The Meadow* .... 5.00 - 8.00
1467 *Just A Blue-Eyed Blonde* .... 7.00 - 10.00

ROYAL TROUBADOURS:
Gennett 3231, 3232, 3257, 3278, 3281, 3287, 3340, 3341, 3346 .... 5.00 - 10.00
Gennett 3359 *Nothing Else Matters But Love* .... 8.00 - 12.00
Gennett 3388, 3390 .... 5.00 - 10.00
Harmony 498-H *Highways Are Happy Ways* .... 5.00 - 10.00
Harmony (most other issues) .... 3.00 - 6.00
(Note: Titles on *Harmony* may also be found on *Diva* and *Velvet Tone*, similarly valued.)

RUTH ROYE:
Columbia 63-D *Big-Hearted Bennie* .... 8.00 - 12.00
Columbia A3714 *I'm Askin' Ye Ain't It The Truth* 8.00 - 12.00
A3881 *Hotsy Totsy Town* .... 8.00 - 12.00

DAVE RUBINOFF:
Perfect 14483 *Fiddlin' The Fiddle* .... 5.00 - 10.00
14502 *Strad' Blues* .... 5.00 - 10.00
14518 *Feelin' Kind Of Blue* .... 5.00 - 10.00
(Note: Above titles, on *Pathe-Actuelle* are similarly valued.)

RUSSELL'S ROVING REVELERS:
Champion 15701 *Alfalfa* .... 25.00 - 35.00

LUIS RUSSELL & HIS BURNING EIGHT/ ORCHESTRA; (LUIS) RUSSELL'S HEEBIE JEEBIE STOMPERS/HOT SIX:
Titles, issued contemporaneously on Banner, Melotone, Oriole, Perfect, Romeo: *At The Darktown Strutters' Ball; Ghost Of The Freaks; Hokus Pocus; My Blue Heaven; Ol' Man River; Primitive* .... 20.00 - 30.00
Melotone 12000 *I Got Rhythm* .... 15.00 - 25.00
Okeh 8424 *Plantation Joys* .... 150.00 - 200.00
8454 *Sweet Mumtaz* .... 150.00 - 200.00
8656 *The Call Of The Freaks* .... 40.00 - 60.00
8734 *Jersey Lightnin'* .... 40.00 - 60.00
8760 *Savoy Shout* .... 40.00 - 60.00
8766 *Feelin' The Spirit* .... 40.00 - 60.00
8780 *Saratoga Shout* .... 40.00 - 60.00
8811 *Louisiana Swing* .... 50.00 - 80.00
8830 *Muggin' Lightly* .... 50.00 - 80.00
8849 *High Tension* .... 50.00 - 80.00
Victor 22789 *Goin' To Town* .... 30.00 - 40.00
22793 *You Rascal, You* .... 30.00 - 40.00
22815 *Freakish Blues* .... 30.00 - 40.00
Vocalion 1010 *29th and Dearborn* .... 150.00 - 250.00
1579 *Saratoga Drag* .... 150.00 - 200.00

PEE WEE RUSSELL'S RHYTHMMAKERS:
Hot Rhythm Society 17, 1000, 1001 .... 7.00 - 10.00

RED RUSSELL'S RHYTHM:

Superior 2719 *Mood Indigo* .... 75.00 - 100.00

TED RUSSELL & HIS ORCHESTRA:
Champion 40040 *I Wished On The Moon* ..... 7.00 - 10.00
  40041 *In The Middle Of a Kiss* .... 7.00 - 10.00
  40042 *Rhythm Is Our Business* .... 7.00 - 10.00
  40056 *Santa Claus Is Comin' To Town* .... 7.00 - 10.00
  40057 *You Are My Lucky Star* .... 7.00 - 10.00
  40066 *Here's To Romance* .... 7.00 - 10.00
  40071 *I Found A Dream* .... 7.00 - 10.00
  40072 *You Took My Breath Away* .... 7.00 - 10.00
  40079 *I Fell Like A Feather In My Breeze* ..... 7.00 - 10.00
  40089 *Dinner For One, Please James* .... 7.00 - 10.00
  40109 *Melody From The Sky* .... 7.00 - 10.00
  40110 *Knick-Knacks on The Mantel* .... 7.00 - 10.00

DAN RUSSO & HIS ORIOLE ORCHESTRA;
DAN RUSSO & HIS ORIOLES:
Brunswick 4490, 4672, 4708 .... 5.00 - 10.00
Columbia 2641-D *I'm a Ding Dong Daddy* ..... 10.00 - 15.00
  2642-D *Noah's Ark* .... 10.00 - 15.00

ST. LOUIS LEVEE BAND:
Okeh 8404 *Soap Suds* .... 150.00 - 250.00

ST. LOUIS RHYTHM KINGS:
Columbia 349-D *Papa De Da Da* .... 20.00 - 30.00

ST. LOUIS SYNCOPATORS:
Majestic 1431 *Way Down Yonder In New Orleans* 15.00 - 20.00
Olympic 1436 *Long Lost Mama* .... 15.00 - 20.00
  1437 *The Snakes' Hips* .... 15.00 - 20.00

HARRY SALTER & HIS ORCHESTRA:
Titles, issued contemporaneously on Cameo,
  Lincoln, Romeo: *Sing Me A Song; Goodness*
  Gracious Gracie; I Ain't Got Nothing For
  Nobody But You; I'm Just A Vagabond Lover;
  Poor People; We Were In The Moonlight ...... 4.00 - 8.00

SAM 'N' HENRY (See CORRELL and
GOSDEN):

EDGAR SAMPSON & HIS ORCHESTRA:
Vocalion 4942 *Pick Your Own Lick* .... 8.00 - 12.00

JOSEPH SAMUELS' JAZZ BAND/
ORCHESTRA:
Banner 1203 *That Red Head Gal* .... 5.00 - 8.00
  1214 *I Ain't Never Had Nobody Crazy Over Me* 5.00 - 8.00
Odeon 20087 *Dangerous Blues* .... 10.00 - 15.00
Okeh 4122 *Marriage Blues* .... 5.00 - 8.00
Okeh 4124 *Slim Trombone* .... 5.00 - 8.00
Okeh 4166 *Hold Me* .... 5.00 - 8.00
Okeh 4167 *Dreaming Blues* .... 5.00 - 8.00
Okeh 4213 *Zowie!* .... 5.00 - 8.00
Okeh 4233 *No Wonder I'm Blue* .... 5.00 - 8.00
Okeh 4250 *Home Again Blues* .... 5.00 - 8.00
Okeh 4252 *Oh, Gee! Say, Gee! You Ought To See*
  My Gee-Gee .... 5.00 - 8.00
Okeh 4255 *Sweet Mama (Papa's Getting Mad)* .. 5.00 - 8.00
Okeh 4260 *Spread Yo' Stuff* .... 5.00 - 8.00
Okeh 4282 *Tropical Blues* .... 5.00 - 8.00
Okeh 4302 *I'm Nobody's Baby* .... 5.00 - 8.00
Okeh 4370 *Pullman Porter Blues* .... 5.00 - 8.00
Okeh 4453 *Mysterious Blues* .... 5.00 - 8.00
Okeh 4460 *Dapper Dan* .... 5.00 - 8.00
Okeh 4477 *I've Got My Habits On* .... 5.00 - 8.00
Okeh 4573 *13 I'm So Unlucky 13* .... 5.00 - 8.00
Okeh 4609 *Boo Hoo Hoo* .... 5.00 - 8.00
Okeh 4663 *Houston Blues* .... 5.00 - 8.00

JOE SANDERS (AND HIS ORCHESTRA):
Decca 658, 659, 676, 692, 843, 850, 952, 955,
  956, ... 5.00 - 10.00
Victor 24033 *Intangibility* .... 10.00 - 15.00

RED SANDERS AND HIS ORCHESTRA:
Gennett 3147 *What Could Be Sweeter Than You?* . 7.00 - 10.00
  3148 *On The Bam Bam Bamy Shore* .... 10.00 - 15.00
  3166 *When You See That Aunt Of Mine* ..... 10.00 - 15.00
  3178 *Show Me The Way To Go Home* .... 7.00 - 10.00

JIMMY SAUTER'S NIGHT OWLS:

Gennett 6755 *Avalon Town* .... 7.00 - 10.00
  6769 *Glad Rag Doll* .... 7.00 - 10.00

HELEN SAVAGE:
Brunswick 4536 *It's Bad For Your Soul* .... 75.00 - 100.00

SAVANNAH NIGHT HAWKS:
Champion 15641 *Nightmare* ....150.00 - 200.00

SAVANNAH SIX:
Harmony 56-H *Hot Aire* .... 10.00 - 15.00
  58-H *Jacksonville Gal* .... 10.00 - 15.00

SAVANNAH SYNCOPATORS:
Brunswick 3245 *Deep Henderson* .... 15.00 - 20.00
  3281 *Jackass Blues* .... 15.00 - 20.00
  3361 *Sugar Foot Stomp* .... 15.00 - 20.00
  3373 *Wa Wa Wa* .... 15.00 - 20.00
  6046 *Who's Blue?* .... 40.00 - 60.00
  6176 *Radio Rhythm* .... 25.00 - 40.00
  7124 *My Melancholy Baby* .... 75.00 - 100.00

JAN SAVITT & HIS TOP HATTERS:
Bluebird 7281, 7283, 7295, 7490, 7493, 7504,
  7593, 7595, 7607, 7666, 7670, 7679, 7733, 7737,
  7748, 7783, 7786, 7797, 10005, 10013, 10018 ... 6.00 - 9.00
Decca, blue label, most issues .... 4.00 - 7.00
Variety 506 *How Could You?* .... 8.00 - 12.00
  542 *Supposing* .... 8.00 - 12.00
  585 *Cross Country Hop* .... 8.00 - 12.00
Victor, most issues .... 4.00 - 7.00

SAVOY BEARCATS:
Victor 20182 *Senegalese Stomp* .... 20.00 - 30.00
  20307 *Bearcat Stomp* .... 20.00 - 30.00
  20406 *Stampede* .... 20.00 - 30.00

THE SCARE CROW:
Gennett 7209 *Traveling Blues* ....150.00 - 200.00
  7229 *Easy Creeping Mama* ....150.00 - 200.00
  7275 *The Scare Crow Ball* ....150.00 - 200.00

REX SCHEPP:
Autograph 630 *Russian Rag* .... 30.00 - 50.00

ELMER SCHOEBEL & HIS FRIARS
SOCIETY ORCHESTRA:
Brunswick 4652 *Copenhagen* .... 30.00 - 40.00

ADRIAN SCHUBERT AND HIS
(DANCE/SALON) ORCHESTRA:
Banner 0804 *Syncopated Jamboree* .... 10.00 - 15.00
Crown 3004, 3007, 3011, 3034, 3036, 3052,
  3062, 3066, 3087, 3088, 3110 .... 5.00 - 10.00
Crown 3129 *Moonlight Saving Time* .... 8.00 - 12.00
Crown 3151, 3164, 3178 .... 5.00 - 10.00
Crown 3181 *This Is The Missus* .... 8.00 - 12.00
Crown 3191, 3206, 3207, 3225, 3226, 3245, 3257,
  3258, 3269, 3274, 3282, 3303, 3316, 3318,
  3335, 3348, 3350, 3359, 3364, 3388, 3408,
  3411, 3439, 3483 .... 5.00 - 10.00
Crown 3484 *I've Got To Sing A Torch Song* ..... 8.00 - 12.00
Crown 3493, 3496, 3508 .... 5.00 - 10.00
Domino 4606 *When Love Comes in the*
  Moonlight .... 5.00 - 8.00
  4609 *Living a Life of Dreams* .... 7.00 - 10.00

BERNIE SCHULTZ & HIS CRESCENT
ORCHESTRA:
Gennett 6216 *Sweet Violets* .... 25.00 - 40.00
  6234 *Hold Everything* .... 25.00 - 40.00
  6235 *Show Me That Kind of a Girl* .... 25.00 - 40.00

ARTHUR SCHUTT (& HIS ORCHESTRA):
Harmony 860-H *Rambling In Rhythm* .... 8.00 - 12.00
(Note: Above, on *Diva* or *Velvet Tone*, is valued
  similarly.)
Okeh 41243 *Piano Puzzle* .... 10.00 - 15.00
Okeh 41345 *Take Everything But You* .... 7.00 - 10.00
Okeh 41346 *My Fate Is In Your Hands* .... 7.00 - 10.00
Okeh 41359 *Cryin' For The Carolines* .... 10.00 - 15.00
Okeh 41360 *I'm Following You!* .... 10.00 - 15.00
Okeh 41391 *The Moon Is Low* .... 7.00 - 10.00
Okeh 41392 *It Must Be You* .... 7.00 - 10.00

Okeh 41400 *'Leven-Thirty Saturday Night* ...... 10.00 - 15.00

**CECIL SCOTT & HIS BRIGHT
BOYS/ORCHESTRA:**

Victor V38098 *In A Corner* .... 100.00 - 150.00
    38117 *Bright Boy Blues* .... 100.00 - 150.00

**LEONARD SCOTT/BLUE SCOTT & HIS
BLUE BOYS:**

Bluebird 6520 *Rubbin' Rubbin'* .... 10.00 - 15.00
    6557 *At The Bottom* .... 10.00 - 15.00
Vocalion 03311 *She's Got Something Good* .... 10.00 - 15.00

LLOYD SCOTT & HIS ORCHESTRA:

Victor 20495 *Happy Hour Blues* .... 40.00 - 60.00
    21491 *Harlem Shuffle* .... 75.00 - 100.00

THE SCRANTON SIRENS ORCHESTRA:

Okeh 40297 *Why Should I Believe In You?* ...... 40.00 - 60.00
    40329 *Common Street Blues* .... 50.00 - 75.00

SEARCY TRIO:

Okeh 8360 *Kansas Avenue Blues* .... 50.00 - 75.00

SEATTLE HARMONY KINGS:

Victor 19772, 20133, 20142 .... 5.00 - 10.00

GENE SEDRIC & HIS HONEY BEARS:

Vocalion 4552, 4576 .... 5.00 - 10.00

BLOSSOM SEELEY:

Columbia 114-D *Don't Mind The Rain* .... 8.00 - 12.00
    136-D *Bringin' Home The Bacon* .... 8.00 - 12.00
Columbia 304-D *Everybody Loves My Baby* .... 5.00 - 8.00
    386-D *Yes Sir, That's My Baby* .... 5.00 - 8.00
    613-D *Spanish Shawl* .... 7.00 - 10.00

RAY SEELEY & HIS ORCHESTRA:

Odeon ONY-36106 *I Love You So Much* .... 20.00 - 30.00
    ONY-36107 *Can I Help It?* .... 20.00 - 30.00
    ONY-36192 *I Found What I Wanted In You* .... 25.00 - 40.00
    ONY-36203 *I'm Crazy 'Bout My Baby* .... 25.00 - 40.00

EMIL SEIDEL & HIS ORCHESTRA:

Gennett 6295 *The Best Things In Life Are Free* .. 30.00 - 50.00
    6309 *Down South* .... 30.00 - 50.00
    6324 *Together, We Two* .... 25.00 - 35.00
    6327 *For My Baby* .... 25.00 - 35.00
    6340 *One More Night* .... 20.00 - 30.00
    6355 *Counting The Days* .... 20.00 - 30.00
    6367 *Beautiful* .... 25.00 - 35.00

BEN SELVIN & HIS ORCHESTRA:

Banner 1586 *Loud Speakin' Papa* .... 7.00 - 10.00
Brunswick 3172 *Betty* .... 5.00 - 8.00
    3213 *Hoodle-Dee-Doo-Dee-Doo-Doo* .... 5.00 - 8.00
Brunswick (most other issues) .... 4.00 - 6.00
Columbia 1274-D, 1285-D, 1321-D, 1399-D,
    1426-D, 1538-D, 1605-D, 1635-D, 1693-D,
    1702-D, 1751-D, 1800-D, 1831-D, 1900-D,
    1937-D, 1956-D, 1964-D, 2014-D, 2024-D,
    2077-D .... 4.00 - 8.00
Columbia 2096-D *'Tain't No Sin* .... 5.00 - 8.00
    2116-D *Happy Days Are Here Again* .... 5.00 - 8.00
Columbia 2150-D *Let Me Sing And I'm Happy* .. 7.00 - 10.00
    2255-D *It's Easy To Fall In Love* .... 7.00 - 10.00
    2287-D *Dixiana* .... 7.00 - 10.00
    2323-D *My Man From Caroline* .... 7.00 - 10.00
    2356-D *Cheerful Little Earful* .... 8.00 - 12.00
    2366-D *Yours And Mine* .... 10.00 - 15.00
    2381-D *Would You Like To Take A Walk?* ...... 10.00 - 15.00
    2400-D *99 Out Of A Hundred Wanna Be Loved* 10.00 - 15.00

2421-D *Smile, Darn Ya, Smile* .... 10.00 - 15.00
2426-D *Lean To Croon* .... 10.00 - 15.00
2463-D *Now You're In My Arms* .... 10.00 - 15.00
2487-D *Let's Drink A Drink To The Future* .... 10.00 - 15.00
2491-D *Sing Another Chorus, Please* .... 10.00 - 15.00
2499-D *Hikin' Down The Highway* .... 10.00 - 15.00
2501-D *My Sweet Tooth Says ''I Wanna''* .... 10.00 - 15.00
2515-D *This Is The Missus* .... 10.00 - 15.00
2554-D *Little Mary Brown* .... 10.00 - 15.00
2661-D *Crazy People* .... 10.00 - 15.00
2669-D *Cabin In The Cotton* .... 10.00 - 15.00
2731-D *Young And Healthy* .... 10.00 - 15.00
2789-D *Morning, Noon and Night* .... 10.00 - 15.00
12126-F *Happy Days Are Here Again*
    (instrumental) .... 15.00 - 30.00
(Above is green label ethnic series)
Columbia 18000-D *''Hot Cha'' medley* .... 15.00 - 20.00
(Note: Above is a "longer playing" record.)
Vocalion 14851 *San* .... 7.00 - 10.00
    14853 *Red Hot Mama* .... 7.00 - 10.00
    14871 *Susquehanna Home* .... 7.00 - 10.00
    15029 *Suite 16* .... 7.00 - 10.00
    15038 *Charleston* .... 7.00 - 10.00
    15083 *Let's Wander Away* .... 7.00 - 10.00
    15110 *Brown Eyes, Why Are You Blue?* ..... 7.00 - 10.00
    15154 *Sleepy Time Gal* .... 7.00 - 10.00

SEMINOLE SYNCOPATORS:

Okeh 40228 *Blue Grass Blues* .... 80.00 - 120.00

**BOYD SENTER (& HIS SENTERPEDES/
ZOBO-KA-ZOOS):**

Titles, on Autograph (unnumbered): *Bucktown
    Blues; Gertie; Laugh; Mobile Blues; Omaha
    Blues; Powder Rag* .... 50.00 - 100.00
Autograph (unnumbered) *Mr. Jelly Lord* .... 75.00 - 100.00
Banner 0620, 0621, 0622, 1633 .... 5.00 - 8.00
Broadway 1337 *Mobile Blues* .... 30.00 - 50.00
Cameo 0222 *Beef Stew* .... 5.00 - 8.00
Clarion 5054-C, 5112-C, 5181-C, ... 8.00 - 12.00
Diva 6034-G, 6044-G .... 8.00 - 12.00
Domino 3604 *Fat Mama Blues* .... 7.00 - 10.00
Okeh 40755, 40777, 40819, 40836, 40861, 40888,
    40949, 41018 .... 7.00 - 10.00
    41059, 41115, 41163 .... 8.00 - 12.00
Pathe-Actuelle 36256, 36270, 36285, 36320,
    36336, 36351, 36359, 36397, 36424, 36483,
    36493, 36528 .... 7.00 - 10.00
Perfect 14437, 14451, 14466, 14501, 14517, 14532,
    14540, 14578, 14605, 14664, 14674, 14709 .... 7.00 - 10.00
Puritan 11341 *Mobile Blues* .... 7.00 - 10.00
Regal 9937 *Fat Mama Blues* .... 7.00 - 10.00
Velvet Tone 7070-V, 7118-V, 7120-V, 7121-V ...... 8.00 - 12.00
Victor 21864, 21912, 22010 .... 8.00 - 12.00
    22303 *Copenhagen* .... 15.00 - 20.00
    22464 *No One* .... 10.00 - 15.00
    22812 *Waterloo* .... 10.00 - 15.00
    23032 *Smiles* .... 30.00 - 50.00

THE SEPIA SERENADERS:

Bluebird 5770 *Ridiculous Blues* .... 15.00 - 20.00
    5782 *Breakin' The Ice* .... 15.00 - 20.00
    5803 *Alligator Crawl* .... 15.00 - 20.00

THE SEVEN ACES (See WARNER'S SEVEN

ACES) THE 7 BLUE BABIES:

Edison 52495 *That's Her Now!*	20.00	-	30.00
52602 *Heigh Ho! Ev'robody, Heigh Ho!*	15.00	-	20.00

SEVEN BROWN BABIES:

Ajax 17011 *Do Doodle Oom*	20.00	-	30.00
17011 *Dicty Blues*	20.00	-	30.00

THE SEVEN GALLON JUG BAND:

Columbia 2087-D *Wipe 'Em Off*	20.00	-	30.00

THE SEVEN HOT AIR MEN:

Columbia 2092-D *Harlem Madness*	10.00	-	15.00
2175-D *Red Hot Chicago*	10.00	-	15.00

SEVEN LITTLE CLOUDS OF JOY:

Brunswick 7180 *You Rascal, You*	75.00	-	100.00

SEVEN LITTLE POLAR BEARS:

Cameo 915 *Someone Is Losin' Susan*	5.00	-	8.00
919 *Show That Fellow The Door*	5.00	-	8.00
952 *I'm Just Wild About Animal Crackers*	5.00	-	8.00
956 *Hi-Ho! The Merrio*	5.00	-	8.00
971 *Fiddle-Dee-Dee-Dee*	5.00	-	8.00
994 *Any Ice To-Day, Lady?*	5.00	-	8.00
1000 *Out in the New Mown Hay*	5.00	-	8.00
1019 *My Girl Has Eye Trouble*	5.00	-	8.00
1045 *If My Baby Cooks (As Good As She Looks)*	5.00	-	8.00
1046 *Gigolo*	5.00	-	8.00
1058 *How Could Red Riding Hood?*	5.00	-	8.00
1059 *Where Do You Work-a, John?*	5.00	-	8.00
Cameo 1060 *Don't Take That Black Bottom Away*	5.00	-	8.00
1071 *How Could Red Riding Hood?*	5.00	-	8.00
1084 *If I Didn't Know Your Husband*	5.00	-	8.00
1088 *You Should See My Tootsie*	5.00	-	8.00
1090 *She Said And I Said*	5.00	-	8.00
1098 *Got No Time To Feel Lonesome*	5.00	-	8.00
1281 *Our Bungalow of Dreams*	5.00	-	8.00
8178 *Hello Montreal*	5.00	-	8.00
8188 *Mississippi Mud*	10.00	-	15.00
8243 *Since She Learned To Ride a Horse*	5.00	-	8.00
8244 *Oh! You Have No Idea*	5.00	-	8.00
8339 *The Cat and The Dog*	5.00	-	8.00
Lincoln 2644 *You Never Get Nowhere Holding Hands*	5.00	-	8.00
Romeo 618 *Mississippi Mud*	10.00	-	15.00
667 *Oh! You Have No Idea*	5.00	-	8.00

SEVEN MISSING LINKS:

Perfect 14480 *Angry*	7.00	-	10.00

SEVEN WILD MEN:

Harmony 191-H, 193-H	5.00	-	8.00

HATCH SEWARD:

Broadway 5063 *Honky Train Blues*	75.00	-	100.00

TERRY SHAND AND HIS ORCHESTRA:

Decca, blue label, most issues	4.00	-	6.00
Vocalion 4113, 4131	5.00	-	10.00

SHARKEY'S NEW ORLEANS BOYS/ SHARKS OF RHYTHM:

Decca 1014 *Everbody Loves My Baby*	6.00	-	10.00
Vocalion 3353 *Mudhole Blues*	7.00	-	12.00
3380 *High Society*	7.00	-	12.00
3400 *When You're Smiling*	7.00	-	12.00
3410 *Blowin Off Steam*	7.00	-	12.00
3450 *Big Boy Blue*	7.00	-	12.00
3470 *Swing Like A Rusty Gate*	7.00	-	12.00

FRED SHARP'S DIXIE PLAYERS:

Champion 15216 *I'm Looking Over a Four-Leaf Clover*	50.00	-	80.00

CHARLIE SHAVERS QUINTET:

Vogue 754 *She's Funny That Way*	30.00	-	40.00
755 *Serenade To A Pair Of Nylons*	30.00	-	40.00
756 *If I Had You*	30.00	-	40.00

ART(IE) SHAW & HIS NEW MUSIC/ ORCHESTRA/STRINGS:

Bluebird 7746, 7759, 7772, 7875, 7889, 7952,

10001, 10054, 10055, 10075, 10079, 10091, 10125, 10126, 10127, 10128, 10134, 10141, 10148, 10178, 10188, 10195, 10202, 10215, 10307, 10319, 10320, 10324, 10334, 10345, 10347, 10385, 10406, 10412, 10430, 10446, 10468, 10482, 10492	4.00	-	8.00
Brunswick 7688, 7698, 7721, 7735, 7741, 7750, 7771, 7778, 7787, 7794, 7806, 7827, 7835, 7841, 7852, 7895, 7899, 7907, 7914, 7934, 7936, 7942, 7947, 7952, 7965, 7971, 7976, 7986, 8010, 8019, 8050, 8054	5.00	-	10.00
Musicraft, most issues	3.00	-	6.00
Victor, most issues	3.00	-	6.00

JOEL SHAW & HIS ORCHESTRA:

Crown 3244 *Who's Your Little Who-Zis?*	8.00	-	12.00
3271 *Business In F*	8.00	-	12.00
3273 *Barnacle Bill, The Sailor*	8.00	-	12.00
3285 *Some Of These Days*	8.00	-	12.00
3302 *Goofus*	5.00	-	10.00
3304 *Business In Q*	5.00	-	10.00
3306 *Minnie The Moocher*	8.00	-	12.00
3311 *Whistle And Blow Your Blues Away*	8.00	-	12.00
3312 *Call Of The Freaks*	10.00	-	15.00
3319 *Dinah*	8.00	-	12.00
3332 *Minnie The Moocher's Wedding Day*	10.00	-	15.00
3333 *How'm I Doin'?*	10.00	-	15.00
3349 *Why Don't You Get Lost?*	8.00	-	12.00
3352 *That's A Plenty*	10.00	-	15.00
3362 *Basin Street Blues*	10.00	-	15.00
3381 *Sing (It's Good For Ya)*	8.00	-	12.00
3382 *Margie*	10.00	-	15.00
3383 *Tiger Rag*	10.00	-	15.00
3413 *White Zombie*	10.00	-	15.00
3414 *Jazz Pie*	10.00	-	15.00
3423 *Reefer Man*	10.00	-	15.00
3442 *The Old Kitchen Kettle*	7.00	-	10.00
3444 *Original Dixieland One Step*	10.00	-	15.00
3451 *Indiana*	10.00	-	15.00
3453 *Forty-Second Street*	10.00	-	15.00

MILT SHAW & HIS DETROITERS:

Columbia 1811-D *Walking With Susie*	5.00	-	8.00
Melotone (most issues)	4.00	-	8.00
Okeh 41158 *Where the Shy Little Violets Grow*	7.00	-	10.00
Okeh 41172 *On The Alamo*	7.00	-	10.00
Okeh 41196 *A Precious Little Thing Called Love*	7.00	-	10.00
Vocalion 15665 *Golden Gate*	15.00	-	25.00
Vocalion 15666 *Borneo*	15.00	-	25.00
Vocalion 15697 *That's My Weakness Now*	15.00	-	20.00

TED SHAWNE & HIS ORCHESTRA:

Parlophone PNY-34126 *I Ain't Got Nobody*	30.00	-	50.00
PNY-34027 *Rockin' Chair*	30.00	-	50.00
PNY-34032 *Song Of The Islands*	30.00	-	50.00
PNY-34033 *Blue, Turning Grey Over You*	30.00	-	50.00
PNY-34129 *I'm In The Market For You*	30.00	-	50.00
PNY-34131 *I'm A Ding Dong Daddy*	30.00	-	50.00
PNY-34172 *The Peanut Vendor*	30.00	-	50.00
PNY-34173 *Sweethearts On Parade*	30.00	-	50.00
Odeon ONY-41276 *Ain't Misbehavin'*	30.00	-	50.00

HARRY "FREDDIE" SHAYNE:

Champion 50061 *Lonesome Man Blues*	25.00	-	40.00

BERT SHEFTER & HIS ORCHESTRA/ RHYTHM OCTET:

Decca 2525, 2584, 2653	5.00	-	10.00
Victor 25614, 25622, 25632	5.00	-	10.00

OLLIE SHEPARD:

Decca, Okeh	5.00	-	10.00

SHERIDAN ENTERTAINERS:

Banner 6024 *You Don't Like It-Not Much*	5.00	-	8.00
Banner 6025 *Sing Me A Baby Song*	5.00	-	8.00
6026 *What Do We Do On A Dew-Dew-Dewy Day*	5.00	-	8.00
6105 *Baltimore*	5.00	-	8.00

Broadway 1105 *Washington & Lee Swing*	5.00 -	8.00
1106 *Sweetheart Of Sigma Chi*	5.00 -	8.00
1107 *Balitmore*	5.00 -	8.00
1114 *Blue Baby*	5.00 -	8.00
Challenge 658 *Dew Dew Dewy Day*	5.00 -	8.00

SHERMAN CLUB ORCHESTRA:

Challenge 715 *Muddy Water* ....100.00 -	150.00

SHERMAN'S GLOBE TROTTERS:

Bell 615 *Louisiana*	15.00 -	20.00

SHERMAN SUNDODGERS/SUNDOWNERS:

Herwin 8057 *Happy-Go-Lucky Lane*	30.00 -	50.00
Silvertone 8057 *Happy-Go-Lucky Lane*	10.00 -	15.00

JACK SHILKRET & HIS ORCHESTRA:

Titles, issued contemporaneously on Banner, Melotone, Oriole, Perfect: *Another Perfect Night is Ending; Dream Awhile; Gee! But You're Swell; Hey, Babe, Hey! Hidden Valley; I Can't Escape From You; Never Should Have Told You; One Hamburger For Madame; San Francisco; Shoe Shine Boy; So Divine; There's Always A Happy Ending; There's A Small Hotel; Twinkle, Twinkle, Little Star* ....

	5.00 -	10.00
Bluebird 5884, 5885, 5886, 5986, 5987, 5988, 6013	5.00 -	10.00
Brunswick 7602, 7603	7.00 -	10.00
Victor 19394 *Africa*	5.00 -	8.00
Victor 19818 *If You Hadn't Gone Away*	5.00 -	8.00
Victor 19922 *Roll 'Em, Girls*	5.00 -	8.00
Victor 19931 *In Your Green Hat*	5.00 -	8.00

NAT SHILKRET & THE VICTOR ORCHESTRA:

Victor 20469 *I Love You But I Don't Know Why* .	35.00 -	50.00
20471 *What Does It Matter?*	5.00 -	8.00
20508 *Ain't She Sweet?*	5.00 -	8.00
20634 *Fifty Million Frenchmen Can't Be Wrong*	5.00 -	8.00
20675 *Me and My Shadow*	5.00 -	8.00
20882 *Baby's Blue*	5.00 -	8.00
20926 *Zulu Wail*	5.00 -	8.00
21080 *Nothin'*	5.00 -	8.00
21515 *When Sweet Susie Goes Steppin' By*	5.00 -	8.00
21603 *Moonlight Madness*	5.00 -	8.00
Victor 21729 *Here's That Party Now In Person* ..	7.00 -	10.00
Victor 21853 *Dream Train*	5.00 -	8.00
21996 *Susianna*	5.00 -	8.00
Victor 22106 *You Made Me Love You-Why Did You?*	8.00 -	12.00
22258 *When I'm Looking At You*	5.00 -	8.00
22306 *Singing A Vagabond Song*	7.00 -	10.00
22472 *Dixiana*	5.00 -	8.00

ALBERT E. SHORT & HIS TIVOLI SYNCOPATORS:

Vocalion 14554 *Wolverine Blues*	7.00 -	10.00
14600 *Long Lost Mama*	7.00 -	10.00
14658 *Bugle Call Rag*	7.00 -	10.00

SHREVEPORT SIZZLERS:

Okeh 8918 *Zonky*	50.00 -	75.00
41561 *You've Got To Be Modernistic*	50.00 -	75.00

AL SIEGEL & HIS ORCHESTRA:

Titles, issued contemporaneously on Broadway, Claxtonola, Paramount, Pennington, Puritan:

Blue Grass Blues; Sooke Hey Hey	25.00 -	40.00
Additional titles: *So Long To You And The Blues; You've Got Ways I'm Crazy About*	50.00 -	100.00
Harmograph 901 *So Long To You And The Blues* .	30.00 -	50.00

SIGLER'S BIRMINGHAM MERRYMAKERS:

Okeh 40280 *Mama's Gone Goodbye*	35.00 -	50.00
40310 *I Love Her*	35.00 -	50.00

FRANK SIGNORELLI AND HIS ORCHESTRA:

Pathe-Actuelle 36518 *She's Still My Baby* ...	10.00 -	15.00
36523 *Don't Be Angry With Me*	10.00 -	15.00
36535 *St. Louis Hop*	15.00 -	20.00
Perfect 14699 *She's Still My Baby*	10.00 -	15.00

14704 *Don't Be Angry With Me*	10.00 -	15.00
14716 *A Blues Serenade*	15.00 -	20.00

SILENT JOE & HIS BOYS:

Champion 15051 *Cooler Hot*	15.00 -	20.00
15052 *Give Me Your Heart*	10.00 -	15.00
15053 *Any Blues (Is Good Enough For Me)* ...	15.00 -	25.00

DAVID H. SILVERMAN & HIS ORCHESTRA:

Victor 19195 *Mean Blues*	5.00 -	8.00
19237 *Blue Grass Blues*	5.00 -	8.00

SILVER SLIPPER ORCHESTRA:

Challenge 801 *A Little Bit Closer* ....150.00 -	200.00
Challenge 806 *There'll Come A Day* ....150.00 -	200.00

JOHNNY SILVESTER AND HIS ORCHESTRA (See JOHNNY SYLVESTER):

OMER SIMEON:

Brunswick 7109 *Beau-Koo Jac* ....100.00 -	150.00

LESTER SIMMONS & HIS ORCHESTRA:

Champion 15475 *I've Got Somebody Now*	20.00 -	30.00

HOWARD SIMMS:

Harmograph 841 *Pensacola Joe*	30.00 -	50.00

JOSEPH SIMPKINS & HIS RUBE BAND:

Champion 15581 *Bass Blues*	50.00 -	80.00

ARTHUR SIMS & HIS CREOLE ROOF ORCHESTRA:

Okeh 8373 *Soapstick Blues*	80.00 -	120.00
40675 *As Long As I Have You* ....125.00 -	175.00

THE SINGING BOYS & THEIR NOVELTY ORCHESTRA:

Harmony 928-H *My Kinda Love*	8.00 -	12.00
1087-H *You'll Recognize My Baby*	10.00 -	15.00

(Note: The above titles, on *Diva* and *Velvet Tone*, are similarly valued.)

SIOUX CITY SIX:

Gennett 5569 *Flock O' Blues* ....100.00 -	150.00

NOBLE SISSLE; (NOBLE) SISSEL/SISSLE & (EUBIE) BLAKE; NOBLE SISSLE & HIS (INTERNATIONAL) ORCHESTRA/ SIZZLIN' SYNCOPATORS SWINGSTERS:

Brunswick 6073 *Got The Bench, Got The Park* ..	15.00 -	25.00
6111 *Roll On, Mississippi, Roll On*	15.00 -	25.00
6129 *Basement Blues*	25.00 -	40.00
Decca 153 *Under The Creole Moon*	8.00 -	12.00
154 *Loveless Love*	8.00 -	12.00
766 *I Wonder Who Made Rhythm*	8.00 -	12.00
778 *That's What Love Did To Me*	8.00 -	12.00
847 *I Take To You*	8.00 -	12.00
2129 *Blackstick*	7.00 -	10.00
7429 *Viper Mad*	8.00 -	12.00
Edison 50754 *Crazy Blues*	15.00 -	20.00
51572 *Broken Busted Blues*	15.00 -	20.00
Emerson 10296 *Broadway Blues*	7.00 -	10.00
10326 *Crazy Blues*	7.00 -	10.00
10357 *Boll Weevil Blues*	8.00 -	12.00
10365 *Low Down Blues*	10.00 -	15.00
10367 *Royal Garden Blues*	10.00 -	15.00
Emerson 10385 *Baltimore Buzz*	7.00 -	10.00
10396 *Oriental Blues*	10.00 -	15.00
10443 *Arkansas Blues*	10.00 -	15.00
10484 *I'm A Doggone Struttin' Fool*	8.00 -	12.00
Okeh 40776 *'Deed I Do*	8.00 -	12.00
40824 *Slow River*	8.00 -	12.00
40859 *Sometimes I'm Happy*	8.00 -	12.00
40877 *Broken Hearted*	8.00 -	12.00
40882 *Give Me A Night In June*	8.00 -	12.00
40917 *Pickaninny Shoes*	10.00 -	15.00
Paramount 12002 *Bandana Days*	20.00 -	30.00
12007 *Crazy Blues*	20.00 -	30.00
Pathe 20210 *Mammy's Little Choc'late Cullud Chile*	7.00 -	10.00
Pathe 20226 *Goodnight, Angeline*	7.00 -	10.00
Pathe 20233 *Stay In Your Own Back Yard*	7.00 -	10.00
Pathe 20267 *There It Goes Again*	7.00 -	10.00

Pathe 20280 *That's The Kind Of A Baby For Me* . 8.00 - 12.00
Pathe 20295 *Mandy Lou* . . . . 7.00 - 10.00
Pathe 20470 *Affectionate Dan* . . . . 7.00 - 10.00
Pathe 22284 *I'm Just Simply Full Of Jazz* . . . . 8.00 - 12.00
Pathe 22357 *Melodious Jazz* . . . . 8.00 - 12.00
Pathe 22394 *Mammy's Little Sugar Plum* . . . . 7.00 - 10.00
Variety 552 *I'm Just Wild About Harry* . . . . 10.00 - 15.00
   648 *Characteristic Blues* . . . . 10.00 - 15.00
Victor 19086, 19253, 19494 . . . . 5.00 - 10.00
Vocalion 3840 *Characteristic Blues* . . . . 10.00 - 15.00

KENN SISSON & HIS ORCHESTRA:
Brunswick (most issues) . . . . 4.00 - 8.00

SIX BLACK DIAMONDS:
Banner 1181 *Farewell Blues* . . . . 5.00 - 8.00
   1217 *Long Lost Mama* . . . . 5.00 - 8.00
   1227 *My Sweetie Went Away* . . . . 5.00 - 8.00
   1265 *Sobbin' Blues* . . . . 5.00 - 8.00
   1318 *Mindin' My Business* . . . . 7.00 - 10.00
   1322 *Lots O'Mama* . . . . 7.00 - 10.00
   1336 *Waitin' Around* . . . . 7.00 - 10.00
   1346 *My Papa Doesn't Two-Time No Time* . . . . 7.00 - 10.00
   1349 *Nobody's Sweetheart* . . . . 7.00 - 10.00
   1385 *Charleston Cabin* . . . . 5.00 - 8.00
   1428 *Dixie Flyer Sam* . . . . 10.00 - 15.00
   1540 *Sweet Georgia Brown* . . . . 5.00 - 8.00
Banner 1656 *Steppin' Fool* . . . . 5.00 - 8.00
   1662 *My Charleston Dancing Man* . . . . 5.00 - 8.00
   1842 *Here Comes Fatima* . . . . 5.00 - 8.00
   6076 *I Can't Fool Around With Someone Who's*
     Foolin . . . . 7.00 - 10.00
   6093 *Hello, Miss Liberty* . . . . 5.00 - 8.00
   6104 *There's Always Somebody Looking For*
     Somebody . . . . 5.00 - 8.00
   6167 *Chloe (Song of the Swamp)* . . . . 5.00 - 8.00
   6289 *She's My Sweet Patootie* . . . . 5.00 - 8.00
   6291 *Copper Colored Sam* . . . . 5.00 - 8.00
   6298 *Susianna* . . . . 5.00 - 8.00
   6300 *Some Of These Days* . . . . 5.00 - 8.00
   6318 *Dixieanna* . . . . 5.00 - 8.00
   6324 *I Can't Stop Lovin' You Now* . . . . 5.00 - 8.00
   6352 *Long Lost Daddy* . . . . 5.00 - 8.00
   6382 *I've Got The San Francisco Blues* . . . . . 7.00 - 10.00
   6383 *Where Has Mammy Gone?* . . . . 5.00 - 8.00
   6384 *The Oliver Twist* . . . . 5.00 - 8.00
   6392 *Why Can't It Be Me?* . . . . 5.00 - 8.00
   6418 *Some Of These Days* . . . . 5.00 - 8.00
   7008 *Stay Out Of The South* . . . . 5.00 - 8.00
Domino 392 *Any Way The Wind Blows* . . . . 5.00 - 8.00
Domino 3510 *Sweet Georgia Brown* . . . . 5.00 - 8.00
   3632 *My Charleston Dancing Man* . . . . 5.00 - 8.00
   3633 *Steppin' Fool* . . . . 5.00 - 8.00
Oriole 497 *Melancholy Lou* . . . . 8.00 - 12.00
Oriole 518 *I'm Gonna Charleston Back To*
   Charleston . . . . 5.00 - 8.00
Regal 8006 *Flamin' Mamie* . . . . 5.00 - 8.00
   8022 *Say Mister! Have You Met Rosie's Sister?* 5.00 - 8.00
   9458 *Farewell Blues* . . . . 5.00 - 8.00
   9503 *Beale Street Mama* . . . . 5.00 - 8.00
   9553 *Sobbin' Blues* . . . . 5.00 - 8.00
   9612 *Lots O' Mama* . . . . 7.00 - 10.00
   9628 *Mindin' My Business* . . . . 7.00 - 10.00
   9643 *Josephine (Who's The Meanest Gal In*
     Town) . . . . 7.00 - 10.00
   9646 *My Papa Doesn't Two-Time No Time* . . . . 7.00 - 10.00
   9706 *Any Way The Wind Blows* . . . . 5.00 - 8.00
Regal 9725 *Dixie Flyer Sam* . . . . 10.00 - 15.00
   9981 *Charleston Baby* . . . . 5.00 - 8.00

SIX BROWN BROTHERS:
Victor 17677 *That Moaning Saxophone Rag* . . . . . 7.00 - 10.00
Victor 17834 *Down Home Rag* . . . . 7.00 - 10.00
Victor 18097 *Bull Frog Blues* . . . . 5.00 - 8.00
Victor 18140 *Walkin' The Dog* . . . . 5.00 - 8.00

Victor 18310 *For Me And My Gal* . . . . 5.00 - 8.00
Victor 18376 *The Darktown Strutters' Ball* . . . . . . 5.00 - 8.00
Victor 18385 *Smiles And Chuckles* . . . . 5.00 - 8.00

THE SIX HOTTENTOTS:
Titles, issued contemporaneously on Banner,
  Domino, Regal: *Hurricane; I'm In Love Again;*
  Melancholy Charlie; The Memphis Blues; Rosy
  Cheeks; Sometimes I'm Happy . . . . 8.00 - 12.00

SIX JOLLY JESTERS:
Vocalion 1449 *Oklahoma Stomp* . . . . 50.00 - 75.00
(Note: Re-issues of above, on black and gold, or
  blue and gold label are valued much lower.)
  15843 *Six Or Seven Times* . . . . 100.00 - 150.00

SIX JUMPING JACKS:
Brunswick 3031 *Wimmin—Aaah!* . . . . 5.00 - 8.00
Brunswick 3064 *Charleston Ball* . . . . 5.00 - 8.00
   3094 *Thanks For The Buggy Ride* . . . . 5.00 - 8.00
   3095 *Masculine Women! Feminine Men!* . . . . . 7.00 - 10.00
   3109 *I'm Gonna Let The Bumble Bee Be* . . . . . 5.00 - 8.00
   3131 *Say Mister! Have You Met Rosie's Sister?* . 5.00 - 8.00
   3169 *Rah-Rah-Rah* . . . . 5.00 - 8.00
   3216 *I'm Just Wild About Animal Crackers* . . . 5.00 - 8.00
   3252 *Out in the New Moon Hay* . . . . 5.00 - 8.00
   3254 *How Could Red Riding Hood?* . . . . 5.00 - 8.00
   3374 *If You Can't Land 'Er on the Old Veranda* 5.00 - 8.00
   3412 *The Coat and Pants Do All The Work* . . . . 5.00 - 8.00
   3434 *I Love The College Girls* . . . . 5.00 - 8.00
   3511 *I Wonder How I Look When I'm Asleep* . . 5.00 - 8.00
   3524 *The More We Are Together* . . . . 5.00 - 8.00
   3582 *Positively—Absolutely* . . . . 5.00 - 8.00
   3603 *She's Got "It"* . . . . 5.00 - 8.00
   3623 *I'm Gonna Dance Wit De Guy Wot*
     Brung Me . . . . 5.00 - 8.00
   3650 *Pastafazoola* . . . . 5.00 - 8.00
   3699 *Here Comes The Show Boat* . . . . 5.00 - 8.00
   3726 *Fair Co-Ed* . . . . 5.00 - 8.00
   3782 *Henry's Made a Lady Out of Lizzie* . . . . . 5.00 - 8.00
   3856 *Get 'Em in a Rumble Seat* . . . . 5.00 - 8.00
   3876 *Hey! Hey! Hazel* . . . . 5.00 - 8.00
   3917 *He Ain't Never Been In College* . . . . 5.00 - 8.00
   3923 *They Landed Over Here From Over There* 5.00 - 8.00
   3930 *I Love That Girl* . . . . 5.00 - 8.00
   3940 *Etiquette Blues* . . . . 5.00 - 8.00
   4011 *Nagasaki* . . . . 5.00 - 8.00
   4073 *The Prune Song* . . . . 5.00 - 8.00
   4196 *I Faw Down An' Go Boom!* . . . . 5.00 - 8.00
   4219 *Olaf (You Oughta Hear Olaf Laff)* . . . . . 5.00 - 8.00
   4220 *Outside* . . . . 5.00 - 8.00
   4362 *She's Got Great Ideas* . . . . 5.00 - 8.00
   4457 *The Woopee Hat Brigade* . . . . 5.00 - 8.00
   4498 *He's a Big, Big Man from the South* . . . . 15.00 - 20.00
Brunswick 4589 *My Wife Is On A Diet* . . . . 5.00 - 8.00
   4590 *It's Unanimous Now* . . . . 5.00 - 8.00
   4759 *Send For Our Free Booklet* . . . . 7.00 - 10.00
   4946 *Football Freddy* . . . . 7.00 - 10.00
   4948 *It's a Great Life* . . . . 7.00 - 10.00
   6007 *Twenty Swedes Ran Through the Weeds* . . 7.00 - 10.00
   6081 *Egyptian Ella* . . . . 7.00 - 10.00
   6137 *When Yuba Plays The Rumba on the Tuba* 7.00 - 10.00

SIX MEN AND A GIRL:
Varsity 8193 *Tea For Two* . . . . 7.00 - 10.00
   8190 *Zonky* . . . . 7.00 - 10.00

THE SIZZLERS:
Edison 52463 *Diga Diga Doo* . . . . 20.00 - 30.00

CHARLEY SKEETE'S ORCHESTRA:
Edison 51775 *Deep Henderson* . . . . 75.00 - 100.00

DUDE SKILES & HIS VINE STREET BOYS:
Variety 516, 584 . . . . 7.00 - 10.00

SKILLET DICK & HIS FRYING PANS:
Champion 15883 *Asphalt Walk* . . . . 125.00 - 175.00
   15996 *Rock and Gravel* . . . . 125.00 - 175.00

SLIM & HIS HOT BOYS:

Victor V38044 *That's A Plenty* . . . . 50.00 - 75.00

SLIM AND SLAM:

Vocalion 3981, 4021, 4110, 4163, 4225, 4346,

4461, 4521, 4594 . . . . 5.00 - 10.00

FATS SMITH & HIS RHYTHM KINGS:

Vocalion 03528 *If I Had You In My Arms* . . . . . 20.00 - 30.00

FRED SMITH & HIS SOCIETY
ORCHESTRA:

Black Swan 2052, 2114, 2119 . . . . 8.00 - 15.00

HARL SMITH AND HIS ORCHESTRA:

Pathe-Actuelle 036158 *Rose Marie* . . . . 8.00 - 12.00

Perfect 14339 *Bring Back Those Rock-A-Bye*

Baby Days . . . . 8.00 - 12.00

JABBO SMITH & HIS RHYTHM ACES:

(see also THE RHYTHM ACES):

Brunswick 7058 *Little Willie Blues* . . . . 80.00 - 120.00

7061 *Take Your Time* . . . . 80.00 - 120.00

7065 *Let's Get Together* . . . . 80.00 - 120.00

7069 *Michigander Blues* . . . . 80.00 - 120.00

7071 *Ace Of Rhythm* . . . . 80.00 - 120.00

7078 *Decatur Street Tutti* . . . . 80.00 - 120.00

7087 *Lina Blues* . . . . 80.00 - 120.00

7101 *Tanguay Blues* . . . . 80.00 - 120.00

7111 *Band Box Stomp* . . . . 80.00 - 120.00

Decca 1712, 1980 . . . . 5.00 - 10.00

JOE SMITH'S MARTHA LEE CLUB
ORCHESTRA:

Okeh 40322 *Don't Bother Me* . . . . 10.00 - 15.00

KATE SMITH:

Brunswick 6496 *Twenty Million People* . . . . 8.00 - 12.00

6497 *Moon Song* . . . . 8.00 - 12.00

Clarion 5015-C *Don't Let Me Hold You, Baby*

Mine . . . . 10.00 - 15.00

5038-C *You'll Be Coming Back To Me* . . . . . 10.00 - 15.00

5074-C *You'll Never Know, Sweetheart* . . . . . 10.00 - 15.00

5123-C *Held By The Spell Of The Moon* . . . . 10.00 - 15.00

5124-C *Morning, Noon And Night* . . . . 10.00 - 15.00

5227-C *You Don't Want Me Any More* . . . . . 10.00 - 15.00

5228-C *Grievin'* . . . . 10.00 - 15.00

5278-C *Dinah Lee From Tennessee* . . . . 10.00 - 15.00

5279-C *Now's The Time* . . . . 10.00 - 15.00

(Note: Above titles, on *Velvet Tone*, are similarly

valued.)

Columbia 810-D *Jersey Walk* . . . . 7.00 - 10.00

Columbia 911-D *One Sweet Letter From You* . . . 10.00 - 15.00

1132-D *Clementine (From New Orleans)* . . . . . 7.00 - 10.00

1348-D *In The Evening* . . . . 7.00 - 10.00

Columbia 2516-D *When The Moon Comes Over*

The Mountain . . . . 7.00 - 10.00

2539-D *I Don't Know Why (I Just Do)* . . . . . 7.00 - 10.00

2563-D *Tell Me With A Love Song* . . . . 8.00 - 12.00

2605-D *Twenty-One Years* . . . . 8.00 - 12.00

2624-D *Snuggled On Your Shoulder* . . . . 8.00 - 12.00

Decca 276, 277, 278 . . . . 5.00 - 10.00

Harmony 970-H *He's A Good Man To Have*

Around . . . . 7.00 - 10.00

999-H *Moanin' Low* . . . . 7.00 - 10.00

1050-H *I May Be Wrong, But I Think You're*

Wonderful . . . . 7.00 - 10.00

1069-H *Chant Of The Jungle* . . . . 7.00 - 10.00

1170-H *Dancing With Tears In My Eyes* . . . . . 5.00 - 8.00

1191-H *Swingin' In A Hammock* . . . . 7.00 - 10.00

1216-H *Maybe It's Love* . . . . 8.00 - 12.00

1235-H *I Got Rhythm* . . . . 8.00 - 12.00

1280-H *Overnight* . . . . 8.00 - 12.00

1303-H *Wabash Moon* . . . . 8.00 - 12.00

1347-H *Makin' Faces At The Man In The Moon* 8.00 - 12.00

1371-H *Shine On, Harvest Moon* . . . . 8.00 - 12.00

(Note: Above titles, on *Diva* or *Velvet Tone*, are

similarly valued.)

Velvet Tone 2465-V *Goodnight, Sweetheart* . . . . 8.00 - 12.00

2483-V *All Of Me* . . . . 10.00 - 15.00

2512-V *Between The Devil And The Deep Blue Sea* 10.00 - 15.00

LEROY SMITH & HIS ORCHESTRA:

Blu-Disc 1001 *Stop And Listen* . . . . 100.00 - 200.00

Everybody's 1020 *Harlem's Araby* . . . . 75.00 - 100.00

1027 *Dixie Dreams* . . . . 75.00 - 100.00

Victor 21328 *St. Louis Blues* . . . . 15.00 - 20.00

21472 *St. Louis Blues* . . . . 10.00 - 15.00

LLOYD SMITH'S GUT-BUCKETEERS:

Vocalion 1560 *Wake Up, Sinners* . . . . 150.00 - 200.00

1573 *That's My Stuff* . . . . 150.00 - 200.00

SAMMY SMITH'S STOMPERS:

Clarion 5417-C *Blues In My Heart* . . . . 20.00 - 30.00

Velvet Tone 2477-V *Blues In My Heart* . . . . . . 20.00 - 30.00

STUFF SMITH & HIS ORCHESTRA/
ONYX CLUB BOYS:

Decca 1279 *Onyx Club Spree* . . . . 8.00 - 12.00

1287 *Where Is The Sun?* . . . . 8.00 - 12.00

Varsity 8063 *Sam The Vegetable Man* . . . . 7.00 - 10.00

8081 *My Blue Heaven* . . . . 7.00 - 10.00

8242 *I've Got You Under My Skin* . . . . 7.00 - 10.00

8251 *It's Up To You* . . . . 7.00 - 10.00

Vocalion 3169 *I'se A Muggin'* . . . . 7.00 - 10.00

3170 *I Hope Gabriel Likes My Music* . . . . . . 7.00 - 10.00

3200 *'Tain't No Use* . . . . 7.00 - 10.00

3201 *After You've Gone* . . . . 7.00 - 10.00

3234 *I've Got A Heavy Date* . . . . 7.00 - 10.00

3270 *It Ain't Right* . . . . 7.00 - 10.00

3300 *Knock Knock, Who's There* . . . . 7.00 - 10.00

3316 *Here Comes The Man With The Jive* . . . . 7.00 - 10.00

TED SMITH'S RHYTHM ACES:

Champion 16321 *Minnie The Moocher* . . . . 75.00 - 100.00

16332 *Boogie Woogie* . . . . 75.00 - 100.00

16420 *New Moten Stomp* . . . . 75.00 - 100.00

40006 *Jig Time* . . . . 20.00 - 30.00

WILLIE "THE LION" SMITH (& HIS
ORCHESTRA): WILLIE SMITH (THE
LION) & HIS CLUBS:

Commodore 518, 519, 521, 522, 523, 524, 525 . . . 5.00 - 10.00

Decca 1291 *The Swampland' Is Calling Me* . . . . 7.00 - 10.00

1308 *More Than That* . . . . 7.00 - 10.00

1366 *Knock Wood* . . . . 7.00 - 10.00

1380 *Get Acquainted With Yourself* . . . . 7.00 - 10.00

1957 *I've Got To Think It Over* . . . . 5.00 - 8.00

7073 *There's Gonna Be The Devil To Pay* . . . 10.00 - 15.00

7074 *Streamline Gal* . . . . 10.00 - 15.00

7086 *Sittin' At The Table* . . . . 10.00 - 15.00

7090 *Swing, Brother, Swing* . . . . 8.00 - 12.00

General 1712 *Peace On You* . . . . 7.00 - 10.00

1713 *Rushin'* . . . . 7.00 - 10.00

MARVIN SMOLEV & HIS SYNCOPATORS:

Titles, issued contemporaneously on Grey Gull,

Radiex: *Apart From You; Because I'm*

Lonesome; Desert Blues; No-One But Betty

Brown; Ring Around The Moon; She's Just The

Baby For Me; Soubrette; The Terror; We'll Be

Married In June . . . . 15.00 - 30.00

SMYTH & WEST ORCHESTRA:

Broadway 1486 *I Need Lovin'* . . . . 7.00 - 10.00

JACK SNEED AND HIS SNEEZERS:

Decca 7522 *Big Joe Louis* . . . . 8.00 - 12.00

HARRY SNODGRASS:

Brunswick 2852 *Blue Evening Blues* . . . . 7.00 - 10.00

3239 *Maple Leaf Rag* . . . . 7.00 - 10.00

SNOOKS & HIS MEMPHIS RAMBLERS/
STOMPERS; SNOOKS & HIS PARAMOUNT
THEATRE ORCHESTRA:

Melotone 12203 *That's My Desire* . . . . 7.00 - 10.00

12210 *Just One More Chance* . . . . 7.00 - 10.00

12245 *Goodnight, Sweetheart* . . . . 7.00 - 10.00

12259 *When It's Sleepy Time Down South* . . . 7.00 - 10.00

Victor 22629 *I'm Happy When You're Happy* . . . 7.00 - 10.00

22662 *Smile, Darn Ya, Smile*	7.00	10.00
22684 *Bon Soir*	7.00	10.00
22704 *You Don't Need Glasses*	7.00	10.00
22720 *Dip Your Brush In The Sunshine*	7.00	10.00
22779 *Sweet Georgia Brown*	10.00	15.00
22813 *Kissable Baby*	7.00	10.00
22815 *Japanese Sandman*	15.00	25.00
22895 *Nothin' To Do But Love*	7.00	10.00
22988 *'Neath The Silvery Moon*	7.00	10.00
23038 *Hello, Beautiful!*	10.00	15.00

BOB SNYDER & HIS ORCHESTRA:

Vocalion 2660 *My Dog Loves Your Dog*	7.00	10.00
2661 *Nasty Man*	7.00	10.00
2707 *Love Thy Neighbor*	7.00	10.00

JOE SODJA'S SWINGTETTE:

Variety 609 *Limehouse Blues*	8.00	12.00

HARRY SOSNIK & HIS (EDGEWATER BEACH HOTEL) ORCH.:

Decca 1466 *Here Comes The Sandman*	5.00	8.00
Decca other issues	3.00	5.00
Nocturne 3135 *Swinging the Jingle*	7.00	10.00
*actually, a Pepsi-Cola commercial!		
Victor 24481 *One Minute To One*	5.00	8.00
24488 *Count Your Blessings*	5.00	8.00
24570 *Let's Put Two And Two Together*	5.00	8.00
24572 *Winter Interlude*	5.00	8.00
24623 *How Do I Know It's Sunday?*	5.00	8.00
24626 *Fool That I Am*	5.00	8.00

JACKIE SOUDERS AND HIS ORCHESTRA:

Columbia 837-D *Every Little Thing*	7.00	10.00
906-D *Maybe Sometime*	7.00	10.00
Columbia (other issues)	4.00	7.00

Sousa's Band

Victor 312 *A Coon Band Contest (one-sided disc)*	15.00	25.00
Victor 315 *At A Georgia Camp Meeting (one-sided disc)*	15.00	25.00
Victor 316 *A Hot Time in the Old Town Tonight (one-sided disc)*	15.00	25.00
Victor 361 *Whistling Rufus (one-sided)*	15.00	25.00
Victor 362 *Who Dat Say Chicken In Dis Crowd (one-sided)*	15.00	25.00
Victor 1182 *Creole Belles (one-sided disc)*	15.00	25.00
Victor 1223 *Trombone Sneeze (one-sided disc)*	15.00	30.00
Victor 1417 *The Passing Of Rag Time (one-sided disc)*	15.00	30.00
Victor 2443 *Hiawatha (one-sided disc)*	15.00	25.00
Victor 4538 *Silence and Fun- A Rag Time Oddity (one-sided)*	20.00	40.00
Victor 16402 *At a Georgia Camp Meeting*	10.00	15.00
Victor 17252 *Creole Belles*	8.00	12.00

(Note: Some of the above titles were issued on the small, primitive *Berliner* records, these are of greater interest and value than the foregoing. Also, some of the above *Victor* records occur as 7-inch records, and/or with label variations (e.g., *Monarch, Victor Monarch, Improved*) found among the earliest products of the Victor Talking Machine Company.)

EDDIE SOUTH & HIS ALABAMIANS/ ORCHESTRA:

Victor 21151 *By The Waters Of Minnetonka*	5.00	8.00
21155 *The Voice Of The Southland*	5.00	8.00
21605 *That's What I Call Keen*	7.00	10.00
24324 *Old Man Harlem*	20.00	30.00
24343 *Gotta Go!*	20.00	30.00
24383 *Nagasaki*	20.00	30.00

SOUTHAMPTON SOCIETY ORCHESTRA:

Pathe-Actuelle 036252 *Ah-Ha!*	5.00	8.00
036253 *Suite 16*	5.00	8.00
036264 *If You Hadn't Gone Away*	5.00	8.00
036276 *I Miss My Swiss*	5.00	8.00
036301 *Loud Speakin' Papa*	5.00	8.00
36312 *Hugo, I Go Where You Go*	5.00	8.00

36318 *Brown Eyes, Why Are You Blue?*	5.00	8.00
36643 *I'm In Love Again*	8.00	12.00
Perfect 14395 *Poplar Street Blues*	15.00	20.00
14433 *Cross Words Between My Sweetie And Me*	5.00	8.00
14445 *Flag That Train*	5.00	8.00
14450 *Flapper Wife*	5.00	8.00
14457 *Oh Say! Can I See You Tonight*	5.00	8.00
14472 *Cecilia*	5.00	8.00
14482 *Loud Speakin' Papa*	5.00	8.00
14493 *Mighty Blue*	5.00	8.00
14824 *I'm In Love Again*	8.00	12.00

THE SOUTHERNERS:

Gennett 3061 *Craving*	10.00	15.00
3198 *Clap Hands! Here Comes Charley*	8.00	12.00
3199 *Rhythm Of The Day*	10.00	15.00
3204 *That Certain Party*	8.00	12.00
3212 *Someone's Stolen My Sweet Sweet Baby*	10.00	15.00
3265 *My Bundle Of Love*	10.00	15.00
3266 *But I Do - You Know I Do*	10.00	15.00

THE SOUTHERN FIVE:

LaBelle 1410 *I Wish I Could Shimmy Like My Sister Kate*	15.00	20.00
Melody 1410 *I Wish I Could Shimmy Like My Sister Kate*	15.00	20.00

SOUTHERN MELODY ARTISTS:

Okeh 41216 *When The World Is At Rest*	8.00	12.00

SOUTHERN MELODY SYNCOPATORS:

Marathon 229 *I'm on the Crest of a Wave*	20.00	up
232 *Sonny Boy*	20.00	up
234 *High Up on a Hill Top*	20.00	up
235 *Roses of Yesterday*	20.00	up

(Note: Above are 7-inch records.)

SOUTHERN ORCHESTRA:

Victor 707 *West Indies Rhythm*	8.00	12.00

SOUTHERN RHYTHM MASTERS:

Van Dyke 81891 *Sweetheart It's You*	10.00	15.00

THE SOUTHERN SERENADERS:

Bluebird 7367 *Goin' To Town*	7.00	10.00
Cameo 310 *Runnin' Wild*	5.00	8.00
Harmony 4-H *I Miss My Swiss*	15.00	20.00
5-H *Alone At Last*	15.00	20.00
Regal 9164 *Lonesome Lovesick Blues*	8.00	12.00
9191 *Satanic Blues*	8.00	12.00
Silvertone 2320 *Oh Sister! Ain't That Hot?*	8.00	12.00
2770 *I've Found A New Baby*	15.00	20.00

SOUTHLAND SIX:

Vocalion 14476 *Runnin' Wild*	7.00	10.00

SOUTHLAND SYNCOPATORS:

Vocalion 15544 *Brown Sugar*	10.00	150.00

SOUTH SHORE MELODY BOYS:

Champion 15036 *Oh Maud*	15.00	25.00
15037 *You Can't Make A Woman Change Her Mind*	15.00	25.00
15068 *Lantern Of Love*	8.00	12.00
15638 *Jo-Anne*	50.00	75.00
15639 *Blue Night*	50.00	75.00

SOUTH STREET RAMBLERS:

Q.R.S. 7019 *Endurance Stomp*	100.00	150.00

SOUTH STREET TRIO: ▶

Victor 20402 *Need More Blues*	75.00	100.00
21135 *Dallas Blues*	100.00	150.00
21249 *Suitcase Breakdown*	100.00	150.00
V38509 *South Street Stomp*	100.00	150.00

BUD SPAIGHT'S HARMONY KINGS:

Broadway 1389 *Don't Lose It*	35.00	50.00

ROY SPANGLER:

Rex 5024 *Cannon Ball Rag*	35.00	50.00
Rex 5026 *Red Onion Rag*	35.00	50.00
Rex 5342 *Red Onion Rag*	35.00	50.00

MUGGSY SPANIER & HIS RAGTIME BAND:

Bluebird 10384, 10417, 10506, 10518, 10532, 10682, 10719, 10766	4.00	8.00

SPARTON SYNCOPATORS:

Okeh 41331 *Sweetheart, We Need Each Other* ...	7.00 -	10.00
Okeh 41345 *I'll Still Go On Wanting You*	7.00 -	10.00
Parlophone PNY34071 *My Mad Moment*	15.00 -	20.00
Parlophone PNY34072 *Mia Cara (My Dear)*	15.00 -	20.00

PAUL SPECHT & HIS ORCHESTRA;
SPECHT'S SOCIETY SERENADERS:

Titles, issued contemporanesouly on Clarion, Harmony, Velvet Tone: *Keepin' Out Of Mischief Now; Sing A New Song; What A Life* .	8.00 -	12.00
Additional titles, issued on Banner, Paramount, Puritan, Triangle: *Hot Lips; You Can Have Him, I Don't Want Him Blues*	10.00 -	20.00
Columbia 554-D *Drifting Apart*	5.00 -	8.00
Columbia 577-D *So Does Your Old Mandarin* ...	5.00 -	8.00
Columbia 619-D *Honey Bunch*	5.00 -	8.00
Columbia 627-D *Static Strut*	8.00 -	12.00
Columbia 819-D *I've Grown So Lonesome, Thinking of You*	5.00 -	8.00
Columbia 853-D *Here Or There (As Long As I'm With You)*	5.00 -	8.00
Columbia 880-D *If All the Stars Were Pretty Babies*	5.00 -	8.00
Columbia 902-D *I'm Looking Over A Four Leaf Clover*	5.00 -	8.00
Columbia 997-D *She Looks Like Helen Brown* ...	8.00 -	12.00
Columbia 1013-D *Echoes of the South*	5.00 -	8.00
Columbia 1064-D *Dreamy Amazon*	5.00 -	8.00
Columbia 1117-D *Who's That Pretty Baby?*	5.00 -	8.00
Columbia 1186-D *Roll Up The Carpets*	8.00 -	12.00
Columbia 1273-D *Let a Smile Be Your Umbrella* .	7.00 -	10.00
Columbia 1307-D *St. Louis Shuffle*	8.00 -	12.00
Columbia 1333-D *Not Too Good - Not Too Bad* ..	7.00 -	10.00
Columbia 1708-D *Sweetheart of All My Dreams* .	5.00 -	8.00
Columbia 1766-D *On With the Dance*	5.00 -	8.00
Columbia 1807-D *The Things That Were Made for Love*	5.00 -	8.00
Columbia 1836-D *Hittin' The Ceiling*	8.00 -	12.00
Columbia 1890-D *At Close Of Day*	5.00 -	8.00
Columbia 1943-D *The World's Greatest Sweetheart Is You*	5.00 -	8.00
Columbia 2056-D *I'm Following You*	5.00 -	8.00
Columbia 2106-D *Keepin' Myself For You*	8.00 -	12.00
2472-D *Falling In Love*	7.00 -	10.00
Columbia 2482-D *I Found a Million Dollar Baby*	7.00 -	10.00
Columbia A3817 *When You and I Were Young Maggie Blues*	5.00 -	8.00
Columbia (most other issues)	3.00 -	6.00

MIKE SPECIALE: & HIS (CARLTON TERRACE) ORCHESTRA:

Edison 51612 *When The Dear Old Summer Goes* .	10.00 -	15.00
52498 *My Inspiration Is You*	15.00 -	20.00
Perfect 14375 *There'll Be Some Changes Made* ..	5.00 -	8.00
14405 *Breakin' The Leg*	7.00 -	10.00
14456 *Row, Row, Rosie*	5.00 -	8.00
14489 *Breezin' Along*	7.00 -	10.00
14491 *Want A Little Lovin'*	7.00 -	10.00
14494 *Walking The Rails*	7.00 -	10.00
14497 *I'm Knee Deep In Daisies*	5.00 -	8.00
14505 *Let's Make Believe*	5.00 -	8.00
14506 *Bam Bam Bamy Shore*	5.00 -	8.00
14526 *Mammy Chasing Blues*	7.00 -	10.00
14536 *I Love My Baby (My Baby Loves Me)* ...	7.00 -	10.00
14568 *Tentin' Down in Tennessee*	10.00 -	15.00
14569 *Dinah*	7.00 -	10.00
Perfect 14579 *Let's Do It*	5.00 -	8.00
Perfect 14581 *But I Do- You Know I Do*	5.00 -	8.00

SPENCER TRIO:

Decca 1873 *John Henry*	7.00 -	10.00
1941 *Baby, Won't You Please Come Home* .	7.00 -	10.00

HERBERT SPENCER AND HIS ORCHESTRA:

Banner 7032 *Why Do I Love You?*	7.00 -	10.00

Banner 7050 *Tin Ear*	7.00 -	10.00
Banner 7054 *I Still Love You*	5.00 -	8.00
Banner 7055 *She's a Great, Great Girl*	7.00 -	10.00
Banner 7057 *Lila*	8.00 -	12.00
Banner 7106 *Collegiana*	7.00 -	10.00
Banner 7107 *Last Night I Dreamed You Kissed Me*	7.00 -	10.00
Banner 7140 *Persian Rug*	7.00 -	10.00
Conqueror 7127 *Persian Rug*	5.00 -	8.00
Domino 4119 *She's a Great, Great Girl*	7.00 -	10.00
Regal 8516 *Lila*	8.00 -	12.00

WALLY SPENCER'S GEORGIANS:

Champion 15304 *Buffalo Rhythm*	50.00 -	75.00
15307 *Rubber Heels*	60.00 -	90.00
15308 *Swamp Blues*	50.00 -	75.00
15362 *Who's That Knockin' At My Door?*	40.00 -	60.00
15363 *The Varsity Drag*	40.00 -	60.00
15366 *Gold Digger*	150.00 -	250.00

SPIKE'S SEVEN PODS OF PEPPER ORCHESTRA:

Nordskog 3009 *Ory' s Creole Trombone*	200.00 -	400.00

REB SPIKES MAJORS AND MINORS:

Columbia 1193-D *My Mammy's Blues*	35.00 -	50.00

PHILIP SPITALNY & HIS ORCHESTRA:

Brunswick 4917 *Maybe It's Love*	7.00 -	10.00
Edison (thin) 14035 *I Want To Meander in the Meadow*	15.00 -	20.00
14050 *Same Old Moon*	15.00 -	20.00
14058 *Waiting at the End of the Road*	15.00 -	20.00
14062 *Just You, Just Me*	15.00 -	20.00
14069 *I May Be Wrong*	15.00 -	25.00
14076 *Bottoms Up*	15.00 -	25.00
14086 *If I Can't Have You*	15.00 -	25.00
Edison 52568 *An Eyeful Of You*	25.00 -	35.00
52577 *To Be In Love*	10.00 -	15.00
52589 *Here We Are*	10.00 -	15.00
52605 *When My Dreams Come True*	10.00 -	15.00
52622 *I Want To Meander in the Meadow*	15.00 -	20.00
52637 *So Sentimental*	10.00 -	15.00
Victor 20115 *Hello Baby*	5.00 -	8.00
20108 *Jackass Blues*	7.00 -	10.00
20475 *Rippin' It Off*	7.00 -	10.00
(See Also: THE HOUR OF CHARM ALL GIRL ORCHESTRA)		

DICK STABILE AND HIS ORCHESTRA:

Bluebird 7388 *In the Shade of the Old Apple Tree*	7.00 -	10.00
Decca 716 *Just Because*	8.00 -	12.00
977 *Ja Da*	8.00 -	12.00
Vocalion 3368 *Riffin' at the Ritz*	7.00 -	10.00

JESS STACY (& HIS ORCHESTRA):

Commodore 506, 507, 529, 1503	5.00 -	10.00
Varsity 8064, 8076, 8121, 8132, 8140	5.00 -	10.00

BILL STAFFON & HIS ORCHESTRA:

Bluebird 6048, 6049, 6082, 6115, 6175	5.00 -	10.00

JESSE STAFFORD & HIS (PALACE HOTEL) ORCHESTRA:

Brunswick 4048 *Cinderella Blues*	5.00 -	8.00
4129 *Doin' The Raccoon*	5.00 -	8.00
4548 *I Don't Want Your Kisses*	5.00 -	8.00
4630 *I'm Following You!*	5.00 -	8.00
Brunswick 4629, 4822, 4823, 4824, 6126	4.00 -	8.00

MARY STAFFORD AND HER JAZZ BAND:

Columbia A-3365 *Royal Garden Blues*	7.00 -	10.00
A3390 *Down Where They Play The Blues*	8.00 -	12.00
A3418 *Strut Miss Lizzie*	8.00 -	12.00
A3426 *Wild Weeping Blues*	10.00 -	15.00
A3493 *Blind man Blues*	10.00 -	15.00
A3511 *Monday Morning Blues*	8.00 -	12.00
Pathe Actuelle 7502 *Take Your Finger Off It*	50.00 -	75.00
Perfect 102 *Take Your Finger Off It*	50.00 -	75.00

AILEEN STANLEY:

Okeh 4326 *I've Got The Traveling Choo Choo Blues*	5.00 -	8.00

Okeh 4358 *It Takes a Good Man To Do That*	5.00 -	8.00
Okeh 4415 *'Tain't Nothin' Else But Jazz*	5.00 -	8.00
Okeh (Most other issues)	4.00 -	7.00
Victor 19373 *Nobody's Sweetheart*	5.00 -	8.00
Victor 19486 *Everybody Loves My Baby*	5.00 -	8.00
Victor 19863 *No Man's Mama*	5.00 -	8.00
Victor 20056 *I Wonder What's Become of Joe?* ..	5.00 -	8.00
Victor 22469 *Swingin' in a Hammock*	7.00 -	10.00
Victor 22524 *Wasn't It Nice?*	7.00 -	10.00
Victor (Most other issues)	3.00 -	6.00

HENRY STARR:

Flexo 148 *Mr. Froggie*	50.00 -	75.00

STATE STREET RAMBLERS:

Champion 16247 *Tiger Moan* ....150.00 -	250.00
16279 *Georgia Grind* ....150.00 -	250.00
16320 *Kentucky Blues*...........150.00 -	250.00
16350 *Richmond Stomp* ....150.00 -	250.00
16464 *Careless Love* ....150.00 -	250.00
40007 *Barrel House Stomp* .... 30.00 -	50.00
40009 *Georgia Grind* .... 30.00 -	50.00
40070 *Sic 'Em Tige* .... 30.00 -	50.00
40086 *Careless Love* .... 30.00 -	50.00
Gennett 6232 *Cootie Stomp* ....150.00 -	250.00
6249 *There'll Come A Day* ....150.00 -	250.00
6454 *My Baby* ....150.00 -	250.00
6485 *Shanghai Honeymoon* ....150.00 -	250.00
6552 *Endurance Stomp* ....150.00 -	250.00
6569 *Brown-Skin Mama* ....150.00 -	250.00
6589 *Tuxedo Stomp* ....150.00 -	250.00
6641 *Yearning And Blue* ....150.00 -	250.00
6692 *Oriental Man* ....150.00 -	250.00
Savoy 503 *Tiger Moan*................200.00 -	300.00

STATE STREET SWINGERS:

Vocalion 03284 *Chicago Rhythm*	15.00 -	25.00
03319 *Whippin' That Jelly*	15.00 -	25.00
03347 *You Waited Too Long*	15.00 -	25.00
03364 *Swing Cat Swing*	15.00 -	25.00
03395 *Rattlesnakin' Daddy*	15.00 -	25.00
03462 *You Drink Too Much*		
03572 *You Can't Do That To Me*	15.00 -	25.00

STEAMBOAT JOE & HIS LAFFIN' CLARINET:

Black Patti 8020 *Texas Shuffle* ....150.00 -	200.00
Gennett 6103 *Mississippi Valley Blues* .... 75.00 -	100.00

BLUE STEELE & HIS ORCHESTRA:

Bluebird 5867 *Sugar Babe, I'm Leavin'!*	5.00 -	8.00
Victor 20971 *Sugar Babe, I'm Leavin'!* ..	7.00 -	10.00
21183 *Betty Jean*	15.00 -	20.00
21262 *Washington And Lee Swing*	10.00 -	15.00
21355 *Be My Baby*	10.00 -	15.00
21400 *Because You Are My Dream Girl*	7.00 -	10.00
21530 *Beyond The Sunset*	7.00 -	10.00
22436 *You Darlin'*	7.00 -	10.00
23002 *Searching*	10.00 -	15.00
23014 *Shooin' Flies*	20.00 -	30.00
23501 *Worries On My Mind*..........	15.00 -	20.00
V-40140 *Coronado (Brings Memories Of You)* .	10.00 -	15.00
V-40161 *Tennessee Memories*................	10.00 -	15.00
V-40182 *Are You Lonesome?*	35.00 -	50.00
V-40288 *How Can You Forget?*	15.00 -	20.00

JOE STEELE & HIS ORCHESTRA:

Victor V-38066 *Coal Yard Shuffle*...........100.00 -	150.00

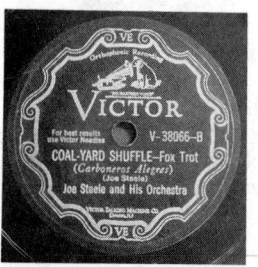

BILLY STENNETT'S CAROLINA STOMPERS:

Broadway 1193 *Down Where The Sun Goes Down*	15.00 -	20.00
1194 *Buffalo Rhythm*	25.00 -	40.00

LEITH STEVENS AND HIS SATURDAY NIGHT SWING CLUB ORCHESTRA:

Vocalion 4210 *Memphis Blues*.................	7.00 -	10.00
4350 *Twelfth Street Rag*	7.00 -	10.00

CARLYLE STEVENSON'S BON TON/EL PATIO ORCHESTRA:

Hollywood 1024 *Eccentric*	75.00 -	100.00
Sunset 1114 *Charleston*	15.00 -	20.00
1117 *Milenburg Joys*	50.00 -	75.00
1119 *Cecilia*.................	10.00 -	15.00
1120 *Collegiate*	10.00 -	15.00
1134 *Remember*	10.00 -	15.00

REX STEWART & HIS FIFTY-SECOND STREET STOMPERS/ORCHESTRA; REX STEWART'S BIG SEVEN:

Bluebird 10946 *Without A Song*	7.00 -	10.00
11057 *Linger Awhile*	7.00 -	10.00
11258 *Some Saturday*	7.00 -	10.00
Hot Record Society 2004 *Diga Diga Doo*	7.00 -	10.00
2005 *Bugle Call Rag*	7.00 -	10.00
Okeh 3831, 3844, 5448, 5510	5.00 -	10.00
Variety 517 *Rexatious*	7.00 -	10.00
618 *Back Room Romp*	7.00 -	10.00
664 *Sugar Hill Shim-Sham*	7.00 -	10.00
Vocalion 2880 *Stingaree*	20.00 -	30.00
3831 *Tea And Trumpets*	7.00 -	10.00
3844 *Sugar Hill Shim-Sham*	7.00 -	10.00
5448 *Fat Stuff Serenade*	5.00 -	8.00
5510 *San Juan Hill*	7.00 -	10.00

SAMMY STEWART & HIS ORCHESTRA; SAMMY STEWART'S TEN KNIGHTS OF SYNCOPATION:

Paramount 20340 *My Man Rocks Me*	35.00 -	50.00
20359 *Copenhagen*	30.00 -	40.00
Puritan 11340 *My Man Rocks Me*	35.00 -	50.00
11359 *Copenhagen*	30.00 -	40.00
Vocalion 15724 *'Cause I Feel Low Down* ....100.00 -	150.00
15734 *Crazy Rhythm*................100.00 -	150.00

JACK STILLMAN'S ORCHESTRA/ ORIOLES/ORIOLE ORCHESTRA; STILLMAN CLUB ORCHESTRA:

Bell 368, 382	5.00 -	8.00
Bell 457 *Gone Again Gal*	8.00 -	12.00
477 *High-High-High Up In The Hills*	8.00 -	12.00
Broadway 1001 *Say It Again*	8.00 -	12.00
1013 *Blue Bonnet*	8.00 -	12.00
Challenge 362 *Go Away And Don't Come Back* ..	7.00 -	10.00
Edison 51471 *Nobody Knows What A Red-Head Mamma Can Do*....................	10.00 -	15.00
51538 *Little Peach*	15.00 -	20.00
51768 *Valentine*.................	20.00 -	30.00
Emerson 3082 *Gone Again Gal*	8.00 -	12.00
3103 *High-High-High Up In The Hills*	8.00 -	12.00
3106 *My Little Bunch of Happiness*	8.00 -	12.00
Gennett 3183 *Cooler Hot*	15.00 -	20.00
3226 *Go Away and Don't Come Back*	7.00 -	10.00
3233 *Where Were You Then?*	8.00 -	12.00
3237 *Charleston of the Evening*	7.00 -	10.00

3244 *Lantern of Love*	7.00 -	10.00
3407 *Faustine*	7.00 -	10.00
Oriole 494 *Any Blues*	'8.00 -	12.00
499 *Mr. Cooler Hot*	8.00 -	12.00
Paramount 20423 *I Wonder Where My Baby Is*		
Tonight	8.00 -	12.00
20427 *Clap Hands, Here Comes Charley*	8.00 -	12.00
20455 *Blue Bonnet (You Make Me Feel Blue)*	8.00 -	12.00
Pathe Actuelle 36304 *Mr. Cooler Hot*	8.00 -	12.00
36305 *Charleston of the Evening*	7.00 -	10.00
36441 *Blue Bonnet*	7.00 -	10.00
36443 *Tonight's My Night with Baby*	7.00 -	10.00
36465 *Come On and Do Your Red Hot*		
Business	10.00 -	15.00
36473 *Nothing But Love*	5.00 -	8.00
36474 *Twilight And You*	5.00 -	8.00
Perfect 14485 *Mr. Cooler Hot*	8.00 -	12.00
14486 *Charleston of the Evening*	7.00 -	10.00
Perfect 14508 *Hip! Hip!*	7.00 -	10.00
Perfect 14510 *Go Away And Don't Come Back*	7.00 -	10.00
14622 *Blue Bonnet*	7.00 -	10.00
14624 *Tonights My Night With Baby*	7.00 -	10.00
14646 *Come On and Do Your Red Hot Business*	10.00 -	15.00
Perfect 14654 *Nothing But Love*	5.00 -	8.00
Perfect 14655 *Twilight And You*	5.00 -	8.00
Puritan 11424 *Dream Pal*	7.00 -	10.00
11427 *Roll 'Em, Girls*	7.00 -	10.00
11429 *If I Had A Girl Like You*	7.00 -	10.00
11443 *Say It Again*	5.00 -	8.00
11446 *Oh, You Lulu Belle*	5.00 -	8.00

BERT STOCK & HIS ORCHESTRA:

Gennett 7059 *Honeysuckle Rose*	25.00 -	40.00
7075 *'Tain't No Sin*	25.00 -	40.00

OCIE STOCKARD & THE WANDERERS:

Bluebird 7208 *Ain't Nobody Truck Like You*	8.00 -	12.00
Bluebird 7296 *One Of Us Was Wrong*	10.00 -	15.00
Bluebird 7459 *Same Thing All The Time*	8.00 -	12.00
Bluebird 7570 *There'll Be Some Changes Made*	10.00 -	15.00
Bluebird 7652 *Black and Blue*	10.00 -	15.00
Bluebird 7716 *Just Blues*	10.00 -	15.00
Bluebird 8021 *Wabash Blues*	10.00 -	15.00

THE STOMPIN' SIX:

Sunset 1098 *Jimtown Blues*	200.00 -	300.00
1099 *Down And Out Blues*	200.00 -	300.00

THE STOMP SIX:

Autograph 626 *Everybody Loves My Baby*	200.00 -	300.00

EDDIE STONE & HIS ORCHESTRA:

Vocalion 3555, 3576, 3585, 3703, 3750, 3984,		
3996, 4101	5.00 -	10.00

JESSE STONE & HIS BLUES SERENADERS/ORCHESTRA:

Okeh 8471 *Boot To Boot*	100.00 -	150.00
Variety 521 *Wind Storm*	15.00 -	20.00

CHARLEY STRAIGHT & HIS ORCHESTRA:

Brunswick 3136 *What A Man!*	5.00 -	8.00
3224 *Hobo's Prayer*	7.00 -	10.00
3324 *Tell Me Tonight*	5.00 -	8.00
3899 *That's What I Call Keen*	5.00 -	8.00
3900 *Sentimental Baby*	5.00 -	8.00
3945 *Too Busy*	5.00 -	8.00
Harmograph 862 *Easy Melody*	30.00 -	50.00
Paramount 20244 *Buddy's Habits*	30.00 -	50.00
Paramount 20264 *Arkansas Mule*	30.00 -	50.00
20266 *That Old Gang Of Mine*	7.00 -	10.00
20270 *Tweet Tweet*	7.00 -	10.00
20271 *Sweet Henry*	30.00 -	50.00

STRAND ROOF ORCHESTRA:

Domino 3456 *Prince of Wails*	15.00 -	20.00

ELLIS STRATAKOS & HIS HOTEL JUNG ORCHESTRA:

Vocalion 15792 *Weary River*	150.00 -	200.00

STRAUN'S PULLMAN PORTERS:

Gennett 3005 *Casey Jones*	8.00 -	12.00

HAL STUART & HIS GANG:

Bell 602 *Hot Coffee*	15.00 -	20.00
Champion 15680 *Avalon Town*	5.00 -	8.00

JOE SULLIVAN:

Columbia 2876-D *Gin Mill Blues*	25.00 -	40.00
2925-D *Onyx Bringdown*	25.00 -	40.00
Commodore 538, 540	5.00 -	10.00
Decca 600 *Little Rock Getaway*	10.00 -	15.00
Okeh 5496, 5531, 5647	5.00 -	10.00
Vocalion 5496, 5531, 5556	5.00 -	10.00

MAXINE SULLIVAN:

Victor 25802, 25810, 25894, 25895, 26124, 26132	5.00 -	10.00
Vocalion 3654, 3679, 3848, 3885, 3993, 4015,		
4068	5.00 -	10.00

SUNNY AND THE D'C'NS:

Blu-Disc 1003 *Oh- How I Love My Darling!*	250.00 -	500.00

SUNSET DANCE ORCHESTRA:

Champion 15038 *High Society*	40.00 -	60.00

THE SUNSHINE BOYS:

Columbia 1834-D, 2303 D	5.00 -	10.00

SUPER SYNCOPATORS:

Autograph (unnumbered) *Jimtown Blues*	100.00 -	Up
625 *South Bound*	100.00 -	Up

SUPERIOR DANCE KINGS:

Superior 2801 *Sweet Georgia Brown*	...	

WILBUR (C.) SWEATMAN'S ORIGINAL JAZZ BAND/ORCHESTRA; WILBUR SWEATMAN'S BROWNIES; WILBUR SWEATMAN (& HIS ACME SYNCOPATORS/ JAZZ BAND/ORCHESTRA):

Columbia A-2611, A-2645, A-2663, A-2682,		
A-2707, A-2721, A-2752, A-2768, A-2775,		
A-2818, A-2994	3.00 -	6.00
Edison 51438 *Battleship Kate*	20.00 -	30.00
Emerson 5163, 7161, (6 and 7 inch records)	8.00 -	12.00
Gennett 5584 *Battleship Kate*	15.00 -	20.00
Pathe 20145, 20147, 20167	7.00 -	10.00
Victor 23254 *Got 'Em Blues*	75.00 -	100.00
V38597 *Sweat Blues*	50.00 -	75.00
Vocalion 2945 *Battleship Kate*	10.00 -	15.00
2983 *The Hooking Cow Blues*	10.00 -	15.00

SAMMY SWIFT'S JAZZ BAND:

Black Swan 2042 *Blue Danube Blues*	25.00 -	35.00
2082 *The Carolina Shout*	25.00 -	35.00
2113 *That Red-Head Gal*	20.00 -	30.00
2117 *Way Down Yonder In New Orleans*	20.00 -	30.00
10078 *The Carolina Shout*	25.00 -	35.00

JOHN(NY) SYLVESTER & HIS ORCHESTRA/ PLAYMATES;

Gennett 3384 *No-One But You*	20.00 -	30.00
6026 *A Blues Serenade*	50.00 -	80.00
6027 *Song Of The Wanderer*	10.00 -	15.00
6056 *Indiana Butterfly*	10.00 -	15.00
6061 *No-One But You*	50.00 -	80.00
6095 *Mine*	10.00 -	15.00
6099 *St. Louis Blues*	50.00 -	80.00
Herschel Gold Seal 2010 *No-One But You*	50.00 -	100.00
Pathe-Actuelle 036086 *Sweet Man Joe*	10.00 -	15.00
036154 *I Wanna Jazz Some More*	10.00 -	15.00
036211 *King Porter Stomp*	10.00 -	15.00
36331 *I'm Goin' Out If Lizzie Comes In*	10.00 -	15.00
36354 *I Would Rather Be Alone in the South*	10.00 -	15.00
36502 *Looking at the World Thru' Rose-*		
Colored Glasses	7.00 -	10.00
36555 *Idolizing*	7.00 -	10.00
36556 *I've Got The Girl*	7.00 -	10.00
36599 *What's The Use?*	7.00 -	10.00
Perfect 14267 *Clearing House Blues*	10.00 -	15.00
14335 *Temperamental Papa*	10.00 -	15.00
14512 *I'm Goin' Out If Lizzie Comes In*	10.00 -	15.00
14535 *I Would Rather Be Alone in the South*	10.00 -	15.00

14683 *Looking at the World Thru' Rose-*
    Colored Glasses .... 7.00 - 10.00
14736 *Idolizing* .... 7.00 - 10.00
14737 *I've Got The Girl* .... 7.00 - 10.00
14780 *Rosie O'Ryan* .... 7.00 - 10.00

SYNCO JAZZ BAND: (See also: NEW SYNCO
JAZZ BAND)
Pathe 20499 *Sweet Mamma (Papa's Getting*
    Mad) .... 5.00 - 8.00
Pathe 22099 *Slim Trombone* .... 5.00 - 8.00
Pathe 22117 *Alcoholic Blues* .... 5.00 - 8.00
Pathe 22122 *At The Jazz Band Ball* .... 7.00 - 10.00
Pathe 22207 *Old Joe Blues* .... 7.00 - 10.00
Pathe-Actuelle 020558 *Satanic Blues* ...... 7.00 - 10.00
   020565 *Mysterious Blues* .... 7.00 - 10.00
   020699 *Carolina Blues* .... 7.00 - 10.00
Pathe-Actuelle (most other issues) .... 5.00 - 8.00

THE SYNCOPATING FIVE:
Gennett (unnumbered) *Lips* .... 10.00 - 20.00

THE SYNCOPATING SEVEN:
Gennett (unnumbered) *Toot-Toot Tootsie* ...... 100.00 - 150.00
(unnumbered) *Strutting At The Strutters' Ball* . 100.00 - 150.00

WILLIAM HOWARD TAFT:
Victor 16143 *Our Army And Navy* .... 5.00 - 8.00
Victor 35255 *A Protective Tariff (12-inch)* ...... 5.00 - 10.00
Victor 35256 *Who Are The People (12-inch)* .... 5.00 - 10.00

BOB TAMMS & HIS ORCHESTRA:
Broadway 1372 *Blue Is the Night* .... 5.00 - 8.00
Broadway 1373 *Strike Up The Band* .... 5.00 - 8.00
Broadway 1374 *Sweeping the Clouds Away* .... 10.00 - 15.00
Broadway 1509 *Every Time My Heart Beats* .... 5.00 - 8.00

TAMPA BLUE JAZZ BAND:
Okeh 4397 *Get Hot* .... 7.00 - 10.00
Okeh 4405 *Bad Land Blues* .... 7.00 - 10.00
Okeh 4425 *I've Got The Joys* .... 7.00 - 10.00
Okeh 4453 *The Missing Link* .... 5.00 - 8.00
Okeh 4461 *Brother Low Down* .... 5.00 - 8.00
Okeh 4485 *Torrid Dora* .... 5.00 - 8.00
Okeh 4499 *Down Home Blues* .... 5.00 - 8.00
Okeh 4522 *Atta Baby* .... 5.00 - 8.00
Okeh 4544 *Hurry Back Home* .... 5.00 - 8.00
Okeh 4573 *Dying With The Blues* .... 7.00 - 10.00
Okeh 4595 *The West Texas Blues* .... 7.00 - 10.00
Okeh 4663 *Hot Lips* .... 5.00 - 8.00
Okeh 4671 *Haunting Blues* .... 5.00 - 8.00
Okeh 4773 *Four O'Clock Blues* .... 7.00 - 10.00
Okeh 4777 *At the Weeping Widow's Ball* .... 7.00 - 10.00
Okeh 4791 *The Cootie Crawl* .... 7.00 - 10.00
Okeh 4803 *Sunny Jim* .... 5.00 - 8.00
Okeh 4816 *Railroad Man* .... 7.00 - 10.00
Okeh 4826 *Maxie Jones* .... 7.00 - 10.00

FRANK TANNER'S RHYTHM KINGS:
Bluebird 6667 *You Don't Love Me* .... 8.00 - 12.00
   6686 *Wrappin' It Up* .... 8.00 - 12.00
   6690 *Sailor Man Rhythm* .... 8.00 - 12.00
   6719 *Death In B Flat* .... 10.00 - 15.00
   6750 *Texas Teaser* .... 8.00 - 12.00

CARROLL C. TATE:
Victor 21061 *You Live On In Memory* .... 20.00 - 30.00

ERSKINE TATE'S VENDOME ORCHESTRA:
Okeh 4907 *Chinaman Blues* .... 150.00 - 200.00
Vocalion 1027 *Static Strut* .... 150.00 - 200.00
   15372 *Static Strut* .... 150.00 - 200.00

ART TATUM (& HIS BAND/SWINGSTERS):
Brunswick 6543 *St. Louis Blues* .... 15.00 - 20.00
   6553 *Tea For Two* .... 15.00 - 20.00
Decca 155 *Moon Glow* .... 8.00 - 12.00
   156 *Cocktails For Two* .... 8.00 - 12.00
   306 *Star Dust* .... 8.00 - 12.00
   468 *The Shout* .... 8.00 - 12.00
   741 *When A Woman Loves A Man* ...... 8.00 - 12.00
   1197 *Body And Soul* .... 8.00 - 12.00

1198 *With Plenty Of Money And You* .... 8.00 - 12.00
1373 *(I Would Do) Anything For You* .... 8.00 - 12.00
1603 *Stormy Weather* .... 8.00 - 12.00
2052 *The Skeik Of Araby* .... 5.00 - 8.00
2456 *Tea For Two* .... 4.00 - 7.00
8526 *Battery Bounce* .... 10.00 - 15.00
8536 *Stompin' At The Savoy* .... 10.00 - 15.00
8563 *Corrine Corrina* .... 10.00 - 15.00
8577 *Rock Me, Mama* .... 10.00 - 15.00

JACKIE TAYLOR & HIS ORCHESTRA
Victor 22500 *We're On The Highway To Heaven* . 8.00 - 12.00

JASPER TAYLOR & HIS ORIGINAL
WASHBOARD BAND/STATE STREET BOYS:
Paramount 12409 *Stomp Time Blues* ....250.00 - 400.00
Vocalion 1196 *Jasper Taylor Blues* ....150.00 - 250.00

RAY/ROY TAYLOR & HIS (SINGING)
ORCHESTRA:
Champion 15323 *Sweetheart Of Sigma Chi* ..... 40.00 - 60.00
   15324 *Sweet Violets* .... 20.00 - 30.00
Champion 15342 *Somebody And Me* .... 20.00 - 30.00
   15343 *Show Me That Kind Of A Girl* .... 25.00 - 35.00
Superior 356 *Sweet Violets* .... 50.00 - 100.00
   359 *Show Me That Kind Of A Girl* .... 50.00 - 100.00

TAYLOR'S DIXIE ORCHESTRA:
Victor 23277 *Everybody Loves My Baby* ....150.00 - 250.00

JACK TEAGARDEN (& HIS CHICAGOANS/
ORCHESTRA):
Brunswick 6716 *A Hundred Years From Today* ... 10.00 - 15.00
   6741 *Blue River* .... 10.00 - 15.00
   6780 *Ol' Pappy* .... 10.00 - 15.00
   6993 *Stars Fell On Alabama* .... 10.00 - 15.00
   7652 *Junk Man* .... 8.00 - 12.00
Columbia 2588-D *You Rascal, You* .... 20.00 - 30.00
   2803-D *Shake Your Hips* .... 20.00 - 30.00
   2913-D *Plantation Moods* .... 20.00 - 30.00
   35206, 35215, 35224, 35233, 35245, 35252,
     35297, 35323 .... 4.00 - 7.00
Crown 3051 *Rockin' Chair* .... 30.00 - 50.00
Domino 4651 *Son Of The Sun* .... 10.00 - 15.00
Hot Record Society 2006, 2007 .... 5.00 - 10.00
Perfect 15361 *You're Simply Delish* .... 10.00 - 15.00
   15363 *Son Of The Sun* .... 10.00 - 15.00

TED & HIS GANG:
Radiex 1531 *Forgetting You* .... 7.00 - 10.00
(Note: Above also issued on *Grey Gull*)

THE TEMPO KINGS:
Pathe-Actuelle 36385 *Rhythm Of The Day* ...... 8.00 - 12.00
Perfect 14566 *Rhythm Of The Day* .... 8.00 - 12.00

TEN BLACK BERRIES:
Titles, issued contemporaneously on Banner,
   Cameo, Challenge, Conqueror, Domino,
   Jewel, Oriole, Perfect, Regal, Romeo: *Jungle*
   Blues; Rent Party Blues; St. James Infirmary;
   When You're Smiling .... 10.00 - 15.00
Banner 0839 *Tiger Rag* .... 8.00 - 12.00
Jewel 6089 *Tiger Rag* .... 8.00 - 12.00
Oriole 2089 *St. Louis Blues* .... 8.00 - 12.00
Regal 10145 *St. Louis Blues* .... 8.00 - 12.00
Romeo 976 *Sorority Stomp* .... 10.00 - 15.00
   1453 *Tiger Rag* .... 8.00 - 12.00

TEN BLACK DIAMONDS:
Freshman Hop, issued contemporaneously on
   Banner, Cameo, Romeo .... 10.00 - 15.00
Banner 6539 *Look What You've Done To Me* .... 5.00 - 8.00
Banner 6542 *That's Why I'm Jealous Of You* .... 5.00 - 8.00

TEN FRESHMEN:
Pathe-Actuelle 37054 *Bag O' Blues* .... 10.00 - 15.00
Perfect 15235 *Bag O' Blues* .... 10.00 - 15.00

TENNESSEE CHOCOLATE DROPS:
Vocalion 1517 *Vine Street Drag* .... 80.00 - 120.00

TENNESSEE HAPPY BOYS:
Edison 51575 *Sweet Georgia Brown* .... 7.00 - 10.00

51613 *Wait'll It's Moonlight*	7.00 -	10.00
51703 *Birdie*	7.00 -	10.00
Edison (most other issues)	4.00 -	8.00

TENNESSEE MUSIC MEN:

Clarion 5389-C *Georgia On My Mind*	20.00 -	30.00
5392-C *You Rascal You*	20.00 -	30.00
5446-C *Loveless Love*	20.00 -	30.00
5461-C *Bugle Call Rag*	20.00 -	30.00
5467-C *Choo Choo*	15.00 -	25.00

5469-C *Baby Won't You Please Come Home*	15.00 -	25.00
5474-C *Shim-Me-Sha- Wabble*	15.00 -	25.00
Harmony 1375-H *Georgia On My Mind*	20.00 -	30.00
1378-H *You Rascal You*	20.00 -	30.00
1406-H *Loveless Love*	20.00 -	30.00
1415-H *Bugle Call Rag*	20.00 -	30.00
1420-H *Choo Choo*	15.00 -	25.00
1422-H *Baby, Won't You Please Come Home*	15.00 -	25.00
1427-H *Shim-Me-Sha-Wabble*	15.00 -	25.00
Velvet Tone 2453-V *Georgia On My Mind*	20.00 -	30.00
2456-V *You Rascal You*	20.00 -	30.00
2506-V *Loveless Love*	20.00 -	30.00
2521-V *Bugle Call Rag*	20.00 -	30.00
2527-V *Choo Choo*	15.00 -	25.00
2529-V *Baby, Won't You Please Come Home*	15.00 -	25.00
2534-V *Shim-Me-Sha-Wabble*	15.00 -	25.00

TENNESSEE TEN:

Victor 19073 *You've Got To See Mama Ev'ry Night*	5.00 -	8.00
Victor 19094 *Down Hearted Blues*	5.00 -	8.00
Victor 19105 *Long-Lost Mama*	5.00 -	8.00
Victor 19109 *Waitin' for The Evenin' Mail*	5.00 -	8.00
Victor 19130 *That Big Blonde Mama*	5.00 -	8.00

THE TENNESSEE TOOTERS:

Vocalion 14952 *Prince Of Wails*	15.00 -	20.00
14967 *Hot-Hot-Hottentot*	15.00 -	20.00
14985 *Everybody Loves My Baby*	15.00 -	20.00
15004 *Red Hot Henry Brown*	10.00 -	15.00
15022 *Jimtown Blues*	10.00 -	15.00
15068 *Milenberg Joys*	10.00 -	15.00
15086 *Charleston*	10.00 -	15.00
15109 *Deep Elm*	10.00 -	15.00
15135 *I Ain't Got Nobody*	10.00 -	15.00
15169 *Hot Aire*	10.00 -	15.00
15201 *Fallin' Down*	25.00 -	40.00
15388 *Hobo's Prayer*	10.00 -	15.00
15487 *Crazy Quilt*	10.00 -	15.00
15488 *You're Burnin' Me Up*	10.00 -	15.00

TENNESSEE TRIO:

Vocalion 5472 *Knox County Stomp*	80.00 -	120.00

MAX TERR & HIS ORCHESTRA:

Pathe-Actuelle 036175 *Have A Little Fun*	40.00 -	60.00
Perfect 14356 *Have A Little Fun*	40.00 -	60.00
14464 *My Dawg*	7.00 -	10.00
14468 *Fascinatin' Baby*	7.00 -	10.00
14469 *When You Do What You Do*	7.00 -	10.00
14475 *Charleston Bound*	7.00 -	10.00
14478 *Farewell*	7.00 -	10.00
14576 *Pensacola*	8.00 -	12.00

BOB TERRY & HIS ORCHESTRA:

Champion 40093 *My Heart And I*	10.00 -	15.00
40094 *It's Been So Long*	10.00 -	15.00

THELMA TERRY & HER PLAY BOYS:

Columbia 1390-D *Voice of the Southland*	8.00 -	12.00
1532-D *Starlight and Tulips*	5.00 -	8.00
1588-D *Dusky Stevedore*	8.00 -	12.00
1706-D *Mama's Gone, Goodbye*	10.00 -	15.00

TEXAS BLUES DESTROYERS:

Ajax 17065 *Lenox Avenue Shuffle*	30.00 -	50.00
Pathe-Actuelle 036160 *Lenox Avenue Shuffle*	20.00 -	30.00
Perfect 14314 *Lenox Avenue Shuffle*	20.00 -	30.00
Vocalion 14913 *Lenox Avenue Shuffle*	20.00 -	30.00

TEXAS TEN:

Banner 1540 *Sweet Georgia Brown*	7.00 -	10.00
Regal 9835 *Charleston*	7.00 -	10.00

TEXAS TODDLERS:

Varsity 5081 *Keepin' Out Of Mischief Now*	7.00 -	10.00

THEM BIRMINGHAM NIGHT OWLS:

Champion 15338 *Sugar*	150.00 -	200.00

HENRY THIES AND HIS (CASTLE FARM/HOTEL SINTON) ORCHESTRA:

Gennett 3118 *Angry*	15.00 -	20.00
Victor 21890 *Sweet Liza*	8.00 -	12.00
22476 *Here Comes Emily Brown*	8.00 -	12.00

THOMAS' DEVILS:

Brunswick 7064 *Boot It, Boy*	100.00 -	150.00

THOMAS' MUSCLE SHOALS DEVILS:

Okeh 8225 *Wash Woman Blues*	75.00 -	100.00

EDDIE THOMAS' COLLEGIANS:

Columbia 1154-D *Sugar*	8.00 -	12.00

GEORGE THOMAS & HIS BOYS:

Champion 15434 *Blue Hawaii*	100.00 -	150.00

HARRY THOMAS:

Victor 18229 *A Classical Spasm*	10.00 -	15.00

HERSAL THOMAS:

Okeh 8227 *Suitcase Blues*	75.00 -	100.00

HOCIEL THOMAS:

Buddy 8020 *I Must Have It*	100.00 -	150.00
8021 *Worried Down With The Blues*	100.00 -	150.00
Gennett 3004 *I Can't Feel Frisky Without My Liquor*	75.00 -	100.00
3006 *I Must Have It*	40.00 -	60.00
Okeh 8222 *Fish Tail Dance*	40.00 -	60.00
8258 *Adam And Eve Got The Blues*	80.00 -	120.00
8289 *Gambler's Dream*	80.00 -	120.00
8297 *Deep Water Blues*	80.00 -	120.00
8326 *Sunshine Baby*	80.00 -	120.00
8346 *Listen To Ma*	80.00 -	120.00

HOWARD THOMAS & HIS ORCHESTRA:

Champion 16380 *Business In F*	40.00 -	60.00
16387 *In The Shade Of The Old Apple Tree*	75.00 -	100.00
16656 *Rose Of Washington Square*	50.00 -	75.00
40080 *Business In F*	20.00 -	30.00

MILLARD G. THOMAS (& HIS CHICAGO NOVELTY ORCHESTRA):

Ajax 17045 *Lazy Drag*	30.00 -	50.00
17052 *More*	30.00 -	50.00
17053 *Hard Luck Blues*	30.00 -	50.00
17056 *Worryin' Blues*	30.00 -	50.00
17074 *Blue Ivories*	30.00 -	50.00

JOHNNY THOMPSON:

Columbia 14285-D *Back In Your Own Backyard*	10.00 -	15.00

KAY THOMPSON AND THE BOYS/HER ORCHESTRA:

Brunswick 7560 *You Hit The Spot*	8.00 -	12.00
7564 *Out Of Sight, Out Of Mind*	8.00 -	12.00
Victor 25564 *There's A Lull In My Life*	5.00 -	8.00
25582 *It Had To Be You*	5.00 -	8.00

CLAUDE THORNHILL AND HIS ORCHESTRA:

Brunswick 7951, 7957	5.00 -	10.00
Columbia, most issues	3.00 -	5.00
Harmony 1038 *Lullaby of the Rain*	5.00 -	8.00
Okeh 6124, 6168, 6178, 6202, 6234	4.00 -	7.00

V-Disc (12-inch) 612 *Stealin' Apples* . . . . 7.00 - 10.00
Vocalion 3595 *Gone With The Wind* . . . . 8.00 - 12.00
  3616 *Stop! You're Breaking My Heart* . . . . 7.00 - 10.00

THE THREE BARBERS:
Pathe-Actuelle 36414 *Down Town Rag* . . . . 15.00 - 20.00
Perfect 14565 *Down Town Rag* . . . . 15.00 - 20.00

THREE BLACK DIAMONDS:
Lincoln 2331 *Freakish Blues* . . . . 7.00 - 10.00

THREE BLUES CHASERS:
Okeh 8595 *Nothin' But Blues* . . . . 30.00 - 40.00

THE THREE BOSWELL SISTERS:
Okeh 41444 *Heebie Jeebies* . . . . 20.00 - 30.00
  41470 *Gee, But I'd Like To Make You Happy* . . 20.00 - 30.00

THE THREE DEUCES:
Commodore 537, 539 . . . . 5.00 - 10.00

THREE HAPPY DARKIES:
Silvertone 3057 *Freakish Blues* . . . . 15.00 - 20.00

THREE HOT ESKIMOS:
Pathe-Actuele 036298 *Black Cat Blues* . . . . 8.00 - 12.00
Perfect 14479 *Black Cat Blues* . . . . 8.00 - 12.00

THE THREE JACKS:
Okeh 41102 *Chile Blues* . . . . 15.00 - 20.00

THREE JOLLY MINERS:
Vocalion 1003 *Pig Alley Stomp* . . . . 15.00 - 20.00
  1004 *Chicago Back Step* . . . . 15.00 - 20.00
  15009 *Freakish Blues* . . . . 15.00 - 20.00
  15051 *Black Cat Blues* . . . . 15.00 - 20.00
  15087 *Lake George Blues* . . . . 15.00 - 20.00
  15111 *Plain Old Blues* . . . . 15.00 - 20.00
  15141 *Texas Shuffle* . . . . 15.00 - 20.00
  15164 *House Party Stomp* . . . . 15.00 - 20.00
  15269 *Pig Alley Stomp* . . . . 15.00 - 20.00
  15271 *Chicago Back Step* . . . . 15.00 - 20.00

THE THREE KEYS:
Brunswick 6388 *Jig Time* . . . . 10.00 - 15.00
  6411 *Nagasaki* . . . . 10.00 - 15.00
  6423 *Wah-Dee-Dah* . . . . 10.00 - 15.00
  6522 *That Doggone Dog of Mine* . . . . 10.00 - 15.00
  6567 *Rasputin* . . . . 10.00 - 15.00
Columbia 2706-D *Mood Indigo* . . . . 15.00 - 20.00
Vocalion 2523 *Heebie Jeebies* . . . . 10.00 - 15.00
  2569 *I Found A New Baby* . . . . 10.00 - 15.00
Vocalion 2730 *Someone Stole Gabriel's Horn* . . . 10.00 - 15.00
  2732 *Fit as a Fiddle* . . . . 10.00 - 15.00
  2744 *Basin Street Blues* . . . . 10.00 - 15.00
  2755 *(I Would Do) Anything For You* . . . . . 10.00 - 15.00
  2765 *Oh! By Jingo* . . . . 10.00 - 15.00

THREE MONKEY CHASERS:
Harmony 23-H *Corn Bread Wiggle* . . . . 8.00 - 12.00
  50-H *Uncle Remus Stomp* . . . . 8.00 - 12.00

THE THREE PEPPERS:
Decca 2239, 2557, 2609, 2751, 3342, 8508 . . . . . 5.00 - 10.00
Variety 523 *Alexander's Ragtime Band* . . . . 7.00 - 10.00
  590 *The Duck's Yas Yas* . . . . 7.00 - 10.00
  630 *Serenade in the Night* . . . . 7.00 - 10.00
  650 *Swingin' at the Cotton Club* . . . . 7.00 - 10.00
Vocalion 3803 *Swing Out Uncle, Wilson* . . . . . 7.00 - 10.00
  3805 *The Midnight Ride of Paul Revere* . . . . . 7.00 - 10.00

THREE'S A CROWD:
Bluebird 10014, 10051, 10160 . . . . 5.00 - 8.00

THE THREE T'S:
Victor 25273 *I'se A Muggin'* . . . . 7.00 - 10.00

THREE-FIFTEEN & HIS SQUARES:
Vocalion 03515 *Three Fifteen Blues* . . . . 15.00 - 20.00
  03560 *Mollie Mae Blues* . . . . 15.00 - 20.00

BUD THURSTON:
Champion 15489 *My Senorita* . . . . 50.00 - 80.00

LE ROY TIBBS & HIS CONNIE'S INN ORCHESTRA:
Columbia 14309-D *One O'Clock Blues* . . . . 50.00 - 75.00

TIM TIMOTHY & HIS FRIVOLITY CLUB ORCHESTRA:

Edison 52311 *My Pet* . . . . 15.00 - 20.00

KLIEN TINDULL'S PARAMOUNT SERENADERS:
Paramount 12377 *Down On The Amazon* . . . . . . 75.00 - 100.00

THE TIN PAN PARADERS:
Gennett 6456 *My Pet* . . . . 10.00 - 15.00
  6488 *Mama's Grown Young, Papa's Grown Old* 10.00 - 15.00
  6504 *Who Wouldn't Be Blue* . . . . 10.00 - 15.00
  6520 *When Sweet Susie Goes Steppin' By* . . . . 10.00 - 15.00
  6849 *She Only Laughs At Me* . . . . 10.00 - 15.00
  6921 *Believe It Or Not* . . . . 10.00 - 15.00
  6965 *If I Were You I'd Fall In Love With Me* . . 10.00 - 15.00
  6967 *I'm Finding The Long Way Home* . . . . . 10.00 - 15.00
  7012 *Clowning* . . . . 10.00 - 15.00
  7072 *Wake Up Your Feet* . . . . 10.00 - 15.00
  7132 *Harmonica Harry* . . . . 15.00 - 20.00
  7146 *You've Got That Thing* . . . . 15.00 - 20.00
  7148 *Puttin' On The Ritz* . . . . 15.00 - 20.00
  7174 *Chinnin' and Chattin' with May* . . . . . 15.00 - 20.00
Supertone 9333 *My Scandinavian Gal* . . . . 8.00 - 12.00
  9416 *She Only Laughs At Me* . . . . 8.00 - 12.00
  9464 *Now I'm In Love* . . . . 10.00 - 15.00
  9477 *I Lift Up My Finger and I Say "Tweet Tweet"* . . . . 10.00 - 15.00
  9544 *I Gotta Have You* . . . . 10.00 - 15.00
  9616 *The Man From The South* . . . . 10.00 - 15.00
  9620 *Just Can't Be Bothered With Me* . . . . . 10.00 - 15.00
  9634 *The Free And Easy* . . . . 10.00 - 15.00

TINSLEY'S WASHBOARD BAND:
Victor 24405 *Shoutin' In The Amen Corner* . . . . . 20.00 - 30.00

BEN TOBIER & HIS CALIFORNIA CYCLONES:
Champion 16425 *Hot And Heavy* . . . . 75.00 - 100.00
Superior 2571 *Hot And Heavy* . . . . 80.00 - 120.00

TOBIN'S MIDNIGHT SERENADERS:
Okeh 40297 *I'm Afraid To Care For You* . . . . . . 40.00 - 60.00

SKEETS TOLBERT AND HIS GENTLEMEN OF SWING:
Decca 7570, 7591, 7630, 7653, 7669, 7717, 7722,
  7751, 7791, 8506, 8516, 8528, 8534, 8565,
  8579, 8589, 8608, 8617, 8631, 8641 . . . . 5.00 - 10.00

TOM AND JERRY:
Champion 15507 *Dustin' The Keys* . . . . 75.00 - 100.00

PINKY TOMLIN:
Brunswick 7377, 7378, 7502, 7525, 7594, 7653,
  7731, 7811, 7849, 7897 . . . . 5.00 - 10.00

TOMMY "RED" TOMPKINS & HIS ORCHESTRA:
Variety 543 *Monopoly Swing* . . . . 7.00 - 10.00
  610 *I Never Had a Dream* . . . . 7.00 - 10.00
Vocalion 3271 *What The Heart Believes* . . . . . . 7.00 - 10.00
  3293 *Viper's Dream* . . . . 7.00 - 10.00

TRACY-BROWN'S ORCHESTRA:
Columbia 1344-D *Chloe (Song of the Swamp)* . . . 5.00 - 8.00
Columbia 1405-D *Sh-h! Here Comes My Sugar* . . 7.00 - 10.00
Columbia 1541-D *Joline* . . . . 5.00 - 8.00

TRAM, BIX & EDDIE:
Okeh 40871 *For No Reason At All In C* . . . . 25.00 - 40.00

TRAM, BIX & LANG:
Okeh 40916 *Wringin' And Twistin'* . . . . 30.00 - 50.00

THE TRAVELERS:
Melotone 12113 *Sweet And Hot* . . . . 8.00 - 12.00
  12148 *I've Got A Sweet Somebody* . . . . 8.00 - 12.00
  12227 *I Apologize* . . . . 6.00 - 10.00
  12230 *I Can't Get Mississippi Off My Mind* . . . 15.00 - 25.00
Okeh 41259 *Am I Blue* . . . . 15.00 - 20.00
  41260 *Breakaway* . . . . 15.00 - 20.00
  41471 *Fine And Dandy* . . . . 15.00 - 20.00

VINCENT TRAVERS AND HIS ORCHESTRA:
Titles, issued contemporaneously on Banner, Melotone,
  Oriole, Perfect, Romeo, Vocalion: *Love Is*
  Good For Anything That Ails You; Was It Rain? 5.00 - 8.00

TRAVIS-CARLTON ORCHESTRA:

Gennett 3099 *Headin' For Home*	8.00	-	12.00
3216 *Somebody's Eyes*	7.00	-	10.00

THE TRAYMORE ORCHESTRA:

Vocalion 15556 *Black And Tan Fantasy*	35.00	-	50.00

PAUL TREMAINE AND HIS ARISTOCRATS/ ORCHESTRA:

Bluebird 5049, 5050	5.00	-	8.00
Columbia 2130-D *Hand Me Down My Walkin' Cane*	7.00	-	10.00
2200-D *Rockin' Chair*	7.00	-	10.00
2229-D *Steamboat Bill*	7.00	-	10.00
2302-D *Gospel Train*	7.00	-	10.00
2462-D *I Wanna Sing About You*	8.00	-	12.00
2510-D *I Can't Get Mississippi Off My Mind*	8.00	-	12.00
Victor V-40176 *Four-Four Rhythm*	30.00	-	40.00
V-40230 *Sarah Lee*	15.00	-	20.00

GEORGE H. TREMER:

Champion 15372 *Some Of These Days*	40.00	-	60.00
15436 *Spirit Of '49 Rag*	150.00	-	200.00
Decca 7137 *Spirit of '49 Rag*	10.00	-	15.00
Gennett 6242 *Spirit Of '49 Rag*	75.00	-	100.00

ALPHONSE TRENT & HIS ORCHESTRA:

Champion 15956 *St. James Infirmary*	150.00	-	200.00
16587 *I've Found A New Baby*	150.00	-	200.00
Gennett 6664 *Louder and Funnier*	150.00	-	250.00
6710 *Nightmare*	150.00	-	250.00

JO TRENT AND THE D'C'NS:

Blu-Disc 1003 *Deacon Jazz*	250.00	-	500.00

TRIANGLE HARMONY BOYS:

Gennett 6275 *Sweet Patootie*	200.00	-	300.00
6322 *Canned Heat Blues*	200.00	-	300.00

BARNEY TRIMBLE & HIS OKLAHOMANS:

Harmony 781-H *Are We Downhearted? No!*	5.00	-	8.00
926-H *Honey*	5.00	-	8.00
948-H *I'm Featuring A Nest*	5.00	-	8.00
958-H *Where The Sweet Forget-Me-Nots Remember*	7.00	-	10.00
987-H *Bashful Baby*	7.00	-	10.00
1093-H *Blue, Turning Grey Over You*	5.00	-	8.00

(Note: Above titles, on *Diva* and *Velvet Tone*, are similarly valued.)

TROMBONE RED AND HIS BLUE SIX:

Columbia 14612-D *Greasy Plate Stomp*	100.00	-	150.00

CHARLIE TROUTT'S MELODY ARTISTS:

Columbia 1030-D *Transportation Blues*	8.00	-	12.00
1265-D *Transportation Blues, Parts 3/4*	10.00	-	15.00
Okeh 40589 *Mountain City Blues*	20.00	-	30.00
40627 *Sweet Child (I'm Wild About You)*	75.00	-	100.00

THE TROY HARMONISTS:

Pathe-Actuelle 7508 *Great Scott*	50.00	-	75.00
Perfect 108 *Great Scott*	50.00	-	75.00

FRANKIE TRUMBAUER & HIS ORCHESTRA; FRANKIE TRUMBAUER'S AUGMENTED ORCHESTRA:

Brunswick 6146 *Crazy Quilt*	10.00	-	15.00
6159 *Honeysuckle Rose*	10.00	-	15.00
6763 *Juba Dance*	8.00	-	12.00
6788 *Emaline*	8.00	-	12.00
6912 *China Boy*	8.00	-	12.00
6997 *In A Mist*	8.00	-	12.00
7613 *Breakin' In A Pair Of Shoes*	8.00	-	12.00
7629 *Announcer's Blues*	8.00	-	12.00
7663 *'S Wonderful*	8.00	-	12.00
7665 *Ain't Misbehavin'*	8.00	-	12.00
7687 *Diga Diga Doo*	8.00	-	12.00
Columbia 2710-D *Business In Q*	15.00	-	20.00
2729-D *The Newest St. Louis Blues*	15.00	-	20.00
2879-D *Bass Drum Dan*	15.00	-	20.00
18002-D *Sizzling One-Step Medley*	20.00	-	30.00
Okeh 40772 *Singin' The Blues*	20.00	-	30.00
40822 *Ostrich Walk*	25.00	-	40.00

40843 *I'm Coming Virginia*	25.00	-	30.00
40871 *Trumbology*	20.00	-	30.00
40879 *Blue River*	20.00	-	30.00
40903 *Three Blind Mice*	20.00	-	30.00
40926 *Humpty Dumpty*	20.00	-	30.00
40966 *A Good Man Is Hard To Find*	25.00	-	40.00
40979 *There'll Come A Time*	25.00	-	40.00
41019 *Lila*	25.00	-	40.00
Okeh 41039 *My Pet*	25.00	-	40.00
41044 *Jubilee*	25.00	-	40.00
41100 *Dusky Stevedore*	25.00	-	40.00
41128 *High Up On A Hill Top*	25.00	-	40.00
41145 *Take Your Tomorrow*	25.00	-	40.00
41209 *Futuristic Rhythm*	25.00	-	40.00
41231 *Louise*	20.00	-	30.00
41252 *Nobody But You*	20.00	-	30.00
41268 *Shivery Stomp*	20.00	-	30.00
41286 *Baby, Won't You Please Come Home?*	25.00	-	40.00
41301 *How Am I To Know?*	15.00	-	20.00
41313 *Turn On The Heat*	15.00	-	20.00
41326 *My Sweeter Than Sweet*	15.00	-	20.00
41330 *What Wouldn't I Do For That Man?*	15.00	-	20.00
41421 *Happy Feet*	15.00	-	20.00
41431 *Deep Harlem*	15.00	-	20.00
41432 *What's The Use?*	15.00	-	20.00
41450 *Choo Choo*	15.00	-	20.00
Victor 24812 *Blue Moon*	15.00	-	20.00
24834 *Troubled*	15.00	-	20.00

TRUMP'S AMBASSADOR BELL HOPS ORCHESTRA:

Okeh 1 *What A Man*		-	

GEORGE TUCKER & HIS NOVELTY BAND:

Champion 15638 *Doin' The New Low Down*	50.00	-	75.00
15639 *Spiked Beer*	50.00	-	75.00

ORRIN TUCKER AND HIS ORCHESTRA:

Columbia, most issues	3.00	-	5.00
Vocalion, most issues	3.00	-	6.00

SOPHIE TUCKER:

Columbia 826-D *Some Of These Days*	7.00	-	10.00
Okeh 4565, 4590, 4617, 4817, 4818, 4837, 4839, 40054, 40895, 40921, 41010, 41058, 41249	5.00	-	10.00
Okeh 40068 *I've Got a Cross-Eyed Papa*	15.00	-	25.00
40129 *Hula Lou*	10.00	-	15.00
40813 *One Sweet Letter From You*	15.00	-	20.00
40837 *Afer You've Gone*	15.00	-	20.00
Victor 21993, 21994, 21995, 22049	5.00	-	10.00

TOMMY TUCKER & HIS CALIFORNIANS/ ORCHESTRA; TOMMY TUCKER TIME:

Crown 3470 *Low Down Upon The Harlem River*	10.00	-	15.00
3497 *Blue Prelude*	10.00	-	15.00
Crown 3471, 3477, 3478, 3479, 3499	4.00	-	8.00
Okeh (most issues)	3.00	-	5.00
Varsity 8070 *Blue Prelude*	5.00	-	8.00
Vocalion (most issues)	3.00	-	6.00

AL TURK'S (PRINCESS) ORCHESTRA:

Okeh 8362 *Snag It*	75.00	-	100.00
8377 *Mean Man*	75.00	-	100.00
40648 *I'm Just Wild About Animal Crackers*	20.00	-	30.00
40653 *Snag It*	75.00	-	100.00
40660 *Shanghai Honeymoon*	20.00	-	30.00
Olympic 1461 *Copenhagen*	75.00	-	100.00
1463 *King Porter Stomp*	75.00	-	100.00

JOE TURNER AND HIS MEMPHIS MEN:

Columbia 1813-D *Freeze And Melt*	15.00	-	20.00

LLOYD TURNER AND HIS (VILLA VENICE) ORCHESTRA:

Okeh 40648 *Blue Bonnet, You Make Me Blue*	20.00	-	30.00
40658 *Let's Forget*	7.00	-	10.00
40674 *My Mama's In Town*	8.00	-	12.00

TUXEDO SYNCOPATORS:

Titles, issued contemporaneously on Globe, Madison: *Horse Feathers, Torrid Rhythm,*

    Zoolithique .... 25.00 - 40.00

TWIN CITIES DANCE ORCHESTRA:
    Challenge 257 *I'm Looking Over A Four-Leaf*
    Clover .... 75.00 - 100.00

TWIN CITY BELL HOPS:
    Champion 15174 *No-One But You (Knows How*
    To Love) .... 30.00 - 50.00

TWO BLACK CROWS (See MORAN & MACK):

SUGAR UNDERWOOD:
    Victor 21538 *Dew Drop Alley Stomp* .... 75.00 - 100.00

UNITED STATES MARINE BAND:
    Victor 16792 *Maple Leaf Rag* .... 10.00 - 15.00
    35880 *Crazy Bone Rag (12-inch)* .... 10.00 - 15.00
    (Note: Earlier issues, on the primitive *Berliner*
    discs, are scarcer and more valuable than the
    foregoing.)

UNITED STATES NAVAL RESERVE BAND:
    Columbia A2627 *A Slippery Place—A Comic Rag* 8.00 - 12.00

UNIVERSAL DANCE ORCHESTRA:
    Madison 1620 *Pepper Blues* .... 10.00 - 15.00

UNIVERSAL SEXTETTE:
    Lincoln 2417 *Milenberg Joys* .... 8.00 - 12.00

UNIVERSITY BOYS:
    Oriole 1069 *Is She My Girl Friend?* .... 5.00 - 8.00
    Oriole 1152 *Changes* .... 7.00 - 10.00
    Oriole 1446 *If You Want the Rainbow* .... 5.00 - 8.00
    Oriole 1627 *Singin' in the Rain* .... 5.00 - 8.00
    Oriole 1668 *Lovable and Sweet* .... 10.00 - 15.00
    Oriole 1692 *Steppin' Along* .... 5.00 - 8.00

UNIVERSITY EIGHT:
    Lincoln 2543 *Ya Gotta Know How To Love* ..... 7.00 - 10.00
    2566 *She Knows Her Onions* .... 7.00 - 10.00
    2606 *Crazy Words-Crazy Tune* .... 7.00 - 10.00
    2626 *Ain't She Sweet?* .... 7.00 - 10.00
    2674 *Arkansas Blues* .... 8.00 - 12.00

UNIVERSITY ORCHESTRA:
    Gennett 6815 *Button Up Your Overcoat* .... 10.00 - 15.00
    6862 *I've Got A Feeling I'm Falling* .... 10.00 - 15.00
    6892 *Singin' in the Rain* .... 10.00 - 15.00
    6920 *I'm In Seventh Heaven* .... 10.00 - 15.00
    6980 *Hang On To Me* .... 10.00 - 15.00
    7011 *Miss Wonderful* .... 15.00 - 20.00
    7042 *Lady Luck* .... 15.00 - 20.00
    7117 *Happy Days Are Here Again* .... 15.00 - 20.00
    7234 *Swingin' in a Hammock* .... 15.00 - 20.00
    7257 *Hullabaloo* .... 15.00 - 20.00

UNIVERSITY SEXTETTE:
    Lincoln 2093, 2105, 2116, 2127, 2130, 2142, 2154,
    2166, 2167, 2176, 2216, 2219, 2229, 2231, 2241,
    2242, 2250 .... 4.00 - 8.00
    Lincoln 2168 *Mean Blues* .... 7.00 - 10.00
    2208 *Doodle Doo Doo* .... 5.00 - 8.00
    2238 *Hard Hearted Hannah* .... 5.00 - 8.00
    2245 *She Loves Me* .... 5.00 - 8.00
    2256 *A New Kind Of Man* .... 5.00 - 8.00
    2264 *Talkin' To Myself* .... 5.00 - 8.00
    2268 *Copenhagen* .... 7.00 - 10.00
    2270 *Them Ramblin' Blues* .... 5.00 - 8.00
    2276 *Dear One* .... 5.00 - 8.00
    2279 *I'm Satisfied Beside That Sweetie O'*
    Mine .... 5.00 - 8.00
    Lincoln 2288 *Doo Wacka Doo* .... 5.00 - 8.00
    2290 *Oh! Mabel* .... 5.00 - 8.00
    2302 *Happy* .... 5.00 - 8.00
    2306 *I Ain't Got Nobody To Love* .... 5.00 - 8.00
    2307 *Ain't My Baby Grand* .... 5.00 - 8.00
    2311 *I Like You Best Of All* .... 5.00 - 8.00
    2315 *No One* .... 5.00 - 8.00
    2328 *Nobody Knows What A Red Head Mama*
    Can Do .... 5.00 - 8.00
    2330 *Don't Bring Lulu* .... 5.00 - 8.00

    2337 *Cheatin' On Me* .... 7.00 - 10.00
    2339 *Lady of the Nile* .... 4.00 - 7.00
    2340 *Sweet Georgia Brown* .... 7.00 - 10.00
    2343 *Ah Ha!* .... 5.00 - 8.00
    2352 *If You knew Susie* .... 7.00 - 10.00
    2355 *Charleston* .... 7.00 - 10.00
    2371 *Yes, Sir! That's My Baby* .... 7.00 - 10.00
    2380 *Oh, Say! Can I See You Tonight?* .... 7.00 - 10.00
    2382 *I Want To See A Little More Of What I*
    Saw In Arkansas .... 5.00 - 8.00
    2387 *Tryin' To Keep Away From You* .... 5.00 - 8.00
    2403 *Sweet Man* .... 7.00 - 10.00
    2435 *Show Me The Way To Go Home* .... 5.00 - 8.00
    2441 *Freshie* .... 5.00 - 8.00
    2463 *In My Gondola* .... 5.00 - 8.00
    2517 *What a Man!* .... 7.00 - 10.00
    2557 *Static Strut* .... 8.00 - 12.00
    2578 *Lay Me Down To Sleep In Carolina* .... 5.00 - 8.00
    2598 *Lonely Eyes* .... 5.00 - 8.00
    2697 *Vo-Do-Do-De-O Blues* .... 8.00 - 12.00
    2745 *Is She My Girl Friend?* .... 7.00 - 10.00
    2795 *Farewell Blues* .... 8.00 - 12.00
    2809 *Steamboat Bill* .... 8.00 - 12.00
    2864 *On The Vagabond Trail* .... 4.00 - 6.00
    2865 *Mother* .... 4.00 - 6.00
    3260 *What Do We Get From Boston?* .... 5.00 - 8.00

UNIVERSITY SIX:
    Harmony 36-H *The Camel Walk* .... 7.00 - 10.00
    37-H *Desdemona* .... 7.00 - 10.00
    71-H *Smile a Little Bit* .... 7.00 - 10.00
    73-H *In Your Green Hat* .... 7.00 - 10.00
    106-H *Fallin' Down* .... 8.00 - 12.00
    134-H *Dustin' The Donkey* .... 8.00 - 12.00
    155-H *Georgianna* .... 7.00 - 10.00
    160-H *Sittin' Around* .... 7.00 - 10.00
    209-H *Ace In The Hole* .... 10.00 - 15.00
    224-H *Tiger Rag* .... 10.00 - 15.00
    230-H *I Ain't Got Nobody* .... 8.00 - 12.00
    Harmony 245-H *St. Louis Hop* .... 8.00 - 12.00
    262-H *That's A Good Girl* .... 7.00 - 10.00
    296-H *My Baby Knows How* .... 7.00 - 10.00
    316-H *It Takes A Good Woman* .... 7.00 - 10.00
    Harmony 367-H *The Cat* .... 8.00 - 12.00
    382-H *It's Ok Katy With Me* .... 8.00 - 12.00
    399-H *Rosy Cheeks* .... 5.00 - 8.00
    414-H *Beale Street Blues* .... 10.00 - 15.00
    425-H *Yes She Do—No She Don't* .... 7.00 - 10.00
    433-H *Lazy Weather* .... 5.00 - 8.00
    444-H *Bless Her Little Heart* .... 5.00 - 8.00
    466-H *Swanee Shore* .... 5.00 - 8.00
    474-H *Pastafazoola* .... 5.00 - 8.00
    489-H *Oh, Doris! Where Do You Live?* .... 7.00 - 7.00
    510-H *Zulu Wail* .... 7.00 - 10.00
    529-H *Manhattan Mary* .... 5.00 - 8.00
    534-H *Is She My Girl Friend?* .... 5.00 - 8.00
    551-H *Changes* .... 8.00 - 12.00
    557-H *Tell Me, Little Daisy* .... 5.00 - 8.00
    565-H *Mine—All Mine* .... 5.00 - 8.00
    570-H *Under The Clover Moon* .... 5.00 - 8.00
    581-H *Let A Smile Be Your Umbrella* .... 7.00 - 10.00
    591-H *What Do You Say?* .... 7.00 - 10.00
    617-H *Stay Out Of The South* .... 7.00 - 10.00
    619-H *Speedy Boy* .... 7.00 - 10.00
    652-H *Chilly-Pom-Pom-Pee* .... 4.00 - 7.00
    653-H *C-O-N-S-T-A-N-T-I-N-O-P-L-E* .... 4.00 - 7.00
    (Note: Above titles, issued also on *Diva* and
    Velvet Tone, are of equal value and interest.)

THE VAGABONDS:
    Cameo 896 *What! No Women?* .... 7.00 - 10.00
    Gennett 3099 *I'm Gonna Charleston Back To*
    Charleston .... 8.00 - 12.00
    3100 *Ukelele Lady* .... 8.00 - 12.00

3128 *Normandy*	7.00 -	10.00
3137 *Sweet Man*	8.00 -	12.00
3282 *Could I? I Certainly Could*	8.00 -	12.00
3283 *I'd Climb The Highest Mountain*	8.00 -	12.00
3361 *The Birth of the Blues*	8.00 -	12.00
3362 *Looking at the World Thru' Rose-Colored Glasses*	8.00 -	12.00
5288 *Rememb'ring*	5.00 -	8.00
5291 *Sittin' In A Corner*	5.00 -	8.00
5362 *California, Here I Come*	5.00 -	8.00
5447 *Shine*	7.00 -	10.00
5448 *Don't Mind The Rain*	7.00 -	10.00
5485 *Where The Dreamy Wabash Flows*	7.00 -	10.00
5501 *Nobody's Child*	7.00 -	10.00
5502 *Knock at the Door*	7.00 -	10.00
5504 *You Know Me, Alabam!*	7.00 -	10.00
5529 *Sing a Little Song*	7.00 -	10.00
5539 *I Want To Be Happy*	7.00 -	10.00
5540 *Rose Marie*	7.00 -	10.00
5568 *Nancy*	7.00 -	10.00
5576 *Southern Rose*	7.00 -	10.00
5602 *Back Where The Daffodils Grow*	7.00 -	10.00
5630 *Somebody Like You*	7.00 -	10.00
Gennett 6398 *You Gotta Be Good To Me*	10.00 -	15.00

SYD VALENTINE & HIS PATENT LEATHER KIDS:

Gennett 7026 *Patent Leather Stomp*	150.00 -	250.00
7071 *Asphalt Walk*	150.00 -	250.00

RUDOLPH VALENTINO:

Special Record (unnumbered) *Kashmiri Song*	30.00 -	40.00

RUDY VALLEE AND HIS CONNECTICUT YANKEES:

Titles, issued contemporaneously on Banner, Conqueror, Melotone, Oriole, Perfect, Romeo: *All's Fair In Love And War; Bojangles of Harlem' Call of the Prairie; The Coronation Waltz; Dream Time; Empty Saddles; A Fine Romance; The Glory of Love; I'm on a Wild Goose Chase; I Was Saying to the Moon; Rhythm on the Range; Seventh Heaven; She Shall Have Music; Speaking of the Weather; That's Southern Hospitality; These Foolish Things; Turn Off the Moon; Us on a Bus; The Waltz In Swing Time; The Way You Look Tonight, The Whiffenpoof Song; Who Loves You? Would You?* ... 7.00 - 12.00

Bluebird 5097 *On The Air*	8.00 -	12.00
5098 *Thank Heaven For You*	8.00 -	12.00
5114 *Lazy Bones*	8.00 -	12.00
5115 *Don't Blame Me*	8.00 -	12.00
5118 *To Be Or Not To Be In Love*	8.00 -	12.00
5132 *Three Wishes*	8.00 -	12.00
5171 *Honeymoon Hotel*	10.00 -	15.00
5172 *Shaghai Lil*	5.00 -	8.00
5175 *Shame On You*	10.00 -	15.00
5177 *Nagasaki*	8.00 -	12.00
5182 *Happy Boy—Happy Girl*	10.00 -	15.00

(Note: Above titles, on *Electradisk* are worth somewhat more; on *Sunrise*, substantially more.)

Bluebird 7067, 7069, 7078, 7120, 7135, 7140, 7226, 7238, 7331, 7342, 7368, 7543, 7645, 7649, 7667	4.00 -	8.00
Clarion 5086-C *Sweetheart Of All My Dreams*	7.00 -	10.00
Columbia 2700-D *Maori*	10.00 -	15.00
2702-D *Strange Interlude*	10.00 -	15.00
2714-D *Say It Isn't So*	10.00 -	15.00
2715-D *Me Minus You*	10.00 -	15.00
2724-D *Please*	10.00 -	15.00
2725-D *Brother, Can You Spare A Dime?*	10.00 -	15.00
2730-D *Till Tomorrow*	10.00 -	15.00
2733-D *The Language Of Love*	10.00 -	15.00

2737-D *I'm Playing With Fire*	10.00 -	15.00
2738-D *A Jug Of Wine, A Loaf Of Bread*	10.00 -	15.00
2744-D *Hey! Young Fella*	10.00 -	15.00
2746-D *Pretending You Care*	10.00 -	15.00
2756-D *Meet Me In the Gloaming*	10.00 -	15.00
2764-D *Old Man Harlem*	10.00 -	15.00
2771-D *I Lay Me Down To Sleep*	10.00 -	15.00
2773-D *I've Got To Sing A Torch Song*	10.00 -	15.00

(Note: Above *Columbia* records are often found pressed of "royal blue" shellac.)

Diva 2825-G *Makin' Whoopee*	8.00 -	12.00
2834-G *Marie*	7.00 -	10.00
2857-G *Outside*	7.00 -	10.00
2881-G *Lover, Come Back To Me!*	7.00 -	10.00
Harmony 724-H *Right Out Of Heaven*	10.00 -	15.00
728-H *Salaaming The Rajah*	10.00 -	15.00
Harmony 759-H *Doin' The Raccoon*	-	
811-H *The Song I Love*	7.00 -	10.00
834-H *Caressing You*	7.00 -	10.00
881-H *Lover, Come Back To Me!*	7.00 -	10.00
1087-H *The Land Of Going To Be*	10.00 -	15.00
1247-H *You'll Do It Someday, So Why Not Now?*	10.00 -	15.00

(Note: See also FRANK MATER, a pseudonym used on some of the above recordings on affiliated labels, and other titles.)

Hit-of-the-Week A-3-4 *Home*	5.00 -	8.00
B-1-2 *By The Sycamore Tree*	5.00 -	8.00
C-1-2 *Was That The Human Thing To Do?*	5.00 -	8.00
C-3-4 *The Wooden Soldier And The China Doll*	7.00 -	10.00
D-2-3 *By The Fireside; Lovable*	7.00 -	10.00
M-4-5 *A Faded Summer Love*	5.00 -	8.00
MM-4-5 *You Try Somebody Else*	5.00 -	8.00

(Note: Above are one-sided cardboard records, which may have a picture of Rudy Vallee on the non-playing side.)

Velvet Tone 1759-V *Bye And Bye Sweetheart*	7.00 -	10.00
Velvet Tone 1808-V *Let's Do It*	8.00 -	12.00
1834-V *Marie*	7.00 -	10.00
1857-V *Outside*	7.00 -	10.00
1905-V *Bye And Bye Sweetheart*	7.00 -	10.00

(Note: See *Diva* and *Harmony* listing, above; and also FRANK MATER, a pseudonym for Rudy Vallee.)

Victor 21868, 21869, 21880, 21924, 21963, 21967, 21983, 21998, 22029, 22034, 22062, 22084, 22090, 22118, 22136, 22193, 22196, 22227, 22261, 22284, 22321, 22361, 22412, 22419, 22435, 22445, 22473, 22489, 22506, 22545, 22560, 22572, 22574, 22585, 22595, 22611, 22615, 22672, 22679, 22742, 22751, 22752	5.00 -	10.00
Victor 22773, 22774, 22784	7.00 -	12.00
Victor 22783 *This Is The Missus*	8.00 -	12.00
Victor 24458 *My Dancing Lady*	8.00 -	12.00
24459 *Flying Down To Rio*	8.00 -	12.00
24475 *Puddin' Head Jones*	8.00 -	12.00
24476 *What Is There To Say?*	8.00 -	12.00
24554 *Goin' To Heaven on a Mule*	8.00 -	12.00
24558 *Carolina*	8.00 -	12.00
24580 *You Oughta Be In Pictures*	10.00 -	15.00
24581 *Nasty Man*	10.00 -	15.00
24642 *The Sweetest Music This Side of Heaven*	10.00 -	15.00
24646 *So Help Me*	10.00 -	15.00
24697 *Panama*	10.00 -	15.00
24702 *Somewhere in Your Heart*	10.00 -	15.00
24721 *The Drunkard Song*	8.00 -	12.00
24722 *Out in the Cold Again*	10.00 -	15.00
24723 *P.S.—I Love You*	10.00 -	15.00
24739 *The Tattooed Lady*	7.00 -	10.00

(Copies of Victor 24739 having white labels with simulated handwriting in red are not particularly scarce).

24827 *Sweet Music*	10.00 -	15.00
24833 *Fare Thee Well, Annabelle*	10.00 -	15.00
24838 *On the Good Ship Lollipop*	10.00 -	15.00
24895 *You Opened My Eyes*	10.00 -	15.00
24899 *Seein' Is Believen'*	10.00 -	15.00
25089 *His Majesty The Baby*	8.00 -	12.00
25092 *The Gentleman Obviously Doesn't Believe*	8.00 -	12.00
25109 *Plain Old Me*	8.00 -	12.00
Victor 25231, 25233, 25234, 25260, 25267, 25313, 25835, 25836	5.00 -	10.00
Victor 27823, 27841, 27842, 27843, 27844	3.00 -	5.00

VALLEY INN ORCHESTRA:

Claxtonola 40421 *Because They All Love You*	10.00 -	15.00

VAN'S COLLEGIANS; VAN & HIS HALF MOON HOTEL ORCHESTRA:

Gennett 6397 *Rainy Day Pal*	8.00 -	12.00
6455 *In My Bouquet of Memories*	7.00 -	10.00
Gennett 6472 *Louisiana*	20.00 -	30.00
6556 *If You Want The Rainbow*	10.00 -	15.00
6594 *Pickin' Cotton*	10.00 -	15.00
6629 *My Blue Ridge Mountain Home*	15.00 -	25.00
Pathe-Actuelle 36422 *Jig Walk*	15.00 -	20.00
36432 *Whose Who Are You*	10.00 -	15.00
36473 *You Gotta Know How To Love*	5.00 -	8.00
36474 *Oh Boy! How It Was Raining*	5.00 -	8.00
36559 *Who Are You Vamping Tonight?*	5.00 -	8.00
36679 *Cornfed*	8.00 -	12.00
36737 *Let a Smile Be Your Umbrella*	7.00 -	10.00
Perfect 14603 *Jig Walk*	15.00 -	20.00
Perfect 14613 *Whose Who Are You*	10.00 -	15.00
Perfect 14654 *You Gotta Know How To Love*	5.00 -	8.00
Perfect 14655 *Oh Boy! How It Was Raining*	5.00 -	8.00
Perfect 14740 *Sweet Thing*	5.00 -	8.00
Perfect 14860 *Cornfed*	8.00 -	12.00
Perfect 14918 *Without You, Sweetheart*	7.00 -	10.00
Perfect 14976 *Happy-Go-Lucky Lane*	8.00 -	12.00

FRED VAN EPS/VAN EPPS; VAN EPS TRIO/BANJO ORCHESTRA; VAN EPS-BANTA DANCE ORCHESTRA:

Columbia A1063 *Pearl of the Harem*	5.00 -	8.00
Columbia A1118 *The White Wash Man*	7.00 -	10.00
Columbia A1294 *Whipped Cream*	8.00 -	12.00
Columbia A1417 *Junk Man Rag*	8.00 -	12.00
Columbia A1593 *Thanks For The Lobster*	7.00 -	10.00
Columbia A1594 *Some Baby*	7.00 -	10.00
Columbia A1629 *Soup To Nuts*	7.00 -	10.00
Columbia A2034 *Hill and Dale*	7.00 -	10.00
Columbia A5613 *As You Please (12-inch)*	7.00 -	10.00
Columbia A5618 *Old Folks Rag (12-inch)*	7.00 -	10.00
D & R 3810 *The White Wash Man*	8.00 -	12.00
Edison 51324 *Ragtime Oriole*	7.00 -	10.00
Edison 51480 *Dancing On The House Top*	7.00 -	10.00
Edison 51514 *A Ragtime Episode*	7.00 -	10.00
Edison 51604 *The New Gaiety*	7.00 -	10.00
Emerson 10206 *Palm Beach Rag*	10.00 -	15.00
Okeh 1140 *Below Deck Rag*	10.00 -	15.00
Pathe 20087 *Teasin' The Cat*	7.00 -	10.00
20094 *Down Home Rag*	7.00 -	10.00
20328 *Stockyard Blues*	8.00 -	12.00
Pathe 29030 *Florida Rag*	10.00 -	20.00
Pathe 29081 *The Smiler Rag*	10.00 -	20.00
Pathe 29082 *The White Wash Man*	10.00 -	20.00
Pathe 29083 *A Rag Time Episode*	10.00 -	20.00
Perfect 11160 *Grace And Beauty*	8.00 -	12.00
Victor 16667 *A Bunch Of Rags*	7.00 -	10.00
Victor 16845 *A Ragtime Episode*	7.00 -	10.00
Valley 16934 *Rag Pickings*	5.00 -	8.00
Victor 16969 *Pearl Of The Harem*	5.00 -	8.00
Victor 17033 *Red Pepper—A Spicy Rag*	5.00 -	8.00
Victor 17168 *Black Diamond Rag*	7.00 -	10.00
Victor 17308 *Florida Rag*	7.00 -	10.00

Victor 17369 *Frolic of the Coons*	5.00 -	8.00
Victor 17575 *The Smiler—A Joplin Rag*	7.00 -	10.00
Victor 17601 *Notoriety Rag*	7.00 -	10.00
Victor 17677 *Original Fox Trot*	5.00 -	8.00
Victor 18085 *Ragging The Scale*	5.00 -	8.00
Victor 18226 *Teasin' The Cat*	5.00 -	8.00
Victor 18376 *Razzberries—One-Step*	5.00 -	8.00
Victor 35400 *Old Folks Rag (12-inch)*	7.00 -	10.00
Zonophone 5828 *Chatterbox Rag*	10.00 -	20.00

PAUL VAN LOAN AND HIS ORCHESTRA:

Cameo 820 *Deep Elm*	5.00 -	8.00
848 *Pretty Little Baby*	5.00 -	8.00
853 *Cross My Heart Mother*	5.00 -	8.00

VARSITY EIGHT:

Titles, issued contemporaneously on Cameo, Lincoln, Romeo: *Sorority Stomp; Dance Your Blues Away*	10.00 -	15.00
Titles, issued contemporaneously on Banner, Conqueror, Domino, Jewel, Oriole, Perfect, Regal, Romeo: *Fraternity Blues; Never Swat A Fly; One Pair Of Pants At A Time; Sweetheart Of My Student Days; Toodle-Oo; When Kentucky Bids The World 'Good Morning!; Who's Calling You Sweetheart Tonight?*	7.00 -	10.00
Cameo 400, 420, 426, 444, 445, 454, 456, 480, 505, 507, 571, 574, 580, 593, 617, 633, 640, 753	4.00 -	8.00
Cameo 498 *Mean Blues*	7.00 -	10.00
556 *San*	5.00 -	8.00
559 *Doodle Doo Doo*	5.00 -	8.00
567 *You Know Me, Alabam'*	5.00 -	8.00
577 *Charleston Cabin*	5.00 -	8.00
588 *Hard Hearted Hannah*	5.00 -	8.00
602 *A New Kind Of Man*	5.00 -	8.00
605 *Them Ramblin' Blues*	5.00 -	8.00
606 *No-One Knows What It's All About*	5.00 -	8.00
620 *Talkin' To Myself*	5.00 -	8.00
622 *Copenhagen*	7.00 -	10.00
632 *I'm Satisfied (Beside That Sweetie O'Mine)*	5.00 -	8.00
635 *Those Panama Mamas*	5.00 -	8.00
641 *Doo Wacka Doo*	5.00 -	8.00
646 *Oh! Mabel*	5.00 -	8.00
680 *Ain't My Baby Grand?*	5.00 -	8.00
694 *No One*	5.00 -	8.00
695 *I Like You Best Of All*	5.00 -	8.00
711 *He's The Kind Of Man You Like*	5.00 -	8.00
714 *Don't Bring Lulu*	5.00 -	8.00
724 *If You Knew Susie*	7.00 -	10.00
725 *Cheatin' On Me*	7.00 -	10.00
730 *Sweet Georgia Brown*	7.00 -	10.00
732 *Ah Ha!*	5.00 -	8.00
741 *Charleston*	7.00 -	10.00
750 *Yes, Sir! That's My Baby*	7.00 -	10.00
772 *Oh, Say! Can I See You Tonight?*	7.00 -	10.00
774 *Row Row Rosie!*	5.00 -	8.00
780 *Tryin' To Keep Away From You*	5.00 -	8.00
782 *Fallin' Down*	7.00 -	10.00
797 *Sweet Man*	7.00 -	10.00
817 *Milenberg Joys*	8.00 -	12.00
824 *I'm Gonna Hang Around My Sugar*	7.00 -	10.00
832 *Show Me The Way To Go Home*	5.00 -	8.00
835 *Freshie*	5.00 -	8.00
837 *She Doesn't*	7.00 -	10.00
870 *T.N.T.*	8.00 -	12.00
925 *What A Man!*	7.00 -	10.00
975 *Static Strut*	8.00 -	12.00
986 *I'd Give A Lot Of Love*	5.00 -	8.00
1016 *Lay Me Down To Sleep in Carolina*	5.00 -	8.00
1017 *Precious*	5.00 -	8.00
1020 *She Knows Her Onions*	7.00 -	10.00
1040 *Susie's Feller*	7.00 -	10.00
1049 *My Baby Knows How*	7.00 -	10.00
1077 *Lonely Eyes*	5.00 -	8.00

1110 *Crazy Words—Crazy Tune*	7.00	-	10.00
1114 *Ain't She Sweet?*	7.00	-	10.00
1209 *Arkansas Blues*	8.00	-	12.00
1232 *Vo-Do-Do-De-O Blues*	8.00	-	12.00
1245 *Clementine*	8.00	-	12.00
1266 *Steamboat Bill*	8.00	-	12.00
1280 *Is She My Girl Friend?*	7.00	-	10.00
8141 *Farewell Blues*	8.00	-	12.00
Cameo 8321 *Talkin' To MySelf*	5.00	-	8.00
Cameo 8324 *Out Side*	5.00	-	8.00
Cameo 9003 *He Ain't Never Been In College*	5.00	-	8.00
Cameo 9143 *I Get The Blues When It Rains*	5.00	-	8.00
Cameo 9208 *Dance Your Blues Away*	10.00	-	15.00
Cameo 9233 *What Do We Get From Boston?*	5.00	-	8.00
Lincoln 2697 *Vo-Do-Do-Dee-O Blues*	8.00	-	12.00
2710 *Clementine*	8.00	-	12.00
Perfect 15473 *Popeye (The Sailor Man)*	7.00	-	10.00
Romeo 900 *Sorority Stomp*	10.00	-	15.00
Romeo 1035 *What Do We Get From Boston?*	5.00	-	8.00
1068 *Send Love Through The Breeze*	5.00	-	8.00

VARSITY SEVEN:

Varsity 8135 *Scratch My Back*	8.00	-	12.00
8147 *It's Tight Like That*	8.00	-	12.00
8173 *How Long, How Long Blues*	8.00	-	12.00
8179 *Shake It And Break It*	8.00	-	12.00

JOE VENUTI (& HIS NEW YORKERS/ ORCHESTRA); JOE VENUTI'S BLUE FOUR; JOE VENUTI & HIS BLUE FIVE; JOE VENUTI-EDDIE LANG BLUE FIVE; JOE VENUTI-EDDIE LANG & THEIR ALLSTAR ORCHESTRA; JOE VENUTI & RUSS MORGAN:

Titles, issued contemporaneously on Banner, Conqueror, Melotone, Oriole, Perfect, Romeo: *Alice In Wonderland; Build A Little House; Cheese And Crackers; Cinderella's Fella; Doin' The Up Town Lowdown: Easter Parade; Everything I Have Is Yours; Heat Wave; I Want To Ring Bells; Moon Glow; My Dancing Lady; No More Love; One Minute To One; You Must Have Taken My Heart; You're My Past, Present and Future* .... 5.00 - 10.00

Bluebird 5293 *Fiddlesticks*	8.00	-	12.00
5520 *Everybody Shuffle*	8.00	-	12.00
10280 *Doin' Things*	5.00	-	8.00
Columbia 914-D *Stringin' The Blues*	10.00	-	15.00
2535-D *There's No Other Girl*	10.00	-	15.00
2589-D *The Wolf Wobble*	10.00	-	15.00
2765-D *Raggin' The Scale*	10.00	-	15.00
2782-D *Vibraphonia*	10.00	-	15.00
2783-D *Isn't It Heavenly?*	8.00	-	12.00
2834-D *Doin' The Uptown Lowdown*	10.00	-	15.00
3103-D *Eeny Meeny Miney Mo*	10.00	-	15.00
3104-D *Stop, Look and Listen*	10.00	-	15.00
3105-D *Red Velvet*	15.00	-	20.00
Decca 624 *Nothing But Notes*	7.00	-	10.00
625 *Tap Room Blues*	7.00	-	10.00
669 *Vibraphonia No. 2*	7.00	-	10.00
Melotone 12277 *Farewell Blues*	20.00	-	30.00
12294 *Beale Street Blues*	20.00	-	30.00
Okeh 40762 *Wild Cat*	10.00	-	15.00
40825 *Doin' Things*	10.00	-	15.00
40853 *Kickin' The Cat*	15.00	-	20.00
40897 *A Mug Of Ale*	15.00	-	20.00
40947 *Penn Beach Blues*	15.00	-	20.00
41025 *The Wild Dog*	15.00	-	20.00
41051 *Tain't So, Honey, Tain't So*	15.00	-	20.00
41056 *Because My Baby Don't Mean "Maybe" Now*	15.00	-	20.00
41076 *The Man From The South*	15.00	-	20.00
41087 *Pickin' Cotton*	15.00	-	20.00
41133 *I Must Have That Man*	15.00	-	20.00

41144 *The Blue Room*	15.00	-	20.00
41192 *Weary River*	15.00	-	20.00
41251 *My Honey's Lovin' Arms*	15.00	-	20.00
41263 *I'm In Seventh Heaven*	15.00	-	20.00
41320 *Chant Of The Jungle*	15.00	-	20.00
41361 *Apple Blossoms*	15.00	-	20.00
41427 *Promises*	15.00	-	25.00
41432 *Raggin' The Scale*	15.00	-	20.00
41451 *Out Of Breath*	15.00	-	20.00
41469 *I've Found A New Baby*	15.00	-	20.00
41506 *Pardon Me, Pretty Baby*	15.00	-	20.00
41586 *Fiddlesticks*	15.00	-	20.00
Victor 21561 *Doin' Things*	10.00	-	15.00
23015 *My Man From Caroline*	20.00	-	30.00
23018 *Wasting My Love On You*	25.00	-	40.00
23021 *The Wild Dog*	20.00	-	30.00
23039 *Gettin' Hot*	75.00	-	100.00
Vocalion 15858 *Farewell Blues*	20.00	-	30.00
15864 *Beale Street Blues*	20.00	-	30.00

VICKSBURG BLOWERS:

Gennett 6089 *Monte Carlo Joys*	150.00	-	200.00

VICKSBURG TEN:

Champion 15477 *Clarinet Marmalade*	50.00	-	75.00

VICTOR MILITARY BAND:

Victor 17006 *Slippery Place Rag*	5.00	-	8.00
Victor 17044 *Ragtime Violin*	7.00	-	10.00
Victor 17362 *Melinda's Wedding Day-Medley One-Step*	7.00	-	10.00
Victor 17489 *The Junk Man Rag*	8.00	-	12.00
Victor 17508 *Stomp Dance*	8.00	-	12.00
Victor 17585 *Swanee Ripples Rag*	8.00	-	12.00
Victor 17619 *Rag-a-Muffin Rag—One-Step*	8.00	-	12.00
Victor 17764 *Blame It On The Blues*	8.00	-	12.00
Victor 18163 *Kansas City Blues*	8.00	-	12.00
Victor 18203 *Brown Skin*	8.00	-	12.00
Victor 18252 *Spooky Spooks One-Step*	8.00	-	12.00
Victor 35405 *Balling The Jack (12-inch)*	8.00	-	12.00
Victor 35429 *Music Box Rag (12-inch)*	8.00	-	12.00
Victor 35431 *Midnight Whirl Rag—One Step (12-inch)*	8.00	-	12.00
Victor 35533 *Bugle Call Rag*	8.00	-	12.00

VICTOR ORCHESTRA:

Victor 16350 *Black And White Rag*	7.00	-	10.00
Victor 16472 *Wild Cherries Rag*	7.00	-	10.00
Victror 16515 *The Cakewalk in the Sky*	7.00	-	10.00
Victor 17063 *The Gaby Glide*	5.00	-	8.00
Victor 35088 *The Cakewalk in the Sky (12-inch)*	8.00	-	12.00

JOHN VINCENT'S CALIFORNIANS:

Conqueror 7209 *Me And The Man In The Moon*	5.00	-	8.00
7235 *I'm Wild About Horns On Automobiles*	5.00	-	8.00
7245 *Dream Train*	7.00	-	10.00
7401 *Moanin' Low*	7.00	-	10.00

THE VIRGINIANS:

Victor 21219 *In the Sing-Song Sycamore Tree*	5.00	-	8.00
Victor 21228 *Away Down South In Heaven*	5.00	-	8.00
Victor 21680 *Low Down*	7.00	-	10.00
Victor (most other issues)	3.00	-	6.00

VOCALION MILITARY BAND:

Aeolian-Vocalion 12000 *America and Star Spangled Banner—Patriotic Medley* .... 50.00 - 100.00
(Note: Above is pressed of red, white and blue shellac; its value is due to its novelty and striking appearance.)

THE VOLUNTEER FIREMEN:

Brunswick 3025 *Why Aren't Yez Eatin' More Oranges?*	5.00	-	8.00
Brunswick 3041 *Keep Your Skirts Down, Mary Ann*	5.00	-	8.00
Brunswick 3045 *In Your Green Hat*	5.00	-	8.00
Brunswick 3077 *Blinky Moon Bay*	7.00	-	10.00

DON VOORHEES & HIS (EARL CARROLL VANITIES) ORCHESTRA:

Cameo 1134 *Pardon The Glove*	10.00	-	15.00
Columbia 765-D, 835-D, 881-D	4.00	-	7.00

Columbia 954-D *Dancing The Devil Away*	7.00 -	10.00
Columbia 990-D, 1078-D	4.00 -	8.00
Columbia 1123-D *Baby's Blue*	8.00 -	12.00
1124-D *Highways Are Happy Ways*	7.00 -	10.00
1126-D *Rain*	5.00 -	8.00
1129-D *My Blue Heaven*	7.00 -	10.00
1180-D *Clementine*	7.00 -	10.00
1284-D *Ol' Man River*	7.00 -	10.00
Edison 51855 *Just One More Kiss*	15.00 -	20.00
51888 *Somebody's Eyes*	10.00 -	15.00
51890 *Sunday*	15.00 -	20.00
51919 *Blue Skies*	10.00 -	15.00
51927 *Muddy Water*	15.00 -	20.00
51962 *Pardon The Glove*	20.00 -	30.00
51963 *Never Without You*	15.00 -	20.00
51997 *I'll Always Remember You*	15.00 -	20.00
51999 *Dancing The Devil Away*	20.00 -	30.00
52024 *Room For Two*	10.00 -	15.00
52070 *Show Me That Kind Of A Girl*	15.00 -	20.00
52072 *Oh! Doris, Where Do You Live?*	15.00 -	20.00
Pathe-Actuelle 36567, 36594	5.00 -	10.00
Perfect 14748, 14775	5.00 -	10.00

WABASH TRIO:

Titles, issued contemporaneously on Grey Gull, Radiex; *Coal Black Blues; Hoppin' Round; Lone Western Blues*	15.00 -	30.00

(JIMMY) WADE'S CLUB ALABAM/MOULIN ROUGE/MOULIN ROUGH ORCHESTRA; JIMMY WADE & HIS DIXIELANDERS:

Black Patti 8019 *Original Black Bottom Dance*	200.00 -	300.00
Gennett 6105 *Original Black Bottom Dance*	150.00 -	200.00
Harmograph 893 *Mobile Blues*	100.00 -	150.00
Paramount 20295 *Someday Sweetheart*	100.00 -	150.00
Puritan 11295 *Someday Sweetheart*	100.00 -	150.00
11363 *You've Got Ways I'm Crazy About*	75.00 -	100.00
Vocalion 1236 *Mississippi Wobble*	150.00 -	200.00

SOL S. WAGNER & HIS ORCHESTRA:

Gennett 5311 *My Sweet Girl*	35.00 -	50.00
5313 *Oklahoma Indian Jazz*	35.00 -	50.00
5323 *Dream Daddy*	75.00 -	125.00
Okeh 40827 *South Wind*	15.00 -	20.00
40838 *You Don't Like It-Not-Much*	15.00 -	20.00
40973 *Countin' The Days*	15.00 -	20.00

HERMAN WALDMAN AND HIS ORCHESTRA:

Bluebird 5437 *Cocktails For Two*	5.00 -	8.00
5439 *Out For No Good*	5.00 -	8.00
5478 *Home on the Range*	5.00 -	8.00
Brunswick 4649 *Marbles*	8.00 -	12.00
6181 *Lazy River*	8.00 -	12.00

JOHNNY WALKER & HIS ORCHESTRA:

Columbia 2380-D *Personally, I Love You*	5.00 -	8.00
2404-D *Walkin' My Baby Back Home*	10.00 -	20.00

ESTHER WALKER:

Brunswick (most issues)	3.00 -	6.00

TED WALLACE & HIS ORCHESTRA/SWING MUSIC/CAMPUS BOYS:

Banner 6231 *She's Funny That Way*	5.00 -	8.00
6236 *All By Yourself In The Moonlight*	5.00 -	8.00
6239 *I'll Get By*	5.00 -	8.00
Bluebird 6251, 6252, 6253, 6254	4.00 -	8.00
Columbia 1756-D *The One That I Love Loves Me*	7.00 -	10.00
1833-D *I've Got A Feeling I'm Falling*	7.00 -	10.00
1970-D *Bigger And Better Than Ever*	7.00 -	10.00
2046-D *Lucky Me—Lovable You*	7.00 -	10.00
2140-D *Get Happy*	7.00 -	10.00
2236-D *Here Comes The Sun*	7.00 -	10.00
Columbia (most other issues)	4.00 -	7.00
Okeh 40749 *When I First Met Mary*	8.00 -	12.00
40751 *Usen't You Used To Be My Sweetie?*	8.00 -	12.00
40760 *Ain't She Sweet?*	8.00 -	12.00
40778 *The Cat*	10.00 -	15.00

40850 *Love and Kisses*	8.00 -	12.00
40915 *Zulu Wail*	10.00 -	15.00
40961 *Changes*	10.00 -	15.00
41014 *Buffalo Rhythm*	25.00 -	40.00
Regal 8688 *I'll Get By (As Long As I Have You)*	5.00 -	8.00
8691 *She's Funny That Way*	5.00 -	8.00

TRIXIE WALLACE:

Claxtonola 40393 *Copenhagen*	80.00 -	120.00

THOMAS ("FATS") WALLER (WITH MORRIS'S HOT BABIES); FATS WALLER & HIS BUDDIES/RHYTHM:

Bluebird (Most issues)	4.00 -	7.00
Columbia 14593-D *I'm Crazy 'Bout My Baby*	50.00 -	75.00
Okeh 4757 *Birmingham Blues*	50.00 -	80.00
Victor 20357 *St. Louis Blues*	7.00 -	10.00
20470 *Soothin' Syrup Stomp*	20.00 -	30.00
20492 *Rusty Pail*	20.00 -	30.00
20655 *Stompin' The Bug*	20.00 -	30.00
20776 *Savannah Blues*	35.00 -	50.00
20890 *Beale Street Blues*	35.00 -	50.00
21127 *I Ain't Got Nobody*	35.00 -	50.00
21202 *He's Gone Away*	35.00 -	50.00
21358 *The Digah's Stomp*	20.00 -	30.00
21525 *Hog Maw Stomp*	20.00 -	30.00
22092 *Ain't Misbehavin'*	7.00 -	10.00
22108 *Sweet Savannah Sue*	10.00 -	15.00
22371 *St. Louis Blues*	5.00 -	10.00
23260 *That's All*	75.00 -	100.00
23331 *Sugar*	30.00 -	50.00
Victor 24641, 24648, 24708, 24714, 24737, 24738, 24742, 24801, 24808, 24826, 24830, 24846, 24853, 24863, 24867, 24888, 24889, 24892, 24898, 25015, 25026, 25037, 25039, 25044, 25063	5.00 -	10.00
25075 *through* 26002	4.00 -	8.00
V38050 *Harlem Fuss*	30.00 -	50.00
V38086 *Lookin' Good But Feelin' Bad*	30.00 -	50.00
V38110 *When I'm Alone*	40.00 -	60.00
V38119 *Ridin' But Walkin'*	30.00 -	50.00
V38508 *Numb Fumblin'*	40.00 -	60.00
V38554 *Valentine Stomp*	50.00 -	75.00
V38568 *Turn On The Heat*	40.00 -	60.00
V38613 *Smashing Thirds*	50.00 -	75.00

EDDIE WALTERS:

Columbia 1763-D, 1969-D	4.00 -	8.00
Columbia 2035-D *Singin' In The Bathtub*	8.00 -	12.00
Columbia 2137-D *'Leven-Thirty Saturday Night*	8.00 -	12.00
2232-D *It Must Be Love*	8.00 -	12.00
Columbia 2290-D *(Since They're All Playing) Miniature Golf*	8.00 -	12.00

THE WANDERERS:

Bluebird 5834 *A Good Man Is Hard To Find*	10.00 -	15.00
5869 *I Ain't Got Nobody*	10.00 -	15.00
5887 *Tiger Rag*	10.00 -	15.00
5921 *Thousand Miles*	8.00 -	12.00
5994 *Footwarmer*	10.00 -	15.00
Cameo 1133 *My Sunday Girl*	5.00 -	8.00

BILLY WARD:

Oriole 4472 *Squeeze Me*	15.00 -	25.00

JOE WARD'S SWANEE CLUB ORCHESTRA:

Cameo 9026 *Traffic Jam*	10.00 -	15.00

WARING'S PENNSYLVANIANS:

Victor L-16016, L-16018 (Program Transcriptions Long Playing)	20.00 -	30.00
Victor 19189 *Stack O'Lee Blues*	5.00 -	8.00
Victor 19254 *Oh Baby!*	5.00 -	8.00
Victor 19257 *Dancin' Dan*	5.00 -	8.00
Victor 19303 *Down Home Blues*	5.00 -	8.00
Victor 19346 *Wa Wa Waddle Walk*	5.00 -	8.00
Victor 19377 *Just Hot!*	5.00 -	8.00
Victor 19533 *Oh! Mabel*	5.00 -	8.00
Victor 19610 *When My Sugar Walks Down The Street*	5.00 -	.8.00

21508 *Stack O'Lee Blues*	5.00 -	8.00
Victor 21715 *What a Night For Spooning*	5.00 -	8.00
Victor 21836 *Glorianna*	5.00 -	8.00
Victor 22266 *Hello Baby*	5.00 -	8.00
Victor 22272 *Crying For The Carolines*	5.00 -	8.00
22325 *Red-Hot Chicago*	8.00 -	12.00
22326 *Good For You, Bad For Me*	7.00 -	10.00
22470 *It Seems To Be Spring*	8.00 -	12.00
22978 *How Am I Doin'?*	10.00 -	15.00
24030 *I Heard*	10.00 -	15.00
Victor 24051 *Holding My Honey's Hand*	8.00 -	12.00
24062 *Old Yazoo*	8.00 -	12.00
24168 *Fit As A Fiddle*	7.00 -	10.00
24179 *More Beautiful Than Ever*	7.00 -	10.00
24181 *Here It Is Monday And I've Still Got A Dollar*	7.00 -	10.00
24214 *You're Getting To Be A Habit With Me*	7.00 -	10.00
Victor (most other issues)	4.00 -	7.00

BUD WARNER & HIS RED CAPS:

Bell 1174 *Down Home Special*	200.00 -	300.00

WARNER'S SEVEN ACES:

Columbia 305-D *Cheatin' On Me*	7.00 -	10.00
336-D *The Blues Have Got Me*	10.00 -	15.00
Columbia 491-D *Go Get'Em, Caroline*	10.00 -	15.00
605-D *Breakin' The Leg*	15.00 -	25.00
656-D *So Is Your Old Lady*	8.00 -	12.00
816-D *Don't Take That Black Bottom Away*	7.00 -	10.00
863-D *Who'll Be The One?*	7.00 -	10.00
1001-D *There's Everything Nice About You*	7.00 -	10.00
1046-D *That's My Hap-Hap-Happiness*	8.00 -	12.00
Okeh 4888 *In a Tent*	10.00 -	15.00
4911 *Dream Girl of P.K.A*	10.00 -	15.00
4924 *Mean Eyes*	15.00 -	20.00
40080 *Ace of Spades*	15.00 -	20.00
40198 *Bessie Couldn't Help It*	15.00 -	20.00
40201 *Love Time*	10.00 -	15.00

WASHBOARD RHYTHM BAND:

Columbia 14680-D *Going, Going, Gone*	50.00 -	75.00

WASHBOARD RHYTHM BOYS/KINGS:

Titles, issued contemporaneously on Banner, Melotone, Oriole, Perfect, Romeo: *Dog and Cat; I Cover The Waterfront; Lazybones; Learn To Croon; Mississippi Basin; Old Man Blues; St. Louis Blues; Some Of These Days*	15.00 -	20.00
Bluebird 6157 *Arlena*	8.00 -	12.00
6186 *Street Walkin' Blues*	8.00 -	12.00
6278 *Hot Nuts*	8.00 -	12.00
Victor 22719 *A Porter's Love Song To A Chambermaid*	40.00 -	60.00
22814 *Shoot 'Em*	40.00 -	60.00
22958 *Pepper Steak*	40.00 -	60.00
23301 *Georgia On My Mind*	40.00 -	60.00
23303 *Boola Boo*	75.00 -	100.00
23323 *If You Don't Love Me*	40.00 -	60.00
23337 *All This World Is Made Of Glass*	75.00 -	100.00
23348 *My Silent Love*	40.00 -	60.00
23357 *Depression Stomp*	150.00 -	200.00
23364 *Say It Isn't So*	50.00 -	80.00
23367 *Ash Man Crawl*	50.00 -	80.00
23368 *The Boy In The Boat*	50.00 -	80.00
23373 *How Deep Is The Ocean?*	50.00 -	80.00
23375 *A Nickel For A Pickel*	50.00 -	80.00
23380 *Sloppy Drunk Blues*	75.00 -	100.00
23403 *Nobody's Sweetheart*	75.00 -	100.00
23405 *Sophisticated Lady*	75.00 -	100.00
23408 *Bug-A-Boo*	75.00 -	100.00
23413 *Move Turtle*	50.00 -	75.00
23415 *Hard Corn*	50.00 -	75.00
Victor 24059 *Tiger Rag*	15.00 -	20.00
24065 *Hummin' To Myself*	15.00 -	20.00
Vocalion 1724 *Sentimental Gentleman From Georgia*	40.00 -	60.00

1725 *The Scat Song*	40.00 -	60.00
1729 *Syncopate Your Sins Away*	40.00 -	60.00
1730 *Oh! You Sweet Thing*	40.00 -	60.00
1731 *Angeline*	40.00 -	60.00
1732 *Blue Drag*	40.00 -	60.00
1733 *Old Yazoo*	40.00 -	60.00
1734 *Spider Crawl*	40.00 -	60.00

WASHBOARD SERENADERS:

Victor V38127 *Kazoo Moan*	100.00 -	150.00
V38610 *Teddy's Blues*	100.00 -	150.00

WASHBOARD TRIO:

Paramount 12682 *Washboard Rag*	100.00 -	150.00
Radiex 1485 *Yellow Dog Blues*		-

WASHBOARD WONDERS:

Silvertone 3548 *Shake That Thing*	75.00 -	125.00
3549 *Skoodlum Blues*	75.00 -	125.00

BENNIE WASHINGTON'S SIX ACES:

Okeh 8269 *Compton Ave. Blues*		-

BUCK WASHINGTON:

Columbia 2925-D *Old Fashioned Love*	25.00 -	40.00

STEVE WASHINGTON & HIS ORCHESTRA:

Vocalion 2598 *Sing A Little Low-Down Tune*	15.00 -	25.00
2607 *Blue River*	15.00 -	25.00

THE WASHINGTONIANS:

Titles issued contemporaneously on Cameo, Lincoln, Romeo: *East St. Louis; Toodle-Oo; Hot and Bothered; Hottentot; Jubilee Stomp; The Mooche; Move Over, Saratoga Swing; Take It Easy; Who Said "It's Tight Like That"?*	10.00 -	20.00
Additional titles, issued contemporaneously on Cameo, Lincoln, Romeo: *It's Tight Like That; Mississippi; Here I Am*	7.00 -	10.00
Blu-Disc 1002 *Choo Choo*	250.00 -	500.00
Brunswick 3526 *Black And Tan Fantasy*	10.00 -	15.00
4009 *Black Beauty*	15.00 -	20.00
4044 *Jubilee Stomp*	15.00 -	20.00
Diva 2577-G *Bugle Call Rag*	15.00 -	20.00
2601-G *Stack O'Lee Blues*	15.00 -	20.00
Harmony 577-H *Bugle Call Rag*	15.00 -	20.00
601-H *Stack O'Lee Blues*	15.00 -	20.00
Pathe-Actuelle 36333 *Trombone Blues*	75.00 -	100.00
Pennington 1437 *Rainy Nights*	75.00 -	100.00
Perfect 14514 *Trombone Blues*	75.00 -	100.00
Puritan 11437 *Rainy Nights*	75.00 -	100.00
Triangle 11437 *Rainy Nights*	75.00 -	100.00
Velvet Tone 1577-V *Bugle Call Rag*	15.00 -	20.00
1601-V *Stack O'Lee Blues*	15.00 -	20.00
Vocalion 15704 *Take It Easy*	35.00 -	50.00
15710 *Jubilee Stomp*	50.00 -	75.00

ETHEL WATERS: ETHEL WATERS' JAZZ MASTERS:

Black Swan 2010 *Down Home Blues*	20.00 -	35.00
2021 *There'll Be Some Changes Made*	20.00 -	35.00
2035 *Royal Garden Blues*	20.00 -	35.00
2037 *Bugle Blues*	20.00 -	35.00
2038 *Dyin' With The Blues*	20.00 -	35.00
2074 *Struggle*	30.00 -	50.00
2077 *Tiger Rag*	30.00 -	50.00
10077 *Struggle*	30.00 -	50.00
10073 *Tiger Rag*	30.00 -	50.00
14117 *Jazzin' Babies Blues*	50.00 -	75.00
14120 *Georgia Blues*	50.00 -	75.00
14128 *At The New Jump Steady Ball*	50.00 -	75.00
14145 *Brown Baby*	50.00 -	75.00
14146 *Memphis Man*	50.00 -	75.00
14148 *Long-Lost Mama*	35.00 -	50.00
14151 *Lost Out Blues*	35.00 -	50.00
14154 *Ethel Sings 'Em*	35.00 -	50.00
14155 *All The Time*	35.00 -	50.00
Brunswick 6517 *I Can't Give You Anything But Love*	8.00 -	12.00

6521 *St. Louis Blues*	10.00 -	15.00
6564 *Stormy Weather*	8.00 -	12.00
6617 *Shadows On The Swanee*	10.00 -	15.00
6885 *You've Seen Harlem At It's Best*	10.00 -	15.00
Cardinal 2036 *The New York Glide*	50.00 -	75.00
Columbia 379-D *Sweet Georgia Brown*	8.00 -	12.00
433-D *Sympathetic Dan*	7.00 -	10.00
472-D *Pickaninny Blues*	7.00 -	10.00
487-D *Sweet Man*	8.00 -	12.00
561-D *I've Found A New Baby*	10.00 -	15.00
1837-D *Birmingham Bertha*	8.00 -	12.00
1871-D *True Blue Lou*	8.00 -	12.00
1905-D *Shoo Shoo Boogie Boo*	8.00 -	12.00
1933-D *Trav'lin All Alone*	7.00 -	10.00
2184-D *Porgy*	10.00 -	15.00
2222-D *My Kind Of Man*	15.00 -	20.00
2288-D *You're Lucky To Me*	10.00 -	15.00
2346-D *I Got Rhythm*	10.00 -	15.00
2409-D *When Your Lover Has Gone*	15.00 -	20.00
2481-D *Without That Gal*	15.00 -	20.00
2511-D *River, Stay 'Way From My Door*	15.00 -	20.00
2826-D *Harlem On My Mind*	20.00 -	30.00
2853-D *A Hundred Years From Today*	20.00 -	30.00
14093-D *Down Home Blues*	10.00 -	15.00
14112-D *Maybe Not At All*	15.00 -	20.00
14116-D *No Man's Mama*	7.00 -	10.00
14125-D *Bring Your Greenbacks*	10.00 -	15.00
14132-D *Throw Dirt In Your Face*	10.00 -	15.00
14134-D *I Wonder What's Become Of Joe?*	10.00 -	15.00
14146-D *You'll Want Me Back*	8.00 -	12.00
14153-D *Heebie Jeebies*	10.00 -	15.00
14162-D *Take What You Want*	10.00 -	15.00
14170-D *I'm Coming, Virginia*	10.00 -	15.00
Columbia 14182-D *Jersey Walk*	10.00 -	15.00
14199-D *Satisfyin' Papa*	10.00 -	15.00
14214-D *Take Your Black Bottom Outside*	15.00 -	20.00
14229-D *Smile!*	20.00 -	30.00
14264-D *Someday, Sweetheart*	15.00 -	20.00
14297-D *I'm Saving It All For You*	15.00 -	25.00
14353-D *My Handy Man*	7.00 -	10.00
14365-D *West End Blues*	15.00 -	20.00
14380-D *Do What You Did Last Night*	15.00 -	20.00
14411-D *Lonesome Swallow*	15.00 -	20.00
14458-D *Long Lean Lanky Mama*	20.00 -	30.00
14565-D *Georgia Blues*	20.00 -	30.00
Decca 140 *Moon Glow*	5.00 -	8.00
141 *I Ain't Gonna Sin No More*	8.00 -	12.00
234 *When It's Sleepy Time Down South*	5.00 -	8.00
Liberty Music Shop 188 *Thief In The Night*	7.00 -	10.00
310 *Taking A Chance On Love*	7.00 -	10.00
311 *Cabin In The Sky*	7.00 -	10.00
Paramount 12169 *Down Home Blues*	20.00 -	30.00
12170 *There'll Be Some Changes Made*	20.00 -	30.00
12171 *Royal Garden Blues*	20.00 -	30.00
12173 *Bugle Blues*	20.00 -	30.00
12174 *Dying With The Blues*	20.00 -	30.00
12175 *Jazzin' Babies Blues*	50.00 -	75.00
12176 *At The New Jump Steady Ball*	50.00 -	75.00
12177 *Georgia Blues*	50.00 -	75.00
12178 *Brown Baby*	50.00 -	75.00
12179 *Memphis Man*	50.00 -	75.00
12180 *Long-Last Mama*	50.00 -	75.00
12181 *Lost Out Blues*	30.00 -	50.00

12182 *Ethel Sings 'Em*	30.00 -	50.00
12189 *Tell 'Em 'Bout Me*	30.00 -	50.00
12230 *Black Spatch Blues*	80.00 -	120.00
12313 *Craving Blues*	100.00 -	150.00
Vocalion 14680 *Pleasure Mad*	8.00 -	12.00

WATSON'S PULLMAN PORTERS:

Gennett 6353 *Barbecue Blues*	150.00 -	250.00
6378 *Down Home Special*	150.00 -	250.00

EL WATSON:

Victor 20951 *Narrow Gauge Blues*	20.00 -	30.00
21440 *El Watson's Fox Chase*	25.00 -	40.00
21585 *Bay Rum Blues*	25.00 -	40.00

LU WATTERS' YERBA BUENA JAZZ BAND:

Jazz Man 1, 2, 3, 4, 5, 6, 7, 13, 14, 15, 17	8.00 -	12.00
Mercury 11026, 11065, 11090	5.00 -	8.00
West Coast 101, 103, 104, 111, 152	5.00 -	10.00

CHICK WEBB & HIS LITTLE CHICKS/ORCHESTRA; CHICK WEBB'S SAVOY ORCHESTRA:

Brunswick 6156 *Blues In My Heart*	20.00 -	30.00
Columbia 2875-D *On The Sunny Side Of The Street*	20.00 -	30.00
2883-D *Let's Get Together*	20.00 -	30.00
2920-D *Imagination*	20.00 -	30.00
2926-D *Stompin' At The Savoy*	15.00 -	25.00
Decca 172 *Blue Minor*	8.00 -	12.00
173 *That Rhythm Man*	8.00 -	12.00
483 *Don't Be That Way*	8.00 -	12.00
494 *Love And Kisses*	8.00 -	12.00
588 *Rhythm And Romance*	8.00 -	12.00
640 *I'll Chase The Blues Away*	8.00 -	12.00
785, 830, 831, 995, 1032, 1065, 1087, 1114, 1115, 1123, 1213, 1220, 1273, 1513, 1521, 1586, 1681, 1716, 1759	5.00 -	10.00
Okeh 41571 *If It Ain't Love*	15.00 -	20.00
41572 *Blue Minor*	15.00 -	20.00
Vocalion 1607 *Heebie Jeebies*	75.00 -	100.00
3100 *If It Ain't Love*	10.00 -	15.00
3101 *True*	10.00 -	15.00
3246 *Stompin' At The Savoy*	7.00 -	12.00

MALCOLM WEBB & HIS GANG:

Champion 15420 *Friday Night*	50.00 -	75.00

CARL WEBSTER'S YALE COLLEGIANS:

Okeh 41393 *Puttin' On The Ritz*	20.00 -	30.00
Personal Record 139-P *If I'm Without You*	30.00 -	50.00

JULIAN WEBSTER AND HIS BAY STATE ACES:

Edison 52061 *Just Once Again*	15.00 -	20.00

ANSON WEEKS AND HIS (HOTEL MARK HOPKINS) ORCHESTRA:

Brunswick 6524, 6526, 6569, 6575, 6604, 6619, 6639, 6661, 6665, 6727, 6730, 6772, 6795, 6944, 6946, 6965, 6969, 6983, 6989, 6990, 6997, 7349, 7350	5.00 -	10.00
Brunswick 7477, 7510, 7515, 7518	5.00 -	10.00
Brunswick 20120 ''Strike Me Pink'' medley	15.00 -	20.00
(Note: Brunswick 20120 is a 12-inch record)		
Columbia 2211-D *Ro-Ro-Rollin' Along*	7.00 -	10.00
40004-D *Susianna*	15.00 -	20.00
Decca 1134, 1139, 1140	5.00 -	8.00

TED WEEMS & HIS ORCHESTRA:

Bluebird 5130 *Trouble In Paradise*	7.00 -	10.00
5131 *Heartaches*	7.00 -	10.00
5148 *If I Had Somebody To Love*	7.00 -	10.00
5235 *In A One-Room Flat*	7.00 -	10.00
5236 *Doin' The Uptown Lowdown*	10.00 -	15.00
5239 *Why Am I Happy?*	7.00 -	10.00
5288 *The Boulevard of Broken Dreams*	7.00 -	10.00
5289 *The Music Man*	7.00 -	10.00
5290 *The Rooftop Serenade*	7.00 -	10.00
5292 *I Guess It Had To Be That Way*	7.00 -	10.00
Columbia 2956-D *Ten Yards To Go*	10.00 -	15.00

2957-D *Blue Sky Avenue* .... 10.00 - 15.00
2975-D *I'm Growing Fonder Of You* .... 10.00 - 15.00
2976-D *Winter Wonderland* .... 10.00 - 15.00
Decca 820 *You Can't Pull The Wool Over My*
  Eyes .... 8.00 - 12.00
  822 *Lazy Weather* .... 5.00 - 8.00
  895 *Until Today* .... 5.00 - 8.00
Decca 921 *Fooled By The Moon* .... 5.00 - 8.00
  958 *Picture Me Without You* .... 5.00 - 8.00
  959 *Darling, Not Without You* .... 5.00 - 8.00
  969 *Rainbow on the River* .... 5.00 - 8.00
Decca (blue Label) Most other issues .... 3.00 - 6.00
Electradisk (same titles as bluebirds, more highly
  valued)
Sunrise (same titles as Bluebird, much more
  highly valued)
Victor L-16025 *Long-Playing "Program*
  Transcription" .... 30.00 - 50.00
  19258 *Nine O'Clock Sal* .... 5.00 - 8.00
  19287 *My Gal Sal* .... 5.00 - 8.00
  19344 *Savannah* .... 5.00 - 8.00
  19377 *Red-Nose Pete* .... 5.00 - 8.00
  19496 *Traveling Blues* .... 5.00 - 8.00
  19722 *Siberia* .... 5.00 - 8.00
  19804 *Lonesome* .... 5.00 - 8.00
  19930 *Smile a Little Bit* .... 5.00 - 8.00
  19938 *The Day That I Met You* .... 5.00 - 8.00
  20033 *Love Bound* .... 5.00 - 8.00
  20120 *My Cutey's Due at Two-to-Two Today* ... 5.00 - 8.00
  20133 *Oh! If I Only Had You* .... 5.00 - 8.00
  20196 *That's My Girl* .... 5.00 - 8.00
  20206 *Chick, Chick, Chick, Chick, Chicken* .. 5.00 - 8.00
  20230 *Climbing Up The Ladder Of Love* ..... 5.00 - 8.00
  20234 *What's The Use of Crying?* .... 5.00 - 8.00
  20829 *She's Got "It"* .... 5.00 - 8.00
  20846 *Miss Annabelle Lee* .... 5.00 - 8.00
  20901 *Marvelous* .... 5.00 - 8.00
  20910 *It Was Only A Sun*
    Shower .... 5.00 - 8.00
  21105 *Cobble-Stones* .... 5.00 - 8.00
  21173 *Everybody Loves My Girl* .... 5.00 - 8.00
  21364 *He's Tall, Dark and Handsome* .... 7.00 - 10.00
  21511 *Who Wouldn't Be Blue?* .... 7.00 - 10.00
  21670 *If You Want The Rainbow (You Must*
    Have the Rain) .... 7.00 - 10.00
  21729 *Come On, Baby!* .... 7.00 - 10.00
  21767 *You're The Cream In My Coffee* ..... 5.00 - 8.00
  21773 *I Found You "Out" When I Found You*
    "In" Somebody Else's Arms .... 7.00 - 10.00
  21809 *Me and the Man in the Moon* .... 5.00 - 8.00
  22032 *Good Morning, Good Evening, Good*
    Night .... 7.00 - 10.00
  22037 *Piccolo Pete* .... 7.00 - 10.00
  22038 *What A Day!* .... 7.00 - 10.00
  22137 *Miss Wonderful* .... 7.00 - 10.00
  22138 *I Don't Want Your Kisses (If I Can't*
    Have Your Love) .... 7.00 - 10.00
  22157 *Remarkable Girl* .... 7.00 - 10.00
  22215 *Sophomore Prom* .... 7.00 - 10.00
Victor 22238 *The Man From The South* ...... 7.00 - 10.00
  22304 *Talk Of The Town* .... 5.00 - 8.00
  22406 *Collegiate Love* .... 8.00 - 12.00
  22411 *Slappin' The Bass* .... 7.00 - 10.00
  22426 *Washing Dishes With My Sweetie* ..... 8.00 - 12.00
  22499 *My Baby Just Cares For Me* .... 7.00 - 10.00
  22515 *I Still Get a Thrill* .... 5.00 - 8.00
  22564 *The One-Man Band* .... 7.00 - 10.00
  22637 *Walkin' My Baby Back Home* .... 7.00 - 10.00
  22644 *Egyptian Ella* .... 8.00 - 12.00
  22646 *Little Joe* .... 7.00 - 10.00
  22648 *When You Were The Blossom of*
    Buttercup Lane .... 5.00 - 8.00

22656 *My Favorite Band* .... 5.00 - 8.00
22822 *Oh! Monah* .... 7.00 - 10.00
22829 *Nobody's Baby Is Somebody's Baby*
  Now .... 7.00 - 10.00
22838 *I'm For You A Hundred Percent* ..... 7.00 - 10.00
22877 *One Of Us Was Wrong* .... 7.00 - 10.00
22881 *She's So Nice* .... 7.00 - 10.00
24053 *Play That Hot Guitar* .... 8.00 - 12.00
24219 *At the Baby Parade* .... 7.00 - 10.00
24227 *When The Morning Rolls Around* ..... 7.00 - 10.00
24265 *Juggling A Jigsaw* .... 8.00 - 12.00
24266 *I Like Mountain Music* .... 8.00 - 12.00
24302 *Panhandle Pete* .... 10.00 - 15.00
24308 *Hats Off, Here Comes a Lady* .... 8.00 - 12.00

GENE WEIMER & HIS PEPPERS:
  Champion 15422 *Clementine* .... 25.00 - 35.00
LEW WEINER'S GOLD AND BLACK ACES:
  Gennett 6540 *Louisiana Bo Bo* .... 30.00 - 50.00
LAWRENCE WELK & HIS ORCHESTRA:
  Broadway 1462 *Smile, Darn Ya, Smile* .... 15.00 - 20.00
  Broadway 1481 *This Is The Missus* ...... 15.00 - 20.00
  Gennett 6697 *Doin' The New Low Down* ..... 60.00 - 80.00
    6712 *Spiked Beer* .... 60.00 - 80.00
    20341 *Shanghai Honeymoon* .... 60.00 - 80.00
DICKEY WELLS' SHIM SHAMMERS;
DICKIE WELLS' ORCHESTRA:
  Columbia 2829-D *Baby, Are You Satisfied?* ..... 30.00 - 40.00
  Signature .... 5.00 - 8.00
PETE WENDLING:
  Okeh 4868, 4984 .... 7.00 - 10.00
MAE WEST:
  Brunswick 6495 *Easy Rider* .... 10.00 - 15.00
    6675 *I'm No Angel* .... 10.00 - 15.00
    6676 *They Call Me Sister Honkey-Tonk* .... 10.00 - 15.00
THEADOR WEST:
  Ajax 17118 *Hot Jelly Blues* .... 25.00 - 40.00
    17129 *Blues, Just Blues* .... 25.00 - 40.00
THE WESTERNERS:
  Harmony 297-H *Take In The Sun, Hang Out the*
    Moon .... 7.00 - 10.00
  Harmony 358-H *There's Everything Nice About*
    You .... 4.00 - 7.00
  Harmony 366-H *My Regular Gal* .... 5.00 - 8.00
  Harmony 447-H *I Ain't That Kind of a Baby* .... 5.00 - 8.00
  Harmony 547-H *Away Down South in Heaven* ... 5.00 - 8.00
  Harmony 611-H *She's a Great, Great Girl* ...... 7.00 - 10.00
  Harmony 638-H *Sweet Sue—Just You* .... 5.00 - 8.00
  Harmony 651-H *The Pay-Off* .... 8.00 - 12.00
  (Note: Above Titles, on Diva and Velvet Tone,
    are similarly valued.)
FRANK WESTPHAL & HIS ORCHESTRA:
  Columbia 17-D *All Wrong* .... 7.00 - 10.00
    22-D *Oh! Sister, Ain't That Hot?* .... 5.00 - 8.00
    32-D *Forgetful Blues* .... 7.00 - 10.00
  Columbia A3571 *She's A Mean Job* .... 5.00 - 8.00
  Columbia A3693 *State Street Blues* .... 5.00 - 8.00
  Columbia A3743 *Choo Choo Blues* .... 5.00 - 8.00
  Columbia A3872 *Bugle Call Rag* .... 5.00 - 8.00
  Columbia A3911 *Wolverine Blues* .... 5.00 - 8.00
  Columbia A3929 *Off Again—On Again Blues* ..... 7.00 - 10.00
  Columbia (Most other issues) .... 3.00 - 6.00
WE THREE:
  Pathe-Actuelle 36464 *Trumpet Sobs* ..... 15.00 - 25.00
    36492 *Plenty Off Center* .... 20.00 - 30.00
  Perfect 14645 *Trumpet Sobs* .... 15.00 - 25.00
    14673 *Plenty Off Center* .... 20.00 - 30.00
WHISTLER & HIS JUG BAND:
  Gennett 5554 *Chicago Flip* .... 100.00 - 150.00
    5614 *Jail House Blues* .... 100.00 - 150.00
  Okeh 8469 *Low Down Blues* .... 100.00 - 150.00
    8816 *Pig Meat Blues* .... 100.00 - 150.00
  Victor 23305 *Hold That Tiger* .... 150.00 - 200.00

BETSY WHITE:

Q.R.S. 1035 *Calamity Jane* . . . . 10.00 - 15.00

BOB WHITE'S DIXIE TRIO:

Puritan 11400 *Alabamy Bound* . . . . 100.00 - 150.00

HAL WHITE'S SYNCOPATORS:

Domino 3444 *Everybody Loves My Baby*
(instrumental) . . . . 15.00 - 20.00
     3444 *Everybody Loves My Baby* (vocal chorus) 75.00 - 100.00

HAROLD WHITE & HIS ORCHESTRA:

Romeo 1833 *Gosh Darn!* . . . . 7.00 - 10.00
Romeo 1891 *Why Little Boy Blue Was Blue* . . . . . 7.00 - 10.00

STEVE WHITE'S DANCELAND ORCHESTRA:

Sunset 1132 *Slippery Elm* . . . . 25.00 - 40.00

TED WHITE'S COLLEGIANS:

Jewel 5073 *Miss Annabelle Lee* . . . . 5.00 - 8.00
     5410 *My Blackbirds Are Bluebirds Now* . . . . . . 5.00 - 8.00
Oriole 931 *Hurricane* . . . . 8.00 - 12.00
     960 *12th Street Rag* . . . . 7.00 - 10.00
     1152 *For My Gal And Me* . . . . 7.00 - 12.00
     1359 *Makin' Whoopee!* . . . . 5.00 - 8.00
     1392 *Crying Blues* . . . . 5.00 - 8.00
     1398 *Come On, Baby* . . . . 5.00 - 8.00
     1503 *Wedding Bells* . . . . 5.00 - 8.00
Oriole 1544 *Shirt Tail Stomp* . . . . 8.00 - 12.00
     1613 *To Be In Love (Espesh'lly With You)* . . . . 5.00 - 8.00
     1634 *Painting The Clouds With Sunshine* . . . . 5.00 - 8.00
     1664 *Sweetness* . . . . 5.00 - 8.00
     1694 *Little By Little* . . . . 5.00 - 8.00

WILLY WHITE:

Perfect 11175 *Try And Play It* . . . . 7.00 - 10.00

PAUL WHITEMAN & HIS (CONCERT) ORCHESTRA:

Columbia 1401-D, 1402-D, 1448-D, 1465-D,
1701-D, 1736-D, 1755-D, 1771-D, 1845-D,
1862-D, 2010-D, 2163-D, 2171-D . . . . 4.00 - 8.00
1441-D *Because My Baby Don't Mean
''Maybe'' Now* . . . . 8.00 - 12.00
1444-D *That's My Weakness Now* . . . . 8.00 - 12.00
1464-D *Pickin' Cotton* . . . . 8.00 - 12.00
1478-D *Felix The Cat* . . . . 15.00 - 25.00
1491-D *Georgie Porgie* . . . . 10.00 - 15.00
1496-D *I'd Rather Cry Over You* . . . . 8.00 - 12.00
1505-D *Out O' Town Gal* . . . . 8.00 - 12.00
1683-D *Makin' Whoopee* . . . . 7.00 - 10.00
1723-D *How About Me?* . . . . 7.00 - 10.00
1822-D *When My Dreams Come True* . . . . 8.00 - 12.00
1877-D *I'm In Seventh Heaven* . . . . 8.00 - 12.00
1945-D *China Boy* . . . . 8.00 - 12.00
1974-D *Waiting At The End Of The Road* . . . . . 8.00 - 12.00
1993-D *When You're Counting The Stars Alone* 8.00 - 12.00
2023-D *Great Day* . . . . 8.00 - 12.00
2047-D *Should I?* . . . . 7.00 - 10.00
2098-D *After You've Gone* . . . . 8.00 - 12.00
2164-D *A Bench In The Park* . . . . 8.00 - 12.00
2170-D *I Like To Do Things For You* . . . . 8.00 - 12.00
2277-D *The New Tiger Rag* . . . . 8.00 - 12.00
2491-D *Choo Choo* . . . . 10.00 - 15.00
Columbia (12-inch) 50068 *My Melancholy Baby* . 15.00 - 20.00
(12-inch) 50103-D *Sweet Sue* . . . . 15.00 - 20.00
Victor L-16001 *George White's Scandals Medley* . 25.00 - 40.00
     L-16002 *I'm Sorry Dear* plus 2 more tunes . . . . 30.00 - 50.00
     L-16017 *Willow, Weep For Me* plus 2 more tunes 30.00 - 50.00
(above are long-playing "Program
Transcriptions")
Victor 19381 *San* . . . . 5.00 - 8.00
Victor 19671 *Charleston* . . . . 5.00 - 8.00
Victor 19720 *Footloose* . . . . 5.00 - 8.00
Victor 19773 *Rhythm Rag* . . . . 5.00 - 8.00
Victor 19785 *Charlestonette* . . . . 5.00 - 8.00
Victor 19920 *Sweet And Low-Down* . . . . 5.00 - 8.00
Victor (Most other issues in the 19000 series) . . . 3.00 - 6.00
Victor 20092 *Bell Hoppin' Blues* . . . . 7.00 - 10.00

20177 *When The Red, Red Robin Comes Bob,
Bob, Bobbin' Along* . . . . 5.00 - 8.00
20418 *Wistful and Blue* . . . . 4.00 - 7.00
20627 *Side By Side* . . . . 7.00 - 10.00
20679 *Magnolia* . . . . 7.00 - 10.00
20751 *I'm Coming, Virginia* . . . . 7.00 - 10.00
20883 *It Won't Be Long Now* . . . . 5.00 - 8.00
21103 *Changes* . . . . 8.00 - 12.00
21119 *Whiteman Stomp* . . . . 7.00 - 10.00
21214 *Lonely Melody* . . . . 5.00 - 8.00
21218 *Ol' Man River* . . . . 7.00 - 10.00
21228 *Smile* . . . . 7.00 - 10.00
21240 *Back In Your Own Backyard* . . . . 7.00 - 10.00
21274 *From Monday On* . . . . 8.00 - 12.00
Victor 21301 *Coquette* . . . . 5.00 - 8.00
21338 *When* . . . . 7.00 - 10.00
21365 *When You're With Somebody Else* . . . . . . 7.00 - 10.00
21388 *My Angel* . . . . 7.00 - 10.00
21389 *My Pet* . . . . 7.00 - 10.00
Victor 21398 *You Took Advantage Of Me* . . . . . . 7.00 - 10.00
21438 *Louisiana* . . . . 8.00 - 12.00
21453 *It Was The Dawn of Love* . . . . 8.00 - 12.00
21464 *Sugar* . . . . 10.00 - 15.00
22883 *'Leven Pounds Of Heaven* . . . . 7.00 - 10.00
22984 *Lawd, You Made the Night Too Long* . . . 8.00 - 12.00
24078 *San* . . . . 15.00 - 20.00
24105 *Love Nest* . . . . 15.00 - 20.00
24140 *You're Telling Me* . . . . 8.00 - 12.00
24400 *It's Only a Paper Moon* . . . . 10.00 - 15.00
24403 *Shanghai Lil* . . . . 10.00 - 15.00
24571 *Fare-Thee-Well To Harlem* . . . . 10.00 - 15.00
24615 *Christmas Night In Harlem* . . . . 10.00 - 15.00
24668 *G Blues* . . . . 10.00 - 15.00
24704 *Pardon My Southern Accent* . . . . 8.00 - 12.00
Victor 25806 *Dodging a Divorcee* . . . . 7.00 - 10.00
25088 *And Then Some* . . . . 7.00 - 10.00
25091 *I'm in the Mood for Love* . . . . 7.00 - 10.00
25113 *The Duke Insists* . . . . 7.00 - 10.00
25150 *Sugar Plum* . . . . 7.00 - 10.00
Victor 25192, 25238, 25319, 25404, 25675, 26415 5.00 - 10.00
25366 *Mississippi Mud* . . . . 8.00 - 12.00
25367 *San* . . . . 8.00 - 12.00
25368 *From Monday On* . . . . 8.00 - 12.00
25369 *Louisiana* . . . . 8.00 - 12.00
25370 *Changes* . . . . 8.00 - 12.00
(*25366 through 25370 were issued as a set)
27685 *Loveable* . . . . 5.00 - 8.00
27686 *Forget-Me-Not* . . . . 5.00 - 8.00
27687 *Dancing Shadows* . . . . 3.00 - 6.00
27688 *From Monday On* . . . . 5.00 - 8.00
27689 *Back In Your Own Back Yard* . . . . 5.00 - 8.00
(*27685 through 27689 were issued as a set)
Victor L-35001 *Grand Canyon Suite* . . . . 25.00 - 40.00
     L-35002 *Grand Canyon Suite* . . . . 25.00 - 40.00
     35822, 35877, 35912, 35933, 35934 . . . . -
     *39000 *A Night With Paul Whiteman At The
Biltmore* . . . . 75.00 - 100.00
     *39003 *Let 'Em Eat Cake—Program* . . . . 75.00 - 100.00
(* 12-inch picture records, in the style of the
more familar Vogue issues)
     55225 *Rhapsody In Blue* (12-inch) record) . . . . 5.00 - 8.00
     *67-2000 *A Night With Paul Whiteman At The
Biltmore* . . . . 75.00 - 100.00

PAUL WHITEMAN'S RHYTHM BOYS:

Columbia 1455-D *Wa Da Da* . . . . 8.00 - 12.00
     1629-D *Rhythm King* . . . . 8.00 - 12.00
     1819-D *Louise* . . . . 8.00 - 12.00
     2223-D *A Bench In The Park* . . . . 8.00 - 12.00
Victor 20783 *Mississippi Mud, etc.* . . . . 5.00 - 8.00
     21302 *From Monday On* . . . . 7.00 - 10.00
     24095 *Bahama Mamas* . . . . 7.00 - 10.00
     24190 *Jig Time* . . . . 7.00 - 10.00
     24240 *Mississippi Mud, etc.* . . . . 7.00 - 10.00
     24349 *From Monday On* . . . . 8.00 - 12.00

WHITE WAY DANCE ORCHESTRA:

Radiex 1325 *Fool Me Nice*	5.00 -	8.00
Supreme 1325 *Fool Me Nice*	5.00 -	8.00

WHITEWAY JAZZ BAND:

Paramount 20014 *Tiger Rag*	15.00 -	20.00

WHITE WAY PLAYERS:

Van Dyke 71816 *Ev'rybody Dance*	10.00 -	15.00

JACK WHITNEY AND HIS ORCHESTRA:

Clarion 5270-C *Please Don't Talk About Me*		
When I'm Gone	8.00 -	12.00
5344-C *You Forgot Your Gloves*	7.00 -	10.00
5366-C *So Sure Of You*	7.00 -	10.00
Harmony 1335-H *You Forgot Your Gloves*	7.00 -	10.00
1354-H *So Sure Of You*	7.00 -	10.00
Parlophone PNY-34194 *If You Should Ever*		
Need Me	20.00 -	30.00
Velvet Tone 2408-V *You Forgot Your Gloves*	7.00 -	10.00
2430-V *So Sure Of You*	7.00 -	10.00

THE WHOOPEE MAKERS:

Titles, issued contemporaneously on Banner,		
Jewel, Oriole, Regal, Romeo: *Rockin' Chair;*		
Them There Eyes	10.00 -	15.00
Banner 0859 *Humpty Dumpty Baby*	10.00 -	15.00
Banner 6548 *Saturday Night Function*	10.00 -	15.00
Cameo 9036 *Hottentot*	10.00 -	15.00
9037 *Misty Mornin'*	10.00 -	15.00
9306 *Saturday Night Function*	10.00 -	15.00
Columbia 14367-D *Sister Kate*	15.00 -	20.00
Conqueror 7428 *Flaming Youth*	10.00 -	15.00
Domino 4428 *Flaming Youth*	10.00 -	15.00
Lincoln 3065 *Hottentot*	10.00 -	15.00
3066 *Misty Mornin'*	10.00 -	15.00
3330 *Saturday Night Function*	10.00 -	15.00
Pathe-Actuelle 36781 *Jubilee Stomp*	12.00 -	16.00
36787 *Take It Easy*	12.00 -	16.00
36899 *The Mooche*	12.00 -	16.00
36915 *Hot and Bothered*	12.00 -	16.00
36923 *Misty Mornin'*	12.00 -	16.00
36945 *Bugle Call Rag*	12.00 -	16.00
37013 *Tiger Rag*	10.00 -	15.00
37036 *Twelfth Street Rag*	10.00 -	15.00
37042 *Dirty Dog*	15.00 -	20.00
37059 *Doin' The Voom Voom*	12.00 -	16.00
Perfect 14962 *East St. Louis Toodle-Oo*	12.00 -	16.00
14968 *Take It Easy*	12.00 -	16.00
15080 *Move Over*	12.00 -	16.00
15096 *Hot And Bothered*	12.00 -	16.00
15104 *Misty Mornin'*	12.00 -	16.00
15126 *Bugle Call Rag*	12.00 -	16.00
15194 *Tiger Rag*	10.00 -	15.00
15217 *Twelfth Street Rag*	10.00 -	15.00
15223 *The Sorority Stomp*	15.00 -	20.00
15240 *Doin' The Voom Voom*	12.00 -	16.00
15376 *Happy Feet*	10.00 -	15.00
15418 *Them There Eyes*	10.00 -	15.00
Perfect 15507 *Slow But Sure*	8.00 -	12.00
Regal 10173 *Humpty Dumpty Baby*	10.00 -	15.00
Romeo 840 *Misty Mornin'*	10.00 -	15.00
Vocalion 15763 *Dardanella*	75.00 -	100.00
15768 *I've Neer Been Loved*	50.00 -	80.00
15769 *Freshman Hop*	75.00 -	100.00

ZACH WHYTE'S CHOCOLATE BEAU BRUMMELS:

Gennett 6781 *Mandy*	150.00 -	200.00
6798 *It's Tight Like That*	125.00 -	175.00
7086 *Good Feelin' Blues*	150.00 -	250.00

HERB WIEDOEFT & HIS (CINDERELLA ROOF) ORCHESTRA:

Brunswick 2542 *Cinderella Blues*	5.00 -	8.00

Brunswick 2627 *Oh, Peter (You're So nice)*	5.00 -	8.00
Brunswick 2647 *Chimes Blues*	5.00 -	8.00
Brunswick 2660 *Stack O'Lee Blues*	5.00 -	8.00
Brunswick 2730 *Clementine*	5.00 -	8.00
Brunswick 2751 *Hard Hearted Hannah*	5.00 -	8.00
Brunswick 2781 *Hot Stuff*	5.00 -	8.00
Brunswick 2795 *Maple Leaf Rag*	5.00 -	8.00
Brunswick 2893 *Roamin' Around*	5.00 -	8.00
Brunswick 2916 *He's Just a Horn-Tootin' Fool*	5.00 -	8.00
Brunswick 2982 *Deep Elm*	5.00 -	8.00
Brunswick 3810 *Ella Cinders*	5.00 -	8.00
Brunswick 3811 *Swing Along*	5.00 -	8.00
Brunswick 3812 *Golden Gate*	5.00 -	8.00

LEE WILEY:

Gala 1 *Baby's Awake Now*	7.00 -	10.00
2 *I've Got Five Dollars*	7.00 -	10.00
3 *You Took Advantage Of Me*	7.00 -	10.00
4 *As Though You Were There*	7.00 -	10.00
Liberty Music Shop 281 *My One And Only*	7.00 -	10.00
282 *I've Got A Crush On You*	7.00 -	10.00
283 *Sam And Delilah*	7.00 -	10.00
284 *Sweet And Low Down*	7.00 -	10.00
294 *You Do Something To Me*	5.00 -	8.00
295 *Easy To Love*	5.00 -	8.00
296 *Find Me A Primitive Man*	7.00 -	10.00
297 *Let's Do It*	7.00 -	10.00

WILLIAMS' COTTON CLUB ORCEHSTRA:

Victor 24083 *Red Blues*	10.00 -	15.00

WILLIAMS' PURPLE KNIGHTS:

Victor 22625 *Dinah*	10.00 -	15.00

WILLIAMS' WASHBOARD BAND:

Bluebird 5183 *I Want To Ring Bells*	15.00 -	20.00
5204 *Hard Corn*	20.00 -	30.00
5230 *Move Turtle*	20.00 -	30.00
(Note: Above titles, on Sunrise, are worth		
substantially more.)		

WILLIAMS & MOORE:

QRS 7016 *Block And Tackle Blues*	150.00 -	200.00

BILL WILLIAMS & HIS GANG:

Champion 15011 *Doo Wacka Doo*	8.00 -	12.00
Champion 15215 *Make Me Know It*	75.00 -	100.00
15216 *Georgia Bo Bo*	80.00 -	120.00
15226 *She Looks Like Helen Brown*	15.00 -	25.00
15253 *Zulu Wail*	10.00 -	20.00
15268 *Go Wash An Elephant (If You Want To*		
Do Something Big)	8.00 -	12.00
Silvertone 3099 *I'm Sitting On Top Of The World*	7.00 -	10.00

CLARENCE WILLIAMS (& HIS WASHBOARD BAND/ORCHESTRA); CLARENCE WILLIAMS' BLUE FIVE/JAZZ KINGS/JUG BAND/NOVELTY BAND/ ORCHESTRA/STOMPERS/TRIO/ WASHBOARD FOUR/WASHBOARD FIVE:

Banner 32021 *Papa De-Da-Da*	20.00 -	30.00
32063 *Shout, Sister, Shout*	20.00 -	30.00
Bluebird 6918, 6919, 6932	7.00 -	10.00
Broadway 1347 *Long, Deep and Wide*	75.00 -	125.00
Broadway 1348 *Squeeze Me*	75.00 -	125.00
Broadway 5067 *Saturday Night Jag*	75.00 -	125.00
Brunswick 3580 *Slow River*	10.00 -	15.00
3664 *Baltimore*	15.00 -	20.00
3667 *Slow River*	10.00 -	15.00
3703 *Baltimore*	12.00 -	18.00
7000 *Cushion Foot Stomp*	20.00 -	30.00
7017 *Baltimore*	20.00 -	30.00
Columbia 1735-D *Have You Ever Felt That Way?*	20.00 -	30.00
2806-D *High Society*	20.00 -	30.00
2829-D *Chizzlin' Sam*	30.00 -	40.00
2863-D *Organ Grinder Blues*	20.00 -	30.00
14193-D *Candy Lips*	40.00 -	60.00
14241-D *Shootin' The Pistol*	35.00 -	50.00
14244-D *I'm Goin' To Bottomland*	25.00 -	40.00

14287-D *Dreaming The Hours Away* . . . . 35.00 - 50.00
14314-D *Any Time* . . . . 35.00 - 50.00
14326-D *Red River Blues* . . . . 50.00 - 75.00
14341-D *Farm Hand Papa* . . . . 40.00 - 60.00
14348-D *Walk That Broad* . . . . 40.00 - 60.00
14422-D *Mountain City Blues* . . . . 40.00 - 60.00
14434-D *In Our Cottage Of Love* . . . . 40.00 - 60.00
14447-D *Whoop It Up* . . . . 40.00 - 60.00
14460-D *Freeze Out* . . . . 40.00 - 60.00
14468-D *Railroad Rhythm* . . . . 40.00 - 60.00
14488-D *Zonky* . . . . 50.00 - 75.00
14502-D *I've Found A New Baby* . . . . 50.00 - 75.00
14555-D *High Society Blues* . . . . 50.00 - 75.00
14666-D *Baby, Won't You Please Come Home?* 50.00 - 75.00
Domino 4687 *Baby, Won't You Please Come*
  Home? . . . . 20.00 - 30.00
Jewel 6164 *Hot Lovin'* . . . . 20.00 - 30.00
Okeh 4893 *Mixing The Blues* . . . . 30.00 - 50.00
  4925 *Wild Cat Blues* . . . . 50.00 - 75.00
  4966 *Achin' Hearted Blues* . . . . 75.00 - 100.00
  4975 *New Orleans Hop Scop Blues* . . . . 80.00 - 120.00
  4993 *Old Fashioned Love* . . . . 50.00 - 75.00
  8020 *Pullman Porter Blues* . . . . 20.00 - 30.00
  8021 *Roumania* . . . . 15.00 - 20.00
  8027 *Brown Skin (Who You For)* . . . . 15.00 - 20.00
  8029 *The Dance They Call The Georgia Hunch* 15.00 - 20.00
  8171 *Texas Moaner Blues* . . . . .100.00 - 150.00
  8181 *Everybody Loves My Baby* . . . . 50.00 - 80.00
  8204 *Temptation Blues* . . . . 15.00 - 25.00
  8215 *Papa De-Da-Da* . . . . .100.00 - 150.00
  8245 *Coal Cart Blues* . . . . 75.00 - 100.00
  8254 *Santa Claus Blues* . . . . .100.00 - 150.00
  8267 *Get It Fixed* . . . . 50.00 - 75.00
  8272 *Livin' High Sometimes* . . . . 75.00 - 100.00
  8286 *I've Found A New Baby* . . . . 75.00 - 100.00
  8440 *Candy Lips* . . . . 40.00 - 60.00
  8443 *Senegalese Stomp* . . . . 50.00 - 80.00
  8462 *Cushion Foot Stomp* . . . . 40.00 - 60.00
  8465 *Black Snake Blues* . . . . 40.00 - 60.00
  8510 *Close Fit Blues* . . . . 35.00 - 50.00
  8525 *Yama Yama Blues* . . . . 35.00 - 50.00
  8572 *Log Cabin Blues* . . . . 35.00 - 50.00
  8584 *Red River Blues* . . . . 50.00 - 75.00
  8592 *Lazy Mama* . . . . 50.00 - 75.00
Okeh 8604 *Wildflower Rag* . . . . 35.00 - 50.00
  8617 *Organ Grinder Blues* . . . . 35.00 - 50.00
  8629 *Walk That Broad* . . . . 35.00 - 50.00
  8645 *In The Bottle Blues* . . . . 50.00 - 80.00
  8663 *Freeze Out* . . . . 35.00 - 50.00
  8672 *Steamboat Days* . . . . 35.00 - 50.00
  8706 *High Society* . . . . 35.00 - 50.00
  8738 *I've Got What It Takes* . . . . 35.00 - 50.00
  8752 *You Don't Understand* . . . . 35.00 - 50.00
  8763 *I've Found A New Baby* . . . . 35.00 - 50.00
  8790 *Worn Out Blues* . . . . 50.00 - 75.00
  8798 *He Wouldn't Stop Doin' It* . . . . 50.00 - 75.00
  8806 *You Rascal, You* . . . . 35.00 - 50.00
  8821 *Shout, Sister, Shout!* . . . . 50.00 - 75.00
  8826 *Kansas City Man Blues* . . . . 50.00 - 75.00
  8842 *Papa De-Da-Da* . . . . 50.00 - 75.00
  40006 *Shreveport* . . . . 35.00 - 50.00
  40172 *My Own Blues* . . . . 25.00 - 40.00
  40260 *Mandy, Make Up Your Mind* . . . . 75.00 - 100.00
  40321 *Cake-Walking Babies From Home* . . . . 75.00 - 100.00
  40541 *Dinah* . . . . 25.00 - 40.00
  40598 *What's The Matter Now?* . . . . 15.00 - 20.00
  41565 *Mister, Will You Serenade?* . . . . 40.00 - 60.00
Oriole 2141 *Papa De-Da-Da* . . . . 20.00 - 30.00
  2164 *Hot Lovin'* . . . . 20.00 - 30.00
Paramount 12435 *Shut Your Mouth* . . . . .100.00 - 150.00
  12517 *Bottomland* . . . . 75.00 - 100.00
  12587 *Jingles* . . . . 75.00 - 125.00

12839 *Midnight Stomp* . . . . .150.00 - 200.00
12870 *Pane In The Glass* . . . . .150.00 - 200.00
12884 *Speakeasy* . . . . .150.00 - 200.00
12885 *Squeeze Me* . . . . .150.00 - 200.00
Perfect 15387 *Baby, Won't You Please Come*
  Home? . . . . 20.00 - 30.00
15403 *Hot Lovin'* . . . . 20.00 - 30.00
QRS 7004 *Speakeasy* . . . . .150.00 - 200.00
  7005 *Squeeze Me* . . . . .150.00 - 200.00
  7039 *Midnight Stomp* . . . .
                                                          150.00 - 200.00
  7034 *Bozo* . . . . .150.00 - 200.00
  7040 *I'm Through* . . . . .150.00 - 200.00
  7044 *Sister Kate* . . . . .150.00 - 200.00
Romeo 1529 *Hot Lovin'* . . . . 20.00 - 30.00
Victor V-38063 *Lazy Mama* . . . . 50.00 - 75.00
  V38524 *Too Low* . . . . 50.00 - 75.00
  V38630 *I'm Not Worryin'* . . . . 75.00 - 100.00
Vocalion 1088 *Cushion Foot Stomp* . . . . 20.00 - 30.00
  1130 *Baltimore* . . . . 20.00 - 30.00
Vocalion 2541 *Breeze* . . . . 5.00 - 8.00
  2563 *The Right Key But The Wrong Keyhole* . . . 10.00 - 15.00
  2584 *Chocolate Avenue* . . . . 10.00 - 15.00
  2602 *Harlem Rhythm Dance* . . . . 10.00 - 15.00
  2616 *Swaller-Tail Coat* . . . . 10.00 - 15.00
  2629 *Jimmy Had A Nickel* . . . . 10.00 - 15.00
  2630 *How Can I Get It?* . . . . 10.00 - 15.00
  2654 *New Orleans Hop Scop Blues* . . . . 10.00 - 15.00
  2674 *As Long As I Live* . . . . 10.00 - 15.00
  2676 *St. Louis Blues* . . . . 10.00 - 15.00
  2689 *I Can't Dance, I Got Ants In My Pants* . . 10.00 - 15.00
  2718 *Pretty Baby, Is It Yes Or No?* . . . . 10.00 - 15.00
  2736 *After Tonight* . . . . 10.00 - 15.00
  2759 *Let's Have A Showdown* . . . . 10.00 - 15.00
  2778 *Bimbo* . . . . 10.00 - 15.00
  2788 *Trouble* . . . . 10.00 - 15.00
  2805 *Ain't Gonna Give You None Of My Jelly*
    Roll . . . . 10.00 - 15.00
  2838 *Big Fat Mama* . . . . 10.00 - 15.00
  2854 *Chizzlin' Sam* . . . . 10.00 - 15.00
  2871 *Organ Grinder Blues* . . . . 10.00 - 15.00
  2889 *Tell The Truth* . . . . 10.00 - 15.00
  2899 *I Saw Stars* . . . . 10.00 - 15.00
  2909 *Jungle Crawl* . . . . 10.00 - 15.00
  2927 *Milk Cow Blues* . . . . 10.00 - 15.00
  2938 *Black Gal* . . . . 10.00 - 15.00
  2958 *I Can See You All Over The Place* . . . . . . 10.00 - 15.00
  2991 *Yama Yama Blues* . . . . 10.00 - 15.00
  3195 *This Is My Sunday Off* . . . . 10.00 - 15.00
  03350 *Mississippi Basin* . . . . 20.00 - 30.00
  25009 *Black-Eyed Susan Brown* . . . . 20.00 - 30.00
  25010 *High Society* . . . . 20.00 - 30.00

**COOTIE WILLIAMS & HIS
ORCHESTRA/RUG CUTTERS:**
Okeh 5618 *Black Butterfly* . . . . 7.00 - 10.00
  5690 *Give It Up* . . . . 7.00 - 10.00
  6224 *Ain't Misbehavin'* . . . . 7.00 - 10.00
  6336 *Top And Bottom* . . . . 7.00 - 10.00
  6370 *West End Blues* . . . . 7.00 - 10.00
Variety 527 *Downtown Uproar* . . . . 10.00 - 15.00
  555 *Diga Diga Doo* . . . . 10.00 - 15.00
Vocalion 3814 *Blue Reverie* . . . . 10.00 - 15.00
  3818 *Diga Diga Doo* . . . . 10.00 - 15.00
  3890 *I Can't Give You Anything But Love* . . . 10.00 - 15.00
  3922 *Pigeons And Peppers* . . . . 10.00 - 15.00
  3960 *Echoes Of Harlem* . . . . 8.00 - 12.00
  4061 *Carnival In Caroline* . . . . 8.00 - 12.00
  4086 *Ol' Man River* . . . . 8.00 - 12.00
  4324 *Blue Is The Evening* . . . . 8.00 - 12.00
  4425 *Swing Pan Alley* . . . . 8.00 - 12.00
  4574 *The Boys From Harlem* . . . . 8.00 - 12.00
  4646 *Mobile Blues* . . . . 8.00 - 12.00

4726	*Boudoir Benny*	8.00 -	12.00
4958	*Black Beauty*	7.00 -	10.00
5411	*Beautiful Romance*	7.00 -	10.00
5618	*Blues A-Poppin'*	7.00 -	10.00
5690	*Give It Up*	7.00 -	10.00

DOUGLAS WILLIAMS (FOUR) (& HIS ORCHESTRA):

Victor 21269	*Roadhouse Stomp*	10.00 -	15.00
21413	*Far Away Texas Blues*	25.00 -	40.00
21695	*Kind Daddy*	25.00 -	40.00
23264	*Darktown Jubilee*	100.00 -	150.00
23303	*Thrill Me*	75.00 -	100.00
23337	*Clarinet Jiggles*	75.00 -	100.00
23362	*Memphis Gal*	100.00 -	150.00
23387	*Leaving Blues*	100.00 -	150.00
V-38031	*Riverside Stomp*	15.00 -	20.00
V-38518	*Neal's Blues*	50.00 -	80.00
V-38850	*P-Wee Strut*	75.00 -	100.00
V-38623	*Louisiana Hop*	100.00 -	150.00

FESS WILLIAMS & HIS JOY BOYS:

Vocalion 15690	*Dixie Stomp*	80.00 -	120.00

FESS WILLIAMS & HIS ROYAL FLUSH (SAVOY) ORCHESTRA:

Brunswick 3532	*Variety Stomp*	10.00 -	15.00
3589	*Alligator Crawl*	10.00 -	15.00
3596	*Razor Edge*	10.00 -	15.00
Champion 15118	*Ya Gotta Know How To Love*	50.00 -	75.00
15120	*It's Breaking My Heart*	50.00 -	75.00
Diva 2189-G	*My Mama's In Town*	15.00 -	20.00
Gennett 3182	*Green River Blues*	30.00 -	50.00
3210	*Caroline*	30.00 -	50.00
3259	*Wimmin—Aah!*	100.00 -	150.00
3336	*Ya Gotta Know How To Love*	25.00 -	40.00
Harmony 189-H	*My Mama's In Town*	15.00 -	20.00
Okeh 8322	*Make Me Know It*	50.00 -	80.00
Velvet Tone 1189-V	*My Mama's In Town*	15.00 -	20.00
Victor 22864	*Hot Mama*	20.00 -	30.00
23003	*Everything's O.K. With Me*	20.00 -	30.00
23005	*Dinah*	20.00 -	30.00
23025	*She's Still Dizzy*	50.00 -	80.00
24153	*Playing My Saxophone*	20.00 -	30.00
V38056	*Here 'Tis*	15.00 -	20.00
V38064	*Betsy Brown*	15.00 -	20.00
V38604	*Do Shuffle*	20.00 -	30.00
V38065	*Sweet Savannah Sue*	20.00 -	30.00
V38077	*Hot Town*	20.00 -	30.00
Victor V38095	*Buttons*	30.00 -	50.00
V38106	*Slide, Mr. Jelly*	30.00 -	50.00
V38128	*Big Shot*	30.00 -	50.00
V38131	*I'm Feelin' Devilish*	30.00 -	50.00
Vocalion 1054	*Heebie Jeebies*	15.00 -	25.00
1058	*High Fever*	50.00 -	75.00
1085	*White Ghost Shivers*	50.00 -	75.00
1087	*Gambler's Blues*	50.00 -	75.00
1117	*Ozark Blues*	20.00 -	30.00
15492	*High Fever*	50.00 -	75.00
15550	*Variety Stomp*	15.00 -	25.00

HOD WILLIAMS AND HIS ORCHESTRA:

Bluebird 7104, 7119, 7141		5.00 -	10.00

JOHN WILLIAMS & HIS MEMPHIS STOMPERS:

Black Patti 8009	*Pee Wee Blues*	200.00 -	400.00
Vocalion 1453	*Lotta Sax Appeal*	150.00 -	200.00

JOHN WILLIAMS' SYNCO JAZZERS:

Paramount 12457	*Goose Grease*	150.00 -	200.00

(DRUMMER MAN) JOHNNY WILLIAMS & HIS BOYS/SWING SEXTETTE:

Variety 594	*Where's My Sweetie Hiding?*	8.00 -	12.00
638	*I'll Build A Stairway To Paradise*	8.00 -	12.00
Vocalion 3826	*Little Old Lady*	8.00 -	12.00
3827	*I'll Build A Stairway To Paradise*	8.00 -	12.00
5077	*Milenberg Joys*	5.00 -	8.00

5213	*Clarinet Marmalade*	5.00 -	8.00

LEONA WILLIAMS & HER DIXIE BAND:

Columbia A-3565	*Cruel Daddy Blues*	8.00 -	12.00
A-3599	*Achin' Hearted Blues*	7.00 -	10.00
A-3642	*Got To Cool My Doggies Now*	7.00 -	10.00
A-3696	*Sugar Blues*	7.00 -	10.00
A-3713	*I Wish I Could Shimmy Like My Sister Kate*	7.00 -	10.00
A-3736	*Mexican Blues*	7.00 -	10.00
A-3815	*Bring It With You When You Come*	7.00 -	10.00
A-3835	*If Your Man Is Like My Man*	7.00 -	10.00

MARY LOU WILLIAMS:

Brunswick 7178	*Night Life*	100.00 -	150.00
Decca 781	*Mary's Special*	8.00 -	12.00
1021	*Isabelle*	8.00 -	12.00
1155	*Clean Pickin'*	8.00 -	12.00
2796, 2797, 18122		5.00 -	8.00

MIDGE WILLIAMS & HER JAZZ JESTERS:

Variety 519	*Walkin' The Dog*	7.00 -	10.00
566	*Let's Begin Again*	7.00 -	10.00
620	*That Old Feeling*	10.00 -	15.00
670	*The One Rose (That's Left In My Heart)*	10.00 -	15.00
Vocalion 3779	*I Know Now*	10.00 -	15.00
3801	*An Old Flame Never Dies*	10.00 -	15.00
3812	*Walkin' The Dog*	7.00 -	10.00
3821	*I'm Getting Sentimental Over You*	7.00 -	10.00
3838	*I Was Born To Swing*	10.00 -	15.00
3865	*Fortune Tellin' Man*	10.00 -	15.00
3900	*Singin' The Blues*	8.00 -	12.00
3961	*Goodnight, Angel*	8.00 -	12.00
04026	*Love Is Like Whiskey*	10.00 -	15.00
4177	*In Any Language*	8.00 -	12.00
4192	*Don't Wake Up My Heart*	8.00 -	12.00

RALPH WILLIAMS & HIS (RAINBO) ORCHESTRA:

Victor 19504, 19528, 19957, 19958		4.00 -	7.00
Victor 19573	*Wait Till You See Me With My Baby*	5.00 -	8.00
19775	*Cocaine dance*	-	

SAMMY WILLIAMS (& HIS THREE NATURALS):

Autograph (unnumbered)	*House Of David Blues*	75.00 -	100.00
	Mandy, Make Up Your Mind	75.00 -	100.00
Vocalion 4197	*All Alone*	7.00 -	10.00
4229	*Some Sweet Day*	7.00 -	10.00
4243	*My Walking Stick*	7.00 -	10.00
4259	*Ain't She Sweet?*	7.00 -	10.00

SID/SIDNEY WILLIAMS:

Champion 15372	*Mississippi Shivers*	40.00 -	60.00
Gennett 6353	*Mississippi Shivers*	150.00 -	250.00
Vocalion 15691	*My Pet*	35.00 -	50.00

SPEED WILLIAMS' ORCHESTRA:

Superior 2818	*Tin Roof Blues*	150.00 -	250.00

TE ROY WILLIAMS & HIS ORCHESTRA:

Titles, issued contemporaneously on Diva, Harmony, Velvet-Tone; *Lindberg Hop; Oh Malinda*		30.00 -	50.00

WILLIAMSON'S BEALE STREET FROLIC ORCHESTRA:

Victor 20555	*Memphis Scrontch*	75.00 -	100.00
21410	*Scandinavian Stomp*	75.00 -	100.00

VIRGINIA WILLRICH & HER TEXAS RANGERS:

Okeh 41328	*Same Old Moon*	50.00 -	80.00

WILSHIRE DANCE ORCHESTRA:

Sunset 1059	*My Best Girl*	15.00 -	20.00
1088	*Charleston Charley*	15.00 -	20.00

WILSON'S T.O.B.A. BAND:

Paramount 12408	*Steady Roll*	100.00 -	150.00

CHICKEN WILSON AND SKEETER HINTON:

QRS 7051	*Myrtle Avenue Stomp*	100.00 -	150.00
7052	*House Snake Blues*	100.00 -	150.00

DUKE WILSON & HIS TEN BLACK
BERRIES:
Banner 32607 *Mary's Idea*	15.00 -	25.00
Banner 32643 *Beale Street Blues*	12.00 -	15.00
32733 *House Of David Blues*	15.00 -	20.00
Domino 0127 *House Of David Blues*	15.00 -	20.00
Melotone 12662 *House Of David Blues*	15.00 -	20.00
Oriole 2466 *How'm I Doin'* (Hey Hey)	15.00 -	20.00
2488 *Beale Street Blues*	12.00 -	15.00
2677 *House Of David Blues*	15.00 -	20.00
Perfect 15603 *How'm I Doin'* (Hey Hey)	15.00 -	20.00
15617 *Beale Street Blues*	10.00 -	15.00
15632 *Bull Fiddle Blues*	10.00 -	15.00
15697 *Once Or Twice*	15.00 -	25.00
15738 *Goodbye Blues*	15.00 -	20.00
15753 *House Of David Blues*	15.00 -	20.00
Romeo 1858 *Beale Street Blues*	12.00 -	15.00

EDITH WILSON (&HER/JOHNNY DUNN'S
JAZZ BAND/HOUNDS):
Brunswick 4685 *Black And Blue*	30.00 -	50.00
Columbia A-3479 *Vampin' Liza Jane*	10.00 -	15.00
A-3506 *Old Time Blues*	10.00 -	15.00
A-3537 *The West Texas Blues*	10.00 -	15.00
A-3558 *Birmingham Blues*	8.00 -	12.00
A-3634 *Mammy, I'm Thinking Of You*	8.00 -	12.00
A-3653 *He May Be Your Man (But He Comes To See Me Sometimes)*	8.00 -	12.00
A-3674 *Lonesome Mama Blues*	8.00 -	12.00
A-3746 *Evil Blues*	8.00 -	12.00
A-3787 *He Used To Be Your Man But He's My Man Now*	8.00 -	12.00
14008-D *Daddy, Change Your Mind*	20.00 -	30.00
14027-D *Muscle Shoals Blues*	15.00 -	20.00
14054-D *Double Crossin' Papa*	25.00 -	40.00
14066-D *There'll Be Some Changes Made*	15.00 -	20.00
Diva 6025-G *I Don't Know And I Don't Care Blues*	20.00 -	30.00
Velvet Tone 7051-V *Daddy, Change Your Mind*	20.00 -	30.00
Victor V38624 *I'll Get Even With You*	75.00 -	100.00

GARLAND WILSON:
Okeh 41556 *Rockin' Chair*	30.00 -	40.00

GEORGE WILSON AND JIMMY HINTON:
Paramount 12843 *Chicken Wilson Blues*	100.00 -	150.00
QRS 7060 *Frog Eye Stomp*	100.00 -	150.00

LENA WILSON:
Ajax 17014 *Down South Blues*	20.00 -	30.00
17025 *He Wasn't Born In Araby*	20.00 -	30.00
Black Swan 14129 *The Wicked Fives' Blues*	25.00 -	40.00
Brunswick 2464, 2590	7.00 -	10.00
Clarion 5036-C *Chiropractor Blues*	25.00 -	40.00
Columbia A3915 *Memphis, Tennessee*	10.00 -	15.00
Columbia 14618-D *My Man O'War*	50.00 -	80.00
Diva 6038-G *Baby, It Upsets Me So*	30.00 -	50.00
6045-G *Chiropractor Blues*	30.00 -	50.00
Emerson 10745 *I Don't Love Nobody*	10.00 -	15.00
Harmograph 2543 *Deceitful Blues*	40.00 -	60.00
Paramount 12029 *Deceitful Blues*	40.00 -	60.00
12042 *Memphis, Tennessee*	40.00 -	60.00
Pathe-Actuelle 020910, 032015	7.00 -	10.00
Perfect 12044, 12094	7.00 -	10.00
Silvertone 3010 *Afternoon Blues*	20.00 -	30.00
Victor 19085 *Triflin' Blues*	7.00 -	10.00
Vocalion 14631 *Your Time Now*	8.00 -	12.00
14651 *Afternoon Blues*	20.00 -	30.00

ROY WILSON & HIS GEORGIA CRACKERS:
Melotone 12026 *Swamp Blues*	25.00 -	40.00

TEDDY WILSON (& HIS ORCHESTRA)
TEDDY WILSON QUARTET:
Brunswick 7498 *What A Little Moonlight Can Do*	8.00 -	12.00
7501 *Miss Brown To You*	8.00 -	12.00
7511, 7520, 7543, 7550, 7554, 7563, 7522, 7572, 7577, 7581, 7599, 7612, 7640, 7663, 7684, 7699,		

7702, 7729, 7736, 7762, 7768, 7781, 7789, 7797, 7816, 7824, 7840, 7844, 7859, 7867, 7877, 7884, 7893, 7903, 7911, 7917, 7926, 7940, 7943, 7954, 7960, 7964, 7973, 8008, 8015, 8025, 8053, 8070, 8112, 8116, 8141, 8153, 8199, 8207, 8259, 8265, 8270, 8281, 8283, 8314, 8319, 8438, 8455	7.00 -	12.00
Columbia 35207, 35220, 35232, 35298, 35354, 35372, 35711, 35737	5.00 -	10.00

WOODROW WILSON:
Victor 35251 *Woodrow Wilson on the Third Party* (12-inch)	5.00 -	8.00
Victor (12-inch) 35252 *Democratic Principles*	5.00 -	8.00
35253 *The Tariff*	5.00 -	8.00

DALE WIMBROW (THE DEL-MAR-VA
SONGSTER) & HIS RUBEVILLE TUNERS:
Columbia 821-D *Country Bred And Chicken Fed*	8.00 -	12.00
1200-D *Oshkosh*	8.00 -	12.00
Edison 51894 *So Long North (I'm Headin' South)*	15.00 -	20.00
52292 *Oshkosh*	15.00 -	20.00
Q.R.S. 1009 *Crying For The Carolines*	10.00 -	15.00
1019 *The Preacher And The Bear*	10.00 -	15.00
1056 *Sing You Sinners*	10.00 -	15.00

WINDY RHYTHM KINGS:
Broadway 1294 *South African Blues*	150.00 -	250.00
Paramount 12770 *Piggly Wiggly Blues*	150.00 -	250.00

WINEGAR'S PENN. BOYS:
Edison 52097 *Shaking The Blues Away*	20.00 -	30.00
52099 *Ooh! Maybe It's You*	15.00 -	20.00
52221 *Since My Best Gal Turned Me Down*	25.00 -	40.00
52224 *Stay Out Of The South*	15.00 -	20.00
52241 *Since My Best Gal Turned Me Down*	20.00 -	30.00
52255 *Say So!*	10.00 -	15.00
52305 *My Gal Sal*	20.00 -	30.00
52321 *Ida! Sweet As Apple Cider*	20.00 -	30.00
52381 *Imagination*	15.00 -	20.00
52596 *Dream Mother*	15.00 -	20.00
(*All copies seen of 52221 play same song both sides, although flip side is labelled *A Good Man Is Hard To Find*)	-	

JACK WINN'S/WYNN'S DALLAS DANDIES:
Melotone 12008 *Lovey Lee*	8.00 -	12.00
12027 *Wild Man Blues*	10.00 -	15.00
12051 *Loved One*	75.00 -	100.00
12064 *Melancholy*	10.00 -	15.00
Vocalion 15860 *Loved One*	75.00 -	100.00

GUS WINSON & HIS ORCHESTRA:
Broadway 1476 *It's The Girl*	7.00 -	10.00

CHIC WINTERS' (HOTEL GRAMATIN)
ORCHESTRA:
Blu-Disc 1004 *Nashville Nightingale*	25.00 -	50.00
Gennett 3294 *Spring Is Here*	7.00 -	10.00
3314 *Will You Be True?*	7.00 -	10.00
3320 *No More Worryin'*	7.00 -	10.00
3340 *Faded Cherry Blossom*	7.00 -	10.00
Hudson 11423 *Nashville Nightingale*	10.00 -	20.00
Triangle 11423 *Nashville Nightingale*	8.00 -	12.00

JULIE WINTZ AND HIS (HOFBRAU/
MAYFLOWER) ORCHESTRA; JULIE
WINTZ AND GEORGE ZIMMER'S JERSEY
COLLEGIANS:
Harmony 436-H *Vo-Do-Do-Deo Blues*	5.00 -	8.00
438-H *Magnolia*	5.00 -	8.00
Harmony 899-H *Perfume Of Roses*	7.00 -	10.00
1040-H *H'lo Baby*	5.00 -	8.00
1044-H *Till Your Happiness Happens Along*	5.00 -	8.00
1051-H *I Gotta Have You*	5.00 -	8.00
1092-H *The Man From The South*	7.00 -	10.00
1104-H *Harmonica Harry*	5.00 -	25.00
1169-H *After You've Gone*	7.00 -	10.00
Pathe-Actuelle 36451 *Deep Henderson*	10.00 -	15.00
36460 *Spanish Mamma*	10.00 -	15.00

Perfect 14632 *Deep Henderson* . . . . 10.00 - 15.00
　14641 *Spanish Mamma* . . . . 10.00 - 15.00
Velvet Tone 2092-V *The Man from the South* . . . . 7.00 - 10.00
　2104-V *Harmonica Harry* . . . . 15.00 - 25.00

BILL WIRGES & HIS ORCHESTRA;
WILLIAM F. WIRGES & HIS ORCHESTRA:
Brunswick (most issues) . . . . 3.00 - 6.00
Perfect 14404 *Cheatin' On Me* . . . . 5.00 - 8.00
　14440 *Yes Sir, That's My Baby* . . . . 5.00 - 8.00
　14443 *Pango Pango Maid* . . . . 7.00 - 10.00
　14474 *So's Your Old Man* . . . . 5.00 - 8.00
　14475 *I Want A Lovable Baby* . . . . 7.00 - 10.00
　14533 *Shake That Thing* . . . . 8.00 - 12.00
　14762 *Where's That Rainbow?* . . . . 5.00 - 8.00
(Note: Above titles, on Pathe-Actuelle, are
　similarly valued.)

WISCONSIN ROOF ORCHESTRA:
Broadway 1063 *There's Everything Sweet About*
　You . . . . 7.00 - 10.00
　1087 *Shanghai Honeymoon* . . . . 7.00 - 10.00
　1142 *Riverboat Blues* . . . . 10.00 - 20.00
　1177 *Wob-A-Ly Walk* . . . . 7.00 - 10.00
　1178 *Whispering* . . . . 7.00 - 10.00
　1180 *When You're Smiling* . . . . 7.00 - 10.00
　1210 *Farewell Blues* . . . . 15.00 - 20.00
　1249 *Dream Train* . . . . 7.00 - 10.00
　1268 *There's A Place In The Sun For You* . . . . . 7.00 - 10.00
Paramount 20561 *Who's That Knockin' At My*
　Door? . . . . 10.00 - 15.00
　20619 *Wob-A-Ly Walk* . . . . 7.00 - 10.00
　20621 *Whispering* . . . . 7.00 - 10.00
　20622 *When You're Smiling* . . . . 7.00 - 10.00

WISCONSIN U SKYROCKETS:
Paramount 12641 *Slow Beef* . . . . 200.00 - 300.00
　12642 *Postage Stomp* . . . . 200.00 - 300.00

WOLVERINE ORCHESTRA; THE
WOLVERINES:
Brunswick 3332 *Crazy Quilt* . . . . 10.00 - 15.00
Gennett 5408 *Jazz Me Blues* . . . . 100.00 - 150.00
　5453 *Copenhagen* . . . . 100.00 - 150.00
　5454 *Riverboat Shuffle* . . . . 100.00 - 150.00
　5542 *Lazy Daddy* . . . . 100.00 - 150.00
　5565 *'Tia Juana* . . . . 100.00 - 150.00
　5620 *Prince Of Wails* . . . . 75.00 - 125.00

WOODING'S GRAND CENTRAL RED CAPS:
Victor 22718 *I Can't Get Enough Of You* . . . . . . 30.00 - 50.00

BABE WOODS & HIS PALS:
Champion 15468 *Let's Misbehave* . . . . 40.00 - 60.00

ALLISTER WYLIE & HIS CORONADO
HOTEL ORCHESTRA:
Brunswick 4143 *Come On, Baby!* . . . . 15.00 - 20.00

(ALBERT) WYNN'S (AND HIS) GUT
BUCKET FIVE/CREOLE JAZZ BAND:
Okeh 8350 *When* . . . . 150.00 - 200.00
Vocalion 1218 *Crying My Blues Away* . . . . 150.00 - 200.00
　1220 *Parkway Stomp* . . . . 150.00 - 200.00
　1252 *She's Crying For Me* . . . . 150.00 - 200.00

JACK WYNN'S DALLAS DANDIES; See JACK
WINN'S DALLAS DANDIES:
ALBERT WYNNE (See: ALBERT WYNN)
BILLY WYNNE & HIS GREENWICH
VILLAGE INN ORCHESTRA:
Edison 51432 *I Want To Be Happy* . . . . 5.00 - 8.00
　51452 *Not Now, Not Yet, But Soon* . . . . 5.00 - 8.00
　51488 *Blue-Eyed Sally* . . . . 5.00 - 8.00
　51501 *Alabamy Bound* . . . . 7.00 - 10.00
　51503 *The Only Only One For Me* . . . . 7.00 - 10.00
　51519 *Yearning (Just For You)* . . . . 5.00 - 8.00
　51549 *Lenore* . . . . 15.00 - 20.00
　51566 *Pango Pango Maid* . . . . 15.00 - 20.00
　51573 *Say, Arabella* . . . . 15.00 - 20.00
　51578 *Nantucket Nan* . . . . 7.00 - 10.00

　51580 *Steppin' In Society* . . . . 10.00 - 15.00
　51603 *Cecilia* . . . . 15.00 - 20.00
　51606 *Charleston Baby O'Mine* . . . . 15.00 - 20.00
　51715 *Everything's Gonna Be All Right* . . . . . . 7.00 - 10.00
Harmony 33-H *The Co-Ed* . . . . 5.00 - 8.00
　34-H *Let's Wander Away* . . . . 5.00 - 8.00
　54-H *Why aren't Yez Eatin' More Oranges?* . . . 5.00 - 8.00
　57-H *Five Foot Two, Eyes Of Blue* . . . . 7.00 - 10.00
　163-H *I'm In Love With You, That's Why* . . . . . 5.00 - 8.00
Pathe-Actuelle 36431 *Dorothy* . . . . 7.00 - 10.00
　36460 *If You Can't Hold The Man You Love* . . . 10.00 - 15.00
Perfect 14612 *No Foolin'* . . . . 7.00 - 10.00
　14641 *If You Can't Hold The Man You Love* . . . 10.00 - 15.00

THE YACHT CLUB BOYS:
Columbia 2887-D *We Own A Salon* . . . . 10.00 - 15.00
　2908-D *The Great American Tourist* . . . . 10.00 - 15.00

YALE COLLEGIANS:
Edison 52108 *You'll Do It Someday* . . . . 20.00 - 30.00
Okeh 41474 *Blue Again* . . . . 25.00 - 40.00

JIMMY YANCEY:
Bluebird 8630 *Death Letter Blues* . . . . 10.00 - 15.00
Session 10001, 10003, 10005 . . . . 7.00 - 10.00
Vocalion 05464, 05490 . . . . 8.00 - 12.00

THE YANKEE SIX:
Okeh 40335 *Oh! Those Eyes* . . . . 30.00 - 50.00
　40348 *Jimtown Blues* . . . . 30.00 - 50.00

THE YANKEE TEN (DANCE) ORCHESTRA:
Oriole 684 *Baby Face* . . . . 7.00 - 10.00
　846 *Ain't She Sweet?* . . . . 7.00 - 10.00
　933 *Sometimes I'm Happy* . . . . 8.00 - 12.00
　1455 *Makin' Whoopee* . . . . 5.00 - 8.00
　1726 *Look What You've Done To Me* . . . . 10.00 - 15.00

DUKE YELLMAN AND HIS ORCHESTRA:
Edison 52076 *The Light House Blues* . . . . 20.00 - 30.00
Edison 52225 *Missouri Squabble* . . . . 20.00 - 30.00
　52227 *I'm More Than Satisfied* . . . . 20.00 - 30.00
　52328 *Fireworks* . . . . 20.00 - 30.00
　52353 *Louisiana* . . . . 15.00 - 20.00
　52470 *If You Want The Rainbow* . . . . 15.00 - 20.00

YERKES' JAZARIMBA ORCHESTRA;
YERKES' MARIMBAPHONE
ORCHESTRA; YERKES' NOVELTY FIVE;
YERKES' SOUTHERN FIVE:
Aeolian-Vocalion 14047 *Railroad Blues* . . . . 8.00 - 12.00
Columbia A2634 *Hear Dem Bells* . . . . 5.00 - 8.00
　A2720 *Bevo Blues* . . . . 5.00 - 8.00
　A2929 *Railroad Blues* . . . . 5.00 - 8.00
　A6166 *Sensation (12-inch)* . . . . 10.00 - 15.00

YOUNG'S CREOLE JAZZ BAND:
Claxtonola 40272 *Tin Roof Blues* . . . . 100.00 - 150.00
Harmograph 863 *Tin Roof Blues* . . . . 100.00 - 150.00
Paramount 12060 *Every Saturday Night* . . . . 125.00 - 175.00
　12088 *Dearborn Street Blues* . . . . 150.00 - 300.00
　20272 *Tin Roof Blues* . . . . 100.00 - 150.00
Puritan 11272 *Tin Roof Blues* . . . . 100.00 - 150.00

CLARENCE YOUNG'S HARMONY
SYNCOPATORS:
Harmograph 874 *Jazzbo Jenkins* . . . . 100.00 - 150.00

MARGARET YOUNG:
Brunswick 2253 *High Brown Blues* . . . . 5.00 - 8.00
　2265 *Oo-Oo Ernest* . . . . 5.00 - 8.00
　2284 *Nobody Loves Me Now* . . . . 5.00 - 8.00
　2297 *Oh! Is She Dumb* . . . . 5.00 - 8.00
　2319 *'Way Down Yonder in New Orleans* . . . . . 5.00 - 8.00
　2346 *Lovin' Sam* . . . . 5.00 - 8.00
　2359 *Jimbo Jambo* . . . . 5.00 - 8.00
　2371 *Whoa, Tillie, Take Your Time* . . . . 5.00 - 8.00
　2386 *Counterfeit Bill* . . . . 5.00 - 8.00
　2413 *Seven Or Eleven* . . . . 5.00 - 8.00
　2442 *Louisville Lou* . . . . 5.00 - 8.00
　2459 *Papa Better Watch Your Step* . . . . 5.00 - 8.00
　2475 *Stingo Stungo* . . . . 5.00 - 8.00

2514 *Mama Goes Where Papa Goes* .... 5.00 - 8.00
2537 *You Better Keep Babying Baby* .... 5.00 - 8.00
2553 *Why Should I Weep About One Sweetie* .. 5.00 - 8.00
2583 *Dancin' Dan* .... 5.00 - 8.00
2596 *Nobody's Sweetheart* .... 5.00 - 8.00
2621 *Oh, Gee, Georgie!* .... 5.00 - 8.00
2652 *Hard Hearted Hannah* .... 5.00 - 8.00
2673 *Doodle-Doo-Doo* .... 5.00 - 8.00
2687 *Africa* .... 5.00 - 8.00
2736 *Big Bad Bill (Is Sweet William Now)* .... 5.00 - 8.00
2806 *Nobody Knows What a Red-Head Mama Can Do* .... 7.00 - 10.00

PATSY YOUNG: (See also: Dot Dare, Annette Hanshaw)
Harmony 878-H *I Want To Be Bad* .... 7.00 - 10.00
Publix 1057-P *I Think You'll Like It* .... 8.00 - 12.00
Velvet Tone 1792-V *Is There Anything Wrong In That?* .... 10.00 - 15.00
1829-V *Don't Be Like That* .... 7.00 - 10.00

VICTOR YOUNG & HIS ORCHESTRA:
Brunswick 6128 *Sing A Little Jingle* .... 15.00 - 20.00
6554 *Two Tickets To Georgia* .... 10.00 - 15.00
6747 *This Little Piggie Went To Market* .... 10.00 - 15.00

20106 (12-inch) *Face The Music* .... 15.00 - 25.00
Decca 279 *Mr. And Mrs. Is The Name* .... 8.00 - 12.00

BARNEY ZEEMAN'S KENTUCKY CARDINALS:
Gennett 3299 *I'd Rather Be Alone* .... 8.00 - 12.00
3360 *Horses* .... 8.00 - 12.00

ZENITH KNIGHTS:
Q.R.S. 1007 *My Blue Ridge Mountain Home* .... 10.00 - 15.00
1020 *Eyes Of Blue* .... 10.00 - 15.00
1021 *Congratulations* .... 10.00 - 15.00
1025 *Get Yourself A Sweetie* .... 10.00 - 15.00
1039 *Keep On The Sunny Side* .... 15.00 - 25.00
1045 *We'll Be Married In June* .... 10.00 - 15.00

ZON-O-PHONE ORCHESTRA:
Zon-o-phone 5285 *Noodles-Rag-Time Two-Step* .. 15.00 - 25.00
5320 *Persian Lamb Rag* .... 15.00 - 25.00

BOB ZURKE & HIS DELTA RHYTHM BAND:
Victor (most issues) .... 5.00 - 10.00

ZUTTY & HIS BAND:
Decca 431 *Look Over Yonder* .... 7.00 - 10.00
432 *Clarinet Marmalade* .... 7.00 - 10.00
465 *Royal Garden Blues* .... 7.00 - 10.00

BLUES; RHYTHM & BLUES

1920s to early 1950s

All records in this section are 78 RPM unless otherwise stated. An Asterisk (*) after price indicates that the record is known or likely to exist in 45 rpm form, with the same label and catalog number. The price of such 45 rpm records usually is substantially higher than the 78 rpm counterpart. Some issues are listed in this section (78 rpm) and in the 45 rpm section.

(PEG LEG) BEN ABNEY:
Bluebird 6496 *Dirty Double Crosser* . . . . 15.00 - 25.00
6628 *I'm Rattlesnakin' Daddy* . . . . 15.00 - 25.00
8121 *'Way Down In Town* . . . . 15.00 - 25.00

KATHERINE ADKINS:
Okeh 8363 *Individual Blues* . . . . 30.00 - 50.00

GARFIELD AKERS:
Vocalion 1442 *Cottonfield Blues* . . . . 150.00 - 200.00
1481 *Dough Roller Blues* . . . . 150.00 - 200.00

ALABAMA FOUR:
Victor 21136 *Queen Street Rag* . . . . 25.00 - 40.00

ALABAMA JIM (AND GEORGE):
Gennett 6905 *Crossin' Beale Street* . . . . 150.00 - 200.00
6918 *All Over You* . . . . 150.00 - 200.00
6949 *Deep Blue Sea* . . . . 150.00 - 200.00

ALABAMA SAM:
Titles, issued contemporaneously on Banner,
Conqueror, Melotone, Oriole, Perfect, Romeo,
Red Cross Blues; You Gonna Need Me . . . . 30.00 - 50.00

ALABAMA SHIEKS:
Victor 23261 *Sittin' On Top Of The World* . . . . . . 150.00 - 200.00
23265 *Travelin' Railroad Man Blues* . . . . 150.00 - 200.00

ALABAMA SLIM:
Savoy 5553 *Boar Hog Blues* . . . . 7.00 - 10.00

MOZELLE ALDERSON (AND BLIND JAMES BECK):
Black Patti 8003 *Mozelle Blues* . . . . 200.00 - 300.00

8004 *Room Rent Blues* . . . . 200.00 - 300.00
8029 *Tall Man Blues* . . . . 250.00 - 400.00
Brunswick 7159 *Tight In Chicago* . . . . 75.00 - 100.00

ALEXANDER BROTHERS:
Champion 16493 *Limehouse Blues* . . . . 50.00 - 100.00
16497 *Tiger Rag* . . . . 50.00 - 100.00
16499 *St. Louis Blues* . . . . 50.00 - 100.00

LITTLE DAVID ALEXANDER:
Ebony 1005 *Dupree Blues* . . . . 20.00 - 30.00

HILDA ALEXANDER:
Brunswick 7069 *He's Tight Like This* . . . . 75.00 - 125.00

ORA ALEXANDER:
Columbia 14626-D *Sweetest Daddy In Town* . . . . 30.00 - 50.00
14646-D *Ugle Man Blues* . . . . 30.00 - 50.00
14651-D *Rider Needs A Fast Horse* . . . . 30.00 - 50.00

TEXAS ALEXANDER:
Freedom 1538 *Crossroads* . . . . 25.00 - 40.00
Okeh 8498 *Section Gang Blues* . . . . 30.00 - 40.00
8511 *Corn-Bread Blues* . . . . 30.00 - 40.00
8526 *Farm Hand Blues* . . . . 30.00 - 40.00
8542 *Sabine River Blues* . . . . 30.00 - 40.00
8563 *Bell Cow Blues* . . . . 30.00 - 40.00
8578 *Death Bed Blues* . . . . 30.00 - 40.00
8591 *Deep Blue Sea Blues* . . . . 30.00 - 40.00
8603 *West Texas Blues* . . . . 30.00 - 40.00
8624 *Sittin' On A Log* . . . . 30.00 - 50.00
8640 *Blue Devil Blues* . . . . 35.00 - 50.00

8658 *'Frisco Train Blues* . . . . 80.00 - 120.00
8673 *Tell Me Woman Blues* . . . . 80.00 - 120.00
8688 *St. Louis Fair Blues* . . . . 30.00 - 90.00
8705 *Gold Tooth Blues* . . . . 35.00 - 50.00
8731 *Awful Moaning Blues* . . . . 35.00 - 50.00
8745 *Double Crossing Blues* . . . . 35.00 - 50.00
8751 *Peaceful Blues* . . . . 35.00 - 50.00
8764 *Broken Yo Yo* . . . . 35.00 - 50.00
8771 *Texas Special* . . . . 35.00 - 50.00
8785 *Thirty Day Blues* . . . . 35.00 - 50.00
8801 *Yellow Girl Blues* . . . . 35.00 - 50.00
8813 *She's So Far* . . . . 50.00 - 85.00
8823 *Last Stage Blues* . . . . *50.00 - 80.00*
8835 *Days Is Lonesome* . . . . 50.00 - 80.00
8890 *Seen Better Days* . . . . 50.00 - 80.00
Vocalion 02743 *Blues In My Mind* . . . . 30.00 - 50.00
02764 *Prairie Dog Hole Blues* . . . . 30.00 - 50.00
02772 *Worried Blues* . . . . 30.00 - 50.00
02856 *Justice Blues* . . . . 30.00 - 50.00
02876 *Lonesome Valley Blues* . . . . 30.00 - 50.00
02894 *Katy Crossing Blues* . . . . 30.00 - 50.00
02912 *Deceitful Blues* . . . . 30.00 - 50.00

MAY ALIX (& HER HARMOGRAPH JAZZ BOYS):
Famous 3193 *Come On Home* . . . . 25.00 - 40.00
3237 *Loveless Love* . . . . 40.00 - 60.00
Harmograph 791 *Aggravatin' Papa* . . . . 25.00 - 40.00
Harmograph 801 *Chirping The Blues* . . . . 15.00 - 25.00
816 *You Shall Reap Just What You Sow* . . . . . . 15.00 - 25.00
873 *Experience Blues* . . . . 100.00 - 150.00
Paramount 20243 *Loveless Love* . . . . 25.00 - 40.00
Puritan 11199 *Come On Home* . . . . 25.00 - 40.00
11243 *Loveless Love* . . . . 25.00 - 40.00

GEORGE ALLISON & WILLIE WHITE:
Paramount 12960 *How I Feel My Love* . . . . 75.00 - 100.00

TESSIE AMES:
Silvertone 3565 *Rider Blues* . . . . 35.00 - 50.00
3576 *High Yellow Blues* . . . . 100.00 - 150.00
3577 *Ada Jane's Blues* . . . . 35.00 - 50.00

AMOS:
Bluebird 5780 *Mean Mistreatin' Woman* . . . . 15.00 - 20.00
5862 *Muddy Water Blues* . . . . 15.00 - 20.00

IRA AMOS:
Modern 817 *Blue And Disgusted* . . . . 8.00 - 15.00
Octave 23-20 *I'm Lonesome* . . . . 8.00 - 15.00

BLIND JOE AMOS:
Vocalion 1116 *C & O Blues* . . . . 150.00 - 200.00

CURTIS AMY:
Gold Star 618 *Sleepin Blues* . . . . 20.00 - 30.00

"TALKING" BILLY ANDERSON:
Columbia 14216-D *Adam And Eve* . . . . 20.00 - 30.00
14274-D *Cow Cow Blues* . . . . 35.00 - 50.00

JELLY ROLL ANDERSON:
Gennett 6135 *Free Woman Blues* . . . . 100.00 - 150.00
6181 *Good Time Blues* . . . . 200.00 - 300.00
6226 *Salt Tear Blues* . . . . 250.00 - 400.00
Herwin 92014 *Salt Tear Blues* . . . . 125.00 - 175.00
92020 *Free Women Blues* . . . . 125.00 - 175.00

JIMMIE ANDERSON:
Broadway 5111 *Ko Ko Mo Blues* . . . . 250.00 - 400.00

LOUISE ANDERSON:
Gennett 6242 *Papa, You're Too Slow* . . . . 75.00 - 100.00

MAYBELLE ANDERSON:
Supertone 9429 *Moanful Wailin' Blues* . . . . 150.00 - 200.00

MISSOURI ANDERSON:

Vocalion 1041 *Somebody Else's Blues* . . . . 75.00 - 125.00

PINK ANDERSON & SIMMIE DOOLEY:
Columbia 14336-D *Gonna Tip Out Tonight* . . . . . 75.00 - 100.00
   14400-D *C.C. & O. Blues* . . . . 75.00 - 100.00

ED ANDREWS:
Okeh 8137 *Barrel House Blues* . . . . 75.00 - 100.00

MOSE ANDREWS:
Decca 7338 *Ten Pound Hammer* . . . . 15.00 - 25.00

ANDY BOY:
Bluebird 6858 *House Raid Blues* . . . . 20.00 - 30.00
   6893 *Jive Blues* . . . . 20.00 - 30.00
   6940 *Yellow Gal Blues* . . . . 20.00 - 30.00
   7075 *Evil Blues* . . . . 20.00 - 30.00

ROOSEVELT ANTRIM:
Bluebird 7149 *Complaint To Make* . . . . 30.00 - 50.00
   7475 *Station Boy Blues* . . . . 30.00 - 50.00

ARCHIBALD:
Colony 105 *Crescent City Bounce* . . . . 7.00 - 10.00
Imperial 5068, 5082, 5089, 5101, 5212 . . . . 5.00 - 10.00

ARKANSAS SHORTY:
Bluebird 6545 *Greyhound Bus* . . . . 20.00 - 30.00
   6571 *Double Crossing Buddy* . . . . 20.00 - 30.00
   6983 *Blue as a Fool Can Be* . . . . 20.00 - 30.00

MAY ARMSTRONG:
Brunswick 7010 *Joe Boy Blues* . . . . 75.00 - 100.00
Vocalion 1129 *Joe Boy Blues* . . . . 75.00 - 100.00

RICHARD ARMSTRONG:
Randy's 104 *Gene Nobel's Boggie* . . . . — - —

SHELLEY ARMSTRONG:
Champion 50008 *How Long How Long Blues* . . . 15.00 - 20.00
   50024 *Chain Gang Bound* . . . . 20.00 - 30.00
   50028 *B & O Blues* . . . . 15.00 - 20.00
   50029 *D.B.A. Blues* . . . . 15.00 - 20.00
Decca 7127 *My Old Pal Blues* . . . . 12.00 - 16.00
   7350 *B & O Blues* . . . . 8.00 - 12.00

KOKOMO ARNOLD:
Decca 7026 *Milk Cow Blues* . . . . 20.00 - 30.00
   7044 *Back To The Woods* . . . . 25.00 - 40.00
   7050 *Sissy Man Blues* . . . . 25.00 - 40.00
   7059 *Milk Cow Blues-No. 2* . . . . 25.00 - 40.00
   7069 *Chain Gang Blues* . . . . 25.00 - 40.00
   7070 *How Long, How Long Blues* . . . . 25.00 - 40.00
   7083 *Feels So Good* . . . . 25.00 - 40.00
   7092 *Slop Jar Blues* . . . . 25.00 - 40.00
   7103 *Tonic Head Blues* . . . . 25.00 - 40.00
   7116 *Milk Cow Blues-No. 3* . . . . 25.00 - 40.00
   7133 *Monday Morning Blues* . . . . 25.00 - 40.00
   7139 *Southern Railroad Blues* . . . . 25.00 - 40.00
   7147 *Policy Wheel Blues* . . . . 25.00 - 40.00
   7156 *Back Door Blues* . . . . 25.00 - 40.00
   7163 *Milk Cow Blues-No. 4* . . . . 25.00 - 40.00
   7165 *Desert Blues* . . . . 25.00 - 40.00
   7172 *Sundown Blues* . . . . 25.00 - 40.00
   7181 *Stop Look and Listen* . . . . 25.00 - 40.00
   7198 *Model 'T' Woman Blues* . . . . 25.00 - 40.00
   7212 *Bull Headed Woman Blues* . . . . 25.00 - 40.00
   7242 *Coffin Blues* . . . . 25.00 - 40.00
   7261 *Lonesome Road Blues* . . . . 25.00 - 40.00
   7267 *Salty Dog* . . . . 25.00 - 40.00
   7275 *Fool Man Blues* . . . . 25.00 - 40.00
   7285 *Laugh And Grin Blues* . . . . 25.00 - 40.00
   7306 *Long And Tall* . . . . 25.00 - 40.00
   7319 *Black Mattie* . . . . 25.00 - 40.00
   7347 *Red Beans And Rice* . . . . 25.00 - 40.00
   7361 *Big Ship Blues* . . . . 25.00 - 40.00
   7390 *Back On The Job* . . . . 25.00 - 40.00
   7417 *Head Cuttin' Blues* . . . . 25.00 - 40.00
   7431 *Neck Bone Blues* . . . . 25.00 - 40.00
   7449 *Rocky Road Blues* . . . . 25.00 - 40.00
   7464 *Kid Man Blues* . . . . 25.00 - 40.00
   7485 *Something's Hot* . . . . 25.00 - 40.00
   7510 *Midnight Blues* . . . . 25.00 - 40.00
   7540 *Bad Luck Blues* . . . . 25.00 - 40.00
Decca 48000 *Milk Cow Blues* . . . . 4.00 - 7.00

MILDRED AUSTIN:
Champion 15530 *Sing That Song With Feeling* . . . 50.00 - 80.00

BABY BONNIE:
Buddy 8021 *I Got Your Water On* . . . . 150.00 - 200.00
   8023 *Home, Sweet Home Blues* . . . . 100.00 - 150.00
Gennett 3041 *Longing Blues* . . . . 40.00 - 60.00
   5593 *I Got Your Water On* . . . . 40.00 - 60.00
   5616 *Backbiting Moan* . . . . 40.00 - 60.00
   5644 *Longing Blues* . . . . 50.00 - 75.00
Silvertone 4031 *Backbiting Moan* . . . . 50.00 - 75.00
   4034 *I Got You Water On* . . . . 30.00 - 50.00

BABY BOY:
Sampson 633 *Taxi Driver* . . . . 30.00 - 50.00

BABY DOO:
Decca 7763 *The Death Of Walter Barnes* . . . . . . 15.00 - 20.00
   7773 *I'm Gonna Walk Your Log* . . . . 15.00 - 20.00

(VOCALIST) BABY FACE (LEROY) (TRIO):
Chess 1447 *Take A Little Walk With Me* . . . . 10.00 - 20.00
J.O.B. 100 *Take A Little Walk With Me* . . . . 50.00 - 75.00
Parkway 104 *Boll Weevil* . . . . 80.00 - 100.00
   501 *Rollin' And Tumblin'* . . . . 80.00 - 100.00
Savoy 1122 *Red Headed Woman* . . . . 10.00 - 20.00

THE BACK PORCH BOYS:
Apollo 392 *Big Hip Mama* . . . . 10.00 - 15.00
   406 *Sweet Woman Blues* . . . . 10.00 - 15.00

DE FORD BAILEY:
Bluebird 5147 *Ice Water Blues* . . . . 8.00 - 12.00
Brunswick 146 *Pan-American Blues* . . . . 15.00 - 20.00
   147 *Muscle Shoals Blues* . . . . 15.00 - 20.00
   148 *Alcoholic Blues* . . . . 15.00 - 20.00
   149 *Fox Chase* . . . . 15.00 - 20.00
   434 *Up Country Blues* . . . . 10.00 - 15.00
Victor 23336 *John Henry* . . . . 150.00 - 200.00
   23831 *John Henry* . . . . 50.00 - 75.00
V38014 *Ice Water Blues* . . . . 30.00 - 50.00

KID BAILEY:
Brunswick 7114 *Rowdy Blues* . . . . 150.00 - 300.00

RED MIKE BAILEY:
Paramount 13077 *Neck Bone Blues* . . . . 150.00 - 200.00

HOUSTON BAINES:
Blues & Rhythm 7001 *Going Home* . . . . 10.00 - 15.00

BLIND BOBBY BAKER:
Pathe-Actuelle 7533 *Macon Georgia Cut-Out* . . . 75.00 - 100.00
Perfect 133 *Macon Georgia Cut-Out* . . . . 75.00 - 100.00

C.B. BAKER:
Sittin' In With 625 *Skin To Skin* . . . . 20.00 - 30.00

DOROTHY BAKER:
Decca 7080 *Steady Grinding Blues* . . . . 30.00 - 50.00

KATHERINE BAKER:
Gennett 6125 *I Helped You, Sick Man* . . . . 150.00 - 200.00
   6157 *Chicago Fire Blues* . . . . 150.00 - 200.00
   6194 *Wild Woman Blues* . . . . 150.00 - 200.00
   6228 *Money Woman Blues* . . . . 150.00 - 200.00
   6321 *Mistreated Blues* . . . . 150.00 - 200.00
Herwin 92017 *My Man Left Me Blues* . . . . 150.00 - 250.00
   92022 *Chicago Fire Blues* . . . . 150.00 - 250.00
   92037 *Daddy Sunshine Blues* . . . . 150.00 - 250.00
   92038 *Wild Woman Blues* . . . . 150.00 - 250.00
   92039 *Mistreated Blues* . . . . 150.00 - 250.00

VIOLA BAKER:
Okeh 8141 *Sweet Man Blues* . . . . 30.00 - 50.00

WILLIE BAKER:
Gennett 6751 *Weak-Minded Blues* . . . . 200.00 - 300.00
   6766 *No No Blues* . . . . 200.00 - 300.00
   6812 *Bad Luck Moan* . . . . 200.00 - 300.00
   6846 *Crooked Woman Blues* . . . . 200.00 - 300.00

BANJO JOE:
Paramount 12571 *Poor Boy, Long Ways From
   Home* . . . . 100.00 - 200.00
   12588 *Jonestown Blues* . . . . 100.00 - 200.00
   12604 *Jazz Gypsy Blues* . . . . 100.00 - 200.00

BARBECUE BOB:

Columbia 14205-D *Barbecue Blues*	20.00	-	30.00
14222-D *Mississippi Heavy Water Blues*	25.00	-	50.00
14246-D *Honey You Don't Know My Mind*	25.00	-	50.00
14257-D *Brown-Skin Gal*	25.00	-	50.00
14268-D *It Won't Be Long Now*	25.00	-	40.00
14280-D *Crooked Woman Blues*	25.00	-	40.00
14299-D *Thinkin' Funny Blues*	25.00	-	40.00
14316-D *Goin' Up The Country*	30.00	-	50.00
14331-D *Waycross Georgia Blues*	30.00	-	50.00
14350-D *My Mistake Blues*	30.00	-	50.00
14372-D *Blind Pig Blues*	30.00	-	50.00
14383-D *Cold Wave Blues*	30.00	-	50.00
14412-D *Dollar Down Blues*	35.00	-	50.00
14424-D *It's Just Too Bad*	35.00	-	50.00
14436-D *It's a Funny Little Thing*	35.00	-	50.00
14449-D *Good Time Rounder*	35.00	-	50.00
14461-D *Bad Time Blues*	35.00	-	50.00
14479-D *Yo Yo Blues*	35.00	-	50.00
14507-D *Me And My Whiskey*	40.00	-	60.00
14523-D *Yo You Blues No. 2*	40.00	-	60.00
14546-D *Telling It To You*	40.00	-	60.00
14588-D *The Spider And The Fly*	40.00	-	60.00
14573-D *California Blues*	50.00	-	75.00
14581-D *Jambooger Blues*	75.00	-	100.00
14591-D *Atlanta Moan*	75.00	-	100.00
14614-D *It Just Won't Quit*	75.00	-	100.00

JOHN HENRY BARBEE:

Vocalion 04417 *Six Weeks Old Blues*	10.00	-	20.00

BAREFOOT BILL:

Columbia 14481-D *Big Rock Jail*	120.00	-	150.00
14510-D *My Crime Blues*	100.00	-	150.00
14526-D *Squabblin' Blues*	100.00	-	150.00
14561-D *One More Time*	125.00	-	175.00

WILEY BARNER:

Gennett 6261 *My Gal Treats Me Mean*	150.00	-	200.00

FAE BARNES:

Black Swan 12153 *I Just Want A Daddy*	20.00	-	30.00
Paramount 12099 *Good-Bye Blues*	20.00	-	30.00
12136 *I Just Want A Daddy*	20.00	-	30.00

WILLIE BARNES:

Champion 15378 *My Gal Treats Me Mean*	80.00	-	120.00
Silvertone 5121 *My Gal Treats Me Mean*	150.00	-	200.00

MARTHA BARR:

Broadway 5017 *Memphis Earthquake*	50.00	-	75.00

BARRELL HOUSE ANNIE:

Vocalion 03542 *Must Get Mine In Front*	20.00	-	30.00

BARREL HOUSE BUCK:

Decca 7013 *Lamp Post Blues*	25.00	-	40.00
7030 *Mercy Mercy Blues*	25.00	-	40.00

BARRELHOUSE FRANKIE:

Paramount 13019 *Smother Me Blues*	100.00	-	150.00

BARRELHOUSE SAMMY (THE COUNTRY BOY):

Atlantic 891 *Kill It Kid*	15.00	-	25.00

VIOLA BARTLETTE:

Paramount 12322 *Tennessee Blues*	75.00	-	125.00
12345 *Quit Knocking On My Door*	100.00	-	150.00
12351 *Anna Mina Forty And St. Louis Shorty*	100.00	-	150.00
12363 *Out Bound Train Blues*	100.00	-	150.00
12369 *Sunday Morning Blues*	100.00	-	150.00

SLIM BARTON (& EDDIE MAPP) (& JAMES MOORE):

Paramount 13114 *Fourth Avenue Blues*	100.00	-	150.00
QRS 7081 *It's Tight Like That*	100.00	-	150.00
7088 *I'm Hot Like That*	100.00	-	150.00
7089 *Fourth Avenue Blues*	100.00	-	150.00

TIPPY BARTON:

Vocalion 1742 *High Brown Cheater*	75.00	-	100.00

BAT THE HUMMING BIRD:

Varsity 6068 *Humming Blues*	15.00	-	25.00

DEACON L. J. BATES:

Paramount 12585 *He Arose From The Dead*	50.00	-	75.00

WILL BATTS:

Vocalion 02531 *Country Woman*	100.00	-	150.00
02542 *Cadillac Baby*	100.00	-	150.00

A. & J. ANDREW AND JIM BAXTER:

Victor 20962 *K. C. Railroad Blues*	125.00	-	175.00
21475 *The Moore Girl*	150.00	-	200.00
23394 *Done Wrong Blues*	200.00	-	300.00
23404 *Operator Blues*	200.00	-	300.00
V38002 *Georgia Stomp*	150.00	-	200.00
V38603 *It Tickles Me*	150.00	-	200.00

HELEN BAXTER:

Banner 1920 *I Wants A Real Man*	20.00	-	30.00
1958 *Scrubbin' Blues*	20.00	-	30.00
Domino 3892 *I Wants A Real Man*	20.00	-	30.00
Domino 3929 *Scrubbin' Blues*	20.00	-	30.00
Regal 8238 *I Wants A Real Man*	20.00	-	30.00
Regal 8283 *Scrubbin' Blues*	20.00	-	30.00

BEALE STREET ROUNDERS:

Vocalion 1555 *I'm Sittin' On Top Of The World*	100.00	-	150.00

BEALE STREET SHEIKS:

Paramount 12518 *It's A Good Thing*	150.00	-	200.00
12531 *Half Cup Of Tea*	150.00	-	200.00
12552 *Blues In 'D'*	150.00	-	200.00
12576 *Beale Town Bound*	150.00	-	200.00
12591 *Jazzin' The Blues*	150.00	-	200.00
12758 *Rockin' On The Hill Blues*	150.00	-	200.00
12774 *Hunting Blues*	150.00	-	200.00
12894 *Fillin' In Blues*	150.00	-	200.00

LOTTIE BEAMAN:

Brunswick 7147 *Going Away Blues*	75.00	-	100.00
Paramount 12201 *Honey Blues*	25.00	-	35.00
12235 *Regular Man Blues*	40.00	-	60.00
12254 *Sugar Daddy Blues*	40.00	-	60.00

HELEN BEASLEY:

Brunswick 7077 *Tia Juana Blues*	35.00	-	50.00

WALTER BEASLEY:

Okeh 8540 *Georgia Skin*	15.00	-	20.00
8564 *Sore Feet Blues*	15.00	-	20.00

CHARLES/ELDER CHARLIE BECK:

Bluebird 8244 *Changes*	10.00	-	15.00
8271 *You Can't Hurry God*	10.00	-	15.00
8317 *Dry Bones*	10.00	-	15.00
8337 *Talk On Talkers*	10.00	-	15.00
Decca 7320 *If I Have To Run*	20.00	-	30.00
Decca 7344 *I'm A Stranger*	15.00	-	20.00
7372 *Love, Oh Love Divine*	15.00	-	20.00
7418 *That's The Way I Do*	15.00	-	20.00
Okeh 8907 *When The World's On Fire*	50.00	-	75.00

JOHNNY BECK (THE BLIND BOY):

Sittin' In With 531 *Locked In Jail Blues*	15.00	-	20.00

SON BECKY:

Vocalion 03942 *Sunrise Blues*	20.00	-	30.00
03967 *Sweet Woman Blues*	20.00	-	30.00
04081 *Cryin' Shame Blues*	20.00	-	30.00

WILLIE BEE:

Vocalion 03907 *Ramblin' Mind Blues*	10.00	-	15.00

BROTHER BELL:

Blues & Rhythm 7002 *If You Feel Froggish*	10.00	-	15.00

ED BELL:

Columbia 14595-D *She's A Fool Gal*	75.00	-	125.00
Paramount 12524 *Ham Bone Blues*	100.00	-	150.00
12546 *Mean Conductor Blues*	100.00	-	150.00

BABY BENBOW:

Okeh 8098 *Down Home Gal*	20.00	-	30.00

ELOISE BENNETT:

Black Patti 8006 *Sting Me, Mr. Strange Man*	150.00	-	200.00
Gennett 6147 *I Can't Be Satisfied With One*	100.00	-	150.00
Paramount 12412 *Effervescent Daddy*	30.00	-	50.00

WILL BENNETT:

Vocalion 1464 *Railroad Bill*	100.00	-	150.00

GLADYS BENTLEY:

Okeh 8610 *Ground Hog Blues*	15.00	-	20.00

8612 *Moanful Wailin' Blues* .... 15.00 - 20.00
8634 *Wild Geese Blues* .... 20.00 - 30.00
8707 *Big Gorilla Man* .... 20.00 - 30.00

GLORY BERNARD:
Grey Gull 7035 *South Bound Blues* .... 15.00 - 20.00
7036 *Cockroach Blues* .... 15.00 - 20.00

BESSEMER MELODY BOYS;
Victor 23252, 38606 .... 25.00 - 50.00

BIDDLEVILLE QUINTETTE;
QRS 7070 *Wasn't That a Mighty Day?* .... 35.00 - 50.00
7071 *Holy Is Thy Name* .... 35.00 - 50.00
7072 *Got The Heaven In My View* .... 35.00 - 50.00
7073 *Didn't It Rain?* .... 35.00 - 50.00
7075 *Jesus Is The Rock* .... 35.00 - 50.00
7076 *The Lord Giveth* .... 35.00 - 50.00

BIG BILL (& HIS JUG BUSTERS/MEMPHIS FIVE/ORCHESTRA) BIG BILL & THOMPS:
Titles, issued contemporaneously on Banner, Melotone, Oriole, Perfect, Romeo: *Ash Hauler; Barrel House When It Rains; Big Bill Blues; Big Bill's Milk Cow No.2; Black Mare Blues; Black Widow Spider; Border Blues; Bricks In My Pillow; Bull Cow Blues No.3; C and A Blues; C.C. Rider; Cherry Hill; Come Home Early; Detroit Special; Dirty No-Gooder; Dying Day Blues; Evil Hearted Me; Falling Rain; Get Away; Good Boy; Hard Headed Woman; Hattie Blues; Hobo Blues; Horny Frog; I'm A Southern Man; It's Too Late Now; I Wanta See My Baby Cry; I Want My Hands On It; I Want You By My Side; Let Her Go- She Don't Know; Let My Be Your Winder; Let's Reel and Rock; Little Bug; Louise, Louise, Blues; Low Down Woman Blues; Low Land Blues; Made A Date With An Angel; Married Life's A Pain; Match Box Blues; Mean Old World; My Big Money; My Gal Is Gone' My Old Lizzie; My Woman Mistreated Me; Of Babe; Play Your Hand; Pneumonia Blues; Prowlin' Groung Hog; Rising Sun Shine On; Serve It To me Right; Seven-Eleven; Somebody's Got To Go; Something Good; Southern Flood Blues; Tell We What You Been Doing; Terrible Flood Blues: These Ants Keep Biting Me; W. P. A. Blues; You Do Me Any Old Way; You Know I Gotta Reason; You know I Need Lovin'; You May Need My Help Someday* 10.00 - 20.00
Titles issued contemporaneously on Banner, Melotone, Oriole, Perfect Romeo:*Bull Cow Blues; How You Want It Done?, Long Tall Mama; M and O Blues; Mistreatin' Mama Blues; Rukus Juice Blues; Shelby County Blues; Too-Too Train Blues; Worrying You Off My Mind* .... 15.00 - 25.00
Bluebird 5476 *Bull Cow Blues* .... 15.00 - 20.00
5535 *Friendless Blues* .... 15.00 - 20.00
5571 *At The Break Of Day* .... 15.00 - 20.00
5674 *Serve It To Me Right* .... 15.00 - 20.00
5706 *Hungry Man Blues* .... 15.00 - 20.00
5998 *The Southern Blues* .... 15.00 - 20.00
6060 *Mountain Blues* .... 10.00 - 15.00
6111 *I'm Just A Bum* .... 10.00 - 15.00
6230 *Down The Line Blues* .... 10.00 - 15.00
Columbia 30002, 30009, 30016, 30135 ... 3.00 - 7.00
Conqueror .... 4.00 - 8.00
Paramount 12656 *House Rent Stomp* .....200.00 - 300.00
12707 *Down In The Basement Blues* ....150.00 - 200.00
Vocalion .... 4.00 - 8.00

BIG BLOKE:
Varsity 6051 *Everybody Likes That Thing* ... 10.00 - 15.00

BIG CHIEF (& HIS) TRIO:
Sittin' In With 523 *Big Chief's Blues* .... 10.00 - 15.00
530 *Poor Man's Blues* .... 10.00 - 15.00

ESTER BIGEOU:
Okeh 8025 *Stingaree Blues* .... 8.00 - 12.00
8026 *The Memphis Blues* .... 8.00 - 12.00
8029 *Nervous Blues* .... 8.00 - 12.00
8053 *Aggravatin' Papa* .... 7.00 - 10.00
8054 *Four O'Clock Blues* .... 7.00 - 10.00
8056 *The Gulf Coast Blues* .... 7.00 - 10.00
8057 *Beale Street Mama* .... 7.00 - 10.00
8058 *Beale Street Blues* .... 7.00 - 10.00
8065 *The Hesitating Blues* .... 7.00 - 10.00
Okeh 8118 *West Indies Blues* .... 25.00 - 40.00
8125 *Panama Limited Blues* .... 15.00 - 20.00

BIG JOE (AND HIS RHYTHM/WASHBOARD BAND):
Bluebird 7022 *Brother James* .... 25.00 - 35.00
7065 *Rootin' Ground Hog* .... 25.00 - 35.00
8814 *We Can't Agree* .... 7.00 - 10.00
8864 *What Will I Do?* .... 7.00 - 10.00
8956 *Got To Go Blues* .... 7.00 - 10.00
8986 *It Ain't No Lie* .... 7.00 - 10.00
9013 *Sleeping By Myself* .... 5.00 - 8.00
Okeh 06141 *I Love You Baby* .... 7.00 - 10.00
06175 *When You Said Goodbye* .... 7.00 - 10.00

BIG JOHN:
Acorn 304 *Too Late Blues* .... — - —

BIG MACEO:
Bluebird 8772, 8798, 8827, 8939, 8973, 9012 .... 5.00 - 8.00
34-0703, 34-0735, 34-0743 .... 3.00 - 6.00
Fortune 137, 805 .... 7.00 - 10.00
Specialty 320, 346 .... 5.00 - 10.00
RCA Victor 20-1870, 20-2028, 20-2173, 20-2353, 20-2505, 20-2687 .... 3.00 - 6.00

BIG OSCAR:
Decca 7067 *Mistreatment Blues* .... 20.00 - 30.00

BIG MEMPHIS MA RAINEY:
Sun 184 Baby, No, No .... 50.00 - 80.00

BIG RICHARD:
Varsity 6055 *Nobody's Business If I Do* .... 10.00 - 15.00

BIG SISTER:
Varsity 6063 *Pig Meat Mama* .... 10.00 - 15.00

BIG THREE TRIO:
Columbia 30019, 30055, 30103, 30108, 30110,30125 . 3.00 - 6.00
Okeh .... 3.00 - 6.00

BIG WILLIE:
Apollo 450 *Bogey Man* .... 8.00 - 12.00

D.H. BILBRO:
Victor 23831 *Chester Blues* .... 50.00 - 75.00

BILL AND SLIM:
Champion 16015 *Papa's Gettin' Hot* ....100.00 - 150.00

BILLY & JESSE:
Brunswick 7099 *Put Your Mind On It* .... 50.00 - 75.00

BILLY BIRD:
Columbia 14381-D *Mill Man Blues* .... 50.00 - 80.00
14418-D *Alabama Blues* .... 50.00 - 80.00

BIRMINGHAM QUARTET:
Columbia 14154-D, 14190-D, 14224-D, 14263-D, 14311-D, 14567-D .... 10.00 - 20.00

BIRMINGHAM SAM:
Savoy 5558 *Landing Blues* .... 7.00 - 10.00

BLACK ACE:
Decca 7281 *Trifling Woman* .... 20.00 - 30.00
7340 *Whiskey And Woman* .... 20.00 - 30.00
7387 *Christmas Time Blues* .... 20.00 - 30.00

BLACK BOY SHINE:
Vocalion 03417 *Sugarland Blues* .... 20.00 - 30.00
03454 *Crazy Woman Blues* .... 20.00 - 30.00
03484 *Back Home Blues* .... 20.00 - 30.00
03551 *Wrong Doing Woman Blues* .... 20.00 - 30.00
03613 *Grey With Worry Blues* .... 20.00 - 30.00
03624 *Bed And Breakfast Blues* .... 20.00 - 30.00

03687 *Business Woman Blues*	20.00 -	30.00
03757 *Coal Woman Blues*	20.00 -	30.00
04003 *Hobo Blues*	20.00 -	30.00
(Note: First four titles issued contemporaneously on Banner, Melotone, Oriole, Perfect, Romeo:	20.00 -	30.00

BLACK DIAMOND:

Jaxyson 50 *Lonesome Blues*	10.00 -	20.00

BLACK IVORY KING:

Decca 7307 *The Flying Crow*	20.00 -	30.00
7355 *Match Box Blues*	20.00 -	30.00

BLACK SPIDER DUMPLIN':

Bluebird 6972 *John D. Blues*	15.00 -	20.00
6995 *Sold It To The Devil*	15.00 -	20.00
7001 *Death Of The Gambler*	15.00 -	20.00

FRANKIE BLACK:

Champion 50000 *Wayback Blues*	25.00 -	50.00
50036 *Bad Liquor Blues*	25.00 -	50.00
50049 *Alley Sally Blues*	25.00 -	50.00

LEWIS BLACK:

Columbia 14291-D *Gravel Camp Blues*	35.00 -	50.00
14429-D *Rock Island Blues*	35.00 -	50.00

MAMIE BLACKBURN:

Herwin 92015 *Bird Nest Blues*	100.00 -	150.00

FRANCIS/SCRAPPER BLACKWELL:

Bluebird 5914 *A Blues*	100.00 -	150.00
Champion 15973 *Springtime Blues*	150.00 -	200.00
Champion 16361 *Back Door Blues*	150.00 -	200.00
16370 *Rambling Blues*	150.00 -	200.00
16452 *Down South Blues*	150.00 -	200.00
Gennett 7158 *Springtime Blues*	200.00 -	300.00
Vocalion 1192 *Kokomo Blues*	150.00 -	200.00
1213 *Trouble Blues*	150.00 -	200.00
1276 *Non-Skid Tread*	150.00 -	200.00
1417 *Mr. Scrapper's Blues*	150.00 -	200.00
02752 *Morning Mail Blues*	100.00 -	150.00

WILLIE "61" BLACKWELL:

Bluebird 8810, 8845, 8876, 8921	10.00 -	15.00

SUNNY BLAIR:

Meteor 5006 *Please Send My Baby Back*	10.00 -	20.00*
RPM 354 *Five Foot Three Blues*	15.00 -	20.00*

BLIND ARTHUR:

Paramount 12892 *Blind Arthur's Breakdown*	150.00 -	200.00

BLIND BLAKE:

Paramount 12387 *Early Morning Blues*	75.00 -	125.00
12413 *Skeedle Loo Doo Blues*	75.00 -	125.00
12431 *Too Tight*	75.00 -	125.00
12442 *Tampa Bound*	75.00 -	125.00
12464 *Buck-Town Blues*	75.00 -	125.00
12479 *One Time Blues*	75.00 -	125.00
12497 *Bad Feeling Blues*	75.00 -	125.00
12565 *Southern Rag*	75.00 -	125.00
12583 *Hard Road Blues*	75.00 -	125.00
12597 *Wabash Rag*	75.00 -	125.00
12606 *Brownskin Mama Blues*	75.00 -	125.00
12634 *C.C. Pill Blues*	100.00 -	150.00
12643 *Tootie Blues*	100.00 -	150.00
12657 *Detroit Bound Blues*	100.00 -	150.00
12673 *Hot Potatoes*	150.00 -	200.00
12681 *South Bound Rag*	150.00 -	200.00
12695 *Low Down Loving Gal*	100.00 -	150.00
12710 *Back Door Slam Blues*	100.00 -	150.00
12723 *No Dough Blues*	100.00 -	150.00
12737 *Search Warrant Blues*	100.00 -	150.00
12754 *Notoriety Woman Blues*	100.00 -	150.00
12767 *Ramblin' Mama Blues*	100.00 -	150.00
12794 *Hookworm Blues*	100.00 -	150.00
12810 *Poker Woman Blues*	100.00 -	150.00
12824 *Georgia Bound*	100.00 -	150.00
12863 *Fightin' The Jug*	150.00 -	200.00
12867 *Third Degree Blues*	100.00 -	150.00
12888 *Police Dog Blues*	100.00 -	150.00
12904 *Ice Man Blues*	100.00 -	150.00

12918 *Cold Love Blues*	100.00 -	150.00
12964 *Keep It Home*	100.00 -	150.00
12994 *Hard Pushing Papa*	100.00 -	150.00
13016 *Ain't Gonna Do That No More*	100.00 -	150.00
13035 *Playing Policy Blues*	100.00 -	150.00
13103 *Rope Stretchin' Blues*	150.00 -	200.00
13115 *Dissatisfied Blues*	150.00 -	200.00
13123 *Night And Day Blues*	150.00 -	200.00
13137 *Depression's Gone From Me Blues*	200.00 -	300.00

BLIND GARY:

Titles, issued contemporaneously on Banner, Melotone, Oriole, Perfect, Romeo: *Cross And Evil Woman Blues; I'm Throwin' Up My Hand*	15.00 -	20.00

BLIND MACK:

Vocalion 03167 *Rootin'Ground Hog Blues*	50.00 -	75.00

BLIND NORRIS:

Decca 7290 *Sundown Blues*	25.00 -	40.00

BLIND PERCY & HIS BLIND BAND:

Paramount 12584 *Coal River Blues*	100.00 -	150.00

BLIND SAMMIE:

Columbia 14484-D *Travelin' Blues*	100.00 -	150.00
14551-D *Razor Ball*	100.00 -	150.00
14632-D *Broke Down Engine Blues*	100.00 -	150.00
14657-D *Atlanta Strut*	100.00 -	150.00

BLIND WILLIE (& PARTNER):

Regal 3260 *How About You*	25.00 -	40.00
Vocalion 02568 *Weary Hearted Blues*	100.00 -	150.00
02577 *Death Cell Blues*	100.00 -	150.00
02595 *Warm It Up To Me*	100.00 -	150.00
02622 *It's A Good Little Thing*	100.00 -	150.00
02623 *Lord Have Mercy If You Please*	100.00 -	150.00
02668 *My Baby's Gone*	100.00 -	150.00

BLUE BELLE:

Okeh 8483 *High Water Blues*	25.00 -	40.00
8538 *Sneakin' Lizard Blues*	25.00 -	40.00
8553 *Dead Sea Blues*	25.00 -	40.00
8588 *Ghost Creepin'Blues*	25.00 -	40.00
8659 *Good Feelin' Blues*	25.00 -	40.00
8704 *Death Valley Moan*	25.00 -	40.00

BLUE BILL:

Bluebird 6795 *More Blues*	15.00 -	25.00

BLUE BOY:

Varsity 6052 *Back-Biter Blues*	10.00 -	15.00
6059 *Electric Chair*	10.00 -	15.00

THE BLUE BOYS:

Okeh 45314 *Memphis Stomp*	75.00 -	100.00

BLUE HARMONY BOYS:

Paramount 12889 *Take It Out Too Deep*	75.00 -	100.00
12901 *Sweet Miss Stella Blues*	75.00 -	100.00
12976 *Ragged But Right*	75.00 -	100.00

THE BLUEJACKS:

Dot 1000 *Late Hour Blues*	7.00 -	10.00

BLUES BIRDHEAD:

Okeh 8824 *Harmonica Blues*	50.00 -	75.00

BLUE SMITTY & HIS STRING MEN:

Chess 1522 *Sad Story*	8.00 -	12.00

THE BLUES KING:

Solo 10-0003 *Me And My Baby*	8.00 -	12.00

THE BLUES MAN:

Specialty 501 *My Baby's Blues*	— -	—

THE BLUES ROCKERS:

Aristocrat 407 *Trouble In My Home*	15.00 -	25.00
413 *Blues Rockers' Bop*	15.00 -	25.00
Chess 1483 *My Mama's Baby Child*	7.00 -	10.00

LOUIS BLUIE AND TED BOGAN:

Bluebird 5490 *I'm Through With You*	125.00 -	200.00
5593 *Ted's Stomp*	125.00 -	200.00

CALVIN BOAZ WITH MARVIN JOHNSON & HIS ORCHESTRA:

G & G 1029 *Saffronia Bee*	8.00 -	12.00

LUCILLE BOGAN:

Brunswick 7051 *New Way Blues*	75.00 -	100.00

7083 *Coffee Grindin' Blues*	75.00 -	100.00
7145 *My Georgia Blues*	75.00 -	100.00
7163 *Dirty Treatin' Blues*	75.00 -	100.00
7186 *Black Angel Blues*	75.00 -	100.00
7193 *Crawlin' Lizard Blues*	75.00 -	100.00
7210 *Alley Boogie*	75.00 -	100.00
Okeh 8071, 8074	15.00 -	20.00
8079 *Pawn Shop Blues*	20.00 -	30.00
Paramount 12459 *Sweet Patunia*	50.00 -	80.00
12504 *Kind Stella Blues*	75.00 -	100.00
12514 *Doggone Wicked Blues*	75.00 -	100.00
12560 *War Time Man Blues*	75.00 -	100.00
12577 *Cravin' Whiskey Blues*	75.00 -	100.00

HOUSTON BOINES:

RPM 364 *Monkey Motion*	10.00 -	15.00*

LELA BOLDEN:

Okeh 8139 *Southern Woman Blues*	30.00 -	50.00

ZU ZU BOLLIN:

Torch 6910 *Headlight Blues*	7.00 -	10.00*
6912 *Stavin' Chain*	10.00 -	15.00*

PILLIE BOLLING (AND BAREFOOT BILL):

Columbia 14544-D *I Don't Like That*	75.00 -	100.00
14654-D *Brown Skin Woman*	75.00 -	100.00

HATTIE BOLTEN:

Vocalion 04470 *Down Home Shake*	10.00 -	15.00

BROTHER SON BONDS; BROWNSVILLE SON BONDS; SON BONDS:

Bluebird 8927 *80 Highway Blues*	15.00 -	20.00
8950 *Come Back Home, Little Girl*	15.00 -	20.00
Champion 50064 *Weary Worried Blues*	30.00 -	40.00
Decca 7022 *All Night Long*	30.00 -	40.00
7024 *In My Father's House*	30.00 -	40.00
7039 *Ain't That News?*	30.00 -	40.00
Decca 7558 *Old Bachelor Blues*	10.00 -	15.00

THE BOOGIE MAN:

Acorn 308 *Do The Boogie*	5.00 -	8.00*

CHARLEY BOOKER:

Blues & Rhythm 7003 *Rabbit Blues*	15.00 -	25.00
Modern 878 *Moonrise Blues*	10.00 -	15.00*

CONNIE MAC/MACK BOOKER:

Freedom 1520 *Come Back Baby*	5.00 -	8.00

JOHN LEE BOOKER:

Chance 1108 *Miss Lorraine*	8.00 -	12.00*
1110 *Graveyard Blues*	8.00 -	12.00*
1122 *609 Boogie*	8.00 -	12.00*
DeLuxe 6004 *Lovin' Guitar Man*	4.00 -	7.00*
6032 *Stuttering Blues*	4.00 -	7.00*
6046 *Real Real Gone*	4.00 -	7.00*
Rockin' 525 *Pouring Down Rain*	5.00 -	8.00*

ALONZO BOONE:

Supertone 9428 *Kansas City Blues*	250.00 -	400.00

CALVIN BOSTICK & HIS TRIO:

Chess 1444 *All Of My Life*	6.00 -	10.00
1451 *Fleetwood Blues*	6.00 -	10.00
1530, 1571	4.00 -	7.00*

EDDIE BOYD (& HIS CHESS MEN): LITTLE EDDIE BOYD (& HIS BOOGIE BAND):

Chess 1523 *Cool Kind Treatment*	5.00 -	8.00
1533, 1541, 1552, 1561	4.00 -	7.00*
J.O.B. 1005 *I'm Pleading*	5.00 -	10.00*
1007 *Five Long Years*	5.00 -	10.00*
RCA Victor	4.00 -	7.00

ERNIE BOYD:

Regal 3305 *I Gotta Find My Baby*	8.00 -	15.00

GEORGIA BOYD:

Bluebird 5573 *I'm Sorry Blues*	50.00 -	75.00

RAYMOND BOYD:

Okeh 8528 *Unkind Mama*	25.00 -	40.00

ROBERT BOYD:

Wasco 201 *East St. Louis Baby*	15.00 -	20.00

CALVIN BOZE:

Aladdin 3055 *Safronia B*	5.00 -	8.00*

3072 *Stinkin; From Drinkin'*	5.00 -	8.00*
3110 *Fish Tail*	5.00 -	8.00*
3122 *Hey Lawdy, Miss Claudie*	5.00 -	8.00*

ISHMAN BRACEY/BRACY (& HIS NEW ORLEANS NEHI BOYS):

Paramount 12941 *Jake Liquor Blues*	200.00 -	400.00
12970 *Suitcase Full Of Blues*	200.00 -	400.00
13038 *Pay Me No Mind*	200.00 -	400.00
Victor 21349 *Saturday Blues*	150.00 -	200.00
21691 *Trouble-Hearted Blues*	150.00 -	200.00
V38560 *The Four Day Blues*	150.00 -	200.00

MISSISSIPPI BRACY:

Okeh 8867 *Cherry Ball*	200.00 -	300.00
8904 *I'll Overcome Someday*	200.00 -	300.00

AUNTIE MARY BRADFORD:

Paramount 12617 *Loafing Blues*	75.00 -	100.00

MARY H. BRADFORD:

Okeh 8102 *Chattanooga Blues*	75.00 -	100.00
8123 *Waco Texas Blues*	75.00 -	100.00

WALTER BRADFORD:

Sun 176 *Dreary Nights*	100.00* -	Up

(The issuance of the above record has not been
verified.)

BIG CHARLEY BRADIX:

Aristocrat 418 *Wee Wee Hours*	80.00 -	120.00
Blue Bonnet 153 *Dollar Diggin' Woman*	35.00 -	50.00
Colonial 108 *Boogie Like You Wanna*	20.00 -	30.00

MARIE BRADLEY:

Paramount 12456 *Down Home Moan*	75.00 -	125.00
12466 *Stormy Hailing Blues*	200.00 -	300.00

TOMMIE BRADLEY (& JAMES COLE):

Champion 16149 *Adam And Eve*	200.00 -	300.00
16308 *When You're Down And Out*	200.00 -	300.00
16339 *Four Day Blues*	200.00 -	300.00
16696 *Window Pane Blues*	200.00 -	300.00
16782 *Where Have You Been So Long?*	200.00 -	300.00
50050 *Adam And Eve*	50.00 -	75.00

VELMA BRADLEY:

Broadway 5075 *Gypsy Glass Blues*	50.00 -	75.00

JEAN BRADY:

Okeh 06254 *My Mellow Man*	7.00 -	10.00

DOBBY BRAGG (AND CHARLIE MCFADDEN):

Paramount 12827 *Fire Detective Blues*	150.00 -	200.00
13004 *We Can Sell That Thing*	150.00 -	200.00
13044 *Little Snow Blues*	150.00 -	200.00
13083 *Don't Look Strange At Me*	150.00 -	200.00
13093 *You Got That Thing*	100.00 -	150.00

FRANK BRASSWELL:

Titles issued comtemporaneously on Banner,
Oriole, Perfect, Romeo: *Mountain Girl Blues;*

Western Blues	15.00 -	20.00

JACKIE BRENSTON:

Chess 1458 *Rocket '88*	7.00 -	10.00*
1469 *My Real Gone Rocket*	5.00 -	10.00*
1472 *Juiced*	5.00 -	10.00*
1496 *Leo The Louse*	5.00 -	10.00*
1532 *Starvation*	5.00 -	10.00*

EVELYN BRICKEY:

Okeh 8256 *Down In The Valley Blues*	35.00 -	50.00

GRACE BRIM:

J.O.B. 117 *Hospitality Blues*	10.00 -	15.00

JOHN BRIM (& HIS COMBO/GARY KINGS/STOMPERS); JOHN BRIM TRIO:

Checker 769 *Rattlesnake*	8.00 -	12.00*
Chess 1588, 1624	5.00 -	8.00*
Fortune 801 *Strange Man*	10.00 -	15.00*
J.O.B. 110 *Trouble In The Morning*	15.00 -	20.00*
Parrot 799 *Gary Stomp*	10.00 -	15.00*
Random 201 *Dark Clouds*	15.00 -	20.00*

MRS. JOHN BRIM:

Randon 202 *Going Down The Line*	7.00 -	12.00

FLORENCE BRISTOL:

Up-To-Date 2019 *How Come You Do Me Like*		
You Do?	150.00 -	300.00
DUSTY BROOKS:		
Sun 182 *Heaven On Fire*	50.00 -	75.00
EMORY BROOKS:		
Champion 15416 *The Worried Man Blues*	150.00 -	200.00
JUNIOR BROOKS:		
RPM 343 *Lone Town Blues*	10.00 -	15.00*
BIG BILL BROOMSLEY:		
Paramount 13084 *Station Blues*	150.00 -	250.00
BIG BILL BROONZY (& HIS FAT FOUR):		
Mercury 8122, 8126, 8139, 8160, 8261, 8271, 8284	5.00 -	8.00
BROTHER BELL; (See BELL):		
BROTHER BLUES & THE BACK ROOM BOYS:		
Abbey 3015 *Day Break*	7.00 -	10.00
BROTHER GEORGE & HIS SANCTIFIED		
SINGERS:		
Conqueror 9361	4.00 -	7.00
Okeh 5671, 5729, 05893, 06019	4.00 -	7.00
Vocalion 05261, 5465	4.00 -	7.00
ADA BROWN:		
Okeh 8101 *Evil Mama Blues*	75.00 -	100.00
8123 *Ill-Natured Blues*	75.00 -	100.00
8694 *Down Home Dance*	15.00 -	20.00
Vocalion 1009 *Panama Limited Blues*	75.00 -	100.00
ALBERTA BROWN:		
Columbia 14321-D *Lonely Blues*	75.00 -	100.00
BESSIE BROWN:		
Banner 1833 *What's The Matter Now?*	10.00 -	15.00
Banner 1859 *Nobody But My Baby Is Getting My*		
Love	10.00 -	15.00
Brunswick 4346 *The Blues Singer From Alabam'*	15.00 -	25.00
4409 *He Just Don't Appeal To Me*	15.00 -	25.00
Domino 3781 *How Could I Be Blue?*	10.00 -	15.00
3829 *Nobody But My Baby Is Getting My Love*	10.00 -	15.00
Regal 8143 *What's The Matter Now?*	10.00 -	15.00
8171 *St. Louis Blues*	10.00 -	15.00
Vocalion 1182 *Arkansas Blues*	35.00 -	50.00
15688 *The Man I Love*	35.00 -	50.00
BILL BROWN:		
Varsity 6064 *Goin' Away And Leavin' My Baby*	10.00 -	15.00
CHOCOLATE BROWN:		
Paramount 12944 *Itching Heel*	100.00 -	150.00
12798 *Cherry Hill Blues*	100.00 -	150.00
DANIEL BROWN:		
Paramount 12663 *Now Is The Needy Time*	125.00 -	175.00
DUDLEY BROWN:		
Supertone 9524 *Western Traveler Blues*	125.00 -	175.00
ELIZA BROWN:		
Columbia 14466-D *Get On Out Of Here*	25.00 -	40.00
14471-D *Peddlin' Man*	25.00 -	40.00
14478-D *Take A Little Bit*	25.00 -	40.00
FLOSSIE (AND DUKE) BROWN:		
Champion 15814 *Shake It Daddy*	40.00 -	60.00
15858 *Pig Meat Mama*	40.00 -	60.00
FREDDIE BROWN:		
Paramount 12910 *Whip It To A Jelly*	80.00 -	120.00
GABRIEL BROWN:		
Beacon 5021	4.00 -	8.00
Joe Davis 5003, 5004, 5006, 5008, 5015, 5016,		
5017, 5020, 5021, 5025, 5026, 5027, 5028	4.00 -	8.00
Gennett 5003, 5004	4.00 -	8.00
GATEMOUTH BROWN:		
Aladdin 198, 199	4.00 -	7.00
Peacock 1500, 1504, 1505, 1508, 1561, 1568	4.00 -	7.00
Peacock (higher numbers)	3.00 -	5.00*
"HI" HENRY BROWN:		
Vocalion 1692 *Skin Man Blues*	200.00 -	300.00
1715 *Hospital Blues*	200.00 -	300.00
1728 *Titanic Blues*	200.00 -	300.00
ELDER J.C. BROWN:		
Herwin 93004 *Where Shall I Be?*	150.00 -	200.00

JAMES "WIDEMOUTH" BROWN-HIS		
GUITAR & ORCHESTRA:		
Jax 306 *Boogie Woogie Night Hawk*	8.00 -	12.00*
JOE BROWN:		
Okeh 8491 *Cotton Patch Blues*	30.00 -	50.00
TEXAS JOHNNY BROWN:		
Atlantic 876 *There Go The Blues*	10.00 -	15.00
JUDSON BROWN:		
Brunswick 7220 *You Don't Know My Mind Blues*	100.00 -	150.00
KITTY BROWN:		
Banner 1436 *Family Skeleton Blues*	10.00 -	15.00
1437 *I Wanna Jazz Some More*	10.00 -	15.00
1452 *Keep On Going*	10.00 -	15.00
Paramount 12223 *Keep On Going*	25.00 -	40.00
Regal 9734 *One Of These Days*	10.00 -	15.00
LEE BROWN:		
Chicago 104 *Bobby Town Boogie*	10.00 -	15.00
Decca 7386 *Pitchin' Boogie*	15.00 -	20.00
7504 *Carpenter Man Blues*	15.00 -	20.00
Decca 7575, 7587	5.00 -	8.00
Decca 7615 *Forsaken Blues*	7.00 -	10.00
7626 *Low Down Feelin'*	7.00 -	10.00
7654 *Lock And Key Blues*	10.00 -	15.00
7686 *My Driving Wheel*	10.00 -	15.00
Decca 7697, 7710, 7726, 7744, 7775, 7790	5.00 -	8.00
King 4157 *New Little Girl*	7.00 -	10.00
Queen 4157 *Brownie's Boogie*	7.00 -	10.00
LIL BROWN:		
Black Patti 8007 *Moanful Mama*	150.00 -	200.00
8008 *Three Card Monte Blues*	150.00 -	200.00
LOTTIE BROWN:		
Supertone 9286 *Wayward Girl Blues*	150.00 -	200.00
9289 *Don't Speak To Me*	150.00 -	200.00
9367 *Goin' Away Blues*	150.00 -	200.00
9429 *Blue World Blues*	150.00 -	250.00
LUCILLE BROWN:		
Superior 2552 *Pay With Money*	150.00 -	250.00
2633 *Can't Get Enough*	150.00 -	250.00
ORA BROWN:		
Paramount 12481 *Jinx Blues*	75.00 -	100.00
12500 *Jailhouse Moan*	75.00 -	100.00
RICHARD "RABBIT" BROWN:		
Victor 20578 *James Alley Blues*	100.00 -	150.00
21475 *Never Let the Same Bee Sting You*		
Twice	150.00 -	200.00
35840 *(12-inch) Sinking Of The Titanic*	100.00 -	150.00
ROY BROWN:		
De Luxe 1098, 1128, 1166, 3154, 3189, 3198, 3212,		
3226, 3300, 3301, 3302, 3304, 3308, 3312,		
3319	3.00 -	6.00
Gold Star 636 *Deep Sea Diver*	7.00 -	10.00
King	3.00 -	5.00*
Miltone 3198	3.00 -	6.00
SAMMY BROWN:		
Gennett 6337 *Barrel House Blues*	200.00 -	300.00
SKEET BROWN:		
Vocalion 1205 *Skeet Skat Blues*	75.00 -	100.00
WILLIE BROWN:		
Campion 50023 *M And O Blues*	100.00 -	150.00
Paramount 13090 *M And O Blues*	250.00 -	500.00
13099 *Kicking In My Sleep Blues*	250.00 -	500.00
YODELING KID BROWN:		
Vocalion 1205 *Policy Blues*	75.00 -	100.00
ALTA BROWNE:		
Gennett 3308 *Couldn't Hear Nobody Pray*	20.00 -	30.00
3318 *Nobody Knows Da Trouble I See*	20.00 -	30.00
BRYANT'S JUBLIEE QUARTET/QUINTETTE:		
Gennett 6608 *Who Stole The Lock Off The Hen*		
House Door?	50.00 -	75.00
QRS 7018 *When The World's On Fire*	50.00 -	75.00
7020 *Do You Call That Religion?*	50.00 -	75.00
GLADYS BRYANT:		

Harmograph 818 *Beale Street Mama*	30.00 -	50.00
2539 *Triflin'Blues*	20.00 -	30.00
2540 *Laughin' Cryin'Blues*	20.00 -	30.00
Paramount 12026 *Laughin' Cryin' Blues*	20.00 -	30.00
12027 *Triflin' Blues*	20.00 -	30.00
12031 *Beale Street Mama*	30.00 -	50.00

ELDER RICHARD BRYANT ('S SANCTIFIED SINGERS):

Okeh 8559 *Come Over Here*	100.00 -	150.00
8579 *How Much I Owe For Love Divine*	100.00 -	150.00
Victor 21357 *The Master Come And Called To Me*	100.00 -	150.00
21694 *A Wild Man In Town*	100.00 -	150.00
V38507 *Everybody Was There*	100.00 -	150.00

JOHN BULLARD (QUARTET):

De Luxe 6019 *Spoiled Hambone Blues*	7.00 -	10.00*
6035 *Mary Lou*	7.00 -	10.00*
Index 300 *Callin' The Blues*	10.00 -	15.00

BULL CITY RED:

Titles, issued contemporaneously on Banner, Melotone, Oriole, Perfect, Romeo: *Black Woman And Poison Blues; I Won't Be Dogged Around; Now I'm Taking To You; Mississippi River; Pick And Shovel Blues; Richmond Blues*   15.00 - 25.00

BUMBLE BEE SLIM (& HIS THREE SHARKS):

Titles, issued contemporaneously on Banner, Melotone, Oriole, Perfect, Romeo; *Big Six; Bumblee Bee's New Muddy Water; Goodbye; I'm Having So Much Trouble; I'm Needing Someone; My Big Moments; Rising River Blues; Rough Treatment; She Never; 12 O'clock Midnight; 12 O'clock Southern Train; Woman For Every Man*   10.00 - 15.00

Bluebird 5563 *Sad And Lonesome*	15.00 -	25.00
6521 *Everybody's Fishing*	25.00 -	40.00
Bluebird 6559, 6586, 6612, 6635, 6649, 6834	7.00 -	12.00
Decca 7021 *Cruel Hearted Woman Blues*	15.00 -	20.00
7031 *Ain't It A Crying Shame?*	15.00 -	20.00
7045 *The Longest Day You Live*	15.00 -	20.00
7053 *Bleeding Heart Blues*	15.00 -	20.00
7054 *Let's Pitch A Boogie Woogie*	15.00 -	20.00
7071 *My Black Gal Blues*	10.00 -	15.00
7079 *Mean Bloody Murder Blues*	10.00 -	15.00
7089 *Good Evening Blues*	10.00 -	15.00
7098 *The Death Of Leroy Carr*	10.00 -	15.00
7101 *Sail On Sail On Blues*	10.00 -	15.00
7121 *I'll Take You Back*	10.00 -	15.00
7126 *Smoky Mountain Blues*	10.00 -	15.00
7138 *Happy Life Blues*	10.00 -	15.00
7145 *Some Old Rainy Days*	10.00 -	15.00
7162 *Deep Bass Blues*	10.00 -	15.00
7170 *No Good Woman*	10.00 -	15.00
Decca (others)	7.00 -	12.00
Fidelity 3004 *Ida Red*	5.00 -	8.00*
Paramount 13102 *Yo Yo String Blues*	100.00 -	150.00
13109 *Chain Gang Bound*	100.00 -	150.00
13132 *Honey Bee Blues*	100.00 -	150.00
Vocalion 1691 *Piney Woods Working Man*	75.00 -	100.00
1719 *Greasy Greens*	75.00 -	100.00
1720 *B And O Blues*	75.00 -	100.00
02713 *Busy Devil*	20.00 -	30.00
02728 *Baby So Long*	20.00 -	30.00
02742 *East St Louis Blues*	20.00 -	30.00
02773 *Wrecked Life Blues*	20.00 -	30.00
02809 *Helping Hand Blues*	20.00 -	30.00
02829 *Rough Road Blues*	20.00 -	30.00
02865 *Cold-Blooded Murder*	20.00 -	30.00
02885 *Burned Down Mill*	20.00 -	30.00
02903 *Running Bad Luck Blues*	20.00 -	30.00
02930 *Blues Before Daylight*	20.00 -	30.00
02970 *Way Down In Georgia*	20.00 -	30.00

03005 *Lemon Squeezing Blues*	20.00 -	30.00
03037 *I Keep On Drinking*	20.00 -	30.00
03054 *When The Sun Goes Down*	20.00 -	30.00
03090 *Big 80 Blues*	20.00 -	30.00
03130 *Sometimes Blues*	20.00 -	30.00
03165 *Cold Blooded Murder No. 2*	20.00 -	30.00
03197 *When Somebody Loses*	15.00 -	20.00
03209 *Can't You Trust Me No More?*	15.00 -	20.00
03221 *Dumb Tricks Blues*	15.00 -	20.00
03242 *Back In Jail Again*	15.00 -	20.00
03267 *Wet Clothes Blues*	15.00 -	20.00
03298 *Any Time At Night*	10.00 -	15.00
03328 *Hard Rocks In My Bed*	10.00 -	15.00
03384 *Meet Me At The Landing*	10.00 -	15.00
03418 *Slave Man Blues*	10.00 -	15.00
03446 *Fast Life Blues*	10.00 -	15.00
Vocalion 03473 *12 O'clock Midnight*	10.00 -	15.00
03506 *She Never*	10.00 -	15.00
03550 *Big Six*	10.00 -	15.00
03582 *Woman For Every Man*	10.00 -	15.00
03611 *Good Bye*	10.00 -	15.00
03637 *Rough Treatment*	10.00 -	15.00
03698 *Just Yesterday*	10.00 -	15.00
03767 *The Old Life I'm Living*	10.00 -	15.00
03870 *When Your Deal Goes Down*	10.00 -	15.00
03929 *Rock Hearted Woman*	10.00 -	15.00
04042 *If I Make It Over*	10.00 -	15.00
04661 *Where Was You Last Night?*	10.00 -	15.00

ALLEN BUNN:

Apollo 436 *She'll Be Sorry*	5.00 -	8.00*
439 *I Got You Covered*	5.00 -	8.00*
442, 447	3.00 -	5.00*

TEDDY BUNN & SPENCER WILLIAMS:

Victor 23253 *Tampa Twirl*	150.00 -	200.00
V38592 *Pattin' Dat Cat*	125.00 -	175.00
V38602 *Goose And Gander*	125.00 -	175.00
V38617 *Blow It Up*	125.00 -	175.00

PINETOP BURKS:

Titles, issued contemporaneously on Banner, Melotone, Oriole, Perfect, Romeo, Vocalion: *Mountain Jack Blues; Shake The Shack*   25.00 - 40.00

Vocalion 03979 *Jack Of All Trades Blues*	25.00 -	40.00
04107 *Fannie Mae Blues*	25.00 -	40.00

HATTIE BURLESON:

Brunswick 7042 *Superstitious Blues*	75.00 -	125.00
7054 *Bye Bye Baby*	75.00 -	125.00
Paramount 13050 *Clearin' House Blues*	100.00 -	150.00
13138 *Dead Lover Blues*	150.00 -	200.00

DAN BURLEY:

Circle 1020 *South Side Shake*	10.00 -	20.00
1021 *Big Cat, Little Cat*	10.00 -	20.00
1022 *Shotgun House Rag*	10.00 -	20.00

EDDIE BURNS:

Deluxe 6024 *Dealing With The Devil*	5.00 -	10.00*

(CHARLIE) BURSE (& HIS MEMPHIS MUD-CATS); CHARLIE CURSE WITH THE MEMPHIS JUG BAND; BURSE & SHADE; BURSE & STEPHEN:

Champion 16481 *I Got Good Taters*	200.00 -	300.00
16599 *Fishing In The Dark*	200.00 -	300.00
16654 *Tapping That Thing*	200.00 -	300.00
Okeh 8959 *Bottle It Up And Go*	100.00 -	150.00
Vocalion 03080 *Bottle It Up And Go*	75.00 -	100.00
05017, 05070, 05123, 05192, 05299, 05393, 05551	8.00 -	12.00

CLARA BURSTON:

Champion 16125 *Try That Man O'Mine*	150.00 -	250.00
16216 *Pay With Money*	150.00 -	250.00
16756 *Good And Hot*	150.00 -	250.00
Gennett 7319 *Pay With Money*	200.00 -	300.00
Paramount 12881 *Georgia Man Blues*	150.00 -	200.00
13003 *C.P. Blues*	100.00 -	150.00

13045 *Ginger Snappin'*	100.00	150.00

BUDDY (BUDDY) BURTON:

Gennett 6453 *Silvery Moon*	100.00	150.00
6471 *It's No-One But You*	100.00	150.00
Paramount 12625 *Ham-Fatchet Blues*	150.00	300.00

W. H. BURTON-MARCUS MOMAN -(CLIFF) MOORE:

Paramount 12787 *St. Louis Blues*	100.00	150.00
12789 *Roll That Jelly*	100.00	150.00

FRANK BUSBY:

Decca 7295 *Prisoner Bound*	8.00	12.00

MARY BUTLER:

Brunswick 7046 *Bungalow Blues*	150.00	200.00
7049 *Mad Dog Blues*	150.00	200.00

SAM BUTLER:

Vocalion 1056 *Heaven Is My View*	100.00	150.00
1057 *Poor Boy Blues*	100.00	150.00

TRIXIE BUTLER:

Bluebird 6392 *Take It Easy Greasy*	10.00	15.00
6429 *You Got The Right Key*	15.00	25.00

BUTTERBEANS AND SUSIE:

Okeh 8147, 8180	15.00	20.00
8163 *Construction Gang*	75.00	125.00
8182 *Kiss Me Sweet*	75.00	125.00
8192, 8199, 8202, 8209, 8219, 8224, 8233, 8241, 8303, 8307, 8319, 8323, 8335	15.00	30.00
8355 *He Likes Is Slow*	75.00	100.00
8392, 8399, 8432, 8520	15.00	30.00
8502 *I Wannt Hot Dog For My Roll*	50.00	75.00
8556 *Gonna Make You Sorry*	50.00	75.00
8598, 8614, 8670, 8687, 8701	20.00	30.00
8769 *Ain't Gonna Do That No More*	50.00	75.00
8833 *Times Is Hard*	50.00	75.00
8893 *Broke Down Mama*	50.00	75.00
8911 *Radio Papa*	50.00	75.00
8950 *Papa Ain't No Santa Claus*	50.00	75.00

JOHN BYRD:

Paramount 12997 *Billy Goat Blues*	150.00	300.00

JOSEPHINE BYRD:

Columbia 14349-D *Mosquito Blues*	25.00	40.00

ROLAND BYRD:

Atlantic 947 *Hey Little Girl*	15.00	20.00

ROY ("BALD HEAD") BYRD; ROY BYRD & HIS BLUES JUMPERS:

Atlantic 897 *She Walks Right In*	15.00	20.00
Federal 12061 *K.C. Blues*	6.00	10.00*
12073 *Rockin' With Fes*	6.00	10.00*
Mercury 8175 *Bald Head*	6.00	10.00
8184 *Oh Well*	6.00	10.00

BOBBY (BOBBIE) CADILLAC:

Columbia 14413-D *Carbolic Acid Blues*	75.00	100.00
14505-D *Easin' In*	75.00	100.00
14604-D *I Can't Stand That*	75.00	100.00

ROBERT CAFFREY:

Chess 1470 *Ida Bee*	10.00	15.00*

PERRY CAIN:

Gold Star 632 *All The Way From Texas*	15.00	25.00

JOE CALICOTT:

Brunswick 7166 *Fare Thee Well Blues*	150.00	200.00

BOB CALL:

Brunswick 7137 *31 Blues*	100.00	150.00
Coral 65009 *Talkin' Baby Blues*	5.00	10.00

BOB CAMP (& HIS BUDDIES/THE NIGHTHAWKS):

Decca 48112, 48118	5.00	8.00
Essex 714 *Pitch A Boogie*	8.00	12.00*
Southern 121,130	7.00	10.00

BOB CAMPBELL:

Vocalion 02798 *Starvation Farm Blues*	150.00	250.00
02830 *Shotgun Blues*	150.00	250.00

CARL CAMPBELL (WITH HENRY HAYES 4 KINGS):

Freedom 1521 *Ooh Wee Baby*	8.00	12.00
Peacock 1538 *Early Morning Blues*	8.00	12.00

CHARLIE CAMPBELL:

Vocalion 03571 *Pepper Sauce Mama*	75.00	100.00

GENE CAMPBELL:

Brunswick 7139 *Bended Knee Blues*	80.00	120.00
7154 *Western Plain Blues*	80.00	120.00
7161 *Freight Train Yodeling Blues*	80.00	120.00
7170 *Wandering Blues*	80.00	120.00
7177 *Wash And Iron Woman Blues*	80.00	120.00
7184 *Lazy Woman Blues*	80.00	120.00
7197 *Wedding Day Blues*	80.00	120.00
7206 *Face To Face Blues*	80.00	120.00
7214 *Doggone Mean Blues*	80.00	120.00
7225 *Crooked Woman Blues*	100.00	150.00
7226 *Turned Out Blues*	100.00	150.00
7227 *Married Life Blues*	100.00	150.00

CANNON & WOODS:

Brunswick 7138 *Fourth And Beale*	100.00	150.00

CAROLINA PEANUT BOYS:

Victor 23267 *Got A Letter From My Baby*	200.00	300.00
23274 *You Got Me Rollin'*	200.00	300.00
23319 *Spider's Nest Blues*	250.00	400.00

CAROLINA SLIM:

Acorn 319 *Pleading Blues*	7.00	10.00
323 *Worry You Off My Mind*	7.00	10.00
324 *Rag Mama*	7.00	10.00
3015 *Mama's Boogie*	7.00	10.00

CAROLINA WASHBOARD TRIO:

Varsity 6036 *That Thing Blues*	20.00	30.00

DORA CARR: DORA CARR-CHAS. DAVENPORT:

Okeh 8130 *You Might Pizen Me*	40.00	60.00
8244 *Good Woman's Blues*	40.00	60.00
8250 *Cow Cow Blues*	50.00	75.00
8284 *Fifth Street Blues*	50.00	75.00

GUNTER LEE CARR:

Decca 48167, 48170	3.00	6.00

LEROY CARR; (AND/WITH SCRAPPER BLACKWELL):

Bluebird 5877 *Ain't It A Shame*	30.00	50.00
5915 *Big Four Blues*	30.00	50.00
5946 *Just A Rag*	30.00	50.00
5963 *Going Back Home*	30.00	50.00
Vocalion 1191 *My Own Lonesome Blues*	30.00	50.00
1200 *Tennessee Blues*	75.00	100.00
1214 *Low Down Dirty Blues*	75.00	100.00
1232 *Truthful Blues*	75.00	100.00
1241 *Prison Bound Blues*	75.00	100.00
1259 *How About Me?*	75.00	100.00
1261 *Tired Of Your Low Down Ways*	75.00	100.00
1279 *You Don't Mean Me No Good*	75.00	100.00
1290 *Straight Alky Blues*	75.00	100.00
1400 *Naptown Blues*	100.00	150.00
1405 *Wrong Man Blues*	100.00	150.00
1412 *Gambler's Blues*	100.00	150.00
1423 *Gettin' All Wet*	75.00	125.00
1432 *Prison Cell Blues*	75.00	125.00
1435 *Love Hides All Faults*	75.00	125.00
1454 *The Dirty Dozen*	75.00	125.00
1460 *I'm Going Back To Tennessee*	75.00	125.00
1473 *Rainy Day Blues*	75.00	125.00
1483 *That's Tellin' 'Em*	75.00	125.00
1499 *Blue With The Blues*	75.00	125.00
1519 *I Know That I'll Be Blue*	75.00	125.00
1527 *Memphis Town*	75.00	125.00
1541 *Papa Wants A Cookie*	75.00	125.00
1574 *Jail Cell Blues*	75.00	125.00
1585 *Big House Blues*	75.00	125.00
1593 *Papa's On The House Top*	75.00	125.00
1605 *Low Down Dog Blues*	75.00	125.00
1624 *Let's Disagree*	75.00	125.00

1636 *Papa's Got Your Water On*	75.00 -	125.00
1651 *What More Can I Do?*	75.00 -	125.00
1693 *The Depression Blues*	75.00 -	125.00
1703 *Midnight Hour Blues*	75.00 -	125.00
1709 *I Keep The Blues*	75.00 -	125.00
1716 *Quittin' Papa*	75.00 -	125.00
02657 *Blues Before Sunrise*	50.00 -	75.00
02681 *Blues She Gave Me*	75.00 -	100.00
02741 *Hurry Down Sunshine*	75.00 -	100.00
02751 *Court Room Blues*	75.00 -	100.00
02762 *Shady Lane Blues*	50.00 -	80.00
02791 *Barrel House Woman*	75.00 -	100.00
02820 *I Believe I'll Make A Change*	75.00 -	100.00
02875 *Longing For My Sugar*	75.00 -	100.00
02893 *Cruel Woman Blues*	75.00 -	100.00
02922 *Stormy Weather Blues*	75.00 -	100.00
02950 *My Woman's Gone Wrong*	75.00 -	100.00
02969 *Bo Bo Stomp*	75.00 -	100.00
02986 *George Street Blues*	75.00 -	100.00
03034 *Tight Time Blues*	75.00 -	100.00
03067 *Black Wagon Blues*	75.00 -	100.00
03107 *Muddy Water*	75.00 -	100.00
03157 *My Good For Nothin' Gal*	75.00 -	100.00
Vocalion 03233 *Blue Night Blues*	75.00 -	100.00
03296 *Good Woman Blues*	75.00 -	100.00
03349 *Big Four Blues*	75.00 -	100.00

ALICE CARTER:

Okeh 8070, 8076	15.00 -	20.00

ALICE LESLIE CARTER:

Titles, issued contemporaneously on Arto, Bell, Globe: *The Also-Ran Blues; Aunt Hagar's Blues. Cry Baby Blues; Dangerouse Blues; Decatur Street Blues; Down Home Blues; Got To Have My Daddy Blues; I Want Some Lovin' Blues; You'll Think Of Me Blues* .... 15.00 - 30.00

BO CARTER (& WALTER JACOBS):

Bluebird 5489 *Bo Carter Special*	30.00 -	40.00
5536 *Howlin' Tome Cat Blues*	30.00 -	40.00
5594 *Pin In You Cushion*	30.00 -	40.00
5629 *Beans*	30.00 -	40.00
5704 *Nobody's Business*	30.00 -	40.00
5825 *Backache Blues*	30.00 -	40.00
5861 *Old Shoe Blues*	30.00 -	40.00
5912 *Mashing That Thing*	30.00 -	40.00
5997 *Skin Ball Blues*	25.00 -	35.00
6024 *Blue Runner Blues*	20.00 -	30.00
6058 *Please Warm My Weiner*	20.00 -	30.00
6124 *When You Left*	20.00 -	30.00
6295 *Cigarette Blues*	20.00 -	30.00
6315 *Ride My Mule*	20.00 -	30.00
6363 *Rolling Blues*	20.00 -	30.00
6407 *It's Too Wet*	15.00 -	25.00
6444 *Fat Mouth Blues*	15.00 -	25.00
6529 *T Baby Blues*	25.00 -	40.00
6589 *I Get The Blues*	40.00 -	60.00
6659 *Doubled Up In A Knot*	15.00 -	25.00
6695 *Sue Cow*	15.00 -	20.00
6735 *Worried G Blues*	15.00 -	30.00
7073 *Got To Work Somewhere*	15.00 -	30.00
7213 *The Ins And Outs Of My Girl*	15.00 -	30.00
7927 *Shake 'Em On Down*	15.00 -	30.00
7952 *Lucille, Lucille*	15.00 -	30.00
7968 *Shoo That Chicken*	15.00 -	30.00
8045 *Let's Get Drunk Again*	15.00 -	20.00
8078 *World In A Jug*	15.00 -	20.00
8093 *Old Devil*	15.00 -	20.00
8122 *Whiskey Blues*	15.00 -	20.00
8147 *Santa Claus*	15.00 -	20.00
8159 *Trouble In Blues*	15.00 -	20.00
8397 *The County Farm Blues*	15.00 -	20.00
8423 *Lock The Lock*	15.00 -	20.00
8459 *Baby Ruth*	15.00 -	20.00

8495 *Policy Blues*	15.00 -	20.00
8514 *My Little Mind*	15.00 -	20.00
8555 *Honey*	15.00 -	20.00
Columbia 14661-D *Pussy Cat Blues*	80.00 -	120.00
14671-D *New Auto Blues*	80.00 -	120.00
Okeh 8852 *I'm An Old Bumble Bee*	80.00 -	120.00
8858 *Times Is Tight Like That*	80.00 -	120.00
8870 *Mean Feeling Blues*	80.00 -	120.00
8887 *Pin In Your Cushion*	80.00 -	120.00
8888 *Loveless Love*	80.00 -	120.00
8889 *Howling Tom Cat Blues*	80.00 -	120.00
8897 *Ants In My Pants*	80.00 -	120.00
8906 *Blue Runner Blues*	80.00 -	120.00
8923 *What Kind Of Scent Is This?*	80.00 -	120.00
8930 *Last Go Round*	80.00 -	120.00
8935 *I Want You To Know*	80.00 -	120.00
8952 *Baby, How Can It Be?*	80.00 -	120.00
Vocalion 03091 *Pussy Cat Blues*	50.00 -	75.00
03259 *Ants In My Pants*	40.00 -	60.00

BUNNY CARTER:

Conqueror 7266 *Midnight Special Blues*	100.00 -	150.00

CHARLIE CARTER:

Broadway 5076 *Long Gone Lost John*	35.00 -	50.00

GEORGE CARTER:

Paramount 12750 *Hot Jelly Roll Blues*	150.00 -	200.00
12769 *Weeping Willow Woman*	150.00 -	200.00

GOREY/GORY CARTER (AND/WITH HIS GUITAR & ROCKIN' RHYTHM ORCHESTRA/HEPCATS):

Coral 65058, 65064	7.00 -	10.00
Freedom 1502, 1506, 1511, 1518, 1522, 1525, 1536	7.00 -	10.00
Modern 819 *Seven Days*	5.00 -	8.00
Sittin' In With 556, 572	7.00 -	10.00

HARRY CARTER:

Bluebird 6009 *Letter From Texas*	30.00 -	40.00
6095 *Hoo Doo Blues*	30.00 -	40.00
6210 *Deep Blues Ocean Blues*	30.00 -	40.00

JOSEPHINE CARTER:

Okeh 8002, 8015	15.00 -	20.00

LEROY CARTER:

Vocalion 03120 *Black Widow Spider*	75.00 -	100.00

NELSON CARTER & HIS GUITAR:

Sittin' In With 557 *My Baby Left Me*	10.00 -	15.00

"SPIDER" CARTER:

Brunswick 7181 *Dry Spell Blues*	90.00 -	120.00
7188 *Don't Leave Me Blues*	90.00 -	120.00

CASEY BILL (AND THE BROWN BOMBERS OF SWING):

Bluebird 6212 *Long-Eared Mule*	15.00 -	20.00
6243 *My Stove Won't Work*	15.00 -	20.00
6262 *Howlin' Dog Blues*	15.00 -	20.00
6356 *Somebody's Got To Go*	15.00 -	20.00
6390 *Let Me Be Your Butcher*	15.00 -	20.00
6465 *I'm A Stranger In Your Town*	15.00 -	20.00
6519 *Casey Blues*	15.00 -	20.00
8004 *You Gotta Do Your Duty*	15.00 -	20.00
8060 *Midnight Blues*	15.00 -	20.00
Vocalion 03186 *W.P.A. Blues*	15.00 -	20.00
03220 *Flood Water Blues*	15.00 -	20.00
03250 *Keyhole Blues*	15.00 -	20.00
03274 *Big Bill Blues*	15.00 -	20.00
03330 *Back Door Blues*	15.00 -	20.00
03373 *Gonna Take My Time*	15.00 -	20.00
03407 *Talkin' To Myself*	15.00 -	20.00
03437 *Streamline Woman*	15.00 -	20.00
03464 *Big Katy Adam*	15.00 -	20.00
03496 *Jinx Blues*	15.00 -	20.00
03529 *Round And Round*	15.00 -	20.00
03561 *I've Been Tricked*	15.00 -	20.00
03592 *No Good Woman*	15.00 -	20.00
03859 *Sales Lady*	15.00 -	20.00
03860 *New Round And Round*	15.00 -	20.00

03930 *Rooster Blues* . . . . 15.00 - 20.00
04001 *Go Ahead, Buddy* . . . . 15.00 - 20.00
04066 *Red Hot Blues* . . . . 15.00 - 20.00
04138 *Spider Blues* . . . . 15.00 - 20.00

CHARLIE CHAPMAN:
Broadway 5079 *Moanin' The Blues* . . . . .125.00 - 175.00
5091 *Back To The Wood Blues* . . . . .125.00 - 175.00
5108 *She's Got Good Stuff* . . . . .125.00 - 175.00

HENRY CHARLES:
Broadway 5094 *Henry Charles Blues* . . . . .100.00 - 150.00

THE CHARLESTON BLUES TRIO:
Champion 15734 *Lighthouse Blues* . . . . .100.00 - 150.00
15755 *Runnin' Wild* .125.00 - 175.00

CHATMAN BROTHERS:
Bluebird 6657 *Stir In Now* . . . . 30.00 - 50.00
6682 *Hold It At The Bottom* . . . . 30.00 - 50.00
6717 *Wake Me Just Before Day* . . . . 30.00 - 50.00
7167 *Radio Blues* . . . . 30.00 - 50.00
8139 *Jumping Out Blues* . . . . 30.00 - 50.00

ANDY CHATMAN:
Brunswick 7185 *Shakin' The Jelly* . . . . 80.00 - 120.00

BO CHATMAN:
Brunswick 7048 *Good Old Turnip Greens* . . . . . .150.00 - 200.00

PETER CHATMAN:
Okeh 05799 *Last Pair Of Shoes Blues* . . . . 10.00 - 15.00
05845 *Miss Ora Lee Blues* . . . . 10.00 - 15.00
05908 *The Jive Blues* . . . . 10.00 - 15.00

HARRY CHATMON:
Vocalion 03143 *Black Ants Blues* . . . . 50.00 - 75.00

CHICAGO FIVE:
Bluebird 6543 *I'm A Gamblin' Man* . . . . 10.00 - 15.00

THE CHICAGO SHEIKS:
Superior 2798 *Beedle Um Bum* . . . . .100.00 - 150.00

CHICAGO SUNNY BOY:
Meteor 5004 *Western Union Man* . . . . 15.00 - 20.00

VIRGIL CHILDERS:
Bluebird 7441 *Somebody Stole My Jane* . . . . 20.00 - 30.00
7464 *Red River Blues* . . . . 20.00 - 30.00
7487 *Travelin' Man* . . . . 20.00 - 30.00

BUDDY CHILES:
Gold Star 660 *Jet Black Woman* . . . . 15.00 - 20.00

ANNA LEE CHISHOLM:
Paramount 12213 *Georgia Sam Blues* . . . . 50.00 - 75.00

BUDDY CHRISTIAN'S FOUR CRY-BABIES:
Okeh 8332 *Nina Lee* . . . . 30.00 - 50.00

BLIND CLYDE CHURCH:
Victor 23271 *Number Nine Blues* . . . . .150.00 - 250.00

DOT CLARK:
Supertone 9288 *Papa, You're Too Slow* . . . . — - —

ETHEL CLARK:
Silvertone 3521 *Black Man Blues* . . . . 75.00 - 100.00
3523 *Jelly Roll Blues* . . . . .100.00 - 150.00

LONNIE CLARK:
Paramount 12871 *Broke Down Engine* . . . . .150.00 - 200.00

GEORGE CLARKE:
Bluebird 7485 *Prisoner Blues* . . . . 20.00 - 30.00

DOCTOR CLAYTON:
Bluebird 8901, 8938, 9003, 9021, 34-0702 . . . . . . 5.00 - 10.00
RCA Victor 20-1995, 20-2153, 20-2323 . . . . . . 4.00 - 7.00

JESSE CLAYTON:
Vocalion 1598 *Neckbone Blues* . . . . 80.00 - 120.00

PETER J. CLAYTON:
Bluebird 6071 *Peter's Blues* . . . . 20.00 - 30.00
6096 *Yo Yo Jive* . . . . 30.00 - 40.00

PETER CLEIGHTON:
Conqueror 9447 *Roaming Gambler* . . . . 5.00 - 8.00
9948 *Back Door Man Blues* . . . . 8.00 - 12.00
Okeh 06375 *Love Is Gone* . . . . 7.00 - 10.00
06398 *Slick Man Blues* . . . . 7.00 - 10.00
06464 *Streamline Love* . . . . 7.00 - 10.00
06514 *Something Going On Wrong* . . . . 7.00 - 10.00

ALBERT CLEMENS:

Bluebird 5930 *Policy Blues* . . . . 35.00 - 50.00

BIG BOY CLEVELAND:
Gennett 6108 *Quill Blues* . . . . .150.00 - 250.00

KAISER CLIFTON:
Victor 23278 *Cash Money Blues* . . . . .200.00 - 300.00
38600 *Teach Me Right From Wrong* . . . . .150.00 - 250.00

JAMES COLE; JAMES COLE'S WASHBOARD
BAND/FOUR:
Champion 16150 *Sweet Lizzie* . . . . .200.00 - 300.00
16308 *I Love My Mary* . . . . .200.00 - 300.00
16718 *Mistreated The Only Friend You Had* . . .200.00 - 300.00
40047 *Runnin' Wild* . . . . 50.00 - 75.00

KID COLE:
Vocalion 1186 *Sixth Street Moan* . . . . 75.00 - 100.00
1187 *Hard Hearted Mama Blues* . . . . 75.00 - 100.00

LUCY COLE:
Champion 15549 *Empty Bed Blues* . . . . 75.00 - 100.00

WALTER COLE:
Champion 16104 *Everybody Got Somebody* . . . . .200.00 - 300.00
Gennett 7318 *Everybody Got Somebody* . . . . . . .200.00 - 300.00

BOB COLEMAN:
Paramount 12731 *Cincinnati Underworld Moan* . .250.00 - 400.00
12791 *Sing Song Blues* . . . . .150.00 - 250.00

ELLEN COLEMAN:
Edison 51200 *Cruel Back Bitin' Blues* . . . . 20.00 - 30.00
51242 *She Walked Right Up And Took* . . . . . . 20.00 - 30.00

JAYBIRD COLEMAN:
Black Patti 8055 *Boll Weevil* . . . . .250.00 - 400.00
Columbia 14534-D *Man Trouble Blues* . . . . . . .100.00 - 150.00
Gennett 6226 *Mill Log Blues* . . . . .250.00 - 400.00
Gennett 6245 *Man Trouble Blues* . . . . .200.00 - 300.00
6276 *No More Good Water* . . . . .200.00 - 300.00

LONNIE COLEMAN:
Columbia 14440-D *Old Rock Island Blues* . . . . . 50.00 - 80.00

WALTER COLEMAN:
Decca 7157 *Smack That Thing* . . . . 20.00 - 30.00
7168 *I'm Going To Cincinnati* . . . . 20.00 - 30.00

CHASEY COLLINS:
Bluebird 6187 *Atlanta Town* . . . . 35.00 - 50.00
6261 *Walking Blues* . . . . 35.00 - 50.00

SAM COLLINS:
Black Patti 8025 *The Jail House Blues* . . . . .250.00 - 400.00
8026 *Yellow Dog Blues* . . . . .200.00 - 300.00
Gennett 6146 *Yellow Dog Blues* . . . . .200.00 - 300.00
6167 *The Jail House Blues* . . . . .200.00 - 300.00
6181 *Devil In The Lion's Den* . . . . .200.00 - 300.00
6260 *Dark Cloudy Blues* . . . . .260.00 - 400.00
6291 *Lead Me All The Way* . . . . .250.00 - 400.00
6307 *Midnight Special Blues* . . . . .250.00 - 400.00
6379 *Hesitation Blues* . . . . .250.00 - 400.00
Herwin 92043 *Riverside Blues* . . . . .250.00 - 400.00
Superior 330 *Midnight Special Blues* . . . . .250.00 - 400.00
350 *Hesitation Blues* . . . . .250.00 - 400.00
369 *Dark Cloudy Blues* . . . . .250.00 - 400.00

BIG TOM COLLINS:
King 4483 *Heartache Blues* . . . . 8.00 - 12.00
4568 *Watchin' My Stuff* . . . . 8.00 - 12.00

VIE COLLINS:
Silvertone 3518 *Nobody Knows* . . . . 75.00 - 100.00
3519 *Who'll Drive My Blues Away* . . . . 75.00 - 100.00
3538 *Confessin' Blues* . . . . 75.00 - 100.00
3539 *Reckless Don't Care Mama Blues* . . . . . . 75.00 - 100.00
3540 *Midnight Special* . . . . 75.00 - 100.00

CONNIE'S/CONNEY'S COMBO (WITH L.C.
WILLIAMS):
Freedom 1508 *Ugly Mae* . . . . 7.00 - 10.00
1510 *That's Alright* . . . . 7.00 - 10.00

BEN CONWAY:
Herwin 93014 *Sing Song Blues* . . . . .150.00 - 250.00

ANN COOK:
Victor 20579 *Mama Cookie* . . . . 75.00 - 125.00

DONALD COOKS (& HIS BAND):

Jade 202 *Dolphin Street Stomp*	7.00	-	10.00

SILVER COOKS WITH THE GONDOLIERS:

Peacock 1510 *Mr. Ticket Agent*	15.00	-	20.00

RATTLESNAKE COOPER:

Talent 804 *Rattlesnake Blues*	40.00	-	60.00

MARTHA COPELAND:

Columbia 14161-D, 14189-D, 14196-D	7.00	-	10.00
14208-D, 14227-D, 14237-D, 14248-D, 14262-D,			
14281-D, 14310-D, 14327-D	10.00	-	20.00
14352-D *Desert Blues*	20.00	-	30.00
14377-D *Mama's Well Has Done Gone Dry*	30.00	-	50.00
Okeh 8091, 8112	10.00	-	15.00
Victor 20548 *Hard-Headed Mama*	30.00	-	50.00
20769 *Stole My Man Blues*	30.00	-	50.00

COTTON TOP MOUNTAIN SACTIFIED SINGER:

Brunswick 7100 *Give Me That Old Time Religion*	100.00	-	150.00
7119 *She's Coming Round The Mountain*	100.00	-	150.00

JAMES COTTON:

Sun 199 *Straighten Up Baby*	30.00	-	50.00
206 *Cotton Crop Blues*	40.00	-	60.00*

SYLVESTER COTTON:

Modern 655 *Ugly Woman Blues*	6.00	-	10.00
Sensation 7000 *Ugly Woman Blues*	8.00	-	15.00

LITTLE WILLIE COTTON:

Swing Time 319 *Gonna Shake It Up And Go*	10.00	-	15.00*

DIPPER BOY COUNCIL:

Titles, issued contemporaneously on Banner, Conqueror, Melotone, Oriole, Perfect, Romeo: *I'm Grievin' and I'm Worryin'; Poor And Ain't Got A Dime; Runaway Man Blues; Working*

Man Blues	15.00	-	20.00

COUNTRY JIM:

Imperial 5062 *Rainy Morning Blues*	7.00	-	10.00
5073 *Old River Blues*	7.00	-	10.00
5091 *Good Looking Mama*	5.00	-	8.00
5095 *Phillipine Blues*	5.00	-	8.00

COUNTRY PAUL:

King 4517 *Your Picture Done Faded*	7.00	-	12.00*
4532 *One More Time*	7.00	-	12.00*
4560 *Black Cat Trail*	7.00	-	12.00*
4573 *Side Walk Boogie*	7.00	-	12.00*

(MISS) COUNTRY SLIM:

Hollywood 1005 *What Wrong Have I Done*	10.00	-	5.00

COUSIN JOE:

Savoy 5527 *Weddin' Day Blues*	5.00	-	8.00
Signature 1013 *Come Down Baby*	5.00	-	8.00

BLIND/BOGUS BEN COVINGTON:

Brunswick 7121 *Boodle-De-Bum Bum*	75.00	-	100.00
Paramount 12693 *Adam And Eve In The Garden*	100.00	-	150.00

BOB CRANE:

Herwin 93018 *Ghost Woman Blues*	150.00	-	200.00

JAMES CRAWFORD:

Gennett 6536 *Flood And Thunder*	75.00	-	100.00

ROSETTA CRAWFORD:

Decca 7567, 7584	10.00	-	15.00
Okeh 8096 *Down On The Levee Blues*	50.00	-	75.00
Pathe-Actuelle 7505 *Misery*	40.00	-	60.00
Perfect 105 *Misery*	40.00	-	60.00

PEE WEE CRAYTON:

Aladdin 3112 *Day Break*	4.00	-	6.00*
Modern 624, 643, 658, 675, 707, 719, 732, 742,			
763, 774, 796, 816, 892	4.00	-	7.00*

KATIE CRIPPEN:

Black Swan 2003 *Blind Man's Blues*	25.00	-	40.00
2018 *That's My Cup Blues*	25.00	-	40.00
Same Titles On Claxtonola, Paramount, Puritan	25.00	-	40.00

DAVID CROSS:

Brunswick 7079 *Then My Gal's In Town*	75.00	-	100.00

(ARTHUR) "BIG BOY" CRUDUP:

Bluebird 8858 *Death Valley Blues*	10.00	-	15.00
8896 *Black Pony Blues*	10.00	-	15.00
9019 *Raised To My Hand*	10.00	-	15.00
Bluebird 34-0704 *Mean Old Frisco Blues*	5.00	-	8.00
34-0717 *My Mamma Don't Allow Me*	5.00	-	8.00
34-0725 *Rock Me Mama*	5.00	-	8.00
34-0738 *Cool Disposition*	5.00	-	8.00
34-0746 *She's Gone*	5.00	-	8.00
RCA Victor 20-1949 *Ethel Mae*	5.00	-	8.00
20-2105 *I Want My Lovin'*	5.00	-	8.00
20-2205 *That's All Right*	5.00	-	8.00
20-2387 *That's Your Red Wagon*	5.00	-	8.00
20-2565 *Train Fore Blues*	5.00	-	8.00
20-2757 *Dirty Road Blues*	5.00	-	8.00
20-2989 *Boy Friend Blues*	5.00	-	8.00
20-3140 *Just Like A Spider*	5.00	-	8.00
20-3261 *Chicago Blues*	5.00	-	8.00
20-4367 *Love Me Mama*	5.00	-	8.00
20-4572 *Goin' Back To Georgia*	5.00	-	8.00
20-4753 *Late In The Evening*	5.00	-	8.00
20-4933 *Second Man Blues*	5.00	-	8.00
20-5070 *Lookin' For My Baby*	5.00	-	8.00
20-5167 *Nelvina*	5.00	-	8.00
20-5563 *The War Is Over*	5.00	-	8.00
22-0007 *Gonna Be Some Changes Made*	5.00	-	8.00
22-0029 *Crudup's Vicksburg Blues*	5.00	-	8.00
22-0048 *Hoodoo Lady Blues*	5.00	-	8.00
22-0061 *Come Back Baby*	5.00	-	8.00
22-0074 *Dust My Broom*	5.00	-	8.00
22-0092 *Mean Old Santa-Fe*	5.00	-	8.00
22-0100 *Lonesome World To Me*	5.00	-	8.00
22-0105 *She's Just Like Caldonia*	5.00	-	8.00
22-0117 *Nobody Wants Me*	5.00	-	8.00
22-0126 *Roberta Blues*	5.00	-	8.00
22-0141 *Too Much Competition*	5.00	-	8.00

(*45 rpm issues have catalog number prefixes 47 or 50 instead of 20 or 22; catalog numbers may / also be different in some cases. See 45 rpm section.)

PERCY LEE CRUDUP:

Checker 754 *Tears In My Eyes*	7.00	-	10.00

DENNIS CRUMPTON & ROBERT SUMMERS:

Titles, issued contemporaneously on Banner, Melotone, Oriole, Perfect, Romeo: *Everybody Ought To Pray Sometime; Go I'll Send Thee*

	30.00	-	90.00

BEN CURRY:

Champion 50019 *You Rascal You*	75.00	-	100.00
Paramount 13118 *Fat Mouth Blues*	200.00	-	300.00
13122 *Hot Dog*	200.00	-	300.00
13140 *The New Dirty Dozen*	200.00	-	300.00

ELDER CURRY:

Okeh 8857 *Memphis Flu*	50.00	-	80.00
8879 *Hard Times*	50.00	-	80.00
8892 *None Good But One*	50.00	-	80.00
8910 *Prove All Things*	50.00	-	80.00

DADDY STOVEPIPE (AND MISSISSIPPI SARAH):

Bluebird 5913 *The Spasm*	100.00	-	150.00
6023 *35 Depression*	100.00	-	150.00
Claxtonola 40335 *Sundown Blues*	100.00	-	150.00
Gennett 5459 *Stove Pipe Blues*	100.00	-	150.00

DUSKY DAILEY:

Titles, issued contemporaneously on Banner, Melotone, Oriole, Perfect, Romeo, Vocalion: *Flying Crow Blues; I Want You, I Need You; I Would Do Anything For You; Screamin' And Hollerin' Blues*

	15.00	-	25.00
Vocalion 04963 *Miss Georgia Blues*	15.00	-	25.00
04977 *Can Cutter Blues*	15.00	-	20.00
05044 *Lost Lovin' Blues*	15.00	-	20.00
05110 *Misunderstandin' Man*	15.00	-	20.00

FLORA DALE:

Domino 360 *Jail House Blues*	25.00	-	40.00
3504 *Everything My Sweetie Does (Pleases Me)*	10.00	-	15.00

SALLY DALE:
Domino 3452 *A Good Man Is Hard To Find* .... 10.00 - 15.00
3453 *Blind Man Blues* .... 10.00 - 15.00

DALLAS RED:
Selective 112 *Cold Blooded Blues* .... 5.00 - 8.00

DALLAS STRING BAND (WITH COLEY JONES)
Columbia 14290-D *Dallas Red* ....100.00 - 150.00
14389-D *Hokum Blues* ....100.00 - 150.00
14410-D *Chasin' Rainbows* ....100.00 - 150.00
14574-D *Sugar Blues* ....125.00 - 175.00

LEROY DALLAS:
Sittin' In With 522 *Jump Little Children* .... 8.00 - 15.00
526 *Good Morning Blues* .... 8.00 - 15.00
537 *Your Sweet Man's Blues* .... 8.00 - 15.00

(JULIUS DANIELS (AND TORRENCE):
Victor 20499 *I'm Gonna Tell God How You Doin'* 100.00 - 150.00
20658 *Ninety Nine Year Blues* .... 100.00 - 150.00
21065 *Richmond Blues* ....100.00 - 150.00
21359 *Can't Put The Bridle On That Mule* ....100.00 - 150.00

BLIND (BLUES) DARBY:
Decca 7328 *Heart Trouble Blues* .... 20.00 - 30.00
7816 *Spike Driver* .... 20.00 - 30.00
Vocalion 02953 *I'm Gonna Wreck Your Vee Eight* 40.00 - 60.00
02988 *Pokino Blues* .... 40.00 - 60.00
03177 *Sweet Memories Blues* .... 40.00 - 60.00

TEDDY DARBY:
Paramount 12828 *My Laona Blues* ....200.00 - 300.00
12907 *What Am I To Do?* ....200.00 - 300.00
Victor 23311 *Deceiving Blues* ....200.00 - 300.00

GENEVIEVE DAVIS:
Victor 20648 *I've Got Something* .... 75.00 - 125.00

GEORGE DAVIS:
Decca 7756, 7799 .... 10.00 - 15.00

BLIND JOHN(NY) DAVIS (TRIO):
MGM 10574 *No Mail Today* .... 7.00 - 10.00
10738 *My Love* .... 7.00 - 00.00
10919 *Telegram To My Baby* .... 7.00 - 10.00
10976 *The Day Will Come* .... 7.00 - 10.00
Vocalion 04079 *Jersey Cow Blues* .... 10.00 - 15.00
04189 *Alley Woman Blues* .... 10.00 - 15.00
04580 *Anna Lou Breakdown* .... 10.00 - 15.00

HENRYETTE DAVIS:
Okeh 8371 *Another Sweet Daddy* .... 35.00 - 50.00
8395 *Mail Box Blues* .... 35.00 - 50.00

SONNY BOY DAVIS:
Talent 802 *I Don't Live Here No More* .... 30.00 - 50.00

WALTER DAVIS:
Bluebird 5031 *M. & O. Blues* .... 50.00 - 80.00
5038 *Blue Sea Blues* .... 50.00 - 80.00
5077 *Howling Wind Blues* .... 50.00 - 80.00
5094 *Hijack Blues* .... 50.00 - 80.00
5129 *Worried Man Blues* .... 50.00 - 80.00
5143 *Red Cross Blues* .... 50.00 - 80.00
5192 *Moonlight Blues* .... 50.00 - 80.00
5228 *Evil Woman* .... 50.00 - 80.00
5305 *Red Cross Blues-No. 2* .... 50.00 - 80.00
5324 *You Don't Smell Right* .... 50.00 - 80.00
5361 *What's The Use Of Worryinn'?* .... 50.00 - 80.00
5390 *Oil Field Blues* .... 50.00 - 80.00
5411 *Stormy Weather Blues-No. 2* .... 75.00 - 100.00
(Note: Above titles, on Sunrise label, are valued more highly.)
5879 *Sloppy Drunk Again* .... 25.00 - 40.00
5931 *Sweet Sixteen* .... 25.00 - 40.00
5965 *Minute Man Blues* .... 25.00 - 40.00
5982 *Sad And Lonesome Blues* .... 25.00 - 40.00
6040 *Dentist Blues* .... 15.00 - 20.00
6059 *I Can Tell By They Way You Smell* .... 15.00 - 20.00
6074 *Pearly May* .... 15.00 - 20.00
6125 *Santa Claus* .... 25.00 - 40.00
6167 *Moonlight Is My Spread* .... 10.00 - 15.00

6201 *Katy Blues* .... 10.00 - 15.00
6228 *Blues At Midnight* .... 10.00 - 15.00
6354 *Carpenter Man* .... 10.00 - 15.00
6410 *Fallin' Rain* .... 8.00 - 12.00
6468 *Jacksonville* .... 8.00 - 12.00
6498 *Think You Need A Shot* .... 10.00 - 15.00
6971 *Nightmare Blues* .... 8.00 - 12.00
6996 *Good Gal* .... 8.00 - 12.00
7021 *Fifth Avenue Blues* .... 8.00 - 12.00
7064 *Angel Child* .... 8.00 - 12.00
7292 *Guiding Rod* .... 8.00 - 12.00
7329 *Holiday Blues* .... 8.00 - 12.00
7375 *Big Jack Engine Blues* .... 8.00 - 12.00
7512 *Walking The Avenue* .... 8.00 - 12.00
7551 *Easy Goin' Mama* .... 8.00 - 12.00
7589 *Million-Dollar* .... 8.00 - 12.00
7643 *Candy Man* .... 8.00 - 12.00
7663 *Friendless Blues* .... 8.00 - 12.00
7693 *13 Highway* .... 8.00 - 12.00
7745 *Call Me Anytime* .... 8.00 - 12.00
7792 *Love Will Kill You* .... 8.00 - 12.00
7836 *Homesick* .... 8.00 - 12.00
7978 *Cuttin' Off My Days* .... 8.00 - 12.00
8002 *Early This Mornin'* .... 8.00 - 12.00
8026 *Smoky Mountain* .... 8.00 - 12.00
8058 *Mercy Blues* .... 8.00 - 12.00
8107 *Troubled And Weary* .... 8.00 - 12.00
8227 *Corinne* .... 8.00 - 12.00
8261 *Big Four Blues* .... 8.00 - 12.00
8282 *Green And Lucky* .... 8.00 - 12.00
8312 *Bachelor Blues* .... 8.00 - 12.00
8343 *Froggy Bottom* .... 8.00 - 12.00
8367 *Doctor Blues* .... 8.00 - 12.00
8393 *Sundown Blues* .... 8.00 - 12.00
8434 *Jungle Blues* .... 8.00 - 12.00
8470 *Western Land* .... 8.00 - 12.00
8510 *Come Back Baby* .... 8.00 - 12.00
8534 *The Way I Love You* .... 8.00 - 12.00
8574 *Four Foot Eleven* .... 8.00 - 12.00
8600 *Can't See Your Face* .... 8.00 - 12.00
8664 *Just Thinking* .... 8.00 - 12.00
8694 *Soon Forgotten* .... 8.00 - 12.00
8737 *Friends Must Part* .... 8.00 - 12.00
8773 *The Only Woman* .... 8.00 - 12.00
8802 *All My Money Gone* .... 8.00 - 12.00
8833 *I'll Be Back After A While* .... 8.00 - 12.00
8860 *You Keep On Crying* .... 8.00 - 12.00
8926 *Teasin' Brown Skin* .... 8.00 - 12.00
8961 *Frisco Blues* .... 8.00 - 12.00
8998 *Hello Baby* .... 5.00 - 8.00
9027 *Goodbye* .... 5.00 - 8.00
Bullet 305 *Move Back To The Woods* .... 5.00 - 10.00
311 *I Would Hate To Hate You* .... 5.00 - 10.00
321 *Santa Claus Blues* .... 5.00 - 10.00
Stop That Train In Harlem .... 5.00 - 10.00
341 *I Just Can't Help It* .... 5.00 - 10.00
Montgomery Ward (many titles same as Bluebird, above)........................ 5.00 - 10.00
Victor 23250 *Blue Sea Blues* ....150.00 - 200.00
23282 *What Made Me Love You So?* ....150.00 - 200.00
23291 *Railroad Man Blues* ....150.00 - 200.00
23302 *Mr. Davis Blues- No. 2* ....150.00 - 200.00
23308 *Howling Wind Blues* ....200.00 - 300.00
23313 *Strange Land Blues* ....200.00 - 300.00
23325 *Lonesome Hill Blues* ....200.00 - 300.00
23333 *Worried Man Blues* ....200.00 - 300.00
23343 *Hijack Blues* ....200.00 - 300.00
23355 *South-West Missouri Blues* ....200.00 - 300.00
23414 *Night Creepin'* ....200.00 - 300.00
23418 *L & N Blues* ....200.00 - 300.00
23423 *Red Cross Blues* ....200.00 - 300.00
V-38618 *Mr. Davis' Blues* ....150.00 - 200.00

BLIND WILLIE DAVIS:
Paramount 12658 *When The Saints Go*
Marching In ....150.00 - 200.00
    12726 *Your Enemy Cannot Harm You* ....150.00 - 200.00
    12979 *I Believe I'll Go Back Home* ....200.00 - 300.00

RUTH DAY:
Columbia 14642-D *Painful Blues* ....150.00 - 200.00

TEXAS BILL DAY (& BILLIKEN JOHNSON):
Columbia 14494-D *Goin' Back To My Baby* ..... 75.00 - 100.00
    14514-D *Elm Street Blues* .... 75.00 - 100.00
    14587-D *Good Mornin' Blues* .... 75.00 - 100.00

WILL DAY:
Columbia 14318-D *Sunrise Blues* .... 75.00 - 100.00

JOE DEAN:
Vocalion 1544 *Mexico Bound Blues* .... 75.00 - 100.00

JAMES/JIMMY DE BERRY (& HIS MEMPHIS
PLAYBOYS):
Okeh 05800 *Spider Bite Blues* .... 10.00 - 15.00
Sun 185 *Take A Little Chance* .... 35.00 - 50.00*
Vocalion 05084 *You Can Go* .... 10.00 - 15.00
    05247 *Insane Jealous Blues* .... 10.00 - 15.00
    05349 *You Played A Trick On Me* .... 10.00 - 15.00

MERCY DEE:
Bayou 003 *Please Understand* .... 10.00 - 15.00*
    013 *Happy Bachelor* .... 10.00 - 15.00
Colony 102 *Straight And Narrow* .... 10.00 - 15.00
    107 *Old Fashioned Ways* .... 10.00 - 15.00
    111 *Birdbrain Baby* .... 10.00 - 15.00
Imperial 5104 *Empty Life* .... 8.00 - 12.00
    5110 *Big Foot Country* .... 8.00 - 12.00
    5118 *Bought Love* .... 8.00 - 12.00
    5127 *Pay Off* .... 8.00 - 12.00
Spire 11-001 *Lonesome Cabin Blues* .... 10.00 - 15.00
    11-002 *Travelin' Alones Blues* .... 10.00 - 15.00

MATTIE DELANEY:
Vocalion 1480 *Tallahatchie River Blues* ....150.00 - 200.00

TOM DELANEY:
Columbia 14082-D *Georgia Stockade Blues* .... 15.00 - 20.00
    14122-D *Bow Legged Mama* .... 15.00 - 20.00

THE DELLS:
Vee Jay 134 *Tell the World* .... 20.00 - 40.00*

DELTA BOYS:
    8891 *When The Saints Go Marching In* .... 20.00 - 30.00
Bluebird 8852 *Black Gal Swing* .... 20.00 - 30.00
    8915 *Get Up And Go* .... 20.00 - 30.00

DELTA JOE:
Chance 1115 *4 O'Clock Blues* .... 25.00 - 40.00*

DELTA JOHN:
Regent 1001 *Goin' Mad Blues* .... 7.00 - 10.00

DELTA RHYTHM BOYS:
Atlantic 889, 899, 900, 905, 1023 .... 5.00 - 10.00
Decca 8514, 8522, 8530, 8542 .... 5.00 - 10.00

DESCRIPTIVE NOVELTY (See BLIND
LEMON JEFFERSON)

DETROIT COUNT:
JVB 75830 *Hastings Street Opera* .... 20.00 - 30.00
    75831 *Hastings St. Woogie Man* .... 20.00 - 30.00
King 4264 *Hastings Street Opera* .... 10.00 - 15.00
    4265 *I'm Crazy About You* .... 15.00 - 20.00
    4279 *Little Tillie Willie* .... 15.00 - 20.00

THE DEVIL'S DADDY-IN-LAW:
Conqueror 9204 *Lookin' For My Baby* .... 15.00 - 20.00
Vocalion 04643 *Lookin' For My Baby* .... 15.00 - 20.00

PEARL DICKSON:
Columbia 14286-D *Little Rock Blues* .... 75.00 - 100.00

PERE DICKSON:
Victor 23335 *Red Hot Papa* ....150.00 - 200.00

TOM DICKSON:
Okeh 8570 *Worry Blues* ....100.00 - 150.00
    8590 *Death Cell Blues* ....100.00 - 150.00

DIRTY RED:
Aladdin 194 *Home Last Night* .... 10.00 - 15.00
    207 *Hotel Boogie* .... 10.00 - 15.00

FLOYD DIXON (TRIO) (WITH JOHNNY
MOOR'S THREE BLAZERS):
Aladdin 3069, 3073, 3074, 3075, 3078, 3082,
    3083, 3084, 3101, 3111, 3135, 3144, 3151, 3166,
    3196, 3230 .... 3.00 - 5.00*
Modern 653, 664, 700, 724, 725, 744, 761, 776,
    797 .... 3.00 - 7.00
Supreme 1528, 1535, 1546, 1547 .... 5.00 - 8.00
Swing Time 261, 287 .... 7.00 - 10.00

MARY DIXON:
Columbia 14415-D *Daddy You Got Ev'rything* ... 35.00 - 50.00
    14442-D *All Around Mama* .... 35.00 - 50.00
    14459-D *Black Dog Blues* .... 40.00 - 60.00
    14532-D *Unhappy Blues* .... 50.00 - 75.00
Vocalion 1199 *Dusky Stevedore* .... 75.00 - 100.00

PERRY DIXON:
Columbia 14522-D *Back To Georgia Blues* ..... 75.00 - 100.00

DOCTOR CLAYTON'S BUDDY:
RCA Vitor 20-2733, 20-2954, 20-3085, 20-3255 . 3.00 - 6.00

DR. HEPCAT (See L. DURST):

FATS DOMINO:
Imperial 5058 *The Fat Man* .... 15.00 - 20.00
    5065 *Boogie Woogie Baby* .... 15.00 - 20.00
    5077 *Hide Away Blues* .... 15.00 - 20.00
    5085 *Brand New Baby* .... 15.00 - 20.00
    5099 *Every Night About This Time* .... 15.00 - 20.00
    5114 *What's The Matter Baby* .... 15.00 - 20.00
    5123 *Don't You Lie To Me* .... 15.00 - 20.00
    5138 *No, No Baby* .... 10.00 - 15.00
    5145 *Rockin' Chair* .... 10.00 - 15.00
    5167 *I'll Be Gone* .... 10.00 - 15.00

BLIND JOE DONNELL:
Broadway 5089 *There's A Hand Writing On the*
Wall ....100.00 - 150.00

MATTIE DORSEY:
Paramount 12521 *Mattie Blues* .... 75.00 - 100.00
    12554 *Stingaree Blues* .... 75.00 - 100.00

BIG BILL DOTSON & HIS GUITAR:
Blues & Rhythm 7004 *Dark Old World* .... 10.00 - 15.00

DAISY DOUGLAS:
Columbia 14175-D *Down-Hearted Blues* .... 30.00 - 50.00

K.C. DOUGLAS:
Down Town 2004 *Mercury Boogie* .... 15.00 - 20.00

DOWN HOME BOYS:
Bluebird 6331 *You Do It* .... 25.00 - 40.00
Victor V38567 *It's All Gone Now* ....150.00 - 200.00

DOWN HOME TRIO:
Down Town 2017 *Down Town Shuffle* .... 20.00 - 30.00

DOWN SOUTH BOYS:
Varsity 6009 *The New Stop And Listen Blues* .... 15.00 - 25.00
    6019 *Down On My Bended Knees* .... 15.00 - 20.00

LITTLE BUDDY DOLE:
Vocalion 05111 *Grief Will Kill You* .... 15.00 - 25.00
    05246 *Sweet Man Blues* .... 15.00 - 25.00
    05771 *Renewed Love Blues* .... 15.00 - 25.00

ARIZONA DRANES:
Okeh 8352 *John Said He Saw A Number* .... 30.00 - 50.00
    8353 *It's All Right Now* ....100.00 - 150.00
    8380 *In That Day* ....100.00 - 150.00
    8419 *I'm Going Home On The Morning Train* . 40.00 - 60.00
    8438 *I'm Glad My Lord Saved Me* .... 40.00 - 60.00
    8600 *I Shall Wear A Crown* .... 40.00 - 60.00
    8646 *Don't You Want To Go?* .... 40.00 - 60.00

DRIFTIN' SLIM/SMITH:
Modern 849 *My Little Machine* .... 8.00 - 15.00*
RPM 370 *Good Morning Baby* .... 10.00 - 15.00*

SLIM DUCKETT & PIG NORWOOD:
Okey 8871 *You Gotta Stand Judgement For*
Yourself ....100.00 - 200.00
    8899 *When The Saints Go Marching In* ......100.00 - 200.00

SIDEWHEEL SALLIE/SALLY DUFFIE:
Paramount 12519 *King Papa Blues* .... 80.00 - 120.00

12545 *Bunker Hill Blues* .... 80.00 - 120.00
12581 *Kid Man Blues* .... 80.00 - 120.00

BERNICE DUKE:
Broadway 5037 *Sawmill Blues* .... 80.00 - 120.00
 5038 *Back Door Blues* .... 80.00 - 120.00
 5088 *Arkansas Mill Blues* .... 80.00 - 120.00

DUKE BAYOU & HIS MYSTIC 6:
Apollo 440 *Rub A LIttle Boogie* .... 7.00 - 10.00

WILLIE DUKES:
Champion 16126 *Snake Hip Twirl* .... 75.00 - 100.00
 16745 *Sweet Poplar Bluff Blues* .... 150.00 - 200.00
 50055 *Snake Hip Twirl* .... 20.00 - 30.00

ANDREW DUNHAM:
Sensation 23 *Hattie Mae* .... 10.00 - 15.00

FRED DUNN & HIS BARRELHOUSE RHYTHM:
Signature 1026, 1027, 32010 .... 5.00 - 10.00

CHAMPION JACK DUPREE; JACK DUPREE & HIS BAND:
Alert 421 *Highway 51* .... 7.00 - 10.00
Apollo 407, 413, 421 .... 5.00 - 8.00
Continental 6064, 6065, 6066......... 5.00 - 8.00
Joe Davis 5100, 5101, 5102, 5103, 5104, 5105,
 5106, 5107, 5108 .... 4.00 - 7.00
Okeh 05656, 05713, 05769, 05823, 06068, 06104,
 06152, 06197, 06597, 06642 .... 5.00 - 10.00

L. DURST (DR. HEPCAT):
Peacock 1509 *Hattie Green* .... 50.00 - 75.00
Uptown 201 *Hattie Green* .... 75.00 - 100.00

JIMMY EAGER & HIS TRIO:
Sabre 100 *Please Mr. Doctor* .... 7.00 - 10.00*

AMOS EASTON (& HIS ORCHESTRA):
Specialty 410 *Strange Angel* .... 7.00 - 10.00
Vocalion 1694 *M and O Blues*............. 80.00 - 120.00

EBONY THREE:
Decca 7503, 7527 .... 8.00 - 12.00

EDDIE AND OSCAR:
Victor 23324 *Flying Crow Blues* ....250.00 - 400.00

EDDY TEDDY:
Brunswick 7223 *Alcohol Mama* ....150.00 - 200.00

BERNICE EDWARDS (BLACK BOY SHINE & HOWLING SMITH):
Paramount 12620 *Southbound Blues*.........100.00 - 150.00
 12633 *Long Tall Mama*..............100.00 - 150.00
 12653 *Sunshine Blues*..............100.00 - 150.00
 12713 *Jack Of All Trades* ....100.00 - 150.00
 12741 *Born To Die Blues* ....100.00 - 150.00
 12766 *Hard Hustlin' Blues* ....100.00 - 150.00
Vocalion 03036 *Bantam Rooster Blues* .... 75.00 - 100.00
 03168 *Hot Mattress Stomp* .... 75.00 - 100.00

BIG BOY EDWARDS:
Titles, issued contemporaneously on Banner,
 Melotone, Oriole, Perfect, Romeo, Vocalion: *It
 Was No Dream; Louise* .... 25.00 - 40.00
Vocalion 02866 *Who Did You Give My Barbecue
 To?* .... 30.00 - 40.00
 02932 *Hoodoo Blues* .... 30.00 - 40.00
 03079 *Dancing The Blues Away* .... 30.00 - 40.00

CARRIE EDWARDS:
Columbia 14652-D *Dirty Mistreater* .... 75.00 - 100.00
Okeh 8938 *Hard Time Blues* .... 50.00 - 75.00

FRANK EDWARDS:
Okeh 06393 *Terraplane Blues* .... 10.00 - 15.00
 06493 *Sweet Man Blues* .... 10.00 - 15.00

HONEYBOY EDWARDS:
Artist 102 *Build A Cave*.................... 8.00 - 15.00

J. D. EDWARDS:
Imperial 5245 *Hobo* .... 5.00 - 8.00*

PIANO KID EDWARDS:
Paramount 13051 *Piano Kid Special* ....150.00 - 250.00
 13086 *Hard Luck Gamblin' Man* ....150.00 - 300.00

(BIG BOY) TEDDY EDWARDS; BIG TEDDY

BOY EDWARDS:
Bluebird 5628 *Who Did You Give My Barbecue
 To?* .... 20.00 - 30.00
 5813 *Love Will Provide For Me* .... 20.00 - 30.00
 5826 *Louise* .... 20.00 - 30.00
Decca 7184 *Louisiana* .... 20.00 - 30.00
Melotone 12037 *Them Things* .... 50.00 - 75.00
 12097 *Lovin' Blues* .... 50.00 - 75.00
Polk 9008 *Lovin' Blues* .... 75.00 - 100.00
 9009 *Them Things* .... 75.00 - 100.00
Vocalion 02698 *Lovin' Blues* .... 50.00 - 75.00

TENDERFOOT EDWARDS
Paramount 12873 *Seven Sister Blues* ....200.00 - 300.00
 12952 *Up On The Hill Blues* ....200.00 - 300.00

W.C. ELKINS & HIS DEXTRA SINGERS:
QRS 7045 *Climbing Up The Mountain* .... 25.00 - 50.00
 7046 *Oh, Mother, Don't You Weep* .... 25.00 - 50.00
 7047 *Roll, Roll Chariot* .... 25.00 - 50.00
 7063 *Eloi* .... 25.00 - 50.00
 7066 *Ride On, Moses* .... 25.00 - 50.00
 7068 *A Wheel In A Wheel* .... 25.00 - 50.00

BIG BOY ELLIS & HIS RHYTHM:
Lenox 521 *Dices Dices* .... 7.00 - 10.00

BILLY (THE KID) EMERSON:
Sun 195 *No Teasin' Around*................ 25.00 - 40.00
 214 *Move Baby Move* .... 10.00 - 15.00
 219 *Red Hot* .... 8.00 - 12.00
 233 *Something For Nothing* .... 8.00 - 12.00

JACK ERBY:
Columbia 14570-D *Hot Peter* .... 35.00 - 50.00

JOHN ERBY:
Columbia 14151-D *Lonesome Jimmy Blues* .... 35.00 - 50.00

LEROY ERVIN:
Gold Star 628 *Rock Island Blues* .... 15.00 - 20.00
Swing 415 *Rock Island Blues*................ 15.00 - 20.00

(SLEEPY) JOHN ESTES; JOHN ESTES JAMES RACHEL:
Bluebird 7677 *Diving Duck Blues* .... 30.00 - .50.00
 7849 *The Girl I Love, She Got Long Curly
 Hair* .... 30.00 - 50.00
Bluebird 8871 *Little Laura Blues* .... 20.00 - 30.00
 8950 *Working Man Blues*............... 20.00 - 30.00
Champion 50001 *Stop That Thing*.............. 20.00 - 30.00
 50048 *Drop Down Mama* .... 20.00 - 30.00
 50068 *Someday Baby Blues*............. 20.00 - 30.00
Decca 7279 *Someday Baby Blues* .... 20.00 - 30.00
 7289 *Married Woman Blues* .... 20.00 - 30.00
 7325 *Down South Blues* .... 20.00 - 30.00
 7342 *Vernita Blues* .... 15.00 - 20.00
 7354 *Hobo Jungle Blues* .... 15.00 - 20.00
 7365 *Need More Blues* .... 15.00 - 20.00
 7414 *Government Money* .... 15.00 - 20.00
 7442 *Floating Bridge* .... 12.00 - 16.00
 7473 *Brownsville Blues* .... 15.00 - 20.00
 7491 *Liquor Store Blues* .... 15.00 - 20.00
 7516 *Easin' Back To Tennessee* .... 15.00 - 20.00
 7561 *Everybody Oughta Make A Change* ..... 15.00 - 20.00
 7766 *Drop Down* .... 15.00 - 20.00
 7789 *Mailman Blues* .... 15.00 - 20.00
 7814 *Jailhouse Blues* .... 15.00 - 20.00
Victor 23318 *Expressman Blues* ....200.00 - 300.00
 23397 *Stack O'Dollars* ....200.00 - 300.00
 V 38549 *Diving Duck Blues* ....100.00 - 150.00
 V 38582 *Black Mattie Blues* ....150.00 - 200.00
 V 38595 *T-Bone Steak Blues* ....150.00 - 200.00
 V 38614 *Milk Cow Blues* ....150.00 - 200.00
 V 38628 *Poor John Blues* ....150.00 - 200.00

CHARLOTTE EVANS:
Domino 3453 *I'm Done, Done, Done With You* .. 10.00 - 15.00

JOE EVANS:
Titles, issued contemporaneously on Oriole,
 Perfect, Romeo: *Boogity Woogity; Down In*

Black Bottom; Early Some Morning Blues;
Georgia Rose; Mill Man Blues; New Huntsville
Jail; Oh You Son Of A Gun; Shook It This
Morning Blues ....100.00 - 200.00
 Gennett 6259 *Little Son Of A Gun* ....150.00 - 200.00

EVANS AND McCLAIN:
 Titles, issued contemporaneously on Banner,
 Oriole, Perfect, Romeo: *So Sorry Dear;*
 Sourwood Mountain ....100.00 - 150.00

DOROTHY EVERETTS:
 Columbia 14444-D *Macon Blues* .... 50.00 - 80.00

LOTTIE EVERSON (& HER BUDDY):
 Champion 15591 *Lost Lover Blues* ....125.00 - 175.00
  15636 *Blue World Blues* ....125.00 - 175.00
  15755 *Wayward Girl Blues* ....125.00 - 175.00

EXCELSIOR (NORFOLK) QUARTETTE:
 Black Swan 2060 *Jelly Roll Blues* .... 25.00 - 40.00
 Gennett 4881 *Kitchen Mechanic Blues* .... 15.00 - 25.00
 Okeh 4481 *Kitchen Mechanic Blues* .... 15.00 - 25.00
  8033 *Roll Them Bones* .... 15.00 - 25.00
  8035 *Down By The Old Mill Stream* .... 15.00 - 25.00
  8038 *Goodbye, My Coney Island Baby* .... 15.00 - 25.00

FAMOUS HOKUM BOYS:
 Titles, issued contemporaneously on Banner,
 Homestead, Jewel, Oriole, Perfect, Romeo:
 Ain't Going There No More; Black Cat Rag;
 Come On In; Come On Mama; Eagle Riding
 Papa; Guitar Rag; It's All Used Up; Nancy
 Jane; Papa's Getting Hot; Pat That Bread; Pie-
 Eating Strut; Pig Meat Strut; Saturday Night
 Rub; Somebody's Been Using That Thing; That
 Stuff I Got; That's The Way She Likes It; You
 Can't Get Enough Of That Stuff; You Do It ... 75.00 - 150.00

Perfect 155 *Do That Thing* ....150.00 - 200.00
 161 *Rollin' Mill* ....150.00 - 200.00

THE FAT MAN:
 J.O.B. 103 *You've Got To Stop This Mess* .... 30.00 - 50.00

FEATHERS AND FROGS:
 Paramount 12812 *How You Get That Way* ......150.00 - 200.00

BEN FERGUSON:
 Victor 23297 *Please Don't Holler, Mama* ......200.00 - 300.00

TROY FERGUSON:
 Columbia 14483-D *College Blues* .... 40.00 - 60.00
  14644-D *You Better Keep It At Home* .... 50.00 - 75.00

ALFRED FIELDS:
 Okeh 06020, 06129 .... 7.00 - 10.00
 Vocalion 05018, 05727 .... 7.00 - 10.00

FINE ART(S) TRIO (SIPPIN AT THE PIANO):
Fine Art 203 *Caught In The Web Of Sin* .... 10.00 - 15.00
 204 *Here I Go Wher The Morning Glories*
 Grow .... 10.00 - 15.00

THE FIVE BREEZES:
 Bluebird 8590 *Sweet Louise* .... 15.00 - 20.00
  8614 *My Buddy Blues* .... 15.00 - 20.00
  8679 *Swingin' The Blues* .... 15.00 - 20.00
  8710 *Just A Jitterbug* .... 15.00 - 20.00

FIVE JINKS:
 Bluebird 6857 *I'm Moaning All Day For You* .... 10.00 - 15.00
  6905 *Cushion Foot* .... 10.00 - 15.00
  6951 *There Goes My Headache* .... 10.00 - 15.00

FIVE ROCQUETTES:

Decca 7848 *Dearie* ....   -

FIVE SCAMPS:
 Columbia (most issues) .... 4.00 - 7.00

THE FIVE SHARPS:
 Jubilee 5104 *Stormy Weather/Sleepy Cowboy*
 (Almost legendary amoung Rhythm & Blues
 collectors, this record was reportedly sold at
 auction for over $3,800.00. Only two or three
 copies are known, despite the seemingly
 inordinate publicity given this record over the
 years) .... Rare -

THE FLAMINGOS:
 Parrot 811 *I Really Don't Want To Know* .... 50.00 - 75.00

NAPOLEON FLETCHER:
 Bluebird 5383 *She Showed It All* ....100.00 - 150.00

NELLIE FLORENCE:
 Columbia 14342-D *Jacksonville Blues* .... 50.00 - 75.00

THE FLORIDA KID:
 Bluebird 8589 *Hitler Blues* .... 10.00 - 15.00
  8625 *Lazy Mule Blues* .... 10.00 - 15.00
  8680 *Back Log Blues* .... 10.00 - 15.00
  8743 *That's All Right Baby* .... 10.00 - 15.00

ELL-ZEE FLOYD:
 Brunswick 7181 *Snow Bound And Blues* .... 90.00 - 130.00

FLYIN' LINDBURG:
 Decca 7066 *No Good Woman Blues* .... 30.00 - 40.00

A.C. FOREHAND:
 Victor 20547 *Mother's Prayer* .... 50.00 - 75.00

BLIND MAMIE FOREHAND:
 Victor 20574 *Honey In The Rock* .... 80.00 - 120.00

FOREST CITY JOE:
 Aristocrat 3101 *Memory of Sonny Boy* .... 40.00 - 60.00

DESSA FOSTER & HOWLING SMITH:
 Melotone 12117 *Tell It To The Judge* .... 35.00 - 50.00

EVELYN FOSTER:
 Champion 15569 *Park No More Mama Blues* ...200.00 - 300.00
  15590 *Beating Blues* ....150.00 - 250.00

JIM FOSTER:
 Champion 15301 *Riverside Blues* ....175.00 - 250.00
  15320 *The Jail House Blues* ....175.00 - 250.00
  15359 *Pork Chop Blues* ....200.00 - 300.00
  15397 *Dark Cloudy Blues* ....175.00 - 250.00
  15453 *It Won't Be Long* ....200.00 - 300.00
  15472 *Hesitation Blues* ....200.00 - 300.00
 Silvertone 5127 *Yellow Dog Blues* ....175.00 - 250.00
  5131 *Do That Thing* ....175.00 - 250.00
  5172 *I Want To Be Like Jesus In My Heart* ...200.00 - 300.00
 Superior 330 *Pork Chop Blues* ....200.00 - Up
  350 *Devil In The Lions Den* ....200.00 - Up

 369 *Dark Cloudy Blues* ....200.00 - Up

LEROY FOSTER & MUDDY WATERS:
 Aristocrat 1234 *Locked Out Boogie* .... 25.00 - 40.00

RUDY FOSTER:
 Paramount 12981 *Corn Trimmer Blues* ....200.00 - 300.00

FOUR BLACKAMOORS:
 Decca 7850 *Break It Up Charlie* .... 7.00 - 10.00
  8512 *Romance in the Dark* .... 7.00 - 10.00

THE FOUR BLUEJACKETS:
 Mercury 8017 *Baby Baby Please Come Home* ... 5.00 - 8.00

THE FOUR BLUES:
 DeLuxe 1002 *The Things You Want Most Of All* .. 5.00 - 8.00

    1004 *Blues Can Jump* . . . . 5.00 - 8.00

4 DEEP TONES:
    Coral 65061 *Just In Case You Change Your Mind*   8.00 - 12.00
    65062 *The Night You Said Goodbye* . . . . 8.00 - 12.00

THE FOUR DOTS:
    Dot 1043 *My Dear* . . . . 7.00 - 10.00

FOUR HARMONY KINGS:
    Black Swan 2016 *Ain't It A Shame* . . . . 15.00 - 20.00

FOUR PODS OF PEPPER:
    Brunswick 7103 *Ain't Got No Mama Now* . . . . . . 30.00 - 50.00

THE FOUR ROCKETS:
    Aladdin 3007 *Travelin' Light* . . . . 8.00 - 12.00

THE FOUR SOUTHERNERS:
    Decca 7291 *Dan The Back Door Man* . . . . 5.00 - 8.00

FOUR SOUTHERN SINGERS:
    Bluebird 8392 *Old Man Harlem* . . . . 10.00 - 15.00
    Victor 24262 *Mammy Lou* . . . . 15.00 - 20.00
    24328 *Hamebone Am Sweet* . . . . 15.00 - 20.00

JOHN D. FOX:
    Gennett 6352 *The Worried Man Blues* . . . . .200.00 - 300.00
    Superior 389 *The Worried Man Blues* . . . . .200.00 - Up

ELI FRAMER:
    Victor 23409 *Framer's Blues* . . . . .250.00 - 400.00

FRANKIE AND CLARA:
    Paramount 13010 *Frankie and Clara* . . . . .100.00 - 150.00

BUCK FRANKLIN:
    Victor 23310 *Crooked World Blues* . . . . 75.00 - 100.00

EMERY FRANKLIN:
    Cava-Tone 251 *Lonesome Day* . . . . 10.00 - 15.00

TINY FRANKLIN:
    Gennett 5345 *Shorty George Blues* . . . . 40.00 - 60.00
    5346 *Up The Country Blues* . . . . 40.00 - 60.00
    Silvertone 4049 *Houston Blues* . . . . 40.00 - 60.00
    4050 *Shorty George Blues* . . . . 40.00 - 60.00

CALVIN FRAZIER:
    Alben 106 *Sweet Lucy (Drinking Woman)* . . . . -

FREEZONE:
    Paramount 12803 *Indian Squaw Blues* . . . . .150.00 - 250.00

JOE (PAPOOSE) FRITZ:
    Modern 750 *Wrong Doing Woman* . . . . 7.00 - 10.00
    Peacock 1606 *Real Fine Girl* . . . . 7.00 - 10.00
    Sittin' In With 559 *Please Get Off My Mind* . . . . 7.00 - 10.00
    574 *I'm So Sorry* . . . . 7.00 - 10.00
    584 *Cool Cool Baby Blues* . . . . 7.00 - 10.00
    591 *Lady Bear Boogie* . . . . 7.00 - 10.00
    602 *Please, My Darling* . . . . 7.00 - 10.00

BLIND BOY FULLER:
    Titles, issued contemporaneously on Banner, Conqueror, Melotone, Oriole, Perfect, Romeo, Vocalion: *Ain't It A Crying Shame?; Babe, You Got To Do Better; Baby, I Don't Have To Worry; Baby You Gotta Change Your Mind; Big Red Blues; Black And Tan; Boots And Shoes; Careless Love; Cat Man Blues; Death Valley; Evil Hearted Woman; Homesick And Lonesome Blues; Hungry Calf Blues; If You Don't Give Me What I Want; I'm A Rattlesnakin' Daddy; I'm Climbin' On Top Of The Hill; I'm Going To Move; Let Me Squeeze Your Lemon; Log Cabin Blues; Looking For My Woman; Mama Let Me Lay It On You; Mamie; Mistreater, You're Going To Be Sorry; Mojo Hidin' Woman; My Baby Don't Mean Me No Good; My Best Gal Gonna Leave Me; My Brownskin Sugar Plum; New Louise, Louise Blues; New Oh Red; Rag, Mama Rag; Shaggy Like A Bear; She's Funny That Way; Somebody's Been Playing With That Thing; Snake Woman Blues; Stealing Bo-Hog; Sweet Honey Hole; Throw You Yas Yas Back In Jail; Tom Cat Blues; Truckin' My Blues Away; Truckin' My Blues Away-No. 2; Untrue Blues; Walking My*

Troubles Away, When You Gal Picks Up And Leaves; Wires All Down; Worried And Evil Man Blues . . . . 10.00 - 20.00
    Conqueror 9038, 9075, 9076, 9157, 9158, 9171, 9202, 9280, 9281, 9310, 9311, 9344, 9373, 9374, 9376, 9377, 9580, 9757, 9758 . . . . 5.00 - 10.00
    Decca 7330, 7878, 7892, 7899, 7903 . . . . 5.00 - 10.00
    Okeh 05657, 05712, 05756, 05685, 05933, 06231   5.00 - 8.00
    Vocalion 04054, 04106, 04137, 04175, 04237, 04343, 04391, 04456, 04519, 04557, 04603, 04675 . . . . 8.00 - 12.00
    04732, 04782, 04843, 04897, 05030, 05083, 05150, 05218, 05273, 05324, 05476, 05527, 05540 . . . . 7.00 - 10.00

ROCKY FULLER:
    Checker 753 *Soon One Morning* . . . . 10.00 - 15.00*

LOWELL FULSON/FULSOM (WITH GUITAR/ORCHESTRA):
    Aladdin 3088, 3104 . . . . 7.00 - 10.00
    Big Town 1068, 1070, 1071, 1072, 1074. 1077 . . . . 5.00 - 10.00
    Down Beat 116, 119, 120, 121 . . . . 5.00 - 10.00
    Down Town 2002, 2021 . . . . 8.00 - 12.00
    Gilt Edge 5041, 5043 . . . . 8.00 - 12.00
    RPM 305 . . . . 8.00 - 12.00
    Scotty's 101 *Scotty's Blues* . . . . 8.00 - 12.00
    SwingTime 110, 111, 112, 113, 114, 115, 116, 117, 119, 120, 121, 122, 123, 133, 134, 167, 196, 197, 201, 202, 203, 219, 220, 226, 227, 230, 231, 237, 243, 272, 295, 301, 308, 315, 320, 325, 330, 335, 338 . . . . 4.00 - 8.00*
    Trilon 185, 186, 192, 193 . . . . 5.00 - 10.00

BOB GADDY & HIS ALLEY CATS:
    Jackson 2303 *Bicycle Boogie* . . . . 5.00 - 8.00*
    Jax 308 *Little Girl's Boogie* . . . . 5.00 - 8.00*

(LITTLE) BILL GAITHER (LEROY'S BUDDY):
    Decca 7141 *Georgia Woman Stomp* . . . . 10.00 - 15.00
    7625 *I Got Your Water On* . . . . 8.00 - 12.00
    Okeh 05655, 05714, 05770, 05824, 06044, 06092, 06128, 06164, 06208, 06561, 06659 . . . 5.00 - 10.00

(PVT.) CECIL GANT (& HIS TRIO):
    Bullet 250, 255, 256, 257, 264, 265, 272, 280, 289, 299, 300, 313, 320 . . . . 3.00 - 6.00
    Decca 48171, 48185, 48190, 48200, 48212, 48231, 48249 . . . . 3.00 - 6.00
    4 Star 1176, 1284, 1339, 1377, 1452, 1526, 1561, 1584, 1606 . . . . 3.00 - 6.00
    Gilt-Edge 501, 502, 503, 504, 505, 506, 508, 509, 510, 511, 512, 513, 514, 515, 516, 517, 518, 519, 525, 534 . . . . 4.00 - 8.00

HATTIE GARLAND:
    Black Patti 8005 *Strange Woman's Dream* . . . . . .150.00 - 200.00

CLARENCE ("BON TON") GARLOW (& HIS GUITAR/ORCHESTRA):
    Aladdin 3179 *New Bon Ton Roula* . . . . 4.00 - 8.00*
    3225 *I'm Hurt* . . . . 4.00 - 8.00*
    Feature 1000 *New Bon Ton Roula* . . . . 10.00 - 15.00
    Lyric 100 *Louisiana Blues* . . . . 10.00 - 15.00
    101 *Wrong Doing Woman* . . . . 10.00 - 15.00
    Macy's 5001 *She's So Fine* . . . . 10.00 - 15.00
    5002 *Bon Ton Roula* . . . . 10.00 - 15.00

CORA GARNER:
    Columbia 14659-D *Wouldn't Stop Doing It* . . . . . 35.00 - 50.00

BOB GEDDINS (& HIS CAVALIERS):
    Cavatone 5, 103 . . . . 6.00 - 12.00
    Trilon 1058 *Irma Jean* . . . . 6.00 - 12.00

GEORGIA BILL:
    Okeh 8924 *Georgia Rag* . . . . .200.00 - 300.00
    8936 *Stomp Down Rider* . . . . .200.00 - 300.00

THE GEORGIA BROWNS:
    Titles, issued contemporaneously on Banner, Melotone, Oriole, Perfect, Romeo: *Decatur*

Street 81; It Must Have Been Her; Tampa
Strut; Who Stole De Lock? . . . . 40.00 - 60.00

GEORGIA COTTON PICKERS:
Columbia 14577-D *Diddle-Da-Diddle* . . . . .100.00 - 150.00
14594-D *She Looks So Good* . . . . .100.00 - 150.00

GEORGIA PINE BOY:
Champion 50009 *One In A Hundred* . . . . 25.00 - 40.00
50041 *Look Who's Coming Down The Road* . . . 25.00 - 40.00
50057 *What's The Matter With You* . . . . 25.00 - 40.00
Decca 7822 *Please Baby* . . . . 20.00 - 30.00

GEORGIA SLIM:
Titles, issued contemporaneously on Banner,
Melotone, Oriole, Perfect, Romeo: *Evil
Hearted Woman; I've Been Mistreated; New
Root Man Blues; Ocean Wide Blues;
Separatin' Blues; Sweet Woman Blues* . . . . 40.00 - 60.00

GEORGIA TOM:
Titles, issued contemporaneously on Banner,
Jewel, Melotone, Oriole, Perfect, Romeo:
*Don't Leave Me Here; Don't Mean To Mistreat
You; The Duck's Yas Yas Yas; Mama's Leaving
Town; My Texas Blues; Pig Meat Strut; Six
Shooter Blues; You Got Me In This Mess* . . . . . 50.00 - 75.00
Champion 16237 *Been Mistreated Blues* . . . . . . .150.00 - 250.00
16360 *Don't Leave Me Blues* . . . . .150.00 - 250.00
Decca 7362 *Levee Bound Blues* . . . . 10.00 - 15.00
Gennett 6919 *My Texas Blues* . . . . .125.00 - 175.00
6933 *Suicide Blues* . . . . .125.00 - 175.00
7008 *Pig Meat Blues* . . . . .125.00 - 175.00
7041 *Rollin' Mill Stomp* . . . . .125.00 - 175.00
7130 *Six Shooter Blues* . . . . .150.00 - 250.00
7190 *Dark Hour Blues* . . . . .150.00 - 250.00
Supertone 9506 *My Texas Blues* . . . . 100.00 - 150.00
9507 *Pig Meat Blues* . . . . .100.00 - 150.00
9508 *Eagle Ridin' Papa* . . . . .100.00 - 150.00
9512 *Rollin' Mill Stomp* . . . . .100.00 - 150.00
9647 *Second-Hand Woman Blues* . . . . .100.00 - 150.00
Vocalion 1216 *Grievin' Me Blues* . . . . 30.00 - 40.00
1246 *Lonesome Man Blues* . . . . 75.00 - 100.00
1282 *If You Want Me To Love You* . . . . 75.00 - 100.00
1685 *Don't Leave Me Here* . . . . 75.00 - 100.00

GEORGIA TOM & JANE LUCAS:
Champion 16171 *Terrible Operation Blues* . . . . . .150.00 - 200.00
16215 *What's That I Smell* . . . . .150.00 - 200.00
16289 *Double Trouble Blues* . . . . .150.00 - 200.00
50015 *Terrible Operation Blues* . . . . 30.00 - 50.00
Decca 7259 *Terrible Operation Blues* . . . . 20.00 - 30.00

GEORGIA TOM & HANNAH MAY:
Titles, issued contemporaneously on Oriole
(8033, 8034, 8041), Perfect (169, 170, 171),
Romeo (5033, 5034, 5041): *Come On Mama;
It's Been So Long; Rent Man Blues; Terrible
Operation Blues; What's That I Smell* . . . . 50.00 - 75.00
Same Titles on Banner, Melotone; and on Oriole
Perfect, Romeo (different numbers than
above): . . . . 50.00 - 75.00

**GEORGIA TOM & TAMPA RED (AND
FRANKIE JAXON) (THE BLACK HILL
BILLIES):)**
Vocalion 1246 *Long Ago Blues* . . . . 75.00 - 100.00
1286 *Pat That Bread* . . . . .100.00 - 150.00
1450 *Kunjine Baby* . . . . .100.00 - 150.00

CLIFFORD GIBSON:
Bluebird 5110 *Jive Me Blues* . . . . 75.00 - 100.00
Paramount 12866 *Tired Of Being Mistreated* . . . .100.00 - 150.00
12923 *Stop Your Rambling* . . . . .150.00 - 200.00
QRS 7079 *Tired Of Being Mistreated* . . . . .100.00 - 150.00
7082 *No No Blues* . . . . .100.00 - 150.00
7083 *Stop Your Rambling* . . . . .150.00 - 250.00
7087 *Whiskey Moan Blues* . . . . .150.00 - 250.00
7090 *Morgan Street Blues* . . . . .150.00 - 250.00
Victor 23255 *Old Timer Rider* . . . . .150.00 - 250.00

23290 *Railroad Man Blues* . . . . .150.00 - 250.00
V38562 *Ice And Snow Blues* . . . . .150.00 - 200.00
V38572 *Don't Put That Thing On Me* . . . . .150.00 - 200.00
V38577 *Levee Camp Moan* . . . . .150.00 - 250.00
V38590 *Bad Luck Dice* . . . . .150.00 - 250.00
V38612 *Society Blues* .150.00 - 250.00

BILL/JAZZ GILLUM (& HIS JAZZ BOYS):
Bluebird 5565 *Early In The Morning* . . . . 15.00 - 25.00
6409 *Jockey Blues* . . . . 10.00 - 15.00
6445 *Sarah Jane* . . . . 10.00 - 15.00
7253, 7341, 7524, 7563, 7615, 7718, 7769, 7821. 6.00 - 10.00
7986, 8027, 8016, 8189, 8221, 8257, 8287, 8505,
8529, 8739; 8778, 8816, 8846, 8872 . . . . 5.00 - 8.00
8943, 8975, 9004, 9034, 9042, 34-0707,
34-0709, 34-0730, 34-0741, 34-0747 . . . . 4.00 - 6.00
RCA Victor . . . . 3.00 - 5.00

BOYD GILMORE:
Modern 860 *Ramblin' On My Mind* . . . . 7.00 - 12.00
872 *Take A Little Walk With Me* . . . . 7.00 - 12.00

GENE GILMORE:
Decca 7661 *Brown Skin Woman* . . . . 8.00 - 12.00
7763 *The Natchez Fire* . . . . 10.00 - 15.00
7773 *She Got Something There* . . . . 10.00 - 15.00

THE GIRL FRIEND:
Varsity 6045 *Good And Hot* . . . . 10.00 - 15.00

GITFIDDLE JIM:
Victor 23268 *Paddlin' Blues* . . . . .250.00 - 400.00

RUBY GLAZE & HOT SHOT WILLIE:
Bluebird 5362 *Rollin' Mama Blues* . . . . 75.00 - 100.00
5391 *Lonesome Day Blues* . . . . 75.00 - 100.00
6007 *Rollin' Mama Blues* . . . . 25.00 - 40.00
Victor 23328 *Rollin' Mama Blues* . . . . .200.00 - 300.00
23353 *Lonesome Day Blues* . . . . .200.00 - 300.00

EMERY GLEN:
Columbia 14283-D *Two Ways To Texas* . . . . 50.00 - 75.00
14472-D *Back Door Blues* . . . . 50.00 - 75.00

LILLIAN GLINN:
Columbia 14275-D *Doggin' Me Blues* . . . . 35.00 - 50.00
14300-D *Come Home Daddy* . . . . 35.00 - 50.00
14315-D *Shake It Down* . . . . 40.00 - 60.00
14330-D *Best Friend Blues* . . . . 40.00 - 60.00
14360-D *Lost Letter Blues* . . . . 40.00 - 60.00
14421-D *Atlanta Blues* . . . . 40.00 - 60.00
14433-D *Black Man Blues* . . . . 40.00 - 60.00
14493-D *Don't Leave Me Daddy* . . . . 40.00 - 60.00
14519-D *Shreveport Blues* . . . . 40.00 - 60.00
14559-D *I Love That Thing* . . . . 50.00 - 75.00
14617-D *Cannon Ball Blues* . . . . 50.00 - 75.00

MAE GLOVER (AND JAMES PARKER):
Champion 16238 *My Man Blues* . . . . .100.00 - 150.00
16244 *Two Timin' Mama* . . . . .100.00 - 150.00
16268 *Hoboken Prison Blues* . . . . .100.00 - 150.00

16351 *Grasshopper Papa* . . . . .150.00 - 200.00
16408 *North Wind Blues* . . . . .150.00 - 200.00
Gennett 6948 *Pig Meat Mama* . . . . .150.00 - 200.00
6964 *Shake It Daddy* .150.00 - 200.00

GOLDEN LEAF QUARTET/QUARTETTE:
Brunswick 7032 *Alabama Camp Meetin'* . . . . 50.00 - 75.00
7050 *I Wouldn't Mind Dying* . . . . 25.00 - 40.00
7150 *Central Georgia Blues* . . . . 75.00 - 100.00
7169 *Let Me Ride* . . . . 75.00 - 100.00

7176 *Shake My Righteous Hand*	30.00 -	50.00
7221 *I Sing Because I'm Happy*	30.00 -	50.00
7228 *Let God Use You*	30.00 -	50.00

GOLDRUSH:

Jaxyson 6 *All My Money Is Gone*	10.00 -	15.00

FANNIE MAE GOOSBY:

Brunswick 7029 *Dirty Moaner Blues*	75.00 -	100.00
7030 *Fortune Teller Blues*	75.00 -	100.00
Okeh 8079 *Grievous Blues*	15.00 -	20.00
8095, 8121, 8128	10.00 -	20.00

JAMES/JIMMIE GORDON:

Bluebird 5661 *Neck Bone Blues*	30.00 -	50.00
Champion 50075 *Graveyard Blues*	15.00 -	25.00
Decca 7007 *Bed Springs Blues*	30.00 -	50.00
7020 *Yo Yo Mama Blues*	20.00 -	30.00
7099 *Bed Springs Blues No. 2*	15.00 -	20.00
Decca 7230, 7250, 7264, 7268, 7282 . . .	7.00 -	10.00
Decca (higher numbers)	5.00 -	10.00

ROSCOE GORDON:

Chess 1487 *Booted*	5.00 -	8.00*
Duke 109 *Too Many Women*	5.00 -	8.00*
Flip 227 *Weeping Blues*	10.00 -	15.00*
RPM 322 *Roscoe's Boogie*	5.00 -	10.00*
324 *Ouch, Pretty Baby*	5.00 -	10.00*
336 *Dime A Dozen*	5.00 -	10.00*
350 *No More Doggin'*	5.00 -	10.00*
365 *Two Kinds Of Women*	5.00 -	10.00*
Sun 227 *Weeping Blues*	15.00 -	20.00*

SLIM GORDON:

Vocalion 1743 *Leg Iron Blues*	75.00 -	100.00

GEORGIA GORHAM:

Black Swan 2017 *Broadway Blues*	20.00 -	35.00

GOSPEL CAMP MEETING SINGERS:

Vocalion 1283 *Come And Go To That Land*	75.00 -	100.00

GOSPEL MINNIE:

Decca 7063 *Let Me Ride*	25.00 -	40.00

EMMA GOVER:

Pathe-Actuelle 021006, 021060, 021061	7.00 -	10.00
Perfect 12065, 12073, 12074	7.00 -	10.00

JACK GOWDLOCK:

Victor 23419 *Rollin' Dough Blues*	250.00 -	Up

RUBY GOWDY:

Champion 15569 *Moanful Wailin' Blues*	200.00 -	300.00
15613 *Florida Flood Blues*	200.00 -	300.00
Champion 15635 *Breath And Britches Blues*	200.00 -	300.00
Gennett 6570 *Moanful Wailin' Blues*	250.00 -	400.00
6708 *Florida Flood Blues*	300.00 -	500.00

GRAND CENTRAL RED CAP QUARTET:

Columbia 14621-D *My Little Dixie Home*	30.00 -	50.00

(COOT) GRANT AND (KID WESLEY)/
(SOCKS/SOX) WILSON:

Titles, issued contemporaneously on Banner,		
Melotone, Oriole, Perfect, Romeo: *Do It*		
Again; Water Trough Blues	40.00 -	60.00
Cameo 9015 *Ducks*	25.00 -	50.00
Columbia 14637-D *You Can't Do That To Me* . . .	50.00 -	80.00
14649-D *Deceiving Man Blues*	50.00 -	80.00
Decca 7500 *Uncle Joe*	10.00 -	15.00
Okeh 8944 *Do Your Duty*	50.00 -	80.00
Paramount 12272 *Rock, Aunt Dinah, Rock*	75.00 -	100.00
12317 *Come On Coot Do That Thing*	100.00 -	150.00
12324 *You Dirty Mistreater*	100.00 -	150.00
12337 *Find Me At The Greasy Spoon*	100.00 -	150.00
12379 *Scoop It*	100.00 -	150.00
12831 *Big Trunk Blues*	75.00 -	100.00
12833 *Uncle Joe*	75.00 -	100.00
Pathe-Actuelle 7540 *Mama Didn't Do It*	25.00 -	50.00
Perfect 140 *Mama Didn't Do It*	25.00 -	50.00
QRS 7065 *Uncle Joe*	75.00 -	125.00
7085 *Big Trunk Blues*	75.00 -	125.00
7092 *Take It Right Back*	75.00 -	125.00
Romeo 819 *Ducks*	25.00 -	50.00

Vocalion 02799 *Whippin' The Wolf*	50.00 -	75.00
03121 *Do Your Duty*	25.00 -	40.00

LEE GRAVES:

Mercury 8214, 8222	5.00 -	8.00

(BLIND) ROOSEVELT GRAVES AND (HIS)
BROTHER:

Paramount 12820 *Guitar Boogie*	200.00 -	300.00
12859 *Bustin' The Jug*	200.00 -	300.00
12891 *Staggerin' Blues*	250.00 -	400.00
12913 *Happy Sunshine*	250.00 -	400.00
12961 *St. Louis Rambler Blues*	250.00 -	400.00
12974 *When I Lay My Burdens Down*	250.00 -	400.00

BETTY GRAY:

Titles, issued contemporaneously on Cameo,		
Lincoln, Romeo: *Loud And Wrong; Mean Old*		
Bed Bug Blues	10.00 -	15.00

CHRISTINA GRAY:

Okeh 8757 *The Reverend Is My Man*	50.00 -	75.00

GENEVA GRAY:

Okeh 8449 *Fortune Teller Blues*	35.00 -	50.00

BOY GREEN:

Regis 120 *A and B Blues*	10.00 -	15.00

L.M./LEE/LEOTHUS GREEN:

Bluebird 7353 *My Best Friend*	20.00 -	30.00
Decca 7016 *Memphis Fives*	30.00 -	50.00
7032 *Doctorin' Fool Blues*	30.00 -	50.00
7062 *Round The World Blues*	30.00 -	50.00
7346 *The Way I Feel*	20.00 -	30.00
7368 *Sealskin Black Woman*	20.00 -	30.00
7437 *Country Gal Blues*	20.00 -	30.00
Gennett 6934 *Pork Chop Stomp*	200.00 -	300.00
Paramount 12865 *Five Minute Blues*	150.00 -	200.00
Vocalion 1401 *Railroad Blues*	100.00 -	150.00
1422 *The Way I Feel Blues*	100.00 -	150.00
1441 *Little Eddie Jones*	100.00 -	150.00
1467 *Dud-Low Joe*	100.00 -	150.00
1485 *Death Bell Blues*	100.00 -	150.00
1501 *Bootleggin' My Jelly*	100.00 -	150.00
1510 *Wash Day And No Soap*	100.00 -	150.00
1533 *Gambling Man Blues*	100.00 -	150.00
1562 *Pork Chop Blues*	100.00 -	150.00
1566 *Train Number 14*	100.00 -	150.00
1648 *Five Minute Blues*	100.00 -	150.00

L.C. GREEN:

Dot 1103 *When The Sun Is Shining*	15.00 -	20.00
1128 *Little School Girl*	15.00 -	20.00
1147 *Little Machine*	15.00 -	20.00
Von 42 *Going Down To The River Blues*	20.00 -	30.00

LIL GREEN:

Bluebird	3.00 -	6.00

PORK CHOP GREEN:

Gennett 7116 *She Walks Like A Maltee Cat*	250.00 -	400.00

R. GREEN & TURNER:

J & M Fullbright 123 *Central Avenue Blues*	10.00 -	15.00

ROSA GREEN:

Oriole 263 *Barrel House Blues*	10.00 -	15.00
281 *The Basement Blues*	10.00 -	15.00

RUTH GREEN:

Okeh 8140 *Sad And Lonely Blues*	30.00 -	50.00

SADIE GREEN:

Oriole 716 *Ain't Much Good In The Best Of Men*		
Now Days	10.00 -	15.00
746 *St. Louis Blues*	10.00 -	15.00
771 *Nobody But My Baby Is Getting My Love* .	10.00 -	15.00
Pathe-Actuelle 7524 *Alley Man (Haul My Ashes)* .	35.00 -	50.00
Perfect 124 *Don't Wear Your Welcome Out*	35.00 -	50.00

SLIM GREEN:

Murray 501 *Tricky Woman Blues*	15.00 -	20.00

FLOYD GRIFFIN:

Supertone 9521 *Ocean Wave Blues*	125.00 -	175.00
9522 *You Broke My Heart Baby*	125.00 -	175.00
9523 *Back-Biter Blues*	125.00 -	175.00

9525 *Easy Papa*	125.00 -	175.00

MARIE GRIFFIN:

Paramount 13015 *Blue And Disgusted*	150.00 -	200.00

TOMMY GRIFFIN:

Bluebird 6696 *I'm Gonna Try That Meat*	25.00 -	35.00
6734 *Young Heifer Blues*	25.00 -	35.00
6756 *Dream Book Blues*	25.00 -	35.00
6793 *On My Way Blues*	25.00 -	35.00
6834 *Dying Sinner Blues—Part 2*	25.00 -	35.00
6872 *Mistreatin' Papa*	25.00 -	35.00
Bluebird 7179 *Hey Hey Blues*	15.00 -	20.00
7194 *Young Heifer Blues*	15.00 -	20.00
Vocalion 1479 *Bell Tolling Blues*	100.00 -	150.00
1507 *Mistreatment Blues*	100.00 -	150.00

MARIE GRINTER:

Buddy 8023 *Morning Dove Blues*	150.00 -	200.00
Gennett 3004 *Morning Dove Blues*	75.00 -	100.00
Gennett 6551 *Road House Blues*	200.00 -	300.00
6738 *St. Louis Man*	250.00 -	400.00
Okeh 8384 *East And West Blues*	75.00 -	100.00
Supertone 9304 *Road House Blues*	150.00 -	250.00
9530 *Charleston Blues*	100.00 -	150.00

BLIND ARTHUR GROOM & BRO.:

Paramount 12874 *Telephone To Glory*	150.00 -	250.00

THE GROOVY FIVE:

Groovy 103 *Wrong Love Blues*	7.00 -	10.00

THE GROOVY TRIO:

Groovy 101 *Too Late Baby*	7.00 -	10.00

HELEN GROSS:

Ajax 17036 *Haunted House Blues*	30.00 -	50.00
17037 *Hard Luck Blues*	30.00 -	50.00
17042 *I Wanna Jazz Some More*	30.00 -	50.00
17046 *Rockin' Chair Blues*	30.00 -	50.00
17049 *What'll I Do?*	30.00 -	50.00
17050 *Strange Man*	30.00 -	50.00
17051 *My Man Ain't Yo' Man*	30.00 -	50.00
17060 *Ticket Agent, Ease Your Window Down*	30.00 -	50.00
Ajax 17062 *Chicago Monkey Man Blues*	35.00 -	50.00
17071 *Neglected Blues*	35.00 -	50.00
17077 *If You Can't Ride Slow And Easy*	35.00 -	50.00
17082 *Conjure Man Blues*	35.00 -	50.00
17086 *Bitter Feelin' Blues*	35.00 -	50.00
17090 *Last Journey Blues*	35.00 -	50.00
17133 *Workin' Woman's Blues*	35.00 -	50.00

CREOLE GEORGE GUESNON:

Bluebird 6706 *Goodbye Good Luck To You*	25.00 -	40.00
Decca 7740, 7792	7.00 -	10.00

GUITAR SLIM:

Titles, issued contemporaneously on Banner, Melotone, Oriole, Perfect, Romeo: *Ain't It A Shame?, Katie May-Katie May*	40.00 -	60.00
Imperial 5278, 5310	4.00 -	7.00*
Specialty 482, 490, 527, 536, 542, 551, 557, 569	4.00 -	7.00*

GULF COAST QUARTET:

Columbia 14012-D *Alabama Blues*	20.00 -	30.00

ELDER J.J. HADLEY:

Paramount 12799 *Prayer Of Death*	200.00 -	300.00

JAMES HALL:

Vocalion 04231 *My Jivin' Woman*	10.00 -	15.00
04316 *Street Walkin' Woman*	10.00 -	15.00

HALLELUJAH JOE (& CONGREGATION):

Decca 7047 *If I Be Lifted Up*	20.00 -	30.00
7118 *The Great Love*	20.00 -	30.00
7302 *Twenty Minutes In Hell*	15.00 -	20.00
7802 *Highway 61*	15.00 -	20.00

HAM GRAVY:

Vocalion 03275 *Mama Don't Allow—No. 1*	15.00 -	20.00
03375 *Mama Don't Allow—No. 2*	15.00 -	20.00

"BEANS" HAMBONE & EL MORROW:

Victor 23280 *Beans*	200.00 -	300.00

GEORGE HAMILTON:

Champion 15726 *Atlanta Rag*	150.00 -	200.00

15756 *Givin' It Away*	150.00 -	200.00

HAMMIE AND SON:

Decca 7040 *Tennessee Worried Blues*	30.00 -	50.00

STICK HORSE HAMMOND:

Gotham 504 *Truck 'em On Down*	20.00 -	30.00
J.O.B. 100 *Gambling Man*	75.00 -	100.00
105 *Highway 51*	50.00 -	75.00
Royalty 906 *Too Late Baby*	50.00 -	75.00

R.T. HANEN:

Victor 23288 *Happy Days Blues*	200.00 -	300.00

GEORGE HANNAH:

Paramount 12786 *The Snitches Blues*	150.00 -	200.00
12788 *Gutter Man Blues*	100.00 -	150.00
13024 *Freakish Man Blues*	150.00 -	200.00
13048 *Alley Rat Blues*	150.00 -	200.00
Vocalion 1047 *Hurry Home Blues*	75.00 -	125.00

LANE HARDIN:

Bluebird 6242 *Hard Time Blues*	75.00 -	100.00

LUCIUS HARDY:

Paramount 12598 *Jelly Bean Man*	80.00 -	120.00

MATTIE HARDY:

Conqueror 9203 *Striped Ape Blues*	10.00 -	15.00
Vocalion 04660 *Striped Ape Blues*	10.00 -	15.00

TRILBY HARGENS:

Herwin 92012 *Goofer Dust Blues*	150.00 -	250.00

HARLEM STARS:

E & W 100 *All Right Baby*	15.00 -	25.00

HARMONICA FRANK:

Chess 1475 *Swamp Root*	15.00 -	25.00*
1494 *Howlin' Tomcat*	15.00 -	25.00*
Sun 205 *The Great Medical Menagerist*	50.00 -	75.00*

JOSIE HARLEY:

Paramount 12025 *2 A.M. Blues*	25.00 -	40.00

HARMONY HOUNDS:

Columbia 14119-D *Done Got De Blues*	25.00 -	40.00

HARRIS & HARRIS:

Victor 21285 *That Same Cat*	75.00 -	100.00
V38594 *Teasing Brown*	150.00 -	250.00

ALFONCY HARRIS:

Vocalion 02902 *All Alone Blues*	75.00 -	100.00
02971 *No Good Guy*	75.00 -	100.00
02996 *Absent Freight Train Blues*	75.00 -	100.00

BOB HARRIS; LITTLE BOBBY HARRIS:

Derby 770, 773	5.00 -	8.00
Jackson 2301 *Friendly Advice*	5.00 -	8.00
Par 1304 *Heavyweight Mama*	7.00 -	10.00

CLARENCE HARRIS:

Bluebird 8138 *Try My Whiskey Blues*	15.00 -	25.00

HELEN HARRIS:

Champion 15510 *You Just Can't Keep A Good Woman Down*	100.00 -	150.00
15529 *Butcher Shop Blues*	100.00 -	150.00

JAMES HARRIS:

Broadway 5061 *Forty-Four Blues*	150.00 -	200.00

JOHN HARRIS:

Victor 23284 *Prowling Wolf Blues*	200.00 -	300.00

MAGNOLIA HARRIS AND HOWLING SMITH:

Melotone 12077 *Mama's Quittin' and Leavin'*	75.00 -	100.00
Vocalion 1602 *Mama's Quittin' and Leavin'*	75.00 -	100.00

MARY HARRIS:

Champion 50045 *Happy New Year Blues*	20.00 -	30.00

MAXINE HARRIS:

Champion 15490 *Satisfied Blues*	100.00 -	150.00

OTIS HARRIS:

Columbia 14428-D *Waking Blues*	75.00 -	100.00

PEPPERMINT HARRIS:

Modern 936 *Black Cat Bone*	5.00 -	8.00
Sittin' In With 543, 554, 568, 576, 578, 587, 597, 612, 623, 638, 650	4.00 -	7.00

WILLIAM HARRIS:

Gennett 6306 *I'm Leavin' Town*	300.00 -	500.00

6661 *Bull Frog Blues*	300.00 -	500.00
6677 *Kitchen Range Blues*	300.00 -	600.00
6693 *Leavin' Here Blues*	300.00 -	600.00
6707 *Kansas City Blues*	300.00 -	600.00
6737 *I'm A Roamin' Gambler*	300.00 -	600.00
6752 *Electric Chair Blues*	300.00 -	600.00
6904 *Nothin' Right Blues*	300.00 -	600.00

WILLIE HARRIS:

Brunswick 7092 *West Side Blues*	150.00 -	200.00
7149 *Lonesome Midnight Dream*	150.00 -	250.00

SMOKEY/SMOKY HARRISON:

Paramount 12920 *Hop Head Blues*	150.00 -	200.00
12936 *St. Peter's Blues*	150.00 -	200.00
12984 *Mail Coach Blues*	150.00 -	200.00

HATTIE HART:

Victor 23273 *You Wouldn't, Would You, Papa?*	200.00 -	300.00
Vocalion 02821 *Coldest Stuff In Town*	100.00 -	150.00
02855 *I'm Missing That Thing*	100.00 -	150.00

HARUM SCARUMS:

Broadway 5097 *I'm The Lonesome One*	100.00 -	150.00
Crown 3324 *I'm The Lonesome One*	100.00 -	150.00
3358 *Where Did You Stay Last Night?*	100.00 -	150.00
Paramount 13054 *Alabama Scratch*	200.00 -	300.00
13104 *Come On In*	200.00 -	300.00

CLEO HARVES WITH LIGHTNING GUITAR:

Okla Tornado 105 *Skinny Woman Boogie*	8.00 -	12.00

WILLIE HATCHER:

Bluebird 8003 *They're Mean To Me*	15.00 -	20.00

BERT (SNAKE-ROOT) HATTON:

Vocalion 1101 *Down In Black Bottom*	75.00 -	100.00

BUDDY BOY HAWKINS:

Paramount 12475 *Number Three Blues*	100.00 -	150.00
12489 *Jailhouse Fire Blues*	100.00 -	150.00
12539 *Awful Fix Blues*	100.00 -	150.00
12558 *Yellow Woman Blues*	100.00 -	150.00

ROY HAWKINS:

Down Town 2018, 2020, 2024, 2025, 2026	5.00 -	8.00
Modern	3.00 -	5.00

WALTER HAWKINS:

Paramount 12802 *Voice Throwin' Blues*	150.00 -	200.00
12814 *A Rag Blues*	150.00 -	200.00

BILL HAYES & HIS BAND/ORCHESTRA:

Jade 211 *I'm Just Another Fool*	5.00 -	8.00
Sittin' In With 551, 560	5.00 -	8.00

DADDY MOON HAYES & HIS BOYS:

Gennett 6122 *Gang Of Brown Skin Women*	250.00 -	400.00
Champion 15283 *Two Little Tommie Blues*	200.00 -	300.00

BLIND ROGER HAYS:

Brunswick 7047 *On My Way To Heaven*	150.00 -	200.00

EDDIE HEAD:

Columbia 14548-D *Down On Me*	75.00 -	100.00
14589-D *Within My Mind*	75.00 -	100.00

JOHNNIE HEAD:

Paramount 12628 *Fare Thee Blues*	100.00 -	150.00

(BIG) BERTHA HENDERSON:

Chance 1143 *Rock, Daddy, Rock*	10.00 -	15.00*
Paramount 12645 *So Sorry Blues*	100.00 -	150.00
12655 *Lead Hearted Blues*	100.00 -	150.00
12697 *Leavin' Gal Blues*	100.00 -	150.00

KATHERINE HENDERSON:

Broadway 5034 *West End Blues*	150.00 -	200.00
Paramount 12840 *If You Like Me*	200.00 -	300.00
QRS 7024 *West End Blues*	150.00 -	200.00
7032 *Lonesome Lovesick Blues*	200.00 -	300.00
7041 *If You Like Me*	200.00 -	300.00
7054 *What Can You Do Without Me?*	200.00 -	300.00

LEROY HENDERSON:

Vocalion 02979 *Good Scuffler Blues*	30.00 -	50.00
03020 *Deep Sea Diver*	30.00 -	50.00

ROSA HENDERSON:

Ajax 17021 *When You Walked Out*	30.00 -	40.00
17049 *I Can't Get The One I Want*	30.00 -	50.00

17055 *Strut Yo' Puddy*	30.00 -	50.00
17060 *Hard Hearted Hannah*	30.00 -	50.00
17069 *Memphis Bound*	30.00 -	50.00
17081 *Twelfth Street Blues*	30.00 -	50.00
17116 *It Takes a Two-Time Papa*	30.00 -	50.00
Banner 1534 *Everything My Sweetie Does (Pleases Me)*	10.00 -	15.00
Brunswick 2589 *I'm A Good Gal*	10.00 -	15.00
2612 *Cleaning House Blues*	10.00 -	15.00
Columbia A-3958 *I Need You*	10.00 -	15.00
Columbia 14130-D *Let's Talk About My Sweetie*	30.00 -	50.00
14627-D *Doggone Blues*	75.00 -	100.00
Edison 51476 *Undertakers Blues*	75.00 -	100.00
51478 *Don't Advertise Your Man*	75.00 -	100.00
Emerson 10747 *West Indies Blues*	10.00 -	15.00
10763 *Four-Flushin' Papa*	20.00 -	30.00
Marathon 045 (7-inch) *Shake It Down.* Rare		
Pathe-Actuelle 7519 *Git Goin'*	20.00 -	30.00
7522 *Slow Up Papa*	20.00 -	30.00
7529 *Black Snake Moan*	35.00 -	50.00
7534 *I'm Saving It All For You*	35.00 -	50.00
7535 *Dyin' Crap Shooters Blues*	35.00 -	50.00
7538 *Police Blues*	35.00 -	50.00
032021 *Every Day Blues*	20.00 -	30.00
Perfect 119 *Some Day You'll Come Back To Me*	20.00 -	30.00
122 *Hock Shop Blues*	20.00 -	30.00
129 *Fortune Teller Blues*	35.00 -	50.00
134 *Gay Catin' Daddy*	35.00 -	50.00
135 *Dyin' Crap Shooters Blues*	35.00 -	50.00
138 *Police Blues*	35.00 -	50.00
Regal 9831 *Everything My Sweetie Does (Pleases Me)*	10.00 -	15.00
Victor 19084, 19157	5.00 -	10.00
Victor 19124 *Midnight Blues*	10.00 -	15.00
Vocalion 1011 *Fulton Street Blues*	100.00 -	200.00
1021 *Chicago Policeman Blues*	75.00 -	100.00
1025 *Daddy, Come Back*	75.00 -	100.00
1038 *Rough House Blues*	75.00 -	100.00
1177 *Get It Fixed*	75.00 -	100.00
14635 *Down South Blues*	8.00 -	12.00
14652 *So Long To You And The Blues*	8.00 -	12.00
14682 *Every Woman's Blues*	10.00 -	15.00
14708 *I Want My Sweet Daddy Now*	10.00 -	15.00
14770 *Do Right Blues*	15.00 -	20.00
14795 *My Papa Doesn't Two-Time No Time*	10.00 -	15.00
14825 *Barbadoes Blues*	15.00 -	20.00
14831 *Barrel House Blues*	10.00 -	15.00
14832 *Chicago Monkey Man Blues*	10.00 -	15.00
14995 *Penitentiary Bound Blues*	15.00 -	20.00
15011 *Low Down Daddy*	25.00 -	40.00
15044 *Get It Fixed*	25.00 -	40.00
15215 *And I Dont Mean If*	25.00 -	40.00

CURTIS HENRY:

Bluebird 6845 *G-Man Blues*	15.00 -	20.00
6888 *The Worried Blues*	15.00 -	20.00

HOUND HEAD HENRY:

Vocalion 1208 *Freight Train Special*	100.00 -	150.00
1209 *Hound Head Blues*	100.00 -	150.00
1210 *Laughin' Blues*	100.00 -	150.00
1288 *My Silver Dollar Mama*	100.00 -	150.00

LENA HENRY:

Vocalion 14873, 14910	8.00 -	12.00
14902 *Sinful Blues*	20.00 -	30.00

ROBERT HENRY:

King 4624 *Miss Anna B*	30.00 -	50.00*
4646 *Old Battle Ax*	30.00 -	50.00*

"SLOPPY" HENRY:

Okeh 8178 *Tom Cat Rag*	50.00 -	75.00
8305 *Traveling Blues*	35.00 -	50.00
8334 *Goose-Pecked Man*	35.00 -	50.00
8368 *Foggy Morning Blues*	35.00 -	50.00
8630 *Canned Heat Blues*	75.00 -	100.00

8683 *Hobo Blues*		75.00	-	100.00
8805 *Say I Do It*		75.00	-	100.00
8845 *Royal Palm Special Blues*		75.00	-	100.00

LAURA HENTON:

Brunswick 7129 *I Can Tell The World About This*	80.00	-	120.00
7144 *Plenty Good Room In My Father's Kingdom*	80.00	-	120.00
Columbia 14388-D *He's Coming Soon*	50.00	-	80.00

CLARA HERRING:

Gennett 6591 *Beating Blues*	200.00	-	300.00

EDNA HICKS:

Ajax 17006 *Just Thinkin'*	35.00	-	50.00
17008 *Mistreatin' Daddy*	25.00	-	40.00
17012 *Kind Lovin' Blues*	25.00	-	40.00
Brunswick 2463 *Gulf Coast Blues*	7.00	-	10.00
Columbia 14001-D *No Name Blues*	10.00	-	15.00
Gennett 5195 *Bleeding Hearted Blues*	10.00	-	15.00
5234 *Tin Roof Blues*	10.00	-	15.00
Paramount 12023 *Hard Luck Blues*	25.00	-	40.00
Paramount 12024 *Mistreatin' Daddy*	20.00	-	30.00
12069 *Uncle Sam Blues*	25.00	-	40.00
12089 *Cemetery Blues*	25.00	-	40.00
12090 *Where Can That Somebody Be?*	25.00	-	40.00
12204 *Down On The Levee Blues*	100.00	-	150.00
Vocalion 14650 *You've Got Everything*	15.00	-	20.00
14659 *Wicked Dirty Fives*	10.00	-	15.00

MINNIE HICKS:

Broadway 5099 *Sweet Rider*	100.00	-	150.00
Melotone 12549 *Jim Jam Blues*	100.00	-	150.00

ROBERT HICKS:

Columbia 14231-D *When The Saints Go Marching In*	30.00	-	50.00

ROBERT AND CHARLIE HICKS:

Columbia 14531-D *Darktown Gamblin'*	75.00	-	100.00

BILLY HIGGINS:

Ajax 17125 *Levee Blues*	25.00	-	40.00
17135 *Ain't Trustin' Nobody No More*	25.00	-	40.00
Regal 9749 *Sweet Mandy*	10.00	-	15.00

BERTHA "CHIPPIE" HILL:

Okeh 8273 *Low Land Blues*	150.00	-	200.00
8312 *Trouble In Mind*	80.00	-	120.00
8339 *Lonesome, All Alone And Blue*	100.00	-	150.00
8367 *Panama Limited Blues*	100.00	-	150.00
8420 *Pratt City Blues*	100.00	-	150.00
8437 *Mess, Katie, Mess*	100.00	-	150.00
8453 *Lovesick Blues*	100.00	-	150.00
8473 *Do Dirty Blues*	100.00	-	150.00
Vocalion 1224 *Weary Money Blues*	75.00	-	100.00
1248 *Hangman Blues*	150.00	-	200.00
1264 *Hard Time Blues*	75.00	-	100.00
1406 *Pratt City Blues*	75.00	-	100.00

CHARLIE HILL:

Gennett 6904 *Papa Charlie Hill Blues*	300.00	-	600.00

CHIPPIE HILL (See BERTHA "CHIPPIE" HILL)

HENRY HILL:

Federal 12030, 12037, 12044, 12083	4.00	-	7.00*

KING SOLOMON HILL:

Champion 50022 *Tell Me Baby*	100.00	-	150.00
Crown 3325 *Whoopee Blues*	75.00	-	100.00
Paramount 13116 *Whoopee Blues*	250.00	-	400.00
13125 *My Buddy Blind Papa Lemon*	250.00	-	500.00
13129 *The Gone Dead Train*	250.00	-	400.00

ROBERT HILL:

Bluebird 6680 *It Is So Good*	20.00	-	30.00
6706 *Pal, How I Miss You Tonight*	25.00	-	40.00
6716 *Just Smilin'*	20.00	-	30.00
6741 *Tell Me What's Wrong With You*	20.00	-	30.00
6776 *Lumber-Yard Blues*	20.00	-	30.00
6795 *G Blues*	20.00	-	30.00
6963 *You Gonna Look Like A Monkey*	15.00	-	25.00

RAYMOND HILL:

Sun 204 *Bourbon Street Jump*	40.00	-	60.00

SAM HILL FROM LOUISVILLE:

Brunswick 7195 *Near The End*	75.00	-	100.00
7216 *Things 'Bout Coming My Way*	75.00	-	100.00

SAMMY HILL:

Victor V38588 *Needin' My Woman Blues*	150.00	-	250.00

OTIS HINTON:

Timely 1003 *Walkin' Down Hill*	7.00	-	12.00*

MATTIE HITE:

Bell 263 *An Awful Moanin' Blues*	8.00	-	12.00
273 *Do Right Blues*	8.00	-	12.00
Columbia 14503-D *Texas Twist*	50.00	-	75.00

CHA CHA HOGAN:

Talent 810 *My Walking Baby*	25.00	-	35.00

WALTER HOGAN:

Herwin 93011 *The Duck's Yas Yas*	150.00	-	250.00

ANDREW HOGG:

Crown 122 *Dark Clouds*	7.00	-	10.00*
Decca 7303 *Family Trouble Blues*	15.00	-	20.00
Exclusive 89 *He Knows How Much We Can Bear*	5.00	-	8.00

JOHN HOGG:

Mercury 8230 *Got A Mean Woman*	7.00	-	10.00
Octive 705, 706	10.00	-	15.00

SMOKEY/SMOKY HOGG:

Bullett 285 *Hard Times*	8.00	-	12.00
Colony 103 *In This World Alone*	10.00	-	15.00
Fidelity 3007 *Crawdad*	8.00	-	12.00
Imperial 5106, 5111	7.00	-	10.00
Independent 300 *Misery Blues*	10.00	-	15.00
Jade 210, 212	7.00	-	10.00
Macy's 5003 *You Gotta Go*	15.00	-	20.00
5008 *Change Your Ways*	15.00	-	20.00
Mercury 8228, 8235	5.00	-	8.00
Ray's 33 *Penitentiary Blues*	10.00	-	15.00
35 *I Used To Be Rich*	10.00	-	15.00
Sittin' In With	5.00	-	10.00
Specialty	5.00	-	8.00
Top Hat 1023 *Baby Shake Your Leg*	10.00	-	15.00

THE HOKUM BOYS (WITH PIANO & GUITAR); THE HOKUM BOYS AND JANE LUCAS:

Broadway 5060 *It's All Worn Out*	50.00	-	75.00
5078 *Cut That Out*	50.00	-	75.00
Brunswick 7070 *You Ain't Livin' Right*	75.00	-	100.00
Champion 16081 *Pig Meat Strut*	150.00	-	250.00
16237 *Hip Shakin' Strut*	150.00	-	250.00
16360 *Hokum Stomp*	150.00	-	250.00
Okeh 8747 *Gin Mill Blues*	100.00	-	150.00
8788 *That's My Business*	100.00	-	150.00
Paramount 12714 *Selling That Stuff*	50.00	-	75.00
12746 *Pat-A-Foot Blues*	100.00	-	150.00
12777 *Better Cut That Out*	75.00	-	100.00
12778 *Selling That Stuff*	75.00	-	125.00
12796 *It's All Worn Out*	50.00	-	80.00
12811 *Hokum Blues*	75.00	-	100.00
12821 *Ain't Goin' That Way*	100.00	-	150.00
12858 *Went To His Head*	100.00	-	150.00
12882 *I Was Afraid Of That*	100.00	-	150.00
12897 *Let Me Have It*	100.00	-	150.00

12919 *Gambler's Blues—No. 2*	100.00 -	150.00
12935 *The Folks Down Stairs*	100.00 -	150.00
Savoy 502 *Hip Shakin' Strut*	200.00 -	400.00

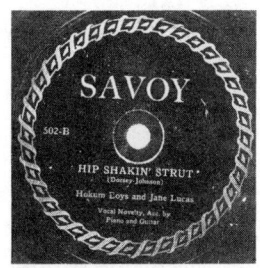

Vocalion 03156 *Caught Us Doing It*	15.00 -	25.00
03232 *Keep Your Mind On It*	15.00 -	25.00
03265 *Nancy Jane*	15.00 -	25.00
03386 *Every Man For Himself*	15.00 -	25.00
03406 *Something Good*	15.00 -	25.00
03463 *Georgia Mule*	15.00 -	25.00
03516 *Just Diddling Around*	15.00 -	25.00
03572 *You Got Your Ribs Out Of Pawn*	15.00 -	25.00

ROSA HOLLEY:
Vocalion 1179 *Lookin' For The Blues*	75.00 -	125.00

TONY HOLLINS:
Okeh 06351, 06523, 06605	8.00 -	12.00

THE HOLLYWOOD FOUR FLAMES:
Recorded In Hollywood 164 *I'll Always Be A Fool*	8.00 -	12.00*
165 *Young Girl*	8.00 -	12.00*

HAPPY HOLMES:
Victor 21075 *Solid Ground*	20.00 -	30.00

SONNY BOY HOLMES:
Recorded in Hollywood 223 *Walking And Crying Blues*	10.00 -	15.00
225 *I Got Them Blues*	10.00 -	15.00

SPEEDY HOLMES:
Supertone 9364 *Mister Mary Blues*	75.00 -	125.00

WINSTON HOLMES AND CHARLIE TURNER:
Paramount 12798 *Rounders Lament*	100.00 -	150.00
12815 *Skinner*	100.00 -	150.00

WRIGHT HOLMES:
Gotham 508 *Drove Home Blues*	15.00 -	20.00
511 *Quinsella*	15.00 -	20.00
Milton 5221 *Alley Special*	15.00 -	20.00

THE HOME WRECKERS:
Bluebird 5341 *Home Wreckin' Blues*	100.00 -	150.00
Sunrise 3422 *Fence Breakin' Blues*	100.00 -	200.00

THE HONEY DRIPPER (ROOSEVELT SYKES):
Decca 7160, 7164, 7173. 7188, 7197, 7252	7.00 -	10.00
7324 and higher numbers	5.00 -	8.00

EARL HOOKER:
King 4600 *Race Track*	7.00 -	10.00*
Rockin' 519 *On The Hook*	7.00 -	10.00*

JOHN LEE HOOKER:
Chart 609, 614	5.00 -	10.00*
Chess 1467, 1482, 1505, 1513	5.00 -	10.00*
JVB 30 *Boogie Rambler*	20.00 -	30.00
Modern 627, 663, 688, 714, 730, 746, 767, 790, 814, 829, 835, 847, 867, 876, 886, 897, 901, 908, 916, 923, 931, 935, 942, 948, 958, 966, 978	4.00 -	7.00*
Regal 3295 *Boogie Chillen*	8.00 -	12.00
3304 *Notoriety Woman*	10.00 -	15.00
Sensation 21, 26, 30, 33, 34	5.00 -	8.00

LIGHTNIN' HOPKINS:
Aladdin 165, 167, 204, 209, 3005, 3015, 3028, 3035, 3052, 3063, 3077, 3096, 3117, 3262	4.00 -	7.00*
Gold Star 613, 616, 634, 637, 640, 641, 646, 652, 656, 662, 664, 665, 666. 669, 673, 3131	7.00 -	15.00
671 *Henny Penny Blues*	35.00 -	50.00

Jax 315, 321, 635, 642, 660	4.00 -	7.00*
Mercury 8276, 8293, 70081, 70191	3.00 -	5.00*
Modern 529, 543, 552, 568, 594, 621, 673	3.00 -	6.00
RPM 337, 346, 351, 359, 378, 388, 398	3.00 -	6.00*
Score 4002 *Whiskey Head Woman*	8:00 -	12.00
Sittin' In With 599, 611, 621, 635, 642, 647, 649, 752, 658, 660, 661	5.00 -	10.00
TNT 8002 *Lightning Jump*	10.00 -	15.00*
8008 *Moanin' Blues*	10.00 -	15.00*

J.D. HORTON:
Bullet 350 *Cadillac Blues*	15.00 -	20.00

SHAKEY/WALTER HORTON:
Chess 1529 *Walter's Boogie*	7.00 -	10.00*
Cobra 5002 *Need My Baby*	7.00 -	10.00*

SON HOUSE:
Paramount 12990 *Dry Spell Blues*	200.00 -	400.00
13013 *Preachin' The Blues*	200.00 -	400.00
13042 *My Black Mama*	200.00 -	400.00
13096 *Clarksdale Moan*	200.00 -	400.00

EMERSON HOUSTON:
Bluebird 5791 *Hard Luck Blues*	75.00 -	100.00

LAWYER HOUSTON:
Atlantic 916 *Dallas Be Bop Blues*	15.00 -	25.00

SOLDIER BOY HOUSTON:
Atlantic 971 *Western Rider Blues*	10.00 -	15.00*

JOHN HENRY HOWARD:
Gennett 3117 *I've Started For The Kingdom*	25.00 -	40.00
3124 *Black Snake*	25.00 -	40.00

JOHNNY HOWARD:
DeLuxe 6044 *Hastings Street Jump*	20.00 -	30.00*

ROSETTA HOWARD:
Decca 7370, 7392, 7410, 7447, 7459, 7515, 7531, 7551, 7618, 7627, 7640, 7658, 7687, 7801	5.00 -	10.00

WHISTLING BOB HOWE & FRANKIE GRIGGS:
Decca 7085 *The Hottest Stuff In Town*	15.00 -	20.00

PEG LEG HOWELL (& HIS GANG): PEG LEG HOWELL & EDDIE ANTHONY/ JIM HILL:
Columbia 14177-D *New Prison Blues*	50.00 -	75.00
14194-D *Coal Man Blues*	50.00 -	75.00
14210-D *New Jelly Roll Blues*	50.00 -	75.00
14238-D *Sadie Lee Blues*	50.00 -	75.00
14270-D *Hobo Blues*	50.00 -	75.00
14298-D *Peg Leg Stomp*	50.00 -	75.00
14320-D *Rock And Gravel Blues*	50.00 -	75.00
14356-D *Fairy Blues*	50.00 -	75.00
14382-D *Turkey Buzzard Blues*	50.00 -	75.00
14426-D *Monkey Man Blues*	75.00 -	100.00
14438-D *Rolling Mill Blues*	75.00 -	100.00
14456-D *Turtle Dove Blues*	75.00 -	100.00
14473-D *Skin Game Blues*	75.00 -	100.00
14535-D *Ball And Chain Blues*	75.00 -	100.00

HOWLIN' WOLF:
Chess 1479, 1497, 1510, 1515, 1528. 1557, 1566	5.00 -	8.00*
RPM 333, 340, 347	4.00 -	8.00*

ED "FATS" HUDSON:
Champion 16414 *Fats' Hard Luck Blues*	150.00 -	250.00

HATTIE HUDSON:
Columbia 14279-D *Black Hand Blues*	40.00 -	60.00

LUTHER HUFF:
Trumpet 132, 141	7.00 -	10.00*

WILLIE B. HUFF:
Big Town 105 *Operator 209*	10.00 -	15.00*

PEE WEE HUGHES & THE DELTA DUO:
Deluxe 3228 *Santa Fe Blues*	10.00 -	15.00

PAPA HARVEY HULL & THE DOWN HOME BOYS & LONG "CLEVE" REED:
Black Patti 8001 *France Blues*	300.00 -	600.00
8002 *Don't You Leave My Here*	300.00 -	600.00

HELEN HUMES:
Okeh 8467 *A Worried Woman's Blues*	30.00 -	50.00

8529 *Alligator Blues* .... 30.00 - 50.00
8545 *If Papa Has Outside Lovin'* .... 30.00 - 50.00
8674 *Garlic Blues* .... 30.00 - 50.00
8825 *Race Horse Blues* .... 30.00 - 50.00

D.A. HUNT:
Sun 183 *Lonesome Ol' Jail* .... 40.00 - 60.00*

HUNTER BROTHERS:
Superior 2836 *Stove Pipe Stomp* ....150.00 - 200.00

ALBERTA HUNTER:
Black Swan 2008 *Bring Back The Joys* ... 20.00 - 35.00
2019 *Someday Sweetheart* .... 20.00 - 35.00
Bluebird 8485, 8539 .... 7.00 - 10.00
Columbia 14450-D *My Particular Man* .... 50.00 - 75.00
Decca 7633, 7644, 7727 .... 7.00 - 10.00
Okeh 8268 *Your Jelly Roll Is Good* .... 50.00 - 75.00
8278 *Everybody Does It Now* .... 50.00 - 75.00
8294 *I'm Hard To Satisfy* .... 50.00 - 75.00
8315 *Empty Cellar Blues* .... 50.00 - 75.00
8365 *You For Me, Me For You* .... 20.00 - 30.00
8383 *Everybody Mess Around* .... 30.00 - 50.00
8393 *Wasn't It Nice?* .... 30.00 - 50.00
8409 *Don't Forget To Mess Around* .... 50.00 - 75.00
Paramount 12001 *Daddy Blues* .... 20.00 - 35.00
12005 *Down Hearted Blues* .... 20.00 - 35.00
12006 *Jazzin' Baby Blues* .... 25.00 - 35.00
12007 *Lonesome Monday Morning Blues* ..... 40.00 - 60.00
12008 *You Can't Have It All* .... 40.00 - 60.00
12010 *After All These Years* .... 25.00 - 40.00
12012 *Someday Sweetheart*.............. 25.00 - 40.00
12014 *Bring Back The Joys* .... 25.00 - 40.00
12016 *'Tain't Nobody's Bizness* ...... 15.00 - 25.00
12017 *Chirping The Blues* .... 15.00 - 25.00
12018 *Bring It With You When You Come* .. 20.00 - 30.00
12019 *Loveless Love* .... 20.00 - 30.00
12020 *Vamping Brown* .... 20.00 - 30.00
12021 *Bleeding Hearted Blues* .... 30.00 - 50.00
12036 *Michigan Water Blues* .... 30.00 - 50.00
12043 *Mistreated Blues* .... 30.00 - 50.00
12049 *Stingaree Blues* .... 30.00 - 50.00
12065 *Experience Blues* ....100.00 - 150.00
12066 *Miss Anna Brown*................100.00 - 150.00
12093 *Old-Fashioned Love* .... 20.00 - 30.00
Victor 20497 *I'll Forgive You 'Cause I Love You* . 20.00 - 30.00
20651 *My Old Daddy's Got A Brand New* .... 20.00 - 30.00
20771 *Sugar* .... 25.00 - 40.00
21539 *I'm Going To See My Ma* .... 40.00 - 60.00

IVORY JOE HUNTER:
Pacific .... 5.00 - 8.00

LOST JOHN HUNTER & THE BLIND BATS:
4 Star 1492 *Cool Down Mama* .... 8.00 - 12.00
1511 *Boogie For Me Baby* .... 8.00 - 12.00

LEE HUNTER:
Gold Star 651 *Lees Boogie* .... 12.00 - 16.00

SLIM HUNTER:
Superior 2808 *Mistreatin' Mama* ....150.00 - 200.00
2837 *Big Bill Blues* ....150.00 - 200.00

HUNTER & JENKINS:
Vocalion 02613 *Meat Cuttin' Blues* .... 15.00 - 20.00
(Note: Above is black & gold label; blue label reissues exist.)

MISSISSIPPI JOHN HURT:
Okeh 8560 *Nobody's Dirty Business* ....100.00 - 150.00
8654 *Stack O'Lee Blues*..............100.00 - 150.00
8666 *Blessed Be The Name* .... 100.00 - 150.00
8692 *Spike Driver Blues* ....100.00 - 150.00
8724 *Louis Collins* ....100.00 - 150.00
8759 *Avalon Blues* ....100.00 - 150.00

J.B. HUTTO:
Chance 1165 *Dim Lights* .... 15.00 - 25.00*

HATTIE HYDE:
Victor 23374 *Special Question Blues* ....150.00 - 200.00

J.B. & HIS BAYOU BOYS:

J.O.B. 1008 *The Mountain* .... 6.00 - 10.00*

J.B. & HIS HAWKS:
Chance 1155 *Combination Boogie* .... 20.00 - 30.00*

JACKIE BOY & LITTLE WALTER:
Sun 174 *Sellin' My Whiskey* (possibly unissued) . — - —

JACK O'DIAMONDS:
Paramount 12786 *The Duck's Yas Yas* ....150.00 - 200.00
12791 *Smiling Blues* ....150.00 - 250.00

JACKSON BLUE BOYS:
Columbia 14397-D *Sweet Alberta* ....100.00 - 150.00

BESSIE JACKSON:
Titles, issued contemporaneously on Banner, Melotone, Oriole, Perfect, Romeo: *Alley Boogie, B.D. Woman Blues; Baking Powder Blues; Barbecue Bess; Black Angel Blues; Boogan Ways Blues; Changed Way Blues; Down In Boogie Alley; Drinking Blues; Forty-Two Hundred Blues; Groceries On The Shelf; House Top Blues; I Hate That Train Called The M. & O; Jump Steady Daddy; Lonesome Midnight Blues; Man Stealer Blues; Mean Twister; My Baby Came Back; My Man Is Boogan Me; New Muscle Shoals Blues; Pig Iron Sally; Reckless Woman; Red Cross Man; Roll And Rattler; Seabord Blues; Shave 'Em Dry; Skin Game Blues; Sloppy Drunk Blues; Stew Meat Blues; Superstitious Blues; That's What My Baby Likes; Tired As I Can Be; Tricks Ain't Walkin' No More; Troubled Mind; Walkin' Blues; You Got To Die Someday* ...... 30.00 - 50.00

BO WEAVIL JACKSON:
Paramount 12389 *Pistol Blues* ....100.00 - 150.00
12390 *When The Saints Come Marching Home* 100.00 - 150.00
12423 *Who Do You Moan?* ....100.00 - 150.00

(PAPA) CHARLIE JACKSON (AND BLIND BLAKE):
Okeh 8954 *Skoodle-Um-Skoo* .... 50.00 - 75.00
8957 *If I Got What You Want* .... 50.00 - 75.00
Paramount 12219 *Papa's Lawdy Lawdy Blues* ... 20.00 - 35.00
12236 *Salty Dog Blues* .... 20.00 - 35.00
12259 *The Cat's Got The Measles* ..... 20.00 - 35.00
12264 *Coffee Pot Blues*.............. 20.00 - 35.00
12281 *Shake That Thing* .... 30.00 - 40.00
12289 *Drop That Sack* .... 30.00 - 40.00
12296 *Take Me Back Blues* .... 30.00 - 40.00
12305 *Mama, Don't You Think I Know?* ...... 30.00 - 40.00
12320 *Maxwell Street Blues* .... 30.00 - 40.00
12335 *Texas Blues* .... 30.00 - 50.00
12348 *Jackson's Blues* .... 30.00 - 50.00
12358 *Butter And Egg Man Blues* ..... 30.00 - 50.00
12366 *The Judge Cliff Davis Blues* .. 30.00 - 50.00
12375 *Up The Way Bound* .... 30.00 - 50.00
12383 *Bad Luck Woman Blues* .... 30.00 - 50.00
12422 *Fat Mouth Blues* .... 30.00 - 50.00
12461 *Coal Man Blues* .... 30.00 - 50.00
12501 *Skoodle Um Skoo* .... 30.00 - 50.00
12553 *Baby Don't You Be So Mean* ... 30.00 - 50.00
12574 *Bright Eyes* .... 30.00 - 50.00
12602 *Long Gone Lost John* .... 30.00 - 50.00
12660 *Ash Tray Blues* .... 40.00 - 60.00
12675 *I Like To Love My Baby* ...... 40.00 - 60.00
12700 *Lexington Kentucky Blues* .... 40.00 - 60.00
12721 *Corn Liquor Blues* .... 40.00 - 60.00
12736 *Don't Break Down On Me* ..... 50.00 - 75.00
12765 *We Can't Buy It No More*..... 75.00 - 100.00
12797 *Tailor Made Lover* .... 75.00 - 100.00
12853 *Forgotten Blues* .... 75.00 - 100.00
12905 *I'll Be Gone Babe* .... 75.00 - 100.00
12911 *Papa Charlie And Blind Blake Talk About It* ....150.00 - 200.00
12956 *Self Experience* ....100.00 - 150.00

DEACON JACKSON:

Herwin 93031 *All I Want Is That Pure Religion* . . 150.00 - 200.00

FRANKIE JACKSON:

Okeh 8359 *Hannah Fell In Love With My Piano* . 75.00 - 100.00

GEORGE JACKSON & BESSIE JONES:

Superior 2555 *I'm Long Gone* . . . . 200.00 - 300.00

HANDY JACKSON:

Sun 177 *Got My Application Baby* . . . . 75.00 - 100.00*

JIM JACKSON:

Victor 21236 *My Monday Woman Blues* . . . . 50.00 - 75.00

  21268 *Bootlegging Blues* . . . . 50.00 - 75.00

  21387 *Old Dog Blue* . . . . 50.00 - 75.00

  21671 *I'm Gonna Move To Louisiana* . . . . . . 75.00 - 100.00

  V-38003 *This Mornin' She Was Gone* . . . . . . 75.00 - 100.00

  V-38505 *What A Time* . . . . 100.00 - 150.00

  V-38517 *Traveling Man* . . . . 100.00 - 150.00

  V-38525 *Going 'Round The Mountain* . . . . . . 100.00 - 150.00

  Vocalion 1144 *Jim Jackson's Kansas City*

  Blues—Part 1/2 . . . . 40.00 - 60.00

  1145 *Mobile Central Blues* . . . . 75.00 - 100.00

  1146 *He's In The Jailhouse Now* . . . . 75.00 - 100.00

  1155 *Jim Jackson's Kansas City Blues—Part 3/4* 50.00 - 75.00

  1164 *I'm A Bad Bad Man* . . . . 75.00 - 100.00

  1284 *Hey Mama, It's Nice Like That* . . . . 75.00 - 100.00

  1295 *Foot Achin' Blues* . . . . 75.00 - 125.00

  1413 *Ain't You Sorry Mama?* . . . . 75.00 - 125.00

  1428 *Jim Jackson's Jamboree* . . . . 100.00 - 150.00

  1477 *Hesitation Blues* . . . . 150.00 - 200.00

LILLIAN JACKSON:

Supertone 9281 *I'm All Broke Out With The*

  Blues . . . . 50.00 - 80.00

  9287 *Sing That Song With Feeling* . . . . 50.00 - 80.00

  9294 *Cow Cow Blues* . . . . 50.00 - 80.00

LIL'/LITTLE SON JACKSON:

Gold Star 638 *Roberta Blues* . . . . 15.00 - 20.00

  642 *Ground Hog Blues* . . . . 15.00 - 20.00

  653 *No Money, No Love* . . . . 15.00 - 20.00

  663 *Cairo Blues* . . . . 15.00 - 20.00

  668 *Gambling Blues* . . . . 15.00 - 20.00

  Imperial 5100 *Ticket Agent Blues* . . . . 5.00 - 8.00*

  5108 *Tough Luck Blues* . . . . 5.00 - 8.00*

  5113 *Rockin' And Rollin'* . . . . 5.00 - 8.00*

  5119 *Rocky Road* . . . . 5.00 - 8.00*

  5125 *Young Woman Blues* . . . . 5.00 - 8.00*

  5131 *Time Changes Things* . . . . 5.00 - 8.00*

  5137 *Restless Blues* . . . . 5.00 - 8.00*

  5144 *Red Light* . . . . 5.00 - 8.00*

  5156, 5165, 5175, 5192, 5204, 5218, 5229, 5237,

  5248, 5259, 5268, 5276, 5286, 5300, 5312,

  5319, 5339 . . . . 3.00 - 5.00*

  Modern 840 *Talkin' Boogie* . . . . 7.00 - 10.00

  Sittin' In With 643 *Gambling Blues* . . . . 10.00 - 15.00

LULU JACKSON:

Vocalion 1193 *Careless Love Blues* . . . . 50.00 - 75.00

  1206 *After You've Had Your Way* . . . . 50.00 - 75.00

  1242 *Lost Lover Blues* . . . . 50.00 - 75.00

  1276 *Little Rosewood Casket* . . . . 50.00 - 75.00

MONROE "MOE" JACKSON:

Mercury 8127 *Move It On Over* . . . . 7.00 - 10.00

ODIS JACKSON:

Fechi 90 *Pretty Baby* . . . . 7.00 - 10.00

PORKCHOP JACKSON:

Supertone 9510 *Lonesome Man Blues* . . . . 150.00 - 300.00

SADIE JACKSON:

Columbia 14181-D *Original Black Bottom Dance* . 50.00 - 80.00

VIOLET JACKSON:

Gennett 6090 *Blue And All By Myself* . . . . 100.00 - 150.00

(BLIND/NEW ORLEANS) WILLIE JACKSON (& BROTHER):

Broadway 5050 *Telephone To Glory* . . . . 150.00 - 200.00

Columbia 14136-D *Willie Jackson's Blues* . . . . . 50.00 - 75.00

  14156-D *Bad, Bad Mama* . . . . 50.00 - 75.00

  14165-D *Who'll Chop Your Suey When I'm Gone* 40.00 - 60.00

14184-D *Numbers on the Brain* . . . . 40.00 - 60.00

14218-D *Railroad Man Blues* . . . . 40.00 - 60.00

14284-D *Kansas City Blues* . . . . 40.00 - 60.00

14432-D *Corn And Bunion Blues* . . . . 50.00 - 80.00

Crown 3326 *Telephone To Glory* . . . . 75.00 - 100.00

Herwin 92035 *Telephone To Glory* . . . . 150.00 - 250.00

  93005 *Rock Of Ages* . . . . 100.00 - 150.00

WALTER JACOBS (& THE CARTER BROTHERS):

Bluebird 6673 *Rats Been On My Cheese* . . . . . . 25.00 - 40.00

Montgomery Ward 7064 *How Did It Happen* . . . . 20.00 - 30.00

Okeh 45468 *Sheiks Special* . . . . 100.00 - 150.00

  45482 *Mississippi Low Down* . . . . 100.00 - 150.00

ELMER JAMES:

Trumpet 186 *Gonna Find My Baby* . . . . 7.00 - 10.00*

ELMO/ELMORE JAMES (& HIS BROOMDUSTERS):

Meteor 5000, 5003 . . . . 5.00 - 8.00*

Trumpet 146 *Dust My Broom* . . . . 5.00 - 8.00*

FRANK JAMES:

Champion 16798 *Mistreated Blues* . . . . 100.00 - 150.00

  16809 *Frank's Lonesome Blues* . . . . 100.00 - 150.00

  50017 *Forsaken Blues* . . . . 50.00 - 75.00

  50018 *Snake Hip Blues* . . . . 50.00 - 75.00

JESSE JAMES:

Decca 7213 *Southern Casey Jones* . . . . 20.00 - 30.00

Sittin' In With 569 *Forgive Me Blues* . . . . 10.00 - 15.00

PAULINE JAMES:

Gennett 6147 *You Used To Be Sugar Blues* . . . . . 100.00 - 150.00

SADIE JAMES:

Victor 20575 *Mama, Fold Your Hands* . . . . 40.00 - 60.00

SKIP JAMES:

Paramount 13065 *Cherry Ball Blues* . . . . 150.00 - 250.00

  13066 *22-20 Blues* . . . . 200.00 - 300.00

  13072 *How Long "Buck"* . . . . 200.00 - 300.00

  13085 *How Long "Buck"* . . . . 200.00 - 300.00

  13083 *Devil Got My Woman* . . . . 200.00 - 300.00

  13098 *Special Rider Blues* . . . . 200.00 - 300.00

  13106 *Hard Luck Child* . . . . 200.00 - 300.00

  13108 *Be Ready When He Comes* . . . . 200.00 - 300.00

  13111 *Drunken Spree* . . . . 250.00 - 400.00

SPRINGBACK JAMES:

Titles, issued contemporaneously on Banner,

  Melotone, Oriole, Perfect, Romeo, Vocalion:

  Hard Driving Mama; Hellish Ways . . . . 50.00 - 75.00

Bluebird 6777 *See For Yourself* . . . . 35.00 - 50.00

  6824 *New Red Cross Blues* . . . . 35.00 - 50.00

  7116 *Poor Coal Passer* . . . . 35.00 - 50.00

Champion 50076 *Lonesome Love Blues* . . . . 50.00 - 80.00

Decca 7091 *Rusty Can Blues* . . . . 35.00 - 50.00

  7119 *Stingaree Mama Blues* . . . . 35.00 - 50.00

SUNNY JAMES:

Down Town 2010 *Excuse Me Baby* . . . . 15.00 - 20.00

ULYSSES JAMES:

Cava-Tone 250 *Poor Boy* . . . . 5.00 - 8.00

W. LAWRENCE JAMES:

Paramount 12450 *Oh Cap'n* . . . . 40.00 - 60.00

JAMMIN' JIM:

Savoy 1106 *Shake Boogie* . . . . 7.00 - 10.00

JAZZBO TOMMY & HIS LOWLANDERS:

Titles, issued contemporaneously on Banner,

Melotone, Oriole, Perfect, Romeo: *Blaze Face
Cow; You Don't Mean Me No Good* .... 75.00 - 100.00

GEORGE JEFFERSON:
Bluebird 7926 *Honey Bee* .... 10.00 - 15.00
Champion 15452 *Why Should I Grieve After
You've Gone* .... 75.00 - 125.00
15472 *When A Man Is Treated Like A Dog* ....200.00 - 300.00

BLIND LEMON JEFFERSON:
Okeh 8455 *Black Snake Moon*. .... 80.00 - 120.00
Paramount 12347 *Booster Blues* .... 75.00 - 100.00
12354 *Got The Blues* .... 50.00 - 80.00
12367 *Black Horse Blues* .... 75.00 - 100.00
12373 *Jack O'Diamond Blues* .... 75.00 - 100.00
12394 *Beggin' Back* .... 75.00 - 100.00
12407 *Stocking Feet Blues* .... 75.00 - 100.00
12425 *Wartime Blues* .... 75.00 - 100.00
12443 *Bad Luck Blues* .... 75.00 - 100.00
12454 *Rabbit Foot Blues* .... 75.00 - 100.00
12474 *Match Box Blues* .... 75.00 - 100.00
12487 *Teddy Bear Blues* .... 75.00 - 100.00
12493 *Weary Dog Blues* .... 75.00 - 100.00
12510 *Right Of Way Blues* .... 75.00 - 100.00
12541 *Rambler Blues* .... 75.00 - 100.00
12551 *Chinch Bug Blues*. .... 75.00 - 100.00
12578 *Gone Dead On You Blues* ...... 75.00 - 100.00
12593 *Lonesome House Blues* .... 75.00 - 100.00
12608 *'Lectric Chair Blues* .... 75.00 - 100.00
12622 *Prison Cell Blues*. .... 75.00 - 100.00
12631 *Mean Jumper Blues* .... 75.00 - 100.00
12639 *Lemon's Cannon Ball Moan* .... 75.00 - 100.00
*12650 *Piney Woods Mama Blues* .... 75.00 - 125.00
12666 *Blind Lemon's Penitentiary Blues* . 75.00 - 100.00
12679 *Lock Step Blues* .... 75.00 - 100.00
12685 *How Long, How Long* ....150.00 - 200.00
12692 *Happy New Year Blues* .... 75.00 - 100.00
12712 *Maltese Cat Blues* .... 75.00 - 100.00
12728 *Competition Bed Blues* .... 75.00 - 100.00
12739 *Eagle Eyed Mama* .... 75.00 - 100.00
12756 *Tin Cup Blues* .... 80.00 - 120.00
12771 *Oil Well Blues*. .... 80.00 - 120.00
12801 *Peach Orchard Mama* .... 80.00 - 120.00
12852 *Long Distance Moan* .... 80.00 - 120.00
12872 *Bed Springs Blues* .... 80.00 - 120.00
12880 *Pneumonia Blues* .... 80.00 - 120.00
**12886 *Hometown Skiffle* .... 75.00 - 100.00
12899 *Mosquito Moan* .... 80.00 - 120.00
12921 *Cat Man Blues* ....100.00 - 150.00
12933 *The Cheaters Spell*. ....100.00 - 150.00
12946 *Empty House Blues* ....100.00 - 150.00

(*Note: Paramount 12650 is designated "Blind
Lemon Jefferson's Birthday Record," and bears
a portrait of the artist.)
(**Note: Paramount 12886 is designated
"Descriptive Novelty," performed by several
artists. Since Blind Lemon Jefferson's name
appears first, it is included in his output.)

JELLY BELLY & SLIM SEWARD:
Apollo 412 *Sorry Woman Blues* .... 7.00 - 10.00

JENKINS AND JENKINS:
Columbia 14040-D *Hen Pecked Man* ...... 15.00 - 25.00
14100-D *Sister, It's Too Bad* .... 15.00 - 25.00
Gennett 3335 *Miserable Blues* .... 20.00 - 30.00

HAZEKIAH JENKINS:
Columbia 14585-D *The Panic Is On* .... 30.00 - 50.00

ROBERT JENKINS:
Parkway 103 *Steelin' Boogie* .... 10.00 - 15.00

JIM JAM:
Varsity 6044 *Diamond Ring Blues* .... 15.00 - 20.00
6054 *Window Pane Blues*. .... 15.00 - 20.00

JOE JOE:
Varsity 6032 *Humming Blues* .... 10.00 - 15.00

JIMMY & WALTER:

Sun 180 *Before Long* .... 50.00 - 75.00

JOHNSON AND JACKSON:
Champion 15835 *Everybody Likes That Thing* ... 75.00 - 100.00

JOHNSON AND SMITH:
Champion 16411 *Brown Skin Shuffle* ....150.00 - 200.00

JOHNSON BOYS:
Okeh 8708 *Violin Blues* .... 75.00 - 100.00

JOHNSON-NELSON-PORKCHOP:
Okeh 8577 *In The Mornin'* .... 75.00 - 100.00

ALEC JOHNSON (& HIS BAND):
Columbia 14378-D *Mysterious Coon* .... 80.00 - 120.00
14416-D *Next Week Sometime* .... 80.00 - 120.00
14446-D *Sundown Blues* .... 80.00 - 120.00

BABE JOHNSON:
Silvertone 3562 *Worried 'Bout Him Blues* ...... 75.00 - 125.00

**BESSIE JOHNSON; BESSIE JOHNSON'S
SANCTIFIED SINGERS:**
Okeh 8725 *No Room At The Hotel* .... 50.00 - 75.00
8765 *The Whole World In His Hand* .... 50.00 - 75.00

BIG BILL JOHNSON:
Champion 16081 *Saturday Night Rub* ....100.00 - 150.00
16172 *That Won't Do*. ....100.00 - 150.00
16327 *The Baker's Blues* ....100.00 - 150.00
16396 *Big Bill Blues* ....100.00 - 150.00
16426 *Mr. Conductor Man* ....150.00 - 200.00
50060 *Big Bill Blues* .... 50.00 - 75.00
50069 *Too Too Train Blues* .... 50.00 - 75.00
Gennett 7210 *Skoodle Do Do* ....175.00 - 250.00
7230 *I Can't Be Satisfed* ....175.00 - 250.00

**BILLIKEN/BILLIKIN JOHNSON & FRED
ADAMS/WITH NEAL ROBERTS:**
Columbia 14293-D *Sun Beam Blues* .... 75.00 - 100.00
14405-D *Wild Jack Blues* .... 75.00 - 100.00

BUD JOHNSON:
Champion 15614 *Kitchen Range Blues* ....250.00 - 400.00
15675 *Hot Time Blues* ....250.00 - 400.00

BUSTER JOHNSON:
Champion 16718 *Undertaker Blues* ....200.00 - 300.00

CONRAD JOHNSON:
Gold Star 622 *Howling On Dowling* .... 7.00 - 10.00

EASY PAPA JOHNSON:
Melotone 12048 *Drinkin' Woman Blues* .... 75.00 - 100.00
12086 *Cotton Seed Blues* .... 75.00 - 100.00
Polk 9010 *No Good Woman Blues* ...... 80.00 - 120.00
9011 *Drinkin' Woman Blues* .... 80.00 - 120.00
Vocalion 02669 *No Good Woman Blues* ...... 75.00 - 100.00
02697 *Papa Sweetback Blues* .... 75.00 - 100.00

EDDIE JOHNSON & HIS ORCHESTRA:
Colony 101 *Juice Head* .... 7.00 - 10.00
Imperial 5120 *Corn Licker Blues* .... 7.00 - 10.00

EDITH (NORTH) JOHNSON:
Okeh 8748 *Heart Aching Blues* .... 80.00 - 120.00
Paramount 12823 *Honey Dripper Blues* ....100.00 - 150.00
12864 *Can't Make Another Day* ....100.00 - 150.00
12915 *Honey Dripper Blues No. 2* ....100.00 - 150.00
12939 *Eight Hour Woman* ....100.00 - 150.00
13032 *Whispering To My Man* ....100.00 - 150.00
QRS 7048 *You Ain't No Good Blues* .... 75.00 - 100.00

EDNA JOHNSON:
Gennet 5367 *I'm Drifting From You Blues* ...... 35.00 - 50.00

ELIZABETH JOHNSON:
Okeh 8593 *Empty Bed Blues* ....100.00 - 150.00
8789 *Be My Kid Blues* .... 75.00 - 100.00

ELNORA JOHNSON:
Black Patti 8033 *Freakish Papa* ....150.00 - 250.00
8039 *Red Cap Porter Blues* ....150.00 - 300.00

ELVIRA JOHNSON:
Gennett 3337 *Numbers on the Brain* ....75.00 - 100.00
Champion 15126 *Numbers on the Brain* ...... 75.00 - 100.00
15127 *How Could I Be Blue* .... 75.00 - 100.00

FANNIE JOHNSON:
Cameo 1066 *I'm Savin' It All For You* .... 10.00 - 15.00

Cameo 1144 *Slow Up Papa*	10.00 -	15.00
1158 *Black Snake Blues*	10.00 -	15.00
Romeo 416 *Back Water Blues*	10.00 -	15.00
453 *Dyin' Crap-Shooter's Blues*	10.00 -	15.00

FRANK JOHNSON:

Herwin 92038 *Trouble 'Bout My Soul*	150.00 -	250.00

GLADYS JOHNSON:

Variety 5033 *I'm Savin' It All For You*	10.00 -	15.00
5048 *Slow Up Papa*	10.00 -	15.00
5085 *Black Snake Blues*	10.00 -	15.00

HARRY "SLICK" JOHNSON:

Peacock 1560 *My Baby's Coming Home*	7.00 -	10.00

JAMES "STEADY ROLL" JOHNSON:

Okeh 8287 *Newport Blues*	30.00 -	50.00

JAMES (STUMP) JOHNSON & HIS PIANO:

QRS 7049 *The Snitchers Blues*	75.00 -	100.00
7050 *My Babe Blues*	100.00 -	150.00

JELLY ROLL JOHNSON:

Champion 15281 *Free Woman Blues*	100.00 -	150.00
Silvertone 5121 *Free Woman Blues*	150.00 -	200.00

JESSE JOHNSON:

Paramount 12829 *I Wish I Had Died In Egyptland*	100.00 -	150.00

JULIA JOHNSON:

Gennett 6519 *Hard Headed Daddy*	75.00 -	100.00

KI KI JOHNSON:

QRS 7001 *Lone Grave*	100.00 -	150.00
7003 *Lady, Your Clock Ain't Right*	100.00 -	150.00

LEROY "COUNTRY" JOHNSON:

Freedom 1509 *Loghouse On The Hill*	10.00 -	15.00

LIL JOHNSON:

Bluebird 6112 *Keep On Knocking*	15.00 -	20.00
Champion 50002 *Get 'Em From The Peanut Man*	15.00 -	20.00
50052 *Snake Man Blues*	20.00 -	30.00
Vocalion 1299 *Never Let Your Left Hand Know*	100.00 -	150.00
1410 *House Rend Scuffle*	100.00 -	150.00
03199 *Press My Button*	10.00 -	15.00
03241 *Get 'Em From The Peanut Man (The New Hot Nuts)*	10.00 -	15.00
03251 *My Stove's In Good Condition*	15.00 -	20.00
03266 *Two Timin' Man*	10.00 -	15.00
03299 *Murder In The First Degree*	15.00 -	20.00
03312 *Hottest Gal In Town*	15.00 -	20.00
03331 *Ramblin' Man Blues*	15.00 -	20.00
03374 *Black And Evil Blues*	15.00 -	20.00
03397 *Crazy About My Rider*	15.00 -	20.00
03428 *New Shave 'Em Dry*	15.00 -	20.00
03455 *River Hip Papa*	15.00 -	20.00
03483 *You Can't Bet On Love*	15.00 -	20.00
03530 *I'm A Sales Lady*	15.00 -	20.00
03562 *Meat Balls*	15.00 -	20.00
03600 *Goofer Dust Swing*	15.00 -	20.00
03604 *Joe Louis Fight*	15.00 -	20.00
03604 *Winner Joe (The Knock Out King)*	15.00 -	20.00
03666 *Mellow Stuff*	15.00 -	20.00
03710 *Broken-Hearted Blues*	15.00 -	20.00
03941 *When Your Troubles Are Like Mine*	10.00 -	15.00
03978 *Ain't That A Shame?*	10.00 -	15.00
04067 *Snake In The Grass*	10.00 -	15.00
Titles, issued contemporaneously on Banner, Melotone, Oriole, Perfect, Romeo: *Get 'Em From The Peanut Man; If You Can Dish It; I'm Bettin' On You; Press My Button; Take It Easy, Greasy; That Bonus Done Gone Through*	8.00 -	15.00

LONNIE JOHNSON (& BLIND WILLIE DUNN/& CLARENCE WILLIAMS/& SPENCER WILLIAMS):

Aladdin 197, 3029, 3047	5.00 -	8.00
Bluebird 8322, 8338, 8363, 8387, 8530, 8564, 8684, 8748, 8779. 8804, 8980, 9006, 9022, 34-0708, 34-0714, 34-0732, 34-0742	7.00 - 5.00 -	12.00 10.00
Columbia 14667-D *Home Wreckers Blues*	50.00 -	75.00

14674-D *Unselfish Love*	50.00 -	75.00
Decca 7388, 7397, 7427, 7445, 7461, 7487, 7509, 7537	7.00 -	12.00
Disc 5060, 5061, 5062, 5063, 5064, 5065	5.00 -	8.00
King	4.00 -	7.00
Okeh 8253 *Mr. Johnson's Blues*	50.00 -	80.00
8282 *Love Story Blues*	50.00 -	80.00
8291 *Bed Of Sand*	50.00 -	80.00
8309 *Lonesome Jail Blues*	50.00 -	80.00
8340 *A Good Happy Home*	40.00 -	60.00
8358 *Good Old Wagon*	40.00 -	60.00
8376 *Baby Please Tell Me*	40.00 -	60.00
8391 *Oh! Doctor, The Blues*	40.00 -	60.00
8411 *Lonnie's Got The Blues*	40.00 -	60.00
8417 *Johnson Trio Stomp*	40.00 -	60.00
8435 *Ball And Chain Blues*	40.00 -	60.00
8451 *You Drove A Good Man A Way*	40.00 -	60.00
8466 *South Bound Water*	40.00 -	60.00
8484 *Treat 'Em Right*	40.00 -	60.00
8497 *Roaming Rambler Blues*	35.00 -	50.00
8505 *Fickle Mamma Blues*	35.00 -	50.00
8512 *St. Louis Cyclone Blues*	35.00 -	50.00
8524 *Tin Can Alley Blues*	35.00 -	50.00
8537 *Kansas City Blues*	35.00 -	50.00
8557 *Life Saver Blues*	35.00 -	50.00
8558 *Playing With The Strings*	50.00 -	75.00
8574 *Crowing Rooster Blues*	35.00 -	50.00
8575 *Blues In G*	50.00 -	75.00
8586 *Bed Bug Blues No. 2*	35.00 -	50.00
8601 *Wrong Woman Blues*	35.00 -	50.00
8618 *Broken Levee Blues*	35.00 -	50.00
8635 *Careless Love*	35.00 -	50.00
8637 *Two Tone Stomp*	35.00 -	50.00
8664 *It Feels So Good Part 1/2*	15.00 -	20.00
8691 *Death Is On Your Track*	35.00 -	50.00
Okeh 8695 *Bull Frog Moan*	50.00 -	75.00
8697 *It Feels So Good—Part 3/4*	15.00 -	20.00
8709 *Mr. Johnson's Blues—No. 2*	35.00 -	50.00
8722 *From Now On Make Your Whoopee At Home*	35.00 -	50.00
8754 *Sundown Blues*	40.00 -	60.00
8762 *Wipe It Off*	40.00 -	60.00
8768 *She's Making Whoopee In Hell Tonight*	50.00 -	75.00
8775 *The Dirty Dozen*	50.00 -	75.00
8786 *Headed For Southland*	50.00 -	75.00
8796 *Don't Drive Me From Your Door*	50.00 -	75.00
8802 *The Bull Frog And The Toad*	50.00 -	75.00
8812 *Keep It To Yourself*	50.00 -	75.00
8822 *Deep Sea Blues*	50.00 -	75.00
8831 *No More Troubles Now*	50.00 -	75.00
8846 *Let All Married Women Alone*	50.00 -	75.00
8875 *Just A Roaming Man*	50.00 -	75.00
8886 *I Just Can't Stand These Blues*	50.00 -	75.00
8898 *Beautiful But Dumb*	50.00 -	75.00
8909 *I Have To Do My Time*	50.00 -	75.00
8916 *The Best Jockey In Town*	50.00 -	75.00
8926 *Sleepy Water Blues*	50.00 -	75.00
8937 *Sam You're Just A Rat*	50.00 -	75.00
8946 *Racketeers Blues*	50.00 -	75.00
40695 *Nile Of Genago*	40.00 -	60.00
Paradise 110 *Tomorrow Night*	8.00 -	12.00
123 *Lonesome Day Blues*	8.00 -	12.00

LOUISE JOHNSON:

Paramount 12992 *All Night Long Blues*	150.00 -	250.00
13008 *On The Wall*	150.00 -	250.00

MARGARET JOHNSON:

Okeh 8107 *E Flat Blues*	75.00 -	100.00
8162 *Absent Minded Blues*	75.00 -	100.00
8185 *Changeable Daddy Of Mine*	150.00 -	200.00
8193 *Who'll Chop Your Suey When I'm Gone?*	80.00 -	120.00
8220 *Nobody's Blues But Mine*	30.00 -	50.00
8230 *I'm A Good Hearted Mama*	75.00 -	100.00

8405 *Mama Papa Don't Wanna Come Back*	
Home .... 35.00 - 50.00	
8418 *Heavy Burden Blues* .... 35.00 - 50.00	
8506 *Stinging Bee Blues* .... 35.00 - 50.00	
Victor 20178 *My Man's Done Done Me Dirty* ... 35.00 - 50.00	
20333 *Graysom Street Blues* .... 35.00 - 50.00	
20652 *Good Woman Blues* .... 75.00 - 100.00	
20982 *Dead Drunk Blues* .... 75.00 - 100.00	

MARTHA JOHNSON:
Superior 2753 *Goin' Away Blues* .... 150.00 - 250.00

MARY JOHNSON:
Brunswick 7081 *Western Union Blues* .... 100.00 - 150.00
7093 *Muddy Creek Blues* .... 100.00 - 150.00
7153 *Dawn Of Day Blues* .... 100.00 - 150.00
7160 *Death Cell Blues* .... 100.00 - 150.00
7175 *Morning Sun Blues* .... 75.00 - 100.00
Champion 16570 *Mary Johnson Blues* .... 150.00 - 200.00
50062 *Mary Johnson Blues* .... 50.00 - 75.00
Decca 7012 *Those Black Man Blues* ...... 50.00 - 75.00
7014 *Black Gal Blues* .... 35.00 - 50.00
7305 *Delmar Avenue* .... 30.00 - 50.00
Paramount 12931 *Dream Daddy Blues.* .... 125.00 - 175.00
12996 *Barrel House Flat Blues* .... 150.00 - 200.00

MERLINE JOHNSON:
Bluebird 6985 *He Roars Like A Lion* .... 20.00 - 30.00
7032 *My Baby Left Me* .... 20.00 - 30.00
7166 *Pallet On The Floor* .... 20.00 - 30.00

PORKCHOP JOHNSON:
Champion 15796 *Pork Chop Stomp* .... 150.00 - 250.00
Supertone 9516 *Pork Chop Stomp* .... 150.00 - 250.00

RAY JOHNSON:
Mercury 70203, 70231 .... 5.00 - 8.00*

RED JOHNSON:
Mercury 70141, 70194 .... 5.00 - 8.00*

ROBERT JOHNSON:
Titles, issued contemporaneously on Banner,
Melotone, Oriole, Perfect, Romeo, Vocalion:
Come On In My Kitchen; Cross Road Blues;
Dead Shrimp Blues; From Four Until Late;
Hell Hound On My Trail; I Believe I'll Dust
My Broom; I'm A Steady Rollin' Man; Kind
Hearted Woman Blues; Last Fair Deal Gone
Down; Malted Milk; Milkcow's Calf Blues;
Ramblin' On My Mind; Stones In My Passway;
Terraplane Blues; They're Red Hot; 32-20
Blues .... 150.00 - 300.00
Vocalion 03601 *Sweet Home Chicago* .... 150.00 - 300.00
04002 *Honeymoon Blues* .... 150.00 - 300.00
04108 *Me And The Devil Blues* .... 150.00 - 300.00
04630 *Love In Vain* .... 150.00 - 300.00

ROCKHEART JOHNSON:
Victor 20-4967, 20-5136 .... 6.00 - 10.00*

RUTH JOHNSON:
Paramount 13060 *Rockin' Chair* .... 50.00 - 75.00

SAM (SUITCASE) JOHNSON:
Sittin' In With 608 *Sam's Boogie* .... 10.00 - 15.00

SARA JOHNSON:
Banner 1882 *Papa If You Can't Do Better* ...... 10.00 - 15.00
Domino 3852 *Papa If You Can't Do Better* ..... 10.00 - 15.00
Regal 8196 *Papa If You Can't Do Better* .... 10.00 - 15.00

SHERMAN JOHNSON (& HIS CLOUDS OF JOY):
Nashboro 507 *Back Alley Boogie* .... 8.00 - 12.00
Trumpet, 198, 190 .... 4.00 - 7.00*

SLIM JOHNSON:
Gennett 6570 *If Mama Has Outside Lovin'* ..... 250.00 - 400.00

SONNY BOY JOHNSON & HIS BLUE BLAZERS:
Murray 505 *Come And Go With Me* .... 10.00 - 15.00
507 *Swimming Pool Blues* .... 10.00 - 15.00

STOVEPIPE JOHNSON:
Vocalion 1203 *Devilish Blues* .... 150.00 - 200.00

1211 *I Ain't Got Nobody* .... 150.00 - 200.00

STUMP JOHNSON: (See also JAMES "STUMP" JOHNSON)
Bluebird 5159 *Don't Give My Lard Away* .... 100.00 - 150.00
5247 *Money Johnson* .... 100.00 - 150.00
Paramount 12862 *Kind Babe Blues* .... 150.00 - 200.00
12906 *Soaking Wet Blues* .... 150.00 - 200.00
12938 *You Buzzard You* .... 150.00 - 200.00
Sunrise 3240 *Steady Grindin'* .... 100.00 - 200.00
3330 *Money Johnson* .... 100.00 - 200.00
Victor 23327 *Barrel Of Whiskey Blues* .... 200.00 - 300.00

T.C. JOHNSON & "BLUE COAT" TOM NELSON:
Okeh 8838 *J.C. Johnson's Blues* .... 75.00 - 125.00

TILLIE JOHNSON:
Gennett 6438 *Chicago Man Blues* .... 100.00 - 150.00
6471 *My Baby* .... 100.00 - 150.00

TOMMY JOHNSON:
Paramount 12950 *Alcohol And Jake Blues* .... 300.00 - 600.00
12975 *Slidin' Delta* .... 300.00 - 600.00
13000 *Black Mare Blues* .... 300.00 - 600.00
Victor 21279 *Big Road Blues* .... 300.00 - 500.00
21409 *Bye-Bye Blues* .... 300.00 - 500.00
V38535 *Canned Heat Blues* .... 400.00 - 700.00

BLIND WILLIE JOHNSON:
Columbia 14276-D *Jesus Make Up My Dying Bed* 50.00 - 75.00
14303-D *Nobody's Fault But Mine* .... 50.00 - 75.00
14343-D *Mother's Children Have A Hard Time* 50.00 - 75.00
14391-D *Jesus Is Coming Soon* .... 50.00 - 75.00
14425-D *Keep Your Lamp Trimmed And Burning* .... 50.00 - 75.00
14490-D *Let Your Light Shine On* .... 50.00 - 75.00
14504-D *You'll Need Somebody On Your Bond* . 50.00 - 75.00
14520-D *God Moves On The Water* .... 50.00 - 75.00
14530-D *John The Revelator* .... 100.00 - 150.00
14537-D *The Rain Don't Fall On Me* .... 50.00 - 80.00
14545-D *When The War Was On* .... 75.00 - 100.00
14556-D *Can't Nobody Hide From God* ...... 75.00 - 100.00
14582-D *The Soul Of A Man* .... 75.00 - 100.00
14597-D *Go With Me To That Land* .... 75.00 - 100.00
14624-D *Take Your Stand* .... 80.00 - 120.00

JOLLY JIVERS:
Vocalion 02532 *Whatcha Gonna Do?* .... 75.00 - 125.00
25015 *Hungry Man's Scuffle* .... 75.00 - 125.00

JOLLY JUG BAND:
Varsity 6037 *Tappin' That Thing* .... 20.00 - 30.00

JOLLY TWO:
Vocalion 25014 *Frisco Blues* .... 75.00 - 125.00
25018 *Guitar Stomp* .... 75.00 - 125.00

ALBERTA JONES (TRIO) AND HER RED PEPPERS):
Buddy 8024 *Sud Bustin' Blues* .... 100.00 - 150.00
8025 *Home Alone Blues* .... 100.00 - 150.00
8033 *It Must Be Hard* .... 100.00 - 150.00
8034 *Take Your Fingers Off It* .... 100.00 - 150.00
Champion 16216 *Bring It Back Daddy* .... 150.00 - 250.00
Gennett 3144 *Home Alone Blues* .... 40.00 - 60.00
3306 *Take Your Finger Off It* .... 60.00 - 90.00
3403 *Lucky Number Blues* .... 100.00 - 150.00
6424 *Dying Blues* .... 75.00 - 100.00
6439 *Shake A Little Bit* .... 100.00 - 150.00
6535 *My Slow and Easy Man* .... 150.00 - 200.00
6642 *Wild Geese Blues* .... 150.00 - 200.00
7252 *On Revival Day* .... 150.00 - 250.00
7274 *I Lost My Man* .... 150.00 - 250.00
Herwin 92001 *Lucky Number Blues* .... 125.00 - 200.00
Silvertone 4052 *Home Alone Blues* .... 35.00 - 50.00
5025 *Lucky Number Blues* .... 100.00 - 150.00

ANNA JONES:
Harmograph 859 *Trixie Blues* .... 75.00 - 100.00
Paramount 12043 *You Can't Do What My Last Man Did* .... 30.00 - 50.00

12052 *Trixie Blues* .... 40.00 - 60.00

BESSIE JONES:

Superior 2633 *Stop Bitin' Other Women In The Back* ....150.00 - 250.00

   Supertone 9474 *I Ain't Givin' Nobody None* ....100.00 - 150.00

   9509 *Pig Meat Mama* ....125.00 - 175.00

"BO" JONES:

Vocalion 1452 *Leavenworth Prison Blues* ....100.00 - 150.00

CLINT JONES:

Columbia 14322-D *Right Or Wrong* .... 20.00 - 30.00

   Okeh 8587 *Blue Valley Blues* .... 30.00 - 50.00

COLEY JONES:

Columbia 14288-D *Traveling Man* .... 75.00 - 100.00

   14489-D *Drunkard's Special* .... 75.00 - 100.00

CURTIS JONES:

Bluebird 7387 *Good Old Easy Street* .... 15.00 - 20.00

   7452 *Schoolmate Blues* .... 15.00 - 20.00

   8412, 8455 .... 10.00 - 15.00

   Conqueror 9030, 9031, 9032, 9077, 9161, 9196,

     9273, 9279, 9358 .... 7.00 - 10.00

     9768, 9944, 9945, 9946 .... 5.00 - 10.00

   Okeh 05744, 05834, 05907, 05947, 05996,

     06069, 06105, 06140, 06186, 06428, 06594,

     06615 .... 5.00 - 10.00

   Parrot 782 *Cool Playing Blues* .... 15.00 - 20.00

   Vocalion 03756, 03953, 03990, 04027, 04080,

     04120, 04162, 04249, 04330, 04392 ... 10.00 - 15.00

EDDIE (GUITAR SLIM) JONES (& HIS PLAYBOYS):

Imperial 5134 *Bad Luck Is On Me* .... 10.00 - 15.00*

Jim Bullet 603 *Feelin' Sad* .... 10.00 - 15.00*

ELIJAH JONES:

Bluebird 7526 *E. Stuff Stomp* .... 20.00 - 30.00

   7565 *Big Boat* .... 20.00 - 30.00

   7616 *Katy Fly* .... 20.00 - 30.00

   7655 *Lonesome Man* .... 20.00 - 30.00

ELSIE JONES WITH SMILIN' JOE:

Flip 1003 *Old Man's Sweetheart* .... —   -   —

FLOYD JONES (& HIS TRIO) (WITH SNOOKY & MOODY):

Chess 1498 *Dark Road* .... 20.00 - 30.00*

   1527 *Early Morning* .... 15.00 - 25.00*

   J.O.B. 1001 *Big World* .... 25.00 - 40.00

   1013 *On The Road Again* .... 25.00 - 40.00*

   Old Swingmaster 22 *Stockyard Blues* ... 35.00 - 50.00

FRANKIE JONES:

Vocalion 04206 *My Lincoln* .... 10.00 - 15.00

   04266 *Jockey Blues* .... 10.00 - 15.00

REV. (GEORGE) JONES (& CONGREGATION):

Champion 15816 *The Heavenly Airplane* .... 75.00 - 100.00

Gennett 6979 *The Heavenly Airplane* .... 80.00 - 120.00

Supertone 9518 *The Heavenly Airplane* .... 75.00 - 100.00

JAKE JONES:

Brunswick 7130 *Monkeyin' Around* .... 80.00 - 120.00

JOSEPHINE JONES:

Ajax 17094 *Just One Word Of Consolation* ..... 20.00 - 30.00

JULIA JONES:

Champion 15265 *Save My Jelly* .... 50.00 - 75.00

Gennett 5177 *That Thing Called Love* .... 15.00 - 20.00

   5233 *Deceitful Blues* .... 15.00 - 20.00

Starr 9407 *That Thing Called Love* .... 15.00 - 20.00

LITTLE HAT JONES:

Okeh 8712 *Two String Blues* .... 75.00 - 125.00

   8735 *Corpus Blues* .... 75.00 - 125.00

   8794 *Little Hat Blues* .... 75.00 - 125.00

   8815 *Kentucky Blues* .... 75.00 - 125.00

   8829 *Cherry Street Blues* .... 75.00 - 125.00

LOUELLA JONES (& JAZZ CASPER):

Banner 1451 *Sweet Mandy* .... 10.00 - 15.00

   1467 *Who Calls You Sweet Mama Now* .... 10.00 - 15.00

Harmograph 983 *Sweet Mandy* .... 15.00 - 20.00

MAGGIE JONES:

Columbia 14044-D, 14047-D, 14070-D, 14081-D,

   14092-D .... 10.00 - 20.00

   14050-D *Poor House Blues* .... 25.00 - 40.00

   14055-D *Screamin' The Blues* .... 30.00 - 50.00

   14059-D *If I Lose, Let Me Lose* .... 30.00 - 40.00

   14063-D *Anybody Here Want To Try My Cabbage?* .... 20.00 - 30.00

   14074-D *Cheatin' On Me* .... 15.00 - 20.00

   14102-D, 14167-D .... 15.00 - 20.00

   14114-D *South Street Blues* .... 25.00 - 40.00

   14127-D *I'm A Back-Bitin' Mama* .... 25.00 - 40.00

   14139-D *I'm Leaving You* .... 25.00 - 40.00

   14243-D *The Man I Love Is Oh So Good* ... 25.00 - 40.00

Pathe-Actuelle 021062, Perfect 12075 .... 10.00 - 15.00

MARY JONES:

Gennett 6860 *You Lied About That Woman* ..... 15.00 - 20.00

ELDER OTIS JONES:

Bluebird 6466 *Repentance* .... 15.00 - 25.00

   6626 *I Am The Vine* .... 15.00 - 25.00

   7720 *O Lord, I'm Your Child* .... 15.00 - 25.00

SONNY JONES:

Vocalion 05056 *Dough Roller* .... 20.00 - 30.00

   05124 *I'm Pretty Good At It* .... 20.00 - 30.00

WILLIE (DOC) JONES:

Peacock 1540 *Do You Want To Roll* .... 5.00 - 10.00

Vocalion 1194 *Willie's Weary Blues* ....100.00 - 150.00

CHARLIE/CHARLEY JORDAN/JORDON:

Decca 7015 *Rolling Moon Blues* .... 20.00 - 30.00

   7065 *Tight Time Blues* .... 20.00 - 30.00

   7130 *Christmas Christmas Blues* .... 20.00 - 30.00

   Victor 23304 *Working Man Blues* ....200.00 - 300.00

   23372 *Greyhound Blues* ....250.00 - 400.00

   Vocalion 1511 *Big Four Blues* .... 75.00 - 100.00

   1528 *Raidin' Squad Blues* .... 75.00 - 100.00

   1543 *Just A Spoonful* .... 75.00 - 100.00

   1551 *Running Mad Blues* .... 75.00 - 100.00

   1557 *Dollar Bill Blues* .... 75.00 - 100.00

   1568 *Tough Times Blues* .... 75.00 - 100.00

   1611 *You Run And Tell Your Daddy* ...... 75.00 - 100.00

   1627 *Starvation Blues* .... 75.00 - 100.00

   1645 *Tight Haired Mama Blues* .... 75.00 - 100.00

   1657 *Hungry Blues* .... 75.00 - 100.00

   1666 *Silver Dollar Blues* .... 75.00 - 100.00

   1696 *Stir It Up* .... 75.00 - 100.00

   1707 *Cherry Wine Woman* .... 75.00 - 100.00

   1717 *Honey Sucker Blues* .... 75.00 - 100.00

   02763 *Bottle Passing Blues* .... 75.00 - 100.00

JENNIE JORDAN:

Champion 15267 *Blue And All By Myself* .... 75.00 - 100.00

JIMMY JORDAN:

Columbia 14622-D *Jelly Killed Old Sam* .... 75.00 - 100.00

   14647-D *She's Dangerous With That Thing* ... 75.00 - 100.00

   14655-D *There Is No Justice* .... 75.00 - 100.00

LUKE JORDAN:

Victor 20957 *Traveling Coon* ....100.00 - 150.00

   21076 *Cocaine Blues* ....100.00 - 150.00

   23400 *If I Call You Mama* ....200.00 - 300.00

   V38564 *My Gal's Done Quit Me* ....150.00 - 200.00

CHARLEY JORDON: (See CHARLIE/ CHARLEY JORDAN)

JUBILEE GOSPEL TEAM:

Paramount 12835 *Dry Bones In The Valley* ...... 30.00 - 50.00

   12836 *Station Will Be Changed* .... 50.00 - 75.00

   12837 *I Know The Lord Has Laid His Hands On Me* .... 50.00 - 75.00

   12838 *I Have Crossed The Separating Line* ... 50.00 - 75.00

   13113 *Jesus Is Mine* .... 50.00 - 75.00

QRS 7013 *Dry Bones In The Valley* .... 50.00 - 75.00

   7014 *Station Will Be Changed* .... 50.00 - 75.00

   7015 *Oh Lord, Remember Me* .... 50.00 - 75.00

   7026 *I Know The Lord Has Laid His Hands*

On Me	50.00 -	75.00
7027 *I Have Crossed The Separating Line*	50.00 -	75.00
7053 *I'm 'Termined To Pray Right On*	50.00 -	75.00
7058 *When The Train Comes Along*	50.00 -	75.00

JUNIOR BLUES:

RPM 320 *Whiskey Head Woman*	10.00 -	15.00

KANSAS CITY BLUES STRUMMERS:

Vocalion 1048 *String Band Blues*	100.00 -	150.00

KANSAS CITY KITTY:

Bluebird 5726 *Christmas Morning Blues*	20.00 -	30.00
5756 *Leave My Man Alone*	20.00 -	30.00
Vocalion 1508 *You Got That Stuff*	75.00 -	100.00
1534 *Room Rent Blues*	75.00 -	100.00
1545 *Fish House Blues*	75.00 -	100.00
1565 *Killing Floor Blues*	75.00 -	100.00
1575 *Who's Been Here Since I Been Gone?*	75.00 -	100.00
1600 *Root Man Blues*	75.00 -	100.00
1612 *Knife Man Blues*	75.00 -	100.00
1632 *Scronchin'*	75.00 -	100.00
1642 *That Thing's A Mess*	75.00 -	100.00

KANSAS JOE (& MEMPHIS MINNIE):

Bluebird 6260 *Something Gonna Happen To You*	15.00 -	25.00
Columbia 14439-D *When The Levee Breaks*	100.00 -	150.00
14542-D *I Want That*	100.00 -	150.00
Vocalion 1500 *What Fault You Find Of Me?*	75.00 -	125.00
1523 *Can I Do It For You?*	75.00 -	125.00
1535 *Cherry Ball Blues*	75.00 -	125.00
1550 *North Memphis Blues*	75.00 -	125.00
1570 *Botherin' That Thing*	75.00 -	125.00
1576 *She Wouldn't Give Me None*	75.00 -	125.00
1612 *Pile Drivin' Blues*	75.00 -	125.00
1631 *I Called You This Morning*	75.00 -	125.00
1643 *Preachers Blues*	75.00 -	125.00
1660 *Pickin' The Blues*	100.00 -	150.00
1668 *My Wash Women's Gone*	100.00 -	150.00
1677 *I'm Fixed For You*	100.00 -	150.00
1686 *Joliet Bound*	100.00 -	150.00
1688 *You Stole My Cake*	100.00 -	150.00
1705 *Dresser Drawer Blues*	100.00 -	150.00

KANSAS KATIE:

Bluebird 8944 *Deep Sea Diver*	10.00 -	15.00
8999 *He's My Man*	10.00 -	15.00

KEGHOUSE:

Okeh 8583 *Keghouse Blues*	50.00 -	75.00
Vocalion 1239 *Canned Heat Blues*	80.00 -	120.00

JACK KELLY (& HIS SOUTH MEMPHIS JUG BAND):

Titles, issued contemporaneously on Banner, Conqueror, Melotone, Oriole, Perfect, Romeo: *Believe I'll Go Back Home; Cold Iron Bed; Highway No. 61 Blues; Highway No. 61 Blues No. 2; Ko-Ko Mo Blues; President Blues; Red Ripe Tomatoes; R.F.C Blues*	75.00 -	125.00
Vocalion 05031 *Diamond Buyer Blues*	30.00 -	50.00
05193 *Neck Bone Blues*	30.00 -	50.00
05312 *Men Fooler Blues*	30.00 -	50.00

WILLIE KELLY:

Victor 23259 *Kelly's Special*	150.00 -	200.00
23263 *Side Door Blues*	150.00 -	200.00
23270 *Big Time Woman*	150.00 -	200.00
23286 *Don't Squeeze Me Too Tight*	150.00 -	200.00
23299 *Nasty But It's Clean*	150.00 -	250.00
23320 *Hard Luck Man Blues*	200.00 -	300.00
23416 *Sad And Lonely Day*	200.00 -	300.00
38608 *Kelly's 44 Blues*	100.00 -	150.00
38619 *32-20 Blues*	100.00 -	150.00

SAM KELLY & HIS HARMONICA:

Von 43 *Ramblin' Around Blues*	20.00 -	30.00

ROBERT KELTON & HIS TRIO:

Aladdin 3054, 3187	5.00 -	8.00

TINY KENNEDY:

Trumpet 187 *Strange Kind Of Feeling*	4.00 -	7.00*

188 *Blues Disease*	4.00 -	7.00*

KID AND COOT:

Columbia 14363-D *Keyhole Blues*	40.00 -	60.00

KID COLEY:

Bluebird 5248 *Clair And Pearley Blues*	100.00 -	150.00
Sunrise 3331 *Clair And Pearly Blues*	100.00 -	200.00
Victor 23293 *Tricks Ain't Walkin' No More*	200.00 -	300.00
23369 *Freight Train Blues*	250.00 -	500.00

KID STORMY WEATHER:

Vocalion 03145 *Short Hair Blues*	75.00 -	125.00

LENA (AND SYLVESTER) KIMBROUGH:

Meritt 2201 *Cabbage Head Blues*	250.00 -	500.00

LOTTIE KIMBROUGH (AND WINSTON HOLMES):

Gennett 6607 *Wayward Girl Blues*	150.00 -	250.00
6624 *Rolling Log Blues*	150.00 -	250.00
6660 *Blue World Blues*	150.00 -	250.00

SYLVESTER KIMBROUGH:

Brunswick 7135 *Garbage Can Blues*	100.00 -	150.00

KING TUT:

Sittin' In With 542, 550	5.00 -	8.00

B.B. ("BLUES BOY") KING:

Bullett 309 *Miss Martha King*	8.00 -	12.00
315 *Got The Blues*	8.00 -	12.00
RPM 304, 311, 318, 323, 330, 339, 348, 355, 360, 363, 374, 380, 386, 391, 395, 403, 408, 411, 412, 416, 421, 425, 430	3.00 -	6.00*

JULIUS KING:

Tennessee 123 *I Want A Slice Of Your Pudding*	7.00 -	10.00

RICHARD KING & HIS ORCHESTRA:

Khoury's 800 *Ride, Daddy, Ride*	5.00 -	8.00

WEE WILLIE KIRK:

Bullet 340 *Your Love Was So Nice And Warm*	10.00 -	15.00

(LITTLE) EDDIE KIRKLAND:

King 4659, 4680	5.00 -	8.00*
RPM 367 *That's All Right*	8.00 -	12.00*

LILLIE MAE KIRKMAN:

Vocalion 04951 *Hop Head Blues*	10.00 -	15.00
04991 *When You Leave Me Honey*	10.00 -	15.00

JESSIE KNIGHT:

Checker 797 *Nothing But Money*	7.00 -	10.00

BIG BOY KNOX:

Bluebird 6904 *Texas Blues*	20.00 -	30.00
6952 *Blue Man Blues*	20.00 -	30.00

CHARLIE KYLE:

Victor 21707 *Kyle's Worried Blues*	100.00 -	150.00
38625 *Walking Blues*	150.00 -	200.00

RUBE LACY:

Paramount 12629 *Mississippi Jail House Groan*	100.00 -	150.00

RUTH LADSON & THREE SHADOWS:

Okeh 06667 *Kicking My Man Around*	8.00 -	12.00

JUSTINE LAMAR:

Decca 7238 *Always Mine*	7.00 -	10.00

ERNEST LANE:

Blues & Rhythm 700 *What's Wrong Baby*	10.00 -	15.00

WILLIE LANE:

Talent 805 *Prowlin' Ground Hog*	35.00 -	50.00
806 *Black Cat Rag*	35.00 -	50.00

SOPHISTICATED JIMMY LA RUE:

Champion 50070 *Money Truckin' Blues*	15.00 -	20.00
50071 *Two Old Maids In A Folding Bed Blues*	20.00 -	30.00

LOUIS LASKY:

Vocalion 02955 *Teasin' Brown Blues*	75.00 -	100.00

LAUGHING CHARLEY:

Columbia 14272-D *Chain Gang Trouble*	50.00 -	80.00

LAZY BILL & HIS BLUE RHYTHMS:

Chance 1148 *I Had A Dream*	15.00 -	25.00*

LAZY SLIM JIM:

Savoy 868 *Sugaree*	5.00 -	8.00

(HUDDIE) LEADBELLY:

Titles, issued contemporaneously on Banner, Melotone, Oriole, Perfect, Romeo: *Becky*

Deem, She Was A Gamblin' Gal; Four Day
Worry Blues; Honey, I'm All Out And Down;
New Black Snake Moan; Packin' Trunk Blues;
Pig Meat Papa .... 50.00 - 100.00
Bluebird 8550 *Sail On, Little Girl Sail On* ...... 10.00 - 15.00
8559 *T.B. Blues* .... 10.00 - 15.00
8570 *Easy Rider* .... 10.00 - 15.00
8709 *Roberta* .... 10.00 - 15.00
8750 *New York City* .... 10.00 - 15.00
8791 *Leaving Blues* .... 10.00 - 15.00

HUDDIE LEDBETTER WITH THE GOLDEN
GATE QUARTET:
Victor 27266, 27267, 27268 .... 5.00 - 10.00

BERTHA LEE:
Vocalion 02650 *Mind Reader Blues* .... 100.00 - 150.00

BESSIE LEE:
Silvertone 3525 *He Likes It Slow* .... 35.00 - 50.00
3534 *Sorrowful Blues* .... 35.00 - 50.00

CAROLINE LEE:
Oriole 353 *Thunderstorm Blues* .... 10.00 - 15.00
698 *What's The Matter Now?* .... 10.00 - 15.00

ELIZA CHRISTMAS LEE:
Gennett 4801 *Arkansas Blues* .... 8.00 - 12.00

EMMA DELL LEE & TRIO:
Khoury's 900 *No Good Daddy* .... 5.00 - 8.00

JERRY LEE:
Herwin 93011 *The Snitches Blues* .... 150.00 - 250.00
93014 *Smiling Blues* .... 150.00 - 250.00

JOHN LEE:
Federal 12054 *Down At The Depot* .... 7.00 - 10.00*
12089 *Blind's Blues* .... 7.00 - 10.00*
Gotham 515 *Mean Old Train* .... 7.00 - 10.00
J.O.B. 114 *Rhythm Rockin' Boogie* .... 15.00 - 20.00

JOHNNY LEE:
DeLuxe 6009 *I Came To See You Baby* .... 7.00 - 10.00

MAE BELLE LEE & GEORGE RAMSEY:
Paramount 13069 *Bumble Bee No. 2* .... 150.00 - 200.00

RUSSELL LEE & DAISY WRIGHT:
Okeh 8263 *Vampire Brown* .... 20.00 - 30.00

TOMMY LEE:
Delta 403 *Highway 80 Blues* .... 10.00 - 15.00*

VERDI LEE (& CHARLEY JORDAN):
Decca 7130 *Christmas Tree Blues* .... 20.00 - 30.00
7142 *Get It If You Can* .... 20.00 - 30.00

J.B. LENOIR/LENORE (& HIS BAYOU
BOYS/COMBO):
Chess 1449 *My Baby Told Me* .... 8.00 - 12.00*
1463 *Deep In Debt Blues* .... 8.00 - 12.00*
J.O.B. 112 *Let's Roll* .... 10.00 - 15.00*
1008 *The Mountain* .... 5.00 - 10.00*
1012 *The Mojo* .... 5.00 - 10.00*
1016 *I'll Die Trying* .... 5.00 - 10.00
1102 *Play A Little While* .... 5.00 - 10.00*
Parrot 802 *Eisenhower Blues/I'm In Korea* ..... 7.00 - 15.00*
802 *Tax Paying Blues/I'm In Korea* .... 7.00 - 10.00*
809 *Mama Talk To Your Daughter* .... 4.00 - 7.00*
814 *What Have I Done* .... 4.00 - 7.00*
821 *I Lost My Baby* .... 4.00 - 7.00*

LEROY'S BUDDY:
Decca 7179, 7180, 7194, 7202, 7223, 7233, 7246,
7258, 7271, 7298, 7308, 7335, 7356, 7374, 7394 ... 7.00 - 12.00
Decca (higher numbers) .... 5.00 - 10.00

LEVEE JOE:
Conqueror 8658 *Flood Water Blues* .... 8.00 - 12.00

LEWIS BRONZEVILLE FIVE:
Bluebird 8433 *Cotton Blossom Blues* .... 10.00 - 15.00
8445 *Natchez Mississippi Blues* .... 10.00 - 15.00
8460 *Low Dow Gal Blues* .... 10.00 - 15.00
8480 *It Can Happen To You* .... 10.00 - 15.00
Montgomery Ward 8898 *Laughing At Life* ...... 10.00 - 15.00
8899 *Linda Brown* .... 10.00 - 15.00
8900 *Mississippi Fire Blues* .... 10.00 - 15.00

8901 *Oh! Mabel Oh!* .... 10.00 - 15.00

ARCHIE LEWIS:
Champion 16677 *Miss Handy Hanks* .... 100.00 - 150.00

BUDDY LEWIS:
Swing Time 312 *You've Got Good Business* ..... 10.00 - 15.00*

ERNEST LEWIS:
Parrot 791 *West Coast Blues* .... 10.00 - 15.00*

FURRY LEWIS:
Victor 21664 *Kassie Jones* .... 150.00 - 200.00
23345 *Cannon Ball Blues* .... 250.00 - 500.00
38506 *Judge Harsh Blues* .... 200.00 - 300.00
38519 *Mistreatin' Mama* .... 200.00 - 300.00
Vocalion 1111 *Rock Island Blues* .... 150.00 - 200.00
1115 *Mr. Furry's Blues* .... 150.00 - 200.00
1116 *Sweet Papa Moan* .... 150.00 - 200.00
1132 *Good Looking Girl Blues* .... 150.00 - 200.00
1133 *Big Chief Blues* .... 150.00 - 200.00
1134 *Mean Old Bedbug Blues* .... 150.00 - 200.00
1474 *John Henry* .... 150.00 - 250.00
1547 *Creeper's Blues* .... 200.00 - 300.00

IDA LEWIS:
Silvertone 3556 *Tennessee Blues* .... 75.00 - 100.00

JOHNNY LEWIS ORCHESTRA:
Rockin' 517 *She's Taking All My Money* .... 10.00 - 15.00*

KATE LEWIS:
Broadway 5016 *Mercy Blues* .... 50.00 - 75.00

PETE (GUITAR) LEWIS:
Federal 12066, 12076, 12103, 12112 .... 4.00 - 8.00*

RAY LEWIS:
Imperial .... 4.00 - 8.00*

SAMMY LEWIS:
Sun 218 *I Feel So Worried* .... 15.00 - 20.00

PAPA LIGHTFOOT:
Aladdin 3171 *P.L. Blues* .... 7.00 - 10.00*
3304 *Jumpin' With Jarvis* .... 7.00 - 10.00*
Imperial 5289 *Mean Old Train* .... 10.00 - 15.00*

PRESTON LILLARD:
Champion 15416 *Barrel House Blues* .... 150.00 - 200.00
15436 *The Jockey Blues* .... 150.00 - 200.00

LILLIE MAE:
Columbia 14600-D *Buggy Jail House Blues* ..... 50.00 - 80.00
Okeh 8920 *Mama Don't Want It* .... 50.00 - 80.00

CHARLEY/CHARLIE LINCOLN:
Columbia 14305-D *Jealous Hearted Blues* ..... 50.00 - 80.00
14332-D *Ugly Papa* .... 50.00 - 80.00
14420-D *Gamblin' Charley* .... 50.00 - 80.00
14475-D *Country Breakdown* .... 50.00 - 80.00
14550-D *Mama Don't Rush Me* .... 75.00 - 100.00

JOE LINTHECOME:
Gennett 7131 *Humming Blues* .... 75.00 - 100.00

VIRGINIA LISTON:
Okeh 8092 *Bed Time Blues* .... 15.00 - 20.00
8115 *Sally Long Blues* .... 15.00 - 20.00
8122 *Shreveport Blues* .... 15.00 - 20.00
8126 *You Can Have It* .... 15.00 - 20.00
8134 *House Rent Stomp* .... 15.00 - 20.00
8138 *I Don't Love Nobody* .... 15.00 - 20.00
8151 *Don't Agitate Me Blues* .... 15.00 - 20.00
8160 *Mississippi Blues* .... 15.00 - 20.00
8173 *You've Got The Right Key, But The*
Wrong Keyhole .... 75.00 - 125.00
8175 *Weeping Willow Blues* .... 15.00 - 20.00
8187 *Early In The Morning* .... 75.00 - 125.00
8196 *Night Latch Key Blues* .... 25.00 - 40.00
8218 *You Can Dip Your Bread In My Gravy,*
But You Can't Have None Of My Chops .... 40.00 - 60.00
8223 *Black Sheep Blues* .... 30.00 - 50.00
8234 *I'm Sick Of Fattening Frogs For Snakes* . 25.00 - 40.00
8247 *Make Me A Pallet* .... 30.00 - 50.00
Vocalion 1031 *Titanic Blues* .... 75.00 - 100.00
1032 *Rolls-Royce Papa* .... 75.00 - 100.00

LITTLE BILL:

Bluebird 6972 *You Can't Love Me And Someone*
  Else Too .... 15.00 - 20.00

LITTLE BROTHER:
Bluebird 6658 *Chinese Man Blues* .... 25.00 - 40.00
  6697 *Louisiana Blues—Part 2* .... 25.00 - 40.00
  6733 *Crescent City Blues* .... 25.00 - 40.00
  6766 *Tantalizing Blues* .... 25.00 - 40.00
  6811 *Santa Fe Blues* .... 25.00 - 40.00
  6825 *Never Go Wrong Blues* .... 25.00 - 40.00
  6894 *Farish Street Jive* .... 25.00 - 40.00
  6916 *Out West Blues* .... 25.00 - 40.00
  7178 *West Texas Blues* .... 25.00 - 40.00
  7277 *Sorrowful Blues* .... 25.00 - 40.00
  7806 *Misled Blues* .... 25.00 - 40.00
  10177 *Farish Street Jive* .... 10.00 - 15.00
  10953 *Crescent City* .... 10.00 - 15.00
Montgomery Ward 7111 *Louisiana Blues* ..... 15.00 - 20.00
  7112 *Tantalizing Blues* .... 15.00 - 20.00

LITTLE DAVID:
Decca 7211 *Standing By A Lamp Post* .... 15.00 - 25.00
  7270 *Ramblin' Mind Blues* .... 15.00 - 25.00
Regal 3271 *Shackles 'Round My Body* .... 15.00 - 20.00
RPM 371 *Crying Blues* .... 7.00 - 10.00

LITTLE HUDSON & HIS RED DEVIL TRIO:
J.O.B. 1015 *Rough Treatment* .... 20.00 - 30.00*

LITTLE JIMMY:
Acorn 301 *Rock That Boogie* ....

LITTLE JOHNNY:
Aristocrat 405 *Shelby County Blues* .... 75.00 - 100.00

LITTLE JUNIOR'S BLUE FLAMES:
Sun 187, 192 .... 6.00 - 10.00*

LITTLE MILTON:
Delta 403 *Little Milton's Boogie* .... 10.00 - 15.00
Sun 194 *Beggin' My Baby* .... 10.00 - 15.00*
  209 *Alone And Blue* .... 25.00 - 40.00*
  220 *Looking For My Baby* .... 15.00 - 20.00*

LITTLE MR. MIDNIGHT:
Regal 3287 *Four O'Clock Blues* .... -

LITTLE PAPA JOE:
Blue Lake 116 *Looking For My Baby* .... 15.00 - 20.00*

LITTLE SISTER:
Varsity 6050 *My Back To The Wall* .... 15.00 - 20.00

LITTLE SON JOE:
Okeh 06707 *Black Rat Swing* .... 5.00 - 8.00
Vocalion 04707 *Diggin' My Potatoes* .... 10.00 - 15.00
  04776 *A.B.C. Blues* .... 10.00 - 15.00
  04978 *My Black Buffalo* .... 10.00 - 15.00
  05004 *Key To The World* .... 10.00 - 15.00

LITTLE T-BONE:
Miltone 5223 *Christmas Blues* .... 8.00 - 12.00

LITTLE WALTER (TRIO) (& HIS JUKES/
NIGHT CAPS):
Chance 1116 *I Just Keep Loving Her* .... 20.00 - 30.00
Checker 758 *Juke* .... 7.00 - 10.00*
  764 *Mean Old World* .... 7.00 - 10.00*
  767 *Tonight With A Fool* .... 5.00 - 8.00*
  770 *Off The Wall* .... 5.00 - 8.00*
Checker 780, 786, 793, 799, 805, 811, 817, 825 ... 4.00 - 7.00*
  833, 838, 845, 852, 859, 867, 890 .... 3.00 - 5.00
Ora Nelle 711 *Ora Nelle Blues* .... 30.00 - 50.00
Regal 3296 *Muskadine Blues* .... 75.00 - 100.00

LITTLE WILLIE LITTLEFIELD:
Eddie's 1202 *Little Willie's Boogie* .... 7.00 - 10.00
  1205 *Chicago Bound* .... 7.00 - 10.00
  1212 *Boogie Woogie Playgirl* .... 7.00 - 10.00
Freedom 1502 *Littlefeld Boogie* .... 5.00 - 8.00
Modern .... 3.00 - 5.00*

JESSE LOCKETT & HIS ORCHESTRA:
Gulf 3000 *Blacker The Berry* .... 10.00 - 15.00

JAMES (BLAZER BOY) LOCKS:
Regal 3231 *Blazer Boy Blues* .... 10.00 - 15.00

ROBERT LOCKWOOD:

Bluebird 8820 *Take A Little Walk With Me* ..... 25.00 - 40.00
  8877 *Black Spider Blues* .... 25.00 - 40.00

ROBERT LOCKWOOD, JR./ROBERT JR.
LOCKWOOD:
J.O.B. 1107 *Sweet Woman From Maine* .... 15.00 - 25.00*
Mercury 8260 *Dust My Broom* .... 7.00 - 10.00

CRIPPLE CLARENCE LOFTON:
Titles, issued contemporaneously on Banner,
  Conqueror, Melotone, Oriole, Perfect: *Brown*
  Skin Girls; You Done Tore Your Playhouse
  Down .... 50.00 - 75.00
Solo Art 12003 *Streamline Train* .... 10.00 - 15.00
  12009 *Pine Top's Boogie Woogie* .... 10.00 - 15.00
Vocalion 02951 *Monkey Man Blues* .... 75.00 - 100.00

POOR BOY LOFTON:
Decca 7010 *Poor Boy Blues* .... 50.00 - 75.00
  7049 *Rainy Day Blues* .... 50.00 - 75.00
  7076 *Jake Leg Blues* .... 50.00 - 75.00

WILLIE LOFTON TRIO:
Bluebird 6229 *Beer Garden Blues* .... 25.00 - 40.00

RAY LOGAN:
Paramount 12310 *Lost John Blues* .... 75.00 - 100.00

CLARENCE LONDON:
Fidelity 3009 *One Rainy Morning* .... 10.00 - 15.00

JOHNNY LONDON:
Sun 175 *Flat Tire* .... 75.00 - 100.00*

LOTTIE AND WINSTON:
Superior 2717 *Wayward Girl Blues* .... 150.00 - 300.00

JOE HILL LOUIS:
Checker 763 *Dorothy May* .... 20.00 - 30.00*
Columbia 30182, 30221 .... 7.00 - 10.00
Modern 795, 813, 822, 828, 839, 856 .... 6.00 - 10.00*
Sun 178 *We All Gotta Go Sometime* .... 75.00 - 100.00*

LESLIE LOUIS:
Rockin' 509 *Ridin' Home* .... 7.00 - 10.00 *

LOUISIANA JOHNNY:
Vocalion 02980 *Policy Blues* .... 25.00 - 40.00
  03497 *Whiskey Head Woman* .... 20.00 - 30.00

HOT SHOT LOVE:
Sun 196 *Wolf Call Boogie* .... 50.00 - 80.00*

WILLIE LOVE & HIS THREE ACES; WILLIE
LOVE'S THREE ACES:
Trumpet 137 *Take It Easy Baby* .... 7.00 - 10.00*
  147 *My Own Boogie* .... 7.00 - 10.00*
  172, 173, 174, 175, 209 .... 5.00 - 8.00*

LOVIN' SAM (FROM DOWN IN 'BAM);
LOVIN' SAM & BURNS CAMPBELL
ORCHESTRA/HIS SWING RASCALS:
Bluebird 7514, 7629, 7916 .... 8.00 - 12.00
Brunswick 7073 *She's Givin' It Away* .... 50.00 - 80.00
  7075 *What You Gonna Do?* .... 50.00 - 80.00
  7090 *Get Your Mind On It* .... 50.00 - 80.00
  7094 *I Ain 't No Ice Man* .... 50.00 - 80.00
  7098 *You Rascal You* .... 50.00 - 80.00
  7117 *Huggin' And Kissin' Gwine On* .... 50.00 - 80.00
  7131 *Get It In Front* .... 50.00 - 80.00
  7167 *You Rascal You—No. 2* .... 75.00 - 100.00
  7183 *Ugly Child* .... 75.00 - 100.00
  7198 *Three Sixes* .... 75.00 - 100.00
  7218 *That New Kinda Stuff* .... 75.00 - 100.00
Vocalion 03686 *Spo-Dee-O-Dee* .... 10.00 - 15.00

FLORENCE LOWERY:
Vocalion 1106 *Poor Girl Blues* .... 75.00 - 100.00
  1107 *Thirty Day Blues* .... 75.00 - 100.00

JANE LUCAS (& GEORGIA TOM):
Champion 16215 *Fix It* .... 100.00 - 150.00
Vocalion 03314 *I Can't Last Long* .... 15.00 - 20.00
  03346 *Mr. Freddie Blues* .... 15.00 - 20.00

LONNIE LYONS (COMBO); LONNIE LYONS,
HIS PIANO & ORCHESTRA:
Freedom 1504, 1507, 1512, 1519, 1523 .... 5.00 - 8.00
Sittin' In With 566 *I Need Romance* .... 5.00 - 8.00

SMILING SMOKEY LYNN:
Peacock 1555, 1579 . . . .   5.00 -   8.00
ALURA MACK:
Gennett 6767 *Old Fashioned Blues* . . . . .100.00 - 150.00
   6797 *My Kitchen Man* .100.00 - 150.00
   6813 *West End Blues* . . . . .100.00 - 150.00
   6876 *Loose Like That* .100.00 - 150.00
   6890 *Beef Blood Blues* . . . . .100.00 - 150.00
   6964 *The Long Lost Blues* . . . . .150.00 - 200.00
   7273 *Monkey Blues* . . . . .150.00 - 200.00
   7295 *Everybody's Man Is Mine* . . . . .150.00 - 200.00
BILLY AND MARY MACK:
Okeh 8195 *My Heart Breakin' Gal* . . . . 80.00 - 120.00
   8274 *Fetch It When You Come* . . . . 50.00 -   75.00
   8296 *You Don't Want Much* . . . . 50.00 -   75.00
   8339 *Oh! Me Oh! My Blues* . . . . .100.00 - 150.00
IDA MAY MACK:
Victor 21690 *Mr. Moore Blues* . . . . 75.00 - 100.00
   V-38030 *Elm Street Blues* . . . . .100.00 - 150.00
   V-38532 *Wrong Doin' Daddy* . . . . .100.00 - 150.00
RED MACK:
Atlas 117 *Black Man's Blues* . . . .   —   -   —
MACON ED (AND TAMPA JOE):
Okeh 8676 *Worrying Blues* . . . . 80.00 - 120.00
   8855 *Try That Thing* . . . . .100.00 - 150.00
   8877 *Tickle Britches* . . . . .100.00 - 150.00
   8896 *Mean Florida Blues* . . . . .100.00 - 150.00
SIDNEY MAIDEN:
Imperial 5189 *Honey Bee Blues* . . . .   7.00 -   10.00
HELENA MANLEY:
Okeh 8111 *Loving Blues* . . . . 20.00 -   30.00
LEOLA MANNING:
Vocalion 1446 *He Fans Me* . . . . 75.00 - 100.00
   1492 *The Arcade Building Moan* . . . . 75.00 - 100.00
   1529 *Laying In The Graveyard* . . . . 75.00 - 100.00
MARTIN AND ROBERT:
Brunswick 7007 *Dollar Blues* . . . . .100.00 - 150.00
Vocalion 1127 *South Street Blues* . . . . .100.00 - 150.00
ARETHA MARTIN:
Champion 15340 *Lost Man Blues* . . . . .150.00 - 200.00
   15360 *Tea-Rollin' Blues* . . . . .150.00 - 200.00
Silvertone 5129 *Lost Man Blues* . . . . .150.00 - 200.00
CARL MARTIN:
Bluebird 5745 *Kid Man Blues* . . . . 50.00 -   80.00
   6139 *Old Time Blues* . . . . 30.00 -   50.00
Champion 50074 *High Water Flood Blues* . . . . . . 30.00 -   50.00
Decca 7114 *Let's Have A New Deal* . . . . 30.00 -   50.00
Okeh 8961 *Badly Mistreated Man* . . . . 75.00 - 100.00
Vocalion 03003 *Badly Mistreated Man* . . . . 40.00 -   60.00
   03047 *Good Morning, Judge* . . . . 40.00 -   60.00
   03496 *That New Kind Of Stuff* . . . . 20.00 -   30.00
DAISY MARTIN:
Banner 1262 *Feelin' Blue* . . . .   7.00 -   10.00
Gennett 4712 *Spread Yo' Stuff* . . . .   5.00 -   12.00
Okeh 8001 *I Won't Be Back 'Til You Change*
   Your Ways . . . . 30.00 -   50.00
   8008 *Everybodys Man Is My Man* . . . . 30.00 -   50.00
   8009 *I Didn't Start In To Love You* . . . . 15.00 -   25.00
   8010 *Sweet Daddy* . . . . 15.00 -   25.00
   8013 *Nightmare Blues* . . . . 15.00 -   25.00
   8027 *If You Don't Want Me Please Don't Dog*
   Me 'Round . . . . 15.00 -   25.00
Regal 9548 *Feelin' Blue* . . . .   7.00 -   10.00
DOLLY MARTIN:
Decca 7080 *All Men Blues* . . . . 30.00 -   50.00
BLIND GEORGE MARTIN:
Broadway 5040 *Worried Blues* . . . . .100.00 - 150.00
   5053 *Southern Rag* .100.00 - 150.00
   5080 *Hookworm Blues* . . . . .100.00 - 150.00
   5084 *Goodbye Mama Moan* . . . . .150.00 - 200.00
OLLIS MARTIN:
Gennett 6306 *Police And High Sheriff Come*

Ridin' Down . . . . .300.00 - 500.00
SARA MARTIN:
Okeh 4904, 8041 8058, 8060, 8062, 8063, 8065,
   8078, 8083, 8084, 8085, 8086, 8087, 8088,
   8093, 8097, 8104, 8117, 8136, 8146, 8161, 8172,
   8191, 8214, 8226, 8237, 8249, 8303, 8354 . . . . . 10.00 -   25.00
   8043 *'Tain't Nobodys Biz-ness If I Do* . . . . 15.00 -   20.00
   8045 *Last Go Round Blues* . . . . 15.00 -   20.00
   8061 *Come Home Papa Blues* . . . . 30.00 -   50.00
   8064 *Laughin' Cryin' Blues* . . . . 30.00 -   50.00
   8067 *Yodeling Blues* . . . . 30.00 -   50.00
   8082 *Hesitation Blues* . . . . 30.00 -   50.00
   8090 *Blind Man Blues* . . . . 50.00 -   75.00
   8099 *Graveyard Dream Blues* . . . . 50.00 -   75.00
   8108 *Squabbling Blues* . . . . 40.00 -   60.00
   8154 *He's Never Gonna Throw Me Down* . . . . . 40.00 -   60.00
   8166 *Jug Band Blues* . . . . 75.00 - 125.00
   8176 *I Got The Crying Blues* . . . . 75.00 - 125.00
   8211 *I Ain't Got No Man* . . . . 75.00 - 125.00
   8203 *Things Done Got Too Much* . . . . 50.00 -   75.00
Okeh 8231 *Papa, Papa Blues* . . . . 75.00 - 125.00
   8262 *Alabamy Bound* . . . . 50.00 -   75.00
   8270 *I'm Gonna Hoodoo You* . . . . 50.00 -   75.00
   8283 *Down At The Razor Ball* . . . . 75.00 - 125.00
   8292 *Forget Me Not Blues* . . . . 75.00 - 125.00
   8304 *Give Me Just a Little Of Your Time* . . . . . 80.00 - 120.00
   8325 *Careless Man Blues* . . . . 75.00 - 100.00
   8336 *What's The Matter Now?* . . . . 75.00 - 100.00
   8374 *Some Sweet Day* . . . . 75.00 - 125.00
   8394 *Look Out Mr. Jazz* . . . . 50.00 -   75.00
   8412 *Shipwrecked Blues* . . . . 50.00 -   75.00
   8427 *Georgia Stockade Blues* . . . . 80.00 - 120.00
   8442 *The Prisoner's Blues* . . . . 75.00 - 100.00
   8461 *Cushion Foot Stomp* . . . . 50.00 -   80.00
   8513 *Orn'ry Blues* . . . . 25.00 -   40.00
Paramount 12841 *Death Sting Me Blues* . . . . . . .200.00 - 300.00
QRS 7035 *Hole In The Wall* . . . . .200.00 - 300.00
   7042 *Death Sting Me Blues* . . . . .200.00 - 300.00
   7043 *Kitchen Man Blues* . . . . .200.00 - 300.00
MARY AND MACK:
Bluebird 6894 *You Gotta Quit Your Low Down*
   Ways . . . . 25.00 -   40.00
   7908 *Black* . . . . 30.00 -   40.00
THE MASKED MARVEL:
Paramount 12805 *Mississippi Bo Weavil Blues* . . .200.00 - 300.00
MINNIE MATHES:
Vocalion 04431 *Ball Game Blues* . . . . 15.00 -   20.00
EMMETT MATHEWS:
Paramount 13087 *Upside Down* . . . . .150.00 - 200.00
LENA MATLOCK:
Champion 16170 *Stop Bitin' Other Women In*
   The Back . . . . .100.00 - 150.00
MAE MATTHEWS:
Gennett 6438 *Dirty Woman Blues* . . . . .100.00 - 150.00
   6439 *Satisfed Blues* . . . . .100.00 - 150.00
CLAUDE MAXWELL:
Sterling 3006 *Bad Woman Blues* . . . .   7.00 -   10.00
HANNAH MAY & THE STATE STREET FOUR:
Titles, issued contemporaneously on Banner,
   Oriole, Perfect, Romeo: *Pussy Cat Blues;*
   What You Call That? . . . . 50.00 -   75.00
Vocalion 03313 *Kansas City Hill* . . . . 15.00 -   20.00
TINY MAYBERRY:
Decca 7496 *Oh That Nasty Man* . . . . 10.00 -   15.00
   7520 *Mayberry Blues* . . . . 10.00 -   15.00
   7593 *Mailman Blues* . . . . 10.00 -   15.00
ETHEL MAYES:
Harmograph 781 *Sugar Blues* . . . . 20.00 -   30.00
   842 *Goin' Down To The Levee* . . . . .100.00 - 150.00
   2544 *Gulf Coast Blues* . . . . 20.00 -   30.00
BERT (M.) MAYS:
Paramount 12614 *Mama's Man Blues* . . . . .100.00 - 150.00

McABEE

12632 *Midnight Rambler's Blues* . . . . .100.00 - 150.00
Vocalion 1223 *Michigan River Blues* . . . . .100.00 - 150.00

PALMER McABEE:

Victor 21352 *McAbee's Railroad Piece* . . . . 20.00 - 30.00

CONNIE McBOOKER:

Eddie's 1928 *Short Baby Boogie* . . . . 15.00 - 20.00

ARTHUR McCLAIN (AND JOE EVANS):

Titles, issued contemporaneously on Banner,
Oriole, Perfect, Romeo: *Cream And Sugar*
Blues; Old Hen Cackle . . . . .100.00 - 150.00

ERNEST McCLAY & HIS TRIO:

Murray 506 *Big Timing Woman* . . . . 15.00 - 20.00

TOMMY McCLENNAN:

Bluebird 8347 *You Can Mistreat Me Here* . . . . . . 10.00 - 15.00
8373 *Bottle It Up And Go* . . . . 7.00 - 10.00
8408 *Cotton Patch Blues* . . . . 10.00 - 15.00
8444 *Brown Skin Girl* . . . . 10.00 - 15.00
8499 *New Highway No. 51* . . . . 10.00 - 15.00
8545 *My Babys Doggin' Me* . . . . 10.00 - 15.00
8605 *My Little Girl* . . . . 10.00 - 15.00
8669 *My Baby's Gone* . . . . 10.00 - 15.00
8689 *Katy Mae Blues* . . . . 10.00 - 15.00
8704, 8725, 8853, 8897, 8957, 9005, 9015,
9037, 34-0706, 34-0716 . . . . 7.00 - 12.00

LILI McCLINTOCK:

Columbia 14575-D *Furniture Man* . . . . 50.00 - 75.00
14602-D *Sow Good Seeds* . . . . 50.00 - 75.00

MATTHEW McCLURE:

Champion 16514 *True Love Blues* . . . . .150.00 - 200.00

McCOY AND JOHNSON:

Bluebird 5385 *I Never Told A Lie* . . . . 75.00 - 100.00
Victor 23313 *I Never Told A Lie* . . . . .200.00 - 300.00
23352 *Georgia Skin* . . . . .250.00 - 400.00

**(''PAPA'') CHARLES/CHARLIE McCOY (AND
BO CARTER/WITH CHATMAN'S
MISSISSIPPI HOT FOOTERS):**

Brunswick 7118 *It Ain't No Good* . . . . .100.00 - 150.00
7141 *Last Time Blues* . . . . .100.00 - 150.00
7156 *Your Valves Need Grinding* . . . . .100.00 - 150.00
7165 *Glad Hand Blues* . . . . .100.00 - 150.00
Okeh 8853 *Mississippi I'm Longing For You* . . . .150.00 - 200.00
8863 *It Is So Good—Part 1* . . . . .150.00 - 200.00
8873 *You Gonna Need Me* . . . . .150.00 - 200.00
8881 *It Is So Good—Part 2* . . . . .150.00 - 200.00
Vocalion 1683 *Boogie Woogie* . . . . .100.00 - 150.00
1712 *Too Long* . . . . .100.00 - 150.00
1726 *Bottle It Up* .100.00 - 150.00

ROBERT/LEE McCOY:

Bluebird 6995 *Prowling Night Hawk* . . . . 20.00 - 30.00
7045 *Lonesome World* . . . . 20.00 - 30.00
7090 *G-Man* . . . . 20.00 - 30.00
7115 *Tough Luck* . . . . 10.00 - 25.00
7303 *Mean Black Cat* . . . . 20.00 - 30.00
7386 *Take It Easy Baby* . . . . 20.00 - 30.00
7416 *My Friend Has Forsaken Me* . . . . 20.00 - 30.00
7440 *CNA* . . . . 15.00 - 25.00

VIOLA/VOLET McCOY:

Ajax 17010 *Lonesome Daddy Blues* . . . . 20.00 - 30.00
17069 *Keep On Going* . . . . 20.00 - 30.00
Banner 1357 *Buzzin' Around* . . . . 8.00 - 12.00
Banner 1371 *You Don't Know My Mind* . . . . 8.00 - 12.00
Banner 1394 *Clearing House Blues* . . . . 8.00 - 12.00
Brunswick 2591 *If Your Good Man Quits You* . . . 10.00 - 15.00
Cameo 1097, 1189, 1225 . . . . 10.00 - 15.00
Columbia 14395-D *I Want A Good Man* . . . . 50.00 - 75.00
Edison 51478 *Memphis Bound* . . . . 75.00 - 100.00
Gennett 5108, 5128, 5162, 5175 . . . . 10.00 - 20.00
5151 *Gulf Coast Blues* . . . . 20.00 - 30.00
Regal 9653, 9667, 9690 . . . . 8.00 - 12.00
Vocalion 1002 *South Street Blues* . . . . 50.00 - 75.00
14632, 14633, 14653, 14689, 14818 . . . . 7.00 - 15.00
Vocalion 14801 *West Indies Blues* . . . . 20.00 - 30.00

14912 *Keep On Going* . . . . 15.00 - 25.00
15245 *Stomp Your Blues Away* . . . . 75.00 - 100.00
15268 *South Street Blues* . . . . 50.00 - 75.00

WILLIAM McCOY:

Columbia 14302-D *Mama Blues* . . . . 25.00 - 40.00
14393-D *How Long Baby* . . . . 50.00 - 75.00
14453-D *Central Tracks Blues* . . . . 50.00 - 75.00
15269-D *Mama Blues* . . . . 25.00 - 40.00

**JIMMY McCRACKLIN (& HIS BLUES
BLASTERS/ORCHESTRA):**

Aladdin 3089 *Bad Luck And Trouble* . . . . 7.00 - 10.00
Cava-Tone 251 *Jimmy's Blues* . . . . 10.00 - 15.00
Courtney 123 *You Had Your Chance* . . . . 8.00 - 12.00
Down Town 2023 *Bad Condition Blues* . . . . 10.00 - 15.00
2027 *Low Down Mood* . . . . 10.00 - 15.00
Excelsior 182 *You Deceived Me* . . . . 7.00 - 10.00
Globe 102 *Miss Mattie Left Me* . . . . 8.00 - 12.00
104 *Highway 101* . . . . 8.00 - 12.00
109 *Street Loafn' Woman* . . . . 8.00 - 12.00
J & M Fullbright 123 *Special For You* . . . . 10.00 - 15.00
124 *Rock And Rye* . . . . 10.00 - 15.00
Modern 722, 728, 741, 762, 806 . . . . 4.00 - 7.00
Old Swingmaster 24, 25 . . . . 8.00 - 12.00
Peacock 1605, 1615, 1639 . . . . 4.00 - 7.00*
RPM 317 *Your Heart Ain't Right* . . . . 8.00 - 12.00
Swing Time 260, 264, 270, 285, 286, 291 . . . . . . 5.00 - 10.00
Trilon 197 *Rock And Rye* . . . . 6.00 - 10.00
231 *Big Foot Mama* . . . . 6.00 - 10.00
244, 245 . . . . 4.00 - 7.00

JAMES McCRAVY:

Columbia 14641-D *Shove It Up It There* . . . . 50.00 - 75.00

ROBERT McCULLUM:

Aristocrat 413 *Jackson Town Woman* . . . . 20.00 - 30.00

HATTIE McDANIEL(S):

Merritt 2202 *Brown-Skin Baby Doll* . . . . .200.00 - 300.00
Okeh 8434 *Boo Hoo Blues* . . . . .150.00 - 200.00
8569 *I Thought I'd Do It* . . . . 50.00 - 75.00
Paramount 12751 *Dentist Chair Blues* . . . . .100.00 - 150.00
12790 *That New Love Maker Of Mine* . . . . .100.00 - 150.00

WILLARD McDANIEL:

Specialty 415, 424 . . . . 5.00 - 10.00

KATHERINE McDAVID:

Okeh 8295 *Underground Blues* . . . . 30.00 - 50.00

HELEN McDONALD:

Gennett 5193 *Squawkin' My Blues* . . . . 20.00 - 30.00

TEE McDONALD:

Decca 7018 *Beef Man Blues* . . . . 50.00 - 75.00

TECUMSEH McDOWELL:

Bluebird 5286 *My Man Blues* . . . . 75.00 - 100.00
Sunrise 3367 *So Called Friend* . . . . .100.00 - 200.00

BLACK PATCH McFADDEN:

Paramount 13021 *Whiskey Head Man* . . . . .200.00 - 300.00

**CHARLES/CHARLIE McFADDEN;
"SPECKS" CHARLIE McFADDEN:**

Bluebird 5160 *Piggly Wiggly Blues* . . . . .100.00 - 150.00
5203 *Times Are So Tight* . . . . .100.00 - 150.00
5325 *Last Journey Blues* . . . . 75.00 - 100.00
5384 *Lonesome Ghost Blues* . . . . 75.00 - 100.00
Decca 7317 *People, People* . . . . 15.00 - 20.00
Okeh 8894 *Don't Bite That Thing* . . . . .100.00 - 150.00
Paramount 12928 *Groceries On The Shelf* . . . . . .200.00 - 300.00
13076 *Groceries On The Shelf No. 2* . . . . .200.00 - 300.00
Sunrise 3241 *People, People* . . . . .100.00 - 200.00
3284 *Friendless Man* . . . . .100.00 - 200.00
3406 *Low Down Rounders Blues* . . . . .100.00 - 200.00
Victor 23420 *Lonesome Ghost Blues* . . . . .250.00 - 400.00

BUCK MacFARLAND:

Paramount 12982 *St. Louis Fire Blues* . . . . .100.00 - 150.00

**BROWNIE McGHEE (& SONNY TERRY/&
HIS JOOK BLOCK BUSTERS):**

Alert 400, 401, 402, 403, 404, 405, 406, 407,
408, 409, 410, 411, 412, 413, 420 . . . . 5.00 - 10.00

Conqueror 9563, 9564, 9566, 9765, 9766, 9937,
9938, 9939, 9940 . . . . 4.00 - 8.00
Derby 776, 783 . . . . 5.00 - 8.00
Disc 6057, 6058, 6059, 6088 . . . . 5.00 - 8.00
Harlem 2323, 2329 . . . . 4.00 - 6.00*
Jax 304, 307, 310, 312, 322 . . . . 8.00 - 12.00*
Savoy 704, 714, 747, 760, 778, 872, 899, 5533,
5534, 5538, 5541, 5548, 5550, 5551, 5557,
5559, 5561, 5565 . . . . 7.00 - 12.00
Sittin' In With 302, 517 . . . . 8.00 - 12.00
Okeh 05875, 05812, 05881, 05933, 06007, 06056,
06265, 06329, 06419, 06437, 06472, 06524,
06579, 06698 . . . . 5.00 - 10.00

STICKS McGHEE (& HIS BUDDIES):
Atlantic 873 *Drinkin' Wine Spo-Dee-O-Dee* . . . . . 8.00 - 12.00
881 *Lonesome Road Blues* . . . . 7.00 - 10.00
898, 909, 912, 926, 937, 955, 991 . . . . 4.00 - 7.00*
Decca 48104 *Drinkin' Wine Spo-Dee-O-Dee* . . . . 8.00 - 12.00
Essex 709 *My Little Rose* . . . . 5.00 - 10.00
Harlem 1018 *Drinkin' Wine Spo-Dee-O-Dee* . . . . 15.00 - 20.00
King 4610, 4628, 4672, 4700, 4783, 4800 . . . . 4.00 - 7.00*

ELDERS McINTORSH & EDWARD; LONNIE McINTORSH:
Okeh 8647 *The 1927 Flood* . . . . 40.00 - 60.00
8671 *Take A Stand* . . . . 40.00 - 60.00
8698 *Since I Laid My Burden Down* . . . . 40.00 - 60.00
Victor 21411 *The Lion And The Tribes Of Judah* . . 75.00 - 100.00
71411 *Arise And Shine* . . . . 75.00 - 100.00

ARTHUR/ART McKAY:
Decca 7068 *Central Limited Blues* . . . . 20.00 - 35.00
7364 *She Squeezed My Lemon* . . . . 15.00 - 20.00

McKENZIE AND CRUMP:
Paramount 12857 *That's A Married Man's Weakness* . . . . 50.00 - 75.00

BILLIE McKENZIE:
Vocalion 03385 *Romeo And Juliet* . . . . 15.00 - 20.00

WILLIE MAE McKENZIE:
Vocalion 03507 *Oh, Babe* . . . . 15.00 - 20.00
03552 *I'm Getting Even With You* . . . . 15.00 - 20.00
03562 *Little Red Wagon* . . . . 15.00 - 20.00

BILL McKINLEY:
Titles, issued contemporaneously on Banner,
Melotone, Oriole, Perfect, Romeo: *I Went To
The Gypsy; She Keeps On Kickin'* . . . . 25.00 - 40.00

(DAVID) PETE McKINLEY:
Fidelity 3008 *Black Snake Blues* . . . . 10.00 - 15.00
Gotham 505 *Shreveport Blues* . . . . 15.00 - 25.00

SADIE McKINNEY:
Victor 20565 *Rock Away* . . . . 50.00 - 75.00

JIMMY McLAIN:
Vocalion 04444 *Tailor Made Blues* . . . . 10.00 - 15.00

CAB McMILLAN & HIS FADEAWAYS:
Macy's 5011 *I'm Young And Able* . . . . 7.00 - 10.00

DENNIS McMILLON:
Regal 3232 *Poor Little Angel* . . . . 15.00 - 25.00
3257 *I Woke Up One Morning* . . . . 15.00 - 25.00

FRED McMULLEN (AND RUTH WILLIS):
Titles, issued contemporaneously on Banner,
Melotone, Oriole, Perfect, Romeo: *De Kalb
Chain Blues; Just Can't Stand It; Poor
Stranger Blues; Rolling Mama; Wait And Listen* 50.00 - 100.00

BLACK BOTTOM McPHAIL:
Vocalion 1690 *Mix That Thing* . . . . 100.00 - 150.00
1721 *Down In Black Bottom* . . . . 100.00 - 150.00
04220 *New Whiskey Man* . . . . 15.00 - 20.00
04317 *Don't Go Down In Black Bottom* . . . . . 15.00 - 20.00

OZIE (DAYBREAK) McPHERSON:
Paramount 12327 *You Gotta Know How* . . . . . . 75.00 - 125.00
12350 *Standing on the Corner Blues* . . . . 75.00 - 125.00
12355 *Nobody Rolls Their Jelly Roll Like Mine* 50.00 - 80.00
12362 *I Want My Loving* . . . . 50.00 - 80.00

BLIND WILLIE McTELL; BLIND WILLIE &

KATE McTELL:
Decca 7078 *Ticket Agent Blues* . . . . 50.00 - 75.00
7093 *Dying Gambler* . . . . 50.00 - 75.00
7117 *Hillbilly Willie's Blues* . . . . 50.00 - 75.00
7140 *We Got To Meet Death One Day* . . . . 50.00 - 75.00
7810 *Cold Winter Day* . . . . 40.00 - 60.00
Regal 3272 *It's My Desire* . . . . 30.00 - 40.00
Victor 21124 *Mr. McTell Got The Blues* . . . . . . 150.00 - 200.00
21474 *Writin' Paper Blues* . . . . 150.00 - 200.00
V38001 *Three Women Blues* . . . . 200.00 - 300.00
V38032 *Dark Night Blues.* . . . . 200.00 - 300.00
V38580 *Drive Away Blues* . . . . 200.00 - 300.00

MEMPHIS EDDIE:
RPM 301, 308, 310, 315 . . . . 5.00 - 10.00

MEMPHIS JIMMY:
RCA Victor 20-1887, 20-2278 . . . . 4.00 - 8.00

MEMPHIS JOE:
Vocalion 1277 *Plenty Gals Blues* . . . . 100.00 - 150.00

MEMPHIS MINNIE & KANSAS JOE (& HER JUG BAND/& HER COMBO/WITH LITTLE JOE & HIS BAND):
Titles, issued contemporaneously on Banner,
Melotone, Oriole, Perect, Romeo: *Bumble
Bee; Bumble Bee No. 2; Fishin' Blues; I'm
Talkin' 'Bout You; Kind Treatment Blues;
Outdoor Blues; Where Is My Good Man* . . . . . 50.00 - 100.00
Bluebird 6187 *When The Sun Goes Down* . . . . . 35.00 - 50.00
6199 *Doctor, Doctor Blues* . . . . 20.00 - 30.00
6202 *Hustlin Woman Blues* . . . . 30.00 - 50.00
Checker 771 *Me And My Chauffeur* . . . . 5.00 - 8.00*
Columbia . . . . 3.00 - 5.00
Conqueror 9025, 9026, 9162, 9198, 9275, 9282,
9372, 9763, 9764, 9934, 9935, 9936 . . . . . 8.00 - 12.00
Decca 7019 *Chickasaw Train Blues* . . . . 30.00 - 50.00
7023 *Hole In The Wall* . . . . 30.00 - 50.00
7037 *Keep It To Yourself* . . . . 30.00 - 50.00
7038 *You Got To Move* . . . . 30.00 - 50.00
7048 *You Can't Give It Away* . . . . 30.00 - 50.00
7084 *Sylvester And His Mule Blues* . . . . 30.00 - 50.00
7102 *Down In New Orleans* . . . . 30.00 - 50.00
7125 *Jockey Man Blues* . . . . 30.00 - 50.00
7146 *Squat It* . . . . 30.00 - 50.00
J.O.B. 1101 *Kissing In The Dark* . . . . 15.00 - 20.00
Okeh 05670, 05728, 05811, 06288, 06410, 06505,
06224, 06707 . . . . 8.00 - 12.00
8948 *My Butcher Man* . . . . 100.00 - 150.00
Regal 3259 *Kidman Blues* . . . . 15.00 - 25.00
Vocalion 1476 *Bumble Bee* . . . . 75.00 - 100.00
1512 *I'm Gonna Bake My Biscuits* . . . . 80.00 - 120.00
1556 *Bumble Bee--No. 2* . . . . 75.00 - 100.00
1588 *Frankie Jean* . . . . 100.00 - 150.00
1601 *Garage Fire Blues* . . . . 150.00 - 200.00
1603 *Good Girl Blues* . . . . 75.00 - 125.00
1618 *New Dirty Dozen* . . . . 75.00 - 125.00
1631 *Plymouth Rock Blues* . . . . 75.00 - 125.00
1638 *Dirt Dauber Blues* . . . . 100.00 - 150.00
1653 *Tricks Ain't Walkin' No More* . . . . 100.00 - 150.00
1658 *Soo Cow Soo* . . . . 100.00 - 150.00
1673 *Don't Bother It* . . . . 100.00 - 150.00
Vocalion 1678 *Crazy Cryin' Blues* . . . . 100.00 - 150.00
1682 *Minnie Minnie Bumble Bee* . . . . 100.00 - 150.00
1688 *Socket Blues* . . . . 100.00 - 150.00
1698 *Outdoor Blues* . . . . 80.00 - 120.00
1711 *Fishin' Blues* . . . . 80.00 - 120.00
1718 *Jailhouse Trouble Blues* . . . . 100.00 - 150.00
02711 *Stinging Snake Blues* . . . . 80.00 - 120.00
Vocalion 03046 *Joe Louis Strut* . . . . 20.00 - 30.00
03144 *Biting Bug Blues* . . . . 20.00 - 30.00
03187 *Ain't Nobody Home But Me* . . . . 20.00 - 30.00
03222 *Ice Man (Come On Up)* . . . . 20.00 - 30.00
03258 *I'm A Gamblin' Woman* . . . . 20.00 - 30.00
03285 *If You See My Rooster (Please Run*

	Him Home)	15.00 -	20.00
03398	*Dragging My Heart Around.*	15.00 -	20.00
03436	*I Don't Want You No More*	15.00 -	20.00
03474	*It's Hard To Be Mistreated*	15.00 -	20.00
03541	*Ball And Chain Blues*	15.00 -	20.00
03581	*Black Cat Blues*	15.00 -	20.00
03612	*Down In The Alley*	10.00 -	15.00
03651	*Keep On Sailing*	10.00 -	15.00
03697	*No Need You Doggin' Me*	10.00 -	15.00
03768	*Living The Best I Can*	10.00 -	15.00
03894	*My Baby Don't Want Me No More*	10.00 -	15.00
03966	*Walking And Crying Blues*	10.00 -	15.00
04250	*I've Been Treated Wrong*	10.00 -	15.00
04295	*Good Biscuits*	10.00 -	15.00
04356	*Keep On Walking*	10.00 -	15.00
04506	*I'd Rather See Him Dead*	10.00 -	15.00
04694	*Good Soppin'*	10.00 -	15.00
04797	*Bad Outside Friends.*	10.00 -	15.00
04858	*Call The Fire Wagon*	10.00 -	15.00
04898	*Don't Lead My Baby Wrong*	10.00 -	15.00
05004	*Poor And Wandering Woman Blues*	10.00 -	15.00

MEMPHIS MOSE:

Brunswick 7102	*Pig Meat Papa*	100.00 -	150.00
7134	*Blue Moanin' Blues*	100.00 -	150.00
7143	*Billie The Grinder*	100.00 -	150.00

MEMPHIS SAM AND JOHN:

Gennett 6987	*It's Just All Right*	100.00 -	150.00

MEMPHIS SLIM (& HIS/THE HOUSE ROCKERS; & HIS SOLID BAND):

Bluebird 8584	*Beer Drinking Woman*	8.00 -	12.00
8615	*Empty Room Blues*	8.00 -	12.00
8645	*Shelby Country Blues*	8.00 -	12.00
8749	*Two Of A Kind*	7.00 -	10.00
8784	*Me, Myself, And I*	7.00 -	10.00
8834	*Whiskey Store Blues*	7.00 -	10.00
8903	*Old Taylor*	7.00 -	10.00
8945	*Whiskey And Gin Blues*	7.00 -	10.00
8974	*Caught The Old Coon At Last*	7.00 -	10.00
9028	*Lend Me Your Love*	7.00 -	10.00
Chess 1491	*Walking Alone*	5.00 -	8.00*
Federal 12007, 12015, 12021, 12033		5.00 -	8.00
Hy-Tone 10, 17, 19		5.00 -	8.00
King 4284, 4312, 4324, 4327		3.00 -	6.00
Master 1010, 1020, 1030		5.00 -	8.00
Mercury 8251, 8266, 8281, 70063		3.00 -	5.00
Miracle 102, 103, 110, 111, 125, 132, 145, 153 . . .		5.00 -	8.00
Old Swingmaster 1010		5.00 -	10.00
Peacock 1517, 1602		5.00 -	8.00
Premium 850, 860, 867, 873, 878, 903		5.00 -	8.00

SARA MESSON:

Oriole 325	*Nobody Knows The Way I Feel*	10.00 -	15.00

ANNA MEYERS:

Pathe-Actuelle 020870	*That Da Da Strain*	7.00 -	10.00
020877	*Evil Minded Blues*	7.00 -	10.00
Perfect 12031	*That Da Da Strain*	10.00 -	15.00
12038	*Last Go Round Blues*	10.00 -	20.00

HAZEL MEYERS:

Ajax 17007	*Love Ain't Blind No More*	15.00 -	20.00
17019	*Mississippi Blues*	15.00 -	20.00
17026	*Heart Breakin' Joe*	25.00 -	40.00
17039	*Papa Don't Ask Mama Where She Was* .	40.00 -	60.00
17040	*I'm Every Man's Mama*	25.00 -	40.00
17047	*War Horse Mama*	25.00 -	40.00
17048	*Hateful Blues*	25.00 -	40.00
17054	*Lonesome for That Man Of Mine*	25.00 -	40.00
17077	*Lost My Sweetie Blues*	35.00 -	50.00
17082	*He Used To Be Mine*	35.00 -	50.00
Banner 1358	*Plug Ugly*	10.00 -	15.00
Bell P-255	*Down Hearted Blues*	10.00 -	15.00
Emerson 10748	*Don't Know and Don't Care Blues*	15.00 -	20.00
Harmograph 925	*'Tain't A Doggone Thing But*		

	The Blues	15.00 -	20.00
967	*Pipe Dream Blues*	20.00 -	30.00
Okeh 8364	*Blackville After Dark*	150.00 -	200.00
Pathe-Actuelle 032053	*Pipe Dream Blues*	20.00 -	30.00
Perfect 12132	*Pipe Dream Blues*	20.00 -	30.00
Regal 9654	*Plug Ugly*	10.00 -	15.00
Silvertone 3011	*Graveyard Dream Blues* . . .	10.00 -	15.00
3012	*Maybe Someday*	15.00 -	20.00
Vocalion 14688	*Graveyard Dream Blues* . . .	10.00 -	15.00
14709	*Awful Moanin' Blues*	15.00 -	25.00
14725	*Mason-Dixon Blues*	15.00 -	25.00
14861	*Maybe Someday.*	30.00 -	50.00

MIDNIGHT RAMBLERS:

Vocalion 03395	*Out With The Wrong Woman*	15.00 -	25.00
03517	*Down In The Alley*	15.00 -	30.00

AMOS MILBURN:

Aladdin 159, 160, 161, 173, 174		5.00 -	10.00
Aladdin (higher numbers)		4.00 -	8.00

JOSIE MILES:

Ajax 17057	*Lovin' Henry Blues*	30.00 -	50.00
17066	*Believe Me Hot Mama*	30.00 -	50.00
17070	*South Bound Blues*	30.00 -	50.00
17076	*Sweet Man Joe*	30.00 -	50.00
17080	*A to Z Blues*	35.00 -	50.00
17083	*Picnic Time*	35.00 -	50.00
17087	*Cross Word Papa.*	35.00 -	50.00
17090	*I'm A Cabaret Nightingale*	35.00 -	50.00
17092	*It Ain't Gonna Rain No Mo*	25.00 -	40.00
17127	*At The Cake Walk Steppers Ball*	50.00 -	80.00
17134	*Give Me Just A Little Bit Of Love* . . .	50.00 -	80.00
Banner 1498	*Bitter Feelin' Blues*	10.00 -	15.00
1499	*Let's Agree To Disagree*	10.00 -	15.00
1516	*Ghost Walkin' Blues*	10.00 -	15.00
1534	*Low Down Daddy Blues*	10.00 -	15.00
Black Swan 14121	*When You're Crazy Over Daddy*	20.00 -	30.00
14130	*If You Want To Keep Your Daddy Home* . .	30.00 -	50.00
14133	*When I Dream Of Old Tennessee Blues* . .	30.00 -	50.00
14136	*Four O'Clock Blues*	30.00 -	50.00
14139	*Low Down 'Bama Blues.*	30.00 -	50.00
Domino 3468	*Bitter Feelin' Blues*	10.00 -	15.00
3469	*Let's Agree To Disagree*	10.00 -	15.00
3485	*Ghost Walkin' Blues.*	10.00 -	15.00
3504	*Low Down Daddy Blues*	10.00 -	15.00
Edison 51476	*Sweet Man Joe*	75.00 -	100.00
51477	*Temper'mental Papa*	75.00 -	100.00
Gennett 5261	*Kansas City Man Blues*	15.00 -	20.00
5292	*Graveyard Dream Blues*	15.00 -	20.00
5307	*I Want My Sweet Daddy Now*	15.00 -	20.00
5339	*Awful Moanin' Blues*	15.00 -	20.00
5359	*War Horse Mamma.*	15.00 -	25.00
5391	*31st. Street Blues*	15.00 -	25.00
Paramount 12156	*When You're Crazy Over Daddy*	15.00 -	25.00
12157	*If You Want To Keep Your Daddy Home* . .	30.00 -	50.00
12158	*When I Dream Of Old Tennessee Blues* . .	30.00 -	50.00
12159	*Four O'Clock Blues*	30.00 -	50.00
12160	*Low Down 'Bama Blues*	30.00 -	50.00
Regal 9796	*Let's Agree To Disagree*	10.00 -	15.00
9797	*Bitter Feelin' Blues*	10.00 -	15.00
9810	*Can't Be Trusted Blues*	10.00 -	15.00
9831	*Low Down Daddy Blues*	10.00 -	15.00
Silvertone 4043, 4048, 4051		10.00 -	20.00

LIZZIE MILES; LIZZIE MILES & THE MELROSE STOMPERS:

Titles, issued contemporaneously on Banner, Conqueror, Domino, Regal: *Banjo Papa; If You Can't Control Your Man; Lonesome Ghost Blues; Mean Old Bed Bug Blues; Police Blues; Second Hand Daddy; Shake It Down; Shootin' Star Blues; When You Get Tired Of Your New Sweetie.*		10.00 -	20.00
Bluebird 5064	*Electrician Blues*	25.00 -	40.00

Brunswick 2462 *My Pillow and Me*	8.00 -	12.00
Columbia A-3897, A-3920	8.00 -	12.00
14335-D *My Diff-rent Kind O'Man*	80.00 -	120.00
Emerson 10586 *Aggravatin' Papa*	15.00 -	25.00
10603 *Tell Me Gypsy*	15.00 -	25.00
10613 *Your Time Now*	15.00 -	25.00
Okeh 8031 *Muscle Shoals Blues*	20.00 -	30.00
8032 *State Street Blues*	20.00 -	30.00
8037 *Wicked Blues*	20.00 -	30.00
8039 *Lonesome Monday Morning Blues.*	20.00 -	30.00
8040 *Hot Lips*	20.00 -	30.00
8048 *Sweet Smellin' Mama*	20.00 -	30.00
8050 *Black Bottom Blues*	15.00 -	20.00
8052 *The Yellow Dog Blues*	20.00 -	30.00
Okeh 8456 *Slow Up Papa*	50.00 -	80.00
Victor 19083, 19124, 19158	5.00 -	10.00
23281 *My Man O'War*	100.00 -	150.00
23298 *Electrician Blues*	100.00 -	150.00
23306 *Good Time Papa*	150.00 -	250.00
V38607 *Good Time Papa*	50.00 -	75.00
V38571 *I Hate A Man Like You*	100.00 -	150.00
Vocalion 05165 *That's All Right Daddy*	8.00 -	12.00
05260 *Mellow Rhythm*	8.00 -	12.00
05325 *He's Red Hot To Me*	8.00 -	12.00
05392 *Twenty Grand Blues*	8.00 -	12.00

MILLER AND RODGERS:

Gennett 6782 *Everyoody's Been Using That Thing*	150.00 -	200.00
Paramount 12778 *I Would If I Could*	75.00 -	125.00

AL MILLER (& HIS MARKET STREET BOYS/SWING STOMPERS); AL MILLER'S STRING BAND:

Black Patti 8047 *Someday Sweetheart*	200.00 -	300.00
8049 *Saturday Night Hymn*	250.00 -	Up
Brunswick 7063 *I Would If I Could*	75.00 -	125.00
7084 *It Ain't Killed Nobody Yet*	75.00 -	125.00
7097 *It Must Be Good*	75.00 -	125.00
7105 *Thirty First And State*	75.00 -	125.00
7140 *That Stuff You Sell*	75.00 -	125.00
7143 *Gimme A Li'l Taste*	100.00 -	150.00
7212 *That Stuff Ain't No Good*	75.00 -	125.00
Champion 50067 *Truckin' Old Fool*	30.00 -	50.00
50072 *Ain't That A Mess?*	25.00 -	40.00
Gennett 6875 *Mister Mary Blues*	150.00 -	200.00

EDDIE MILLER:

Titles, issued contemporaneously on Banner, Melotone, Oriole, Perfect, Romeo: *I'd Rather Drink Muddy Water; Whoopie*	50.00 -	75.00
Brunswick 7133 *Freight Train Blues*	100.00 -	150.00
7213 *School Day Blues*	100.00 -	150.00

JIM MILLER:

Vocalion 1735 *Bye Bye Mama*	75.00 -	100.00
1737 *Joker Man Blues*	100.00 -	150.00
1741 *Hard Times Blues*	75.00 -	100.00

LILLIAN MILLER:

Gennett 6486 *Butcher Shop Blues*	100.00 -	150.00
6518 *Dead Drunk Blues*	100.00 -	150.00
Okeh 8381 *Kitchen Blues*	75.00 -	100.00

LUELLA MILLER (& HER DAGO HILL STRUTTERS:

Vocalion 1044 *Dago Hill Blues*	75.00 -	100.00
1080 *Down in the Alley*	75.00 -	100.00
1081 *Rattle Snake Croan*	75.00 -	100.00
1102 *Carrier Pigeon Blues*	100.00 -	150.00
1103 *Jackson's Blues*	100.00 -	150.00
1104 *Smiling Rose Blues*	100.00 -	150.00
1105 *North Wind Blues*	100.00 -	150.00
1147 *Tornado Groan*	100.00 -	150.00
1151 *Tombstone Blues.*	100.00 -	150.00
1202 *'Frisco Blues*	100.00 -	150.00
1234 *Chicago Blues*	100.00 -	150.00

MAE BELLE MILLER:

Paramount 12985 *Long Tall Man Blues*	150.00 -	200.00

SODARISA/SODARISSA MILLER:

Paramount 12231 *Hot Springs Water Blues.*	50.00 -	80.00
12243 *Don't Dog Me 'Round*	75.00 -	125.00
12261 *Broadway Daddy Blues.*	75.00 -	125.00
12276 *Be Yourself*	75.00 -	100.00
12293 *Nobody Knows*	75.00 -	100.00
12306 *Midnight Special*	75.00 -	100.00
Victor 20404 *Lonesome Room Blues*	40.00 -	60.00

JOSIE MILLS:

Emerson 10874 *Low Down Daddy Blues*	15.00 -	25.00

MAUDE MILLS:

Titles, issued contemporaneously on Banner, Domino, Regal: *Anything That Happens Just Pleases Me; Black Snake Blues; Golden Brown Blues; Hard Headed Mama*	25.00 -	40.00
Emerson 10624 *Triflin' Blues.*	20.00 -	30.00
Pathe-Actuelle 7526 *Somebody's Been Loving My Baby*	25.00 -	40.00
Perfect 126 *Somebodys Been Loving My Baby*	25.00 -	40.00

VIOLET MILLS:

Domino 437 *Worried Blues*	10.00 -	15.00
438 *Mad Mama's Blues*	10.00 -	15.00

IRENE MIMS:

Vocalion 1183 *Dirty Blues*	50.00 -	75.00

MISS FRANKIE:

Titles, issued contemporaneously on Banner, Domino, Regal: *Kissin' Mule Blues; Peepin' Jim Blues*	10.00 -	20.00

MISSISSIPPI BLACKSNAKES:

Brunswick 7196 *It's So Nice And Warm*	150.00 -	200.00
7202 *Five Pound Ax Blues*	150.00 -	200.00
7215 *Easy Going Woman Blues*	150.00 -	200.00
7222 *Bye Bye Baby Blues*	150.00 -	200.00

MISSISSIPPI JOOK BAND:

Titles, issued contemporaneously on Banner, Melotone, Oriole, Perfect, Romeo: *Barbecue Bust; Dangerous Woman; Hittin' The Bottle Stomp; Skippy Whippy*	75.00 -	100.00

MISSISSIPPI MATILDA:

Bluebird 6812 *Hard Working Woman*	30.00 -	40.00
7908 *A. & V Blues*	30.00 -	40.00

THE MISSISSIPPI MOANER:

Vocalion 03166 *Mississippi Moan*	100.00 -	200.00

MISSISSIPPI MUD MASHERS:

Bluebird 5845 *Bring In On Home To Grandma*	20.00 -	30.00
5988 *Take My Seat And Sit Down*	20.00 -	30.00
7316 *Tiger Rag.*	15.00 -	25.00

MISSISSIPPI MUD STEPPERS:

Okeh 45504 *Jackson Stomp*	150.00 -	200.00
45519 *Vicksburg Stomp*	150.00 -	200.00
45532 *Farewell Waltz*	150.00 -	200.00

MISSISSIPPI MUDDER:

Decca 7008 *I Got To Have A Little More*	50.00 -	75.00
7009 *Meat Cutter Blues*	35.00 -	50.00
7036 *Candy Man Blues*	30.00 -	50.00
7046 *Chanty Blues*	30.00 -	50.00
7087 *Motherless And Fatherless Blues*	30.00 -	50.00

MISSISSIPPI SARA (& DADDY STOVEPIPE):

Vocalion 1662 *Greenville Strut*	150.00 -	200.00
1667 *Do You Love Him?*	150.00 -	200.00
1670 *Jail Cell Blues*	150.00 -	250.00
1676 *Jake Leg Blues*	150.00 -	250.00

MISSISSIPPI SHEIKS (WITH BO CARTER):

Bluebird 5452 *Pop Skull Blues*	35.00 -	50.00
5453 *Sales Tax*	35.00 -	50.00
5474 *Hitting The Numbers*	35.00 -	50.00
5516 *I Am The Devil*	35.00 -	50.00
5564 *Blues On My Mind*	35.00 -	50.00
5618 *She's Got Something Crazy*	35.00 -	50.00
5659 *Somebody's Got To Help Me*	35.00 -	50.00
5847 *Do Right Blues*	35.00 -	50.00

5881 *I Can't Go Wrong*	35.00 -	50.00
5949 *Lean To One Woman*	35.00 -	50.00
6006 *Dead Wagon Blues*	35.00 -	50.00
Champion 50003 *Tell Me To Do Right*	50.00 -	100.00
50004 *Please Baby*	50.00 -	100.00
50007 *Don't Wake It Up*	50.00 -	100.00
50013 *New Shake That Thing*	50.00 -	100.00
50021 *The New Stop And Listen Blues*	50.00 -	100.00
50030 *Shooting High Dice*	50.00 -	100.00
Columbia 14660-D *The World Is Going Wrong*	150.00 -	200.00
14672-D *Kind Treatment*	150.00 -	200.00
Okeh 8773 *Wintertime Blues*	80.00 -	120.00
8784 *Sitting On Top Of The World*	50.00 -	75.00
8807 *Driving That Thing*	80.00 -	120.00
8810 *Back To Mississippi*	100.00 -	150.00
8820 *Bootleggers' Blues*	100.00 -	150.00
8834 *Jail Bird Love Song*	150.00 -	200.00
8843 *River Bottom Blues*	150.00 -	200.00
8854 *Sitting On Top Of The World—No. 2*	100.00 -	150.00
8859 *Unhappy Blues*	150.00 -	200.00
8876 *Church Bell Blues*	150.00 -	200.00
8885 *She Ain't No Good*	150.00 -	200.00
8905 *Ram Rod Blues*	150.00 -	200.00
8922 *Please Baby*	150.00 -	200.00
8927 *Bed Spring Poker*	150.00 -	200.00
8933 *She's A Bad Girl*	150.00 -	200.00
8939 *Jake Leg Blues*	150.00 -	200.00
8947 *Kitty Cat Blues*	150.00 -	200.00
8951 *Shake Hands And Tell Me Goodbye*	150.00 -	200.00
8953 *Too Long*	150.00 -	200.00
Paramount 13134 *The New Stop And Listen Blues*	250.00 -	400.00
13142 *Shooting High Dice*	250.00 -	400.00
13143 *New Shake That Thing*	250.00 -	400.00
13152 *Don't Wake It Up*	250.00 -	400.00
13152 *Please Baby*	250.00 -	400.00
13156 *Tell Me To Do Right*	250.00 -	400.00

WALTER MITCHELL:

JVB 75827 *Pet Milk Blues*	35.00 -	50.00

MONARCH JAZZ QUARTET:

Okeh 8736 *Four Or Five Times*	30.00 -	50.00
8761 *I Ain't Got Nobody*	30.00 -	50.00
8931 *Pleading Blues*	40.00 -	60.00

MONKEY JOE (& HIS MUSIC GRINDERS):

Bluebird 6061 *Sweet Petunia Stomp*	30.00 -	50.00
6114 *Monkey Joe Got The Blues*	25.00 -	40.00
Okeh 05685, 06153	8.00 -	12.00
Vocalion 04161 *O.K. With Me Baby*	10.00 -	15.00
04219 *Hair Parted In The Middle*	10.00 -	15.00
04294 *Some Sweet Day*	10.00 -	15.00
04416 *Preach, Pray And Moan*	10.00 -	15.00
04471 *Rabbit Foot Blues*	10.00 -	15.00
04618 *New York Central*	10.00 -	15.00
04814 *Tailor Made Woman*	10.00 -	15.00
04871 *Good Business No. 2.*	10.00 -	15.00
04926 *Wise To The Jive*	10.00 -	15.00
04978 *Mobile And K.C. Line*	10.00 -	15.00
05166 *Carry My Business On*	10.00 -	15.00
05274 *That Same Cat*	10.00 -	15.00
05348 *Mountain Baby Blues*	10.00 -	15.00

ALEX MONROE:

Bell 1190 *The Worried Man Blues*	200.00 -	300.00

"E" MONTGOMERY:

Melotone 12548 *Louisiana Blues*	75.00 -	100.00
Vocalion 02706 *Louisiana Blues*	75.00 -	100.00

LITTLE BROTHER MONTGOMERY:

Bluebird 6072 *Vicksburg Blues No. 2.*	35.00 -	50.00
6140 *Pleading Blues*	35.00 -	50.00
Century 4009, 4010	5.00 -	10.00
Paramount 13006 *Vicksburg Blues*	200.00 -	300.00

SAM MONTGOMERY ("KING OF SPADES"):

Titles, issued contemporaneously on Banner,
Melotone, Oriole, Perfect, Romeo: *Baby*

Please Don't Go; Blue Devil Blues; Honey Dripper; I'm Through With You; Kind Of Knave; King of Knave No. 2.; Low In Mind Blues; Mercy Mercy Blues	30.00 -	50.00

JULIA MOODY:

Titles, issued contemporaneously on Banner,
Regal: *Don't Forget, You'll Regret; Mad*

Mama's Blues; Worried Blues	10.00 -	15.00
Black Swan 14122 *The Cootie Crawl*	40.00 -	60.00
14140 *Starvin' For Love*	40.00 -	60.00
14144 *Good Man Sam*	40.00 -	60.00
Columbia 14087-D *Strivin' Blues*	25.00 -	40.00
14103-D *Midnight Dan*	40.00 -	60.00
14121-D *That Chicago Wiggle*	40.00 -	60.00
Paramount 12153 *That Cootie Crawl*	40.00 -	60.00
12154 *Starvin' For Love*	40.00 -	60.00
12155 *Good Man Sam*	40.00 -	60.00

ETTA MOONEY:

Black Swan 14118 *Early Every Morn*	50.00 -	75.00
14134 *Cootie For Your Tootie*	50.00 -	75.00
Paramount 12151 *Early Every Morn*	50.00 -	75.00
12152 *Cootie For Your Tootie*	50.00 -	75.00

(WHISTLIN') ALEX (ANDER) MOORE:

Columbia 14496-D *West Texas Woman*	50.00 -	80.00
14518-D *Ice Pick Blues*	50.00 -	80.00
14596-D *Blue Bloomer Blues*	75.00 -	100.00
Decca 7288 *Blue Bloomer Blues*	20.00 -	30.00
7552 *Hard Hearted Woman*	20.00 -	30.00
RPM 326 *Neglected Woman*	10.00 -	15.00

ALICE MOORE:

Decca 7028 *Riverside Blues*	50.00 -	75.00
7056 *Lonesome Woman Blues*	50.00 -	75.00
7109 *Just Sitting Here Wondering*	20.00 -	30.00
7132 *Blue Black And Evil Blues*	20.00 -	30.00
7153 *Daddy Calling Mama*	20.00 -	30.00
7190 *Grass Cutter Blues*	20.00 -	30.00
7227 *Money Tree Man*	20.00 -	30.00
7253 *I'm Going Fishing Too*	20.00 -	30.00
7293 *New Blue Black And Evil Blues*	10.00 -	15.00
7327 *Midnight Creepers*	10.00 -	15.00
7369 *Don't Deny Me Baby*	10.00 -	15.00
7380 *Doggin' Man Blues*	10.00 -	15.00
7393 *Push Cart Pusher*	10.00 -	15.00
Paramount 12819 *Black And Evil Blues*	150.00 -	200.00
12868 *My Man Blues*	150.00 -	200.00
12947 *Serving Time Blues*	150.00 -	200.00
12973 *Have Mercy Blues*	150.00 -	200.00
13107 *Lonesome Dream Blues*	150.00 -	200.00

ARAH "BABY" MOORE:

Victor 20553 *Drop Down Blues*	75.00 -	100.00

BILL MOORE:

Paramount 12613 *Barbershop Rag*	100.00 -	150.00
12636 *Ragtime Millionaire*	100.00 -	150.00
12648 *One Way Gal*	100.00 -	150.00

(KID) PRINCE MOORE:

Titles, issued contemporaneously on Banner,
Melotone, Oriole, Perfect, Romeo: *Bug Juice
Blues; Church Bells; Honey Dripping Papa;*

Sign Of Judgement	50.00 -	75.00
Decca 7475 *Single Man Blues*	30.00 -	40.00
7514 *Ford V-8 Blues*	30.00 -	40.00
7539 *That's Lovin' Me*	30.00 -	40.00

MONETTE MOORE:

Ajax 17124 *Memphis Blues*	30.00 -	50.00
Columbia 14105-D *Get It Fixed*	40.00 -	60.00
Decca 7161 *Rhythm Shop Swing*	10.00 -	15.00
Paramount 12015 *Sugar Blues*	20.00 -	30.00
12028 *I Just Want A Daddy*	20.00 -	30.00
12030 *Gulf Coast Blues*	20.00 -	30.00
12046 *I'll Go To My Grave With The Blues*	100.00 -	150.00
12067 *Muddy Water Blues*	20.00 -	30.00
12210 *Friendless Blues*	20.00 -	30.00

Victor 20356 *If You Don't Like Potatoes* . . . . 50.00 - 75.00
20484 *Moaning Sinner Blues* . . . . 50.00 - 75.00
Vocalion 14903 *I Wanna Jazz Some More* . . . . . . 25.00 - 40.00
14911 *Death Letter Blues* . . . . 25.00 - 40.00

ROSIE MAE MOORE:
Victor 21280 *Staggering Blues* . . . . 75.00 - 100.00
21408 *School Girl Blues* . . . . 75.00 - 100.00

WILLIAM MOORE:
Paramount 12761 *Raggin' The Blues* . . . . .100.00 - 150.00

EDDIE MORGAN:
Bluebird 5757 *Rock House Blues* . . . . 35.00 - 50.00

CLARA MORRIS:
Bluebird 8700 *I Stagger In My Sleep* . . . . 10.00 - 15.00
8767 *Poker Playing Daddy* . . . . 10.00 - 15.00

MOSBY AND SYKES:
Champion 16513 *Mosby Stomp* . . . . .150.00 - 200.00

BUDDY MOSS:
Titles, issued contemporaneously on Banner,
Conqueror, Melotone, Oriole, Perfect, Romeo:
*Bachelors' Blues; Back To My Used-To-Be;
Best Gal; B & O Blues No. 2; Broke Down
Engine; Bye Bye Mama; Can't Use You No
More; Cold Country Blues; Daddy Don't Care;
Dough Rolling Papa; Evil Hearted Papa;
Going To Your Funeral In A Vee-Eight Ford;
Gravy Server; Hard Road Blues; Hard Times
Blues; Insane Blues; Jealous Hearted Man;
Jinx Man Blues; Love Me Baby; Love Me;
Married Man's Blues; Misery Man Blues;
Mistreated Boy; My Baby Wont's Pay Me No
Mind; New Lovin' Blues; Oh Lordy Mama; Oh
Lordy Mama No. 2; Prowlin' Gambler Blues;
Prowling Woman; Red River Blues; Restless
Night Blues; See What You Done Done; Shake
It All Night Long; Sleepless Night; Somebody
Keeps Calling Me; Someday Baby; Some
Lonesome Day; Stinging Bull Nettle; Stop
Hanging Around; T.B.'s Killing Me; Too
Doggone Jealous; Travelin' Blues; Tricks Ain't
Walking No More; Undertaker Blues; Unkind
Woman; When I'm Dead And Gone; When The
Hearse Rolls Me From My Door; Worrysome
Woman: You Got To Give Me Some Of It; Your
Hard Head Will Bring You Sorrow Some Day* . 50.00 - 75.00
Okeh 06473, 06515, 06679 . . . . 8.00 - 12.00

TEDDY MOSS:
Gennett 6993 *Texas Dream Blues* . . . . .150.00 - 200.00
7010 *You Broke My Hear Baby* . . . . .150.00 - 200.00
7055 *Ocean Wave Blues* . . . . .150.00 - 200.00
7084 *Back-Biter Blues* . . . . .150.00 - 200.00
7158 *Rocky Luck Blues* . . . . .200.00 - 300.00

MR. FREDDIE:
Bluebird 5995 *4A Highway* . . . . 35.00 - 50.00
6025 *Your Good Man Is Gone* . . . . 35.00 - 50.00
6261 *Let's Go Riding* . . . . 35.00 - 50.00

MUDDY WATERS:
Aristocrat 406 *Screamin' And Cryin'* . . . . 75.00 - 100.00
412 *Rollin' And Tumblin'* . . . . 15.00 - 25.00
1302 *Little Anna Mae* . . . . 20.00 - 30.00
1304 *She Ain't Nowhere* . . . . 20.00 - 30.00
1305 *I Feel Like Going Home* . . . . 12.00 - 18.00
1306 *Train Fare Home* . . . . 15.00 - 20.00
1307 *Mean Red Spider* . . . . 15.00 - 25.00
1310 *Muddy Jumps One* . . . . 15.00 - 20.00
1311 *Little Geneva* . . . . 25.00 - 35.00
Chess 1426 *Rollin' Stone* . . . . 8.00 - 12.00
1434 *You're Gonna Need My Help I Said* . . . . . 8.00 - 12.00
1441 *Louisiana Blues* . . . . 8.00 - 12.00*
1452 *Long Distance Call* . . . . 8.00 - 12.00*
1468 *Honey Bee* . . . . 8.00 - 12.00*
1480 *My Fault* . . . . 8.00 - 12.00*
1490 *Early Morning Blues* . . . . 8.00 - 12.00*

1509 *All Night Long* . . . . 5.00 - 8.00*
1514 *Please Have Mercy* . . . . 5.00 - 8.00*
1526 *Gone To Main Street* . . . . 5.00 - 8.00*
1537 *Sad, Sad Day* . . . . 5.00 - 8.00*

MUMBLES:
Modern 809 *Little Boy Blue* . . . . 10.00 - 15.00
RPM 338 *Black Gal* . . . . 10.00 - 15.00

GLADYS MURRAY:
Banner 1464 *Everybody Loves My Baby* . . . . 15.00 - 20.00
Banner 1479 *Nobody Knows What a Red Head
Mama Can Do* . . . . 10.00 - 15.00
Regal 9760 *Everybody Loves My Baby* . . . . 15.00 - 20.00
Regal 9779 *Nobody Knows What A Red Head
Mama Can Do* . . . . 10.00 - 15.00

MABEL NANCE:
Silvertone 3547 *The Stomps* . . . . .150.00 - 200.00

(CHARLIE) DAD NELSON (& HIS GUITAR):
Paramount 12401 *Red River Blues* . . . . .100.00 - 150.00
12430 *Mississippi Strut* . . . . .100.00 - 150.00
12467 *Traveling Daddy* . . . . .100.00 - 150.00
12492 *Cleveland Stomp* . . . . .100.00 - 150.00

PEPPERMINT NELSON:
Gold Star 626 *Peppermint Boogie* . . . . 10.00 - 20.00

RED NELSON:
Bluebird 7265 *Relief Blues* . . . . 15.00 - 20.00
7918 *Black Gal Stomp* . . . . 15.00 - 20.00
7960 *Working Man Blues* . . . . 15.00 - 20.00
Decca 7136 *Grand Trunk Blues* . . . . 25.00 - 40.00
7154 *Detroit Special* . . . . 25.00 - 40.00
7155 *Sweetest Thing Born* . . . . 25.00 - 40.00
7171 *Streamline Train* . . . . 25.00 - 40.00
7185 *Empty Bed Blues* . . . . 15.00 - 20.00
7256 *Gambling Man* . . . . 15.00 - 20.00
7263 *Gravel In My Bed* . . . . 15.00 - 20.00
Vocalion 03001 *Six Cold Feet In The Ground* . . . . 35.00 - 50.00

ROMEO NELSON:
Vocalion 1447 *Head Rag Hop* . . . . .150.00 - 200.00
1494 *Dyin' Rider Blues* . . . . .150.00 - 200.00

SONNY BOY NELSON:
Bluebird 6672 *Street Walkin'* . . . . 30.00 - 50.00
6718 *Lovin' Blues* . . . . 30.00 - 50.00
7091 *Low Down* . . . . 30.00 - 50.00
7849 *Long Tall Woman* . . . . 30.00 - 50.00

"BLUE COAT" TOM NELSON:
Okeh 8838 *Blue Coat Blues* . . . . 75.00 - 125.00

BLIND (GUSSIE) NESBIT/NESBITT:
Columbia 14576-D *Pure Religion* . . . . 50.00 - 75.00
Decca 7113 *He's The Joy Of My Salvation* . . . . . 20.00 - 30.00
7131 *Motherless Children* . . . . 20.00 - 30.00

SCOTTIE NESBITT:
Bluebird 7125 *Sundown Blues* . . . . 10.00 - 15.00
7155 *Troubled And Blue* . . . . 10.00 - 15.00

HAMBONE WILLIE NEWBERN:
Okeh 8679 *Roll And Tumble Blues* . . . . .150.00 - 200.00
8693 *Way Down In Arkansas* . . . . .150.00 - 200.00
8740 *She Could Toddle-Oo* . . . . .150.00 - 200.00

JACK NEWMAN:
Vocalion 04265 *Blackberry Wine* . . . . 10.00 - 15.00
04344 *New Prison Blues* . . . . 10.00 - 15.00

NEW ORLEANS NEHI BOYS:
Paramount 12980 *Mobile Stomp* . . . . .200.00 - 300.00

MANNY NICHOLS:
FCB 125 *Walkin Talkin Blues* . . . . 30.00 - 50.00
Imperial 5162 *No One To Love Me* . . . . 15.00 - 25.00
5173 *Worried Life Blues* . . . . 15.00 - 25.00

NICK NICHOLS:
Columbia 2071-D *Frankie And Johnny* . . . . 30.00 - 50.00
14512-D *Riverside Blues* . . . . 50.00 - 75.00

FREDDIE "REDD" NICHOLSON:
Brunswick 7152 *Dirty No Gooder* . . . . 75.00 - 125.00
7204 *Freddie's Got The Blues* . . . . 75.00 - 125.00
7220 *Tee Roller's Rub* . . . . .100.00 - 150.00

"BOZO" NICKERSON:
Vocalion 1487 *What's The Matter Now? Part 1/2*	100.00 -	150.00
1525 *Bozo's Blues*	100.00 -	150.00
1604 *What's The Matter Now? Part 3/4*	100.00 -	150.00

THE NIGHTHAWKS:
Aristocrat 413 *Jackson Town Gal*	30.00 -	50.00
2301 *Black Angel Blues*	30.00 -	50.00

ROBERT NIGHTHAWK (& HIS NIGHTHAWKS BAND):
Chess 1484 *Return Mail Blues*	10.00 -	15.00*
States 131 *Maggie Campbell*	10.00 -	15.00*
United 102 *Kansas City Blues*	15.00 -	25.00
105 *Take It Easy Baby*	15.00 -	25.00

WILLIE NIX (& HIS COMBO):
Chance 1163 *Nervous Wreck*	20.00 -	30.00
Checker 756 *Truckin' Little Woman*	7.00 -	10.00*
RPM 327 *Lonesome Bedroom Blues*	8.00 -	12.00
Sabre 104 *All By Myself*	15.00 -	20.00*
Sun 179 *Baker Shop Boogie*	75.00 -	100.00*

ELMORE NIXON:
Mercury 70061 *Playboy Blues*	5.00 -	10.00*
Peacock 1537, 1572	5.00 -	8.00
Savoy 878, 889, 1105	4.00 -	7.00
Sittin' In With 546, 580, 601	6.00 -	10.00

GEORGE NOBLE:
Titles, issued contemporaneously on Banner, Melotone, Oriole, Perfect, Romeo: *If You Lose Your Good Gal, Don't Mess With Mine; The Seminole Blues*	150.00 -	200.00
Vocalion 02905 *New Milk Cow Blues*	150.00 -	200.00
02923 *Bed Spring Blues*	150.00 -	200.00
02954 *On My Death Bed*	150.00 -	200.00

DIXIE NOLAN—JOHNNY HARDGE:
Victor V38556 *Worried Love*	125.00 -	175.00

NORA AND DELLE:
Decca 7852 *Army Camp Blues*	10.00 -	15.00
7858 *Keep A Knockin'*	10.00 -	15.00

NORFOLK JAZZ QUARTET:
Decca 7333, 7349, 7383, 7443	7.00 -	15.00
Okeh 4318, 4345, 4366, 4380, 4391, 8007, 8019, 8022, 8028, 8034	20.00 -	30.00
Paramount 12032 *Ain't It A Shame?*	25.00 -	40.00
12054 *Sad Blues*	25.00 -	40.00
12055 *Dixie Blues*	25.00 -	40.00
12218 *Jelly Roll's First Cousin*	25.00 -	40.00
12453 *Louisiana Bo Bo*	40.00 -	60.00
12844 *Please Give Me Some Of That*	40.00 -	60.00

BEN NORSINGLE:
Brunswick 7041 *Rover's Blues*	150.00 -	200.00
7043 *Black Cat Blues*	150.00 -	200.00

HATTIE NORTH:
Vocalion 1433 *Honey Dripper Blues*	100.00 -	150.00

NUGRAPE TWINS:
Columbia 14187-D *I Got Your Ice Cold Nugrape*	20.00 -	30.00
14251-D *The Road Is Rough And Rocky*	20.00 -	30.00

OAK CLIFF T-BONE:
Columbia 14506-D *Trinity River Blues*	150.00 -	200.00

JIMMIE/JIMMY ODEN:
Bluebird 5260 *My Dream Blues*	80.00 -	120.00
Champion 16540 *I Have Made Up My Mind*	150.00 -	250.00
16613 *Patrol Wagon Blues*	150.00 -	250.00
50044 *Patrol Wagon Blues*	50.00 -	80.00
Sunrise 3343 *Warning Spirit Blues*	100.00 -	150.00

OLD MAN ODEN:
Decca 7017 *Six Feet In The Ground*	40.00 -	60.00
7412 *Silk Worm Blues*	25.00 -	40.00
7545 *Thick And Thin*	25.00 -	40.00

OLD CED ODOM:
Decca 7241 *Hotter Than Fire*	8.00 -	12.00
7247 *Break 'Er Down*	8.00 -	12.00
7276 *Fore Day In The Morning*	8.00 -	12.00

OLD PAL SMOKE SHOP FOUR:

Vocalion 1046 *Black Cat Blues*	150.00 -	200.00

OLD SOUTH QUARTETTE:
Broadway 5031 *Pussy Cat Rag*	75.00 -	125.00
QRS 7006 *Pussy Cat Rag*	75.00 -	125.00
7025 *No Hiding Place Down Here*	75.00 -	125.00
7029 *Watermelon Party*	75.00 -	125.00

ONE ARM SLIM:
Bluebird 7806 *Howling Man Blues*	25.00 -	40.00
Vocalion 04676 *Crap Shootin' Blues*	15.00 -	20.00

ONE STRING SAM:
J.V.B. 40 *I Need A Hundred Dollars*	30.00 -	50.00

THE ORIOLES:
Jubilee 5000 *Barbra Lee*	8.00 -	12.00
5001 *Dare To Dream*	10.00 -	15.00
5002 *It Seems So Long Ago*	10.00 -	15.00
5005 *Tell Me So*	8.00 -	12.00*
5008 *I Challenge Your Kiss*	8.00 -	12.00*
Natural 5000 *Barbra Lee*	10.00 -	15.00

JOHN OSCAR:
Brunswick 7080 *In The Gutter*	150.00 -	200.00
7104 *Mama Don't Allow No Easy Riders Here*	75.00 -	100.00
7203 *Whoopee Mama Blues*	150.00 -	200.00
Decca 7029 *Got To Be Worried Now*	25.00 -	40.00

DUKE OWENS & BUD WILSON:
Gennett 6366 *When A Man Is Treated Like A Dog*	100.00 -	150.00
Gennett 6423 *It's Hot—Let It Alone*	100.00 -	150.00

"BIG BOY" GEORGE OWENS:
Gennett 6006 *Kentucky Blues*	100.00 -	150.00

MARSHALL OWENS:
Paramount 13117 *Texas Blues*	150.00 -	200.00
13131 *Texas Blues—Part 2*	150.00 -	200.00

WILLIE "SCARE CROW" OWENS:
Brunswick 7213 *Cut It Out*	100.00 -	150.00

STAR PAGE:
Paramount 12684 *Georgia Blues*	80.00 -	120.00

DUKE PAIGE:
Juke Box 520 *Two Faced Woman Blues*	7.00 -	10.00

SYLVESTER PALMER:
Columbia 14492-D *Lonesome Man Blues*	50.00 -	75.00
14524-D *Broke Man Blues*	50.00 -	75.00

FRANK PALMES:
Paramount 12893 *Troubled 'Bout My Soul*	150.00 -	200.00

PALMETTO JAZZ QUARTET:
Okeh 8011 *My Jazz Gal*	20.00 -	30.00
8016 *Sweet Mamma (Papa's Getting Mad)*	20.00 -	30.00
8023 *Baseball Blues*	20.00 -	30.00
8028 *"U" Need Some Loving*	20.00 -	30.00
8034 *Norfolk Religion*	20.00 -	30.00

PAPA CHARLIE'S BOYS:
Bluebird 6408 *Let My Peaches Be*	15.00 -	20.00
6602 *Gypsy Woman Blues*	15.00 -	20.00

PAPA EGG SHELL:
Brunswick 7082 *I'm Goin' Up In The Country*	75.00 -	100.00
7095 *Whole Soul Blues*	75.00 -	100.00

PAPA FREDDIE:
Okeh 8422 *Muddy Water Blues*	125.00 -	175.00

PAPA TOO SWEET:
Okeh 8651 *Big Fat Mama*	75.00 -	100.00

EVA PARKER:
Victor 20414 *You Got Yourself Another Woman*	20.00 -	30.00
V-38020 *Careless Love*	50.00 -	75.00

LITTLE JUNIOR PARKER & HIS BLUE FLAMES:
Modern 864 *You're My Angel*	7.00 -	10.00

MONISTER PARKER:
Nucraft 100 *Black Snake Blues*	20.00 -	30.00

SHORTY BOB PARKER:
Decca 7470 *Death Of Slim Green*	25.00 -	40.00
7488 *Tired Of Being Drug Around*	25.00 -	40.00
7526 *Rain And Snow*	25.00 -	40.00

TURNER PARRISH:

Champion 16509 *Four Day Blues* ....150.00 - 200.00
   16629 *Graveyard Blues* ....150.00 - 200.00
   16645 *Trenches* ....150.00 - 200.00
   50027 *Graveyard Blues* .... 50.00 - 75.00
   50046 *Fives* .... 35.00 - 50.00

LILA PATTERSON:
Broadway 5005 *Grievin' Hearted Blues* ....100.00 - 150.00
   5010 *Don't Fish In My Sea* ....100.00 - 150.00
   5018 *Dead Drunk Blues* ....100.00 - 150.00

PATTON AND LEE:
Vocalion 02904 *Troubled 'Bout My Mother* ...150.00 - 200.00

CHARLEY PATTON:
Paramount 12792 *Banty Rooster Blues* ....200.00 - 300.00
   12854 *It Won't Be Long* ....200.00 - 300.00
   12869 *A Spoonful Blues* ....200.00 - 300.00
   12877 *Pea Vine Blues* ....200.00 - 300.00
   12883 *Lord I'm Discouraged* ....200.00 - 300.00
   12909 *High Water Everywhere* ....200.00 - 300.00
   12924 *Rattlesnake Blues* ....200.00 - 300.00
   12943 *Magnolia Blues* ....200.00 - 300.00
   12953 *Mean Black Moan* . ...200.00 - 300.00
   12972 *Green River Blues* ....200.00 - 300.00
Paramount 12986 *I Shall Not Be Moved* ......200.00 - 300.00
   12998 *Hammer Blues* ....200.00 - 300.00
   13014 *Moon Going Down* ....200.00 - 300.00
   13031 *Some Happy Day* ....250.00 - 400.00
   13040 *Devil Sent The Rain* ....250.00 - 400.00
   13070 *Dry Well Blues* ....250.00 - 400.00
   13080 *Some Summer Day* ....250.00 - 400.00
   13110 *Frankie And Albert* ....250.00 - 400.00
   13133 *Joe Kirby* ....250.00 - 400.00
Vocalion 02651 *Poor Me* ....150.00 - 200.00
   02680 *High Sheriff Blues* ....150.00 - 200.00
   02782 *Love My Stuff* ....150.00 - 200.00
   02931 *Revenue Man Blues* ....150.00 - 200.00

RUBY PAUL:
Paramount 12592 *Red Letter Blues* .... 75.00 - 100.00

GUILFORD (PEACHTREE) PAYNE:
Okeh 8103 *Peachtree Man Blues* .... 25.00 - 40.00

PEANUT THE KIDNAPPER:
Titles, issued contemporaneously on Banner,
Conqueror, Melotone, Oriole, Perfect, Romeo:
Eighth Avenue Blues; Silver Spade Blues;
Suicide Blues; Swagger Woman Blues .... 50.00 - 100.00

ALICE PEARSON:
Paramount 12507 *Memphis Earthquake* .... 50.00 - 75.00
   12523 *Greyhound Blues* .... 50.00 - 75.00
   12547 *Black Sow Blues* .... 50.00 - 75.00

BILL PEARSON:
Brunswick 7053 *Detroit Blues* .... 75.00 - 100.00

DAVID PEARSON:
Okeh 8847 *Friendless Blues* .... 80.00 - 120.00

MEMPHIS EDDIE PEE:
Globe 103, 108 .... 8.00 - 12.00

ROBERT PEEPLES:
Paramount 12995 *Fat Greasy Baby* ....100.00 - 150.00
   13033 *Mama's Boy* ....100.00 - 150.00

PEETIE'S BOY:
Decca 7767 *Gonna Keep It For My Daddy* ...... 8.00 - 12.00
   7819 *Friar's Point Blues* .... 8.00 - 12.00

PEETIE WHEATSTRAW'S BUDDY:
Hy-Tone 38 *Miss Irene* .... 10.00 - 15.00

MORRIS PEJOE:
Checker 766 *Gonna Buy Me A Telephone* ...... 5.00 - 8.00*

CORA PERKINS:
Okeh 8348 *Today Blues* .... 50.00 - 75.00

DOLLY PERKINS:
Emerson 10761 *My Doggone Lazy Man* .... 15.00 - 20.00

CHARLES "SPECK" PERTUM:
Brunswick 7128 *Broken Down Blues* ....100.00 - 150.00
   7146 *Gambler's Blues* ....100.00 - 150.00

PETE AND REPEAT:

Brunswick 7055 *Hymn-Singing Bill* .... 50.00 - 75.00
   7104 *Toodle-Oodle-Oo* .... 75.00 - 100.00

CHARLEY PETERS:
Herwin 92036 *Lord I'm Discouraged* ....200.00 - 300.00

ARTHUR PETTIES/PETTIS:
Brunswick 7182 *Good Boy Blues* ....100.00 - 150.00
   7209 *Qarrellin' Mama Blues* ....150.00 - 200.00
Victor 21282 *Two Time Blues* .... 75.00 - 100.00

ROBERT PETWAY:
Bluebird 8726 *Rockin' Chair Blues* .... 10.00 - 15.00
   8756 *Sleepy Woman Blues* .... 10.00 - 15.00
   8786 *My Little Girl* .... 10.00 - 15.00
   8838 *Catfish Blues* .... 10.00 - 15.00
   8987 *Boogie Woogie Woman* .... 7.00 - 10.00
   9008 *My Baby Left Me* .... 10.00 - 15.00

WASHINGTON PHILLIPS:
Columbia 14277-D *Lift Him Up That's All* ...... 30.00 - 50.00
   14333-D *Denomination Blues* .... 30.00 - 50.00
   14369-D *Paul And Silas In Jail* .... 30.00 - 50.00
   14404-D *Jesus Is My Friend* .... 30.00 - 50.00
   14448-D *Train Your Child* .... 30.00 - 50.00
   14511-D *I've Got The Key To The Kingdom* .... 40.00 - 60.00
   14566-D *The Church Needs Good Deacons* ... 40.00 - 60.00

PIANO RED:
RCA Victor .... 4.00 - 7.00

PICANINNY/PICKANINNY JUG BAND:
Champion 15995 *Diamond Ring Blues* ....200.00 - 300.00
   16615 *Bottle It Up And Go* ....250.00 - 400.00

WALTER/FATS PICHON:
DeLuxe 3069 *Pinetop's Boogie* .... 10.00 - 15.00
   3072 *Cherry* .... 8.00 - 12.00
Raynac 1101 *Fat And Greasy* .... 10.00 - 15.00

CHARLIE PICKETT:
Decca 7707 *Down The Highway* .... 20.00 - 30.00
   7762 *Trembling Blues* .... 20.00 - 30.00

DAN PICKETT:
Gotham 201 *Laughing Rag* .... 15.00 - 25.00
   510 *Early One Morning* .... 15.00 - 25.00
   512 *Chicago Blues* .... 15.00 - 25.00
   516 *Lemon Man* .... 15.00 - 25.00
   542 *Baby How Long* .... 15.00 - 25.00

PIG 'N' WHISTLE BAND:
Regal 3277 *Talking To You Mama* .... 25.00 - 40.00

PIGMEAT PETE (AND CATJUICE CHARLIE):
Columbia 14452-D *Can You Do That To Me?* ... 50.00 - 75.00
   14463-D *Do It Right* .... 50.00 - 75.00
   14485-D *My Friend John* .... 50.00 - 75.00
   14513-D *Our Family Doctor* .... 50.00 - 75.00
   14563-D *In Kentucky* .... 50.00 - 75.00
   14588-D *Hard Times* .... 75.00 - 100.00
   14598-D *Honey You Done Gone Too Far* ...... 75.00 - 100.00
   14640-D *Rockin' Chair Mary* .... 75.00 - 100.00

PIGMEAT TERRY:
Champion 50043 *Black Sheep Blues* .... 25.00 - 40.00
Decca 7829 *Moaning The Blues* .... 25.00 - 40.00

PINETOP:
Bluebird 6041 *Workhouse Blues* .... 30.00 - 50.00
   6125 *Every Day I Have The Blues* ...... 25.00 - 40.00
   6202 *Got The Blues About My Baby* ..... 30.00 - 50.00

PINETOP AND LINDBERG:
Victor 23330 *East Chicago Blues* ....250.00 - 400.00
   23359 *Louisiana Bound* ....200.00 - 300.00

PINETOP SLIM:
Colonial 106 *Applejack Boogie* .... 20.00 - 30.00

PINEWOOD TOM (& HIS BLUES HOUNDS):
Titles, issued contemporaneously on Banner,
Conqueror, Melotone, Oriole, Perfect, Romeo:
Badly Mistreated Man; Bed Springs Blues;
Black Gal; Black Man; Broad Players Blues;
Cherry Picker; D.B.A. Blues; Did You Read
That Letter?; Evil Man Blues; Friendless City

Blues; Gone Dry Blues; Gone Mother Blues; Good Gal; Greenville Sheik; Homeless and Hungry Blues; Mean Mistreater Mama; Milk Cow Blues; New D.B.A. Blues; New Mean Mistreater Blues; New Milk Cow Blues; No More Ball And Chain; Pigmeat And Whiskey Blues; Prodigal Son; She's Alright With Me; Silicosis Is Killin' Me; Sissy Man; Stormy Weather No. 1; Talking About My Time; Tweet Tweet Mama Blues; Welfare Blues; When The Sun Goes Down .... 40.00 - 60.00

JAMES PLATT:
Champion 15860 *Sympathizin' Blues* .....150.00 - 200.00
  15880 *Easy Papa* ....150.00 - 200.00
  15927 *Back-Biter Blues* ....150.00 - 200.00
  16059 *Texas Dream Blues* ....200.00 - 300.00

FRANK PLUITT:
Bluebird 5383 *Found A Note On My Door* .....100.00 - 150.00
Sunrise 3464 *Found A Note On My Door* ......100.00 - 200.00
Victor 23428 *Meningitis Blues* ....250.00 - 400.00

POOR BILL:
Varsity 6020 *A Hundred Women* .... 10.00 - 15.00

POOR CHARLIE:
Vocalion 03652 *My Little Machine* .... 15.00 - 20.00

POOR JAB:
Champion 16483 *Poor Jab Blues* ....200.00 - 300.00
  16630 *Get It From Behind* ....200.00 - 300.00
  16654 *Come Along Little Children* .....200.00 - 300.00

POOR JIM (WITH DAN JACKSON):
Titles, issued contemporaneously on Banner, Conqueror, Melotone, Oriole, Perfect, Romeo: *Blue And Worried Woman; Squeaky Work Bench Blues; Stack O'Dollars Blues; Sugar Farm Blues* .... 75.00 - 100.00

JENNY POPE:
Vocalion 1438 *Whiskey Drinkin' Blues* ....100.00 - 150.00
  1489 *Mr. Postman Blues* ....100.00 - 150.00
  1522 *Bull Frog Blues* ....100.00 - 150.00

FLOSSIE PORTER:
Champion 15101 *Ain't Got Nobody to Grind My Coffee* .... 50.00 - 80.00
  15102 *Mama's Losin' A Mighty Good Chance* . 50.00 - 80.00

SONNY PORTER:
Columbia 14366-D *Deck Hand Blues* .... 50.00 - 80.00

NETTIE POTTER:
Banner 1483 *A Good Man Is Hard To Find* ..... 10.00 - 15.00
  1484 *Blind Man Blues* .... 10.00 - 15.00
Pathe-Actuelle 032122 *Nobody Knows The Way I Feel* .... 10.00 - 15.00
  032124 *Meat Man Blues* .... 10.00 - 15.00
Regal 9764 *Who Calls You Sweet Mama Now?*... 10.00 - 15.00
  9781 *Blind Man Blues* .... 10.00 - 15.00
  9782 *A Good Man Is Hard To Find* .... 10.00 - 15.00

LOUIS POWELL:
Vocalion 04040 *Mushmouth Blues* .... 10.00 - 15.00

JULIA/JULIUS POWERS:
Harmograph 827 *Weary Way Blues* .... 75.00 - 100.00
  829 *Bama Bound Blues* .... 25.00 - 35.00
  847 *Any Woman's Blues* .... 25.00 - 35.00
  858 *Chicago Bound Blues* .... 25.00 - 35.00
  872 *Chattanooga Blues* .... 75.00 - 100.00
  883 *Moanin' Groanin' Blues* .... 75.00 - 100.00
  897 *Mama Doo Shee Blues* .... 75.00 - 100.00

BUD PRESTON'S STRING BAND:
Champion 15509 *Those Next Mornin' Blues* ....150.00 - 200.00

L.C. PRIGETT:
Victor 20953 *Sure As You Take A Woman From Somebody Else* .... 50.00 - 75.00
  21359 *Frogtown Blues* ....100.00 - 150.00

WES PRINCE & HIS RHYTHM PRINCES:
Excelsior 167, 170 .... 6.00 - 10.00

HELEN PROCTOR:

Decca 7666 *Cheatin' On Me* .... 10.00 - 15.00
  7703 *Let's Call It A Day* .... 10.00 - 15.00

SNOOKY PRYOR:
J.O.B. 101 *Boogy Fool* .... 50.00 - 75.00
  115 *Going Back On The Road* .... 20.00 - 30.00
Parrot 807 *Crosstown Blues* .... 10.00 - 15.00

PULLMAN PORTERS QUARTETTE:
Paramount 12607 *Pullman Passenger Train* ..... 25.00 - 40.00

JOE PULLEM/PULLUM (& HIS ORCHESTRA/ROBERT COOPER):
Bluebird 5459 *Black Gal What Makes Your Head So Hard?* .... 15.00 - 20.00
  5534 *Cows, See That Train Comin'* ...... 15.00 - 25.00
  5592 *Black Gal What Makes Your Head So Hard No. 2* .... 20.00 - 30.00
  5661 *McKinney Street Stomp* .... 30.00 - 50.00
  5844 *Mississippi Flood Blues* .... 20.00 - 30.00
  5859 *Careful Drivin' Mama* .... 20.00 - 30.00
  5898 *Rack It Back And Tell It Right* ... 20.00 - 30.00
  5947 *Black Gal No. 4* .... 15.00 - 25.00
  6071 *Joe Louis Is The Man* .... 20.00 - 30.00
  6093 *Bad Break Blues* .... 15.00 - 25.00
  6123 *I Can't Control Myself* .... 15.00 - 25.00
  6185 *Ice Man Blues* .... 15.00 - 25.00
  6276 *Hard Working Man Blues* .... 15.00 - 25.00
  6298 *Telephone Blues* .... 15.00 - 25.00
Bluebird 6314 *Swing Them Blues* .... 8.00 - 12.00
  6372 *Woman Trouble Blues* .... 8.00 - 12.00
  6426 *Hattie Green* .... 8.00 - 12.00
Montgomery Ward 4833 *I Believe In You* ... 15.00 - 20.00
  4986 *Traveling Blues* .... 15.00 - 20.00
Swing Time 267 *My Woman* .... 8.00 - 12.00

DOUG QUATTLEBAUM:
Gotham 519 *Lizzie Lou* .... 15.00 - 20.00*

SIS QUANDER:
Pathe-Actuelle 7528 *Mama Is Waiting For You* ... 20.00 - 30.00
  7530 *Black Snake Blues* .... 20.00 - 30.00
Perfect 128 *Mama Is Waiting For You* ..... 20.00 - 30.00
  130 *Black Snake Blues* .... 20.00 - 30.00

RUFUS AND BEN QUILLIAN (WITH JAMES McCRAVY):
Columbia 14560-D *Keep It Clean* .... 50.00 - 75.00
  14584-D *Working It Slow* .... 50.00 - 75.00
  14616-D *It's Dirty But Good* .... 50.00 - 75.00
  14639-D *Workin' It Fast* .... 75.00 - 100.00

YANK RACHELL (AND DAN SMITH):
Bluebird 7525 *Rachel Blues* .... 20.00 - 30.00
  7602 *Lake Michigan Blues* .... 20.00 - 30.00
  7694 *It's All Over* .... 20.00 - 30.00
  7731 *Texas Tommy* .... 20.00 - 30.00
Bluebird 8732 *38 Pistol Blues* .... 8.00 - 12.00
  8768 *Biscuit Baking Woman* .... 8.00 - 12.00
  8796 *Insurance Man Blues* .... 8.00 - 12.00
  8840 *Army Man Blues* .... 8.00 - 12.00
  8951 *Yellow Yam Blues* .... 8.00 - 12.00
  8993 *Rainy Day Blues* .... 8.00 - 12.00
  9033 *Peach Tree Blues* .... 8.00 - 12.00
  34-0715 *Katy Lee Blues* .... 8.00 - 12.00
RCA Victor 20-2955 *38 Pistol Blues* ...... 5.00 - 8.00
Vocalion 02649 *Gravel Road Woman* .... 75.00 - 100.00

CARL RAFFERTY:
Bluebird 5429 *Mr. Carl's Blues* .... 75.00 - 100.00

RAILROAD BILL:
Melotone 12373 *M And O Blues* .... 50.00 - 80.00

RAINEY, BIG MEMPHIS MA:
Sun 184 *Baby No No* .... 50.00 - 75.00*

RAMBLIN' BOB:
Bluebird 7987 *Big Apple Blues* .... 15.00 - 25.00
  8020 *Ol' Mose* .... 15.00 - 25.00
  8059 *Good Gamblin'* .... 15.00 - 25.00
  8067 *Freight Train Blues* .... 15.00 - 25.00

GEORGE RAMSEY (AND MAE BELLE LEE):

Paramount 13067 *Times Done Get Hard* . . . . 150.00 - 200.00
   13068 *Bumble Bee No. 1* . . . . 150.00 - 200.00
   13071 *Perfect Mess Blues* . . . . 150.00 - 200.00
JACK RANGER:
  Okeh 8795 *Thieving Blues* . . . . 75.00 - 100.00
   8847 *Lonesome Grave Blues* . . . . 80.00 - 120.00
RUBY RANKIN (and GEORGE HAMILTON):
  Champion 15736 *Shadow Blues* . . . . 150.00 - 200.00
   15756 *Mistreated Mama Blues* . . . . 150.00 - 200.00
   15857 *Got Jelly On My Mind* . . . . 150.00 - 200.00
   15902 *Doin That Thing* . . . . 150.00 - 200.00
   16057 *Southern High Water Blues* . . . . 150.00 - 200.00
HERMAN RAY:
  Decca 48105, 48107 . . . . 7.00 - 10.00
RED AND HIS WASHBOARD BAND:
  Vocalion 03965 *Prowling Groundhog No. 2* . . . . . 15.00 - 20.00
THE RED DEVIL:
  Vocalion 03954 *Huntsman Blues* . . . . 15.00 - 20.00
RED HOT OL MOSE:
  Paramount 12605 *Shrimp Man* . . . . 75.00 - 100.00
RED ONION JOE AND HIS UKE
THUMPERS:
  Champion 15928 *Humming Blues* . . . . 60.00 - 90.00
JIMMY REED:
  Chance 1142 *High And Lonesome* . . . . 8.00 - 12.00*
  Vee Jay 100 *High And Lonesome* . . . . 5.00 - 8.00*
   105 *Jimmy's Boogie* . . . . 5.00 - 8.00*
  Vee Jay 119, 132, 153, 168, 186, 203, 226, 237 . . . 3.00 - 5.00*
LONG CLEVE REED & THE DOWN-HOME
BOYS:
  Black Patti 8030 *Mama You Don't Know How* . . . 400.00 - Up
SADIE REED:
  Champion 15435 *Fall Or Summer Blues* . . . . 100.00 - 150.00
WILLIE REED:
  Columbia 14407-D *Dreaming Blues* . . . . . 75.00 - 100.00
  Vocalion 03093 *All Worn Out And Dry Blues* . . . . 75.00 - 100.00
SLIM REESE:
  Sittin' In With 581 *Got The World In A Jug* . . . . . 10.00 - 15.00
BLIND JOE REYNOLDS:
  Broadway 5106 *Outside Woman Blues* . . . . 150.00 - 200.00
  Paramount 12927 *Nehi Blues* . . . . 150.00 - 200.00
   12983 *Cold Woman Blues* . . . . 150.00 - 200.00
TEDDY REYNOLDS:
  Sittin' In With 558, 571, 586, 594, 613 . . . . 5.00 - 8.00
BLIND WILLIE REYNOLDS:
  Victor 23258 *Third Street Woman Blues* . . . . . . 200.00 - 300.00
MACK RHINEHART & BROWNIE
STUBBLEFIELD:
  Titles, issued contemporaneously on Banner,
   Melotone, Oriole, Perfect, Romeo: *Blues After*
   Sundown; Broke And Hungry; Clay County
   Blues; Dirty No Gooder; I Can't Take It Any
   More; If I Leave Here Running; Lonesome
   House Blues; Lost Woman Blues; Open Back
   Door Blues; T.P.N. Moaner; Up-town Blues;
   You Don't Know My Mind . . . . 50.00 - 100.00
WALTER RHODES:
  Columbia 14289-D *The Crowing Rooster* . . . . . . 75.00 - 100.00
RHYTHM WILLIE (& HIS GANG):
  Okeh 05856 *Bedroom Stomp* . . . . 15.00 - 20.00
   05960 *Boarding House Blues* . . . . 15.00 - 20.00
  Premium 866 *Wailin' Willie* . . . . 15.00 - 20.00
RICHARD BROTHERS:
  Strate-8 1500 *Stolen Property* . . . . 50.00 - 75.00*
ROBERT RICHARD:
  JVB 75828 *Cadillac Woman* . . . . 50.00 - 75.00
  King 4274 *Wigwam Woman* . . . . 15.00 - 25.00
SETH RICHARD:
  Columbia 14325-D *Lonely Seth Blues* . . . . 50.00 - 75.00
UNCLE CHARLIE RICHARDS:
  Pathe-Actuelle 7521 *Levee Blues* . . . . 50.00 - 75.00
   7527 *Sore Bunion Blues* . . . . 50.00 - 75.00

Perfect 121 *Levee Blues* . . . . 50.00 - 75.00
  127 *Sore Bunion Blues* . . . . 50.00 - 75.00
"MOOCH" RICHARDSON:
  Okeh 8554 *T And T Blues* . . . . 50.00 - 75.00
   8576 *Big Kate Adams Blues* . . . . 50.00 - 75.00
   8611 *Helena Blues* . . . . 50.00 - 75.00
RICHMOND STARLIGHT (JAZZ) QUARTET:
  QRS 7028 *Gone Jazz Crazy* . . . . 35.00 - 50.00
   7056 *Oh, You Better Mind* . . . . 35.00 - 50.00
EHTEL RIDLEY:
  Ajax 17126 *Get It Fixed* . . . . 35.00 - 50.00
   17131 *He Was A Good Man* . . . . 35.00 - 50.00
  Columbia A-3941, A-3965 . . . . 8.00 - 12.00
  Victor 19111 *Memphis Tennessee* . . . . 20.00 - 30.00
WILLIE (BOODLE IT) RIGHT:
  Okeh 05959 *Down South Blues* . . . . 8.00 - 12.00
   06008 *Sunny Land Blues* . . . . 8.00 - 12.00
   06057 *West Texas Blues* . . . . 8.00 - 12.00
ISSIE RINGGOLD:
  Columbia 14509D *He's A Good Meat Cutter* . . . 50.00 - 75.00
SALLY RITZ:
  Banner 1394, 1437, 1452 . . . . 10.00 - 15.00
HUBERT ROBERTSON & HIS ORCHESTRA:
  Eddies 1211 *Lonely Traveler* . . . . 7.00 - 10.00
GIP ROBERTS:
  JVB 29 *Sandman* . . . . 10.00 - 15.00
HELEN ROBERTS:
  Silvertone 3570 *Lonely Blues* . . . . 80.00 - 120.00
SISTER MINNIE PEARL ROBERTS:
  Brunswick 7179 *You Make Your Troubles So Hard* 50.00 - 80.00
SALLY ROBERTS:
  Okeh 8485 *Gonna Ramble Blues* . . . . 40.00 - 60.00
   8500 *Black Hearse Blues* . . . . 40.00 - 60.00
SNITCHER ROBERTS:
  Okeh 8750 *Low Moaning Blues* . . . . 100.00 - 150.00
   8781 *Snitcher's Blues* . . . . 100.00 - 150.00
ROBINSON BROTHERS:
  Black & White 107, 108 . . . . 7.00 - 10.00
ROBINSON & MACK:
  Okeh 8259 *I Beg To Be Excused* . . . . 50.00 - 75.00
   8298 *It's All The Same To Me* . . . . 50.00 - 75.00
   8321 *Booze* . . . . 50.00 - 75.00
ALEXANDER ROBINSON:
  Paramount 12649 *My Baby* . . . . 100.00 - 150.00
HUBERT ROBINSON (& HIS YARDBIRDS):
  Jade 206 *Hard Lovin' Daddy* . . . . 7.00 - 10.00
  Macy's 5005, 5007, 5010, 5015 . . . . 7.00 - 10.00
JAMES "BAT" ROBINSON:
  Champion 16236 *Bat's Own Blues* . . . . 150.00 - 200.00
   16745 *Humming Blues* . . . . 150.00 - 200.00
MABEL ROBINSON:
  Decca 8568, 8580, 8601 . . . . 4.00 - 7.00
MUSHMOUTH ROBINSON:
  Black & White 105 *Boogie Boo Blues* . . . . 5.00 - 8.00
NETTIE ROBINSON:
  Pathe-Actuelle 7523 *I've Got The Right Man Now* 25.00 - 40.00
  Perfect 123 *I've Got The Right Man Now* . . . . . . 25.00 - 40.00
JIMMY ROGERS (& HIS TRIO/ROCKING
FOUR):
  Chess 1435 *That's All Right* . . . . 8.00 - 15.00*
   1442 *Going Away Baby* . . . . 8.00 - 15.00*
   1453, 1476 . . . . 7.00 - 10.00*
   1506, 1519, 1543, 1574, 1616, 1643 . . . . 3.00 - 6.00*
   1659, 1687, 1721 . . . . 3.00 - 5.00
MAE ROGERS:
  Champion 16530 *My Time Blues* . . . . 150.00 - 250.00
MAY ROGERS:
  Champion 15590 *Road House Blues* . . . . 150.00 - 250.00
WALTER ROLAND:
  Titles, issued contemporaneously on Banner,
   Conqueror, Melotone, Oriole, Perfect, Romeo:
   Back Door Blues; Bad Dream Blues: Big

*Mama; Club Meeting Blues; Cold Blooded
Murder; Collector Man Blues; C.W.A. Blues;
Dices' Blues; Early This Morning; Early In
The Morning No. 2; Every Morning Blues; 45
Pistol Blues; House Lady Blues; Last Year
Blues; Man, Man, Man; Money Taker Woman;
O.B.O. Blues; Overall Blues; Penniless Blues;
Red Cross Blues No. 2; Sail On Little Girl No.
2; Schoolboy Blues; Screw Worm; Slavin'
Blues; S.O.L. Blues; Talkin' Low Blues; T
Model Blues; Worn Out Man Blues; You Gonna
Want Me* .... 50.00 - 75.00

MAMIE ROMER:
  Oriole 325 *A Good Man Is Hard To Find* .... 10.00 - 15.00

BAYLESS ROSE:
  Champion 16037 *Black Dog Blues* .... 100.00 - 150.00
  16772 *Frisco Blues* .... 150.00 - 250.00
  Gennett 7250 *Black Dog Blues* .... 125.00 - 175.00

LUCY ROSE:
  Champion 15471 *Papa, You're Too Slow* .... 75.00 - 100.00

BERTHA ROSS:
  Gennett 6227 *My Jelly Blues* .... 200.00 - 300.00
  6243 *Lost Man Blues* .... 200.00 - 300.00
  Superior 331 *Tea Rollin' Blues* .... 250.00 - Up

DOCTOR/DR. ROSS (& HIS JUMP & JIVE BOYS):
  Chess 1504 *Dr. Ross Boogie* .... 25.00 - 40.00*
  Sun 193 *Chicago Breakdown* .... 40.00 - 60.00*
  212 *The Boogie Disease* .... 50.00 - 75.00*

DOLLY ROSS:
  Brunswick 7005 *Hootin' Owl Blues* .... 50.00 - 75.00
  Vocalion 1166 *Hootin' Owl Blues* .... 50.00 - 75.00

LOUISE ROSS:
  Columbia 14118-D *No Home Blues* .... 30.00 - 50.00

LUCY ROSS:
  Champion 15715 *West End Blues* .... 90.00 - 130.00
  15754 *Loose Like That* .... 90.00 - 130.00
  15775 *Cotton Belt Blues* .... 90.00 - 130.00

OLLIE ROSS:
  Brunswick 7045 *Ox Meat Blues* .... 100.0 - 150.00

TED ROSS:
  Champion 15859 *Mother-In-Law Blues* .... 150.00 - 200.00
  15882 *Clickety-Clack Blues* .... 150.00 - 200.00

WILL ROWLAND & HIS BAND (Vocal, JESSE LOCKETT):
  Gold Star 657 *Don't Lose Your Mind* .... 7.00 - 10.00

LAURA RUCKER:
  Paramount 13030 *I'm The Lonesome One* ...... 150.00 - 200.00
  13075 *Little Joe* .... 150.00 - 200.00
  13138 *Fancy Tricks* .... 150.00 - 200.00

OLLIE RUPERT:
  Victor 20577 *Ain't Goin' To Be Your Low Down
  Dog* .... 100.00 - 150.00

LILLIAN RUSH:
  Champion 15510 *Do What You Did Last Night* ... 100.00 - 150.00
  15529 *There's Been Some Changes Made* ..... 100.00 - 150.00

BLIND TIM RUSSELL:
  Herwin 93008 *I've Crossed The Separation Line* 100.00 - 150.00

GEORGE "HAMBONE" RUTHERS:
  Champion 15795 *Street Walkin' Blues* .... 100.00 - 150.00

ST. LOUIS BESSIE:
  Vocalion 1559 *Sugar Man Blues* .... 150.00 - 200.00
  1615 *Meat Cutter Blues* .... 150.00 - 200.00

ST. LOUIS JIMMY:
  Apollo 420 *Chicago Woman Blues* .... 7.00 - 10.00
  Aristocrat 7001 *Florida Hurricane* .... 15.00 - 25.00
  Bluebird 8889 *Going Down Slow* .... 10.00 - 15.00
  8933 *Lost Ball Blues* .... 10.00 - 15.00
  9016, 9040, 34-0718, 34-0727 .... 7.00 - 10.00
  Bullet 270 *Going Down Slow* .... 10.00 - 15.00
  278 *Sittin' And Thinkin'* .... 8.00 - 12.00
  291 *Mr. Brown Boogie* .... 8.00 - 12.00

Herald 407 *Hard Luck Boogie* .... 10.00 - 15.00*
J.O.B. 101 *Mother's Day* .... 50.00 - 75.00
Mercury 8137 *Shame On You Baby* .... 5.00 - 8.00
Miracle 134 *Biscuit Roller* .... 5.00 - 8.00
RCA Victor 20-2650 *Dog House Blues* .... 3.00 - 6.00

ST. LOUIS JOHNNY:
  Champion 50071 *Sister Kelly Blues* .... 20.00 - 30.00

ST. LOUIS RED MIKE:
  Bluebird 7744 *Red Mike Blues* .... 15.00 - 20.00
  7781 *Wash My Hands Nice And Clean* ...... 15.00 - 20.00
  7896 *Gamblin' Man Blues* .... 15.00 - 20.00

SALLY SAD:
  Varsity 6033 *Don't Say Goodbye* .... 10.00 - 20.00
  6040 *Gin House Blues* .... 10.00 - 20.00
  6058 *Mistreated Mamma Blues* .... 10.00 - 20.00
  6066 *Gypsy Woman Blues* .... 10.00 - 20.00

SALTY DOG SAM:
  Titles, issued contemporaneously on Banner,
  Melotone, Oriole, Perfect, Romeo: *Graveyard
  Digger's Blues; I'm Still Sitting On Top Of The
  World; Lonesome Road Blues; New Salty Dog;
  Signifying Blues; Slow Mama Slow* .... 100.00 - 200.00

SAM AND OSCAR:
  Brunswick 7208 *You Can't Get That Stuff No
  More* .... 75.00 - 100.00
  7212 *I Done Caught That Rascal Now* .... 75.00 - 100.00

SAMMY SAMPSON:
  Titles, issued contemporaneously on Banner,
  Oriole, Perfect, Romeo: *I Got The Blues For
  My Baby; Meanest Kind Of Blues; Police
  Station Blues; State Street Woman; Tadpole
  Blues; They Can't Do That* .... 50.00 - 75.00

CLARENCE SAMUELS:
  Aristocrat 1001 *Boogie Woogie Blues* .... 10.00 - 15.00
  DeLuxe 3219 *Stompin' At The Jubilee* .... 4.00 - 8.00
  Freedom 1533, 1541, 1544 .... 4.00 - 8.00
  Swing Time 131, 149 .... 4.00 - 8.00

BESSIE SANDERS (& HER DIXIE DUDES):
  Champion 15101 *It Must Be Hard* .... 50.00 - 80.00
  15102 *Take Your Fingers Off It* .... 50.00 - 80.00
  15106 *Home Alone Blues* .... 35.00 - 50.00
  15180 *Lucky Number Blues* .... 80.00 - 120.00
  15471 *Shake A Little Bit* .... 75.00 - 100.00
  15490 *Dying Blues* .... 100.00 - 150.00
  15550 *Where Have All The Black Men Gone?* .. 100.00 - 150.00
  15613 *Wild Geese Blues* .... 200.00 - 300.00
  15635 *Red Beans And Rice* .... 200.00 - 300.00
  16058 *I Lost My Man* .... 150.00 - 200.00

GERTRUDE SAUNDERS:
  Vocalion 1131 *Don't Let Your Love Come Down* .. 40.00 - 60.00

THE SCARE CROW:
  Champion 16014 *Easy Creeping Mama* .... 150.00 - 200.00
  16036 *Traveling Blues* .... 150.00 - 200.00
  16103 *Ornery Blues* .... 150.00 - 200.00
  16194 *That Black Bottom Dance* .... 150.00 - 200.00

BEVERLY SCOTT & HIS TRIO:
  Murray 503 *Shaking The Boogie* .... 10.00 - 20.00

ELLIE SCOTT:
  Vocalion 1461 *Sunshine Special* .... 150.00 - 200.00

LANNIE SCOTT TRIO:
  Savoy 614 *Lannie's Boogie Woogie* .... 5.00 - 8.00

LULU SCOTT:
  Bluebird 7706 *Baby Can I Holler* .... 15.00 - 20.00

MAE SCOTT:
  Paramount 12048 *Squawkin' The Blues* .... 35.00 - 50.00

ROOSEVELT SCOTT:
  Vocalion 05137 *Do You Call That Right?* ...... 15.00 - 20.00
  05206 *Brownskin Woman Swing* .... 15.00 - 20.00
  05371 *Tender Foot Blues* .... 15.00 - 20.00
  05415 *Look Up And Down* .... 15.00 - 20.00
  05502 *Doctor Bill Blues* .... 15.00 - 20.00
  05550 *Down In The Gutter* .... 15.00 - 20.00

SONNY SCOTT:

Vocalion 02533 *No Good Biddie* . . . . 75.00 - 100.00
    02586 *Black Horse Blues* . . . . 75.00 - 100.00
    02614 *Fire Wood Man* . . . . 75.00 - 100.00
    25012 *Noal Mountain Blues* . . . . 75.00 - 100.00
    25013 *Working Man's Moan* . . . . 75.00 - 100.00
    25016 *Naked Man Blues* . . . . 75.00 - 100.00
    25017 *Red Rooster Blues* . . . . 75.00 - 100.00

IRENE SCRUGGS:
Champion 16102 *Borrowed Love* . . . . .150.00 - 200.00
    16148 *My Back To The Wall* . . . . .150.00 - 200.00
    16756 *The Voice of the Blues* . . . . .150.00 - 250.00
Gennett 7296 *You've Got What I Want* . . . . .150.00 - 200.00
Okeh 8142 *Why He Left Me I Don't Know* . . . . . 30.00 - 50.00
    8156 *My Daddy's Calling Me* . . . . 30.00 - 50.00
    8476 *Lonesome Valley Blues* . . . . 50.00 - 75.00
Paramount 13023 *Good Meat Grinder* . . . . .200.00 - 300.00
    13046 *Back To The Wall* . . . . .200.00 - 300.00
Vocalion 1017 *Home Town Blues* . . . . .200.00 - 300.00

CHARLIE SEGAR:
Decca 7027 *Southern Hospitality* . . . . 35.00 - 50.00
    7075 *Cow Cow Blues* . . . . 35.00 - 50.00
Vocalion 05441 *Key To The Highway* . . . . 15.00 - 25.00
    05539 *Lonesome Graveyard Blues* . . . . 15.00 - 25.00

HOWARD SERRATT:
Sun 198 *Troublesome Waters* . . . . 50.00 - 75.00*

TOMMY SETTLERS & HIS BLUES MOANER:
Paramount 13049 *Low Down Blues Moan* . . . . . .200.00 - 300.00
    13056 *Big Bed Bug* . . . . .200.00 - 300.00
    13120 *Blowing The Bugle Blues* . . . . .250.00 - 400.00

TOMMY SETTLES WITH EZIEKIEL LOWE
& LEE BUNKLEY:
Titles, issued contemporaneously on Banner,
    Melotone, Oriole, Perfect, Romeo: *Don't Want*
    You No More; Pearlie Mae Blues . . . . 50.00 - 100.00

SLIM SEWARD & FAT BOY HAYES:
MGM 10306, 10770 . . . . 7.00 - 10.00

GEORGE SEYMOUR:
Herwin 93016 *Southland Blues* . . . . .100.00 - 150.00

WILL SHADE:
Champion 16599 *She Done Sold It Out* . . . . . . .200.00 - 300.00
    16630 *Get It From The Front* . . . . .200.00 - 300.00
Victor 21725 *Better Leave That Stuff Alone* . . . . .150.00 - 250.00

ALLEN SHAW:
Vocalion 02844 *Moanin' The Blues* . . . . 90.00 - 120.00

THE SHA-WEEZ:
Aladdin 3170 *No One To Love Me* . . . . 40.00 - 60.00*

JOHNNY SHINES:
J.O.B. *116 Cool Driver* . . . . 50.00 - 75.00*
    1010 *Brutal Hearted Woman* . . . . 50.00 - 75.00*

SHOE SHINE JOHNNY:
Chess 1443 *Joliet Blues* . . . . 15.00 - 25.00

JAYDEE SHORT:
Paramount 13040 *Drafted Mama* . . . . .150.00 - 200.00
    13043 *Telephone Arguin' Blues* . . . . .150.00 - 200.00
    13091 *Flaggin' It To Georgia* . . . . .150.00 - 200.00

JELLY JAW SHORT:
Vocalion 1704 *Snake Doctor Blues* . . . . .100.00 - 150.00
    1708 *Let Me Mash That Thing* . . . . .100.00 - 150.00

SHORTY GEORGE:
Brunswick 7106 *Jones Law Blues* . . . . .125.00 - 175.00

SHREVEPORT HOME WRECKERS:
Victor 23275 *Home Wreckin' Blues* . . . . .300.00 - 500.00

SHUFFLIN' SAM & HIS RHYTHM:
Vocalion 03329 *Good Liquor* . . . . 15.00 - 20.00

BILL SIMPSON:
Lin 100 *Jelly Roll Man* . . . . 7.00 - 10.00

COLETHA SIMPSON:
Brunswick 7089 *Riverside Blues* . . . . 75.00 - 100.00
    7112 *Black Man Blues* . . . . 75.00 - 100.00

FRANKIE LEE SIMS:
Blue Bonnet 147 *Home Again Blues* . . . . 40.00 - 60.00
    148 *Single Man Blues* . . . . 40.00 - 60.00

HENRY SIMS:
Paramount 12912 *Farrell Blues* . . . . .200.00 - 300.00
    12940 *Be True Be True Blues* . . . . .200.00 - 300.00

JOE SIMS AND CLARENCE WILLIAMS:
Paramount 12435 *Shut Your Mouth* . . . . .100.00 - 150.00

SKOODLE DUM DOO AND SHEFFIELD:
Manor 1056 *West Kinney Street Blues* . . . . 15.00 - 20.00
Regis 107 *Gas Ration Blues* . . . . 15.00 - 20.00

SLEEPY JOE & HIS WASHBOARD BAND:
Savoy 753 *Amen Blues* . . . . 10.00 - 15.00

SLOKE & IKE:
Decca 7315 *Chocolate Candy Bars* . . . . 15.00 - 20.00
    7375 *Slocum Blues* . . . . 15.00 - 20.00

SLUEFOOT JOE:
QRS 7080 *House Top Blues* . . . . .150.00 - 200.00
    7084 *Grab It And Run* . . . . .150.00 - 200.00
    7086 *Shouting Baby Blues* . . . . .150.00 - 200.00
    7091 *Rocky Road Moan* . . . . .150.00 - 200.00

SMITH AND HARPER:
Titles, issued contemporaneously on Banner,
    Melotone, Oriole, Perfect, Romeo: *Insurance*
    Policy Blues; Poor Girl . . . . 50.00 - 80.00

ANNIE SMITH:
Harmograph 896 *Moonshine Blues* . . . . 80.00 - 120.00

BESSIE SMITH:
Columbia A-3844 *Down Hearted Blues* . . . . 8.00 - 12.00
    A-3877 *Beale Street Mamma* . . . . 10.00 - 15.00
    A-3888 *Oh Daddy Blues* . . . . 8.00 - 12.00
    A-3898 *'Tain't Nobody's Business If I Do* . . . . 10.00 - 15.00
    A-3900 *Mama's Got The Blues* . . . . 10.00 - 15.00
    A-3936 *Bleeding Hearted Blues* . . . . 10.00 - 15.00
    A-3939 *Lady Luck Blues* . . . . 10.00 - 15.00
    A-3942 *Nobody In Town Can Bake A Sweet*
      Jelly Roll Like Mine . . . . 10.00 - 15.00
    A-4001 *Graveyard Dream Blues* . . . . 10.00 - 15.00
    13000-D *My Sweetie Went Away* . . . . 15.00 - 20.00
    13001-D *Any Woman's Blues* . . . . 15.00 - 20.00
    13005-D *Sam Jones Blues* . . . . 15.00 - 20.00
    13007-D *Far Away Blues* . . . . 15.00 - 20.00
    14000-D *Chicago Bound Blues* . . . . 15.00 - 20.00
    14005-D *Frosty Mornin' Blues* . . . . 15.00 - 20.00
    14010-D *Eavesdropper's Blues* . . . . 15.00 - 20.00
    14018-D *Moonshine Blues* . . . . 10.00 - 15.00
    14020-D *Sorrowful Blues* . . . . 10.00 - 15.00
    14023-D *Hateful Blues* . . . . 10.00 - 15.00
    14025-D *Pinchbacks-Take 'Em Away* . . . . 10.00 - 15.00
    14031-D *Mountain Top Blues* . . . . 15.00 - 20.00
    14032-D *House Rent Blues* . . . . 15.00 - 20.00
    14037-D *Rainy Weather Blues* . . . . 15.00 - 20.00
    14042-D *Weeping Willow Blues* . . . . 15.00 - 20.00
    14051-D *Dying Gambler's Blues* . . . . 15.00 - 20.00
    14052-D *Sinful Blues* . . . . 10.00 - 15.00
    14056-D *Sobbin' Hearted Blues* . . . . 30.00 - 50.00
    14064-D *Cold In Hand Blues* . . . . 30.00 - 50.00
    14075-D *Soft Pedal Blues* . . . . 25.00 - 40.00
    14079-D *You've Been A Good Old Wagon* . . . . . 25.00 - 40.00
    14083-D *Careless Love* . . . . 50.00 - 75.00
    14090-D *Nashville Woman's Blues* . . . . 50.00 - 75.00
    14095-D *J.C. Holmes Blues* . . . . 50.00 - 75.00
    14098-D *Nobody's Blues But Mine* . . . . 25.00 - 40.00
    14109-D *New Gulf Coast Blues* . . . . 25.00 - 40.00
    14115-D *Red Mountain Blues* . . . . 30.00 - 50.00
    14123-D *Lonesome Desert Blues* . . . . 30.00 - 50.00
    14129-D *What's The Matter Now?* . . . . 25.00 - 40.00
    14133-D *Jazzbo Brown From Memphis Town* . . . 25.00 - 40.00
    14137-D *Hard Driving Papa* . . . . 25.00 - 40.00
    14147-D *Baby Doll* . . . . 30.00 - 50.00
    14158-D *Lost Your Head Blues* . . . . 30.00 - 50.00
    14172-D *One And Two Blue* . . . . 30.00 - 50.00
    14179-D *Young Woman's Blues* . . . . 30.00 - 50.00
    14195-D *Back Water Blues* . . . . 30.00 - 50.00
    14197-D *After You've Gone* . . . . 30.00 - 50.00

14209-D *Them's Graveyard Words* .... 40.00 - 60.00
14219-D *Alexander's Ragtime Band* .... 30.00 - 50.00
14232-D *Trombone Cholly* .... 40.00 - 60.00
14250-D *Mean Old Bed Bug Blues* .... 30.00 - 50.00
14260-D *Sweet Mistreater* .... 30.00 - 50.00
14273-D *Foolish Man Blues* .... 50.00 - 75.00
14292-D *Thinking Blues* .... 30.00 - 50.00
14304-D *Pickpocket Blues* .... 30.00 - 50.00
14312-D *Empty Bed Blues* .... 10.00 - 15.00
14324-D *Spider Man Blues* .... 30.00 - 50.00
14338-D *Standin' In The Rain Blues* ...... 30.00 - 50.00
14354-D *Devil's Gonna Git You* .... 30.00 - 50.00
14375-D *Washwoman's Blues* .... 30.00 - 50.00
14384-D *Slow And Easy Man* .... 30.00 - 50.00
14399-D *You Ought To Be Ashamed* .... 30.00 - 50.00
14427-D *I'm Wild About That Thing* .... 15.00 - 20.00
14435-D *I've Got What It Takes* .... 30.00 - 50.00
14451-D *Take It Right Back* .... 40.00 - 60.00
14464-D *He's Got Me Goin'* .... 40.00 - 60.00
14476-D *Wasted Life Blues* .... 40.00 - 60.00
14487-D *You Don't Understand* .... 40.00 - 60.00
14516-D *Keep It To Yourself* .... 40.00 - 60.00
14527-D *Blue Spirit Blues* .... 40.00 - 60.00
14538-D *Moan, You Moaners* .... 50.00 - 75.00
14554-D *Hustlin' Dan* .... 50.00 - 75.00
14569-D *Hot Springs Blues* .... 75.00 - 100.00
14611-D *In The House Blues* .... 75.00 - 100.00
14634-D *Safety Mama* .... 75.00 - 100.00
14663-D *Shipwreck Blues* .... 75.00 - 100.00
Okeh 8945 *Do Your Duty* .... 50.00 - 75.00
8949 *Gimme a Pigfoot* .... 50.00 - 75.00

BESSIE MAE SMITH:
Paramount 12922 *St. Louis Daddy* .... 80.00 - 120.00

CLARA SMITH:
Black Patti 8034 *Sand Raisin' Blues* ....100.00 - 200.00
8035 *Clara Blues* ....100.00 - 200.00
Columbia 12-D *Kansas City Man Blues* ..... 10.00 - 15.00
A-3943 *Every Woman's Blues* .... 8.00 - 12.00
A-3961 *Kind Lovin' Blues* .... 8.00 - 12.00
A-3966 *All Night Blues* .... 8.00 - 12.00
A-3991 *Irresistible Blues* .... 10.00 - 15.00
A-4000 *Awful Moanin' Blues* .... 8.00 - 12.00
Columbia 13002-D *Don't Never Tell Nobody* .... 10.00 - 15.00
13007-D *Far Away Blues* .... 10.00 - 15.00
14006-D *It Won't Be Long Now* .... 10.00 - 15.00
14009-D *31st. Street Blues* .... 20.00 - 30.00
14013-D *I'm Gonna Tear Your Playhouse Down* 15.00 - 20.00
14016-D *My Doggone Lazy Man* .... 10.00 - 15.00
14019-D *The Clearing House Blues* .... 10.00 - 15.00
14021-D *Cold Weather Papa* .... 10.00 - 15.00
14022-D *Mean Papa, Turn In Your Key* .... 10.00 - 15.00
14026-D *Don't Advertise Your Man* .... 10.00 - 15.00
14034-D *Deep Blues Sea Blues* .... 20.00 - 30.00
14039-D *Basement Blues* .... 10.00 - 15.00
14041-D *Freight Train Blues* .... 15.00 - 20.00
14045-D *Death Letter Blues* .... 15.00 - 20.00
14049-D *San Francisco Blues* .... 15.00 - 20.00
14053-D *Steel Drivin' Sam* .... 15.00 - 20.00
14058-D *Nobody Knows The Way I Feel Dis
Mornin'* .... 30.00 - 50.00
14062-D *Broken Busted Blues* .... 30.00 - 50.00
14069-D *When I Steps Out* .... 10.00 - 15.00
14073-D *Courthouse Blues* .... 30.00 - 50.00
14077-D *Shipwrecked Blues* .... 30.00 - 50.00
14085-D *Different Way Blues* .... 15.00 - 20.00
14097-D *Kitchen Mechanic Blues* .... 15.00 - 20.00
14098-D *My Man Blues* .... 25.00 - 40.00
14104-D *Alley Rat Blues* .... 20.00 - 30.00
14108-D *The Market Street Blues* .... 20.00 - 30.00
14117-D *I'm Tired Of Bein' Good* .... 20.00 - 30.00
14126-D *Disappointed Blues* .... 20.00 - 30.00
14138-D *Rock, Church, Rock* .... 20.00 - 30.00

14143-D *Salty Dog* .... 20.00 - 30.00
14150-D *Whip It To A Jelly* .... 20.00 - 30.00
14160-D *Separation Blues* .... 20.00 - 30.00
14183-D *Get On Board* .... 20.00 - 30.00
14192-D *Cheatin' Daddy* .... 20.00 - 30.00
14202-D *Percolatin' Blues* .... 20.00 - 30.00
14223-D *Black Woman's Blues* .... 20.00 - 30.00
14240-D *Black Cat Moan* .... 20.00 - 30.00
14256-D *Troublesome Blues* .... 20.00 - 30.00
14294-D *Race Track Blues* .... 20.00 - 30.00
14319-D *It's All Coming Home To You* ... 20.00 - 30.00
14344-D *Steamboat Man Blues* .... 25.00 - 40.00
14368-D *Ain't Got Nobody To Grind My Coffee* 25.00 - 40.00
14398-D *It's Tight Like That* .... 25.00 - 40.00
14409-D *Empty House Blues* .... 25.00 - 40.00
14419-D *Got My Mind On That Thing* .... 25.00 - 40.00
14462-D *Papa I Don't Need You Now* .... 30.00 - 50.00
14536-D *Where Is My Man?* .... 35.00 - 50.00
14553-D *Don't Fool Around On Me* ...... 35.00 - 50.00
14568-D *You're Getting Old On Your Job* .... 50.00 - 75.00
14580-D *Woman To Woman* .... 50.00 - 75.00
14592-D *Good Times* .... 40.00 - 60.00
14619-D *Ol' Sam Tages* .... 50.00 - 75.00
14633-D *You Dirty Dog* .... 50.00 - 75.00
14645-D *Street Department Papa* .... 50.00 - 75.00
14653-D *So Long Jim* .... 50.00 - 75.00

CLEMENTINE SMITH:
Banner 1483 *I'm Done Done Done With You* .... 10.00 - 15.00
1484 *Nobody Knows The Way I Feel This
Morning* .... 10.00 - 15.00
Pathe-Actuelle 032067 *Hard Luck Blues* ... 10.00 - 15.00
Perfect 12146 *Hard Luck Blues* .... 10.00 - 15.00
Regal 9779 *Nobody Knows What A Red Head
Mama Can Do* .... 10.00 - 15.00
9781 *Nobody Knows The Way I Feel This
Morning* .... 10.00 - 15.00

EITHEL SMITH:
Champion 16613 *Jelly Roll Mill* ....150.00 - 250.00

ELIZABETH SMITH:
Victor 20297 *No Sooner Blues* .... 20.00 - 30.00
20334 *When My Wants Run Out* .... 40.00 - 60.00
21539 *Police Done Tore My Playhouse Down* .. 40.00 - 60.00

FLOSSIE SMITH & THE RED HOTS TWINS:
Superior 2603 *Hokum Stomp* ....150.00 - 250.00
2699 *That's The Way She Likes It* ....150.00 - 250.00

"FUNNY PAPER" SMITH:
Vocalion 1558 *Howling Wolf Blues—No. 1/2* ....100.00 - 150.00
1590 *Good Coffee Blues* ....100.00 - 150.00
1614 *Howling Wolf Blues—No. 3/4* ......100.00 - 150.00
1633 *Corn Whiskey Blues* ....100.00 - 150.00
1641 *Seven Sisters Blues—Part 1/2* .....100.00 - 150.00
1655 *Hungry Wolf* ....100.00 - 150.00
1664 *Forty-Five Blues* ....100.00 - 150.00
1674 *Fool's Blues* ....100.00 - 150.00
1679 *County Jail Blues* ....100.00 - 150.00

GRACE SMITH:
National 9051 *What's on the Rail for the Lizard* . 5.00 - 8.00

GUY SMITH:
Paramount 12806 *Southland Blues* ....100.00 - 150.00

HAZEL SMITH:
Okeh 8620 *West End Blues* ....125.00 - 175.00

HENRY SMITH:
Dot 1220 *Good Rocking Mama* .... 7.00 - 10.00*
Fortune 802 *Dog Me Blues* .... 7.00 - 10.00*

HORACE SMITH:
Gennett 7025 *Mother-n-Law Blues* ....150.00 - 250.00
7056 *Clickety-Clack Blues* ....150.00 - 250.00

IKE SMITH'S CHICAGO BOYS:
Champion 50040 *Fighting Joe Louis* ...... 15.00 - 20.00

**IVA/IVY SMITH (AND CHARLIE
DAVENPORT/AND HER BUDDIES):**
Champion 16080 *Milkman Blues* ....150.00 - 250.00

Gennett 6829 *Shadow Blues*	150.00 -	200.00
6861 *Gin House Blues*	150.00 -	200.00
6875 *Mistreated Mama Blues*	150.00 -	200.00
7024 *Wringin' And Twistin' Papa*	150.00 -	200.00
7040 *Doin' That Thing*	150.00 -	200.00
7101 *Cheating Only Blues*	150.00 -	200.00
7251 *Milkman Blues*	200.00 -	300.00
Paramount 12436 *Rising Sun Blues*	150.00 -	200.00
12447 *Sad And Blue*	150.00 -	200.00
12472 *Barrel House Mojo*	150.00 -	200.00
12496 *Ninety-Nine Years Blues*	150.00 -	200.00
Supertone 9509 *Shadow Blues*	125.00 -	175.00
9515 *No Good Man Blues*	125.00 -	175.00
9527 *Wringing And Twistin' Papa*	125.00 -	175.00
9531 *Mistreated Mama Blues*	125.00 -	175.00
9533 *Southern High Waters Blues*	125.00 -	175.00

JANE SMITH:

Silvertone 3563 *Kentucky Blues*	50.00 -	75.00

JULIA SMITH:

Oriole 771 *Crap Shootin' Papa, Mama Done Caught Your Dice*	10.00 -	15.00
772 *I Needs Plenty Of Grease In My Frying Pan*	10.00 -	15.00
816 *Harlem Blues*	15.00 -	20.00

LAURA SMITH:

Don't You Leave Me Here, issued contemporaneously on Banner, Domino, Regal	15.00 -	25.00
Okeh 8157 *Texas Moaner Blues*	75.00 -	100.00
8169 *Two-Faced Woman Blues*	75.00 -	100.00
8179 *Gravier Street Blues*	50.00 -	80.00
8186 *I'm Gonna Get Myself A Real Man*	75.00 -	100.00
8246 *Disgusted Blues*	75.00 -	100.00
8252 *Face To Face*	50.00 -	80.00
8316 *I'll Get Even With You*	75.00 -	100.00
8331 *Them Has Been Blues*	30.00 -	50.00
8366 *Cool Can Blues*	75.00 -	100.00
8445 *Hateful Blues*	50.00 -	80.00
Pathe-Actuelle 7520 *When A Gator Hollers*	50.00 -	75.00
7525 *I'm Gonna Kill Myself*	50.00 -	75.00
Perfect 120 *When A Gator Hollers*	50.00 -	75.00
125 *I'm Gonna Kill Myself*	50.00 -	75.00
Victor 20775 *Lonesome Refugee*	40.00 -	60.00
20945 *Red River Blues*	40.00 -	60.00

MAMIE SMITH (& HER JAZZ BAND/ HOUNDS); MAMIE SMITH'S JAZZ HOUNDS:

Ajax 17058 *Good Time Ball*	35.00 -	50.00
17063 *Remorseful Blues*	30.00 -	50.00
Okeh 4113 *That Thing Called Love*	10.00 -	15.00
4169 *Crazy Blues*	8.00 -	12.00
4194 *Fare Thee Honey Blues*	8.00 -	12.00
4228 *If You Don't Want Me Blues*	10.00 -	15.00
4253 *Don't Care Blues*	10.00 -	15.00
4254 *Royal Garden Blues*	15.00 -	25.00
4295 *Jazzbo Ball*	15.00 -	25.00
4296 *That Thing Called Love*	15.00 -	25.00
4305 *You Can't Keep A Good Man Down*	15.00 -	25.00
4351 *Dangerous Blues*	10.00 -	15.00
4416 *Sax-O-Phoney Blues*	10.00 -	15.00
4427 *Mamma Whip! Mamma Spank!*	10.00 -	15.00
4445 *The Wang Wang Blues*	10.00 -	15.00
4446 *Down Home Blues*	10.00 -	15.00
4471 *Weepin'*	10.00 -	15.00
4511 *Sweet Man O'Mine*	10.00 -	15.00
4542 *Oh, Joe (Please Don't Go)*	10.00 -	15.00
4578 *Doo-Dah Blues*	10.00 -	15.00
4600 *A-Wearin' Away The Blues*	10.00 -	15.00
4623 *I Want A Jazzy Kiss*	10.00 -	15.00
4630 *Lonesome Mama Blues*	15.00 -	20.00
4631 *Mean Daddy Blues*	15.00 -	20.00
4658 *Alabama Blues*	10.00 -	15.00
4670 *Got To Cool My Doggies Now*	10.00 -	15.00

4689 *That Da Da Strain*	10.00 -	15.00
4752 *I Ain't Gonna Give Nobody None O'This Jelly Roll*	10.00 -	15.00
4767 *The Darktown Flappers Ball*	15.00 -	20.00
4781 *I'm Gonna Get You*	10.00 -	15.00
4856 *Mean Man*	15.00 -	25.00
4926 *Kansas City Man Blues*	50.00 -	75.00
4935 *Good Looking Papa*	10.00 -	15.00
4960 *Mistreatin' Daddy Blues*	10.00 -	15.00
8024 *Rambling Blues*	15.00 -	20.00
8030 *Carolina Blues*	20.00 -	30.00
8036 *Strut Your Material*	20.00 -	30.00
8072 *Those Longing For you Blues*	20.00 -	30.00
8864 *Don't Advertise Your Man*	50.00 -	75.00
8915 *Golfing Papa*	50.00 -	75.00
Victor 20210 *Goin' Crazy With The Blues*	30.00 -	50.00
20233 *Sweet Virginia Blues*	30.00 -	50.00

MANDY SMITH:

Jewel 5138, 5188, 5207, 5230, 5254, 5309	8.00 -	15.00
Oriole 1059, 1118, 1147, 1170, 1197, 1249	8.00 -	15.00

PINE TOP SMITH:

Vocalion 1245 *Pine Top's Boogie Woogie*	80.00 -	120.00
1256 *Big Boy They Can't Do That*	80.00 -	120.00
1266 *I'm Sober Now*	100.00 -	150.00
1298 *Jump Steady Blues*	100.00 -	150.00

ROBERT SMITH:

Independent 301 *Freeway Boogie*	8.00 -	12.00

RUBY SMITH:

Bluebird 7654 *Dream Man Blues*	10.00 -	15.00
7794 *Flyin' Mosquito Blues*	10.00 -	15.00
7864 *Hard Up Blues*	10.00 -	15.00
Vocalion 04903 *Back Water Blues*	15.00 -	20.00

SIX CYLINDER SMITH:

Paramount 12968 *Pennsylvania Woman Blues*	100.00 -	150.00

SPARK PLUG SMITH:

Titles, issued contemporaneously on Banner, Melotone, Oriole, Perfect, Romeo: *Deserted Man Blues; In A Shanty In Old Shanty Town; Make It Tight; Mama's Doughnut; Motherless Boy; New Blues Heaven; Stopped Clock Blues; Sweet Evening Breeze; Vampire Woman; You Put That Thing On Me*	40.00 -	60.00

SUSIE SMITH:

Ajax 17064 *House Rent Blues*	30.00 -	50.00
17073 *Salt Water Blues*	30.00 -	50.00
17075 *Bullet Wound Blues*	30.00 -	50.00
17079 *The Bye Bye Blues*	30.00 -	50.00
17081 *Meat Man Pete*	30.00 -	50.00
17086 *Nobody Knows The Way I Feel Dis Mornin'*	30.00 -	50.00
17089 *Sore Bunion Blues*	30.00 -	50.00
17093 *Scandal Blues*	30.00 -	50.00
17095 *How Can I Miss You*	30.00 -	50.00
17127 *Texas Special Blues*	50.00 -	80.00
17132 *Undertaker's Blues*	30.00 -	50.00
17134 *Crepe Hanger Blues*	50.00 -	80.00

THUNDER SMITH (AND ROCKIE):

Aladdin 166 *Little Mama Boogie*	10.00 -	15.00
Down Town 2011 *Thunder's Unfinished Boogie*	15.00 -	25.00
2012 *New Worried Life Blues*	15.00 -	25.00
2013 *Low Down Dirty Ways*	15.00 -	25.00
Gold Star 615 *Cruel Hearted Woman*	15.00 -	25.00
644 *Santa Fe Blues*	15.00 -	25.00

TRIXIE SMITH:

Black Swan 2039 *Trixie's Blues*	20.00 -	30.00
2044 *Long Lost Weary Blues*	20.00 -	30.00
14114 *Pensacola Blues*	20.00 -	30.00
14127 *My Man Rocks Me*	20.00 -	30.00
14132 *I'm Through With You*	20.00 -	30.00
14138 *I'm Gonna Get You*	20.00 -	30.00
14142 *Log Cabin Blues*	20.00 -	30.00
14149 *Triflin' Blues*	20.00 -	30.00

Decca 7469 *Trixie Blues*	8.00 -	12.00
7489 *My Unusual Man*	8.00 -	12.00
7528 *Jack, I'm Mellow*	8.00 -	12.00
7617 *No Good Man*	8.00 -	12.00
Paramount 12161 *Trixie's Blues*	20.00 -	30.00
12162 *Long Lost Weary Blues*	20.00 -	30.00
12163 *Pensacola Blues*	20.00 -	30.00
12164 *My Man Rocks Me*	20.00 -	30.00
12165 *I'm Through With You*	20.00 -	30.00
12166 *I'm Gonna Get You*	20.00 -	30.00
12167 *Log Cabin Blues*	20.00 -	30.00
12168 *Triflin' Blues*	20.00 -	30.00
12208 *Sorrowful Blues*	40.00 -	60.00
12211 *Freight Train Blues*	40.00 -	60.00
12232 *Praying Blues*	40.00 -	60.00
12245 *Choo Choo Blues*	40.00 -	60.00
12256 *Mining Camp Blues*	100.00 -	150.00
12262 *Railroad Blues*	100.00 -	150.00
12330 *Love Me Like You Used To Do*	50.00 -	75.00
12336 *Black Bottom Hop*	50.00 -	75.00

WILLIAM & VERSEY SMITH:

Paramount 12505 *When That Great Ship Went Down*	40.00 -	60.00
12516 *I Believe I'll Go Back Home*	40.00 -	60.00

SMOKEHOUSE CHARLEY:

Champion 15794 *My Texas Blues*	100.00 -	150.00
15815 *Pig Meat Blues*	100.00 -	150.00
15834 *Broke Man's Blues*	100.00 -	150.00
15903 *Rollin' Mill Stomp*	100.00 -	150.00
15950 *Six Shooter Blues*	150.00 -	200.00
15994 *Second Hand Love*	150.00 -	200.00
16682 *Levee Bound Blues*	200.00 -	300.00
50014 *Gee, But It's Hard*	50.00 -	75.00

SMOKEY JOE:

Flip 502 *Split Personality*	25.00 -	35.00*
Sun 228 *Split Personality*	15.00 -	20.00*

SNOOKY AND MOODY:

Old Swing-Master 18 *Calling Up My Baby Blues*	25.00 -	40.00

EDDIE SNOW:

Sun 226 *Ain't That Right*	30.00 -	40.00*

HATTIE SNOW:

Gennett 7039 *Don't Say Goodbye*	150.00 -	250.00
7070 *Make That Gravel Fly*	150.00 -	250.00
7115 *Two Train Blues*	150.00 -	250.00

Q. ROSCOE SNOWDEN:

Okeh 8119 *Misery Blues*	30.00 -	50.00

SONNY BOY & LONNIE:

Continental 6050, 6052, 6053, 6054	7.00 -	10.00

SONNY BOY & SAM:

Continental 6055 *Mama Blues*	7.00 -	10.00

SOUTH CAROLINA QUARTETTE:

QRS 7012 *Paul And Silas*	30.00 -	50.00
7061 *I'm A Pilgrim*	30.00 -	50.00

SOUTHERN BLUES SINGERS:

Gennett 6828 *Lighthouse Blues*	125.00 -	175.00
6845 *Runnin' Wild*	125.00 -	175.00

SOUTHERN JUBILEE QUARTET:

Black Patti 8036 *Listen To The Lambs*	100.00 -	Up

SOUTH MEMPHIS JUG BAND:

Vocalion 02585 *Doctor Medicine*	100.00 -	150.00

SOUTHERN (NEGRO) QUARTETTE:

Columbia A-3444 *I'm Wild About Moonshine*	10.00 -	20.00
A-3450 *I Ain't Givin' Nothin' Away*	10.00 -	20.00
A-3489 *He Took It Away From Me*	10.00 -	20.00
14038-D *Hampton Road Blues*	10.00 -	20.00
14043-D *Moanin' Croanin' Blues*	15.00 -	25.00
14048-D *My Man Rocks Me (With One Steady Roll)*	15.00 -	25.00

SOUTHERN SANCTIFIED SINGERS:

Brunswick 7074 *Soon We'll Gather At The River*	75.00 -	100.00

SOUTHERN UNIVERSITY QUARTET:

Bluebird 5846 *All Over The World*	15.00 -	20.00

5932 *I'm Tired Of Living In The Country*	15.00 -	20.00
6142 *I'm Troubled In Mind*	15.00 -	20.00

CHARLIE SPAND:

Okeh 05699 *Rock And Rye*	20.00 -	30.00
05757 *Gold Tooth Mama*	20.00 -	30.00
05894 *Big Alley Rat Blues*	20.00 -	30.00
05946 *Gone Mother Blues*	20.00 -	30.00
Paramount 12790 *Soon This Morning*	150.00 -	200.00
12817 *Back To The Woods Blues*	150.00 -	200.00
12856 *Moanin' The Blues*	150.00 -	200.00
12887 *In The Barrel Blues*	150.00 -	200.00
12917 *Mississippi Blues*	150.00 -	200.00
12930 *Room Rent Blues*	150.00 -	200.00
13005 *She's Got Good Stuff*	150.00 -	200.00
13022 *Mistreatment Blues*	150.00 -	250.00
13047 *Thirsty Woman Blues*	150.00 -	250.00
13101 *Georgia Mule Blues*	200.00 -	300.00
13112 *Hard Times Blues*	200.00 -	300.00

THE SPANIELS:

Chance 1141 *Baby It's You*	15.00 -	20.00*

SPARKLING FOUR QUARTETTE:

QRS 7011 *Keep On To Galilee*	25.00 -	40.00

SPARKS BROTHERS:

Bluebird 5193 *61 Highway*	100.00 -	150.00
5247 *Chicago's Too Much For Me*	100.00 -	150.00
Sunrise 3273 *Down on the Levee*	100.00 -	200.00
3330 *Chicago's Too Much For Me*	100.00 -	200.00

MILTON SPARKS:

Bluebird 6096 *Grinder Blues*	30.00 -	40.00
6126 *I Wake Up In The Morning*	25.00 -	40.00
6521 *Ina Blues*	25.00 -	40.00
6529 *Erie Train Blues*	25.00 -	40.00

HENRY SPAULDING:

Brunswick 7085 *Cairo Blues*	75.00 -	125.00

BLOSSOM SPEARS:

Champion 15267 *Indian Brown Blues*	75.00 -	100.00

SPECKLED RED:

Bluebird 7985 *St. Louis Stomp*	10.00 -	15.00
8012 *Try Me One More Time*	10.00 -	15.00
8036 *You Got To Fix It*	10.00 -	15.00
8069 *Welfare Blues*	10.00 -	15.00
8113 *Down On The Levee*	10.00 -	15.00
Brunswick 7116 *The Dirty Dozen*	100.00 -	150.00
7137 *House Dance Blues*	100.00 -	150.00
7151 *The Dirty Dozen—Part No. 2*	100.00 -	150.00
7164 *Speckled Red's Blues*	100.00 -	150.00
7200 *We Got To Get That Thing Fixed*	100.00 -	150.00

MAMIE SPENCER:

Oriole 795 *Scrubbin' Blues*	20.00 -	30.00

BIG BOY SPIRES & HIS TRIO:

Chance 1137 *About To Lose My Mind*	15.00 -	25.00*
Checker 752 *One Of These Days*	7.00 -	10.00*

SWEET PEASE SPIVEY & HER/DOT SCOTT'S RHYTHM DUKES:

Decca 7204 *Grievin' Me*	10.00 -	15.00
7237 *410 Blues*	10.00 -	15.00

(ORIGINAL) VICTORIA SPIVEY (AND CHICAGO FOUR/DOT SCOTT'S RHYTHM DUKES/HER HALLELUJAH BOYS):

Decca 7203 *Black Snake Swing*	10.00 -	15.00
7222 *T.B.'s Got Me Blues*	10.00 -	15.00
Okeh 8338 *No More Jelly Bean Blues*	50.00 -	75.00
8351 *Dirty Woman's Blues*	50.00 -	75.00
8370 *Hoodoo Man Blues*	40.00 -	60.00
8389 *Humored And Petted Blues*	50.00 -	75.00
8401 *Big Houston Blues*	50.00 -	75.00
8410 *Santa Fe Blues*	50.00 -	75.00
8464 *Idle Hour Blues*	50.00 -	75.00
8481 *The Alligator Pond Went Dry*	50.00 -	75.00
8494 *T.B. Blues*	50.00 -	75.00
8517 *Garter Snake Blues*	30.00 -	50.00
8531 *Blood Thirst Blues*	30.00 -	50.00

8550 *Red Lantern Blues*	30.00 -	50.00
8565 *Your Worries Ain't Like Mine*	30.00 -	50.00
8581 *Murder In The First Degree*	30.00 -	50.00
8615 *Organ Grinder Blues*	75.00 -	125.00
8626 *New Black Snake Blues, Part 1/2*	25.00 -	40.00
8634 *Mosquito, Fly And Flea*	30.00 -	50.00
8652 *Furniture Man Blues—Part 1/2*	20.00 -	30.00
8713 *How Do You Do It That Way?*	75.00 -	100.00
8733 *You Done Lost Your Good Thing Now—Part 1/2*	25.00 -	40.00
8744 *Toothache Blues—Part No. 1/2*	25.00 -	40.00
Victor 23349 *Baulin Water Blues*	200.00 -	300.00
V38546 *Telephoning The Blues*	100.00 -	150.00
Victor V-38570 *Dirty T.B. Blues*	100.00 -	150.00
V38584 *New York Blues*	75.00 -	100.00
V38598 *Haunted By The Blues*	75.00 -	100.00
V38609 *You've Gotta Have What It Takes*	80.00 -	120.00
Vocalion 1606 *Nebraska Blues*	100.00 -	150.00
1640 *Low Down Man Blues*	100.00 -	150.00
03243 *Toothache Blues—Part 1/2*	8.00 -	12.00
03260 *Furniture Man Blues—Part 1/2*	8.00 -	12.00
03366 *I Ain't Gonna Let You See My Santa Claus*	15.00 -	20.00
03405 *Detroit Moan*	15.00 -	20.00
03505 *One Hour Mama*	15.00 -	20.00
03639 *Good Cabbage*	15.00 -	20.00

"MR. FREDDIE" SPRUELL:

Paramount 12665 *Tom Cat Blues*	150.00 -	250.00

STABLE BOY SAM:

Vocalion 1739 *Mama's Doughnut*	—	—

STATE STREET BOYS:

Okeh 8962 *Don't Tear My Clothes*	40.00 -	60.00
8964 *Crazy About You*	40.00 -	60.00
8965 *Sweet To Mama*	40.00 -	60.00
Vocalion 03002 *She Caught The Train*	25.00 -	40.00
03004 *Crazy About You*	30.00 -	50.00
03049 *Sweet To Mama*	30.00 -	50.00
03131 *Mobile And Western Line*	30.00 -	50.00

STEAMBOAT BILL & HIS GUITAR:

Champion 15674 *No No Blues*	150.00 -	200.00
15694 *Weak-Minded Blues*	150.00 -	200.00
15716 *Bad Luck Moan*	150.00 -	200.00
15735 *Rag Baby*	150.00 -	200.00

STEELE AND JOHNSON:

Champion 16395 *Selling That Stuff*	100.00 -	150.00

VOL STEVENS:

Victor 21356 *Vol Stevens Blues*	150.00 -	200.00

DAN STEWART:

Vocalion 1536 *New Orleans Blues*	80.00 -	120.00

MAE STEWART:

Silvertone 3518 *I Was Born A Brownskin*	75.00 -	100.00
3520 *You Ain't Foolin' Me*	75.00 -	100.00
3541 *Going To The Nation*	50.00 -	75.00

PRISCILLA STEWART:

Paramount 12205 *True Blues*	75.00 -	100.00
12224 *Mecca Flat Blues*	75.00 -	100.00
12240 *Delta Bottom Blues*	75.00 -	100.00
12253 *The Woman Ain't Born*	100.00 -	150.00
12286 *Priscilla Blues*	75.00 -	100.00
12299 *Going To The Nation*	50.00 -	80.00
12360 *It Must Be Hard*	75.00 -	100.00
12402 *Biscuit Roller*	100.00 -	150.00
12463 *Lonesome Hour Blues*	75.00 -	100.00
12465 *P.D.Q Blues*	80.00 -	120.00
12740 *A Little Bit Closer*	80.00 -	120.00

ARBEE STIDHAM:

Abco 100, 107	4.00 -	6.00*
Checker 751, 758	4.00 -	7.00*
RCA Victor	3.00 -	5.00
Sittin' In With 596, 606, 617	5.00 -	8.00

FRANK STOKES:

Victor 21272 *Downtown Blues*	150.00 -	200.00
21672 *Mistreatin' Blues*	150.00 -	200.00
21738 *Stomp That Thing*	150.00 -	200.00
23341 *I'm Going Away Blues*	250.00 -	500.00
23411 *Frank Stoke' Dream*	250.00 -	400.00
V38500 *Tain't Nobody's Business If I Do*	150.00 -	200.00
V38512 *I Got Mine*	150.00 -	200.00
V38531 *Take Me Back*	150.00 -	200.00
V38548 *South Memphis Blues*	200.00 -	300.00
V38589 *Right Now Blues*	200.00 -	300.00

JOE STONE:

Bluebird 5169 *Back Door Blues*	75.00 -	125.00
Sunrise 3250 *It's Hard Time*	100.00 -	150.00

LUTHER STONEHAM:

Mercury 8275 *Sittin' And Wonderin'*	8.00 -	12.00*

STOVEPIPE No. 1 (AND DAVID CROCKETT):

Columbia 201-D *Turkey In The Straw*	40.00 -	60.00
15011-D *Lonesome John*	75.00 -	100.00
Okeh 8514 *Court Street Blues*	75.00 -	100.00
8543 *Bed Slats*	75.00 -	100.00

FREEMAN STOWERS:

Gennett 6814 *Railroad Blues*	75.00 -	100.00
Gennett 6830 *Texas Wildcat Chase*	75.00 -	100.00
Supertone 9396 *Sunrise on the Farm*	50.00 -	80.00

MARY STRAINE:

Black Swan 14115 *Ain't Got Nothing Blues*	25.00 -	40.00
14123 *Last Go Round Blues*	20.00 -	30.00
14150 *Chirpin' The Blues*	20.00 -	30.00
Paramount 12132 *Ain't Got Nothing Blues*	25.00 -	40.00
12149 *Last Go Round Blues*	20.00 -	30.00
12150 *Chirpin' The Blues*	20.00 -	30.00

JIMMY STRANGE:

Victor 23317 *No Limit Blues*	200.00 -	300.00

JOHNNIE STRAUSS:

Decca 7035 *Old Market Street Blues*	30.00 -	50.00
7081 *Hard Working Woman*	30.00 -	50.00

STREAMLINE MAE:

Okeh 06045 *Romance In The Dark*	10.00 -	15.00
06093 *School Boy Blues*	10.00 -	15.00

SUGAR CANE JOHNNY:

Bluebird 5948 *Who Pumped The Wind In The Doughnuts?*	50.00 -	75.00

THE SUGARMAN:

Sittin' In With 609 *Which Woman Do I Love*	10.00 -	15.00

ANNIE SUMMERFORD:

Okeh 8174 *'Fo Day Blues*	75.00 -	100.00

SUNNY BOY & HIS PALS:

Champion 15283 *Don't You Leave Me Here*	200.00 -	300.00
Gennett 6106 *France Blues*	250.00 -	400.00

SUNNY JIM AND WHISTLIN' JOE:

Champion 15361 *Black Snake Blues*	150.00 -	200.00

SUNNYLAND SLIM & HIS SUNNY (LAND) BOYS/TRIO; SUNNYLAND SLIM & MUDDY WATERS (COMBO); SUNNYLAND TRIO:

Apollo 416 *Bad Times*	8.00 -	12.00
Aristocrat 1301 *Fly Right, Little Girl*	20.00 -	30.00
1304 *She Ain't Nowhere*	20.00 -	30.00
Blue Lake 105 *Going Back To Memphis*	10.00 -	15.00*
107 *Shake It Baby*	10.00 -	15.00
Ebony 1009 *Shake It Baby*	—	
Hytone 32 *Jivin' Boogie*	8.00 -	12.00
33 *My Heavy Load*	8.00 -	12.00
33 *Miss Bessie Mae*	8.00 -	12.00
37 *I've Done You Wrong*	8.00 -	12.00
J.O.B. 102 *Down Home Child*	50.00 -	75.00
1002 *Pet Rabbit*	40.00 -	60.00
1003 *Mary Lee*	40.00 -	60.00
1105 *Shake It Baby*	15.00 -	20.00*
1108 *Four Day Bounce*	15.00 -	20.00*
Mercury 8132, 8264, 8277	7.00 -	10.00*
Regal 3327 *Orphan Boy Blues*	20.00 -	30.00
Sunny 101 *Back To Korea Blues*	30.00 -	50.00

Tempo Tone 1001 *Hard Times* . . . . 20.00 - 30.00
1002 *Blue Baby* . . . . 20.00 - 30.00

THE SWALLOWS:
King 4458, 4466, 4501, 4515, 4521, 4612, 4632 . . 7.00 - 10.00*

SWAN AND LEE:
Okeh 8732 *Fishy Little Thing* . . . . 50.00 - 75.00

SWEET PAPA STOVEPIPE:
Paramount 12404 *Mama's Angel Child* . . . . 75.00 - 125.00

SWEET PAPA TADPOLE:
Vocalion 1592 *Have You Ever Been Worried In*
Mind . . . . .100.00 - 150.00
1680 *Black Spider Blues* . . . . .100.00 - 150.00
1687 *Your Baby Can't Get Enough* . . . . .100.00 - 150.00

SWEET PEA(S):
Bluebird 7224 *Cold In Hand* . . . . 15.00 - 20.00
8114 *Blood Drippin' Blues* . . . . 15.00 - 20.00
8146 *Disgusted Blues* . . . . 15.00 - 20.00
Victor 23361 *Day Breakin' Blues* . . . . .200.00 - 300.00
V38565 *Heart-Breakin' Blues* . . . . .150.00 - 250.00

SYKES AND JOHNSON:
Champion 16558 *Steady Grinding* . . . . .150.00 - 250.00

ISABEL SYKES:
Bluebird 5170 *Don't Rush Yourself* . . . . 75.00 - 125.00

ROOSEVELT SYKES:
Black & White 100 *This Tavern Boogie* . . . . 8.00 - 12.00
Bluebird 5323 *New 44 Blues* . . . . 80.00 - 120.00
5342 *Working Dollar Blues* . . . . 80.00 - 120.00
34-0721, 34-0729 . . . . 4.00 - 7.00
Bullet 319 *Candy Man Blues* . . . . 10.00 - 15.00
Champion 16586 *Highway 61 Blues* . . . . .150.00 - 200.00
50012 *Highway 61 Blues* . . . . 50.00 - 75.00
Decca 7011 *Ethel Mae Blues* . . . . 50.00 - 75.00
7280 *Mister Sykes Blues* . . . . 20.00 - 30.00
7586 *Have You Seen Ida B* . . . . 10.00 - 15.00
7597 *Love Will Wear You Down* . . . . 10.00 - 15.00
Okeh 06219, 06387, 06455, 06542, 06709 . . . . . . 5.00 - 10.00
8702 *Boot That Thing* . . . . 75.00 - 100.00
8727 *The Way I Feel Blues* . . . . 75.00 - 100.00
8742 *Henry Ford Blues* . . . . 75.00 - 100.00
8749 *Skeet And Garret* . . . . 75.00 - 100.00
8776 *Roosevelt's Blues* . . . . 75.00 - 100.00
8787 *Poor Boy Blues* . . . . 75.00 - 100.00
8819 *Bury That Thing* . . . . 75.00 - 100.00
RCA Victor . . . . 5.00 - 8.00
Regal 3269 *Rock It* . . . . 10.00 - 15.00
3286 *Drivin' Wheel* . . . . 10.00 - 15.00
3306 *Mailbox Blues* . . . . 10.00 - 15.00
3324 *Green Onion Top* . . . . 10.00 - 15.00
Sunrise 3404 *New 44 Blues* . . . . .100.00 - 200.00
3423 *Devil's Island Gin Blues* . . . . .100.00 - 200.00
United 101, 120, 129, 139, 152 . . . . 5.00 - 8.00

HANNAH SYLVESTER:
Emerson 10625 *Midnight Blues* . . . . 20.00 - 30.00
Famous 3237 *Farewell Blues* . . . . 40.00 - 60.00
Paramount 12033 *Midnight Blues* . . . . 40.00 - 60.00
12034 *The Wicked Fives* . . . . 40.00 - 60.00
20243 *Farewell Blues* . . . . 40.00 - 60.00
Puritan 11243 *Farewell Blues* . . . . 40.00 - 60.00

BLIND JOE/JOEL TAGGART (&
BERTHA/EMMA/JAMES TAGGART):
Decca 7033 *I Wonder Will My Mother Be On*
That Train? . . . . 50.00 - 75.00
7034 *I Ain't No Sinner Now* . . . . 50.00 - 75.00
Paramount 12611 *Been Listening All The Day* . . . .100.00 - 150.00
12717 *I've Crossed The Separation Line* . . . . . .100.00 - 150.00
12744 *Mother's Love* . . . . .100.00 - 150.00
12780 *Scandulous And A Shame* . . . . .100.00 - 150.00
13020 *Wonder Will My Troubles Then Be Over* .100.00 - 150.00
13059 *Pressin' Up That Shiny Way* . . . . .100.00 - 150.00
13081 *Satan Your Kingdom Must Come Down* .100.00 - 150.00
13094 *I Ain't No Sinner Now* . . . . .100.00 - 150.00
Vocalion 1061 *Take Your Burden To The Lord* . . . 75.00 - 100.00

1062 *I Will Not Be Removed* . . . . 75.00 - 100.00
1063 *I'll Be Satisfed* . . . . 75.00 - 100.00
1070 *Keep On The Firing Line* . . . . 75.00 - 100.00
1123 *The Storm Is Passing Over* . . . . 75.00 - 100.00

TALLAHASSEE TIGHT:
Titles, issued contemporaneously on Banner,
Comqueror, Domino, Melotone, Oriole,
Perfect, Romeo: *Black Gal; Black Snake*
Blues; Coast Line Blues; Homesick Blues;
Jealous Man; Lonesome And Worried Blues;
Quincey Wimmems; Ramblin' Mind Blues;
Screaming Woman; Tallahassee Women . . . . . . 60.00 - 100.00

TAMPA KID:
Decca 7278 *Keep On Trying* . . . . 20.00 - 30.00

TAMPA RED, "THE GUITAR WIZARD",
TAMPA RED'S HOKUM JUG BAND;
TAMPA RED & THE CHICAGO
FIVE/HOKUM JUG BAND:
Titles, issued contemporaneously on Banner,
Melotone, Oriole, Perfect, Romeo: *Dead Cats*
On The Line; Georgia Hound Blues; How Long
How Long Blues; Mama Don't Allow No Easy
Riders Here; New Strangers Blues; Reckless
Man Blues . . . . 50.00 - 75.00
Bluebird 5450 *I'll Find My Way* . . . . 35.00 - 50.00
5515 *I'll Kill Your Soul* . . . . 35.00 - 50.00
5546 *Mean Mistreater Blues* . . . . 30.00 - 50.00
5572 *Somebody's Been Using That Thing* . . . . . 30.00 - 50.00
5617 *Kingfish Blues* . . . . 30.00 - 50.00
5673 *I'm Just Crazy Bout You* . . . . 30.00 - 50.00
5723 *Witchin' Hour Blues* . . . . 30.00 - 50.00
5744 *Worried Devil Blues* . . . . 30.00 - 50.00
5779 *Happy Jack* . . . . 30.00 - 50.00
5812 *Stockyard Fire* . . . . 30.00 - 50.00
5878 *Shake It Up A Little* . . . . 30.00 - 50.00
5929 *Don't Dog Your Woman* . . . . 30.00 - 50.00
5981 *Worthy Of You* . . . . 40.00 - 60.00
6037 *My Baby Said Yes* . . . . 15.00 - 20.00
6059 *Keep On Dealin'* . . . . 15.00 - 20.00
6126 *Rowdy Woman Blues* . . . . 25.00 - 40.00
6166 *You Missed A Good Man* . . . . 15.00 - 20.00
6211 *Drinkin' My Blues Away* . . . . 15.00 - 20.00
6241 *Waiting Blues* . . . . 15.00 - 20.00
6353 *Let's Get Drunk And Truck* . . . . 7.00 - 10.00
Bluebird 6388 *She Don't Know My Mind* . . . . . 10.00 - 15.00
6245 *Nutty And Buggy Blues* . . . . 15.00 - 20.00
6443 *When You Were A Gal Of Seven* . . . . 7.00 - 10.00
6498 *She Don't Know My Mind—Part 2* . . . . . . 10.00 - 15.00
6532 *All Night Long* . . . . 7.00 - 10.00
6578 *That's The Way I Do* . . . . 10.00 - 15.00
6620 *You Stole My Heart* . . . . 7.00 - 10.00
6681 *Blue And Evil Blues* . . . . 10.00 - 15.00
6755 *Stop Truckin' And Suzi-Q* . . . . 7.00 - 10.00
6787 *If It Wasn't For You* . . . . 7.00 - 10.00
6825 *Someday I'm Bound To Win* . . . . 25.00 - 40.00
6832 *Cheatin' On Me* . . . . 7.00 - 10.00
6968 *You Got To Learn To Do It* . . . . 8.00 - 12.00
6990 *I See You Can't Take It* . . . . 7.00 - 10.00
7010 *My Gal Is Gone* . . . . 15.00 - 20.00
7058 *I Give My Love To You* . . . . 8.00 - 12.00
7091 *When Love Comes In* . . . . 30.00 - 50.00
7115 *Taking It And Make My Get Away* . . . . . . 15.00 - 25.00
7225 *Harlem Swing* . . . . 8.00 - 12.00
7236 *I'm Gonna Get High* . . . . 10.00 - 15.00
7269 *Oh Babe, Oh Baby* . . . . 10.00 - 15.00
7276 *Wrong Idea* . . . . 10.00 - 15.00
7315 *Deceitful Friend Blues* . . . . 10.00 - 15.00
7364 *Whoopee Mama* . . . . 10.00 - 15.00
7499 *The Most Of Us Do* . . . . 7.00 - 10.00
7538 *We Gonna Get High Together* . . . . 7.00 - 10.00
7591 *A Lie In My Heart* . . . . 7.00 - 10.00
7642 *Grouchy Hearted Woman* . . . . 10.00 - 15.00

7675 *Got To Leave My Woman*	10.00	-	15.00
7743 *Rock It In Rhythm*	7.00	-	10.00
7793 *Sweetest Gal In Town*	7.00	-	10.00
7822 *When I Had A Good Woman*	8.00	-	12.00
7879 *Crazy With The Blues*	8.00	-	12.00
7976 *Checkin' Up On You*	7.00	-	10.00
8011 *Mr. Rhythm Man*	7.00	-	10.00
8046 *Blues For My Baby*	8.00	-	12.00
8086 *Hellish Old Feeling*	8.00	-	12.00
8179 *Please Don't Throw Me Down*	8.00	-	12.00
8205 *Poor Old Gal Blues*	8.00	-	12.00
8238 *No Good Woman Blues*	8.00	-	12.00
8266 *Booze Head Woman*	8.00	-	12.00
8291 *Sad Letter Blues*	8.00	-	12.00
8327 *Sweet Mellow Woman Blues*	8.00	-	12.00
8353 *Ready For Rhythm*	8.00	-	12.00
8368 *I Got A Big Surprise For You*	8.00	-	12.00
8407 *Dangerous Woman Blues*	8.00	-	12.00
8454 *I Don't Care No More*	8.00	-	12.00
8475 *You Say We're Through*	7.00	-	10.00
8575 *Baby Take A Chance With Me*	7.00	-	10.00
8635 *It Hurts Me Too*	7.00	-	10.00
8654 *Anna Lou Blues*	7.00	-	10.00
8715 *I Want To Swing*	8.00	-	12.00
8744 *This Ain't No Place For Me*	8.00	-	12.00
8780 *Hard Road Blues*	8.00	-	12.00
8821 *Noonday Hour Blues*	8.00	-	12.00
8890, 8919, 8962, 8991, 9009, 9024, 34-0700, 34-0711, 34-0724, 34-0731, 34-0740	5.00	-	10.00
Paramount 12685 *Through Train Blues*	150.00	-	200.00
Vocalion 1216 *It's Tight Like That*	30.00	-	40.00
1228 *It's Tight Like That*	30.00	-	40.00
1237 *You Can't Come In*	100.00	-	150.00
1244 *It's Tight Like That—No. 2*	75.00	-	100.00
1251 *Jelly Whippin' Blues*	100.00	-	150.00
1254 *Down In The Alley*	100.00	-	150.00
1258 *It's Tight Like That*	75.00	-	100.00
1268 *Juicy Lemon Blues*	100.00	-	150.00
1274 *Boot It Boy*	100.00	-	150.00
1277 *The Duck Yas-Yas-Yas*	100.00	-	150.00
1281 *Mess, Katie, Mess*	100.00	-	150.00
1294 *It's So Nice*	100.00	-	150.00
1404 *Prison Bound Blues*	100.00	-	150.00
1409 *Givin' It Away*	100.00	-	150.00
1418 *Strange Woman Blues*	100.00	-	150.00
Vocalion 1420 *Come On, Mama, Do That Dance*	100.00	-	150.00
1426 *You Better Tighten Up On It*	100.00	-	150.00
1429 *Strewin' Your Mess*	100.00	-	150.00
1430 *Saturday Night Scrontch*	100.00	-	150.00
1450 *Corrine Corrina*	100.00	-	150.00
1456 *That Stuff You Sell*	100.00	-	150.00
1469 *Mrs. Baker's Blues*	100.00	-	150.00
1484 *Moanin' Heart Blues*	100.00	-	150.00
1491 *Dying Mercy Blues*	100.00	-	150.00
1496 *Corrine Corrina—No.2*	75.00	-	100.00
1521 *You Rascal You*	75.00	-	100.00
1538 *The Dirty Dozen—No. 2*	75.00	-	100.00
1540 *You Rascal You*	50.00	-	75.00
1571 *Poor Old Bachelor Blues*	100.00	-	150.00
1572 *Dying Mercy Blues*	100.00	-	150.00
1577 *It's My Time Blues*	100.00	-	150.00
1596 *Jinx Doctor Blues*	100.00	-	150.00
1608 *Bear Cat's Kittens*	100.00	-	150.00
1619 *Boogie Woogie Dance*	100.00	-	150.00
1623 *Cryin' Shame Blues*	100.00	-	150.00
1628 *They Call It Boogie Woogie*	100.00	-	150.00
1637 *Cotton Seed Blues*	100.00	-	150.00
1654 *Georgia Hound Blues*	75.00	-	100.00
1656 *Depression Blues*	100.00	-	150.00
1661 *Stop And Listen Blues*	100.00	-	150.00
1671 *Please Mister Blues*	100.00	-	150.00
1685 *Dead Cats On The Line*	80.00	-	120.00

1699 *No Matter How She Done It*	100.00	-	150.00
1700 *Turpentine Blues*	100.00	-	150.00
1706 *Reckless Man Blues*	80.00	-	120.00
02720 *That Stuff Is Here*	80.00	-	120.00
02753 *Black Angel Blues*	80.00	-	120.00
02774 *Denver Blues*	100.00	-	150.00

FRANK TANNEHILL:
Titles, issued contemporaneously on Banner, Melotone, Oriole, Perfect, Romeo, Vocalion:

I.G.N Blues; Steel Mill Blues	35.00	-	50.00
Bluebird 7945 *Warehouse Blues*	20.00	-	30.00
8028 *Door Bell Blues*	20.00	-	30.00
8762 *Lillie Mae*	15.00	-	20.00
8803 *Sweet Jelly Roll*	15.00	-	20.00

SAM TARPLEY:

Champion 16327 *Try Some Of That*	100.00	-	150.00
16782 *That Stuff*	200.00	-	300.00
Superior 2584 *Try Some Of That*	200.00	-	300.00

SLIM TARPLEY:

Paramount 13062 *Alabama Hustler*	150.00	-	200.00

TARTER AND GAY:

Victor V38017 *Brownie Blues*	100.00	-	150.00

TASKIANA FOUR:

Victor 20183, 20184	8.00	-	12.00
20852 *Dixie Bo-Bo*	20.00	-	30.00

HATTIE TATE:

Supertone 9288 *There's Been Some Changes Made*		-	

ROSE TATE:

Champion 15302 *My Man Left Me Blues*	125.00	-	175.00
15319 *Wild Woman Blues*	125.00	-	175.00
15417 *Money Woman Blues*	125.00	-	175.00
Silvertone 5133 *My Man Left Me Blues*	125.00	-	175.00
5168 *Mistreated Blues*	125.00	-	175.00

TAYLOR'S WEATHERBIRDS:

Victor 23309 *Coal Camp Blues*	200.00	-	300.00

TAYLOR AND ANDERSON:

Champion 15951 *Corrine Corrina*	150.00	-	250.00
50016 *You Rascal, You*	50.00	-	75.00
Supertone 9646 *You Rascal, You*	150.00	-	250.00

CHARLES/CHARLEY TAYLOR:

Paramount 12949 *Where My Shoes At?*	150.00	-	250.00
12967 *Heavy Suitcase Blues*	150.00	-	250.00
13121 *C.P. Railroad Blues*	200.00	-	300.00

EDNA TAYLOR:

Paramount 12057 *Good Man Blues*	150.00	-	200.00

ETHEL TAYLOR:

Supertone 9285 *Empty Bed Blues*	75.00	-	100.00

EVA TAYLOR (& HER BOY FRIENDS):
Titles, issued contemporaneously on Banner, Melotone, Oriole, Perfect, Romeo: *Crazy Blues; The Stuff Is Here And It's Mellow*

Blues; The Stuff Is Here And It's Mellow	15.00	-	20.00
Black Swan 2103 *New Moon*	20.00	-	30.00
Edison 14046 *West End Blues*	50.00	-	75.00
52646 *West End Blues*	50.00	-	75.00
Okeh 3055 (12-inch) *Farewell Blues*	75.00	-	100.00
4740 *Baby, Won't You Please Come Home*	15.00	-	20.00
4805 *Down Hearted Blues*	15.00	-	20.00
4927 *Oh! Daddy Blues*	50.00	-	75.00
8047 *You Missed A Good Woman When You Picked All Over Me*	15.00	-	20.00
8049 *12th Street Rag*	15.00	-	20.00
8050 *You Can Have My Man*	15.00	-	20.00
8051 *My Pillow And Me*	15.00	-	20.00
8067 *Yodeling Blues*	30.00	-	50.00
8068 *You'll Never Have No Luck By Quittin' Me*	15.00	-	20.00
8069 *Church Street Sobbin' Blues*	15.00	-	20.00
8073 *Barefoot Blues*	50.00	-	75.00
8089 *Original Charleston Strut*	50.00	-	75.00
8114 *Old Fashioned Love*	50.00	-	75.00
8129 *Jazzin' Babies Blues*	50.00	-	75.00

8145 *Ghost Of The Blues*	50.00 -	75.00
8183 *Terrible Blues*	50.00 -	75.00
8342 *You Can't Shush Katie (The Gabbiest Gal In Town)*	100.00 -	150.00
8407 *Morocco Blues*	75.00 -	100.00
8414 *Scatter Your Smiles*	75.00 -	100.00
8444 *I Wish You Would*	75.00 -	100.00
8463 *Red Hot Flo*	75.00 -	100.00
8518 *May We Meet Again*	25.00 -	35.00
8585 *Chloe*	40.00 -	60.00
8665 *Happy Days And Lonely Nights*	40.00 -	60.00
40330 *Pickin' On Your Baby*	80.00 -	120.00
40655 *Senorita Mine*	20.00 -	30.00
40671 *When The Red, Red Robin Comes Bob, Bob*	20.00 -	30.00
40715 *Candy Lips*	60.00 -	90.00
Victor V38575 *Don't You Understand*	80.00 -	120.00

BLIND JEREMIAH TAYLOR:

Herwin 93027 *Mother's Love*	125.00 -	175.00

MONTANA TAYLOR (& THE JAZOO BOYS):

Circle 1008 *In The Bottom*	7.00 -	10.00
1009 *Low Down Boogie*	7.00 -	10.00
1010 *Sweet Sue*	7.00 -	10.00
1015 *Montana's Blues*	7.00 -	10.00
Vocalion 1275 *Whoop And Holler Stomp*	100.00 -	150.00
1419 *Detroit Rocks*	100.00 -	150.00

SALLIE TAYLOR:

Supertone 9365 *Seven Men Blues*	90.00 -	130.00
9392 *West End Blues*	90.00 -	130.00
9426 *Old Fashioned Blues*	90.00 -	130.00
9440 *Loose Like That*	90.00 -	130.00
9530 *The Long Lost Blues*	100.00 -	150.00

WALTER TAYLOR:

Champion 15972 *Yo-Yo Blues*	200.00 -	300.00
16059 *Broadcasting Blues*	200.00 -	300.00
Gennett 7144 *Corrine Corrina*	200.00 -	300.00
7157 *Broadcasting Blues*	250.00 -	350.00
7171 *Deal Rag*	250.00 -	350.00
7189 *It Ain't No Good*	250.00 -	350.00
Supertone 9681 *Yo-Yo Blues*	200.00 -	300.00
9682 *Thirty-Eight And Plus*	200.00 -	300.00

"BIG ROAD" WEBSTER TAYLOR:

Vocalion 1271 *Sunny Southern Blues*	80.00 -	120.00

T.C.I. SECTION CREW:

Paramount 12478 *Section Gang Song*	50.00 -	75.00

TEARDROPS:

Sampson 634 *Come Back To Me*	15.00 -	30.00

JOHNNIE/JOHNNY TEMPLE:

Bluebird 8913 *Sundown Blues*	10.00 -	15.00
8968 *Big Woman Blues*	10.00 -	15.00
Decca 7244 *Louise Louise Blues*	15.00 -	20.00
7316 *Peepin' Through The Keyhole*	15.00 -	20.00
7337 *So Lonely And Blue*	15.00 -	20.00
7385 *Hoodoo Women*	8.00 -	12.00
7416 *Snapping Cat*	8.00 -	12.00
7444 *Mean Baby Blues*	8.00 -	12.00
7456 *County Jail Blues*	8.00 -	12.00
7495 *Fare You Well*	8.00 -	12.00
7532 *Stavin' Chain*	8.00 -	12.00
7547 *Big Leg Woman*	8.00 -	12.00
7564 *Mississippi Woman's Blues*	8.00 -	12.00
7573 *What A Fool I've Been*	8.00 -	12.00
7583 *Grinding Mill*	8.00 -	12.00
7599 *If I Could Holler*	8.00 -	12.00
7632 *The Sun Goes Down In Blood*	8.00 -	12.00
7643 *Down In Mississippi*	8.00 -	12.00
7660 *Streamline Blues*	8.00 -	12.00
7678 *Cherry Ball*	8.00 -	12.00
7735 *Good Woman Blues*	8.00 -	12.00
7750 *Skin And Bones Woman*	8.00 -	12.00
7772 *Lovin' Woman Blues*	8.00 -	12.00
7782 *Roomin' House Blues*	8.00 -	12.00
7800 *Fix It Up And Go*	8.00 -	12.00
7817 *Bow Leg Woman*	8.00 -	12.00
7825 *Corrine Corrina*	8.00 -	12.00
Vocalion 02987 *Jacksonville Blues*	50.00 -	75.00
03068 *Big Boat Whistle*	50.00 -	75.00

TENNESSEE SHAKERS:

Brunswick 7199 *Grind So Fine*	150.00 -	200.00

NAT TERRY:

Imperial 5150 *Take It Easy*	10.00 -	15.00

SONNY ("HOOTIN") TERRY (& HIS BUCKSHOT FIVE/NIGHT OWLS):

Capitol 931, 15237, 40003, 40043, 40061, 40097, 40121	4.00 -	8.00
Gotham 517, 518	7.00 -	10.00
Gramercy 1004/1005 *Hootin' Blues*	7.00 -	10.00
Harlem 2327 *Dangerous Woman*	7.00 -	10.00*
Jackson 2327 *Harmonica Train*	7.00 -	10.00*
Jax 305 *I Don't Worry*	7.00 -	10.00*
Okeh 05453 *Harmonica Blues*	10.00 -	15.00
05538 *Harmonica Stomp*	10.00 -	15.00
05684 *Blowing The Blues*	10.00 -	15.00
Red Robin 110 *Harmonica Hop*	7.00 -	10.00*

TEXAS RED & JIMMY:

Viceroy 3333 *Black Snake Blues*	15.00 -	20.00*

TEXAS SLIM:

King 4283, 4315, 4323, 4329, 4334, 4366, 4377	5.00 -	10.00

TEXAS TOMMY:

Brunswick 7044 *Jail Break Blues*	40.00 -	60.00
Varsity 6035 *Ridin' Papa*	15.00 -	20.00
6039 *Broke and Hungry*	15.00 -	20.00

SAM THEARD ("LOVIN" SAM FROM DOWN IN 'BAM):

Decca 7025 *That Rhythm Gal*	15.00 -	20.00
7146 *Till I Die*	30.00 -	50.00
(See also LOVIN' SAM)		

AL "FATS" THOMAS:

Checker 759 *Dog Days*	7.00 -	10.00*

ANDREW THOMAS:

Swing With The Stars 1038 *Chicago Blues*	10.00 -	20.00

ANDY THOMAS:

Gold Star 645 *My Baby Quit Me Blues*	15.00 -	25.00
659 *In Love Blues*	15.00 -	25.00

BESSIE THOMAS:

Supertone 9282 *Harbor Blues*	90.00 -	130.00

BUD THOMAS:

Supertone 9511 *Street Walkin' Blues*	100.00 -	150.00

EARL THOMAS:

Decca 7195 *Sugar Girl Blues*	20.00 -	30.00
7221 *Rent Day Blues*	20.00 -	30.00

ELVIE THOMAS:

Paramount 12977 *Motherless Child Blues*	90.00 -	130.00

F.T. THOMAS:

Gennett 6963 *Street Walkin' Blues*	125.00 -	175.00

GEORGE THOMAS:

Paramount 12826 *Fast Stuff Blues*	100.00 -	150.00

HENRY THOMAS:

Bluebird 5343 *My Sweet Candy*	75.00 -	100.00
5411 *Sick With The Blues*	75.00 -	100.00
Sunrise 3424 *She's Got What I Want*	100.00 -	150.00
Vocalion 1094 *John Henry*	100.00 -	150.00
1137 *Red River Blues*	100.00 -	150.00
1138 *The Little Red Caboose*	100.00 -	150.00
1139 *Woodhouse Blues*	100.00 -	150.00
1140 *Jonah In The Wilderness*	100.00 -	150.00
1141 *Run, Mollie, Run*	100.00 -	150.00
1197 *Texas Easy Street Blues*	100.00 -	150.00
1230 *Bull Doze Blues*	100.00 -	150.00
1249 *Texas Worried Blues*	100.00 -	150.00
1286 *Arkansas*	100.00 -	150.00
1443 *Don't Leave Me Here*	100.00 -	150.00
1468 *Lovin' Babe*	100.00 -	150.00

JESSE THOMAS; JESSE (BABYFACE)

THOMAS:

Club (unnumbered) *You Are My Dreams*	15.00 -	20.00
(unnumbered) *I Wonder Why*	7.00 -	10.00
Freedom 1513 *Guess I'll Walk Alone*	7.00 -	10.00
Hollywood 1072 *Cool Kind Lover*	3.00 -	6.00*
Miltone 232 *Same Old Stuff*	20.00 -	30.00
233 *Mountain Key Blues*	20.00 -	30.00
Modern 710 *Texas Blues*	10.00 -	15.00
Specialty 419 *When You Say I Love You*	7.00 -	10.00
Swing Time 240 *I Can't Stay Here*	8.00 -	12.00
241 *Now's The Time*	8.00 -	12.00
Victor 23381 *Down In Texas Blues*	200.00 -	300.00
V-38555 *Blue Goose Blues*	150.00 -	200.00

JOSEPHINE THOMAS:

Pathe-Actuelle 032122 *Memphis Bound*	10.00 -	15.00
Perfect 12201 *Memphis Bound*	10.00 -	15.00

L.J. THOMAS:

Chess 1493 *Sam's Drag*	5.00 -	8.00*

RAMBLIN' THOMAS:

Paramount 12609 *Back Gnawing Blues*	100.00 -	150.00
12616 *Sawmill Moan*	100.00 -	150.00
12637 *Lock And Key Blues*	100.00 -	150.00
12670 *No Baby Blues*	100.00 -	150.00
12708 *Ramblin' Man*	100.00 -	150.00
12752 *Good Time Blues*	100.00 -	150.00

RAMBLING THOMAS:

Victor 23332 *Ground Hog Blues*	200.00 -	300.00
23365 *Ground Hog Blues No. 2*	250.00 -	350.00

RUFUS THOMAS:

Chess 1466 *Night Walkin' Blues*	15.00 -	25.00*
1492 *No More Doggin' Around*	15.00 -	25.00*
1517 *Juanita*	15.00 -	25.00*
Sun 181 *Walkin' In The Rain*	10.00 -	15.00*
188 *Tiger Man*	10.00 -	15.00*
Talent 807 *I'm So Worried*	40.00 -	60.00

SIPPIE THOMAS:

Victor V-38502 *I'm A Mighty Tight Woman*	150.00 -	250.00

WASHINGTON THOMAS:

Champion 15489 *Time Enough*	50.00 -	80.00
15511 *Silvery Moon*	50.00 -	80.00

JIM THOMPKINS:

Brunswick 7200 *Bedside Blues*	100.00 -	150.00

EDWARD THOMPSON:

Paramount 13018 *West Virginia Blues*	200.00 -	300.00

EVELYN THOMPSON:

Vocalion 1075 *Someday, Sweetheart*	40.00 -	60.00
1083 *After You've Gone*	40.00 -	60.00
1084 *One More Kiss*	40.00 -	60.00
15529 *One More Kiss*	35.00 -	50.00
15548 *One Sweet Letter From You*	35.00 -	50.00

MARGARET THORNTON:

Black Patti 8041 *Jockey Blues*	250.00 -	Up

WILLIE MAE (BIG MAMA) THORNTON:

Peacock	5.00 -	10.00*

THE THRILLERS:

Big Town 109 *The Drunkard*	7.00 -	10.00*

ANDY TIBBS:

Aristocrat 1104 *Going Down Fast*	5.00 -	8.00

SLIM TINSLEY:

Globe 117 *606 Blues*	8.00 -	12.00
118 *Big Shot Mama*	8.00 -	12.00

JAMES TISDOM:

Universal-Fox 100 *Last Affair Blues*	20.00 -	30.00
101 *Throw This Dog A Bone*	20.00 -	30.00
102 *Overhaul Blues*	20.00 -	30.00

KINGFISH BILL TOMLIN:

Paramount 13034 *Hot Box*	100.00 -	150.00
13057 *Dupree Blues*	100.00 -	150.00

TOMMY AND JIMMY:

Superior 2555 *Where You Been So Long?*	200.00 -	300.00

THE TOO BAD BOYS:

Paramount 12861 *Ballin' The Jack*	50.00 -	100.00

TOO TIGHT HENRY:

Brunswick 7189 *Squinch Owl Moan*	150.00 -	200.00
Columbia 14374-D *Charleston Contest*	75.00 -	100.00

GEORGE TOREY:

Titles, issued contemporaneously on Banner, Melotone, Oriole, Perfect, Romeo: *Lonesome Man Blues; Married Woman Blues*	50.00 -	75.00

JIM TOWEL:

Brunswick 7060 *Buckwheat Cakes*	75.00 -	100.00

HENRY TOWNSEND:

Bluebird 5966 *She's Got A Mean Disposition*	40.00 -	60.00
6589 *She's Got A Mean Disposition*	40.00 -	60.00
7453 *Lose Your Man*	20.00 -	30.00
7474 *A Ramblin' Mind*	20.00 -	30.00
Columbia 14491-D *Mistreated Blues*	75.00 -	125.00
14529-D *Henry's Worry Blues*	75.00 -	125.00
Paramount 13097 *Doctor, Oh Doctor*	150.00 -	200.00

JESSE TOWNSEND:

Victor 23322 *No Home Blues*	200.00 -	300.00

SAM TOWNSEND:

Brunswick 7116 *Curbstone Blues*	250.00 -	400.00
Columbia 14571-D *I'm Missing That*	75.00 -	100.00

TRIANGLE QUARTETTE:

Broadway 5071 *She Done Quit Me Blues*	50.00 -	80.00
Paramount 12781 *She Done Quit Me Blues*	50.00 -	80.00

RICH TRICE:

Decca 7701 *Come On Baby*	15.00 -	25.00

WELLY TRICE:

Decca 7358 *Come On In Here Mama*	15.00 -	25.00

DORETHEA TROWBRIDGE:

Bluebird 5431 *Bad Luck Blues*	75.00 -	100.00

TUB JUG WASHBOARD BAND:

Paramount 12671 *Tub-Jug Rag*	125.00 -	175.00

BESSIE TUCKER:

Bluebird 5128 *Bogy Man Blues*	75.00 -	100.00
Sunrise 3208 *Bogy Man Blues*	100.00 -	150.00
Victor 21692 *Black Name Moan*	75.00 -	100.00
21708 *The Dummy*	75.00 -	100.00
23385 *Bogey Man Blues*	250.00 -	350.00
23392 *T.B Moan*	250.00 -	400.00
V-38018 *Fryin' Pan Skillet Blues*	100.00 -	150.00
V38526 *Bessie's Moan*	150.00 -	200.00
V38538 *Old Black Mary*	150.00 -	200.00
V38542 *Katy Blues*	150.00 -	200.00

ANNIE TURNER:

Bluebird 6707 *Black Pony Blues*	35.00 -	50.00
6788 *Workhouse Blues*	35.00 -	50.00

BABY FACE TURNER:

Modern 882 *Gonna Let You Go*	10.00 -	15.00*

BEE TURNER:

Paramount 13017 *Rough Treatin' Daddy*	200.00 -	300.00

CHARLIE TURNER AND WINSTON HOLMES:

Paramount 12793 *The Death Of Holmes Mule*	100.00 -	150.00

IKE TURNER:

Chess 1459 *I'm Lonesome Baby*	5.00 -	8.00*

(BIG) JOE TURNER (& THE ALL STARS):

Bayou 015 *Blues Jump The Rabbit*	7.00 -	10.00
Coral 65004 *Blues On Central Avenue*	7.00 -	10.00
Decca 4093 *Rocks In My Bed*	10.00 -	15.00
7824 *Doggin' The Dog*	10.00 -	15.00
7827 *Jumpin' Down Blues*	10.00 -	15.00
7856 *Somebody's Got To Go*	10.00 -	15.00
7868 *Nobody In Mind*	10.00 -	15.00
7885 *Blues In The Night*	10.00 -	15.00
7889 *Sun Risin' Blues*	10.00 -	15.00
Excelsior	3.00 -	5.00
Freedom 1531 *Still In The Dark*	10.00 -	15.00
National 9011 *Watch That Jive*	7.00 -	10.00
Vocalion 4607 *Goin' Away Blues*	15.00 -	20.00

LAVINIA TURNER:

Pathe-Actuelle 020544, 020572, 020627, 020705,

020878	7.00 -	12.00
Perfect 12005, 12032, 12033, 12034, 12039	7.00 -	12.00

SMILEY TURNER:

Mercury 8161 *Lonely Boy Blues*	5.00 -	8.00

BLIND SQUIRE TURNER:

Bluebird 5307 *She Thinks She's Slick*	100.00 -	150.00
5412 *Low Mellow*	100.00 -	150.00
5491 *Pitty Pat Blues*	100.00 -	150.00

JOHN D. TWITTY:

Titles, issued contemporaneously on Banner,
Melotone, Oriole, Perfect, Romeo, Vocalion: *A
Gang Of Trouble; Walking Blues* . . . . 40.00 - 60.00

TWO BOYS FROM SAVANNAH:

Supertone 9485 *It's Just All Right*	75.00 -	100.00
9529 *Messed Up Blues*	80.00 -	120.00

THE TWO CHARLIES:

Titles, issued contemporaneously on Banner,
Melotone; Oriole; Perfect; Romeo: *Don't Put
Your Dirty Hands On Me; Got Your Water On;
I Couldn't Stay Here; Pork Chops Blues* . . . . . . 50.00 - 75.00

THE TWO OF SPADES:

Columbia 14072-D *Meddlin' With The Blues*	20.00 -	30.00

TWO POOR BOYS:

Titles, issued contemporaneously on Banner,
Oriole, Perfect, Romeo: *John Henry Blues;
Sitting On Top Of The World; Take A Look At
That Baby; Two White Horses In A Line* . . . . . 100.00 - 200.00

TYUS & TYUS:

Columbia 14638-D *Dad's Ole Mule*	75.00 -	100.00

CHARLES (& EFFIE) TYUS:

Okeh 8133 *Omaha Blues*	25.00 -	40.00
8149 *I Want To Go Back To The Farm*	25.00 -	40.00
8200 *Cuddle Up Closer, It's Winter Time*	40.00 -	60.00
8330 *Good Old Bygone Days*	40.00 -	60.00
8459 *Alibi-ing Papa*	75.00 -	100.00

UMBRIAN GLEE CLUB:

Vocalion 1012 *Swing Along*	20.00 -	30.00
1013 *Rain Song*	20.00 -	30.00

UNCLE SKIPPER:

Decca 7353 *Cutting My A B C's*	20.00 -	30.00
7455 *Look What Shape I'm In*	20.00 -	30.00

LOUISE VANT:

Okeh 8264 *Show Me The Way To Go Home*	50.00 -	75.00
8275 *I'm Tired Of Everything But You*	75.00 -	100.00
8281 *Just A Little Bit Bad*	75.00 -	100.00
8293 *Do Right Blues*	75.00 -	100.00
8310 *Pensacola Blues*	75.00 -	100.00
8341 *Daddy, Don't You Try To Pull That Two*		
Time Thing On Me	30.00 -	50.00

CALLIE VASSAR:

Gennett 5172 *All Night Blues*	50.00 -	75.00
5173 *Original Stomps*	50.00 -	75.00

EDITH VAUGHAN:

Oriole 298 *Mad Mama's Blues*	10.00 -	15.00
311 *Broken Busted Can't Be Trusted Blues*	10.00 -	15.00

THE VELVETONES:

Columbia 30224 *I'm Disillusioned*		-

JOHN P. VIGAL:

Black Swan 14115 *Fowler Twist*	25.00 -	40.00
Paramount 12132 *Fowler Twist*	25.00 -	40.00

WALTER VINCENT:

Brunswick 7126 *Your Friends Gonna Use It Too* .	100.00 -	150.00
7141 *Overtime Blues*	100.00 -	150.00
7190 *Mississippi Yodelin' Blues*	100.00 -	150.00
Decca 7169 *Losin' Blues*	40.00 -	60.00
7178 *The Wrong Man*	40.00 -	60.00

WALTER VINCSON:

Bluebird 8828 *Every Dog Must Have His Day* . . .	15.00 -	20.00
8908 *Gulf Coast Boy*	15.00 -	20.00
8963 *Rosa Lee Blues*	15.00 -	20.00

OTTO VIRGIAL:

Bluebird 6213 *Bad Notion Blues*	15.00 -	25.00

6279 *Seven Year Itch*	15.00 -	25.00

THE VIRGINIA FOUR:

Decca 7662 *Dig My Jelly Roll*	10.00 -	15.00
7808 *Queen Street Rag*	10.00 -	15.00

THE VOCALEERS:

Red Robin 130 *Shim Sham Shimmy* . . . . -
(The existence of this record has not been
verified. It Is known that labels for such issue
were printed. Offers of hundreds of dollars
have been made. Note that the title was issued
on Red Robin 130 by CHAMPION JACK
DUPREE, and a simple printing error may be
all that's involved.)

VON BATTLE, JOSEPH:

JVB 75828 *Looking For My Woman*	15.00 -	20.00

UNCLE BUD WALKER:

Okeh 8828 *Stand Up Suitcase Blues*	75.00 -	100.00

JAMES WALKER:

Silvertone 3553 *Lost John Blues*	60.00 -	80.00

MONROE WALKER:

Columbia 14549-D *High Powered Mama*	40.00 -	60.00

PRETTY BOY WALKER:

Vocalion 1713 *The Break I'm Gettin'*	50.00 -	75.00

T-BONE WALKER:

Black & White 110, 111, 115, 121, 122, 123, 125,		
126, 127	5.00 -	10.00
Capitol 10033 *Mean Old World*	7.00 -	10.00
Capitol (others)	3.00 -	5.00
Comet 50, 51, 52, 53	5.00 -	8.00
Imperial 5071, 5081, 5086, 5094, 5103, 5116, 5147,		
5153, 5161, 5171, 5181, 5193	5.00 -	10.00
Imperial (5202 through 5330)	4.00 -	8.00
Mercury 8016 *My Baby Left Me*	5.00 -	8.00
Old Swing-Master 11 *She Is Going To Ruin Me* . .	8.00 -	12.00
Rhumboogie 4000, 4002, 4003	7.00 -	12.00

WILLIAM WALKER:

Gennett 7100 *I'll Remember You*	35.00 -	50.00

WILLIE WALKER:

Columbia 14578-D *South Carolina Rag*	75.00 -	100.00

FRANCES WALLACE:

Brunswick 7076 *Low Down Man Blues*	75.00 -	100.00

INEZ WALLACE:

Black Swan 14137 *Radio Blues*	20.00 -	30.00
14144 *Come Back Dear*	20.00 -	30.00
14147 *Kissin' Daddy*	30.00 -	50.00
Paramount 12145 *Radio Blues*	20.00 -	30.00
12146 *Kissin' Daddy*	30.00 -	50.00
12155 *Come Back Dear*	20.00 -	30.00

MINNIE WALLACE:

Bluebird 5144 *Dirty Butter*	100.00 -	150.00
Victor V38547 *Dirty Butter*	150.00 -	250.00
Vocalion 03106 *Field Mouse Stomp*	125.00 -	200.00
03154 *Let's All Do That Thing*	125.00 -	200.00

SIPPIE WALLACE:

Okeh 8106 *Up The Country Blues*	40.00 -	60.00
8144 *Underworld Blues*	25.00 -	40.00
8159 *Stranger's Blues*	25.00 -	40.00
8168 *Mama's Gone, Goodbye*	25.00 -	40.00
8177 *Sud Bustin' Blues*	50.00 -	80.00
8190 *Let My Man Alone Blues*	40.00 -	60.00
8197 *Off And On Blues*	50.00 -	80.00
8205 *Every Dog Has His Day*	150.00 -	200.00
8206 *Devil Dance Blues*	150.00 -	200.00
8212 *Trouble Everywhere I Roam*	100.00 -	150.00
8232 *Section Hand Blues*	100.00 -	150.00
8243 *Murder's Gonna Be My Crime*	50.00 -	80.00
8251 *The Man I Love*	50.00 -	80.00
8276 *Advice Blues*	50.00 -	80.00
8288 *I'm Leaving You*	40.00 -	60.00
8301 *A Jealous Woman Like Me*	150.00 -	200.00
8328 *Jack O'Diamonds Blues*	100.00 -	150.00
8345 *The Mail Train Blues*	150.00 -	200.00

8381 *I Must Have It*	75.00 -	100.00
8439 *Bedroom Blues*	75.00 -	100.00
8470 *Lazy Man Blues*	150.00 -	200.00
8499 *Dead Drunk Blues*	150.00 -	200.00

WESLEY WALLACE:

Paramount 12958 *Fanny Lee Blues*	150.00 -	200.00

PEGGY WALLER AND GEORGE RAMSEY:

Paramount 13037 *Blacksnake Wiggle*	150.00 -	200.00

CHARLOTTE WALSH:

Silvertone 3567 *Cool Daddy Blues*	50.00 -	75.00

WALTER & BYRD:

Paramount 12945 *Wasn't It Sad About Lemon*	125.00 -	175.00

LORRAINE WALTON:

Bluebird 7577 *Whiskey Blues*	10.00 -	15.00
7630 *Freight Train Blues*	10.00 -	15.00
Vocalion 03989 *If You're A Viper*	15.00 -	20.00

SQUARE WALTON:

RCA Victor 20-5493 *Pepper Head Woman*	7.00 -	10.00*
20-5584 *Bad Hangover*	7.00 -	10.00*

AMY WARD:

Silvertone 3566 *Uptown Daddy*	60.00 -	100.00
3568 *Riverside Blues*	60.00 -	100.00
3573 *Nobody Knows*	60.00 -	100.00

EDDIE WARE & HIS BAND:

Chess 1461, 1507	5.00 -	8.00*
States 130 *That's The Stuff I Like*	7.00 -	10.00*

REV. I.B. WARE:

Vocalion 1235 *You Better Quit Drinking Shine*	100.00 -	150.00

OZIE WARE:

Titles, issued contemporaneously on Cameo, Lincoln, Pathe-Actuelle, Perfect, Romeo: *He Just Don't Appeal To Me; Hit Me In The Nose Blues*	35.00 -	50.00
Victor 21777 *I Done Caught You Blues*	150.00 -	200.00

PETER WARFIELD:

Miltone 5249 *Morning Train Blues*	20.00 -	30.00

BABY BOY WARREN (& HIS BUDDY):

Blue Lake 106 *Mattie Mae*	15.00 -	20.00*
Drummond 3002 *Baby Boy Blues*	10.00 -	15.00*
3003 *Stop Breakin' Down*	10.00 -	15.00*
Federal 12008 *Forgive Me Darling*	10.00 -	15.00*
Gotham 507 *My Special Friend Blues*	15.00 -	25.00
JVB 26 *Hello Stranger*	30.00 -	50.00
Staff 706 *My Special Friend Blues*	30.00 -	50.00
707 *Lonesome Cabin Blues*	30.00 -	50.00
709 *Forgive Me Darling*	30.00 -	50.00

WASHBOARD PETE:

Savoy 5556 *Christmas Blues*	7.00 -	12.00

WASHBOARD SAM (& HIS WASHBOARD BAND); WASHBOARD SAM'S BAND:

Bluebird 5983 *Ocean Blues*	50.00 -	75.00
6355 *You Done Tore Your Playhouse Down*	10.00 -	15.00
6518 *Give Me Lovin'*	10.00 -	15.00
6556 *Cherry Hill Blues*	10.00 -	15.00
6765 *Razor Cuttin' Man*	10.00 -	15.00
6794 *Out With The Wrong Woman*	10.00 -	15.00
6870 *Big Woman*	10.00 -	15.00
6970 *Easy Ridin' Mama*	9.00 -	12.00
7001 *We Gonna Move*	8.00 -	12.00
7048 *I Drink Good Whiskey*	8.00 -	12.00
7096 *Lowland Blues*	8.00 -	12.00
7148 *Out With The Wrong Woman*	10.00 -	15.00
7179 *I Love All My Women*	15.00 -	20.00
7194 *You Done Tore Your Playhouse Down*	15.00 -	20.00
7291 *Washboard's Barrel House Song*	8.00 -	12.00
7328 *Beer Garden Blues*	8.00 -	12.00
7365 *Gonna Be Some Walkin' Done*	8.00 -	12.00
7403 *Second Story Man*	10.00 -	15.00
7440 *Want To Woogie Some More*	15.00 -	25.00
7501 *Don't Leave Me Here*	8.00 -	12.00
7526 *Down At The Old Village Store*	20.00 -	30.00
7552 *My Woman's A Sender*	8.00 -	12.00

7601 *Phantom Black Snake*	8.00 -	12.00
7655 *The Gal I Love*	20.00 -	30.00
7664 *Yellow, Black And Brown*	8.00 -	12.00
7732 *Serve It Right*	8.00 -	12.00
7780 *Sophisticated Mama*	8.00 -	12.00
7834 *Policy Writer's Blues*	8.00 -	12.00
7866 *Jumpin' Rooster*	8.00 -	12.00
7906 *Bucket's Got A Hole In It*	8.00 -	12.00
7977 *Walkin' In My Sleep*	8.00 -	12.00
7993 *Warehouse Blues*	8.00 -	12.00
8018 *Gonna Kill My Baby*	7.00 -	10.00
8044 *Rack 'Em Back*	7.00 -	10.00
8076 *Suspicious Blues*	7.00 -	10.00
8184 *That Will Get It*	7.00 -	10.00
8211 *Diggin' My Potatoes*	7.00 -	10.00*
8243 *Good Old Easy Street*	7.00 -	10.00*
8270 *This Time Is My Time*	7.00 -	10.00
8323 *Has My Gal Been By Here?*	7.00 -	10.00
8342 *Jersey Cow Blues*	7.00 -	10.00
8358 *So Early In The Morning*	7.00 -	10.00
8377, 8424, 8450, 8469, 8500, 8525, 8540, 8554, 8569, 8599, 8644, 8675, 8699, 8727, 8761, 8792, 8815, 8844, 8878, 8909, 8937, 8967, 8997, 9007, 9018, 9039, 34-0705, 34-0710	5.00 -	10.00
Chess 1545 *Diggin' My Potatoes*	7.00 -	10.00*
Montgomery Ward 7050 *Don't 'Low*	7.00 -	10.00
7062 *Razor Cuttin' Man*	7.00 -	10.00
7497 *Towboat Blues*	7.00 -	10.00
7498 *Barbecue*	7.00 -	10.00
7499 *Want To Woogie Some More*	7.00 -	10.00
7500 *Down At The Old Village Store*	15.00 -	20.00
7588, 7790, 7759, 7760, 7761, 8801, 8804	4.00 -	8.00
RCA Victor	3.00 -	5.00
Vocalion 02937 *Don't Tear My Clothes*	15.00 -	20.00
03365 *Mixed Up Blues*	15.00 -	20.00
Titles, issued contemporaneously on Banner, Conqueror, Melotone, Oriole, Perfect, Romeo: *Don't Tear My Clothes; I'm A Prowlin' Groundhog*	15.00 -	20.00

WASHBOARD WALTER (& HIS BAND):

Paramount 12954 *Narrow Face Blues*	200.00 -	300.00
12991 *Disconnected Mama*	200.00 -	300.00
13100 *Wuffin' Blues*	200.00 -	300.00

WASHBOARD WILLIE & HIS SUPER SUDS OF RHYTHM:

JVB 59 *Cherry Red Blues*	15.00 -	20.00
70 *Washboard Blues*	15.00 -	20.00*

ALBERTA WASHBURN:

Superior 2668 *Skeeter Blues*	150.00 -	250.00
2739 *Pig Meat Mama*	150.00 -	250.00
2783 *Forty-Four Blues*	150.00 -	250.00
2826 *Hoboken Prison Blues*	150.00 -	300.00

BOOKER T. WASHINGTON:

Bluebird 8352 *Just Want To Think*	15.00 -	20.00
8378 *Cotton Club Blues*	15.00 -	20.00
8413 *Cozy Corner Blues*	15.00 -	20.00
8449 *Wrapped Up In Bad Luck*	15.00 -	20.00

D.C. WASHINGTON:

Gold Star 661 *Happy Home Blues*	20.00 -	30.00

ELIZABETH WASHINGTON:

Bluebird 5229 *Riot Call Blues*	75.00 -	125.00
Sunrise 3312 *You Put That Thing On Me*	100.00 -	150.00
Victor 23425 *Mistreated Blues*	250.00 -	400.00

ISABELLE WASHINGTON:

Black Swan 14141 *I Want To*	20.00 -	30.00
Paramount 12135 *I Want To*	20.00 -	30.00

LIZZIE WASHINGTON:

Black Patti 8054 *Mexico Blues*	200.00 -	Up
Champion 15282 *Skeleton Key Blues*	100.00 -	150.00
15303 *East Coast Blues*	100.00 -	150.00
15319 *Sport Model Mamma Blues*	125.00 -	175.00

Gennett 6126 *Working Man Blues*	150.00	-	200.00
6134 *Skeleton Key Blues*	150.00	-	200.00
6195 *Fall Or Summer Blues*	150.00	-	200.00
6321 *Brick Flat Blues*	150.00	-	200.00
6408 *Lord Have Mercy Blues*	150.00	-	200.00
Herwin 92013 *East Coast Blues*	150.00	-	200.00
92021 *My Low Down Brown*	150.00	-	200.00
92039 *Lord Have Mercy Blues*	150.00	-	250.00
92040 *Mexico Blues*	150.00	-	250.00
92041 *Brick Flat Blues*	150.00	-	200.00
92042 *Ease Away Blues*	200.00	-	300.00
Vocalion 1459 *Whiskey Head Blues*	100.00	-	150.00

LOUIS WASHINGTON:

Vocalion 02634 *Run, Sinner, Run*	75.00	-	100.00
02658 *Standin' On A Rock*	75.00	-	100.00

WALTER (COWBOY) WASHINGTON:

Bluebird 6917 *Ice Pick Mama*	15.00	-	25.00
7314 *I Need You Blues*	15.00	-	25.00

CROWN PRINCE WATERFORD:

Aladdin 534, 535	4.00	-	6.00
Capitol 40074, 40103, 40132, 40137	4.00	-	6.00
King 4310, 4374, 4393	4.00	-	6.00
Torch 6911 *Eatin' Watermelon*	10.00	-	15.00

KITTY WATERS:

Pathe-Actuelle 7531 *Back Water Blues*	25.00	-	40.00
7537 *Loud And Wrong*	25.00	-	40.00
Perfect 131 *Back Water Blues*	25.00	-	40.00
137 *Loud And Wrong*	25.00	-	40.00

KATIE WATKINS:

Viceroy 3333 *Trying To Get You Off My Mind*	15.00	-	20.00*

VIOLA WATKINS:

Jubilee 5007 *Jelly And Bread*	7.00	-	10.00

DEEK WATSON & THE BROWN DOTS:

Manor	4.00	-	8.00

YOUNG JOHN WATSON:

Federal 12120 *Highway 60*	7.00	-	10.00*
12131 *Motor Head Baby*	7.00	-	10.00*
12143 *Walkin' To My Baby*	5.00	-	8.00*
12157 *What's Going On*	5.00	-	8.00*
12175 *Space Guitar*	5.00	-	8.00*

MOJO WATSON:

Atlas 1080 *All Alone*	7.00	-	10.00

JAMES WAYNE/WAYNES:

Imperial 5151, 5160, 5166, 5258	5.00	-	8.00*
Sittin' In With 573, 588, 607, 622, 639	6.00	-	10.00

WEAVER AND BEASLEY:

Okeh 8530 *Bottleneck Blues*	40.00	-	60.00

CURLEY WEAVER (& HIS GUITAR/& EDDIE MAPP/& CLARENCE MOORE/& RUTH WILLIS):

Title,. issued contemporaneously on Banner, Melotone, Oriole, Perfect, Romeo: *Birmingham Gambler, Black Woman; City Cell Blues; Early Morning Blues; Leg Iron Blues; No No Blues; Some Cold Rainy Day; Tippin'*

Tom	50.00	-	75.00
Champion 50065 *Two Faced Woman*	50.00	-	75.00
50077 *Fried Pie Blues*	50.00	-	75.00
Columbia 14386-D *No No Blues*	75.00	-	125.00
Decca 7077 *Early Morning Blues*	50.00	-	75.00
7664, 7906	15.00	-	25.00
Okeh 8928 *Baby Boogie Woogie*	80.00	-	120.00
QRS 7077 *Dirty Deal Blues*	150.00	-	200.00
Sittin' In With 547 *My Baby's Gone*	15.00	-	20.00
646 *Some Rainy Day*	8.00	-	12.00

SYLVESTER WEAVER:

Okeh 8109 *Guitar Rag*	75.00	-	100.00
8152 *Smoketown Strut*	75.00	-	100.00
8207 *Weaver's Blues*	75.00	-	100.00
8460 *True Love Blues*	50.00	-	75.00
8480 *Guitar Rag*	50.00	-	75.00
8504 *Penitentiary Bound Blues*	35.00	-	50.00

8522 *What Makes A Man Blue?*	35.00	-	50.00
8534 *Black Spider Blues*	40.00	-	60.00
8549 *Rock Pile Blues*	40.00	-	60.00
8608 *Polecat Blues*	40.00	-	60.00

BOOGIE BILL WEBB:

Imperial 5257 *Bad Dog*	8.00	-	12.00*

TINY WEBB TRIO:

Globe 108 *G.I. Blues*	5.00	-	8.00

MARGARET WEBSTER:

Diva 6040-G *How Can I Get It*	20.00	-	30.00
Velvet Tone 7066-V *How Can I Get It*	20.00	-	30.00
7076-V *Wipe 'Em Off*	20.00	-	30.00

BARREL HOUSE WELCH:

Paramount 12759 *Dying Pickpocket Blues*	75.00	-	100.00

KANSAS CITY BILL WELDON:

Vocalion 03078 *Race Horse Filly Blues*	20.00	-	30.00
03198 *Doctor's Blues*	20.00	-	30.00

WILL WELDON:

Victor 21134 *Turpentine Blues*	75.00	-	100.00

TUDIE WELLS:

Pathe-Actuelle 032006 *Uncle Sam Blues*	10.00	-	15.00
Perfect 12085 *Uncle Sam Blues*	10.00	-	15.00

NOLAN WELSH:

Okeh 8372 *St. Peter Blues*	150.00	-	200.00
8425 *Bouncing Blues*	40.00	-	60.00

CHARLEY WEST:

Bluebird 7033 *Poor Boy Blues*	10.00	-	15.00
8085 *Rollin' Stone Blues*	10.00	-	15.00

WESTERN KID:

Gennett 7210 *Mountain Girl Blues*	175.00	-	250.00
7230 *Western Blues*	175.00	-	250.00

PERRY WESTON:

Vocalion 03699 *Border Blues*	15.00	-	20.00

LITTLE DAVID WHEATON:

Capitol 40009, 40034, 40139	12.00	-	18.00

PEETIE WHEATSTRAW:

Titles, issued contemporaneously on Banner, Conqucror, Melotone, Oriole, Perfect, Romeo; Vocalion: *Froggie Blues; Good Whiskey Blues; Kidnappers Blues; The Last Dime; Letter Writing Blues; Long Lonesome Drive; Mistreated Love Blues; Remember And Forget*

Blues	15.00	-	30.00
Bluebird 5451 *Devil's Son-In-Law*	20.00	-	30.00
Conqueror 8858, 8925, 9027, 9028	6.00	-	10.00
Decca 7007 *Doin' The Best I Can*	30.00	-	50.00
7018 *Throw Me In The Alley*	50.00	-	75.00
7061 *Good Home Blues*	25.00	-	40.00
7082 *Numbers Blues*	25.00	-	40.00
7111 *Whiskey Head Blues*	20.00	-	30.00
7123 *Good Hustler Blues*	20.00	-	30.00
7129 *Santa Claus Blues*	20.00	-	30.00
7144 *King Spider Blues*	20.00	-	30.00
7159 *Coon Can Shorty*	20.00	-	30.00
7167 *Deep Sea Love*	20.00	-	30.00
7177 *Poor Millionaire Blues*	20.00	-	30.00
7187 *Meat Cutter Blues*	15.00	-	20.00
7200 *Low Down Rascal*	15.00	-	20.00
7228 *Country Fool Blues*	15.00	-	20.00
7243 *False Hearted Woman*	15.00	-	20.00
7257 *I Don't Want No Pretty-Faced Woman*	15.00	-	20.00
7272 *Beggar Man Blues*	15.00	-	20.00
7292 *Crapshooter's Blues*	8.00	-	12.00
7311 *Working On The Project*	8.00	-	12.00
7348 *Crazy With The Blues*	8.00	-	12.00
7379 *New Working On The Project*	8.00	-	12.00
7391 *Give Me Black Or Brown*	8.00	-	12.00
7403 *Sick Bed Blues*	8.00	-	12.00
7422 *Devilment Blues*	8.00	-	12.00
7441, 7453, 7465, 7479, 7498, 7529, 7544, 7568, 7578, 7589, 7605, 7641, 7657, 7676, 7692, 7738, 7753, 7778, 7788, 7798, 7815, 7823,			

7837, 7844, 7857, 7879, 7886, 7894, 7901	5.00	-	10.00
7904 *Southern Girl Blues*	15.00	-	20.00

Vocalion 1552 *Tennessee Peaches Blues* .... 75.00 - 125.00
   1569 *School Days* .... 75.00 - 125.00
   1597 *Strange Man Blues* .... 75.00 - 125.00
   1620 *Mama's Advice* .... 75.00 - 125.00
   1649 *Ain't It A Pity And A Shame* ..... 75.00 - 125.00
   1672 *C And A Blues* .... 75.00 - 125.00
   1722 *Police Station Blues* .... 75.00 - 125.00
   1727 *Can't See Blues* .... 75.00 - 125.00
   02783 *Back Door Blues* .... 50.00 - 80.00
   02810 *C And A Train Blues* .... 50.00 - 80.00
   02843 *Keyhole Blues* .... 50.00 - 80.00
   02942 *Blues At My Door* .... 20.00 - 30.00
   02978 *Good Whiskey Blues* .... 20.00 - 30.00
   03035 *Up The Road Blues* .... 20.00 - 30.00
   03066 *King Of Spades* .... 15.00 - 25.00
   03119 *Sorrow Hearted Blues* .... 15.00 - 25.00
   03155 *Johnnie Blues* .... 15.00 - 25.00
   03185 *True Blue Woman* .... 15.00 - 25.00
   03231 *Jungle Man Blues* .... 15.00 - 25.00
   03249 *Froggie Blues* .... 15.00 - 20.00
   03273 *Mistreated Love Blues* .... 15.00 - 20.00
   03348 *Block And Tackle* .... 15.00 - 20.00
   03396 *Sweet Home Blues* .... 15.00 - 20.00
   03444 *Cut Out Blues* .... 15.00 - 20.00

LULU WHIDBY:
Black Swan 2005 *Home Again Blues* .... 20.00 - 30.00
Home Again Blues also issued
   contemporaneously on Claxtonola, Paramount,
   Puritan .... 15.00 - 30.00

WHISTLIN' PETE AND DADDY STOVEPIPE:
Gennett 6212 *Black Snake Blues* ....150.00 - 250.00

WHISTLIN' RUFUS:
Bluebird 5306 *Sweet Jelly Rollin'* .... 35.00 - 50.00
   5360 *Sweet Thing* .... 50.00 - 75.00

BOB WHITE:
Bluebird 8595 *I'm The Woogie Man* .... 10.00 - 15.00

BUKKA WHITE:
Conqueror 9072 *Shake 'Em On Down* ...... 10.00 - 15.00
Okeh 05625 *Good Gin Blues* .... 10.00 - 20.00
   05683 *District Attorney Blues* .... 10.00 - 20.00
   05743 *Sleepy Man Blues* .... 10.00 - 20.00
Vocalion 03711 *Shake 'Em On Down* ...... 20.00 - 30.00
   05489 *High Fever Blues* .... 15.00 - 20.00
   05526 *Strange Place Blues* .... 15.00 - 20.00
   05588 *Black Train Blues* .... 15.00 - 20.00

CLARA WHITE (Accompanied by SAM HILL/HARRY SIMS):
Oriole 263 *Clearing House Blues* .... 10.00 - 15.00
   264 *Buzzin' Around* .... 10.00 - 15.00
   265 *You Don't Know My Mind* .... 10.00 - 15.00

FLORENCE WHITE:
Victor 20584 *Cold Rocks Was My Pillow* .... 50.00 - 75.00

GEORGIA WHITE:
Decca 7072 *Your Worries Ain't Like Mine* ...... 10.00 - 15.00
   7100 *Dupree Blues* .... 10.00 - 15.00
   7122 *Honey Dripper Blues* .... 10.00 - 15.00
   7135 *Easy Rider Blues* .... 10.00 - 15.00
   7143 *Your Worries Ain't Like Mine No. 2* ..... 8.00 - 12.00
   7149 *If You Can't Get Five, Take Two* .... 8.00 - 12.00
   7152 *Tell Me Baby* .... 8.00 - 12.00
   7166 *Can't Read, Can't Write* .... 8.00 - 12.00
   7174 *Rattlesnakin' Daddy* .... 8.00 - 12.00
   7183 *New Hot Nuts (Get 'Em From The Peanut Man)* .... 7.00 - 10.00
Decca 7192 *Trouble In Mind* .... 7.00 - 10.00
   7199 *I Just Want Your Stingaree* .... 7.00 - 10.00
   7209 *Pigmeat Blues* .... 7.00 - 10.00
   7216 *No Second Hand Woman* .... 7.00 - 10.00
   7254 *Your Hellish Ways* .... 5.00 - 8.00
   7269 *Sinking Sun Blues* .... 5.00 - 8.00

   7277 *You Don't Know My Mind* .... 5.00 - 8.00
   7287 *Little Red Wagon* .... 5.00 - 8.00
   7309 *Toothache Blues* .... 5.00 - 8.00
   7323 *When My Love Comes Down* ...... 5.00 - 8.00
   7332 *New Trouble In Mind* .... 5.00 - 8.00
   7357 *Biscuit Roller* .... 5.00 - 8.00
   7377 *Georgia Man* .... 5.00 - 8.00
   7389 *Red Cap Porter* .... 5.00 - 8.00
   7405 *All Night Blues* .... 5.00 - 8.00
   7419 *Strewin' Your Mess* .... 5.00 - 8.00
   7436 *The Stuff Is Here* .... 5.00 - 8.00
   7450 *Almost Afraid To Love* .... 5.00 - 8.00
   7477 *Too Much Trouble* .... 5.00 - 8.00
   7521 *Trouble In Mind Swing* .... 5.00 - 8.00
   7534 *Dead Man's Blues* .... 5.00 - 8.00
   7562 *My Worried Mind Blues* .... 5.00 - 8.00
   7596 *Married Woman Blues* .... 5.00 - 8.00
   7608 *Fire In The Mountain* .... 5.00 - 8.00
   7620 *Beggin' My Daddy* .... 5.00 - 8.00
   7631 *Hydrant Love* .... 5.00 - 8.00
   7652 *Do It Again* .... 5.00 - 8.00
   7672 *I'm Doing What My Heart Says Do* ..... 5.00 - 8.00
   7689 *Furniture Man* .... 5.00 - 8.00
   7741 *Jazzin' Babies Blues* .... 7.00 - 10.00
   7754 *Sensation Blues* .... 7.00 - 10.00
   7783 *Papa Pleaser* .... 7.00 - 10.00
   7807 *Worried Head Blues* .... 5.00 - 8.00
   7841 *Come Around To My House* .... 5.00 - 8.00
   7853 *Territory Blues* .... 5.00 - 8.00
   7866 *Mail Plane Blues* .... 5.00 - 8.00

GLADYS WHITE:
Oriole 746 *I'm Saving It All For You* .... 10.00 - 15.00
   772 *Papa, If You Can't Do Better* .... 10.00 - 15.00

GRACE WHITE:
Silvertone 3542 *Friendless Blues* .... 15.00 - 20.00

JOSH/JOSHUA WHITE:
Titles, issued contemporaneously on Banner,
   Conqueror, Melotone, Oriole, Perfect, Romeo:
   Baby, Won't You Doodle-Doo Doo; Bad
   Depression Blues, Big House Blues, Black And
   Evil Blues; Blood Red River; Can't Help But
   Crying Sometimes, Crying Blues; Death's
   Coming Back After You; Double Crossing
   Women; Downhearted Man Blues; Down On
   Me; Four And Twenty Elders; Got A Key To
   The Kingdom; High Brown Cheater; How
   About You?; Howlin' Wolf Blues; I Don't Intend
   To Die In Egyptland; I Got A Home In That
   Rock; Jesus Gonna Make Up My Dying Bed;
   Lay Some Flowers On My Grave; Lazy Black
   Snake Blues; Little Brother Blues; Lord, I Want
   To Die Easy; Motherless Children; My Father
   Is A Husbandman; My Soul Is Gonna Live
   With God; On My Way; Paul And Silas Bound
   In Jail; Pickin' Low Cotton; Pure Religion
   Hallilu; So Sweet, So Sweet; That Suits Me;
   There's A Man Going round Taking Names;
   Things About Coming My Way; This Heart Of
   Mine; While The Blood Runs Warm In Your
   Veins; You Sinner You .... 30.00 - 50.00

WASHINGTON WHITE:
Victor 23295 *The Panama Limited* ....200.00 - 300.00
   V38615 *Promise True And Grand* ....150.00 - 200.00

ELSIE WHITMAN:
Paramount 12172 *Sweet Daddy It's You I Love* ... 25.00 - 35.00

ESSIE WHITMAN:
Black Swan 2036 *If You Don't Believe I Love You* 25.00 - 40.00

MARGARET WHITMIRE:
Brunswick 7024 *Tain't A Cow In Texas* ...... 50.00 - 75.00
Vocalion 1173 *Tain't A Cow In Texas* .... 50.00 - 75.00

(JAMES) "BOODLE IT" WIGGINS:
Paramount 12662 *Evil Woman Blues* ....150.00 - 200.00

12860 *Forty-Four Blues*	150.00 -	200.00
12878 *Weary Heart Blues*	150.00 -	200.00
12916 *Gotta Shave 'Em Dry*	150.00 -	200.00

BILL WILBER:

Champion 50053 *Greyhound Blues*	50.00 -	80.00

WILEY AND WILEY:

Brunswick 7022 *The Dixie Drug Store Down On*	75.00 -	100.00
Columbia 14610-D *Irenes Bakershop Blues*	50.00 -	80.00
14630-D *Jumpin Judy Blues*	50.00 -	80.00
Okeh 8385 *Dear Old Campanion*	40.00 -	60.00
Vocalion 1171 *The Dixie Drug Store Down On*	75.00 -	100.00

ARNOLD WILEY:

Apollo 391 *Wiley's Boogie*	7.00 -	10.00
Brunswick 7113 *Windy City*	50.00 -	120.00
Paramount 12955 *Jumping Blues*	100.00 -	150.00

DOC WILEY:

Bullet 323 *Play our Hand*	7.00 -	10.00

GEESHIE WILEY:

Paramount 12951 *Skinny Leg Blues*	80.00 -	100.00
13074 *Pick Poor Robin Clean*	80.00 -	100.00

ROBERT WILKINS:

Brunswick 7125 *Falling Down Blues*	100.00 -	150.00
7158 *Get A way Blues*	100.00 -	150.00
7168 *Police Sergeant Blues*	100.00 -	150.00
7205 *Long Train Blues*	100.00 -	150.00
Victor 21741 *Rolling Stone*	80.00 -	100.00
23379 *Jail House Blues*	200.00 -	300.00

TIM WILKINS:

Vocalion 03176 *Black Rat Blues*	75.00 -	100.00
03223 *Dirty Deal Blues*	75.00 -	100.00

B. WILLIAMS:

Top Tunes 101 *Mortgaged Love*	8.00 -	12.00

BESSIE WILLIAMS:

Domino 361, 362, 363, 364	8.00 -	15.00
412 *I Wanna Jazz Some More*	10.00 -	15.00
413 *Family Skeleton Blues*	10.00 -	15.00
424 *Deep River Blues*	10.00 -	15.00

BILL WILLIAMS (& SAMMY SAMPSON):

Titles, issued contemporaneously on Banner, Oriole, Perfect, Romeo: *Mr. Conductor Man; No Good Buddy*	40.00 -	60.00

BILYE WILLIAMS:

Acorn 310 *Disgusted Blues*	7.00 -	10.00

BLIND BOY WILLIAMS:

Sittin' In With 538 *Just Drifting*	10.00 -	15.00

EDDIE WILLIAMS & THE BROWN BUDDIES:

Selective 121 *Unfaithful Woman*	5.00 -	8.00
Supreme 1528, 1535, 1542, 1546, 1547, 1548	4.00 -	6.00

BOODLE IT WILLIAMS:

Broadway 5086 *Evil Woman Blues*	125.00 -	175.00

BROTHER WILLIAMS' MEMPHIS SANCTIFIED SINGERS:

Vocalin 1482 *He's Got The Whole World In His Hands*	50.00 -	80.00

ELLIS WILLIAMS:

Columbia 14482-D *Smokey Blues*	40.00 -	60.00

ELSIE WILLIAMS:

Decca 7399 *Bind It Back*	7.00 -	10.00

GEORGE ("BULLET") WILLIAMS:

Broadway 5085 *Frisco Leaving Birmingham*	60.00 -	90.00
Paramount 12651 *The Escaped Convict*	75.00 -	100.00
12680 *Touch Me Light Mama*	75.00 -	100.00

GEORGE WILLIAMS (AND BESSIE BROWN):

Columbia A-3974 *Satisfied Blues*	10.00 -	15.00
Columbia 13006-D *If Mama Quits Papa, What Will Papa Do?*	10.00 -	15.00
14002-D *A Woman Gets Tired Of One Man All Of The Time*	10.00 -	15.00
14011-D *You Ain't Quittin' Me Without Two Weeks' Notice*	8.00 -	12.00
Columbia 14015-D *I Won't Stand No Leavin' Now*	10.00 -	15.00

14017-D *You Need Stome Lovin's*	10.00 -	15.00
14030-D *Hard Headed Gal*	10.00 -	15.00
14033-D *If You Hit My Dog I'll Kick Your Cat*	15.00 -	20.00
14046-D *I Can Do What You Do*	15.00 -	20.00
14065-D *Bald-Headed Mama Blues*	10.00 -	15.00
14071-D *Cheatin' Blues*	15.00 -	20.00
14078-D *Oh! Dark Gal*	10.00 -	15.00
14135-D *Hit Me But Don't Quit Me*	25.00 -	40.00
14148-D *West Virginia Blues*	20.00 -	30.00
14543-D *Yodelin' The Blues Away*	30.00 -	50.00
Diva 6027-G *You Ain't Quittin' Me Without Two Weeks' Notice*	8.00 -	12.00
Velvet Tone 7053-V *It Takes A Brownskin Man To Make A High Yellow Blue*	8.00 -	12.00

GUSSIE WILLIAMS:

Okeh 8934 *Its Too Slippery*	30.00 -	50.00

HENRY WILLIAMS AND EDDIE ANTHONY:

Columbia 14328-D *Georgia Crawl*	50.00 -	75.00

"JABO" WILLIAMS:

Paramount 13127 *Ko Ko Mo Blues*	250.00 -	400.00
13130 *Fat Mama Blues*	250.00 -	400.00
13136 *House Lady Blues*	250.00 -	400.00
13141 *Pratt City Blues*	250.00 -	400.00

(BIG) JOE WILLIAMS (& HIS 9-STRING GUITAR); JOE WILLIAMS' WASHBOARD BLUES SINGERS:

Bluebird 5900 *Little Leg Woman*	35.00 -	50.00
5930 *Providence Help The Poor People*	35.00 -	50.00
5948 *My Grey Pony*	50.00 -	75.00
5996 *40 Highway Blues*	35.00 -	50.00
6200 *Wild Cow Blues*	30.00 -	40.00
6231 *Worried Man Blues*	30.00 -	40.00
7719 *Get Your Head Trimmed Down*	25.00 -	35.00
7770 *Peach Orchard Mama*	25.00 -	35.00
8738 *Crawlin King Snake*	10.00 -	15.00
8774 *I'm Getting Wild About Her*	10.00 -	15.00
8969 *Please Don't Go*	10.00 -	15.00
9025 *Highway 49*	8.00 -	12.00
34-0739 *Vitamin A*	5.00 -	8.00
Bullet 337 *Jivin' Woman*	8.00 -	12.00
Columbia 30099, 30107, 30119, 30129, 30191, 37945, 38055, 38190	4.00 -	7.00
Trumpet 151 *Delta Blues*	7.00 -	10.00*
169 *Overhauling Blues*	7.00 -	10.00*
171 *She Left Me A Mule*	7.00 -	10.00*
Vocalion 1457 *Mr. Devil Blues*	150.00 -	200.00

JOHNNY WILLIAMS:

Gotham 506 *Wandering Blues*	8.00 -	12.00
Staff 704 *Highway Blues*	10.00 -	15.00
710 *Wandering Blues*	10.00 -	15.00
717 *I Got Lucky*	25.00 -	40.00
718 *Prison Bound*	10.00 -	15.00
Swing Time 225 *I Got Lucky*	7.00 -	10.00
266 *Prison Bound*	7.00 -	10.00

L.C. WILLIAMS (with J.C. CONNEY'S COMBO); L.C. (LIGHTNIN' JR.) WILLIAMS:

Bayou 008 *All Through My Dreams*	10.00 -	15.00*
Dot 1052 *You Never Miss The Water*	8.00 -	12.00
Freedom 1501, 1517, 1524	5.00 -	8.00
1529 *All Through My Dreams*	6.00 -	10.00
Gold Star 614 *Trying, Trying*	10.00 -	15.00
623 *Hole In The Wall*	10.00 -	15.00
648 *I Won't Be Here Long*	10.00 -	15.00
Imperial 5195 *Mean And Evil Blues*	5.00 -	8.00*
Jax 640 *Baby Child*	8.00 -	12.00
648 *Fannie Mae*	8.00 -	12.00
Mercury 8276 *Don't Want No Woman*	5.00 -	8.00
Sittin' In With 640 *So Sorry*	8.00 -	12.00
648 *Fannie Mae*	8.00 -	12.00

LESTER WILLIAMS:

Macy's 5000, 5004, 5006, 5009, 5016	7.00 -	12.00

Specialty 422, 431, 437, 450	4.00 -	6.00*

LIGHTNIN' JR. WILLIAMS (see L.C. WILLIAMS); (PAPA) LONNIE WILLIAMS; (& GEORGE HOLMES):

Champion 15695 *Somebody's Been Using That Thing*	75.00 -	125.00
Sittin' In With 567 *New Road Blues*	8.00 -	15.00
593 *Wavin' Sea Blues*	8.00 -	15.00

LULU WILLIAMS:

Titles. issued contemporaneously on Banner, Oriole, Perfect, Romeo: *Careless Love Blues; You're Going To Leave The Old Home, Jim* ...	35.00 -	50.00

MAMIE WILLIAMS:

Silvertone 5134 *Ease Away Blues*	100.00 -	150.00

RABBITS FOOT WILLIAMS:

Black Patti 8052 *Mistreatin'Mama*	300.00 -	Up
Champion 15339 *Mill Log Blues*	200.00 -	300.00
15379 *Man Trouble Blues*	200.00 -	300.00
Silvertone 5172 *I'm Gonna Cross The River*	200.00 -	300.00

SONNY BOY WILLIAMS:

Decca 7888, 7898, 8513, 8532, 8643, 8651	5.00 -	10.00

SUNNY WILLIAMS TRI0:

Super Disc 1030, 1058	5.00 -	10.00

SUSAN WILLIAMS:

Lincoln 2612 *Someday You'll Come Back To Me* .	10.00 -	15.00
2651 *Black Water Blues*	10.00 -	15.00
2690 *Gay-Cattin' Daddy*	10.00 -	15.00

JAMES WILLIAMSON & HIS TRIO:

Chance 1121 *Lonesome Ole Train*	20.00 -	30.00*
1131 *Homesick*	20.00 -	30.00*

SONNY BOY WILLIAMSON:

Ace 511 *Boppin' With Sonny*	4.00 -	6.00*
Bluebird 7012 *Skinny Woman*	20.00 -	30.00
7059 *Sugar Mama Blues*	20.00 -	30.00
7098 *Blue Bird Blues*	20.00 -	30.00
7302 *Early In The Morning*	15.00 -	20.00
7352 *Suzanna Blues*	15.00 -	20.00
7404 *Frigidaire Blues*	15.00 -	20.00
7428 *Collector Man Blues*	15.00 -	20.00
7500 *Sunny Land*	15.00 -	20.00
7536 *You Can Lead Me*	15.00 -	20.00
7576 *Miss Louisa Blues*	15.00 -	20.00
7603 *Beauty Palor*	15.00 -	20.00
7665 *Decoration Blues*	15.00 -	20.00
7707 *Honey Bee Blues*	15.00 -	20.00
7756 *You Give An Account*	15.00 -	20.00
7805 *Deep Down In The Ground*	15.00 -	20.00
7847 *Shannon Street Blues*	15.00 -	20.00
7979, 7995	8.00 -	12.00
8010 *Number Five Blues*	10.00 -	15.00
8034, 8094	8.00 -	12.00
8237 *Good For Nothing Blues*	10.00 -	15.00
8265 *Bad Luck Blues*	10.00 -	15.00
8307 *Doggin' My Love Around*	10.00 -	15.00
8333 *T.B. Blues*	10.00 -	15.00
8357 *Good Gal Blues*	10.00 -	15.00
8383 *New Jail House Blues*	10.00 -	15.00
8403 *Joe Louis And John Henry Blues*	10.00 -	15.00
8439 *Miss Ida Lee*	10.00 -	15.00
8474 *Honey Bee Blues*	10.00 -	15.00
8580 *War Time Blues*	8.00 -	12.00
8610 *Welfare Store Blues*	8.00 -	12.00
8674 *My Little Machine*	8.00 -	12.00
8731 *Western Union Man*	8.00 -	12.00
8766 *Big Apple Blues*	8.00 -	12.00
8797 *Mattie Mae Blues*	8.00 -	12.00
8822 *Sloppy Drunk Blues*	8.00 -	12.00
8866 *Million years Blues*	8.00 -	12.00
8914 *She Was A Dreamer*	7.00 -	10.00
8955 *Drink On, Little Girl*	7.00 -	10.00
8992 *My Black Name Blues*	5.00 -	8.00
9031 *Ground Hog Blues*	5.00 -	8.00

34-0701 *She Don't Love Me That Way*	5.00 -	8.00
34-0713, 34-0722, 34-0736, 34-0744	4.00 -	8.00
Checker 824, 834, 847, 864, 883	3.00 -	6.00*
RCA Victor	3.00 -	6.00
Trumpet 129 *Eyesight To The Blind*	8.00 -	12.00*
139 *Do It If You Wanna*	8.00 -	12.00*
140 *Stop Crying*	8.00 -	12.00*
114 *West Memphis Blues*	8.00 -	12.00*
145 *Pontiac Blues*	8.00 -	10.00*
166, 168, 212, 215, 228	5.00 -	8.00*

WILLIE MAE:

Vocalion 03404 *I'd Rather Drink Muddy Water* ..	15.00 -	25.00

LITTLE SON WILLIS:

Swing Time 304 *Bad Luck And Trouble*	15.00 -	25.00*
305 *Harlem Blues*	15.00 -	25.00*
306 *Nothing But The Blues*	15.00 -	25.00*
341 *Roll Me Over Slow*	15.00 -	25.00*

MAC WILLIS:

Elko 254 *Pretty Woman*	10.00 -	20.00

MARY WILLIS:

Okeh 8921 *Rough Alley Blues*	80.00 -	120.00
8932 *Merciful Blues*	80.00 -	120.00

MILTON WILLIS COMBO:

Lucky 7 5001 *Little Joe's Boogie*	5.00 -	8.00

RALPH ('BAMA) WILLIS (& HIS ALABAMA TRIO); RALPH WILLIS' COUNTRY BOYS:

Abbey 3002 *Cool That Thing*	15.00 -	20.00
Jubilee 5034, 5044, 5078	6.00 -	10.00*
King 4611, 5631	7.00 -	10.00*
Prestige 919, 923	7.00 -	10.00
Regis 118 *Worried Blues*	10.00 -	15.00
Signaure 32012, 32016	7.00 -	10.00
20th Century 20-09, 20-11, 20-12	7.00 -	10.00

RUTH WILLIS:

Titles. issued contemporaneously on Banner, Melolone, Oriole, Perfect, Romeo: *I'm Still Sloppy Drunk; Man Of My Own*	40.00 -	60.00

TURNER WILLIS:

Trilon 1058 *Re-Enlistment Blues*	6.00 -	12.00

WILSON AND REED:

Champion 15264 *France Blues*	200.00 -	300.00

JIMMY WILSON (& HIS ALL STARS):

Aladdin 3087, 3140, 3169, 3241	5.00 -	8.00*
Cavatone 252 *Mistake In Life*	7.00 -	10.00

LEOLA WILSON WITH WESLEY WILSON AND COOT GRANT:

Columbia 14669-D *I Can't Get Enough*	75.00 -	100.00
14675-D *Dirty Spoon Blues*	75.00 -	100.00

LEOLA B. WILSON:

Paramount 12392 *Ashley St. Blues*	100.00 -	150.00
12403 *Dishrag Blues*	100.00 -	150.00
12426 *Wilson Dam*	100.00 -	150.00
12444 *Down The Country*	100.00 -	150.00

EDNA WINSTON:

Victor 20407 *Peepin Jim*	25.00 -	40.00
20424 *Pail In My Hand*	25.00 -	40.00
20654 *Joogie Blues*	35.00 -	50.00
20857 *Rent Man Blues*	35.00 -	50.00

KATIE WINTERS:

Gennett 6107 *Indian Brown Blues*	75.00 -	125.00

BIG BOY WOODS:

Bell 1173 *The Jail House Blues*	175.00 -	250.00
1180 *Do That Thing*	200.00 -	300.00
1181 *Dark Cloudy Blues*	200.00 -	300.00

BUDDY WOODS:

Vocalion 03906 *Muscat Hill Blues*	20.00 -	30.00
04604 *Jam Session Blues*	20.00 -	30.00
04745 *Low Life Blues*	20.00 -	30.00

EVA WOODS:

Silvertone 3522 *You Gotta Know How*	75.00 -	100.00
3557 *He's My Man*	75.00 -	100.00

OSCAR WOODS:

Decca 7219 Lone Wolf Blues . . . . 20.00 - 30.00
7904 *Evil Hearted Woman Blues* . . . . 15.00 - 20.00

EMMA WRIGHT:
Columbia 14413-D *Lonesome Trail Blues* . . . . 75.00 - 100.00

THE YAS YAS GIRL:
Titles, issued contemporaneously on Banner,
Conqueror, Melotone. Oriole, Perfect, Romeo,
Vocalion: *Blues Everywhere; Crime Don't Pay;
Got A Man In The 'Bama Mines; Grandma
And Grandpa; I'd Rather Drink Muddy Water--
No. 2; I Drink Good Whiskey; Jackass For
Sale; New Drinking My Blues Away; Patrol
Wagon Blues; Sold It To The Devil; Working On
The Project; You Got To Pay* . . . . 10.00 - 15.00
Conqueror 9079 *Don't You Leave Me Here* . . . . . 7.00 - 10.00
9147 *Don't You Make Me High* . . . . 7.00 - 10.00
9205 *Breakin' 'Em Down Tonight* . . . . 7.00 - 10.00
9375 *Want To Woogie Some More* . . . . 5.00 - 8.00
9449 *You're A Pain In The Neck To Me* . . . . . 5.00 - 8.00
9451 *I'll Try To Forget* . . . . 5.00 - 8.00
9601 *I Won't Sell My Love* . . . . 5.00 - 8.00
9949 *Good Old Easy Street* . . . . 5.00 - 8.00
9950 *Milk Man Blues* . . . . 5.00 - 8.00
Okeh 05870 *Worried Heart Blues* . . . . 5.00 - 8.00
05932 *You Know It Ain't Right* . . . . 5.00 - 8.00
05984 *Got The Blues For My Baby* . . . . 5.00 - 8.00
06032 *Evil Old Nightmare* . . . . 5.00 - 8.00
06340 *Blues Before Daybreak* . . . . 5.00 - 8.00
06446 *Good Old Easy Street* . . . . 5.00 - 8.00
06570 *Froggy Bottom* . . . . 5.00 - 8.00
Vocalion 04013 *He May Be Your Man* . . . . 8.00 - 12.00
04094 *Love Shows Weakness* . . . . 8.00 - 12.00
04150 *About My Time To Check* . . . . 8.00 - 12.00

04188 *Jelly Bean Blues* . . . . 7.00 - 10.00
04331 *You Can't Shoot Your Pistol* . . . . 7.00 - 10.00
04455 *Don't You Make Me High* . . . . 7.00 - 10.00
04545 *Whiskey Fool* . . . . 7.00 - 10.00
04719 *Reckless Life Blues* . . . . 7.00 - 10.00
04775 *Grieving Heart Blues* . . . . 7.00 - 10.00
04830 *Easy Towing Mama* . . . . 7.00 - 10.00
04885 *Got A Mind To Ramble* . . . . 7.00 - 10.00
05105 *Fine And Mellow* . . . . 7.00 - 10.00
05180 *I'd Rather Be Drunk* . . . . 5.00 - 8.00
05219 *I Need You By My Side* . . . . 7.00 - 10.00
05286 *I Got To Have It Daddy* . . . . 5.00 - 8.00
05337 *I'll Try To Forget* . . . . 5.00 - 8.00
05382 *Mama's Bad Luck Child* . . . . 7.00 - 10.00
05501 *You Don't Know My Mind* . . . . 5.00 - 8.00
05576 *Stop And Listen* . . . . 5.00 - 8.00
05614 *Black Gypsy Blues* . . . . 5.00 - 8.00

BLIND RICHARD YATES:
Black Patti 8021 *Sore Bunion Blues* . . . . .100.00 - Up
Champion 15264 *I'm Gonna Moan My Blues
Away* . . . . .200.00 - 300.00
15281 *Sore Bunion Blues* . . . . .100.00 - 150.00
Gennett 6104 *Sore Bunion Blues* . . . . 50.00 - 75.00

BILLE YOUNG:
Victor 23339 *You Done Played Out Blues* . . . . . .250.00 - 350.00

JOHNNY YOUNG:
Ora Nelle 712 *Womed Man Blues* . . . . 15.00 - 20.00

MAN YOUNG:
Old Swing Master 19 *Let Me Ride Your Mule* . . . 20.00 - 30.00

THE ZA ZU GIRL:
Titles, issued contemporaneously on Banner,
Melotone, Oriole, Perfect, Romeo, Vocalion:
He Left Me; My Righteous Man . . . . 8.00 - 12.00

COUNTRY/WESTERN; OLD TIME SINGING; STRING BANDS; ETC.

1920s to early 1950s—78 RPM
(All Records in this section are 78 RPM)

(Note: * after listing means that the record may exist also in 45 RPM form.)

ROY ACUFF & HIS CRAZY
TENNESSEANS/SMOKY MOUNTAIN BOYS:
Titles, issued contemporaneously on Banner,
Conqueror, Melotone, Oriole, Perfect, Romeo:
All Night Long; Charmin' Betsy 'Gonna Have
A Big Time Tonight; Gonna Raise A Ruckus
Tonight; Great Speckle Bird; Great Speckle
Bird No. 2; My Gal Sal; My Mountain Home
Sweet Home; New Greenback Dollar; Sailing
Along; Red Lips; Sailing Along; She No Longer
Belongs To Me; Steamboat Whistle Blues; Steel
Guitar Blues; Steel Guitar Chimes; Tell Mother
I'll Be There; Trouble Trouble; Yes Sir, That's
My Baby; You're The Only Star (In My Blue
Heaven); You've Gotta See Mama Every Night . 5.00 - 8.00
Conqueror 9123, 9170, 9255, 9257, 9324, 9404,
9432 . . . . 4.00 - 7.00
Vocalion 03255, 04252, 04374, 04376, 04466,
04505, 04531, 04590, 04657, 04730, 04795,
04867, 04909, 04915, 05041 . . . . 4.00 - 8.00

CHARLIE ADAMS & THE LONE STAR
PLAYBOYS:
Decca 28397, 46335, 46358, 46373, 46391 . . . . . 4.00 - 7.00*
Imperial 8100, 8113 . . . . 5.00 - 10.00

CLARENCE ADAMS:
Challenge 229, 232 . . . . 5.00 - 8.00

AIKEN COUNTRY STRING BAND:
Okeh 45143 *Carolina Stompdown* . . . . 50.00 - 75.00
45219 *Charleston Rag* . . . . 50.00 - 75.00
45294 *Harrisburg Itch* . . . . 50.00 - 75.00

AKINS BIRMINGHAM BOYS:
Columbia 15348-D *I Walked And Walked* . . . . . . 10.00 - 15.00

ALABAMA FOUR:
Broadway 8209 *Looking This Way* . . . . 15.00 - 25.00

ALEXANDER & MILLER:
Supertone 9398 *Medley* . . . . 5.00 - 8.00

WELDON ALLARD:
Imperial 8117 *Too Late You Say* . . . . 7.00 - 10.00

ALLEGHENY HIGHLANDERS:
Brunswick 324, 325 . . . . 8.00 - 12.00

ALLEN BROTHERS:
Bluebird 5001 *Fruit Jar Blues* . . . . 5.00 - 8.00
5104 *Tiple Blues* . . . . 15.00 - 20.00
5165 *Shake It, Ida, Shake It* . . . . 15.00 - 20.00
5224 *Reckless Night Blues* . . . . 10.00 - 15.00
5317 *Slide, Daddy, Slide* . . . . 10.00 - 15.00
5380 *New Chattanooga Blues* . . . . 10.00 - 15.00
5403 *Browns Ferry Blues* . . . . 5.00 - 8.00
5448 *No Low Down Hanging Around* . . . . 7.00 - 10.00
5470 *Chattanooga Mama* . . . . 10.00 - 15.00
5533 *It Can't Be Done* . . . . 10.00 - 15.00
5668 *Shanghai Rooster Blues* . . . . 10.00 - 15.00
5700 *Roll Down The Line* . . . . 10.00 - 15.00
5701 *Glorious Night Blues* . . . . 10.00 - 15.00
5702 *When You Leave, You'll Leave Me Sad* . . 10.00 - 15.00
5772 *Skipping And Flying* . . . . 10.00 - 15.00
Bluebird 6148, 6149, 6195 . . . . 5.00 - 10.00
Columbia 15175-D *Salty Dog Blues* . . . . 75.00 - 100.00
15270-D *Ain't That Skippin?* . . . . 75.00 - 100.00
Victor 23507 *Price Of Cotton Blues* . . . . 30.00 - 40.00
23514 *New Salty Dog* . . . . 15.00 - 25.00
23536 *No Low Down Hanging Around* . . . . 15.00 - 25.00
23551 *Roll Down The Line* . . . . 30.00 - 50.00
23567 *Chattanooga Mama* . . . . 30.00 - 50.00
23578 *Pile Drivin' Papa* . . . . 30.00 - 50.00
23590 *Slide, Daddy, Slide* . . . . 30.00 - 50.00

23607 *Mother-In-Law Blues* . . . . 30.00 - 50.00
23623 *Unlucky Man* . . . . 30.00 - 50.00
23631 *Moonshine Bill* . . . . 30.00 - 50.00
23662 *It Can't Be Done* . . . . 30.00 - 50.00
23678 *Maybe Next Week Some Time No. 2* . . . . 30.00 - 50.00
23692 *Window Shade Blues* . . . . 60.00 - 80.00
23707 *Glorious Night Blues* . . . . 80.00 - 120.00
23756 *Rough Neck Blues* . . . . 50.00 - 75.00
23773 *Slipping Clutch Blues* . . . . 75.00 - 100.00
23786 *Red Hot Rambling Dan* . . . . 75.00 - 100.00
23805 *Warm Knees Blues* . . . . 75.00 - 100.00
23817 *Midnight Mama* . . . . 75.00 - 100.00
V40003 *Frisco Blues* . . . . 25.00 - 40.00
V40210 *Prisoner's Dream* . . . . 30.00 - 50.00
V40266 *Skipping And Flying* . . . . 30.00 - 50.00
V40276 *Enforcement Blues* . . . . 35.00 - 50.00
V40303 *Jake Walk Blues* . . . . 35.00 - 50.00
V40326 *Shanghai Rooster Blues* . . . . 35.00 - 50.00
Vocalion 02817 *Red Pajama Sal* . . . . 40.00 - 60.00
02818 *Salty Dog Blues* . . . . 40.00 - 60.00
02841 *Midnight Mama* . . . . 40.00 - 60.00
02853 *Daddy Park Your Car* . . . . 40.00 - 60.00
02874 *The Prisoner's Dream* . . . . 40.00 - 60.00
02890 *New Deal Blues* . . . . 40.00 - 60.00
02891 *Tiple Blues* . . . . 30.00 - 50.00
02939 *Allen Brothers' Rag* . . . . 30.00 - 50.00

CLAY ALLEN:
Decca 46324, 46360 . . . . 3.00 - 6.00*

ALLEN, LEE & AUSTIN:
Columbia 14266-D *Chattanooga Blues* . . . . 75.00 - 100.00

ALLEN, JULES (THE SINGING COWBOY):
Victor 21470 *Jack O'Diamonds* . . . . 5.00 - 8.00
21627 *Home On The Range* . . . . 5.00 - 8.00
23598 *Sweetie Dear* . . . . 20.00 - 30.00
23757 *The Cow Trail To Mexico* . . . . 25.00 - 40.00
23834 *The Dying Cowboy* . . . . 25.00 - 40.00
V40022 *Zebra Dun* . . . . 8.00 - 12.00
V40068 *The Texas Cowboy* . . . . 10.00 - 15.00
V40118 *Two Fragments* . . . . 10.00 - 15.00
V40167 *Chisholm Trail* . . . . 10.00 - 15.00
V40178 *The Cowboy's Dream* . . . . 15.00 - 20.00
V40263 *Punchin' The Dough* . . . . 15.00 - 20.00

ALLEY, SHELLEY LEE & HIS ALLEY CATS:
Globe 112 *Low Down Blues* . . . . 7.00 - 10.00
Vocalion 03891, 03939, 03975, 04145, 04201,
04276, 04371, 04451, 04600, 04670, 04728,
04793, 04879, 04986, 05053 . . . . 5.00 - 10.00

ALLISON'S SACRED HARP SINGERS:
Gennett 6499 *Sweet Canaan* . . . . 15.00 - 20.00
Gennett 6583 *Weeping Pilgrim* . . . . 15.00 - 20.00

ANDERSON, LEROY (THE RED HEADED
BRIER HOPPER):
Champion 45024 *The Pine Tree On The Hill* . . . . 8.00 - 12.00
45045 *The Fatal Derby Day* . . . . 8.00 - 12.00
45055 *A Mother's Wayward Son* . . . . 8.00 - 12.00
45059 *Gambling On The Sabbath* . . . . 8.00 - 12.00

LES "CARROT TOP" ANDERSON:
Cormac 1107 *Queen of the Saddle* . . . . 8.00 - 12.00
1108 *He's Just A Hobo* . . . . 8.00 - 12.00
Decca 46250, 26259, 46303, 46326, 46352 . . . . . 4.00 - 8.00

ANGLIN BROTHERS/TWINS:
Vocalion 02963, 04078, 04579, 04692, 04774,
04896 . . . . 5.00 - 10.00

ANN, JUDY AND ZEKE WITH PETE:
Okeh 45576 *Me And My Still* . . . . 8.00 - 12.00
45578 *Mississippi Waters* . . . . 8.00 - 12.00

APPALACHIAN VAGABOND:
Vocalion 5450 *The Peddler And His Wife* .... 20.00 - 30.00

APPLEBLOSSOM, CAPTAIN:
Okeh 45373 *Time Table Blues* .... 8.00 - 12.00
     45416 *The Book Of Etiquette* .... 8.00 - 12.00

ARKANSAS BAREFOOT BOYS:
Okeh 45217 *Eighth Of January* .... 30.00 - 50.00

ARKANSAS CHARLIE:
Vocalion 5270 *Goodbye Old Paint* .... 10.00 - 15.00
     5292 *The Texas Trail* .... 10.00 - 15.00
     5298 *He Was A Travelin' Man* .... 10.00 - 15.00
     5355 *The Poor Fish* .... 10.00 - 15.00
     5367 *We All Grow In Time* .... 10.00 - 15.00
     5384 *Old Zip Coon* .... 10.00 - 15.00
     5401 *The Sheriff And The Robber* ...... 10.00 - 15.00

ARKANSAS WOODCHOPPER:
Champion 45058 *Frankie And Johnny* .... 7.00 - 10.00
     45192 *Old And Only In The Way* .... 7.00 - 10.00
Columbia 15463-D *The Dying Cowboy* .... 10.00 - 15.00
Gennett 7036 *In The Jailhouse Now* .... 15.00 - 20.00
     7065 *Home On The Range* .... 15.00 - 20.00
     7095 *Zeb Tuney's Gal* .... 15.00 - 20.00
     7126 *Take Me Back To Colorado* ...... 15.00 - 20.00
     7154 *Old And Only In The Way* .... 15.00 - 20.00
     7184 *A Hard Luck Guy* .... 20.00 - 30.00
     7264 *The Little Green Valley* .... 20.00 - 30.00
Supertone 9569 *Barney McCoy* .... 10.00 - 15.00
     9570 *In The Jailhouse Now* .... 10.00 - 15.00
     9571 *The Cowboy's Dream* .... 10.00 - 15.00
     9628 *If Brother Jack Were Here* ...... 10.00 - 15.00
     9639 *Prisoner At The Bar* .... 10.00 - 15.00
     9643 *The Little Green Valley* .... 10.00 - 15.00
     9664 *A Hard Luck Guy* .... 15.00 - 20.00
     9665 *Write Me A Song About Father* ...... 15.00 - 20.00

ARMSTRONG'S PLAYERS: (see also NICHOLSON'S PLAYERS):
Supertone 9644 *Medley* .... 5.00 - 8.00
     9661 *Sweet Bunch Of Daisies* .... 5.00 - 8.00
     9733 *Muskakatuck Waltz* .... 7.00 - 10.00

ARMSTRONG & ASHLEY:
Paramount 3291 *No More Dying* .... 35.00 - 50.00

ARMSTRONG & JACOBS:
Supertone 9661 *Let Me Call You Sweetheart* .... 5.00 - 10.00

ARNOLD, GENE:
Victor 23785, 23777, 23780, 23803, 23818,
     23827, 23839 .... 5.00 - 10.00

ARTHUR & REXROAT:
Vocalion 5323 *I Tickled Her Under The Chin* ... 20.00 - 30.00
     5335 *The White Rose* .... 20.00 - 30.00

CHARLINE ARTHUR:
Bullet 707 *I've Got The Boogie Blues* .... 5.00 - 8.00

EMRY ARTHUR (& HENRY ARTHUR & THE CUMBERLAND SINGERS/ & DELLA HATFIELD):
Paramount 3221 *The Broken Wedding* .... 35.00 - 50.00
     3222 *The Bluefield Murder* .... 35.00 - 50.00
     3237 *She Lied To Me* .... 35.00 - 50.00
     3243 *Blood Stained Dress* .... 35.00 - 50.00
     3249 *Jennie My Own True Love* ...... 35.00 - 50.00
     3251 *Sunshine And Shadows* .... 35.00 - 50.00
     3289 *The Married Man* .... 35.00 - 50.00
     3290 *Short Life Of Trouble* .... 35.00 - 50.00
     3295 *She Lied To Me* .... 35.00 - 50.00
     3298 *Careless Love* .... 35.00 - 50.00
     3301 *I Tickled Her Under The Chin* .... 35.00 - 50.00
Vocalion 5225 *In The Heart Of The City That
     Has No Heart* .... 30.00 - 50.00
     5228 *Where Gates Swing Outward Never* ..... 30.00 - 50.00
     5229 *Let That Liar Alone* .... 30.00 - 50.00
     5230 *Nobody's Business* .... 30.00 - 50.00
     5234 *Wandering Gypsy Girl* .... 30.00 - 50.00
     5249 *The Rich Man And Joseph Smith.* ...... 30.00 - 50.00

     5264 *Train Whistle Blues* .... 30.00 - 50.00
     5288 *My Girl-She's A Lulu* .... 30.00 - 50.00
     5340 *Frankie Baker* .... 40.00 - 60.00
     5351 *Prison Bound Blues* .... 40.00 - 60.00
     5354 *My Mother-In-Law* .... 40.00 - 60.00
     5358 *The Blind Boy* .... 40.00 - 60.00
     5385 *The Bootleggers Song* .... 40.00 - 60.00
     5396 *Remember The Old Folks Back Home* ... 40.00 - 60.00

ASHFORD QUARTET:
Brunswick 393, 402, 456 .... 5.00 - 10.00

ASHLEY'S MELODY MAKERS/MEN:
Victor 23661 *I Never Felt So Blue* .... 50.00 - 75.00
     23767 *Come Back Lottie* .... 50.00 - 75.00
     V40158 *Bath House Blues* .... 25.00 - 40.00
     V40199 *Sweetest Flower Waltz* .... 25.00 - 40.00
     V40300 *Somewhere In Arkansas* ...... 25.00 - 40.00

ASHLEY & FOSTER:
Vocalion 02554 *Greenback Dollar* .... 7.00 - 10.00
     02611 *Sideline Blues* .... 30.00 - 50.00
     02647 *Frankie Silvers* .... 30.00 - 50.00
     02666 *Faded Roses* .... 30.00 - 50.00
     02750 *One Dark And Stormy Night* ... 30.00 - 50.00
     02780 *Baby, All Night Long* .... 30.00 - 50.00
     02789 *Ain't No Use To High Hat Me* .... 30.00 - 50.00
     02900 *My North Carolina Home* ...... 30.00 - 50.00

CLARENCE ASHLEY:
Columbia 15489-D *Dark Holler Blues* .... 40.00 - 60.00
     15522-D *Little Sadie* .... 40.00 - 60.00
     15654-D *Old John Hardy* .... 50.00 - 80.00

CLYDE ASHLEY:
Superior 2558 *Down In Arkansas* .... 15.00 - 25.00
     2605 *The Ramblin' Railroad Boy* ...... 15.00 - 25.00
     2636 *The Hand Car Yodel* .... 15.00 - 25.00
     2676 *High Silk Hat And Gold Top Walking
     Cane* .... 15.00 - 25.00
     2711 *The Bootlegger's Plea* .... 15.00 - 25.00
     2723 *Leaving Town Blues* .... 15.00 - 25.00
Superior 2751 *My Alabama Home* .... 15.00 - 25.00
     2778 *Alimony Woman* .... 15.00 - 25.00
     2833 *In 1992* .... 15.00 - 25.00

THOMAS C./TOM ASHLEY:
Conqueror 8103 *The Fiddlers Contest* .... 7.00 - 10.00
Gennett 6404 *Four Night's Experience* .... 30.00 - 50.00
Romeo 5113 *Haunted Road Blues* .... 15.00 - 20.00

ASPARAGUS JOE:
Champion 15688 *Hand Me Down My Walking
     Cane* .... 7.00 - 10.00
     15709 *Asleep At The Switch* .... 7.00 - 10.00
     15752 *Boston Burglar* .... 7.00 - 10.00
     15970 *Waiting For The Railroad Train* ... 7.00 - 10.00
     16012 *Nutty Song* .... 6.00 - 10.00
     16071 *The Lightning Express* .... 10.00 - 15.00
     16118 *The Roving Gambler* .... 10.00 - 15.00

BOB ATCHER & BONNIE BLUE EYES:
Vocalion 04882, 04898, 05001, 05069 .... 3.00 - 5.00

AUGUSTA TRIO:
Champion 15729 *Down Yonder* .... 15.00 - 20.00
     15768 *Back Up And Push* .... 15.00 - 20.00
     45159 *Whistlin' Rufus* .... 10.00 - 15.00

AUSTIN AND LEE ALLEN (See ALLEN)
GENE AUTRY (& JIMMY LONG); GENE AUTRY TRIO:
Titles, issued contemporaneously on Banner,
    Conqueror, Melotone, Oriole, Perfect, Romeo:
    *Always Dreaming Of You; Atlanta Bound; Bear
    Cat Papa Blues; Birmingham Daddy; Blue
    Days; Cowboy's Yodel; The Crime I Didn't Do;
    Dallas County Jail Blues; The Death Of
    Jimmie Rodgers; Don't Take Me Back To The
    Chain Gang; Do Right Daddy Blues; Eleven
    Months In Leavenworth; A Gangster's
    Warning; He's In The Jail House Now No. 2;*

High Steppin' Mama Blues; I'll Always Be A Rambler; Jailhouse Blues; Methodist Pie; Missouri I'm Calling; My Alabama Home; My Cross-Eyed Girl; Night Time; Pistol Packin' Papa; Rheumatism Blues; T.B. Blues; That's How I Got My Start; True Blue Bill; Uncle Noah's Ark; Wild Cat Mama Blues; The Yodeling Hobo .... 10.00 - 15.00

Additional titles, issued contemporaneously on Banner, Conqueror, Melotone, Oriole, Perfect, Romeo: *After 21 Years; Alone With My Sorrows; Angel Baby; The Answer To Nobody's Darling; The Answer To Red River Valley; The Answer To 21 Years; At The Old Barn Dance; Back To Old Smokey Mountain; Beautiful Texas; The Convict's Dream; Cowboy's Heaven; Don't Waste Your Tears On Me; Dust Pan Blues; The End Of The Trail; Good Luck Old Pal; Gosh! I Miss You All The Time; Guns And Guitars; Have You Found Someone Else; A Hill Billy Wedding In June; Hold On Little Dogies; If I Could Bring Back My Buddy; I Hate To Say Goodbye To The Prairie; I'll Be Thinking Of You Little Girl; I'll Be True While You're Gone; I'll Go Riding down That Texas Trail; I'm Always Dreaming Of You; It's Roundup Time In Reno; The Last Round Up; Little Farm Home; Little Ranch House On The Circle B; Louisana Moon; Memories Of That Silver Haired Daddy Of Mine; Mexicali Rose; Mississippi Valley Blues; Moonlight And Skies; My Carolina Mountain Rose; My Old Pal Of Yesterday; My Old Saddle Pal; Nobody's Darling But Mine; Old Buckaroo Goodbye; The Old Covered Wagon; The Old Folks Back Home; Old Missouri Moon; Ole Faithful; The One Rose; Rhythm Of The Range; Ridin' The Range; Sail Along Silv'ry Moon; Seven More Days; Silver Haired Daddy Of Mine; Some Day In Wyomin'; The Stump Of The Old Pine Tree; Texas Plains; That Old Feather Bed On The Farm; That Ramshackled Shack; That's Why I'm Nobody Darling; There's A Gold Mine In The Sky; There's A Little Old Lady In Waiting; There's An Empty Cot In The Bunkhouse Tonight; Tumbling Tumbleweeds; Watching The Clouds Roll By; Way Out West In Texas; When The Golden Leaves Are Falling; When It's Springtime In The Rockies; When Jimmie Rodgers Said Goodbye; When The Tumbleweeds Come Tumbling Down Again; Why Don't You Come Back To Me; With A Song In My Heart; The Yellow Rose Of Texas; You're The Only Star* .... 5.00 - 10.00

Titles, issued contemporaneously on Clarion, Diva, Velvet Tone: *Blue Yodel No. 5; Dust Pan Blues; Hobo Yodel; Left My Gal In The Mountains* .... 15.00 - 25.00

California Blues; Cowboy Yodel; Daddy And Home; Frankie And Johnny; A Gangster's Warning; I'll Be Thinking Of You Little Girl; Lullaby Yodel; My Alabama Home; My Rough And Rowdy Ways; No One To Call Me Darling; Pictures Of My Mother; Slue Foot Lue; Stay Away From My Chicken House; That's How I Got My Start; That's Why I Left The Mountains; True Blue Bill; Waiting For A Train; Why Don't You Come Back To Me...... 20.00 - 30.00

Champion 16030 *I'll Be Thinking Of You Little Girl*................................. 30.00 - 50.00
16050 *In The Shadow Of The Pine*........... 30.00 - 50.00
16073 *Hobo Bill's Last Ride* .... 30.00 - 50.00

16096 *Hobo Yodel*........................ 30.00 - 50.00
16119 *Dust Pan Blues* .... 30.00 - 50.00
16166 *High Powered Mama* .... 30.00 - 50.00
16210 *Mean Mama Blues* .... 30.00 - 50.00
16230 *Any Old Time* .... 30.00 - 50.00
16245 *Blue Days*.......................... 30.00 - 50.00
16275 *T. B. Blues* .... 40.00 - 60.00
16328 *True Blue Bill* .... 50.00 - 75.00
16372 *Dad In The Hills* .... 50.00 - 75.00
16485 *That's How I Got My Start* .... 50.00 - 75.00
Champion 45025 *Pistol Packin' Papa*......... 15.00 - 20.00
45027 *Bear Cat Papa Blues*.............. 15.00 - 20.00
45060 *Dad In The Hills* .... 15.00 - 20.00
45071 *In The Shadow Of The Pine* .... 15.00 - 20.00
45073 *T.B. Blues* .... 15.00 - 20.00
45156 *Money Ain't No Use Anyway* ...... 8.00 - 12.00
45172 *Yodeling Hobo* .... 10.00 - 15.00
45183 *I'll Always Be A Rambler* .... 15.00 - 25.00
Columbia (red label), most issues .... 3.00 - 5.00
Decca 5426, 5464, 5488, 5501, 5517, 5527...... 5.00 - 10.00
Gennett 7243 *Cowboy Yodel* ....100.00 - 150.00
7265 *In The Shadow Of The Pine* ....100.00 - 150.00
7290 *Hobo Bill's Last Ride* ....100.00 - 150.00
7310 *Train Whistle Blues* ....150.00 - 200.00
Q.R.S. 1044 *Living In The Mountains* ....200.00 - 300.00
Superior 2561 *The Girl I Left Behind* ....150.00 - 200.00
2596 *Dad In The Hills* ....100.00 - 150.00
2637 *Pistol Packin' Papa* ....100.00 - 150.00
2660 *Mean Mama Blues* ....100.00 - 150.00
2681 *That's How I Got My Start* ......100.00 - 150.00
2710 *Blue Days* ....100.00 - 150.00
2732 *Money Ain't No Use Anyway* .....100.00 - 150.00
2769 *Hobo Bill's Last Ride* ....100.00 - 150.00
Supertone 9702 *Hobo Bill's Last Ride* .... 35.00 - 50.00
9704 *They Cut Down The Old Pine Tree* ...... 35.00 - 50.00
9705 *Whisper Your Mother's Name* .... 35.00 - 50.00
9706 *Train Whistle Blues* .... 35.00 - 50.00
Victor 23530 *Bear Cat Papa* .... 80.00 - 120.00
23548 *Do Right Daddy* .... 80.00 - 120.00
23561 *There's A Good Gal In The Mountains*.. 75.00 - 100.00
23589 *High Steppin' Mama* .... 80.00 - 120.00
23617 *She's A Low Down Mamma* .... 80.00 - 120.00
23630 *Rheumatism Blues* .... 80.00 - 120.00
23642 *Wild Cat Mama*................. 80.00 - 120.00
23673 *I'm Always Dreaming Of You* ..... 80.00 - 120.00
23707 *Black Bottom Blues* .... 80.00 - 120.00
23720 *Kentucky Lullaby* .... 80.00 - 120.00
23725 *The Gangster's Warning* .... 80.00 - 120.00
23726 *Back To Old Smoky Mountain* .... 80.00 - 120.00
23783 *Cowboy's Heaven* ....100.00 - 150.00
23792 *Louisiana Moon* ....100.00 - 150.00
23810 *Your Voice Is Calling* ....100.00 - 150.00
V40200 *My Alabama Home* .... 80.00 - 120.00
Vocalion 02991, 03007, 03070, 03097, 03101, 03138, 03229, 03262, 03291, 03317, 03358, 03448 .... 7.00 - 10.00
04091, 04146, 04172, 04246, 04262, 04267, 04274, 04340, 04375, 04415 .... 5.00 - 10.00

HARVEY AYERS (See GROVER RANN)
GREEN BAILEY:
Gennett 6702 *The Santa Barbara Earthquake* ... 25.00 - 40.00
6732 *If I Die A Railroad Man* .... 25.00 - 40.00
MR. & MRS. BAKER:
Victor 20863 *The Newmarket Wreck*........... 15.00 - 20.00
BUDDY BAKER:
Victor 21549 *Box Car Blues* .... 10.00 - 15.00
V-40017 *Matrimonial Intentions* .... 15.00 - 20.00
CHARLES BAKER (THE WYOMING COWBOY):
Champion 16614 *Just Plain Folks* .... 20.00 - 30.00
45044, 45052 .... 7.00 - 10.00
ELDON BAKER'S BROWN COUNTY

REVELERS:
Vocalion 04217 *Lost John*	7.00	-	10.00
04279 *I Will Meet You*	7.00	-	10.00
04355 *Happy Cowboy*	5.00	-	8.00
04441 *Dear Old Dixieland*	5.00	-	8.00

LUKE BALDWIN:
Champion 15792 *Hungry Hash House Blues*	10.00	-	15.00
15811 *Daddy And Home*	10.00	-	15.00
15853 *California Blues*	10.00	-	15.00
15877 *Alabama Blues*	10.00	-	15.00
15945 *I Love The Jailer's Daughter*	10.00	-	15.00
16009 *The Yodeling Cowboy*	15.00	-	20.00
16075 *The Handcar Yodel*	15.00	-	20.00
16142 *It Won't Happen Again*	15.00	-	20.00
16162 *Don't Ever Marry A Widow*	15.00	-	20.00
16186 *The Bootlegger's Plea*	15.00	-	20.00
16232 *The Ramblin' Railroad Boy*	15.00	-	20.00
16254 *When The Roses Bloom In Dixie*	15.00	-	20.00
16313 *Leaving Town Blues*	15.00	-	25.00
16317 *Alimony Woman*	15.00	-	25.00
16343 *Travelin' Blues*	15.00	-	25.00
16443 *In 1992*	15.00	-	25.00

BENTLEY BALL:
Columbia A-3084 *The Gallows Tree*	—		—

WOLFE BALLARD (& CLAUDE SAMUELS):
Broadway; Paramount	4.00	-	8.00
Herwin 75545 *I Want A Pardon For Daddy*	15.00	-	20.00

JOHN BALTZELL ("CHAMPION OLD TIME FIDDLER"):
Banner 2151 *Turkey in the Straw*	7.00	-	10.00
2159 *Sailor's Hornpipe*	7.00	-	10.00
Conqueror 7741 *The Girl I Left Behind*	5.00	-	8.00
Edison 51236, 51354, 51548, 51995, 52022	7.00	-	10.00
52281 *Emmett Quadrille*	10.00	-	15.00
52294 *Arkansas Traveler*	10.00	-	15.00
52313 *Flowers Of Edinburgh Hornpipe*	10.00	-	15.00
52370 *Soldier's Joy Hornpipe*	10.00	-	15.00
52395 *My Highland Fling*	10.00	-	15.00
52425 *Starlight Waltz*	15.00	-	20.00
52450 *S.J. Rafferty Reel*	15.00	-	20.00
Paramount 3015 *Turkey In The Straw*	7.00	-	10.00
3017 *Sailor's Hornpipe*	7.00	-	10.00

BANG BOYS:
Vocalion 03372 *When Lulu's Gone*	25.00	-	40.00

BANJO JOE:
Columbia 15238-D *Engineer Joe*	20.00	-	30.00

(See also: WILLARD HODGIN)

EMMETT BANKSTON & RED HENDERSON:
Okeh 45292 *Six Nights Drunk*	25.00	-	40.00

GLEN BARBER:
Hallmark 1110 *Styles And Ways Of The World*	5.00	-	8.00*
Stampede 104 *Ring Around The Moon*	5.00	-	8.00*

JOHNNY BARFIELD (& HOYT BRYANT, ACC. BY BERT LAYNE & HIS GEORGIA SERENADERS):
Bluebird	3.00	-	5.00
Bullet 620 *Doin' The Boogie Woogie*	5.00	-	8.00
Champion 16406 *Back To My Georgia Home*	50.00	-	75.00
16415 *Highway Hobo*	50.00	-	75.00

JERRY BARLOW:
Lyric 703 *Just Thinking Of You*	4.00	-	6.00
O.T. 103 *Louisiana Baby*	4.00	-	7.00

(YODELING) FRANKIE BARNES:
Champion 16366 *Hokey Pokey*	7.00	-	10.00
Superior 2746 *Nervy Bum*	15.00	-	20.00

H.M. BARNES & HIS BLUE RIDGE RAMBLERS:
Brunswick 310 *Who Broke The Lock On The Hen House Door?*	7.00	-	10.00
313 *Old Joe Clark*	7.00	-	10.00
327 *Goin' Down The Road Feelin' Bad*	10.00	-	15.00
361 *Our Director March*	8.00	-	12.00

397 *Mandolin Rag*	15.00	-	20.00
463 *Honolulu Stomp*	15.00	-	20.00

THE BARNSTORMERS:
Silverton 5401 *Party Quadrille*	7.00	-	10.00

BARNYARD STEVE:
Okeh 45366 *Out On The Farm*	7.00	-	10.00

BARTLETT'S BOOSTERS:
Paramount 3245 *The Bumble Bee*	10.00	-	15.00

JOHN BARTON:
Broadway 8051, 8052	5.00	-	8.00

KENNETH BARTON: (See BORTON)

DR. HUMPHREY BATE & HIS POSSUM HUNTERS:
Brunswick 232 *Goin' Up Town*	35.00	-	50.00
239 *Billy In The Low Ground*	35.00	-	50.00
243 *Bill Pickle Rag*	35.00	-	50.00
271 *Old Joe*	35.00	-	50.00
275 *Greenback Dollar Bill*	35.00	-	50.00
Vocalion 5238 *Ham Beats All Meat*	40.00	-	60.00

RAY BATTS:
Bullet 754 *Bear Cat Daddy*	10.00	-	15.00

BAXTER FAMILY TRIO:
Superior 2557 *I Am Coming Home*	15.00	-	20.00

JOHNNY BAXTER:
Superior 2811 *I Want My Rib*	20.00	-	30.00

MUMFORD BEAN & HIS ITAWAMBIANS:
Okeh 45303 *Flow Rain Waltz*	50.00	-	75.00

JOHNNIE BEE:
Talent 744 *Hang-Over Blues*	7.00	-	10.00

JERRY BEHRENS:
Okeh 45535 *Drifting Along*	15.00	-	25.00
45564 *Nobody's Business*	15.00	-	25.00

DICK BELL:
Challenge 425 *Shut Up In Coal Creek Mine*	5.00	-	8.00

BENTLEY BOYS:
Columbia 15565-D *Henhouse Blues*	30.00	-	50.00

BEVERLY HILL BILLIES: (See also GLEN RICE)
Brunswick 421 *Red River Valley*	5.00	-	8.00
441 *My Pretty Quadroon*	5.00	-	8.00
455 *Mellow Mountain Moon*	5.00	-	8.00
462 *Peek A Boo*	5.00	-	8.00
506 *Wonder Valley*	5.00	-	8.00
514 *Strawberry Roan*	5.00	-	8.00
519 *Prairie Skies*	5.00	-	8.00

BIG JEFF & THE RADIO PLAYBOYS:
Dot 1004 *Juke Box Boogie*	10.00	-	15.00
1058 *Step It Up And Go*	10.00	-	15.00
1064 *Fast Women, Slow Horses And Wine*	8.00	-	12.00
1088 *Move On Baby*	8.00	-	12.00
World Records 1520 *Poppin' Bubble Gum*	5.00	-	8.00*

BUD & JOE BILLINGS; BUD BILLINGS TRIO:
Victor 23500, 23534, 23539, 23556, 23706, 23709, 23715	7.00	-	15.00
23725 *I Wonder If He's Singing*	80.00	-	120.00
23740, 23744, 23784	10.00	-	15.00
V40082, V40267, V40299, V40322	5.00	-	10.00

DOUG BINE & HIS DIXIE RAMBLERS:
Bluebird 6677, 6705, 6789, 6847, 8133	4.00	-	8.00

BINKLEY BROTHERS' DIXIE CLODHOPPERS:
Victor 21758 *All Go Hungry Hash House*	30.00	-	50.00
V40048 *Give Me Back My Fifteen Cents*	35.00	-	50.00
V40129 *When I Had But Fifty Cents*	35.00	-	50.00

BIRD'S KENTUCKY CORN CRACKERS:
Victor 23608 *Ship That's Sailing High*	75.00	-	100.00

CONNIE BIRD:
Gennett 6929 *Little Mamie*	30.00	-	50.00

ELMER BIRD'S HAPPY FOUR/STRING BAND:
Champion 16421 *Kentucky Stomp*	75.00	-	100.00
45168 *Kentucky Stomp*	30.00	-	50.00
Gennett 7064 *Kentucky Stomp*	75.00	-	100.00

7182 *Muscle Shoals Blues* .... 75.00 - 100.00
Superior 2598 *Sleepy Creek* .... 75.00 - 100.00

LOUIS BIRD:
Vocalion 5428 *It's Funny What Whiskey Will Do* . 15.00 - 25.00

NAT BIRD & TOM COLLINS:
Brunswick 376 *Hornpipe Medley* .... 10.00 - 15.00

L.O. BIRKHEAD & R.M. LANE:
Columbia 15757-D *Robinson County* .... 75.00 - 100.00

JASPER BISBEE:
Edison 51381, 51382 .... 5.00 - 10.00

BILLY BISHOP:
Champion 15331 *Medley Of Old Favorites* ...... 4.00 - 7.00
Gennett 6203 *Medley Of Old Favorites* .... 5.00 - 8.00
Supertone 9171 *Medley Of Old Favorites* ...... 4.00 - 7.00

LESTER PETE BIVINS:
Bluebird 6886, 6950 .... 5.00 - 8.00

BLACK BROTHERS:
Okeh 45244, 45253, 45270, 45296, 45312,
45336, 45345, 45374, 445487, 45493, 45572 .. 5.00 - 10.00

JIMMY BLACK:
Okeh 45275, 45298 .... 5.00 - 10.00

DAD BLACKARD'S MOONSHINERS:
Victor 21130 *Sandy River Belle* .... 30.00 - 50.00

CHARLEY BLAKE:
Supertone 9476 *Daddy And Home* .... 10.00 - 15.00
9489 *Back Home In Tennessee* .... 10.00 - 15.00
9534 *California Blues* .... 10.00 - 15.00
9540 *Go 'Long Mule No. 2* .... 10.00 - 15.00
9556 *She'll Be Coming 'Round The Mountain* . 10.00 - 15.00
9559 *Jackson County* .... 10.00 - 15.00
9600 *Alabama Blues* .... 10.00 - 15.00
9641 *I Love The Jailer's Daughter* .... 10.00 - 15.00
9714 *My Old Log Cabin Home* .... 10.00 - 15.00
9722 *The Yodeling Cowboy* .... 10.00 - 15.00
9724 *My Rough And Rowdy Ways* .... 10.00 - 15.00

CURLEY BLAKE (See CHARLEY BLAKE):

**GUY BLAKEMAN & HIS BLUE GRASS
   SERENADERS:**
Chess 1525 *I Ain't Gonna Give Nobody None Of
My Jelly Roll* .... 7.00 - 10.00*

BLALOCK & YATES:
Columbia 15576-D *Pride Of The Ball* .... 25.00 - 40.00

DAN BLANCHARD:
Champion 15526 *The West Plains Explosion* .... 7.00 - 10.00
15578 *Just A Little West Of West Virginia* ..... 7.00 - 10.00

BLANKENSHIP FAMILY:
Victor 23583 *Jack And Mae* .... 30.00 - 50.00

FRANK BLEVINS' TAR HEEL RATTLERS:
Columbia 15210-D *Old Aunt Betsy* .... 100.00 - 150.00
15280-D *Nine Pound Hammer* .... 100.00 - 150.00
15765-D *I've Got No Honey Babe Now* ..... 150.00 - 250.00
Velvet Tone 7101-V *Old Aunt Betsy* .... 100.00 - 150.00
7103-V *Fly Around My Pretty Little Miss* .... 100.00 - 150.00

RUBYE BLEVINS:
Bluebird 5404, 5973 .... 5.00 - 10.00

BLIND ANDY: (See also ANDREW JENKINS)
Okeh 40393 *Floyd Collins In The Sand Cave* .... 5.00 - 8.00
45007 *The Little Newsboy* .... 5.00 - 8.00
45043 *Charming Billy* .... 5.00 - 8.00
45197 *Little Marian Parker* .... 5.00 - 8.00
45319 *The Alabama Flood* .... 7.00 - 10.00
45343 *Tragedy On Daytona Beach* .... 8.00 - 12.00
45347 *Ramblin' Yodel Sam* .... 8.00 - 12.00
45454 *Stop And Look For The Train* .... 10.00 - 15.00

BLUE BOYS:
Okeh 45314 *Memphis Stomp* .... 75.00 - 100.00

BLUE MOON MELODY BOYS:
Champion 15542 *My Blue Ridge Mountain Home* 7.00 - 10.00

BLUE RIDGE CORNSHUCKERS:
Victor 20835 *Old Time Corn Shuckin'* .... 15.00 - 20.00

**BLUE RIDGE DUO (GENE AUSTIN &
   GEORGE RENEAU):**

Edison 51422 *Little Brown Jug* .... 7.00 - 10.00
51498 *Life's Railway To Heaven* .... 7.00 - 10.00
51502 *Turkey In The Straw* .... 7.00 - 10.00
51515 *Blue Ridge Blues* .... 7.00 - 10.00

**BLUE RIDGE HIGHBALLERS (Led by
 Charley La Prade, Fiddler):**
Columbia 15070-D *Under The Double Eagle* .... 15.00 - 25.00
15081-D *Fourteen Days In Georgia* .... 15.00 - 25.00
15089-D *Round Town Girls* .... 15.00 - 25.00
15096-D *Going Down To Lynchburg Town* .... 15.00 - 25.00
15132-D *Darned* .... 15.00 - 25.00
15168-D *Soldier's Joy* .... 15.00 - 25.00
Paramount 3077 *I'm Tired Of Living Here Alone* . 15.00 - 25.00
3083 *Red Wing* .... 15.00 - 25.00

BLUE RIDGE HILLBILLIES:
Bluebird 6541, 6609, 6786, 7070 .... 5.00 - 8.00

BLUE RIDGE MOUNTAINEER:
Edison 51832 *The Sinking Of The Titanic* ...... 15.00 - 20.00

BLUE RIDGE MOUNTAINEERS:
Gennett 6870 *Old Flannigan* .... 25.00 - 40.00

BLUE RIDGE MOUNTAIN ENTERTAINERS:
Conqueror 7942 *Goodnight Waltz* .... 7.00 - 10.00

BLUE RIDGE MOUNTAIN GIRLS:
Champion 16701 *The First Whippoorwill Song* .. 30.00 - 50.00
16715 *Woman's Answer To 21 Years* .... 30.00 - 50.00
16743 *She Came Rolling Down The Mountain* . 30.00 - 50.00
16752 *New Answer To 21 Years* .... 30.00 - 50.00
16763 *My Heart Is Where The Mohawk Flows* . 30.00 - 50.00
16778 *When It's Prayer Meetin' Time In The
   Hollow* .... 30.00 - 50.00
16795 *Memories of That Silver Haired Daddy* . 30.00 - 50.00
Champion 45077, 45083, 45090, 45100, 45198 ... 7.00 - 10.00

BLUE RIDGE MOUNTAIN SINGERS:
Columbia 15550-D *Lorena* .... 20.00 - 30.00
15580-D *Give My Love To Nell* .... 20.00 - 30.00
15647-D *The Engineer's Last Run* .... 20.00 - 30.00
15678-D *Mansion Of Aching Hearts* .... 20.00 - 30.00

BLUE RIDGE PLAYBOYS:
Vocalion 03425, 03526, 03558, 03765 .... 5.00 - 10.00

BLUE SKY BOYS TRIO:
Bluebird 6480, 6538, 6567, 6621, 6669, 6714,
6764, 6808, 6854, 6901, 7113, 7132, 7173, 7311,
7348, 7411, 7472, 7550, 7661, 7755, 7803, 7878,
7933, 7984 .... 5.00 - 10.00
Bluebird (higher numbers) .... 4.00 - 8.00
Montgomery Ward .... 4.00 - 8.00

BUD BLUE:
Okeh 45254 *A Blind Mother's Prayer* .... 7.00 - 10.00

BOA'S PINE CABIN BOYS:
Vocalion 02594 *Hurry, Johnny, Hurry* .... 15.00 - 20.00

BOB & MONTE:
Vocalion 5279 *The Utah Trail* .... 4.00 - 6.00
5343 *Old Virginia Lullaby* .... 5.00 - 8.00
5373 *Back To Hawaii And You* .... 5.00 - 8.00
5387 *From The Heart Of The West* .... 5.00 - 8.00

(LOY) BODINE (& HOWARD KEESEE):
Champion 16305 *I Still Got Ninety-Nine* .... 50.00 - 75.00
16391 *Where The Old Red River Flows* .... 50.00 - 75.00
Superior 2608 *Wabash Cannon Ball* .... 50.00 - 75.00
2809 *A Gangster's Warning* .... 50.00 - 75.00

"DOCK" BOGGS:
Brunswick 118 *Down South Blues* .... 35.00 - 50.00
131 *Country Blues* .... 35.00 - 50.00
132 *Danville Girl* .... 35.00 - 50.00
133 *Hard Luck Blues* .... 35.00 - 50.00
Vocalion 5144 *Hard Luck Blues* .... 40.00 - 60.00

CAP. M.J. BONNER (THE TEXAS FIDDLER):
Victor 19699 *Medley—Yearling's In The
   Canebreak etc.* .... 10.00 - 20.00

BOONE COUNTY ENTERTAINERS:
Supertone 9163 *Arkansas Traveler* .... 5.00 - 8.00

9177 *Fiddlin' Bootleggers*	10.00 -	15.00
9181 *The Blind Man And His Child*	7.00 -	10.00
9182 *Something Wrong With My Gal*	7.00 -	10.00
9492 *Virginia Bootleggers*	7.00 -	10.00

CLAUDE BOONE (& WALTER HURDT):

Bluebird 7817 *The Poor Widow*	5.00 -	8.00
7008 *The Hobo Blues*	5.00 -	8.00

REV. EDWARD (& MRS.) BOONE (& MISS OLIVE BOONE):

Gennett 6903 *Will David Play His Harp*	20.00 -	30.00
7208 *Springing Up Within My Soul*	25.00 -	40.00
7225 *Flowers On The Open Grave*	25.00 -	40.00
7248 *Salvatin Is For All*	25.00 -	40.00
7321 *A Mansion There For Me*	35.00 -	50.00

JIMMY BOONE:

Superior 2638 *The Brakeman's Reply*	20.00 -	30.00
2661 *Crazy Blues*	20.00 -	30.00
2698 *Box Car Blues*	20.00 -	30.00
2742 *The Fatal Run*	20.00 -	30.00
2775 *Hobo Jack's Last Ride*	20.00 -	30.00
2831 *The Cowboy Song*	20.00 -	30.00

BOOTS & HIS BUDDIES:

Talent 709 *Poor Little Joe*	7.00 -	10.00

BENNY BORG (THE SINGING SOLDIER):

Columbia 15148-D *I Want A Pardon For Daddy*	5.00 -	8.00
15183-D *Pictures From Life's Other Side*	5.00 -	8.00

GODFREY BORTON:

Bell 1186 *Don't Forget Me, Little Darling*	5.00 -	8.00
1187 *Two Little Orphans*	5.00 -	8.00

KENNETH BORTON:

Challenge 331 *That's What The Old Bachelor's Made Of*	5.00 -	8.00

LEO BOSWELL (& DEWEY BOSWELL):

Columbia 15290-D *The Fatal Rose Of Red*	7.00 -	10.00
15469-D *Memory That Time Cannot Erase*	8.00 -	12.00

(MR. & MRS.) CHRIS BOUCHILLON:

Columbia 15120-D *Talking Blues*	8.00 -	12.00
15151-D *Born In Hard Luck*	8.00 -	12.00
15178-D *Let It Alone*	10.00 -	15.00
15213-D *Christ Visits The Barber Shop*	10.00 -	15.00
15244-D *You Look Awful Good To Me*	10.00 -	15.00
15262-D *New Talking Blues*	10.00 -	15.00
15289-D *I've Been Married Three Times*	10.00 -	15.00
15317-D *Oyster Stew*	15.00 -	20.00
15345-D *Adam And Eve*	15.00 -	20.00
15373-D *Speed Maniac*	15.00 -	20.00
15508-D *Girls Of Today*	15.00 -	20.00

BOWERS & LEWIS:

Superior 2659 *Put On Your Old Gray Bonnet*	15.00 -	25.00

EARL BOWERS:

Superior 2526 *I Tickled Her Under The Chin*	15.00 -	25.00
2607 *The Contented Hobo*	15.00 -	25.00

BOWMAN SISTERS:

Columbia 15473-D *My Old Kentucky Home*	7.00 -	10.00
15621-D *Old Lonesome Blues*	15.00 -	20.00

CHARLIE BOWMAN & HIS BROTHERS:

Columbia 15357-D *Gonna Raise The Ruckus Tonight*	20.00 -	30.00
15387-D *The Moonshiner And His Money*	20.00 -	30.00
Vocalion 5118 *Hickman Rag*	30.00 -	50.00
15377 *Hickman Rag*	30.00 -	50.00

DONNIE BOWSHIER:

King 1219 *We'll Never Part*	— -	—

AARON BOYD:

Champion 15652 *The Santa Barbara Earthquake*	12.00 -	18.00

BILL BOYD & HIS COWBOY RAMBLERS:

Bluebird 5608, 5667, 5740, 5788, 5945, 6109,
6119, 6161, 6177, 6235, 6308, 6323, 6328, 6346,
6351, 6384, 6420, 6486, 6492, 6523, 6599,
6670, 6694, 6715, 6731, 6772, 6807, 6889,
6959, 7004, 7006, 7053, 7088, 7128, 7189,
7260, 7299, 7345, 7437, 7507, 7521, 7531, 7573,

7624, 7662, 7691, 7739, 7754, 7788, 7880, 7867, 7910, 7921, 7940, 7971, 7989, 8081	4.00 -	7.00

JOHN BOYD AND HIS SOUTHERNERS:

Vocalion 03661 *Doin' The Raccoon*	5.00 -	8.00

BOYS FROM WILDCAT HOLLOW:

Champion 15633 *The Fiddlin' Bootleggers*	10.00 -	15.00
45010 *The Fiddlin' Bootleggers*	5.00 -	8.00

VIRGEL BOZMAN & CIRCLE C BOYS:

O.T. 112 *Troubles, Troubles*	4.00 -	7.00

BRANCH & COLEMAN:

Okeh 45556 *My Free Wheelin' Baby*	20.00 -	30.00
45561 *Telegraph Shack*	20.00 -	30.00
45568 *Since My Darling Went Away*	20.00 -	30.00

ERNEST BRANCH:

Champion 16286 *Lulu Love*	20.00 -	30.00

HOMER BRIARHOPPER:

Bluebird 6903 *If You Ever Had The Blues*	10.00 -	15.00

BRIER HOPPER (BROTHERS); (See also RED HEADED BRIER HOPPER):

Champion 16648 *Answer To Ninety-Nine Years*	30.00 -	50.00
16692 *Bring Back My Blue-Eyed Boy*	30.00 -	50.00
16708 *Lorena*	50.00 -	75.00
Champion 45032, 45066	8.00 -	12.00

BILLY BRIGGS:

Imperial 8102, 8104, 8111	5.00 -	10.00

BRITT BROTHERS; BRITT & FORD; ELTON BRITT:

Titles, issued contemporaneously on Banner,
Melotone, Oriole, Perfect, Romeo: *Alpine
Milkman Yodel; Answer To 99 Years; Chime
Bells, Dear Old Daddy; Good Night, Little
Girl Of My Dreams; In The Hills Of
Pennsylvania; I Was Born In The Mountains;
My Mother's Tears; Old Fashioned Dipper;
There's A Home In Wyomin'; When It's Harvest
Time In Old New England; When You Played
The Old Church Organ; The Wrong Man And

The Wrong Woman	5.00 -	10.00

MAYNARD BRITTON:

Champion 16543 *The Drunkard's Hell*	50.00 -	75.00
45051 *The Drunkard's Hell*	15.00 -	20.00
Superior 2563 *I Don't Want No Woman*	50.00 -	75.00
2524 *Always Blue, Lonesome Too*	50.00 -	75.00

BROCK SISTERS:

Paramount 3163 *Bring Me Back My Darling*	20.00 -	30.00

BROCK & DUDLEY:

Columbia 15645-D *I'll Remember You Love*	15.00 -	20.00

BILLY BROOKS:

Columbia 15614-D *Freight Train Blues*	20.00 -	30.00

BOB BROOKS:

Columbia 15676-D *Wandering Lamb*	8.00 -	12.00
15689-D *Red River Valley*	8.00 -	12.00

CHARLIE (C.S.) BROOKS (& CHARLIE TURNER):

Columbia 15733-D *My Mammy's Cabin*	15.00 -	20.00
15756-D *Will You Love Me When I'm Old*	15.00 -	20.00

(RICHARD) BROOKS (& REUBEN PUCKETT):

Brunswick 273 *Long Gone*	10.00 -	15.00
281 *She's More To Be Pitied Than Censured*	10.00 -	15.00
301 *The Longest Way Home*	10.00 -	15.00
317 *All In, Down And Out*	10.00 -	15.00
Victor 20541 *Something's Going To Happen*	10.00 -	15.00
20542 *Hello Central, Give Me Heaven*	10.00 -	15.00

BROWN'S MUSICAL BROWNIES (See MILTON BROWN):

BROWN'S HAPPY FOUR:

Champion 16549 *Bootlegger's Dream*	25.00 -	40.00

BROWN & BUNCH:

Supertone 9375 *Let Her Go, I'll Meet Her*	8.00 -	12.00
9443 *My Carolina Home*	8.00 -	12.00

BROWN, GRAY & DILLY:

Vocalion 5432 *A Fiddlers Tryout In Georgia* .... 75.00 - 100.00

HERSAL/HERSHAL/HERSCHEL BROWN &
HIS BOYS/HAPPY FIVE/WASHBOARD
BAND; HERSCHEL BROWN & L.K.
SENTELL:
Okeh 45247 *New Talking Blues*.............. 25.00 - 40.00
   45250 *Home Brew Party* .... 35.00 - 50.00
   45286 *I Wish That Gal Was Mine* .... 35.00 - 50.00
   45337 *New Talking Blues No. 2* .... 35.00 - 50.00
   45354 *Alabama Breakdown* .... 50.00 - 75.00
   45484 *Spanish Rag* .... 50.00 - 75.00
   45494 *County Fair* .... 50.00 - 75.00
Victor 21403 *Down Yonder* .... 20.00 - 30.00
   V-40070 *Shanghai Rag* .... 50.00 - 75.00

JIMMY BROWN:
Champion 16812 *Keep A Light In Your Window*
   Tonight .... 30.00 - 50.00
   45074 *Keep A Light In Your Window Tonight* .... 8.00 - 12.00

(MILTON) BROWN'S (MUSICAL) BROWNIES:
Bluebird 5444 *Oh You Pretty Woman* .... 7.00 - 10.00
(Note: Some copies issued as by FORT
   WORTH BOYS)
Bluebird 5484, 5558, 5610, 5654, 5690, 5715,
   5775, 5808 .... 5.00 - 8.00

OSCAR BROWN:
Champion 15523 *You're A Little Too Small* ..... 10.00 - 15.00

THOMAS BROWN:
Brunswick 593 *On The Plains Of Texas* .... 7.00 - 10.00

BILL BRUNER:
Okeh 45400 *My Pal Of Yesterday* .... 15.00 - 25.00
   45438 *He's In The Jailhouse Now* .... 20.00 - 30.00
   45463 *A Gal Like You* .... 25.00 - 40.00
   45497 *My Old Home Town Girl* .... 25.00 - 40.00

(HOYT) "SLIM" BRYANT (& HIS
RIVERSIDERS):
Champion 16407 *Peach Picking Time In Georgia* 50.00 - 75.00
Crown 3384 *Wreck Of The Old 97* .... 15.00 - 20.00
Superior 2812 *The Rabbit Hunt* .... 50.00 - 75.00

BUCKEYE BOYS:
Champion 16168 *Duck Foot Sue* .... 7.00 - 10.00
   45160, 45200 .... 3.00 - 6.00
Superior 2616 *That Old Fashioned Phonograph* .. 15.00 - 20.00

BUCK MOUNTAIN BAND:
Okeh 45428 *Don't Let The Blues Get You Down* . 50.00 - 75.00

ALVIN BUNCH:
Supertone 9180 *Only A Miner Killed In The*
   Ground .... 8.00 - 12.00

CARL BUNCH:
Bell 1186 *True And Trembling Brakeman* .... 8.00 - 12.00

SAM BUNCH:
Supertone 9372 *My Sarah Jane*.............. 7.00 - 10.00

JACK & JIM BURBANK:
Superior 2741 *Try Not To Forget* .... 15.00 - 20.00
   2761 *On The Banks Of The Brandywine* ..... 15.00 - 20.00
   2825 *Oh Mary Don't You Weep* .... 15.00 - 20.00

JACK BURDETTE & BERT MOSS:
Superior 2696 *That Old Tiger Rag* .... 50.00 - 75.00

BURKE BROTHERS:
Victor V40294 *Lonesome And Lonely* .... 15.00 - 20.00

(FIDDLIN') JIM BURKE (& JESSE COAT):
Champion 15396 *Cripple Creek* .... 5.00 - 8.00
   15449 *Waynesburgh* .... 7.00 - 10.00
   15500 *Billy In The Low Ground* .... 7.00 - 10.00
   15564 *Smoky Row* .... 8.00 - 12.00
   15603 *Brick Yard Joe* .... 8.00 - 12.00
   15668 *Shoot That Turkey Buzzard* .... 8.00 - 12.00
   15690 *Knoxville Rag*................. 10.00 - 15.00
   15749 *Jack's Creek Waltz* .... 8.00 - 12.00
   15788 *The Devil In Georgia* .... 7.00 - 10.00
   15783 *Johnny Inchin' Along* .... 7.00 - 10.00
   15921 *Sally Gooden* .... 7.00 - 10.00
   16027 *Rye Straw* .... 10.00 - 15.00

   16208 *The Drunken Man's Dream*........... 10.00 - 15.00
Silvertone 8179 *And The Cat Came Back* ...... 6.00 - 10.00
   8185 *Arkansas Traveler* .... 6.00 - 10.00
Supertone 9164 *Buck Creek Gal* .... 6.00 - 10.00
   9165 *And The Cat Came Back* .... 6.00 - 10.00
   9168 *Cripple Creek* .... 6.00 - 10.00
   9169 *Dance With The Girl With The Hole* .... 6.00 - 10.00
   9172 *Arkansas Traveler* .... 6.00 - 10.00
   9173 *Brick Yard Joe* .... 6.00 - 10.00
   9176 *Billy In The Low Ground* .... 6.00 - 10.00
   9260 *Knoxville Girl* .... 8.00 - 12.00
   9311 *Run Smoke Run* .... 7.00 - 10.00
   9355 *New Money* .... 7.00 - 10.00
   9390 *The Devil In Georgia* .... 7.00 - 10.00
   9650 *Chicken Reel* .... 7.00 - 10.00

PETE BURKE TRIO:
Humming Bird 1007 *Super Boogie Woogie* ...... — - —

ABNER BURKHARDT:
Champion 15261, 15279, 15356, 15669 .... 5.00 - 8.00

BURNETT BROTHERS:
Victor 23727 *Old Shoes A-Draggin'* .... 15.00 - 20.00
   23730 *Countin' Cross Ties* .... 15.00 - 20.00
   23745 *Rockin' Chair* .... 15.00 - 20.00

BURNETTE & MILLER:
Superior 2764 *Twenty-One Years* .... 15.00 - 20.00

BURNETT & RUTHERFORD:
Columbia 15113-D *Pearl Bryan* .... 10.00 - 15.00
   15122-D *Lost John* .... 8.00 - 12.00
   15133-D *A Short Life Of Trouble* .... 8.00 - 12.00
   15187-D *My Sweetheart In Tennessee* ...... 8.00 - 12.00
   15209-D *Ladies On A Steamboat* .... 8.00 - 12.00
   15204-D *Curley Headed Woman* .... 12.00 - 15.00
   15314-D *All Night Long Blues* .... 15.00 - 20.00

BURNETTE & RUTTLEDGE:
Columbia 15567-D *Blackberry Blossoms* ...... 10.00 - 15.00

SMILIE BURNETTE:
Titles issued contemporaneously on Banner,
   Melotone, Oriole, Perfect, Romeo, include: *He*
   Was A Traveling Man; Mama Don't Like
   Music; Matilda Higgins; Peg Leg Jack .... 8.00 - 12.00

DAPHNE BURNS:
Paramount 3032 *Weeping Willow Tree* .... 10.00 - 15.00

RUBEN BURNS:
Champion 15376 *The Burglar Man* .... 10.00 - 15.00
Gennett 6222 *The Burglar Man* .... 15.00 - 20.00

(JOHN) BURTON (& BODINE):
Superior 2522 *I Don't Want You Mama* .... 50.00 - 75.00
   2573 *Memphis Special Blues* .... 50.00 - 75.00
   2618 *Little Old Home Down In New Orleans* .. 50.00 - 75.00
   2672 *Treasure Untold* .... 50.00 - 75.00
   2810 *Pal Of My Sunny Days* .... 50.00 - 75.00
   2823 *The Longest Train I Ever Saw* .... 75.00 - 100.00

RUSSELL & LOUIS BURTON:
Champion 16454 *Down In Tennessee* .... 35.00 - 50.00
Superior 2703 *The Old Corn Mill*............. 50.00 - 75.00

BUSTER & JACK:
Montgomery Ward 4084 *Guitar Duet Blues* ..... 15.00 - 20.00
Victor 23257 *Guitar Duet Blues* .... 75.00 - 100.00

DWIGHT BUTCHER:
Champion 45187 *Broken Hearted Cowboy* ...... 5.00 - 8.00
Victor 23772 *Lonesome Cowboy* .... 20.00 - 30.00
   23794 *By A Little Bayou* .... 20.00 - 30.00
   23802 *Alarm Clock Blues* .... 25.00 - 40.00
   23810 *Your Voice Is Calling* .... 100.00 - 150.00
   23819 *Pistol Pete* .... 25.00 - 35.00
   23826 *My Rambling Days Are Over* .... 25.00 - 35.00

ALBERT CAIN:
Okeh 45557 *Pickin' On The Old Guitar* .... 25.00 - 40.00
   45567 *Runnin' Wild* .... 25.00 - 40.00

CALDWELL BROTHERS:
Supertone 9343 *Somebody's Waiting For Me* .... 7.00 - 10.00

CALDWELL & BUNCH:

Superior 2791 *My Bones Is Gonna Rise Again* . . . 15.00 - 20.00

BOB CALEN:
Okeh 45372 *Carolina Rolling Stone* . . . . 10.00 - 15.00

HANK CALDWELL & THE SADDLE KINGS:
D'Oro 103 *Alibi* . . . . — - —

SAM CALDWELL:
Supertone 9185 *The Prisoner's Lament* . . . . 7.00 - 10.00

CALLAHAN BROTHERS; HOMER
CALLAHAN; WALTER CALLAHAN:
Titles, issued contemporaneously on Banner,
Conqueror, Melotone, Oriole, Perfect, Romeo:
include: *Asheville Blues; Brown's Ferry Blues;*
Cowboy Jack; Days Are Blue; Don't You
Remember The Time; Going To Heaven On My
Own Expense; Gonna Quit Drinkin' When I
Die; Gonna Quit My Rowdy Ways; Green Back
Dollar; I Don't Want To Hear Your Name;
Katie Dear; Little Poplar Log House On The
Hill; Lonesome And Wear Blues; Maple On
The Hill; Mean Mama; New Birmingham Jail
No. 3; North Carolina Moon; Once I Had A
Darling Mother Rattle Snake Daddy;
Rounder's Luck; St. Louis Blues; She's Killing
Me; She's My Curley Headed Baby No. 2; T.B.
Blues No. 2; True Lover . . . . 5.00 - 10.00
Vocalion 02973 *Take The News To Mother* . . . . . . 10.00 - 15.00
03108 *Just One Year* . . . . 10.00 - 15.00
03171 *Freight Train Blues* . . . . 10.00 - 15.00
03335 *She's My Curley Headed Baby No. 3* . . . 10.00 - 15.00
04358, 04359, 04360, 04361, 04362, 04363 . . . 5.00 - 10.00

CALOWAY'S WEST VIRGINIA
MOUNTAINEERS:
Gennett 6546 *The Corn Shuckers' Frolic* . . . . 20.00 - 30.00

AARON CAMPBELL'S MOUNTAINEERS:
Champion 16689 *The Flying Trapeze* . . . . 10.00 - 15.00
16740 *Mother's Knee* . . . . 10.00 - 15.00
16751 *Daisies Won't Tell* . . . . 15.00 - 20.00
45008, 45038, 45086 . . . . 4.00 - 8.00

ORAN CAMPBELL:
Champion 15429, 15502 . . . . 5.00 - 8.00

HARMON CANADA:
Gennett 6961 *My Little Home In Tennessee* . . . . . 15.00 - 20.00
6972 *Born In Hard Luck* . . . . 15.00 - 20.00

WARREN CAPLINGER & CUMBERLAND
MOUNTAIN ENTERTAINERS/THE DIXIE
HARMONIZERS:
Brunswick 224 *Nobody's Business* . . . . 30.00 - 50.00
241 *Big Ball In Town* . . . . 30.00 - 50.00
Gennett 6915 *The Music Man* . . . . 75.00 - 100.00
Vocalion 5222 *Chicken Reel* . . . . 35.00 - 50.00
5237 *When The Redeemed Are Gathered In* . . . 35.00 - 50.00
5240 *Jerusalem Mourn* . . . . 35.00 - 50.00

KEN CARD:
Champion 45148 *The Last Flight Of Wiley Post* . . 7.00 - 10.00

CARLISLE BROTHERS:
Titles, issued contemporaneously on Banner,
Melotone, Oriole, Perfect, Romeo, include:
The Little Dobie Shack; Looking For
Tomorrow; Ramshackled Shack On The Hill;
Sunshine And Daisies . . . . 5.00 - 10.00
Bluebird . . . . 4.00 - 8.00

(SMILING) BILL CARLISLIE:
Bluebird 6478, 6568, 6600, 6608, 6775, 6938,
7019, 7087, 7153, 7414, 7613 . . . . 4.00 - 8.00
Melotone 7-02-64 *House Cat Mama* . . . . 7.00 - 10.00
(Note: Also issued on Banner, Oriole, Perfect,
Romeo)
Vocalion 02520 *Rattle Snake Daddy* . . . . 15.00 - 25.00
02946 *I'm Gonna Kill Myself* . . . . 15.00 - 25.00

CLIFF/CLIFFORD CARLISLE:
Titles, issued contemporaneously on Banner,
Conqueror, Melotone, Oriole, Perfect, Romeo

include: *Birmingham Jail No. 2; Blue Eyes;*
Chicken Roost Blues; Desert Blues; Don't
Marry The Wrong Woman; Fussin' Mama;
Gamblin' Dan; Going Back To Alabama; Hen
Pecked Man; I Don't Mind; I'm Glad I'm A
Hobo; Just A Lonely Hobo; Louisiana Blues;
My Two Time Mama; On The Banks of The Rio
Grande; Shanghai Rooster Yodel; Wreck Of No.
52; Written Letter . . . . 7.00 - 12.00
Additional titles: *The Bunch Of Cactus On The*
Wall; Casey County Jail; Childhood Dreams;
Dang My Rowdy Soul; Dream A Little Dream
Of Me; Georgia Moon; Goodbye Old Pal;
Lonely Valley; Lonesome For Caroline;
Longing For You; Memories That Haunt Me;
Memories That Make Me Cry; On The Prairie;
Seven Years With The Wrong Woman; When It's
Roundup Time In Texas; Where Romance
Calls; Won't Somebody Pal With Me . . . . 5.00 - 10.00
Bluebird 6350 *Rambling Yodeler* . . . . 5.00 - 10.00
6405 *A Stretch Of 28 Years* . . . . 5.00 - 10.00
6439 *Cowboy Johnny's Last Ride* . . . . 5.00 - 10.00
6458 *You'll Miss Me When I'm Gone* . . . . 5.00 - 10.00
6493 *When I Feel Froggie, I'm Gonna Hop* . . . 5.00 - 10.00
6524 *Wigglin' Mama* . . . . 5.00 - 10.00
6540, 6631, 6647 . . . . 5.00 - 8.00
6754, 6791, 6830, 6855, 6980, 7031, 7094,
7147, 7290, 7702, 7717, 7740, 7790, 7817, 8199,
8228 . . . . 4.00 - 7.00
Champion 15969 *Memphis Yodel* . . . . 15.00 - 20.00
15992 *Desert Blues* . . . . 15.00 - 20.00
16028 *Virginia Blues* . . . . 15.00 - 20.00
Champion *I'm Lonely And Blue* . . . . 15.00 - 20.00
16140 *Crazy Blues* . . . . 15.00 - 20.00
16165 *No Daddy Blues* . . . . 15.00 - 20.00
16212 *Box Car Blues* . . . . 20.00 - 30.00
16239 *High Steppin' Mama* . . . . 20.00 - 30.00
16270 *Hobo Jack's Last Ride* . . . . 20.00 - 30.00
16329 *Nobody Wants Me* . . . . 20.00 - 30.00
16419 *Memories That Haunt Me* . . . . 20.00 - 30.00
16434 *She's Waiting For Me* . . . . 20.00 - 30.00
16447 *The Fatal Run* . . . . 20.00 - 30.00
45029, 45042, 45132, 45134, 45139, 45140,
45147, 45155, 45162, 45179, 45186 . . . . 5.00 - 10.00
Gennett 7153 *Down In The Jailhouse On My*
Knees . . . . 20.00 - 30.00
7187 *Desert Blues* . . . . 20.00 - 30.00
7206 *Memphis Yodel* . . . . 20.00 - 30.00
7244 *Virginia Blues* . . . . 20.00 - 30.00
7288 *I'm Lonely And Blue* . . . . 20.00 - 30.00

CAROLINA BUDDIES:
Columbia 15537-D *The Murder Of The Lawson*
Family . . . . 8.00 - 12.00
15641-D *The Story That The Crow Told Me* . . . . 10.00 - 15.00
15652-D *Otto Wood The Bandit* . . . . 10.00 - 15.00
15663-D *Work Don't Bother Me* . . . . 10.00 - 15.00
15770-D *Mistreated Blues* . . . . 15.00 - 25.00

CAROLINA MANDOLINE BAND:
Okeh 45191 *Georgia Camp Meeting* . . . . 10.00 - 15.00

CAROLINA NIGHT HAWKS:
Columbia 15256-D *Governor Al Smith For*
President . . . . — - —

CAROLINA RAMBLERS STRING BAND:
Melotone 13047 *Chinese Breakdown* . . . . 7.00 - 10.00

CAROLINA TAR HEELS:
Victor 20544 *I'm Going To Georgia* . . . . 15.00 - 20.00
20545 *Bring Me A Leaf From The Sea* . . . . 15.00 - 20.00
20931 *I Love My Mountain Home* . . . . 15.00 - 20.00
20941 *Bulldog Down In Sunny Tennessee* . . . . 15.00 - 20.00
21193 *My Mamma Scolds Me* . . . . 30.00 - 50.00
23516 *Farm Girl Blues* . . . . 30.00 - 50.00
23546 *The Hen House Door Is Locked* . . . . . . 30.00 - 50.00

23611 *Got The Farm Land Blues*	50.00 -	75.00
23671 *Nobody Cares If I'm Blue*	50.00 -	75.00
23682 *Times Ain't Like They Used To Be*	50.00 -	75.00
V40007 *Peg And Awl*	30.00 -	50.00
V40024 *Roll On, Boys*	30.00 -	50.00
V40053 *I Don't Like The Blues No More*	30.00 -	50.00
V40077 *Rude And Rambling Man*	30.00 -	50.00
V40100 *My Home's Across The Blue Ridge Mountains*	30.00 -	50.00
V40128 *Somebody's Tall And Handsome*	30.00 -	50.00
V40177 *The Old Gray Goose*	30.00 -	50.00
V40219 *I'll Be Washed*	30.00 -	50.00

CAROLINA TWINS:

Victor 21363 *Off To War I'm Going*	20.00 -	30.00
21575 *One Dark And Rainy Night*	20.00 -	30.00
23502 *Since My Baby's Gone Away*	25.00 -	40.00
V40044 *When You Go A-Courtin'*	20.00 -	30.00
V40098 *Mr. Brown, Here I Come*	20.00 -	30.00
V40123 *New Orleans Is The Town I Like Best*	20.00 -	30.00
V40243 *Change In Business All Around*	20.00 -	30.00
V40310 *Southern Jack*	25.00 -	40.00

BOYDEN CARPENTER:

Champion 16519 *The Hobos Convention*	15.00 -	25.00

JOHN CARPENTER:

Bell 1178 *Sourwood Mountain*	5.00 -	8.00

CARROLL COUNTY RAMBLERS:

Vocalion 5433 *Georgia Wobble Blues*	50.00 -	75.00

CARSON BROTHERS & SMITH/SPRINKLE:

Okeh 45013, 45023	5.00 -	8.00
45398 *The Highway Man*	7.00 -	10.00

BERT CARSON:

Superior 2520 *My Red Haired Lady*	15.00 -	20.00

FIDDLIN' JOHN CARSON (& HIS VIRGINIA REELERS/with MOONSHINE KATE):

Bluebird 5401 *New Comin' Round The Mountain*	10.00 -	15.00
5447 *Stockade Blues*	10.00 -	15.00
5483 *The Storm That Struck Miami*	10.00 -	15.00
5560, 5652, 5742, 5787, 5959, 6022, 6247	5.00 -	10.00
Montgomery Ward 4848, 4849, 4851, 4852	4.00 -	7.00
Okeh 4890 *The Little Old Log Cabin In The Lane*	10.00 -	15.00
(Note: The existence of an unnumbered issue of the above record, of which 500 copies were supposedly pressed, has not been confirmed.)		
Okeh 4994 *Papa's Billy Goat*	10.00 -	15.00
7003 (12-inch) *Sugar In The Gourd*	40.00 -	60.00
7004 12-inch *John Henry Blues*	40.00 -	60.00
7006 (12-inch) *The Baggage Coach Ahead*	40.00 -	60.00
7008 12-inch *The Lightning Express*	40.00 -	60.00
40020 *Billy In The Low Ground*	8.00 -	15.00
40038 *Casey Jones*	8.00 -	15.00
40050 *Tom Wason Special*	8.00 -	15.00
40071 *The Kickin' Mule*	8.00 -	15.00
40095 *Dixie Boll Weevil*	8.00 -	15.00
40108 *Arkansas Traveler*	8.00 -	15.00
40181 *Ode And In The Way*	10.00 -	15.00
40196 *I'm Nine Hundred Miles From Home*	10.00 -	15.00
40204 *Alabama Gal*	10.00 -	15.00
40230 *Turkey In The Straw*	10.00 -	15.00
40238 *Nancy Rowland*	10.00 -	15.00
40263 *Old Dan Tucker*	10.00 -	15.00
40306 *Steamboat Bill*	10.00 -	15.00
40343 *My North Georgia Home*	10.00 -	15.00
40363 *Charming Betsy*	10.00 -	15.00
40411 *The Honest Farmer*	10.00 -	15.00
40419 *The Boston Burglar*	10.00 -	15.00
40444 *Bully Of The Town*	10.00 -	15.00
40446 *Little Mary Phagan*	10.00 -	15.00
45001 *Run Along Home With Lindy*	10.00 -	15.00
45011 *Soldier's Joy*	10.00 -	15.00
45018 *Hell Broke Loose In Georgia*	10.00 -	15.00
45028 *The Grave Of Little Mary Phagan*	10.00 -	15.00
45032 *The Drunkard's Hiccoughs*	10.00 -	15.00

45035 *Liberty*	10.00 -	15.00
45040 *Georgia Wagner*	10.00 -	15.00
45045 *Everybody Works But Father*	10.00 -	15.00
45049 *Good-Bye Liza Jane*	10.00 -	15.00
45056 *The Batchelor's Hall*	10.00 -	15.00
45068 *Fire In The Mountain*	10.00 -	15.00
45077 *Long Way To Tipperary*	10.00 -	15.00
45096 *Don't Let Your Deal Go Down*	10.00 -	15.00
45122 *Cotton-Eyed Joe*	10.00 -	15.00
45139 *Swanee River*	10.00 -	15.00
45159 *Hell Bound For Alabama*	10.00 -	15.00
45167 *Turkey In The Hay*	10.00 -	15.00
45176 *Engineer On The Mogull*	10.00 -	15.00
45186 *Quit That Ticklin' Me*	10.00 -	15.00
45198 *Old Joe Clark*	10.00 -	15.00
45214 *Going Dcwn To Cripple Creek*	15.00 -	20.00
45249 *Ain't No Bugs On Me*	15.00 -	20.00
45273 *Old And In The Way*	15.00 -	20.00
45290 *John Makes Good Licker*	15.00 -	20.00
45301 *Be Kind To A Man When He's Down*	20.00 -	30.00
45321 *Going To The County Fair*	20.00 -	30.00
45338 *Hawk And Buzzard*	20.00 -	30.00
45353 *My Ford Sedan*	20.00 -	30.00
45369 *John Makes Good Licker, Part 3/4*	15.00 -	20.00
45384 *You'll Never Miss Your Mother, No. 2*	20.00 -	30.00
45402 *Times Are Not Like They Used To Be*	25.00 -	40.00
45415 *Corn Licker And Barbecue, Part 1/2*	25.00 -	40.00
45434 *Sunny Tennessee*	30.00 -	50.00
45440 *Kate's Snuff Box*	30.00 -	50.00
45445 *The Raccoon And The Possum*	30.00 -	50.00
45448 *Who's The Best Fiddler?*	30.00 -	50.00
45458 *John In The Army*	30.00 -	50.00
45471 *The Last Old Dollar Is Gone*	30.00 -	50.00
45488 *On The Banks Of Old Tennessee*	30.00 -	50.00
45498 *The Dominicker Duck*	30.00 -	50.00
45513 *My Home In Dixie-Land*	30.00 -	50.00
45542 *Take The Train To Charlotte*	30.00 -	50.00
45555 *I Intend To Heaven My Home*	30.00 -	50.00
45569 *Didn't He Ramble*	30.00 -	50.00

ROSA LEE CARSON:

Okeh 45005 *The Drinker's Child*	8.00 -	12.00

CARTER BROTHERS (& SON):

Okeh 45202 *Saddle Up The Grey*	15.00 -	25.00
45289 *Give The Fiddler A Dream*	15.00 -	25.00
Vocalion 5295 *Give Me A Chaw Tobacco*	30.00 -	50.00
5297 *Jenny On The Railroad*	30.00 -	50.00

CARTER FAMILY:

Titles, issued contemporaneously on Banner, Conqueror, Melotone, Oriole, Pertect, Romeo: *Broken Hearted Lover; By The Touch Of Her Hand; Cannon Ball Blues; Can The Circle Be Unbroken; East Virginia Blues No. 2; The Fate Of Dewey Lee; Gathering Flowers on the Hillside; Glory To The Lamb; God Gave Noah The Rainbow Sign; He Took A White Rose From Her Hair; I'm Thinking Tonight Of My Blue Eyes; Keep On The Sunny Side; Kissing Is A Crime; Let's Be Lovers Again; Little Darling Pal Of Mine; On The Rocks Where Moses Stood; River Of Jordan; Worried Man Blues*	8.00 -	12.00
Bluebird 5006 *Keep On The Sunny Side*	8.00 -	12.00

5058 *Where We'll Never Grow Old*	8.00	-	12.00
5096 *Meet Me By The Moonlight Alone*	8.00	-	12.00
5122 *When The Spnngtime Comes Again*	8.00	-	12.00
5161 *Will The Roses Bloom In Heaven?*	8.00	-	12.00
5185 *Amber Tresses*	8.00	-	12.00
5243 *Mid The Green Fields Of Virginia*	8.00	-	12.00
5272 *God Gave Noah The Rainbow Sign*	8.00	-	12.00
5301 *My Clinch Mountain Home*	8.00	-	12.00
5356 *Wildwood Flower*	7.00	-	10.00
5406 *Anchored In Love*	7.00	-	10.00
5468 *Sow 'Em On The Mountain*	7.00	-	10.00
5529 *I'll Be All Smiles Tonight*	7.00	-	10.00
5543 *A Distant Land To Roam*	7.00	-	10.00
5586 *Darling Daisies*	7.00	-	10.00
5650 *The East Virginia Blues*	7.00	-	10.00
5716 *I'm Working On A Building*	7.00	-	10.00
5771 *One Little Word*	7.00	-	10.00
5817 *I'll Aggravate Your Soul*	7.00	-	10.00
5856 *Longing For Old Virginia*	7.00	-	10.00
5908 *My Heart's Tonight In Texas*	7.00	-	10.00
5911 *I'll Be Home Some Day*	7.00	-	10.00
5924 *Little Moses*	7.00	-	10.00
5927 *Lulu Wall*	7.00	-	10.00
5956 *The Mountains Of Tennessee*	7.00	-	10.00
5961 *On a Hill Lone And Gray*	7.00	-	10.00
5974 *Sailor Boy*	7.00	-	10.00
5990 *Kitty Waltz*	7.00	-	10.00
5993 *The Church In The Wildwood*	7.00	-	10.00
6000 *Lonesome For You*	7.00	-	10.00
6020 *Worried Man Blues*	7.00	-	10.00
6033 *Diamonds In The Rough*	7.00	-	10.00
6036 *Carter's Blues*	7.00	-	10.00
6053 *When I'm Gone*	7.00	-	10.00
6055 *Where Shall I Be?*	7.00	-	10.00
6106 *Two Sweethearts*	7.00	-	10.00
6117 *Lonesome Valley*	7.00	-	10.00
6176 *Fond Affection*	7.00	-	10.00
6223 *Engine One-Forty-Three*	7.00	-	10.00
6257 *I Never Loved But One*	7.00	-	10.00
6271 *Little Log Cabin By The Sea*	7.00	-	10.00
6762 *The Carter Family & Jimmie Rodgers In Texas*	10.00	-	15.00
8350 *Wabash Cannon Ball*	7.00	-	10.00
8868 *Dark And Stormy Weather*	7.00	-	10.00
Decca 5240 *My Dixie Darling*	7.00	-	10.00
5241 *My Native Home*	7.00	-	10.00
5242 *No Depression*	7.00	-	10.00
5254 *Just Another Broken Heart*	7.00	-	10.00
5263 *My Honey Lou*	7.00	-	10.00
5283 *You've Been A Friend To Me*	7.00	-	10.00
5304 *Bonnie Blue Eyes*	7.00	-	10.00
5318 *Sweet Heaven In My View*	7.00	-	10.00
5359 *In The Shadow Of The Pines*	7.00	-	10.00
5386 *The Last Move For Me*	7.00	-	10.00
5411 *The Only Girl*	7.00	-	10.00
5430 *Lover's Lane*	7.00	-	10.00
5447 *He Never Came Back*	7.00	-	10.00
5452 *Honey In The Rock*	7.00	-	10.00
5467 *Jim Blake's Message*	7.00	-	10.00
5479 *Hello Stranger*	7.00	-	10.00
5494 *Lord I'm In Your Care*	7.00	-	10.00
5518 *Broken Down Tramp*	7.00	-	10.00
5532 *Goodbye To The Plains*	7.00	-	10.00
5565 *Stern Old Bachelor*	7.00	-	10.00
5579 *Happy In The Prison*	7.00	-	10.00
5596 *Coal Miner's Blues*	7.00	-	10.00
5612 *Who's That Knockin' On My Window*	7.00	-	10.00
5632 *Little Joe*	7.00	-	10.00
5649 *Bring Back My Boy*	7.00	-	10.00
5662 *Cuban Soldiers*	7.00	-	10.00
5677 *Farewell Nellie*	7.00	-	10.00
Decca 5692 *You Are My Flower*	7.00	-	10.00

5702 *Charlie And Nellie*	7.00	-	10.00
5722 *Reckless Motorman*	7.00	-	10.00
Montgomery Ward (Many titles, same as on Bluebird and Victor, valued approximately the same as Bluebird issues)	5.00	-	10.00
Victor 20877 *The Poor Orphan Child*	10.00	-	15.00
20937 *Storms Are On The Ocean*	10.00	-	15.00
21074 *Little Log Cabin By The Sea*	10.00	-	15.00
21434 *Keep On The Sunny Side*	10.00	-	15.00
21517 *Chewing Gum*	10.00	-	15.00
21638 *Will You Miss Me When I'm Gone?*	10.00	-	15.00
23513 *On The Rock*	25.00	-	40.00
23523 *Where Shall I Be?*	25.00	-	40.00
23541 *Lonesome Valley*	25.00	-	40.00
23554 *There's Someone A Waiting For Me*	30.00	-	50.00
23569 *Can't Feel At Home*	30.00	-	50.00
23574 *Jimmie Rodgers Visits The Carter Family*	30.00	-	50.00
23585 *Sow 'Em On The Mountain*	30.00	-	50.00
23599 *My Old Cottage Home*	40.00	-	60.00
23618 *Let The Church Roll On*	40.00	-	60.00
23626 *Weary Prodigal Son*	40.00	-	60.00
23641 *Dying Soldier*	40.00	-	60.00
23656 *I Have Never Loved But One*	40.00	-	60.00
23672 *Where We'll Never Grow Old*	40.00	-	60.00
23686 *'Mid The Green Fields Of Virginia*	50.00	-	75.00
23701 *Amber Tresses*	50.00	-	75.00
23716 *Carter's Blues*	50.00	-	75.00
23731 *Wabash Cannon Ball*	75.00	-	100.00
23748 *Will The Roses Bloom In Heaven?*	75.00	-	100.00
23761 *Sweet As The Flowers In May Time*	75.00	-	100.00
23776 *The Church In The Wildwood*	75.00	-	100.00
23791 *Two Sweet Hearts*	75.00	-	100.00
23807 *I Wouldn't Mind Dying*	80.00	-	120.00
23821 *Gold Watch And Chain*	80.00	-	120.00
23835 *I Loved You Better Than I Know*	100.00	-	150.00
23845 *On The Sea Of Galilee*	100.00	-	150.00
V40000 *Wildwood Flower*	15.00	-	25.00
V40036 *I Have No One*	15.00	-	25.00
V40058 *Foggy Mountain Top*	20.00	-	30.00
V40089 *Engine One-Forty-Three*	20.00	-	30.00
V40110 *Little Moses*	20.00	-	30.00
V0126 *Sweet Fern*	20.00	-	30.00
V0150 *Diamonds In The Rough*	20.00	-	30.00
V40190 *Bring Back My Blue-Eyed Boy*	25.00	-	40.00
V40207 *The Homestead On The Farm*	30.00	-	50.00
V40229 *When The Roses Bloom In Dixieland*	30.00	-	50.00
V40255 *Western Hobo*	30.00	-	50.00
V40277 *Lover's Farewell*	30.00	-	50.00
V40293 *When The World's On Fire*	30.00	-	50.00
V40317 *Worried Man Blues*	40.00	-	60.00
V40328 *Don't Forget This Song*	50.00	-	75.00
Vocalion 02990 *Broken Hearted Lover*	20.00	-	30.00
03027 *Can The Circle Be Unbroken*	15.00	-	20.00
03112 *Lonesome Valley*	15.00	-	20.00
03160 *The Storms Are On The Ocean*	15.00	-	20.00
04390 *Don't Forget Me Little Darling*	15.00	-	20.00

(BUSTER) CARTER & (PRESTON) YOUNG:

Columbia 15690-D *I'll Roll In My Sweet Baby's Arms*	50.00	-	75.00
15702-D *It Won't Hurt No More*	50.00	-	75.00
15758-D *Bill Morgan And His Gal*	50.00	-	75.00

FLOYD CARTER:

Oriole 8847 *Flemington Kidnap Trial*	7.00	-	10.00

WILF CARTER:

Bluebird 5536, 5545, 5871, 6009, 6107, 6208, 6380, 6814, 6826, 6827	5.00	-	10.00
Bluebird (lower numbers/Canadian issues)	5.00	-	10.00
Bluebird (higher numbers)	3.00	-	6.00

CARTWRIGHT BROTHERS:

Columbia 15220-D *Kelly Waltz*	5.00	-	10.00
15346-D *On The Old Chisholm Trail*	8.00	-	12.00

15410-D *Utah Carroll*	8.00	-	12.00
15677-D *Over The Waves*	15.00	-	20.00
Victor V40147 *San Antonio*	10.00	-	15.00
V40198 *The Dying Ranger*	10.00	-	15.00
V40247 *The Wandering Cowboy*	15.00	-	20.00

CARVER BOYS:

Broadway 8151 *Wang Wang Harmonica Blues*	80.00	-	120.00
Paramount 3182 *No One To Welcome Me Home*	75.00	-	100.00
3198 *The Brave Engineer*	75.00	-	100.00
3199 *Tim Brook*	75.00	-	100.00
3233 *Simpson County*	75.00	-	100.00
12822 *Sisco Harmonica Blues*	80.00	-	120.00

CASEY'S OLD TIME FIDDLERS:

Victor 23560 *Casey's Old Time Waltz*	30.00	-	50.00

CLAUDE CASEY (& THE PINE STATE PLAYBOYS):

Bluebird 7863, 7883	5.00	-	8.00

ELRY CASH:

Columbia 15399-D *My Old New Hampshire Home*	10.00	-	15.00
15457-D *Then My Love Began To Wane*	10.00	-	15.00

CASS COUNTY BOYS:

Bluebird 8006, 8824	5.00	-	10.00

BILLY CASTEEL WITH SILVER SAGE BUCKAROOS:

Hot Wax 1614 *Hollywood Mama*	7.00	-	10.00
1615 *Trifling On Me*	7.00	-	10.00

THOMPSON CATES:

Paramount 3103 *Curse Of An Aching Heart*	15.00	-	20.00

CAULEY FAMILY:

Melotone 13113 *New River Train*	8.00	-	12.00
13114 *Duplin County Blues*	8.00	-	12.00
(Note: Probably also issued on Banner Oriole, Perfect, Romeo)			

ROLAND CAULEY & LAKE HOWARD:

Meltone 6-04-54 *Grey Eagle*	8.00	-	12.00
(Note: Also issued on Perfect)			

(JACK) CAWLEY'S (OKLAHOMA) RIDGE RUNNERS:

Victor 23521 *White River Stomp*	50.00	-	80.00
23540 *Cross Tie Blues*	75.00	-	100.00
23570 *The Vine-Covered Cottage*	75.00	-	125.00
V40175 *Ft. Worth Rag*	75.00	-	100.00
V40254 *Oklahoma Waltz*	75.00	-	100.00

CEDAR CREEK SHEIK:

Bluebird 6467 *Don't Use That Stuff*	15.00	-	25.00
6528 *She's Totin' Something Good*	15.00	-	25.00
6587 *What A Pity*	15.00	-	25.00
6634 *Don't Credit My Stuff*	15.00	-	25.00
6939 *Ford V-8*	15.00	-	25.00

CEDAR CREST SINGERS (See also WILLIAM REXROAT):

Vocalion 5294 *Dying For Someone To Love Me*	20.00	-	35.00

LEON CHAPPELEAR (THE LONE STAR COWBOY):

Champion 16497 *Little Joe The Wrangler*	30.00	-	50.00
45068 *Little Joe The Wrangler*	8.00	-	12.00
45167 *Trifling Mama Blues*	8.00	-	12.00

CHARLESTON ENTERTAINERS:

Supertone 9718 *Wait Till The Sun Shines Nellie*	5.00	-	8.00

CHEZZ CHASE:

Paramount 3178 *Log Cabin Blues*	5.00	-	8.00

CHENOWETH'S CORNFIELD SYMPHONY ORCHESTRA:

Okeh 45025 *Arkansaw Wampus Cat*	30.00	-	50.00

CHEROKEE RAMBLERS:

Decca 5402 *Back Up And Push*	5.00	-	8.00

TED CHESNUT:

Gennett 6480 *The Letter From Home*	15.00	-	20.00
6513 *The Death Of J.B. Marcum*	15.00	-	20.00
6603 *Bring Back My Boy*	15.00	-	20.00
6638 *The Drunkard's Doom*	15.00	-	20.00

6673 *Only A Tramp*	15.00	-	20.00

CHIEF SHUNATONA, DOUG MaTAGUE, AND SNOOKUM:

Columbia 15781-D *Cowboy Tom's Roundup*	75.00	-	125.00

CHILDERS & WHITE:

Okeh 45208 *Red River Valley*	7.00	-	10.00
45213 *Don't Grieve Your Mother*	7.00	-	10.00

BILL CHILDERS:

Okeh 45203 *Bury Me Not On The Lone Prairie*	7.00	-	10.00

(MR. & MRS.) W.C. CHILDERS:

Champion 16467 *Strawberry Roan*	15.00	-	20.00
45103, 45166	4.00	-	7.00
Gennett 6931 *The Grand Roundup*	15.00	-	20.00
6943 *Over The Hills To The Poor House*	15.00	-	20.00
6973 *Our Mother's Always Waiting*	15.00	-	20.00
7021 *Workin' Habits*	15.00	-	20.00
7066 *Crepe On The Little Cabin Door*	15.00	-	20.00
7113 *I'll Smoke My Long Stemmed Pipe*	20.00	-	30.00
7223 *Two Little Girls In Blue*	20.00	-	30.00
7292 *The Prison Warden's Secret*	20.00	-	30.00
Paramount 3181 *Amber Tresses Tied In Blue*	15.00	-	20.00

LEW CHILDRE:

Champion 16011 *Moonshine Blues*	30.00	-	50.00
Gennett 7183 *Moonshine Blues*	40.00	-	60.00
7312 *The Old Grey Mare*	40.00	-	60.00

BILL CHITWOOD (& GEORGIA MOUNTAINEERS/BUD LANDRESS):

Brunswick 2884 *Furniture Man*	5.00	-	8.00
Okeh 45100 *Fourth Of July At The County Fair*	10.00	-	15.00
45110 *Smiling Watermelon*	10.00	-	15.00
45131 *Preacher Blues*	10.00	-	15.00
45162 *Kitty Hill*	10.00	-	15.00
45236 *Bill Wishes He Was Single Again*	10.00	-	15.00
Silvertone 3048 *Howdy Bill*	7.00	-	10.00
3049 *Over The Sea*	7.00	-	10.00
3050 *Hen Cackle*	7.00	-	10.00

HARRY CHOATES:

Allied 103, 104	5.00	-	10.00
Cajun Classics 1007/1010 *Hackberry Hop*	8.00	-	12.00
Gold Star 1314, 1319, 1326, 1330, 1333, 1335, 1336, 1343, 1380, 1385, 1388	5.00	-	10.00
Macy's 124, 134, 141, 147, 158	7.00	-	10.00

BEN CHRISTIAN & HIS TEXAS COWBOYS:

Four Star 1270 *Moonlight Island*	7.00	-	10.00
Melody 501 *You Played The Game And Lost*	7.00	-	10.00
502 *Moonlight Island*	7.00	-	10.00

HOMER CHRISTOPHER (& RANEY VAN WINK/& WIFE):

Okeh 45041 *Southern Railroad*	5.00	-	8.00
45097 *Red Wing*	5.00	-	8.00
45117 *Going Slow*	5.00	-	8.00
45138 *Hilo March*	5.00	-	8.00
45147 *Home Town Rag*	5.00	-	8.00
45195 *Old Fashioned Waltz*	5.00	-	8.00
45277 *March In "D"*	5.00	-	8.00
Victor 20656 *Lost Mamma Blues*	7.00	-	10.00
Victor 21128 *Going Slow*	5.00	-	8.00

CHUCK WAGON GANG:

Banner, Canqueror, Melotone, Oriole, Perfect, Romeo (various titles)	5.00	-	10.00
Vocalion 02938, 03028, 03224, 03434, 03472, 04105, 04342	5.00	-	10.00

CHUMBLER'S BREAKDOWN GANG:

Q.R.S. 9016 *May I Sleep In Your Barn Tonight?*	75.00	-	100.00

CHUMBLER FAMILY:

Columbia 15481-D *Jacobs Ladder*	8.00	-	12.00
15513-D *I'm Going Home To My Wife*	8.00	-	12.00

GENE CLARDY & STAN CLEMENTS:

Vocalion 5418 *Black Mustache*	10.00	-	15.00
5462 *Sleeping Time Waltz*	10.00	-	15.00

CLARK BROTHERS (See JOHN CLARK):

DUKE CLARK:

Champion 16470 *Make A Change In Business* . . . 50.00 - 80.00
16565 *Thirty Minutes Behind The Time* . . . . 50.00 - 80.00
16624 *11:29 Blues* . . . . 75.00 - 100.00
Superior 2687 *The Wreck Of The F.F. & V* . . . . 50.00 - 100.00

FRANK CLARK:
Champion 15946 *Sad And Lonely Blues* . . . . 15.00 - 25.00

JOHN CLARK:
Champion 15565 *The Prisoner's Lament* . . . . . . 8.00 - 12.00
15586 *Falling By The Wayside* . . . . 8.00 - 12.00

LUTHER B. CLARK (Acc. by BLUE RIDGE HIGHBALLERS):
Columbia 15069-D *Bright Sherman Valley* . . . . . . 10.00 - 15.00
15096-D *Wish To Lord I Had Never Been Born* 10.00 - 15.00

THEO. & GUS CLARK:
Okeh 45339 *Wimbush Rag* . . . . 35.00 - 50.00

CLARKE & HOWELL:
Supertone 9500 *Flop Eared Mule* . . . . 10.00 - 15.00
9536 *Birmingham Jail* . . . . 10.00 - 15.00

AL CLAUSER & HIS OKLAHOMANS:
Gulf 105 *Soldier's Return* . . . . 5.00 - 8.00

CLAYTON & HIS MELODY MOUNTAINEERS:
Vocalion 5434 *Lookout Valley Waltz* . . . . 20.00 - 30.00

CLEM & HARRY:
Champion 16667 *In The Old Town Hall* . . . . 10.00 - 15.00

HARMON CLEM & PRINCE ALBERT HUNT:
Okeh 45360 *Oklahoma Rag* . . . . 75.00 - 100.00

STANLEY CLEMENTS:
Okeh 45562 *The Habit I Never Have Had* . . . . . . 8.00 - 12.00

CLIFF & RAY:
Vocalion 03721, 04204, 04293, 04743 . . . . 5.00 - 10.00

BOB CLIFFORD:
Vocalion 5488 *My Two Time Mama* . . . . 15.00 - 20.00
5492 *Shanghai Rooster Yodel No. 2* . . . . 15.00 - 20.00
5499 *Hobo Jack's Last Ride* . . . . 15.00 - 20.00

CLINCH VALLEY BOYS:
Challenge 302 *Forked Deer* . . . . 20.00 - 30.00
Champion 15297 *Little Red Caboose Behind The Train* . . . . 7.00 - 10.00
15316 *Just As The Sun Went Down* . . . . 7.00 - 10.00
Supertone 9248 *Just As The Sun Went Down* . . . . 7.00 - 10.00

FRANK CLOUTIER & HIS VICTORIA CAFE ORCHESTRA:
Gennett 6305 *Moonshiner's Dance* . . . . 10.00 - 15.00

JESSE COAT (& JOHN BISHOP):
Champion 15585 *East Bound Train* . . . . 10.00 - 15.00
15611 *The Dying Girl's Message* . . . . 10.00 - 15.00
15712 *She Ain't Built That Way* . . . . 10.00 - 15.00
15854 *The Virginia Moonshiner* . . . . 10.00 - 15.00
15922 *The Fellow That Looks Like Me* . . . . . . 10.00 - 15.00

COBB & PROW:
Champion 16167 *My Pretty Snow Dear* . . . . 15.00 - 20.00

COBB & UNDERWOOD:
Champion 16144 *Black Sheep Blues* . . . . 30.00 - 50.00
45146 *Black Sheep Blues* . . . . 10.00 - 15.00
Gennett 7311 *Black Sheep Blues* . . . . 40.00 - 60.00

OSCAR L. COFFEY:
Gennett 6481 *My Dear Old Mountain Home* . . . 15.00 - 20.00
6496 *Six Feet Of Earth* . . . . 15.00 - 20.00

TINY COLBERT & HIS ENTERTAINERS:
Blue Bonnet 133 *Bumble Bee Baby* . . . . 10.00 - 15.00
150 *Our Own Sweet Baby Boy* . . . . 7.00 - 10.00

JAMES COLE STRING BAND:
Vocalion 5226 *I Got A Gal* . . . . 50.00 - 75.00

JIM COLE'S (TENNESSEE) MOUNTAINEERS:
Crown 3102 *I'm Pining For The Pines And Caroline* . . . . 15.00 - 20.00
3122 *Rocky Mountain Sal* . . . . 15.00 - 20.00
3142 *Down In The Valley* . . . . 15.00 - 20.00
3158 *Old Folks' Dance Medley* . . . . 15.00 - 20.00
Paramount 3279 *Rocky Mountain Sal* . . . . 25.00 - 40.00

REX COLE'S MOUNTAINEERS:

Melotone 12055 *Wilderness* . . . . 5.00 - 8.00

BERNICE COLEMAN acc. by WEST VIRGINIA RAMBLERS:
Champion 16456 *The Ring My Mother Wore* . . . . 30.00 - 50.00

DUTCH COLEMAN:
Vocalion 5391 *New Ground Blues* . . . . 30.00 - 50.00
5408 *The Clayton Case* . . . . 30.00 - 50.00
5467 *Gonna Raise Some Bacon At Home* . . . . 30.00 - 50.00

BIFF COLLIE:
Macy's 126 *I Want A Gal (To Cook For Me)* . . . . 10.00 - 15.00

BILL COLLINS:
Victor 20673 *When The Moon Shines* . . . . 7.00 - 10.00

POP COLLINS & HIS BOYS:
Edison 52426 *The Train That Never Arrived* . . . . 10.00 - 15.00
52507 *Pappy's Buried On The Hill* . . . . 10.00 - 15.00

UNCLE TOM COLLINS:
Okeh 45119 *Four Sons Of A Gun* . . . . 10.00 - 15.00
45132 *Little Brown Jug* . . . . 10.00 - 15.00
45140 *Chicken You Can't Roost Too High For Me* . . . . 10.00 - 15.00

COLT BROTHERS:
Melotone 12106 *Eleven More Months & Ten More Days* . . . . 5.00 - 8.00
12314 *Eleven More Months...part ¾* . . . . 5.00 - 8.00
12333 *That Goes On For Days And Days* . . . . . 5.00 - 8.00
12348 *Hang It On The Hen House* . . . . 5.00 - 8.00
12449 *In 1992* . . . . 5.00 - 8.00
12458 *Our Home Town Mountain Band* . . . . . 5.00 - 8.00
12483 *Somethin' I Et* . . . . 5.00 - 8.00
12506 *After The Old Barn Dance* . . . . 5.00 - 8.00
12601 *The Last Words I Said* . . . . 5.00 - 8.00
(Note: Above probably issued contemporaneon Banner, Oriole, Perfect, Romeo.)

FIDDLIN' COLVIN:
Victor V40271 *Old Lady Blues* . . . . 30.00 - 50.00

HITER COLVIN:
Victor 23815 *Indian War Woop* . . . . 75.00 - 100.00
V40239 *Rabbit Up The Gum Stump* . . . . 30.00 - 50.00

PETER J. CONLON:
Okeh 45030 *Barn Dance* . . . . 5.00 - 8.00

CARL CONNER:
Columbia 15076-D *The Story Of Gerald Chapman* . . . . 8.00 - 12.00

HERB COOK:
Columbia 15729-D *Arkansas Sweetheart* . . . . . . 10.00 - 15.00
15778-D *Just A Little Happiness* . . . . 10.00 - 15.00

JAMES COOK'S OLD TIME FIDDLERS:
Vocalion 5265 *Medley Of Old Fiddler's Favorites* 15.00 - 20.00

JOE COOK:
Bluebird 5135 *Got That Old Fashioned Love* . . . 10.00 - 15.00
6884 *Sweet Little Girl In Blue* . . . . 5.00 - 8.00
7362 *Nobody Knows My Name* . . . . 5.00 - 8.00

COON CREEK GIRLS:
Vocalion 04278, 04413, 04504, 04659 . . . . 4.00 - 8.00

COON HOLLOW BOYS:
Champion 15748 *Coon Hollow Boys At The Still* . 10.00 - 15.00

WALTER COON (& HIS JOY BOYS):
Gennett 7002 *Huskin' Bee* . . . . 20.00 - 30.00
7005 *The Boys Best Friend* . . . . 20.00 - 30.00
7079 *Polly Wolly Doodle* . . . . 20.00 - 30.00
7097 *Fly Away Birdie To Heaven* . . . . 25.00 - 40.00

CORN COB CRUSHERS:
Champion 16373 *Dill Pickle Rag* . . . . 30.00 - 50.00
16449 *Lonesome Road Blues* . . . . 40.00 - 60.00
45178 *Lonesome Road Blues* . . . . 15.00 - 20.00

ARTHUR CORNWALL & JOHN GIBSON:
Champion 16429 *Walking The Highway* . . . . 30.00 - 50.00

COUCH & WILKS RAMBLERS:
Bluebird 7552 *Fourteen Days In Georgia* . . . . . . 7.00 - 10.00

COURVILLE & McGEE:
Vocalion 5315 *Courville & McGee Waltz* . . . . . . 30.00 - 50.00

COX & HENSON:

Champion 16694 *National Blues* . . . . 50.00 - 75.00

(BILL) COX & (CLIFF) HOBBS:

Titles, issued contemporaneously on Banner,
Conqueror, Melotone, Oriole, Perfect, Romeo,
include: *Alimony Woman; Barefoot Boy With
Boots On; Best Friend I Ever Had; Blue Eyed
Sally; Blue Ridge Mountain Blues; Bring Back
The Sunshine And Roses; Brown Eyes; Brown's
Ferry Blues; The Clouds Gwine Roll Away; The
Democratic Donkey; Down In Dixie Land; East
Cairo Street Blues; The Fate Of Will Rogers
And Wiley Post; Fiddling Soldier; The
Ganster's Yodel; Hard Luck Blues; I Get Those
Drunken Blues; I Long For Your Love Each
Day; Lay My Head Beneath The Rose; Long
Chain Charlie Blues; Married Life Blues;
Midnight Special; My Gamblin' Days; New
Mama; N.R.A. Blues; Ramblin' Hobo; Sally
Let Your Bangs Hang Down; Sweethearts And
Kisses; Sweet Kentucky Lou; The Trial Of
Bruno Hauptmann; When The Women Get In
Power; Where The Red Roses Grow; Will And
Wiley's Last Flight* . . . . 7.00 - 12.00

Champion 45007, 45021, 45092, 45106, 45141,
45157 . . . . 8.00 - 12.00

Gennett 6928 *California Blues* . . . . 25.00 - 35.00

6946 *Daddy And Home* . . . . 25.00 - 35.00

6974 *Hungry Hash House Blues* . . . . 25.00 - 35.00

7004 *When We Meet On That Beautiful Shore* . 25.00 - 35.00

7037 *Back Home In Tennessee* . . . . 25.00 - 40.00

7052 *When We Sing Of Home* . . . . 25.00 - 40.00

7080 *Alabama Blues* . . . . 30.00 - 50.00

7155 *I Love The Jailer's Daughter* . . . . 30.00 - 50.00

7226 *My Rough And Rowdy Ways* . . . . 35.00 - 50.00

7266 *The Hand Car Yodel* . . . . 35.00 - 50.00

Vocalion 03043, 03161, 03253, 03380 . . . . 7.00 - 12.00

04077, 04148, 04235, 04341, 04454, 04641,
04811, 04869, 05055 . . . . 5.00 - 10.00

**RICHARD COX (& HIS NATIONAL
FIDDLERS):**

Champion 16475 *Sleeping Lulu* . . . . 40.00 - 60.00

16563 *East Tennessee Blues* . . . . 40.00 - 60.00

16693 *Chewing Chawin' Gum* . . . . 50.00 - 75.00

Champion 45040 *It Ain't No Good* . . . . 15.00 - 20.00

GENE CRABB:

Richtone 353 *Truck Stop Lucy* . . . .   -

RILEY CRABTREE:

(Star) Talent 719, 724, 756, 761 . . . . 5.00 - 10.00

EDWARD L. CRAIN (THE TEXAS COWBOY):

Columbia 15710-D *Bandit Cole Younger* . . . . 50.00 - 80.00

Crown 3238 *Twenty-One Years* . . . . 20.00 - 30.00

3239 *Little Joe The Wrangler* . . . . 20.00 - 30.00

3250 *Cowboy's Home Sweet Home* . . . . 20.00 - 30.00

3275 *The Old Chisholm Trail* . . . . 20.00 - 30.00

CRAMER BROTHERS:

Broadway 8058 *Love Always Has It's Way* . . . . . 20.00 - 30.00

8059 *Sara Jane* . . . . 20.00 - 30.00

Broadway 8060 *In The Good Old Summertime* . . 20.00 - 30.00

8071 *On Top Of Old Smoky* . . . . 20.00 - 30.00

8180 *Simpson County* . . . . 20.00 - 30.00

**(BOB) CRANFORD (ERNEST) THOMPSON
(with THE RED FOX CHASERS):**

Champion 16243 *That Sweetie Of Mine* . . . . 25.00 - 40.00

16261 *Otto Wood* . . . . 25.00 - 40.00

16490 *Sweet Fern* . . . . 30.00 - 50.00

16676 *Katy Cline* . . . . 50.00 - 75.00

16768 *Two Babes In The Woods* . . . . 50.00 - 75.00

45061, 45097 . . . . 10.00 - 15.00

Gennett 6636 *Stolen Love* . . . . 40.00 - 60.00

6672 *Something Wrong With My Gal* . . . . 40.00 - 60.00

6901 *Little Sweetheart Pal Of Mine* . . . . 40.00 - 60.00

6945 *Devilish Mary* . . . . 40.00 - 60.00

6959 *How I Love My Mabel* . . . . 40.00 - 60.00

AL CRAVER (& CHARLIE WELLS):

Columbia 15031-D, 15034-D, 15044-D, 15046-D,
15049-D, 15053-D, 15056-D, 15060-D,
15065-D, 15086-D, 15098-D, 15109-D, 15121-D,
15126-D, 15135-D, 15146-D, 15169-D, 15192-D,
15218-D, 15223-D, 15251-D, 15256-D . . . . 5.00 - 10.00

15449-D,15512-D, 15530-D,15546-D, 15561-D,
15585-D . . . . 7.00 - 12.00

ALVIN CRAWFORD:

Superior 2528 *I Sit Broken Hearted* . . . . 20.00 - 30.00

CRAZY HILL BILLIES BAND:

Okeh 45575 *Danced All Night With A Bottle In
My Hand* . . . . 25.00 - 40.00

45579 *Going Down The Road Feeling Bad* . . . . 25.00 - 40.00

CROCKER & CANNON:

Challenge 423 *Two Faithful Lovers* . . . . 5.00 - 8.00

**CROCKETT FAMILY MOUNTAINEERS;
CROCKETT'S KENTUCKY
MOUNTAINEERS:**

Brunswick 290 *Hard Cider Song* . . . . 15.00 - 20.00

291 *Medley* . . . . 15.00 - 20.00

353 *Bonaparte's Retreat* . . . . 15.00 - 20.00

394 *After The Ball* . . . . 15.00 - 20.00

Crown 3074 *Lightnin' Express* . . . . 20.00 - 30.00

3075 *Buffalo Gals Medley* . . . . 20.00 - 30.00

3121 *Sweet Betsy From Pike* . . . . 20.00 - 30.00

3172 *Cripple Creek* . . . . 20.00 - 30.00

3188 *Skip To My Lou* . . . . 20.00 - 30.00

Paramount 3277 *Granny's Old Arm Chair* . . . . . 50.00 - 75.00

3302 *Roving Gambler* . . . . 50.00 - 75.00

3303 *Take Me Back To Old Kentucky* . . . . 50.00 - 75.00

**JOHNNY (& ALBERT) CROCKETT (&
CROCKETT'S KENTUCKY
MOUNTAINEERS:**

Brunswick 372 *Fresno Blues* . . . . 20.00 - 30.00

Crown 3101 *I Was Born About 10,000 Years Ago* . 20.00 - 30.00

Paramount 3278 *The Blind Man's Lament* . . . . . 50.00 - 75.00

Specialty 702 *Just A Minute* . . . . 7.00 - 10.00

BALLARD CROSS:

Vocalion 5359 *My Poodle Dog* . . . . 10.00 - 15.00

5377 *The Wabash Cannon Ball* . . . . 10.00 - 15.00

5402 *Down Where The Swanee River Flows* . . . 10.00 - 15.00

BOB CROSS & HIS TROUBADOURS:

Personality 321/322 *Black Mountain Rag* . . . . . . 8.00 - 12.00

323/324 *Combination Rag* . . . . 8.00 - 12.00

**(HUGH) CROSS (& McCARTT/BOB
NICHOLS/RILEY PUCKETT):**

Columbia 15143-D *Sweet Rosie O'Grady* . . . . 5.00 - 8.00

15182-D *I'm Going Away From The Cotton
Fields* . . . . 5.00 - 8.00

15206-D *Red River Valley* . . . . 5.00 - 8.00

15231-D *The Mansion Of Aching Hearts* . . . . . . 5.00 - 8.00

15266-D *Where The Morning Glories Grow* . . . 5.00 - 8.00

15337-D *Clover Blossoms* . . . . 8.00 - 12.00

15365-D *Never No More Blues* . . . . 15.00 - 20.00

15421-D *Go Feather Your Nest* . . . . 15.00 - 20.00

15439-D *Wabash Cannon Ball* . . . . 15.00 - 20.00

15455-D *Gonna Raise A Ruckus Tonight* . . . . . . 15.00 - 20.00

15458-D *Prett Little Blue-Eyed Sally* . . . . 10.00 - 15.00

15478-D *Smiles* . . . . 10.00 - 15.00

15480-D *I Left My Gal In The Mountains* . . . . . 10.00 - 15.00

15482-D *Kickapoo Medicine Show* . . . . 15.00 - 20.00

15613-D *My Little Home In Tennessee* . . . . 20.00 - 30.00

CROWDER BROTHERS:

Titles, issued contemporaneously on Banner,
Conqueror, Melotone, Oriole, Perfect, Romeo,
include: *Blonde Headed Baby; Depot Blues;
Dying In Ashville Jail; Got No Use For Women;
Lonesome Lost Gal Blues; New Maple On The
Hill; The Sailing Ship* . . . . 10.00 - 15.00

Vocalion 03030 *Got No Use For Women* . . . . 10.00 - 15.00

(PAUL) CRUTCHFIELD (& CLOTWORTHY):

Okeh 45261 *Death's River*	10.00	-	15.00
45266 *Uncle Hiram's Trip To The City*	10.00	-	15.00

CRUTHERS BROTHERS:

Okeh 45307 *Carolina Moon*	7.00	-	10.00

CRYSEL BOYS with ALLEN BULLARD:

Titles, issued contemporaneously on Banner, Melotone, Oriole, Perfect, Romeo: *Crazy Blues; My Gal Kate* .... 10.00 - 15.00

CRYSTAL SPRING RAMBLERS:

Vocalion 03856 *Down In Arkansas*	7.00	-	10.00

CUMBERLAND RIDGE RUNNERS:

Conqueror 8310 *I'm Here To Get My Baby Out Of Jail*	5.00	-	8.00
Melotone 12981 *Roundin' Up The Yearlings*	5.00	-	8.00
Perfect 12993 *Roundin' Up The Yearlings*	5.00	-	8.00

CUMBERLAND STRING BAND:

Superior 2536 *Wink The Other Eye*	20.00	-	30.00

DAVE CUTRELL:

Okeh 45057 *Pistol Pete's Midnight Special*	15.00	-	20.00

DA COSTA WOLTZ'S SOUTHERN BROADCASTERS (featuring FRANK JENKINS/PRICE GOODSON):

Gennett 6187 *Lost Train Blues*	30.00	-	50.00
6220 *John Brown's Dream*	30.00	-	50.00
6223 *Roving Cowboy*	30.00	-	50.00
6240 *Evening Star Waltz*	30.00	-	50.00

VERNON DALHART:

This artist recorded for almost every label during the 1920's. Most of his records command minimal premiums. The selective listing following represents only a tiny fraction of his recorded output.

Black Patti 8027 *The Mississippi Flood*	75.00	-	125.00
8028 *Barbara Allen*	75.00	-	125.00
Buddy 8037 *The Great Titanic*	50.00	-	75.00
Edison (thin) 11002 *The West Plains Explosion*	25.00	-	40.00
20001 *Eleven Cent Cotton*	25.00	-	40.00
20003 *Big Rock Candy Mountain*	25.00	-	40.00
20010 *Dixie Way*	30.00	-	50.00

Edison (thick) 51459, 51541, 51557, 51584, 51597, 51605, 51607, 51608, 51609, 51610, 51611, 51620, 51621, 51637, 51643, 51649, 51669, 51670, 51693, 51741, 51718, 51729, 51735, 51749, 51807, 51827, 51856, 51883, 51901, 51949, 51974, 52020, 52029, 52088, 52095, 52118, 52134, 52144, 52174, 52229, 52248, 52307, 52335. 52423, 52434, 52457, 52472, 52487, 52533, 52558, 52566, 52599,

52628	7.00	-	15.00
52077 *My Horses Ain't Hungry*	20.00	-	30.00
Herschel Gold Seal 2005 *The Miami Storm*	30.00	-	50.00
2018 *Just A Melody*	30.00	-	50.00
Herwin 75501 *Blue Ridge Mountain Blues*	25.00	-	50.00
75505 *The Prisoner's Song*	25.00	-	50.00
Herwin 75506 *The New River Train*	25.00	-	50.00
75507 *Jesse James*	25.00	-	50.00
75517 *The Life Of Tom Watson*	25.00	-	50.00
75531 *Papa's Billy Goat*	25.00	-	50.00
75540 *The Wreck Of The Royal Palm*	25.00	-	50.00
75546 *The Mississippi Flood*	25.00	-	50.00

(TOMMY) DANDURAND & THE BARN DANCE FIDDLERS/HIS BARN DANCE GANG OF WLS/HIS GANG;

Gennett 6273 *Buffalo Gal*	12.00	-	18.00
6351 *McLeod's Reel*	12.00	-	18.00
Supertone 9156 *Big Town Fling*	6.00	-	10.00
9157 *Buffalo Girl*	6.00	-	10.00
9158 *Haste To The Wedding*	6.00	-	10.00
9159 *McLeod's Reel*	6.00	-	10.00
9160 *The Irish Washerwoman*	6.00	-	10.00
9162 *Devil's Dream*	6.00	-	10.00

(TOM) DARBY (JIMMIE) TARLTON:

Columbia 15197-D *Birmingham Town*	15.00	-	20.00
15212-D *Birmingham Jail*	10.00	-	15.00
15254-D *After The Ball*	20.00	-	30.00
15293-D *The Irish Police*	20.00	-	30.00
15319-D *Mexican Rag*	25.00	-	40.00
15330-D *Heavy Hearted Blues*	25.00	-	40.00
15360-D *The Rainbow Division*	25.00	-	40.00
15375-D *Birmingham Jail No. 2*	25.00	-	40.00
15388-D *If You Ever Learn To Love Me*	25.00	-	40.00
15403-D *Down In The Old Cherry Orchard*	30.00	-	50.00
15419-D *Slow Wicked Blues*	30.00	-	50.00
15436-D *Sweet Sarah Blues*	30.00	-	50.00
15452-D *Black Jack Moonshine*	30.00	-	50.00
15477-D *All Bound Down In Texas*	30.00	-	50.00
15492-D *Little Bessie*	30.00	-	50.00
15511-D *Freight Train Ramble*	30.00	-	50.00
15528-D *Jack And May*	30.00	-	50.00
15552-D *Faithless Husband*	30.00	-	50.00
15572-D *My Little Blue Heaven*	30.00	-	50.00
15591-D *The Maple On The Hill*	30.00	-	50.00
15611-D *Hard Time Blues*	50.00	-	75.00
15624-D *Beggar Joe*	50.00	-	75.00
15674-D *The Black Sheep*	50.00	-	75.00
15684-D *Gamblin' Jim*	50.00	-	75.00
15701-D *Rising Sun Blues*	50.00	-	75.00
15715-D *Going Back To My Texas Home*	75.00	-	100.00

MOUNTAIN DEW DARE:

Okeh 45170 *Don't Love A Smiling Sweetheart*	8.00	-	12.00

CHUCK DARLING:

Bluebird 5285 *Harmonica Rag*	7.00	-	10.00
Victor V40330 *Blowin' The Blues*	25.00	-	40.00

DAVE AND HOWARD:

Victor 23566 *Bay Rum Blues*	50.00	-	75.00
23577 *Serves 'Em Fine*	50.00	-	75.00

CARL DAVENPORT & HIS GANG:

Vocalion 5371 *Broken Hearted Lover*	15.00	-	20.00
5394 *Double Eagle March*	15.00	-	20.00

EMMETT DAVENPORT:

Supertone 9178 *The Dingy Miner's Cabin*	8.00	-	12.00
9179 *The Dying Girl's Message*	8.00	-	12.00
9388 *She Ain't Built That Way*	8.00	-	12.00
9539 *The Virginia Moonshiner*	8.00	-	12.00
9642 *Johnny The Drunkard*	8.00	-	12.00
9774 *An Old Fashioned Picture Of Mother*	8.00	-	12.00

HOMER DAVENPORT & THE YOUNG BROTHERS:

Silvertone 4089 *Down In Tennessee Blues*	10.00	-	15.00

DAVIS & NELSON:

Paramount 3186 *I Shall Not Be Moved*	20.00	-	30.00
3187 *I Don't Bother Work*	20.00	-	30.00
3188 *I Don't Want Your Greenback Dollar*	20.00	-	30.00
3227 *Charming Betsy*	25.00	-	50.00
Q.R.S. 9014 *I Don't Want Your Greenback Dollar*	25.00	-	50.00
9018 *I Don't Bother Work*	25.00	-	50.00

DAVIS, STOKES & LAYNE:

Gennett 6548 *Way Down In Alabam'*	30.00	-	50.00

DAVIS TRIO:

Paramount 3238 *Sleepy Hollow*	15.00	-	20.00

C.W./CHARLIE DAVIS:

Gennett 6637 *Sweet Bunch Of Daisies*	15.00	-	20.00
Timely Tunes 1559 *Down In A Southern Town*	15.00	-	20.00

CLAUDE DAVIS (TRIO) (& BOB NICHOLS):

Brunswick 503 *Over In The Hills Of California*	5.00	-	8.00
Columbia 15397-D *We Were Pals Together*	5.00	-	8.00
15466-D *Underneath The Southern Moon*	5.00	-	8.00
15740-D *Standing By The Highway*	8.00	-	12.00

EVA DAVIS:

Columbia 129-D *Wild Bill Jones*	7.00	-	10.00

JEWELL DAVIS:

Okeh 45152 *Thinking Of The Days I've Done Wrong*	7.00	-	10.00

JIMMIE DAVIS:

Bluebird 5005 *She's A Hum-Dum Dinger*	20.00 -	30.00
5156 *The Keyhole In The Door*	30.00 -	50.00
5187 *I Wonder If She's Blue*	30.00 -	50.00
5359 *I Want Her Tailor-Made*	30.00 -	50.00
5394 *Beautiful Texas*	8.00 -	12.00
5425 *Alimony Blues*	40.00 -	60.00
5496 *Arabella Blues*	25.00 -	40.00
5570 *Easy Rider Blues*	25.00 -	40.00
5635 *Triflin' Mama Blues*	25.00 -	40.00
5697 *I'll Get Mine Bye And Bye*	25.00 -	40.00
5699 *Red Nightgown Blues*	50.00 -	75.00
5751 *Sewing Machine Blues*	25.00 -	40.00
5806 *I'll Be Happy Today*	25.00 -	40.00
5965 *Minute Man, Part ½*	25.00 -	40.00
6040 *Dentist Blues*	25.00 -	40.00
6167 *Moonlight*	20.00 -	30.00
6236 *Sweet Sixteen*	15.00 -	20.00
6249 *The Davis Limited*	15.00 -	20.00
6272 *Organ Grinder Blues*	15.00 -	20.00
6437 *Yo Yo Mama*	15.00 -	20.00
7071 *My Dixie Sweetheart*	15.00 -	20.00
Victor 23517 *Arabella Blues*	50.00 -	75.00
23525 *In Arkansas*	50.00 -	75.00
23544 *Penitentiary Blues*	50.00 -	75.00
23559 *Before You Say Farewell*	50.00 -	75.00
23573 *Pea Pickin' Papa*	50.00 -	75.00
23587 *She's A Hum-Dinger*	50.00 -	75.00
23601 *The Davis Limited*	50.00 -	75.00
23620 *Market House Blues*	75.00 -	100.00
23628 *Wild And Reckless John*	75.00 -	100.00
23648 *Lonely Hobo*	75.00 -	100.00
23659 *Red Nightgown Blues*	100.00 -	150.00
23674 *Davis' Salty Dog*	100.00 -	150.00
23688 *1982 Blues*	100.00 -	150.00
23703 *High Behind Blues*	100.00 -	150.00
23718 *Cowboy's Home Sweet Home*	100.00 -	150.00
23746 *Shotgun Wedding*	100.00 -	150.00
23749 *Bury Me In Old Kentucky*	100.00 -	150.00
23752 *Hold 'Er Newt*	75.00 -	100.00
23763 Organ Grinder Blues	100.00 -	150.00
23778 *The Gambler's Return*	100.00 -	150.00
23793 *Yo Yo Mama*	100.00 -	150.00
V40154 *The Barroom Message*	75.00 -	100.00
V40215 *Out Of Town Blues*	75.00 -	100.00
V40286 *Doggone That Train*	75.00 -	100.00
V40302 *My Louisiana Girl*	75.00 -	100.00
V40332 *Settling Down For Life*	75.00 -	100.00

STAN DAVIS:

Okeh 45401 *The Body In The Bag*	10.00 -	15.00

DAVE DAWSON'S STRING BAND:

Superior 2517 *Over The Waves*	15.00 -	20.00
2575 *Grey Eagle*	15.00 -	20.00

DECKERS:

Paramount 3281 *When It's Night Time In Nevada*	10.00 -	20.00
3323 *That Little Boy Of Mine*	10.00 -	20.00

ROSCOE & SAM DELLINGER:

Bluebird 6852 *The Ohio River Floods*	5.00 -	10.00
6868 *Tellin' The Stars*	5.00 -	10.00

DELMORE BROTHERS:

Bluebird 5299 *Lonesome Yodel Blues*	10.00 -	15.00
5338 *The Frozen Girl*	10.00 -	15.00
5258 *I'm Leaving You*	10.00 -	15.00
5403 *Browns Ferry Blues*	5.00 -	8.00
5467 *Ramblin' Minded Blues*	8.00 -	12.00
5531 *Blue Railroad Train*	8.00 -	12.00
5589 *Smoky Mountain Bill*	8.00 -	12.00
5653 *I'm Mississippi Bound*	8.00 -	12.00
5741 *Lonesome Jailhouse Blues*	8.00 -	12.00
5857 *Hey! Hey! I'm Memphis Bound*	8.00 -	12.00
5893 *Brown's Ferry Blues, Part 2*	8.00 -	12.00
5925 *Lorena, The Slave*	7.00 -	10.00

5957 *I Long To See My Mother*	7.00 -	10.00
6002 *I Got The Kansas City Blues*	7.00 -	10.00
6019 *The Fugitive's Lament*	7.00 -	10.00
6034 *Alabama Lullaby*	7.00 -	10.00
6312 *The Nashville Blues*	7.00 -	10.00
6349 *I'm Worried Now*	7.00 -	10.00
6386 *Lonesome Yodel Blues No. 2*	7.00 -	10.00
6401 *Carry Me Back To Alabama*	7.00 -	10.00
6522 *The Lover's Warning*	7.00 -	10.00
6841 *Southern Moon*	7.00 -	10.00
6915 *No Drunkard Can Enter There*	7.00 -	10.00
6949 *False Hearted Girl*	7.00 -	10.00
6998 *No One*	7.00 -	10.00
7029 *Don't Forget Me, Darling*	7.00 -	10.00
7129 *Singing My Troubles Away*	7.00 -	10.00
7192 *They Say It Is Sinful To Flirt*	7.00 -	10.00
7262 *The Budded Rose*	7.00 -	10.00
7300 *Weary Lonesome Blues*	7.00 -	10.00
7337 *Lead Me*	7.00 -	10.00
7383 *The Farmers Girl*	7.00 -	10.00
7436 *Goodbye Booze*	7.00 -	10.00
7496 *'Cause I Don't Mean To Cry*	5.00 -	10.00
7560 *Big Ball In Texas*	5.00 -	10.00
7672 *Wonderful There*	5.00 -	10.00
7741 *Brother, Take Warning*	5.00 -	10.00
7778 *Alcatraz Island Blues*	5.00 -	10.00
7913 *Leavin' On That Train*	5.00 -	10.00
7957 *Where Is My Sailor Boy?*	5.00 -	10.00
7991 *The Cannon Ball*	5.00 -	10.00
8031 *Fifteen Miles From Birmingham*	5.00 -	10.00
8052 *Home On The River*	5.00 -	10.00
8177 *Baby, You're Throwing Me Down*	5.00 -	10.00
8204 *Wabash Blues*	5.00 -	10.00
8215 *I Loved You Better Than You Knew*	5.00 -	10.00
8230 *Gambler's Yodel*	5.00 -	10.00
8247 *Nothing But The Blues*	5.00 -	10.00
8264 *I'm Alabama Bound*	5.00 -	10.00
8290 *A Better Range Is Home*	5.00 -	10.00
8404 *Scatterbrain Mama*	5.00 -	10.00
8418 *Back To Birmingham*	5.00 -	10.00
8451 *Over The Hills*	5.00 -	10.00
8488 *The Eastern Gate*	5.00 -	10.00
8557 *Rainin' On The Mountain*	5.00 -	10.00
8613 *Storms Are On The Ocean*	5.00 -	10.00
8637 *Heart Of Sorrow*	5.00 -	10.00
8687 *That Yodelin' Gal, Miss Julie*	5.00 -	10.00
(Note: Some of above titles were also issued on Montgomery Ward label.)		
Columbia 15724-D *Got The Kansas City Blues*	75.00 -	125.00
Decca 5878, 5890, 5897, 5907, 5925, 5970, 6000, 6051, 6080	3.00 -	6.00
King 509, 514, 518, 525, 527, 533	3.00 -	5.00

MORGAN DENMON:

Okeh 45075 *Naomi Wise*	7.00 -	10.00
45105 *I've Still Got Ninety-Nine*	7.00 -	10.00
45306 *The Two Drummers*	8.00 -	12.00
45327 *The Drunkard's Dream*	8.00 -	12.00

DICK DEVALL:

Timely Tunes 1563 *Out On The Lone Star Cow Trail*	15.00 -	20.00

CHARLES M. (BUDDY) DE WITTE (THE SINGING MOONSHINER/ MOUNTAINEER; THE VAGABOND YODELER):

Champion 16371 *Vagabond Yodel*	35.00 -	50.00
16444 *Vagabond Yodel No. 2*	35.00 -	50.00
16658 *My Kentucky Cabin*	35.00 -	50.00
16680 *Rose Of Mother's Day*	50.00 -	75.00
16759 *The Girl I Met In Bluefield*	50.00 -	75.00
16825 *The Sad, Sad Story*	50.00 -	75.00

AL DEXTER & HIS TROOPERS:

Vocalion 03435 *New Jellyroll Blues*	7.00 -	10.00

03569, 03719, 03927, 03988 . . . . 5.00 - 8.00
04174, 04277, 04327, 04405, 04988, 05042 . . . 4.00 - 7.00

DEZURIK SISTERS:
Vocalion 04616, 04704, 04781 . . . . 4.00 - 7.00

DICKSON & CARROLL:
Superior 2523 *Advice To Husband Seekers* . . . . . . 15.00 - 20.00

BOB DICKSON:
Victor 23633, 23679 . . . . 7.00 - 12.00

M.S. DILLEHAY:
Victor V40155 *Mother-In-Law* . . . . 20.00 - 30.00

JOHN DILLESHAW & THE STRING MARVEL:
Okeh 45328 *Cotton Patch Rag* . . . . 75.00 - 100.00

(SEVEN FOOT) DILLEY (see DILLY) JOHN DILLINGSHAW:
Vocalion 5459 *Farmer's Blues* . . . . 35.00 - 50.00

DILLY, LINDSEY, LINDSEY, GRAY & BROWN; DILLY, TUCKER, LEE, STOKES & MELVIN; (SEVEN FOOT) DILLY & HIS DILL PICKLES:
Brunswick 489 *A Bootlegger's Joint In Atlanta* . . 30.00 - 50.00
575 *Kenesaw Mountain Rag* . . . . 30.00 - 50.00
Vocalion 5419 *Square Dance Fight On Bald Top Mountain* . . . . 50.00 - 75.00
5421 *Bust Down Stomp* . . . . 50.00 - 75.00
5436 *Georgia Bust Down* . . . . 50.00 - 75.00
5446 *Lye Soap* . . . . 50.00 - 75.00
5454 *A Georgia Barbecue At Stone Mountain* . 50.00 - 75.00

DIX & WILSON:
Bluebird 5397, 5472 . . . . 5.00 - 10.00

DIXIE CRACKERS:
Paramount 3151 *The Old Bell Cow* . . . . 20.00 - 30.00

DIXIE HARMONIZERS:
Gennett 6872 *Gonna Raise A Ruckus Tonight* . . . . 25.00 - 40.00

DIXIE MOUNTAINEERS:
Edison 52057 *Hop Light Ladies* . . . . 15.00 - 20.00

DIXIE STRING BAND:
Paramount 3164 *Atlanta Special* . . . . 25.00 - 40.00
3166 *Show Me The Way To Go Home* . . . . 20.00 - 30.00

DIXIELAND SWINGSTERS:
Bluebird 7857, 7882, 7899, 7948 . . . . 4.00 - 6.00

DIXIE RAMBLERS: (see also DOUG BINE)
Bluebird 6118, 6179, 6248, 6352. 6442 . . . . 4.00 - 8.00

DIXIE REELERS:
Bluebird 6461, 6713, 6738, 6831 . . . . 4.00 - 8.00

DIXIE STRING BAND:
Columbia 15273-D *Dixie Waltz* . . . . 10.00 - 15.00
Silvertone 3516 *Soldier's Joy* . . . . 7.00 - 10.00

DIXON'S CLOD HOPPERS:
Melotone 12007 *Steamboat Bill* . . . . 5.00 - 8.00
12052 *Wreck On The Southern Old 97* . . . . 5.00 - 8.00

DIXON BROTHERS:
Bluebird 6327 *Intoxicated Rat* . . . . 5.00 - 10.00
6441 *Weave Room Blues* . . . . 5.00 - 10.00
6462 *Answer To Maple On The Hill* . . . . 5.00 - 10.00
6582 *My Girl In Sunny Tennessee* . . . . 5.00 - 10.00
6630, 6691, 6809, 6867, 6979, 7020, 7263, 7449, 7674, 7767, 7801 . . . . 4.00 - 8.00

DIXON TRIO:
Victor 23790 *Carolina Lullaby* . . . . 10.00 - 20.00

BOB DIXON:
Victor 23752 *There Ain't No Man In The Moon* . . 75.00 - 100.00
23764 *Old Bill Smith* . . . . 10.00 - 15.00
23787 *What Are We Gonna Use For Money* . . . 10.00 - 15.00

JOHNNY DODDS:
Okeh 45417 *The Railroad Boomer* . . . . 75.00 - 100.00
45462 *No One To Call Me Darling* . . . . 75.00 - 100.00
45472 *Slu Foot Lue* . . . . 75.00 - 100.00
45560 *Cowboy Yodel* . . . . 75.00 - 100.00

DONALDSON QUARTET:
Victor 23788 *Hannah From Panama* . . . . 7.00 - 10.00

DONALDSON TRIO:
Bluebird 5003, 5035, 5060, 5134, 5166, 5221 . . . . 3.00 - 6.00

LOUIE DONALDSON & HOKE RICE:
Gennett 6885 *The Gang's All Here* . . . . 30.00 - 50.00

BUSTER DOSS & HIS ARKANSAS PLAYBOYS:
Talent 734 *Playboy Boogie* . . . . 10.00 - 15.00

EVAN DOUGLAS & NATE SMITH:
Champion 15651 *If I Could Only Blot Out The Past* . . . . 10.00 - 15.00
15711 *If I Only Had A Home* . . . . 10.00 - 15.00

THE DOWN HOMERS: (see also WOWO DOWN HOMERS)
Vogue 736 *Out Where The West Winds Blow* . . . . 25.00 - 40.00

DOYLE BROS:
TNT 113 *T.N.T. Baby* . . . . -

FRANK DUDGEON:
Champion 16532 *Atlanta Bound* . . . . 50.00 - 75.00
16575 *Sweet Betsy From Pike* . . . . 50.00 - 75.00
16580 *The Crime I Didn't Do* . . . . 50.00 - 75.00
16602 *Birmingham Jail No. 2* . . . . 50.00 - 75.00

FRANK DUNBAR:
Superior 2538 *Nobody's Darling On Earth* . . . . . 15.00 - 20.00

DUNCAN BOYS:
Supertone 9676 *Kentucky Stomp* . . . . 20.00 - 30.00

DUNCAN SISTERS:
Columbia 15745-D *Dusty Roads* . . . . 7.00 - 10.00

UNCLE ECK DUNFORD:
Victor 20880 *The Whip-Poor-Will Song* . . . . 10.00 - 15.00
20938 *Barney McCoy* . . . . 8.00 - 12.00
21131 *My First Bicycle Ride* . . . . 15.00 - 20.00
21244 *The Taffy-Pulling Party* . . . . 15.00 - 20.00
21578 *Sweat Summer Has Gone Away* . . . . 10.00 - 15.00
V40060 *Old Shoes And Leggin's* . . . . 20.00 - 30.00

BARNEY DUNROE:
Champion 15523 *Six Feet Of Earth* . . . . 10.00 - 15.00

DUPREE'S ROME BOYS:
Okeh 45320 *Wedding Bells Waltz* . . . . 30.00 - 50.00
45356 *Cat Rag-Breakdown* . . . . 30.00 - 50.00

DYE'S SACRED HARP SINGERS:
Gennett 6889 *Amazing Grace* . . . . 15.00 - 20.00

DYKES' MAGIC CITY TRIO:
Brunswick 120 *Cotton-Eyed Joe* . . . . 30.00 - 50.00
125 *Ida Red* . . . . 30.00 - 50.00
127 *Poor Ellen Smith* . . . . 30.00 - 50.00
128 *Hook And Line* . . . . 30.00 - 50.00
129 *Huckleberry Blues* . . . . 30.00 - 50.00
130 *Far Beyond The Blue Sky* . . . . 30.00 - 50.00
Vocalion 5143 *Frankie* . . . . 35.00 - 50.00
5181 *Callahan's Reel* . . . . 35.00 - 50.00

DICK DYSON (& HIS MUSICAL TEXANS):
Blue Bonnet 126 *Waited Too Long Blues* . . . . 7.00 - 10.00
Tri-State 113 *Hell's Fire* . . . . — - —

EARL & BILL:
Vocalion 15014 *On The Oregon Trail* . . . . 5.00 - 8.00

EAST TEXAS SERENADERS:
Brunswick 282 *Acorn Stomp* . . . . 7.00 - 10.00
298 *Deacon Jones* . . . . 10.00 - 15.00
379 *Three-In-One Two Step* . . . . 10.00 - 15.00
429 *Mckinney Waltz* . . . . 10.00 - 15.00
453 *Babe* . . . . 15.00 - 20.00
538 *Ozark Rag* . . . . 15.00 - 20.00
562 *Mineola Rag* . . . . 15.00 - 20.00
Columbia 15229-D *Combination Rag* . . . . 10.00 - 15.00

GARNER ECKLER & ROLAND GAINES (YODELING TWINS):
Champion 45043 *Moonlight And Skies* . . . . 5.00 - 8.00
45087 *Mountain Rangers Lullaby* . . . . 5.00 - 8.00

GEORGE EDGIN'S CORN DODGERS:
Columbia 15754-D *My Ozark Mountain Home* . . 50.00 - 80.00

DAVE EDWARDS & HIS ALABAMA BOYS:
Decca 5470, 5478, 5493, 5507, 5522, 5536, 5564, ... 5.00 - 10.00

HAROLD EDWARDS:

Champion 15702 *Who Cares What You Have
  Been* .... 7.00 - 10.00
ELK CREEK TRIO:
  Champion 15584 *Silvery Bell* .... 5.00 - 8.00
ELKINS' STRINGED STEPPERS:
  Okeh 45079 *Speed* .... 50.00 - 75.00
RAY ELKINS:
  Champion 15831 *The Boy's Best Friend* .... 8.00 - 12.00
ELLIOTT (& MITCHELL):
  Victor 23646 *When It's Springtime In The Blue
    Ridge Mountains* .... 15.00 - 20.00
    23652 *When The Oriole Sings Again* .... 15.00 - 20.00
ELM CITY QUARTET:
  Champion 16827 *The Tree Song* .... 7.00 - 10.00
ELMER & JUD:
  Broadway 8052 *Turkey In The Straw* .... 5.00 - 8.00
  Conqueror 7332 *Turkey In The Straw* .... 5.00 - 8.00
  Oriole 1414 *Turkey In The Straw* .... 5.00 - 8.00
EVANS' OLD TIMERS:
  Champion 16512 *Honeysuckle Time* .... 50.00 - 80.00
    16531 *The Old Elm Tree* .... 50.00 - 80.00
    16709 *No Low Down Hanging Around* .... 75.00 - 100.00
CLYDE EVANS BAND:
  Columbia 15597-D *How I Got My Gal* .... 20.00 - 30.00
JOHN B. EVANS:
  Brunswick 237 *Three Night's Experience* ...... 8.00 - 12.00
    276 *The Last Mile Of The Way* .... 8.00 - 12.00
  Supertone 2051 *Mother's Grave* .... 7.00 - 10.00
**CLAY EVERHEART & THE NORTH
CAROLINA COOPER BOYS:**
  Columbia 15737-D *Standing By A Window* ...... 75.00 - 100.00
BOB FAGAN:
  Challenge 839 *She Was A Moonshiner's
    Daughter* .... 7.00 - 10.00
JIMMIE FAIR:
  Kentucky 532 *I'll Walk Alone* .... 4.00 - 7.00
    533 *Just A Little Lovin'* .... 4.00 - 7.00
    538 *Anytime* .... 4.00 - 7.00
J.D. FARLEY:
  Victor V40269 *Bill Was A Texas Lad* .... 25.00 - 35.00
FARM HANDS:
  Paramount 3294 *The Old Hayloft Waltz* .... 20.00 - 30.00
HARVEY FARR:
  Supertone 9320 *The Santa Barbara Earthquake* . 8.00 - 12.00
    9372 *The Fate Of Ellen Smith* .... 8.00 - 12.00
FAY & THE JAYWALKERS:
  Paramount 3100 *My Baby Don't Love Me* .... 20.00 - 30.00
    3156 *Longing For Home* .... 20.00 - 30.00
BOB FERGUSON (& HS SCALAWAGGERS):
  Columbia 15297-D, 15433-D, 15476-D,
    15529-D, 15553-D, 15616-D, 15664-D .... 4.00 - 8.00
    15677-D *The Strawberry Roan* .... 8.00 - 12.00
    15704-D, 15727-D, 15732-D, 15739-D,
    15759-D, 15782-D .... 4.00 - 8.00
  Victor 23697, 23704, 23715 .... 10.00 - 15.00
JOHN FERGUSON:
  Challenge 158 *Wild Bill Jones* .... 10.00 - 15.00
    159 *Railroad Daddy* .... 10.00 - 15.00
    324 *Wild Bill Jones* .... 10.00 - 15.00
    325 *Frankie's Gamblin' Man* .... 8.00 - 12.00
  Supertone 9259 *Down Where The Swanee River
    Flows* .... 6.00 - 10.00
FIDDLER JOE & HIS BOYS:
  Okeh 45042 *Turkey In The Straw* .... 10.00 - 15.00
FLANNERY SISTERS:
  Decca 5000, 5256, 5284 .... 4.00 - 7.00
ALAN FLATT & HIS BAND:
  Jamboree 508 *It's All Over Now* .... 5.00 - 8.00
    511 *I'm Movin' On* .... 5.00 - 8.00
FLEMING & TOWNSEND:
  Bluebird 5002, 5106, 5186, 5256, 5378, 5426,
    5470, 5497, 5566, 5634, 5694, 5695, 5696,

5821, 5874 .... 7.00 - 10.00
Decca 5419, 5427, 5445, 5463, 5487, 5516 ...... 5.00 - 8.00
Melotone 13231 *She's Just That Kind* .... 8.00 - 12.00
(Note: Probably issued also on Banner, Oriole,
  Perfect, Romeo.)
Victor 23509 *She's Always On My Mind* .... 25.00 - 40.00
  23520 *I'll Tell You About Women* .... 25.00 - 40.00
  23543 *Gonna Quit Dnnkin'* .... 25.00 - 40.00
  23557 *Ramblin' Boy* .... 25.00 - 40.00
  23563 *I'm Leavin' This Town* .... 30.00 - 50.00
  23575 *Sweet Daddy From Tennessee* .... 30.00 - 50.00
  23594 *How Can You Be Mean To Me* .... 30.00 - 50.00
  23604 *Come And Drift With Me* .... 30.00 - 50.00
  23625 *I Feel So Blue* .... 30.00 - 50.00
  23635 *Blowin' The Blues* .... 35.00 - 50.00
  23666 *First Time In Jail* .... 35.00 - 50.00
  23676 *Yes, I Got Mine* .... 35.00 - 50.00
  23694 *Bad Reputations* .... 40.00 - 60.00
  23710 *That Lonesome Train* .... 50.00 - 75.00
  23758 *Blues Have Gone* .... 50.00 - 75.00
  23771 *When It's Hottest Doun South* .... 50.00 - 75.00
  23789 *Picture On My Dresser* .... 50.00 - 75.00
  23793 *Do-Do-Daddling Thing* .... 50.00 - 75.00
  23814 *Right Always Wins* .... 75.00 - 100.00
  23829 *Gambler's Advice* .... 75.00 - 100.00
  V40297 *She's Just That Kind* .... 30.00 - 50.00
  V40321 *I'm Blue And Lonesome* .... 35.00 - 50.00

FLETCHER & FOSTER:
  Champion 16121 *Travelin' North* .... 35.00 - 50.00
  Victor V40232 *Charlotte Hot Step* .... 30.00 - 50.00
OTTO & JIM FLETCHER:
  Superior 2669 *True And Trembling Brakeman* ... 35.00 - 50.00
    2726 *When The Cactus Is In Bloom* .... 35.00 - 50.00
    2749 *Columbus Stockade Blues* .... 35.00 - 50.00
    2777 *The Chicken Roost Blues* .... 35.00 - 50.00
**TEX FLETCHER (& JOE ROGERS); TEX
FLETCHER'S LONELY COWBOYS:**
  Decca 5300, 5302, 5320, 5332, 5391, 5403,
    5441, 5460, 5489, 5500, 5520 .... 4.00 - 8.00
TIM FLORA & RUFUS LINGO:
  Okeh 45311 *Stuttering Billy* .... 10.00 - 15.00
FLOYD COUNTY RAMBLERS:
  Victor 23759 *Barn Dance* .... 50.00 - 75.00
  V40307 *Sunny Tennessee* .... 25.00 - 40.00
  V40331 *Aunt Dinah's Quilting Party* .... 30.00 - 50.00
ELZIE FLOYD & LEO BOSWELL:
  Columbia 15150-D *Nellie Dare* .... 7.00 - 10.00
    15167-D *The Two Orphans* .... 7.00 - 10.00
DAVID FOLEY:
  Challenge 393 *I'll Never Be Yours* .... 8.00 - 12.00
    394 *Poor Little Joe* .... 8.00 - 12.00
    397 *Train No. 45* .... 8.00 - 12.00
**(RAMBLING) RED FOLEY (Acc. by THE
CUMBERLAND RIDGE RUNNERS):**
Titles, issued contemporaneously on Banner,
  Melotone, Oriole, Periect, Romeo: *Blonde
  Headed Girl; The Dying Rustler, Echoes of My
  Plantation Home; I Got The Freight Train
  Blues; Just One Little Kiss; The Lone Cowboy;
  Seven Long Years; Single Life Is Good Enough
  For Me* .... 7.00 - 12.00

FORD & GRACE:
Okeh 45157 *Kiss Me Cindy* . . . . 10.00 - 15.00
  45237 *Hide Away* . . . . 10.00 - 15.00

JACK FORD:
Chess 4858 *That's All You Gotta Do* . . . . 5.00 - 8.00

OSCAR FORD:
Columbia 15437-D *Henry Ford's Model A* . . . . . . 8.00 - 12.00
  15554-D *Me And My Gal* . . . . 8.00 - 12.00
  15599-D *The Farmer's Dream* . . . . 10.00 - 15.00
  15634-D *Georgia Is My Home* . . . . 10.00 - 15.00
  15673-D *Little Nan* . . . . 10.00 - 15.00

FORT WORTH BOYS (see MILTON BROWN)

FORT WORTH DOUGHBOYS:
Bluebird 5257 *Nancy Jane* . . . . 40.00 - 60.00
Montgomery Ward 4416 *Nancy Jane* . . . . 40.00 - 60.00
Victor 23653 *Nancy Jane* . . . . 80.00 - 120.00

JOE FOSS & HIS HUNGRY SANDLAPPERS:
Columbia 15268-D *Oh! How She Lied* . . . . 10.00 - 15.00

(J.D.) FOSTER (& J.D. JAMES); FOSTER & (T.S.) YOUNG; JOHN FOSTER:
Champion 16733 *My Boyhood Happy Days* . . . . 20.00 - 30.00
  16753 *Some Day I'll Wander Back Again* . . . . . 20.00 - 30.00
  45037, 45102 . . . . 7.00 - 10.00
Gennett 6434 *When I Was Single, My Pockets*
  Would Jingle . . . . 20.00 - 30.00
  6791 *My Sarah Jane* . . . . 20.00 - 30.00

OWEN FOSTER:
Victor 20934 *Wilkes County Blues* . . . . 20.00 - 30.00

SALLY FOSTER & THE TRAVELERS:
Decca 5229, 5308, 5333, 5352, 5387 . . . . 4.00 - 8.00

FOUR BUZZ SAWS:
Vocalion 5471 *The Tree Song* . . . . 7.00 - 10.00

FOUR PICKLED PEPPERS:
Bluebird . . . . 4.00 - 8.00

FOUR VIRGINIANS:
Okeh 45163 *Two Little Lads* . . . . 15.00 - 20.00
  45181 *Swing Your Partner* . . . . 15.00 - 20.00

FOX CHASERS:
Okeh 45477 *Red Wing* . . . . 15.00 - 25.00
  45496 *Forked Deer* . . . . 15.00 - 25.00

FOX & DAVIS:
Supertone 9406 *Monroe County Quickstep* . . . . . 10.00 - 15.00

CODY FOX & HIS YELLOW JACKETS:
Vocalion 03493 *I Only Want A Buddy* . . . . 5.00 - 8.00

CURLEY FOX:
Decca 5169 *Tennessee Roll* . . . . 7.00 - 10.00
  5185 *Yum Yum Blues* . . . . 7.00 - 10.00
  5213 *Listen To The Mockingbird* . . . . 7.00 - 10.00

GLEN FOX & JOE WILSON:
Vocalion 5490 *My Dixie Home* . . . . 5.00 - 8.00
  5495 *The Old Covered Bridge* . . . . 5.00 - 8.00
  5496 *The Roundup In The Spring* . . . . 5.00 - 8.00

OSCAR FOX:
Supertone 9325 *My Dear Old Mountain Home* . . 7.00 - 10.00

DUEL FRADY:
Victor 20930 *Leavenworth* . . . . 7.00 - 10.00

LEE FRAZIER:
Champion 16626 *The Ice Man Blues* . . . . 50.00 - 80.00

FREDERICK & MASON:
Victor 20965 *Missouri Waltz* . . . . 5.00 - 10.00

FREED & MOORE:
Vocalion 14865 *Harmonica Blues* . . . . 7.00 - 10.00
  14917 *Banjo Blues* . . . . 7.00 - 10.00
  15116 *Plantation Medley* . . . . 7.00 - 10.00

FREEMAN & ASHCRAFT:
Columbia 15442-D *Alabama Rag* . . . . 30.00 - 50.00

FREENY'S BARN DANCE BAND:
Okeh 45508 *Don't You Remember The Time* . . . . 30.00 - 50.00
  45524 *The Leake County Two Step* . . . . 30.00 - 50.00
  45533 *Mississippi Square Dance* . . . . 30.00 - 50.00

THE FRONTIERSMEN:
Bullet 708 *Honky Tonk Hop* . . . . 4.00 - 7.00

FRUIT JAR GUZZLERS:
Paramount 3095 *Sourwood Mountain* . . . . 35.00 - 50.00
  3099 *Black Sheep Of The Family* . . . . 35.00 - 50.00
  3106 *Yes, I'm Free* . . . . 35.00 - 50.00
  3113 *Kentucky Bootlegger* . . . . 35.00 - 50.00
  3116 *Cripple Creek* . . . . 35.00 - 50.00
  3121 *Steel Driving Man* . . . . 35.00 - 50.00
  3148 *Old Joe Clark* . . . . 25.00 - 50.00

JEP FULLER:
Vocalion 5074, 15125 . . . . 4.00 - 7.00

CLARENCE (& CLAUDE) GANUS:
Vocalion 5272 *Memories Of Floyd Collins* . . . . . 15.00 - 20.00
  5284 *Down In Indiana* . . . . 15.00 - 20.00
  5312 *Just The Thought Of Mother* . . . . 15.00 - 20.00
  5385 *I Love Nobody But You* . . . . 15.00 - 20.00
  5386 *Sleeping At The Foot Of The Bed* . . . . . 15.00 - 20.00
  5396 *The Dying Soldier* . . . . 15.00 - 20.00
  5409 *Take A Tater And Wait* . . . . 15.00 - 20.00
  5417 *I'm Going Away* . . . . 15.00 - 20.00
  5452 *Won't The Angels Let Mama Come* . . . . 15.00 - 20.00

GARDNER & DAVID:
Diva 6010-G *John Hardy* . . . . 5.00 - 8.00

BLIND UNCLE GASPARD:
Vocalion 5320 *Markeville Blues* . . . . 50.00 - 75.00
  5333 *Natchitocheo* . . . . 50.00 - 75.00

AUBREY GASS:
Capitol 1427 *K.C Boogie* . . . . 5.00 - 8.00
Gold Star 1318 *Delivery Man Blues* . . . . 5.00 - 8.00

JOHNNIE GATES:
Columbia 15573-D *Saw Mill Blues No. 1* . . . . . 10.00 - 15.00
  15661-D *Saw Mill Blues No. 2* . . . . 10.00 - 15.00

GATWOOD SQUARE DANCE BAND:
Columbia 15363-D *Third Party* . . . . 15.00 - 20.00

RED GAY & JACK WELLMAN:
Brunswick 523 *Flat Wheel Train Blues* . . . . 15.00 - 20.00

WHIT GAYDON:
Victor V40315 *Tennessee Coon Hunt* . . . . 15.00 - 20.00

NORMAN GAYLE:
Champion 15447 *Train No. 45* . . . . 10.00 - 15.00
  15465 *She's Mine All Mine* . . . . 10.00 - 15.00
  15501 *Sally Gooden* . . . . 10.00 - 15.00

GEORGE'S HOT SHOTS:
Victor 23729 *We Do It Just The Same* . . . . 10.00 - 15.00

GEORGIA CRACKERS:
Okeh 45098 *Diamond Joe* . . . . 20.00 - 30.00
  45111 *Georgia Black Bottom* . . . . 15.00 - 20.00
  45192 *Stockade Blues* . . . . 20.00 - 30.00

GEORGIA MELODY BOYS:
Broadway 8119 *Cabin Home* . . . . 7.00 - 10.00

GEORGIA ORGAN GRINDERS:
Columbia 15394-D *Back Up And Push* . . . . 25.00 - 40.00
  15415-D *Charming Betsy* . . . . 25.00 - 40.00
  15445-D *Georgia Man* . . . . 30.00 - 50.00

GEORGIA POT LICKERS:
Brunswick 595 *Up Jumped The Rabbit* . . . . 15.00 - 20.00

GEORGIA SERENADERS:
Supertone 9473 *Gonna Raise a Ruckus Tonight* . . 10.00 - 15.00

GEORGIA WILDCATS:
Victor 23640 *She's Waiting For Me* . . . . 30.00 - 50.00

GEORGIA YELLOW HAMMERS:
Victor 20549 *Fourth Of July* . . . . 8.00 - 12.00
  20550 *Pass Around The Bottle* . . . . 7.00 - 10.00
  20928 *Mary, Don't You Weep* . . . . 10.00 - 15.00
  20943 *My Carolina Girl* . . . . 7.00 - 10.00
  21073 *Tennessee Coon* . . . . 15.00 - 20.00
  21195 *G Rag* . . . . 20.00 - 30.00
  21362 *The Song Of The Doodle Bug* . . . . 20.00 - 30.00
  21486 *The Old Rock Jail* . . . . 20.00 - 30.00
  21626 *Moonshine Hollow Band* . . . . 20.00 - 30.00
  23542 *No One To Welcome Me* . . . . 50.00 - 75.00
  23547 *Child Hood Days* . . . . 50.00 - 75.00
  23683 *Peaches Down In Georgia* . . . . 75.00 - 100.00

V40004 *Warhorse Game*	30.00 -	50.00
V40069 *The Sale Of Simon Slick*	30.00 -	50.00
V40091 *Kiss Me Quick*	30.00 -	50.00
V40138 *Big Ball In Memphis*	40.00 -	60.00

FRANK GERARD-HOWARD DIXON-MUTT EVANS:

Bluebird 7895 *Honey, Baby Mine*	7.00 -	10.00

GIBBS BROTHERS & CLYDE DAVIS:

Vocalion 5447 *I Love My Toodlum-Doo*	25.00 -	40.00
5464 *Strolling Home With Jenny*	25.00 -	40.00

HUGH GIBBS STRING BAND:

Paramount 3001 *I'm Goin' Crazy*	25.00 -	40.00
3002 *Almost Persuaded*	25.00 -	40.00
3003 *Chicken Feed*	25.00 -	40.00
3004 *In The Good Old Summertime*	25.00 -	40.00

GRINNELL GIGGERS:
(see GRINNELL)

CECIL GILL (YODELING COUNTRY BOY):

Silver Star 100, 101	5.00 -	10.00

GIRLS OF THE GOLDEN WEST:

Bluebird 5155, 5167, 5189, 5226, 5288, 5318, 5382, 5394, 5427, 5718, 5719, 5737, 5732, 6004, 6054, 6163, 6164, 6178, 6255	5.00 -	10.00
Victor 23857 *The Cowgirl's Dream*	35.00 -	50.00
Vocalion 04022, 04053, 04103, 04147, 04234, 04292, 04373	4.00 -	7.00

SHORTY GODWIN:

Columbia 15411-D *Turnip Greens*	8.00 -	12.00

GOLDEN MELODY BOYS:

Paramount 3068 *The Cross Eyed Butcher*	5.00 -	8.00
3074 *Would You Ever Think Of Me*	5.00 -	8.00
3081 *Cabin Home*	5.00 -	8.00
3087 *Way Down In Arkansas*	5.00 -	8.00
3107 *Freak Melody*	10.00 -	15.00
3124 *Jack And May*	10.00 -	15.00
3137 *When The Lilac Blooms*	10.00 -	15.00
3153 *Uncle Ebner & Ebner At The Rehersal*	10.00 -	15.00
3169 *Guitar Rag*	12.00 -	15.00

DAN GOLDEN:

Champion 15525 *Good Old Turnip Greens*	10.00 -	15.00

GOOD'S BOX WHITTLERS:

Vocalion 5352 *Election Day In Kentucky*	10.00 -	15.00

HERALD GOODMAN & HIS TENNESSEE VALLEY BOYS:

Bluebird 7868, 7935, 7999, 8033	5.00 -	8.00

PRICE GOODSON:

Gennett 6154 *Lonesome Road Blues*	35.00 -	50.00

GOOSE CREEK GULLY JUMPERS:

Superior 2639 *Let Me Call You Sweetheart*	15.00 -	20.00
2738 *Medley*	15.00 -	20.00

ALEX GORDON:

Conqueror 7269 *A Message From Home Sweet Home*	10.00 -	15.00
7270 *The Burial Of Wild Bill*	10.00 -	15.00

TOMMY GORDON & HIS CORN HUSKERS:

Superior 2614 *Halfway To Arkansas*	25.00 -	40.00
2712 *Wild Hog In The Woods*	25.00 -	40.00

TED GOSSETT'S BAND:

Champion 16116 *Fox Chase*	15.00 -	25.00
16310 *Bow Legged Irishman*	20.00 -	30.00
Gennett 7308 *Fox Chase*	30.00 -	50.00

GRADY FAMILY:

Columbia 15633-D *Carolina's Best*	10.00 -	15.00

GRAHAM BROTHERS:

Victor 23654 *Ninety-Nine Years*	8.00 -	12.00
23664 *Gene, The Fighting Marine*	8.00 -	12.00
23668 *Spring's Tornado*	8.00 -	12.00
23670 *Don't Hang Me*	8.00 -	12.00
23690 *Bobby Boy*	8.00 -	12.00

HENRY GRAHAM:

Bell 1167 *The Marion Parker Murder*	7.00 -	10.00
1177 *The Sinking Of The Submarine S-4*	7.00 -	10.00

GRANT BROTHERS & THEIR MUSIC:

Columbia 15322-D *Tell It To Me*	15.00 -	20.00
15460-D *Goodbye My Honey, I'm Gone*	15.00 -	20.00

GRANT TRIO:

Victor 23667 *Under The Old Umbrella*	8.00 -	12.00
23743 *Say A Prayer For Baby*	8.00 -	12.00

GRAPEVINE COON HUNTERS:

Brunswick 584 *The Broan Waltz*	15.00 -	20.00

GRAVES & TANNER:

Vocalion 5342 *The Bum's Rush*	15.00 -	20.00

GRAY & NELSON:

Supertone 9309 *Mandolin Rag*	8.00 -	12.00
9377 *Farewell Waltz*	8.00 -	12.00
9397 *Martha Campbell*	8.00 -	12.00
9670 *Waltz The Hall*	8.00 -	12.00

A.A. GRAY & SEVEN FOOT DILLY:

Vocalion 5430 *Streak O'Lean-Streak O'Fat*	50.00 -	75.00
5458 *The Old Ark's A 'Moving*	50.00 -	75.00

"MOMMIE" GRAY/OWEN GRAY/OTTO GRAY'S (OKLAHOMA) COWBOY BAND:

Champion 16027 *It Can't Be Done*	15.00 -	25.00
Gennett 6376 *It Can't Be Done*	25.00 -	40.00
6387 *In The Baggage Coach Ahead*	25.00 -	40.00
Gennett 6405 *The Drunkard's Lone Child*	25.00 -	40.00
7222 *Down Where The Swanee River Flows*	30.00 -	50.00
Superior 2550 *It Can't Be Done*	20.00 -	30.00
Vocalion 5250 *It Can't Be Done*	30.00 -	50.00
5267 *Tom Cat Blues*	30.00 -	50.00
5301 *Be Home Early Tonight, My Dear*	30.00 -	50.00
5327 *The Terrible Marriage*	30.00 -	50.00
5337 *Midnight Special*	30.00 -	50.00
5479 *Who Stole The Lock*	30.00 -	50.00

(G.B.) GRAYSON & (HENRY) WHITTER (See also WHITTER & GRAYSON):

Bluebird 5498, 7072	4.00 -	8.00
Gennett 6304 *Nobody's Darling*	30.00 -	50.00
Victor 21139 *Don't Go Out Tonight My Darling*	15.00 -	20.00
21189 *Train Forty-Five*	15.00 -	20.00
21625 *Rose Conley*	15.00 -	20.00
23565 *Going Down The Lee Highway*	40.00 -	60.00
V40038 *Joking Henry*	15.00 -	20.00
V40063 *Red And Green Signal Lights*	15.00 -	25.00
V40268 *I Have Lost You Darling*	20.00 -	30.00
V40324 *I've Always Been A Rambler*	25.00 -	40.00

GREAT GAP ENTERTAINERS:

Broadway 8137 *Barn Dance On The Mountain*	10.00 -	15.00
8140 *Pussy Cat Rag*	10.00 -	15.00
8200 *O Wasn't I Getting Away*	10.00 -	15.00

GREEN'S STRING BAND:

Champion 16115 *Zenda Waltz*	15.00 -	20.00
16249 *Gray Eagle*	15.00 -	20.00
16489 *Rickett's Hornpipe*	20.00 -	30.00
Gennett 7307 *Glide Waltz*	15.00 -	25.00

GREEN & RUSSELL:

Supertone 9377 *Goodnight Waltz*	10.00 -	15.00

UNCLE GEORGE GREEN & HIS BOYS:

Champion 15828 *Louisiana Hop*	8.00 -	12.00
15896 *Polly Wolly Doodle*	8.00 -	12.00

JERRY GREEN:

Specialty 712 *Naggin' Women And Braggin' Men*	8.00 -	12.00
714 *Are You Goin' My Way?*	— -	—

AMOS GREENE:

Supertone 9651 *Down In The Jailhouse On My Knees*	12.00 -	18.00
9671 *Memphis Yodel*	12.00 -	18.00
9707 *I'm Lonely And Blue*	12.00 -	18.00
9708 *Yodeling Them Blues Away*	12.00 -	18.00
9709 *Just A Lonely Hobo*	12.00 -	18.00

CLARENCE GREENE (& THE WISE BROTHERS):

Columbia 15311-D *Fond Affection*	20.00 -	30.00

15461-D *Johnson City Blues*	20.00 -	30.00
15580-D *Pride Of The Ball*	20.00 -	30.00
Victor V40141 *Little Bunch Of Roses*	20.00 -	30.00

LEM GREEN:

Okeh 45418 *Eleven More Months & Ten More Days*	8.00 -	12.00

PROFESSOR & MRS. GREER:

Paramount 3195 *Black Jack Davy*	25.00 -	40.00
3236 *Sweet William And Fair Ellen*	25.00 -	40.00

BOBBY GREGORY:

Okeh 45350 *The Runaway Boys*	10.00 -	15.00
45473 *Hoopee Scoopee*	10.00 -	15.00
45500 *Little Pal Of Mine*	10.00 -	15.00

WALLACE GREY:

Champion 15832 *Little Mamie*	8.00 -	12.00

REX GRIFFIN:

Decca 5088, 5089, 5118, 5147, 5202, 5227, 5250, 5269, 5294, 5383, 5395	4.00 -	7.00

TAYLOR GRIGGS MELODY MAKERS (See TAYLOR'S MELODY MAKERS):

GRINNELL GIGGERS:

Bluebird 5284 *Ruth's Rag*	15.00 -	25.00
Victor 23511 *Duck Shoes Rag*	50.00 -	80.00
23632 *Cotton Picker's Rag*	75.00 -	100.00
23675 *Plow Boy Hop*	75.00 -	100.00
V40275 *Giggers Waltz*	50.00 -	80.00

BILL GRUBBS & HIS OKLAHOMA RAMBLERS:

Blue Bonnet 101 *My Gal Alice*	5.00 -	8.00
105 *I'm Gonna Wake Up In Waco*	5.00 -	8.00

GUNBOAT BILLY & THE SPARROW:

Crown 3077 *Eleven More Months And Ten More Days*	7.00 -	10.00
Paramount 3273 *Eleven More Months And Ten More Days*	7.00 -	10.00
Victor 23698 *I'm Glad I'm A Bum*	10.00 -	15.00
23714 *Four Stone Walls*	10.00 -	15.00
24024 *Oh Lord The Life Of A Hobo*	7.00 -	10.00

HARDROCK GRUNTER & THE PEBBLES:

Bama 104 *Birmingham Bounce*	5.00 -	8.00
202 *Lonesome Blues*	5.00 -	8.00

(E.E) HACK'S STRING BAND:

Champion 16292 *Kentucky Plow Boy's March*	30.00 -	50.00
45149 *Wink The Other Eye*	10.00 -	15.00
Columbia 15418-D *Too Tight Rag*	25.00 -	40.00
15466-D *Black Lake Waltz*	30.00 -	50.00

HACKBERRY RAMBLERS:

Bluebird 2002 *Bring It Down To The Jailhouse, Honey*	8.00 -	12.00
2003 *Jolie Blonde*	8.00 -	12.00
2005 *Vinton High Society*	8.00 -	12.00
2010 *Rambling*	8.00 -	12.00
2013 *Cajun Crawl*	8.00 -	12.00
2017 *Rice City Stomp*	8.00 -	12.00
2019 *Dobie Shack*	8.00 -	12.00
2021, 2066, 6069, 6110, 6120, 6136, 6181, 6289, 6368	8.00 -	12.00

RED HADLEY'S WRANGLERS:

Meteor 5017 *Brother, That's All*	5.00 -	8.00*

EWEN HAIL:

Brunswick 141 *Cowboy's Lament*	5.00 -	8.00
433 *Cowboy's Lament*	5.00 -	8.00
Vocalion 5146 *Cowboy's Lament*	5.00 -	8.00

THERON HALE & DAUGHTERS:

Victor V40019 *Turkey Gobbler*	25.00 -	40.00
V40046 *Jolly Blacksmith*	25.00 -	40.00

TRAVIS B. HALE (& E.J. DERRY, JR.):

Victor 20796 *Oh Bury Me Out On The Prairie*	5.00 -	8.00
20866 *Long Gone*	7.00 -	10.00

AMBROSE HALEY'S OZARK RAMBLERS:

Vocalion 03590 *It Looks Like Rain In Cherry Blossom Lane*	7.00 -	10.00

03648 *How's Your Folks & My Folks*	7.00 -	10.00
03709 *I Can't Lose That Longing For You*	7.00 -	10.00

HALL BROTHERS:

Bluebird 6843 *Little Mohee*	5.00 -	8.00
6925 *Whistle, Honey, Whistle*	7.00 -	10.00
7103 *Little Girl, You've Done Me Wrong*	7.00 -	10.00
7363 *Spartanburg Jail*	7.00 -	10.00
7462 *Alcatraz Prisoner*	7.00 -	10.00
7728 *The Wrong Road*	7.00 -	10.00
7801 *Hitch-Hike Blues*	7.00 -	10.00
Clarion 5183-C *That Goes On For Days And Days*	5.00 -	8.00

HALL TRIO:

Victor 23782 *The Answer To 21 Years*	10.00 -	15.00
23797 *It Makes No Difference*	10.00 -	15.00
23799 *I'm Twisting Loops In Pretzels*	10.00 -	15.00
23836 *Absolutely Free*	10.00 -	15.00
23838 *Shepherd Of The Air*	10.00 -	15.00

ROY HALL (& HIS BLUE RIDGE ENTERTAINERS):

Bluebird 8561 *New San Antonio Rose*	5.00 -	8.00
8656 *Don't Let Your Sweet Love Die*	5.00 -	8.00
8863 *Polecat Blues*	5.00 -	8.00
8959 *I Wonder Where You Are Tonight*	5.00 -	8.00
Bullet 704 *Mule Boogie*	5.00 -	8.00
712 *Ain't You Afraid*	5.00 -	8.00
Vocalion 04627 *Good For Nothing Gal*	5.00 -	10.00
04717 *Lonesome Dove*	5.00 -	10.00
04771 *Where The Roses Never Fade*	5.00 -	10.00
04842 *Come Back Little Pal*	5.00 -	10.00

HALTON BROTHERS:

Champion 16628 *Hook And Line*	50.00 -	75.00

STUART HAMBLEN (COWBOY JOE) (& HIS COVERED WAGON JUBILEE):

Bluebird 5242 *Boy In Blue*	8.00 -	12.00
Decca 5001, 5077, 5109, 5145	5.00 -	10.00
Victor 23685 *My Brown-Eyed Texas Rose*	20.00 -	30.00
V40109 *Boy In Blue*	20.00 -	30.00
V40242 *Wrong Keyhole*	20.00 -	30.00
V40306 *Standin' On The Pier In The Rain*	25.00 -	40.00
Victor V40311 *Sailor's Farewell*	25.00 -	40.00
V40319 *Drifting Back To Dixie*	25.00 -	40.00

PAUL HAMBLIN:

Victor V40260 *Strawberry Roan*	10.00 -	15.00
V40280 *Prairie Maiden*	10.00 -	15.00

WYZEE HAMILTON (Acc. by HAMILTON HARMONIANS):

Gennett 6272 *Old Sefus Brown*	15.00 -	25.00

HAMLIN QUARTETTE:

Herwin 75572 *Darling Nellie Gray*	15.00 -	25.00

JOHN HAMMOND:

Champion 15356 *Drunken Hiccoughs*	8.00 -	12.00
Gennett 6256 *Little Birdie*	15.00 -	20.00
Supertone 9249 *Little Birdie*	7.00 -	10.00

SID HAMPTON (THE YODELIN' MAN FROM DIXIE LAND):

Columbia 15555-D *Kicking Mule*	8.00 -	12.00
15583-D *The Hills Of Tennessee*	8.00 -	12.00

WILLIAM HANSON:

Okeh 45506 *Stop And Listen Blues*	30.00 -	50.00
45523 *Gambling On The Sabbath*	30.00 -	50.00

HAPPY HOLLOW HOODLUMS:

Decca 5098 *Down Home Rag*	5.00 -	8.00

HAPPY HAYSEEDS:

Victor 23722 *Ladies' Quadrille*	15.00 -	25.00
23774 *Cottonwood Reel*	15.00 -	25.00

HAPPY JACK:

Columbia 15720-D *I'm Only Suggesting This*	7.00 -	10.00

HAPPY VALLEY FAMILY:

Vocalion 04251 *Lily Of The Valley*	5.00 -	8.00
04296 *My Clinch Mountain Home*	5.00 -	8.00
04484 *Going Down To The Valley*	5.00 -	8.00

(Note: Above titles and others were also issued on Banner, Melotone, Oriole, Perfect, and Romeo.)

TEX HARDIN:

Champion 16552 *The Trail To California* . . . . 15.00 - 20.00

BILLY HARDISON (See TENNESSEE DRIFTERS):

HARKINS & MORAN:

Broadway 8055 *Hand Me Down My Walking Cane*	8.00	-	12.00
8056 *Bully Of The Town*	8.00	-	12.00
8064 *Lazy Tennessee*	10.00	-	15.00
8081 *Land Where We'll Never Grow Old*	10.00	-	15.00
8114 *John Henry*	10.00	-	15.00
8115 *The Gambler's Dying Words*	10.00	-	15.00
8117 *In The Sweet Bye And Bye*	10.00	-	15.00
8157 *Kitty Wells*	10.00	-	15.00

HARKINS & OWENS:

Broadway 8214 *A Mother's Plea* . . . . 8.00 - 12.00

HARKINS & PERRY:

Broadway 8129 *Life's Railway To Heaven* . . . . 8.00 - 12.00

(SID) HARKREADER & (GRADY) MOORE; HARKREADER & (BLYTHE) POTEET:

Paramount 3022 *Bully Of The Town*	10.00	-	15.00
3023 *John Henry*	10.00	-	15.00
3024 *There's A Little Rosewood Casket*	10.00	-	15.00
3025 *The Gambler's Dying Words*	10.00	-	15.00
3033 *Mockingbird Breakdown*	25.00	-	40.00
3035 *Only As Far As The Gate*	10.00	-	15.00
3043 *Kitty Wells*	10.00	-	15.00
3044 *Bits Of Blues*	25.00	-	40.00
3052 *Land Where We'll Never Grow Old*	10.00	-	15.00
3054 *It Looks To Me Like A Big Night Tonight* .	25.00	-	40.00
3061 *The Old Rugged Cross*	10.00	-	15.00
3063 *Lazy Tennessee*	25.00	-	40.00
3094 *Life's Railway To Heaven*	10.00	-	15.00
3104 *Take Me Back To Carolina Home*	15.00	-	20.00
3112 *Sweet Bird*	15.00	-	20.00
3118 *Wang Wang Blues*	25.00	-	40.00
3141 *Red River Valley*	15.00	-	20.00
3183 *On The Bowery*	15.00	-	20.00
3296 *Land Where We'll Never Grow Old*	10.00	-	15.00
Vocalion 5063 *Never River Train*	15.00	-	20.00
5066 *Oh, Where Is My Boy Tonight*	15.00	-	20.00
5082 *Struttin' Round*	15.00	-	20.00
5114 *Dark Eyes*	15.00	-	20.00
14887 *Soldier's Joy*	15.00	-	20.00
15035 *New River Train*	15.00	-	20.00
15075 *The Dying Girl's Message*	15.00	-	20.00
15193 *Struttin' Round*	15.00	-	20.00
15366 *Dark Eyes*	15.00	-	20.00

HARMONICA BILL:

Champion 16393 *The Prisoner's Radio*	20.00	-	30.00
16399 *Answer To The Gypsy's Warning*	20.00	-	30.00
16425 *Georgia The Dear Old State I Love*	20.00	-	30.00

HARMONICA JIM:

| Superior 2789 *The Prisoner's Radio* . . . . | 25.00 | - | 35.00 |
| 2806 *Great Grandad And Grandma* . . . . | 25.00 | - | 35.00 |

RICHARD HAROLD:

| Columbia 15426-D *Sweet Bird* . . . . | 8.00 | - | 12.00 |
| 15586-D *The Battleship Maine* . . . . | 8.00 | - | 12.00 |

HARPER BROTHERS:

| Brunswick 469 *Dreamy Rock Mountain Moon* . . . | 5.00 | - | 8.00 |
| 505 *Blue Pacific Moonlight* . . . . | 5.00 | - | 8.00 |

HARPER FAMILY TRIO:

Supertone 9645, 9649, 9656, 9729 . . . . 4.00 - 7.00

HARPER & HALL:

| Superior 2678 *Down The Lane To Home Sweet Home* . . . . | 15.00 | - | 20.00 |
| 2799 *Life's Railway To Heaven* . . . . | 15.00 | - | 20.00 |

HARPER & PAGE :

Supertone 9314 *Sweet William* . . . . 7.00 - 10.00

HARPER & TURNER:

Supertone 9262, 9266, 9316, 9353, 9391, 9658 . .	4.00	-	8.00
9640 *Sweet Adeline At The Still*	5.00	-	10.00
9656 *There's A Vacant Chair At Home Sweet Home*	5.00	-	10.00
9678 *No Never Alone*	5.00	-	10.00
9725 *I Surrender All*	5.00	-	10.00
9726 *Beautiful Garden Of Prayer*	5.00	-	10.00

DIXIE HARPER & HER BLUEBONNET BRATS:

| Royalty P-31 *Sweeter Than The Flowers* . . . . . | 8.00 | - | 12.00 |
| P-38/39 *Lovesick Blues* . . . . | 8.00 | - | 12.00 |

AUNT IDY HARPER & THE COON CREEK GIRLS:

Vocalion 04203, 04354 . . . . 7.00 - 10.00

JACK HARPER:

Vocalion 5494 *The Tramp's Last Ride* . . . . 7.00 - 10.00

OSCAR HARPER'S TEXAS STRING BAND:

| Okeh 45227 *Bouquet Waltz* . . . . | 25.00 | - | 40.00 |
| Vocalion 5403 *Sally Johnson* . . . . | 25.00 | - | 40.00 |

OSCAR & DOC HARPER:

Okeh 45397 *Beaumont Rag*	35.00	-	50.00
45420 *Terrell Texas Blues*	35.00	-	50.00
45485 *Bitter Creek*	35.00	-	50.00

ROY HARPER & EARL SHIRKEY: (See also SHIRKEY & HARPER):

| Columbia 15429-D *Bootlegger's Dream* . . . . . . | 30.00 | - | 50.00 |
| Columbia 15467-D *Cowboy's Lullaby* . . . . | 30.00 | - | 50.00 |

KELLY HARRELL (& HENRY NORTON):

Okeh 40486 *Wild Bill Jones*	8.00	-	12.00
Victor 19596 *New River Train*	5.00	-	8.00
20103 *My Horses Ain't Hungry*	5.00	-	8.00
20171 *Rovin' Gambler*	5.00	-	8.00
20242 *Butcher's Boy*	5.00	-	8.00
20527 *Bright Sherman Valley*	5.00	-	8.00
20535 *Bye And Bye You Will Forget*	5.00	-	8.00
20657 *I'm Nobody's Darling On Earth*	5.00	-	8.00
20797 *Charles Giteau*	6.00	-	10.00
20867 *I Love My Sweetheart The Best*	6.00	-	10.00
20935 *Row Us Over The Tide*	6.00	-	10.00
21069 *For Seven Long Years*	8.00	-	12.00
21520 *My Wife, She Has Gone*	8.00	-	12.00
23741 *I Heard Somebody Call*	20.00	-	30.00
V40047 *Oh, My Pretty Monkey*	15.00	-	20.00
V40095 *She Just Kept Kissing On*	15.00	-	20.00

EARL HARRIS:

Okeh 45566 *Gene, The Fighting Marine* . . . . . . 5.00 - 8.00

GEORGE HARRIS:

Columbia 15543-D *That's The Blue Heaven For Me* . . . . 10.00 - 15.00

J.D. HARRIS:

Okeh 45024 *Cackling Hen* . . . . 15.00 - 20.00

SIM HARRIS:

Oriole 916 *Pass Around The Bottle*	7.00	-	10.00
946 *The Fatal Wedding*	7.00	-	10.00
947 *Bully Of The Town*	7.00	-	10.00

HAPPY BUD HARRISON:

Vocalion 5344 *Mail Man Blues*	15.00	-	20.00
5350 *I'm Glad I'm Free*	15.00	-	20.00
5370 *Ball And Chain Blues*	15.00	-	20.00
5405 *Mama Don't Allow No Easy Riders*	15.00	-	20.00

HART BROTHERS:

Paramount 3162 *The Miner's Prayer*	10.00	-	15.00
3176 *The Empty Cradle*	10.00	-	15.00
3262 *Lamp Lighting Time In The Valley*	10.00	-	15.00
3265 *The Prodigal Son*	10.00	-	15.00

HART & CATES:

Okeh 45499 *In The Valley Of Broken Hearts* . . . . 15.00 - 20.00

HART & OGLE:

Paramount 3297 *They Cut Down The Old Pine Tree* . . . . 15.00 - 20.00

HARTMAN'S HEARTBREAKERS; DICK

HARTMAN'S TENNESSEE RAMBLERS:
Bluebird 5796, 5797, 5837, 5875, 5876, 5891,
5909, 5962, 5992, 6003, 6089, 6105, 6122,
6135, 6162, 6180, 6207, 6226, 6227, 6274,
6481, 6494, 6516, 6542, 6566, 6622, 6656 .... 4.00 - 8.00

BOB HARTSELL:
Bluebird 7439 *Rambling Freight Train Yodel* .... 7.00 - 10.00
7473 *Rock Me To Sleep In My Rocky Mountain*
Home .... 7.00 - 10.00

(ROY) HARVEY (& COLEMAN/LEONARD HOKE COPELAND/BOB HOKE/JESS JOHNSON/HIS NORTH CAROLINA RAMBLERS/POSEY RORER):
Brunswick 223 *There'll Come A Time* .... 15.00 - 20.00
234 *I'll Be There Mary Dear* .... 15.00 - 20.00
250 *The Bluefield Murder* .... 15.00 - 20.00
268 *Budded Roses* .... 15.00 - 20.00
Champion 16187 *No Room For A Tramp* ... 30.00 - 50.00
16213 *When The Bees Are In The Hive's* ... 30.00 - 50.00
16255 *Railroad Blues* .... 50.00 - 75.00
16281 *Gambling Blues* .... 50.00 - 75.00
16312 *Called To The Foreign Fields* ...... 50.00 - 75.00
16331 *You're Bound To Look Like A Monkey*... 50.00 - 75.00
16662 *The Great Reaping Day* .... 50.00 - 75.00
16781 *Jefferson Street Rag* .... 80.00 - 120.00
45011, 45035, 45117 .... 10.00 - 20.00
Columbia 15155-D *Daisies Won't Tell* ...... 10.00 - 15.00
15514-D *Beckley Rag* .... 50.00 - 75.00
15582-D *Lonesome Weary Blues* .... 50.00 - 75.00
15637-D *Greasy Wagon* .... 75.00 - 100.00
15714-D *Dark Eyes* .... 75.00 - 100.00
Gennett 6303 *The Old Clay Pipe* .... 50.00 - 75.00
6350 *We Will Outshine The Sun* .... 50.00 - 75.00
Vocalion 5243 *Sweet Refrain* .... 35.00 - 50.00

OVERTONE HATFIELD:
Columbia 15687-D *A Gangster's Warning* ......100.00 - 150.00

HAUULEA ENTERTAINERS:
Okeh 45461 *Twelfth Street Rag* .... 20.00 - 30.00
45490 *Railroad Blues* .... 20.00 - 30.00

HAWAIIAN PALS:
Victor 23588 *It's Awful What Whiskey Will Do* .. 25.00 - 40.00

BUDDY HAWK & HIS BUDDIES:
Atlantic 7074 *Painting The Big Town* .... —   —

HAWKINS & PUCKETT:
Bluebird 5691 *Down In The Valley* .... 10.00 - 15.00

UNCLE BEN HAWKINS (& HIS BOYS):
Challenge 244 *The Poor Tramp Has To Live* .... 7.00 - 10.00
Champion 15248 *Round Town Gals* ...... 7.00 - 10.00
Silvertone 5001 *The Poor Tramp Has To Live* ... 7.00 - 10.00
5003 *Long Eared Mule* .... 7.00 - 10.00
Supertone 9255 *When The Roses Bloom Again* .. 7.00 - 10.00
9400 *The New River Train* .... 7.00 - 10.00

UNCLE BILLY HAWKINS:
Champion 15084 *Turkey In The Straw* .... 5.00 - 8.00

UNCLE JIM HAWKINS:
Challenge 101 *Hell Broke Loose In Georgia* ..... 5.00 - 8.00
109 *Turkey In The Straw* .... 5.00 - 8.00
111 *Dixie* .... 5.00 - 8.00
112 *Billy In The Low Ground* .... 5.00 - 8.00
301 *Arkansas Traveler* .... 5.00 - 8.00
304 *Hell Broke Loose In Georgia* .... 5.00 - 8.00
Champion 15098 *Seneca Square Dance* ... 7.00 - 10.00

TED HAWKINS' MOUNTAINEERS:
Columbia 15752-D *Roamin' Jack* .... 50.00 - 75.00

HAYES & JENKINS:
Superior 2537 *I Played On My Spanish Guitar* .. 25.00 - 35.00

DEWEY HAYES (THE CAROLINA TROUBADOUR):
Columbia 15753-D *Bring Back The One I Love* .. 25.00 - 40.00

ED HAYES:
Okeh 45025 *Big White Rooster And The Little*
Brown Hen .... 15.00 - 20.00

SELMA & DEWEY HAYES:
Victor 23629 *Broken Heart* .... 15.00 - 20.00

HAYWOOD COUNTY RAMBLERS:
Victor 23779 *Buncombe Chain Gang* .... 75.00 - 100.00

BILL HELMS & HIS UPSON COUNTY BAND:
Victor 21649 *Georgia Blues* .... 10.00 - 15.00
V40079 *Alabama Jubilee* .... 8.00 - 12.00

BILL HELMS & RILEY PUCKETT:
Columbia 15774-D *Lost Love* .... 75.00 - 125.00

ERNEST HELTON:
Okeh 45010 *Royal Clog* .... 15.00 - 20.00

HENDERSON BROTHERS:
Vocalion 03128 *The Grave Beneath The Pines* ... 7.00 - 10.00

RED HENDERSON:
Okeh 45283 *Auto Ride Through Alabama* ...... 7.00 - 10.00

(FISHER) HENDLEY (& HIS ARISTOCRATIC PIGS/CAROLINA TAR HEELS/& SMALL)
Bluebird 6555 *Another Man's Wife* .... 7.00 - 10.00
Okeh 45012 *Let Your Shack Burn Down* .... 40.00 - 60.00
Victor 23528 *Shuffle Feet, Shuffle* .... 75.00 - 100.00
Vocalion 02530 *Greasy Possum* .... 30.00 - 50.00
02543 *Answer To Big Rock Candy Mountain* .. 30.00 - 50.00
02612 *Going Down Town* .... 25.00 - 40.00
02679 *Hook And Line* .... 25.00 - 40.00
04516, 04556, 04658, 04718, 04780, 04881,
04937, 05016 .... 4.00 - 7.00

(CHIEF) HENRY'S STRING BAND:
Victor V40195 *Cherokee Rag* .... 50.00 - 75.00
V40225 *Choctow Waltz* .... 50.00 - 75.00
V40281 *Indian Tom Tom* .... 50.00 - 75.00

HENSLEY, TAYLOR & WALKER:
Vocalion 02639 *It's Hard To Make Gertie* ...... 30.00 - 50.00
02640 *Scottdale Stomp* .... 30.00 - 50.00
02678 *Match Box Blues* .... 30.00 - 50.00

HERMAN BROTHERS:
Broadway 8165 *Turkey In The Straw* .... 5.00 - 8.00

HERNANDEZ BROTHERS:
Victor V40081 *When You And I Were Young,*
Maggie .... 5.00 - 10.00

ZEB HERRELSON & M.B. PADGETT:
Okeh 45078 *Soldier's Joy* .... 10.00 - 15.00

BENNIE HESS (& HIS NATION'S PLAY BOYS):
Opera 102 *I'm Not Gonna Fool With You* .... 5.00 - 10.00
104 *Drink Drink Drink* .... 5.00 - 10.00
1013 *Bennie Hess Boogie* .... 5.00 - 10.00
1015 *Novelty Yodel No. 1* .... 5.00 - 8.00
1018 *To Be Loved* .... 5.00 - 8.00
1019 *Texas Stars* .... 5.00 - 8.00

HICKORY NUTS:
Okeh 45169 *The Louisville Burglar* .... 10.00 - 15.00
45220 *There'll Be No Liars There* .... 10.00 - 15.00

HI-FLYERS:
Vocalion 03684, 03964, 04011, 04093, 04589,
04671, 04703, 05000, 05054 .... 4.00 - 8.00

LEN & JOE HIGGINS:
Columbia 15243-D *Kentucky Wedding Chimes* ... 8.00 - 12.00
15354-D *Slippery Elm Tree* .... 10.00 - 15.00

HIGHLANDERS:
Paramount 3171 *Flop-Eared Mule* .... 30.00 - 50.00
3184 *Richmond Square* .... 30.00 - 50.00
3200 *Tennessee Blues* .... 30.00 - 50.00

HIGH NEIGHBOR BOYS:
Vocalion 04555, 04691, 04773, 04895 .... 4.00 - 7.00

LUKE HIGHNIGHT & HIS OZARK STRUTTERS:
Vocalion 5325 *There's No Hell In Georgia* ..... 50.00 - 80.00
5339 *Fort Smith Breakdown* .... 50.00 - 80.00

HILL'S VIRGINIA MOUNTAINEERS:
Supertone 9170 *Forked Deer* .... 30.00 - 50.00

BOB HILL:

Victor 23718 *He Was A Good Man* .... 30.00 - 40.00

EZRA HILL & HENRY JOHNSON:

Champion 15750 *Birmingham Jail* .... 20.00 - 30.00

FRANK HILL:

Supertone 9319 *Lonely Village Churchyard* ..... 6.00 - 10.00

     9612 *I'll Not Forget You Daddy* .... 6.00 - 10.00

JESS HILLARD (See HILLIARD)

     HILLBILLIES:

Vocalion 5016 *East Tennessee Blues* .... 7.00 - 10.00

     5017 *Blue Eyed Girl* .... 7.00 - 10.00

     5018 *Kitty Wells* .... 7.00 - 10.00

     5019 *Sally Ann* .... 7.00 - 10.00

     5020 *Cluck, Old Hen* .... 7.00 - 10.00

     5021 *Texas Gals* .... 7.00 - 10.00

     5022 Sourwood Mountains .... 7.00 - 10.00

     5023 *Buck-Eyed Rabbits* .... 7.00 - 10.00

     5024 *Cumberland Gap* .... 7.00 - 10.00

     5025 *Bristol Tennessee Blues* .... 7.00 - 10.00

     5115 *Cripple Creek* .... 7.00 - 10.00

     5116 *Mississippi Sawyer* .... 7.00 - 10.00

     5117 *Old Joe Clark* .... 7.00 - 10.00

     5173 *Hear Dem Bells* .... 7.00 - 10.00

     5178 *Sweet Bunch Of Daisies* .... 7.00 - 10.00

     5179 *Black-Eyed Susie* .... 7.00 - 10.00

     5182 *Baby, Your Time Ain't Long* .... 7.00 - 10.00

     5183 *Wasn't She A Dandy* .... 7.00 - 10.00

Vocalion 5186 *Darling Nellie Gray* .... 7.00 - 10.00

     15367 *Cripple Creek* .... 7.00 - 10.00

     15368 *Mississippi Lawyer* .... 7.00 - 10.00

     15369 *Old Joe Clark* .... 7.00 - 10.00

HARRY HILLIARD:

Champion 16337 *Blue Yodel No. 9* .... 60.00 - 90.00

Superior 2663 *The Mystery Of No 5* .... 75.00 - 100.00

JESS HILLIARD (& HIS ACES/WEST

VIRGINIA HILLIBILLIES):

Champion 16333 *Cackling Hen* .... 50.00 - 75.00

     16347 *Pea Pickin Papa* .... 50.00 - 75.00

     16368 *Penitentiary Blues* .... 50.00 - 75.00

     16398 *Ninety-Nine Years* .... 50.00 - 75.00

     16525 *Red Night Gown Blues* .... 50.00 - 75.00

     16564 *Mississippi Moon* .... 50.00 - 75.00

     16571 *The Barnyard Stomp* .... 50.00 - 75.00

     16617 *99 Years Blues.* .... 50.00 - 75.00

     16638 *Hell Up Flat Rock* .... 50.00 - 75.00

     16640 *Tall Mamma Blues* .... 50.00 - 75.00

     16651 *Austin Breakdown* .... 50.00 - 75.00

     16670 *Dixie Rag* .... 50.00 - 75.00

Champion 45001, 45003, 45026, 45047, 45091,

     45095 .... 10.00 - 20.00

Superior 2695 *The Ramblers Blues* .... 80.00 - 120.00

HINSON, PITTS & COLEY:

Bluebird 7438 *Whoa, Mule, Whoa* .... 5.00 - 8.00

W.A. HINTON:

Victor 23555 *Leather Breeches* .... 75.00 - 100.00

HOBBS BROTHER:

Conqueror 7332 *Patty On The Turnpike* .... 4.00 - 7.00

Paramount 3219 *Devils Dream* .... 7.00 - 10.00

     3220 *Patty On The Turnpike* .... 7.00 - 10.00

     3224 *Hell Among The Yearlings* .... 7.00 - 10.00

Q.R.S. 9003 *Turkey In The Straw* .... 20.00 - 30.00

GEORGE HOBSON:

Silvertone 3045 *The Lighting Express* .... 5.00 - 8.00

     3047 *The Baggage Coach Ahead* .... 5.00 - 8.00

WILLARD HODGIN (BANJO JOE):

Edison 52204 *Courtin' The Widow* .... 15.00 - 20.00

     52243 *Girl That Lived On Polecat Creek* ..... 15.00 - 20.00

     52278 *Judge Done Me Wrong* .... 15.00 - 20.00

     52332 *Ugly Gals Got Something Hard To Beat* 15.00 - 20.00

Victor 21485 *Don't Get One Woman* .... 15.00 - 20.00

ADOLPH HOFNER & HIS TEXANS:

Bluebird 7597, 7641, 7701, 7752, 7833, 7900,

     7931, 7955, 7988, 8071 .... 5.00 - 10.00

GEORGE HOLDEN:

Challenge 385 *The Marion Parker Murder* ..... 7.00 - 10.00

     392 *The Preacher And The Bear* .... 7.00 - 10.00

HOLMES & TAYLOR:

Superior 2713 *The Pretty Quadroon* .... 15.00 - 20.00

GEORGE HOLMES:

Superior 2525 *A Mother's Plea* .... 15.00 - 20.00

SALTY HOLMES:

Bluebird 5303 *I Want My Mama* .... 8.00 - 12.00

HOME TOWN BOYS:

Columbia 15736-D *Still Got Ninety-Nine* .... 25.00 - 40.00

     15762-D *Home Town Rag* .... 25.00 - 40.00

HONEYBOY & SASSAFRAS:

Brunswick 417 *The Lighthouse Song* .... 7.00 - 10.00

     509 *The Chicken Sermon* .... 7.00 - 10.00

     585 *Some Family* .... 7.00 - 10.00

HONOLULU STROLLERS:

Okeh 45226 *Ole Oaken Bucket* .... 8.00 - 12.00

     45239 *Mighty Lak' A Rose* .... 8.00 - 12.00

Victor 23600 *Don't Say No* .... 25.00 - 40.00

HOOSIER HOT SHOTS:

This largely corn-ball but popular group
recorded many titles during the 1930's which
were issued on Banner, Conqueror, Melotone,
Oriole, Perlect, Romeo, Vocalion. Since the
records are generally of minimal value, no
detailed listing is presented.

AL HOPKINS & HIS BUCKLE BUSTERS:

Brunswick 103 *Round Town Girls* .... 7.00 - 10.00

     104 *Bristol Tennessee Blues* .... 7.00 - 10.00

     105 *Sally Ann* .... 7.00 - 10.00

     106 *Governor Alf Taylor's Fox Chase* .... 7.00 - 10.00

     174 *Sweet Bunch Of Daisies* .... 5.00 - 8.00

     175 *Black Eyed Susie* .... 5.00 - 8.00

     176 *Down The Meadow Lane* .... 5.00 - 8.00

     177 *The Nine Pound Hammer* .... 5.00 - 8.00

     179 *Johnson Boys* .... 5.00 - 8.00

     180 *Echoes Of The Chimes* .... 5.00 - 8.00

     181 *Hear Dem Bells* .... 5.00 - 8.00

     182 *Bug In The Taters* .... 5.00 - 8.00

     183 *Baby Your Time Ain't Long* .... 5.00 - 8.00

     184 *Down To The Club* .... 5.00 - 8.00

     185 *Sleep Baby Sleep* .... 5.00 - 8.00

     186 *Ride That Mule* .... 5.00 - 8.00

     187 *Wasn't She A Dandy?* .... 5.00 - 8.00

     189 *Hear Dem Bells* .... 5.00 - 8.00

     295 *Old Dan Tucker* .... 5.00 - 8.00

     318 *Carolina Moonshiner* .... 5.00 - 8.00

     321 *Polka Medley* .... 5.00 - 10.00

     335 *Wild Hoss* .... 5.00 - 10.00

ANDY HOPKINS:

Supertone 9490 *Put Me Off At Buffalo* .... 8.00 - 12.00

     9601 *Crepe On The Little Cabin Door* .... 8.00 - 12.00

     9655 *I'll Smoke My Long Stemmed Pipe* ..... 8.00 - 12.00

     9713 *The Prison Wardens Secret* .... 8.00 - 12.00

DOC HOPKINS:

Broadway 8337 *Methodist Pie* .... 7.00 - 10.00

DAN HORNSBY (NOVELTY)

ORCH./QUARTETTE/(LION'S DEN) TRIO:

Columbia 15276-D *On Mobile Bay* .... 5.00 - 8.00

     15321-D *The Shelby Disaster* .... 7.00 - 10.00

     15381-D *She Was Bred In Old Kentucky* ...... 7.00 - 10.00

     15444-D *Hinky Dinky Dee* .... 7.00 - 10.00

     15578-D *I'm Sorry I Made You Cry* .... 7.00 - 10.00

     15628-D *The Lunatics Lullaby* .... 7.00 - 10.00

     15769-D *Dear Old Girl* .... 15.00 - 20.00

     15771-D *Three Blind Mice* .... 15.00 - 20.00

JOHNNY HORTON:

Abbott 100 *Candy Jones* .... 8.00 - 12.00*

     101 *Happy Millionaire* .... 8.00 - 12.00*

     102 *Plaid And Calico* .... 8.00 - 12.00*

     103 *Birds And Butterflies* .... 8.00 - 12.00*

104 *In My Home In Shelby County*	8.00 –	12.00*
105 *Shadows On The Bayou*	8.00 –	12.00*
106 *Smokey Joes Barbeque*	8.00 –	12.00*
107 *It's A Long Rocky Road*	8.00 –	12.00*
108 *Betty Lorraine*	8.00 –	12.00*
109 *Rhythm In My Baby's Walk*	8.00 –	12.00*
Cormac 1193 *Plaid And Calico*	15.00 –	25.00
Cormac 1197 *Birds And Butterflies*	15.00 –	25.00

WILLIAM B. HOUCHENS:

Gennett 5240 *Turkey In The Straw*	7.00 –	10.00

KENNETH HOUCHiNS (& SLIM COX):

Champion 16473 *Fancy Nancy*	35.00 –	50.00
16484 *Do Right Daddy Blues*	40.00 –	60.00
16501 *Tennessee Blues*	40.00 –	60.00
16553 *T7he Wanderer's Warning*	40.00 –	60.00
16584 *The Yodeling Drifter*	40.00 –	60.00
16603 *Mean Old Ball And Chain Blues*	40.00 –	60.00
16619 *Bay Rum Blues*	40.00 –	60.00
16636 *I'm Just A Yodeling Rambler*	40.00 –	60.00
16637 *The Old Missouri Moon*	40.00 –	60.00
16650 *Back To Old Smoky Mountain*	40.00 –	60.00
16669 *Behind These Grey Walls*	40.00 –	60.00
16679 *Homesick For Heaven*	40.00 –	60.00
16695 *Our Old Family Album*	40.00 –	60.00
16755 *Louisiana Moon*	50.00 –	75.00
16775 *My Little Ozark Mountain Home*	50.00 –	75.00
16787 *Blue Ridge Lullaby*	50.00 –	75.00
16793 *When Jimmie Rodgers Said Goodbye*	50.00 –	75.00
16807 *The Gangsters Brother*	50.00 –	75.00
Champion 45028 *Cowboys Meditation*	8.00 –	12.00
45030 *Blue Ridge Lullaby*	8.00 –	12.00
45049 *Louisiana Moon*	8.00 –	12.00
45054 *The End Of Memory Lane*	8.00 –	12.00
45062 *When Jimmie Rodgers Said Goodbye*	15.00 –	20.00
45078 *Back To Old Smoky Mountain*	8.00 –	12.00

LAKE HOWARD:

Titles, issued contemporaneously on Banner, Melotone, Oriole, Perfect, Romeo: *Chewing Chewing Gum; Don't Let our Deal Go Down; Forsaken Love; Get Your Head In Here; I Have No One To Leave Me; It's None Of Your Business; Little Annie; Love Me Darling; Love Me; Lover's Farewell; New Chattanooga Mama; Streamlined Mama; Within My Fathers House* .... 10.00 – 15.00

J.H. HOWELL'S CAROLINA HILLBILLIES:

Bluebird 7162 *Lost John*	8.00 –	12.00
7409 *The Burning Of Cleveland School*	8.00 –	12.00
8219 *Mollie Married a Travelin Man*	8.00 –	12.00

UNCLE STEVE HUBBARD (& HIS BOYS):

Gennett 6088 *Big Town Fling*	10.00 –	15.00
6101 *Two Step Quadrille*	10.00 –	15.00
6121 *Devil's Dream*	10.00 –	15.00
6436 *Over The Ocean Waves*	10.00 –	15.00
Supertone 9161 *Soldiers Joy*	7.00 –	10.00

HUGH & SHUG'S RADIO PALS:

Decca 5406, 5407, 5428, 5431, 5451, 5466, 5506, 5534	5.00 –	10.00

DAN HUGHEY:

Champion 15428 *The Fatal Wedding*	7.00 –	10.00
15466 *Froggie Went A-Courtin*	7.00 –	10.00
15502 *Sweet Kitty Wells*	7.00 –	10.00
15631 *An Old Camp Meeting*	7.00 –	10.00
15687 *Four Thousand Years Ago*	7.00 –	10.00
15710 *The Red River Valley*	7.00 –	10.00
15731 *The Little Mohee*	7.00 –	10.00
15771 *Will The Angels Play Their Harps For Me*	8.00 –	12.00
15851 *Cindy*	8.00 –	12.00
15876 *After The Ball*	8.00 –	12.00
15923 *Old Number Three*	10.00 –	15.00
16029 *Charlie Brooks*	10.00 –	15.00

HUMPHRIES BROTHERS:

Okeh 45464 *Black And White Rag*	35.00 –	50.00
45478 *After The Ball*	35.00 –	50.00
45489 *Ragged Ann Rag*	35.00 –	50.00
45501 *What Made The Wild Cat Wild*	35.00 –	50.00

PRINCE ALBERT HUNT'S TEXAS RAMBLERS:

Okeh 45230 *Blues In A Bottle*	75.00 –	100.00
45375 *Wake Up Jacob*	75.00 –	100.00
45446 *Houston Slide*	75.00 –	100.00

DAVE HUNT:

Champion 15565 *Katy Lee*	10.00 –	15.00
15610 *Wake Up In The Morning*	10.00 –	15.00

WALTER HURDT & HIS BOYS/ SINGING COWBOYS:

Bluebird 7915 *My Skinny Sarah Jane*	5.00 –	8.00
7959 *I've Always Loved My Old Guitar*	5.00 –	8.00

ZACK HURT:

Okeh 45212 *Gamblers Lament*	5.00 –	8.00

HUTCHENS BROTHERS:

Champion 15464 *Praise The Lord, Its So*	7.00 –	10.00
15485 *I'm On The Sunny Side*	7.00 –	10.00
15567 *Climbing Up The Golden Stairs*	7.00 –	10.00
15588 *I'm Free Again*	7.00 –	10.00
15632 *I Feel Like Traveling On*	7.00 –	10.00
15671 *I Wants My Lulu*	7.00 –	10.00
15693 *Why Not Tonight*	8.00 –	12.00
15753 *At The Battle Front*	8.00 –	12.00
15900 *No Never Alone*	8.00 –	12.00
15944 *Old Kentucky Dew*	8.00 –	12.00
15971 *Life's Railway To Heaven*	8.00 –	12.00
16101 *I Surrender All*	8.00 –	12.00
16122 *Down The Lane To Home Sweet Home*	10.00 –	15.00

JOHN HUTCHENS:

Champion 15414 *The Preacher And The Bear*	7.00 –	10.00
15427 *The Sinking Of The Submarine S-4*	7.00 –	10.00
15467 *The Wreck Of The Virginian Train*	7.00 –	10.00
15483 *The Volunteer Organist*	7.00 –	10.00
15503 *I Got Mine*	7.00 –	10.00
15549 *He Included Me*	7.00 –	10.00
15550 *The Vestris Disaster*	10.00 –	15.00
15751 *Hard Luck Jim*	10.00 –	15.00

FRANK HUTCHISON (& SHERMAN LAWSON):

Okeh 45064 *Worried Blues*	25.00 –	40.00
45083 *The West Virginia Rag*	25.00 –	40.00
45089 *The C & O Excursion Train*	25.00 –	40.00
45093 *The Wild Horse*	25.00 –	40.00
45106 *Stackalee*	25.00 –	40.00
45114 *Worried Blues*	25.00 –	40.00
45121 *Logan County Blues*	25.00 –	40.00
45144 *All Night Long*	25.00 –	40.00
45258 *The Miners Blues*	25.00 –	40.00
45274 *Hutchisons Rag*	25.00 –	40.00
45313 *The Burglar Man*	25.00 –	40.00
45361 *Johnny And Jane*	30.00 –	50.00
45378 *Cannon Ball Blues*	30.00 –	50.00
45425 *Railroad Bill*	30.00 –	50.00
45452 *Hell Bound Train*	30.00 –	50.00
45570 *Cumberland Gap*	40.00 –	60.00
Velvet-Tone 7107-V *Worried Blues*	20.00 –	30.00

H.K. HUTCHISON:

Gennett 6464 *Good Old Turnip Greens*	20.00 –	30.00

JERRY IRBY (& THE TEXAS RANCHERS):

Cireco 101 *Almost Every Time*	8.00 –	12.00
Globe 113 *Nails In My Coffin*	8.00 –	12.00
114 *Steel Guitar Special*	8.00 –	12.00
115 *Don't You Weep*	8.00 –	12.00
120 *Super Boogie Woogie*	8.00 –	12.00
Gulf 103 *Nails In My Coffin*	10.00 –	15.00
Imperial 8014 *Hillbilly Boogie*	8.00 –	12.00

HARVEY IRWIN:

Okeh 45014 *The Blind Child*	10.00	-	15.00
45052 *Sunny Tennessee*	10.00	-	15.00

WALLIE & TEX ISABELL:

Eddie's 1219 *Sugar Cain Gal*	8.00	-	12.00

JACK & BILL:

Okeh 45368 *The Lonesome Road*	10.00	-	15.00

JACK HARMONICA PLAYERS:

Vocalion 5353 *Mouth Harp Blues*	20.00	-	30.00

JACK & TONY:

Okeh 45421 *Since I Gave My Heart To You*	10.00	-	15.00
45422 *The Burial Of The Miners Child*	10.00	-	15.00

JACKSON COUNTY BARN OWLS:

Champion 16031 *Bake That Chicken Pie*	20.00	-	30.00

JACKSON COUNTY RAMBLERS:

Champion 16284 *Carolina Girl*	15.00	-	20.00

JACK JACKSON:

Columbia 15497-D *I'm Just A Black Sheep*	10.00	-	15.00
15662-D *Flat Tire Blues*	15.00	-	20.00

AUNT MOLLY JACKSON:

Columbia 15731-D *Kentucky Miner's Wife*	15.00	-	20.00

JACOBY BROS.:

TNT 1002 *There's No Use To Go Wrong*	7.00	-	10.00
1004 *Cannonball*	7.00	-	10.00
1009 *Bicycle Wreck*	7.00	-	10.00*

BEN JARRELL (Acc. by DA COSTA WOLTZ'S SOUTHERN BROADCASTERS):

Gennett 6143 *Merry Girl*	15.00	-	20.00
6164 *I Know My Name Is Written There*	15.00	-	20.00
6176 *When You Ask A Girl To Leave Her Happy Home*	15.00	-	20.00

JARVIS & JUSTICE:

Brunswick 333 *Guian Valley Waltz*	8.00	-	12.00
358 *Muskrat Rag*	10.00	-	15.00

(BLIND ANDREW) JENKINS (& FRANK HICKS/CARSON ROBINSON/ WHITWORTH):

Okeh 45232 *On The Banks Of The Old Omaha*	5.00	-	8.00
45234 *In The Baggage Coach Ahead*	5.00	-	8.00
45246 *Silver Threads Among The Gold*	5.00	-	8.00
45264 *My Dixie Home*	5.00	-	8.00
45331 *I'll Be All Smiles Tonight*	5.00	-	8.00
45443 *Don't Stop Praying*	5.00	-	8.00
45481 *The Little Flower Girl*	6.00	-	10.00

FRANK JENKINS (& HIS PILOT MOUNTAINEERS):

Gennett 6165 *Home Sweet Home*	15.00	-	20.00
7034 *Sunny Home In Dixie*	20.00	-	30.00

"GOOBY" JENKINS:

Okeh 45069 *Fiddlin' Bill*	15.00	-	20.00
45082 *The Prisoners Dream*	15.00	-	20.00
45088 *Georgia Girl*	15.00	-	20.00
45115 *Hopeful Walter Booth*	15.00	-	20.00

OSCAR JENKINS' MOUNTAINEERS:

Broadway 8249 *Burial of Wild Bill*	7.00	-	10.00
Paramount 3240 *The Railway Flagman's Sweetheart*	7.00	-	10.00

JENNINGS BROS.:

Champion 15148 *Cripple Creek*	5.00	-	8.00

HERB JENNINGS:

Champion 15198 *The Death Of John Henry*	7.00	-	10.00
15209 *The Roving Gambler*	7.00	-	10.00

JESSE'S STRING FIVE:

Bluebird 6443 *River Blues*	7.00	-	10.00

JOHNNY & SLIM:

Superior 2752 *Back To My Georgia Home*	25.00	-	40.00

WHITEY JOHNS:

Challenge 852 *The Farm Relief Song*	5.00	-	8.00
895 *The Prisoners Rosary*	5.00	-	8.00
Paramount 3190 *The Little Old Sod Shanty*	7.00	-	10.00

JOHNSON BROTHERS:

Vicior 20661 *Down In Happy Valley*	12.00	-	16.00
20662 *Sweet Nellie Brown*	12.00	-	16.00
20891 *The Soldiers Poor Little Boy*	12.00	-	16.00
20940 *Careless Love*	12.00	-	16.00
21243 *Two Brothers Are We*	12.00	-	16.00
21532 *Old Timer From Caroliner*	12.00	-	16.00
21646 *The Crime Of The D'Autremount Brothers*	12.00	-	16.00

JOHNSON & HARVEY:

Champion 16449 *Birdie*	40.00	-	60.00

EARL JOHNSON (& HIS CLODHOPPERS/ DIXIE ENTERTAINERS):

Okeh 45092 *Ain't Nobody's Business*	20.00	-	30.00
45101 *John Henry Blues*	20.00	-	30.00
45112 *Shortenin' Bread*	20.00	-	30.00
45123 *Johnson's Old Grey Mule*	20.00	-	30.00
45129 *I'm Satisfied*	20.00	-	30.00
45156 *Twinkle Little Star*	20.00	-	50.00
45171 *Johnnie Get Your Gun*	30.00	-	50.00
45183 *They Don't Roost Too High For Me*	30.00	-	50.00
45209 *Red Hot Breakdown*	30.00	-	50.00
45223 *Mississippi Jubilee*	30.00	-	50.00
45269 *Wire Grass Drag*	50.00	-	75.00
45300 *G Rag*	50.00	-	75.00
45383 *All Night Long*	50.00	-	75.00
45406 *Poor Little Joe*	50.00	-	75.00
45412 *Bringing In The Sheaves*	50.00	-	75.00
45528 *Take Me Back To My Old Mountain Home*	50.00	-	75.00
45545 *There's No Place Like Home*	50.00	-	75.00
45559 *Way Down In Georgia*	50.00	-	75.00
Victor 23638 *I Lost My Gal*	75.00	-	100.00
V40212 *Fiddlin Rufus*	50.00	-	75.00
V40304 *Green Mountain Polka*	50.00	-	75.00

EDWARD JOHNSON:

Champion 15048 *Sand Cave*	4.00	-	7.00

GENE JOHNSON:

Timely Tunes 1550 *TB Blues*	50.00	-	75.00
1551 *Jimmie The Kid*	50.00	-	75.00
1552 *Do Right Daddy Blues*	75.00	-	100.00

HENRY JOHNSON:

Champion 15732 *When The Snowflakes Fall Again*	20.00	-	30.00

JAMES JOHNSON:

Columbia 15453-D *Papa Please Buy Me An Airship*	10.00	-	15.00

JESS JOHNSON (& ROY HARVEY):

Champion 16255 *The Ding Brakeman*	35.00	-	50.00
16780 *By A Cottage In The Twilight*	50.00	-	75.00

JIMMIE/JIMMY JOHNSON'S STRING BAND:

Champion 16389 *Washington Ouadrille*	30.00	-	50.00
16430 *Ching Chovw*	40.00	-	60.00
16506 *Bury Me On The Prairie*	40.00	-	60.00
16516 *Drink More Cider*	40.00	-	60.00
16541 *Old Blind Dog*	40.00	-	60.00
16559 *Jennie Baker*	40.00	-	60.00
Superior 2821 *Step Lively*	75.00	-	100.00

JULIAN JOHNSON & LEON HYATT:

Bluebird 7510 *T.B. Killed My Daddy*	10.00	-	15.00

PAUL (AND CHARLES) JOHNSON:

Gennett 7313 *Wild Cat Hollow*	50.00	-	75.00
Superior 2612 *Wild Cat Hollow*	50.00	-	100.00

SMILIN' TUBBY JOHNSON:

Champion 15247 *I'm A Stern Old Bachelor*	5.00	-	8.00
15260 *Whoa, Mule, Whoa*	5.00	-	8.00
15278 *Oh, Suzanna*	5.00	-	8.00
15298 *Little Brown Jug*	5.00	-	8.00
15430 *Oh, Dem Golden Slippers*	5.00	-	8.00

JONES BROTHERS:

Melotone 12017 *The Memory That Time Cannot Erase*	5.00	-	8.00
12179 *The Little Green Valley*	5.00	-	8.00

BUDDY JONES:

Decca 5345, 5372, 5414, 5476, 5490, 5521, 5538,
5539 .... 5.00 - 10.00

CARL JONES:
Okeh 45516 *The Wild Man Of Borneo* .... 20.00 - 30.00
45540 *My Tennessee Girl* .... 20.00 - 30.00

COLON JONES & RILEY PUCKETT:
Columbia 15774-D *That Saxophone Waltz* ...... 50.00 - 75.00

DEMPSEY JONES:
Champion 16356 *The Cross-Eyed Butcher* ...... 10.00 - 15.00
16416 *Jack And May* .... 10.00 - 20.00
16697 *Cabin Home* .... 10.00 - 20.00

FLOYD JONES:
Paramount 3029 *My Dream Of The Big Parade* .. 10.00 - 15.00
3030 *Someone Is Waiting Your Light* .... 10.00 - 15.00

GENE JONES:
Gold Star 1382 *Stop, Look And Listen* .... 5.00 - 8.00

GRANDPA JONES:
King 502, 508, 513, 517, 524 .... 3.00 - 5.00

HIRAM JONES:
Homestead 16492 *Sailor's Hornpipe* .... 15.00 - 20.00

ROY JONES:
Columbia 15428-D *Southern Yodel Blues* .... 20.00 - 30.00

JORDAN BROTHERS:
Bluebird 7123 *Answer To Birmingham Jail* ...... 8.00 - 12.00
7235 *Goin' Back Home* .... 8.00 - 12.00

JORDAN & RUPERT:
Supertone 9494 *It Won't Be Long Till My Grave
Is Made* .... 7.00 - 10.00

JERRY JORDAN:
Supertone 9407 *The Cat's Got The Measles And
The Whooping Cough* .... 10.00 - 15.00
9454 *The Baldheaded End Of A Broom* ..... 7.00 - 10.00

**JUDY & JEN, ACCOMP. BY THE
HILLTOPPERS:**
Vogue 744 *Flat River, Missouri* .... 25.00 - 40.00

JUERLING & JUSTIS:
Supertone 9099 *Grasshopper Polka* .... 7.00 - 10.00

DICK JUSTICE:
Brunswick 336 *Brown Skin Blues* .... 15.00 - 20.00
367 *Henry Lee* .... 15.00 - 20.00
395 *Cocaine* .... 15.00 - 20.00

BOB KACKLEY (& BEN WEAVER):
Okeh 45531 *The Strawberry Roan* .... 10.00 - 15.00

KARL (DAVIS) & HARTY (TAYLOR):
Banner, Conqueror, Melotone, Perfect, Oriole,
Romeo .... 5.00 - 10.00

ALFRED G. KARNES:
Victor 20840 *Where We'll Never Grow Old* ..... 5.00 - 8.00
20933 *To The Work* .... 5.00 - 8.00
V40076 *Days Of My Childhood Plays* .... 15.00 - 20.00
V40327 *Called To The Foreign Field* .... 15.00 - 20.00

KAY BROTHERS:
Victor 23508 *Got The Jake Leg Too* .... 50.00 - 75.00

BUELL KAZEE (& SOOKIE HOBBS):
Brunswick 144 *John Hardy* .... 7.00 - 10.00
145 *Rock Island* .... 7.00 - 10.00
154 *East Virginia* .... 7.00 - 10.00
155 *The Ship That's Sailing High* .... 7.00 - 10.00
156 *The Little Mohee* .... 7.00 - 10.00
157 *The Old Maid* .... 7.00 - 10.00
206 *The Faded Coat Of Blue* .... 7.00 - 10.00
210 *Red Wing* .... 7.00 - 10.00
211 *The Orphan Girl* .... 7.00 - 10.00
212 *The Cowboy's Farewell* .... 7.00 - 10.00
213 *The Butcher's Boy* .... 7.00 - 10.00
215 *Little Bessie* .... 7.00 - 10.00
216 *In The Shadow Of The Pines* .... 7.00 - 10.00
217 *Poor Boys Long Ways From Home* ...... 7.00 - 10.00
218 *Gambling Blues* .... 7.00 - 10.00
330 *The Hobo's Last Ride* .... 7.00 - 10.00
338 *A Mountain Boy Makes His First Record* .. 7.00 - 10.00
351 *The Blind Man* .... 7.00 - 10.00

436 *The Little Mohee* .... 7.00 - 10.00
437 *The Old Maid* .... 7.00 - 10.00
481 *The Cowboy Trail* .... 7.00 - 10.00
Vocalion 5221 *In The Shadow Of The Pines* .... 8.00 - 12.00
5231 *Little Bessie* .... 8.00 - 12.00

**HANK KEENE (& HIS CONNECTICUT
HILLBILLIES):**
Bluebird 5241, 5254, 5339, 6035 .... 4.00 - 7.00
Brunswick 516 *The Run Away Boy* .... 7.00 - 10.00

**(HOWARD) KEESE/KEESEE (& LOY
BODINE):**
Champion 16097 *Indiana Pal Of Mine* .... 20.00 - 30.00
16260 *The Mystery Of Number 5* .... 25.00 - 35.00
16374 *The Longest Train I Ever Saw* .... 25.00 - 35.00
16446 *Pal Of My Sunny Days* .... 25.00 - 35.00
Gennett 7082 *Blue Yodel No. 5* .... 25.00 - 40.00
7113 *My Dear Old Sunny South By The Sea* .. 25.00 - 40.00
7166 *Memphis Special Blues* .... 35.00 - 50.00
7315 *A Sailor's Plea* .... 35.00 - 50.00

KELLY BROTHERS:
Decca 5027 *Precious One* .... 7.00 - 10.00
Victor 23822 *After You've Gone* .... 15.00 - 20.00
23828 *Floating Down A River* .... 15.00 - 20.00
23833 *Always Remember* .... 15.00 - 20.00
23853 *Stormy Hawaiian Weather* .... 20.00 - 30.00

R.D. KELLY & JULIUS DUNN:
Okeh 45510 *Moonlight On The Colorado* ...... 15.00 - 25.00
45543 *Harem Scarem* .... 15.00 - 25.00

REX KELLY:
Paramount 3319 *Down By The Railroad Track* ... 25.00 - 40.00

KEN, CHUCK & JIM:
Champion 16579 *I Like Mountain Music* .... 10.00 - 15.00
16672 *Cattesburg* .... 20.00 - 30.00
45131 *Home On The Range* .... 5.00 - 8.00

KENTUCKY GIRLS:
Columbia 15364-D *Old And Only In The Way* ... 10.00 - 15.00

KENTUCKY MOUNTAIN BOYS:
Supertone 2026 *The Two Orphans* .... 5.00 - 8.00
2260 *Many Happy Returns Of The Day* ...... 5.00 - 8.00

KENTUCKY RAMBLERS:
Paramount 3283 *With My Mother Dead And
Gone* .... 25.00 - 35.00
3284 *The Prisoner's Sweetheart* .... 25.00 - 35.00
3285 *The Unfortunate Brakeman* .... 25.00 - 35.00
3300 *Some Mother's Boy* .... 25.00 - 35.00

KENTUCKY SERENADERS:
Champion 15770 *Gonna Raise A Ruckus Tonight* . 10.00 - 15.00

KENTUCKY STRING TICKLERS:
Champion 16577 *Stove Pipe Blues* .... 50.00 - 75.00
16581 *Georgia Bust Down* .... 50.00 - 75.00
16681 *Leaving Here Blues* .... 75.00 - 100.00
45014 *Leaving Here Blues* .... 15.00 - 20.00

KENTUCKY THOROBREDS:
Paramount 3010 *I Love You Best Of All* .... 15.00 - 20.00
3011 *Mother's Advice* .... 15.00 - 20.00
3014 *This World Is Not My Home* .... 15.00 - 20.00
3036 *The Preacher And The Bear* .... 15.00 - 20.00
3059 *Till We Meet Again* .... 15.00 - 20.00
3071 *I've Waited Long For You* .... 15.00 - 20.00
3080 *I'll Not Marry At All* .... 15.00 - 20.00

KESSINGER BROTHERS:
Brunswick 220 *Wednesday Night Waltz* .... 7.00 - 10.00
235 *Turkey In The Straw* .... 7.00 - 10.00
238 *Garfield March* .... 7.00 - 10.00
247 *Arkansas Traveler* .... 7.00 - 10.00
256 *Devil's Dream* .... 7.00 - 10.00
267 *Sixteen Days In Georgia* .... 7.00 - 10.00
308 *Sourwood Mountain* .... 7.00 - 10.00
309 *Mississippi Sawyer* .... 10.00 - 15.00
315 *Dill Pickle* .... 10.00 - 15.00
323 *Old Jake Gillespie* .... 10.00 - 15.00
331 *Wild Goose Chase* .... 10.00 - 15.00

344 *Black Hawk Waltz*	8.00	-	12.00
352 *Midnight Serenade Waltz*	8.00	-	12.00
364 *Durang Hornpipe*	8.00	-	12.00
396 *Chinky Pin*	10.00	-	15.00
411 *Sopping The Gravy*	10.00	-	15.00
458 *Rat Cheese Under The Hill*	10.00	-	15.00
468 *Little Brown Jug*	8.00	-	12.00
480 *Chicken Reel*	10.00	-	15.00
484 *Mary Jane Waltz*	10.00	-	15.00
518 *Dixie*	10.00	-	15.00
521 *Liza Jane*	10.00	-	15.00
540 *Ragtime Annie*	10.00	-	15.00
554 *Shoo, Fly*	10.00	-	15.00
563 *Steamboat Bill*	10.00	-	15.00
567 *Mexican Waltz*	10.00	-	15.00
580 *Little Betty Brown*	10.00	-	15.00
592 *Regal March*	10.00	-	15.00
Vocalion 02565 *Brownstown Girl*	35.00	-	50.00
02566 *Kanawha County Rag*	35.00	-	50.00
5248 *Patty On The Turnpike*	15.00	-	20.00
5481 *Hot Foot*	35.00	-	50.00

KIDOODLERS:

Vocalion 03717, 03866, 03925, 03974, 04063, 04133, 04202, 04260, 04338, 04404, 04503, 04907, 04960 .... 4.00 - 8.00

B.F. KINCAID (THE BRIER HOPPER OF WFIW):

Gennett 7309 *Lane County Bachelor* .... 25.00 - 40.00

BRADLEY KINCAID:

Titles, issued contemporaneously on Banner, Conqueror, Melotone, Oriole, Perfect, Romeo, Vocalion: *After The Ball; Bury Me Out On The Prairie; The Fatal Derby Day; The Fatal Wedding; For Sale, A Baby; Gooseberry Pie; The Innocent Prisoner; I Wish I Had Someone To Love Me; The Lightning Express; A Picture From Life's Other Side; Red River Valley; Somewhere Somebody's Waiting For You; Sourwood Mountain, The True And Trembling Brakeman; Two Little Girls In Blue .* 5.00 - 10.00

Bluebird 5179 *Long Long Ago*	7.00	-	10.00
5201 *The Old Wooden Bucket*	7.00	-	10.00
5255 *House Carpenter*	8.00	-	12.00
5321 *Sweet Betsy From Pike*	7.00	-	10.00
5377 *The Death Of Jimmie Rodgers*	10.00	-	15.00
5423 *Mrs. Jimmie Rodgers Lament*	10.00	-	15.00
5486 *The Life Of Jimmie Rodgers*	10.00	-	15.00
5569 *The Ship That Never Returned*	5.00	-	8.00
5895 *The Letter Edged In Black*	5.00	-	8.00
5971 *In The Hills Of Kentucky*	5.00	-	8.00
8410 *Zeh Turney's Gal*	5.00	-	8.00
8478 *Mammy's Precious Baby*	5.00	-	8.00
8501 *The Blind Girl*	5.00	-	8.00
Brunswick 403 *Give My Love To Neil*	7.00	-	10.00
420 *Methodist Pie*	7.00	-	10.00
464 *Cindy*	7.00	-	10.00
485 *Old Coon Dog*	7.00	-	10.00
Bullet 615 *Ain't We Crazy*	5.00	-	8.00
Champion 45039 *On Top Of Old Smoky*	5.00	-	8.00
45057 *Four Thousand Years Ago*	5.00	-	8.00
45098 *Wreck On The C & O Road*	5.00	-	8.00
45130 *Angels In Heaven Know I Love You*	5.00	-	8.00
Decca 5025 *Ain't We Crazy*	8.00	-	12.00
5026 *The Old Wooden Rocker*	8.00	-	12.00
5048 *The Cowboy's Dream*	8.00	-	12.00
Gennett 6363 *The Fatal Wedding*	15.00	-	20.00
6417 *Methodist Pie*	15.00	-	20.00
6462 *The Swapping Song*	15.00	-	20.00
6620 *The Cuckoo Is A Pretty Bird*	15.00	-	20.00
6761 *Four Thousand Tears Ago*	15.00	-	20.00
6823 *Pearl Bryan*	15.00	-	20.00
6856 *The Little Mohee*	15.00	-	20.00

6900 *Angels In Heaven Know I Love You*	15.00	-	20.00
6944 *Let That Mule Go Aunk! Aunk!*	15.00	-	20.00
6958 *Charlie Brooks*	15.00	-	25.00
7020 *Old Number Three*	20.00	-	30.00
7053 *On Top Of Old Smoky*	20.00	-	30.00
7081 *After The Ball*	20.00	-	30.00
7112 *Cindy*	20.00	-	30.00
Superior 366 *Sourwood Mountain*	25.00	-	50.00
2656 *Four Thousand Years Ago*	15.00	-	20.00
2770 *On Top Of Old Smoky*	20.00	-	30.00
2788 *Old Number Three*	20.00	-	30.00
Supertone 9208 *Bury Me On The Prairie*	7.00	-	10.00
9209 *Froggie Went A-Courting*	7.00	-	10.00
9210 *Methodist Pie*	7.00	-	10.00
9211 *The Fatal Wedding*	7.00	-	10.00
9212 *Two Sisters*	8.00	-	12.00
9350 *Give My Love To Nell*	7.00	-	10.00
9362 *Four Thousand Years Ago*	7.00	-	10.00
9402 *The Little Mohee*	7.00	-	10.00
9403 *The Red River Valley*	7.00	-	10.00
9404 *Pearl Bryan*	7.00	-	10.00
9452 *Angels In Heaven Know I Love You*	7.00	-	10.00
9471 *Happy Lays Long Ago*	7.00	-	10.00
9505 *Old Number Three*	7.00	-	10.00
9566 *On Top Of Old Smoky*	7.00	-	10.00
9648 *After The Ball*	7.00	-	10.00
9666 *Pretty Little Pink*	7.00	-	10.00

9565 *The Blind Girl* .... 7.00 - 10.00

CHICKIE KING:

Speed 108 *Lov-ie Lov-ie* .... — - —

MARTIN KING:

Superior 2530 *We Parted By The Riverside*	15.00	-	20.00
2574 *Lane County Bachelor*	15.00	-	20.00

RANDY KING:

TNT 108 *Tied And Bound* .... — - —

KIRBY & PHILLIPS:

Bluebird 6367, 7056 .... 4.00 - 6.00

FRED KIRBY:

Bluebird 6325 *In The Shade Of The Pine*	5.00	-	8.00
6419 *I'm A Gold Diggin' Papa*	5.00	-	8.00
6597 *My Heavenly Sweetheart*	5.00	-	8.00
6763, 7009, 7164, 7190, 7261, 7310	4.00	-	7.00

FRED KIRBY (& DON WHITE/CLIFF CARLISLE):

Bluebird 6540 *My Old Saddle Horse Is Missing* . 5.00 - 8.00

ROCKY KIRKLAND:

J-B 1503 *Candy Baby* .... — - —

BERT KNOWLES:

Okeh 45427 *Blue Undertaker's Blues No. 2* .... 20.00 - 30.00

VANCE KNOWLES & RED LAY:

Bluebird 6585 *A Thousand Miles From Texas* ... 5.00 - 8.00

DON KUTTER:

Challenge 326 *Two Little Orphans*	7.00	-	10.00
327 *That Bad Man Stackalee*	8.00	-	12.00

PIEREE LA DIEU:

Columbia 15278-D *The Shanty-Man's Life* ..... 20.00 - 30.00

SLIM LAKE:

Superior 2819 *Peach Picking Time In Georgia* ... 75.00 - 100.00

BELLA LAM & HIS GREENE COUNTY SINGERS:

Okeh 45126, 45136, 45145, 45177, 45228, 45407, 45456 .... 5.00 - 10.00

LAMBERT & HILLPOT:

Paramount 3013 *My Carolina Home* .... 4.00 - 7.00

G.E. LANCASTER:

Superior 2538 *Tennessee Yodel* .... 25.00 - 40.00

LEE LANDERS:

Champion 15727 *Blue Yodel No. 3*	10.00	-	15.00
15767 *Lullaby Yodel*	10.00	-	15.00

UNCLE BUD LANDRESS:

Victor 21036 *Candy Pulling Time*	8.00	-	12.00
21354 *Coon Hunting In Moonshine Hollow*	8.00	-	12.00

23606 *The Daddy Song*	15.00 -	20.00
V40252 *Rubber Doll Rag*	15.00 -	20.00

DUKE LANE:

Supertone 9425 *Blue Yodel No. 4*	8.00 -	12.00
9496 *Waiting For A Train*	8.00 -	12.00

LAND & MILES:

Supertone 9314 *The Old New Hampshire Village*	7.00 -	10.00

(FIDDLIN') BOB LARKAN/LARKIN (FAMILY/IS MUSIC MAKERS):

Okeh 45205 *Kansas City Reel*	20.00 -	30.00
45229 *Beautiful Belle*	20.00 -	30.00
45349 *The Woman Wear No Clothes At All*	30.00 -	40.00
Vocalion 5277 *Saturday Night Waltz*	20.00 -	30.00
5313 *McLeod's Reel*	20.00 -	30.00
5329 *Arkansas Waltz*	20.00 -	30.00

CHARLIE LAWMAN:

Crown 3144 *There Must Be A Bright Tomorrow*	5.00 -	8.00
Paramount 3304 *There Must Be A Bright Tomorrow*	7.00 -	10.00

JIMMIE LAWSON:

Victor 20477 *Tennessee Blues*	10.00 -	15.00

ZORA LAYMAN:

Decca 5033, 5034	5.00 -	10.00

BERT LAYNE (& HIS GEORGIA SERENADERS/MELODY BOYS):

Brunswick 502 *Nights Of Gladness*	15.00 -	20.00
582 *I Ain't Got No Sweetheart*	15.00 -	20.00
Champion 16346 *The Rabbit Hunt*	35.00 -	50.00

BENNIE LEADERS:

Freedom 5012 *Boots Don't Leave Me*	7.00 -	10.00
5020 *I'll Be Jumped Up And Down*	7.00 -	10.00
5029 *Naggin' Woman*	7.00 -	10.00
Nucraft 105 *Clean Town Blues*	8.00 -	12.00
Ok'ed 1050 *Hey Miss Fannie*	8.00 -	12.00

LEAKE COUNTY REVELERS:

Columbia 15149-D *Johnson Gal*	15.00 -	20.00
15189-D *Wednesday Night Waltz*	5.00 -	8.00
15205-D *The Old Hat*	8.00 -	12.00
15227-D *My Bonnie Lies Over The Ocean*	8.00 -	12.00
15264-D *Merry Widow Waltz*	8.00 -	12.00
15292-D *They Go Wild Over Me*	10.00 -	15.00
15318-D *Crow Black Chicken*	15.00 -	20.00
15353-D *Rockin' Yodel*	15.00 -	20.00
15380-D *Bring Me A Bottle*	15.00 -	20.00
15409-D *Georgia Camp Meeting*	15.00 -	20.00
15427-D *Memories Waltz*	10.00 -	15.00
15441-D *Dry Town Blues*	15.00 -	20.00
15470-D *Saturday Night Breakdown*	15.00 -	20.00
15501-D *Beautiful Bells*	15.00 -	20.00
15520-D *Leake County Blues*	15.00 -	20.00
15569-D *Mississippi Moon*	15.00 -	20.00
15625-D *Birds In The Brook*	15.00 -	20.00
15648-D *When It's Springtime In The Rockies*	10.00 -	15.00
15668-D *Mississippi Breakdown*	25.00 -	40.00
15691-D *Texas Fair*	25.00 -	40.00
15767-D *Lazy Kate*	30.00 -	50.00
15776-D *Listen To The Mockingbird*	30.00 -	50.00

LEATHERMAN SISTERS:

Bluebird 6490, 6590	4.00 -	7.00

STEVE LEDFORD & HIS MOUNTAINERS:

Bluebird 7626, 7742	5.00 -	8.00

LEE BROTHERS TRIO:

Brunswick 501 *Cotton Mills Blues*	20.00 -	30.00

A. LEE, B. BROWN, P. MELVIN, H. RICE, P. LINDSEY & JUDGE LEE:

Brunswick 419 *A Bootlegger's Joint In Atlanta*	15.00 -	20.00

NANCY LEE & THE HILLTOPPERS:

Vogue 744 *Don't Tetch It*	25.00 -	40.00

WOODY LEFTWICH & ROY LILLY:

Champion 16345 *Lonesome Road Blues*	40.00 -	60.00

MALCOLM LEGETTE:

Columbia 15424-D *Song Of The Tramp*	7.00 -	10.00

LEON'S LONE STAR COWBOYS:

Champion 45151 *Mistreated Blues*	7.00 -	10.00
45152 *Sweet Sue*	7.00 -	10.00
45165 *Weary Blues*	7.00 -	10.00
45169 *Bugle Call Rag*	7.00 -	10.00
45174 *Dinah*	7.00 -	10.00
45185 *White River Stomp*	7.00 -	10.00
45195 *Just Forget*	7.00 -	10.00
45196 *Milenburg Joys*	7.00 -	10.00
Decca 5280, 5288, 5289, 5301, 5323, 5328, 5340, 5361, 5377, 5388, 5396, 5511, 5530	4.00 -	8.00

JOE (& MARY) LESTER (& DICK MOSS);

Superior 2606 *My Old Cottage Home*	15.00 -	20.00
2632 *That Silver Haired Daddy Of Mine*	15.00 -	20.00
2654 *Missouri Is Calling*	15.00 -	20.00
2675 *Yodel Your Troubles Away*	20.00 -	30.00
2683 *Down And Out Blues*	20.00 -	30.00
2702 *By The Ozark Trail*	20.00 -	30.00

LEWIS BROTHERS:

Victor V40172 *Sally Johnson*	20.00 -	30.00
V40187 *When Summer Comes Again*	20.00 -	30.00

ARCHIE LEWIS:

Champion 16677 *Miss Handy Hanks*	20.00 -	30.00

TEXAS JIM LEWIS & LONE STAR COWBOYS:

Vocalion 03754, 03915, 03977	5.00 -	8.00

LIGHT CRUST DOUGHBOYS:

Okeh, most issues	3.00 -	6.00
Vocalion 02992 *My Pretty Quadroon*	8.00 -	12.00
03017 *El Rancho Grande*	8.00 -	12.00
03065, 03141, 03239, 03610, 03660, 03867, 03926, 04158, 04216, 04261, 04326, 04403, 04468, 04559, 04560, 04638, 04701, 04702, 04770, 04825, 04921, 04965, 04973, 04974, 05039	5.00 -	10.00

ADD LINDSAY:

Victor 21401 *Whoa Mule*	10.00 -	15.00

RED LINDSEY:

Talent 711 *Penitentiary Blues*	10.00 -	15.00

W.A. LINDSEY & ALVIN CONDER:

Okeh 45346 *Good Old Turnip Greens*	15.00 -	20.00

LITTLE JIMMIE (See ASHER SIZEMORE**TOBE LITTLE:**

Okeh 40460, 40479, 45090	5.00 -	10.00

DOCTOR LLOYD & HOWARD MAXEY:

Okeh 45150 *Western Union*	30.00 -	50.00

RUSTY LOCKE:

TNT 1012 *Milk Cow Blues*	5.00 -	8.00

HANK LOCKLIN:

Gold Star 1341 *Rio Grande Waltz*	15.00 -	20.00
Royalty 603 *Please Come Back And Stay*	15.00 -	20.00
604 *You've Been Talking In Your Sleep*	15.00 -	20.00

GEORGE E. LOGAN ("PETE THE HIRED MAN"):

Champion 45036 *By The Ozark Trail*	7.00 -	10.00

LOGAN COUNTY TRIO:

Challenge 302 *The Buckin' Mule*	5.00 -	8.00
325 *Hand Me Down My Walking Cane*	5.00 -	8.00

LOG CABIN BOYS:

Banner 32903 *Ole Bill Jackson Brown*	5.00 -	8.00
Decca 5035, 5036, 5103, 5110	15.00 -	20.00

LONESOME COWBOY:

Champion 16767 *Memphis Gal*	50.00 -	75.00
45080 *Memphis Gal*	10.00 -	15.00
Perfect 12591 *I'm Just A Black Sheep*	5.00 -	8.00
Superior 2652 *The Yodeling Cowboy*	50.00 -	75.00

LONESOME COWGIRL:

Champion 16767 *Lonesome Cowboy*	50.00 -	75.00
Superior 2631 *Livin' In The Mountains*	20.00 -	30.00
2652 *My Mother Was A Lady*	50.00 -	75.00

LONESOME LUKE (& HIS FARMS BOYS):

Champion 16229 *Dogs In The Ash Can*	20.00 -	30.00

16269 *Beaver Valley Breakdown* .... 20.00 - 30.00

LONESOME PINE TWINS:
Banner 6041 *A Picture From Life's Other Side* ... 4.00 - 7.00

LONE STAR COWBOYS:
Bluebird 5283 .... 4.00 - 7.00
6001, 6052 .... 4.00 - 7.00
Champion 45046 *Dillinger's Warning* .... 7.00 - 10.00
Victor 23846 *Deep Elm Blues* .... 25.00 - 40.00
23850 *Wonderful Child* .... 25.00 - 40.00

LONE STAR RANGERS:
Broadway 8141 *The Prison Warden's Secret* ..... 7.00 - 10.00
8142 *The Train That Never Arrived* ..... 7.00 - 10.00
8144 *Farm Relief Song* .... 7.00 - 10.00
8150 *Eleven More Months And Ten More Days*. 7.00 - 10.00
3202 *The Train That Never Arrived* .... 7.00 - 10.00
3208 *Farm Relief Song* .... 7.00 - 10.00
3218 *Eleven More Months And Ten More Days*. 7.00 - 10.00
Regal 8973 *Eleven More Months And Ten More Days* .... 5.00 - 8.00

LONG BROTHERS:
Victor 23622 *Cross-Eyed Gal That Lived Upon The Hill* .... 20.00 - 30.00
23637 *Missouri Is Calling* .... 20.00 - 30.00

BEVERLY & JIM/JIMMIE/JIMMY LONG:
Bluebird 5139, 5188 .... 3.00 - 6.00
Champion 16659 *Two Little Orphans* .... 20.00 - 30.00

CLAY LONG & HIS LONG HORNS:
Vocalion 04602, 04731, 04812 .... 7.00 - 10.00

JIMMIE/JIMMY LONG (& BEVERLY LONG/CLIFF KEISER):
Champion 16099 *Missouri I'm Calling You* ..... 10.00 - 15.00
16117 *That's Why I Left The Mountains* .... 10.00 - 15.00
16164 *My Alabama Home* .... 15.00 - 20.00
16190 *My Old Pal Of Yesterday* .... 10.00 - 15.00
16214 *Listen To The Voice* .... 10.00 - 15.00
16233 *Yodel Your Troubles Away* .... 15.00 - 20.00
16280 *Have You Found Somebody Else To Love* 15.00 - 20.00
16296 *Down And Out Blues* .... 20.00 - 30.00
16311 *Let's Get Together* .... 20.00 - 30.00
16632 *The Answer To 21 Years* .... 25.00 - 40.00
16641 *Hang It In The Hen House* .... 30.00 - 50.00
16663 *The Old Folks Back Home* .... 30.00 - 50.00
16671 *My California Mountain Rose* .... 30.00 - 50.00
45022, 45023, 45084, 45089 .... 5.00 - 10.00
Gennett 7287 *Blue Pining For You* .... 30.00 - 50.00
7314 *Missouri Is Calling* .... 30.00 - 50.00
Victor 23705 *Doggone Blues* .... 40.00 - 60.00
23724 *Down And Out* .... 40.00 - 60.00
23824 *Alone With My Sorrows* .... 50.00 - 75.00

LOOKOUT MOUNTAIN BOYS:
Paramount 3164 *Down In Atlanta* .... 20.00 - 30.00
3264 *Down In Atlanta* .... 20.00 - 30.00

LOOKOUT MOUNTAIN REVELERS:
Paramount 3105 *Barn Dance On The Mountain* .. 15.00 - 20.00
3111 *Pussy Cat Rag* .... 15.00 - 20.00
3123 *Dreaming Of Mother* .... 10.00 - 15.00
3143 *Bury Me Beneath The Willow* .... 10.00 - 15.00

LOUISIANA LOU:
Bluebird 5424 *Sinful To Flirt* .... 15.00 - 20.00
5484 *A Package Of Love Letters* .... 15.00 - 20.00
5636 *With A Banjo On My Knee* .... 15.00 - 20.00
5749 *Go 'Long Mule* .... 15.00 - 20.00
Victor 23848 *Go 'Long Mule* .... 50.00 - 80.00

LOUISIANA ROUNDERS:
Decca 5483, 5495 .... 4.00 - 8.00

LOUISIANA STROLLERS:
Champion 45199 *Strollers Waltz* .... 7.00 - 10.00

(DADDY) JOHN LOVE:
Bluebird 6294 *My Little Red Ford* .... 15.00 - 20.00
6491 *Cotton Mill Blues* .... 15.00 - 20.00
6583 *Blue Days* .... 15.00 - 20.00
6624 *Railroad Blues* .... 15.00 - 20.00

6675 *Over The Hills In Carolina* .... 15.00 - 20.00

RAMBLIN' RED LOWERY:
Vocalion 02665 *Ramblin' Red's Memphis Yodel* .. 25.00 - 40.00

LUKE THE DRIFTER (See HANK WILLIAMS):

LULLABY LARKERS:
Champion 16257 *Shine On Harvest Moon* ...... 20.00 - 30.00
16295 *The True And Trembling Breakman* ... 20.00 - 30.00
16322 *When The Cactus Is In Bloom* .... 20.00 - 30.00
16364 *The Chicken Roost Blues* .... 25.00 - 40.00
16417 *My Lonely Boyhood Days* .... 25.00 - 40.00
45132, 45186 .... 8.00 - 12.00

LULU BELLE: & SCOTTY:
Vocalion 04690, 04772, 04841, 04910, 04962 .... 4.00 - 7.00
Vogue 718 *Some Sunday Morning* .... 20.00 - 35.00
719 *I Get A Kick Out Of Corn* .... 20.00 - 35.00
720 *Time Will Tell* .... 25.00 - 40.00

BASCOM LAMAR LUNSFORD:
Brunswick 219 *Mountain Dew* .... 8.00 - 12.00
227 *Lost John Dean* .... 8.00 - 12.00
228 *Darby's Ram* .... 8.00 - 12.00
229 *Lulu Wall* .... 8.00 - 12.00
Brunswick 230 *Kidder Cole* .... 8.00 - 12.00
231 *Dry Bones* .... 8.00 - 12.00
314 *Dry Bones* .... 8.00 - 12.00
Columbia 15595-D *Speaking The Truth* ...... 20.00 - 30.00
40155 *Jesse James* .... 15.00 - 20.00
45008 *Fate Of Santa Barbara* .... 15.00 - 20.00
Vocalion 5246 *Lost John Dean* .... 10.00 - 15.00
5252 *Little Turtle Dove* .... 10.00 - 15.00

TED LUNSFORD:
Champion 16287 *The Hobo's Return* .... 20.00 - 30.00

FRANK LUTHER:
This artist recorded for many labels in the 1920s and 1930s. Most of his records are of minimal value or interest to the collector. Following are a few possible exceptions.
Broadway 8102 *Memphis Yodel* .... 5.00 - 8.00
Columbia 15588-D *Oklahoma Charley* .... 5.00 - 8.00
15768-D *Carry Me Back To The Mountains* ... 10.00 - 15.00
Edison (thick) .... 4.00 - 8.00
Edison (thin) .... 10.00 - 15.00
Timely Tunes 1558 *Divorce Blues* .... 10.00 - 15.00
Victor 23737 *Sweetest Of All My Dreams* .... 7.00 - 10.00
Vocalion 5227, 5278 .... 4.00 - 8.00

"MAC" (AND HIS HAYWIRE ORCHESTRA): (See also "RADIO MAC")
Victor 21343, 21420, 21421, 21487, 21704, 21761 .. 5.00 - 10.00
Victor V-40016 *Trail To Mexico* .... 10.00 - 15.00

W.W. MacBETH:
Brunswick 373 *Southern Melodies* .... 5.00 - 8.00
443 *Red Wing* .... 5.00 - 8.00
571 *Darling Nellie Gray* .... 5.00 - 8.00

BOB MacGIMSEY:
Victor 23562 *Religion Ain't Nothin' To Play With* 8.00 - 12.00
23584 *Bob's Medley* .... 8.00 - 12.00
23612 *Southern Melodies* .... 8.00 - 12.00

MACK BROTHERS:
Decca 5073, 5086, 5125 .... 5.00 - 10.00

BILL MACK:
Imperial 8114 *Crazy Baby Boogie* .... 7.00 - 10.00
8151 *Big Bad Daddy* .... 7.00 - 10.00
8174 *Play My Boogie* .... 7.00 - 10.00
8192 *Forever I'll Wait For You* .... 5.00 - 8.00

MACON QUARTETTE:
Columbia 15211-D *Uncle Joe* .... 8.00 - 12.00

UNCLE DAVE MACON; MACON & (SID) HARKREADER; UNCLE DAVE MACON & KIRK/SAM McGEE; UNCLE DAVE MACON & HIS FRUIT JAR DRINKERS:

Bluebird 5842 One More River To Cross	20.00 -	30.00
5873 I'll Tickle Nancy	20.00 -	30.00
5926 Just One Way To The Pearly Gates	20.00 -	30.00
7174 From Jerusalem To Jericho	15.00 -	20.00
7234 Travelin Down The Road	15.00 -	20.00
7350 Bum Hotel	15.00 -	20.00
7385 Fame Apart From God's Approval	15.00 -	20.00
7549 She's Got The Money Too	15.00 -	20.00
7779 Peek-A-Boo	15.00 -	20.00
7951 Country Ham And Red Gravy	15.00 -	20.00
8279 Working For My Lord	15.00 -	20.00
8325 Railroadin' And Gamblin'	15.00 -	20.00
8341 Beautiful Love	15.00 -	20.00
8379 Johnny Grey	15.00 -	20.00
8422 They're After Me	15.00 -	20.00
Brunswick 112 On The Dixie Bee Line	15.00 -	20.00
114 The Cross Eyed Butcher & The Cackling Hen	15.00 -	20.00
263 Governor Al Smith	20.00 -	30.00
266 Worthy Of Estimation	20.00 -	30.00
292 I'm The Child To Fight	20.00 -	30.00
329 From Earth To Heaven	20.00 -	30.00
340 Uncle Dave's Travels-Part 1	20.00 -	30.00
349 Uncle Dave's Travels-Part 2	20.00 -	30.00
355 Uncle Dave's Travels-Part 3	20.00 -	30.00
362 Uncle Dave's Travels-Part 4	20.00 -	30.00
425 Coming Round The Mountains	20.00 -	30.00
Champion 16805 When The Train Comes Along	100.00 -	150.00
16822 Don't Get Weary Children	100.00 -	150.00
45048 Don't Get Weary Children	15.00 -	25.00
45105 When The Train Comes Along	15.00 -	25.00
Decca 5369 Don't Get Weary Children	10.00 -	15.00
5373 Thank God For Everything	10.00 -	15.00
Montgomery Ward 4819 One More River To Cross	10.00 -	15.00
7347 The Bum Hotel	10.00 -	15.00
7348 Honest Confession Is Good For The Soul	10.00 -	15.00
7349 From Jerusalem To Jericho	10.00 -	15.00
7350 Two-In-One Chewing Gum	10.00 -	15.00
7884 She's Got The Money Too	10.00 -	15.00
7885 Johnny Grey	10.00 -	15.00
8029 Don't Get Weary Children	10.00 -	15.00
Okeh 45507 Tennessee Red Fox Chase	75.00 -	125.00
45522 Mysteries Of The World	75.00 -	125.00
45552 She's Got The Money Too	75.00 -	125.00
Vocalion 5001 Deliverance Will Come	20.00 -	30.00
5002 Arcade Blues	20.00 -	30.00
5003 The Old Man's Drunk Again	20.00 -	30.00
5004 Something's Always Sure To Tickle Me	20.00 -	30.00
5005 Sourwood Mountain Medley	20.00 -	30.00
5006 Sassy Sam	20.00 -	30.00
5007 My Girl's A High Born Lady	20.00 -	30.00
5008 Them Two Gals Of Mine	20.00 -	30.00
5009 I Ain't Got Long To Stay	20.00 -	30.00
5010 Sho' Fly, Don't Bother Me	20.00 -	30.00
5011 Uncle Ned	20.00 -	30.00
5012 Diamond In The Rough	20.00 -	30.00
5013 Tossing The Baby So High	20.00 -	30.00
5014 Never Make Love No More	20.00 -	30.00
5040 (She Was Always) Chewing Gum	20.00 -	30.00
5041 Papa's Billie Goat	20.00 -	30.00
5042 Down By The River	20.00 -	30.00
5043 The Fox Chase	20.00 -	30.00
5046 Jonah And The Whale	20.00 -	30.00
5047 Soldier's Joy	20.00 -	30.00
5051 All I've Got's Gone	20.00 -	30.00
5060 Run Nigger, Run	20.00 -	30.00
5061 Old Dan Tucker	20.00 -	30.00
5062 The Girl I Left Behind Me	20.00 -	30.00
5065 Southern Whistling Coon	20.00 -	30.00
Vocalion 5066 Oh, Where Is My Boy Tonight	20.00 -	30.00
5067 All-Go-Hungry Hash House	20.00 -	30.00
5070 Save My Mother's Picture From The Sale	20.00 -	30.00
5071 Muskrat Medley	20.00 -	30.00
5075 Down By The Old Mill Stream	20.00 -	30.00
5081 Arkansas Travelers	20.00 -	30.00
5082 Struttin' Round	20.00 -	30.00
5095 I've Got The Mourning Blues	20.00 -	30.00
5096 On The Dixie Bee Line	20.00 -	30.00
5097 Way Down The Old Plank Road	20.00 -	30.00
5098 He Won The Heart Of My Sarah Jane	20.00 -	30.00
5099 Whoop 'Em Up Cindy	20.00 -	30.00
5100 Poor Sinners, Fare You Well	20.00 -	30.00
5104 Old Ties	20.00 -	30.00
5109 I Tickled Nancy	20.00 -	30.00
5148 Bake That Chicken Pie	25.00 -	40.00
5149 In The Shade Of The Old Apple Tree	25.00 -	40.00
5151 Carve That Possum	25.00 -	40.00
5152 Rockabout My Sara Jane	25.00 -	40.00
5153 Tell Her To Come Back Home	25.00 -	40.00
5154 Walk, Tom Wilson, Walk	25.00 -	40.00
5155 Sail Away, Ladies	25.00 -	40.00
5156 Sleepy Lou	25.00 -	40.00
5157 I's Gwine Back To Dixie	25.00 -	40.00
5159 Poor Old Dad	25.00 -	40.00
5161 The Mockingbird Song Medley	25.00 -	40.00
5163 When Ruebin Comes To Town	25.00 -	40.00
5164 Backwater Blues	25.00 -	40.00
5165 Go Along Mule	25.00 -	40.00
5172 More Like Your Dad Every Day	25.00 -	40.00
5261 The New Ford Car	25.00 -	40.00
5316 Jesus, Lover Of My Soul	25.00 -	40.00
5341 Farm Relief	25.00 -	40.00
5356 The Life And Death Of Jesse James	25.00 -	40.00
5374 We Need A Change In Business All Around	25.00 -	40.00
5380 Susie Lee	25.00 -	40.00
5397 Put Me In My Little Bed	25.00 -	40.00
14847 (She Was Always) Chewing Gum	20.00 -	30.00
14848 Keep My Skillet Good And Greasy	20.00 -	30.00
14849 Down By The River	20.00 -	30.00
14850 Old Maid's Last Hope (A Burglar Song)	20.00 -	30.00
14864 Jonah And The Whale	20.00 -	30.00
14904 All I've Gots Gone	20.00 -	30.00
15032 Run, Nigger, Run	20.00 -	30.00
15033 Old Dan Tucker	20.00 -	30.00
15034 Down In Arkansaw	20.00 -	30.00
15063 Walermelon Smilin' On The Vine	20.00 -	30.00
15076 All-Go-Hungry Hash House	20.00 -	30.00
15100 Save My Mother's Picture From The Sale	20.00 -	30.00
15101 Muskrat Medley	20.00 -	30.00
15143 Down By The Old Mill Stream	20.00 -	30.00
15192 Arkansas Travelers	20.00 -	30.00
15319 I've Got The Mourning Blues	20.00 -	30.00
15320 On The Dixie Bee Line	20.00 -	30.00
15321 Rise When The Rooster Crows	20.00 -	30.00
15322 He Won The Heart Of My Sarah Jane	20.00 -	30.00
15323 Whoop 'Em Up Cindy	20.00 -	30.00
15324 Poor Sinners, Fare You Well	20.00 -	30.00
15325 Old Ties	20.00 -	30.00
15341 I Tickled Nancy	20.00 -	30.00
15439 Uncle Dave's Beloved Solo	20.00 -	30.00
15441 In The Good Old Summer Time	20.00 -	30.00
15442 Something's Always Sure To Tickle Me	20.00 -	30.00
15443 Sourwood Mountain Medley	20.00 -	30.00
15444 Sassy Sam	20.00 -	30.00
15445 My Girls A High Born Lady	20.00 -	30.00
15446 Them Two Girls Of Mine	20.00 -	30.00
15447 We Are Up Against It Now	20.00 -	30.00
15448 Sho' Fly Don't Bother Me	20.00 -	30.00

15450 *Uncle Ned*	20.00 -	30.00
15451 *Hold On To The Sleigh*	20.00 -	30.00
15452 *Kissin' On The Sly*	20.00 -	30.00
15453 *Never Make Love No More*	20.00 -	30.00

MADDOX BROS. & ROSE:

4-Star 1184 *Midnight Train*	5.00 -	8.00
1185 *Milk Cow Blues*	5.00 -	8.00

MADDUX FAMILY:

Decca 5393 *Stone Rag*	4.00 -	7.00

MADISONVILLE STRING BAND:

Champion 16452 *B Flat Rag*	20.00 -	30.00
16503 *Next To Your Mother, Who Do You Love*	20.00 -	30.00
45005 *B Flat Rag*	7.00 -	10.00
Decca 5437 *B Flat Rag*	5.00 -	8.00
Superior 2756 *B Flat Rag*	25.00 -	40.00

MAGNOLIA TRIO:

Okeh 45505 *My Carolina Sweetheart*	10.00 -	15.00
45521 *'Neath The Old Pine Tree At Twilight*	10.00 -	15.00

JACK MAHONEY:

Columbia 15685-D *The Convict And The Bird*	15.00 -	20.00
15712-D *The Convict's Return*	15.00 -	20.00

**J.E. MAINER (& HIS MOUNTAINEERS);
WADE MAINER & SONS; WADE MAINER
& ZEKE MORRIS; WADE MARINER &
SON OF THE MOUNTAINEERS; MAINERS
MOUNTAINEERS; MAINER'S SMILIN
RANGERS:**

Bluebird 6065 *Maple On The Hill*	5.00 -	8.00
6088 *This World Is Not My Home*	7.00 -	10.00
6090 *Broken Hearted Blues*	7.00 -	10.00
6104 *Let Her Go, God Bless Her*	7.00 -	10.00
6160 *The City On The Hill*	7.00 -	10.00
6194 *Write A Letter To Mother*	7.00 -	10.00
6222 *Longest Train*	7.00 -	10.00
6290 *Fatal Wreck Of The Bus*	7.00 -	10.00
6293 *Maple On The Hill-Part 2*	7.00 -	10.00
6324 *Satisfied*	7.00 -	10.00
6347 *A Leaf From The Sea*	7.00 -	10.00
6383 *Just As The Sun Went Down*	7.00 -	10.00
6385 *When I Reach My Home Eternal*	7.00 -	10.00
6424 *New Lost Train Blues*	7.00 -	10.00
6440 *Behind The Parlor Door*	7.00 -	10.00
6460 *Nobody's Darling On Earth*	7.00 -	10.00
6479 *The Old And Faded Picture*	7.00 -	10.00
6489 *Cradle Days*	7.00 -	10.00
6539 *Got A Home In That Rock*	7.00 -	10.00
6551 *Come Back To Your Dobie Shack*	7.00 -	10.00
Bluebird 6584 *Watermelon On The Vine*	7.00 -	10.00
6596 *Shake Hands With Mother*	7.00 -	10.00
6624 *What Makes Him Do It?*	7.00 -	10.00
6629 *John Henry Was A Little Boy*	7.00 -	10.00
6653 *Cowboy's Pony In Heaven*	7.00 -	10.00
6675 *Budded Roses*	7.00 -	10.00
6704 *Been Foolin' Me Baby*	7.00 -	10.00
6738 *Won't Be Worried Long*	7.00 -	10.00
6752 *Hop Along Peter*	7.00 -	10.00
6784 *Just One Way To The Pearly Gates*	7.00 -	10.00
6792 *Seven And A Half*	7.00 -	10.00
6840 *Little Birdie*	7.00 -	10.00
6890 *Always Born A Gambler*	7.00 -	10.00
6936 *In The Land Beyond The Blue*	7.00 -	10.00
6993 *Little Rosebuds*	7.00 -	10.00
7114 *Answer To Two Little Rosebuds*	7.00 -	10.00
7151 *Answer To Greenback Dollar*	7.00 -	10.00
7165 *I'm Not Turning Backward*	7.00 -	10.00
7201 *Little Maggie*	7.00 -	10.00
7222 *In The Little Village Churchyard*	7.00 -	10.00
7249 *Wild Bill Jones*	7.00 -	10.00
7274 *Memory Lane*	5.00 -	10.00
7289 *Kiss Me Cindy*	5.00 -	10.00
7298 *Riding On Train 45*	5.00 -	10.00
7349 *Don't Go Out*	5.00 -	10.00
7384 *What Are You Goin' To Do, Brother?*	5.00 -	8.00
7412 *Lamp Lightin' Time In Heaven*	5.00 -	8.00
7424 *All My Friends*	5.00 -	8.00
7471 *If I Lose, Let Me Lose*	5.00 -	8.00
7483 *Don't Get To Deep In Love*	5.00 -	8.00
7523 *Floating Down The Stream Of Time*	5.00 -	8.00
7561 *I Won't Be Worried*	5.00 -	8.00
7586 *Your Best Friend Is Always Near*	5.00 -	8.00
7587 *Mountain Sweetheart*	5.00 -	8.00
7659 *I Once Loved A Young Man*	5.00 -	8.00
7730 *Just Over In Glory Land*	5.00 -	8.00
Bluebird 7753 *Where Romance Calls*	5.00 -	8.00
7845 *Mitchell Blues*	5.00 -	8.00
7965 *Great Reaping Day*	5.00 -	8.00
7965 *More Good Women Gone Wrong*	5.00 -	8.00
8042 *Sparkling Blue Eyes*	5.00 -	8.00
Bluebird (higher numbers)	4.00 -	7.00
King	3.00 -	5.00

JACK MAJOR:

Brunswick 252 *Tennessee Mountain Girl*	15.00 -	20.00
Columbia 15362-D *My Kentucky Mountain Sweetheart*	20.00 -	30.00

BLIND JOE MANGUM & FRED SHRIBER:

Okeh 40018 *Bacon And Cabbage*	15.00 -	20.00

MAPLE CITY FOUR:

Supertone 9193 *Roll Dem Bones*	5.00 -	8.00

MARKHAM BROS.:

Challenge 399 *I Am Resolved*	5.00 -	8.00
400 *Constantly Abiding*	5.00 -	8.00
401 *I'm On The Sunny Side*	7.00 -	10.00

ANDY MARLOW:

Champion 15875 *My Little Lady*	15.00 -	20.00
15899 *Blue Yodel No. 5*	15.00 -	20.00

MARLOW AND YOUNG:

Champion 15691 *Let Her Go I'll Meet Her*	7.00 -	10.00
15732 *My Carolina Home*	20.00 -	30.00
15750 *Six Months Ain't Long*	20.00 -	30.00

CHARLIE MARSHALL:

Vocalion 03045 *The Old Hitchin' Rail*	10.00 -	15.00

MARTIN BROTHERS:

Paramount 3194 *The Marion Massacre*	30.00 -	50.00
3217 *Whistling Rufus*	30.00 -	50.00
3248 *Don't Marry A Man If He Drinks*	30.00 -	50.00

MARTIN MELODY BOYS:

Columbia 15413-D *The Donald Rag*	25.00 -	40.00

**(ASA) MARTIN & (JAMES) ROBERTS;
MARTIN & ROSE; MARTIN & HOBBS:**

Titles, issued contemporaneously on Banner,
Conqueror, Melotone, Oriole, Perfect, Romeo:
*Aged Mother; Bronco Bill; Budded Roses; Bury
Me Neath The Weeping Willow; Careless Love;
The Contented Hobo; Crawdad Song; Darling
Nellie Gray. Down On The Farm; The Dying
Cowboy; The East Bound Train; Give My Love
To Nellie, Jack; Good Bye Bett; Hang Down
Your Head And Cry; Hot Corn; I Tickled Her
Under The Chin; The Knoxville Girl; A Letter
From Home Sweet Home; Lillie Dale; The
Little Old Jail House; Little Shack Around The
Corner; Low Down Hanging Around; Message
Of A Broken Heart; My Blue Eyed Boy; My
Dixie Home; My Lover On The Deep Blue Sea;
My Old Homestead By The Sea; My Rocky
Mountain Queen; Ninety Nine Years; The Pine
Tree On The Hill; Prisoner No. 999; The
Roundup In The Spring; The Rovin'
Moonshiner; Rycove Cyclone; Shadows And
Dreams; She Ain't Built That Way; The Ship
That Never Returned; Sunny Tennessee; Sweet
Florine; There's A Little Box Of Pine On The
7:29; There's No Place Like Home; There's
Someone Waiting For You; The Wandering*

Hobo; When Its Lamp Lighhng Time In The			
Valley; When The Roses Bloom In Dixie;			
Where's My Sweetie Now	5.00	-	10.00
Champion 16049 *An Old Fashioned Picture Of*			
Mother	12.00	-	16.00
16272 *Mind Your Own Business*	12.00	-	16.00
16299 *The Contented Hobo*	12.00	-	16.00
16520 *Hot Corn*	20.00	-	30.00
16529 *Prisoner No. 949*	20.00	-	30.00
16536 *Wild Cat Rag*	25.00	-	40.00
16539 *The Little Old Jailhouse*	25.00	-	40.00
16557 *The Roving Moonshiner*	25.00	-	40.00
16568 *I Must See My Mother*	20.00	-	30.00
16589 *I'm On My Way Back Home*	20.00	-	30.00
16597 *Shadows And Dreams*	20.00	-	30.00
16610 *Wolf County Blues*	30.00	-	50.00
16611 *Gamblin' Cowboy*	30.00	-	50.00
16627 *Jakewalk Papa*	30.00	-	50.00
16769 *It's Funny When You Feel That Way*	30.00	-	50.00
Champion 45034 *Bronco Bill*	8.00	-	12.00
45065 *Hot Corn*	8.00	-	12.00
45067 *My Cabin Home Among The Hills*	7.00	-	10.00
45129 *She Ain't Built That Way*	7.00	-	10.00
45133 *Red River Valley Rose*	7.00	-	10.00
45142 *Take Those Lips Away*	7.00	-	10.00
Champion 45175 *The Dying Girls Message*	8.00	-	12.00
45176 *Prisoner No. 949*	8.00	-	12.00
Decca 5444 *Take Those Lips Away*	5.00	-	8.00
Gennett 6531 *The Dingy Miner's Cabin*	20.00	-	30.00
6601 *The Old New Hampshire Valley*	20.00	-	30.00
6621 *The Dying Girls Message*	20.00	-	30.00
6762 *Bad Campanions*	20.00	-	30.00
6808 *She Ain't Built That Way*	20.00	-	30.00
6975 *The Virginia Moonshiner*	20.00	-	30.00
7050 *Gwine Down To Town*	25.00	-	40.00
7068 *Down On The Farm*	25.00	-	40.00
7207 *Johnny The Drunkard*	25.00	-	40.00
7242 *Put On Your Old Gray Bonnet*	25.00	-	40.00
Vocalion 04529, 04569, 04673, 04759, 04827,			
04894	4.00	-	8.00

CLYDE MARTIN & HIS HOOSIER RANGERS:
Champion 16409 *Shuber's Hoe Down*	25.00	-	40.00

DAN MARTIN:
Superior 2824 *The Cross-Eyed Butcher*	10.00	-	20.00

JOHN MARTIN:
Superior 2626 *Railroad Blues*	20.00	-	30.00
2658 *The Hobos Pal*	20.00	-	30.00
2701 *The Wreck Of The C & O Sportsman*	20.00	-	30.00

JOHNNY MARTIN:
Supertone 9721 *Sweet Wimmin'*	25.00	-	40.00

MARVIN FAMILY:
Columbia 15474-D *Yodeling Them Blues Away*	15.00	-	20.00

MARVIN'S STRING BAND:
Supertone 9738 *Fox Chase*	7.00	-	10.00

FRANKIE MARVIN (& HIS GUITAR & JIMMIE SMITH):
Following is a selective listing form the large
number of records, mostly of minimal value,
by the artist:
Crown 3125, 3204	5.00	-	8.00
Edison (thin) 11006 *Away Out On The Mountain*	15.00	-	20.00
20002 *Ben Dewberry's Final Run*	15.00	-	20.00
20011 *Oklahoma, Land Of The Sunny West*	—	-	—
(Note: 20011 was not officially issued, but copies			
have been reported.)			
Edison (thick) 52436, 52451, 52460, 52490,			
52523, 52576, 52607	10.00	-	20.00
52650 *Blue Yodel No. 4*	20.00	-	30.00
Paramount 3275 *T.B. Blues*	10.00	-	15.00
3276 *The Gangster's Warning*	10.00	-	15.00
Timely Tunes 1553 *She's Just That Kind*	15.00	-	20.00
1554 *She's Always On My Mind*	15.00	-	20.00

1555 *I'm Blue And Lonesome*	15.00	-	20.00
Victor 23553 *Old Man Duff*	10.00	-	15.00
23561 *When It's Night Time In Nevada*	75.00	-	100.00

JOHNNY MARVIN:
Most of the records by this artist are of little
value or interest as country/western music.
Victor 23691 *I'm Gonna Yodel My Way To*			
Heaven	10.00	-	15.00
23708 *Seven Come Eleven*	10.00	-	20.00
23728 *Go Along Bum*	10.00	-	20.00

MASSEY FAMILY:
Vocalion 02993 *Sweet Mama Tree Top Tall*	8.00	-	12.00

JACK MATHIS:
Columbia 15344-D *Your Mother Still Prays For*			
You	8.00	-	12.00
15450-D *Charming Bessie Lee*	8.00	-	12.00

JOHNNY MATHIS:
Talent 738 *Tell Me Why*	10.00	-	15.00

JIMMIE MATTOX:
Gennett 7227 *Good Bye Mama*	35.00		50.00

BILLIE MAXWELL (THE COWGIRL SINGER):
Victor V40148 *Billy Venero*	8.00	-	12.00
V40188 *The Cowboy's Wife*	10.00	-	15.00
V40241 *Haunted Hunted*	10.00	-	15.00

KEN MAYNARD:
Columbia 2310-D *The Cowboy's Lament*	75.00	-	100.00

DAVID McCARN:
Victor 23506 *Poor Man, Rich Man*	50.00	-	80.00
23532 *Hobo Life*	50.00	-	80.00
23555 *Gastonia Gallop*	75.00	-	100.00
V40274 *Cotton Mill Colic*	50.00	-	80.00

McCARTT BROTHERS & PATTERSON:
Columbia 15454-D *Green Valley Waltz*	5.00	-	8.00

McCLAIN & HARPOLD:
Gennett 7224 *Bake That Chicken Pie*	20.00	-	30.00
Supertone 9716 *Bake That Chicken Pie*	15.00	-	20.00

McCLENDON BROTHERS:
Bluebird 6961 *My Little Mountain Lady*	5.00	-	8.00
7339 *Free As I Can Be*	8.00	-	12.00
7832 *Corns On My Feet*	5.00	-	8.00

HARRY McCLINTOCK (See "RADI0 MAC" AND "MAC"
McCLUNG BROTHERS (& CLEVE CHAFFIN):
Brunswick 134 *Birdie*	15.00	-	20.00
135 *Chicken*	15.00	-	20.00
136 *It's A Long, Long Way To Tipperary*	15.00	-	20.00
Paramount 3161 *Alabama Jubilee*	20.00	-	30.00
3179 *Rock House Gamblers*	20.00	-	30.00

(SMILIN') ED McCONNELL:
Bluebird 5075, 5105, 5140, 5200, 5275	3.00	-	6.00
Champion 16209 *The Hell Bound Train*	10.00	-	15.00
16263 *Leave It There*	10.00	-	15.00
45137 *The Devil Song*	4.00	-	6.00
Victor 23808 *Tiny Toys*	8.00	-	12.00
23812 *The Royal Telephone*	8.00	-	12.00
23823 *Life's Railway To Heaven*	8.00	-	12.00
23825 *Where Is My Boy Tonight*	8.00	-	12.00
23844 *The Old Rugged Cross*	8.00	-	12.00
23848 *Leave It There*	8.00	-	12.00

EARL McCOY (& JESSIE BROCK/ALFRED MENG & CLEM GARNER):
Columbia 15499-D *Cotton Mill Girl*	30.00	-	50.00
15604-D *Off To War*	30.00	-	50.00
15622-D *Forty Per Cent*	30.00	-	50.00

FRANK & JAMES McCRAVY:
Brunswick 192, 193, 194, 424, 444, 452, 465,			
467, 504, 515, 528, 535, 566, 572, 589	3.00	-	6.00
Columbia 15617-D *No More Dying*	5.00	-	8.00
15764-D *I Love You In The Same Old Way*	7.00	-	10.00
Okeh 45128, 45135, 45433, 45435, 45447, 45457,			
45466	4.00	-	7.00

Vocalion 5193, 5194, 5195, 5255, 5293	4.00 -	7.00

LEWIS/LOUIS McDANIEL (& GID SMITH):

Timely Tunes 1560 *One More Kiss Before I Go* . .	15.00 -	20.00
Victor 23505 *I've Loved You So True*	15.00 -	20.00
40287 *We'll Talk About One Another*	10.00 -	15.00

McDONALD BROTHERS:

Vocalion 5406 *Poor Little Joe*	10.00 -	15.00

(LESTER) McFARLAND & (BOB) GARDNER:

Brunswick 107, 108, 109, 110, 111, 116, 160, 163, 164, 167, 168, 169, 170, 171, 190, 195, 199, 200, 201, 202, 203, 286, 293, 305, 307, 311, 316, 322, 326, 332, 334, 339, 350, 356, 366, 398, 409, 426, 432, 438, 439, 451, 454, 461, 466, 475, 479, 483, 492, 499, 520, 524, 525, 527, 537, 541, 548, 551, 553, 561, 568, 570, 578, 586, 588, 594, 596	4.00 -	7.00
Vocalion 5026, 5027, 5028, 5120, 5121, 5122, 5123, 5124, 5125, 5126, 5127, 5128, 5129, 5130, 5174, 5177, 5184, 5187, 5191, 5192, 5259, 5285, 5307, 5322, 5364, 5369, 5381, 5392	4.00 -	8.00
(Note: Other records by this duo usually command similar premiums.)		

J.D. McFARLANE & DAUGHTER:

Okeh 45027 *Devil In The Wood Pile*	10.00 -	20.00

ALPHUS McFAYDEN:

Victor 21128 *Medley*	5.00 -	8.00

DENNIS McGEE:

Vocalion 5334 *Allen And Tassone*	15.00 -	25.00
5348 *Myself*	15.00 -	25.00

SAM (& KIRK) McGEE; KIRK & SAM McGEE; KIRK McGEE (& BLYTHE POTEET):

Champion 16804 *Browns Ferry Blues*	75.00 -	100.00
45033 *Brown's Ferry Blues*	10.00 -	15.00
Decca 5348 *Brown's Ferry Blues*	10.00 -	15.00
Gennett 6704 *If I Only Had A Home*	30.00 -	50.00
6731 *If I Could Hear My Mother Pray Again* . .	30.00 -	50.00
6778 *Only A Step To The Grave*	30.00 -	50.00
6960 *My Wife Left Me*	30.00 -	50.00
7022 *Kickin' Mule*	30.00 -	50.00
Vocalion 5094 *The Franklin Blues*	20.00 -	30.00
5101 *Knoxville Blues*	20.00 -	30.00
5150 *Salty Dog Blues*	20.00 -	30.00
5166 *Charming Bill*	20.00 -	30.00
5167 *Old Master's Runaway*	20.00 -	30.00
5169 *Salt Lake City Blues*	20.00 -	30.00
5254 *Easy Rider*	20.00 -	30.00
5310 *The Ship Without A Sail*	20.00 -	30.00
15318 *Buck Dancer's Choice*	20.00 -	30.00
15326 *Knoxville Blues*	20.00 -	30.00

McGHEE & COGER:

Gennett 6703 *The Vestris Disaster*	15.00 -	25.00
6795 *He Included Me*	15.00 -	25.00
6932 *Calling The Prodigal*	15.00 -	25.00

(JOHN) McGHEE & (FRANK WELLING: (See also WELLING & McGHEE)

Brunswick 222 *He Abides*	7.00 -	10.00
251 *I Would Not Be Denied*	7.00 -	10.00
258 *Dwelling In Beulah Land*	7.00 -	10.00
272 *I Am Coming Home*	7.00 -	10.00
Champion 16479 *My Burdens Rolled Away*	15.00 -	20.00
16542 *He Abides*	15.00 -	20.00
Gennett 6334 *I've Been Redeemed*	15.00 -	20.00
6389 *Praise The Lord, It's So*	15.00 -	20.00
6435 *I Am Resolved*	15.00 -	20.00
6533 *I'm Free Again*	15.00 -	20.00
6657 *Get A Transfer*	15.00 -	20.00
6671 *I Wants My Lulu*	15.00 -	25.00
6690 *Why Not Tonight*	15.00 -	25.00
6749 *At The Battle Front*	15.00 -	25.00
6874 *I Have To Tell The Story*	15.00 -	25.00

7083 *Beautiful Garden Of Prayer*	15.00 -	25.00
7114 *No Never Alone*	20.00 -	30.00
7128 *Old Kentucky Dew*	20.00 -	30.00
7143 *He'll Understand*	20.00 -	30.00
7156 *Life's Railway To Heaven*	20.00 -	30.00
7185 *Where Is My Mamma*	20.00 -	30.00
7228 *Sweeping Through The Gates*	20.00 -	30.00
7247 *I'm Drifting Back To Dreamland*	20.00 -	30.00
7294 *I Surrender All*	20.00 -	30.00
7316 *I'm Forever Blowing Bubbles*	30.00 -	50.00
Paramount 3234 *The Prisoners Child*	20.00 -	30.00
Superior 323 *He Keeps Me Singing*	30.00 -	50.00
345 *I Am Resolved*	30.00 -	50.00
Supertone 9626 *Down The Lane To Home Sweet Home*	7.00 -	10.00
Vocalion 5251 *The Lily Of The Valley*	10.00 -	15.00

JOHN McGHEE:

Gennett 6362 *The Sinking Of Submarine S-4* . . .	7.00 -	10.00
6103 *The Preacher And The Bear*	10.00 -	15.00
6149 *Aged Mother*	10.00 -	15.00
6450 *The Volunteer Organist*	10.00 -	15.00
6479 *Bill Bailey, Ain't That A Shame*	10.00 -	15.00
6546 *Hard Luck Jim*	10.00 -	15.00
6587 *The Hatfield-McCoy Feud*	15.00 -	25.00
6960 *Life Ain't Worth Living When You're Broke*	25.00 -	35.00
7096 *The Great Airplane Crash*	20.00 -	30.00
7168 *You're As Welcome As The Flowers In May*	20.00 -	30.00
Superior 325 *The Preacher And The Bear*	30.00 -	50.00
344 *The Marian Parker Murder*	30.00 -	50.00
367 *The Sinking Of Submarine S-4*	30.00 -	50.00

KIRK McGHEE; SAM McGHEE (See McGEE)

MERLE McGINNIS:

Gennett 6990 *Highway Blues*	30.00 -	50.00

McGINTY'S OKLAHOMA COWBOY BAND:

Champion 15446 *It Can't Be Done*	8.00 -	12.00
15482 *Adam And Eve*	8.00 -	12.00
Okeh 45057 *The Cowboy's Dream*	10.00 -	15.00

LEON McGUIRE:

Vocalion 5393 *When The Blue Eyes Meet The Brown*	7.00 -	10.00

McKINNEY BROTHERS:

Champion 16830 *Old Uncle Joe*	10.00 -	15.00

McLAUGHLIN'S (OLD TIME) MELODY MAKERS:

Victor 21286 *Dill Pickles Rag*	8.00 -	12.00
V40117 *Whistlin' Rufus*	10.00 -	15.00
Vocalion 5296 *Mississippi Shadows*	10.00 -	15.00
5330 *Hilarious Zeb*	10.00 -	15.00

McMANN & ROBERTS:

Supertone 9318 *If I Could Hear My Mother Pray Again*	7.00 -	10.00

(CLAYTON) McMICHEN'S MELODY MEN; McMICHEN LAYNE STRING ORCHESTRA; CLAYTON McMICHEN & DAN HORNSBY/RILEY PUCKETT; CLAYTON McMICHEN & HIS GEORGIA WILDCATS/HARMONY BOYS/HOME TOWN BAND:

Columbia 15111-D *Sweet Bunch Of Daisies*	7.00 -	10.00
15130-D *House Of David Blues*	7.00 -	10.00
*15140-D *A Fiddlers Convention In Georgia* . . .	7.00 -	10.00
15190-D *St. Louis Blues*	10.00 -	15.00
*15201-D *A Corn Licker Still In Georgia*	7.00 -	10.00
15202-D *The Missouri Waltz*	7.00 -	10.00
15224-D *Fifty Years Ago*	8.00 -	12.00
15247-D *Silver Threads Among The Gold*	5.00 -	8.00
15253-D *The Original Arkansas Traveler*	10.00 -	15.00
*15258-D *A Corn Licker Still In Georgia*	7.00 -	10.00
15288-D *Home Sweet Home*	7.00 -	10.00
15310-D *Ain't She Sweet*	10.00 -	15.00

15333-D *The Blind Child's Prayer*	10.00 -	15.00
15340-D *Lonesome Mama Blues*	15.00 -	20.00
15356-D *Down The Ozark Trail*	15.00 -	20.00
*15366-D *Corn Licker Still Part 5/6*	8.00 -	12.00
15391-D *When You're Far From The Ones Who Love You*	10.00 -	15.00
*15432-D *Corn Licker Still Part 7/8*	10.00 -	15.00
15464-D *The Dying Hobo*	15.00 -	20.00
*15503-D *A Night In A Blind Tiger*	15.00 -	20.00
15521-D *McMichen's Reel*	15.00 -	20.00
*15531-D *Corn Licker Still Part 9/10*	15.00 -	20.00
15540-D *Honolulu Moon*	15.00 -	20.00
*15549-D *Taking The Census*	15.00 -	20.00
*15598-D *Jeremiah Hopkins' Store At Sand Mountain*	15.00 -	20.00
*15618-D *Corn Licker Still Part 11/12*	20.00 -	30.00
*15632-D *Prohibition—Yes Or No*	20.00 -	30.00
*15667-D *Fiddler's Convention Part 3/4*	20.00 -	30.00
15686-D *The Arkansas Sheik*	30.00 -	50.00
*15700-D *A Bee Hunt On Hell For Sartin Creek*	30.00 -	50.00
*15703-D *Corn Licker Still Part 13/14*	40.00 -	60.00
15723-D *Yum Yum Blues*	75.00 -	100.00
15775-D *Wild Cat Rag*	80.00 -	120.00

(*These "descriptive novelty" records credit several or more artists on the labels; since McMichen's name appears first, all are included in this listing.)

Crown 3384 *Singing An Old Hymn*	20.00 -	30.00
3385 *Georgia Wildcat Breakdown*	20.00 -	30.00
3386 *Way Down In Caroline*	20.00 -	30.00
3397 *Arkansas Traveler*	15.00 -	20.00
3416 *Old Joe Clarke*	15.00 -	20.00
3419 *When The Bloom Is On The Sage*	15.00 -	20.00
3432 *Countin' Cross Ties*	20.00 -	30.00
Decca 5418, 5424, 5436, 5448, 5491	5.00 -	8.00
Okeh 45022 *Alabama Jubilee*	15.00 -	25.00
45034 *Bully Of The Town*	15.00 -	20.00
45330 *Ain't She Sweet?*	20.00 -	30.00

WHITEY McPHERSON:

Vocalion 03883 *Little Lady*	7.00 -	10.00
03937 *Brakeman Blues*	7.00 -	10.00
04245 *Blue Ridge Mountain Blues*	7.00 -	10.00
04339 *Am I Blue*	7.00 -	10.00

ODDIE McWINDERS:

Crown 3398 *Down In Old Kentucky*	20.00 -	30.00

GRACE MEANS:

Supertone 9244 *Your Mother Still Prays For You*	5.00 -	8.00

"THE MEDICINE SHOW" (See EMMETT MILLER DAVID MEEK & HIS BOYS:

Champion 15376 *Old Sefus Brown*	7.00 -	10.00

DICK MEEKS:

Supertone 9306 *Poor, But A Gentleman Still*	8.00 -	12.00

MELTON & MINTER/WAGGONER:

Columbia 15423-D *In The Hills Of Old Kentucky*	7.00 -	10.00
Vocalion 5435 *Let Me Call You Sweetheart*	7.00 -	10.00

MEMPHIS BOB:

Columbia 15735-D *Little Marion McLean*	7.00 -	10.00

MERIDIAN HUSTLERS:

Paramount 3173 *Queen City Square Dance*	25.00 -	40.00

MERT'S HOMETOWN SERENADERS:

Vocalion 5338 *We Gotta Look Into This*	7.00 -	10.00

ARTHUR MILES:

Victor V40156 *The Lonely Cowboy*	8.00 -	12.00

PAUL MILES & THE RED FOX CHASERS:

Gennett 6461 *Under The Double Eagle*	15.00 -	20.00
6516 *The Arkansas Traveler*	15.00 -	20.00
6547 *Weeping Willow Tree*	15.00 -	20.00
6568 *Mississippi Sawyer*	15.00 -	20.00
6866 *The Red Fox... Makin' Licker, Part 1/2*	20.00 -	30.00
6912 *The Red Fox... Makin' Licker, Part 3/4*	20.00 -	30.00
6930 *Virginia Bootleggers*	20.00 -	30.00

MILLER'S BULL FROG ENTERTAINERS:

Okeh 45348, 45358, 45386	5.00 -	10.00

MILLER & BURNETT:

Champion 15963 *Missouri Joe*	7.00 -	10.00
15985 *Long White Robe*	7.00 -	10.00
Gennett 7164 *Missouri Joe*	10.00 -	15.00
7220 *Twenty-One Years*	10.00 -	15.00
Okeh 45442, 45541	5.00 -	10.00

BOB MILLER (& HIS HINKY DINKERS/TRIO); CHARLOTTE MILLER & HINKY DINKERS:

Brunswick 404, 428, 4431	5.00 -	10.00
Champion 16008 *The Ohio Prison Fire*	10.00 -	15.00
7239 *Five Cent Glass Of Beer*	10.00 -	15.00
Okeh 45475 *Little Cotton Mill Girl*	10.00 -	15.00
45497 *Nebuchudneezer*	10.00 -	15.00
Victor 23693 *Twenty-One Years, Part 2*	8.00 -	12.00

DAVID MILLER:

Champion 15298 *Don't Forget Me, Little Darling*	8.00 -	12.00
15317 *The Lonesome Valley*	5.00 -	8.00
15334 *The Bad Man Stackalee*	5.00 -	8.00
Gennett 6175 *The Lonesome Valley*	15.00 -	20.00
6188 *The Bad Man Stacklee*	15.00 -	20.00
6333 *Sweet Floetta*	15.00 -	20.00
6349 *A Little Child Shall Lead Them*	15.00 -	20.00
6388 *Give My Love To Nellie, Jack*	15.00 -	20.00
Superior 324 *Sweet Floetta*	25.00 -	50.00
368 *Give My Love To Nellie, Jack*	12.00 -	18.00
384 *Two Little Orphans*	25.00 -	50.00
Supertone 9258 *Two Little Orphans*	12.00 -	18.00

EMMETT MILLER:

Okeh 45380 *The Medicine Show, Act 1/2*	8.00 -	12.00
45391 *The Medicine Show, Act 3/4*	8.00 -	12.00
45413 *The Medicine Show, Act 5/6*	10.00 -	15.00

(Note: Although the labels of the above "descriptive novelty" records credit several artists, they are listed here, since Emmett Miller's name appears first.)

Okeh 45546 *Sam's New Job*	15.00 -	20.00

(Note: Other records by Emmett Miller are listed in the jazz and dance bands section.)

JOHN MILLER:

Superior 2839 *Highway Hobo*	15.00 -	25.00

STANLEY MILLER:

Champion 15297 *Be Kind To A Man When He Is Down*	15.00 -	20.00
15315 *Lost Train Blues*	25.00 -	40.00

OWEN MILLS & FRANK WELLING (& McGHEE):

Paramount 3155 *A Mother's Plea*	8.00 -	12.00
3158 *Don't Forget Me Darling*	10.00 -	15.00
3159 *It's Hard To Be Shut Up In Prison*	10.00 -	15.00

MILNER & CURTIS WITH THE MAGNOLIA RAMBLERS:

Vocalion 5426 *Northeast Texas*	50.00 -	75.00

BILLY MILTON & ONE MAN BAND:

Gennett 6318 *Dill Pickles*	20.00 -	30.00

FLOYD MING'S PEP STEPPERS:

Victor 21294 *Indian War Whoop*	30.00 -	50.00
21534 *Tupelo Blues*	35.00 -	50.00

MISSISSIPPI 'POSSUM HUNTERS:

Victor 23595 *Mississippi Breakdown*	75.00 -	100.00

MITCHELL FAMILY TRIO:

Superior 2641 *Picture On The Wall*	10.00 -	20.00
2657 *The Old Rugged Cross*	10.00 -	20.00
2700 *Hide Me*	10.00 -	20.00
2776 *There Is Power In The Blood*	10.00 -	20.00

MOATSVILLE STRING TICKLERS:

Columbia 15491-D *Moatsville Blues*	20.00 -	30.00

MODERN MOUNTAINEERS:

Bluebird 6911, 6976, 6997, 7047, 7247, 7323, 7423, 7470, 7671, 8558	5.00 -	10.00

MONROE BROTHERS:

Bluebird 6309 *This World Is Not My Home*	8.00	-	12.00
6363 *What Is Home Without Love?*	8.00	-	12.00
6422 *My Long Journey Home*	8.00	-	12.00
6477 *God Holds The Future In His Hands*	8.00	-	12.00
6512 *Six Months Ain't Long*	8.00	-	12.00
6552 *Just A Song Of Old Kentucky*	8.00	-	12.00
6607 *On Some Foggy Mountain Top*	8.00	-	12.00
6645 *New River Train*	8.00	-	12.00
6676 *The Old Crossroad*	8.00	-	12.00
6729 *My Savior's Train*	8.00	-	12.00
6762 *Where Is My Sailor Boy?*	10.00	-	15.00
6773 *Roll In My Sweet Baby's Arms*	6.00	-	10.00
6820 *Will The Circle Be Unbroken*	6.00	-	10.00
6829 *Forgotten Soldier Boy*	6.00	-	10.00
6866 *I Am Ready To Go*	6.00	-	10.00
6912 *What Would The Profit Be?*	6.00	-	10.00
6960 *Katy Cline*	6.00	-	10.00
7007 *I Am Going That Way*	6.00	-	10.00
7055 *Do You Call That Religion*	6.00	-	10.00
7093 *Weeping Willow Tree*	6.00	-	10.00
7122 *What Would You Give In Exchange?*	6.00	-	10.00
7145 *On My Way To Glory*	6.00	-	10.00
7191 *Let Us Be Lovers*	6.00	-	10.00
7273 *My Last Moving Day*	6.00	-	10.00
7326 *Sinner, You Better Get Ready*	6.00	-	10.00
7385 *On The Banks Of The Ohio*	8.00	-	12.00
7425 *I've Still Got Ninety-Nine*	5.00	-	8.00
7460 *On My Way Back Home*	5.00	-	8.00
7508 *Goodbye, Maggie*	5.00	-	8.00
7562 *A Beautiful Life*	5.00	-	8.00
7598 *Rollin' On*	5.00	-	8.00
Montgomery Ward (some titles as above.)	4.00	-	7.00

MONROE COUNTY BOTTLE TIPPERS:

Gennett 6585 *The Fiddlin' Bootleggers*	25.00	-	40.00

BILL MONROE & THE BLUE GRASS BOYS:

Bluebird 8568 *Mule Skinner Blues*	7.00	-	10.00
8611 *No Letter In The Mail*	7.00	-	10.00
8692 *Dog House Blues*	5.00	-	8.00
8813 *Tennessee Blues*	7.00	-	10.00
8861 *Blue Yodel No. 7*	7.00	-	10.00
Columbia (red label)	3.00	-	5.00

CHARLIE MONROE'S BOYS:

Bluebird 7862 *Great Speckled Bird*	5.00	-	8.00
7922 *Farther Along*	5.00	-	8.00
7949 *You're Gonna Miss Me*	5.00	-	8.00
7990 *When The World's On Fire*	5.00	-	8.00
8050 *Guided By Love*	5.00	-	8.00
8118 *Joy Bells In My Soul*	5.00	-	8.00

MONTANA SLIM:

Bluebird 6515 *Midnight, The Unconquered*			
Outlaw	5.00	-	8.00
6814 *Prairie Sunset*	5.00	-	8.00
6826 *Round-Up Time In Heaven*	5.00	-	8.00
6827 *Yodeling Cowgirl*	5.00	-	8.00
7618 *By The Grave Of Nobody's Darling* ...	5.00	-	8.00
8150, 8202, 8241, 8313, 8329, 8361, 8374,			
8425, 8441, 8456, 8472, 8517, 8531, 8566,			
8696, 8875, 8924, 8983	4.00	-	7.00

(Note: See also WILF CARTER:)

PATSY MONTANA (with THE PRAIRIE RAMBLERS):

Titles, issued contemporaneously on Banner,
Conqueror, Melotone, Oriole, Perfect, Romeo,
include: *Blazin' The Trail; A Cowboy
Honeymoon: Give Me A Home In Montana;
Gold Coast Express; I Wanna Be A Cowboy's
Sweetheart; Lone Star; Pride Of The Prairie;
Ridin' The Sunset Trail; Sweetheart Of The
Saddle; Swingtime Cowgirl; With A Banjo On

My Knee	5.00	-	8.00
Vocalion 03010, 03135, 03268, 03292, 03377,			
03422	5.00	-	8.00

04023, 04076, 04135, 04247, 04291, 04469,			
04482, 04518, 04568, 04689, 04742, 05081 .	4.00	-	7.00
Vogue 721 *When I Gets To Where I'm Going*	20.00	-	35.00

PHIL MONTGOMERY:

Superior 2542 *That Old Covered Bridge*	15.00	-	20.00

**TOMMY MOONEY (WITH BOBBY
MOONEY) & HIS AUTOMOBILE BABIES:**

Floto 78001 *Bingo Boogie*	—		—
78003 *Rose Covered Garden*	—		—

MOONSHINE DAVE:

Champion 15789 *Biscuit Jim*	10.00	-	15.00

MOONSHINE HARRY:

Supertone 9553 *Son Of A Gun*	10.00	-	15.00

MOONSHINE KATE (& HER PALS):

Okeh 45444 *Texas Blues*	50.00	-	80.00
45515 *Texas Bound*	50.00	-	80.00
45547 *The Poor Girl's Story*	50.00	-	80.00
45555 *My Man's A Jolly Railroad Man*	50.00	-	80.00

MOONSHINERS:

Victor V40223 *Fulton County*	15.00	-	25.00
V40284 *Midnight Waltz*	15.00	-	25.00

MOORE, BURNETTE & RUTHERFORD:

Gennett 6706 *Cumberland Gap*	15.00	-	20.00

**MOORE & FREED: (See also FREED
& MOORE):**

Vocalion 5131 *Harmonica Blues*	8.00	-	12.00
5132 *Plantation Medley*	8.00	-	12.00

MOORE & GREENE:

Champion 16357 *Cincinnati Rag*	30.00	-	50.00

MOORE & SMECK:

Vocalion 5133 *Dear Old Pal Of Mine*	7.00	-	10.00

BYRD MOORE (& HIS HOT SHOTS):

Champion 16498 *Oh Take Me Back*	50.00	-	75.00
Columbia 15496-D *Careless Love*	50.00	-	75.00
15536-D *Frankie Silvers*	50.00	-	75.00
Gennett 6549 *Hobo's Paradise*	35.00	-	50.00
6586 *Mama Toot Your Whistle*	40.00	-	60.00
6686 *Back Water Blues*	40.00	-	60.00
6763 *Snatch 'Em Back Blues*	40.00	-	60.00
6841 *When The Snowflakes Fall Again*	40.00	-	60.00
6991 *Mama Don't Allow No Low Down*			
Hanging Round	75.00	-	100.00

JOHN MOORE:

Broadway 8188 *Columbus Prison Fire*	8.00	-	12.00

LATTIE MOORE:

Speed 101 *Juke Joint Johnny*	7.00	-	10.00

O. MOORE:

Challenge 422 *The Drunkard's Doom*	7.00	-	10.00

SAM MOORE & HORACE DAVIS:

Vocalion 14430 *Annie Laurie*	8.00	-	12.00

PEG MORELAND:

Victor 21548 *The Prisoner At The Bar*	7.00	-	10.00
21653 *Going Back To Dixie*	7.00	-	10.00
21724 *Maple In The Lane*	7.00	-	10.00
23510 *I Got Mine*	10.00	-	15.00
Victor 23539 *In Berry Picking Time*	10.00	-	15.00
23593 *Cowboy Jack*	10.00	-	15.00
V40008 *Stay In The Wagon Yard*	7.00	-	10.00
V40101 *He Never Came Back*	7.00	-	10.00
V40137 *You're Gonna Miss Me*	10.00	-	15.00
V40209 *When I Had But Fifty Cents*	10.00	-	15.00
V40272 *Make Me A Cowboy Again*	10.00	-	15.00
V40296 *In The Town Where I Was Born*	10.00	-	15.00

EVERETT MORGAN:

Champion 16616 *Texas Home*	25.00	-	40.00

MORRIS BROTHERS:

Bluebird 7903 *The Story Of Charlie Lawson*	8.00	-	12.00
7967 *Let Me Be Your Salty Dog*	8.00	-	12.00

FRANK MORRIS:

Paramount 3070 *Old Brown Pants*	7.00	-	10.00

WALTER MORRIS:

Columbia 15079-D *Crazy Coon*	10.00	-	15.00

15101-D *The Railroad Tramp*	8.00 -	12.00
15115-D *Sweet Marie*	7.00 -	10.00
15186-D *In The Time Of Long Ago*	7.00 -	10.00

ZEKE MORRIS:

Bluebird 7362 *Garden Of Prayer*	7.00 -	10.00

MORRISON BROTHERS BAND:

Victor V40323 *Dry And Dusty*	30.00 -	50.00

MORTON, BOND & WILLIAMS:

Champion 15653 *Cumberland Gap*	10.00 -	15.00

MORTON & CRANE:

Supertone 9497 *Budded Roses*	8.00 -	12.00
9535 *Put My Little Shoes Away*	8.00 -	12.00

JACK MOSER & HIS OKLAHOMA CAVALIERS:

Bluebird 6728, 6751	4.00 -	7.00

(BERT) MOSS & (JOE) LONG:

Superior 2539 *My Trouble Blues*	50.00 -	80.00
2559 *Jake Leg Blues*	50.00 -	80.00
2838 *Pig Ankle*	100.00 -	150.00

OTIS MOTE (& TOM):

Okeh 45389 *Tight Like That*	15.00 -	20.00
45429 *Home In The Rock*	10.00 -	15.00

BILL MOUNCE:

Bluebird	4.00 -	8.00

MURPHY BROTHERS:

Champion 16455 *When Katie Comes Down To The Gate*	15.00 -	20.00

CHARLES NABELL:

Okeh 40252 *The Great Round Up*	10.00 -	15.00
45021 *After The War Is Over*	10.00 -	15.00
45031 *The Hills Of Old Kentucky*	10.00 -	15.00
45039 *The Scopes Trail*	10.00 -	15.00

NANCE FAMILY (& CLARENCE DOOLEY/with THE TRAPHILL TWINS:

Brunswick 542 *The Lawson Murder*	10.00 -	15.00
565 *Sweet Freedom*	10.00 -	15.00
Champion 16316 *A Mother's Advice*	10.00 -	15.00
16330 *I'm On My Way To Heaven*	10.00 -	15.00
16369 *Somebody's Knocking At Your Door*	10.00 -	15.00

NARMOUR & SMITH:

Bluebird 5615 *New Carroll County Blues No. 2*	20.00 -	30.00
5616 *Sweet Milk And Peaches*	20.00 -	30.00
5637 *Someone I Love*	20.00 -	30.00
5669 *Gallop To Georgia*	20.00 -	30.00
5720 *New Carroll County Blues No. 2*	20.00 -	30.00
5754 *Rose Waltz*	20.00 -	30.00
5810 *New Charleston No. 3*	20.00 -	30.00
6234 *New Charleston No. 2*	15.00 -	20.00
Okeh 45242 *The Sunny Waltz*	25.00 -	35.00
45263 *Whistling Coon*	25.00 -	35.00
45276 *Little Star*	25.00 -	35.00
45317 *Carroll County Blues*	20.00 -	30.00
45329 *Someone I Love*	25.00 -	35.00
45344 *Gallop To Georgia-Breakdown*	35.00 -	50.00
45377 *Charleston No. 2*	35.00 -	50.00
45390 *Dry Gin Rag*	35.00 -	50.00
45414 *Avalon Blues*	40.00 -	60.00
45424 *Sweet Milk And Peaches-Breakdown*	40.00 -	60.00
45459 *Charleston No. 3*	40.00 -	60.00
45469 *Jake Leg Rag*	50.00 -	80.00
45480 *Where The Southern Crosses The Dog*	50.00 -	80.00
45492 *Texas Breakdown*	75.00 -	100.00
45536 *Tequila Hop Blues*	75.00 -	100.00
45548 *Limber Neck Blues*	75.00 -	100.00

LEN NASH (& HIS COUNTRY BOYS):

Brunswick 354 *On The Road To California*	8.00 -	12.00
387 *The Ozark Trail*	8.00 -	12.00
440 *Goin' Down To Town*	8.00 -	12.00
Supertone 2069 *The Trail To Mexico*	8.00 -	12.00

BUCK NATION (& RAY WHITLEY):

Decca 5065, 5066, 5075, 5081, 5105, 5114, 5124, 5172	5.00 -	10.00

NATIONAL BARN DANCE ORCHESTRA:

Bluebird 5212, 5213, 5214, 5215, 5216, 5217	3.00 -	6.00

AMOS NEAL:

Champion 15692 *She'll Be Coming 'Round The Mountain*	8.00 -	12.00

FIDDLIN' DAVE NEAL:

Challenge 102 *Seneca Square Dance*	5.00 -	8.00
103 *Sandy Land*	5.00 -	8.00
301 *Seneca Square Dance*	5.00 -	8.00

DAVID NEAL:

Supertone 9184 *Good Old Turnip Greens*	8.00 -	12.00

RUSH NEAL & WANDA NEAL:

Okeh 45124 *The Two Orphans*	7.00 -	10.00

FIDDLIN' FRANK NELSON:

Challenge 303 *Cripple Creek*	5.00 -	8.00

NELSTONE'S HAWAIIANS:

Victor V40273 *Mobile County Blues*	10.00 -	15.00

NETTLE BROS. STRING BAND:

Bluebird, most issues	4.00 -	8.00

BILL NETTLES (& HIS DIXIE BLUE BOYS):

Bullet 637 *High Falutin' Mama*	5.00 -	8.00
Vocalion 03634 *My Cross-Eyed Nancy Jane*	7.00 -	10.00
03662 *No Daddy Blues*	7.00 -	10.00
Vocalion 03694, 03903, 03952, 04012, 04075, 04615, 04655, 04757	5.00 -	10.00

JIM NEW:

Timely Tunes 1564 *Wreck Of The Six Wheeler*	10.00 -	15.00

NEW ARKANSAS TRAVELERS:

Victor 21288 *Handy Man*	8.00 -	12.00

NEW DIXIE DEMONS:

Decca 5140, 5141, 5148, 5163, 5171, 5253, 5257, 5259, 5264, 5271, 5277, 5292, 5314, 5343, 5362, 5363, 5392	4.00 -	8.00

THE NEWMAN BROTHERS (HANK & SLIM):

Vocalion 02807 *Mississippi River Blues*	— -	—
02808 *How Beautiful Heaven Must Be*	— -	—
02840 *Dear Old Mother*	— -	—
02852 *Good Old Country Town*	— -	—

CHARLIE NEWMAN (& BUD NEWMAN):

Okeh 45072 *Sweet Bunch Of Daisies*	5.00 -	8.00
45095 *Pretty Little Dear*	5.00 -	8.00
45116 *Susie Ann*	7.00 -	10.00
45184 *Blue Ridge Mountain Blues*	8.00 -	12.00
45200 *My Blues Ridge Mountain Queen*	8.00 -	12.00
45431 *The Old Traveling Man*	8.00 -	12.00

FRED NEWMAN:

Paramount 3177 *San Antonio*	10.00 -	15.00
3267 *San Antonio*	10.00 -	15.00

ROY NEWMAN & HIS BOYS:

Vocalion 03117 *I Can't Dance*	8.00 -	12.00
03598, 03752, 03878, 03938, 03963, 04025, 04578, 04639, 04740, 04792, 04866, 04959, 05014, 05066	5.00 -	10.00

NEWTON COUNTY HILLBILLIES:

Okeh 45520 *Happy Hour Breakdown*	35.00 -	50.00
45544 *Nine O'Clock Breakdown*	35.00 -	50.00
45549 *Going To The Wedding To Get Some Cake*	35.00 -	50.00

NICHOLS BROTHERS:

Victor 23582 *She's Killing Me*	75.00 -	100.00
23596 *Dear Old Tennessee*	40.00 -	60.00

BOB NICHOLS (& HUGH CROSS/RILEY PUCKETT):

Columbia 15114-D, 15136-D, 15161-D	7.00 -	10.00
15198-D *Let The Rest Of The World Go By*	8.00 -	12.00
15216-D *In The Shade Of The Old Apple Tree*	8.00 -	12.00
15304-D *The Trail Of The Lonesome Pine*	8.00 -	12.00
15350-D *Dear Old Dixieland*	10.00 -	15.00
15480-D *Corrine Corrina*	20.00 -	30.00
15556-D *Smoky Mountain Home*	20.00 -	30.00
15590-D *The Killing Of Tom Slaughter*	20.00 -	30.00

15698-D *When It's Peach Pickin' Time In*
Georgia . . . . 30.00 - 50.00

JOE & BOB NICHOLS:
Crown 3399 *Smoky Mountain Home* . . . . 7.00 - 10.00
3419 *Red Wing* . . . . 10.00 - 15.00
3447 *Blue Hills Of Virginia* . . . . 7.00 - 10.00

NICHOLSON'S PLAYERS:
Champion 15942 *Muskakatuck Waltz* . . . . 10.00 - 15.00
16007 *Sweet Bunch Of Daisies* . . . . 10.00 - 15.00
16137 *My Honey* . . . . 10.00 - 15.00
45193 *Let Me Call You Sweetheart* . . . . 4.00 - 7.00
Gennett 7125 *Muskakatuck Waltz* . . . . 10.00 - 15.00
7151 *Sweet Bunch Of Daisies* . . . . 10.00 - 15.00
7241 *Let Me Call You Sweetheart* . . . . 12.00 - 18.00

NITE OWLS:
Vocalion 03621, 03675, 03706, 03879, 03905,
03951, 03987, 04064, 04118, 04159, 04233,
04312, 04372, 04452, 04517, 04626, 04715,
04794, 04853, 04935 . . . . 4.00 - 8.00

HOYLE/HOYAL NIX & HIS WEST TEXAS
COWBOYS:
Talent 709 *A Big Ball's In Cowtown* . . . . 10.00 - 15.00

EDDIE NOACK:
Gold Star 1352 *Triflin' Mama Blues* . . . . 10.00 - 15.00

FLORA NOLES:
Okeh 45037 *Little Mohee* . . . . 7.00 - 10.00

FATE NORRIS (& HIS PLAYBOYS/& THE
TANNER BOYS):
Columbia 15124-D *New Dixie* . . . . 15.00 - 20.00
15332-D *A Day At The County Fair* . . . . 10.00 - 15.00
15435-D *Johnnie Get Your Gun* . . . . 20.00 - 30.00
(Note: The label of Columbia 15332-D credits
several artists, but since Fate Norris' name
appears first, the record is listed here.)

LAND NORRIS:
Okeh 40096 *Groundhog* . . . . 15.00 - 20.00
45006 *Ida Red* . . . . 10.00 - 15.00
45017 *Pat That Butter Down* . . . . 15.00 - 20.00
45033 *Charming Betsy* . . . . 15.00 - 20.00
45047 *The Old Grey Mare* . . . . 15.00 - 20.00
45058 *Getting Into Trouble* . . . . 15.00 - 25.00

LYMON NORRIS:
Champion 16431 *In A Lonely Jail* . . . . 20.00 - 30.00
45070 *In A Lonely Jail* . . . . 10.00 - 15.00

NORTH CAROLINA COOPER BOYS:
Okeh 45174 *Red Rose Of Texas* . . . . 15.00 - 20.00

NORTH CAROLINA FOX CHASERS:
Supertone 9322 *Mountain Sweetheart* . . . . 10.00 - 15.00

NORTH CAROLINA HAWAIIANS:
Okeh 45248 *Soldier's Joy* . . . . 7.00 - 10.00
45297 *Bully Of The Town* . . . . 7.00 - 10.00
45405 *Chinese Breakdown* . . . . 20.00 - 30.00

NORTH CAROLINA RAMBLERS (& ROY
HARVEY):
(See also ROY HARVEY)
Columbia 15106-D *Flyin' Clouds* . . . . 25.00 - 40.00
15127-D *Rag Time Annie* . . . . 25.00 - 40.00
15279-D *Mountain Reel* . . . . 25.00 - 40.00
Gennett 6288 *Poor Little Joe* . . . . 50.00 - 75.00
Paramount 3064 *Take Back The Ring* . . . . 40.00 - 60.00
3065 *Give My Love To Nell* . . . . 40.00 - 60.00
3072 *Blue Eyes* . . . . 40.00 - 60.00
3079 *Bill Mason* . . . . 40.00 - 60.00
3136 *Sweet Sunny South* . . . . 50.00 - 75.00

NORTH CAROLINA RIDGE RUNNERS:
Columbia 15650-D *Nobody's Darling* . . . . 30.00 - 50.00

NORTH GEORGIA FOUR:
Paramount 3135 *I Can, I Do, I Will* . . . . 25.00 - 40.00
3149 *Amazing Grace* . . . . 25.00 - 40.00
3174 *She Was A Lulu* . . . . 25.00 - 40.00

NORTHLANDERS:
Vocalion 5274 *Over The Waves* . . . . 6.00 - 10.00

FRANK NOVACK & HIS ROOTIN' TOOTIN'
BOYS:
Vocalion 03525, 03557, 03588, 03658, 03877,
03913, 03936, 03962, 03998, 04052, 04117,
04171, 04232, 04290, 04370, 04467, 04567,
04744, 04777 . . . . 4.00 - 8.00

SLIM OAKDALE:
Crown 3433 *Lonesome Road Blues* . . . . 10.00 - 15.00
3461 *No Hard Times* . . . . 10.00 - 15.00
3476 *Roll Along Kentucky Moon* . . . . 10.00 - 15.00
3503 *Cowboy's Heaven* . . . . 10.00 - 15.00
3516 *When Jimmie Rodgers Said Goodbye* . . . . 15.00 - 20.00

JESSE OAKLEY:
Supertone 9243 *Aged Mother* . . . . 8.00 - 12.00
9256 *I Got Mine* . . . . 5.00 - 8.00
9257 *Sinking Of The Submarine S-4* . . . . 5.00 - 8.00
9674 *You're As Welcome As The Flowers In*
May . . . . 5.00 - 8.00

OAK MOUNTAIN FOUR:
Champion 15874 *Medley* . . . . 7.00 - 10.00

CHARLIE OAKS:
Vocalion 5068 *The John T. Scopes Trail* . . . . . . 5.00 - 8.00
5069 *Little Mary Phagan* . . . . 5.00 - 8.00
5072 *Poor Little Joe* . . . . 5.00 - 8.00
5073 *The Kaiser And Uncle Sam* . . . . 5.00 - 8.00
5076 *The Fatal Wedding* . . . . 5.00 - 8.00
5105 *The Old Cottage Home* . . . . 5.00 - 8.00
5110 *Darling Nellie Gray* . . . . 5.00 - 8.00
5111 *Ginger Blues* . . . . 5.00 - 8.00
5112 *Home Of The Soul* . . . . 5.00 - 8.00
15094 *The John T. Scopes Trial* . . . . 7.00 - 10.00
15099 *Little Mary Phagan* . . . . 7.00 - 10.00
15103 *Poor Little Joe* . . . . 7.00 - 10.00
15104 *The Kaiser And Uncle Sam* . . . . 7.00 - 10.00
15144 *The Fatal Wedding* . . . . 7.00 - 10.00
15195 *Moonshine* . . . . 7.00 - 10.00
15342 *Boll Weevil* . . . . 7.00 - 10.00
15343 *Darling Nellie Gray* . . . . 5.00 - 8.00
15344 *Ginger Blues* . . . . 5.00 - 8.00
15345 *Home Of The Soul* . . . . 5.00 - 8.00
15346 *The Old Cottage Home* . . . . 5.00 - 8.00

W. LEE O'DANIEL & HILLBILLY BOYS/THE
LIGHT CRUST DOUGHBOYS:
Vocalion 02842 *Saturday Night Rag* . . . . 20.00 - 30.00
03196 *Peach Pickin' Time In Georgia* . . . . 8.00 - 12.00
03412 *Everybody Kiss Your Partner* . . . . 7.00 - 10.00
03538 *Keep A Light In Your Window Tonight* . 7.00 - 10.00
03568 *Back To Old Smoky Mountain* . . . . 7.00 - 10.00
03674 *When You Hear Me Call* . . . . 7.00 - 10.00
03753, 03902, 03950, 03986, 04049, 04102,
04185, 04244, 04311, 04353, 04388, 04440,
04542, 04588, 04656, 04727, 04778, 04852 . 5.00 - 10.00

CHESTER ODOM & HIS WESTERN
RHYTHM BOYS:
Blue Bonnet 128 *You've Done Broke My Heart* . . 7.00 - 10.00
144 *That's All* . . . . 7.00 - 10.00
Royalty 301 *Don't Rob Another Man's Castle* . . . 10.00 - 15.00
329 *Rag Time Annie* . . . . 10.00 - 15.00

OKLAHOMA WRANGLERS (with THE
WILLIS BROTHERS):
Sterling 202 *I Can't Go On This Way* . . . . 10.00 - 15.00

OLIVER & ALLEN:
Bluebird 7124, 7175, 7327, 7402 . . . . 5.00 - 10.00

OWENS BROTHERS:
Columbia 15416-D *If You Don't Like My Ford*
Coupe, Don't You Cadillac Me . . . . 15.00 - 20.00
Victor V40283 *Right Upon The Firing Line* . . . . . 15.00 - 20.00
V40309 *Harvest Field* . . . . 15.00 - 20.00

E.B. OWENS:
Columbia 15414-D *Sweet Carlyle* . . . . 15.00 - 20.00

TEX OWENS:
Decca 5015, 5187 . . . . 5.00 - 10.00

TOM OWENS' WLS BARN DANCE TRIO:

Challenge 104 *Ocean Waves*	5.00 -	8.00
105 *Kings Head*	5.00 -	8.00
106 *Hell On The Wabash*	5.00 -	8.00
107 *Buckwheat Batter*	5.00 -	8.00
306 *Ocean Waves*	5.00 -	8.00
Silvertone 3104 *Kings Head*	5.00 -	8.00
3105 *Buffalo Girls*	5.00 -	8.00
3106 *Buckwheat Batter*	5.00 -	8.00
3107 *McLeod's Reel*	5.00 -	8.00

OZARKERS:

Okeh 45573 *There's More Pretty Girls Than One*	20.00 -	30.00

OZARK RAMBLER:

Paramount 3322 *The Wreck Of The 1262*	15.00 -	20.00

OZARK WARBLERS:

Paramount 3127 *Memories Of Floyd Collins*	15.00 -	20.00

JACK PADGETT:

Talent 729 *Boogie Woogie Gal*	10.00 -	15.00

BUTTERBALL PAIGE:

Bullet 695 *I'm Too Old To Boogie Anymore*	7.00 -	10.00

BILL PALMER (TRIO):

Bluebird 1824 *Free Wheelin' Hobo*	15.00 -	20.00
1825 *Duck Foot Sue*	15.00 -	20.00
Bluebird 5009, 5010, 5012, 5013, 5034	5.00 -	8.00
Electradisk 1938 *Duck Foot Sue*	10.00 -	15.00
Victor 23723 *In The Hills Of Arkansas*	10.00 -	15.00

PAPPY, ZEKE, EZRA & ELTON:

Decca 5097, 5126, 5153	5.00 -	10.00

GEO. R. PARISEAU'S ORCHESTRA:

Champion 15987 *Moonshiner's Serenade*	15.00 -	20.00
16802 *Falling Leaf*	30.00 -	50.00
45009 *Falling Leaf*	10.00 -	15.00
Gennett 6899 *Waggoner's Hornpipe*	20.00 -	30.00
7033 *Fisher's Hornpipe*	20.00 -	30.00
7203 *Moonshiner' Serenade*	25.00 -	40.00

CHARLIE PARKER (& MACK WOOLBRIGHT):

Columbia 15154-D *Rabbit Chase*	15.00 -	20.00
15236-D *Ticklish Reuben*	15.00 -	20.00
15694-D *Will, The Weaver*	25.00 -	40.00

CHUBBY PARKER (& HIS OLD TIME BANJO):

Champion 15393 *Uncle Ned*	5.00 -	8.00
16143 *I'm A Stern Old Bachelor*	8.00 -	12.00
16163 *The Old Wooden Rocker*	8.00 -	12.00
16211 *Get Away Old Maids Get Away*	10.00 -	15.00
Columbia 15296-D *Down On The Farm*	15.00 -	20.00
Gennett 6077 *Nickety Nackety Now Now Now*	10.00 -	15.00
6097 *I'm A Stern Old Bachelor*	10.00 -	15.00
6120 *Little Brown Jug*	10.00 -	15.00
6287 *Uncle Ned*	10.00 -	15.00
6319 *My Little Old Sod Shanty*	10.00 -	15.00
6374 *A Rovin' Little Darky*	10.00 -	15.00
Melotone 12524 *Get Away, Old Maids*	8.00 -	12.00
12525 *Walking The Last Mile*	8.00 -	12.00
12526 *Many Times I've Wondered*	8.00 -	12.00
12653 *Bringing In The Sheaves*	8.00 -	12.00
Silvertone 5011 *Whoa, Mule, Whoa*	5.00 -	8.00
5013 *Little Brown Jug*	5.00 -	8.00
Supertone 9187 *Darling Nellie Gray*	5.00 -	8.00
9188 *Whoa, Mule, Whoa*	5.00 -	8.00
9190 *Oh, Dem Golden Slippers*	5.00 -	8.00
9191 *Oh, Susanna*	5.00 -	8.00
9192 *Uncle Ned*	5.00 -	8.00
9723 *In Kansas*	5.00 -	8.00
9731 *You'll Hear The Bell In The Morning*	5.00 -	8.00
9732 *Grandfather's Clock*	5.00 -	8.00

DAN PARKER & BILL PARKER:

Crown 3248 *They Cut Down The Old Pine Tree*	10.00 -	15.00
3265 *That Silver Haired Daddy Of Mine*	10.00 -	15.00
3266 *Fifty Years Repentin'*	10.00 -	15.00
3279 *Carry Me Back To The Mountains*	10.00 -	15.00

3291 *Ninety-Nine Years*	10.00 -	15.00

SILVIA PARKER-THE HAPPY BUCKEYE:

Champion 45094 *Old Bill Mosher's Ford*	7.00 -	10.00

(DICK) PARMAN (OF KENTUCKY); PARMAN & SMITH:

Champion 16010 *I Love You Best Of All*	15.00 -	20.00
16055 *The Trail Of The Lonesome Pine*	15.00 -	20.00
16300 *In The Hills Of Old Kentucky*	15.00 -	20.00
45189 *I Love You Best Of All*	7.00 -	10.00
Gennett 6718 *She'll Be Coming Around The Mountain*	15.00 -	25.00
6747 *Many Trouble Blues*	20.00 -	30.00
6792 *Seven Long Years Of Trouble*	20.00 -	30.00
7127 *Are You From Dixie*	20.00 -	30.00
7204 *I Love You Best Of All*	20.00 -	30.00
Paramount 3138 *We've Been Chums For Fifty Years*	15.00 -	20.00

V.D. PARMAN & SNYDER:

Okeh 45302 *Blue Bell*	10.00 -	15.00

FIDDLIN' IKE PATE:

Champion 15085 *Medley*	5.00 -	8.00

FIDDLIN' JIM PATE:

Victor V40170 *Texas Farewell*	15.00 -	20.00

LUTHER PATRICK:

Gennett 6448 *Cornbread*	15.00 -	20.00

COLONEL JOHN A. PATTEE:

Columbia 231-D *Old Money Must Quadrille*	8.00 -	12.00

PATTERSON'S PIEDMONT LOG ROLLERS:

Victor 20936 *I'll Never Get Drunk Anymore*	15.00 -	20.00
21132 *Sweet Sunny South*	15.00 -	20.00
21187 *My Sweetheart Is Shy*	15.00 -	20.00
35874 (12-inch) *Poor Little Joe*	20.00 -	30.00

PATTERSON & CAPLINGER:

Gennett 7003 *The Black Sheep*	30.00 -	50.00

PATT PATTERSON (& LOIS DEXTER):

Romeo 5022 *A Home On The Range*	4.00 -	6.00
5031 *The Cowboy's Love Song*	4.00 -	6.00

RED PATTERSON'S PIEDMONT LOG ROLLERS (See PATTERSON'S PIEDMONT LOG ROLLERS)

SAM PATTERSON TRIO:

Edison 51644 *Old MacDonald Had A Farm*	7.00 -	10.00
52085 *Pictures From Life's Other Side*	7.00 -	10.00

PAUL & JOHN:

Okeh 45280 *Band Rehersal For Old Settler's Union*	10.00 -	15.00

EZRA PAULETTE & THE BEVERLY HILLBILLIES:

Titles, issued contemporaneously on Banner, Melotone, Oriole, Perfect, Romeo: *The Old Arapahoe Trail; On The Texas Prairie; The Prisoner's Song 'Rosalie; When The Wild Flowers Are In Bloom*

	5.00 -	8.00
Conqueror 8954, 8955, 8956, 9011	5.00 -	8.00
Vocalion 03164, 03263, 03882, 04104	5.00 -	8.00

PHIL PAVEY:

Okeh 45308 *Broncho Bustin' Blues*	8.00 -	12.00
45355 *Utah Mormon Blues*	8.00 -	12.00

LEON PAYNE:

Bullet 649, 670, 671, 679	5.00 -	8.00

PECK'S MALE QUARTET:

Q.R.S. 9029 *There Is Power In The Blood*	20.00 -	30.00
9030 *The Home Over There*	20.00 -	30.00

BERT PECK:

Brunswick 522 *Over The Hills To The Poor House*	7.00 -	10.00

FRED PENDLETON & HIS MELODY BOYS:

Champion 16457 *Come Take A Trip In My Airship*	20.00 -	30.00

JACK PENEWELL:

Paramount 3130 *When Irish Eyes Are Smiling*	5.00 -	8.00
3131 *Last Night I Was Dreaming*	5.00 -	8.00

BESS PENNINGTON:
Vocalion 5423 *Jake And May* . . . . 15.00 - 20.00

(OLD) HANK PENNY (& HIS RADIO COWBOYS):
Columbia 15766-D *My Blue Ridge Mountain Bride* . . . . 75.00 - 100.00
King 507, 512, 519, 521, 528, 534 . . . . 3.00 - 5.00
Okeh, most issues . . . . 3.00 - 5.00
Vocalion 04543, 04640, 04741, 04826, 04922, 05067 . . . . 4.00 - 8.00

PERRY COUNTY MUSIC MAKERS:
Vocalion 5425 *Madaline* . . . . 20.00 - 30.00
5443 *Got A Buddy I Must See* . . . . 20.00 - 30.00

PETE THE HIRED MAN (GEORGE E. LOGAN):
Champion 45004 *Will The Roses Bloom In Heaven* . . . . 5.00 - 8.00

PETERSON'S HOBO ORCHESTRA:
Victor 20677 *Submarine Waltz* . . . . 5.00 - 8.00

W.C./WALTER PETERSON:
Champion 45000, 45018 . . . . 3.00 - 5.00
Gennett 6078 *Medley* . . . . 8.00 - 12.00
6102 *Over The Waves* . . . . 8.00 - 12.00
6221 *Medley* . . . . 8.00 - 12.00
6274 *One-Two-Three-Four* . . . . 8.00 - 12.00
6406 *Marching Through Georgia* . . . . 8.00 - 12.00
6463 *Where The River Shannon Flows* . . . . . . 8.00 - 12.00
6674 *Medley* . . . . 8.00 - 12.00
Superior 349 *Over The Waves* . . . . 10.00 - 15.00
9194 *Lazy Old Man* . . . . 5.00 - 8.00
9195 *Bummelpetrus* . . . . 5.00 - 8.00
9196 *Medley Of Old Timers* . . . . 5.00 - 8.00
9197 *Medley* . . . . 5.00 - 8.00
9198 *Over The Waves* . . . . 5.00 - 8.00
9199 *One-Two-Three-Four* . . . . 5.00 - 8.00
9200 *Medley* . . . . 5.00 - 8.00
9201 *Marching Through Georgia* . . . . 5.00 - 8.00

NORMAN PHELPS' VIRGINIA ROUNDERS:
Decca 5191, 5192, 5193, 5204, 5212, 5224, 5225, 5237, 5245, 5252, 5268, 5307 . . . . 5.00 - 10.00

WILLIE PHELPS:
Decca 5223 *The Terrible Tupelo Storm* . . . . 7.00 - 10.00

PHILYAW BROTHERS:
Vocalion 02974, 02997, 03011, 03111, 03379, 03419, 04065, 04119, 04186, 04218, 04314 . . . . . 5.00 - 10.00

PICKARD FAMILY:
Banner 6283 *Down In Arkansas* . . . . 5.00 - 8.00
Broadway 8179 *Thompson's Old Gray Mare* . . . . 5.00 - 8.00
Brunswick 348 *Down In Arkansas* . . . . 7.00 - 10.00
363 *Buffalo Gals* . . . . 7.00 - 10.00
385 *Get Me Out Of This Birmingham Jail* . . . . 7.00 - 10.00
Conqueror 7251 *Down In Arkansas* . . . . 5.00 - 8.00
Oriole 1502 *Rabbit In The Pea Patch* . . . . 5.00 - 8.00
Paramount 3213 *Rabbit In The Pea Patch* . . . . . 5.00 - 8.00
3214 *Down In Arkansas* . . . . 5.00 - 8.00
3218 *On The Dummy Line* . . . . 7.00 - 10.00
3231 *Thompson' Old Gray Mare* . . . . 5.00 - 8.00
Q.R.S. 9022 *Down In Arkansas* . . . . 10.00 - 20.00
9006 *Thompson's Old Grey Mare* . . . . 10.00 - 20.00

OBED PICKARD:
Columbia 15141-D *Kitty Wells* . . . . 8.00 - 12.00
15246-D *The Old Gray Horse* . . . . 8.00 - 12.00

JACK PICKELL:
Columbia 15117-D *Don't You Love Your Daddy Too* . . . . 10.00 - 15.00

WILL PICKETT:
Bell 1169 *It Can't Be Done* . . . . 10.00 - 15.00

PIEDMONT MELODY BOYS:
Victor 23660 *Tell Him Now* . . . . 30.00 - 50.00

JOHNNY PIEMONTE:
Gennett 6348 *Over The Waves* . . . . 7.00 - 12.00

PIE PLANT PETE:

Champion 16770 *Medley Of Old Familiar Tunes* . 12.00 - 16.00
45015, 45063, 45064, 45093 . . . . 5.00 - 10.00
Decca 5014, 5030 . . . . 5.00 - 8.00
Gennett 6748 *Boston Burglar* . . . . 10.00 - 15.00
6776 *Ben Tucker Reel* . . . . 10.00 - 15.00
6810 *Asleep At The Switch* . . . . 10.00 - 15.00
7167 *Waiting For The Railroad Train* . . . . 10.00 - 15.00
7205 *Nutty Song* . . . . 10.00 - 15.00
7289 *The Lightning Express* . . . . 15.00 - 20.00
Melotone 13277 *Stay On The Farm* . . . . 5.00 - 8.00
13278 *Do You Hear The Goldfish Sing?* . . . . . 5.00 - 8.00
6-06-52 *Prairie Moon* . . . . 5.00 - 8.00
(Note: Above titles, and others, were also issued on Banner, Oriole, Perfect, Romeo.)
Process 1014 *I'm Gonna Ride That Train* . . . . . — - —
Supertone 9351 *Boston Burglar* . . . . 5.00 - 8.00
9363 *The Letter That Never Came* . . . . 6.00 - 10.00
9405 *Ben Tucker Reel* . . . . 6.00 - 10.00
9652 *Nutty Song* . . . . 6.00 - 10.00
9667 *Medley Of Old Familiar Tunes* . . . . 6.00 - 10.00
9668 *0 Jailer Bring Back That Key* . . . . 6.00 - 10.00
9669 *Sand Will Do It* . . . . 6.00 - 10.00
9701 *The Lightning Express* . . . . 8.00 - 12.00
9712 *Good Old Turnip Greens* . . . . 8.00 - 12.00
9717 *Little Brown Jug* . . . . 7.00 - 10.00

JACK PIERCE'S OKLAHOMA (COW) BOYS:
Bluebird 6610, 6632, 6646, 6785, 6822 . . . . 4.00 - 7.00

WEBB PIERCE:
4 Star . . . . 3.00 - 5.00
Pacemaker 1015 *In The Jailhouse* . . . . 10.00 - 15.00

PINE KNOB SERENADERS:
Superior 2556 *Apple Cider* . . . . 15.00 - 25.00

PINE MOUNTAIN BOYS:
Victor 23582 *She Wouldn't Be Still* . . . . 75.00 - 100.00
23592 *Wild Woman Blues* . . . . 75.00 - 100.00
23605 *Apron String Blues* . . . . 75.00 - 100.00

PINE MOUNTAIN RAMBLERS:
Champion 15610 *Ramblin' Reckless Hobo* . . . . . . 10.00 - 15.00

PINE RIDGE BOYS:
Bluebird 8360 *The Convict And The Rose* . . . . . . 5.00 - 8.00
Bluebird 8671 *Railroad Boomer* . . . . 5.00 - 8.00
8940 *Lonesome For You* . . . . 5.00 - 8.00

PINE STATE PLAYBOYS: (See Also CLAUDE CASEY)
Bluebird 7451, 7535, 7704 . . . . 4.00 - 7.00

PIPERS GAP RAMBLERS:
Okeh 45185 *I Ain't Nobody's Darling* . . . . 15.00 - 20.00

PLAINSMEN & RUFUS HALL:
Broadway 8183 *Bill Mason* . . . . 15.00 - 25.00

PLANTATION BOYS:
Bluebird 6678, 6981 . . . . 5.00 - 10.00

PLEASANT FAMILY:
Broadway 8148 *Rabbit In The Pea Patch* . . . . . . 5.00 - 8.00
8149 *Down In Arkansas* . . . . 5.00 - 8.00
8150 *On The Dummy Line* . . . . 7.00 - 10.00

PLYMOUTH VERMONT OLD TIME BARN DANCE ORCHESTRA:
Okeh 45073 *Portland Fancy* . . . . 15.00 - 20.00

POHLMANN & HATHAWAY:
Supertone 9139 *Throw Out The Life Line* . . . . . . — - —

DOUG POINDEXTER:
Sun 202 *Now She Cares No More* . . . . 25.00 - 40.00*

TALMADGE POLLARD:
Bluebird 7176 *Mind Your Own Business* . . . . 7.00 - 10.00

CHARLIE POOLE (& ROY HARVEY/& THE NORTH CAROLINA RAMBLERS):
Columbia 15038-D *Don't Let Your Deal Go Down Blues* . . . . 10.00 - 15.00
15043-D *The Girl I Left In Sunny Tennessee* . . . 8.00 - 12.00
15099-D *White House Blues* . . . . 8.00 - 12.00
15116-D *There'll Come A Time* . . . . 8.00 - 12.00
15138-D *Good Bye Booze* . . . . 10.00 - 15.00

15160-D *The Highwayman*	10.00 -	15.00
15179-D *Falling By The Wayside*	10.00 -	15.00
15193-D *You Ain't Talkin' To Me*	10.00 -	15.00
15215-D *If You Lose I Don't Care*	10.00 -	15.00
15286-D *Ramblin' Blues*	15.00 -	20.00
15307-D *I Cannot Call Her Mother*	15.00 -	20.00
15342-D *Jealous Mary*	15.00 -	20.00
15385-D *Hangman, Hangman, Slack The Rope*	20.00 -	30.00
15407-D *Bill Mason*	20.00 -	30.00
15425-D *Sweet Sunny South*	20.00 -	30.00
15456-D *The Wayward Boy*	20.00 -	30.00
15509-D *The Baltimore Fire*	25.00 -	40.00
15519-D *Sweet Sixteen*	25.00 -	40.00
15545-D *If The River Was Whiskey*	30.00 -	50.00
15584-D *A Young Boy Left His Home One Day*	30.00 -	50.00
Columbia 15601-D *Look Before You Leap*	30.00 -	50.00
15615-D *Southern Medley*	30.00 -	50.00
15636-D *Just Keep Waiting Till The Good Time Comes*	30.00 -	50.00
15672-D *Took My Gal A-Walkin'*	50.00 -	75.00
15688-D *Milwaukee Blues*	50.00 -	75.00
15711-D *Write A Letter To My Mother*	50.00 -	75.00

POPE'S ARKANSAS MOUNTAINEERS:

Victor 21295 *Hog Eye*	15.00 -	20.00
21469 *Cotton-Eyed Joe*	20.00 -	30.00
21577 *Jaw Bone*	25.00 -	40.00

POPLIN-WOODS TENNESSEE STRING BAND:

Victor V40080 *Are You From Dixie?*	20.00 -	30.00

ARCHIE PORTER & HIS HAPPY BUCKEYES:

Champion 16729 *Log Cabin Call*	50.00 -	75.00

POTTER & JAMES:

Supertone 9541 *Down On The Farm*	8.00 -	12.00

POWDER RIVER JACK & KITTY LEE:

Victor 23527 *Tying A Knot In The Devils Tail*	40.00 -	60.00

JACK & JOHNNIE POWELL:

Victor 23568 *By The Old Garden Gate*	30.00 -	50.00
V40259 *You Ain't Talking To Me*	30.00 -	50.00

FIDDLIN' POWERS (& FAMILY):

Edison 51662 *Old Joe Clark*	10.00 -	15.00
51789 *Sourwood Mountains*	15.00 -	20.00
52083 *Cluck Old Hen*	15.00 -	20.00
Okeh 45154 *Old Virginia Reel*	10.00 -	15.00
45268 *Did You Ever See The Devil, Uncle Joe?*	15.00 -	20.00
Victor 19448 *Sour Wood Mountains*	5.00 -	8.00
Victor 19449 *Cripple Creek*	5.00 -	8.00

PRAIRIE RAMBLERS:

Titles, issued contemporaneously on Banner, Conqueror, Melotone, Oriole, Perfect, Romeo, include: *Deep Elem Blues; Gonna Have a Feast Here Tonight; I'm Looking For The Bully Of The Town; Isle Of Capri; Jim's Windy Mule; Jug Rag; Just Come On In; The Lady In Red; Mistook In The Woman I Love; Nobody's Darling But Mine; On Treasure Island; The Oregon Trail; Put On An Old Pair Of Boots; Snowflakes; Swingin' Down The Old Orchard Lane; Truckin; Uncle Oph's Got The Coon; When I Grow Too Old To Dream; Woman's Answer To Nobody's Dream*

	5.00 -	10.00
Bluebird 5302 *Blue River*	20.00 -	30.00
5320 *Go Easy Blues*	20.00 -	30.00
5322 *Gonna Have A Feast Here Tonight*	20.00 -	30.00
5395 *Next Year*	15.00 -	20.00
Okeh 05851, 05878, 06053, 06102, 06230, 06243, and others	3.00 -	5.00
Victor 23856 *Go Easy Blues*	75.00 -	100.00
23859 *Kentucky Blues*	75.00 -	100.00
Vocalion 03061 *Maple On The Hill, Part 2*	10.00 -	15.00
03085 *You Look Pretty In An Evening Gown*	10.00 -	15.00
03100 *This World Is Not My Home*	10.00 -	15.00

03115 *Jesus Hold My Hand*	10.00 -	15.00
03332, 03422, 03469, 04039, 04092, 04134, 04427, 04601, 04672, 04796, 04868, 04899, 04936, 05002, 05081	5.00 -	8.00

PRAIRIE SERENADERS:

Champion 45164 *The Lonely Cowboy*	7.00 -	10.00
45190 *I'm The Last Of The Texas Rangers*	7.00 -	10.00

CHARLIE PRESCOTT:

Challenge 335 *The Dixie Cowboy*	20.00 -	30.00

RAY PRICE:

Bullet 701 *Jealous Lies*	35.00 -	50.00

WILLIAM PRICE:

Challenge 332 *Little Birdie*	5.00 -	8.00

B.L./SUNSHINE PRITCHARD:

Gennett 6902 *Son Of A Gun*	25.00 -	40.00
Paramount 3320 *Stone Mountain Wobble*	35.00 -	50.00

HOLLAND PUCKETT:

Gennett 6144 *Weeping Wilow Tree*	10.00 -	15.00
6163 *A Mother's Advice*	10.00 -	15.00
6189 *Drunken Hiccoughs*	10.00 -	15.00
6206 *He Lives On High*	10.00 -	15.00
6271 *The Dying Cowboy*	10.00 -	15.00
6433 *Come And Kiss Me Baby Darling*	10.00 -	15.00
6532 *The Maple On The Hill*	10.00 -	15.00
6720 *Little Bessie*	10.00 -	15.00
Silvertone 25065 *The Dying Cowboy*	10.00 -	15.00
Supertone 9324 *Little Bessie*	10.00 -	15.00

RILEY PUCKETT (& TED HAWKINS/RED JONES/CLAYTON McMICHEN):

Bluebird 5432 *The Old Spinning Wheel*	10.00 -	20.00
5471 *K.C Railroad*	10.00 -	20.00
5473 *Texas Hop*	10.00 -	20.00
5514 *Kimball Blues*	10.00 -	20.00
5532 *Careless Love*	10.00 -	20.00
5587 *I'm Gettin' Ready To Go*	10.00 -	20.00
5607 *Renfro Valley Home*	10.00 -	20.00
5656 *Tokio Rag*	10.00 -	20.00
5666 *Lost Love*	10.00 -	20.00
5691 *Down In The Valley*	10.00 -	20.00
5738 *Puckett Blues*	10.00 -	20.00
5786 *Four Day Blues*	10.00 -	20.00
5818 *Chain Gang Blues*	10.00 -	20.00
6064 *Roll Back The Carpet*	10.00 -	15.00
6067 *Don't Let Your Deal Go Down*	7.00 -	10.00
6103 *Nobody's Business*	7.00 -	10.00
6134 *Curly Headed Baby*	7.00 -	10.00
6196 *Blue Ridge Mountain Blues*	7.00 -	10.00
6291 *When I Grow Too Old To Dream*	7.00 -	10.00
6313 *Ole Faithful*	7.00 -	10.00
6348 *Back To My Home In The Smoky Montains*	7.00 -	10.00
6404 *My Old Mule*	7.00 -	10.00
7303 *Carolina Sunshine Girl*	7.00 -	10.00
7717 *Old Maid's Brown Ferry*	7.00 -	10.00
Columbia 107-D *Rock All Your Babies To Sleep*	8.00 -	12.00
110-D *Hen Cackle*	8.00 -	12.00
113-D *Casey Jones*	8.00 -	12.00
119-D *Black-Eyed Alabama Gal*	8.00 -	12.00
150-D *Johnson's Old Grey Mule*	8.00 -	12.00
240-D *Just As The Sun Went Down*	7.00 -	10.00
254-D *Blue Ridge Mountain Blues*	10.00 -	15.00
405-D *Let Me Call You Sweetheart*	8.00 -	12.00
15003-D *Swanee River*	15.00 -	20.00
15015-D *Burglar Man*	15.00 -	20.00
15033-D *Jesse James*	10.00 -	15.00
15035-D *Just Break The News To Mother*	10.00 -	15.00
15036-D *I Wish I Was Single Again*	10.00 -	15.00
15045-D *Long Tongue Woman*	10.00 -	15.00
15050-D *The Orphan Girl*	10.00 -	15.00
15055-D *When I'm Gone You'll Soon Forget*	10.00 -	15.00
15058-D *Down By The Old Mill Stream*	8.00 -	12.00
15063-D *You'd Be Surprised*	10.00 -	15.00

15068-D *Hello Central Give Me Heaven*	10.00	-	15.00
15073-D *Wait Till The Sun Shines Nellie*	7.00	-	10.00
15074-D *Bully Of The Town*	7.00	-	10.00
15078-D *Everybody Works But Father*	7.00	-	10.00
15088-D *Sauerkraut*	7.00	-	10.00
15095-D *My Carolina Home*	7.00	-	10.00
15102-D *Ida Red*	7.00	-	10.00
15125-D *Put My Little Shoes Away*	7.00	-	10.00
15139-D *Down In Arkansas*	8.00	-	12.00
15163-D *Fuzzy Rag*	10.00	-	15.00
15171-D *Little Log Cabin In The Lane*	7.00	-	10.00
15185-D *Alabama Gal*	10.00	-	15.00
15196-D *My Poodle Dog*	10.00	-	15.00
15198-D *That Old Irish Mother Of Mine*	7.00	-	10.00
15226-D *Red Wing*	7.00	-	10.00
15232-D *Little Brown Jug*	7.00	-	10.00
15250-D *All Bound 'Round With The Mason-Dixon Line*	10.00	-	15.00
15261-D *Blue Yodel*	10.00	-	15.00
15277-D *Little Maumee*	10.00	-	15.00
15295-D *Slim Gal*	10.00	-	15.00
15324-D *The Moonshiner's Dream*	15.00	-	20.00
15358-D *Bill Johnson*	15.00	-	20.00
15374-D *I'm Going To Georgia*	15.00	-	20.00
15392-D *Don't Try It For It Can't Be Done*	15.00	-	20.00
15393-D *Carolina Moon*	15.00	-	20.00
15408-D *Waiting For A Train*	20.00	-	30.00
15448-D *McKinley*	20.00	-	30.00
15505-D *Frankie And Johnny*	20.00	-	30.00
15563-D *Dark Town Strutters Ball*	20.00	-	30.00
15605-D *Waitin' For The Evenin' Mail*	25.00	-	40.00
15631-D *Somewhere In Old Wyoming*	25.00	-	40.00
15656-D *The Cat Came Back*	25.00	-	40.00
15708-D *There's A Hard Time Coming*	30.00	-	50.00
15719-D *All Bound Down In Prison*	30.00	-	50.00
15747-D *East Bound Train*	50.00	-	80.00
Decca 5438 *There's More Pretty Girls Than One*	7.00	-	10.00
5442 *Short Life Of Trouble*	7.00	-	10.00
5455 *Altoona Freight Wreck*	7.00	-	10.00
5472 *Gulf Coast Blues*	7.00	-	10.00
5523 *Somebody's Waiting For You*	5.00	-	8.00
5540 *Moonlight On The Colorado*	5.00	-	8.00

SI PUCKETT:

Supertone 9186 *The Maple On The Hill*	7.00	-	10.00
9254 *The Bright Sherman Valley*	7.00	-	10.00

PETE PYLE:

Bluebird 8581, 8711	4.00	-	7.00
Bullet 602 *Talking The Blues*	5.00	-	8.00

QUADRILLERS:

Paramount 3008 *Drunk Man Blues*	15.00	-	20.00
3009 *Cumberland Blues*	15.00	-	20.00

FRANK QUINN:

Okeh 45030 *Pop Goes The Weasel*	7.00	-	10.00

RADIO MAC:

Victor 23510 *Home Spun Gal*	10.00	-	15.00
23586 *He Sure Can Play*	10.00	-	15.00
24690 *Last Old Dollar*	10.00	-	15.00
23704 *Sweet Betsy From Pike*	8.00	-	12.00
23829 *Bald Top Mountain*	30.00	-	50.00
V40101 *Ain't We Crazy*	7.00	-	10.00
V40264 *Roamin'*	10.00	-	15.00

JAMES RAGAN & OLIVER BECK:

Challenge 390 *Please Papa Come Home*	8.00	-	12.00
401 *Walking On The Streets Of Glory*	7.00	-	10.00

RAGGEDY ANN'S MELODY MAKERS:

Okeh 45235 *Zenda Waltz*	8.00	-	12.00

RAILROAD BOYS:

Superior 2684 *By A Cottage In The Twilight*	15.00	-	20.00
2779 *You're Bound To Look Like A Monkey*	20.00	-	30.00

RAINEY OLD TIME BAND:

Columbia 15675-D *Engineer Frank Hawk*	50.00	-	75.00

RALEY BROTHERS:

Bluebird 7062 *Chicken Roost Blues*	7.00	-	10.00

RAMBLING DUET:

Bluebird 7131, 7233, 7450, 7484, 7534, 7574	5.00	-	10.00

RAMBLING KID & PROFESSOR:

Melotone 7-07-54 *Little Home In Tennessee*	10.00	-	15.00

RAMBLING RAMBLERS:

Vocalion 04628, 04758, 04949	5.00	-	10.00

RANCH BOYS:

Decca 5016, 5017, 5040, 5045, 5046, 5061, 5074, 5113, 5128, 5167, 5319, 5341, 5354	5.00	-	10.00

RAND & FOSTER'

Supertone 9326 *The Vestris Disaster*	8.00	-	12.00
9373 *Only A Step To The Grave*	8.00	-	12.00

GROVER RANN & HIS LOOKOUT MOUNTAINEERS:

Columbia 15638-D *Don't Stay After Ten*	40.00	-	60.00

RAY BROTHERS:

Bluebird 5789 *Winona Rag*	20.00	-	30.00
Victor 23552 *Mississippi Echoes*	50.00	-	75.00
23713 *Winona Rag*	75.00	-	100.00
V40291 *Jake Leg Wobble*	40.00	-	60.00
V40313 *Choctaw County Rag*	40.00	-	60.00

AULTON RAY/RAYL:

Champion 15332 *Maxwell Girl*	25.00	-	40.00
Gennett 6129 *True And Trembling Brakeman*	25.00	-	40.00
6177 *The Dixie Cowboy*	25.00	-	40.00
6205 *Maxwell Girl*	40.00	-	60.00
Herwin 75550 *Maxwell Girl*	35.00	-	50.00
Herwin 75552 *True And Trembling Brakeman*	25.00	-	50.00
Silvertone 8150 *The Dixie Cowboy*	25.00	-	40.00
Superior 385 *The Dixie Cowboy*	30.00	-	60.00
Supertone 9250 *The Maxwell Girl*	35.00	-	50.00

REAVES' WHITE COUNTY RAMBLERS:

Vocalion 5218 *Ten Cent Piece*	75.00	-	100.00
5219 *Rattler Tree'd A Possum*	75.00	-	100.00
5224 *Down In Arkansas*	75.00	-	100.00
5247 *Drunkard's Hiccups*	75.00	-	100.00
5260 *Arkansas Pullet*	75.00	-	100.00

RECORD BOYS:

Vocalion 5136 *Harmonica Jim*	8.00	-	12.00

RECTOR TRIO:

Columbia 15658-D *Skyland Rag*	15.00	-	20.00

RED BRUSH ROWDIES/SINGERS:

Paramount 3122 *The Hatfield-McCoy Feud*	30.00	-	50.00
3140 *The Third Of July*	30.00	-	50.00
3143 *Beyond The Starry Plane*	30.00	-	50.00
3150 *Midnight Serenade*	30.00	-	50.00

RED HEADED BRIER HOPPER (LEROY ANDERSON):

Champion 16578 *Gooseberry Pie*	30.00	-	50.00
16668 *Three Wishes*	30.00	-	50.00
16678 *The Fatal Derby Day*	40.00	-	60.00
16708 *Is There No Chance For Me Tonight, Love*	40.00	-	60.00
16797 *The Wrong Man And The Wrong Woman*	50.00	-	75.00
16811 *A Mother's Wayward Son*	50.00	-	75.00
16820 *Gambling On The Sabbath*	50.00	-	75.00

RED HEADED FIDDLERS:

Brunswick 285 *Texas Quickstep*	15.00	-	20.00
388 *Rag Time Annie*	15.00	-	20.00
460 *The Fatal Wedding*	15.00	-	20.00
470 *Cheat 'Em*	15.00	-	20.00
526 *The Steeley Rag*	15.00	-	20.00

RED MOUNTAIN TRIO:

Columbia 15260-D *The Wang Wang Blues*	10.00	-	15.00
15369-D *Dixie*	10.00	-	15.00
15462-D *Carolina Sunshine*	15.00	-	20.00

RED RIVER COON HUNTERS:

Superior 2647 *The Wreck Of The West Bound Airliner*	20.00	-	30.00
2754 *By And By You Will Forgive Me*	20.00	-	30.00

RED & SON RAYMOND:

Champion 16797 *Mother' Beautiful Hands* ..... 15.00 - 20.00

REED CHILDREN:

Columbia 15525-D *I'll Be All Smiles Tonight* .... 7.00 - 10.00

ALFRED & ORVILLE REED:

Victor 23550 *Beware* .... 40.00 - 60.00

   23650 *Old Fashioned Cottage* .... 40.00 - 60.00

BLIND ALFRED REED:

Victor 20836 *The Wreck Of The Virginia* .... 25.00 - 40.00

   20939 *You Must Unload* .... 25.00 - 40.00

   21191 *Explosion In The Fairmount Mines* ..... 30.00 - 50.00

   21360 *Why Do You Bob Your Hair, Girls?* .... 30.00 - 50.00

   21533 *The Fate Of Chris Lively And Wife* ..... 35.00 - 50.00

   V40196 *Woman's Been After Man Ever Since* .. 40.00 - 60.00

   V40236 *Money Cravin' Folks* .... 40.00 - 60.00

   V40290 *Black And Blue Blues* .... 50.00 - 75.00

L.K. REEDER:

Okeh 45026 *Falling Leaf* .... 5.00 - 8.00

JACK REEDY & HIS WALKER MOUNTAIN STRING BAND:

Brunswick 221 *Chinese Breakdown* .... 20.00 - 30.00

JIMMY REESE:

Supertone 9613 *Blue Yodel No. 5* .... 10.00 - 15.00

   9627 *You And My Old Guitar* .... 10.00 - 15.00

REEVES & MOODY:

Victor 20540 *Down Where The Watermelon Grows* .... 10.00 - 15.00

   20929 *Rock All Our Babies To Sleep* .... 8.00 - 12.00

   21188 *Sweet Evelina* .... 10.00 - 15.00

GOEBEL REEVES (THE TEXAS DRIFTER):

Titles, issued contemporaneously on Banner, Conqueror, Melotone, Oriole, Perfect, Romeo: *The Bar None Ranch; Big Rock Candy Mountain; The Cowboy's Dizzy Sweetheart; It's True I'm Just A Convict; Reckless Tex From Texas; The Wandering Boy; Where The Mississippi Washes* .... 7.00 - 12.00

Brunswick 539 *Station H.O.B.O* .... 10.00 - 15.00

Champion 16139 *The Hobo's Grave* .... 15.00 - 20.00

   16189 *Station H.O.B O* .... 15.00 - 20.00

   16234 *The Drifter* .... 15.00 - 20.00

   45181 *The Drifter's Buddy* .... 5.00 - 8.00

   45194 *I Learned About Women From Her* ..... 5.00 - 8.00

Conqueror 8442 *Cold And Hungry* .... 7.00 - 10.00

   8443 *The Bar None Ranch* .... 7.00 - 10.00

Okeh 45365 *The Drifter* .... 10.00 - 15.00

   45381 *The Tramp's Mother* .... 15.00 - 20.00

   45408 *Blue Undertaker's Blues* .... 15.00 - 20.00

   45449 *The Texas Drifter's Warning* .... 15.00 - 20.00

   45491 *In The Land Of Never Was* .... 15.00 - 20.00

JIM REEVES:

Macy's 115 *Teardrops Of Regret* .... 40.00 - 60.00

   132 *I've Never Been So Blue* .... 35.00 - 50.00

WALTER REGAN:

Superior 2524 *Just As Your Mother Was* ...... 15.00 - 25.00

   2585 *Moundsville Prisoner* .... 25.00 - 40.00

DICK REINHART:

Brunswick 386 *Rambling Lover* .... 10.00 - 15.00

GEORGE RENEAU ("THE BLIND MUSICIAN OF THE SMOKEY MOUNTAINS"):

Vocalion 5029 *Lonesome Road Blues* .... 6.00 - 10.00

   5030 *Life's Railway To Heaven* .... 6.00 - 10.00

   5031 *Little Brown Jug* .... 6.00 - 10.00

   5032 *Arkansas Traveler* .... 6.00 - 10.00

   5033 *Here, Rattler, Here* .... 6.00 - 10.00

   5034 *Blue Ridge Blues* .... 6.00 - 10.00

   5049 *Red Wing* .... 6.00 - 10.00

   5050 *C & O Wreck* .... 6.00 - 10.00

   5052 *The Baggage Coach Ahead* .... 6.00 - 10.00

   5054 *The New Market Wreck* .... 6.00 - 10.00

   5055 *I've Got The Railroad Blues* .... 6.00 - 10.00

   5056 *The Prisoner's Song* .... 6.00 - 10.00

   5057 *Little Rosewood Casket* .... 6.00 - 10.00

   5058 *Wild Bill Jones* .... 6.00 - 10.00

   5059 *Wild And Reckless Hobos* .... 6.00 - 10.00

   5064 *My Redeemer* .... 6.00 - 10.00

   5077 *Rovin' Gambler* .... 6.00 - 10.00

   5078 *Gambling On The Sabbath Day* .... 6.00 - 10.00

   5079 *Bad Companions* .... 6.00 - 10.00

   5080 *The Hand Of Fate* .... 6.00 - 10.00

   5083 *Railroad Lover* .... 6.00 - 10.00

   5106 *Old Man On The Hill* .... 6.00 - 10.00

   5107 *Old Rugged Cross* .... 6.00 - 10.00

   5108 *Two Orphans* .... 6.00 - 10.00

   14809 *Lonesome Road Blues* .... 6.00 - 10.00

   14811 *Life's Railway To Heaven* .... 6.00 - 10.00

   14812 *Little Brown Jug* .... 6.00 - 10.00

   14813 *Arkansas Traveler* .... 6.00 - 10.00

   14814 *Here, Rattler, Here* .... 8.00 - 12.00

   14815 *Blue Ridge Blues* .... 8.00 - 12.00

   14896 *Red Wing* .... 6.00 - 10.00

   14897 *C & W Wreck* .... 8.00 - 12.00

   14918 *The Baggage Coach Ahead* .... 6.00 - 10.00

   14930 *The New Market Wreck* .... 8.00 - 12.00

   14946 *I've Got The Railroad Blues* .... 8.00 - 12.00

   14991 *The Prisoner's Song* .... 6.00 - 10.00

   14997 *The Little Rosewood Casket* .... 6.00 - 10.00

   14998 *Wild Bill Jones* .... 8.00 - 12.00

   14999 *Wild And Reckless Hobos* .... 8.00 - 12.00

   15046 *My Redeemer* .... 7.00 - 10.00

   15148 *Rovin' Gambler* .... 7.00 - 10.00

   15149 *Gambling On The Sabbath Day* ...... 7.00 - 10.00

   15150 *Bad Companions* .... 7.00 - 10.00

   15182 *The Hand Of Fate* .... 7.00 - 10.00

   15194 *Railroad Lover* .... 7.00 - 10.00

   15347 *Old Man On The Hill* .... 7.00 - 10.00

   15348 *The Old Rugged Cross* .... 7.00 - 10.00

   15349 *Two Orphans* .... 7.00 - 10.00

   15366 *On Top Of Old Smoky* .... 15.00 - 20.00

RENFRO VALLEY BOYS:

Paramount 3311 *Twenty-One Years* .... 15.00 - 20.00

   3315 *My Renfro Valley Home* .... 15.00 - 20.00

   3316 *The Yellow Rose Of Texas* .... 15.00 - 20.00

   3321 *Loreena* .... 25.00 - 40.00

JIMMIE REVARD & THE OKLAHOMA PLAYBOYS:

Bluebird 6654, 6679, 6712, 6739, 6753, 6774, 6823, 6842, 6877, 6935, 6992, 7028, 7061, 7085, 7172, 7199, 7248, 7309, 7370, 7371, 7481, 7520, 7559, 7610, 7727, 7776, 7911, 7939, 7964 .... 4.00 - 8.00

Bluebird (higher numbers) .... 4.00 - 6.00

Everstate 1011 *Holdin' The Sack* .... 5.00 - 8.00

WILLIAM REXROAT (& HIS CEDAR CREST SINGERS):

Vocalion 5290 *Fading Away* .... 15.00 - 25.00

   5323 *Build Me A Bungalow* .... 15.00 - 25.00

   5345 *We Shall Wear A Crown* .... 15.00 - 25.00

REYNOLDS & ROBINSON:

Superior 2653 *Rocky Mountain Rose* .... — - —

RALPH REYNOLDS & HIS DUDE RANCH WRANGLERS:

Globe 127, 128 .... 5.00 - 10.00

RICE BROTHERS' GANG:

Decca, most issues .... 5.00 - 10.00

RICE, DAVIS & THOMAS:

Paramount 3309 *Circus Day Rag* .... 25.00 - 40.00

Q.R.S. 9019 *Circus Day Rag* .... 35.00 - 50.00

EDD RICE:

Vocalion 5220 *Cricket On The Hearth* .... 10.00 - 15.00

GLEN RICE & HIS BEVERLY HILLBILLIES:
(See also BEVERLY HILLBILLIES)

Brunswick 506 *My Old Iowa Home* .... 5.00 - 8.00

   519 *Prairie Skies* .... 5.00 - 8.00

   597 *Swiss Yodel* .... 5.00 - 8.00

598 *The Big Corral*	5.00 -	8.00
599 *Ridge Runnin' Roan*	5.00 -	8.00
600 *Cowboy Joe*	5.00 -	8.00

HOKE RICE & HIS HOKY POKY BOYS/
SOUTHERN BAND/STRING BAND;
HOKE RICE & HARRY STARK:

Brunswick 416 *Georgia Jubilee*	10.00 -	15.00
473 *Wabash Blues*	10.00 -	15.00
482 *Georgia Gal*	10.00 -	15.00
552 *Floating Down To Cotton Town*	10.00 -	7.00
Gennett 6839 *Waiting For A Train*	25.00 -	40.00
6855 *Blue Yodel No. 4*	25.00 -	40.00
7067 *Unexplained Blues*	25.00 -	40.00
Paramount 3212 *I'm Lonely And Blue*	25.00 -	40.00
3229 *Chinese Breakdown*	25.00 -	40.00
3239 *Down In A Southern Town*	25.00 -	40.00
3308 *Macon Georgia Breakdown*	30.00 -	50.00
Q.R.S. 9012 *Waiting For A Train*	35.00 -	50.00
9015 *Down In A Southern Town*	35.00 -	50.00
9022 *Way Down South By The Sea*	35.00 -	50.00

RENUS RICH & CARL BRADSHAW:

Columbia 15341-D *Sleep Baby Sleep*	7.00 -	10.00

FRED RICHARDS:

Columbia 15483-D *Danville Blues*	10.00 -	15.00

RALPH RICHARDSON:

Okeh 45267 *Little Dog Yodel*	5.00 -	8.00

RIDGEL'S FOUNTAIN CITIANS:

Vocalion 5363 *Be Ready*	50.00 -	75.00
5389 *Little Bonnie*	50.00 -	75.00
5427 *Baby, Call Your Dog Off*	50.00 -	75.00
5455 *The Bald Headed End Of The Broom*	50.00 -	75.00

RILEY'S MOUNTAINEERS:

Supertone 9677 *Sunny Home In Dixie*	7.00 -	10.00

GEORGE RILEY:

Perfect 12653 *The Texas Drifter's Warning*	7.00 -	10.00
(Probably also issued on Melotone, Oriole, Romeo.)		

TEX RITTER:

Titles, issued contemporaneously on Banner,
Conqueror, Melotone, Oriole, Perfect, Romeo,
Vocalion: *A-Ridin' Old Paint; Every Day In
The Saddle; Goodbye Old Paint; Rye Whiskey,*

Rye Whiskey	10.00 -	15.00
Champion 45153 *Nobody's Darling But Mine*	8.00 -	12.00
45154 *The Oregon Trail*	8.00 -	12.00
45191 *Bill The Bar Fly*	8.00 -	12.00
45197 *Answer To Nobody's Darling But Mine*	8.00 -	12.00
45198 *The Hills Of Old Wyomin'*	8.00 -	12.00
Decca 5076 *Lady Killin' Cowboy*	10.00 -	15.00
5112 *Thirty-Three Years In Prison*	10.00 -	15.00
5305 *Bill The Bar Fly*	8.00 -	12.00
5306 *Jailhouse Lament*	8.00 -	12.00
5315 *High, Wide And Handsome*	7.00 -	10.00
5389 *Down The Colorado Trail*	7.00 -	10.00
5405 *I'm Hittin' The Trail (For Home)*	7.00 -	10.00
5639, 5648, 5922	5.00 -	10.00
Montgomery Ward 8020, 8032	8.00 -	12.00

RIVERSIDE RAMBLERS:

Bluebird 6926, 7063, 7202, 7251, 7846, 7942, 7974	4.00 -	8.00

ROANE COUNTY RAMBLERS:

Columbia 15328-D *Home Town Blues*	30.00 -	50.00
15377-D *Tennessee Waltz*	30.00 -	50.00
15398-D *Roane County Rag*	30.00 -	50.00
15438-D *McCarroll's Breakdown*	40.00 -	60.00
15498-D *Johnson City Rag*	40.00 -	60.00
15570-D *Alabama Trot*	50.00 -	80.00

ROANOKE JUG BAND:

Okeh 45393 *Home Brew Rag*	75.00 -	125.00
45423 *Stone Mountain Rag*	75.00 -	125.00

GEORGE ROARK:

Columbia 15383-D *I Ain't A Bit Drunk*	8.00 -	12.00

SHORTBUCKLE ROARK & FAMILY:

Victor V40023 *My Mother's Hands*	15.00 -	20.00

FIDDLIN' DOC ROBERTS (TRIO):

Titles, issued contemporaneously on Banner,
Conqueror, Melotone, Oriole, Perfect. Romeo:
*Blue Grass Rag; Carroll County Blues;
Charleston No. 1; Coal Tipple Blues;
Cumberland Blues; Did You Ever See The
Devil, Uncle Joe?; Down Yonder; Farewell
Waltz; A Good Man Is Waiting For You; I Don't
Love Nobody; In The Shadow Of The Pines;
Ninety-Nine Years; Over The Waves; Pickin'
And Playin'; Ragtime Chicken Joe; Sally Ann;
Shortenin' Bread; Turkey In The Straw; The
Waggoner; 'Way Down South; Wednesday Night*

Waltz	7.00 -	12.00
Challenge 501 *All I've Got Is Done Gone*	8.00 -	12.00
Champion 45099, 45135, 45136	5.00 -	10.00
Gennett 3152 *Martha Campbell*	10.00 -	15.00
3162 *All I've Got Is Done Gone*	10.00 -	15.00
3235 *Billy In The Low Ground*	10.00 -	15.00
6025 *In The Shadow Of The Pine*	12.00 -	16.00
6257 *Waynesburgh*	12.00 -	16.00
6336 *Old Buzzard*	12.00 -	16.00
6390 *Billy In The Low Ground*	10.00 -	15.00
6495 *Old Zip Coon & Medley Of Reels*	15.00 -	20.00
6588 *My Old Coon Dog*	15.00 -	20.00
6635 *Brickyard Joe*	15.00 -	20.00
6689 *Shippin' Sport*	15.00 -	20.00
6717 *Farewell Waltz*	15.00 -	20.00
6750 *Mandolin Rag*	15.00 -	20.00
6775 *Shoot That Turkey Buzzard*	15.00 -	20.00
6826 *Who's Been Here Since I Been Gone*	15.00 -	20.00
6942 *The Devil In Georgia*	15.00 -	25.00
7017 *Jack's Creek Waltz*	15.00 -	25.00
7049 *Johnny Inchin' Along*	15.00 -	25.00
7094 *My Baby Don't Love Me*	20.00 -	30.00
7110 *Hawk's Got A Chicken*	20.00 -	30.00
7221 *Rye Straw*	20.00 -	30.00
Superior 348 *And The Cat Came Back*	50.00 -	75.00
386 *Billy In The Low Ground*	50.00 -	75.00
2762 *Sally Gooden*	25.00 -	35.00
Supertone 9252 *In The Shadow Of The Pine*	7.00 -	10.00
9397 *Martha Campbell*	7.00 -	10.00

JAMES ROBERTS:

Titles, issued contemporaneously on Banner,
Conqueror, Melotone, Oriole, Perfect, Romeo,
include: *The Crepe On The Cabin Door; Down
And Out Blues; Duval County Blues; May I
Sleep In Your Barn Tonight, Mister?; String*

Bean Mama	7.00 -	12.00

A.C. (ECK) ROBERTSON (& DR. J.B.
CRANFILL/& FAMILY):

Victor 18956 *Arkansas Traveler*	5.00 -	8.00
19149 *Turkey In The Straw*	5.00 -	8.00
19372 *Sally Johnson*	5.00 -	8.00
V40145 *Texas Wagoner*	10.00 -	15.00
V40166 *The Island Unknown*	10.00 -	15.00
V40205 *Great Big Taters*	10.00 -	15.00
V40298 *Amarillo Waltz*	15.00 -	20.00
V40334 *Brown Kelly Waltz*	15.00 -	20.00

TEXAS JIM ROBERTSON:

Bluebird 8186, 8606, 8706	3.00 -	6.00

MELVIN ROBINETTE & BYRD MOORE:

Gennett 6841 *Birmingham Jail*	50.00 -	80.00
6884 *Flop Eared Mule*	50.00 -	80.00
6957 *That Old Tiger Rag*	50.00 -	80.00
7068 *Goodbye Sweetheart*	50.00 -	80.00

CARSON ROBINSON (& VERNON
DALHART/FRANK LUTHER THE
PIONEERS):

This artist recorded seemingly countless records

for many labels from the 1920s to the 1950s. Most of his records are of minimal value and interest to collectors of country music. A few selected exceptions are listed following (and also see the Jazz and the Rockabilly/Rock & Roll, etc., sections!)

Columbia 15548-D, 15627-D, 15644-D, 15768-D .	5.00 -	10.00
15773-D *Old Familiar Tunes*	10.00 -	15.00
15779-D *Missouri Valley*	10.00 -	15.00
Okeh 45537 *So I Joined The Navy*	8.00 -	12.00
Superior 2546 *When The Sun Goes Down Again* .	15.00 -	25.00
2580 *Cross Eyed Sue*	15.00 -	25.00

ROCKY MOUNTAIN RANGERS:
Bluebird 6907, 6908	4.00 -	7.00

HUGH RODEN (& ROY ROGERS/HIS TEXAS NIGHTHAWKS):
Okeh 45430 *Deep Sea Waltz*	30.00 -	50.00
45465 *Tulsa Waltz*	30.00 -	50.00
45540 *Hogs In The Potato Patch*	30.00 -	50.00

RODEO TRIO:
Victor V40136 *Arkansas Traveler*	5.00 -	8.00
V40186 *Medley*	5.00 -	8.00

JESSIE RODGERS:
Bluebird 5443 *The Ramblers' Yodel*	7.00 -	10.00
5499 *Way Down In Mississippi*	7.00 -	10.00
5632 *Roughneck Blues*	7.00 -	10.00
5839 *Rattlesnake Daddy*	7.00 -	10.00
5853 *Headin' Home*	7.00 -	10.00
5910 *An Old Rugged Road*	7.00 -	10.00
5942 *Leave Me Alone*	25.00 -	40.00
5958 *Lonely Days In Texas*	7.00 -	10.00
6066 *Hummin' To My Honey*	7.00 -	10.00
6087 *Window Shopping Mama*	7.00 -	10.00
6116 *When I Was A Boy*	7.00 -	10.00
6143 *Jessie's Talking Blues*	7.00 -	10.00
6196 *Give Your Love*	7.00 -	10.00
6256 *When The Texas Moon Is Shining*	5.00 -	8.00
6311 *Little Prairie Town*	5.00 -	8.00
6364 *San Antonio Blues*	5.00 -	8.00
6402 *Tell You About A Gal Named Sal*	5.00 -	8.00
6924 *Troubled In Mind And Blues*	5.00 -	8.00
7018 *Just One Little Kiss*	5.00 -	8.00
7042 *Back In Jail Again*	5.00 -	8.00
7209 *I'm A Roaming Cowboy*	5.00 -	8.00

JIMMIE RODGERS:
Bluebird 5000 *Moonlight And Skies*	7.00 -	10.00
5037 *Gambling Bar Room Blues*	10.00 -	15.00
5057 *Happy Till She Met You*	10.00 -	15.00
5061 *You've Got Me Crying Again*	10.00 -	15.00
5076 *Prairie Lullaby*	10.00 -	15.00
5080 *Mother, Queen Of My Heart*	10.00 -	15.00
5081 *Down The Old Road To Home*	10.00 -	15.00
5082 *Roll Along, Kentucky Moon*	10.00 -	15.00
5083 *My Time Ain't Long*	10.00 -	15.00
5084 *What's It*	10.00 -	15.00
5085 *Blue Yodel*	7.00 -	10.00
5136 *Mississippi Moon*	8.00 -	12.00
5163 *Waiting For A Train*	7.00 -	10.00
5199 *When It's Harvest Time*	10.00 -	15.00
5223 *In The Jailhouse Now*	6.00 -	10.00
5281 *Jimmie Rodgers' Last Blue Yodel*	20.00 -	30.00
5393 *My Blue-Eyed Jane*	10.00 -	15.00
5482 *Ben Dewberry's Final Run*	6.00 -	10.00
5556 *Yodeling Ranger*	6.00 -	10.00
5609 *My Old Pal*	6.00 -	10.00
5739 *I'm Lonesome Too*	8.00 -	12.00
5784 *In The Hills Of Tennessee*	8.00 -	12.00
5838 *Treasures Untold*	5.00 -	8.00
5892 *Why Did You Give Me Your Love*	10.00 -	15.00
5942 *My Good Gal's Gone*	25.00 -	40.00
5991 *Daddy And Home*	5.00 -	8.00
6198 *Old Love Letters*	15.00 -	20.00

6225 *Sleep, Baby, Sleep*	5.00 -	8.00
6246 *The Sailor's Plea*	5.00 -	8.00
6275 *Mule Skinner Blues*	15.00 -	20.00
6698 *Why There's A Tear In My Eye*	15.00 -	25.00
6762 *The Carter Family & Jimmie Rodgers In Texas*	10.00 -	15.00
6810 *I've Only Loved Three Women*	10.00 -	15.00

(Note: First pressings of above are "buff" Bluebird label; subsequent pressings with blue label are worth less.)

7280 *Yodeling My Way Back Home*	10.00 -	15.00
7600 *Take Me Back Again*	10.00 -	15.00
Montgomery Ward (many titles as on Bluebird) .	7.00 -	10.00
4209 *Blue Yodel No. 9*	15.00 -	20.00
5014 *My Good Gal's Gone Blues*	15.00 -	20.00
Victor 20864 *Soldier's Sweetheart*	10.00 -	15.00
21142 *Away Out On The Mountain*	10.00 -	15.00
21245 *Ben Dewberry's Final Run*	10.00 -	15.00
21291 *Blue Yodel No. 2*	15.00 -	20.00
21433 *Treasures Untold*	15.00 -	20.00
21531 *Blue Yodel No. 3*	15.00 -	20.00
21574 *Dear Old Sunny South By The Sea*	15.00 -	20.00

21636 *Memphis Yodel*	15.00 -	20.00
21757 *Daddy And Home*	15.00 -	20.00
22072 *Blue Yodel No. 5*	15.00 -	25.00
22143 *Frankie And Johnny*	15.00 -	25.00
22220 *My Rough And Rowdy Ways*	20.00 -	30.00
22271 *Blue Yodel No. 6*	20.00 -	30.00
22319 *The Drunkard's Child*	20.00 -	30.00
22379 *Train Whistle Blues*	20.00 -	30.00
22421 *Hobo Bill's Last Ride*	20.00 -	30.00
22488 *Any Old Time*	20.00 -	30.00
22523 *High Powered Mama*	20.00 -	30.00
22554 *Pistol Packin' Papa*	20.00 -	30.00
23503 *Blue Yodel No. 8*	25.00 -	40.00
23518 *Nobody Knows But Me*	25.00 -	40.00
23535 *T.B. Blues*	30.00 -	50.00
23549 *Jimmie, The Kid*	30.00 -	50.00
23564 *I'm Lonesome, Too*	30.00 -	50.00
23574 *Moonlight And Skies*	30.00 -	50.00
23580 *Blue Yodel No. 9*	50.00 -	80.00
23609 *What's It*	50.00 -	80.00
23621 *Rodgers Puzzle Record*	50.00 -	80.00
23636 *Gambling Polka Dot Blues*	50.00 -	80.00
23651 *Roll Along Kentucky Moon*	50.00 -	80.00
23669 *My Time Ain't Long*	50.00 -	80.00
23681 *Home Call*	50.00 -	80.00
23696 *Blue Yodel No. 10*	50.00 -	80.00
23711 *Hobo's Meditation*	50.00 -	80.00
23721 *Mother, The Queen Of My Heart*	50.00 -	80.00
23736 *Miss The Mississippi And You*	75.00 -	100.00
23751 *Whippin' That Old T.B.*	75.00 -	100.00
23766 *Gambling Bar Room Blues*	75.00 -	100.00
23781 *Peach Pickin' Time In Georgia*	75.00 -	100.00
23796 *Blue Yodel No. 11*	80.00 -	120.00
23811 *The Southern Cannon Ball*	100.00 -	150.00
23816 *Mississippi Delta Blues*	100.00 -	150.00
23830 *The Yodeling Ranger*	100.00 -	150.00
23840 *Old Love Letters*	125.00 -	175.00
24456 *Blue Yodel No. 12*	75.00 -	100.00
V40014 *Blue Yodel No. 4*	10.00 -	15.00

V40054 *The Sailor's Plea* .... 10.00 - 15.00
V40072 *My Little Lady* .... 15.00 - 20.00
V40096 *My Carolina Sunshine Girl* .... 10.00 - 15.00
18-6000 (picture record) *Blue Yodel No. 12* ....200.00 - Up
(Note: Valuations of several hundred dollars and
up have been placed on this sought-after disc;
however, only one actual transaction at such a
lofty figure has been verified.)

MRS. JIMMIE RODGERS:
Bluebird 6698 *We Miss Him When The Evening*
Shadows Fall .... 10.00 - 15.00
7339 *My Rainbow Trail* .... 10.00 - 15.00

ROE BROTHERS (& MORRELL):
Columbia 15156-D *The Ship That Never Returned* 8.00 - 12.00
15199-D *Goin' Down The Road Feelin' Bad* ... 10.00 - 15.00

ERNEST ROGERS:
Victor 20502 *Willie, The Chimney Sweeper* ..... 5.00 - 8.00
20672 *The Flight of "Lucky" Lindberg* ...... 10.00 - 15.00
20798 *Steamboat Bill* .... 8.00 - 12.00
20870 *My Red-Haired Lady* .... 8.00 - 12.00
21361 *Mythological Blues* .... 8.00 - 12.00

ROY ROGERS:
Vocalion 04050 *When A Cowboy Sings A Song* .. 8.00 - 12.00
04051 *Listen To The Rhythm Of The Range* .... 8.00 - 12.00
04091 *Hi-Yo Silver* .... 8.00 - 12.00
04263 *I'm A Lonely Ranger* .... 8.00 - 12.00
04389 *When The Sun Is Setting On The Prairie* 8.00 - 12.00
04453 *Colorado Sunset* .... 8.00 - 12.00
Vocalion 04544 *Born To The Saddle* .... 8.00 - 12.00
04840 *Somebody's Smile* .... 8.00 - 12.00
04923 *Headin' For Texas And Home* ...... 8.00 - 12.00
04961 *Let Me Build A Cabin* .... 8.00 - 12.00

ROLLING STONES:
Victor V40316 *Down By The Old Rio Grande* ... 15.00 - 20.00

POSEY RORER & THE NORTH CAROLINA RAMBLERS:
Edison (thin) 11009 *A Wild And Reckless Hobo* .. — - —
20005 *As We Sat Beneath The Maple On The Hill* .... — - —
(Note: The above two discs were never officially
released, but copies may have gotten out.)
Edison (thick) 52414 *As We Sat Beneath The*
Maple On The Hill .... 50.00 - 75.00

ROSE FAMILY:
Bluebird 5004, 5036, 5074 .... 4.00 - 7.00
JACK ROSE:
Okeh 45370 *Jack And Babe Blues* .... 10.00 - 15.00
ROSS' RHYTHM RASCALS:
Decca 5344, 5384, 5399, 5410, 5446, 5480, 5512,
5528 .... 5.00 - 10.00
CARTER ROWLAND & SON:
Vocalion 5349 *Cotton-Eyed Joe* .... 20.00 - 30.00
GEORGE RUNNELS:
Champion 15394 *Write A Letter To My Mother* .. 15.00 - 25.00
FLOYD RUSSELL:
Supertone 9167 *Coal Creek March* .... 7.00 - 10.00
RUSTIC REVELERS:
Decca 5059 *Dixie Get Together* .... 7.00 - 10.00
5062 *Chicken Reel* .... 7.00 - 10.00
5063 *Fiddlin' Away* .... 7.00 - 10.00

RUTHERFORD & BURNETT/FOSTER/

MOORE:
Brunswick 490 *Six Months Ain't Long* .... 15.00 - 20.00
581 *My Boyhood Happy Days* .... 15.00 - 20.00
Gennett 6688 *Under The Pale Moonlight* ...... 25.00 - 40.00
6746 *Let Her Go, I'll Meet Her* .... 25.00 - 40.00
6760 *Good Night Waltz* .... 25.00 - 40.00
6807 *Six Months Ain't Long* .... 25.00 - 40.00
6873 *My Carolina Home* .... 25.00 - 40.00
6913 *Taylor's Quickstep* .... 25.00 - 40.00
6976 *Richmond Blues* .... 25.00 - 40.00
Superior 2640 *My Carolina Home* .... 50.00 - 75.00

J.P./JOE RYAN:
Champion 16342 *It Just Suits Me* .... 25.00 - 40.00
Gennett 7006 *Bed Bug Groan* .... 30.00 - 50.00
7140 *Worried Daddy Blues* .... 30.00 - 50.00
Supertone 9542 *Sad And Lonely Blues* .... 15.00 - 20.00

SADDLE TRAMPS:
Vocalion 03609, 03649, 03940, 04037 .... 4.00 - 8.00

SALEM HIGHBALLERS:
Okeh 45455 *Going On To Town* .... 15.00 - 20.00

CURLEY SANDERS:
Talent 749 *Last On Your List* .... 7.00 - 10.00

DILLIARD SANDERS:
Supertone 9247 *I'll Never Be Yours* .... 8.00 - 12.00

IRENE SANDERS (Acc. by AARON CAMPBELL'S MOUNTAINEERS):
Champion 16719 *Fond Affection* .... 40.00 - 60.00
45056 *Fond Affection* .... 10.00 - 15.00

LITTLE TOMMIE SANDS:
Freedom 5022 *Syrup Soppin' Blues* .... 7.00 - 10.00

SANDY CREEK WOOD CHOPPERS:
Supertone 9543 *Huskin' Bee* .... 7.00 - 10.00
9680 *Polly Wolly Doodle* .... 7.00 - 10.00

SANFORD & McCONNELL:
Victor 23765 *Over The Bar* .... 10.00 - 15.00

SAXTON BROTHERS:
Superior 2537 *Going-A-Courtin'* .... 25.00 - 35.00

JIMMIE SCOTT:
Star Talent 781 *Rocky Road* .... 7.00 - 10.00

RAMBLIN' TOMMY SCOTT:
Macy's 130 *Smoky Mountain Sunset* .... 5.00 - 8.00

SCOTT COUNTY TRIO:
Supertone 9308 *Silvery Bell* .... 5.00 - 8.00

SCOTTSDALE STRING BAND:
Okeh 45074 *Aunt Hager's Blues* .... 15.00 - 20.00
45103 *Chinese Breakdown* .... 10.00 - 15.00
45118 *Stone Mountain Wobble* .... 10.00 - 15.00
45142 *Carolina Glide* .... 10.00 - 15.00
45158 *Hiawatha Breakdown* .... 10.00 - 15.00
45173 *Scottdale Stomp* .... 10.00 - 15.00
45188 *Down Yonder* .... 10.00 - 15.00
45201 *Goin' Crazy Blues* .... 15.00 - 20.00
45256 *Share 'Em* .... 15.00 - 20.00
45279 *Silver Bell* .... 15.00 - 20.00
45341 *Coughdrop Blues* .... 20.00 - 30.00
45352 *The Moonshiner's Waltz* .... 20.00 - 30.00
45379 *Honolulu Moon* .... 20.00 - 30.00
45509 *Japanese Breakdown* .... 25.00 - 40.00
45527 *Charleston Wobble* .... 35.00 - 50.00

SCOTTY THE DRIFTER:
Decca 5296 *Gooseberry Pie* .... 7.00 - 10.00

LISTON SCROGGINS:
Brunswick 378 *Goodbye To Friends And Home* .. 8.00 - 12.00

JOHN SEAGLE---LEONARD STOKES:
Victor 22060 *Life's Railway To Heaven* .... 7.00 - 10.00
22289 *Will There Be Any Stars* .... 7.00 - 10.00

(UNCLE) JIM SEANY:
Challenge 324 *The Poor Tramp Has To Live* .... 7.00 - 10.00
398 *The Poor Tramp Has To Live* .... 7.00 - 10.00
Champion 15222 *Kenney Wagner's Surrender* ... 8.00 - 12.00
15233 *Sweet Bunch Of Violets* .... 8.00 - 12.00

JILSON SETTERS:

Victor 21353 *The Wild Wagoner* .... 10.00 - 15.00
   21407 *Forked Deer* .... 8.00 - 12.00
   21635 *Way Up On Clinch Mountain* .... 10.00 - 15.00
   V40025 *Wild Horse Of Stoney Point* .... 15.00 - 20.00
   V40127 *Black Eyed Susie* .... 15.00 - 20.00

BILL SHAFER:
Vocalion 5413 *Kicking Mule* .... 10.00 - 15.00

"TED" SHARP, HINMAN & SHARP:
Champion 16712 *Hell Among The Yearlings* ..... 30.00 - 50.00
   16739 *Where's My Other Foot* .... 30.00 - 50.00
   16766 *Goin' On Up To Town* .... 30.00 - 50.00
   45002, 45012, 45182 .... 10.00 - 15.00

BERT/BURT SHAW:
Superior 2733 *Pea Pickin' Papa* .... 75.00 - 100.00
   2760 *Doggone Them Blues* .... 80.00 - 120.00
   2805 *Ninety-Nine Years* .... 75.00 - 100.00

MIKE SHAW & HIS ALABAMA
ENTERTAINERS:
Okeh 45518 *Tennessee River Bottom Blues* ...... 35.00 - 50.00
   45529 *Going Crazy* .... 35.00 - 50.00

SHELOR FAMILY:
Victor 20865 *Big Bend Gal* .... 10.00 - 15.00

SHELTON BROTHERS (BOB & JOE):
Decca 5079, 5087, 5099, 5100, 5135, 5137, 5161,
5170, 5173, 5177, 5180, 5184, 5187, 5190, 5198,
5219, 5244, 5261, 5339, 5353, 5367, 5381,
5397, 5409, 5422, 5440, 5456, 5471, 5475,
5484, 5496, 5508, 5519, 5533 .... 5.00 - 10.00

B.F. SHELTON:
Victor V40107 *Cold Penitentiary Blues* .... 30.00 - 50.00

BILL SHEPARD (Acc. by SHEPARD BROS. &
ED WEBB):
Champion 16383 *Aunt Jane Blues* .... 50.00 - 75.00

ARKEY SHIBLEY:
Gilt-Edge 5021, 5030 .... 5.00 - 10.00

UNCLE JOE SHIPPEE:
Pathe 21164 *Old Time Fiddler* .... 7.00 - 10.00
Perfect 11237 *Old Time Fiddler* .... 7.00 - 10.00

EARL SHIRKEY & ROY HARPER:
15376-D *Poor Little Joe* .... 25.00 - 40.00
15490-D *My Yodeling Sweetheart* .... 30.00 - 50.00
15535-D *The Virginian Strike of '23* .... 30.00 - 50.00
15642-D *We Have Moonshine In The West*
   Virginia Hills .... 50.00 - 75.00

CHESLEY SHIRLEY (THE TEXAS
RAMBLER):
Champion 16826 *The Last Great Roundup* ...... 25.00 - 40.00
   45075 *Only Flirting* .... 8.00 - 12.00

SHORE'S SOUTHERN TRIO:
Gennett 6842 *Whistling Rufus* .... 25.00 - 40.00
   6927 *Goin' Crazy* .... 25.00 - 40.00

BILL SHORES & MELVIN DUPREE:
Columbia 15506-D *West Texas Breakdown* ...... 20.00 - 35.00

SHORT BROTHERS:
Okeh 45206 *Whistling Coon* .... 10.00 - 15.00

SHORT CREEK TRIO:
Gennett 6272 *Hand Me Down My Walking Cane* 10.00 - 15.00
   6364 *The Buckin' Mule* .... 10.00 - 15.00

CHIEF SHUNATONA, ET AL. (See CHIEF)...

CONNIE SIDES:
Columbia 15009-D *In The Shadow Of The Pine* . 8.00 - 12.00

BILL SIMMON (S' COWBOYS):
Victor 23533 *The Cowboy's Plea* .... 15.00 - 20.00
   23603 *Rocky Mountain Blues* .... 15.00 - 20.00

MATT SIMMONS & FRANK MILLER:
Okeh 45148 *That Little Old Hut* .... 7.00 - 1.00

OLIVER SIMS:
Columbia 15103-D *Lost John* .... 10.00 - 15.00

ALLEN SISSON:
Edison 51522 *Farewell Ducktown-Reel* .... 8.00 - 12.00
   51559 *Walking Water* .... 8.00 - 12.00
   51690 *Katy Hill-Reel* .... 8.00 - 12.00
   51720 *Gray Eagle-Reel* .... 8.00 - 12.00

ASHER SIZEMORE (& LITTLE JIMMY):
Bluebird 5445 *Goodbye To Jimmie Rodgers* ..... 30.00 - 50.00
   5495 *Cowboy Jim* .... 25.00 - 40.00
Bluebird 5568 *Shake Hands With Mother* ...... 25.00 - 40.00
Bluebird 5717 *My West Virginia Home* .... 25.00 - 40.00
Bluebird 5774 *Memories Of Kentucky* .... 25.00 - 40.00
Bluebird 6021 *I Dreamed I Searched* .... 25.00 - 40.00

BILL SKIDMORE:
Columbia 15761-D *Behind The Big White House* 10.00 - 15.00

BOB SKILES (4 OLD TUNERS):
Okeh 45211 *Rye Waltz* .... 5.00 - 10.00
   45225 *Casey Jones* .... 5.00 - 10.00
   45243 *Wagner* .... 5.00 - 8.00

SKYLAND & SCOTTY:
Bluebird 5357 *Great Grandad* .... 15.00 - 20.00
   5906 *Two Little Frogs* .... 10.00 - 15.00

BOB SKYLES & HIS SKYROCKETS:
Bluebird (most issues) .... 4.00 - 8.00

SLOAN & THREADGILL:
Brunswick 284 *Clover Blossoms* .... 8.00 - 12.00
   299 *When The Harvest Is Shining* .... 8.00 - 12.00

LESTER SMALLWOOD:
Victor V40181 *Cotton Mill Girl* .... 40.00 - 60.00

(DR.) SMITH'S (CHAMPION) HOSS HAIR
PULLERS:
Victor 21711 *Going Down The River* .... 40.00 - 60.00
   V40059 *Save My Mother's Picture From The*
   Sale .... 40.00 - 60.00
   V40124 *Just Give Me The Leavings* .... 40.00 - 60.00

SMITH'S GARAGE FIDDLE BAND:
Vocalion 5268 *Beaumont Rag* .... 25.00 - 40.00
   5287 *Done Gone* .... 25.00 - 40.00
   5306 *Dill Pickle Rag* .... 25.00 - 40.00
   5336 *Miss Lola* .... 25.00 - 40.00
   5375 *Tom & Jerry* .... 25.00 - 40.00

SMITH & WOODLIEFF:
Gennett 6809 *The Old Schoolhouse Playground* . 30.00 - 50.00
   6840 *I Ain't Gonna Grieve My Lord Anymore* . 30.00 - 50.00
   6858 *I'd Rather Be With Rosy Nell* .... 30.00 - 50.00

ARTHUR SMITH (TRIO) (& HIS DIXIE
LINERS):
Bluebird 5896 *Blackberry Blossom* .... 7.00 - 10.00
   6322 *Chittlin' Cookin' Time* .... 7.00 - 10.00
   6369 *Cheatham County Breakdown* .... 7.00 - 10.00
   6442 *Fiddler's Blues* .... 7.00 - 10.00
   6514 *Take Me Back To Tennessee* .... 7.00 - 10.00
   6844 *Florida Blues* .... 7.00 - 10.00
   6869 *Never Alone* .... 7.00 - 10.00
   6913 *The Girl I Love Don't Pay Me No Mind* . 7.00 - 10.00
   6927 *Sugar Tree Stomp* .... 7.00 - 10.00
   6994 *It's Hard To Please Your Mind* .... 7.00 - 10.00
   7043 *Walking In My Sleep* .... 7.00 - 10.00
   7146 *Lonesome For You* .... 5.00 - 8.00
   7203 *Beautiful Memories* .... 5.00 - 8.00
   7221 *Across The Blue Ridge Mountains* ...... 5.00 - 8.00
   7325 *Nellie's Blues Eyes* .... 5.00 - 8.00
   7351 *Cheatham County Breakdown No. 2* ..... 7.00 - 10.00
   7437 *Answer To More Pretty Girls Than One* .. 7.00 - 10.00
   7498 *Henpecked Husband Blues* .... 7.00 - 10.00
   7511 *Smith's Breakdown* .... 7.00 - 10.00

7547 *Her Little Brown Hand* . . . . 7.00 - 10.00
7651 *Lost Love* . . . . 7.00 - 10.00
7893 *The Gypsy's Warning* . . . . 7.00 - 10.00
7943 *Why Should I Wonder?* . . . . 7.00 - 10.00
7982 *Give Me Old Time Music* . . . . 5.00 - 8.00
Bluebird (higher numbers) . . . . 4.00 - 7.00

BLAINE & CAL SMITH:
Vocalion 04705, 04855, 04976 . . . . 5.00 - 10.00

CHARLES B. SMITH:
Columbia 15755-D *Walkin' Georgia Rose* . . . . . . 15.00 - 20.00

HANK SMITH:
Vocalion 5318 *Eleven Cent Cotton And Forty
Cent Meat* . . . . 10.00 - 15.00

HARRY SMITH:
Okeh 45260 *The Death Of Floyd Collins* . . . . . . 10.00 - 15.00

TRAVELIN' J. SMITH:
Columbia 15547-D *So I Joined The Navy* . . . . . . 7.00 - 10.00

JIMMIE SMITH:
Timely Tunes 1556 *She's A Low Down Mama* . . . 75.00 - 100.00
1557 *There's A Good Gal In The Mountains* . . . 75.00 - 100.00

JOE SMITH (THE COLORADO COWBOY):
Bluebird 5522 *John Dillinger* . . . . 5.00 - 8.00
5530 *Pining For The Pines In Caroline* . . . . . . 5.00 - 8.00
5651 *That Silver-Haired Mother* . . . . 5.00 - 8.00
Champion 15808 *The Talkin' Blues* . . . . 8.00 - 12.00
45173 *Born In Hard Luck* . . . . 5.00 - 8.00

KID SMITH'S FAMILY:
Victor 23576 *Little Bessie* . . . . 35.00 - 50.00
Vocalion 03414 *I'm Not Angry With You Darling* . 10.00 - 15.00
03415 *Mississippi Freight Train Blues* . . . . 10.00 - 15.00
03443 *Ten Is Served And Ten To Serve* . . . . . . 10.00 - 15.00

MARSHALL SMITH:
Columbia 15080-D *Jonah And The Whale* . . . . . 5.00 - 8.00

(MERRITT) SMITH & (KEITH) POOSER:
Okeh 45318 *Carolina Moon* . . . . 5.00 - 8.00
45326 *Softly And Tenderly* . . . . 5.00 - 8.00
45362 *The Lonesome Road* . . . . 5.00 - 8.00
45474 *Death Is Only A Dream* . . . . 5.00 - 8.00

MERRITT SMITH & LEO BOSWELL:
Champion 16335 *On The Banks Of The
Brandywine* . . . . 7.00 - 10.00
16344 *Oh Mary Don't You Weep* . . . . 7.00 - 10.00
16433 *Daisies Never Tell* . . . . 7.00 - 10.00
Columbia 15748-D *Try Not To Forget* . . . . 8.00 - 12.00

R.B. SMITH & S.J. ALLGOOD:
Okeh 45010 *American And Spanish Fandango* . . . 10.00 - 15.00

SLIM SMITH:
Crown 3118 *Bread Line Blues* . . . . 15.00 - 20.00
Victor 23526 *Bread Line Blues* . . . . 10.00 - 15.00
Vocalion 05082 *Sad And Alone* . . . . 8.00 - 12.00

WALTER SMITH:
Gennett 6825 *The Cat's Got The Measles, The
Dogs Got The Whoopin' Cough* . . . . 20.00 - 30.00

SMOKY MOUNTAIN BOYS:
Gennett 6871 *The Smoky Mountain Boys At The
Still* . . . . 25.00 - 40.00

SMOKY MOUNTAIN FIDDLER TRIO:
Bluebird 6387 *Bonaparte's Retreat* . . . . 5.00 - 8.00

SMOKY MOUNTAIN RAMBLERS:
Vocalion 5422 *San Antonio* . . . . 30.00 - 50.00
5437 *Bear Mountain Rag* . . . . 30.00 - 50.00
5451 *Born In Tennessee* . . . . 30.00 - 50.00

SMYTH'S COUNTY RAMBLERS:
Victor V40144 *Way Down In Alabama* . . . . 50.00 - 75.00

**(LEO) SOILEAU & LAFLEUR/(MOISE)
ROBIN:**
Decca 5101, 5102, 5116, 5117, 5133, 5157, 5182,
5210, 5215, 5236, 5262, 5279, 5299, 5326 . . . . . 5.00 - 10.00
Paramount 12808 *Easy Rider* . . . . 75.00 - 100.00
Victor 21769 *Basile* . . . . 15.00 - 25.00
21770 *The Criminal* . . . . 15.00 - 25.00
22183 *Penitentiary Waltz* . . . . 15.00 - 25.00

22207 *Grosse Mama* . . . . 15.00 - 25.00

SOLOMON & HUGHES:
Victor V40244 *Ragtime Annie* . . . . 10.00 - 15.00

SONS OF THE PIONEERS:
Decca 5013 *Ridin' Home* . . . . 8.00 - 12.00
5047 *Moonlight On The Prairie* . . . . 7.00 - 10.00
5082, 5083, 5168, 5178, 5218, 5232, 5243,
5247, 5248, 5275, 5358 . . . . 5.00 - 10.00
Vocalion 03399 *Power In The Blood* . . . . 8.00 - 12.00
03880 *Open Range Ahead* . . . . 8.00 - 12.00
03881 *Smilin' Through* . . . . 7.00 - 10.00
03916 *I Love You, Nelly* . . . . 7.00 - 10.00
04136 *Billie The Kid* . . . . 7.00 - 10.00
04187 *Hear Dem Bells* . . . . 7.00 - 10.00
04264 *Cajon Stomp* . . . . 7.00 - 10.00
04328 *Send Him Home To Me* . . . . 7.00 - 10.00

SOUTHERN KENTUCKY MOUNTAINEERS:
Supertone 9310 *Cumberland Gap* . . . . 8.00 - 12.00

SOUTHERN MOONLIGHT ENTERTAINERS:
Vocalion 5372 *My Blue Ridge Mountain Queen* . . 15.00 - 20.00
5388 *My Carolina Girl* . . . . 15.00 - 20.00
5407 *Buckin' Mule* . . . . 15.00 - 20.00
5440 *Then I'll Move To Town* . . . . 15.00 - 20.00
5460 *Lost John* . . . . 15.00 - 20.00

SOUTH GEORGIA HIGHBALLERS:
Okeh 45155 *Bibb County Grind* . . . . 35.00 - 50.00

SPANGLE & PEARSON:
Okeh 45287 *Patrick County Blues* . . . . 40.00 - 60.00

SPOONEY FIVE:
Columbia 15234-D *Chinese Rag* . . . . 15.00 - 20.00

CARL T. SPRAGUE:
Aurora 418 *Cowboy Love Song* . . . . 20.00 - 30.00
Bluebird 6258 *The Prisoner's Meditation* . . . . . . 7.00 - 10.00
Victor 19747 *Bad Companions* . . . . 5.00 - 8.00
20067 *Cowboy Love Song* . . . . 5.00 - 8.00
20122 *The Cowboy's Dream* . . . . 5.00 - 8.00
20534 *The Boston Burglar* . . . . 7.00 - 10.00
20932 *The Last Great Roundup* . . . . 7.00 - 10.00
21194 *Utah Carroll* . . . . 8.00 - 12.00
21402 *Cowman's Prayer* . . . . 8.00 - 12.00
V40066 *Here's To The Texas Ranger* . . . . 10.00 - 15.00
V40197 *The Last Longhorn* . . . . 10.00 - 15.00
V40246 *The Wayward Daughter* . . . . 10.00 - 15.00

FRED STANLEY:
Columbia 15559-D *The Tie That Binds* . . . . 8.00 - 12.00

JOHN STANLEY'S ORCHESTRA:
Superior 2691 *Moonshiner's Serenade* . . . . 25.00 - 40.00

ROBA STANLEY & WILLIAM PATTERSON:
Okeh 40213 *Devilish Mary* . . . . 10.00 - 15.00
45036 *Old Maid Blues* . . . . 10.00 - 15.00

STANTON'S JOY BOYS:
Superior 2671 *Huskin' Bee* . . . . 35.00 - 50.00

FRANK STANTON:
Superior 2521 *Creole Girl* . . . . 35.00 - 50.00
2544 *Poor Old Dad* . . . . 35.00 - 50.00

STAPLETON BROTHERS:
Columbia 15284-D *In A Cool Shady Nook* . . . . . 8.00 - 12.00
Victor 23591 *Won't You Take Me Back Again* . . . 20.00 - 30.00

STEAMBOAT BILL & HIS GUITAR:
Champion 15674 *No, No, Blues* . . . . 10.00 - 15.00
15694 *Weak Minded Blues* . . . . 10.00 - 15.00
15752 *Boston Burglar* . . . . 10.00 - 15.00

JOE STEEN:
Bluebird 5567 *I'll Love Ya Till The Cows
Come Home* . . . . 5.00 - 8.00
Champion 16258 *Railroad Jack* . . . . 10.00 - 15.00
Victor 23634 *Crazy Engineer* . . . . 20.00 - 30.00

UNCLE "BUNT" STEPHENS:
Columbia 15071-D *Louisburg Blues* . . . . 10.00 - 15.00
15085-D *Left In The Dark Blues* . . . . 10.00 - 15.00

STEVE'S HOT SHOTS:
Victor 23699 *Sour Apple Cider* . . . . 30.00 - 50.00

V40308 *The Press* .... 20.00 - 30.00

OTIS STEWART:
Supertone 9242 *Adam And Eve* .... 8.00 - 12.00

CHARLES LEWIS STINE:
Columbia 15027-D *The Wreck On The C & O* ... 7.00 - 10.00

STOKES, MILLER, McKINNEY, MARTIN, WILLIAMS & BROWN:
Brunswick 422 *The Great Hatfield-McCoy Feud, Part 1/2* .... 15.00 - 20.00
423 *The Great Hatfield-McCoy Feud, Part 3/4* 15.00 - 20.00

LEONARD STOKES:
Bluebird 7349 *Will You Miss Me When I'm Gone* 7.00 - 10.00
7401 *There's A Green Hill Far Away* .... 5.00 - 8.00
Electradisk 1920 *He's Too Far Gone* .... 8.00 - 12.00

LOWE STOKES & HIS NORTH GEORGIANS/ POT LUCKERS; LOWE STOKES & RILEY PUCKETT/MIKE WHITTEN:
Brunswick 491 *Prohibition Is A Failure* .... 20.00 - 30.00
549 *Four Cent Cotton* .... 20.00 - 30.00
Columbia 15241-D *Home Brew Rag* .... 25.00 - 40.00
15369-D *Wave That Frame* .... 25.00 - 40.00
15486-D *Take Me Back To Georgia* .... 30.00 - 50.00
15557-D *Left All Alone Again Blues* .... 30.00 - 50.00
15620-D *Everybody's Doing It* .... 40.00 - 60.00
15660-D *Bone Dry Blues* .... 50.00 - 75.00
15693-D *Sailing On The Robert E. Lee* ... 50.00 - 75.00

JIMMY STONE:
Imperial 8137 *Midnight Boogie* .... 7.00 - 10.00

STONEMAN FAMILY:
Victor V40030 *Broken-Hearted Lover* .... 15.00 - 20.00
V40116 *Going Up The Mountain After Liquor* .. 15.00 - 20.00
V40206 *Too Late* .... 15.00 - 20.00

MR. & MRS. ERNEST V. STONEMAN & HIS DIXIE MOUNTAINEERS/GRAYSON COUNTY BOYS; ERNEST V. STONEMAN (TRIO) (& FIDDLER JOE):
Banner 1993 *Hand Me Down My Walking Cane* .. 5.00 - 8.00
2157 *Pass Around The Bottle* .... 5.00 - 8.00
2158 *It's Sinful To Flirt* .... 5.00 - 8.00
Broadway 8054 *Pass Around The Bottle* .... 5.00 - 8.00
8055 *Hand Me Down My Walking Cane* ... 5.00 - 8.00
Challenge 151 *Katy Cline* .... 5.00 - 8.00
152 *Barney McCoy* .... 5.00 - 8.00
153 *Silver Bell* .... 5.00 - 8.00
309 *Barney McCoy* .... 5.00 - 8.00
312 *May I Sleep In Your Barn Tonight Mister* .. 5.00 - 8.00
665 *Pass Around The Bottle* .... 5.00 - 8.00
Conqueror 7064 *Pass Around The Bottle* .... 5.00 - 8.00
7755 *Bully Of The Town* .... 5.00 - 8.00
Domino 0187 *The Old Hickory Cane* ...... 5.00 - 8.00
3964 *Hand Me Down My Walking Cane* ...... 5.00 - 8.00
3984 *The Fatal Wedding* .... 5.00 - 8.00
3985 *Pass Around The Bottle* .... 5.00 - 8.00
Edison (thin) 20004 *He Is Coming After Me* .... -
(There is some question as to whether the above disc was issued.)
Edison (thick) 51788 *Bad Companions* .... 20.00 - 30.00
51864 *Watermelon Hanging On The Vine* ..... 20.00 - 30.00
51869 *Wild Bill Jones* .... 20.00 - 30.00
51909 *Bury Me Beneath The Weeping Willow Tree* .... 20.00 - 30.00
51935 *Once I Had A Fortune* .... 20.00 - 30.00
51938 *Hand Me Down My Walking Cane* ..... 20.00 - 30.00
51951 *Bully Of The Town* .... 20.00 - 30.00
51994 *Kitty Wells* .... 20.00 - 30.00
52026 *The Fate Of Talmadge Osborne* ...... 20.00 - 30.00
52077 *The Orphan Girl* .... 20.00 - 30.00
52290 *When The Redeemed Are Gathered In* .. 20.00 - 30.00
52299 *Unlucky Road To Washington* ..... 25.00 - 40.00
52312 *Down On The Banks Of The Ohio* ..... 25.00 - 40.00
52350 *All Go Hungry Hash House* .... 25.00 - 40.00
52369 *The Old Maid And The Burglar* ..... 25.00 - 40.00

52386 *It's Sinful To Flirt* .... 25.00 - 40.00
52461 *The Prisoner's Lament* .... 30.00 - 50.00
52479 *He Is Coming After Me* .... 30.00 - 50.00
52489 *All I've Got's Gone* .... 30.00 - 50.00
Gennett 3368 *May I Sleep In Your Barn Tonight Mister?* .... 7.00 - 10.00
3369 *Pretty Snow Deer* .... 7.00 - 10.00
3381 *Barney McCoy* .... 7.00 - 10.00
6044 *Kenney Wagner's Surrender* .... 10.00 - 15.00
6052 *Long Eared Mule* .... 10.00 - 15.00
6065 *Sweet Bunch Of Violets* .... 10.00 - 15.00
Herwin 75528 *Barney McCoy* .... 20.00 - 30.00
75529 *Silver Bell* .... 20.00 - 30.00
75530 *Pretty Snow Deer* .... 20.00 - 30.00
75535 *The Poor Tramp Has To Live* .... 20.00 - 30.00
75541 *Sweet Bunch Of Violets* .... 20.00 - 30.00
Homestead 16490 *Pass Around The Bottle* ...... 20.00 - 30.00
16498 *The Fatal Wedding* .... 20.00 - 30.00
16500 *Bully Of The Town* .... 20.00 - 30.00
Okeh 7011 (12-inch) *John Hardy* .... 35.00 - 50.00
40288 *The Titanic* .... 10.00 - 15.00
40312 *Freckled Face Mary Jane* .... 10.00 - 15.00
40384 *Dying Girl's Farewell* .... 10.00 - 15.00
40405 *The Long Eared Mule* .... 10.00 - 15.00
40408 *The Lightning Express* .... 10.00 - 15.00
40430 *Uncle Sam And The Kaiser* ...... 10.00 - 15.00
45009 *All I've Got's Gone* .... 10.00 - 15.00
45015 *The Fancy Ball* .... 10.00 - 15.00
45036 *The Kicking Mule* .... 10.00 - 15.00
45044 *Asleep At The Switch* .... 10.00 - 15.00
45048 *In The Shadow Of The Pine* ...... 10.00 - 15.00
45051 *The Religious Critic* .... 10.00 - 15.00
45054 *The Texas Ranger* .... 10.00 - 15.00
45059 *The Old Hickory Cane* .... 10.00 - 15.00
45060 *My Pretty Snow Dear* .... 10.00 - 15.00
45062 *The All Go Hungry Hash House* ...... 10.00 - 15.00
45065 *Katie Cline* .... 10.00 - 15.00
45084 *The Fatal Wedding* .... 10.00 - 15.00
45094 *Lonesome Road Blues* .... 10.00 - 15.00
45125 *The Mountaineer's Courtship* .... 10.00 - 15.00
Paramount 3021 *Pass Around The Bottle* .... 5.00 - 8.00
Pathe-Actuelle 32271 *The Old Hickory Cane* ... 5.00 - 8.00
32278 *The Fatal Wedding* .... 5.00 - 8.00
32279 *Bully Of The Town* .... 5.00 - 8.00
Perfect 12350 *Sinful To Flirt* .... 5.00 - 8.00
12357 *Pass Around The Bottle* .... 5.00 - 8.00
12358 *Bully Of The Town* .... 5.00 - 8.00
Regal 8324 *Hand Me Down My Walking Cane* ... 5.00 - 8.00
8346 *Sinful To Flirt* .... 5.00 - 8.00
8347 *The Fatal Wedding* .... 5.00 - 8.00
8369 *The Old Hickory Cane* .... 5.00 - 8.00
Romeo 597 *Bully Of The Town* .... 5.00 - 8.00
600 *Sinful To Flirt* .... 5.00 - 8.00
Silvertone 5004 *Sweet Bunch Of Violets* .... 7.00 - 10.00
Supertone 9255 *The Poor Tramp Has To Live* ... 7.00 - 10.00
Victor 20223 *In The Golden Bye And Bye* ..... 7.00 - 10.00
20224 *Hallelujah Side* .... 7.00 - 10.00
20235 *The Little Old Log Cabin In The Lane* .. 7.00 - 10.00
20237 *All Go Hungry Hash House* .... 7.00 - 10.00
20294 *Sugar In The Gourd* .... 7.00 - 10.00
20302 *Old Joe Clark* .... 7.00 - 10.00
20531 *Going Down The Valley* .... 10.00 - 15.00
20532 *The Great Reaping Day* .... 10.00 - 15.00
20533 *I'll Be Satisfed* .... 10.00 - 15.00
20540 *Peekaboo* .... 10.00 - 15.00
20671 *The Story Of The Mighty Mississippi* .. 10.00 - 15.00
20672 *The Fate Of Talmadge Osborne* .... 10.00 - 15.00
20799 *The Old Hickory Cane* .... 10.00 - 15.00
20844 *Are You Washed In The Blood?* .... 10.00 - 15.00
20880 *The Mountaineer's Courtship* .... 10.00 - 15.00
21071 *I Am Resolved* .... 10.00 - 15.00
21129 *The Dying Girl's Farewell* .... 10.00 - 15.00

21186 *I Know My Name Is There*	10.00 -	15.00
21264 *Possum Trot School Exhibition*	12.00 -	18.00
21518 *Serenade In The Mountains*	12.00 -	18.00
21648 *The Raging Sea, How It Roars*	12.00 -	18.00
V40078 *There's A Light Lit Up In Galilee*	15.00 -	20.00
Vocalion 02632 *Texas Ranger*	20.00 -	30.00
02655 *Nine Pound Hammer*	20.00 -	30.00
02901 *All I Got's Gone*	20.00 -	30.00

WILLIE STONEMAN:

Gennett 6565 *Katy Lee*	15.00 -	25.00

STONE MOUNTAIN BOYS:

Supertone 9456 *Makin' Licker In North Carolina*	10.00 -	15.00

STONE MOUNTAIN ENTERTAINERS:

Broadway 8159 *Red Wing*	6.00 -	10.00

STONE MOUNTAIN TRIO:

Brunswick 543 *Maple Leaf Waltz*	10.00 -	15.00
Vocalion 5457 *Stone Mountain Waltz*	10.00 -	15.00

SMOKEY STOVER:

Specialty 715 *What A Shame*	—	—

DICK STRATTON & THE NITE OWLS:

Tennessee 795 *Pistol Boogie*	—	—

HARLEY STRATTON:

Superior 2588 *The Red River Valley*	15.00 -	20.00

STRIPLING BROTHERS:

Decca 5018, 5019, 5041, 5049, 5069, 5207, 5246, 5267, 5291, 5313, 5417	5.00 -	10.00
Melotone 12173 *Moonlight Waltz*	5.00 -	8.00
12181 *Big Footed Nigger In The Sandy Lot*	5.00 -	8.00
Vocalion 02738 *June Rose Waltz*	30.00 -	50.00
02739 *Coal Mine Blues*	30.00 -	50.00
5321 *The Lost Child*	20.00 -	30.00
5365 *Railroad Bum*	20.00 -	30.00
5366 *Red River Waltz*	20.00 -	30.00
5382 *New Born Blues*	20.00 -	30.00
5395 *Dance All Night With A Bottle In My Hand*	20.00 -	30.00
5412 *Wolves Howling*	25.00 -	40.00
5441 *Lost John*	25.00 -	40.00
5453 *Coal Mine Blues*	25.00 -	40.00
5468 *Midnight Waltz*	25.00 -	40.00

UNCLE "AM" STUART:

Vocalion 5035 *Cumberland Gap*	8.00 -	12.00
5036 *Sourwood Mountain*	8.00 -	12.00
5037 *Leather Breeches*	8.00 -	12.00
5038 *Billie In The Low Ground*	8.00 -	12.00
5039 *Forked Deer*	8.00 -	12.00
5048 *Dixie*	8.00 -	12.00
5053 *George Boker*	8.00 -	12.00
14839 *Cumberland Gap*	8.00 -	12.00
14840 *Sourwood Mountain*	8.00 -	12.00
14841 *Leather Breeches*	8.00 -	12.00
14843 *Billie In The Low Ground*	8.00 -	12.00
14846 *Forked Deer*	8.00 -	12.00
14888 *Dixie*	8.00 -	12.00
14919 *George Boker*	8.00 -	12.00

SUE & RAWHIDE (Acc. by THE CRAZY HILLBILLIES BAND):

Okeh 45577 *Falling Leaf*	25.00 -	40.00

SWAMP ROOTERS:

Brunswick 556 *Swamp Cat Rag*	15.00 -	20.00

SWEET BROTHERS:

Gennett 6620 *I Got A Bull Dog*	20.00 -	30.00
6655 *Falling By The Wayside*	20.00 -	30.00

HERBERT SWEET:

Gennett 6567 *The Prisoner's Lament*	15.00 -	20.00

SWEET VIOLET BOYS:

Vocalion 03110, 03218, 03219, 03256, 03281, 03327, 03402, 03587, 03663, 03766, 04010, 04428, 04528, 04714, 04756	5.00 -	10.00

SWING BILLIES:

Bluebird 7121, 7143, 7161, 7338	4.00 -	7.00

CHARLES ROSS TAGGART:

Edison 51001 *A Country Fiddler At Home*	7.00 -	10.00
51048 *A Country Fiddler At The Telephone*	7.00 -	10.00
51448 *Sister Sorrowful*	7.00 -	10.00
Victor 18036 *Old Country Fiddler At The Party*	5.00 -	8.00

ARTHUR TANNER & HIS CORNSHUCKERS/ & RILEY PUCKETT:

Columbia 15145-D *Knoxville Girl*	15.00 -	20.00
15180-D *Two Little Children*	10.00 -	15.00
15352-D *Sleep On Blue Eyes*	10.00 -	15.00
15479-D *Dr. Ginger Blue*	30.00 -	50.00
15577-D *Gather The Flowers*	30.00 -	50.00
Paramount 3159 *Devilish Mary*	20.00 -	30.00
3160 *The Lightening Express Train*	20.00 -	30.00
3161 *The Little Old Log Cabin In The Lane*	20.00 -	30.00
3162 *The Knoxville Girl*	20.00 -	30.00
3163 *When I Was Single My Pockets Would Jingle Jingle*	20.00 -	30.00
Silvertone 3514 *The Burglar Man*	15.00 -	20.00
3515 *The Knoxville Girl*	15.00 -	20.00

GID TANNER & HIS GEORGIA BOYS/SKILLET LICKERS; GID TANNER & FATE NORRIS/RILEY PUCKETT; TANNER, McMICHEN, PUCKETT, STOKES & NORRIS:

Bluebird 5433 *Mississippi Sawyer*	10.00 -	15.00
5434 *Cumberland Gap On A Buckin' Mule*	10.00 -	15.00
5435 *Skillet Licker Breakdown*	10.00 -	15.00
5446 *Prosperity And Politics*	10.00 -	15.00
5488 *Ida Red*	10.00 -	15.00
5559 *Practice Night With The Skillet Lickers*	10.00 -	15.00
5562 *Down Yonder*	8.00 -	12.00
5591 *Cotton Patch*	10.00 -	15.00
5633 *Hinkey-Dinkey-Dee*	10.00 -	15.00
5657 *Tanner's Rag*	10.00 -	15.00
5658 *Soldier's Joy*	8.00 -	12.00
5665 *On Tanner's Farm*	10.00 -	15.00
5748 *Three Nights Drunk*	10.00 -	15.00
5805 *I Ain't No Better Now*	10.00 -	15.00
Columbia 119-D *Black Eyed Susie*	8.00 -	12.00
15010-D *Don't Grieve Your Mother*	10.00 -	15.00
15017-D *Fox Chase*	10.00 -	15.00
15019-D *Georgia Railroad*	10.00 -	15.00
15059-D *Just Gimme The Leavings*	10.00 -	15.00
15084-D *Turkey In The Straw*	7.00 -	10.00
15091-D *Hand Me Down My Walking Cane*	7.00 -	10.00
15104-D *Alabama Jubilee*	10.00 -	15.00
15105-D *Goodbye, Booze*	10.00 -	15.00
15108-D *Old Joe Clark*	10.00 -	15.00
15123-D *Shortening Bread*	10.00 -	15.00
15134-D *I Got Mine*	10.00 -	15.00
15142-D *John Henry*	10.00 -	15.00
15158-D *Dixie*	10.00 -	15.00
15165-D *Football Rag*	15.00 -	20.00
15170-D *The Old Gray Mare*	10.00 -	15.00
15188-D *The Darktown Strutters Ball*	10.00 -	15.00
15200-D *She'll Be Coming 'Round The Mountain*	10.00 -	15.00
15204-D *Big Ball In Town*	15.00 -	20.00
15217-D *Please Do Not Get Offended*	10.00 -	15.00
15221-D *Uncle Bud*	10.00 -	15.00
15237-D *Casey Jones*	10.00 -	15.00
15249-D *Bile Them Cabbage Down*	10.00 -	15.00
15267-D *Slow Buck*	10.00 -	15.00
15283-D *Cotton-Eyed Joe*	10.00 -	15.00
*15298-D *Possum Hunt On Stump Mountain*	10.00 -	15.00
15303-D *Cumberland Gap*	8.00 -	12.00
15315-D *Settin' In The Chimney Jamb*	8.00 -	12.00
15334-D *Liberty*	10.00 -	15.00
15382-D *Old Dan Tucker*	10.00 -	15.00
15404-D *Cotton Baggin'*	15.00 -	20.00
15420-D *Mississippi Sawyer*	15.00 -	20.00
15447-D *The Rovin' Gambler*	15.00 -	20.00

*15468-D *Hog Killing Day* .... 15.00 - 20.00
15472-D *Flatwoods* .... 15.00 - 20.00
15485-D *Cripple Creek* .... 15.00 - 20.00
15516-D *Hell's Broke Loose In Georgia* ..... 20.00 - 30.00
15562-D *Sal's Gone To The Cider Mill* ...... 20.00 - 30.00
15589-D *Devilish Mary* .... 20.00 - 30.00
15612-D *Sugar In The Gourd* .... 20.00 - 30.00
15623-D *New Arkansas Traveler* .... 20.00 - 30.00
15640-D *Bully Of The Town No. 2* .... 25.00 - 40.00
15665-D *Don't You Cry My Honey* .... 25.00 - 40.00
15682-D *Ricketts Hornpipe* .... 25.00 - 40.00
15695-D *Giddup Napoleon* .... 30.00 - 50.00
15709-D *Fly Around My Pretty Little Miss* .... 30.00 - 50.00
15716-D *You've Got To Stop Drinking 'Shine* .. 30.00 - 50.00
15730-D *Miss McLeod's Reel* .... 30.00 - 50.00
15746-D *Four Cent Cotton* .... 40.00 - 60.00
15777-D *McMichen's Breakdown* .... 50.00 - 80.00
(These "descriptive novelty" records credit
several or more artists on the labels; since
Tanner's name appears first, they are listed
here.)

LUCY TANNER & THE SKILLET LICKERS:
Columbia 15538-D *Rock That Cradle Lucy* ..... 20.00 - 30.00

JIMMIE TARLTON (& DARBY); LOUISE J. TARLTON:
Columbia 15629-D *New Birmingham Jail* ...... 50.00 - 75.00
15651-D *Moonshine Blues* .... 75.00 - 100.00
15763-D *By The Old Oaken Bucket* .... 80.00 - 120.00
Montgomery Ward 4335 *Once I Had A Fortune* . 10.00 - 15.00
Victor 23665 *Dixie Jail* .... 100.00 - 150.00
23680 *13 Years In Kilby Prison* ...... 100.00 - 150.00
23700 *Ooze Up To Me* .... 100.00 - 150.00

TATE BROTHERS & (RHODA) HICKS:
Champion 15965 *Medley* .... 10.00 - 15.00
Gennett 7165 *Medley* .... 15.00 - 20.00

TAYLOR'S KENTUCKY BOYS:
Gennett 6130 *Forked Deer* .... 50.00 - 75.00

TAYLOR'S (LOUISIANA) MELODY MAKERS:
Victor 21768 *Big Ball Uptown* .... 15.00 - 20.00
23613 *'Mid The Shamrock Of Shannon* ...... 20.00 - 30.00
V40261 *On The Bridge At Midnight* .... 20.00 - 30.00

TAYLOR & BUNCH:
Supertone 9352 *Six Months Ain't Long* .... 8.00 - 12.00

TAYLOR-GRIGGS LOUISIANA MELODY MAKERS:
Victor V40083 *Ione* .... 20.00 - 30.00
V40184 *The Yodler's Serenade* .... 20.00 - 30.00

TAYLOR, MOORE & BURNETT:
Gennett 6760 *Knoxville Rag* .... 15.00 - 20.00

JIM TAYLOR & BILL SHELBY:
Champion 15730 *It's Sad To Leave You
Sweetheart* .... 10.00 - 15.00
15772 *The Bald-headed End Of A Broom* ..... 10.00 - 15.00
15812 *I Ain't Gonna Grieve My Lord Anymore* . 10.00 - 15.00
15855 *The Old Schoolhouse Playground* ...... 10.00 - 15.00
45072 *It's Sad To Leave You Sweetheart* ...... 7.00 - 10.00

UNCLE FRANK TEMPLETON:
Bell 1172 *Over The Waves* .... 7.00 - 10.00

TENNESSEE DRIFTERS:
Dot 1001 *Boogie Beat Rag* .... 7.00 - 10.00
1002 *Mean Ole Boogie* .... 7.00 - 10.00

TENNESSEE FIDDLERS:
Timely Tunes 1562 *Cottonwood Reel* .... 15.00 - 20.00

TENNESSEE RAMBLERS:
Brunswick 255 *Arkansas Traveler* .... 8.00 - 12.00
252 *Medley Of Mountain Songs* .... 10.00 - 15.00
257 *A Fiddlers Contest* .... 10.00 - 15.00
Vocalion 5362 *Give The Fiddler A Dram* ...... 20.00 - 30.00
5398 *In My Dear Old Sunny South* .... 20.00 - 30.00

TENNESSEE TRAVELERS:
Champion 15300 *Forked Deer* .... 25.00 - 40.00

TENNEVA RAMBLERS:

Victor 20861 *The Longest Train* .... 10.00 - 15.00
21141 *Miss Liza, Poor Gal* .... 15.00 - 20.00
21289 *The Curtains Of Night* .... 15.00 - 20.00
21406 *Seven Long Years In Prison* .... 15.00 - 20.00
21645 *I'm Goin' To Georgia* .... 15.00 - 20.00

JACK TETER:
Paramount 3235 *Silver Threads Among The Gold* 10.00 - 15.00

NORWOOD TEW:
Bluebird 6553 *Sailorman Blues* .... 10.00 - 15.00
6892 *My Old Crippled Daddy* .... 10.00 - 15.00
7288, 7618, 7791, 7950 .... 7.00 - 10.00

TEXAS COWBOY BAND:
Supertone 9673 *New Harmony Waltz* .... 8.00 - 12.00

TEXAS DRIFTER:
(See also: GOEBEL REEVES)
Decca 5020 *The Yodeling Teacher* .... 8.00 - 12.00
5021 *Cowboy's Lullaby* .... 8.00 - 12.00
Melotone 12016 *The Texas Drifter* .... 7.00 - 10.00
12047 *The Oklahoma Kid* .... 7.00 - 10.00
12186 *Bright Sherman Valley* .... 7.00 - 10.00
12214 *Little Joe, The Wrangler* .... 7.00 - 10.00
12232 *Mother-In-Law Blues* .... 7.00 - 10.00
12242 *The Tramp's Mother* .... 7.00 - 10.00
12290 *John Law And The Hobo* .... 8.00 - 12.00
12302 *The Cowboy's Secret* .... 8.00 - 12.00
Vocalion 5484 *The Drifter* .... 10.00 - 15.00

TEXAS NIGHT HAWKS:
Okeh 45363 *Possum Rag* .... 20.00 - 30.00

TEXAS RANGER:
Superior 2774 *Eleven Cent Cotton-Forty Cent
Meat* .... 35.00 - 50.00
2792 *All Aboard For Blanket Bay* .... 35.00 - 50.00
Supertone S-2055 *The Brakeman's Blues* .... 7.00 - 10.00

TEXAS RANGERS:
Decca 5022, 5107, 5139, 5183 .... 5.00 - 10.00

TEXAS RHYTHM BOYS:
Royalty 600 *Benzedrine Blues* .... 15.00 - 20.00

GEORGE THOMAS & HIS BOYS/MUSIC:
Champion 15262 *Big Town Fling* .... 5.00 - 8.00
15280 *Larry O'Gaff* .... 5.00 - 8.00
15354 *Haste To The Wedding* .... 5.00 - 8.00
15410 *Leather Breeches* .... 5.00 - 8.00
15434 *Blue Hawaii* .... 5.00 - 8.00

GRAYSON THOMAS & WILL LOTTY:
Champion 15395 *Nobody's Darling* .... 15.00 - 20.00

THOMPSON, CRANFORD & MILES:
Gennett 6602 *The Blind Man And His Child* .... 20.00 - 30.00

THOMPSON & MILES WITH THE RED FOX CHASERS:
Gennett 6914 *Put My Little Shoes Away* .... 25.00 - 40.00
6930 *The Girl I Loved In Sunny Tennessee* .... 30.00 - 50.00

BUD THOMPSON:
Crown 3418 *Five Cent Cotton* .... 8.00 - 12.00
3430 *I'm A Fugitive From A Chain Gang* ..... 8.00 - 12.00
3489 *The Lie He Wrote Home* .... 8.00 - 12.00
3502 *When The White Azaleas Start Blooming* . 8.00 - 12.00

ERNEST THOMPSON:
Columbia 130-D *Are You From Dixie* .... 8.00 - 12.00
145-D *Lightning Express* .... 8.00 - 12.00
147-D *Little Brown Jug* .... 8.00 - 12.00
153-D *Life's Railway To Heaven* .... 8.00 - 12.00
189-D *Mississippi Sawyer* .... 8.00 - 12.00
190-D *Red Wing* .... 8.00 - 12.00
216-D *In The Baggage Coach Ahead* .... 7.00 - 10.00
15001-D *Weeping Willow Tree* .... 10.00 - 15.00
15002-D *Silly Bill* .... 10.00 - 15.00
15006-D *Whistlin' Rufus* .... 10.00 - 15.00
15007-D *The Old Time Religion* .... 10.00 - 15.00

ERNEST E. THOMPSON:
Gennett 7139 *Medley* .... 20.00 - 30.00

FLOYD THOMPSON & HIS HOMETOWNERS:
Vocalion 5233 *Sidewalks Of New York* .... 10.00 - 15.00

5236 *Little Brown Jug* .... 10.00 - 15.00
5242 *Oh My Darling Clementine* .... 10.00 - 15.00
5253 *The Trail Of The Lonesome Pine* .... 10.00 - 15.00
5258 *Billy Boy* .... 10.00 - 15.00
5266 *I Wonder How She Did It* .... 10.00 - 15.00
5300 *When The Sunset Turns The Ocean Blue*
   To Gold .... 10.00 - 15.00
5317 *Mountains Of Virginia* .... 10.00 - 15.00
5331 *Red Wing* .... 10.00 - 15.00

GEORGIA THOMPSON:
Columbia 15532-D *Cross Eyed Sue* .... 7.00 - 10.00

HANK THOMPSON (& HIS BRAZOS
  VALLEY BOYS):
Blue Bonnet 107 *My Starry-Eyed Texas Gal* ..... 8.00 - 12.00
  123 *California Women* .... 8.00 - 12.00
Globe 124 *Whoa Sailor!* .... 7.00 - 12.00

HUGH THOMPSON:
Crystal 385 *Naggin' Wife* .... — - —

UNCLE JIMMIE THOMPSON:
Columbia 15118-D *Billy Wilson* .... 10.00 - 15.00
Vocalion 5456 *Lynchburg* .... 20.00 - 30.00

THREE 'BACCER TAGS:
Victor 23571 *Ain't Gonna Do It* .... 25.00 - 40.00

THREE GEORGIA CRACKERS:
Columbia 15630-D *I've Been Hoodooed* .... 7.00 - 10.00
  15653-D *Hannah-My Love* .... 7.00 - 10.00

THREE HOWARD BOYS:
Challenge 110 *Down In Tennessee Blues* .... 7.00 - 10.00
  304 *Down In Tennessee Blues* .... 7.00 - 10.00

THREE KENTUCKY SERENADERS:
Supertone 9246 *Pearl Bryant* .... 8.00 - 12.00
  9251 *Please, Papa, Come Home* .... 8.00 - 12.00
  9269 *We Will Outshine The Sun* .... 8.00 - 12.00

THREE MUSKETEERS:
Bluebird 8129 *Chattanooga Mama* .... 5.00 - 8.00

THREE OLD CRONIES:
Vocalion 5134 *Turkey In The Straw* .... 7.00 - 10.00
  15305 *Turkey In The Straw* .... 7.00 - 10.00

THREE STRIPPED GEARS:
Okeh 45553 *Depression Blues* .... 75.00 - 100.00
  45571 *Alabama Blues* .... 75.00 - 100.00

THREE TOBACCO TAGS:
Bluebird 6668, 6730, 6853, 6902, 6948, 6999,
  7044, 7130, 7163, 7211, 7250, 7312, 7361, 7400,
  7448, 7482, 7533, 7692, 7715, 7777, 7877, 7912,
  7973 .... 5.00 - 10.00
Champion 16480 *The Teacher's Hair Was Red* ... 20.00 - 30.00
  16674 *Reno Blues* .... 35.00 - 50.00

THREE TWEEDY BOYS/BROTHERS:
Champion 15486 *The Bully Of The Town* .... 7.00 - 10.00
  15548 *Sugar In The Gourd* .... 7.00 - 10.00
  15689 *Ida Red* .... 7.00 - 10.00

THREE VIRGINIANS:
Okeh 45451 *June Tenth Blues* .... 30.00 - 50.00

THREE WILLIAMSONS:
Bluebird 7819 *Fiddlers Blues* .... 7.00 - 10.00

TOBACCO TAGS:
Bluebird 8396, 8420 .... 5.00 - 8.00

TOM & CHUCK:
Victor V40305 *White River Road* .... 15.00 - 25.00

TOM & ROY:
Bluebird 5073, 5138, 5198, 5245 .... 4.00 - 7.00
Victor 23800 *Grandfather's Clock* .... 7.00 - 10.00
  23804 *In My Old Cabin Home* .... 7.00 - 10.00
  23813 *Chant Of The Jungle* .... 7.00 - 10.00

TOMMIE & WILLIE:
Champion 16034 *By The Old Oak Tree* .... 8.00 - 12.00
  16231 *I'm The Last One Left On The Corner* .. 10.00 - 15.00
  16240 *By My Side* .... 10.00 - 15.00
  16259 *My Canary Has Circles Under His Eyes* 10.00 - 15.00
  16276 *Rocky Mountain Rose* .... 10.00 - 15.00
  16301 *When It's Night Time In Nevada* .... 10.00 - 15.00

16314 *If You Can't Sing Whistle* .... 10.00 - 15.00
16432 *There's A Little Box Of Pine On*
  The 7:29 .... 10.00 - 15.00
45006, 45180 .... 5.00 - 10.00
Gennett 7246 *By The Old Oak Tree* .... 15.00 - 25.00

JED THOMPKINS:
Harmony 5096-H *Life's Railway To Heaven* ..... 4.00 - 6.00
  5099-H *Mississippi Sawyer* .... 4.00 - 6.00
  5101-H *Coon Crap Game* .... 4.00 - 6.00
Velvet Tone 7034-V *Mississippi Sawyer* .... 4.00 - 6.00

JACK TOOMBS:
Excello 2033 *Two Cheaters In Love* .... 5.00 - 10.00
  2041 *My Imagination* .... 5.00 - 10.00
Speed 111 *Pin Ball Fever* .... 10.00 - 15.00

WELBY TOOMEY:
Gennett 6005 *Roving Gambler* .... 12.00 - 16.00
  6025 *Little Brown Jug* .... 12.00 - 16.00
Silvertone 8151 *Roving Gambler* .... 7.00 - 10.00
Supertone 9245 *Little Brown Jug* .... 7.00 - 10.00
  9252 *Roving Gambler* .... 7.00 - 10.00

GEORGE TOON & THE TENNESSEE
  DRIFTERS:
Dot 1008 *That There Gal O'Mine* .... 8.00 - 12.00
(Note: See also TENNESSEE DRIFTERS)

MITCHELL TOROK:
FBC 102 *Nacogdoches County Line* .... 15.00 - 20.00
  115 *Piney Woods Boogie* .... 15.00 - 20.00

TRAVELERS:
Decca 5453, 5461 .... 5.00 - 8.00

CARL TRIMBLE:
Champion 16717 *Down On The Old Plantation* .. 20.00 - 30.00
  45050 *In A Lonely Little Cottage* .... 7.00 - 10.00

ERNEST TUBB:
Bluebird 6693 *The Passing Of Jimmie Rodgers* ..100.00 - 150.00
  7000 *Since That Black Cat Crossed My Path* ..100.00 - 150.00
  8899 *Mean Old Bed Bug Blues* .... 80.00 - 120.00
  8966 *My Mother Is Lonely* .... 75.00 - 100.00
Decca 5825, 5846, 5900, 5910, 5920, 5938, 5958,
  5976, 5993, 6007, 6023, 6040 .... 5.00 - 10.00

TUNE WRANGLERS:
Bluebird 6310, 6326, 6365, 6403, 6421, 6438,
  6513, 6554, 6655, 6692, 6703, 6828, 6856,
  6900, 6947, 6962, 6982, 7030, 7076, 7089,
  7200, 7272, 7336, 7413, 7571, 7612, 7673, 7703,
  7766, 7830, 7867, 7947, 7966, 7972, 7992,
  8014 .... 5.00 - 10.00

BUCK TURNER:
Title, issued contemporaneously on Banner,
  Melotone, Oriole, Perfect Romeo: *Sing Sing*
  Blues .... 8.00 - 12.00

CAL TURNER:
Champion 15524 *The Rowan County Feud* ...... 12.00 - 18.00
  15544 *The Death Of J.B. Marcum* .... 12.00 - 18.00
  15587 *Only A Tramp* .... 12.00 - 18.00
  15630 *By The Silvery Rio Grande* .... 12.00 - 18.00

DAVE TURNER:
Supertone 9318 *She'll Be Comin 'Round The*
  Mountain .... 7.00 - 10.00
  9319 *That Old Covered Bridge* .... 7.00 - 10.00
  9374 *Many Troubles Blues* .... 8.00 - 12.00
  9560 *We've Been Chums For Fifty Years* ...... 8.00 - 12.00

HOBO JACK TURNER:
Various recordings issued on Diva, Harmony and
  Velvet Tone under this name are of little
  interest or value.

JACK TURNER:
Gennett 7305 *Honey Stay In Your Own Back Yard* 20.00 - 30.00

LEMUEL TURNER:
Victor 21292 *'Way Down Yonder Blues* .... 20.00 - 30.00
  V40052 *Jake Bottle Blues* .... 20.00 - 30.00

BILL TUTTLE:
Columbia 15697-D *Gamblin' Bill Driv' On* ... 10.00 - 15.00

FRANK TUTTLE:

Velvet Tone 2148-V *The Prison Fire* . . . . 5.00 - 8.00

TWEEDY BROTHERS: (See also THREE TWEEDY BOYS/BROTHERS)

Champion 16048 *Home Brew Rag*	15.00	-	25.00
Gennett 6447 *The Bully Of The Town*	8.00	-	12.00
6483 *Sugar In The Gourd*	8.00	-	12.00
6529 *Shortnin' Bread*	8.00	-	12.00
6604 *Buckwheat Batter*	8.00	-	12.00
6734 *Dixie*	8.00	-	12.00
7240 *Home Brew Rag*	20.00	-	30.00
Superior 2784 *Home Brew Rag*	20.00	-	30.00
Supertone 9166 *Ida Red*	8.00	-	12.00
9174 *Shortnin' Bread*	8.00	-	12.00

UNCLE BUD & HIS PLOWBOYS:

Oriole 8170 *Five Cent Cotton* . . . . 5.00 - 8.00

CHAS. UNDERWOOD (Acc. by HACK'S STRING BAND)

Champion 16144 *Black Snake Moan*	30.00	-	50.00
16362 *I Want My Rib*	30.00	-	50.00

MARION UNDERWOOD (& SAM HARRIS):

Gennett 6155 *A Picture From Life's Other Side* . .	20.00	-	30.00
6177 *Just As The Sun Went Down*	20.00	-	30.00
6240 *Coal Creek March*	35.00	-	50.00

VAGABONDS:

Bluebird 5072, 5103, 5124, 5137, 5197, 5282, 5297, 5300, 5315, 5335, 5381, 5402, 5588, 6184	5.00	-	12.00
Victor 23801 *In The Sleepy Hills Of Tennessee* . .	20.00	-	30.00
23809 *The Old Rugged Cross*	20.00	-	30.00
23820 *Ninety-Nine Years*	30.00	-	50.00
23849 *My Pretty Quadroon*	30.00	-	50.00
23855 *In The Valley Of Yesterday*	30.00	-	50.00

VAGABOND YODELER:

Superior 2793 *No More To Ride The Rails* . . . . . 40.00 - 60.00

VAL & PETE:

Okeh 45224 *Yodel Blues* . . . . 5.00 - 8.00

VANCE'S TENNESSEE BREAKDOWNERS:

Okeh 45151 *Tennessee Breakdown* . . . . 25.00 - 40.00

VASS FAMILY:

Decca 5425 *Jimmy Randall*	5.00	-	10.00
5432 *Deep Blue Sea*	5.00	-	10.00

BILLY VEST:

Titles, issued on Banner, Conqueror, Melotone, Oriole, Perfect, Romeo, include: *Big City Jail; Dear Old Texas*	6.00	-	10.00
Columbia 15669-D *She'll Never Find Another Daddy Like Me*	10.00	-	15.00
15692-D *Billy's Blue Yodel*	10.00	-	15.00

VIRGINIA DANDIES:

Crown 3145 *God's Getting Worried*	15.00	-	20.00
Paramount 3305 *Mid The Green Fields Of Virginia*	20.00	-	30.00

VIRGINIA MOUNTAIN BOOMERS:

Gennett 6567 *Ramblin' Reckless Hobo*	20.00	-	30.00
6687 *Cousin Sally Brown*	20.00	-	30.00
Supertone 9305 *Rambling Reckless Hobo*	15.00	-	20.00
9406 *East Tennessee Polka*	15.00	-	20.00

VIRGINIA POSSUM TAMERS:

Champion 15484 *The Wreck On The Mountain Road*	10.00	-	15.00
15522 *Turkey In The Straw*	10.00	-	15.00
15566 *Weeping Willow Tree*	10.00	-	15.00
15609 *The Blind Man And His Child*	10.00	-	15.00
15672 *Something Wrong With My Gal*	10.00	-	15.00
15769 *The Virginia Possum Tamers Makin' Licker*	12.00	-	18.00
15790 *Virginia Bootleggers*	12.00	-	18.00
15809 *The Virginia Possum Tamers Makin' Licker Part ¾*	12.00	-	18.00
15925 *Put My Little Shoes Away*	10.00	-	15.00
45079 *Virginia Bootleggers*	7.00	-	10.00

VIRGINIA RAMBLERS:

Timely Tunes 1561 *Rag Time Annie* . . . . 15.00 - 20.00

WILD BILL WADE:

Okeh 45550 *Weeping Daddy Blues* . . . . 10.00 - 15.00

GEORGE WADE & CAROLINIANS:

Bluebird 7904 *Long And Bony*	7.00	-	10.00
Columbia 15515-D *When We Go A-Courtin'*	10.00	-	15.00

GEORGE WALBURN'S FOOT-SCORCHERS; GEORGE WALBURN & EMMETT HETHCOX:

Columbia 15721-D *Dixie Flyer*	75.00	-	100.00
Okeh 45024 *Lee County Blues*	30.00	-	50.00
45066 *Home Brew*	30.00	-	50.00
45178 *Kansas City Railroad Blues*	30.00	-	50.00
45305 *Decatur Street Rag*	40.00	-	60.00

WALKER'S CORBIN RAMBLERS:

Vocalion 02468 *Nobody's Business*	15.00	-	20.00
02667 *Ned Went A-Fishin'*	15.00	-	20.00
02678 *The Dying Tramp*	15.00	-	20.00
02719 *I Had A Dream*	15.00	-	20.00
02771 *Dark Town Strutters Ball*	15.00	-	20.00
02790 *Stone Mountain Toddle*	15.00	-	20.00

DAVE WALKER:

Superior 2688 *Someone Owns A Cottage* . . . . . . 15.00 - 20.00

FRANCIS/FRANKIE WALLACE:

(Note: Most records issued under these names—pseudonyms for Frank Marvin—are of minimal value.)

Edison 52356 *Away Out On The Mountain*	10.00	-	15.00
52387 *Drowsy Moonlight*	10.00	-	15.00
Paramount 3180 *Yodeling Them Blues Away*	8.00	-	12.00
3190 *Mississippi Moonshine*	8.00	-	12.00
3203 *I'm Riding The Blinds On A Train Headed West*	10.00	-	15.00
3209 *I Don't Work For A Living*	5.00	-	8.00
3211 *Blue Yodel No. 5*	7.00	-	10.00
3272 *Jimmie Rodger's Blue Yodel*	5.00	-	8.00
Supertone 9082 *Blue Yodel No. 2*	5.00	-	8.00

JERRY WALLACE:

Superior 2577 *Waiting For The Railroad Train* . .	15.00	-	20.00
2643 *O Jailer Bring Back That Key*	15.00	-	20.00
2677 *Hand Me Down My Walking Cane*	15.00	-	20.00

"DOCK" WALSH:

Columbia 15047-D *The East Bound Train*	10.00	-	15.00
15057-D *The Educated Man*	10.00	-	15.00
15075-D *We Courted In The Rain*	10.00	-	15.00
15094-D *In The Pines*	10.00	-	15.00
15105-D *Traveling Man*	10.00	-	15.00
Victor V40237 *Bathe In The Beautiful Pool*	25.00	-	40.00
V40325 *We're Just Plain Folks*	30.00	-	50.00

WALTER FAMILY:

Champion 16595 *Too Young To Get Married*	40.00	-	60.00
16622 *Flying Cloud Waltz*	40.00	-	60.00
16643 *Patty On The Turn Pike*	40.00	-	60.00
16653 *Shaker Ben*	40.00	-	60.00

WANNER & JENKINS/WHITE:

Champion 16306 *The Pretty Quadroon*	20.00	-	30.00
16348 *The Little Old Church In The Valley*	20.00	-	30.00
Columbia 15728-D *A Sweetheart's Promise*	20.00	-	30.00
Superior 2734 *That Little Boy Of Mine*	15.00	-	25.00

ENOS WANNER:

Champion 15791 *Over The Hills To The Poor House*	8.00	-	12.00
15810 *Don't Grieve Your Mother*	8.00	-	12.00
15830 *Put Me Off At Buffalo*	8.00	-	12.00
15898 *Crepe On The Little Cabin Door*	8.00	-	12.00
16052 *The Prison Warden's Secret*	10.00	-	15.00
16098 *Two Little Girls In Blue*	10.00	-	15.00
Superior 2722 *Strawberry Roan*	20.00	-	30.00

A.E WARD & HIS PLOW BOYS:

Columbia 15734-D *Going To Leave Old Arkansas* 75.00 - 100.00

CROCKETT WARD & HIS BOYS:

Okeh 45179 *Deadheads And Suckers* .... 35.00 - 50.00
    45304 *Ain't That Trouble In Mind?* .... 35.00 - 50.00

PRESTON WARD:
Kentucky 540, 541 .... 3.00 - 6.00

TOMMY WARD:
Superior 2689 *Mississippi River Blues* .... 40.00 - 60.00

PAUL WARMACK & HIS GULLY JUMPERS:
Victor V40009 *Robertson County* .... 30.00 - 50.00
    V40067 *Little Red Caboose Behind The Train* . 25.00 - 40.00

HANK WARNER:
Banner 5-11-61 *The Death Of Hughey P. Long* ... 7.00 - 10.00
(Note: Probably also issued on Melotone, Oriole,
    Perfect, and Romeo.)

YODELIN' JIMMY WARNER:
Champion 15562 *Blue Yodel No. 2* .... 7.00 - 10.00

WASHBOARD WONDERS:
Bluebird 6455 *You Gotta Eat Your Spinach, Baby* 6.00 - 10.00
    6463 *All Quiet On The Old Front Porch* ...... 6.00 - 10.00
    6464 *It Ain't Right* .... 6.00 - 10.00
    6495 *Feather Your Nest* .... 6.00 - 10.00
    6526 *Meet Me At The Ice House* .... 6.00 - 10.00
    6648 *Apple Tree* .... 6.00 - 10.00
    6671 *Roll Your Own* .... 6.00 - 10.00
    6737 *You're Everything Sweet* .... 6.00 - 10.00
    6761 *Breeze* .... 4.00 - 6.00

W.L. "RUSTIC" WATERS:
Columbia 15705-D *Sweet Nora Shannon* .... 8.00 - 12.00

WATKINS BAND:
Victor 21405 *Gideon* .... 7.00 - 10.00

DR. CLAUDE WATSON & L.W. McCREIGHTON:
Okeh 45020 *Chicken Reel* .... 15.00 - 20.00
    45034 *Ballin' The Jack And Nigger Blues* ..... 15.00 - 20.00

GEORGE P. WATSON:
Edison 51530 *Love's A Magic Spell* .... 5.00 - 8.00
    51691 *Medley Of J.K. Emmett's Yodel Songs* .. 5.00 - 8.00
Victor 20190, 20247 .... 3.00 - 5.00

HARVEY WATSON:
Challenge 328 *Drunken Hiccoughs* .... 8.00 - 12.00
    329 *Bright Sherman Valley* .... 8.00 - 12.00
    330 *Weeping Willow Tree* .... 8.00 - 12.00
Champion 15299 *A Mother's Advice* .... 7.00 - 10.00
    15333 *He Lives On High* .... 7.00 - 10.00
    15334 *Weeping Willow Tree* .... 8.00 - 12.00
    15356 *Drunken Hiccoughs* .... 8.00 - 12.00
    15428 *The Dying Cowboy* .... 7.00 - 10.00
Supertone 9243 *Weeping Willow Tree* .... 8.00 - 12.00
    9263 *He Lives On High* .... 7.00 - 10.00

LUIS WATSON:
Supertone 9167 *Home Sweet Home* .... 7.00 - 10.00
    9175 *Wandering Boy* .... 7.00 - 10.00

TOM WATSON:
Silvertone 3262 *Georgia Railroad* .... 7.00 - 10.00

WATTS & WILSON:
Paramount 3006 *The Sporting Cowboy* .... 75.00 - 100.00
    3007 *The Night Express* .... 75.00 - 100.00
    3019 *The Chain Gang Special* .... 75.00 - 100.00

OLD POP WATTS:
Phamous 701 *Kissin And Huggin'* .... — -- —

WILMER WATTS & THE LONELY EAGLES:
Broadway 8248 *Knockin' Down Casey Jones* .... 40.00 - 70.00
Paramount 3210 *Knockin' Down Casey Jones* ... 50.00 - 80.00
    3232 *Charles Gitaw* .... 75.00 - 100.00
    3242 *Banjo Sam* .... 75.00 - 100.00
    3247 *She's A Hard Boiled Rose* .... 75.00 - 100.00
    3254 *Cotton Mill Blues* .... 75.00 - 100.00
    3271 *Banjo Sam* .... 75.00 - 100.00
    3282 *Sleepy Desert* .... 75.00 - 100.00
    3299 *Bonnie Bess* .... 75.00 - 100.00

WEAVER BROTHERS:
Columbia 15487-D *Prison Sorrows* .... 10.00 - 15.00

WEAVER & WIGGINS:

Broadway 8112 *The Sporting Cowboy* .... 75.00 - 100.00
    8113 *The Night Express* .... 75.00 - 100.00
    8114 *The Chain Gang Special* .... 75.00 - 100.00

J.D. WEAVER:
Okeh 45016 *Arkansas Traveler* .... 8.00 - 12.00

WEBER & BROOKS:
Superior 2740 *The Utah Trail* .... 20.00 - 30.00

DAN WEBER:
Superior 2527 *Fair Florella* .... 25.00 - 40.00
    2582 *Worried Daddy Blues* .... 35.00 - 50.00

SAM WEBER:
Superior 2822 *My Ozark Mountain Home* ...... 30.00 - 50.00

WEEMS STRING BAND:
Columbia 15300-D *Greenback Dollar* .... 20.00 - 30.00

WELLING TRIO:
Champion 16035 *Will The Circle Be Unknown* .. 10.00 - 15.00
    16054 *Wait Till The Sun Shines Nellie* ..... 10.00 - 15.00
    16078 *Halleluiah All The Way* .... 10.00 - 15.00
    16120 *School Days* .... 10.00 - 15.00
Champion 45123, 45171 .... 5.00 - 10.00
Gennett 7291 *Tie Me To Your Apron Strings
    Again* .... 15.00 - 25.00

WELLING & McGHEE: (See also McGHEE & WELLING)
Champion 16585 *The Hallelujah Side* .... 20.00 - 30.00
    16598 *Nothing But The Blood* .... 20.00 - 30.00
    16660 *Ring The Bells Of Heaven* .... 20.00 - 30.00
Gennett 6719 *Lonely Village Churchyard* ...... 15.00 - 20.00
    7096 *Picture From Life's Other Side* ...... 15.00 - 20.00
Melotone 5-12-59 *The Maple On The Hill* ..... 7.00 - 10.00
Oriole 8056 *The Lonely Village Churchyard* .... 7.00 - 10.00
(Note: The above titles on Melotone and Oriole,
    and those on Perfect, below, probably were
    issued contemporaneously on Banner,
    Conqueror, Melotone, Oriole, Perfect,
    Romeo.)
Paramount 3084 *In The Garden* .... 10.00 - 15.00
    3093 *Haven Of Rest* .... 10.00 - 15.00
    3102 *Are You Washed In The Blood* .... 10.00 - 15.00
    3108 *My Mother's Bible* .... 10.00 - 15.00
    3115 *At The Cross* .... 10.00 - 15.00
    3157 *Too Many Parties And Too Many Pals* .... 15.00 - 20.00
    3175 *I Love To Walk With Jesus* .... 10.00 - 15.00
    3286 *Where Is My Mama* .... 15.00 - 20.00
    3310 *Almost Persuaded* .... 15.00 - 20.00
Perfect 12769 *The Crime At Quiet Dell* .... 7.00 - 10.00
Perfect 12801 *Sweet Hour Of Prayer* .... 7.00 - 10.00
Vocalion 5241 *The Hallelujah Side* .... 10.00 - 15.00
    5251 *The Lilly Of The Valley* .... 10.00 - 15.00
    5263 *The Nearer, The Sweeter* .... 10.00 - 15.00
    5299 *Go By The Way Of The Cross* .... 10.00 - 15.00

WELLING & SCHANNEN/SHANNON:
Paramount 3127 *S.O.S. Vestris* .... 10.00 - 15.00
    3134 *I'm A Child Of The King* .... 10.00 - 15.00
    3142 *Are You A Christian?* .... 10.00 - 15.00

FRANK WELLING (& THE RED BRUSH ROWDIES):
Champion 16474 *My Little Mountain Home* ..... 30.00 - 50.00
    16562 *I Can't Think Of Everything* .... 30.00 - 50.00
    16588 *The Old Man's Story* .... 30.00 - 50.00
    16590 *Shake Hands With Mother Again* ...... 30.00 - 50.00
    16594 *The Little Old Cross Road Store* ..... 30.00 - 50.00
    16618 *Roll It Down Baby* .... 50.00 - 75.00
    16652 *Daddy's Lullaby* .... 50.00 - 75.00
    16697 *Daddy And Son* .... 50.00 - 75.00
Gennett 6616 *Yodelin' Daddy Blues* .... 25.00 - 40.00
    6671 *I Wants My Lulu* .... 20.00 - 30.00
    7111 *Little Pal* .... 20.00 - 30.00
    7142 *That's A Plenty* .... 40.00 - 60.00
Paramount 3119 *The Last Mile* .... 35.00 - 50.00
    3125 *She's My Mama, And I'm Her Daddy* .... 35.00 - 50.00
    3216 *A Plea To Young Wives* .... 35.00 - 50.00

3287 *Busted Bank Blues* . . . . 40.00 - 60.00
Supertone 9083 *Yodelin' Daddy Blues* . . . . 10.00 - 15.00

WELLS BROTHERS STRING BAND:
Bluebird 7588 *Snow White Stone* . . . . 5.00 - 8.00

WENATCHEE MOUNTAINEERS:
Titles, issued contemporaneously on Banner,
Conqueror, Melotone, Oriole, Perfect. Romeo,
include: *Bring Your Roses To Your Mother;
Britt's Reel; By The Sleepy Rio Grande; Dear
Old Southern Moon; I Like Mountain Music;
The Little Rose Covered Shack; Texas Rag;
When It's Harvest Time* . . . . 5.00 - 8.00

JOE WERNER & THE RAMBLERS:
Bluebird 7539, 7575, 7639, 7690, 7923 . . . . 5.00 - 8.00

C.A. WEST:
Gennett 7098 *A Mother's Advice* . . . . 12.00 - 16.00
Supertone 9650 *Oh Willie Come Back* . . . . 5.00 - 8.00

CAL WEST:
Vocalion 5361 *Cal West's Yodeling Blues* . . . . 8.00 - 12.00

ED "JAKE" WEST:
Broadway 8109 *Waiting For The Train* . . . . 4.00 - 7.00
Challenge 813 *Waiting For The Train* . . . . 5.00 - 8.00
Paramount 3154 *Waiting For The Train* . . . . 5.00 - 8.00

WALTON WEST:
Champion 45161 *'Leven Miles From Leavenworth* . 7.00 - 10.00
45170 *In That Vine Covered Chapel* . . . . 7.00 - 10.00

WESTERNERS:
Titles, issued contemporaneously on Banner,
Conqueror, Melotone, Oriole, Perfect, Romeo,
include: *Carry Me Back To The Lone Prairie;
The Cowboy's Dream; Goin' Down To Santa Fe
Town; Gol Darn Wheel; Good Old Turnip
Greens; If Jesse James Rode Again; Is It True
What They Say About Dixie?; My Gal On The
Rio Grande; My Herdin' Song; Nobody To
Love; Out On The Loco Range; Pretty Boy
Floyd; Rancho Grande; Ridin' Down That Old
Texas Trail; Roundup Time In Heaven; The
Santa Fe Trail; Texas Star* . . . . 5.00 - 10.00

DON WESTON:
Champion 16748 *That Old Feather Bed On
The Farm* . . . . 15.00 - 20.00
16764 *The Dying Cowgirl* . . . . 15.00 - 20.00
16779 *'Way Out West In Texas* . . . . 15.00 - 20.00
16825 *That Mother And Daddy Of Mine* . . . . . 20.00 - 30.00
45053, 45101, 45107, 45110 . . . . 5.00 - 10.00

WEST VIRGINIA COON HUNTERS:
Victor 20862 *Greasy String* . . . . 20.00 - 30.00

WEST VIRGINIA NIGHT OWLS:
Victor 21190 *Sweet Bird* . . . . 15.00 - 25.00
21533 *I'm Goin' To Walk On The Streets
Of Glory* . . . . 15.00 - 25.00

WEST VIRGINIA RAIL SPLITTER:
Champion 15852 *In The Jail House Now* . . . . . . 10.00 - 15.00
15897 *Barney McCoy* . . . . 10.00 - 15.00
15943 *Old And Only In The Way* . . . . 10.00 - 15.00
15990 *The Habit* . . . . 10.00 - 15.00
16053 *Zeb Turney's Gal* . . . . 10.00 - 15.00
16095 *The Dying Ranger* . . . . 10.00 - 15.00

WEST VIRGINIA RAMBLERS:
Champion 16757 *O Dem Golden Slippers* . . . . . 20.00 - 30.00
45017 *O Dem Golden Slippers* . . . . 7.00 - 10.00

WEST VIRGINIA RIDGE RUNNERS:
Superior 2794 *Dill Pickle Rag* . . . . 25.00 - 40.00

WEST VIRGINIA SNAKE HUNTERS:
Brunswick 119 *Standin' In The Need Of Prayer* . 15.00 - 25.00

JIM WHALEN:
Champion 15545 *May I Sleep In Your Barn
Tonight Mister?* . . . . 8.00 - 12.00

(FRANK) WHEELER & (MONROE) LAMB:
Victor 23537 *Jim Blake, The Engineer* . . . . 10.00 - 15.00
23755 *Will You Sometimes Think Of Me* . . . . . 20.00 - 30.00

V40169 *Jolly Group Of Cowboys* . . . . 10.00 - 15.00
V40248 *Since The Preacher Made Us One* . . . . 10.00 - 15.00

WEBB WHIPPLE:
Okeh 45574 *Don't Hang Me In The Morning* . . . 10.00 - 15.00

WHITE & DAWSON:
Superior 9541 *On The Banks Of The Silvery
Stream* . . . . 8.00 - 12.00

FIDDLIN' BOB WHITE:
Bell 1171 *Cripple Creek* . . . . 5.00 - 8.00
1188 *Billy In The Low Ground* . . . . 5.00 - 8.00

CLYDE WHITE:
Champion 16318 *Beside A Lonely River* . . . . . . 10.00 - 15.00

GEORGE WHITE:
Okeh 45241, 45257, 45287, 45335, 45351 . . . . . 5.00 - 10.00
45382 *Dust Pan Blues* . . . . 7.00 - 10.00
45432 *Living' In The Mountains* . . . . 7.00 - 10.00
45502 *I Am Just A Gambler* . . . . 7.00 - 10.00

JOHN WHITE:
Romeo 5066 *Strawberry Roan* . . . . 5.00 - 8.00

**JOHNNIE/JOHNNY WHITE & HIS RHYTHM
RIDERS:**
Citation 102 *My Home In Tennessee* . . . . 7.00 - 10.00
Fortune 145 *Mean And Evil Blues* . . . . 5.00 - 8.00

REUBEN WHITE:
Challenge 336 *Old Sefus Brown* . . . . 7.00 - 10.00

ZEB WHITE:
Vocalion 5189 *When You Were Sweet Sixteen* . . . 8.00 - 12.00

RED WHITEHEAD & DUTCH COLEMAN:
Vocalion 5414 *Booneville Stomp* . . . . 30.00 - 50.00

WHITE MOUNTAIN ORCHESTRA:
Victor 23619 *Maxwell's Old Rye Waltz* . . . . 30.00 - 50.00
V40185 *Leather Britches* . . . . 20.00 - 30.00

**RAY WHITELY (& ODIS ELDER);
WHITLEY'S RANGE RAMBLERS:**
Titles, issued contemporaneously on Banner,
Conqueror, Melotone, Oriole, Perfect, Romeo:
*Have You Written Your Mother Lately; The
Morror Castle Disaster; Pretty Boy Floyd; Old
Wishing Well; Singing A Song In Sing Sing;
Sittin' On The Old Settee* . . . . 8.00 - 12.00
Decca 5078 *Big Bad Blues* . . . . 8.00 - 12.00
5132 *Wiley Post* . . . . 8.00 - 12.00
5195 *Wah-Hoo* . . . . 7.00 - 10.00
5205 *Blue Yodel Blues* . . . . 7.00 - 10.00
5285 *Travelin'* . . . . 5.00 - 8.00
5293 *You Took My Candy* . . . . 5.00 - 8.00

J.B. WHITMIRE & THE BLUE SKY TRIO:
Bluebird 7132, 7844 . . . . 5.00 - 10.00

**(HENRY) WHITTER (& G.B. GRAYSON):
WHITTER'S VIRGINIA BREAKDOWNERS;
HENRY WHITTER & FIDDLER JOE: (See
also GRAYSON & WHITTER)**
Champion 15629 *Cluck Old Hen* . . . . 8.00 - 12.00
Gennett 6320 *Train Forty-Five* . . . . 15.00 - 20.00
6373 *I'll Never Be Yours* . . . . 15.00 - 20.00
6418 *Red Or Green* . . . . 15.00 - 20.00
6436 *Old Jimmy Sutton* . . . . 15.00 - 20.00
6656 *Cluck Old Hen* . . . . 15.00 - 20.00
6733 *Sally Goodin* . . . . 15.00 - 20.00
Herwin 75537 *Snow Storm* . . . . 20.00 - 30.00
Okeh 40015 *Lonesome Road Blues* . . . . 15.00 - 20.00
40029 *Last Train Blues* . . . . 10.00 - 15.00
40063 *Little Brown Jug* . . . . 10.00 - 15.00
40064 *Tippy Two Step Blues* . . . . 10.00 - 15.00
40077 *Western County* . . . . 10.00 - 15.00
40109 *Sydney Allen* . . . . 10.00 - 15.00
40120 *Double Headed Train* . . . . 10.00 - 15.00
40143 *New River Train* . . . . 10.00 - 15.00
40169 *The Drunkard's Child* . . . . 10.00 - 15.00
40187 *Rain Crow Bill Blues* . . . . 10.00 - 15.00
40211 *Nellie Gray* . . . . 10.00 - 15.00
40229 *Broken Engagement Blues* . . . . 10.00 - 15.00

40237 *Ellen Smith*	10.00 -	15.00
40269 *Rabbit Race*	10.00 -	15.00
40296 *Keep My Skillet Good And Greasy*	10.00 -	15.00
40320 *Round-Town Girl*	10.00 -	15.00
40352 *The Long Tongued Woman*	10.00 -	15.00
40375 *Butcher Boy*	10.00 -	15.00
40395 *My Darling's Black Mustache*	12.00 -	18.00
40403 *Good-Bye, Old Booze*	12.00 -	18.00
45003 *Liza Jane*	10.00 -	15.00
45045 *The Heart Of Old Galax*	10.00 -	15.00
45046 *Put My Little Shoes Away*	10.00 -	15.00
45053 *Many Times With You I've Wondered*	10.00 -	15.00
45061 *Hand Me Down My Walking Cane*	10.00 -	15.00
45063 *The Burglar Man*	10.00 -	15.00
45081 *George Collins*	10.00 -	15.00
Victor 20878 *Whitter's Fox Chase*	7.00 -	10.00
V40061 *Poor Lost Boy*	15.00 -	20.00
V40105 *Short Life Of Trouble*	15.00 -	20.00
V40135 *Little Maggie With A Dram Glass*	15.00 -	20.00
V40235 *Tom Dooley*	15.00 -	20.00
V40292 *Fox Chase No. 2*	15.00 -	20.00

PETE WIGGINS:

Okeh 45295 *The Gay Caballero*	5.00 -	8.00
45412 *Everybody Does It In Hawaii*	5.00 -	8.00

MILLER WIKEL:

Gennett 6566 *Frail Wildwood Flower*	15.00 -	20.00
Paramount 3205 *Young Charlotte*	15.00 -	25.00

RILEY WILCOX:

Bell 1179 *The Broken Engagement*	7.00 -	10.00

WILEY, ZEKE & HOMER:

Bluebird 7426 *Greenback Dollar, Part 3*	5.00 -	8.00
7452 *Someone To Love You When You're Old*	5.00 -	8.00
7572 *I Will Never Turn Back*	5.00 -	8.00
7628 *Under The Old Kentucky Moon*	5.00 -	8.00

WILKINS & SHARON:

Broadway 8204 *My Mother's Bible*	7.00 -	10.00

FRANK WILKINS:

Broadway 8205 *The Last Mile*	8.00 -	12.00

"DAD" WILLIAMS:

Brunswick 306 *Money Musk*	10.00 -	15.00

HANK WILLIAMS:

(Note: Some issues on MGM label are credited
as by LUKE THE DRIFTER.)

MGM 10033, 10073, 10124, 10171, 10212, 10226, 10271	7.00 -	12.00
10328, 10352,10832	5.00 -	10.00
10401, 10434, 10461, 01506, 01560, 10609, 10645, 10696, 10760, 10813, 10904, 10961, 11000, 11054, 11100, 11160, 11202, 11283, 11318, 11366, 11416	5.00 -	10.00
11479, 11533, 11574, 11628, 11707, 11768, 11861	7.00 -	12.00
11975 *Message To My Mother*	8.00 -	12.00
12029 *Alone And Forsaken*	8.00 -	12.00
12077 *Someday You'll Call My Name*	8.00 -	12.00
12127 *Thank God*	8.00 -	12.00
12185 *Thy Burdens Are Greater Than Mine*	8.00 -	12.00
12244 *I Wish I Had A Nickel*	10.00 -	15.00

(Note: Early issues, to about—10401, designated
"Metrolite," are later pressings; little
difference in premium between the "original"
and subsequent pressings exist.)

Sterling 201 *Never Again (Will I Knock On Your Door)*	100.00 -	150.00
204 *Wealth Won't Save Your Soul*	100.00 -	150.00
208 *I Don't Care (If Tomorrow Never Comes)*	100.00 -	150.00
210 *Pan American*	75.00 -	100.00

MARC WILLIAMS:

Brunswick 240 *Willie The Weeper*	8.00 -	12.00
244 *The Cowboy's Dream*	8.00 -	12.00
269 *Jesse James*	8.00 -	12.00
304 *Sam Bass*	8.00 -	12.00
377 *The Cowboy's Last Wish*	8.00 -	12.00

430 *Cowboy Jack*	8.00 -	12.00
497 *The Dying Ranger*	8.00 -	12.00
544 *Cole Younger*	8.00 -	12.00
564 *The Boys In Blue*	8.00 -	12.00
Decca 5010 *Roy Bean*	7.00 -	10.00
5011 *Sioux Indians*	7.00 -	10.00
5012 *Old Montana*	7.00 -	10.00
5106 *Old Chism Trail*	5.00 -	8.00
5196 *When They Changed My Name To A Number*	5.00 -	8.00
5216 *My Blue Heaven*	5.00 -	8.00
5327 *William And Mary*	5.00 -	8.00
Supertone 2051 *The Crepe Upon The Little Cabin Door*	8.00 -	12.00

MARVIN WILLIAMS (THE SUNSHINE YODELER):

Okeh 45467 *Can't Sleep In Your Barn Tonight, Mister*	7.00 -	10.00
45483 *Back Where The Blue Bonnets Grow*	7.00 -	10.00

WILLIAMSON BROTHERS & CURRY:

Okeh 45108 *Cumberland Gap*	50.00 -	75.00
45127 *Gonna Die With My Hammer In My Hand*	50.00 -	75.00
45146 *Lonesome Road Blues*	50.00 -	75.00

BOB WILLS & SLEEPY JOHNSON:

Titles, issued on Banner, Melotone, Oriole,
Perfect, Romeo (all numbered 6-11-58):

Harmony; Smith's Reel	30.00 -	50.00

BOB WILLS & HIS TEXAS PLAYBOYS:

The Antones 501 *Have I Stayed Away Too Long?*	10.00 -	15.00

(Note: Above is limited issue for Bob Wills Fan
Club. There are others, of like value and
interest.)

Columbia, most issues	3.00 -	6.00
MGM, most issues	3.00 -	6.00
Okeh, most issues	4.00 -	8.00
Vocalion 03076 *St. Louis Blues*	10.00 -	15.00
03086 *Mexicali Rose*	10.00 -	15.00
03096 *Osage Stomp*	10.00 -	15.00
03139 *Black And Blue Rag*	10.00 -	15.00
03173 *Wang Wang Blues*	10.00 -	15.00
03206 *I Ain't Got Nobody*	8.00 -	12.00
03230 *Blue River*	8.00 -	12.00
03264 *Never No More Blues*	8.00 -	12.00
03295 *Oklahoma Rag*	8.00 -	12.00
03343 *Trouble In Mind*	7.00 -	10.00
03344 *Basin Street Blues*	7.00 -	10.00
03361 *Fan It*	7.00 -	10.00
03394 *Steel Guitar Rag*	7.00 -	10.00
03424 *She's Killing Me*	7.00 -	10.00
03451 *Right Or Wrong*	7.00 -	10.00
03492 *Mean Mama Blues*	7.00 -	10.00
03537 *Too Busy*	7.00 -	10.00
03578 *Swing Blues No. 2*	7.00 -	10.00
03597 *Bleeding Hearted Blues*	7.00 -	10.00
03614 *White Heat*	7.00 -	10.00
03659 *Rosetta*	7.00 -	10.00
03693 *The New St. Louis Blues*	7.00 -	10.00
03924 *Maiden's Prayer*	6.00 -	10.00
03977 *Sunbonnet Sue*	6.00 -	10.00
04132 *Black Rider*	6.00 -	10.00
04184 *Empty Bed Blues*	6.00 -	10.00
04275 *Gambling Polka Dot Blues*	6.00 -	10.00
04325 *Tulsa Stomp*	5.00 -	8.00
04387 *Loveless Love*	5.00 -	8.00
04439 *Moonlight And Roses*	5.00 -	8.00
04515 *Oh, Lady Be Good*	5.00 -	8.00
04566 *That's What I Like 'Bout The South*	5.00 -	8.00
04625 *Whoa, Babe*	5.00 -	8.00
04755, 04839, 04934, 04999, 05079, 05161, 05228, 05282	5.00 -	10.00

JOHNNIE LEE WILLIS:

Bullet 696, 700, 710, 711, 717, 721, 724, 726, 737, 741, 743 .... 5.00 - 10.00

FRANK WILSON & HIS BLUE RIDGE MOUNTAIN TRIO:
Columbia 15372-D *Katy-Did Waltz* .... 15.00 - 20.00

JIMMIE WILSON'S CATFISH STRING BAND; JIMMIE WILSON:
Okeh 45019 *Let Me Call You Sweetheart* .... 10.00 - 15.00
45029 *Over The Waves* .... 10.00 - 15.00
Victor V40163 *Catfish Whiskers* .... 10.00 - 15.00
V40216 *Catfish Medley March* .... 15.00 - 20.00
V40240 *Polecat Creek* .... 20.00 - 30.00

TOMMY WILSON:
Vocalion 5262 *The Sinking Of The Vestris* ...... 8.00 - 12.00

JUSTIN WINFIELD:
Gennett 6619 *The New River Train* .... 25.00 - 40.00
6733 *Say, Darling, Say* .... 25.00 - 40.00

WING'S ROCKY MOUNTAIN RAMBLERS:
Champion 16808 *Jackson County Rag* .... 50.00 - 75.00
16819 *Whiskers* .... 50.00 - 75.00
45019 *Ragged Ann* .... 15.00 - 20.00

F. WINGATE:
Supertone 9121 *Sleep, Baby, Sleep* .... 5.00 - 8.00
9122 *Emmett's Cuckoo Song* .... 5.00 - 8.00

WISE STRING BAND:
Vocalion 5360 *Yellow Dog Blues* .... 15.00 - 20.00

HASKELL WOLFBERGER:
Vocalion 5390 *My Little Girl* .... 10.00 - 15.00

WONDER STATE HARMONISTS:
Vocalion 5275 *Turnip Greens* .... 8.00 - 12.00
5291 *On The Wing* .... 8.00 - 12.00
5346 *My Castle On The Nile* .... 8.00 - 12.00

SMOKY WOOD & HIS WOOD CHIPS:
Bluebird 7660, 7729 .... 5.00 - 10.00

JACK WOODCLIFF:
Paramount 3280 *I Wonder If She Cares To See Me Now* .... 20.00 - 30.00

JAKE WOODFIELD:
Crown 3103 *There's A Mother Old And Gray Who Needs Me Know* .... 10.00 - 15.00

WOODIE BROTHERS:
Victor 23579 *Like Likker Better Than Me* ...... 40.00 - 60.00

EPPHRIAM WOODIE & THE HENPECKED HUSBANDS:
Columbia 15564-D *Last Gold Dollar* .... 10.00 - 15.00

NORMAN WOODLIEFF:
Gennett 6824 *Brace Up And Be A Man* .... 25.00 - 40.00

FRANK WOODS:
Okeh—*Canadian Husking Bee/Money Musk* .... — - —

LAWRENCE WOODS:
Champion 16517 *The Cyclone Of Rycove* .... 40.00 - 60.00

SHEB WOOLEY (& THE CALUMET INDIANS):
Blue Bonnet 124 *Lazy Mazy* .... 7.00 - 10.00
125 *Peeping Through The Key Hole* .... 7.00 - 10.00
126 *Your Papa Ain't Steppin' Anymore* .... 7.00 - 10.00
Bullet 603 *Oklahoma Honky-Tonk Gal* .... 7.00 - 10.00

KYLE WOOTEN:
Okeh 45511 *Lumber Camp Blues* .... 30.00 - 50.00
45526 *Choking Blues* .... 30.00 - 50.00

WORKMAN, RAMSEY & WOLFE:
Gennett 6659 *The South Salon Quadrille* .... 20.00 - 30.00

W O W O DOWN HOMERS: (See also THE DOWN HOMERS)
Vogue 786 *Boogie Woogie Yodel* .... 75.00 - 125.00

WRIGHT & McNEW (THE HOOSIER HAWAIIANS):
Champion 16336 *The Utah Trail* .... 15.00 - 20.00

EARL WRIGHT (Acc. by THE ARKANSAS CORN DODGERS):
Champion 16382 *My Ozark Mountain Home* .... 25.00 - 40.00

WYATT & BRANDON:

Columbia 15523-D *Evalina* .... 15.00 - 20.00

WYOMING COWBOY (CHARLES BAKER):
Champion 16724 *Utah Carroll* .... 20.00 - 30.00
16737 *Curly Joe* .... 25.00 - 40.00
45044, 45052 .... 7.00 - 10.00

IRA & EUGENE YATES:
Columbia 15581-D *Sarah Jane* .... 30.00 - 50.00

JIMMY YATES' BOLL WEEVILS:
Victor 21723 *Smiles* .... 20.00 - 30.00
V40065 *Bloody War* .... 25.00 - 40.00

YELLOW JACKETS:
Champion 16070 *Heel And Toe Polka* .... 10.00 - 15.00
16161 *Medley* .... 10.00 - 15.00
Gennett 7262 *Medley* .... 10.00 - 15.00

YODELING TWINS (GARNER ECKLER & ROLAND GAINES):
Champion 16723 *Mountain Rangers Lullaby* .... 20.00 - 30.00
16747 *Moonlight And Skies* .... 20.00 - 30.00

YOUNG BROTHERS TENNESSEE BAND:
Columbia 15219-D *Are You From Dixie?* .... 15.00 - 20.00

BUDDY YOUNG'S KENTUCKIANS:
Superior 2519 *Fire On The Mountain* .... 30.00 - 50.00
2655 *Eighth Of January* .... 30.00 - 50.00
2731 *Rocky Mountain Goat* .... 30.00 - 50.00

CLARENCE YOUNG:
Champion 15550 *The Lonely Village Churchyard* 10.00 - 15.00
15582 *Yodelin' Daddy Blues* .... 10.00 - 15.00
15924 *Little Pal* .... 10.00 - 15.00
15991 *That's A Plenty* .... 10.00 - 15.00

JACKSON YOUNG:
Champion 15318 *Take Me Back To The Sweet Sunny South* .... 8.00 - 12.00
15333 *I Know My Name Is There* .... 7.00 - 10.00

JESS YOUNG'S TENNESSEE BAND:
Columbia 15338-D *Fiddle Up* .... 15.00 - 20.00
15400-D *Sweet Bunch Of Daisies* .... 15.00 - 20.00
15431-D *Lovin' Henry* .... 15.00 - 20.00
15493-D *Old Weary Blues* .... 20.00 - 30.00

ZACK & GLENN:
Okeh 45212 *The Gambler's Lament* .... 5.00 - 8.00
45240 *Love's Old Sweet Song* .... 5.00 - 8.00

ZORA & THE HOMETOWNERS:
Decca 5459, 5460 .... 5.00 - 10.00

RHYTHM & BLUES; ROCK & ROLL; ROCKABILLY; BLUES; ETC.

1950s through Early 1960s

All records in this section are 45 rpm unless otherwise indicated. Albums and Extended-Play records are denoted by (LP) or (EP) between the name of the label and the record/catalog number. LPs and EPs must be in their original jackets; LPs and EPs lacking jackets or having damaged or defaced jackets are worth substantially less than the prices listed (and may, in fact, be virtually unsalable in many cases).

Collectors of 1950s records are particularly fussy about labels. The color, logo or style of type may distinguish first from subsequent pressings. An effort has been to designate, where repressings involving label variations are notorious, the label color (or other determinant) of the original or earliest pressing. In addition, the presence of writing, stickers, tears, or other damage to labels detracts from desirability and value moreso than with earlier 78 rpm records.

Although most of the records listed in this section are 45RPM, LPs and EPs selected 78 RPM records are listed. These are the 78 RPM counterparts (having the same label and catalog/record number) of big-selling 45 RPM rock and roll hits of the late 1950s. Such records, common and of minimal value as 45s (and therefore not listed herein), are often quite scarce as 78s. By the late 1950s, the process of phasing out 78s in favor of 45s had nearly concluded. The major companies discontinued 78s in 1957-1958; some smaller labels continued to produce 78s as late as 1960. The market for these "late 78s" is in its formative stage, and prices are necessarily speculative. The greatly increased demand for these records parallels the rise in popularity of antique 78 rpm jukeboxes, whose owners often seek to fill them with 1950s oldies. But they are also the focus of increasing attention by record collectors. Perhaps the listing of "late 78s" will be greatly expanded as interested collectors discover additional (and even later!) 78s.

While the "late 78s" may be worth more than their 45 rpm counterparts, the opposite is generally true of records from the early to mid-50s. During this period, 45s, being relatively new, had not yet supplanted 78s, and often were issued in smaller quantities than 78s. This is particularly true of Rhythm and Blues, Blues, and Country records, whose purchasers were among the last to discard their old 78s and record players in favor of the new format. Thus, for most of the records listed is this section, a 78 RPM copy would be worth less than its 45 RPM counterpart.

Readers will note the presence of a number of incomplete listings which lack label, catalog/record number, title, or price. These records are deemed worthy of inclusion notwithstanding missing information due to their having appeared in want lists or auction lists of knowledgeable collectors and dealers. It is expected that collectors will supply some of the missing information, or in some cases will advise the deletion of a record, in time for a fifth edition of this book.

THE ACADEMICS:
Ancho 101 *Too Good To Be True*	8.00	-	12.00
103 *Darla, My Darling*	8.00	-	12.00

THE ACCENTS:
Brunswick 55100 *Wiggle Wiggle* (78rpm)	5.00	-	8.00
55100 *Wiggle Wiggle*	15.00	-	20.00
55123 *Ching A Ling*	5.00	-	8.00

JOHNNY ACE:
Duke (EP) 80 *Memorial Album*; (EP) 81	30.00	-	40.00
Duke (LP) DLP-70 (10") "Memorial Album for *Johnny Ace*"	80.00	-	120.00
(LP) DLP 71 *Memorial Album*	50.00	-	75.00
102 *My Song*	15.00	-	20.00
107 *Cross My Heart*	15.00	-	20.00
112 *The Clock*	10.00	-	15.00
118 *Saving My Love For You*	10.00	-	15.00
128 *Please Forgive Me*	8.00	-	12.00
136 *Pledging My Love*	8.00	-	12.00
144 *Anymore*	5.00	-	8.00
148 *So Lonely*	5.00	-	8.00
Flair 1015 *Midnight Hours Journey*	15.00	-	20.00

SONNY ACE:
TNT 153 *If My Teardrops Could Talk*	10.00	-	15.00

JOHNNY ACEY:
Fling 728 *I Go Into Orbit*	8.00	-	12.00

ACORNS:
Unart 2006, 2015	7.00	-	10.00

ROY ACUFF:
Capitol (LP) T-617	10.00	-	15.00
Columbia (LP) 9004 (10") *Songs Of The Smoky Mountains*	20.00	-	30.00
(LP) 9010 (10") *Old Time Barn Dance*	20.00	-	30.00
Harmony (LP) 7082 *Great Speckled Bird*	10.00	-	15.00
MGM (LP) 3707 *Favorite Hymns*	10.00	-	15.00

ART ADAMS:
Cherry 1005 *Rock Crazy Baby*	30.00	-	50.00

ARTHUR K. ADAMS:

Jetstar 102 *Beetle Bust Out*		-	

BILLY ADAMS (& THE ROCK-A-TEERS):
Decca 30724 *Baby I'm Bugged*	7.00	-	10.00
Dot 15689 *You Heard Me Knocking*	10.00	-	15.00
Nau-Voo 805 *That's My Baby*	20.00	-	30.00

CHARLIE ADAMS:
Columbia 21239, 21355	5.00	-	8.00
21445 *Pistol Packin' Mama has Laid Her Pitol Down*	7.00	-	10.00
21524 *Black Land Blues*	7.00	-	10.00
Decca 46335, 46358, 46373	6.00	-	10.00

FAYE ADAMS:
Herald 416 *Shake A Hand*	7.00	-	10.00
416 *Shake A Hand* (red plastic)	20.00	-	30.00
419 *I'll Be True*	5.00	-	8.00
423 *Say A Prayer*	5.00	-	8.00
429 *Crazy Mixed Up World*	5.00	-	8.00
434 *Ain't Gonna Tell*	5.00	-	8.00
439 *Love Ain't Nothin' To Play With*	5.00	-	8.00
Herald 444, 450, 457, 462, 470, 480, 489, 512	4.00	-	7.00
Warwick (LP) 2031 "*Shake A Hand*"	30.00	-	40.00

JO JO ADAMS:
Chance 1127 *Didn't I Tell You*	20.00	-	30.00

WOODROW ADAMS (& THE BOOGIE BLUES BLASTERS/THE THREE B'S):
Checker 757 *Pretty Baby Blues*	30.00	-	50.00
Meteor 5018 *Wine Head Woman* (Red Label)	40.00	-	60.00

ADELPHIS:
Rim 2022 *Shine Again*	10.00	-	15.00

THE ADMIRALS:
King 4772 *Left With A Broken Heart*	20.00	-	30.00
4782 *Close Your Eyes*	20.00	-	30.00

ADMIRAL TONES:
Felsted 8563 *Rocksville, Pa*	10.00	-	15.00
Pretty Baby	8.00	-	12.00

THE ADVENTURERS:
Columbia 42227 *Rock And Roll Uprising*	7.00	-	10.00

RAY AGEE:
Spark 119 *Another Fool Sings The Blues* . . . . 10.00 - 15.00
AGGIE DUKES:
Aladdin 3364 *Swing Low Sweet Cadillac* . . . . — - —
JIM AKINS:
Marlo 1517 *Floating On A Cloud* . . . . 5.00 - 8.00
THE ALADDINS:
Aladdin 3275 *Cry Cry Baby* . . . . 20.00 - 30.00
    3298 *I Had Dream Last Night* . . . . 20.00 - 30.00
    3314 *All Of My Life* . . . . 20.00 - 30.00
STEVE ALAIMO & THE RED COATS:
Lifetime 6112 *The Girl Can't Help It* . . . . 7.00 - 10.00
Marlin 6064 *I Want You To Love Me* . . . . 5.00 - 8.00
DENNI ALAN:
Academy 434 *Turn-A-Bout Date* . . . . 15.00 - 20.00
MEL ALBERT:
Apollo 530 *Sugar Plum* . . . . 8.00 - 12.00
MAX ALEXANDER:
Caprock 116 *Rock, Rock, Rock Everybody* . . . . . 20.00 - 30.00
ANNIE ALFORD:
Groove 0172 *It's Heavenly* . . . . 15.00 - 20.00
THE ALGERS:
Nothern 3730 *Heavenly Father* . . . . 10.00 - 15.00
BILL(Y) ALLEN (& THE BACK BEATS):
Eldorado 505 *Oo-Wee-baby* . . . . 7.00 - 10.00
Imperial 5500 *Please Give Me Something* . . . . . 20.00 - 30.00
CHARLIE ALLEN:
Portrait 107 *Wheelin' And Dealin'* . . . . 7.00 - 10.00
CONNIE ALLEN:
King 4528 *Rocket 69* . . . . 10.00 - 15.00
DANNY ALLEN:
Valley 101 *Teenage Blues* . . . . 7.00 - 10.00
HAROLD ALLEN:
Mar Vel 1200 *Honky Tonkin Women* . . . . 15.00 - 20.00
    1021 *If You Were Mine Again* . . . . 15.00 - 20.00
IRA ALLEN:
Mav-Rick 105 *Nursery Rock.* . . . . 50.00 - 75.00
LEE ALLEN:
Ember (LP) ELP 200 *Walkin' With Mr. Lee* . . . . 30.00 - 40.00
MILTON ALLEN:
RCA Victor 6994 *Just Look, Don't Touch* . . . . . . 8.00 - 12.00
    7116 *Don't Bug Me Baby* . . . . 8.00 - 12.00
    Robin 61824 *Anything Goes* . . . . 10.00 - 15.00
RAY ALLEN:
Blast (LP) 6004 *Tribute To Six* . . . . 20.00 - 30.00
REX ALLEN:
Decca (LP) 8402 *Under Western Skies* . . . . 10.00 - 15.00
    30674 *Knock Knock Rattle* . . . . 7.00 - 10.00
RONNIE ALLEN:
San 208 *Juvenile Delinquent* . . . . 15.00 - 20.00
    209 *High School Love* . . . . 15.00 - 20.00
    300 *Gonna Get My Baby* . . . . 15.00 - 20.00
TONY ALLEN (& THE CHAMPS/ TWILIGHTERS/WONDERS):
(See also THE CHIMES)
Bethlehem 3002 *Just Like Before* . . . . 5.00 - 8.00
Crown (LP) CLP 5231 *Rock And Roll with* . . . . . 15.00 - 20.00
Dig 109 *I Found An Angel* . . . . 10.00 - 15.00
Jamie 1119 *Looking For My Baby* . . . . 7.00 - 10.00
Kent 364 *Dreamin'* . . . . — - —
Ultra 104 *It Hurts Me So* . . . . 5.00 - 8.00
JOE ALLISON:
Dot 15714 *Baby Doll* . . . . 10.00 - 15.00
"ALL STAR ROCK & ROLL REVUE":
King (LP) 513 (various artists) . . . . 50.00 - 75.00
"ALL TIME COUNTRY & HILLBILLY FAVORITES":
Capitol (LP) 9103, 9107, (10") . . . . 15.00 - 20.00
"ALL TIME COUNTRY & WESTERN HITS":
King (LP) 537 . . . . 15.00 - 20.00
HERSCHEL ALMOND:
Ace 558 *Let's Get It On* . . . . 15.00 - 20.00

LUCKY JOE ALMOND:
Trumpet 199 *Rock Me* . . . . 10.00 - 15.00
    221 *Gonna Roll And Rock* . . . . 10.00 - 15.00
HENRY ALSTON:
Skyline 551 *Once In A Beautiful Lifetime* . . . . . . 7.00 - 10.00
ALTON & THE FLAMES:
Dutchess 1568 *Nothing Sweeter* . . . . 8.00 - 12.00
ALVANS:
May 102 *What Can It Be?* . . . . 5.00 - 8.00
THE AMBASSADORS: .
Bon 001 *Power Of Love* . . . . 8.00 - 12.00
Timely 1001 *Darling, I'm Sorry* . . . . 8.00 - 12.00
THE AMBERS:
Ebb 142 *Never Let You Go* . . . . 7.00 - 10.00
JOHNNY AMELIO:
Blue Moon 405 *Jugue* . . . . 40.00 - 60.00
Blue Moon 408 *Jo-Ann, Jo-Ann* . . . . 40.00 - 60.00
AMERICAN BEETLES:
Mammoth 102 *You're Getting To Me* . . . . 7.00 - 10.00
DOUG AMERSON:
IntraState 25 *Bop Man Bop* . . . . 30.00 - 50.00
ANDY ANDERSON (& THE DAWNBREAKERS/ROLLING STONES):
Apollo 535 *You Shake Me Up* . . . . 15.00 - 20.00
Century 601 *Gimme A Lock-A Yo' Hair* . . . . 15.00 - 20.00
    602 *Gonna Sit Right Down And Cry* . . . . . 15.00 - 20.00
Felsted 8508 *I-I-I- Love You* . . . . 8.00 - 12.00
BILL ANDERSON:
TNT 9015 *City Lights* . . . . 20.00 - 30.00
ELTON ANDERSON:
Trey 1002 *Wanta Come Back Home* . . . . 7.00 - 10.00
Vin 1001 *Roll On Train* . . . . 5.00 - 8.00
GENE ANDERSON & THE KEYNOTES:
Sage 329 *Wizard Rock* . . . . 7.00 - 10.00
Top Ten 252 *I've Got It Bad* . . . . 7.00 - 10.00
JIMMY ANDERSON (& HIS JOY JUMPERS):
Excello 2220, 2227, 2257 . . . . 5.00 - 8.00
Zynn 1014 *I Wanna Boogie* . . . . 10.00 - 15.00
DEBBIE ANDREWS (with the MUSKETEERS):
United 144 *Don't Make Me Cry* . . . . 10.00 - 15.00
GARY ANDREWS:
Artic---*Rockin' The Blues* . . . . — - —
LEE ANDREWS & THE HEARTS:
Casino 110 *Baby Come Back* . . . . 15.00 - 20.00
Chess 1665 *Long Lonely Nights* . . . . 5.00 - 8.00
Gotham 318 *Bluebird Of Happiness* . . . . 20.00 - 30.00
    320 *Lonely Room* . . . . 20.00 - 30.00
    321 *Just Suppose* . . . . 20.00 - 30.00
Mainline 105 *Teardrops* . . . . 10.00 - 15.00
Rainbow 250 *White Cliffs Of Dover* (red plastic) . 100.00 - 150.00
    252 *Maybe You'll Be There* (red plastic) . . . . . . 75.00 - 100.00
    259 *The Fairest* . . . . 40.00 - 60.00
Rivera 965 *Maybe You'll Be There* . . . . 75.00 - 100.00
UnArt 151 *Maybe You'll Be There* . . . . 5.00 - 8.00
ANDY & THE LIVE WIRES:
Applause 1249 *Maggie* . . . . 10.00 - 15.00
Liberty 55321 *You've Done It Again* . . . . 7.00 - 10.00
JOHNNY ANGEL:
Excello 2077 *Baby I'm Confessin'* . . . . 10.00 - 15.00
THE ANGELOS:
Tollie 9003 *Bad Motorcycle* . . . . 7.00 - 10.00
THE ANGELS:
Caprice (LP) *And The Angels Sing* . . . . 50.00 - 75.00
Gee 1024 *The Glory Of Love* . . . . 10.00 - 15.00
PAUL ANKA:
ABC Paramount (LP) 240 *Paul Anka* . . . . 15.00 - 20.00
    (LP) 296 *My Heart Sings* . . . . 15.00 - 20.00
    (LP) 420 *Diana* . . . . 15.00 - 20.00
ABC Paramount (LP) 323, 360, 390, 409 . . . . . . 10.00 - 15.00
    9831 *Diana* (78 RPM) . . . . 15.00 - 20.00
    9880 *You Are My Destiny* (78 RPM) . . . . . . 12.00 - 16.00
RPM 499 *I Confess* . . . . 15.00 - 20.00

PATTI ANN:
Aladdin 3198 *Sorrowful Heart*	20.00 -	25.00
3280 *Shtiggy Boom*	8.00 -	12.00

ANNETTE & CECIL NULL:
Epic 9829 *Moment Of Silence*	— -	—

THE ANNUALS:
Marconn 1 *Once In A Lifetime*	15.00 -	20.00

THE ANSWERS:
United 214 *Have No Fear*	15.00 -	25.00

PAUL ANTHONY:
Roulette 4099 *Bop Bop Bop!*	10.00 -	15.00

VINCE ANTHONY:
Hilton 0007 *Too Hot To Handle*	10.00 -	15.00
Viking 1018 *Clarabel*	10.00 -	15.00

THE APOLLOS:
Harvard 803 *I Love You Darling*	35.00 -	50.00

DAVE APPELL:
President 1013 *Applejack*	7.00 -	10.00

THE AQUA-NITES:
Astra 1000, 2001 *Lover Don't You Weep*	8.00 -	12.00

THE AQUATONES:
Fargo 1001 *You*	5.00 -	8.00
1002 *So Fine*	7.00 -	10.00
1003 *Our First Kiss*	7.00 -	10.00
1005 *My One Desire*	7.00 -	10.00
1015 *Every Time*	7.00 -	10.00
1016 *Crazy For You*	7.00 -	10.00
1022 *My Treasure*	7.00 -	10.00
Fargo (LP) FLP 3001 *"The Aquatones Sing"*	75.00 -	100.00

THE ARABIANS:
Carrie 1516 *My One Possession*	— -	—
JAM 3738 *Heaven Sent You*	15.00 -	20.00
Magnificent 102 *My Heart Beats Over*	10.00 -	15.00
114 *Teardrops In The Night*	10.00 -	15.00
Teek 4824 *Condition Your Heart*	15.00 -	25.00
Twin Star 1018 *Heaven Sent You*	15.00 -	25.00

ARCHIBALD:
Imperial 5212 *Great Big Eyes*	20.00 -	30.00
Imperial 5358 *Stack-A-Lee*	15.00 -	20.00

ARIST-O-KATS:
Vita 168 *I Don't See Me In Your Eyes*	10.00 -	15.00

SMOKEY ARMEN:
Peek-A-Boo 102 *Baby What Am I Gonna Do*	15.00 -	20.00

BILLY BOY ARNOLD:
Cool 103 *Hello Stranger*	10.00 -	20.00

EDDY ARNOLD:
Camden (LP) 471, 563	7.00 -	10.00
RCA Victor (LP) 1111 *Wanderin'*	20.00 -	30.00
1223 *All-Time Favorites*	15.00 -	20.00
1224 *Anytime*	15.00 -	20.00
1225 *Chapel On The Hill*	20.00 -	30.00
1293 *A Dozen Hits*	10.00 -	15.00
1377 *A Little On The Lonely Side*	15.00 -	20.00
1484 *When They Were Young*	15.00 -	20.00
(LP) 3027 (10") *Country Classics*	30.00 -	40.00
3031 (10") *All-Time Hits*	20.00 -	30.00
3117 (10") *Eddy Arnold*	20.00 -	30.00
3230 (10") *An American Institution*	20.00 -	30.00
3249 (10") *When It's Round-Up Time In Heaven*	20.00 -	30.00
Tops (LP) 1612 *Cowboy Songs Of The West*	8.00 -	12.00

JACK ARNOLD & THE CHALECOS:
Wildcat W-00018 *Pistol Packing Mama*	10.00 -	15.00

JAMES ARP:
Vellez 1515 *Let It Rock*	10.00 -	15.00

THE ARROGANTS:
Lute 6226 *Canadian Sunset*	7.00 -	10.00

THE ARROWS:
Flash 132 *Annie Mae*	15.00 -	20.00
Hugo 11172 *No Other Arms*	15.00 -	20.00

RICHIE ARTHUR:
Platter—*Walkin' Down A Lonesome Road*	7.00 -	10.00

THE ARTISTICS:

S & G—*One Way*	8.00 -	12.00

LITTLE JOE ARTWOOD:
Kingsport 105 *Cue Ball Blues*	10.00 -	15.00

THE ASCOTS:
Ace 650 *Perfect Love*	10.00 -	15.00
J & S 1628/1629 *What Love Can Do*	15.00 -	20.00

JOHN ASHLEY:
Dot 15775 *Born To Rock*	10.00 -	15.00

ASTRONAUTS:
Palladium 610 *Come Along Baby*	30.00 -	40.00

BOB ATCHER:
Columbia (LP) 9006 (10") *Early American Folksongs*	15.00 -	20.00
(LP) 9013 (10") *Songs Of The Saddle*	15.00 -	20.00

CHUCK ATHA:
Fox 1169 *Just Me And My Baby*	15.00 -	20.00

CHET ATKINS:
RCA Victor (LP) 1090 *Session*	20.00 -	30.00
1197 *In Three Dimensions*	20.00 -	30.00
1236 *Stringin' Along*	20.00 -	30.00
1383 *Finger—Style Guitar*	20.00 -	30.00
1544 *At Home*	15.00 -	20.00
1577 *Hi-Fi In Focus*	15.00 -	20.00
(LP) 3079 (10") *Galloping Guitar*	30.00 -	50.00
3163 (10") *Stringin' Along*	30.00 -	50.00

DAVE ATKINS AND HIS OFFBEATS:
Back Beat 511 *Shake—Kum—Down*	8.00 -	12.00

THE ATLANTICS:
Linda 107 *Remember The Night*	8.00 -	12.00

AUDREY:
Plus 104 *Dear Elvis*	10.00 -	15.00

LITTLE AUGIE AUSTIN (& THE CHROMATICS):
Brunswick 55080 *My Heart Let Me Be Free*	15.00 -	25.00
Pontiac 101 *I Thank My Lucky Star*	— -	—

BILLY AUSTIN & THE HEARTS:
Apollo 444 *Night Has Gone*	80.00 -	100.00

DON AUSTIN & THE SENSATIONAL DELLOS:
U-C 1031 *Why Did You Leave Me*	60.00 -	90.00
Mida 106 *So Shy*	15.00 -	20.00
109 *So Don't Go*	20.00 -	30.00

GENE AUTRY:
Columbia (LP) 9001 (10") *Western Classics*	15.00 -	20.00
(LP) 9002 (10") *Western Classics, Vol. 2*	15.00 -	20.00

FRANKIE AVALON:
Chancellor 1011 *De De Dinah* (78 RPM)	15.00 -	20.00
(LP) 5001 *Frankie Avalaon*	15.00 -	20.00
(LP) 5002 *Young Frankie Avalon*	15.00 -	20.00
(LP) 5004, 5009, 5011	10.00 -	15.00
(LP) 5022, 5027, 5031, 5032	10.00 -	15.00

THE AVALONS:
Casino 108 *You Do Something To Me*	15.00 -	20.00
Grove 0141 *Chains Around My Heart*	25.00 -	35.00
0174 *It's Funny But It's True*	25.00 -	35.00
NPC 302 *Begin The Beguine*	5.00 -	8.00
UnArt 2007 *Heart's Desire*	8.00 -	12.00

THE AVONS:
Groove 0039 *Whatever Happened To Our Love*	10.00 -	15.00
Hull 717 (black label) *Our Love Will Never End*	15.00 -	20.00
717 (orange label) *Our Love Will Never End*	8.00 -	12.00
722 *Baby*	15.00 -	20.00
726 *You Are So Close To Me*	10.00 -	15.00
728 *What Will I Do*	10.00 -	15.00
731 *What Love Can Do*	10.00 -	15.00
744 *Whisper (Softly)*	10.00 -	15.00
754 *A Girl To Call My Own*	10.00 -	15.00
(LP) HLP *The Avons*	100.00 -	150.00

BABY DEE:
MGM 1179 *Hold The Light For Me*	7.00 -	10.00

THE BACHELORS:
Earl 101 *Delores*	15.00 -	30.00

102 *Tell Me Now*	15.00 -	30.00

GAR BACON:
Baton 248 *There's Gonna Be Rocking Tonight* . . . 5.00 - 8.00

SHORTY BACON:
Ozark 1237 *Fire Of Love* . . . . 7.00 - 10.00

JACK BAILEY & THE NATURALS:
Ford 105 *Oh What Love Is* . . . . 30.00 - 40.00

LITTLE MARIE BAILEY:
Excello 2007 *Brownskin Woman Blues* . . . . 15.00 - 20.00
2016 *My Baby's Blues* . . . . 15.00 - 20.00

MORRIS BAILEY:
Bailey 500 *Calendar Hanging On The Wall* . . . . . 8.00 - 12.00

BOB BAKER:
Veeda 4006 *Turned On The Ice* . . . . — - —

CHARLIE BAKER:
Mun Rab 106 *You Crack Me Up* . . . . 15.00 - 20.00

DONNY BAKER:
Rainbow 219 *Drinking Wine Spo-Dee-O-Dee* . . . . 15.00 - 20.00

LAVERNE BAKER:
Atlantic (EP) 566, 588 . . . . 20.00 - 30.00
1004, 1030, 1047 . . . . 4.00 - 8.00
(LP) 1281 *Sings Bessie Smith* . . . . 30.00 - 40.00
(LP) 8007 *Lavern Baker* . . . . 30.00 - 40.00
(LP) 8030 *Blues Ballads* . . . . 35.00 - 50.00
(LP) 8036 *Precious Memories* . . . . 30.00 - 40.00
(LP) 8071 *See See Rider* . . . . 15.00 - 20.00
King 4556 *Trying* . . . . 10.00 - 15.00

RONNIE BAKER & THE DELTONES:
Laurie 3128 *My Story* . . . . 5.00 - 8.00

WILLIE BAKER:
DeLuxe 6023 *Before She Leaves Town* . . . . 20.00 - 35.00
Rockin' 527 *Before She Leaves Town* . . . . 20.00 - 35.00

EARL BALL:
Pathenon 101 *Party Of One* . . . . 7.00 - 10.00

THE BALLADS:
Franwil 5028 *Before You Fall In Love* . . . . 15.00 - 20.00
Ron-Cris 1003 *Somehow* . . . . 10.00 - 15.00
Veltone 1738 *I Hope I Never Fall In Love* . . . . . 20.00 - 30.00

FRANK BALLARD:
Phillips Int. (LP) 198 *"Rhythm—Blues Party"* . . 100.00 - Up

HANK BALLARD (& THE MIDNIGHTERS):
(See also: THE MIDNIGHTERS)
Federal (EP) 333, 435, 451 . . . . 30.00 - 50.00
King (LP) 541 *Their Greatest Juke Box Hits* . . . 100.00 - 150.00
(LP) 581 *Hank Ballard & The Midnighters* . . . 100.00 - 150.00
(LP) 618, 674, ... 30.00 - 50.00
(LP) 700, 748, 759, 781, 793 . . . . 20.00 - 30.00
King 5171 *The Twist* . . . . 5.00 - 8.00
5195 *Kansas City* . . . . 5.00 - 8.00
5215 *Sugaree* . . . . 7.00 - 10.00
King 5275, 5312, 5341, 5459 . . . . 4.00 - 7.00

JERRY BALLARD:
Skippy 120 *Pinch Me* . . . . 5.00 - 8.00

THE BALTINEERS:
Teenage 1000 *Moments Like This* . . . . 20.00 - 30.00
1002 *Tears In My Eyes* . . . . 20.00 - 30.00

JAMES BANISTER & HIS COMBO:
States 141 *Gold Digger* . . . . 20.00 - 30.00

DICK BANKS:
Liberty 55145 *Dirty Dog* . . . . 10.00 - 15.00

MACK BANKS:
Fame 580 *Be Boppin' Daddy* . . . . 30.00 - 40.00

OTIS BANKS:
Bow 304 *She's My Baby* . . . . 7.00 - 10.00

THE BANNERS:
MGM 12810 *My Own True Love* . . . . 8.00 - 12.00
12862 *Fortune Teller* . . . . 8.00 - 12.00

DON BARBER & THE DUKES:
Personality 3505 *Henrietta* . . . . 7.00 - 10.00

GLENN BARBER:
D 1098 *Go Home Letter* . . . . 10.00 - 15.00
Pic 1143 *I Created A Monster* . . . . 8.00 - 12.00

Starday 166 *Ice Water* . . . . 15.00 - 25.00
196 *Poor Man's Baby* . . . . 15.00 - 20.00
249 *Shadow My Baby* . . . . 20.00 - 30.00

PHIL BARCLAY & THE SLIDERS:
Doke 101 *Young Long John* . . . . 20.00 - 30.00
102 *I Love 'Em All* . . . . 20.00 - 30.00

BOBBY BARE:
Fraternity 861 *That's Where I Want To Be* . . . . 5.00 - 8.00

BARKER BROS:
Decca 30811 *Lovin' Honey* . . . . 7.00 - 10.00
Kent 302 *Hey Little Mama* . . . . 10.00 - 15.00

DELBERT BARKER:
King 4951 *No Good Robin Hood* . . . . 20.00 - 30.00

AL BARKLE:
Frantic 108 *Muscle Beach* . . . . 8.00 - 12.00
M&M 4041 *Jumpin' From Six To Six* . . . . 20.00 - 30.00

DEAN BARLOW (featured with THE
CRICKETS, which also see):
Jay-Dee 799, 803 . . . . 4.00 - 7.00

DEAN BARLOW & THE MONTEREYS:
Onyx 513 *Dearest One* . . . . 10.00 - 15.00

JUKE BOY BARNER:
Irma 111 *Well Baby* . . . . 15.00 - 20.00

BENNY BARNES:
D 1052 *Happy Little Blue Bird* . . . . 7.00 - 10.00
Starday 401 *You Gotta Pay* . . . . 15.00 - 20.00

DAVID BARNES:
San 302 *Lovin' On My Mind* . . . . 10.00 - 15.00

JIMMY BARNES & THE GIBRALTARS:
Gibraltar 102 *Be Careful With My Love* . . . . . . 5.00 - 8.00

THE BARONS:
Decca (EP) ED-2400 . . . . 10.00 - 15.00
29293 *Forget About Me* . . . . 15.00 - 20.00
48323 *A Year And A Day* . . . . 15.00 - 20.00
Imperial 5343 *Eternally Yours* . . . . 15.00 - 20.00
5359 *I Know I Was Wrong* . . . . 15.00 - 20.00
5370 *Searching For You* . . . . 15.00 - 20.00
5383 *So Long My Darling* . . . . 15.00 - 20.00
5397 *Once In A Lifetime* . . . . 15.00 - 20.00
Spartan 400 *I've Been Hurt* . . . . 7.00 - 10.00

CHUCK BARR & THE ROCKABILLIES:
Elsan 100 *Susie Or Mary Lou* . . . . 8.00 - 12.00

THE BARRETT SINGERS:
Reserve 124 *Lonesome Road* . . . . 10.00 - 15.00

HUGH BARRETT:
Lucky Four 1015 *Devil's Love* . . . . 15.00 - 20.00

RICHARD BARRETT:
Seville 104 *Dream On* . . . . 7.00 - 10.00

BILLY BARRIX:
Chess 1662 *Cool Off Baby* . . . . 75.00 - 100.00

LONNIE BARRON:
Sage 230 *Teenage Queen* . . . . 8.00 - 12.00

DAVE BARRY & SARA BERNER:
RPM 469 *Out Of This World With Flying Saucers* 5.00 - 8.00

JAY BARRY:
ABC Paramount 10226 *Love Spell* . . . . 7.00 - 10.00

JEFF BARRY:
RCA Victor 7477 *It's Called Rock And Roll* . . . . 7.00 - 10.00
7797 *Lonely Lips* . . . . 7.00 - 10.00
7821 *All You Need Is A Quarter* . . . . 7.00 - 10.00

JOE BARRY:
Jin 144, 152 . . . . 4.00 - 7.00

TEDDY BART:
Felsted 8514 *Headin' For A Weddin'* . . . . — - —

DAVE BARTHOLOMEW:
Bayou 005 *Country Gal* . . . . 20.00 - 30.00
Imperial 5322 *Another Mule* . . . . 7.00 - 10.00
(LP) 9162 *Fats Domino Presents* . . . . 20.00 - 30.00
(LP) 9217 *New Orleans House Party* . . . . . . 20.00 - 30.00

BART BARTON:
E & M 1651 *Ain't I'm A Mess* . . . . 10.00 - 15.00

BILLY (BOY) BARTON:

Gulf Reef 1001 *Monkey Business*	7.00 -	10.00
King 1478 *Do You Love Me*	7.00 -	10.00
Radio 117 *Doorway To Heaven*	7.00 -	10.00
Sims 176 *Even Steven*	7.00 -	10.00
Vidor 1007 *Crazy Lover*	7.00 -	10.00

DICK BARTON & THE REBELS:

Anthem 61712 *I Get The Blues*	15.00 -	20.00

OTTO BASH with THE RHYTHM ROCKERS:

Hidus 2008 *My Babe*	8.00 -	12.00
RCA Victor 6585 *The Elvis Blues*	8.00 -	12.00
RCA Victor most other issues	4.00 -	7.00

NORVEN BASKERVILLE & THE ADMIRATIONS:

X-tra 100 *Gonna Find My Pretty Baby*	10.00 -	15.00

TONY BASSETT:

Orchid 873 *Rocking Little Mama*	15.00 -	20.00

THE BATCHELORS:

Aladdin 3210 *Can't Help Lovin' You*	15.00 -	20.00

"BATTLE OF THE BLUES":

King (LP) 607 *Vol. 1 Roy Brown, Wynonie, Harris, Eddie Vinso*	75.00 -	100.00
King (LP) 627 *Vol. 2*	75.00 -	100.00
King (LP) 634 *Vol. 3 (Eddie Vinson, Jimmy Witherspoon)*	100.00 -	150.00
King (LP) 668 *Vol. 4*	150.00 -	250.00

RAY BATTS:

Bullet—*Wild Man Boogie*	-	
Excello 2028 *Stealin' Sugar*	10.00 -	15.00

DAVE BAUCOM:

Giant 1101 *That'll Be The Day*	10.00 -	15.00

ALLEN BAUM:

Red Robin 124 *My Kinda Woman*	25.00 -	35.00

THE BAY BOPS:

Coral 61975 *Joanie*	7.00 -	10.00

BILL BEACH:

King 4940 *Peg Pants*	25.00 -	35.00

RUFUS BEACHAM:

Chart 617 *Don't Say You Love Me*	10.00 -	15.00
627 *I Can't Believe*	10.00 -	15.00

THE BEACH BOYS:

Candix 301 *Surfin'*	50.00 -	75.00
301 (same, but bears notation: "Dist. by ERA RECORD SALES, INC.")	30.00 -	50.00
331 *Surfin'*	30.00 -	50.00
Capitol (Custom) KFWB Promotional Souvenir *Spirit Of America*	40.00 -	60.00
SXA-1981 (7-inch, for juke boxes) *Surfer Girl*	30.00 -	40.00
DU 2269 (7-inch, for juke boxes) *The Beach Boys Today*	30.00 -	40.00
PRO 2937 (Courtesy Of Downtown Salt Lake City Stores) *Salt Lake City*	75.00 -	100.00
(EP) PRO 2993 *Barbara Ann + 3*	40.00 -	60.00
4880 *Ten Little Indians*	5.00 -	8.00
(Note: Picture Sleeves for Cap. 4880 are scarce.)		
Capitol (EP) 5267 *4 by the Beach Boys*	30.00 -	50.00
"X" 301 *Surfin'*	75.00 -	100.00

DEAN BEARD (WITH THE CREW CATS/FOX FOUR SEVENS):

Atlantic 1137 *Rakin' And Scrapin'*	8.00 -	12.00
Atlantic 1137 *Rakin' And Scrapin'* (78 RPM)	10.00 -	20.00
1162 *Party Party*	8.00 -	12.00
1182 *Hold Me Close*	8.00 -	12.00
Challenge 59033 *Egad Charlie Brown*	5.00 -	8.00
Edmoral 1011 *Rakin' And Scrapin'*	15.00 -	25.00
Fox 405 *Red Rover*	15.00 -	20.00
408 *Sing Sing Sing*	15.00 -	20.00
Sangelo I *Party Party*	15.00 -	20.00

JIMMY BEASLEY:

Crown (LP) CLP 5014 *The Fabulous*	20.00 -	30.00

GOOD ROCKIN' (SAM) BEASLEY: (see also KID KING'S COMBO)

Excello 2011 *Happy Go Lucky*	15.00 -	20.00

2051 *Now Listen Baby*	8.00 -	12.00

THE BEATLES:

Atco (LP) 169 *Ain't She Sweet* (MONO)	30.00 -	50.00
(LP) 169 *Ain't She Sweet* (STEREO)	50.00 -	75.00
(LP) 169 (DJ) *Ain't She Sweet*	100.00 -	150.00
Atco 6302 *Sweet Georgia Brown*	7.00 -	10.00
6302 (DJ) *Sweet Georgia Brown*	30.00 -	40.00
6308 *Ain't She Sweet*	7.00 -	10.00
6308 (DJ) *Ain't She Sweet*	30.00 -	40.00
(Note: Picture sleeve to Atco 6308 is very scarce; originals have sold for as much as $75.00)		
Capitol SXA 2047 (7-inch, 33-1/3 rpm) *Meet The Beatles*	30.00 -	50.00
2056 (DJ) *Hello Goodbye*	20.00 -	30.00
SXA 2080 (7-inch, 33-1/3 rpm) *Beatles Second Album*	30.00 -	50.00
SXAS 2108 (7-inch, 33 1/3 rpm) *Something New*	40.00 -	60.00
(EP) EAP-2121 *Four By The Beatles*	50.00 -	75.00
2138 (DJ) *Lady Madonna*	20.00 -	30.00
(LP) ST-2553 *Yesterday and Today* (STEREO, with "first state" "Butcher" cover: Beatles are sitting among doll parts and pieces of raw meat. Withdrawn shortly after issue, and replaced with a more tasteful depiction of the Beatles gathered around a trunk. Prices as high as $5,000.00 have been quoted for this issue.)	1,000.00 -	Up
(LP) ST-2553 (same as foregoing, but with new cover pasted over "butcher" cover, traces of which are visible.*)	250.00 -	Up
(LP) T-2553 (MONO, with "first state" "butcher" cover. Prices as high as $1,500.00 have been seen for this issue)	300.00 -	Up
(LP) T-2553 (same as foregoing, but new cover pasted over "butcher" cover, traces of which are visible.*)	150.00 -	Up
*beware of "peeled" paste-overs being offered as "first state" issues.		
2637 (DJ) *KFW Beatles*	75.00 -	100.00
(Note: Picture sleeve for above is valuable)		
5150 *Can't Buy Me Love* (picture sleeve is quite scarce—record is of minimal value)		
(EP) EPR 5365 *4 By The Beatles*	50.00 -	75.00
5810 (DJ) *Penny Lane*	20.00 -	30.00
5964 (DJ) *All You Need Is Love*	20.00 -	30.00
(Note: Certain Capitol, reissues, including some of fairly recent vintage, are valued far more highly than original issues)		
Clarion (LP) 601 *The Amazing Beatles And Other Great English Group Sounds*	25.00 -	35.00
MGM 13213 *My Bonnie*	7.00 -	10.00
13213 (DJ) *My Bonnie*	30.00 -	50.00
13227 *Why*	10.00 -	15.00
13227 (DJ) *Why*	30.00 -	50.00
(Note: Picture sleeve for MGM 13227 is scarce)		
Radio Pulsebeat (LP) *The American Tour With Ed Rudy*	20.00 -	30.00
#Swan 4152 (white label, red printing, without legend *Don't Drop Out*) *She Loves You*	50.00 -	80.00
4152 (white label, red printing, with legend "*Don't Drop Out*") *She Loves You*	30.00 -	40.00
4152 (DJ) *She Loves You*	75.00 -	100.00
Tollie 9008 (DJ) *Love Me Do*	30.00 -	50.00
#Tollie (most other issues)	5.00 -	15.00
United Artists (LP) UAL-336 *A Hard Day's Night* (MONO)	100.00 -	Up
#Vee Jay 498 *Please Please Me*	80.00 -	120.00
498 (DJ) *Please Please Me*	100.00 -	150.00
(Note: Some issues of Vee Jay 498 have the group's name as by THE BEATTLES)		
522 *From Me To You*	30.00 -	40.00

522 (DJ) *From Me To You* . . . . 40.00 - 60.00
581 *Please Please Me* (purple label) . . . . 40.00 - 60.00
581 *Please Please Me* (white label) . . . . 30.00 - 40.00
581 (DJ) *Please Please Me* . . . . 40.00 - 60.00
(Note: Picture sleeve for Vee Jay 581 is very
scarce)
587 *Do You Want To Know A Secret* . . . . 8.00 - 12.00
587 (DJ) *Do You Want To Know a Secret* . . . . . 30.00 - 50.00
(Note: Picture sleeve for Vee Jay 587 is scarce)
(EP) 1-903 *Souvenir Of Their Visit To America* . . 20.00 - 30.00
Vee Jay (LP) LP-1062 *Introducing The Beatles*
  (Mono, black label, reverse of jacket depicts
  "other fine albums of significant interest") . . . .250.00 - Up
(LP) LP-1062 *Introducing The Beatles*
  (MONO, black label, reverse of jacket is
  blank) . . . . .100.00 - Up
(LP) LPS-1062 *Introducing The Beatles*
  (STEREO, black label, reverse of jacket has
  ads for other albums) . . . . .500.00 - Up
(LP) LPS-1062 *Introducing The Beatles*
  (STEREO, black label, reverse of jacket is
  blank) . . . . .200.00 - Up
(LP) LP-1085 *The Beatles and Frank Ifield On
Stage* MONO, picture of Beatles on cover; not
  to be confused with nominally-valued version
  having drawing of an old man on cover) . . . . . .200.00 - Up
(LP) LPS-1085 *The Beatles and Frank Ifield On
Stage* (STEREO, picture of Beatles on cover) . .500.00 - Up
(LP) LPS-1092 *Songs, Pictures and Stories of
  the Fabulous Beatles* (STEREO) . . . . .200.00 - Up
(Note: Prices far in excess of those listed above
  have been quoted for most of these top-drawer
  Beatles collectibles, with an occasional "still-
  sealed" copy being valued at as much as ten
  times the foregoing estimates. Whether such
  lofty figures are ever actually realized is not
  known. Also, how does the purchaser of a
  "still sealed" album satisfy himself that the
  appropriate LP is actually contained by the
  jacket?)
Note: These records (and others) occur with
  seemingly minute variations in label and/or
  covers, which may affect prices drastically.
  One interesting variation of Vee Jay 498 has the
  group designated as "THE BEATTLES."
IMPORTANT: The generally applicable caveat
  concerning bootlegs and reissues deserves
  particular emphasis in the case of the
  BEATLES' records. Also note that in many
  instances picture sleeves are worth far more
  than the record. Mentioned above are some of
  the most sought-after sleeves, but there are
  others which, although of lesser scarcity and
  value, are desirable (even where the record,
  unlisted here, is of nominal value). Finally,
  where a record listed is a promotional copy
  ("DJ" after record number), it should not be
  inferred that the regular issue is of comparable
  value; the regular issue, unless it is also listed,
  is common and of little value.
Those interested in pursuing the intricacies of
  Beatle records (and peripheral collectibles)
  should consult one of the books dealing with
  same, such as "The Official Price Guide to
  Memorabilia of Elvis Presley and The
  Beatles," by Osborne, Cox, and Lindsay.

THE BEATNICKS:
Key-Lock 913 *Blue Angel* . . . . 10.00 - 15.00
E.C. BEATTY:
Colonial 7009 *Little Blue Eyes* . . . . 5.00 - 8.00
THE BEAU-MARKS:
Rust 5035 *School Is Out* . . . . 5.00 - 8.00
Shad 5017 *Clap Your Hands* . . . . 5.00 - 8.00

5021 *'Cause We're In Love* . . . . 7.00 - 10.00
Time 1032 *Rockin' Blues* . . . . 15.00 - 20.00
STAN BEAVER:
Petal 1012 *I Got a Rocket In My Pocket* . . . . 5.00 - 8.00
THE BEAVERS:
Brunswick 65018 *If You See Tears In My Eyes* . . . 75.00 - 100.00
65026 *I'd Rather Be Wrong Than Blue* . . . . . . 75.00 - 100.00
THE BEES:
Imperial 5314 *Toy Bell* . . . . 25.00 - 35.00
THE BEL-AIRES/BELAIRES:
Flip 303 *This Paradise* . . . . 15.00 - 20.00
Raft 604 *Are You My Girl* . . . . 7.00 - 10.00
CARL BELEW:
Decca 30947 *Cool Gator Shoes* . . . . 7.00 - 10.00
Sowder 248 *I'm Long Gone* . . . . 8.00 - 12.00
BILL BELL & THE FOUR UNKNOWNS:
Mida 112 *Little Bitty Girl* . . . . 15.00 - 20.00
CARL BELL & THE NOVAIRS:
Laurie 3014 *Birth of The Beat* . . . . 7.00 - 10.00
DWAIN BELL:
Summit 110 *Rock & Roll On A Saturday Night* . . . 75.00 - 100.00
EDDIE/EDDY BELL:
Coed 512 *Countin' The Days* . . . . 5.00 - 8.00
Mercury 71677 *The Masked Man* . . . . 7.00 - 10.00
FREDDIE BELL & THE BELL BOYS:
Mercury (LP) 20289 *Rock and Roll* . . . . 20.00 - 30.00
Teen 101 *Hound Dog* (78 RPM) . . . . 10.00 - 15.00
JOHNNY BELL:
Brunswick 55142 *Flip Flop And Fly* . . . . 15.00 - 20.00
TOMMY BELL:
Zil 9001 *Swamp Gal* . . . . 25.00 - 40.00
THE BEL-LARKS:
Ransom 5001 *A Million And One Dreams* . . . . . . 35.00 - 50.00
THE BELL NOTES:
Madison 141 *Real Wild Child* . . . . 8.00 - 12.00
Time (EP)100 *I've Had It* . . . . 50.00 - 75.00
Time 1013 *Bettty Dear* . . . . 7.00 - 10.00
THE BELLS:
Rama 166 *What Can I Tell Her Now* . . . . 75.00 - 100.00
THE BELLTONES:
Grand (blue) 102 *Estelle* (red plastic) . . . . .300.00 - Up
TONY BELLUS:
NRC (LP) LPA 8 *Robbin The Cradle* . . . . 75.00 - 100.00
THE BELMONTS:
Sabrina 500 *Tell Me Why* . . . . 10.00 - 15.00
  501 *Searching For A New Love* . . . . 10.00 - 15.00
Sabina 502 *I Need Someone* . . . . 10.00 - 15.00
  503 *I Confess* . . . . 7.00 - 10.00
  505 *Come On Little Angel* . . . . 7.00 - 10.00
  507 *Diddle-Dee-Dum* . . . . 8.00 - 12.00
  509 *Ann Marie* . . . . 8.00 - 12.00
  513 *Let's Call It A Day* . . . . 8.00 - 12.00
  517 *Walk On By* . . . . 10.00 - 15.00
  519 *C'mon Everybody* . . . . 10.00 - 15.00
  521 *Summertime* . . . . 15.00 - 20.00
THE BELTONES:
Hull 721 *I Talk To My Echo* . . . . 15.00 - 20.00
Jell 188 *I Want To Be Loved* . . . . 15.00 - 20.00
THE BELVEDERES:
Baton 217 *Pepper Hot Baby* . . . . 10.00 - 15.00
Lucky Four 1003 *Wage Assignment Blues* . . . . . . 10.00 - 15.00
Trend 30-009 *Let's Get Married* . . . . 8.00 - 12.00
THE BELVIDEERS:
Buena Serra 1771 *Walking In The Garden* . . . . . . 35.00 - 50.00
JESSE BELVIN:
Cash 1056 *Beware* . . . . 8.00 - 12.00
J.R.M. 003/004 *Going Away Baby* . . . . 7.00 - 10.00
Modern 1005 *Goodnight My Love* . . . . 7.00 - 10.00
RCA Victor (LP) 2089 . . . . 20.00 - 30.00
  (LP) 2105 *Mr. Easy* . . . . 20.00 - 30.00
Specialty 550 *Gone* . . . . 5.00 - 8.00
559 *Where's My Girl* . . . . 5.00 - 8.00

ARNOLD BENNETT:
Sharp 110 *Wahoo* .... 7.00 - 10.00

BARBARA BENNETT:
Swade 101 *Big Daddy Rabbit* .... — - —

BOYD BENNETT (& HIS ROCKETS):
King (EP) 383 *Rock And Roll* .... 20.00 - 30.00
(LP) 532 *Boyd Bennett* .... 150.00 - 200.00
(LP) 594 *Boyd Bennett* .... 150.00 - 200.00
1413 *I've Had Enough* .... 7.00 - 10.00
1432 *You Upset Me Baby* .... 7.00 - 10.00
1275 *Tennessee Rock And Roll* .... 10.00 - 15.00
1494 *My Boy Flat Top* .... 4.00 - 7.00
4903 *Blue Suede Shoes* .... 7.00 - 10.00
4985 *Rockin' Up A Storm* .... 8.00 - 12.00
5094 *Put The Chain On The Door* .... 7.00 - 10.00
5115 *Move* .... 10.00 - 15.00
Mercury 71479 *Boogie Bear* .... 5.00 - 8.00

CLIFF BENNETT:
Capitol 4621 *You Got What I Like* .... 10.00 - 15.00

CHUCK BENNETT:
Bonnie 101 *I Went To Your House* .... 8.00 - 12.00

JOE BENSON:
DeLuxe 6146 *Rock And Roll Jungle* .... 7.00 - 10.00

BROOK BENTON (& THE SANDMEN):
Camden (LP) 564 .... 8.00 - 12.00
Epic (LP) LN-3573 *At His Best* .... 20.00 - 30.00
Mercury (LP) 20421 *It's Just A Matter Of Time* . 20.00 - 30.00
(LP) 20464 *Endlessly* .... 20.00 - 30.00
(LP) 20565 *So Many Ways* .... 15.00 - 20.00
Okeh 7058 *Ooh* .... 10.00 - 15.00
Vik 0311 *A Million Miles From Nowhere* .... 7.00 - 10.00

BUSTER BENTON:
Melloway 20668 *Hole In My Head* .... 7.00 - 10.00

MERV BENTON:
MarVel 401 *Twenty Hole In My Head* .... 20.00 - 30.00

WALT BENTON (& THE SNAPPERS):
20th Fox 143 *Big Wheel* .... 15.00 - 20.00

SHIRLEY BERGERON:
Lanor 510 *French Rocking Boogie* .... 10.00 - 15.00

ROD BERNARD (& THE TWISTERS):
Argo 5327 *Pardon Mr. Gordon* .... 7.00 - 10.00
Argo 5327 *Pardon Mr. Gordon* (78 RPM) ... 10.00 - 15.00
5338 *My Life Is A Mystery* .... 7.00 - 10.00
Jin 105 *Pardon Mr. Gordon* .... 12.00 - 16.00
(LP) 1007 *Rod Bernard* .... 20.00 - 30.00
Mercury 71654 *Dance Fool Dance* .... 7.00 - 10.00
Mercury (most other issues) .... 4.00 - 7.00

THE BERRY CUPS:
Khoury's 710 *Delores Darlin'* .... 8.00 - 12.00

THE BERRY KIDS:
MGM 12379 *Go, Go, Go, Right Into Town* ...... 15.00 - 20.00
MGM 12496 *You're My Teen Age Baby* ...... 15.00 - 20.00

CHUCK BERRY:
Chess (LP) 1426 *After School Session* ...... 30.00 - 50.00
(LP) 1432 *One Dozen Berrys* .... 30.00 - 50.00
(LP) 1435 *Chuck Berry Is On Top* ...... 30.00 - 50.00
(LP) 1448 *Rockin' At The Hops* .... 30.00 - 50.00
(Note: LPs must have black labels with silver
printing.)
Chess 1604 *Maybelline* (silver top label) ...... 8.00 - 12.00
1604 *Maybelline* (78 RPM) .... 10.00 - 15.00
1610 *Thirty Days* .... 8.00 - 12.00
1615 *No Money Down* .... 8.00 - 12.00
1626* *Roll Over Beethoven* .... 8.00 - 12.00
1635* *Brown Eyed Handsome Man* ..... 7.00 - 10.00
1645 *You Can't Catch Me* .... 5.00 - 8.00
1653 *School Day* .... 5.00 - 8.00
1664 *Oh Baby* .... 5.00 - 8.00
(Note: Foregoing have "silver top" labels)
Chess 1671* *Rock & Roll Music* .... 7.00 - 10.00
1683* *Reelin' And Rockin'* .... 7.00 - 10.00
1691* *Johnny B. Goode* .... 7.00 - 10.00

1697 *Vacation Time* .... 5.00 - 8.00
1700 *Carol* .... 7.00 - 10.00
1709* *Sweet Little Rock And Roller* ..... 10.00 - 15.00
1714 *Run Rudolph Run* .... 12.00 - 18.00
1716 *That's My Desire* .... 7.00 - 10.00
1722* *Little Queenie* .... 7.00 - 10.00
1729* *Back In The U.S.A.* .... 7.00 - 10.00
1737 *Childhood Sweetheart* .... 7.00 - 10.00
1747* *Let It Rock* .... 7.00 - 10.00
(Note: Any of the foregoing, in 78 RPM format,
are valued about the same as the 45s, except
that those with asterisk might being
substantially more-possibly twice as much)
Chess (most issues, higher numbers) .... 4.00 - 7.00
Chess (EP) 5118 *After School Session* .... 30.00 - 40.00
(EP) 5119 *Rock & Roll Music* .... 35.00 - 50.00
(EP) 5121 *Sweet Little Sixteen* .... 35.00 - 50.00
(EP) 5124 *Pickin' Berries* .... 30.00 - 40.00

DOROTHY BERRY:
Planetary 101 *Ain't That Love* .... 7.00 - 10.00

LOU BERRY & THE BELL RAVES:
Dreem 1001 *What A Dolly* .... 50.00 - 75.00
20th Fox 169 *What A Dolly* .... 15.00 - 25.00

MIKE BERRY & THE OUTLAWS:
Coral 62341 *Tribute To Buddy Holly* .... 10.00 - 15.00
62357 *Don't You Think It's Time* .... 8.00 - 12.00
62483 *Gonna Fall In Love* .... 8.00 - 12.00

RED BERRY & THE BELL RAVES: (See LOU
BERRY, sbove)

RICHARD BERRY (& THE DREAMERS/
PHARAOHS):
Crown (LP) 5371 *Richard Berry & The Dreamers* 30.00 - 40.00
Flair 1016 *I'm Still In Love With You* .... 15.00 - 20.00
1055 *What You Do To Me* .... 15.00 - 20.00
1058 *Baby Darling* .... 15.00 - 20.00
1064 *Please Tell Me* .... 15.00 - 20.00
1068 *God Gave Me You* .... 15.00 - 20.00
Flip 318 *Take The Key* .... 8.00 - 12.00
321 *Louie Louie* .... 8.00 - 12.00
327 *Rock Rock Rock* .... 8.00 - 12.00
331 *You're The Girl* .... 8.00 - 12.00
336 *Heaven On Wheels* .... 8.00 - 12.00
Flip other issues .... 4.00 - 8.00
RPM 448 *Rockin' Man* .... 8.00 - 12.00
452 *I Am Bewildered* .... 8.00 - 12.00
465 *Angel Of My Life* .... 8.00 - 12.00
476 *Wait For Me* .... 8.00 - 12.00

THE BEST OF RHYTHM AND BLUES:
Jubilee (LP) 1014 .... 30.00 - 50.00

BIG BOPPER: (See also: JAPE RICHARDSON)
D1008 *Chantilly Lace* .... 30.00 - 40.00
Mercury (LP) MG-20402 *Chantilly Lace* (black
& silver label) .... 100.00 - 150.00
(LP) MG-20402 *Chantilly Lace* (red label) ... 20.00 - 30.00
Mercury 71343 *Chantilly Lace* .... 5.00 - 8.00
71343 *Chantilly Lace* (78 RPM) .... 75.00 - 100.00
71375 *Big Bopper's Wedding* .... 5.00 - 8.00
71416 *Walking Through My Dreams* .... 10.00 - 15.00
71451 *It's The Truth, Ruth* .... 10.00 - 15.00
71482 *The Clock* .... 10.00 - 15.00

BIG CONNIE:
Groove 0142 *Mumbles Blues* .... 10.00 - 15.00

BIG DADDY:
Gee (LP) 704 *Big Daddy's Blues* .... — - —

BIG ED & HIS COMBO:
Checker 790 *Biscuit Baking Mama* .... 75.00 - 100.00

THE BIG FIVE:
Shad 5019 *Blue Eyes* .... 8.00 - 12.00

BIG FOUR:
Moon 306 *Outa Tune* .... 10.00 - 15.00

BIG MAC:
Tri-Mac 501 *Someday You're Gonna Sing The Blues* 10.00 - 15.00

BIG MACEO (with TAMPA RED):
Groove 5001 *Worried Life Blues* . . . . 10.00 - 15.00
RCA Victor 50-0002 (orange plastic) *If You Ever*
Change Your Ways . . . . 20.00 - 30.00

BIG MAYBELLE:
Okeh 7060 *Whole Lotta Shakin' Goin On* . . . . . . 15.00 - 20.00
(LP) 14005 *Big Maybelle Sings* . . . . 20.00 - 30.00
Savoy (LP) 14011 *Blues, Candy And Big Maybelle* 20.00 - 30.00

BIG MEMPHIS MA RAINEY: (See MARAINEY)

BIG WALTER (& HIS COMBO/THE THUNDERBIRDS):
Global 409 *Watusie Freeze* . . . . 5.00 - 8.00
Goldband 1080 *Crazy Dream* . . . . 7.00 - 10.00
Myrl 406 *Feelin' A Little Worried* . . . . 5.00 - 8.00
Peacock 1661 *Gamblin' Woman* . . . . 7.00 - 10.00
States 145 *Hard Hearted Woman* . . . . 15.00 - 20.00
Teardrop 3130 *Get To Gitten'* . . . . 5.00 - 8.00
TNT 8005 *Calling Margie* . . . . 20.00 - 30.00
8006 *Oh No, No Blues* . . . . 20.00 - 30.00

DICK BILLS:
Crest 1089 *Rockin' And Rollin'* . . . . 15.00 - 20.00

BILLY & LILLIE:
Casino 105 *La Dee Dah* . . . . 5.00 - 8.00
Swan 4002 *La Dee Dah* (78 rpm) . . . . 15.00 - 20.00

BILLY BOY:
Vee Jay 146 *I Was Fooled* . . . . 8.00 - 12.00
171 *I Ain't Got You* . . . . 5.00 - 8.00
192 *Here's My Picture* . . . . 5.00 - 8.00
238, 260 . . . . 4.00 - 6.00

BILLY GUITAR & HIS NIGHTHAWKS:
Decca 30634 *Here Comes The Night* . . . . 10.00 - 15.00

BILLY THE KID:
Kapp 261 *Apron Strings* . . . . 10.00 - 15.00

LONG MAN BINDER:
United 194 *I'm A Lover* . . . . 15.00 - 20.00

BING BONGS:
Dragon 10205 *Ding-A-Ling-A-Ling-Ding-Dong* . . — - —

BIP AND BOP:
Aladdin 3287 *Ding Dong Ding* . . . . 5.00 - 8.00

LARRY BIRDSONG:
Excello 2064, 2076 . . . . 5.00 - 8.00

OTIS BLACKWELL:
Davis (LP) 109 *Singin' The Blues* . . . . 75.00 - 100.00
Davis 455 *Daddy Rollin' Stone* . . . . 10.00 - 15.00
Jay-Dee 784 *Daddy Rollin' Stone* . . . . 10.00 - 15.00
787 *Bartender, Fill It Up Again* . . . . 8.00 - 12.00
791 *On That Power Line* . . . . 8.00 - 12.00
792 *I'm Standing At The Doorway* . . . . 8.00 - 12.00
794 *Ain't Got No Time* . . . . 8.00 - 12.00
798 *Go Away Mr. Blues* . . . . 8.00 - 12.00
802 *You More Me Baby* . . . . 7.00 - 10.00
808 *Let The Daddy Hold You* . . . . 10.00 - 15.00

THE BLACKWELLS:
GB 125 *Here's The Question* . . . . 15.00 - 20.00

TOMMY BLAKE:
Buddy 107 *Cool It (Baby)* . . . . 100.00 - 150.00
RCA Victor 6925 *Freedom* . . . . 5.00 - 8.00
Sun 278 *Flat Foot Sam* . . . . 10.00 - 15.00
300 *I Dig You Baby* . . . . 100.00 - 150.00

CLIFF BLAKELEY:
Starday 352 *High Steppin'* . . . . 20.00 - 30.00
369 *Get Off My Toes* . . . . 20.00 - 30.00

CORNELL BLAKELY:
Fulton 2453 *Don't Touch The Moon* . . . . 15.00 - 20.00

JIMMY BLAKELEY:
Starday 299 *Crazy Blues* . . . . 20.00 - 30.00

WELLINGTON BLAKELY:
Vee Jay 104 *Sailor Joe* . . . . 15.00 - 25.00

JACKIE BLANCHARD with THE ROCKING IMPALAS:
Mida 111 *The King O'Hearts* . . . . 15.00 - 20.00

BILLY BLAND:
Old Town 1016 *The Fat Man* . . . . 7.00 - 10.00

BOBBY BLUE BLAND:
Crown (LP) 5258 *Two In Blues* . . . . 20.00 - 30.00
Duke (LP) 74 *Two Steps From The Blues* . . . . . . 20.00 - 30.00
(LP) 77 *Call On Me* . . . . 20.00 - 30.00
(LP) 78 *Ain't Nothing You Can Do* . . . . . . 20.00 - 30.00
(Above LPs are MONO issues)
Duke 141, 153, 170, 182, 185 . . . . 5.00 - 10.00
Duke 105 *I.O.U. Blues* . . . . 30.00 - 50.00
115 *Army Blues* . . . . 20.00 - 30.00

GLENN BLAND:
Sarg 159 *Mean Gene* . . . . 15.00 - 20.00
164 *When My Baby Passes By* . . . . 20.00 - 30.00

BLANKENSHIP BROTHERS:
Skyline 106 *That's Why I'm Blue* . . . . 10.00 - 15.00

THE BLASERS:
United 191 *She Needs To Be Loved* . . . . 10.00 - 15.00

JULES BLATTNER:
Bobbin 105 *Rock And Roll Blues* . . . . 20.00 - 30.00
K-Ark 609 *Lonesome* . . . . 10.00 - 15.00
Norman 509 *Slip 'N Slide* . . . . 5.00 - 8.00

BLAZER BOY (See also JAMES LOCKS):
Imperial 5199 *Mornin' Train* . . . . 20.00 - 30.00

STEVE BLEDSOE:
Scope 8266 *Cool Steppin' Baby* . . . . 20.00 - 30.00
Witch 102 *Dumb Dumb Bunny* . . . . 20.00 - 30.00

THE BLENDAIRS:
Tin Pan Alley 252 *My Love Is Just For You* . . . . 10.00 - 15.00

THE BLENDERS:
Class 236 *Little Rose* . . . . 10.00 - 15.00
Decca 31284 *Tell Me What's On Your Mind* . . . . 15.00 - 20.00
48156 *Gone* . . . . 15.00 - 20.00
48244 *You Do The Dreamin'* . . . . 15.00 - 20.00
Paradise 111 *I Won't Tell The World* . . . . 15.00 - 20.00

THE BLENDS:
Casa Grande 5000 *A Thousand Miles Away* . . . . 10.00 - 15.00
5037 *Someone To Care* . . . . 8.00 - 12.00
Talent 110 *Tell Me* . . . . 7.00 - 10.00

THE BLENDTONES:
MGM 12782 *Lilly* . . . . 15.00 - 20.00

MARV BLIHOVE:
Lindy 113 *Cigarettes And Coffee Blues* . . . . 10.00 - 15.00

THE BLOCKBUSTERS:
Aladdin 3319 *Why Baby Why* . . . . 10.00 - 15.00

THE BLUE ANGELS:
Edsel 781 *Deserie* . . . . 10.00 - 15.00

THE BLUE BELLES:
Atlantic 987 *The Story Of A Fool* . . . . 5.00 - 8.00

BLUE CHARLIE:
Nasco 6002 *I'm Gonna Kill That Hen* . . . . 15.00 - 25.00

THE BLUE CHIPS:
Groove 0006 *Promise* . . . . 5.00 - 8.00

THE BLUE DIAMONDS:
Savoy 1134 *No Money* . . . . 15.00 - 20.00

THE BLUE DOTS:
Ace 596 *Please Don't Tell 'Em* . . . . 7.00 - 10.00
De Luxe 6052 *You've Got To Live For Yourself* . . 20.00 - 30.00
6055 *Street Of Sorrow* . . . . 20.00 - 30.00
6061 *Save All Your Love For Me* . . . . 20.00 - 30.00
6067 *Hold Me Tight* . . . . 20.00 - 30.00
NRC 504 *All You Gotta Do* . . . . 5.00 - 8.00

BLUE FLAMES (See LITTLE JUNIOR)

THE BLUE JAYS:
Blue Jay 102 *Write Me A Letter* . . . . 35.00 - 50.00
Checker 782 *White Cliffs Of Dover* . . . . 100.00 - 150.00
Milestone 2008 *Lover's Island* . . . . 4.00 - 7.00
2010 *Let's Make Love* . . . . 5.00 - 8.00
Roulette 4169 *Barbara* . . . . 7.00 - 10.00

THE BLUE NOTES:
Josie 800 *If You Love Me* . . . . 15.00 - 20.00
823 *The Retribution Blues* . . . . 15.00 - 20.00

Lost—*She Is Mine*	15.00 -	20.00
Port 70021 *If You Love Me*	8.00 -	12.00
TNT 150 *Darling Of Mine*	7.00 -	10.00
20th Century 1213 *Pucker Your Lips*	5.00 -	8.00
Value 213 *My Hero*	7.00 -	10.00

"THE BLUES":
Argo (LP) 4026	20.00 -	30.00

THE BLUES ROCKERS:
Excello 2062 *Calling All Cows*	10.00 -	15.00

BLUES SLIM:
Five-Four 5435 *Drivin' Me, Baby*	7.00 -	10.00

THE BLUES TOPPERS:
Duke 172 *Sleeping In An Ocean Of Tears*	10.00 -	15.00

THE BLUE TONES:
King 5088 *Shake Shake*	15.00 -	20.00

TOOTER BOATMAN:
Twinkle 501 *More And More*	75.00 -	100.00

HARMON BOAZEMAN:
Sarg 145 *No Love In You*	20.00 -	30.00

BOB AND LUCILLE:
Ditto 121 *Eenie Meenie Miney Moe*	25.00 -	40.00
126 *What's The Password*	8.00 -	12.00
Imperial 5631 *Eenie Meenie Miney Moe*	10.00 -	15.00

BOB AND RAY:
Nasco 6023 *Shorty Shorty*	8.00 -	12.00
Nasco 6029 *Sweet Nancy*	8.00 -	12.00

BOB & THE ROCKABILLIES:
Blue Chip 011 *Your Kind Of Love*	10.00 -	15.00

BOB AND SHERI:
Safari 101 *The Surfer Moon*	100.00	Up

(DJ: white label; regular issue; blue label.
   Caution: Bootlegs exist of this early BEACH
   BOYS related disc.)

THE BOBBETTES:
Atlantic 1144 *Mr. Lee* (78 RPM)	10.00 -	15.00

BOBBY & THE ORBITS:
Seeco 6067 *Felicia*	7.00 -	10.00

BILL BODAFORD & THE ROCKETS:
Back Beat 507 *Little Girl*	15.00 -	20.00

THE BON-AIRES
Dootone 325 *It's Xmas Time*	10.00 -	15.00
King 4975 *Stop The World*	7.00 -	10.00

EDDIE BOND (& HIS STOMPERS):
Coral 62200 *Little Black Book*	15.00 -	20.00
D 1016 *The Blues Got Me*	15.00 -	20.00
Diplomat 8566 *The Monkey And The Baboon*	15.00 -	20.00
Ekko 1015 *Talkin' Off The Wall*	50.00 -	75.00
1016 *Love Makes A Fool*	30.00 -	40.00
Memphis 115 *Here Comes The Train*	20.00 -	30.00
Mercury 70826 *Rockin' Daddy*	15.00 -	20.00
70882 *Slip Slip Slippin' In*	15.00 -	20.00
70941 *Boppin' Bonnie*	15.00 -	25.00
71067 *You're Part Of Me*	10.00 -	15.00
71153 *Hershey Bar*	10.00 -	15.00
71237 *Backslidin'*	10.00 -	15.00
Stomper Time 1156 *You'll Never Be A Stranger*	10.00 -	15.00

JOHNNY BOND:
Columbia 21521 *The Little Rock Roll*	7.00 -	10.00
Republic 2005 *Hot Rod Lincoln*	5.00 -	8.00
2008 *The Way A Star Is Born*	8.00 -	12.00
2010 *Side Car Cycle*	8.00 -	12.00
2022 *Sadie Was A Lady*	7.00 -	10.00

LUTHER BOND & HIS EMERALDS:
Federal 12279 *He Loves You Baby*	15.00 -	20.00
12368 *Old Mother Nature*	15.00 -	20.00
Savoy 1124 *What If You*	15.00 -	20.00
1131 *Starlight, Starbright*	10.00 -	15.00
1159 *It's Written In The Stars*	10.00 -	15.00

GARY U.S. BONDS (See U.S. BONDS)

LEE BONDS:
Decca 29338 *I'm Lookin' For Some Lovin'*	5.00 -	8.00
Tennessee 804 *Oh-Huh Honey*	10.00 -	15.00

826 *Wild Cattin' Woman*	10.00 -	15.00

U.S. BONDS:
Legrand (LP) 3001 *Dance Til Quarter To Three*	30.00 -	40.00
(LP) 3002 *Twist Up Calypso*	20.00 -	30.00

JOHNNY BONI:
Black-Crest 108 *Ruby Baby*	10.00 -	15.00

JUKE BOY BONNER:
Goldband 1102 *Call Me Juke Boy*	15.00 -	20.00

THE BONNEVILLES:
Barry 104 *Lorraine*	5.00 -	8.00
Munich 103 *Lorraine*	30.00 -	40.00

BOOGALOO:
Crest 1030 *Cops and Robbers* (red plastic)	15.00 -	20.00

BOOGIE JAKE:
Chess 1746 *Bad Luck And Trouble*	10.00 -	15.00
Instant 3314 *Early Morning Blues*	8.00 -	12.00

BOOGIE KINGS:
Pic 1 133 *Let It Be Me*	8.00 -	12.00

JOHN LEE BOOKER:
De Luxe 6004 *Blue Monday*	20.00 -	30.00
6032 *Pouring Down Rain*	15.00 -	20.00
6046 *Real Real Gone*	15.00 -	20.00
Rockin' 525 *Pouring Down Rain*	30.00 -	40.00

CONNIE BOOKS:
Citation 5001 *Black Magic And Witchcraft*	7.00 -	10.00

PAT BOONE:
Dot (LP) 3050 *Pat*	10.00 -	15.00
Republic 7049, 7062, 7084	5.00 -	8.00

THE BOP-CHORDS:
Holiday 2601 *Castle In The Sky*	15.00 -	20.00
2603 *When I Woke Up This Morning*	15.00 -	20.00
2608 *Baby*	12.00 -	16.00

**"BOPPIN" (With THE ORIOLES, THE
   MARYLANDERS, etc al.)**
Jubilee (LP) 1118	30.00 -	50.00

BOSSTONES:
Boss 501 *Mope-Itty Mope*	8.00 -	12.00
V-Tone 208 *Mope-Itty Mope*	5.00 -	8.00

BOBBY BOSTON:
Starwin 7001 *Lazy Daisy*	8.00 -	12.00

BILL BOWEN & THE ROCKETS:
Meteor 5033 *Have Myself A Ball*	40.00 -	60.00

JIMMY BOWEN:
Blue Moon 402 *I'm Stickin' With You*	50.00 -	75.00
Roulette 4001, 4010	4.00 -	7.00
Roulette 4010 *I'm Sticking' With You* (78rpm)	10.00 -	15.00
4010 *Warm Up To Me Baby* (78rpm)	10.00 -	15.00
4023 *It's Shameful*	4.00 -	7.00
4023 *It's Shameful* (78rpm)	10.00 -	15.00
(LP) 25004 *Jimmy Bowen*	30.00 -	50.00
Triple-D 797 *I'm Stickin' With You*	75.00 -	100.00

CHUCK BOWERS:
Decca 30356 *Til My Baby Comes Home*	7.00 -	10.00

DOUG BOWLES:
Tune 206 *Cadillac Baby*	15.00 -	25.00

CECIL BOWMAN:
D 1048 *Man-A- Waitin'*	7.00 -	10.00
Saturday 336 *Blues Around My Door*	15.00 -	20.00

DONNIE BOWSER:
Era 3029 *Stone Heart*	7.00 -	10.00
Sage 265 *I Love You Baby*	10.00 -	15.00
276 *Got The Best Of Me*	10.00 -	15.00

LITTLE DONNIE BOWSHIER:
Dess 7002 *Rock And Roll Joys*	60.00 -	90.00

DAVID BOX:
Joed 717 *Do The Best I Can*	15.00 -	20.00

EDDIE BOYD:
Bea & Baby 101, 107, 108	7.00 -	10.00
Chess 1523 *Cool Kind Treatment*	15.00 -	20.00
1533 *The Tickler*	10.00 -	15.00
1541, 1552, 1561, 1573, 1576, 1582, 1595, 1606, 1621, 1634	7.00 -	10.00
1660, 1674	5.00 -	8.00

Herald 406 *I'm Goin' Downtown*	30.00 -	40.00
J.O.B. 1005 *I'm Pleading*	50.00 -	80.00
1007 *Five Long Years*	30.00 -	50.00
1009 *I'm Pleading*	50.00 -	75.00
1114 *I Love You*	50.00 -	80.00
Oriole 1316/1317 *Five Long Years*	10.00 -	15.00

JIMMY BOYD:

Columbia 21571 *Shakin' Down The Mississippi*	7.00 -	10.00

ROBERT BOYD:

Wasco 201 *Boyd's Bounce*	75.00 -	100.00

HELEN BOZEMAN:

Sandy 1011 *Sugar Baby*	15.00 -	20.00

TOMMY BRADEN:

United 177 *Do The Do*	8.00 -	12.00

ROCKIN' BRADLEY:

Fire 1007 *Look Out*	15.00 -	20.00

JACK BRADSHAW:

Mar Vel 750 *Don't Tease Me*	8.00 -	12.00
752 *Naughty Girls*	8.00 -	12.00

JIMMY BRADSHAW:

McBrad 1000 *When School's Out*	7.00 -	10.00

TINY BRADSHAW:

King (LP) 501 *Selections*	15.00 -	20.00
4497 *Train Kept-A-Rollin'*	8.00 -	12.00

DOUG BRAGG:

Coral 61716 *Barbed Wire Love*	10.00 -	15.00
D 1045 *Calling Me Back*	8.00 -	12.00
Dixie 2002 *Lovin' On My Mind*	15.00 -	20.00
Pretty Little Thing	15.00 -	20.00

JOHNNY BRAGG & THE MARIGOLDS:

Excello 2078 *Foolish Me*	15.00 -	20.00
2091 *Juke Box Rock 'n' Roll*	15.00 -	20.00

RONNIE BRANHAM:

Pep 117 *You Treat Me Like A Fool*	15.00 -	20.00

BOBBY BRANT:

East West 124 *Piano Nellie*	10.00 -	15.00
White Rock 1114 *Piano Nellie*	40.00 -	60.00

NICKY BRAZZELL:

Sparr—*Betty Joe*	— -	—

JIMMY BREEDLOVE:

Atco 6094 *That's My Baby*	7.00 -	10.00
Diamond 144 *Jealous Fool*	7.00 -	10.00

JACKIE BRENSTON:

Federal 12283 *Gonna Wait For My Chance*	10.00 -	15.00
12291 *The Mistreater*	10.00 -	15.00

FRANKIE BRENT (& THE COUNTS):

Calvert 201 *No Rock 'n' Rollin' Here*	15.00 -	20.00
Strand 25014 *No Rock 'n' Rollin' Here*	10.00 -	15.00
Vik 0322 *Cold As Ice*	10.00 -	15.00

RONNIE BRENT:

Colt 45 101 *Shirley Ann*	15.00 -	20.00

BRENTWOODS:

Dore 559 *Midnight Star*	7.00 -	10.00

ROBIN HOOD BRIANS:

Fraternity 803 *Dis a Itty Bit*	30.00 -	50.00

JAY BRINKLEY:

Kliff 101 *Guitar Smoke*	30.00 -	40.00

LARRY BRINKLEY:

Magic—*Right String But The Wrong Yo Yo*	— -	—
Westwood—*Jackson Dog*	— -	—

DARRYL BRITT:

Blue 1199 *Lover Lover*	10.00 -	15.00

ELTON BRITT:

ABC Paramount (LP) 293 *Wandering Cowboy*	15.00 -	20.00
(LP) 322 *Beyond The Sunset*	15.00 -	20.00
RCA Vitor (LP) 1288 *Yodel Songs*	15.00 -	20.00

BOBBY BROOKES:

RCA Victor 7238 *You'd Better Move*	5.00 -	8.00

BROOKLYN BOYS:

Ferris 902 *Every Night*	7.00 -	10.00

CHUCK BROOKS:

Dub 2844 *Spinning My Wheels*	10.00 -	15.00

LILLIAN BROOKS (& THE MOROCCOS):

King 4934 *For Only You*	10.00 -	15.00
4956 *Sweet Sweet William*	10.00 -	15.00

LOUIS BROOKS (& HIS HI-TOPPERS)

Excello 2042, 2056, 2063, 2100, 2119	7.00 -	10.00
2141, 2159	5.00 -	8.00

SONNY BROOKS:

Tip Top 1008 *I'm So Downhearted*	8.00 -	12.00

BIG BILLY BROONZY:

Columbia (LP) 111 *Big Bill's Blues*	15.00 -	20.00
EmArcy (LP) 20634 (10") *Folk Blues*	40.00 -	60.00
Folkways (LP) 2326 *Sings Country Blues*	10.00 -	15.00
(LP) 3586 *Songs And Story*	10.00 -	15.00
Mercury (LP) 36137 *Blues*	30.00 -	50.00
Period (LP) 1114 (10") *Sings*	50.00 -	80.00

THE BROTHERS:

Argo 5318 *Deep Sleep*	7.00 -	10.00

BILLY BROWN:

Columbia 41029 *Did We Have A Party*	8.00 -	12.00
41100 *Meet Me In The Alley, Sally*	8.00 -	12.00
41297 *Flip Out*	8.00 -	12.00
41380 *Run 'Em Off*	7.00 -	10.00
Republic 2007 *Lost Weekend*	7.00 -	10.00

BOBBY BROWN & THE CURIOS:

Vaden 100 *Down At Big Mary's Place*	30.00 -	40.00

BUSTER BROWN:

Fire (LP) 102 *The New King Of The Blues*	75.00 -	100.00
1008 *Fannie Mae* (78rpm)	75.00 -	100.00

This is one of the last 78 rpm records to be issued, and as such, is much sought-after. Rumors of prices far in excess of those here quote remain unconfirmed.)

CHARLES BROWN:

Ace 561 *Educated Fool*	7.00 -	10.00
Aladdin (LP) 702 (10") *Mood Music* (pressed of red vinyl)	150.00 -	250.00
(LP) 702 (10") *Mood Music* (black vinyl)	100.00 -	150.00
(LP) 809 (12") *Mood Music*	150.00 -	200.00
Aladdin 3091 *The Message*	10.00 -	15.00
3092 *Seven Long Days*	10.00 -	15.00
3116 *Hard Times*	10.00 -	15.00
3120 *My Last Affair*	10.00 -	15.00
3138 *Without Your Love*	10.00 -	15.00
3157 *Rollin' Like a Pebble in the Sand*	10.00 -	15.00
3163 *Moonrise*	10.00 -	15.00
3176 *Rising Sun*	10.00 -	15.00
3191 *Lonesome Feeling*	10.00 -	15.00
3200 *All My Life*	10.00 -	15.00
3209 *Cryin' And Driftin' Blues*	10.00 -	15.00
3220 *Everybody's Got Troubles*	10.00 -	15.00
3235 *Crying Mercy*	10.00 -	15.00
3254 *My Silent Love*	10.00 -	15.00
Aladdin 3284, 3290, 3316, 3339, 3342, 3348	7.00 -	12.00

(Note: Aladdin numbers prior to 3091 may be found as 45rpm records, but they are scarce, and would command prices higher than earliest issues listed above. Aladdin 78 RPM records by Charles Brown are usually valued at $5.00 to $10.00.)

Hollywood 1006 *Pleading For Your Love*	8.00 -	12.00
1021 *Merry Christmas Baby*	8.00 -	12.00
Imperial (LP) 9257 *The Best of The Blues*	40.00 -	60.00
Score (LP) 4011 *Drifting Blues*	75.00 -	100.00
Swing Time 238 *Lost in the Night*	15.00 -	20.00
259 *Be Fair With Me*	15.00 -	20.00
276 *Moonrise*	15.00 -	20.00

CHARLIE BROWN & HIS CISCO KIDS:

Rose 101 *Mean, Mean, Mama*	15.00 -	20.00
102 *Have You Heard The Gossip*	15.00 -	20.00

DANNY BROWN:

Earth 702 *Standing On The Corner*	7.00 -	10.00

DUSTY BROWN:
Bandera 2503 *Please Don't Go*	8.00 -	12.00
Parrot 820 *Yes She's Gone*	15.00 -	20.00

EARL "GOOD ROCKING" BROWN:
Kappa 207 *Turn Back The Time*	15.00 -	20.00

GATEMOUTH BROWN: (See also Blues 78 rpm section)
Cue 1050 *Leftover Blues*	7.00 -	10.00
Peacock 1617 *Boogie Uproar*	10.00 -	15.00
1619 *Please Tell Me Baby*	10.00 -	15.00
1633 *Midnight Hour*	10.00 -	15.00
1637 *Depression Blues*	10.00 -	15.00
1653 *Gate's Salty Blues*	10.00 -	15.00
1662 *September Song*	8.00 -	12.00

GENE BROWN:
Gene Brown 28 *Big Door*	15.00 -	20.00
Dot 15709 *Big Door*	10.00 -	15.00

GUY BROWN with RED CAMPI & HIS BAND:
Echo 5002 *How Long Will It Be*	20.00 -	30.00

HYLO BROWN:
Capitol (LP) 1168	15.00 -	20.00

J.T. BROWN:
Meteor 5016 *Dumb Woman Blues*	30.00 -	40.00

JAMES BROWN (& THE FAMOUS FLAMES):
King (LP) 610 *Please, Please*	30.00 -	50.00
(LP) 743 *The Amazing James Brown*	20.00 -	30.00
(LP) 826 *Live at the Apollo*	30.00 -	50.00

JIM EDWARD & THE BROWNS:
RCA Victor (LP) 1438	10.00 -	15.00
(LP) 2144 *Sweet Sounds*	10.00 -	15.00
(LP) 2174 *Town & Country*	10.00 -	15.00

JIMMY BROWN:
Capitol 3255 *It's Over*	10.00 -	15.00

MARCUS BROWN:
Khoury's 734 *Lover Lee*	10.00 -	15.00

MILTON BROWN & HIS BROWNIES:
Decca (LP) 5561 (10″) *Dance-O-Rama*	30.00 -	50.00

NAPPY BROWN:
Savoy most issues	3.00 -	6.00
Savoy (LP) 14002 *Nappy Brown Sings*	15.00 -	20.00
(LP) 14025 *The Right Time*	15.00 -	20.00

ROY BROWN:
(See Also: "Battle of The Blues")
Home of the Blues 107 *Don't Break My Heart*	7.00 -	10.00
110 *Rocking All The Time*	7.00 -	10.00
115 *Sugar Baby*	7.00 -	10.00
Imperial 5422, 5427, 5439	5.00 -	8.00
5510 *Hip Shakin' Baby*	10.00 -	15.00
King (EP) 254 *Blues Boogie*	30.00 -	50.00
4602 *Travelin' Man*	10.00 -	15.00
4609 *Money Can't Buy Love*	10.00 -	15.00
4627 *Gamblin' Man*	10.00 -	15.00
4637 *Old Age Boogie*	10.00 -	15.00
4669 *Caldonia's Wedding Day*	10.00 -	15.00
4704, 4715, 4731, 4761, 4834	8.00 -	12.00
King (higher numbers)	5.00 -	8.00

RUTH BROWN:
Atlantic (EP) 535 *Ruth Brown Sings*	30.00 -	40.00
Atlantic 919 *Teardrops From My Eyes*	20.00 -	30.00
941 *I Know*	10.00 -	15.00
973 *Have A Good Time*	8.00 -	12.00
978 *Three Letters*	8.00 -	12.00
1005, 1023, 1027, 1036, 1044	5.00 -	8.00
(LP) 1308 *Late Date With*	30.00 -	40.00
(LP) 8004 *Ruth Brown*	35.00 -	50.00
(LP) 8026 *Miss Rhythm*	30.00 -	40.00
(LP) 8080 *The Best Of Ruth Brown*	10.00 -	15.00
(Note: Above must be original MONO issues)		
King (LP) 115 (10″) (reported; existence not verified)	300.00 -	Up

TOMMY BROWN:
Imperial 5476 *Rock Away My Blues*	8.00 -	12.00
5533 *Just For You*	7.00 -	10.00

WALTER BROWN:
Zip 4686 *Alley Cat*	30.00 -	40.00

LITTLE WILLIE BROWN:
Chart 1485 *Things Ain't Like They Use To Be*	10.00 -	15.00
Do-Ra-Me 1404 *Cut It Out*	10.00 -	15.00
Suntan 1112 *Going Back To The Country*	10.00 -	15.00
Topic 223 *Do It Like That*	10.00 -	15.00

WINI BROWN & HER BOYFRIENDS:
Mercury 5870 *Here In My Heart*	15.00 -	20.00
8270 *Heaven Knows Why*	10.00 -	15.00

DORIS BROWNE:
Gotham 290 *Please Believe Me*	10.00 -	15.00
296 *Until The End Of Time*	10.00 -	15.00
298 *My Cherie*	10.00 -	15.00
303 *When The Moon Is High*	10.00 -	15.00

BILL BROWNING:
Island 3 *One Day A Month*	8.00 -	12.00
10 *Lay Me Low*	8.00 -	12.00
Starday 432 *Don't Push Don't Shove*	10.00 -	15.00

EDWIN BRUCE:
Sun 276 *Rock Boppin' Baby*	7.00 -	10.00
292 *Sweet Woman*	15.00 -	20.00

FRANK BRUNSON:
Groove 0173 *Charmaine*	7.00 -	10.00

BILLY BRYAN:
Blaze 351 *Cradle Of Your Arms*	7.00 -	10.00
Everest 19420 *All Summer Long*	5.00 -	8.00
Festival 25002 *Please, Come Back Baby*	5.00 -	8.00

DAVE BRYAN:
Speck 103 *Let's Make It Real*	15.00 -	20.00

WES BRYAN:
Clock 1013 *Honey Baby*	10.00 -	15.00
Roulette 4289 *I Guess I'll Never Know*	7.00 -	10.00
United Artist 102 *Tiny Spaceman*	7.00 -	10.00
122 *Wait For Me Baby*	7.00 -	10.00

GENE BUA:
ABC Paramount 9928 *Well Honey*	7.00 -	10.00
Warner Bros. *Once Upon A Time*	7.00 -	10.00

THE BUCCANEERS:
Rama 21 *The Stars Will Remember*	150.00 -	200.00
24 *In The Mission Of St. Augustine*	100.00 -	150.00
Southern 101 *Fine Brown Frame*	150.00 -	200.00

BUCHANAN & ANCELL:
Flying Saucer 501 *The Creature*	8.00 -	12.00

BUCHANAN & GOODMAN:
Luniverse 100 *Flying Saucer*	5.00 -	8.00
101 *Back To Earth*	5.00 -	8.00
102 *Buchanan & Goodman On Trial*	5.00 -	8.00
103 *The Mystery*	7.00 -	10.00
105 *Flying Saucer The 2nd*	7.00 -	10.00
107 *Santa & The Satellite*	7.00 -	10.00
108 *The Flying Saucer Goes West*	7.00 -	10.00
(Note: 78 RPM issues of above are worth more)		
Radioactive 101 *Flying Saucer*	15.00 -	20.00

BUCHANAN & GREENFIELD:
Novel 711 *The Invasion*	7.00 -	10.00

WES BUCHANAN:
Pep 114 *Give Some Love My Way*	30.00 -	40.00

ART BUCHANON:
Dixie 823 *Queen From Bowling Green*	— -	—

GARY BUCK:
Petal 1011 *Savin' All My Love For You*	5.00 -	8.00

PETER BUCK:
Drew-Blan 1005 *That's Enough*	7.00 -	10.00

THE BUCKEYES:
De Luxe 6110 *Since I Fell For You*	20.00 -	30.00
6126 *Dottie Baby*	12.00 -	16.00

BUCKY & THE PREMIERES:
Nu-Phi 701 *Cruisin'*	8.00 -	12.00

JOHN BULLARD:
De Luxe 6019 *Spoiled Hambone Blues* .... 35.00 - 50.00
NORMAN BULLOCK:
M & J 1-2 *Moanin' The Blues* .... 20.00 - 30.00
  1108 *Lies, Lies, Lies* .... 20.00 - 30.00
BUNCH OF GOODIES:
Chess (LP) 1441 .... 15.00 - 20.00
BILLY BUNN & HIS BUDDIES:
RCA Victor 4483 *I Need A Shoulder To Cry On* . 35.00 - 50.00
  4657 *That's When Your Heartaches Begin* .... 30.00 - 40.00
RAY BURDEN:
Adonis 112 *A Hot Rodder's Dream* .... 20.00 - 30.00
Cullman 6403 *That Kind Of Carrying On* ...... 25.00 - 35.00
DAVE BURGESS:
Challenge 1018 *Maybelle* .... 5.00 - 8.00
  59027 *I Don't Want To Know* .... 5.00 - 8.00
  59032 *Lovey Dovey Baby* .... 5.00 - 8.00
Challenge 59037, 59045 .... 4.00 - 7.00
SONNY BURGESS:
Phillips 3551 *Sadie's Back In Town* .... 8.00 - 12.00
Razorback 136 *Odessa* .... 10.00 - 15.00
Sun 247 *Red Headed Woman* .... 15.00 - 20.00
  263 *Ain't Got A Thing* .... 20.00 - 30.00
  285 *My Bucket's Got A Hole In It* .... 10.00 - 15.00
  304 *Thunderbird* .... 20.00 - 30.00
JIM BURGETT:
GO 6565 *Pick-Up-A-Coupla' Records* .... 15.00 - 20.00
Oro 1502 *Live It Up* .... 15.00 - 20.00
TOMMY BURK & THE COURTS:
Nat 100 *You'll Feel It Too* .... 5.00 - 8.00
Rich Rose 1003 *You Took My Heart* .... 7.00 - 10.00
BUDDY BURKE:
Bullseye 1002 *That Big Old Moon* .... 15.00 - 20.00
EDDIE BURKE:
D 1063 *Rock Mop* .... 7.00 - 10.00
THE BURNETTE BROTHERS:
Imperial 5509 *Warm Love* .... 15.00 - 20.00
DORSEY BURNETTE:
Abbott 190 *At A Distance* .... 5.00 - 8.00
Cee-Jam 16 *Bertha Lou* .... 10.00 - 15.00
Imperial 5668 *Way In The Middle Of The Night* . 10.00 - 15.00
  5561, 5597 .... 7.00 - 10.00
JOHNNY BURNETTE (& THE ROCK 'N' ROLL TRIO):
JOHNNY BURNETTE TRIO:
Coral (LP) 57080 *Johnny Burnette & The Rock*
  'N' Roll Trio ....200.00 - 300.00
  61651 *Tear It Up* .... 20.00 - 30.00
  61675 *Midnight Train* .... 15.00 - 20.00
  61719 *The Train Kept A-Rollin'* .... 15.00 - 20.00
  61758 *Lonesome Train* .... 15.00 - 20.00
  61829 *Eager Beaver Baby* .... 30.00 - 40.00
  61869 *Drinkin' Wine Spo-Dee-O-Dee* ..... 30.00 - 40.00
  61918 *If You Want It Enough* .... 30.00 - 40.00
  62190 *Midnight Train* .... 15.00 - 20.00
Freedom 44001 *I'm Restless* .... 8.00 - 12.00
  44011 *Me And The Bear* .... 8.00 - 12.00
  44017 *Sweet Baby Doll* .... 10.00 - 15.00
Liberty (EP) 1011 *"Hits"* .... 35.00 - 50.00
Liberty (LPs) 3179, 3183, 3190, 3206, 7183, 7190,
  7197, 7206 .... 15.00 - 20.00
LINDA BURNETTE:
Perry 5 *Rattle Bones Rock* .... 15.00 - 25.00
MAC BURNEY & THE FOUR JACKS:
Aladdin 3274 *Tired Of Your Sexy Ways* (blue
  label) .... 15.00 - 25.00
EDDIE BURNS:
Chess 1672 *Treat Me Like I Treat You* .... 5.00 - 8.00
De Luxe 6024 *Dealing With The Devil* .... 15.00 - 20.00
Harvey 111, 115, 118 .... 5.00 - 8.00
JVB 82 *Treat Me Like I Treat You* .... 20.00 - 30.00
JACKIE BURNS:

Del-Fi 4102 *Hey Then There Now* .... 7.00 - 10.00
SONNY BURNS:
Starday 209 *A Real Cool Cat* .... 30.00 - 40.00
HAROLD BURRAGE:
Cobra 5004, 5012, 5018, 5022, 5026 .... 7.00 - 10.00
BOB BURTON:
Mar-Vel 953 *Tired Of Rocking* .... 15.00 - 20.00
DAVE BURTON:
RCA Victor 6535 *Rock And Roll Ruby* .... 7.00 - 10.00
WAYNE BUSBY:
Empire 506 *Goin' Back To Dixie* .... 20.00 - 30.00
EDDIE BUSH:
Jaxon 503 *Little Darling* .... 30.00 - 40.00
THE BUTANES:
Enrica 1007 *That's My Desire* .... 7.00 - 10.00
SAM BUTERA & THE WITNESSES:
Capitol 4014 *Bim Bam* .... 10.00 - 15.00
CLIFF BUTLER & THE DOVES:
States 123 *When You Love* .... 30.00 - 40.00
JERRY BUTLER & THE IMPRESSIONS:
Abner 1013, 1017, 1023 .... 5.00 - 8.00
  1013 *For Your Precious Love* (78rpm) ...... 15.00 - 20.00
Falcon 1013 *For Your Precious Love* .... 10.00 - 15.00
Vee Jay 280 *For Your Precious Love* (Rare) .....100.00 - Up
BOBBY BYRD & THE BIRDS:
Cash 1031 *Let's Live Together As One* .... 15.00 - 20.00
ROBERT BYRD:
Jamie 1039 *Bippin' And Boppin'* .... 8.00 - 12.00
Spark 501 *Bippin' And Boppin'* .... 15.00 - 20.00
ROY BYRD:
Federal 12061 *Curly Haired Baby* .... 30.00 - 50.00
  12073 *Rockin' With Fes* .... 30.00 - 50.00
JERRY BYRNE:
Specialty 635 *Lights Out* .... 7.00 - 10.00
EDD BYRNES:
Warner Bros. (LP) 1309 *Kookie* .... 10.00 - 15.00
JIMMIE BYRON:
Teen 113 *Sidewalk Rock* .... 8.00 - 12.00
WILLIE C,:
Ruler 5000 *Slow Down Baby* .... 5.00 - 8.00
THE CABINEERS:
Prestige 904 *Each Time* ....150.00 - 200.00
  917 *Baby Mine* ....150.00 - 200.00
FREDDIE CADDELL:
Ardent 12-001 *At the Rockhouse* .... 15.00 - 20.00
THE CADETS:
Crown (LP) 5015 *Rockin' n' Rollin'* .... 30.00 - 50.00
  (LP) 5370 *The Cadets* .... 20.00 - 30.00
  (LP) CST 370 *The Cadets* .... 15.00 - 25.00
Jan Lar 102 *Car Crash* .... 7.00 - 10.00
Modern 956 *Don't Be Angry* .... 15.00 - 20.00
  960 *Rollin' Stone* .... 10.00 - 15.00
  963 *I Cried* .... 10.00 - 15.00
  969 *Annie Met Henry* .... 10.00 - 15.00
  971 *Do You Wanna Rock* .... 10.00 - 15.00
  985 *Church Bells May Ring* .... 10.00 - 15.00
  994 *Stranded in the Jungle* .... 7.00 - 10.00
  1000 *I Got Loaded* .... 8.00 - 12.00
  1006 *Fools Rush In* .... 7.00 - 10.00
  1012 *Heaven Help Me* .... 7.00 - 10.00
  1017 *You Belong To Me* .... 8.00 - 12.00
  1019 *Pretty Evey* .... 8.00 - 12.00
  1024 *Hands Across The Table* .... 8.00 - 12.00
  1026 *Baby Ya Know* .... 8.00 - 12.00
THE CADILLACS:
Capitol 4825 *White Gardenia* .... 10.00 - 15.00
Josie 759 *Carelessly* .... -
  765 *Gloria* .... 50.00 - 75.00
  769 *Wishing Well* .... 50.00 - 75.00
  773 *Sympathy* .... 20.00 - 30.00
  778 *Down The Road* .... 20.00 - 30.00
  785 *Speedo* .... 5.00 - 8.00

785 *Speedo* (78rpm)	10.00	-	15.00
792 *Zoom*	5.00	-	8.00
792 *Zoom* (78rpm)	10.00	-	15.00
798, 805, 812, 820, 821, 846, 866	7.00	-	10.00
*Jubilee (LP) 1045 *The Fabulous Cadillacs*	100.00	-	125.00
*(LP) 1089 *The Crazy Cadillacs*	75.00	-	100.00
*(LP) 1117 *The Cadillacs Meet The Orioles*	40.00	-	60.00
(LP) 5009 *Twisting With The Cadillacs*	10.00	-	15.00

(*original issues have blue label)

CAESER & THE ROMANS:

Hi-Note 602 *Your True Love*	10.00	-	15.00

AUBREY CAGLE:

Glee 1001 *Come Along Little Girl*	30.00	-	50.00
1013 *Bop 'N' Stroll*	30.00	-	50.00
Be Bop Blues	30.00	-	50.00
House Of Sound 504 *Real Cool*	30.00	-	50.00

ANDY CALDWELL:

Liberty 55142 *She's So Fine*	10.00	-	15.00

JOE CALDWELL:

Esta 1001 *Rowdy Mae*	20.00	-	30.00

THE CALENDARS:

Swingin' 649 *One-Week Romance*	5.00	-	8.00

THE CALIFORNIANS:

Federal 12231 *My Angel*	15.00	-	20.00

MIKE CALLAHAN:

Protone 204 *I Can't Help It*	15.00	-	20.00

BOB CALLAWAY:

Big Red 102 *Tick Tock*	30.00	-	40.00
U B C 1013 *Wake Up Little Boy Blue*	30.00	-	40.00

DUDLEY CALLICUT & THE "GO" BOYS:

"DC" 0412 *Get Ready Baby*	15.00	-	20.00

BABY CALLOWAY:

Bay-Tone 106 *Midnight Blues*	8.00	-	12.00

THE CALVAES:

Checker 928 *So Bad*	8.00	-	12.00
Cobra 5003 *Fine Girl*	30.00	-	40.00
5014 *Lonely Lonely Village*	25.00	-	35.00

THE CALVANES:

Deck 579 *Dreamworld*	5.00	-	8.00
Dootone (EP) 205	30.00	-	50.00
380 *Florabelle*	10.00	-	15.00

THE CALVEYS:

Comma 445 *The Wind*	5.00	-	8.00

THE CAMELOTS:

Aanko 1001, 1004	7.00	-	10.00
Ember 1108 *Searchin' For My Baby*	7.00	-	10.00

THE CAMEOS:

Dean 504 *Lost Lover*	15.00	-	20.00

THE CAMERONS:

Felsted 8638 *Guardian Angel*	7.00	-	10.00

DAVID CAMPANELLA & THE DELLCHORDS:

Kane 5593 *Over The Rainbow*	7.00	-	10.00

CECIL CAMPBELL:

MGM 12482 *Rock & Roll Fever*	20.00	-	30.00

DICK CAMPBELL:

Great 4703 *She's My Girl*	7.00	-	10.00

GLEN CAMPBELL:

Capitol 5441 *Guess I'm Dumb*	7.00	-	10.00
Capitol (most other issues)	3.00	-	5.00
Crest 1087 *Turn Around Look At Me*	7.00	-	10.00
1096 *The Miracle Of Love*	7.00	-	10.00

JO ANN CAMPBELL:

End (LP) 306 *I'm Nobody's Baby*	30.00	-	50.00
Gone 5014 *Wait A Minute*	7.00	-	10.00
5021 *Rock And Roll Love*	7.00	-	10.00
5027 *Whatsa Matter With You*	7.00	-	10.00
5037 *I'm Nobody's Baby Now*	7.00	-	10.00
5049 *Happy New Year Baby*	7.00	-	10.00
5055 *Nervous*	7.00	-	10.00
5068 *I Ain't Got No Steady Date*	7.00	-	10.00

LOUIS CAMPBELL:

Excello 2035 *The Natural Facts*	20.00	-	30.00

RAY CAMPI:

D 1047 *The Ballad Of Donna And Peggy Sue*	10.00	-	15.00
Domino 700 *My Screamin' Mimie*	20.00	-	30.00
Dot 15617 *It Ain't Me*	20.00	-	30.00
TNT 145 *Catapillar*	50.00	-	75.00

CAMP MEETING CHOIR:

Mercury (LP) 25084 (10″) *Negro Spirituals*	30.00	-	40.00

THE CAMPS:

Parkway 974 *The Ballad Of Batman*	5.00	-	8.00

FREDDY CANNON:

Swan (LP) 502 *The Explosive Freddy Cannon*	40.00	-	60.00
(LP) 504 *Freddy Cannon Sings Happy Shades Of Blue*	40.00	-	60.00
(LP) 505 *Solid Gold Hits*	20.00	-	30.00
(LP) 506 *Twistin' All Night Long*	20.00	-	30.00
(LP) 507 *Palisades Park*	30.00	-	50.00
(LP) 511 *Freddy Cannon Steps Out*	30.00	-	50.00

THE CANUCKS with RAY PARK:

Diadon 60-116 *Rock Around The Barn*	15.00	-	20.00

JERRY CAPEHART:

Cash 1021 *Walking Stick Boogie*	12.00	-	16.00

THE CAPISTRANOS:

Duke 179 *Now Darling*	15.00	-	20.00

THE CAPITOLS:

Cindy 3002 *Rose-Marie*	20.00	-	30.00
Gateway 721 *Day By Day*	15.00	-	20.00
Pet 807 *Angel Of Love*	15.00	-	20.00

THE CAPRIS:

Gotham 7304 *God Only Knows*	30.00	-	40.00
7306 *It Was Moonglow*	30.00	-	40.00
7308 *It's A Miracle*	30.00	-	40.00
Lifetime 1001/1002 *Oh, My Darling*	15.00	-	20.00
Old Town 1094 *There's A Moon Out Tonight*	5.00	-	8.00
1099 *Some People Think*	5.00	-	8.00
1103 *Tears In My Eyes*	7.00	-	10.00
1107 *Girl In My Dreams*	7.00	-	10.00
Planet 1010 *There's A Moon Out Tonight*	30.00	-	40.00
20th Century 1201 *My Weakness*	10.00	-	15.00

THE CAPS:

White Star 102 *Daddy Dean*	5.00	-	8.00

CAPTAIN & TENILLE:

Butter-Castle 001 *The Way I Want To Teach You*	—		—

THE CAP-TANS:

Anna 1122 *I'm Afraid*	10.00	-	15.00
Dot 15114 *With All My Love*	30.00	-	50.00

BOBBY & TERRY CARAWAY:

Crest 1065 *Ballin' Keen*	15.00	-	20.00

LEONARD CARBO:

Vee Jay 291 *Pigtails And Blue Jeans*	7.00	-	10.00

THE CARDELLS:

Middle tone 011 *Helen*	10.00	-	15.00

JACK CARDELL:

Rama 227 *Rock-A-Billy Yodler*	8.00	-	12.00

THE CARDINALS:

Atlantic 938 *Shouldn't I Know*	80.00	-	100.00
952 *I'll Always Love You*	30.00	-	50.00
958 *Wheel Of Fortune*	30.00	-	50.00
972 *She Rocks*	30.00	-	50.00
995 *You Are My Only Love*	20.00	-	30.00
1025 *Under A Blanket Of Blues*	12.00	-	18.00
1054, 1067, 1076, 1079	8.00	-	12.00

(Note: Above are yellow label)

1090, 1126	7.00	-	10.00
Rose 835 *Why Don't You Write Me?*	—	-	—

THE CARIANS:

Magenta 04 *Only A Dream*	10.00	-	15.00

THE CARIBBEANS:

20th Fox 112 *Keep Her By My Side*	8.00	-	12.00

STEVE CARL:

Meteor 5046 *Curfew*	30.00	-	40.00

CARLISLE BROTHERS:

King (LP) 643 *Fresh From The Country*	20.00 -	30.00
"CARL, LEFTY AND MARTY"		
Columbia (LP) 2544 (10")	40.00 -	60.00
CARLO:		
Laurie 3151, 3157	4.00 -	7.00
CARLOS BROS.		
Zen 106 *I Realize*	7.00 -	10.00
THE CARNATIONS:		
Lescay 3002 *Long Tall Girl*	15.00 -	20.00
Music City 736 *You Gave Peace Of Mind*	15.00 -	20.00
Savoy 1172 *The Angels Sent You To Me*	10.00 -	15.00
PAUL CARNES:		
P.R.C. 4417 *I'm A Mean, Mean Daddy*	10.00 -	15.00
CAROLINA SLIM:		
Sharp (LP) 2002 *Blues From The Cotton Fields*	75.00 -	100.00
THE CAROLS:		
Lamp 2001 *My Search Is Over*	15.00 -	20.00
Savoy 896 *Fifty Million Women*	12.00 -	16.00
THE CAROUSELS:		
Gone 5118 *If You Want To*	7.00 -	10.00
Jaguar 3029 *Rendezvous*	10.00 -	15.00
THE CARPETS:		
Federal 12257 *Why Do I*	15.00 -	20.00
12269 *Lonely Me*	15.00 -	20.00
CATHY CARR:		
Fraternity 734 *Ivory Tower* (78 rpm)	7.00 -	10.00
(LP) 1005 *Ivory Tower*	20.00 -	30.00
CARRIBIANS:		
Brooks 2000 *Wonderland*	— -	—
CURTIS CARRINGTON:		
Fury 1018 *I'm Gonna Catch You*	5.00 -	8.00
THE CARROLL BROS.:		
Cameo 140 *Red Hot*	10.00 -	15.00
BILL(Y) CARROLL:		
Dixie 2010 *I Feel So Good*	30.00 -	40.00
CHUCK CARROLL:		
Happy Heart 133 *Mean Ole Blues*	— -	—
EARL CARROLL & THE ORIGINAL		
CADILLACS:		
Josie 829 *Buzz-Buzz-Buzz*	5.00 -	8.00
JIMMY CARROLL:		
Fascination 2000 *Big Green Car*	20.00 -	30.00
JOHNNY CARROLL (& HIS HOT ROCKS):		
Decca 29940 *Rock 'N' Roll Ruby*	20.00 -	30.00
29941 *Wild Wild Women*	20.00 -	30.00
30013 *Hot Rock*	20.00 -	30.00
Phillips 3520 *That's The Way I Love*	15.00 -	20.00
WA 112 *Trudy*	10.00 -	15.00
Warner Bros. 5042 *Bandstand Doll*	10.00 -	15.00
WAYNE CARROLL:		
King 5123 *Chicken Out*	10.00 -	15.00
5134 *Rockin' Chair Mama*	10.00 -	15.00
5146 *He Cheated*	7.00 -	10.00
THE CARTER KIDS:		
Gambler 1638 *Gotta Rock*	7.00 -	10.00
THE CARTER RAYS:		
Gone 5006 *My Secret Love*	15.00 -	20.00
Jubilee 5142 *Goodnight, Sweetheart, Goodnight*	10.00 -	15.00
BILL CARTER:		
Ozark 1234 *Cool Tom Cat*	20.00 -	30.00
Tally 111 *I Wanna Feel Good*	15.00 -	20.00
BOB CARTER:		
Den 11229 *The Fortunate Few*	7.00 -	10.00
DEAN CARTER:		
Milky Way 0111 *Jailhouse Rock*	— -	—
HARRY CARTER:		
Mar-Vel 1300 *Jump Baby Jump*	15.00 -	20.00
1301 *You Made Me Love You Baby*	15.00 -	20.00
WILF CARTER:		
Camden (LP) 527 *Montana Slim*	15.00 -	20.00
RIC CARTEY & JIVA TONES:		
ABC Paramount 10415 *Something In My Eye*	8.00 -	12.00

NRC 503 *Scratchin' On My Screen*	30.00 -	40.00
RCA Victor 6751 *Ooh Eee*	10.00 -	15.00
6828 *Heart Throb*	10.00 -	15.00
6920 *Let Me Tell You About Love*	10.00 -	15.00
7011 *My Babe*	10.00 -	15.00
CASANOVA & THE CHANTS:		
Sapphire 2254 *Geraldine*	8.00 -	12.00
CASANOVA, JR.:		
Port 7001 *Sally Mae*	10.00 -	15.00
TONY CASANOVA:		
American International 532 *Dairy Of A High School Bride*	7.00 -	10.00
Crest 1053 *Yea! Yea! Come Another Day*	15.00 -	20.00
Dore 535 *Boogie Woogie Feeling*	15.00 -	20.00
THE CASANOVAS:		
Apollo 471 *That's All*	20.00 -	30.00
474 *Hush-A-Mecca*	20.00 -	30.00
477 *Please Be My Love*	20.00 -	30.00
483 *My Baby's Love*	20.00 -	30.00
519 *Please Be Mine*	15.00 -	20.00
523 *You Are My Queen*	15.00 -	20.00
Planet 1027 *In My Land Of Dreams*	15.00 -	20.00
THE CASCADES:		
Renee 105 *Pains In My Heart*	7.00 -	10.00
Valiant (LP) 405 *Rhythm Of The Rain*	30.00 -	50.00
AL CASEY:		
Dot 15563 *Guitar Man*	8.00 -	12.00
Highland 1002 *Teenage Blues*	10.00 -	15.00
Liberty 55117 *She Gotta Shake*	8.00 -	12.00
EDDIE CASH:		
Peak 1001 *Doin' All Right*	20.00 -	30.00
JOHNNY CASH:		
Sun (EP) 111 *Sing's Hank Williams*	15.00 -	20.00
(EP) 112 *Country Boy*	15.00 -	20.00
221 *Hey Porter*	10.00 -	15.00
232 *Folsom Prisom Blues*	5.00 -	8.00
241 *I Walk The Line*	5.00 -	8.00
241 *I Walk The Line* (78rpm)	10.00 -	15.00
258, 266, 279, 295, (78rpm)	7.00 -	10.00
283, 302, 309, 316, (78rpm)	10.00 -	15.00
(LP) 1240 *Greatest!*	30.00 -	50.00
(LP) 1270 *All Aboard The Blue Train*	30.00 -	40.00
(LP) 1275 *The Original Sun Sound Of*	15.00 -	20.00
THE CASHMERES:		
Herald 474 *Little Dream Girl*	10.00 -	15.00
Josie 894 *Where Have You Been*	5.00 -	8.00
Laurie 3088 *Singing Waters*	5.00 -	8.00
Mercury 70501 *My Sentimental Heart*	7.00 -	10.00
70617 *Don't Let It Happen Again*	10.00 -	15.00
70679 *There's A Rumor*	10.00 -	15.00
THE CASINOS:		
Fraternity (LP) 1019	35.00 -	50.00
THE CASLONS:		
Seeco 6078 *Anniversary Of Love*	8.00 -	12.00
TOMMY CASSELL:		
Cassell 58½ *Go Ahead On*	15.00 -	20.00
THE CASTALEERS:		
Donna 1349 *That's Why I Cry*	7.00 -	10.00
Felsted 8504 *Come Back*	8.00 -	12.00
8512 *Lonely Boy*	10.00 -	15.00
8585 *You're My Dream*	10.00 -	15.00
(GEORGE CASTELLE &) THE CASTELLES:		
Atco 6069 *Hey Baby, Baby*	8.00 -	12.00
Grand 101 *My Girl Awaits Me*	30.00 -	50.00
103 *This Silver Ring*	40.00 -	60.00
105 *Do You Remember*	40.00 -	60.00
109 *Over A Cup Of Coffee*	75.00 -	100.00
114 *Marcella*	40.00 -	60.00
118 *Over The Rainbow*	30.00 -	40.00
122 *Heavenly Father*	30.00 -	40.00
JOE(Y) CASTLE (& DADDY-O's):		
Headline 1008 *Rock And Roll Daddy-O*	30.00 -	50.00

RCA Victor 7283 *That Ain't Nothin' But Right* .. 10.00 - 15.00

THE CASTLE-TONES:
Rift 502 *Goodnight* .... 8.00 - 12.00
   504 *We Met At A Dance* .... 8.00 - 12.00

JIMMY CASTOR & THE JUNIORS:
Wing 90078 *I Know The Meaning Of Love* ..... 8.00 - 12.00

THE CASTROES:
Lasso *Lucky Me* .... —

CASUAL-AIRES:
Brunswick 55064 *Thunderbird.* .... 10.00 - 15.00

THE CASUALS (See also: THE ORIGINAL CASUALS):
Dot 15557 *My Love Song For You* .... 7.00 - 10.00

THE CASUALTEENS:
Felsted 8529 *Need You So* .... 7.00 - 10.00

THE CASUAL THREE:
Luniverse 109 *The Invisible Thing* .... 7.00 - 10.00

THE CATALINAS:
Back Beat 513 *Speechless* .... 20.00 - 30.00
Glory 285 *With Your Girl—Yeah!* .... 8.00 - 12.00
Little 812 *Castle Of Love* .... 8.00 - 12.00

CATHY JEAN & THE ROOMATES:
Valmor (LP) 789 *At The Hop* ....100.00 - Up

THE CATS:
Federal 12238 *After I Gave You My Heart* ..... 15.00 - 20.00
   12248 *You're So Nice* .... 15.00 - 20.00

THE CATS & THE FIDDLE:
RCA Victor 50-0077 *I Miss You So* .... 10.00 - 15.00

JOHNNY CAVALIER:
Hi Class 105 *Knock Off The Rock* .... 10.00 - 15.00

JIM CAVALLO:
Sunnyside 3105 *Don't Move Me No More* ...... 15.00 - 20.00

JIMMY CAVELLO & HOUSE ROCKERS:
Coral 61689 *Soda Shoppe Rock* .... 10.00 - 15.00
   61728 *Rock, Rock, Rock* .... 15.00 - 20.00
   61787 *Ooh Wee* .... 15.00 - 20.00
Coral 61868 *Yo-Yo Baby* .... 10.00 - 15.00
   61919 *Cherry Pie* .... 10.00 - 15.00

JOHN W. CAVES:
Mem'ry Lane 102 *Rocket To The Moon* .... — - —

THE CELLOS:
Apollo 510 *You Took My Love* .... 8.00 - 12.00
   515 *Under Your Spell* .... 8.00 - 12.00
   516 *The Be-Bop Mouse* .... 8.00 - 12.00
   524 *I Beg For Your Love* .... 10.00 - 15.00

THE CELTICS:
Al Jacks 2 *Can You Remember?* .... 50.00 - 80.00
War Conn 2216 *Darlene Darling* .... 30.00 - 50.00

THE CENTURIES:
Life 501 *In This Whole World* .... 15.00 - 20.00

THE CENTURY'S:
Fortune 533 *Take My Hand* .... 10.00 - 15.00

ERNIE CHAFFIN:
Hickory 1024 *I Can't Lose The Blues* .... 5.00 - 8.00
Sun 262, 275 .... 5.00 - 8.00

THE CHALETS:
Tru-Lite 101 *Who's Laughin?* .... 8.00 - 12.00

THE CHALONS:
Dice 89 *Oh You* .... — - —

THE CHAMBERLAIN BROS:
Columbia 41227 *Baby Walked Out* .... 10.00 - 15.00

EDDIE CHAMBLEE:
United 160, 181 .... 5.00 - 8.00

HOLLIS CHAMPION:
Stripe 501 *Long Gone Lonesome Blues* .... — - —

JOHNNY CHAMPION:
Natural Sound 2004 *Beer Drinking Daddy* ...... 5.00 - 8.00

THE CHAMPIONS:
Ace 541 *I'm So Blue* .... 7.00 - 10.00
Chart 602 *Annie Met Henry* .... 10.00 - 15.00
   611 *Mexico Bound* .... 10.00 - 15.00
   620 *Pay Me Some Attention* ...... 15.00 - 20.00

   631 *Come On* .... 15.00 - 20.00

THE CHAMPS:
Challenge (LP) 601 *Go Champs Go* .... 30.00 - 40.00
  (LP) 601 (same, but pressed of blue vinyl) ....100.00 - Up
  1016 *Tequila* (78rpm) .... 10.00 - 15.00
  59007 *El Rancho Rock* (78rpm) .... 8.00 - 12.00

THE CHANCELLORS:
XYZ 104 *I'm Coming Home* .... 7.00 - 10.00
   105 *Seaport At Sunset* .... 7.00 - 10.00

THE CHANCETEERS:
Chess 1636 *Night Beat* .... 10.00 - 15.00

THE CHANDELIERS:
Angel Tone 521 *Blueberry Sweet* .... 15.00 - 20.00
Do-Well 102 *Once More* .... 7.00 - 10.00

ELAINE CHANDLER:
4 Star 1700 *Tiptoin' Thru The Teepee* .... — - —

LEE CHANDLER:
Band Box 224 *Tree-Top* .... 10.00 - 15.00
   250 *Sweet Dreams* .... 10.00 - 15.00

WAYLAND CHANDLER:
4 Star 1716 *Little Lover* .... 8.00 - 12.00

CLISTON CHANIER:
Post 2010 *Rockin' The Bop* .... 10.0 - 15.00
  2016 *Rockin' Hop* .... 10.00 - 15.00

BRUCE CHANNEL:
Le Cam 953 *Hey! Baby* .... 15.00 - 20.00
Manco 1035 *Run, Romance, Run* .... 10.00 - 15.00
Teen Ager 601 *Run, Romance, Run* .... 7.00 - 10.00

THE CHANNELS:
Fire 1001 *The Girl Next Door* .... 15.00 - 20.00
Fury 1021 *Bye Bye Baby* .... 10.00 - 15.00
Gone 5012 *That's My Desire* .... 15.00 - 20.00
  5019 *Altar Of Love* .... 15.00 - 20.00
Port 70014 *The Closer You Are* .... 8.00 - 12.00
  70017 *The Gleam In Your Eye* .... 8.00 - 12.00
  70022 *Flames In My Heart* .... 8.00 - 12.00
  70023 *I Really Love* .... 8.00 - 12.00
Whirlin Disc 100 *The Closer You Are* .... 15.00 - 20.00
  102 *The Gleam In Your Eyes* .... 15.00 - 20.00
  107 *I Really Love You* .... 15.00 - 20.00
  109 *Flames In My Heart* .... 15.00 - 20.00

CHANTAYS:
Dot (LP) 3516 *Pipeline* (MONO) .... 20.00 - 30.00
  (LP) 3771 *Two Sides of...* (MONO) .... 20.00 - 30.00
  (LP) 25516 *Pipeline* (STEREO) .... 30.00 - 40.00
  (LP) 25571 *Two Sides of...* (STEREO) ...... 20.00 - 30.00
Downey 104 *Pipeline* .... 7.00 - 10.00
  108 *Monsoon* .... 7.00 - 10.00
Downey (LP) 1002 *Pipeline* .... 75.00 - 100.00

CHANTELS:
End (EP) 201 *I Love You So* .... 50.00 - 75.00
  (EP) 202 *"C'est Si Bon"* .... 50.00 - 75.00
End (LP) 301 *We Are The Chantels* (group photo) 100.00 - 150.00
  (LP) 301 *The Chantels* (juke box) .... 20.00 - 30.00
  (LP) 312 *There's Our Song Again* .... 20.00 - 30.00
  1001 *He's Gone* (black label) .... 7.00 - 10.00
  1005 *Maybe* (black label) .... 7.00 - 10.00
  1005 *Maybe* (78rpm) .... 15.00 - 20.00
  1015 *Every Night* .... 5.00 - 8.00
  1015 *Every Night* (78rpm) .... 10.00 - 15.00
  1020 *I Love You So* .... 5.00 - 8.00
  1020 *I Love You So* (78rpm) .... 10.00 - 15.00
Ludix 101 *Eternally* .... 5.00 - 8.00
Verve 10435 *It's Just Me* .... 7.00 - 10.00

THE CHANTERS:
Combo 78 *Why* .... 30.00 - 40.00
  92 *I Love You* .... 30.00 - 40.00
De Luxe 6162, 6166, 6172, 6177, 6191, 6194,
  6200 .... 8.00 - 12.00
Kem 2740 *Lonesome Me* .... 15.00 - 20.00
RPM 415 *Tell Me, Thrill Me* .... 25.00 - 35.00

THE CHANTICLEERS:

Lyric 103 *To Keep Your Love*	20.00	-	30.00
THE CHANTONES:			
TNT 167 *Dear Diary*	10.00	-	15.00
THE CHANTS:			
Nite Owl 40 *Heaven And Paradise*	—	-	—
JEAN CHAPEL:			
RCA Victor 6892 *Oo-Ba La Baby*	8.00	-	12.00
Sun 244 *I Won't Be Rockin' Tonight*	15.00	-	20.00
THE CHAPERONES:			
Josie 885 *Shining Star*	7.00	-	10.00
PAUL CHAPLAIN:			
Harper 100 *Nicotine*	5.00	-	8.00
GENE CHAPMAN:			
Westport 145 *Don't Come Cryin'*	5.00	-	8.00
LEON CHAPPEL:			
Capitol 1954 *Booger Blues*	7.00	-	10.00
2065 *True Detective*	7.00	-	10.00
2167 *Automatic Mama*	7.00	-	10.00
2526 *I'm Getting Mighty Tired*	5.00	-	8.00
2611 *New Do Right Daddy*	5.00	-	8.00
BILL CHAPPELL:			
Yucca 121 *Lovey Dove*	10.00	-	15.00
Yucca 156 *Down On the Farm Boogie*	—	-	—
THE CHARIOTEERS:			
Columbia (LP) CL 6014 (10″) *Sweet And Low*	75.00	-	100.00
Harmony (LP) 7089	30.00	-	50.00
Josie 787 *I've Got My Heart On My Sleeve*	10.00	-	15.00
MGM 12569 *The Candles*	15.00	-	20.00
CHARIOTS:			
Time 1006 *Gloria*	10.00	-	15.00
ANDY CHARLES & THE BLUES KINGS:			
D 1061 *Baby Don't Go*	20.00	-	30.00
BOBBY CHARLES:			
Chess 1609 *Later Alligator*	10.00	-	15.00
1617 *Why Did You Leave*	8.00	-	12.00
1628 *Take It Easy Greasy*	8.00	-	12.00
1638 *No Use Knocking*	8.00	-	12.00
1647 *Why Can't You, Honey*	5.00	-	8.00
1658 *No More*	5.00	-	8.00
1670 *One-Eyed Jack*	7.00	-	10.00
RAY CHARLES:			
ABC Paramount (LP) 385 ''...& Betty Carter''	50.00	-	75.00
ABC Parmount (most issues)	3.00	-	6.00
Atlantic 976 *The Midnight Hour* (yellow label)	10.00	-	15.00
984 *The Sun's Gonna Shine Again* (yellow label)	10.00	-	15.00
999 *Mess Around* (yellow label)	10.00	-	15.00
1154 *Swanee River Rock* (78rpm)	10.00	-	15.00
(LP) 1289 *At Newport*	15.00	-	20.00
(LP) 1312 *Genius*	15.00	-	20.00
(LP) 1369 *The Genius After Hours*	15.00	-	20.00
2006 *Rockhouse* (78rpm)	15.00	-	20.00
2031 *What'd I Say* (78rpm)	20.00	-	30.00
2043 *I'm Movin' On* (78rpm)	20.00	-	30.00
(LP) 8006 *Ray Charles* (black label)	30.00	-	40.00
(LP) 8025 *Yes Indeed!* (black label)	20.00	-	30.00
(LP) 8029 *What'd I Say*	10.00	-	15.00
CHARLIE BOP TRIO:			
Capitol 4100 *Mr. Big Feet*	7.00	-	10.00
THE CHARMERS:			
Allison 921 *Magic Rose*	8.00	-	12.00
Central 1002 *The Beating Of My Heart*	20.00	-	30.00
Laurie 3142 *My Kind Of Love*	8.00	-	12.00
Timely 1011 *The Church On The Hill*	—	-	—
THE CHARMS: (See also OTIS WILLIAMS)			
Chart 608 *Love's Our Inspiration*	15.00	-	20.00
613 *I Offer You*	15.00	-	20.00
623 *I'll Be True*	20.00	-	30.00
De Luxe (EP) 357, 364	30.00	-	40.00
6000 *Heaven Only Knows*	30.00	-	50.00
6014 *Happy Are We*	20.00	-	30.00
6034 *Please Believe Me*	20.00	-	30.00

6050 *Quiet Please*	15.00	-	20.00
6056 *My Baby Dearest Darling*	15.00	-	20.00
De Luxe 6062 *Hearts Of Stone*	8.00	-	12.00
6065 *Two Hearts*	8.00	-	12.00
6072 *Crazy, Crazy Love*	8.00	-	12.00
6076 *Ling Ting Tong*	8.00	-	12.00
6080 *Ko Ko Mo*	8.00	-	12.00
6082 *Whadaya Want?*	8.00	-	12.00
6087 *When We Get Together*	8.00	-	12.00
6089 *One Fine Day*	8.00	-	12.00
Rockin' 516 *Heaven Only Knows*	40.00	-	60.00
THE CHARTERS:			
Merry-Go-Round 103 *Lost In A Dream*	7.00	-	10.00
THE CHARTS:			
Everlast 5001 *Deserie*	7.00	-	10.00
5002 *Why Do You Cry*	10.00	-	15.00
5006 *You're The Reason*	8.00	-	12.00
5008 *All Because Of Love*	8.00	-	12.00
5010 *My Diane*	7.00	-	10.00
5026 *Deserie*	4.00	-	7.00
Guyden 2021 *For The Birds*	6.00	-	10.00
JODY CHASTAIN:			
Kay 1002 *Jody's Beat*	15.00	-	20.00
THE CHATEAUS:			
Coral 62364 *Honest I Will*	5.00	-	8.00
Warner Bros 5043, 5071	5.00	-	8.00
CHRISTINE CHATMAN:			
Million 2002 *Wino's Lament*	7.00	-	10.00
EARL CHATMAN:			
Fortune 844 *Take Two Steps Back*	7.00	-	10.00
THE CHAVELLES:			
Vita 127 *Valley Of Love*	15.00	-	20.00
THE CHAVIS BROTHERS:			
Ascot 2177 *Humpty Dumpty*	5.00	-	8.00
BOOZOO CHAVIS:			
Folk Star 1197 *Paper In My Shoe*	15.00	-	20.00
1201 *Forty One Days*	15.00	-	20.00
Goldband 1161 *Hamburgers And Popcorn*	5.00	-	8.00
Imperial 5374 *Boozoo Stomp*	15.00	-	20.00
CHUBBY CHECKER:			
Parkway 804 *The Class* (78rpm)	75.00	-	Up
(Note: the existence of this record in 78rpm form has not been confirmed.)			
965 *You Just Don't Know*	10.00	-	15.00
THE CHECKER DOTS:			
Peacock 1688 *Alpha Omega*	7.00	-	10.00
THE CHECKERS:			
Federal 12375 *White Cliffs Of Dover*	15.00	-	20.00
King 4558 *Flame In My Heart*	50.00	-	75.00
4581 *Night Curtains*	40.00	-	60.00
4626 *Ghost Of My Baby*	20.00	-	30.00
4673 *I Promise You*	20.00	-	30.00
4675 *White Cliffs Of Dover*	15.00	-	20.00
4710 *House With No Windows*	15.00	-	20.00
4719 *Over The Rainbow*	20.00	-	30.00
4751 *Mama's Daughter*	20.00	-	30.00
4764 *Trying To Hold My Gal*	20.00	-	30.00
5156 *Heaven Only Knows*	15.00	-	20.00
Skyla 1120 *Blue Saturday*	7.00	-	10.00
CHELMARS:			
Select 712 *Confess*	8.00	-	12.00
BIG CHENIER & HIS NIGHT OWLS/THE R.B. ORCHESTRA:			
Goldband 1051 *Let Me Hold Your Hand*	7.00	-	10.00
1131 *The Dog And His Puppies*	5.00	-	8.00
CLIFTON CHENIER:			
Argo 5262 *The Big Wheel*	5.00	-	8.00
Bayou 707 *Black Gal*	10.00	-	15.00
710 *Louisiana Rock*	10.00	-	15.00
Checker 939 *Bayou Drive*	5.00	-	8.00
Elko 920 *Louisiana Stomp*	20.00	-	30.00
Imperial 5352 *Louisiana Stomp*	10.00	-	15.00

Specialty 552, 556, 568	5.00 -	8.00
Zynn 506 *Goodbye Baby*	7.00 -	10.00
1004 *Worried Life Blues*	7.00 -	10.00
1011 *Rockin' Accordion*	7.00 -	10.00

THE CHEROKEES:

Grand 106 *Rainbow Of Love*	30.00 -	40.00
Peacock 1656 *Is She Real*	20.00 -	30.00
United Artists 367 *My Heavenly Angel*	8.00 -	12.00

FRANKIE CHER-VALI:

Dot 15674 *My First Impression Of You*	10.00 -	15.00

THE CHESTERFIELDS:

Chess 1559 *I'm In Heaven*	— -	—

THE CHESTERS:

Apollo 521 *The Fires Burn No More*	15.00 -	20.00

THE CHESTNUTS:

Aladdin 3444 *This Is My Love*	10.00 -	15.00
Davis 447 *Love Is True*	15.00 -	20.00
452 *Forever I Vow*	15.00 -	20.00
Mercury 70489 *Don't Go*	15.00 -	20.00
Standard 100 *Who Knows Better Than I*	20.00 -	30.00

THE CHEVELLES:

Infinity 1007 *I'm Sorry*	7.00 -	10.00

THE CHEV-RONS:

Galt 100 *The Defense Rests*	10.00 -	15.00

CHICK & THE HOT RODS:

King 5537 *Jimmy Caught The Dickens*	7.00 -	10.00

THE CHIFFONS:

Laurie (LP) 2018 *He's So Fine*	35.00 -	50.00
(LP) 2036 *Sweet Talkin' Guy*	35.00 -	50.00

BUDDY CHILDRESS:

Dub 2838 *My Lovin' Arms*	8.00 -	12.00

THE CHIMES:

Flair 1051 *My Heart's Crying For You*	15.00 -	20.00
House Of Beauty 3 *Tears From An Angel's Eyes* .	-	
Royal Roost 577 *Dearest Darling*	10.00 -	15.00
Specialty 555 *Zindy Lou*	10.00 -	15.00
570, 574	7.00 -	10.00

THE CHIPPENDALES:

Andie 5013 *What A Night*	5.00 -	8.00
Rust 5023 *The Day Will Come*	5.00 -	8.00

THE CHIPS:

Josie 803 *Rubber Biscuit*	15.00 -	20.00

CHOCOLATEERS:

Parrot 781 *Bartender Blues*	50.00 -	80.00

THE CHORALS:

Decca 29914 *In My Dream*	15.00 -	20.00

THE CHORDCATS:

Cat 112 *A Girl To Love*	10.00 -	15.00

THE CHORDELLS:

Jaro 77005 *At Last*	10.00 -	15.00
Onyx 504 *Here's A Heart For You*	10.00 -	15.00

THE CHORDS:

Casino 451 *Tears In Your Eyes*	7.00 -	10.00
Cat 104, 109	5.00 -	8.00
Metro 20015 *Elephant Walk*	5.00 -	8.00

"A CHRISTMAS GIFT FOR YOU":

Philles (LP) 4005 (various artists)	30.00 -	50.00

JOHN CHRISTMON:

Excello 2031 *My Baby's Gone*	15.00 -	20.00

THE CHROMATICS: (See also LITTLE AUGIE AUSTIN)

Million 2010 *Here In The Darkness*	7.00 -	10.00

CHUCK & BILL:

Brunswick 55011 *Watch Your Step*	15.00 -	20.00
55034 *Wanna Move A Little Closer*	15.00 -	20.00

THE CHUCKLES:

West Side 1019 *On The Street Where You Live* . . .	7.00 -	10.00

CHUCK WAGON GANG:

Columbia (LP) 922 *Sacred Songs*	10.00 -	15.00
(LP) 9022 (10")	15.00 -	20.00

EUGENE CHURCH:

Class 235, 254	5.00 -	8.00
235 *Pretty Girls Everywhere* (78rpm)	10.00 -	15.00
254 *Miami* (78rpm)	10.00 -	15.00

THE CINCINNATIANS:

Emerald 16116 *Magic Genie*	5.00 -	8.00

CINDY & SANDY:

Tailspin 102 *Make Believe Baby*	—	—

THE CINERAMAS:

Rhapsody 71964 *Crying For You*	7.00 -	10.00

PETE CIOLINO:

Recorte 401 *Daddy Joe*	10.00 -	15.00

CIRCLE C BAND:

Melco 105 *Ramshackled Shack*	—	—

JIMMY CLANTON:

Ace 546 *Just A Dream* (78rpm)	15.00 -	20.00
668 *Heart Hotel*	7.00 -	10.00
(LP) 1001 *Just A Dream*	30.00 -	40.00
(LP) 1007 *Jimmy's Happy*	20.00 -	30.00
(LP) 1008 *Jimmy's Blue*	20.00 -	30.00
(LP) 1011 *My Best To You*	15.00 -	20.00
(LP) 1014 *Teenage Millionaire*	20.00 -	30.00
(LP) 1026 *Venus In Blue Jeans*	20.00 -	30.00

THE CLAREMONTS:

Apollo 517 *Angel Of Romance*	15.00 -	20.00

CHARLES CLARK:

Artistic 1500 *Row Your Boat*	10.00 -	15.00

DEE CLARK:

Falcon 1002, 1005	5.00 -	8.00
1009 *Oh Little Girl*	15.00 -	20.00
Vee Jay (LP) 1037 *Hold On...It's Dee Clark* .	30.00 -	40.00

FRED CLARK:

Federal 12136 *Ground Hog Snooper*	30.00 -	40.00

LEONARD CLARK & LAND OF SKY BOYS:

Klub 3108 *Come To Your Tommy Now*	8.00 -	12.00

RAY CLARK & THE DEMONS:

Crystal 01 *Little Betty Twist*	20.00 -	30.00

SANFORD CLARK:

Dot 15534, 15556	5.00 -	8.00
Jamie 1107 *Sing 'Em Some Blues*	7.00 -	10.00
1120 *Bad Luck*	7.00 -	10.00
MCI 1003 *The Fool*	15.00 -	20.00
Project *Tennessee Walk*	—	—

THE CLASSICS:

Class 219 *If Only The Sky Was A Mirror*	8.00 -	12.00
Dart 1015 *Cinderella*	8.00 -	12.00
1024 *Life Is But A Dream, Sweetheart*	8.00 -	12.00
1032 *Angela Angela*	8.00 -	12.00
Mercury 71829 *Life Is But a Dream Sweetheart* . .	8.00 -	12.00
Musicnote 118, 1116	7.00 -	10.00
Promo 1010 *Blue Moon*	7.00 -	10.00

THE CLASSMATES:

Marquee 102 *Pretty Little Pet*	5.00 -	8.00

JOE CLAY:

Vik 0211 *Duck Tail*	20.00 -	30.00
0218 *Cracker Jack*	20.00 -	30.00

DOCTOR CLAYTON:

Groove 5006 *Honey Stealin' Blues*	10.00 -	15.00

DOUG CLAYTON:

Pure Gold *Sally Ann*	—	—

JOHNNY CLAYTON:

Dixie 838 *Never Again*	15.00 -	20.00

CLEAR WATERS:

Atomic H 203 *Boogie Woogie Baby*	15.00 -	20.00

EDDIE CLEARY:

Kawana 102 *Think It Over Baby*	10.00 -	15.00

THE CLEFS:

Chess 1521 *We Three*	50.00 -	80.00
Peacock 1643 *I'll Be Waiting*	30.00 -	40.00

THE CLEFTONES:

Gee (LP) 705 *Heart And Soul*	75.00 -	100.00
(LP) 707 *For Sentimental Reasons*	75.00 -	100.00
1000 *You Baby You*	8.00 -	12.00
1000 *You Baby You* (78 rpm)	7.00 -	10.00

1011 *Little Girl Of Mine*	7.00 -	10.00
1016 *Neki-Hokey*	4.00 -	7.00
1016 *Neki-Hokey* (78rpm)	7.00 -	10.00
1064, 1067	3.00 -	5.00
Old Town 1011 *The Masquerade Is Over*	50.00 -	75.00

HENRY CLEMENT:

Spot 1000 *Late Hour Blues*	10.00 -	15.00
Zynn 1006 *I'll Be Waiting*	8.00 -	12.00

JACK CLEMENT:

Sun 291 *Ten Years*	5.00 -	8.00

CLEO & THE CRYSTALIERS:

Cindy 3003 *Please Be My Guy*	20.00 -	30.00

THE CLICKS:

Josie 780 *Come Back To Me*	20.00 -	30.00

THE CLIMBERS:

J & S 1652 *My Darlin' Dear*	30.00 -	40.00

CECIL CLINE:

Blue Hen 612 *Do Drop In*	15.00 -	20.00

PATSY CLINE:

Coral 61523 *Turn The Cards Slowly*	5.00 -	8.00
61583 *Come On In*	5.00 -	8.00
Coral (EP) 81159 *Songs by Patsy Cline*	30.00 -	50.00
(LP) 4202 *Patsy Cline Showcase*	20.00 -	30.00
Decca (LP) 4282 *Sentimentally Yours*	20.00 -	30.00
(EP) DXSB 7176 *The Patsy Cline Story* (7") (STEREO)	15.00 -	20.00
(LP) 8611 *Patsy Cline*	20.00 -	30.00
Decca 29963 *Stop, Look And Listen*	7.00 -	10.00
Decca (most other issues)	4.00 -	7.00
Everest 2011 *Hungry For Love*	7.00 -	10.00
2020 *Walking After Midnight*	7.00 -	10.00
2031 *Just Out Of Reach*	7.00 -	10.00
2039 *I've Loved And Lost Again*	5.00 -	8.00
2045 *In Care Of The Blues*	5.00 -	8.00
2052 *Got A Lot of Rhythm* (In My Soul)	7.00 -	10.00
2060 *Crazy Dream*	7.00 -	10.00
2005 *I Can't Forget*	5.00 -	8.00
Everest (LP) ST-90070 *Patsy Cline's Golden Hits* (STEREO)	30.00 -	50.00
Patsy Cline 1 *A Church, A Courtroom, Then Goodbye*	10.00 -	15.00
2 *Turn The Cards Slowly*	8.00 -	12.00
Patsy Cline (EP) 11 *Come On In* + 3	15.00 -	20.00
(EP) 14 *A Poor Man's Roses* + 3	15.00 -	20.00
(EP) 16 *Try Again* + 3	15.00 -	20.00
(EP) 21 *Three Cigarettes* + 3	15.00 -	20.00

LOY CLINGMAN:

Dot 15567 *I'm Low, Low, Low*	7.00 -	10.00

THE CLINTONIAN CUBS:

My Brothers 7 *She's Just My Style*	75.00 -	100.00

THE CLIPS:

Calvert-*Let Me Get Close To You Baby*	10.00 -	15.00

THE CLIQUES:

Modern 987, 995	7.00 -	10.00

THE CLOUDS:

Cobra 1005 *I Do*	75.00 -	100.00

THE CLOVERS:

Atlantic (EP) 504 *One Mint Julep*	30.00 -	50.00
(EP) 537 *Good Lovin'*	30.00 -	50.00
(EP) 590 *The Clovers*	30.00 -	50.00
934 *Don't You Know I Love You*	50.00 -	80.00
944 *Fool Fool Fool*	30.00 -	50.00
963 *One Mint Julep*	20.00 -	30.00
969 *Ting-A -Ling*	20.00 -	30.00
977 *I Played The Fool*	20.00 -	30.00
989 *Crawlin'*	10.00 -	15.00
1000 *Good Lovin'*	8.00 -	12.00
1001 *The Feeling Is So Good*	8.00 -	12.00
1022 *Lovey Dovey*	8.00 -	12.00
1035 *Your Cash Ain't Nothin' But Trash*	7.00 -	10.00
1046 *I Confess*	7.00 -	10.00
1052 *Blue Velvet*	7.00 -	10.00

1060 *Love Bug*	7.00 -	10.00
1073 *Nip Sip*	7.00 -	10.00
1083 *Devil Or Angel*	7.00 -	10.00
(Above are yellow label)		
Atlantic (higher number, red label)	5.00 -	8.00
(LP) 1248 *The Clovers* (black label)	100.00 -	150.00
(LP) 8009 *The Clovers* (black label)	80.00 -	120.00
(LP) 8034 *Clovers' Dance Party*	30.00 -	45.00
Popular (LP) 1001 *The Clovers In Clover*	30.00 -	50.00
Rainbow 122 *When You Came Back To Me* (78 RPM)	— -	—
United Artists 174 *That Old Black Magic* (78 RPM)	15.00 -	20.00
180 *Love Potion Number Nine* (78 RPM) (existence of this has not been verified)	— -	—
United Artists (most issues, 45 rpm)	4.00 -	8.00
United Artists (LP) UAS-609 *Love Potion Number Nine* (STEREO)	60.00 -	90.00
(LP) 3033 *The Clovers In Clover* (MONO)	30.00 -	40.00
(LP) 3099 *Love Potion Number Nine* (MONO)	40.00 -	60.00

THE CLUSTERS:

Tee Gee 102 *Pardon My Heart*		-

THE COASTERS:

Atco (LP) 101 *The Coasters*	30.00 -	40.00
(LP) 111 *The Coasters' Greatest Hits*	20.00 -	30.00
(LP) 123 *One By One*	25.00 -	35.00
(LP) 135 *Coast Along With The Coasters*	15.00 -	20.00
6064 *Turtle Dovin'* (maroon label)	7.00 -	10.00
6073 *Brazil* (maroon label)	7.00 -	10.00
6087 *Searchin'* (maroon label)	7.00 -	10.00
Atco (higher numbers, yellow label)	— -	—
6098 *My Baby Comes To Me*	7.00 -	10.00
6104 *What Is The Secret Of Your Success?*	7.00 -	10.00
6111 *Gee, Golly* (78rpm)	8.00 -	12.00
6116 *Yakety Yak* (78rpm)	15.00 -	20.00
6126 *The Shadow Knows* (78rpm)	10.00 -	15.00
6132 *Charlie Brown* (78rpm)	20.00 -	30.00
6146 *Poison Ivy* (78 rpm)	30.00 -	50.00
(EP) 4501 *Rock & Roll With*	20.00 -	30.00
(EP) 4502 *Keep Rockin' With The Coasters*	20.00 -	30.00
(EP) 4506 *The Coasters*	20.00 -	30.00
(EP) 4507 *The Coasters' Top Hits*	20.00 -	30.00

THE COBRAS:

Modern 964 *Sindy*	30.00 -	40.00

WILLIE COBBS:

C & F 300/301 *Five Long Years*	5.00 -	8.00
J.O.B. 1127 *Come On Home*	30.00 -	50.00

KIMBALL COBURN:

Hi 2010 *Please, Please*	7.00 -	10.00

THE COCHRAN BROTHERS:

Cash 1021 *Walkin' Stick Boogie*	20.00 -	30.00
Ekko 1003 *Two Blue Singing Stars*	40.00 -	60.00
1005 *Guilty Conscience*	50.00 -	75.00
3001 *Fool's Paradise*	50.00 -	75.00

EDDIE COCHRAN:

Crest 1026 *Skinny Jim*	30.00 -	50.00
Liberty (EP) 3061 *Singin To My Baby*	50.00 -	80.00
(LP) 3061 *Singin' To My Baby*	90.00 -	130.00
(LP) 3172 *Eddie Cochran*	40.00 -	60.00
(LP) 3220 *Never To Be Forgotten*	40.00 -	60.00
Liberty 55056 *Sittin' In The Balcony*	5.00 -	8.00
55056 *Sittin' in the Balcony* (78 RPM)	20.00 -	30.00
55070 *Mean When I'm Mad*	8.00 -	12.00
50087 *Drive In Slow*	5.00 -	8.00
55112 *Twenty Flight Rock*	8.00 -	12.00
55123 *Jeannie Jeannie Jeannie*	8.00 -	12.00
55138 *Pretty Girl*	8.00 -	12.00
55144 *Summertime Blues*	5.00 -	8.00
55166 *C'mon Everybody*	7.00 -	10.00
55177 *Teenage Heaven*	7.00 -	10.00
55203 *Somethin' Else*	7.00 -	10.00

55217 *Little Angel*	7.00 -	10.00
55242 *Cut Across Shorty*	7.00 -	10.00
55278 *Sweetie Pie*	7.00 -	10.00

JACK(IE) (LEE) COCHRAN:
ABC Paramount 9930 *Buy A Car*	15.00 -	20.00
Decca 30206 *Mama Don't You Think I Know*	25.00 -	35.00
Jaguar 3031 *Georgia Lee Brown*	30.00 -	40.00
Sims 107 *Hip Shakin' Mama*	50.00 -	80.00
Spry 120 *Pity Me*	40.00 -	60.00
Viv 988 *Buy A Car*	20.00 -	30.00

WAYNE COCHRAN:
Gala 117 *Last Kiss*	5.00 -	8.00
Scottie 1303 *My Little Girl*	5.00 -	8.00

JIMMY COE (& HIS GAY CATS OF RHYTHM):
States 129 *Raid On The After Hour Joint* (red plastic)	10.00 -	15.00
155 *The Jet*	8.00 -	12.00

THE CO-EDS:
Dwain 802 *With All My Heart*	10.00 -	15.00
Old Town 1027 *Love You Baby All The Time*	10.00 -	15.00
1033 *I Love An Angel*	10.00 -	15.00
Swing 101 *Mark My Words*	8.00 -	12.00

THE COINS:
Gee 10 *Can't Get No Place With You*	150.00 -	200.00

COKE JINGLES (with THE SHIRELLES, THE FOUR SEASONS, JAN & DEAN, and ROY ORBISON):
	20.00 -	30.00

AL COKER with THE COKER FAMILY:
Decca 30053 *Don't Go Baby*	8.00 -	12.00

ALVADEAN COKER:
Abbott 176 *We're Gonna Bop*	7.00 -	10.00

ANN COLE (& THE SUBURBANS):
Baton 232, 237, 240	5.00 -	8.00

DON COLE:
Kent 305 *Sweet Lovin' Honey*	20.00 -	30.00
RPM 502 *Snake-Eyed Mama*	20.00 -	30.00

JOHNNY COLE:
Dore 605 *Jenny Lou and Susie May*	—	—

LEE COLE:
Mist 1010 *Cool Baby*	20.00 -	30.00

LES COLE with THE ECHOES:
D 1010 *Bee Boppin' Daddy*	30.00 -	50.00

SONNY COLE:
Excell 124 *Robinson Crusoe Bop*	30.00 -	50.00

HONEY COLEMAN:
Combo 3 *Daddy Why Did You Leave Me*	15.00 -	20.00

HOOKS COLEMAN:
Excello 2193 *Teen-Age Baby*	8.00 -	12.00

RAY COLEMAN:
Arcade 147 *Jukebox Rock & Roll*	20.00 -	30.00

COLLAY & THE SATELLITES:
Sho-Biz 102 *Little Girl Next Door*	10.00 -	15.00

THE COLLEGIANS:
Winley 224 *Zoom, Zoom, Zoom*	5.00 -	8.00
261 *Oh, I Need Your Love*	5.00 -	8.00
263 *Right Around The Corner*	5.00 -	8.00
Winley (LP) 6004 *Sing Along With The Collegians*	50.00 -	75.00
X-Tra 108 *Let's Go For A Ride*	15.00 -	20.00

GUS COLLETTI:
Tin Pan Alley *Sample Kiss*	—	—

BIFF COLLIE:
Starday 178 *Lonely*	10.00 -	15.00
203 *Look On The Good Side*	10.00 -	15.00
230 *Empty Kisses*	10.00 -	15.00
251 *All Of A Sudden*	10.00 -	15.00

THE COLLINS KIDS:
Columbia 21470 *Beetle Bug Bop*	10.00 -	15.00
21514 *The Rockaway Rock*	7.00 -	10.00
21543 *I'm In My Teens*	10.00 -	15.00
21560 *Rock And Roll Polka*	7.00 -	10.00

40824 *Move A Little Closer*	8.00 -	12.00
40921 *Hop, Skip And Jump*	8.00 -	12.00
41012 *Party*	10.00 -	15.00
41087 *Mama Worries*	10.00 -	15.00
41149 *Mercy*	10.00 -	15.00
41225 *Rock Boppin' Baby*	10.00 -	15.00
41329 *Sugar Plum*	8.00 -	12.00

AL COLLINS:
Ace 500 *I Got The Blues For You*	30.00 -	40.00

EDDIE COLLINS:
Fernwood 104 *Patience Baby*	10.00 -	15.00

LORRIE & LARRY COLLINS (See THE COLLINS KIDS)

MARTY COLLINS:
Ammons 6083 *I'm Gonna Walk*	7.00 -	10.00
Renner 227 *She's Fine*	10.00 -	15.00

TOMMY COLLINS:
Capitol (LP) 776	15.00 -	20.00
(LP) 1196 *This Is*	15.00 -	20.00

THE COLONAIRS:
Ember 1017 *Can't Stand To Lose You*	15.00 -	20.00
Tru-Lite 127 *Do-Pop-Si*	25.00 -	30.00

THE COLTS:
Vita 112 *Adorable*	10.00 -	15.00
121 *Sweet Sixteen*	15.00 -	20.00
130 *Never, No More*	15.00 -	20.00

CHUCK COMER:
Vaden—*Shall We Dance/Little More Lovin*	—	—

THE COMIC BOOKS:
Dynamic Sound 2005 *The First Time In My Life*	8.00 -	12.00

THE COMMODORES:
Dot 15372 *Uranium*	10.00 -	15.00
RPM 488 *Hello Baby*	10.00 -	15.00

THE COMPANIONS:
Federal 12397 *Why Oh Why Baby*	15.00 -	20.00
Gina 722 *It's Too Late*	7.00 -	10.00

THE COMPOSERS:
Era 3118 *I Had A Dream*	7.00 -	10.00

BOBBY COMSTOCK & THE COUNTS:
Mohawk 124 *Everyday Blues*	7.00 -	10.00
Triumph 602 *Jealous Fool*	5.00 -	8.00

THE CONCORDS:
Ember 1007 *I'll Always Say Please*	10.00 -	15.00
Epic 9697 *Should I Cry*	7.00 -	10.00
Gramercy 304 *Cross My Heart*	7.00 -	10.00
Harlem 2328 *Monticello*	75.00 -	100.00
Herald 576 *Marlene*	10.00 -	15.00
578 *Cold And Frosty Morning*	10.00 -	15.00

TONY CONN:
Decca 30813 *Like Wow*	30.00 -	40.00
30865 *You Pretty Thing*	30.00 -	40.00

CONNY & THE BELLHOPS:
R 505 *Shot Road*	10.00 -	15.00
R 511 *Fafine/Are You Ashamed*	10.00 -	15.00

THE CONSTELLATIONS:
Groove 0140 *Come Sit By Me*	10.00 -	15.00

CONTENDERS:
Saxony 1001 *Whenever I Get Lonely*	20.00 -	30.00

THE CONTINENTALS:
Hunter 3502 *It Doesn't Matter*	20.00 -	30.00
Port 70018 *Fine Fine Frame*	10.00 -	15.00
Whirlin' Disc 101 *Dear Lord*	15.00 -	20.00
105 *Picture Of Love*	15.00 -	20.00

THE CONTOURS:
Motown 1012 *Funny*	10.00 -	15.00

DALE COOK:
Specialty 596 *Forever*	5.00 -	8.00

L.C. COOKE:
Checker 903, 925	7.00 -	10.00

SAM COOKE:
Keen (LP) 2001, 2003, 2004	20.00 -	40.00
4-4002 *Desire Me* (78rpm)	8.00 -	12.00

4-4009 *Lonely Island* (78rpm)	8.00	-	12.00
44013 *You Send Me* (78rpm)	15.00	-	20.00
RCA Victor (EP) 437 *Another Saturday Night*	30.00	-	50.00
Specialty 619 *Forever*	4.00	-	7.00
627 *I Don't Want To Cry*	5.00	-	8.00

COOKIE & THE CUPCAKES:

Khoury's 703 *Mathilda*	10.00	-	15.00
Lyric 1008 *All My Lovin'*	8.00	-	12.00

THE COOKIES:

Josie 822 *King Of Hearts*	7.00	-	10.00

COOL BREEZE (See LITTLE COOL BREEZES)

THE COOLBREEZERS:

ABC Paramount 9865 *You Know I Go For You*	10.00	-	15.00
Bale 100 *The Greatest Love Of All*	15.00	-	20.00
102 *Christmas Ring*	15.00	-	20.00

EDDIE COOLEY & THE DIMPLES:

Roost 621 *Priscilla* (78rpm)	10.00	-	15.00

SPADE COOLEY:

Columbia (LP) 9007 (10") *Sagebrush Swing*	20.00	-	30.00

DOLLY COOPER:

Dot 15495 *Big Rock Inn*	7.00	-	10.00
Ebb 109 *Wild Love*	5.00	-	8.00

LITTLE COOPER & THE DRIFTERS:

Stevens 105 *Evening Train*	7.00	-	10.00

COWBOY COPAS:

Starday 501, 528, 542, 641	5.00	-	8.00

JOHNNY COPELAND:

Mercury 71280 *Rock 'n Roll Lilly*	15.00	-	20.00

KEN COPELAND:

Dot 15686 *Where The Rio De Rosa Flows*	10.00	-	15.00
Lin 5017 *Fanny Brown*	15.00	-	20.00

THE COPESETICS:

Premium 409 *Collegian*	10.00	-	15.00

PAT CORDEL & THE CRESCENTS:

Club 1011 *Darling Come Back*	15.00	-	20.00
Victory 1001 *Darling Come Back* (red plastic)	10.00	-	15.00

THE CORDELLS:

Bullseye 1017 *Believe In Me*	10.00	-	15.00

THE CORDIALS:

Reveille 106 *Eternal Love*	7.00	-	10.00
Seven Arts 707 *Dawn Is Almost Here*	8.00	-	12.00
Whip 276 *My Heart's Desire*	7.00	-	10.00

THE CORONETS:

Chess 1549 *Nadine*	20.00	-	30.00
1549 *Nadine* (red plastic)	100.00	-	Up
1553 *It Would Be Heavenly*	30.00	-	40.00
1553 *It Would Be Heavenly* (red plastic)	100.00	-	UP
Groove 014 *I Love You More*	20.00	-	30.00
0116 *Hush*	20.00	-	30.00

THE CORSAIRS:

Hytone 110 *Goodbye Darling*	75.00	-	125.00

THE CORVAIRS:

Comet 2145 *True True Love*	5.00	-	8.00

THE CORVELLS:

ABC Paramount 10324 *Take My Love*	7.00	-	10.00
Lido 509 *We Made A Vow*	10.00	-	15.00

THE CORVETS:

ABC Paramount 9891 *String Band Hop*	—	-	—

THE COSMIC RAYS:

Satum 222 *Bye Bye*	—	-	—

NED COSTNER:

Hamilton 50030 *Jeopardy*	7.00	-	10.00

ERNEST COTTON:

J.O.B 1120 *Going Back To Memphis*	75.00	-	100.00

JAMES COTTON:

Loma 2042 *Laying In The Weeds*	7.00	-	10.00
Sun 199 *Straighten Up Baby*	75.00	-	100.00
206 *Cotton Crop Blues*	75.00	-	100.00

JERRY COULSTON & THE JADES:

Christy 131 *Bon-Bon Baby*	7.00	-	10.00

THE COUNTRY DUDES (with CLAY ALLAN):

Azalea 121 *Have A Ball*	10.00	-	15.00

THE COUNTRY G-J's:

Valley—*Go, Girl, Go*	—	-	—

FRED COUPLAND (See BLUE TONES) THE COUNTS:

Dot 1188 *Darling Dear*	10.00	-	15.00
1199 *Baby Don't You Know*	10.00	-	15.00
1210 *She Won't Say Yes*	10.00	-	15.00
1226 *Baby I Want You*	8.00	-	12.00
1235 *Let Me Go Lover*	8.00	-	12.00
1243 *Love And Understanding*	8.00	-	12.00
1265 *I Need You Tonight*	8.00	-	12.00
1275 *To Our Love*	8.00	-	12.00

KEITH COURDALE:

Steelwork Blues		-	

COUSIN LEROY:

Ember 1016 *Highway 41*	15.00	-	20.00
1023 *Up The River*	10.00	-	15.00
Groove 0123 *Catfish*	10.00	-	15.00
Herald 546 *Waitin' At The Station*	8.00	-	12.00

BUDDY COVELLE:

Coral 62181 *Lorraine*	75.00	-	100.00

RICKY COYNE:

Event 4298 *Little Darleen*	10.00	-	15.00

C-QUINS/C-QUINNS:

Chess 1815 *My Only Love*	7.00	-	10.00
Ditto 501 *You've Been Crying*	10.00	-	15.00

RILEY CRABTREE:

Ekko 1019 *Don't Turn Away From Me*	7.00	-	10.00

BILL(Y) "CRASH" CRADDOCK:

Colonial 721 *Birddoggin'*	10.00	-	15.00
Columbia 41316 *I Miss You So Much*	5.00	-	8.00
41367 *Blabbermouth*	5.00	-	8.00
41470 *Boom Boom Baby*	5.00	-	8.00
41536 *I Want That*	5.00	-	8.00
41619, 41677	4.00	-	7.00
Date 1007 *Ah, Poor Little Baby*	7.00	-	10.00

JIMMY CRAIG:

Imperial 5592 *Oh! Little Girl!*	15.00	-	20.00
Prism 1002 *Rocka Socka Hop*	15.00	-	20.00

PEE WEE CRAIG:

Choice 1000 *Rambling Man*	10.00	-	15.00

JIMMY CRAIN:

Spangle 2009 *Shig-A-Shag*	10.00	-	15.00
Vincent 5047/5048 *Why Worry*	15.00	-	25.00

BLACKIE CRAWFORD:

Coral 64118, 64128, 64161	5.00	-	8.00

FRED CRAWFORD:

Starday 170 *You Gotta Wait*	15.00	-	25.00
243 *Rock Candy Rock*	20.00	-	30.00

SUGAR BOY CRAWFORD:

Imperial 5424, 5468	7.00	-	10.00

PEE WEE CRAYTON:

Crown (LP) 5175 *Pee Wee Crayton*	20.00	-	30.00
Fox 102 *Look Up And Live*	10.00	-	15.00
Imperial 5288 *Every Dog Has His Day*	10.00	-	15.00
5297 *Hurry Hurry*	10.00	-	15.00
5321 *I Need Your Love*	8.00	-	12.00
5338 *I Got News For You*	8.00	-	12.00
5345 *Eyes Full Of Tears*	8.00	-	12.00
5353 *Be Faithful*	8.00	-	12.00
Post 2007 *Don't Go*	10.00	-	15.00
Recorded in Hollywood 408 *Pappy's Blues*	15.00	-	20.00
426 *I'm Your Prisoner*	15.00	-	20.00
Vee Jay 214 *The Telephone Is Ringing*	5.00	-	8.00
252 *I Don't Care*	5.00	-	8.00
266 *Fiddle De Dee*	5.00	-	8.00

THE CREATIONS:

Jamie 1197 *The Bells*	7.00	-	10.00
Meridian 6283, 7552 *The Wedding*	10.00	-	15.00
Penny 9022 *We're In Love*	5.00	-	8.00
Radiant 103 *Don't Listen To What Others Say*	7.00	-	10.00
Tip Top 400 *Mommy and Daddy*	15.00	-	20.00

THE CREATORS:

Dootone 463 *I've Had You*	10.00 -	15.00
Dore 653 *Too Far To Turn Around*	8.00 -	12.00
Hi-Q 5021 *Wear My Ring*	8.00 -	12.00

THE CRESCENDOS:

Music City 831 *My Heart's Desire*	10.00 -	15.00
Nasco 6005 *Oh Julie*	5.00 -	8.00
6005 *Oh Julie* (78 RPM)	15.00 -	20.00
6009 *Crazy Hop*	8.00 -	12.00
6021 *Rainy Sunday*	8.00 -	12.00
Scarlet 4007 *Strange Love*	10.00 -	15.00
TAP 7027 *Oh Julie*	10.00 -	15.00

THE CRESCENTS:

Hamilton 50033 *When You Wish Upon A Star*	7.00 -	10.00
Joyce 102 *Everybody Knew But Me*	15.00 -	20.00

THE CRESTS:

Coed (EP) 101 *The Angels Listened In*	75.00 -	100.00
Coed 501 *Pretty Little Angel*	15.00 -	20.00
506 *Sixteen Candles*	5.00 -	8.00*
509 *Six Nights A Week*	5.00 -	8.00
511 *Flower Of Love*	7.00 -	10.00
515 *The Angels Listened In*	5.00 -	8.00
421 *A Year Ago Tonight*	5.00 -	8.00
525 *Step By Step*	5.00 -	8.00
531 *Trouble In Paradise*	5.00 -	8.00
535 *Journey Of Love*	5.00 -	8.00
537 *Isn't It Amazing*	7.00 -	10.00
543 *Good Golly Miss Molly*	7.00 -	10.00
561 *Little Miracles*	7.00 -	10.00

*(Note: 78 RPM pressings may exist of THE CRESTS' Coed records; these would be of value. Canadian 78 RPM pressings have been seen.)

Coed (LP) 901 *The Crests Sing All Biggies*	50.00 -	75.00
(LP) 904 *The Best of The Crests* (MONO)	50.00 -	75.00
(LP) LPS-904 *The Best Of The Crests* (STEREO) (existence not confirmed)	200.00 -	Up
Coral 62403 *You Blew Out The Candles*	10.00 -	15.00
Joyce 103 *Sweetest One*	15.00 -	20.00
105 *No One To Love*	15.00 -	20.00

THE CREW CUTS:

Mercury (LP) 20144 *Rock And Roll Bash*	20.00 -	30.00

THE CRICKETS (featuring DEAN BARLOW)

Beacon 104 *Be Faithful*	10.00 -	15.00
Davis (EP) 211 *The Crickets*	30.00 -	40.00
459 *I'm Going To Live My Life Alone*	15.00 -	20.00
Jay Dee 777 *Dreams And Wishes*	15.00 -	20.00
781 *Fine As Wine*	15.00 -	20.00
785 *Your Love*	15.00 -	20.00
786 *Just You*	15.00 -	20.00
789 *Are You Looking For A Sweetheart?*	15.00 -	20.00
795 *I'm Going To Live My Life Alone*	15.00 -	20.00
Junior 396 *I Sold My Heart To The Junkman*	20.00 -	30.00
MGM 11428 *You're Mine*	20.00 -	30.00
11507 *For You I Have Eyes*	20.00 -	30.00

THE CRICKETS (with BUDDY HOLLY):

Brunswick (LP) 54038 *The Chirping Crickets*	100.00 -	150.00
55009 *That'll Be The Day*	7.00 -	10.00
55009 *That'll Be The Day* (78 RPM)	50.00 -	75.00
55035 *Oh Boy!*	7.00 -	10.00
55035 *Oh Boy!* (78 RPM)	50.00 -	75.00
55053 *Maybe Baby*	7.00 -	10.00
55053 *Maybe Baby* (78 RPM)	50.00 -	75.00
55072 *Think It Over*	7.00 -	10.00
55072 *Think It Over* (78 RPM)	50.00 -	75.00
55094 *It's So Easy*	7.00 -	10.00
55094 *It's So Easy* (78 RPM)	50.00 -	75.00
Brunswick (EP) 71036 *The Chirping Crickets*	75.00 -	100.00
(EP) 71038 *The Sound of The Crickets*	75.00 -	100.00
Coral (LP) 57320 *In Style with The Crickets*	75.00 -	100.00
Coral 62198 *More Than I Can Say*	10.00 -	15.00
62238 *Don't Cha Know*	10.00 -	15.00

Coral (EP) 81192 *The Crickets*	50.00 -	75.00

(Note: Promotional copies of above may be of substantially greater interest and value.)

HOWARD CROCKET:

Solar 500 *Seven Cards From Now*	15.00 -	20.00

G. DAVY CROCKETT:

Checker 1121 *Look Out Mabel*	7.00 -	10.00
Chief 7010 *Look Out Mabel*	20.00 -	30.00
U.S.A. 816 *Look Out Mabel*	8.00 -	12.00

GEORGE CROMWELL:

Brunswick 55131 *Washed Up*	8.00 -	12.00

JERRY CRONIN:

Flame 113 *A-Rock-A Me Baby*	7.00 -	10.00

DILLAR CROOM & THE CROOM BROTHERS:

Vee Jay 283 *It's You Love*	25.00 -	35.00

HAROLD CROSBY & THE PINE TREE BOYS:

Lorida 3/4 *The Bastille Blues*	8.00 -	12.00

HANK CROW:

Southwest 204 *Crazy 'Bout You*	15.00 -	20.00

BOBBY CROWN & THE KAPERS:

Felco 102 *One Way Ticket*	15.00 -	20.00

THE CROWNS: (See also ARTHUR LEE MAYE & THE CROWNS)

R n B 6901 *I'll Forget About You*	15.00 -	20.00

THE CROWS:

Gee 1 *Perfidia*	75.00 -	100.00
Rama 3 *Seven Lonely Days*	80.00 -	120.00
5 Gee (red plastic)	30.00 -	50.00
5 Gee (black plastic)	10.00 -	15.00
10 *Heartbreaker*	50.00 -	75.00
29 *Untrue*	30.00 -	50.00
30 *Miss You*	50.00 -	80.00
50 *Sweet Sue*	50.00 -	80.00
Tico 1082 *Mambo Shevitz*	75.00 -	100.00

(ARTHUR) "BIG BOY" CRUDUP:

Ace 503 *My Baby Boogies All The Time*	20.00 -	30.00
Fire (LP) 103 *Mean Old Frisco*	75.00 -	125.00
1502, 1503	5.00 -	8.00
Groove 0011 *I Love My Baby*	15.00 -	20.00
0026 *She's Got No Hair*	15.00 -	20.00
5005 *Rock Me Mama*	10.00 -	15.00
RCA Victor 5070 *Pearly Lee*	25.00 -	35.00
5167 *Keep On Drinkin'*	25.00 -	35.00
5563 *My Wife And Women*	25.00 -	35.00
50-0000 *That's All Right*	20.00 -	30.00
50-0001 *Katie May*	20.00 -	30.00
50-0013 *Crudup's Vicksburg Blues*	20.00 -	30.00
50-0032 *Hoodoo Lady Blues*	20.00 -	30.00
50-0046 *Mercy Blues*	20.00 -	30.00

(Note: RCA Vic 50-0000—50-0046, inclusive, are made of vivid orange plastic.)

RCA Victor 50-0074 *Dust My Broom*	15.00 -	20.00
50-0092 *Mean Old Santa Fe*	15.00 -	20.00
50-0100 *Lonesome World To Me*	15.00 -	20.00
50-0101 *She's Just Like Caldonia*	15.00 -	20.00
50-0117 *Nobody Wants Me*	15.00 -	20.00
50-0126 *Roberta Blues*	15.00 -	20.00
50-0141 *Too Much Competition*	15.00 -	20.00

THE CRUISERS:

Finch 353 *The Moon Is Yours*	15.00 -	20.00
V-Tone 207 *If I Knew*	10.00 -	15.00
213 *Cryin' Over You*	8.00 -	12.00
Zebra 119 *Foolish Me*	20.00 -	30.00

AL CRUM:

Glenn 3800 *Turn 'Em Up*	5.00 -	8.00

SIMON CRUM:

Capitol (LP) 1880 *The Unpredictable Simon Crum*	20.00 -	30.00
3460 *Bop Cat Bop*	7.00 -	10.00
4073 *Stand Up, Sit Down, Shut Your Mouth*	5.00 -	8.00

MANNY CRUSE & THE SOUNDS
QUARTETTE:
Dart 127 *Any Time Any Place* .... 7.00 - 10.00
THE CRYSTALIERS:
Johnson 103 *Don't Cry* .... 20.00 - 30.00
THE CRYSTALS:
Aladdin 3355 *I Do Believe* .... 20.00 - 30.00
De Luxe 6013 *My Dear* .... 50.00 - 75.00
   6037 *Have Faith In Me* .... 30.00 - 50.00
   6077 *God Only Knows* .... 30.00 - 50.00
Felsted 8566 *Blind Date* .... 7.00 - 10.00
Luna 5001 *Come To Me Darling* ..... 30.00 - 50.00
Philles 100 *Oh Yeah, Maybe Baby* ... 7.00 - 10.00
   103 *Uptown* .... 7.00 - 10.00
Rockin' 518 *Don't You Go* .... 50.00 - 75.00
THE C TONES:
Everlast 5005 *On Your Mark* ...... 7.00 - 10.00
THE CUBANS:
Flash 133 *Tell Me* .... 10.00 - 15.00
THE CUBS:
Savoy 1502 *Why Did You Make Me Cry* ...... 10.00 - 15.00
THE CUES:
Capitol 3245 *Oh My Darling* .... 10.00 - 15.00
   3310 *You're On My Mind* ..... 10.00 - 15.00
   3483 *Crackerjack* .... 10.00 - 15.00
THE CUFF LINKS:
Dootone 413 *How You Lied* .... 15.00 - 20.00
   422 *It's Too Late Now* .... 10.00 - 15.00
   409 *Guided Missiles* .... 10.00 - 15.00
Gait 543 *Only One Love* .... 15.00 - 20.00
THE CUFFLINX:
Dootone 433 *So Tough* .... 10.00 - 15.00
   435 *A Fool's Fortune* .... 10.00 - 15.00
   438 *Lawful Wedding* .... 10.00 - 15.00
BRUCE CULVER:
M M.I 1235 *Square Record* .... 10.00 - 15.00
THE CUPIDS:
Aladdin 3404 *Lillie Mae* .... 10.00 - 15.00
Decca 30279 *The Answer To Your Prayer* ...... 8.00 - 12.00
PAT CUPP:
Crown (LP) 5364 *Pat Cupp and Ray Smith* .... 30.00 - 50.00
RPM 461 *Do Me No Wrong* ...... 20.00 - 30.00
   473 *Long Gone Daddy* .... 20.00 - 30.00
That's My Girl .... -
CURLEY JIM (MORRISON):
Mida 100 *Rock 'N' Roll Itch* ..... 20.00 - 30.00
   108 *Sloppy Sloppy Suzie* ..... 20.00 - 30.00
EARL CURRY:
Post 2001 *Somebody Stole My Girl* ... 20.00 - 30.00
   2011 *Hobo* .... 20.00 - 30.00
R & B 1313 *Try And Get Me* ..... 10.00 - 15.00
RPM 402 *One Whole Year Baby* ... 15.00 - 20.00
JAMES CURRY:
Flash 110 *My Promise* .... 8.00 - 12.00
C.C. CURTIS:
Audicon 109 *Aunt Minnie* .... 5.00 - 8.00
DON CURTIS:
Kliff 104 *Rough Tough Man* ...... 30.00 - 50.00
EDDIE CURTIS:
Dot 15505 *You're Much Too Pretty For Me* ..... 5.00 - 8.00
EDDIE "TEX" CURTIS:
Gee 9 *Shake, Pretty Baby, Shake* ... 75.00 - 100.00
MAC CURTIS:
King 4927 *If I Had Me A Woman* ... 20.00 - 30.00
   4949 *Grandaddy's Rockin'* ...... 25.00 - 35.00
   4965 *You Ain't Treatin' Me Right* ... 20.00 - 30.00
   4995 *That Ain't Nothin' But Right* ...... 20.00 - 30.00
   5059 *Say So* .... 15.00 - 20.00
   5107 *What You Want* .... 15.00 - 20.00
   5121 *Little Miss Linda* .... 10.00 - 15.00
Shalimar 103 *Come On Back* .... 5.00 - 8.00

SONNY CURTIS:
Dot 15799 *Willa May Jones* .... 15.00 - 20.00
THE CYCLONES: (See also BILL TAYLOR &
THE CYCLONES)
Flip 324 *My Dear* .... 7.00 - 10.00
Trophy 503 *Aftermath* .... 7.00 - 10.00
JOHNNY CYMBAL:
Kapp (LP) 3324 *Mr. Bass Man* ..... 20.00 - 30.00
THE CYMBALS:
Amazon 709 *One Step Too Far* ..... 7.00 - 10.00
BUDDY CYPRESS:
Flash 118 *I'm In Love With You* ..... 7.00 - 10.00
CZARS OF RHYTHM:
De'Voice 782 *Please Don't Leave Me* .... 10.00 - 15.00
DADDY CLEANHEAD:
Specialty 541 *Back Home* .... 7.00 - 10.00
DICK D'AGOSTIN:
Accent 1046 *I'm Your Daddy-O* .... 10.00 - 15.00
Dot 15773 *Nancy Lynne* .... 10.00 - 15.00
   15867 *Night Walk* .... 7.00 - 10.00
Liberty 55218 *It's You* .... 7.00 - 10.00
DICK DALE & THE DEL-TONES:
Deltone (LP) 1001 *Surfer's Choice* ..... 50.00 - 75.00
   5012 *Ooh-Whee-Marie* .... 10.00 - 15.00
   5014 *Jessie Pearl* .... 10.00 - 15.00
   5019 *Eight Till Midnight* .... 7.00 - 10.00
   5020 *Surf Beat* .... 5.00 - 8.00
JIMMIE DALE:
Drew-Blan 1003 *Emma Lee* ...... 8.00 - 12.00
KENNY DALE:
Picture 310 *Cincy Lee* .... 7.00 - 10.00
LARRY DALE (& THE KING NOTES):
Atlantic 2133 *Drinkin' Wine Spo-Dee-O-Dee* .... 5.00 - 8.00
Elbridge 12763 *Crying Over You* .... 10.00 - 15.00
THE DALES:
Onyx 509 *If You Are Meant To Be* .... 15.00 - 20.00
JIMMY DALEY & THE DING-A-LINGS:
Decca (EP) 2431, 2432, 2480 .... 15.00 - 20.00
   (LP) 8429 *Rock Pretty Baby* ...... 30.00 - 40.00
Decca 30163 *Rock, Pretty Baby* .... 7.00 - 10.00
CHUCK DALLAS:
K-C 102 *Come On Let's Go* ..... 7.00 - 10.00
JACKIE DALLAS:
Fawn 6002 *Lorraine* .... 15.00 - 20.00
CHUCK DALLIS:
Glenn 2201 *Come On Let's Go* ..... 15.00 - 20.00
   2203 *Good Show, But No Go* ..... 15.00 - 20.00
Mar-Vel 2204 *Joni Kaye* .... 15.00 - 20.00
BIG LLOYD DALTON:
Yucca 135 *Jenny* .... 7.00 - 10.00
DURWOOD DALY:
Caprock 108 *That's The Way It Goes* .... 7.00 - 10.00
TERRY DALY:
Mark 122 *You Don't Bug Me* ...... 15.00 - 20.00
JOE D'AMBRA & THE EMBERS:
Mercury 71725 *Please Come Home* .... 5.00 - 8.00
DONNA DAMERON:
Dart 113 *Bopper 486609* .... 10.00 - 20.00
"DANCE THE ROCK & ROLL":
Atlantic (LP) 8013 (various artists) .... 20.00 - 30.00
"DANCE TUNES FROM THE VAULT":
Chess (LP) 1476 (various artists) .... 20.00 - 30.00
THE DANDERLIERS:
B & F 1344 *Chop Chop Boom* ...... 15.00 - 20.00
States 147 *My Autumn Love* .... 15.00 - 20.00
   150 *My Loving Partner* .... 30.00 - 40.00
   152 *May God Be With You* ..... 30.00 - 40.00
   160 *My Love* .... 30.00 - 40.00
DANDEVILLES:
Guyden 2014 *There's A Reason* ...... 8.00 - 12.00
THE DANDIES:
Peach 121 *Red Light* .... 7.00 - 10.00

EDDIE DANIELS:
Ebb 108 *Whoa-Whoa Baby* . . . . 10.00 - 15.00

JEFF DANIELS:
Astro 108 *Foxy Dan* . . . . 15.00 - 20.00
Big B 555 *Uh Uh Uh* . . . . 15.00 - 20.00
Big Howdy 777 *Switch Blade Sam* . . . . 15.00 - 20.00
Caravan *Go Daddyo (?)* . . . .   —   -   —
Meladee 117 *Daddy-O Rock* . . . . 30.00 - 50.00

THE DANLEERS:
Amp-3 2115 *One Summer Night* . . . . 15.00 - 20.00
Epic 9367 *If You Don't Care* . . . . 8.00 - 12.00
   9421 *Little Lover* . . . . 8.00 - 12.00
Everest 19412 *Foolish* . . . . 8.00 - 12.00
Lemans 008 *I'm Sorry* . . . . 8.00 - 12.00
Mercury 71356 *I Really Love You* . . . . 7.00 - 10.00
   71401 *A Picture Of You* . . . . 7.00 - 10.00
   71441 *I Can't Sleep* . . . . 7.00 - 10.00
Smash 1872 *If* . . . . 7.00 - 10.00

DANNY & THE JUNIORS:
ABC Paramount (EP) 11 *At The Hop* . . . . 50.00 - 75.00
ABC Paramount 9871 *At The Hop* . . . . 5.00 - 8.00
   9871 *At The Hop* (78 RPM) . . . . 20.00 - 30.00
   9888 *Rock & Roll Is Here To Stay* . . . . 7.00 - 10.00
   9888 *Rock & Roll Is Here To Stay* (78
     RPM) (Existence of this has not been
     confirmed) . . . .   —   -   —
ABC Paramount (most other issues) . . . . 4.00 - 8.00
Singular 711 *At The Hop* . . . . 30.00 - 40.00

DANNY & THE MEMORIES:
Valiant 705 *Can't Help Lovin' That Girl Of Mine* 5.00 - 8.00

DANNY BOY (& HIS BLUE GUITAR):
Dot 16140 *Send Me Some Lovin'* . . . . 10.00 - 15.00
Kent 300 *Don't Go Pretty Baby* . . . . 15.00 - 20.00
Tifco 824 *Wild Women* . . . . 15.00 - 20.00

CHARLES BUD DANT:
Decca (LP) 8430 *Holiday In The Golden West* . . 15.00 - 20.00

DANTE & THE EVERGREENS:
Madison (LP) 1002 *Dante & The Evergreens* . . . . 50.00 - 75.00

THE DAPPERS:
Epic 9423 *My Love Is Real* . . . . 10.00 - 15.00
Groove 0156 *Unwanted Love* . . . . 30.00 - 50.00
Peacock 1651 *Come Back To Me* . . . . 25.00 - 40.00
Rainbow 373 *Bop Bop Bu* . . . . 8.00 - 12.00
Star-X 505 *We're In Love* . . . . 10.00 - 15.00

THE DAPS:
Marterry 5249 *Down And Out* . . . . 7.00 - 10.00

BOBBY DARIN (& THE JAYBIRDS):
Atco (LP) 102 *Bobby Darin* . . . . 15.00 - 20.00
   (LP) 104 *That's All* . . . . 15.00 - 20.00
   (LP) 115 *This Is Bobby Darin* . . . . 15.00 - 20.00
Atco (EP) 4508 *This Is Darin* . . . . 15.00 - 20.00
   6117 *Splish Splash* (78rpm) . . . . 15.00 - 25.00
   6127 *Queen Of The Hop* (78 rpm) . . . . . . 15.00 - 20.00
   6133 *Plain Jane* (78 rpm) . . . . 15.00 - 20.00
Decca 29983 *Rock Island Line* . . . . 8.00 - 12.00
   29922 *Sully Willie* . . . . 8.00 - 12.00
   30031 *Hear Them Bells* . . . . 8.00 - 12.00
   30225 *Dealer In Dreams* . . . . 8.00 - 12.00

DENVER DARLING:
Audio Lab (LP) 107 . . . . 20.00 - 30.00

JOHNNY DARLING:
De Luxe 6167 *Baseball Baby* . . . .   —   -   —

DARNELL & THE DREAMS:
West Side 1030 *I Had A Love* . . . . 5.00 - 8.00

DON DARNELL:
Brunswick 55144 *In My Own Little Way* . . . . . . 8.00 - 12.00

DARREL & THE OXFORDS:
Roulette 4174 *Picture In My Wallet* . . . . 8.00 - 12.00

JAMES DARREN:
Colpix (LP) 406 *Album No. 1* . . . . 20.00 - 30.00
   (LP) 418 *Sings The Movies* . . . . 15.00 - 20.00
   (LP) 424 *Sings For All Sizes* . . . . 15.00 - 20.00

   (LP) 428 *Love Among The Young* . . . . 15.00 - 20.00

THE DARTS:
Apt 25023 *On My Mind* . . . . 7.00 - 10.00

CHUCK DARTY:
Chart 642 *My Steady Girl* . . . . 15.00 - 20.00
Rama 229 *My Steady Girl* . . . . 8.00 - 12.00

FRANKIE DASH:
Cool 106 *Rock Rhythm Roll* . . . . 40.00 - 60.00

DAVE & THE STEREOS:
Pennant 1001 *Roamin' Romeo* . . . . 8.00 - 12.00

DAVEY & THE DOO RAYS:
Guyden 2002 *It's The Beat* . . . . 7.00 - 10.00

BOB DAVIES & THE RHYTHM JESTERS:
Rama 224 *Never Anymore* . . . . 7.00 - 10.00

AL DAVIS:
Manco—*Go Baby Go* . . . .   —   -   —

BO DAVIS:
Crest 1027 *Let's Coast Awhile* . . . . 20.00 - 30.00

BOB DAVIS:
Bandera 2505 *I Was Wrong* . . . . 5.00 - 8.00

DALE DAVIS & THE TOMCATS:
Stardale 100/101 *Gotta Rock* . . . . 15.00 - 25.00
   104/105 *Why'd You Leave Me Blues* . . . . . 15.00 - 25.00
   701/702 *Bearcat Mama* . . . . 15.00 - 25.00

EDDIE DAVIS:
Fable *Tick Tock Rock* . . . .   —   -   —

EMMETT/EMMIT DAVIS:
Fling 721 *One Last Chance* . . . . 7.00 - 10.00
M and B 101 *How About It Baby* . . . . 7.00 - 10.00

EUNICE DAVIS:
De Luxe 6068 *24 Hours A Day* . . . . 15.00 - 20.00
Grand 130 *Let's Have A Party* . . . . 10.00 - 15.00

GENE DAVIS:
Challenge 59091 *The Facts Of Life* . . . . 7.00 - 10.00
King 5076 *Who'll Dry My Tears* . . . . 7.00 - 10.00
R-Dell 107 *Curfew* . . . . 15.00 - 20.00

HARLEY DAVIS:
Cindy 3011 *Calling All Cats* . . . . 15.00 - 20.00

"HAPPY JACK" DAVIS with PIANO SLIM &
THE STEREO-TONES:
Lluvia 5052 *Ten Cents Stew* . . . . 5.00 - 8.00

JIMMIE DAVIS:
Decca (LP) 5500 (10″) . . . . 20.00 - 30.00
   (LP) 8896 *You Are My Sunshine* . . . . 15.00 - 20.00

JUDGE DAVIS:
Flash 120 *Sawmill Section* . . . . 7.00 - 10.00

KEN DAVIS:
Pfau 3057 *Bundle Of Lovin'* . . . .   —   -   —
Star-Light 1006 *Shook Shake* . . . . 20.00 - 30.00

KING DAVIS:
Hollywood 422 *Waggin' Your Tail* . . . . 10.00 - 15.00

LARRY DAVIS:
Duke 192, 313, 328 . . . . 5.00 - 8.00

LARRY & DIXIE DAVIS:
Kangaroo 13 *Gonna Live It Up* . . . . 30.00 - 40.00

LENNY DAVIS:
Do-Ra-Me 1413 *Santan's Got You* . . . . 7.00 - 10.00

LINK DAVIS:
Al's 1503 *Johnny Be Good* . . . .   —   -   —
All Star 7171 *Bon Ton Rula* . . . . 4.00 - 7.00
Nucraft 2026 *Grasshopper Rock* . . . . 7.00 - 10.00
Okeh 7046 *Mama Say No* . . . . 7.00 - 10.00
   18048 *Crawfish Crawl* . . . . 7.00 - 10.00
Sarg 136 *Cockroach* . . . . 8.00 - 12.00
Starday 235 . . . . 15.00 - 20.00
   242 *Grasshopper Rock* . . . . 15.00 - 20.00
   255 *Don't Big Shot Me* . . . . 15.00 - 20.00
   275 *Bayou Buffalo* . . . . 10.00 - 15.00
   293 *Slippin' And Slidin' Sometimes* . . . . . . 15.00 - 20.00

LITTLE SAM DAVIS:
De Luxe 6025 *Goin' To New Orleans* . . . . 40.00 - 60.00
Rockin' 512 *1958 Blues* . . . . 50.00 - 75.00

519 *Goin' To New Orleans* . . . . 50.00 - 75.00

JIMMIE DAVISON:
Target 861 *Froggie Went A-Courtin'* . . . . 5.00 - 8.00

THE DAWNBREAKERS:
Century 600 *Deep In The Heart Of Texas* . . . . . . — - —

THE DAWNS:
Climax 104 *Why Did You Let Me Love You* . . . . . . 7.00 - 10.00

JIMMY DAWSON (THE DIXIE DRIFTER):
K-Ark 774 *Mean Woman Blues* . . . . 15.00 - 20.00

RONNIE DAWSON:
Rockin' Records 1 *Rockin' Bones* . . . . 40.00 - 60.00

BING DAY:
Apex 7761 *Poor Stagger Lee* . . . . 15.00 - 20.00
Federal 12320 *Ponytail Partner* . . . . 15.00 - 20.00
Mercury 71446 *I Can't Help It* . . . . 8.00 - 12.00
71494 *How Do I Do It.* . . . . 8.00 - 12.00

BOBBY DAY:
Class 211 *Little Bitty Pretty One* (78 rpm) . . . . . . 15.00 - 25.00
229 *Rockin' Robin* (78 rpm) . . . . 20.00 - 30.00
(LP) 5002 *Rockin' With Robin* . . . . 75.00 - 100.00

DAVE (Y) (SONNY) DAY:
Fee-Bee 213 *Jelly Belly* . . . . 10.00 - 15.00
219 *Motorcycle Mike* . . . . 10.00 - 15.00

DAVE DIDDLE DAY:
Mercury 71114 *Blue Moon Baby* . . . . 15.00 - 20.00

JACK DAY:
Arcade 155 *Rattle Bone Boogie* . . . . 15.00 - 25.00

MARGIE DAY:
Cat 118 *Ho Ho* . . . . 5.00 - 7.00

THE DAYBREAKERS:
Aladdin 3434 *I Wonder Why* . . . . 8.00 - 12.00

THE DAYLIGHTERS:
Astra 1001 *This Heart Of Mine* . . . . 10.00 - 15.00
Bea & Baby 103 *You're Breaking My Heart* . . . . . 15.00 - 20.00
Dot 16326 *On What A Way To Be Loved* . . . . 7.00 - 10.00
Tip Top 2002 *Baby I Love You* . . . . 10.00 - 15.00

THE DAZZLERS:
Lee—*Gee Whiz* . . . . — - —

DEACON & THE ROCK AND ROLLERS:
Nau-Voo 804 *Rockin' On The Moon* . . . . 30.00 - 40.00

AL DEAN & HIS ALL STARS:
Warnor 506 *Fragile Heart* . . . . 35.00 - 50.00

BOB/BOBBY DEAN:
Arcade 195 *Hot Rod Daddy* . . . . 10.00 - 15.00
Chess 1673 *Just Go Wild Over Rock And Roll* . . . 30.00 - 40.00
1710 *I'm Ready* . . . . 20.00 - 30.00
Profile 4006 *It's A Fad, Ma* . . . . 15.00 - 25.00

CHARLES DEAN & RONDELLS:
Benton 102 *Train Whistle Boogie* . . . . 20.00 - 30.00

EDDIE DEAN:
Design (LP) 89 *Tribute To Hank Williams* . . . . . . 10.00 - 15.00
Sage 226 *Rock & Roll Cowboy* . . . . 8.00 - 12.00

FRANK DEAN:
Trend 30-008 *Bubblin'* . . . . 7.00 - 10.00

JERRY DEAN:
Creole 1002 *Walkin' In My Sleep* . . . . 15.00 - 20.00

LENNY DEAN & THE ROCKIN' CHAIRS:
(See ROCKIN' CHAIRS)

WALLY DEANE:
Artic 103 *Saddle Up A Satellite* . . . . 7.00 - 10.00
Globe 238 *Cool Cool Daddy* . . . . 10.00 - 15.00
— *Rockin' With Rosie* . . . . — - —

THE DEANS:
Mohawk 126 *It's You* . . . . 7.00 - 10.00

FRANK DEATON & HIS MAD LADS:
Alta 2000 *Framed* . . . . 15.00 - 20.00
Bally 1042 *Just A Little Bit More* . . . . 15.00 - 20.00

JIMMY DEBERRY:
Sun 185 *Take A Little Chance* . . . . 100.00 - 150.00

THE DE'BONAIRS:
Ping 1001 *Say A Prayer For Me* . . . . 15.00 - 20.00

THE DEBONAIRES:

Combo 129 *As Other Lovers Are* . . . . 40.00 - 50.00
Dore 592 *Every Once In Awhile* . . . . 5.00 - 8.00

BUD DECKLEMAN & THE DAYDREAMERS:
Meteor 5014 *Daydreamin'* . . . . 20.00 - 30.00

THE DECOYS:
Aanko 1005 *I Want Only You* . . . . 10.00 - 15.00

THE DEDICATIONS:
C & A 506 *Shining Star* . . . . 10.00 - 15.00
Ramdrca 602 *Someone To Love* . . . . 7.00 - 10.00

DEE & PATTY:
D 1020 *Sweet Lovin' Baby* . . . . 20.00 - 30.00
Mercury 71252 *Our First Date* . . . . 7.00 - 10.00

FERN DEE:
Ember 1035 *You'll Never Know* . . . . 7.00 - 10.00

FRANKIE DEE with CARTER RAYS:
RCA Victor 7276 *Shake It Up Baby* . . . . 10.00 - 15.00

JIMMY DEE (& THE OFFBEATS):
Ace 627 *Wanda* . . . . 15.00 - 20.00
Dot 15664 *Henrietta* . . . . 5.00 - 8 00
15721 *You're Late Miss Kate* . . . . 10.00 - 15.00
TNT 148 *Henrietta* . . . . 10.00 - 15.00
152 *You're Late, Miss Kate* . . . . 15.00 - 20.00
161 *Rick Tick Tock* . . . . 50.00 - 80.00

JOE DEE:
Clix 811 *Satan's Angel* . . . . — - —

JOHNNY DEE:
Colonial 430 *Sittin' In The Balcony* . . . . 5.00 - 8.00
430 *Sittin' In The Balcony* (78 rpm) . . . . 10.00 - 15.00
433 *Teenage Queen* . . . . 5.00 - 8.00
433 *Teenage Queen* (78 rpm) . . . . 7.00 - 10.00

MERCY DEE:
Flair 1073 *Romp And Stomp Blues* . . . . 15.00 - 20.00
1077 *Come Back Maybelline* . . . . 15.00 - 20.00
1078 *Stubborn Woman* . . . . 15.00 - 20.00
Rhythm 1774 *Trailing My Baby* . . . . 15.00 - 20.00
Specialty 458 *One Room Country Shack* . . . . . . 10.00 - 15.00
466 *Rent Man Blues* . . . . 10.00 - 15.00
481 *Dark Muddy Bottom* . . . . 10.00 - 15.00

RONNIE DEE:
Back Beat 522 *Action Packed* . . . . 7.00 - 10.00

THE DEE CALS:
Co-Ed 1960 *Stars In The Blue What Shall I Do* . . 10.00 - 15.00
Mayhams 1960 *Stars In The Blue What Shall I Do* 7.00 - 10.00

THE DEEJAYS:
SRC— *Love Me Baby* . . . . 75.00 - 100.00

THE DEEP RIVER BOYS:
Camden (LP) 303 *Presenting The Deep River*
 Boys . . . . 30.00 - 50.00
Jay-Dee 788 *Truthfully* . . . . 5.00 - 8.00
Que (LP) 104 *Midnight Magic* . . . . 75.00 - 100.00
RCA Victor 47-5268 *The Biggest Fool* . . . . 10.00 - 15.00
Vik 0205 *All My Love Belongs To You* . . . . 10.00 - 15.00
(LP) LXA-1019 . . . . 100.00 - 150.00
Waldorf (LP) 108 (10″) *Spiritual And Jubilees* . . 30.00 - 50.00
(LP) 120 (10″) *Spirituals* . . . . 30.00 - 50.00

THE DEE-VINES:
Lano 2001 *I Believe* . . . . 7.00 - 10.00

THE DEFENDERS:
Parkway 926 *I Laughed So Hard* . . . . 7.00 - 10.00

THE DELACARDOS:
Elgey 1001 *Letter To A School Girl* . . . . 8.00 - 12.00
Shell 308, 311 . . . . 7.00 - 10.00

THE DEL-AIRS:
Delsey 302 *Mam Ma Marie* . . . . 8.00 - 12.00
M.R.S. 001 *While Walking* . . . . 8.00 - 12.00

THE DELATONES:
TNT 9027 *Little Jeanie* . . . . 20.00 - 30.00

THE DELCOS:
Ebony 01 *These Three Little Words* . . . . 7.00 - 10.00
Showcase 2501 *Arabia* . . . . 7.00 - 10.00

THE DELEGATES:
Vee Jay 212 *The Convention* . . . . 15.00 - 20.00

243 *Mother's Son*	15.00 -	20.00

THE DELICATES:
Unart 2017 *Black And White Thunderbird*	8.00 -	12.00

WAILIN' BILL DELL:
O.J. 1003 *You Gotta Be Loose*	15.00 -	20.00

DANNY DELL:
World Pacific 824 *Froggy Went A-Courtin*	15.00 -	20.00

JIMMY DELL:
RCA Victor 7194 *Cool It Baby*	7.00 -	10.00
7355 *I've Got A Dollar*	7.00 -	10.00

TONY DELL:
King 5766 *My Girl*	5.00 -	8.00

THE DEL LARKS:
East-West 116 *Remember The Night*	15.00 -	20.00

THE DEL LOURDS:
Solar 1001 *All Alone*	10.00 -	15.00
1003 *Gloria*	10.00 -	15.00

THE DELLS:
Vee Jays 134 *Tell The World*	250.00 -	500.00
166 *Dreams Of Contentment*	20.00 -	30.00
204 *Oh What A Night*	10.00 -	15.00
230 *Movin' On*	10.00 -	15.00
236 *Why Do You Have To Go*	10.00 -	15.00
251 *A Distant Love*	15.00 -	20.00
258 *Pain In My Heart*	10.00 -	15.00
274 *The Springer*	8.00 -	12.00
292 *I'm Calling*	10.00 -	15.00
300 *My Best Girl*	10.00 -	15.00
(LP) 1010 *Oh What A Night* (black label)	15.00 -	25.00
(LP) 1010 (same, but maroon label)	100.00 -	150.00

THE DELL-VIKINGS (See THE DEL VIKINGS):

THE DELLWOODS:
Big Top 3137 *Don't Put Onions On Hamburgers*	7.00 -	10.00

THE DELMONICOS:
Acu 6318 *You Can Call*	5.00 -	8.00
Musictone 6122 *The Worlds Biggest Fool*	5.00 -	8.00

THE DELMORE BROTHERS:
King (LP) 589 *Sixteen Favorites*	20.00 -	30.00

ALTON DELMORE:
Linco 1315 *Good Times In Memphis*	10.00 -	15.00

THE DEL-PRADOS:
Lucky Four 1021 *Oh Baby*	15.00 -	20.00

THE DEL RAYS:
Carousel 213 *Girl In My Heart*	10.00 -	15.00
Chord 101 *Our Love Is True*	10.00 -	15.00
Future 7209 *When We're Alone*	10.00 -	15.00
Moon 110 *Have A Heart*	10.00 -	15.00

THE DEL RIOS:
Meteor 5038 *Alone On A Rainy Night*	20.00 -	30.00
Neptune 108 *I'm Crying*	10.00 -	15.00

THE DEL ROYALS:
Minit 610 *Who Will Be The One*	7.00 -	10.00

THE DEL-SATINS:
Laurie 3132 *Teardrops Follow Me*	7.00 -	10.00

THE DELTAIRS:
Ivy 101 *Lullaby Of The Bells* (yellow label)	15.00 -	20.00
105 *Standing At The Altar*	7.00 -	10.00

THE DELTA RHYTHM BOYS:
Camden (LP) 313 *The Delta Rhythm Boys*	50.00 -	75.00
Decca 29273, 29329	7.00 -	10.00
Elektra (LP) 138 *The Delta Rhythm Boys Sing*	15.00 -	20.00
Jubilee (LP) 1022 *The Delta Rhythm Boys In Sweden*	30.00 -	40.00
Mercury (LP) 25153 (10")	30.00 -	50.00
RCA Victor (LP) 3085 (10") *Dry Bones*	40.00 -	60.00
2828, 5094, 5217	7.00 -	10.00

THE DEL-TONES:
Oro-Ann 1001 *Best Wishes*	15.00 -	20.00

DEL VETTS:
End 1106 *Repeat After Me*	7.00 -	10.00

THE DEL-VICTORS:

Hi-Q 5028 *Baby Sitter I Love You*	—	—

THE DEL VIKINGS (THE DELL VIKINGS):
Alpine 66 *The Sun*	15.00 -	20.00
Crown (LP) 5368 *The Del Vikings & The Sonnets*	15.00 -	20.00
Dot (LP) 1003 *The Best Of The Del Vikings*	50.00 -	75.00
(EP) 1058 *Come Go With Us*	50.00 -	75.00
(LP) 3695 *Come Go With Me*	75.00 -	100.00
Dot 15538 *Come Go With Me*	5.00 -	8.00
15538 *Come Go With Me* (78 rpm)	30.00 -	40.00
15636 *When I Come Home*	5.00 -	8.00
Fee Bee 205 *Come Go With Me*	20.00 -	30.00
206 *Down In Bermuda*	15.00 -	20.00
210 *When I Come Home*	15.00 -	20.00
214 *Whispering Bells*	15.00 -	20.00
218 *I'm Spinning*	15.00 -	20.00
221 *Woke Up This Morning*	15.00 -	20.00
227 *Tell Me*	15.00 -	20.00
902 *True Love*	15.00 -	20.00
Luniverse 106 *Somewhere Over The Rainbow*	15.00 -	20.00
(LP) 1000 *Come Go With The Del Vikings* (has eight songs)	100.00 -	150.00
Mercury (EP) 3362 *They Sing-They Swing*	30.00 -	40.00
(EP) 35 *The Del Vikings*	30.00 -	40.00
(LP) 20314 *They Sing-They Swing*	50.00 -	75.00
(LP) 20353 *Swinging Singing Record Session*	50.00 -	75.00
71132 *Cool Shake* (78 rpm)	10.00 -	15.00
71241 *Your Book Of Love*	8.00 -	12.00
71345 *You Cheated*	8.00 -	12.00

JERRY DEMAR:
Ford 501 *Cross-Eyed Alley Cat*	30.00 -	50.00

THE DEMENS:
Teenage 1006 *You Broke My Heart*	7.00 -	10.00

THE DEMENSIONS:
Coral 62323 *Your Cheatin' Heart*	7.00 -	10.00
62359 *Fly Me To The Moon*	7.00 -	10.00
62392 *A Little White Gardenia*	7.00 -	10.00
Coral (LP) 757430 *My Foolish Heart*	50.00 -	75.00

THE DEMILLES:
Laurie 3230 *Donna Lee*	8.00 -	12.00

THE DE MIRES:
Lunar 519 *Wheels Of Love*	8.00 -	12.00

THE DEMOLYRS:
V W R 900 *Rain*	—	—

LITTLE JIMMY DEMPSEY:
Fox--*Bop Hop*	—	—
--*Bouncing Back*	—	—

GALEN DENNY:
Liberty 55164 *What Ya Gonna Do*	8.00 -	12.00

DENNIS & THE EXPLORERS:
Coral 62295 *Remember*	15.00 -	20.00

THE DENOTATIONS:
Lawn 253 *Lone Stranger*	7.00 -	10.00

LEE DENSON:
Kent 306 *High School Bop*	20.00 -	30.00
Vik 0251 *Heart Of A Fool*	20.00 -	30.00
0281 *New Shoes*	15.00 -	20.00

BOB (BY) DENTON:
Dot 15743 *Skinny Minnie*	7.00 -	10.00
15833 *Twenty-Four Hour Night*	5.00 -	8.00
Judd 1011 *Sweet And Innocent*	5.00 -	8.00
1013 *I'll Always Be Yours*	5.00 -	8.00

RAY DE PAUL:
ABC Paramount 9903 *Ready To Rip*	7.00 -	10.00

THE DERBYS:
Mercury 71437 *Night After Night*	7.00 -	10.00

TOMMY DEREK:
Flag 120 *Meet Me At The Hop*	15.00 -	20.00

ARNIE DERKSEN:
Decca 30906 *She Wanna Rock*	10.00 -	15.00

THE DERRINGERS:
Capitol 4532 *Sheree*	7.00 -	10.00

THE DESIRES:

Hull 730 *Let It Please Be You*	8.00 -	12.00
733 *Rendezvous With You*	8.00 -	12.00
20th Fox 195 *I Don't Know Why*	5.00 -	8.00

THE DESTINATIONS:

Fortune 864 *Valley Of Tears*	7.00 -	10.00

DETROIT JUNIOR:

Bea & Baby 111 *Money Tree*	10.00 -	15.00
CJ 636, 637	7.00 -	10.00
Foxy 002 *Christmas Day*	7.00 -	10.00
USA 807, 814	5.00 -	8.00

THE DE VILLES:

Aladdin 3423 *Kiss Me Again And Again*	10.00 -	15.00
Arrawak 201 *I Do Believe*	7.00 -	10.00

JAY DE VORE:

Bodark 004 *Doggone Mean*	8.00 -	12.00

THE DEVOTIONS:

Cub 9020 *Silly Milly*	5.00 -	8.00
Delta 1001 *Rip Van Winkle*	15.00 -	20.00

AL DEXTER:

Columbia (LP) 9005 (10") *Songs Of The Southwest*	15.00 -	20.00
Ekko 1020 *Pistol Packin' Mama*	10.00 -	15.00

THE DIABLOS (See NOLAN STRONG & THE DIABLOS)

THE DIADEMS:

Star 514 *Why Don't You Believe Me*	10.00 -	15.00

THE DIALS:

Hilltop 219 *No Hard Feelings*	8.00 -	12.00

THE DIALTONES:

Goldisc 3005 *Till I Heard It From You*	5.00 -	8.00
Lawn 203 *So Young*	5.00 -	8.00

THE DIAMONDS:

Atlantic 1003 *Two Loves Have I* (yellow label)	30.00 -	40.00
1017 *Cherry* (yellow label)	30.00 -	40.00
Mercury (LP) 20309 *The Diamonds*	50.00 -	75.00
(LP) 20368 *The Diamonds Meet Pete Rugolo*	40.00 -	60.00
70835, 70934, 71021, 71060 (maroon label)	5.00 -	8.00
70835 *The Church Bells May Ring* (78 rpm)	7.00 -	10.00
70934 *Ka-Ding Dong* (78rpm)	7.00 -	10.00
71021 *A Thousand Miles Away* (78 rpm)	7.00 -	10.00
71060 *Little Darlin'* (78 rpm)	10.00 -	15.00
71128 *Words Of Love* (78 rpm)	7.00 -	10.00
71165 *Zip Zip* (78 rpm)	7.00 -	10.00
71242 *The Stroll* (78 rpm)	15.00 -	20.00
Wing (LP) 12178 *Pop Hits*	30.00 -	40.00

THE DIATONES:

Bandera 2509 *Ruby Has Gone*	15.00 -	20.00

(LITTLE) JIMMY DICKENS:

Columbia (LP) 1047 *Raisin' The Dickens*	20.00 -	30.00
(LP) 1545 *Big Songs By Little Jimmy Dickens*	20.00 -	30.00
21206 *Rock Me*	8.00 -	12.00
41173 *(I Got) A Hole In My Pocket*	7.00 -	10.00

DUKE DICKSON & THE JIVIN 5:

Global *Walkin' Shoes*	-	

BO DIDDLEY:

Checker 814, *Bo Diddley*	7.00 -	10.00
819, 827, 832, 842, 850, 860	5.00 -	8.00
878, 896, 931, 936, 942, 951, 1045	5.00 -	8.00
878 *Say! (Boss Man)* (78 rpm)	10.00 -	15.00
896 *Hush Your Mouth* (78 rpm)	10.00 -	15.00
924 *Crackin' Up* (78 rpm)	15.00 -	20.00
931 *Say Man* (78 rpm)	15.00 -	20.00
Chess (LP) 1431 *Bo Diddley* (black label)	40.00 -	60.00
(LP) 2974 *Have Guitar Will Travel*	40.00 -	60.00
(EP) 5125 *Bo Diddley*	30.00 -	50.00

ELROY DIETZEL:

Bo-Kay 101 *Teenage Ball*	30.00 -	50.00
103 *Rock-N-Bones*	30.00 -	50.00

THE DIKES:

Federal 12249 *Light Me Up*	7.00 -	10.00

DANNY DILL:

ABC Paramount 9681 *My Girl And His Girl*	10.00 -	15.00

9734 *I'm Hungry For Your Lovin'*	15.00 -	20.00
Cub 9045 *He's Biding His Time*	8.00 -	12.00

ARTIE DILLON:

Kandy Kane *In My Teens*	-	

ZIG DILLON:

"R" 501 *On Down The Line*	15.00 -	20.00
512 *Bird Song Boogie*	15.00 -	20.00

THE DING DONGS:

Brunswick 50073 *Early In The Morning*	15.00 -	20.00

MARK DINNING:

MGM (LP) 3838 *Teen Angel*	20.00 -	30.00

ANDY DIO:

Johnson 114 *You Are My Sunshine*	12.00 -	18.00
Thor 104 *Rough And Bold*	15.00 -	20.00

DION & THE BELMONTS:

Laurie (LP) 1002 *Presenting Dion & The Belmonts*	20.00 -	30.00
Laurie 3013 *I Wonder Why*	5.00 -	8.00
I Can't Go On (Rosalie)	5.00 -	8.00
Don't Pity Me	5.00 -	8.00
Laurie other issues	3.00 -	6.00

DION & THE TIMBERLANES:

Mohawk 105 *The Chosen Few*	10.00 -	15.00
Jubilee 5294 *The Chosen Few*	10.00 -	15.00

THE DIPPERS:

Epic 9453 *Such A Fool Was I*	8.00 -	12.00

THE DISCIPLES:

Fortune 573 *I Found Out/12th Street*		

DIXIE BLUES BOYS:

Flair 1072 *My Baby Left Town*	15.00 -	20.00

THE DIXIELANDERS:

Do-Ra-Me 1412 *Uncle John's Bongos*	7.00 -	10.00

BILLY DIXON & THE TOPICS:

Topix 6002 *I Am All Alone*	20.00 -	30.00
6008 *Lost Lullaby*	20.00 -	30.00

FLOYD DIXON:

Aladdin 3101 *Time And Place*	15.00 -	20.00
3121 *Bad Neighborhood*	15.00 -	20.00
3135 *Wine Wine Wine*	15.00 -	20.00
3144 *Red Cherries*	15.00 -	20.00
3151 *Come Back Baby*	15.00 -	20.00
3166 *Broken Hearted Traveler*	15.00 -	20.00
3196 *Married Woman*	10.00 -	15.00
Cash 1057 *Oh Baby*	5.00 -	8.00
Cat 106 *Moonshine*	7.00 -	10.00
114 *Hey Bartender*	7.00 -	10.00
Checker 857 *Alarm Clock Blues*	5.00 -	8.00
Ebb 105 *Ooh Little Girl*	7.00 -	10.00
Kent 311 *Change Your Mind*	7.00 -	10.00
Specialty 468 *Hard Living Alone*	7.00 -	10.00
477 *Hole In The Wall*	7.00 -	10.00
486 *Nose Trouble*	7.00 -	10.00
Swingin' 626 *Tight Skirts*	5.00 -	8.00

HELENE DIXON:

Vik 0212 *Roll Over Beethoven*	7.00 -	10.00

WEBB DIXON:

Astro 101 *Rock Awhile*	15.00 -	20.00

WILLIE DIXON:

Checker 822, 828, 851	5.00 -	8.00
Prestige (LP) 1003 *Blues*	30.00 -	50.00

CARL DOBKINS, JR.:

Decca (LP) 8938 *Carl Dobkins, Jr*	30.00 -	40.00

LEROY DOBSON:

Ludwig 1006 *I Wanna Make Love*	7.00 -	10.00

CHUCK DOCKERY:

Dearborn *Rock While We Ride*		

THE DODGERS:

Aladdin 3259 *You Make Me Happy*	15.00 -	20.00
3271 *Drip Drop*	35.00 -	50.00

BILL DOGGETT:

King 4950 *Honky Tonk* (78 rpm)	8.00 -	12.00

RAY DOGGETT:

Decca 30295 *It Hurts The One Who Loves You* ..	8.00 -	12.00
Ken-Lee 101 *Beach Party*	8.00 -	12.00
Kix 102 *Love Is Made Of This*	7.00 -	10.00
Pearl 716 *No Doubt About It*	15.00 -	20.00
Spade 1928 *Go Go Heart*	15.00 -	20.00
1932 *It Hurts The One Who Loves You*	15.00 -	20.00
TNT 159 *Whirlpool Of Love*	10.00 -	15.00

ANDY DOLL:

AD 101 *Hey Ba Ba Re Bop*	7.00 -	10.00
Starday 345 *You Can't Stop Me From Dreaming* .	20.00 -	30.00

THE DOLPHINS:

Empress 102 *Rainbow's End*	10.00 -	15.00
Shad 5020 *I Found True Love*	7.00 -	10.00

FATS DOMINO:

Imperial (EP) 127 *Fats Domino*	20.00 -	30.00
Imperial (EP) 138, 139, 140 *Rockin' & Rollin' with Fats Domino*	15.00 -	20.00
Imperial (EP) 141, 142, 143 *Rock And Rollin'* ...	15.00 -	20.00
Imperial (EP) 144, 145, 146 *This Is Fats Domino* .	15.00 -	20.00
Imperial (EP) 147 *Here Comes Fats*	15.00 -	20.00
Imperial (EP) 148, 149, 150 *Here Stands Fats Domino*	15.00 -	20.00
Imperial (EP) 151 *Cookin' With Fats*	15.00 -	20.00
Imperial (EP) 152 *Rockin' With Fats*	15.00 -	20.00
Imperial 5180 *Reeling And Rocking*	20.00 -	30.00
5197 *Poor Poor Me*	20.00 -	30.00
5209 *How Long*	20.00 -	30.00
5209 *How Long* (red plastic)	40.00 -	60.00
5220 *Cheatin'*	15.00 -	20.00
5220 *Cheatin'* (red plastic)	40.00 -	60.00
5231 *Going To The River*	15.00 -	20.00
5231 *Going To The River* (red plastic)	40.00 -	60.00
5240 *Please Don't Leave Me*	10.00 -	15.00
5251 *Rose Marie*	10.00 -	150.00
5262 *Something's Wrong*	10.00 -	15.00
5272 *Little School Girl*	10.00 -	15.00
5283 *Baby Please*	10.00 -	15.00
5301 *I Lived My Life*	10.00 -	15.00
5313 *Love Me*	8.00 -	12.00
5223 *Thinking Of You*	7.00 -	10.00
5348 *Ain't It A Shame*	5.00 -	8.00
Imperial 5357, 5369, 5375	5.00 -	8.00
Imperial 5586, 5396	4.00 -	6.00
Imperial 5407, 5417, 5428, 5442, 5454, 5477, 5492, 5515, 5526, 5537, 5553	4.00 -	8.00
Imperial 5407, 5417, 5428, 5442, 5454, 5477, (78rpm)	8.00 -	12.00
Imperial 5492 *Don't You Know I Love You* (78rpm)	8.00 -	12.00
5515 *Sick And Tired* (78 rpm)	8.00 -	12.00
5526 *Little Mary* (78 rpm)	8.00 -	12.00
5537 *Young School Girl* (78 rpm)	8.00 -	12.00
5553 *Whole Lotta Lovin'* (78 rpm)	10.00 -	15.00
5569 *Telling Lies* (78 rpm)	10.00 -	15.00
Imperial (LP) 9004 *Rockin' And Rollin With Fats Domino*	30.00 -	40.00
Imperial (LP) 9000 *Rock And Rollin'*	30.00 -	40.00
Imperial (LP) 9028 *This Is Fats Domino*	20.00 -	30.00
Imperial (LP) 9038 *Here Stands Fats Domino* ...	20.00 -	30.00
(LP) 9040 *This Is Fats*	20.00 -	30.00
Imperial (LP) 9055 *The Fabulous Mr. Domino* ..	15.00 -	20.00
Imperial (LP) 9062 *Fats Domino Swings*	15.00 -	20.00
Imperial (LP) 9065 *Let's Play Fats Domino*	15.00 -	20.00
Imperial (LP) 9103 *Fats Domino Sings*	15.00 -	20.00
Imperial (LP) 9138 *A Lot Of Dominoes*	10.00 -	15.00

Note: LP's are all MONO. Early issues have maroon labels; later issues and reissues of early issues have multi-colored labels.

THE DOMINOES: (See also BILLY WARD)

Federal 12001 *Do Something For Me*	75.00 -	100.00
12010 *Harbor Lights*	100.00 -	200.00
12022 *Sixty Minute Man*	35.00 -	50.00

12039 *Weeping Willow Blues*	50.00 -	75.00
12059 *That's What You're Doing To Me*	50.00 -	75.00
12068 *Have Mercy Baby*	50.00 -	75.00
12072 *Love Love Love*	50.00 -	75.00
12105 *I'll Be Satisfed*	40.00 -	60.00
12106 *Yours Forever*	40.00 -	60.00
12114 *The Bells*	30.00 -	50.00
12129 *These Foolish Things Remind Me Of You*	15.00 -	20.00

(Above have "gold top" labels)

CHARLIE DONALD:

ABC Paramount 9820 *Bop With Me, Baby*	7.00 -	10.00

THE DON CLAIRS:

Amp-3 1001 *I Lost My Job*	10.00 -	15.00

DON & DEWEY:

Rush 1002 *Soul Motion*	5.00 -	8.00
Shade 1000 *My Heart Is Aching*	5.00 -	8.00
Spot 101 *Fiddlin' The Blues*	10.00 -	15.00

DON & HIS ROSES:

Dot 15755 *Right Now*	10.00 -	15.00
15874 *Leave Those Cats Alone*	10.00 -	15.00

DON, DICK & JIMMY:

Dot (LP) 3152	30.00 -	50.00

THE DON JUANS: (See also LITTLE EDDIE)

Fortune 824, 825	7.00 -	10.00
Jaguar 3020 *Kickin' My Hound Around*	-	

JOHNNY DONN:

Crest 1058 *What Happened Last Night*	8.00 -	12.00

LARRY DONN:

Vaden 113 *Honey-Bun*	30.00 -	40.00

RAL DONNER:

Crown (LP) 5335 *Ral Donner & Ray Smith & Bobby Dale*	15.00 -	20.00
Gone (LP) 2002 *Takin' Care Of Business*	75.00 -	100.00
Gone 5102 *Girl Of My Best Friend*	5.00 -	8.00
5114 *I Didn't Figure On Him*	5.00 -	8.00
5121 *She's Everything*	5.00 -	8.00
5125 *To Love Someone*	5.00 -	8.00
5129 *Loveless Life*	5.00 -	8.00
Red Bird 10-057 *Love Isn't Like That*	12.00 -	16.00

GEORGE DOOLEY:

Chan 104 *Train Ride*	7.00 -	10.00

THE DOOTONES:

Dootone 366 *Teller Of Fortunes*	10.00 -	15.00
470 *Strange Love Affair*	8.00 -	12.00
471 *Down The Road*	8.00 -	12.00

LEE DORSEY:

Fury (LP) 1002 *Ya Ya*	30.00 -	50.00

MEL DORSEY (& CHUCK WAYNE):

Black Jack 103 *Little Lil*	10.00 -	15.00
Orbit 106 *Ain't Gonna Take It No More*	10.00 -	15.00

SLIM DORTCH:

Eugenia 1001 *Big Boy Rock*	50.00 -	75.00

BOB DOSS:

Lynn 505 *I've Got You*	10.00 -	15.00
Starday 265 *Somebody's Knocking*	30.00 -	40.00

BUSTER DOSS:

Wizard 1640 *Messing Around*	7.00 -	10.00

THE DOTS:

Caddy 101 *I Confess*	10.00 -	15.00

JIMMY DOTSON (& THE BLUES BOYS):

Rocko 516 *I Need Your Love*	8.00 -	12.00
Zynn 511 *Looking For My Baby*	8.00 -	12.00

BIG BOB DOUGHERTY:

KCM 3701 *Dizzy Miss Lizzie*	-	
Westport 137 *Movin'*	7.00 -	10.00
139 *Teen-Age Flip*	7.00 -	10.00

DAVEY DOUGLAS:

Ditto 110 *Shivers*	15.00 -	20.00
Liberty 55165 *Party Crashin'*	10.00 -	15.00

DICK DOUGLAS:

Northway 1005 *Rocket Ride*	10.00 -	15.00

GLENN DOUGLAS:

Decca (LP) 8748 *Heartbreak*	30.00 -	40.00
Decca 29815 *Let It Roll*	7.00 -	10.00
30119 *Used Up Love*	7.00 -	10.00
30311 *I Can Love Enough*	5.00 -	8.00
30602 *You Sure Look Lonesome*	5.00 -	8.00

K.C. DOUGLAS:

Cook (LP) 5002	30.00 -	40.00

MEL DOUGLAS:

San 1506 *Cadillac Boogie*	20.00 -	30.00

SHERI LEE DOUGLAS:

Maverick 601 *Chime Bells*	10.00 -	15.00

SHY GUY DOUGLAS:

Excello 2008 *Detroit Arrow*	20.00 -	30.00
2024 *I'm Your Country Man*	20.00 -	30.00
2032 *No Place Like Home*	20.00 -	15.00

JERRY DOVE & HIS STRING BUSTERS:

TNT 122, 144, 162, 173	5.00 -	8.00
141 *Pink Bow Tie*	20.00 -	30.00

LARRY DOWD (& THE ROCK-A-TONES):

Damion 6532 *Tell Me No Lies*	7.00 -	10.00
Spinning 6004 *Why Oh Why*	7.00 -	10.00
6009 *Pink Cadillac*	10.00 -	15.00

THE DOWLANDS:

Tollie 9002 *All My Loving*		

THE DOWNBEATS: (See also O.S. GRANT; SONNY WOODS):

Sarg 168 *Darling Of Mine*	10.00 -	15.00
173 *I Need Your Love*	10.00 -	15.00
186 *I Couldn't See*	7.00 -	10.00
197 *I Just Can't Understand*	7.00 -	10.00

("BIG") AL DOWNING:

Carlton 489 *Miss Lucy*	7.00 -	10.00
507 *It Must Be Love*	5.00 -	8.00
Challenge 59006 *Down On The Farm*	7.00 -	10.00
Columbia 43185 *Georgia Slop*	5.00 -	8.00
V-Tone 215 *Please Come Home*	5.00 -	8.00
220 *Words Of Love*	5.00 -	8.00
230 *There'll Come A Time*	5.00 -	8.00
White Rock 1111 *Down On The Farm*	40.00 -	60.00
1113 *Miss Lucy*	40.00 -	60.00

WAYNE DOWNING:

Big J 164 *Rattlesnake Daddy*		

THE DOZIER BOYS:

Fraternity 767 *Early Morning Blues*	15.00 -	20.00
United 143 *I Keep Thinking Of You*	20.00 -	30.00

RUSTY DRAPER:

Mercury 70921 *Pink Cadillac*	5.00 -	8.00

THE DREAMERS: (See also RICHARD BERRY)

Aladdin 3303 *Charles My Darling*	10.00 -	15.00
Cousins 1005 *Because Of You*	7.00 -	10.00
Flair 1052 *At Last*	15.00 -	20.00
Flip 319 *Since You've Been Gone*	5.00 -	8.00
Goldisc 3015 *Teenage Vows Of Love*	7.00 -	10.00
Grand 131 *Tears In My Eyes*	10.00 -	15.00
Mercury 70019 *Please Don't Love Me*	10.00 -	15.00
Rollin 1001 *No Man Is An Island*	15.00 -	20.00

THE DREAM KINGS:

Checker 858 *MTYLTT*	8.00 -	12.00

THE DREAMLOVERS:

Heritage 102 *When We Get Married*	8.00 -	12.00
104 *Welcome Home*	8.00 -	12.00
107 *Zoom Zoom Zoom*	8.00 -	12.00
V-Tone 211 *Annabelle Lee*	7.00 -	10.00
229 *May I Kiss The Bride*	7.00 -	10.00

THE DREAMS:

Savoy 1130 *Darlene*	15.00 -	20.00
1140 *Under The Willow*	15.00 -	20.00
1157 *I'll Be Faithful*	10.00 -	15.00

THE DREAMTONES:

Astra 551 *A Lover's Answer*	10.00 -	15.00
Express 501 *Praying For A Miracle*	10.00 -	15.00

Klik 8505 *Love Me In The Afternoon*	15.00 -	20.00

THE DRIFTERS (featuring CLYDE McPHATTER):

Atlantic (EP) 534 *The Drifters Featuring Clyde McPhatter*	30.00 -	40.00
1006 *Money Honey*	10.00 -	15.00
1019 *Such A Night*	10.00 -	15.00
1029 *Honey Love*	10.00 -	15.00
1043 *Bip Bam*	7.00 -	10.00
1048 *White Christmas*	7.00 -	10.00
1055 *Gone*	7.00 -	10.00
1070 *Hot Ziggety*	7.00 -	10.00
(Note: above are yellow label)		
2025 *There Goes My Baby* (78 rpm)	15.00 -	20.00
(LP) 8003 *Clyde McPhatter & The Drifters*	50.00 -	75.00
(LP) 8013 *The Good Life With The Drifters*	50.00 -	75.00
(LP) 8022 *Rockin' And Driftin'*	50.00 -	75.00
(above are black label)		
(LP) 8059 *Save The Last Dance For Me*	20.00 -	30.00
Crown 108 *The World Is Changing*	40.00 -	60.00

DRIFTING CHARLES:

Lanor 515 *Drifting Cloud*	7.00 -	10.00

DRINK SMALL & HIS GUITAR:

Sharp 101 *Cold Cold Rain*	7.00 -	10.00

THE DRIVERS:

Alton 252 *Doe Doe*	7.00 -	10.00
De Luxe 6094 *Smooth, Slow And Easy*	10.00 -	15.00
6104 *My Lonely Prayer*	10.00 -	15.00
6117 *Dangerous Lips*	10.00 -	15.00
Drive 101 *No One For Me*		-
RCA Victor 7023 *Blue Moon*	8.00 -	12.00

THE DUALS:

Arc 4446 *Nearest To My Heart*	8.00 -	12.00

THE DUBS:

Gone 5002 *I Found Out*	10.00 -	15.00
5011 *Could This Be Magic*	5.00 -	8.00
5011 *Could This Be Magic* (78 RPM)	15.00 -	20.00
5020 *Beside My Love*	7.00 -	10.00
5034 *Be Sure (My Love)*	7.00 -	10.00
5046 *Chapel Of Dreams*	7.00 -	10.00
Josie (LP) 4001 *The Dubs Meet The Shells*	50.00 -	75.00
Mark-X 8008 *Be Sure My Love*	8.00 -	12.00

DUCES OF RHYTHM & THE TEMPOS TOPPERS (Lead, LITTLE RICHARD):

Peacock 1616 *Ain't That Good News*	15.00 -	20.00

THE DUDADS:

De Luxe 6083 *I Heard You Call Me Dear*	20.00 -	30.00

DAVE DUDLEY:

King 4933 *Rock & Roll Nursery Rhyme*	7.00 -	10.00

THE DU DROPPERS:

Groove 0001 *Laughing Blues*	5.00 -	8.00
0013 *Just Whisper*	7.00 -	10.00
0036 *Boot 'Em Up*	7.00 -	10.00
0104 *Talk That Talk*	7.00 -	10.00
0120 *You're Mine Already*	7.00 -	10.00
(LP) *DuDroppin'*	75.00 -	100.00
RCA Victor 5321 *I Found Out*	7.00 -	10.00
5425 *Whatever You're Doing*	7.00 -	10.00
5543 *The Note In The Bottle*	10.00 -	15.00
Red Robin 108 *Can't Do Sixty No More*	15.00 -	20.00

ARLIE DUFF:

Decca 29987 *Alligator Come Across*	10.00 -	15.00
Starday 104 *You All Come*	7.00 -	10.00
132 *Let Me Be Your Salty Dog*	7.00 -	10.00
176 *Fifteen Cents a Sop*	7.00 -	10.00
Starday 302 *You've Done It Again*	7.00 -	10.00

TAM DUFFILL:

Groove 58-0004 *Cooly Dooly*	8.00 -	12.00

EDDIE DUGOSH:

Award 116 *One Mile*	7.00 -	10.00
Sarg 135 *Strange Kinda Feeling*	15.00 -	20.00

DUKE & NULL (See: DENVER DUKE &

JEFFREY NULL)
BILLY DUKE & HIS DUKES:
Casino 138 *Fun Lovin' Woman* . . . . 10.00 - 15.00
Teen 110 *I Know I Was Wrong* . . . . 15.00 - 20.00
DENVER DUKE & JEFFERY NULL:
Blue Hen 214 *Hank Williams That Alabama Boy* . 7.00 - 10.00
Mercury 70970 *Rock And Roll Blues* . . . . 7.00 - 10.00
71065 *A Million Tears* . . . . 5.00 - 8.00
Starday 446 *I'll Say I Do* . . . . 5.00 - 8.00
479 *I'm Gonna Get You* . . . . 5.00 - 8.00
ROY DUKE:
Decca 29962 *Behave, Be Quiet, Or Be Gone* . . . . 15.00 - 20.00
30095 *Honky Tonk Queen* . . . . 15.00 - 20.00
30325 *I Mean, I'm Mean* . . . . 15.00 - 20.00
DUKE OF EARL (Gene Chandler):
Vee Jay (LP) 1040 *Duke Of Earl* . . . . 20.00 - 30.00
THE DUKES:
Imperial 5401 *Teardrop Eyes* . . . . 15.00 - 20.00
5415 *Baby Please* . . . . 10.00 - 15.00
5480 *Loving You* . . . . 10.00 - 15.00
Specialty 543 *Oh Kay* . . . . 7.00 - 10.00
THE DU MAURIERS:
Fury 1011 *All Night Long* . . . . 10.00 - 15.00
SHELTON DUNAWAY:
Lync 1010 *Shake 'Em Up* . . . . 5.00 - 8.00
BILL DUNCAN:
D B C 1232 *Whirlin' Twerlin' Rock* . . . . 30.00 - 50.00
DON DUNCAN:
Venture 111 *Somethin' Special* . . . . 20.00 - 30.00
HERBIE DUNCAN:
Mar-Vel 1400 *Hot Lips Baby* . . . . 30.00 - 40.00
1402 *That's All* . . . . 10.00 - 15.00
BILL DUNIVEN:
Vaden 306 *Knocking On The Backside (of Your
Heart)* . . . . 30.00 - 40.00
GENE DUNLAP:
Made In The Shade . . . . -
JOHN DUNN:
Spar 720 *If A Woman Answers* . . . . 7.00 - 10.00
WEBSTER DUNN, JR.:
Dunmar 101 *Go Go Baby* . . . . 30.00 - 40.00
THE DUPONTS:
Roulette 4060 *Half Past Nothing* . . . . 10.00 - 15.00
Royal Roost 627 *Somebody* . . . . 15.00 - 20.00
Winley 212 *Must Be Falling In Love* . . . . 10.00 - 15.00
**CHAMPION JACK DUPREE: JACK DUPREE
(& MR. BEAR):**
Atlantic (LP) 8019 *Blues From The Gutter* . . . . . 50.00 - 75.00
(LP) 8045 *Natural & Soulful Blues* . . . . 20.00 - 30.00
(LP) 8056 *Champion Of The Blues* . . . . 20.00 - 30.00
Groove 0171 *Lonely Road Blues* . . . . 7.00 - 10.00
King (LP) 735 *Champion Jack Dupree Sings
The Blues* . . . . 20.00 - 30.00
4633 *Tongue Tied Blues* . . . . 8.00 - 12.00
4651 *Please Tell Me Baby* . . . . 8.00 - 12.00
4695 *Walkin' Upside Your Head* . . . . 8.00 - 12.00
4706 *Hard Feeling* . . . . 7.00 - 10.00
4779 *Two Below Zero* . . . . 7.00 - 10.00
4792 *Harelip Blues* . . . . 7.00 - 10.00
Okeh (LP) 12103 *Cabbage Greens* . . . . 30.00 - 40.00
Red Robin 109 *Stumblin' Block Blues* . . . . 15.00 - 20.00
112 *Highway Blues* . . . . 15.00 - 20.00
130 *Shim Sham Shimmy* . . . . 15.00 - 20.00
Vik 0260, 0279, 0304 . . . . 5.00 - 8.00
THE DUPREES:
Coed 569 *You Belong To Me* . . . . 5.00 - 8.00
571 *My Own True Love* . . . . 5.00 - 8.00
574 *I Wish You Could Believe Me* . . . . 5.00 - 8.00
Coed 576, 580, 584, 585, 587, 591, 593, 595, 596 . 4.00 - 7.00
Coed (LP) 905 *You Belong To Me* . . . . 50.00 - 75.00
(LP) 906 *Have You Heard* . . . . 50.00 - 75.00
Heritage 804 *My Special Angel* . . . . 5.00 - 8.00

805 *Goodnight My Love* . . . . 5.00 - 8.00
808 *My Love, My Love* . . . . 5.00 - 8.00
811 *Two Different Worlds* . . . . 5.00 - 8.00
826 *Have You Heard* . . . . -
NELDA DUPRY:
United 157 *Riding With The Blues* . . . . 15.00 - 20.00
TOMMY DURDEN:
Holiday 777 *A-Weepin' And A-Wailin'* . . . . 15.00 - 20.00
PAUL DURHAM:
Sand Spur 15302 *She Lied* . . . . -
THE DUSTERS:
Cuspid 5003 *She's Mine* . . . . -
HUELYN DUVALL:
Challenge 1012 *Comin' Or Goin'* . . . . 10.00 - 15.00
59002 *Hum-Dinger* . . . . 10.00 - 15.00
59014 *Three Months To Kill* . . . . 10.00 - 15.00
59025 *Friday Night On A Dollar Bill* . . . . . . 10.00 - 15.00
59069 *Pucker Paint* . . . . 7.00 - 10.00
Starfire 600 *It's No Wonder* . . . . 7.00 - 10.00
Twinkle *Beautiful Dreamer* . . . . -
THE DUVALS:
Boss 2117 *Cotton* . . . . 7.00 - 10.00
THE DWELLERS:
Howard- *Tell Me Why* . . . . 25.00 - 35.00
Oasis 101 *Oh Sweetie* . . . . 30.00 - 40.00
CONNIE DYCUS:
Mercury 71376 *Rock-A-Bye Baby Rock* . . . . -
JERRY DYKE & THE VENDELLS:
Saturn- *Mean Woman Blues* . . . . -
BOB DYLAN:
Columbia (LP) CL-1986 *The Freewheelin' Bob
Dylan* (MONO, red label, containing, as cut 3,
side 1, *Let Me Die In My Footsteps*) . . . . 500.00 - up
42656 *Corrina Corrina* . . . . 50.00 - up
42856 *Blowin' In The Wind* . . . . 50.00 - up
(Note: Prices on above are very speculative.
Promotional copies of other 45s have premium
value.)
THE DYNAMICS:
Dynamic 1002 *Delsinia* . . . . 7.00 - 10.00
Emjay 1928 *This Love Of Ours* . . . . 10.00 - 15.00
Herald 569 *Betty My Own* . . . . 8.00 - 12.00
Impala 501 *Moonlight* . . . . 10.00 - 15.00
LiBan 1006 *If I Give My Heart To You* . . . . 10.0 - 15.00
JOHNNY EAGER (& HIS TRIO):
Design 818 *The Howl* . . . . 7.00 - 10.00
Sabre 100 *Please Mr. Doctor* . . . . 20.00 - 30.00
THE EAGLES:
Mercury 70391 *Please, Please* . . . . 7.00 - 12.00
70464 *Such A Fool* . . . . 7.00 - 12.00
70524 *I Told Myself* . . . . 7.00 - 12.00
FORD EAGLIN:
Imperial 5671, 5692, 5736, 5765, 5802, 5823,
5857, 5866, 5890, 5946 . . . . 5.00 - 10.00
THE EARLS:
ABC Paramount 11109 *It's Been A Long Time
Comin'* . . . . -
Old Town (LP) 104 *Remember Me Baby* . . . . . . 75.00 - 100.00
Old Town 1130 *Remember Then* . . . . 5.00 - 8.00
1133 *Never* . . . . 5.00 - 8.00
1145 *Cry Cry Cry* . . . . 5.00 - 8.00
1149 *I Believe* . . . . 5.00 - 8.00
1169 *Ask Anybody* . . . . 5.00 - 8.00
1182 *Remember Me Baby* . . . . 5.00 - 8.00
Rome 101 *Life Is But A Dream* . . . . 8.00 - 12.00
102 *Lookin' For My Baby* . . . . 8.00 - 12.00
112 *Little Boy And Girl* . . . . 7.00 - 10.00
115 *Whoever You Are* . . . . 7.00 - 10.00
5117 *My Heart's Desire* . . . . 7.00 - 10.00
JACK EARLS & THE JIMBOS:
Sun 240 *Slow Down* . . . . 15.00 - 20.00
THE EARTHQUAKES:

Fortune 534, 538, 549	5.00 -	10.00
EDDIE EAY:		
Echo 5911 *Dancin' Girl*	30.00 -	50.00
THE EBBTIDES: (See also: David Ford)		
Jan Lar 101 *Lonesome*	10.00 -	15.00
Marco 105 *Little Miss Blue*	7.00 -	10.00
Recorte 405 *Puppy Love*	10.00 -	15.00
Teen 121 *What Is Your Name, Dear?*		-
THE EBBTONES:		
Crest 1016 *I Want You Only*	10.00 -	15.00
Ebb 100 *I've Got A Feeling*	15.00 -	20.00
Port 70026 *Rockin' On the Range*	7.00 -	10.00
THE EBONAIRES:		
Aladdin 3211 *Three O'Clock In The Morning* . . .	20.00 -	30.00
Lena 1001 *Love Call*	10.00 -	15.00
Money 220 *The Very Best Luck In The World*	8.00 -	12.00
THE EBONIERS:		
Port 70013 *Hand In Hand*	7.00 -	10.00
THE EBONY MOODS:		
Theron 108 *I've Got News For You*		-
THE ECHOES:		
Andex 22102 *Dee-Dee-Di Oh*	7.00 -	10.00
Ascot 2188 *I Love Candy*	7.00 -	10.00
Combo 128 *My Little Honey*	20.00 -	30.00
Gee 1028 *Ding Dong*	8.00 -	12.00
Rockin' 523 *Please Say You're Mine*	40.00 -	60.00
Seg-Way 103, 106	3.00 -	6.00
Specialty 601 *Over The Rainbow*	10.00 -	15.00
ECHOMORES:		
Rocket 1041 *Little Chick*		-
THE ECHOTONES:		
Dart 1009 *So In Love*	5.00 -	8.00
THE ECHO VALLEY BOYS:		
Island 1/2 *Wash Machine Boogie*	75.00 -	100.00
DUANE EDDY:		
Jamie (EP) 100, 301, 302, 304	7.00 -	10.00
1104 *Rebel-'Rouser* (78 rpm)	10.00 -	15.00
CORKY EDMINSTER:		
Raynor 10820 *Chili Dippin' Baby*		-
THE EDSELS:		
Capitol 4675 *If Your Pillow Could Talk*	8.00 -	12.00
Dub 2843 *Rama Lama Ding Dong*	10.00 -	15.00
Ember 1078 *Three Precious Words*	8.00 -	12.00
Tammy 1010 *What Brought Us Together*	8.00 -	12.00
1014 *Three Precious Words*	8.00 -	12.00
1023 *The Girl I Love*	8.00 -	12.00
1031 *Another Lonely Night*		-
Twin 700 *Rama Lama Ding Dong*		-
CHUCK EDWARDS (& THE FIVE		
CROWNS/& HIS GUITAR):		
Alanna 557 *If I Were King*	10.00 -	15.00
Duke 159, 163, 174	5.00 -	8.00
EDDIE ALVIS EDWARDS:		
Real Gone Baby		-
GWEN EDWARDS & THE CO-EDS (See:		
CO-EDS)		
JIMMY EDWARDS:		
Mercury 71209 *Love Bug Crawl*	7.00 -	10.00
71209 Same, but 78 rpm	10.00 -	15.00
JOHNNY EDWARDS & THE WHITE CAPS:		
Northland 7002 *Rock 'N' Roll Saddles*		-
TIBBY EDWARDS:		
Mercury 70591 *Flip Flop And Fly*	5.00 -	8.00
TOMMY EDWARDS:		
MGM (EP) 1003 *It's All In The Game*	20.00 -	30.00
CHARLES EDWINS:		
Duke 124 *I Got Loose*	7.00 -	10.00
WILLIE EGAN/EGANS; LITTLE WILLIE		
EGANS:		
Dash 55001 *Rock & Roll Fever*	7.00 -	10.00
Mambo 102 *What A Shame*	10.00 -	15.00
111 *Come On*	10.00 -	15.00

Spry 107 *Treat Me Right*	10.00 -	15.00
Vita 125 *Wear Your Black Dress*	7.00 -	10.00
COZY EGGLESTON:		
States 133 *Big Heavy*	8.00 -	12.00
BOB EHRET:		
Aladdin 3377 *Stop The Clock*	20.00 -	30.00
DONNIE ELBERT:		
DeLuxe 6125, 6143, 6148, 6156, 6161, 6164, 6168	4.00 -	8.00
King (LP) 629 *The Sensational Donnie Elbert* . . .	50.00 -	75.00
THE EL CAPRIS:		
Bullseye 102 *Oh, But She Did*	20.00 -	30.00
Fee Bee 216 *Your Star*	15.00 -	20.00
Hi-Q 5006 *Girl Of Mine*	8.00 -	12.00
Paris 525 *They're Always Laughin' At Me*	7.00 -	10.00
THE ELCHORDS, Featuring BUTCHY		
SAUNDERS:		
Good 544 *Peppermint Stick*	7.00 -	10.00
THE EL DARADOS (See THE EL DORADOS)		
THE EL DOMINGOS:		
Chelsea 1609 *Lucky Me, I'm In Love*	15.00 -	20.00
THE EL DORADOS: (See HAZEL		
McCOLLUM):		
Vee Jay 115 *My Loving Baby*	50.00 -	80.00
115 *My Loving Baby* (red plastic)	100.00 -	up
127 *One More Chance*	30.00 -	50.00
147 *At My Front Door*	7.00 -	10.00
165 *I'll Be Forever Loving You*	8.00 -	12.00
180 *Rock 'N' Roll's For Me*	8.00 -	12.00
197 *Chop Ling Soon*	15.00 -	20.00
211 *Bim Bam Boom*	10.00 -	15.00
250 *Tears On My Pillow*	15.00 -	20.00
263 *Boom Diddle Boom*	10.00 -	15.00
302 *Lights Are Low*	10.00 -	15.00
Vee Jay (LP) 1001 *Crazy Little Mama* (maroon		
label)	100.00 -	150.00
(LP) 1001 same, but black label	15.00 -	20.00
BILLY ELDRIDGE:		
Unart 2011 *Let's Go Baby*	15.00 -	20.00
Vulco 1580 *It's Over*		-
ELECTRAS:		
Infinity 012 *You Lied*	10.00 -	15.00
THE ELEGANTS:		
Apt 25005 *Little Star* (black label)	8.00 -	12.00
25005 *Little Star* (78 rpm)	20.00 -	30.00
25017 *Please Believe Me*	7.00 -	10.00
25029 *True Love Affair*	7.00 -	10.00
Hull 732 *Little Boy Blue*	10.00 -	15.00
Photo 2662 *A Dream Can Come True*	10.00 -	15.00
LES ELGART & HIS ORCHESTRA:		
Columbia 40180 *Bandstand Boogie*	6.00 -	10.00
JOHNNY ELGIN:		
Roulette 7005 *Sittin' At Home With The Blues* . . .	7.00 -	10.00
THE ELGINS:		
Congress 214 *Ritha Mae*	7.00 -	10.00
Titan 1724 *My Illness*	7.00 -	10.00
THE ELITES:		
Chief 7040 *The Blues*	10.00 -	15.00
THE ELLIS BROTHERS:		
ABC Paramount 9954 *Sneaky Alligator*		-
REX ELLIS:		
Rivermont 1160		-
RAY ELLSWORTH:		
Ellsworth 101 *Rock 'N' Roll Show*	10.00 -	15.00
101/102 *I Wanna Hold You Baby*	10.00 -	15.00
JOHNNY ELMORE:		
Jar 105 *War Chant Boogie*	10.00 -	15.00
THE EL POLLOS:		
Neptune 1001 *Why Treat Me This Way*	15.00 -	20.00
THE EL RAYS:		
Checker 794 *Darling I Know*	100.00 -	150.00
M & M 104 *Till The End Of Time*		-
THE EL REYES:		

Jade 501 *Mr. Moonglow* .... 15.00 - 20.00
Josie 801 *Blue Moon* .... 10.00 - 15.00
Winley 226 *We Teenagers* .... 8.00 - 12.00
EL TEMPOS:
Vee Jay 580 *My Love Goes Deep Within* .... 7.00 - 10.00
THE EL TONES:
Cub 9011 *Little Mattie* .... 7.00 - 10.00
THE EL TORROS:
Fraternity 811 *All The Tears Is Gone* .... 10.00 - 15.00
THE EL VENOS:
Groove 0170 *Geraldine* .... 15.00 - 20.00
Vik 0305 *My Heart Beats Faster* .... 15.00 - 20.00
EMANON 4:
Flash 106 *Oh That Girl* .... 15.00 - 20.00
THE EMANONS:
ABC Paramount 9913 *We Teenagers* ...... 7.00 - 10.00
G.G.S. 443 *No I Miss You* ....   -
THE EMBERS:
Columbia 40287 *Sweet Lips* .... 15.00 - 20.00
Dot 16101 *Couldn't Wait Any Longer* ...... 10.00 - 15.00
Empress 101 *Solitaire* .... 10.00 - 15.00
    104 *I Was Too Careful* .... 10.00 - 15.00
    107 *Abigail* .... 10.00 - 15.00
    108 *What A Surprise* .... 10.00 - 15.00
Herald 410 *Paradise Hill* .... 15.00 - 20.00
    410 *Paradise Hill* (red vinyl) .... 40.00 - 60.00
THE EMBRACEABLES:
Sandy 1025 *From Someone Who Loves You* ..... 7.00 - 10.00
TED EMBRY:
Ac'cent 1057 *New Shoes* .... 10.00 - 15.00
THE EMCEES:
Cimarron 4044 *Wine, Wine, Wine* .... 10.00 - 15.00
THE EMERALDS: (See also LUTHER BOND)
Allied 10002 *Why Must I Wonder* .... 8.00 - 12.00
Bobbin 107 *That's The Way It's Got To Be* ...... 15.00 - 20.00
    121 *Lover's Cry* .... 15.00 - 20.00
Rex 1004 *All The Time* .... 8.00 - 12.00
    1013 *I Kneel At Your Throne* .... 8.00 - 12.00
Showboat 1501 *Gold Will Never Do* .... 5.00 - 8.00
BILLY (THE KID) EMERSON:
Sun 195 *No Teasin' Around* .... 50.00 - 75.00
    214 *Move Baby Move* .... 20.00 - 30.00
    219 *Red Hot* .... 20.00 - 30.00
    233 *Something For Nothing* .... 15.00 - 20.00
THE EMERSONS:
Newport 7004 *Joannie Joannie* ....   -
THE EMOTIONS:
Fury 1010 *Candlelight* .... 10.00 - 15.00
THE EMPERORS:
Haven 511 *Come Back, Come Back* .... 75.00 - 100.00
THE EMPIRES:
Calico 121 *Definition Of Love* .... 10.00 - 15.00
Chavis 1026 *Love You So Bad* .... 10.00 - 15.00
Epic 9527 *Time And A Place* .... 7.00 - 10.00
Harlem 2333 *Magic Mirror* .... 50.00 - 75.00
Whirlin' Disc 104 *Whispering Heart* .... 15.00 - 20.00
Wing 90023 *Shirley* .... 10.00 - 15.00
    90050 *By The Riverside* .... 8.00 - 12.00
    90080 *My First Discovery* .... 8.00 - 12.00
THE ENCHANTERS:
Coral 61756 *True Love Gone* .... 5.00 - 8.00
    61832 *There Goes* .... 5.00 - 8.00*
    61916 *Bottle It Up And Go* .... 10.00 - 15.00
    62373 *The Day* .... 7.00 - 10.00
Ep-Som *I Need Your Love* .... 7.00 - 10.00
J.J & M. 1562 *Oh Rosemarie* .... 10.00 - 15.00
Mercer 992 *True Love Gone* .... 30.00 - 40.00
Musitron 1071/1072 *I Lied To My Heart* ...... 7.00 - 10.00
Sharp 105 *We Make Mistakes* .... 7.00 - 10.00
Stardust 102 *Spellbound By The Moon* .... 50.00 - 80.00
*A Longer version is of higher value.
THE ENCHANTMENTS:

Romac 1001 *Lonely Heart* ....   -
THE ENCHORDS:
Laurie 3089 *I Need You Baby* .... 7.00 - 10.00
THE ENCORES:
Bow 302 *Barbara* .... 7.00 - 10.00
Checker 760 *When I Look At You* ....150.00 - 200.00
THE ENDORSERS:
Moon 109 *Crying (Over You)* ....   -
SCOTT ENGEL:
Orbit 506 *Good For Nothin'* .... 7.00 - 10.00
    545 *Comin' Home* .... 5.00 - 8.00
Orbit (other issues) .... 4.00 - 7.00
BENNY ENGLAND:
Zenith 103 *Eloping* .... 10.00 - 15.00
HANK ENGLAND:
Process 148 *Truck Driving Buddy* .... 7.00 - 10.00
ENSENATORS:
Tar-X 101 *Just Like Before* ....   -
EPICS:
Lifetime 1004 *Lonely* .... 10.00 - 15.00
AL EPP:
Wildcat 0018 *Breaking My Heart* .... 8.00 - 12.00
DON EPPERSON:
Excell *You're Gone Again* ....   -
EARL EPPS:
Minor 103 *Be Bop Blues* .... 50.00 - 75.00
ERIK & THE VIKINGS:
Karate 5031 *Heaven And Paradise* .... 7.00 - 10.00
ERLENE & HER GIRLFRIENDS:
Old Town 1150 *My Dada Say* .... 7.00 - 10.00
THE ERMINES:
Loma 701 *True Love* .... 20.00 - 30.00
FRANKIE ERVIN with JOHNNY MOORE'S
    THREE BLAZERS:
Blaze 103 *Hot Rod* .... 8.00 - 12.00
Hollywood 1031 *Johnny Ace's Last Letter* ...... 8.00 - 12.00
ODIE ERVIN:
Big Town 111 *Note Pinned To My Bed* .... 15.00 - 20.00
THE ESCORTS:
Coral 62302 *Seven Wonders Of The World* ...... 7.00 - 10.00
Judd 1014 *My First Year* .... 8.00 - 12.00
Premium 407 *Sorry* .... 20.00 - 30.00
RCA Victor 6834 *Bad Boy* .... 7.00 - 10.00
Scarlet 4005 *I Will Be Home Again* .... 8.00 - 12.00
ESQUERITA:
Capitol (LP) 1186 *Esquerita* ....150.00 - 200.00
    (EP) 1186 *Esquerita* .... 75.00 - 100.00
    4007 *Oh Baby* .... 15.00 - 20.00
    4058 *Rockin' The Joint* .... 15.00 - 20.00
    4145 *Laid Off* .... 15.00 - 20.00
THE ESQUIRE BOYS:
Guyden 705 *Rock-A-Beatin' Boogie* .... 7.00 - 10.00
    705 *Rock-A-Beatin' Boogie* (78 rpm) ...... 10.00 - 15.00
THE ESQUIRES:
Meridian *Mission Bells* .... 15.00 - 20.00
When I Fall In Love .... 15.00 - 20.00
THE ESSEX:
Roulette (LP) 25235 *A Walkin' Miracle* .... 20.00 - 30.00
SIDNEY ESTER & THE DREAMERS:
Dangold 2001 *Let Me Walk With You* .... 7.00 - 10.00
THE ETERNALS:
Hollywood 68 *Rockin' in the Jungle* .... 10.00 - 15.00
    70 *Babalu's Wedding Day* .... 10.00 - 15.00
ETTA & HARVEY:
Chess 1760, 1771 .... 4.00 - 8.00
ROY ETZEL:
Time 1029 *Jeeny Oh Jenny* ....   -
BILLY EUSTIS:
"R" 506 *I'm Sorry You're Gone* ....   -
JIMMY EVANS (& THE JESTERS)
Clearmont 492 *The Joint's Really Jumpin'* ...... 50.00 - 75.00
Shimmy 1054 *Messy Bessy* .... 8.00 - 12.00

MARK EVANS:
Tab 101 *It's Love* .... 7.00 - 10.00
MARTY EVANS:
Coral 62192 *Poor Me* .... 7.00 - 10.00
PAUL EVANS:
Guaranteed (LP) 1000 *Fabulous Teens* .... 30.00 - 50.00
RUSTY EVANS:
Brunswick 55103 *(Let The Midnight Special)*
Shine Its Light On Me .... 7.00 - 10.00
THE EVENTUALS:
Okeh 7142 *Just The Things That You Do* .... 10.00 - 15.00
BETTY EVERETT:
CJ 611 *Please Come Back* .... 5.00 - 8.00
BRACEY EVERETT:
Atlantic 2013 *The Lover's Curse* .... 8.00 - 12.00
VINCE EVERETT:
ABC Paramount 10313 *Such A Night* .... 7.00 - 10.00
   10360 *Ain't Gonna Be Your Low Down Dog* ... 7.00 - 10.00
   10472 *Baby Let's Play House* .... 7.00 - 10.00
   10624 *Big Brother* .... 7.00 - 10.00
Jam 1067 *Love Me* .... 8.00 - 12.00
Royalty 505 *I'm Snowed* .... 8.00 - 12.00
Town 1964 *Buttercup* .... 8.00 - 12.00
THE EVERGREENS:
Chart 605 *Every Truly Yours* .... 20.00 - 30.00
THE EVERLY BROTHERS:
Cadence (EP) 104, 111, 118, 121, 134 .... 15.00 - 20.00
   (EP) 333 *Rockin' with The Everly Brothers* ... 20.00 - 30.00
   1315 *Bye Bye Love* (78 rpm) .... 15.00 - 20.00
   1337 *Wake Up Little Susie* (78 rpm) .... 15.00 - 20.00
   1342 *This Little Girl Of Mine* (78 rpm) ...... 15.00 - 20.00
   1348 *Claudette* (78 rpm) .... 15.00 - 20.00
   1350 *Bird Dog* (78 rpm) .... 20.00 - 30.00
   1355 *Problems* (78 rpm) .... 15.00 - 20.00
   (LP) 3003 *Everly Brothers* .... 20.00 - 30.00
   (LP) 3016 *Songs Our Daddy Taught Us* ...... 20.00 - 30.00
   (LP) 3025 *Everly Brothers Best* .... 15.00 - 20.00
   (LP) 3040 *The Fabulous Style Of* .... 15.00 - 20.00
   (LP) 3059 *Folk Songs* .... 20.00 - 30.00
   (LP) 3062 *15 Everly Hits* .... 10.00 - 15.00
Columbia 21496 *Keep A-Loving Me* .... 50.00 - 75.00
Warner Bros. (EP) 550 .... 20.00 - 30.00
"EVERYBODY DIGS THE BOSS
RECORD HOP":
Winley (LP) 6001 *Paragons, Jesters, et al* ...... 30.00 - 40.00
THE EXCELLENTS:
Blast 207 *I Hear A Rhapsody* .... 8.00 - 12.00
THE EXCELS:
Central 2601 *Baby Doll* .... 15.00 - 20.00
THE EXCITERS:
United Artists (LP) 326 *Tell Him* .... 20.00 - 30.00
THE EXCLUSIVES:
K&C *It's Over* .... 10.00 - 15.00
THE EXECS:
Fargo 1055 *Walking In The Rain* .... 10.00 - 15.00
THE EXTREMES:
Paro 733 *The Bells* .... 8.00 - 12.00
DENNY EZBA (& THE GOLDENS):
Renner 213 *Mary Diane* .... 10.00 - 15.00
   217 *Come Home Baby* .... 10.00 - 15.00
   225 *Dirty Dirty Feeling* .... 10.00 - 15.00
   228 *Lover Boy* .... 10.00 - 15.00
   234 *Jailbird* .... 10.00 - 15.00
   236 *Love Me* .... 10.00 - 15.00
   238 *C.C. City* .... 10.00 - 15.00
   242 *It's My Way* .... 10.00 - 15.00
   244 *Susie-O* .... 10.00 - 15.00
   245 *Little Girl* .... 8.00 - 12.00
   246 *Just You And Me* .... 8.00 - 12.00
   250 *Please Just Say So* .... 8.00 - 12.00
EZRA & THE IVIES:
United Artists 165 *Comic Book Crazy* .... 15.00 - 20.00

SHELLEY FABARES:
Colpix (LP) 431 *The Things We Did Last*
Summer .... 20.00 - 30.00
FABIAN:
Chancellor (EP) 5003 *Hold That Tiger* ...... 20.00 - 30.00
   (LP) 5003 *Hold That Tiger* .... 30.00 - 40.00
   (LP) 5005 *Fabulous Fabian* .... 15.00 - 25.00
   (LP) 5009 *Fabian & Avalon—The Hit Makers* . 20.00 - 30.00
   (LP) 5012 *Good Old Summertime* ...... 20.00 - 30.00
   (LP) 5019 *Rockin' Hot* .... 30.00 - 40.00
   (LP) 5024 *16 Fabulous Hits* .... 15.00 - 20.00
THE FABULAIRES:
Main-Line 103 *While Walking* .... 10.00 - 15.00
THE FABULONS:
Benson 100 *Connie* .... 7.00 - 10.00
Ember 1069 *Give Me Back My Ring* .... 10.00 - 15.00
THE FABULOUS EGYPTIANS:
Cindy *End Of Time* .... -
THE FABULOUS ENCHANTERS:
Fine Arts 1007 *Why Are You Crying* .... 7.00 - 10.00
THE FABULOUS FABULIERS:
Angeltone 539 *She Is The Girl For Me* .... 8.00 - 12.00
THE FABULOUS FIVE FLAMES:
Time 1023 *No More Tears* .... -
THE FABULOUS FLAMES:
Bay-Tone 102 *Do You Remember* .... 10.00 - 15.00
   105 *I'm So All Alone* .... 10.00 - 15.00
Harlem 114 *So Long My Darling* .... 7.00 - 10.00
Rex 3000 *My Joan* .... 15.00 - 20.00
THE FABULOUS FOUR:
Chancellor 1078 *Why Do Fools Fall In Love* ...... 10.00 - 15.00
   1085 *Betty Ann* .... 15.00 - 20.00
Melic 4114 *Welcome Me Home* .... 10.00 - 15.00
THE FABULOUS GARDENIAS:
Liz 1004 *It's You You You* .... 15.00 - 25.00
THE FABULOUS PEARLS:
Dooto 448 *My Heart's Desire* .... 7.00 - 10.00
THE FABULOUS PLAYBOYS:
Apollo 460 *Tears, Tears, Tears* .... 20.00 - 30.00
THE FABULOUS THREE:
Hale 501 *Cross Every Mountain* .... 7.00 - 10.00
THE FABULOUS TWILIGHTS:
Fortune 542 *My Little Darling* .... 10.00 - 15.00
THE FABULOUS WINDS:
Celestial 111 *Rock & Roll Radio* .... 8.00 - 12.00
TOMMY FACENDA:
Legrande 1001 *High School U.S.A* .... 10.00 - 15.00
Nasco 6018 *Little Baby* .... 7.00 - 10.00
DICK FAGAN & THE SCORES:
Sarg 160 *Nothing Really Shakes Me* .... 10.00 - 15.00
TOMMY FAILE:
Lawn 104 *That's All Right* .... 15.00 - 20.00
Silver Star 1001 *Long Gone* .... 15.00 - 20.00
WERLY FAIRBURN:
Capitol 2770 *Good Deal Lucille* .... 7.00 - 10.00
   2844 *Nothin' But Lovin'* .... 7.00 - 10.00
   2963 *I Feel Like Cryin'* .... 7.00 - 10.00
   3101 *Spiteful Heart* .... 5.00 - 8.00
Columbia 21432 *I Guess I'm Crazy* .... 7.00 - 10.00
   21483 *Stay Close To Me* .... 7.00 - 10.00
   21528 *Everybody's Rockin'* .... 10.00 - 15.00
Savoy 1503 *All The Time* .... 8.00 - 12.00
   1509 *Speak To Me Baby* .... 10.00 - 15.00
   1521 *Telephone Baby* .... 10.00 - 15.00
JOHNNY FAIRE:
Fable 601 *You Gotta Walk The Line* .... 10.00 - 15.00
Surf 5019 *Bertha Lou* .... 10.00 - 15.00
   5024 *Betcha I Getcha* .... 10.00 - 15.00
THE FAIRLANES:
Argo 5357 *Comin' After You* .... 5.00 - 8.00
Lucky Seven 102 *Seventeen Steps* .... 15.00 - 20.00
Radiant 101 *Baby Baby* .... 7.00 - 10.00
THE FALCONS:
Anna 1110 *This Heart Of Mine* .... 15.00 - 20.00
Cash 1002 *I Miss You Darling* .... 40.00 - 60.00

Falcon 1006 *Now That It's Over*	15.00 -	20.00
Flick 001 *You're So Fine*	8.00 -	12.00
008 *You Must Know I Love You*	15.00 -	20.00
Mercury 70940 *Baby That's It*	8.00 -	12.00
Quality 1721 *My Only Love*	10.00 -	15.00
Savoy 843 *You're The Beating Of My Heart*	75.00 -	100.00
Silhouette 521 *Can This be Christmas*	8.00 -	12.00

THE FALLEN ANGELS:

Tollie 9049 *Up On The Mountain*	10.00 -	15.00

JOHNNY FALLIN:

Capitol 4216 *Party Kiss*	10.00 -	15.00
4283 *Wild Streak*	7.00 -	10.00

JAY FANNING:

Acme 2032 *It's Love*	10.00 -	15.00
2035 *Church Bells*	8.00 -	12.00

THE FANTASTICS:

Copa 8005 *That One*	5.00 -	8.00
RCA Victor 7572 *There Goes My Love*	5.00 -	8.00

THE FANTASYS:

Guyden 2029 *No One But You*	7.00 -	10.00

WAYNE FARMER & THE TEEN-BEATS:

Dodge 802 *Yeah! Yeah! My Baby*	7.00 -	10.00

THE FARMER BOYS:

Capitol 3077 *You're A Humdinger*	5.00 -	8.00
3162 *Lend A Helping Hand*	5.00 -	8.00
3246 *It Pays To Advertise*	5.00 -	8.00
3322 *Flip Flop*	5.00 -	8.00
3476 *My Baby Done Left Me*	7.00 -	10.00
3569 *Cool Down Mame*	7.00 -	10.00
3732 *Flash Crash And Thunder*	7.00 -	10.00

LITTLE JOEY FARR:

Band Box 286 *Big White Cadillac*	10.00 -	15.00

BILLY FARRELL:

Imperial 7001 *Slippin' And Slidin'*	10.00 -	15.00

MICKEY FARRELL & THE DYNAMICS:

Bethlehem 3080 *I'm Calling On You*	7.00 -	10.00

THE FASCINATIONS:

Sure 106 *Midnight*	15.00 -	20.00

THE FASCINATORS:

Blue Lake 112 *Can't Stop*	125.00 -	175.00
Capitol 4053 *Chapel Bells*	15.00 -	20.00
4137 *Come To Paradise*	15.00 -	20.00
4247 *Oh Rosemarie*	15.00 -	20.00
King 5119 *Tee Vee*	8.00 -	12.00
Your Copy 1135 *The Bells Of My Heart*	100.00 -	150.00
1136 *Don't Give It Away*	100.00 -	150.00

JOHNNY FAYE:

Dani 1539 *Sweet Linda Brown*	15.00 -	20.00

THE FEATHERS:

Aladdin 3267 *Johnny Darling*	40.00 -	60.00
3277 *I Need A Girl*	40.00 -	60.00
Hollywood 1051 *Dear One*	-	
Show Time 1103 *Desert Winds*	20.00 -	30.00
1104 *Johnny Darling*	20.00 -	30.00
1105 *Why Don't You Write Me*	20.00 -	30.00
1106 *Love Only You*	20.00 -	30.00

CHARLIE FEATHERS:

Flip 503 *I've Been Deceived*	100.00 -	150.00
Holiday Inn 114 *Deep Elm Blues*	10.00 -	15.00
Kay 1001 *Why Don't You*	75.00 -	100.00
King 4971 *Everybody's Lovin' My Baby*	25.00 -	40.00
4997 *Bottle To The Baby*	40.00 -	60.00
5022 *Nobody's Woman*	30.00 -	40.00
5043 *When You Come Around*	30.00 -	40.00
Memphis 103 *Wild Wild Party*	20.00 -	30.00
Meteor 5032 *Tongue-Tied Jill*	100.00 -	150.00
Sun 231 *Defrost Your Heart*	100.00 -	150.00
503 *I've Been Deceived*	80.00 -	120.00

THE FEDERALS:

De Luxe 6112 *Come Go With Me*	10.00 -	15.00
Fury 1009 *Dear Loraine*	10.00 -	15.00

DON FEGER:

Ebony 102 *Date On The Corner*	20.00 -	30.00
103 *Lookout Baby*	20.00 -	30.00

TERRY FELL:

"X" 0114 *Mississippi River Shuffle*	5.00 -	8.00
"X" 0149 *I'm Hot To Trot*	5.00 -	8.00

DERRELL FELTS:

Dixie 2008 *Playmates*	-	
Okeh 7118 *Lookie Lookie Lookie*	10.00 -	15.00

NARVEL FELTS:

Mercury 71140 *Kiss-A-Me Baby*	5.00 -	8.00
Pink 701 *Cutie Baby*	7.00 -	10.00

FREDDY FENDER:

Agro 5375 *A Man Can Cry*	5.00 -	8.00
Duncan 1000 *Mean Woman*	15.00 -	20.00
1001 *Wasted Days & Wasted Nights*	10.00 -	15.00
1002 *Wild Side Of Life*	7.00 -	10.00
1004 *Little Mama*	10.00 -	15.00
Imperial 5659, 5670	7.00 -	10.00
Norco 102, 104, 108	7.00 -	10.00
103 *Going Out With The Tide*	7.00 -	10.00
107 *Bony Moronie*	10.00 -	15.00

THE FENDERMEN:

Soma (LP) 1240 *Mule Skinner Blues*	100.00 -	150.00

FENDERS:

QQ 245 *Honky Tonk Hardwood Floor*	-	

FENTION & THE CASTLE ROCKERS:

Duke 190 *The Freeze*	5.00 -	8.00

H BOMB FERGUSON & HIS MAD LADS:

Arc 9001 *Little Tiger*	-	

TROY FERGUSON:

Flame 101 *At The Jamboree*	7.00 -	10.00

AL FERRIER (& HIS BOPPIN' BILLIES):

Excello 2105 *Hey Baby*	10.00 -	15.00
Goldband 1031 *No No Baby*	20.00 -	30.00
1035 *It's Too Late Now*	15.00 -	20.00
1072 *Let's Go Boppin' Tonight*	35.00 -	50.00
Rocko 502 *Kiss Me Baby*	7.00 -	10.00
Zynn 510 *Chisholm Trail Rock*	7.00 -	10.00
1013 *Blues Stop Knockin'*	7.00 -	10.00

FERRIS & THE WHEELS:

Bambi 801 *Chop, Chop*	5.00 -	8.00

THE FIDELITY'S:

Baton 252 *The Things I Love*	7.00 -	10.00
256 *Memories Of You*	7.00 -	10.00
261 *My Greatest Thrill*	7.00 -	10.00
Sir 271, 276	4.00 -	7.00

THE FIELD BROS.:

Carlton 475 *Time And Time Again*	10.00 -	15.00

THE FIESTAS:

1062 *So Fine*	5.00 -	8.00
1062 *So Fine* (78 RPM)	20.00 -	30.00
1067 *I'm Your Slave*	5.00 -	8.00
1069 *Our Anniversary*	5.00 -	8.00
1074 *Good News*	7.00 -	10.00
1080 *Dollar Bill*	7.00 -	10.00
1090 *You Could Be My Girlfriend*	7.00 -	10.00
1104 *Look At That Girl*	7.00 -	10.00
1111 *She's Mine*	7.00 -	10.00
1122 *Broken Heart*	7.00 -	10.00
1127 *Look At That Girl*	7.00 -	10.00
1134 *The Gypsy Said*	7.00 -	10.00
1140 *The Party's Over*	7.00 -	10.00
1148 *Foolish Dreamer*	7.00 -	10.00
1166 *All That's Good*	7.00 -	10.00
1178 *Anna*	7.00 -	10.00
1187 *Love Is Strange*	7.00 -	10.00
1189 *Ain't She Sweet*	7.00 -	10.00
Vigor 712 *So Fine*	-	

HERBIE FIELDS:

Parrott 806 *Mr. Jump*	5.00 -	8.00

LINCOLN FIG & THE DATES:

Worthy 1006 *Kiss Me Tenderly*	8.00 -	12.00

LEE FINN & RHYTHM MEN:
Westport 141 *High Class Feelin'* . . . . -
THE FIREBALLS:
Top Rank (EP) 1000 *Bulldog, + 3* . . . . 50.00 - 75.00
BRIEN FISHER:
Spangle 2001 *Fingertips* . . . . 8.00 - 12.00
United Artists 115 *It's Up To You* . . . . 8.00 - 12.00
SONNY FISHER:
Starday 179 *Rockin' Daddy* . . . . 20.00 - 30.00
    190 *Sneaky Pete* . . . . 35.00 - 50.00
    207 *Rockin' & Rollin'* . . . . 30.00 - 40.00
    244 *Pink And Black* . . . . 30.00 - 40.00
TOMMY FISHER:
B&D 1314 *Rock & Roll Robin Hood* . . . . 15.00 - 20.00
THE FI-TONES:
Angle Tone 525 *You'll Be The Last* . . . . 10.00 - 15.00
Atlas 1050 *Foolish Dreams* . . . . 20.00 - 30.00
    1051 *It Wasn't A Lie* . . . . 20.00 - 30.00
    1052 *I'll Call To You* . . . . 20.00 - 30.00
    1055 *I Belong To You* . . . . 20.00 - 30.00
Old Town 1042 *My Faith* . . . . 10.00 - 15.00
FIVE ARROWS:
Parrot 816 *Pretty Little Thing* . . . . -
THE FIVE BARS:
Money 224 *Stormy Weather* . . . . -
FIVE BELLS
Clock 1017 *It's You* . . . . 15.00 - 20.00
THE FIVE BILLS:
Brunswick-*Can't Wait For Tomorrow* . . . . 15.00 - 20.00
THE FIVE BLUE NOTES:
Onda 108 *My Special Prayer* . . . . 20.00 - 30.00
Sabre 103 *My Gal Is Gone* . . . . 90.00 - 130.00
    108 *The Beat Of Our Hearts* . . . . 100.00 - 150.00
FIVE BOPS:
Hamilton 50023 *Unforgotten Love* . . . . 10.00 - 15.00
THE FIVE BUDDS:
Rama 1 *I Was Such A Fool* . . . . 40.00 - 60.00
    2 *I Guess It's All Over Now* . . . . 40.00 - 60.00
FIVE CAMPBELLS:
Music City 794 *Morrine* . . . . 30.00 - 40.00
THE FIVE CHANCES:
Chance 1157 *I May Be Small* . . . . 200.00 - 300.00
Federal 12303 *My Days Are Blue* . . . . 20.00 - 30.00
States 156 *Gloria* . . . . 100.00 - 150.00
THE 5 CHANELS:
Deb 500 *The Reason* . . . . 8.00 - 12.00
THE FIVE CHORDS:
Cuca 1031 *Red Wine* . . . . 15.00 - 20.00
Jamie 1110 *Love Is Like Music* . . . . 20.00 - 30.00
THE FIVE CLASSICS:
A 317 *Come On Baby* . . . . 7.00 - 10.00
Arc 4454 *My Imagination* . . . . 7.00 - 10.00
THE FIVE CROWNS:
Alanna 576 *If I Were King* . . . . 7.00 - 10.00
Caravan 15609 *I Can't Pretend* . . . . 8.00 - 12.00
Gee 1001 *God Bless You* . . . . 10.00 - 15.00
Old Town 790 *You Could Be My Love* . . . . 150.00 - 250.00
    792 *Lullaby Of The Bells* . . . . 150.00 - 250.00
Rainbow 179 *A Star* (red plastic) . . . . 100.00 - 150.00
    184 *Who Can Be True* . . . . 75.00 - 100.00
    202 *Keep It A Secret* . . . . 100.00 - 150.00
    206 *Alone Again* . . . . 100.00 - 150.00
    335 *You Came To Me* . . . . 75.00 - 100.00
Riviera 990 *You Came To Me* . . . . 100.00 - 150.00
Transworld 717 *I Can't Pretend* . . . . 40.00 - 60.00
THE FIVE CRYSTALS:
Delcro 827 *Path Of Broken Hearts* . . . . 15.00 - 20.00
Kane 25592 *Hey Landlord* . . . . 7.00 - 10.00
Music City 821 *Path Of Broken Hearts* . . . . . . 10.00 - 15.00
FIVE CRYSTELS (See: FIVE CRYSTALS)
THE FIVE C'S:
United 172 *Tell Me* . . . . 40.00 - 60.00

THE FIVE DAPPS:
Brax 207/208 *You're So Unfaithful* . . . . 30.00 - 40.00
THE FIVE DEBONAIRES:
Herald 509 *Whispering Blues* . . . . 15.00 - 20.00
THE FIVE DELIGHTS;
Newport 7002 *There'll Be No Goodbye* . . . . 15.00 - 20.00
THE FIVE DIAMONDS:
Treat 501 *Ten Commandments Of Love* . . . . 40.00 - 60.00
THE FIVE DIPS:
Original 1005 *Teach Me Tonight* . . . . — - —
FIVE DISCS:
Calo 202 *My Baby Loves Me* . . . . 7.00 - 10.00
Cheer 1000 *That Was The Time* . . . . 7.00 - 10.00
Dwain 803 *Roses* . . . . 10.00 - 15.00
Emge 1004 *I Remember* . . . . 10.00 - 15.00
Vik 0327 *I Remember* . . . . 5.00 - 8.00
Yale 243 *Come On Baby* . . . . 7.00 - 10.00
FIVE DOLLARS:
Fortune 821 *Harmony Of Love* . . . . 15.00 - 20.00
    826 *So Strange* . . . . 12.00 - 18.00
    830 *I Will Wait* . . . . 10.00 - 15.00
    833 *You Fool* . . . . 10.00 - 15.00
    845 *Yellow Moon* . . . . 10.00 - 15.00
    854 *That's The Way It Goes* . . . . 10.00 - 15.00
FIVE DOTS:
Note 1003 *I Just Love The Things She Does* . . . . 15.00 - 20.00
THE FIVE DUKES:
Atlas 1040 *I Cross My Fingers* . . . . 100.00 - 150.00
FIVE ECHOES/ECHOS:
Sabre 102 *Lonely Moon* (red plastic) . . . . 100.00 - 200.00
    105 *So Lonesome* . . . . 75.00 - 100.00
Vee Jay 129 *I Really Do* . . . . 75.00 - 100.00
    156 *Fools Prayer* . . . . 50.00 - 75.00
FIVE EMERALDS:
S.R.C. 106 *I'll Beg* . . . . 100.00 - 150.00
    107 *Darling* . . . . 100.00 - 150.00
FIVE ENCORES:
Rama 180 *Double Date* . . . . 15.00 - 20.00
    185 *Readin' Ritin' 'Rithmetic & Rock 'n' Roll* . 15.00 - 20.00
THE FIVE FLEETS:
Felsted 8513 *Oh What A Feeling* . . . . 8.00 - 12.00
FIVE FORTUNES:
Ranson—*Time Out For Love* . . . . 50.00 - 75.00
FIVE HEARTS:
Arcade 107 *Unbelieveable* . . . . — - —
Flair 1026 *The Fine One* . . . . — - —
FIVE J'S:
Fulton 2454 *My Darling* . . . . 15.00 - 20.00
THE FIVE JADES:
Duke 188 *Without Your Love* . . . . 10.00 - 15.00
Your Choice 908 *My Reverie* . . . . 10.00 - 15.00
FIVE JETS:
De Luxe 6018 *I Am In Love* . . . . 30.00 - 40.00
    6053 *I'm Stuck* . . . . 15.00 - 20.00
    6058 *Tell Me You're Mine* . . . . 15.00 - 20.00
    6064 *Crazy Chicken* . . . . 15.00 - 20.00
    6071 *Please Love Me Baby* . . . . 15.00 - 20.00
Fortune 833 *I'm Wanderin'* . . . . 15.00 - 20.00
THE FIVE KEYS:
Aladdin (LP) 806 *Best Of The Five Keys*
  (blue label) . . . . 150.00 - 200.00
    3085 *With A Broken Heart* . . . . 150.00 - 200.00
    3099 *The Glory Of Love* . . . . 125.00 - 175.00
    3113 *It's Christmas* . . . . 150.00 - 200.00
    3118 *Yes, Sir, That's My Baby* . . . . 150.00 - 200.00
    3127 *Red Sails In The Sunset* . . . . 150.00 - 200.00
    3136 *I Hadn't Any One Til You* . . . . 150.00 - 200.00
    3158 *I Cried For You* . . . . 150.00 - 200.00
    3167 *Can't Keep From Crying* . . . . 150.00 - 200.00
    3186 *I'll Always Be In Love With You* . . . . . 150.00 - 200.00
    3190 *These Foolish Things* . . . . 150.00 - 200.00
    3204 *Tear Drops In Your Eyes.* . . . . 150.00 - 200.00

3214 *My Saddest Hour*	150.00 -	200.00
3228 *Love My Loving*	100.00 -	150.00
3245 *Deep In My Heart*	100.00 -	150.00
3263 *Why, Oh Why*	80.00 -	120.00
3312 *Story Of Love*	80.00 -	120.00

(Note: Above are to have blue labels; maroon label issues are worth somewhat less)

Capitol (EP) 572 *The Five Keys*	50.00 -	75.00
Capitol (EP) 828 *The Five Keys On Stage*	30.00 -	40.00
(LP) 828 *The Five Keys On Stage*	75.00 -	100.00
(LP) 1769 *The Fantastic Five Keys*	75.00 -	100.00
3318 *You Broke The Rules*	5.00 -	8.00
Capitol (45 rpm—others)	4.00 -	8.00
King (LP) 688 *The Five Keys*	75.00 -	100.00
(LP) 692 *Rhythm & Blues Hits—Past & Present*	30.00 -	50.00
King (45 rpm)	4.00 -	8.00
Score (LP) 4003 *On The Town With The Five Keys*	100.00 -	150.00

THE FIVE KIDS:

Maxwell 101 *Carolyn*	— -	—

THE FIVE KINGS:

Columbia 43060 *Light Bulb*	10.00 -	15.00
Yvette 101 *Here Comes My Baby*	15.00 -	20.00

FIVE KNIGHTS:

Specialty 675 *Miracle*	10.00 -	15.00

FIVE LETTERS:

Ivy 102 *Hold My Baby*	20.00 -	30.00

THE FIVE LYRICS:

Music City 799 *I'm Traveling Light*	— -	—

THE FIVE MASKS:

Jan 101 *Forever And A Day*	10.00 -	15.00

THE FIVE MASTERS:

Bumble Bee 502 *We Are Like One*	8.00 -	12.00

FIVE MEMBERS:

Gem 224 *Please Come Home*	50.00 -	75.00

FIVE NOTES:

Chess 1614 *Show Me The Way*	20.00 -	30.00
Jen-D—*You Are So Beautiful*	15.00 -	20.00
Josie 784 *You Are So Beautiful*	15.00 -	75.00
Specialty 461 *Thrill Me Baby*	50.00 -	75.00

FIVE OWLS:

Vulcan 303 *Pleading To You*	50.00 -	75.00

FIVE PEARLS:

Aladdin 3265 *Please Let Me Know*	30.00 -	50.00

FIVE PENNIES:

Savoy 1182 *Let It Rain*	7.00 -	10.00
1190 *My Heart Trembles*	7.00 -	10.00

THE FIVE PLAYBOYS:

Fee Bee 213 *Pages Of My Scrapbook*	— -	—
232 *Angel Mine*	— -	—

FIVE REASONS:

Cub 9006 *Three O'Clock Rock*	10.00 -	15.00

FIVE ROVERS:

Music City 798 *Down To The Sea*	15.00 -	20.00

FIVE ROYALES:

Apollo 441 *Courage To Love* (red plastic)	30.00 -	50.00
441 *Courage To Love* (black plastic)	15.00 -	20.00
443 *Take All Of Me*	15.00 -	20.00
446 *Crazy, Crazy, Crazy*	12.00 -	18.00
488 *I Want To Thank You*	12.00 -	18.00
449 *All Righty*	12.00 -	18.00
452 *I Do*	15.00 -	20.00
454 *Cry Some More*	15.00 -	20.00
458 *Let Me Come Back Home*	15.00 -	20.00
467 *With All Your Heart*	15.00 -	25.00

(Note: The foregoing, if pressed of red vinyl, command substantially higher prices)

(LP) 488 *The Rockin' 5 Royales*	150.00 -	200.00
Home of The Blues 112, 232, 234	4.00 -	8.00
King (LP) 580 *Dedicated To You*	75.00 -	100.00
(LP) 616 *Sing For You*	75.00 -	100.00

(LP) 678 *Five Royales*	50.00 -	75.00
4785 *How I Wonder*	7.00 -	10.00
4830 *Someone Made You For Me*	7.00 -	10.00
King (others)	4.00 -	8.00

FIVE SATINS:

Chancellor 1110 *Raining In My Heart*	8.00 -	12.00
Cub 9090 *Can I Come Over Tonight*	7.00 -	10.00
Ember (EP) 101 *To The Aisle*	30.00 -	50.00
(EP) 102 *Our Anniversary*	30.00 -	50.00
(LP) 101 *The Five Satins Sing*	150.00 -	200.00
(LP) 401 *Five Satins Encore*	75.00 -	125.00
1005 *In The Still Of The Nite*	5.00 -	8.00
1005 *In The Still Of The Nite* (78 rpm)	15.00 -	20.00
1014 *Our Love Is Forever*	7.00 -	10.00
1019 *To The Aisle*	5.00 -	8.00
1019 *To The Aisle* (78 rpm)	10.00 -	15.00
1025 *Our Anniversary*	7.00 -	10.00
1028 *A Million To One*	7.00 -	10.00
1038 *A Night To Remember*	7.00 -	10.00
1056 *Shadows*	7.00 -	10.00
1061 *I'll Be Seeing You*	7.00 -	10.00
1070 *Wishing Ring*	7.00 -	10.00
First 104 *When Your Love Comes Along*	8.00 -	12.00
Klik 7905 *She's Gone*	15.00 -	20.00
Musictone 1108 *Just To Be Near You*	8.00 -	12.00
Standord 1005 *In The Still of the Night*	50.00 -	75.00
1015 *All Mine*	30.00 -	40.00

FIVE SCALDERS:

Drummond 3000 *If Only You Were Mine*	75.00 -	100.00
3001 *Willow Blues*	75.00 -	100.00

FIVE SCAMPS:

Okeh 7049 *With All My Heart*	20.00 -	30.00

FIVE SHADES:

Ember 1074 *Lonely Boy*	8.00 -	12.00

FIVE SHARPS:

Jubilee 5104 *Stormy Weather*	.00 -	.00

(Unknown in 45 rpm format. See Blues, etc. section for listing and comments on 78 rpm issue.)

Jubilee 5478 *Stormy Weather*	7.00 -	10.00

(Note: This is a later rendition by a different group, and should not be confused with the legendary recording, above.)

FIVE SHILLINGS:

Decca 30722 *Letter To An Angel*	20.00 -	30.00

FIVE SOUNDS:

Aljon 115 *Tonight Must Live On*	20.00 -	30.00

THE FIVE SPOTS:

Future 2201 *Get With It*	20.00 -	30.00
Soma 1147 *Mr. Fortune*	10.00 -	15.00

FIVE STARS:

Blues Boy Kingdom 106 *So Lonely Baby*	75.00 -	100.00
Columbia 42056 *Baby, Baby*	10.00 -	15.00
Dot 15579 *Atom Bomb Baby*	7.00 -	10.00
Hunt 318 *Dreaming*		
Show Time 1102 *Walkin' And Talkin'*	100.00 -	150.00
Treat 505 *We Danced In The Moonlight*	100.00 -	150.00

FIVE STRINGS: (See also SID KING)

Columbia 21361 *I Like It*	7.00 -	10.00
21403 *Drinking Wine Spoli Oli*	10.00 -	15.00

FIVE SWANS:

Music City 795 *Little Girl Of My Dreams*	15.00 -	20.00

FIVE THRILLS:

Parrot 796 *My Baby's Gone*	200.00 -	300.00
800 *Gloria*	150.00 -	200.00
Parrot 800 *Gloria* (red vinyl)	200.00 -	300.00

FIVE TINOS:

Sun 222 *Sitting By My Window*	50.00 -	80.00

FIVE TROJANS:

Edison International 410 *I Hear Those Bells*	15.00 -	20.00
412 *Little Doll*	15.00 -	20.00

FIVE VETS:

Allstar 713 *Right Now*	10.00 -	15.00

FIVE WILLOWS:

Allen 1000 *My Dear Dearest Darling*	80.00 -	120.00
1002 *Dolores*	100.00 -	150.00
1003 *White Cliffs Of Dover*	100.00 -	150.00
Herald 433 *Lay Your Head On My Shoulder*	30.00 -	40.00
442 *Look Me In The Eyes*	30.00 -	40.00
Pee Dee 290 *Love Bells*	100.00 -	125.00

FIVE WINGS (See also: BILLY NELSON):

King 4778 *Johnny Has Gone*	30.00 -	50.00
4781 *Teardrops Are Falling*	30.00 -	50.00

BILL FLAGG:

MGM 12637 *Doin' My Time*	15.00 -	20.00
Tetra 4445 *Go Cat Go*	15.00 -	20.00
4448 *Guitar Rock*	15.00 -	20.00

SONNY FLAHERTY:

Spangle 2011 *My Baby's Casual*	8.00 -	12.00

FLAIRS: (See also SHIRLEY GUNTER; FATSO THEUS)

ABC Paramount 9740 *Steppin' Out*	7.00 -	10.00
Crown (LP) 5356 *The Flairs*	30.00 -	50.00
Epic 9447 *Shake Shake Sherry*	7.00 -	10.00
Flair 1012 *I Had A Love*	30.00 -	40.00
1028 *Love Me Girl*	20.00 -	30.00
1044 *This Is The Night For Love*	20.00 -	30.00
Palms 726 *Roll Over Beethoven*		

FLAMES:

Aladdin 3349 *So Alone*	20.00 -	30.00
G.M. 101 *Darling Jane*	7.00 -	10.00
7-11 2106 *Keep On Smiling*	25.00 -	35.00
2107 *Together*	20.00 -	30.00
2108 *Let's Talk It Over*	20.00 -	30.00
2109 *Sorrowful Heart*	20.00 -	30.00
2110 *I'll Hide My Tears*	20.00 -	30.00

FLAMINGOS:

Chance 1133 *If I Can't Have You* (red plastic)	300.00 -	400.00
1140 *That's My Desire*	100.00 -	150.00
1145 *Golden Teardrops*	100.00 -	150.00
1149 *Plan For Love*	200.00 -	300.00
1154 *Cross Over The Bridge*	200.00 -	300.00
1162 *Blues In A Letter*	300.00 -	400.00
Checker 815 *That's My Baby*	15.00 -	20.00
821 *Please*	15.00 -	20.00
830 *I'll Be Home*	15.00 -	20.00
837 *Get With It*	10.00 -	15.00
846 *The Vow*	10.00 -	15.00
853 *Would I Be Crying*	15.00 -	20.00
Chess (LP) 1433 *The Flamingos* (black label)	100.00 -	150.00
End (LP) 205 *Flamingos*	50.00 -	75.00
(LP) 304 *Flamingo Serenade*	50.00 -	75.00
(LP) 307 *Flamingo Favorites*	30.00 -	40.00
(LP) 316 *Sound Of The Flamingos*	40.00 -	60.00
Decca 30335 *Ladder Of Love*	7.00 -	10.00
30454 *My Faith In You*	7.00 -	10.00
30948 *Jerri-Lee*	7.00 -	10.00
Parrott 808 *Dream Of A Lifetime* (red plastic)	90.00 -	130.00
811 *I Really Don't Want To Know*	Very	Rare
812 *I'm Yours* (red plastic)	90.00 -	120.00
Vee Jay (LP) 1052 *Flamingos Meet The Moonglows*	30.00 -	50.00

FLARES:

Felsted 8604 *Loving You*	7.00 -	10.00
Press 2803 *Make It Be Me*	7.00 -	10.00

FLATT & SCRUGGS:

Columbia (LP) 1019 *Foggy Mountain Jamboree*	15.00 -	20.00
Mercury (LP) 20358 *Country Music*	15.00 -	20.00

THE FLEETWOODS:

Dolton 2001 *Mr. Blue*	15.00 -	20.00

GEORGE FLEMING:

Fleming 501 *I'm Gonna Tell On You/The Shake*		

WADE FLEMONS:

Vee Jay 295 *My Baby Likes To Rock*	7.00 -	10.00
Vee Jay (most other issues)	4.00 -	7.00
Vee Jay (LP) 1011 *Wade Flemons*	20.00 -	30.00

FLIPS:

Sapphire *Why Should I*	20.00 -	30.00

FLORESCENTS:

Bethlehem 3079 *Being In Love*	7.00 -	10.00

PHIL FLOWERS:

Domino 501 *Whole Lotta Woman*	7.00 -	10.00
Hollywood 1070 *I'm A Lover Man*	8.00 -	12.00
Sway 903 *No More Tossin' And Turnin'*	8.00 -	12.00
Wing 596 *No Kissin' At The Hop*	10.00 -	15.00

BILL FLOYD:

Topic 8034 *I'll Huff And I'll Puff*	7.00 -	10.00

HARMONICA FRANK FLOYD:

F & L 100 *Rock A Little Baby*	150.00 -	200.00

MERDELL FLOYD:

Erwin 100 *Juke Box Mama*	30.00 -	40.00

FLUORESCENTS:

Hanover 4520 *The Facts Of Love*	10.00 -	15.00

THE FLYERS:

Atco 6088 *My Only Desire*	15.00 -	20.00

RED FOLEY:

Decca (LP) 5303 (10") *Souvenir*	20.00 -	30.00
(LP) 5338 (10") *Lift Up Your Voice*	15.00 -	20.00
(LP) 8294 *Souvenir Album*	15.00 -	20.00
(LP) 8296 *Beyond The Sunset*	15.00 -	20.00
(LP) 8298 *And Ernest Tubb*	20.00 -	30.00
(LP) 8767, 8806, 8847, 8903	10.00 -	15.00
29517 *Plantation Boogie*	5.00 -	8.00

"FOLK FESTIVAL OF THE BLUES":

Argo (LP) 4031 (various artists)	30.00 -	40.00

EDDIE FONTAINE:

Argo 5309 *Nothin' Shakin'*	7.00 -	10.00
Chancellor 1018 *Goodness, It's Gladys*	7.00 -	10.00
Decca 30042, 30108	5.00 -	8.00
30256 *Homesick Blues*	5.00 -	8.00
30446 *Honky Tonk Man*	5.00 -	8.00
Jalo 102 *It Ain't Gonna Happen No More*	10.00 -	15.00
Sunbeam 105 *Nothin' Shakin*	8.00 -	12.00
112 *Nobody Else Can Handle This Job*	5.00 -	8.00
Vik 0193 *Here 'Tis*	5.00 -	8.00

FRANK FONTAINE:

MGM 12129 *Everybody Rock*		

DAVID FORD & THE EBBTIDES:

Specialty 588 *My Confession*	10.00 -	15.00

EARLSON FORD:

Mercury 71108 *Ain't Nothin' Shakin'*	10.00 -	15.00

TENNESSEE ERNIE FORD:

Capitol (LP) 888 *Ol' Rockin' 'Ern*	15.00 -	20.00
3262 *Sixteen Ton s* (78 rpm)	7.00 -	10.00
(unnumbered) Special Commemorative Pressing celebrating artist's 20th anniversary (1949-1969) with Capitol Records. *Sixteen Tons/I've Got The Milk Man In The Mornin' Blues* (78rpm)		

FRANKIE FORD:

Ace (LP) 1005 *On A Sea Cruise With Frankie Ford*	40.00 -	60.00

JIMMIE FORD:

Stylo 2102 *You're Gonna Be Sorry*	8.00 -	12.00
2105 *We Belong Together*	8.00 -	12.00

EARL FOREST/FORREST:

Duke 108 *Whoopin' And Hollerin'*	15.00 -	20.00
113 *53*	15.00 -	20.00
121 *Out On A Party*	10.00 -	15.00
131 *Oh Ooh Wee*	10.00 -	15.00
Meteor 5005 *I Wronged A Woman*	30.00 -	40.00

FORTES:

Current 103 *Waiting For My Baby*	8.00 -	12.00

JESSIE FORTUNE:

U.S.A. 738, 747	4.00 -	6.00

JOHNNY FORTUNE:

Park Avenue 130 *Dragster*		-	
FORTUNES:			
Checker 818 *Believe In Me*	15.00	-	20.00
Decca 30541 *Tarnished Angel*	7.00	-	10.00
30688 *How Clever Of You*	7.00	-	10.00
Top Rank 2019 *Steady Vows*	7.00	-	10.00
THE FORTUNE TELLERS:			
Sheryl 340 *Just A Little Bit Of Your Love*	7.00	-	10.00
THE FOSTER BROS.:			
Hi Mi 3005 *Never Again*	10.00	-	15.00
Profile 4004 *Trust In Me*	10.00	-	15.00
CECIL FOSTER & THE AUDIOS:			
Time 1 *Why Did You Do It To Me?*	10.00	-	15.00
Ultra 105 *Honest I Do*	15.00	-	20.00
JERRY FOSTER & HIS BAND:			
Back Beat 520 *What Would I Do*	7.00	-	10.00
LITTLE WILLIE FOSTER:			
Blue Lake 113 *Falling Rain Blues*	75.00	-	100.00
Cobra 5011 *Crying The Blues*	30.00	-	50.00
Parrot 813 *Falling Rain Blues*	50.00	-	75.00
FOUR ARCS:			
Boulevard 102 *Life Of Ease*	50.00	-	75.00
FOUR BARS:			
Josie 762 *Grief By Day, Grief By Night*	50.00	-	75.00
768 *I'll Give My Heart To You*	25.00	-	40.00
783 *Why Treat Me This Way*	25.00	-	35.00
Republic 7101 *When Did You Leave Heaven*	40.00	-	60.00
THE FOUR BELLS:			
Gem 220 *My Tree*	.00	-	.00
FOUR BLAZES:			
United 114 *Mood Indigo*	7.00	-	10.00
125 *Night Train*	7.00	-	10.00
127 *Stop Boogie Woogie*	7.00	-	10.00
146 *Not Any More Tears*	7.00	-	10.00
158 *Ella Louise*	7.00	-	10.00
168 *My Great Love Affair*	7.00	-	10.00
(Note: All of above exist as red vinyl pressings,			
which command substantially higher prices.)			
FOUR BROTHERS & A COUSIN:			
Jaguar 3005 *Trust In Me*	50.00	-	75.00
FOUR BUDDIES/4 BUDDIES:			
Club-51 105 *Look Out*	75.00	-	100.00
Savoy 769 *I Will Wait*	30.00	-	50.00
779 *Sweet Slumber*	30.00	-	50.00
789 *My Summer's Gone*	50.00	-	75.00
817 *Heart And Soul*	50.00	-	75.00
823 *Simply Say Goodbye*	50.00	-	75.00
845 *You're Part Of Me*	30.00	-	40.00
866 *What's The Matter With Me*	30.00	-	40.00
888 *My Mother's Eyes*	30.00	-	50.00
891 *I'd Climb The Highest Mountain*	30.00	-	40.00
FOUR CHICKADEES:			
Checker 849 *Teenage Blues*	7.00	-	10.00
FOUR CLIPPERS:			
Fox 960/961 *Rain*	35.00	-	50.00
FOUR COUSINS:			
20th Century 75020 *Time And Time Again*	35.00	-	50.00
THE FOUR CRUISERS:			
Chess 1547 *On Account Of You*	50.00	-	80.00
FOUR DATES:			
Chancellor 1014 *Eloise*	5.00	-	8.00
1019 *I Say Babe*	7.00	-	10.00
1027 *Feel Good*	7.00	-	10.00
FOUR DEUCES:			
Music City 790 *W-P-L-J* (maroon label)	10.00	-	15.00
(Above is found with various flip sides, and			
pressed of colored plastic)			
796 *Down It Went*	10.00	-	15.00
FOUR DOTS:			
Bullseye 103 *Rita*	15.00	-	25.00
104 *Peace Of Mind*	15.00	-	20.00
Freedom 44002 *It's Heaven*	10.00	-	15.00
FOUR DUKES:			
Duke 116 *Crying In The Chapel*	30.00	-	50.00
FOUR ELDORADOS:			
Academy 8138 *Little Susie*		-	
FOUR EPICS:			
Heritage 109 *When The Music Ends*	7.00	-	10.00
Laurie 3155 *Again*	8.00	-	12.00
3183 *Dance, Jo-Ann*	8.00	-	12.00
FOUR FELLOWS:			
Ad Lib 208 *That's Why I Pray*	8.00	-	12.00
Glory 231 *I Know Love*	10.00	-	15.00
234 *Soldier Boy*	5.00	-	8.00
236 *In The Rain*	7.00	-	10.00
244 *I Sit In My Window*	7.00	-	10.00
248 *You Don't Know Me*	7.00	-	10.00
250 *Give Me Back My Broken Heart*	7.00	-	10.00
Pop 0208 *That's Why I Pray*	8.00	-	12.00
FOUR FLICKERS:			
Lee 1002 *Is There A Way*	8.00	-	12.00
FOUR GEMS:			
Broadcast *Outside Of Paradise*	10.00	-	15.00
FOUR GENTS:			
Park 113 *On Bended Knee*	40.00	-	60.00
FOUR GUYS:			
Stride 5001 *Tear Drops From My Eyes*	10.00	-	15.00
FOUR HAVEN KNIGHTS:			
Atlas 1066 *In My Lonely Room*	20.00	-	30.00
1092 *Why Go On Pretending*	20.00	-	30.00
Josie 824 *In My Lonely Room*	8.00	-	12.00
FOUR IMPERIALS:			
Chant 101 *Teen Age Fool*	10.00	-	15.00
Dial 101 *Valley Of Tears*	10.00	-	15.00
Twirl 2005 *Seven Lonely Days*	10.00	-	15.00
4/FOUR J'S:			
Impra 1267/1268 *Class Ring*	—	-	—
Jamie 1267 *Here Am I—Broken Hearted*	8.00	-	12.00
1274 *By Love Possessed*	8.00	-	12.00
United Artists 125 *Rock & Roll Age*	10.00	-	15.00
FOUR JACKS:			
Allen 21000 *I Challenge Your Kiss*	—	-	—
Federal 12075 *You Met A Fool*	40.00	-	60.00
12087 *I'll Be Home Again*	40.00	-	60.00
Hollywood 1058 *Walking And Crying*	40.00	-	60.00
Pel 601 *I've Waited Long Enough*	—	-	—
Rebel 1313 *I Can't Forget*	15.00	-	20.00
FOUR JOKERS:			
Diamond 3004 *Transfusion*	7.00	-	10.00
Sue 703 *Written In The Stars*	7.00	-	10.00
FOUR KINGS:			
Fortune 807 *Hurry Home Baby*	20.00	-	30.00
811 *You Don't Mean Me Right*	20.00	-	30.00
817 *Do-Li-Op*	20.00	-	30.00
Stomper Time 1163 *Walkin' Along*	—	-	—
FOUR KNIGHTS:			
Capitol (LP) 346 (10") *Spotlight Songs*	50.00	-	75.00
(LP) 346 *Spotlight Songs*	50.00	-	75.00
Capitol (most issues)	4.00	-	7.00
Coral (LP) 57221	40.00	-	60.00
62045 *Foolish Tears*	5.00	-	8.00
FOUR LOVERS:			
Epic 9255 *Pucker Up*	25.00	-	40.00
RCA (EP) 869 *The Four Lovers*	40.00	-	60.00
(EP) 871 *Joyride*	50.00	-	80.00
(LP) 1317 *Joy Ride*	150.00	-	200.00
6518 *The Girl In My Dreams*	6.00	-	9.00
6519 *Honey Love*	6.00	-	9.00
6646 *Lovey Dovey*	7.00	-	10.00
6648 *Never Never*	7.00	-	10.00
6812 *Shake A Hand*	8.00	-	12.00
Night Train (unissued?)	—	-	—
RAY FOURNIA & ROCKING RELS:			
Diamond Disk *Settle Down*	—	-	—

FOUR NOTES:
Blue Key-*I Didn't Mean To Be So Mean* .... 20.00 - 30.00
FOUR PAGES:
Plateau 101 *Autograph Book* .... 7.00 - 10.00
FOUR PALS:
Roulette 4127 *Yours To Possess* .... 7.00 - 10.00
Royal Roost 610 *If I Can't Have The One I Love* . 10.00 - 15.00
    616 *No One Ever Loved Me* .... 10.00 - 15.00
FOUR PEARLS:
Dolton 26 *Look At Me* .... 7.00 - 10.00
FOUR PENNIES:
Brunswick 55304 *You Have No Time To Lose* ... 7.00 - 10.00
Brunswick 55324 *'Tis The Season* .... 7.00 - 10.00
FOUR PHAROAHS:
Ransom 109 *Give Me Your Love* .... 30.00 - 50.00
FOUR PLAID THROATS:
Mercury 70143 *My Inspiration* .... 80.00 - 100.00
FOUR SEASONS:
Gone 5122 *Bermuda* .... 15.00 - 20.00
Vee Jay 576 *Peanuts* .... 10.00 - 15.00
    (EP) 901 *Special Gift from Vee Jay* .... 15.00 - 25.00
THE FOUR SENSATIONS:
Rainbow 157 *Heaven Knows Why* .... -
FOUR SONS:
Linco 1316 *Little Rock* .... 10.00 - 15.00
FOUR SPEEDS:
De Luxe 6070 *I Need You Baby* .... 15.00 - 20.00
FOUR TEENS:
Challenge 59021 *Go Little Go Cat* .... 10.00 - 15.00
FOUR TOPS:
Chess 1623 *Could It Be You* .... 20.00 - 30.00
Riverside (LP) 217 *Jazz Impressions* .... 100.00 - up
Riverside 4534 *Where You Are* .... 15.00 - 20.00
FOUR TROYS:
Freedom 40013 *In The Moonlight* .... 10.00 - 15.00
FOUR TUNES:
Jubilee (LP) 1039 *12 by 4* .... 80.00 - 120.00
Jubilee 5128, 5132, 5135, 5152, 5165, 5174, 5183,
    5200, 5212, 5218, 5232, 5239, 5245, 5255,
    5276 .... 4.00 - 8.00
RCA Victor 3967 *Cool Water* .... 7.00 - 10.00
    4102 *Wishing You Were Here Tonight* .... 8.00 - 12.00
    4307 *Early In The Morning* .... 8.00 - 12.00
    4427 *Tell Me Why* .... 8.00 - 12.00
    4489 *Come What May* .... 8.00 - 12.00
    4663 *I Wonder* .... 8.00 - 12.00
    4828 *They Don't Understand* .... 8.00 - 12.00
    4968 *Let's Give Love Another Chance* ...... 8.00 - 12.00
    5532 *Water Boy* .... 7.00 - 10.00
    50-0008 *Careless Love* .... 20.00 - 30.00
    50-0016 *My Last Affair* .... 20.00 - 30.00
    50-0042 *The Lonesome Road* .... 20.00 - 30.00
    (Above three are orange plastic)
    50-0085 *Old Fashioned Love* .... 10.00 - 15.00
    50-0131 *May That Day Never Come* .... 10.00 - 15.00
THE FOUR VAGABONDS:
Lloyds 102 *P.S. I Love You* .... -
FOUR VANES:
Vik 0246 *So Young And So Pretty* .... 10.00 - 15.00
THE FOUR VOICES:
Mr. Peacock 106 *Lovely One* .... -
JIMMY FOWLER:
Dart 118 *Let's Rock & Roll* .... -
THE FOX:
RPM 420 *The Dream* .... 20.00 - 30.00
EUGENE FOX:
Checker 792 *Sinner's Dream* .... 30.00 - 40.00
NORMAN FOX & THE ROB-ROYS:
Back Beat 501 *Tell Me Why* .... 10.00 - 15.00
    508 *My Dearest One* .... 10.00 - 15.00
Capitol 4128 *Pizza Pie* .... 20.00 - 30.00
ORVILLE FOX:

Ellis 101 *Don't Do Me This Way* .... 15.00 - 20.00
STEVE FRANCE:
Renown 110 *Dream Boy* .... 10.00 - 15.00
FRANKIE & JOHNNY:
Liberty 55271 *My First Love* .... 5.00 - 8.00
JOE FRANKLIN:
Renown 113 *Who Put The Pep In The Punch* .... 10.00 - 15.00
TILLMAN FRANKS:
Gotham 6412 *High Tone Poppa* .... 10.00 - 15.00
Pacemaker 1101 *Hayride Boogie* .... 10.00 - 15.00
CALVIN FRAZIER:
Checker 908 *Track Down* .... 7.00 - 10.00
JVB 86 *Have Blues Must Travel* .... 20.00 - 30.00
Savoy 858 *Little Baby Child* .... 7.00 - 10.00
RAY FRAZIER & THE MOONRAYS:
Excell 111 *Days* .... 5.00 - 8.00
    112 *All My Love* .... 5.00 - 8.00
STAN FREBERG:
Capitol (EP) 496 *Any Requests?* .... 8.00 - 12.00
    (LP) 777 *Child's Garden Of Freberg* .... 10.00 - 15.00
    (LP) 1242 *With Original Cast* .... 10.00 - 15.00
    2125, 2279, 2596, 2929 .... 3.00 - 5.00
DOTTY FREDERICK:
20th Fox 115 *Just Wait* .... 7.00 - 10.00
ALAN FREED:
Brunswick (LP) 54043 *The Alan Freed Rock &*
    Roll Show .... 40.00 - 60.00
Coral (LP) 57063 *Rock & Roll Dance Party* .... 30.00 - 40.00
    (LP) 57115 *R & R Dance Party—Vol. 2* .... 30.00 - 40.00
    (LP) 57177 *TV Record Hop* .... 20.00 - 30.00
    (LP) 57213 *Rock Around The Block* .... 15.00 - 20.00
Coral 61626 *Right Now, Right Now* .... 7.00 - 10.00
    61714 *Rock 'N' Roll Boogie* .... 7.00 - 10.00
BOBBY FREEMAN:
Jubilee (LP) 1086 *Do You Wanna Dance* .... 30.00 - 40.00
ERNIE FREEMAN:
Imperial 5474 *Raunchy* (78 rpm) .... 7.00 - 10.00
    5486 *The Tuttle* (78 rpm) .... 5.00 - 8.00
DON FRENCH:
Lancer 104 *Lonely Saturday Night* .... 7.00 - 10.00
    105 *Little Blond Girl* .... 7.00 - 10.00
HAL FRITZ & HIS PLAYBOYS:
Soma 1089 *Three Bad Habits* .... 30.00 - 40.00
LEFTY FRIZZELL:
Columbia (LP) 9019 *Sings Jimmy Rodgers Songs* . 15.00 - 20.00
    (LP) 9021 *Listen To Lefty* .... 15.00 - 20.00
FRANK FROST:
Jewel 765, 771, 778 .... 4.00 - 7.00
Phillips Int. (LP) 197 *Hey Boss Man* .... 80.00 - 120.00
BOBBY FULLER:
Exeter 124 *I Fought The Law* .... 10.00 - 15.00
Yucca 140 *You're In Love* .... 8.00 - 12.00
    144 *My Heart Jumped* .... 7.00 - 10.00
JERRY FULLER:
Challenge 59085 *Anna From Louisiana* .... 5.00 - 8.00
LIN 5011 *Blue Memories* .... 8.00 - 12.00
    5012 *Teenage Love* .... 8.00 - 12.00
    5015 *A Certain Smile* .... 8.00 - 12.00
    5016 *The Door Is Open* .... 8.00 - 12.00
    5019 *Lipstick And Rouge* .... 10.00 - 15.00
JESSE FULLER:
Cavalier (LP) 5006 (10") *Frisco Bound* .... 40.00 - 60.00
    (LP) 6009 *Frisco Bound* .... 50.00 - 75.00
JOHNNIE FULLER:
Irma 110 *First Stage Of The Blues* .... 10.00 - 15.00
JOHNNY FULLER:
Aladdin 3278 *Johnny Ace's Last Letter* .... 15.00 - 20.00
Flair 1054 *Hard Times* .... 10.00 - 15.00
Hollywood 1043 *Train, Train Blues* .... 12.00 - 18.00
    1057 *Mean Old World* .... 10.00 - 15.00
    1063 *Roughest Place In Town* .... 10.00 - 15.00
    1077 *Too Late To Change* .... 10.00 - 15.00

1084 *I Can't Succeed*	10.00	-	15.00
Money 206 *These Young Girls*	7.00	-	10.00
Rhythm 1767 *Fool's Paradise*	15.00	-	25.00
1773 *Train, Train Blues*	15.00	-	20.00
1777 *Lovin' Lovin' Man*	15.00	-	20.00
1779 *Mean Old World*	15.00	-	20.00
1782 *Johnny Ace's Last Letter*	15.00	-	20.00
Specialty 655 *Haunted House*	5.00	-	8.00

LOWELL FULSOM/FULSON:

Aladdin 3217 *Chuck With The Boys*	10.00	-	15.00
3233 *You've Got To Reap*	10.00	-	15.00
Checker 804 *Reconsider Baby*	7.00	-	10.00
812 *Check Yourself*	7.00	-	10.00
820 *Lonely Hours*	7.00	-	10.00
829 *Trouble Trouble*	7.00	-	10.00
841, 854, 865, 882	5.00	-	8.00
937, 952, 959, 972, 992, 1027, 1046	4.00	-	8.00
Hollywood 1022 *Lonesome Christmas*	8.00	-	12.00
1029 *Guitar Shuffle*	8.00	-	12.00
1103 *Guitar Shuffle*	5.00	-	8.00
Kent (LP) 5016 *Lowell Fulsom*	15.00	-	20.00
(LP) 5020 *Lowell Fulsom*	15.00	-	20.00
Swing Time 289 *Best Wishes*	20.00	-	30.00
295 *Guitar Shuffle*	20.00	-	30.00
391 *The Highway Is My Home*	20.00	-	30.00
308 *Black Widow Spider*	20.00	-	30.00
315 *Raggedy Daddy Blues*	20.00	-	30.00
320 *Good Party Shuffle*	15.00	-	20.00
325 *Upstairs*	15.00	-	20.00
330 *I Love My Baby*	12.00	-	16.00
335 *Cash Box Boogie*	12.00	-	16.00
338 *Juke Box Shuffle*	12.00	-	16.00

SONNY FULTON:

Hit 1133/1144 *Pardon Me Baby (Did I Hear You Right)*		-	

FURNESS BROTHERS:

Melmar 114 *Only Fate*	7.00	-	10.00
116 *Please Don't Call Me Fool*	7.00	-	10.00

GADABOUTS:

Wing 90008 *Two Things I Have*		-	

BOB GADDY (& HIS ALLEY CATS/KEYS):

Harlem 2330 *Slow Down Baby*	30.00	-	50.00
Jax 308 *Little Girl's Boogie*	30.00	-	50.00
(Note: Above, pressed on red vinyl, command higher prices)			
Old Town 1031, 1039, 1050, 1057, 1064, 1070, 1077, 1085	3.00	-	5.00

GAIL TONES:

Decca 30726 *Lover Boy*	8.00	-	12.00

EDDIE GAINES & HIS ROCKIN' FIVE:

Summit 101 *Be Bop Battlin' Ball*	50.00	-	75.00

ROY GAINES:

De Luxe 6119 *Gainesville*	7.00	-	10.00
6132 *You're Right I'm Left*	7.00	-	10.00
Groove 0146 *Right Now Baby*	10.00	-	15.00

GENE GAITHER:

Astro 232 *Cute Little Chicky*		-	

GALAXY'S:

Carthay 103 *A Lover's Prayer*	15.00	-	20.00

BARBARA GALE & THE LARKS:

Lloyds 111 *When You're Near*	30.00	-	40.00

GALES:

J.O.B. 3001 *Darling Patricia*	100.00	-	150.00
JVB 34 *My Eyes Keep Me In Trouble*	100.00	-	150.00
JVB 35 *Darling Patricia*	100.00	-	150.00

JAMES GALLAGHER:

Decca 29984 *Crazy Chicken*	8.00	-	12.00

JAY GALLAGHER:

Dixie 2023 *Steady Flame*	10.00	-	15.00

THE GALLAHADS:

Jubilee 5252 *The Fool*	5.00	-	8.00
Starla 15 *Keeper Of Dreams*	8.00	-	12.00

BOB GALLION:

MGM 12195 *My Square Dancin' Mamma*	15.00	-	20.00

CECIL GANT:

Sound (LP) 601 *The Incomparable Cecil Gant*	50.00	-	75.00

DAVE GARDNER:

OJ 1002 *White Silver Sands* (78 rpm)	7.00	-	10.00

CLARENCE (BON TON) GARLOW:

Aladdin 3179 *New Bon Ton Roula*	30.00	-	40.00
3325 *I'm Hurt*	15.00	-	20.00
Feature 3005 *I Called You Up Daddy*	15.00	-	20.00
Flair 1021 *Crawfishin'*	15.00	-	20.00
Folk Star 1130 *Made Me Cry*	15.00	-	20.00
1199 *No, No Baby*	15.00	-	20.00
Goldband 1043 *Sundown*	10.00	-	15.00
1065 *Bon Ton Roule*	10.00	-	15.00

BILLY GARNER:

Mojo 2171 *Little Schoolgirl*	5.00	-	8.00

GABBY GARNER:

Erald 2052 *Smokin' Heart*	20.00	-	30.00

JOHNNY GARNER:

Imperial 5536 *Kiss Me Sweet*	15.00	-	20.00
5548 *Didi Didi*	15.00	-	20.00

JIM GARNETT:

Manco 1029 *I Could Be Had*	7.00	-	10.00

BOBBY GARRETT:

E & M 1602 *Short Skirts*	5.00	-	8.00

ROBERT GARRETT:

Excello 2216 *Quit My Drinkin'*	7.00	-	10.00

GLEN GARRISON (& THE NOTE KINGS):

Crest 1047 *Lovin' Lorene*	15.00	-	20.00
Lode 106 *Pony Tail Girl*	12.00	-	18.00

JIMMY GARTIN:

Hi-Q 5014 *Gonna Ride That Satellite*	8.00	-	12.00

GASSERS:

Cash 1035 *Tell Me*	10.00	-	15.00
Encino 1011 *Dody Mighty*		-	

DAVE/DAVID GATES (& THE ACCENTS):

Del-Fi 4206 *You Had It Comin' To You*	7.00	-	10.00
East West 123 *Swingin' Baby Doll*	15.00	-	20.00
Mala 413 *What's This I Hear*	7.00	-	10.00
418 *The Happiest Man Alive*	5.00	-	8.00
427 *Teardrops In My Heart*	5.00	-	8.00
Robbins 1008 *Lovin' At Night*	15.00	-	20.00

GATORVETTES:

Thunder 1001 *It It's Tonight*	10.00	-	15.00

DEE DEE GAUDET:

Dodge 805 *Where's The Law*	7.00	-	10.00

DEE DEE GAUDET:

Dodge 805 *Where's The Law*	7.00	-	10.00

TONY GAVIN:

Sims 165 *It's Never Seven Or Eleven*	7.00	-	10.00

BOBBY GAY & THE SPARKLETONES:

Mida 104 *You're Nice*	7.00	-	10.00

GAY KNIGHTS:

Pet 801 *Angel*	7.00	-	10.00

GAY LARKS:

Music City 792 *Tell Me Darling*	15.00	-	20.00
793 *Lil Dream Girl*	15.00	-	20.00
809 *Church On The Hill*	20.00	-	30.00
812 *Somewhere In This World*	15.00	-	20.00
819 *Ivy League Clothes*	10.00	-	15.00

THE GAYLES:

ABC Paramount 9707 *You Fool*		-	

BILLY GAYLES:

Federal 12265 *I'm Tore Up*	8.00	-	12.00

GAY NOTES:

Drexel 905 *For Only A Moment*	50.00	-	80.00
Post 2006 *Hear My Plea*	20.00	-	30.00
Zynn 504 *Plea Of Love*		-	

THE GAY POPPERS:

Fire 1024 *I Want To Know*	8.00	-	12.00
Savoy 1573 *I Need Your Love*	7.00	-	10.00

GAY TUNES:
Joyce 101 *I Love You* . . . . 10.00 - 15.00
Timely 1002 *Thrill OF Romance* . . . . 40.00 - 60.00

GAZELLES:
Gotham 315 *Honest* . . . . 30.00 - 40.00

THE G-GLEFS:
Paris 502 *Symbol Of Love* . . . . 10.00 - 15.00
506 *Zing Zang Zoo* . . . . 10.00 - 15.00
Pilgrim 715 *Ka-Ding-Dong* . . . . 5.00 - 8.00
715 *Ka-Ding-Dong (78 RPM)* . . . . 15.00 - 20.00
720 *'Cause You're Mine* . . . . 7.00 - 10.00
Terrace 7500 *I Understand (Just How You Feel)* . . 10.00 - 15.00
7503 *A Girl Has To Know* . . . . 10.00 - 15.00
7507 *Make Up Your Mind* . . . . 10.00 - 15.00
7510 *Sitting in the Moonlight* . . . . 10.00 - 15.00
7514 *All My Trials* . . . . 10.00 - 15.00

GEMS:
Drexel 901 *Talk About The Weather* (red plastic) . 100.00 - 150.00
903 *I Thought You'd Care* . . . . 125.00 - 175.00
904 *You're Tired Of Love* . . . . 150.00 - 200.00
915 *Till The Day I Die* . . . . 100.00 - 150.00
Recorte 407 *Please Change Your Mind* . . . . 10.00 - 15.00

GENE & EUNICE:
Combo 64 *Ko Ko Mo* . . . . 8.00 - 12.00
Score (LP) 4018 *Rock & Roll Sock Hop* . . . . . . 100.00 - 150.00

GENIES:
Hollywood 69 *No More Knockin'* . . . . -

SONNY GENO:
Rip 130 *Rumble Rock* . . . . 8.00 - 12.00

J.C. GENT:
Marlo 1501 *Bad Gal Blues* . . . . 5.00 - 10.00

GENTLEMEN:
Apollo 464 *Tired Of You* . . . . 15.00 - 20.00
470 *Baby Don't Go* . . . . 15.00 - 20.00

BILL GENTRY:
Universal Artist 1001 *Baby What' Ya Say* . . . . . . 15.00 - 20.00

GEORGE & EARL:
Dixie *Done Gone* . . . . 20.00 - 30.00
Mercury 70605 *Got Anything Good?* . . . . 4.00 - 7.00
70632 *Goin' Steady* . . . . 8.00 - 12.00
70683 *Don't Don't Don't* . . . . 5.00 - 8.00
70852 *Done Gone* . . . . 7.00 - 10.00

BARBARA GEORGE:
A.F.O. (LP) 5001 *I Know* . . . . 20.00 - 30.00

LLOYD GEORGE:
Imperial 5837 *Lucy Lee* . . . . 5.00 - 8.00
Post 1006 *Come On Train* . . . . 5.00 - 8.00

THE GEORGETTES:
Ebb 125 *Love Like A Fool* . . . . 5.00 - 8.00

RAY GERDSEN:
Bye Bye Baby . . . . -

GEORGIA GIBBS:
RCA Victor 7098 *Great Balls Of Fire* . . . . 5.00 - 8.00

DADDYO GIBSON:
Checker 848 *Night Train* . . . . 5.00 - 8.00

DON GIBSON:
MGM 12393 *I'm Gonna Fool Everybody* . . . . . . 7.00 - 10.00
12494 *I Ain't A-Studyin' You Baby* . . . . 7.00 - 10.00
RCA Victor (LP) 1743 *Lonesome Me* . . . . 15.00 - 20.00
(LP) 1918, 2038 . . . . 10.00 - 15.00
48-0424 *Carolina Breakdown* . . . . 10.00 - 15.00
(Note: Above is made of translucent green
plastic.)

GRANDDADDY GIBSON:
Bobbin 124 *I Don't Want No Woman* . . . . 15.00 - 20.00
127 *The Monkey Likes To Boogie* . . . . 15.00 - 20.00

JOE D. GIBSON:
Tetra 4450 *Good Morning Captain* . . . . 10.00 - 15.00

STEVE GIBSON & THE RED CAPS:
Jay Dee 796 *It Hurts Me But I Like It* . . . . 7.00 - 10.00
Mercury (LP) 25116 (10″) . . . . 30.00 - 50.00
RCA Victor (Most issues) . . . . 4.00 - 8.00

Rose 5534 *I Miss You So* . . . . 5.00 - 8.00

DARLENE GILLESPIE:
Disneyland (LP) 3010 *Darlene Of The Teens* . . . 30.00 - 40.00

MICKEY GILLEY:
Astro (LP) 101 *Lonely Wine* . . . . 125.00 - 175.00
102 *Down The Line* . . . . 10.00 - 15.00
103 *Is It Wrong* . . . . 10.00 - 15.00
104 *Susie-Q* . . . . 15.00 - 20.00
106 *Lotta Lovin'* . . . . 15.00 - 20.00
110 *A Certain Smile* . . . . 15.00 - 20.00
112 *Little Egypt* . . . . 15.00 - 20.00
Astro 5002 *Don't Throw A Good Love Away* . . 10.00 - 15.00
10003 *She Called Me Baby* . . . . 10.00 - 15.00
Daryl 101 *What Have I Done* . . . . 7.00 - 10.00
Dot 15706 *Call Me Shorty* . . . . 30.00 - 40.00
Eric 7021 *Whole Lot Of Twistin' Goin On* . . . . . 7.00 - 10.00
Khoury's 712 *Drive-In Movie* . . . . 50.00 - 75.00
Lynn 503 *Your Selfish Pride* . . . . 10.00 - 15.00
508 *My Baby's Been Cheating Again* . . . . 10.00 - 15.00
512 *Slippin' And Slidin'* . . . . 15.00 - 20.00
515 *My Babe* . . . . 15.00 - 20.00
Minor 106 *Ooh Wee Baby* . . . . 100.00 - 150.00
Potomac 901 *No Greater Love* . . . . 8.00 - 12.00
Princess 4004 *Drive In Movie* . . . . 10.00 - 15.00
4006 *Caught in the Middle* . . . . 10.00 - 15.00
4011 *I'll Keep On Dreaming* . . . . 10.00 - 15.00
4015 *World Of My Own* . . . . 15.00 - 20.00
Sabra 518 *Valley Of Tears* . . . . 10.00 - 15.00
San 1513 *I Ain't No Bo Diddley* . . . . 15.00 - 20.00
Supreme 101 *Now That I Have You* . . . . 10.00 - 15.00
No One Wlll Ever Know . . . . -

EARL GILLIAM:
Ivory 343 *Just You And I* . . . . 5.00 - 8.00
Sarg 128 *Nobody' Blues* . . . . 10.00 - 15.00
133 *Wrong Doing Woman* . . . . 10.00 - 15.00

JAZZ GILLUM:
Groove 5002 *Key To The Highway* . . . . 8.00 - 12.00
RCA Victor 50-0004 *Signifying Woman* . . . . . . 20.00 - 30.00
50-0017 *Look What You Are Today* . . . . 20.00 - 30.00
50-0035 *A Lie Is Dangerous* . . . . 20.00 - 30.00
(Note: Above are made of orange plastic)

LOU GIORDANO:
Brunswick 55115 *Stay Close To Me* . . . . 30.00 - 50.00

WILD CHILD GIPSON:
Hit 2002 *Uncle John* . . . . 20.00 - 30.00

THE GLADIOLAS:
Excello 2101 *Little Darlin'* . . . . 8.00 - 12.00
2120 *I Wanta Know* . . . . 10.00 - 15.00

GLAD RAGS:
Excello 2121 *My China Doll* . . . . 10.00 - 15.00

BILLY GLASSER:
Ozark 1236 *I Left The Dance* . . . . 10.00 - 15.00

DICK GLASSER:
Argo 5279 *Crazy Love (ship logo)* . . . . 8.00 - 12.00
5283 *Go Along baby* . . . . 7.00 - 10.00
Columbia 41472 *Crazy Alligator* . . . . 8.00 - 12.00

DARRELL GLENN:
Valley 105 *Crying In The Chapel* . . . . 7.00 - 10.00
109 *Only A Pastime* . . . . 3.00 - 5.00

GLEN GLENN:
Dore 523 *Goofin' Around* . . . . 8.00 - 12.00
Era 1061 *Everybody's Movin'* . . . . 10.00 - 15.00
1074 *One Cup Of Coffee* . . . . 10.00 - 15.00

THE GLENNS:
Rendezvous 118 *In The Chapel* . . . . 10.00 - 15.00

GLITTERS:
Rubaiyat 413 *You Don't Know* . . . . 10.00 - 15.00

THE G NOTES:
Tender 510 *Ronnie* . . . .

GO BOYS: (See also DUDLEY CALLICUTT)
"DC" 0418 *Flippin'* . . . . 15.00 - 20.00

THE GO-CARTS:

Hope 1003 *Rockin' Liza*	-	

"GO, JOHNNY, GO" (Soundtrack):
(with Chuck Berry, Eddie Cochran, Jimmy
Clanton, The Cadillacs, Richie Valens, et al.

No designation of issuing record company) ...100.00	-	Up

GOLDEN GATE QUARTET:

Camden (LP) 308	15.00	-	20.00
Columbia (LP) 6102 (10″)	30.00	-	50.00
Harmony (LP) 7018 *That Golden Chariot*	30.00	-	50.00
Mercury 5385 *Didn't That Man Believe* ...	7.00	-	10.00
Mercury (LP) 25063 (10″) *Look Up!*	75.00	-	100.00

GOLDEN RODS:

Vee Jay 307 *Wish I Was Back In School*	8.00	-	12.00

GOLDENTONES:

Hush 102 *Ocean Of Tears*	10.00	-	15.00
Jay-Dee 806 *The Meaning Of Love*	10.00	-	15.00
Lifetime 1004 *Stand By Me*	10.00	-	15.00
Samson 107 *I'm Wrong*	15.00	-	25.00

GOOD JELLY BESS:

Hermitage 775 *Come And Get It*	5.00	-	8.00

DICKIE GOODMAN:

Mark-X 8009 *The Touchables*	5.00	-	8.00
8010 *The Touchables In Brooklyn*	5.00	-	8.00
Rori (LP) 3301 *The Many Heads Of Dickie*			
Goodman	30.00	-	50.00
701 *Santa And The Touchables*	7.00	-	10.00

GOOD ROCKIN' BOB:

Goldband 1067 *Take It Easy Katy*	15.00	-	20.00

GOOD ROCKIN' SAMMY T.:

Junior 500 *Good Rockin' Mama*	30.00	-	50.00

HAL GOODSON:

Solo 108 *Who's Gonna Be The Next One Honey* .	10.00	-	15.00

BILL GOODWIN:

Star-*Teenage Blues*	-	

THE GOOFERS:

Coral 61383 *Flip Flop And Fly*	7.00	-	10.00
61650 *Tennessee Rock And Roll*	7.00	-	10.00
61664 *I'm Gonna Rock & Roll Till I Die*	7.00	-	10.00

CURTIS GORDON:

Mercury 70861 *Draggin'*	8.00	-	12.00
71037 *So Tied of Crying*	7.00	-	10.00
71097 *Out To Win Your Heart*	7.00	-	10.00
71121 *Sixteen*	8.00	-	12.00
71183 *Please Baby Please*	8.00	-	12.00
RCA Victor 5356 *Rompin' And Stompin'*	8.00	-	12.00

MIKE GORDON & THE EL TEMPOS:

Cat 101 *Why Don't You Do Right?*	5.00	-	8.00

ROSCO/ROSCOE GORDON:

Duke 109 *Too Many Women*	15.00	-	20.00
114 *Ain't No Use*	15.00	-	20.00
Flip 227 *Weeping Blues*	30.00	-	40.00
237 *The Chicken*	7.00	-	10.00
RPM 350 *No More Doggin'*	15.00	-	20.00
365 *Two Kinds Of Women*	15.00	-	20.00
Sun 227 *Weeping Blues*	50.00	-	75.00

SONNY GORDON & THE ANGELS:

Grand 115 *Wedding Bells Are Ringing*	20.00	-	30.00

STOMP GORDON:

Decca 48287 *Fat Mama Blues*	15.00	-	20.00

CHARLIE GORE:

Audio Lab (LP) 1526 *Country Gentleman*	20.00	-	30.00

JACKIE GOTROE:

Rhythm 111 *Raised On Rock & Roll*	75.00	-	100.00
Rhythm 1024 *Rock It To The Moon*	75.00	-	100.00
Vortex 102 *Lobo Jones*	30.00	-	40.00

SAMMY GOWANS:

United Artists 114 *Rockin' By Myself*	15.00	-	20.00

CHARLIE GRACIE:

Cadillac *No Sin In Rhythm*	-		
141 *Boogie Boogie Blues*	15.00	-	20.00
144 *Rockin' An' Rollin'*	20.00	-	30.00
Cameo 105 *Butterfly* (78 rpm)	10.00	-	15.00

111 *Wanderin' Eyes* (78 rpm)	10.00	-	15.00
111, 118, 127	5.00	-	8.00
Town & Country 5033 *My Baby Loves Me*	15.00	-	20.00
5035 *Wildwood Boogie*	15.00	-	20.00
20th Century 5033 *My Baby Loves Me*	15.00	-	20.00
5035 *Wildwood Boogie*	15.00	-	20.00

LOU GRAHAM:

Coral 61931 *Wee Willie Brown*	7.00	-	10.00

BILLY GRAMMER:

Monument (LP) 40000 *Travelin' On*	35.00	-	50.00

GERRY GRANAHAN:

Sunbeam 108 *Baby Wait*	5.00	-	8.00

O.S. GRANT AND THE DOWNBEATS:
(See also DOWNBEATS)

Sarg 200 *You Did Me Wrong*	7.00	-	10.00

JUNIOR GRAVELY:

Velatone 796 *Take My Hands*	5.00	-	8.00

ARVELLA GRAY:

Gray 13, 14, 100	5.00	-	8.00

BILLY GRAY:

Decca 29800 *Tennessee Toddy*	7.00	-	10.00

CLAUDE GRAY:

Minor 109 *Barricade*	20.00	-	30.00

PHIL GRAY:

Robbins 1002 *Somebody's Got My Baby*	15.00	-	20.00

RUDY GRAY:

Capitol 2946, 3044, 3149	5.00	-	8.00

RUDY GRAYZELL:

Abbott 145, 147, 157	5.00	-	8.00
Starday 229 *The Moon Is Up*	10.00	-	15.00
241 *Duck Tail*	15.00	-	20.00
270 *Jig-Ga-Lee-Ga*	20.00	-	30.00
321 *Let's Get Wild*	20.00	-	30.00
Sun 290 *Judy*	7.00	-	10.00

"THE GREATEST ROCK & ROLL"

Atlantic (LP) 8001 (various artists)	20.00	-	30.00

"THE GREATEST WESTERN HITS"

Columbia (LP) 1257, 1408	8.00	-	12.00

BOBBY GREEN:

Oak 4429/4430 *Little Heart Attacks*	50.00	-	75.00

GEORGE GREEN:

Chance 1135 *Brand New Rockin' Chair*	15.00	-	20.00

LIL GREEN:

Groove 5004 *Why Don't You Do Right*	7.00	-	10.00

RUDY GREEN:

Excello 2074 *Cool Lovin' Mama*	20.00	-	30.00
2090 *Teeny Weeny Baby*	20.00	-	30.00

(GUITAR) SLIM GREEN:

Canton 1789 *Shake 'Em Up*	8.00	-	12.00
Dig 142 *My Woman Done Quit Me*	7.00	-	10.00
Geenote 907 *Rock The Nation*	8.00	-	12.00

VERNON GREEN & THE MEDALLIONS:

Dooto 446 *Magic Mountain*	10.00	-	15.00
Dootone 407 *Did You Have Fun?*	10.00	-	15.00

RUDY GREENE (& THE 4 BUDDIES):

Club 51 103 *You Mean Everything To Me*	75.00	-	100.00
Ember 1012 *Juicy Fruit*	20.00	-	30.00

LIL GREENWOOD (& THE FOUR JACKS):

Federal 12093 *Grandpa Can Boogie Too*	40.00	-	60.00
12158 *I'll Go*	20.00	-	30.00

**(BIG) JOHN GREER (& HIS RHYTHM
ROCKERS):**

Groove 0119 *Come Back Maybelline*	7.00	-	10.00
RCA Victor 5375 *Rhythm In The Breeze*	8.00	-	12.00
50-0007 *Drinkin' Wine, Spo-Dee-O-Dee*	20.00	-	30.00
50-0029 *I Found A Dream*	15.00	-	20.00
50-0051 *Rockin' Jenny Jones*	15.00	-	20.00
50-0096 *Cheatin'*	15.00	-	20.00
(Note: Above are orange plastic)			
50-0108, 50-0113, 50-10125, 50-0137	7.00	-	10.00

CHUCK GREY & THE PANICS:

Fable 616 *Push The Panic Button*	10.00	-	15.00

GRIFFIN BROS.:

Dot 1117 *Slow And Mellow*	30.00	-	50.00
1145 *My Baby's Done Me Wrong*	20.00	-	30.00
1152 *Fare Thee Well Pretty Baby*	20.00	-	30.00
1171 *Move It On Over*	15.00	-	20.00

(Note: Numbers lower than the above, i.e. earlier issues, are usually found as 78 RPM records, which are valued at $5 to $10 each; 45 RPM issues of these earlier numbers would be valued at $30 to $50.00, or higher, particularly if pressed of colored vinyl.)

BUCK GRIFFIN:

Holiday Inn 109 *Pretty Lou*	7.00	-	10.00
Lin 1005 *It Don't Make No Never Mind*	15.00	-	20.00
1007 *Rollin' Tears*	7.00	-	10.00
1008 *Going Home, All Alone*	7.00	-	10.00
1014 *Next To Mine*	7.00	-	10.00
1015 *Ballin' And Squallin'*	30.00	-	40.00
1016 *Cochise*	7.00	-	10.00
1018 *Neither Do I*	7.00	-	10.00
Metro 20007 *The Party*	10.00	-	15.00
MGM 12284 *Stutterin' Papa*	20.00	-	30.00
12439 *Bow My Back*	20.00	-	30.00
12597 *Jessie Lee*	20.00	-	30.00

CURLEY GRIFFIN:

Atomic 303 *You Gotta Play Fair*	15.00	-	20.00
305 *Got Rockin' On My Mind*	20.00	-	30.00

GRIFFINS:

Mercury 70558 *I Swear By All The Stars Above*	20.00	-	30.00
70650 *Scheming*	20.00	-	30.00
70913 *My Baby's Gone*	15.00	-	20.00
Wing 90067 *Forever More*	20.00	-	30.00

JOE GRIFFITH & HIS TEENAGE REBELS:

Reelfoot 1250 *Crazy Sack*	10.00	-	15.00

PEGGY GRIFFITH:

Now 1008 *Rockin' The Blues*		-	

SANDRA GRIMES:

Red Robin 129 *You Didn't*		-	

TINY GRIMES:

Red Robin 123 *Juicy Fruit*	7.00	-	10.00

BIG GOY GROVES:

Money 217 *Traffic Ticket*	7.00	-	10.00
Spark 114 *I Gotta New Car*	10.00	-	15.00
Vita 120 *You Can't Beat The Horses*	8.00	-	12.00

CARL GROVES:

Musicale 116 *Canteen Baby*		-	
MAV 468 *Let's Rock Tonight*	30.00	-	50.00

DON GUESS:

Brunswick 55101 *Shirl-Lee*	8.00	-	12.00

DANNY GUGLIELMI:

Encino 1001 *Hotrod*		-	

THE GUIDES:

Guyden 2023 *You Must Try*	7.00	-	10.00

GUITAR DAVE:

Central 291 *Zoro*	5.00	-	8.00

GUITAR FRANK:

Bridges 2203/2204 *Wild Track*	15.00	-	20.00

GUITAR JR.:

Goldband 1058 *I Got It Made*	10.00	-	15.00
Goldband 1076 *Now You Know*	8.00	-	12.00
Mercury 71602 *Knocks Me Out*	8.00	-	12.00

GUITAR SHORTY (with BOB TATE & HIS ORCH.):

Cobra 5017 *Irma Lee*	15.00	-	20.00
Pull 301 *Hard Life*	10.00	-	15.00
302 *How Long Can It Last*	10.00	-	15.00

GUITAR SLIM:

Atco 6072 *Down Through The Years*	7.00	-	10.00
6097 *If I Should Lose You*	5.00	-	8.00
6108 *I Won't Mind At All*	5.00	-	8.00
6120 *If I Had My Life To Live Over*	5.00	-	8.00
Diamond 204 *Broke And Lonely*	10.00	-	15.00

Imperial 5278 *Cryin' In The Mornin'*	10.00	-	15.00
5310 *Standin' At The Station*	10.00	-	15.00
Specialty 482 *The Things That I Used To Do*	7.00	-	10.00
490 *The Story Of My Life*	7.00	-	10.00
527 *Later For You Baby*	7.00	-	10.00
536 *Sufferin' Mind*	7.00	-	10.00
542 *Stand By Me*	7.00	-	10.00
551 *You're Gonna Miss Me*	7.00	-	10.00
557 *Think It Over*	7.00	-	10.00
569 *You Gave Me Nothin' But The Blues*	7.00	-	10.00
(LP) 2120 *Things That I Used To Do*	50.00	-	80.00

THE GUM DROPS:

King 1496 *Don't Take It So Hard*	10.00	-	15.00
4913 *I Wonder And Wonder*	10.00	-	15.00
4963 *Chapel Of Hearts*	10.00	-	15.00

ARTHUR GUNTER:

Excello 2047 *Baby Let's Play House*	10.00	-	15.00
2053 *She's Mine All Mine*	10.00	-	15.00
2058 *Honey Babe*	15.00	-	20.00
2073 *Baby You Better Listen*	15.00	-	20.00
2084 *Love Has Got Me*	15.00	-	20.00
2125 *Baby Can't You See*	8.00	-	12.00
2137 *We're Gonna Shake*	8.00	-	12.00
2147 *Don't Leave Me Now*	8.00	-	12.00
2164 *I Want Her Back*	8.00	-	12.00
2191 *Mind Your Own Business Babe*	8.00	-	12.00
2201 *My Heart's Always Lonesome*	8.00	-	12.00
2204 *Working For My Baby*	8.00	-	12.00
(LP) 8017 *Black And Blues*	30.00	-	50.00

CORNEL GUNTER:

Eagle 301 *I Want You Madly*	7.00	-	10.00
Liberty 55096 *If We Should Meet Again*	5.00	-	8.00

HARDROCK GUNTER:

Decca 46300 *Boogie Woogie On Saturday Night*	10.00	-	15.00
46350 *I've Done Gone Hog Wild*	10.00	-	15.00
46363 *Sixty Minute Man*	10.00	-	15.00
46367 *Dixieland Boogie*	8.00	-	12.00
King 1505 *I'll Give 'Em Rhythm*	10.00	-	15.00
Sun 201 *Gonna Dance All Night*	50.00	-	80.00

SHIRLEY GUNTER (& THE FLAIRS/QUEENS):

Flair 1050 *Ooop Shoop*	10.00	-	15.00
1060 *You're Mine*	10.00	-	15.00
1070 *That's The Way I Like It*	7.00	-	10.00
1076 *How Can I Tell You*	15.00	-	20.00
Modern 989 *Headin' Home*	7.00	-	10.00

BUDDY GUY (& HIS BAND):

Artistic 1501, 1503	7.00	-	10.00
Chess 1735, 1759, 1784, 1812, 1838, 1878	5.00	-	8.00

GUYTONES:

De Luxe 6114 *You Won't Let Me Go*	10.00	-	15.00
6159 *This Is Love*	10.00	-	15.00
6169 *Tell Me*	10.00	-	15.00

GYPSIES:

Atlas 1073 *Why*	15.00	-	20.00
Groove 0137 *Rockin' Pretty Baby*	7.00	-	10.00

WAYNE HAAS:

Choice 5607 *Betty Ann*	10.00	-	15.00

VELINE HACKERT:

Brunswick 55151 *Show Me How*	8.00	-	12.00

JIM HADLEY:

Buddy 117 *Midnight Train*	20.00	-	30.00

SAM HAGAN:

Capitol 3818 *Don't Cry*	7.00	-	10.00
3885 *Tail-Light*	7.00	-	10.00

DON HAGER:

Oak 0357 *Bebop Boogie*	50.00	-	75.00
0358 *Little Liza Jane Bop*	50.00	-	75.00

JAY HAGGARD:

Daja 503 *Tom Cat*	15.00	-	20.00

MERLE HAGGARD:

Tally 155, 178, 179	7.00	-	10.00

JIMMY HAGGETT:

Caprock 107 *All I Have Is Love*	7.00 -	10.00
Meteor 5043 *Gonna Shut Off Baby*	50.00 -	75.00
Sun 236 *They Call Our Love A Sin*	100.00 -	150.00
Vaden 116 *Don't Let Me Go*	10.00 -	15.00

RONNIE HAIG:

ABC Paramount 9912 *Traveler Of Love*	10.00 -	15.00
Note 10014 *Rocking With Rhythm And Blues*	10.00 -	15.00

REX HALE:

Rhythm 303 *Down At The Big Mama's House*	— -	—

BILL HALEY AND/WITH (HIS/THE COMETS/SADDLEMEN):

APT 25087 *Tongue-Tied Tony*	8.00 -	12.00
Atlantic 727 *I'm Gonna Dry Ev'ry Tear With A Kiss* (78 RPM)	100.00 -	150.00
Center 102 *Stand Up And Be Counted* (78 RPM)	— -	—
Cowboy 1202 *Candy Kissses* (78 RPM)	— -	—
1203 *Yodel Your Blues Away* (78 RPM)	— -	—
1204 *Behind The 8-Ball* (78 RPM)	— -	—
1700 *Four Leaf Clover Blues* (78 RPM)	— -	—
1701 *My Palomino And I* (78 RPM)	— -	—
1705 *Four Leaf Clover Blues* (78 RPM)	— -	—
Decca (EP) 2168 *Shake, Rattle And Roll*	20.00 -	30.00
(EP) 2209 *Dim, Dim The Lights*	20.00 -	30.00
(EP) 2322 *Rock 'N' Roll*	20.00 -	30.00
(EP) 2398, 2399, 2400 *He Digs Rock 'N' Roll*	15.00 -	25.00
(EP) 2416, 2417, 2418 *Rock 'N' Roll Stage Show*	15.00 -	20.00
(EP) 2532 *Rockin' The Oldies*	15.00 -	20.00
(EP) 2564 *Rockin' Around The World*	15.00 -	20.00
(EP) 2615, 2616 *Rockin' The Joint*	20.00 -	30.00
(EP) 2670 *Bill Haley & His Comets*	20.00 -	30.00
(EP) 2671 *Top Teen Hits*	20.00 -	30.00
(LP) 5560 (10") *Shake, Rattle And Roll*	100.00 -	150.00
(LP) 8225 *Rock Around The Clock*	50.00 -	75.00
(LP) 8315 *He Digs Rock 'N' Roll*	30.00 -	40.00
(LP) 8345 *Rock 'N' Roll Stage Show*	30.00 -	40.00
(LP) 8569 *Rockin' The Oldies*	30.00 -	40.00
(LP) 8655 *Let's Have A Party*	30.00 -	40.00
(LP) 8692 *Rockin' Around The World*	20.00 -	30.00
(LP) 8775 *Rockin' The Joint*	30.00 -	40.00
Decca 29124 *Rock Around The Clock* (black label)	7.00 -	10.00
29124 *Rock Around The Clock* (DJ copy)	10.00 -	15.00
Decca (most other issues)	4.00 -	8.00
Essex (EP) 102 *Bill Haley's Dance Party*	50.00 -	75.00
(EP) 117, 118 *Rock With Bill Haley And The Comets*	50.00 -	75.00
(LP) 202 *Rock With Bill Haley And The Comets*	100.00 -	150.00
303 *Rock The Joint*	15.00 -	20.00
305 *Rocking Chair On The Moon*	15.00 -	20.00
310 *Real Rock Drive*	15.00 -	20.00
321 *Crazy Man Crazy*	15.00 -	20.00
327 *Fractured*	10.00 -	15.00
332 *Live It Up*	10.00 -	15.00
340 *I'll Be True*	10.00 -	15.00
348 *Straight Jacket*	15.00 -	20.00
374 *Sundown Boogie*	20.00 -	30.00
381 *Rocket 88*	20.00 -	30.00
399 *Rock The Joint*	10.00 -	15.00
Gone 5116 *War Paint*	10.00 -	15.00
Holiday 105 *Rocket 88*	100.00 -	150.00
108 *Green Tree Boogie*	100.00 -	150.00
110 *Pretty Baby*	100.00 -	150.00
111 *A Year Ago This Christmas*	100.00 -	150.00
113 *Jukebox Cannonball*	100.00 -	150.00
Keystone 5101 *Deal Me A Hand* (78 RPM)	150.00 -	Up
5102 *I'm Not To Blame* (78 RPM)	150.00 -	Up
Radioactive 45 *Rock The Joint*	— -	—
46 *Rock-A-Beatin' Boogie*	— -	—
50 *Crazy Man Crazy*	— -	—
Someset (LP) *Rock with Billy Haley*	30.00 -	50.00

Transworld (LP) 202	— -	—
318 *Rocket 88*	30.00 -	50.00
718 *Yes Indeed*	15.00 -	25.00
Warner Bros. (LP) 1378 *Comets*	30.00 -	40.00
Warner Bros. 5145 *Candy Kisses*	8.00 -	12.00
5154 *Chick Safari*	7.00 -	10.00
5171 *So Right Tonight*	7.00 -	10.00
5228 *Flip, Flop And Fly*	7.00 -	10.00

HALL BROTHERS:

Arc 4444 *My White Convertible*	8.00 -	12.00

BOBBY HALL & THE KINGS:

Harlem 2322 *Fire In My Heart* (red plastic)	100.00 -	150.00
2322 *Fire In My Heart* (black plastic)	50.00 -	75.00
Jax 314 *Why? Oh, Why?* (red plastic)	80.00 -	120.00
316 *You Made Me Cry*	75.00 -	100.00
320 *Sunday Kind Of Love*	75.00 -	100.00

FOX HALL:

Limelight 3003 *Do The Rock And Roll*	8.00 -	12.00

FREDDIE HALL (& THE NIGHT ROCKERS):

Abco 103 *Playin' Hard To Get*	20.00 -	30.00
Chance 1159 *Knock Me Out*	30.00 -	50.00
C.J. 601 *She's A Upsetter* (blue label)	15.00 -	20.00
610 *Love And Affection* (red label)	15.00 -	20.00

LARRY HALL:

Strand (LP) 1005 *Sandy*	30.00 -	40.00

ROY HALL (& HIS JUMPING CATS); ROY HALL'S ALLEY CATS:

Decca 29696 *Whole Lotta Shakin'*	15.00 -	25.00
29786 *See You Later, Alligator*	15.00 -	25.00
29820 *Blue Suede Shoes*	20.00 -	30.00
30060 *Three Alley Cats*	15.00 -	25.00
Fortune *Goin' Down The Road Feelin' Bad*	— -	—
Hi-Q 5045 *Three Alley Cats*	10.00 -	15.00
5050 *Go Go, Little Queenie*	10.00 -	15.00
Pierce *One Monkey Can't Stop The Show*	— -	—

SONNY HALL:

D 1035 *The Day You Walked Away*	10.00 -	15.00

ROY HALLAWAY:

CM 12964 *I Received Your Letter*	7.00 -	10.00

THE HALLIQUINS:

Juanita 102 *Confession Of Love*	— -	—

JOHNNY HALO:

Angeltone 538 *Little Annie*	8.00 -	12.00

THE HALOS:

Warwick (LP) 2046 *The Halos*	30.00 -	50.00

STUART HAMBLEN:

Coral (LP) 57254 *Remember Me*	15.00 -	20.00
Harmony (LP) 7009 *Hymns*	10.00 -	15.00
RCA Victor (LP) 1253 *It Is No Secret*	12.00 -	16.00
(LP) 1436 *Grand Old Hymns*	10.00 -	15.00

GEORGE HAMILTON IV:

ABC Paramount (LP) 220, 251	15.00 -	20.00
9765 *If You Don't Know* (78 rpm)	10.00 -	15.00
Colonial 420 *If You Don't Know*	10.00 -	15.00

MACK HAMILTON:

Feature 1087 *I'm A Honky-Tonk Daddy*	15.00 -	20.00

WALTER HAMILTON:

Fortune 849 *Sherry Blues*	8.00 -	12.00

JACK HAMMER:

Milestone 2001 *Black Widow Spider Woman*	— -	—

CURLEY HAMNER:

Fling 720 *Piano Tuner*	20.00 -	30.00

JOHN HAMPTON:

United 210 *Honey Hush*	15.00 -	20.00

PAUL HAMPTON:

Columbia 41037 *Play It Cool*	7.00 -	10.00
41145 *Slam Bam Thank Ya Ma'm*	7.00 -	10.00

WAYNE HANDY (& THE MELODY MASTERS):

Renown 102 *Say Yeah*	5.00 -	8.00
104 *Betcha' Didn't Know*	7.00 -	10.00
Trend 30-006 *Betcha Didn't Know*	5.00 -	8.00

30-015 *I Think You Oughta Look Again*	5.00 -	8.00

HANK & THE ELECTRAS:

Dauphin 106 *Get Lost Baby*	10.00 -	15.00

MIKE HANKS & THE CONTOURS:

Braz 22 *Can I Be Your Lover Boy*	10.00 -	15.00

TYE TONGUE HANLEY:

JVB 88 *I'll Try To Understand*	20.00 -	30.00

RUDY HANSEN:

Decca (most issues)	4.00 -	7.00
Rudy Hansen 1226 *Saturday Jump*	10.00 -	15.00

KIRK HANSERD WITH BILL CARRIGAN'S TOP BOP BAND:

Dot 1281 *My Heart's Broke Baby*	7.00 -	10.00

HAPPY TEENS:

Paradise 114 *One More Kiss*	7.00 -	10.00

DOUG HARDEN & THE DESERT SONS:

Liberty Bell 9006 *Dig That Ford*	10.00 -	15.00

JIM HARDIN:

Volcano 100 *High Stepping Woman*	15.00 -	20.00

PETE HARDIN:

Peach 748 *Baby Be My Chicadee*	15.00 -	20.00

BILL HARDY:

Rita 1001 *Rockin At The Zoo*	15.00 -	20.00

RON HARGRAVE:

MGM 12422 *Latch On*	10.00 -	15.00

FREDDIE HARKEY:

Hillcrest 1805 *Marooned On An Island*	8.00 -	12.00

BILLY HARLAN:

Brunswick 55066 *I Wanna Bop*	15.00 -	20.00

BOB HARMON:

Decca 29872 *Kentucky Home Boogie*	7.00 -	10.00

HARMONAIRES:

Holiday 2602 *Lorraine*	20.00 -	30.00

HARMONICA FATS:

Darcel 5000, 5003	4.00 -	7.00

HARMONICA FRANK:

F & L 100 *Rock A Little Baby*	75.00 -	100.00
Sun 205 *Rockin' Chair Daddy*	100.00 -	150.00

HARMONICA JOE:

Skymac 1008 *Look Here Mama*	7.00 -	10.00

HARMONICA KID:

Nucraft 114 *Martha Lee*	10.00 -	15.00
2022 *Jole Blon*	10.00 -	15.00

HARMONICA KING:

Lapel 103 *Hot Rolls*	7.00 -	10.00

HARMONICA SLIM:

Aladdin 3317 *Lonely Hours*	10.00 -	15.00
Cenco 1001 *I'll Take Love*	7.00 -	10.00
Spry 103 *Going Back Home*	10.00 -	15.00
Vita 138 *You Better Believe It*	7.00 -	10.00
146 *Drop Anchor*	7.00 -	10.00

THE HARMONY BROTHERS:

Bobbin 109 *Baby, Tonight*	15.00 -	20.00
116 *Saturday Night Bop*	15.00 -	25.00

HARMONY GRITS:

End 1051 *I Could Have Told You*	7.00 -	10.00
1063 *Gee*	7.00 -	10.00

BEN HARPER & THE CINCO'S:

Skylark 112 *Union Station Blues*	8.00 -	12.00
Talent 106 *Drive Way Blues*	5.00 -	8.00

BIG BUD HARPER WITH O.S. GRANT & THE DOWNBEATS:

Harlem 117 *Never Let Me Go*	7.00 -	10.00

SONNY HARPER:

Ball 1011 *Lonely Stranger*	5.00 -	8.00

SLIM HARPO:

Excello 2113 *I'm A King Bee*	8.00 -	12.00
2138 *Strange Love*	8.00 -	12.00
2162, 2171, 2184, 2194	5.00 -	8.00
(LP) 8003 *Raining In My Heart*	30.00 -	50.00
(LP) 8005 *Baby Scratch My Back*	30.00 -	50.00

HARPTONES:

Andrea 100 *What Is Your Decision*	8.00 -	12.00
Bruce 101 *A Sunday Kind Of Love*	10.00 -	15.00
102 *My Memories Of You*	10.00 -	15.00
104 *I Depend On You*	10.00 -	15.00
109 *Forever Mine*	15.00 -	20.00
113 *Since I Fell For You*	10.00 -	15.00
123 *Loving A Girl Like You*	10.00 -	15.00
128 *I Almost Lost My Mind*	10.00 -	15.00
Cub 9097 *Your Love Is A Good Love*	5.00 -	8.00
Gee 1045 *Cry Like I Cried*	8.00 -	12.00
Paradise 101 *Life Is But A Dream*	10.00 -	15.00
103 *It All Depends On You*	10.00 -	15.00
Rama 203 *Three Wishes*	10.00 -	15.00
214 *On Sunday Afternoon*	10.00 -	15.00
221 *The Shrine Of St. Cecilia*	10.00 -	15.00
Raven 8001 *Mambo Boogie*	10.00 -	15.00
Tip Top 401 *My Memories Of You*	10.00 -	15.00
Warwick 500 *I Remember*	8.00 -	12.00
512 *Love Me Completely*	8.00 -	12.00
551 *No Greater Miracle*	8.00 -	12.00

HANK HARRAL:

Caprock 100 *Fabulous Oklahoma*	5.00 -	8.00
102 *The D.J. Blues*	15.00 -	20.00
104 *Tank Town Boogie*	20.00 -	30.00
114 *Oklahoma Land*	5.00 -	8.00

BILL HARRIS:

Eagle 1002 *Danny Boy*	15.00 -	20.00

GENEE HARRIS:

ABC Paramount 9900 *Bye Bye Elvis*	8.00 -	12.00

JOHNNY RAY HARRIS:

Ray's 100 *Cajun Weekend*	

PEPPERMINT HARRIS:

Aladdin 3097 *I Got Loaded*	15.00 -	20.00
Aladdin (others)	7.00 -	10.00
Dart 103 *You Got Me Wonderin'*	7.00 -	10.00
Duke 319 *Angel Child*	5.00 -	8.00
Money 214 *Cadillac Funeral*	10.00 -	15.00
"X" 0142 *Need Your Lovin'*	10.00 -	15.00

RAY HARRIS:

Sun 254 *Come On Little Mama*	15.00 -	20.00
272 *Greenback Dollar*	10.00 -	15.00

THURSTON HARRIS:

Aladdin 3398 *Little Bitty Pretty One* (78 rpm)	10.00 -	15.00
3415, 3428	5.00 -	8.00

WILLARD HARRIS:

Ekko 20001 *Talking Off The Wall*	-

WYNONIE HARRIS:

(See also: Battle of The Blues and Party After Hours)

Atco 6081 *Destination Love*	5.00 -	8.00
King (EP) 260 *Good Rockin' Tonight*	40.00 -	60.00
4210 *Good Rockin' Tonight*	10.00 -	15.00
4461 *Blood Shot Eyes*	8.00 -	12.00
4485 *Loving Machine*	8.00 -	12.00
4526 *Keep On Churnin'*	10.00 -	15.00
4565 *Night Train*	10.00 -	15.00
4592 *Drinkin' Blues*	8.00 -	12.00
4592 *Rot-Gut*	8.00 -	12.00
4620 *Wasn't That Good?*	8.00 -	12.00
4685 *Quiet Whiskey*	8.00 -	12.00
4763 *Christina*	7.00 -	10.00
4774 *Git To Gettin' Baby*	7.00 -	10.00
4814 *Drinkin' Sherry Wine*	7.00 -	10.00
5050 *Big Old Country Fool*	7.00 -	10.00

(Note: Some distinction is made, with regard to the earliest numbers, between "original" and subsequent pressings which lack the suffixes "A" or "AA" after the catalog numbers, the later pressings bringing somewhat less.)

DANNY & AUDREY HARRISON:

Event 4273 *Rock-A-Billy Boogie*	15.00 -	25.00

JOHNNY HARRISON:

Starday 373 *I Don't Want A Sweetheart* . . . .   -

LEE HARRISON (Backed by THE KOUNTS):

Pearl 717 *So Unimportant* . . . . 10.00 -   15.00

WILBERT HARRISON:

De Luxe 6002 *The Letter* . . . . 10.00 -   15.00

    6031 *Gin And Coconut Milk* . . . . 10.00 -   15.00

Fury 1023 *Kansas City* (78 rpm) . . . . 20.00 -   30.00

    1028 "*1960*" (78 rpm) . . . . 20.00 -   30.00

Rockin' 526 *The Letter* . . . . 10.00 -   15.00

Savoy 1149 *Women And Whiskey* . . . . 5.00 -   8.00

    1164 *Florida Special* . . . . 5.00 -   8.00

Savoy 1198, 1517, 1531, 1571 . . . . 4.00 -   8.00

Sphere (LP) 7000 *Kansas City* . . . . 15.00 -   25.00

BILLY HART:

Roulette 4133 *Rock Bop-A-Lina* . . . . 10.00 -   15.00

CASEY HART:

Choice 14 *Blues For My Baby* . . . . 8.00 -   12.00

FREDDIE HART:

Columbia (LP) 1792 *The Spirited Freddie Hart* . . 30.00 -   40.00

    21512, 21550, 41005 . . . . 5.00 -   8.00

LARRY HART:

Goldband 1070 *I'm Just A Mender* . . . . 10.00 -   15.00

Okeh 7077 *Looka Looka* . . . . 10.00 -   15.00

HARVEY (& THE MOONGLOWS):

Chess 1705 *Ten Commandments of Love* . . . . 7.00 -   10.00

    1713 *I Want Somebody* . . . . 7.00 -   10.00

    1725 *Twelve Months of the Year* . . . . 7.00 -   10.00

    1738 *Mama Loocie* . . . . 7.00 -   10.00

    1749 *Blue Skies* . . . . 7.00 -   10.00

    1781 *The First Time* . . . . 7.00 -   10.00

WAYNE HASS (See HAAS)

SHIRLEY HAVEN & THE FOUR JACKS:

Federal 12092 *Troubles Of My Own* . . . . 30.00 -   40.00

"HAVING A BALL"

End (LP) 302 *(The Chantels, The Dubs, et al)* . . 30.00 -   40.00

HAWK:

Phillips 3559 *In The Mood* . . . . 10.00 -   15.00

HAWKETTES:

Chess 1591 *Your Time's Up* . . . . 30.00 -   40.00

DALE HAWKINS:

Checker 843 *See You Soon Baboon* . . . . 8.00 -   12.00

    863 *Susie-Q* (78 RPM) . . . . 15.00 -   20.00

    863 *Susie-Q* . . . . 7.00 -   10.00

    876 *Baby, Baby* . . . . 8.00 -   12.00

    876 *Baby, Baby* (78 RPM) . . . . 15.00 -   20.00

    892 *Tornado* . . . . 7.00 -   10.00

    900 *Cross-Ties* . . . . 7.00 -   10.00

    906 *My Babe* (78 RPM) . . . . 15.00 -   20.00

    906 *My Babe* . . . . 8.00 -   12.00

    913 *Someday One Day* . . . . 7.00 -   10.00

    916 *Class Cutter (Yeah Yeah)* . . . . 7.00 -   10.00

    923 *Ain't That Lovin' You Baby* . . . . 8.00 -   12.00

    929 *Our Turn* . . . . 7.00 -   10.00

    934 *Liza Jane* . . . . 7.00 -   10.00

    940 *Hot Dog* . . . . 7.00 -   10.00

    944 *Every Little Girl* . . . . 7.00 -   10.00

    962 *Linda* . . . . 7.00 -   10.00

    970 *I Want To Love You* . . . . 7.00 -   10.00

    (LP) 1429 *Oh! Suzy-Q* (black label, yellow

      cover) . . . . .125.00 - 175.00

Tilt 781 *Money Honey* . . . . 4.00 -   7.00

HAWKSHAW HAWKINS:

King (LP) 587, 592 . . . . 15.00 -   20.00

SCREAMIN' JAY HAWKINS:

Epic (LP) 3448 *At Home With Screamin' Jay* . . . 90.00 - 130.00

RONNIE HAWKINS (& THE HAWKS):

Roulette 4154 *Forty Days* . . . . 7.00 -   10.00

    4209 *Love Me Like You Can* . . . . 7.00 -   10.00

    4228 *Lonely Hours* . . . . 7.00 -   10.00

Roulette 4231, 4249, 4267, 4311, 4483, 4502 . . . 5.00 -   8.00

Roulette (LP) 25078 *Ronnie Hawkins* . . . . 30.00 -   50.00

    (LP) 25102 *Mr. Dynamo* . . . . 30.00 -   50.00

ROY HAWKINS:

Rhythm 120 *I Hate To Be Alone* . . . . 8.00 -   12.00

RPM 440 *Is It Too Late* . . . . 8.00 -   12.00

HAWKS:

Imperial 5266 *Candy Girl* . . . . 35.00 -   50.00

    5292 *It Ain't That Way* . . . . 30.00 -   40.00

    5306 *Nobody But You* . . . . 25.00 -   35.00

Modern 990 *It's All Over* . . . . 20.00 -   30.00

Post 2004 *These Blues* . . . . 30.00 -   40.00

MICKEY HAWKS (With MOON MULLINS &
HIS NIGHT RAIDERS):

Profile 4002 *Bip Bop Boom* . . . . 10.00 -   15.00

    4007 *Hidi Hidi Hidi* . . . . 8.00 -   12.00

    4010 *Screamin' Mimi Jeanie* . . . . 10.00 -   15.00

RUDY HAYDEN:

Aragon 279 *Want Me A Woman* . . . . 8.00 -   12.00

WILLIE HAYDEN:

Dooto (LP) 293 *Blame It One The Blues* . . . . -

RON HAYDOCK:

Cha Cha 701 *Be-Bop-A-Jean* . . . . 15.00 -   20.00

JIMMY HAYES:

Happy Hearts 141 *Tom Cat Boogie* . . . . 10.00 -   15.00

LINDA HAYES & THE PLATTERS:

King 4752 *My Name Ain't Annie* . . . . 8.00 -   12.00

    4773 *Please Have Mercy* . . . . 8.00 -   12.00

DON HEAD:

Dub 2840 *Goin' Strong* . . . . 10.00 -   15.00

ROY HEAD & THE TRAITS: (See also THE
TRAITS)

Suave 712 *Teen-Age Letter* . . . . 7.00 -   10.00

TNT (LP) 101 *Roy Head And The Traits* . . . . . . 50.00 -   75.00

JIMMY HEAP:

Capitol 3156 *Sebbin Come Elebbin* . . . . 7.00 -   10.00

Fame 502 *Little Jewell* . . . . 10.00 -   15.00

BUDDY HEARD & HIS COMBO:

Red Top 501 *Let's Rock With Me* . . . . 10.00 -   15.00

HEARTBEATS; HEART BEATS:

Gee 1043 *When I Found You* . . . . 8.00 -   12.00

    1047 *After New Year's Eve* . . . . 8.00 -   12.00

    1061 *People Are Talking* . . . . 5.00 -   8.00

    1062 *Hurry Home Baby* . . . . 5.00 -   8.00

Guyden 2011 *One Million Tears* . . . . 5.00 -   8.00

Hull 711 *Crazy For You* (pink label) . . . . 15.00 -   20.00

    713 *Darling How Long* . . . . 15.00 -   20.00

    716 *People Are Talking* . . . . 15.00 -   20.00

    720 *A Thousand Miles Away* . . . . 20.00 -   30.00

Network 71200 *Tormented* . . . . 30.00 -   40.00

Rama 216 *A Thousand Miles Away* . . . . 5.00 -   8.00*

*Label variations exist; some bring higher prices.

    216 *A Thousand Miles Away* (78 rpm) . . . . . . 15.00 -   20.00

    222 *Wedding Bells* . . . . 10.00 -   15.00

    231 *Everybody's Somebody's Fool* . . . . 10.00 -   15.00

Roulette 4054 *Down On My Knees* . . . . 5.00 -   8.00

    4091 *One Day Next Year* . . . . 5.00 -   8.00

    4194 *Crazy For You* . . . . 5.00 -   8.00

Roulette (LP) 25017 *A Thousand Miles Away* . . . 50.00 -   75.00

HEARTBREAKERS:

RCA Victor 4327 *Heartbreaker* . . . . 75.00 - 100.00

    4662 *Why Don't I* . . . . 50.00 -   75.00

    4849 *There Is Time* . . . . 40.00 -   60.00

Vik 0261 *One, Two, I Love You* . . . . 25.00 -   30.00

    0299 *My Love* . . . . 25.00 -   30.00

HEARTS: (See also LEE ANDREWS; BILLY
AUSTIN)

Baton 208 *Lonely Nights* . . . . 5.00 -   10.00

    211 *All My Love Belongs To You* . . . . 5.00 -   10.00

    228 *I Had A Guy* . . . . 5.00 -   10.00

Chancellor 1057 *On My Honor* . . . . 5.00 -   8.00

J & S 995 *A Thousand Years From Today* . . . . . . 5.00 -   8.00

    1180 *You Weren't Home* . . . . 5.00 -   8.00

Tuff 370 *Dear Abby* . . . . 5.00 -   8.00

HEARTSPINNERS:

X-tra 109 *Oh So Much* . . . .   -

HEART-THROBS:

Lamp 2010 *So Glad* . . . .   15.00 -   20.00

BOBBY HELMS:

Decca (LP) 8638 *Sings* . . . .   20.00 -   30.00

   30423 *My Special Angel* (78 rpm) . . . .   15.00 -   20.00

Decca (most other issues) . . . .   4.00 -   7.00

BIG BERTHA HENDERSON:

Chance 1143 *Rock, Daddy, Rock* (red plastic) . . .   30.00 -   40.00

JOCKO HENDERSON:

Wand 112 *Blast Off To Love* . . . .   8.00 -   12.00

R.D. HENDON:

4 Star 1644 *Blues Boogie* . . . .   10.00 -   15.00

Starday 167 *You Traveled Too Far* . . . .   7.00 -   10.00

   194 *Big Black Cat* . . . .   10.00 -   15.00

   228 *Don't Push Me* . . . .   7.00 -   10.00

BOBBY HENDRICKS:

Sue 708 *Molly B. Good* . . . .   5.00 -   8.00

AL HENDRIX (With JOLLY JODY & HIS GO DADDIES):

ABC Paramount 9901 *Rhonda Lee* . . . .   7.00 -   10.00

Lagree 701 *Young And Wild* . . . .   10.00 -   15.00

Tally 119 *Rhonda Lee* . . . .   15.00 -   20.00

CLARENCE (FROGMAN) HENRY:

Argo (LP) 4009 *You Always Hurt The One You Love* . . . .   30.00 -   40.00

   5259 *Ain't Got No Home* (78 rpm) . . . .   8.00 -   12.00

Argo (most issues) . . . .   4.00 -   7.00

ROBERT HENRY:

King 4624 *Miss Anna B* . . . . .100.00 -   150.00

   4646 *Old Battle Ax* . . . . .100.00 -   150.00

GENE HENSLEE:

Imperial 8227 *Dig'n And Datin'* . . . .   10.00 -   15.00

   8277 *Rockin' Baby* . . . .   10.00 -   15.00

HERALDS:

Herald 435 *Eternal Love* . . . .   30.00 -   40.00

HERBY JOE:

Abco 101 *Smokestack Lightning* . . . .   20.00 -   30.00

"HERE ARE THE HITS"

Fire (LP) 100 *The Scarlets, The Velvets, et al)* . . .   30.00 -   50.00

STICKS HERMAN:

Dootone 358 *Bad Luck* 00   .00

Goldband 1047 *I'm Long Gone Baby* . . . .   8.00 -   12.00

   1050 *Beautiful Doll* . . . .   8.00 -   12.00

   1056 *Wipe The Tears From Your Eyes* . . . .   8.00 -   12.00

Hollywood 1080 *Cry Cry Cry* . . . .   7.00 -   10.00

   1085 *Natural Thing To Do* . . . .   7.00 -   10.00

LITTLE JULIAN HERRERA:

Dig 118 *Lonely Lonely Nights* . . . .   10.00 -   15.00

   137 *Symbol Of Heaven* . . . .   15.00 -   20.00

DENNIS HERROLD:

Imperial 5482 *Hip Hip Baby* . . . .   15.00 -   20.00

BENNIE HESS:

Major 1001 *Wild Hog Hop* . . . .   50.00 -   75.00

BEN HEWITT:

Mercury 71413, 71472 . . . .   5.00 -   8.00

   71612 *Whirlwind Blues* . . . .   10.00 -   15.00

ERSEL HICKEY:

Epic 9263 *Hangin' Around* . . . .   8.00 -   12.00

   9278 *Goin' Down That Road* . . . .   8.00 -   12.00

   9298 *You Never Can Tell* . . . .   8.00 -   12.00

   9309 *You Threw A Dart* . . . .   8.00 -   12.00

   9320 *People Gotta Talk* . . . .   8.00 -   12.00

   9357 *What Do You Want* . . . .   7.00 -   10.00

   9395 *Another Wasted Day* . . . .   7.00 -   10.00

Epic (EP) 7202 *In Lovers' Land* . . . .   75.00 -   100.00

BOBBY HICKS:

Skyway 116 *Hassle It Jack* . . . .   -

HIDE-A-WAYS:

MGM 55004 *Cherie* . . . . .100.00 -   150.00

Ronni 1000 *Can't Help Loving That Girl Of Mine*   rare   -

(Note: Prices of up to $800.00 have been quoted

as the value of this record.)

HI-FIDELITIES:

Fortune 528 *Last Night I Cried* . . . .   10.00 -   15.00

HIFIDELITY'S:

Hi-Q 5000 *Help, Murder, Police* . . . .   10.00 -   15.00

HI-FI's:

Montel 1005 *I'm So Lonely* . . . .   -

HI-FIVES:

Decca 30576 *My Friend* . . . .   8.00 -   10.00

   30657 *A Shoulder To Cry On* . . . .   8.00 -   12.00

   30744 *Lonely* . . . .   10.00 -   15.00

CHUCK HIGGINS:

Aladdin 3215 *Chuck-A-Buck* . . . .   7.00 -   10.00

Caddy 108 *The Blacksmith Blues* . . . .   -

Combo 12 *Pachuko Hop* . . . .   7.00 -   10.00

   144 *Long Long Time* . . . .   7.00 -   10.00

   (LP) 300 *Pachuka Hop* . . . .   80.00 -   120.00

Dootone 387 *Gambling Woman* . . . .   7.00 -   10.00

Lucky 005 *Greasy Pig* . . . .   7.00 -   10.00

Money 214 *Rock And Roll* . . . .   10.00 -   15.00

Specialty 532 *Broke* . . . .   7.00 -   10.00

DONNA HIGHTOWER:

RPM 432 *Love Me Again* . . . .   10.00 -   15.00

   481 *I Ain't Gonna Tell* . . . .   8.00 -   12.00

WILLIE HIGHTOWER:

Fury 5002 *If I Had A Hammer* . . . .   5.00 -   8.00

"HIGHWAY OF BLUES":

Audio Lab (LP) 1520 *(Brownie McGhee, John Lee Hooker)* . . . .   30.00 -   50.00

THE HI-LITERS:

Mercury 71342 *Dance Me To Death* . . . .   5.00 -   8.00

HILITES:

Okeh 7046 *I Found A Love* . . . .   30.00 -   40.00

HARVEY HILL, JR.:

SRC 104 *Boogie Woogie Woman* . . . .   30.00 -   50.00

HENRY HILL:

Federal 12030 *Sunday Morning Blues* . . . .   20.00 -   30.00

   12037 *Hold Me Baby* . . . .   20.00 -   30.00

   12044 *If You Love Me* . . . .   20.00 -   30.00

   12053 *My Baby Is Back Home* . . . .   20.00 -   30.00

J.C. HILL:

Argo 5311 *Only True Love* . . . .   5.00 -   8.00

JAYCEE HILL:

Epic 9105 *Romp Stompin' Boogie* . . . .   15.00 -   20.00

JOEL HILL:

Trans Amer. 519 *Little Lover* . . . .   25.00 -   35.00

RAYMOND HILL:

Sun 204 *The Snuggle* .100.00 -   150.00

"HILLBILLY JAMBOREE":

Starday (LP) 101 *(various artists)* . . . .   20.00 -   30.00

CLAYTON HILLIS:

Linco 1319 *Rock City Rock* . . . .   8.00 -   12.00

JOE HINTON:

Back Beat 519 *Ladder Of Prayer* . . . .   5.00 -   8.00

OTIS HINTON:

Timely 1003 *Walkin' Down Hill* . . . .   50.00 -   75.00

THE HI-TONES:

Fonsca 201 *Just For You* . . . .   5.00 -   8.00

CURTIS HOBECK:

Lu 508 *China Rock* . . . .   15.00 -   20.00

GARY HODGE:

Dolton 7 *Not For Love Or Money* . . . .   5.00 -   8.00

RALPH HODGES:

Whispering Pines 61 *Honey Talk* . . . .   7.00 -   10.00

SILAS HOGAN:

Excello 2221, 2231, 2241, 2251, 2255, 2266, 2270, 2271 . . . .   4.00 -   8.00

SMOKEY/SMOKY HOGG:

Combo 4 *Bottle Up And Go* . . . .   20.00 -   30.00

   9 *My Woman* . . . .   20.00 -   30.00

Crown (LP) 5226 *Smokey Hogg Sings The Blues* .   15.00 -   25.00

Ebb 127 *Good Mornin' Baby* . . . .   7.00 -   10.00

Federal 12109 *Keep-A-Walkin'*	20.00 -	30.00
12117 *Your Little Wagon*	20.00 -	30.00
12127 *Gone, Gone, Gone.*	20.00 -	30.00
Imperial 5269 *Tear Me Down*	30.00 -	40.00
5290 *Train Whistle*	20.00 -	30.00
Meteor 5021 *Dark Clouds*	20.00 -	30.00
Modern 924 *Can't Do Nothin'*	10.00 -	15.00
Ray's 33 *Penitentiary Blues*	30.00 -	40.00
Show Time 1101 *No More Whiskey*	20.00 -	30.00

ROY HOGSED:

Capitol 1529 *Shuffleboard Shuffle*	7.00 -	10.00
1635 *Cocaine Blues*	7.00 -	10.00
1854 *The Snake Dance Boogie*	7.00 -	10.00
1987 *Mean Mean Woman*	7.00 -	10.00

JAY HOLIDAY & THE GIANTS:

CMI 1001 *I'm Gonna Be a Wheel Someday*	— -	—

THE HOLIDAYS:

Robbee 103 *Miss You*	15.00 -	20.00
Specialty 533 *Irene*	10.00 -	15.00

EDDIE HOLLAND:

Mercury 71290 *Little Miss Ruby*	7.00 -	10.00
Tamla 102 *It Moves Me*	50.00 -	75.00

HOLLIES:

Imperial (LP) 9265 *Here I Go Again*	35.00 -	50.00

THE HOLLY TWINS:

Liberty 55048 *I Want Elvis For Christmas*	8.00 -	12.00

BUDDY HOLLY:

Coral (LP) 57210 *Buddy Holly* (maroon label) ...	50.00 -	75.00
(LP) 57279 *The Buddy Holly Story*	40.00 -	60.00
(LP) 57326 *The Buddy Holly Story Vol. 2*	35.00 -	50.00
(LP) 57426 *Reminiscing*	30.00 -	50.00
(LP) 57463 *Holly in the Hills*	30.00 -	50.00
Coral 61852 *Words of Love*	30.00 -	40.00
Coral 61885 *Peggy Sue* (78 rpm)	50.00 -	75.00
61885 *Peggy Sue*	7.00 -	10.00
61947 *Listen To Me*	8.00 -	12.00
61985 *Rave On*	8.00 -	12.00
62006 *Early In The Morning*	8.00 -	12.00
62051 *Well, All Right*	8.00 -	12.00
62074 *It Doesn't Matter Anymore*	8.00 -	12.00
62134 *Peggy Sue Got Married*	10.00 -	15.00
62210 *True Love Ways*	10.00 -	15.00
62283 *You're So Square*	15.00 -	20.00

(Note: DJ copies of above are of substantially
higher values)

Coral 62329 *Reminiscing*	10.00 -	15.00
62352 *True Love Ways*	10.00 -	15.00
62369 *Brown Eyed Handsome Man*	10.00 -	15.00
62390 *Rock Around With Ollie Vee*	15.00 -	20.00
62407 *Maybe Baby*	15.00 -	20.00
62448 *Slippin' And Slidin'*	20.00 -	30.00
62554 *Rave On*	10.00 -	15.00
Coral 65000 series (most issues, including DJ copies—which, indeed, may be more common than commercial issues)	8.00 -	12.00
Coral (EP) 81169 *Listen To Me*	40.00 -	60.00
(EP) 81182 *The Buddy Holly Story*	35.00 -	50.00
(EP) 81191 *Peggy Sue Got Married*	40.00 -	60.00
(EP) 81193 *Brown Eyed Handsome Man*	50.00 -	75.00
Decca (EP) 2575 *That'll Be The Day*	125.00 -	175.00
(LP) 8707 *That'll Be The Day* (black label) ...	100.00 -	150.00
(LP) 8707 *That'll Be The Day* (multi-colored label)	30.00 -	40.00
29854 *Love Me*	40.00 -	60.00
30166 *Modern Don Juan*	30.00 -	40.00
30434 *That'll Be The Day*	30.00 -	50.00
30543 *Love Me*	10.00 -	15.00
30650 *Ting A Ling*	15.00 -	20.00

(Note: DJ copies of above are more highly
valued.)

Vocalion (LP) 73811 *The Great Buddy Holly*	30.00 -	50.00

HOLLYWOOD ARGYLES:

Lute (LP) 9001 *The Hollywood Argyles*	50.00 -	75.00

HOLLYWOOD ARIST-O-KATS:

Recorded In Hollywood 406 *I'll Be Home Again* .	20.00 -	30.00

HOLLYWOOD FLAMES:

Atco 6155, 6164, 6171	5.00 -	8.00
Decca 29285 *Peggy*	15.00 -	20.00
48331 *I Know*	15.00 -	20.00
Ebb 119 *Buzz-Buzz-Buzz*	5.00 -	8.00
119 *Buzz-Buzz-Buzz* (78 rpm)	8.00 -	12.00
131 *Give Me Back My Heart*	8.00 -	12.00
144 *Strollin' on the Beach*	5.00 -	8.00
146 *Chains Of Love*	5.00 -	8.00
149 *A Star Fell*	5.00 -	8.00
153 *I'll Be Seeing You*	5.00 -	8.00
158 *So Good*	5.00 -	8.00
162 *Now That You're Gone*	5.00 -	8.00
163 *In The Dark*	5.00 -	8.00
Lucky 006 *Peggy*	75.00 -	100.00
009 *I Know*	50.00 -	75.00
Money 202 *Fare Thee Well*	15.00 -	20.00
Swing Time 345 *Let's Talk It Over*	50.00 -	75.00

HOLLYWOOD SAXONS:

Elf 103 *It's You*	7.00 -	10.00
Entra 1214 *Diamonds*	20.00 -	30.00

TOMMY HOLMES:

Cherry 112 *Wa-Chic-Ka-Noka*	20.00 -	30.00

DAVEY HOLT & THE HUBCAPS:

United Artist 110 *You Move Me*	— -	—

JIM HOLT:

Gulfstream 1064 *Oh! My Linda*	8.00 -	12.00

COUNTRY HOMES:

De Luxe 6036 *Come On And Put Me In The Alley*	20.00 -	30.00
6048 *It Can't Be*	20.00 -	30.00

HOMESICK JAMES:

Atomic H—*Johnnie Mae*	— -	—
Colt 632 *Set A Date*	7.00 -	10.00
U.S.A. 746 *Crossroads*	7.00 -	10.00

THE HONEY BEARS:

Spark 111 *I Shall Not Fail*	30.00 -	50.00

THE HONEY BEES:

Imperial 5400 *Endless*	7.00 -	10.00
5416 *Whats To Become Of Me*	7.00 -	10.00

HONEYBOY:

Specialty 476 *Bloodstains On The Wall*	15.00 -	20.00

GLEN HONEYCUTT:

Sun 264 *I'll Be Around*	7.00 -	10.00

HONEYS:

Capitol 4952 *Shoot The Curls*	15.00 -	20.00
5034 *Pray For Surf*	15.00 -	20.00
5093 *The One You Can't Have*	15.00 -	25.00
Warner Bros. 5430 *He's A Doll*	15.00 -	25.00

EARL HOOKER (& HIS ROADMASTERS):

Age 29101, 29106, 29111, 29114	4.00 -	7.00
Bea & Baby 106 *Dynamite*	7.00 -	10.00
Chief 7016 *Blues In D Natural*	8.00 -	12.00
CJ 613 *Do The Chicken.*	5.00 -	8.00
King 4600 *Race Track*	12.00 -	16.00
Rockin' 519 *Sweet Angel*	20.00 -	30.00

JOHN LEE HOOKER:

Atco (LP) 151 *Don't Turn Me From Your Door* ..	40.00 -	60.00
Chart 609 *Wobbling Baby*	10.00 -	15.00
614 *Misbelieving Baby*	10.00 -	15.00
Chess (LP) 1438 *House Of The Blues* (black label)	50.00 -	75.00
(LP) 1454 *Plays And Sings The Blues*	30.00 -	50.00
Chess 1505 *High Priced Woman*	75.00 -	100.00
1513 *Walkin' The Boogie*	75.00 -	100.00

(Note: Earlier issues, usually found in 78 rpm
format, would command prices *at least* as high
as the above, as 45 rpm records.)

Chess 1562 *It's All My Fault*	15.00 -	20.00

Crown (LP) 5157 *The Blues* .... 20.00 - 30.00
   (LP) 5232 *John Lee Hooker Sings The Blues* .. 15.00 - 20.00
   (LP) 5295 *Folk Blues* .... 15.00 - 20.00
King (LP) 727 *John Lee Hooker Sings Blues* .... 40.00 - 60.00
Modern 835 *I'm In The Mood* (black label) ..... 15.00 - 20.00
   897 *It's Been A Long Time Baby* .... 8.00 - 12.00
   901 *Ride Till I Die* .... 8.00 - 12.00
   916 *Too Much Boogie* .... 8.00 - 12.00
   923 *Down Child* .... 8.00 - 12.00
   935 *Let's Talk It Over* .... 8.00 - 12.00
   942, 948, 958, 966 .... 7.00 - 10.00
Riverside (LP) 12-838 *Folk Blues* .... 20.00 - 30.00
Specialty 528 *I'm Mad* .... 7.00 - 10.00
Vee Jay 164, 188, 205, 233, 255, 265, 293 ..... 5.00 - 8.00
   308, 319, 331, 349, 366 .... 3.00 - 6.00
   (LP) 1007 *I'm John Lee Hooker* (maroon label) 30.00 - 50.00
   (LP) 1023 *Travelin'* .... 20.00 - 30.00
   (LP) 1033 *The Folk Lore Of John Lee Hooker* . 20.00 - 30.00

JESS HOOPER:
Cherry *All Messed Up* .... -
Meteor 5025 *All Messed Up* .... 100.00 - 150.00

EDDIE HOPE & THE MANISH BOYS:
Marlin 804 *Lost Child* .... 15.00 - 20.00

HOPELESS HOMER:
Goldband 1040 *New Way Of Rockin'* .... 15.00 - 20.00

FORD HOPKINS:
Apex 7757 *Ya Fine, Fine, Fine* .... 15.00 - 20.00

LIGHTNIN'/LIGHTNING HOPKINS:
Bluesville (LP) 1019 *Lightnin'* .... 15.00 - 20.00
   (LP) 1057 *Walkin' This Road By Myself* ... 15.00 - 20.00
Candid (LP) 8010 *In New York* (mono) .... 15.00 - 20.00
Chart 636 *Mussy Haired Woman* .... 8.00 - 12.00
Crown (LP) 5224 *Sings The Blues* .... 15.00 - 20.00
Decca 48306 *Happy New Year* .... 8.00 - 12.00
   48312 *Highway Blues* .... 10.00 - 15.00
   48321 *Bad Things On My Mind* .... 10.00 - 15.00
Herald 425 *Lightnin's Boogie* .... 8.00 - 12.00
   428 *Lightnin's Special* .... 8.00 - 12.00
   436 *Sick Feeling Blues* .... 8.00 - 12.00
   443 *Early-Mornin' Boogie* .... 7.00 - 10.00
   449 *They Wonder Who I Am* .... 7.00 - 10.00
   456 *Don't Need No Job* .... 6.00 - 10.00
   465 *Blues For My Cookie* .... 5.00 - 8.00
   571 *Hopkins Sky Hop* .... 5.00 - 8.00
   476 *Grandma's Boogie* .... 5.00 - 8.00
   483 *That's All Right Baby* .... 5.00 - 8.00
   490 *Shine On Moon* .... 5.00 - 8.00
   497 *Remember Me* .... 5.00 - 8.00
Herald (higher numbers) .... 3.00 - 6.00
   (LP) 1012 *Lightnin' Hopkins* .... 50.00 - 75.00
Imperial (LP) 9180 *On Stage* .... 35.00 - 50.00
   (LP) 9186 *Lightning Hopkins Sings The Blues* . 35.00 - 50.00
   (LP) 9211 *Lightnin' Hopkins And The Blues* ... 30.00 - 40.00
Jax 315 *No Good Woman* .... 30.00 - 40.00
   318 *Organ Blues* .... 30.00 - 40.00
   321 *Contrary Mary* .... 30.00 - 40.00
(Note: Above, if pressed of red vinyl, bring
   substantially higher prices.)
Lightning 104 *Grieving Blues* .... 50.00 - 75.00
Score (LP) 4022 *Lightnin' Hopkins Strums The*
   Blues .... 75.00 - 100.00
TNT 8002 *Lightnin's Jump* .... 15.00 - 20.00
   8003 *Leavin' Blues* .... 15.00 - 20.00
Tradition (LP) 1035 *Country Blues* .... 20.00 - 30.00
   (LP) 1040 *Autobiography In Blues* .... 20.00 - 30.00

BIG JACK HORNER:
Trel 1001 *If I Can* .... 8.00 - 12.00

THE HORNETS:
Flash 125 *Crying Over You* .... 15.00 - 20.00
States 127 *I Can't Believe* (red vinyl) .... 300.00 - Up

JOHNNY HORTON:
Columbia (EP) B-2130 *Honky Tonk Man* .... 50.00 - 75.00

Columbia 21504, 21538, 40813, 40919, 40986,
41210 .... 5.00 - 8.00
   41043 *Lover's Rock* .... 7.00 - 10.00
   41110 *Honky Tonk Hardwood Floor* ...... 8.00 - 12.00
Dot (LP) 3221 *Johnny Horton* .... 30.00 - 40.00
Mercury 6418 *This Won't Be The First Time* ... 10.00 - 15.00
   (LP) 20478 *The Fantastic Johnny Horton* ... 30.00 - 50.00
   70100 *Tennessee Jive* .... 10.00 - 15.00
   70156 *S.S. Lure-Line* .... 10.00 - 15.00
   70198 *Red Lips And Warm Red Wine* ...... 10.00 - 15.00
   70227 *The Love Of A Girl* .... 10.00 - 15.00
   70325 *Move Down The Line* .... 10.00 - 15.00
   70462 *No True Love* .... 8.00 - 12.00
   70636 *Ridin' The Sunshine Special* .... 8.00 - 12.00
Sesac (EP) 26 *Free 'N' Easy Songs* .... 20.00 - 30.00

SHAKEY (WALTER) HORTON:
Argo (LP) 4037 *The Soul Of Blues Harmonica* .. 35.00 - 50.00
Chess 1529 *Walter's Boogie* .... 75.00 - 100.00
Cobra 5002 *Have A Good Time* .... 25.00 - 40.00

THE HOT-TODDYS:
Corsican 0056 *Shakin' And Stompin'* ....
Shan-Todd 0056 *Shakin' And Stompin'* .... 5.00 - 8.00

DAVID HOUSTON:
RCA Victor 6917 *Hackin' Around* .... 5.00 - 8.00

JOE HOUSTON:
Bayou 004 *Sabre Jet* .... 10.00 - 15.00
   012 *Pig Tails* .... 10.00 - 15.00
   017 *Landslide* .... 10.00 - 15.00
Cash 1018 *Rockin' And Boppin'* .... 5.00 - 8.00
Crown (LP) 5006 *Rocks And Rolls All Night*
   Long .... 10.00 - 15.00

JOHNNY HOUSTON & THE CAPITALS:
East-West 100 *But It's Too Late* .... -

CAMILLE HOWARD:
Specialty 433 *Old Baldy Boogie* .... 8.00 - 12.00

CHUCK HOWARD:
ESV 1017 *Don't Let It Bother You* .... 7.00 - 10.00
Port 70002 *Crazy, Crazy Baby* .... 7.00 - 10.00

JOHNNY HOWARD:
De Luxe 6044 *Hastings Street Jump* .... 50.00 - 75.00

VAN HOWARD:
ABC Paramount *Maybe Baby* .... -
Hi-Q 3756 *Truck Driving Jack* .... 7.00 - 10.00
Imperial 8202 *Lonesome And Blue* .... 7.00 - 10.00
   8213 *Maybe Baby* .... 7.00 - 10.00

HOWIE & THE SAPPHIRES:
Okeh 7112 *More Than The Day Before* .... 8.00 - 12.00

HOWLIN' WOLF:
Chess (LP) 1434 *Moanin' In The Moonlight*
   (black label) .... 75.00 - 100.00
   (LP) 1469 *Howlin' Wolf* .... 40.00 - 60.00
   (LP) 1502 *The Real Folk Blues* .... 30.00 - 40.00
   1510 *Mr. Highway Man* .... 75.00 - 100.00
   1528 *My Last Affair* .... 75.00 - 100.00
   1557 *All Night Boogie* .... 15.00 - 20.00
   1566 *Rockin' Daddy* .... 15.00 - 20.00
   1575 *Baby How Long* .... 10.00 - 15.00
   1584 *Forty Four* .... 10.00 - 15.00
   1593 *Who Will Be Next* .... 10.00 - 15.00
   1607 *Come To Me Baby* .... 10.00 - 15.00
   1618 *Smoke Stack Lightning* .... 10.00 - 15.00
   1632 *So Glad* .... 8.00 - 12.00
   1648 *My Life* .... 8.00 - 12.00
   1668 *Somebody In My Home* .... 8.00 - 12.00
   1679 *Sitting On Top Of The World* .... 8.00 - 12.00
   1695, 1712, 1726, 1735, 1744, 1750, 1762, 1777,
   1793, 1804, 1813, 1823, 1870, 1890, 1911 ..... 5.00 - 8.00

ORANGIE RAY HUBBARD:
Dixie 662 *Sweet Love* ....
Lucky 0007 *Look What I Found* .... 25.00 - 35.00

JACK HUDDLE:
Petsey 1002 *Believe Me* .... 30.00 - 50.00

JOE HUDGINS:
Robbins 1005 *Where'd You Stay Last Night* ..... 15.00 - 20.00
TOMMY HUDSON:
D 1073 *Band Stand Stomp* .... 10.00 - 15.00
White Rock 1110 *Rock-It* .... 10.00 - 15.00
HUDSON VALLEY BOYS:
Sessions 807 *Stop! I Like It* .... 8.00 - 12.00
JIMMY HUFF:
RPM 366 *She's My Baby* .... 30.00 - 40.00
RPM 390 *Big City Bound* .... 25.00 - 35.00
WILLIE HUFF:
Big Town 105 *Operator 209* .... 30.00 - 40.00
Rhythm 1770 *Beggar Man Blues* .... 35.00 - 50.00
PAUL HUFFMAN & THE REBEL COMBO:
Winston 1015 *She's Mine* .... 15.00 - 20.00
JOE HUGHES:
Kangaroo 105/106 *Make Me Dance Little Ant* ... 15.00 - 20.00
WALLY HUGHES:
Ember 1024 *Convertible Car* .... 5.00 - 8.00
1024 *Convertible Car* (78 rpm) .... 7.00 - 10.00
DENNIS HUNT & THE HUNTERS:
Say 11 *A Story Untold* .... 15.00 - 20.00
SLIM HUNT:
Excello 2055 *Welcome Home Baby* .... 30.00 - 50.00
FLUFFY HUNTER & JESSIE POWELL's
ORCHESTRA:
Federal 12056 *Love's A Fortune* .... 10.00 - 15.00
12161 *Climb The Wall* .... 8.00 - 12.00
12172 *Leave It To Me* .... 8.00 - 12.00
IVORY JOE HUNTER:
Atlantic 1049, 1066, 1086, 1095 .... 4.00 - 8.00
(LP) 8008 *Rock And Roll* (black label) ...... 30.00 - 40.00
(LP) 8015 *Ivory Joe Hunter Sings The Old &*
The New .... 30.00 - 40.00
King (LP) 605 *16 Of His Greatest Hits* .... 20.00 - 30.00
MGM (EP) 1376, 1377, 1378 .... 15.00 - 20.00
(LP) 3488 *I Get That Lonesome Feeling* ...... 50.00 - 75.00
LONG JOHN HUNTER:
Yucca 132 *Paso Rock* .... 5.00 - 8.00
138 *Ole Rattler* .... 5.00 - 8.00
TY HUNTER & THE VOICE MASTERS (See
VOICE MASTERS) HURRICANES:
King 4817 *Poor Little Dancing Girl* .... 20.00 - 30.00
4867 *Maybe It's All For The Best* ...... 20.00 - 30.00
4898 *Raining In My Heart* .... 20.00 - 30.00
4926 *Your Promise To Me* .... 20.00 - 30.00
4947 *Dear Mother* .... 20.00 - 30.00
5018 *Fallen Angel* .... 20.00 - 30.00
5042 *Priceless* .... 20.00 - 30.00
HUSKIES:
Klik 205 *Sorry* .... 15.00 - 25.00
FERLIN HUSKY:
Capitol (LP) 718 *Ferlin Husky* .... 15.00 - 20.00
(LP) 880 *Boulevard Of Broken Dreams* ...... 15.00 - 20.00
(LP) 976 *Sittin' On A Rainbow* ...... 15.00 - 20.00
(LP) 1204 *Born To Lose* .... 15.00 - 20.00
(LP) 1280 *Ferlin's Favorites* .... 10.00 - 150.00
3310 *Slow Down, Brother* .... 7.00 - 10.00
HYTONES:
Hytone 121 *Let Me Hold Your Hand* .... -
IDEALS:
Cool 108 *Do I Have The Right* .... 30.00 - 40.00
Decca 30720 *My Girl* .... 7.00 - 10.00
30800 *Don't Be a Baby, Baby* .... 7.00 - 10.00
Paso 6401 *Together* .... 7.00 - 10.00
6402 *Magic* .... 8.00 - 12.00
I DIG ROCK AND ROLL:
Score (LP) 4002 (various artist) .... 50.00 - 75.00
IMAGINATIONS:
Duel 507 *Guardian Angel* .... 15.00 - 20.00
Music Makers 103 *The Search Is Over* .... 10.00 - 15.00
108 *Guardian Angel* .... 10.00 - 15.00

IMPALAS:
Cub (LP) 8003 *Sorry (I Ran All The Way Home)* 40.00 - 60.00
IMPERIALS:
End 1091 *Traveling Stranger* .... 10.00 - 15.00
Great Lakes 1201 *Life Of Ease* .... 75.00 - 100.00
1212 *You'll Never Walk Alone* .... 75.00 - 100.00
Savoy 1104 *My Darling* .... 75.00 - 100.00
IMPLACABLES:
Kain 1004 *My Foolish Pride* .... -
IMPRESSIONS: (See also JERRY BUTLER):
Abner 1017 *Come Back My Love* .... 7.00 - 10.00
1017 *Come Back My Love* (78 rpm) ..... 10.00 - 15.00
1023 *The Gift Of Love* .... 7.00 - 10.00
1034 *A New Love* .... 7.00 - 10.00
Bandera 2504 *Listen To Me* .... 10.00 - 15.00
Swirl 107 *I Need Your Love* .... -
Vee Jay (LP) 1075 *For Your Precious Love* ..... 35.00 - 50.00
IMPRESSORS:
Cub 9010 *Do You Love Her* .... 10.00 - 15.00
Onyx 514 *Is It Too Late* .... 15.00 - 20.00
INDIVIDUALS:
Chase 1300 *Pillow Wet With Tears* .... 10.00 - 15.00
Music City 838 *Beverly My Darling* .... 10.00 - 15.00
Showtime 595 *Met Her At A Dance* .... 8.00 - 12.00
598 *Dear One* .... 8.00 - 12.00
INFATUATORS:
Destiny 504 *I Found My Love* .... 10.00 - 15.00
BENNY INGRAM:
Bandera 1302 *Jello Sal* .... 10.00 - 15.00
INK SPOTS:
King (LP) 535 *Something Old, Something New* .. 35.00 - 50.00
(LP) 642 *Songs That Will Live Forever* ..... 20.00 - 30.00
1297 *Ebb Tide* .... 10.00 - 15.00
1304 *Changing Partners* .... 10.00 - 15.00
1336 *Melody Of Love* .... 10.00 - 15.00
1378 *Yesterdays* .... 10.00 - 15.00
1429 *There Is Something Missing* .... 10.00 - 15.00
1512 *Keep It Movin'* .... 10.00 - 15.00
4670 *Here In My Lonely Room* .... 15.00 - 20.00
4857 *I'll Walk A Country Mile* .... 10.00 - 15.00
Waldorf (LP) 144 (10") .... 35.00 - 50.00
AUTRY INMAN:
Decca 29936 *Be Bop Baby* .... 10.00 - 15.00
JIMMY INMAN & IMPOLLOS:
Aladdin 3426 *You Never Realized* .... 10.00 - 15.00
INSPIRATIONS:
Apollo 494 *Raindrops* .... 20.00 - 30.00
Jamie 1034 *Dry Your Eyes* .... 10.00 - 15.00
Lamp 2109 *Don't Cry* .... 15.00 - 20.00
Old Town 1053 *Starlight Tonight* .... 15.00 - 20.00
Sultan 1 *The Feeling Of Her Kiss* .... 8.00 - 12.00
INSPIRATORS:
Treat 502 *If Loving You Is Wrong* .... 50.00 - 75.00
INTENTIONS:
Jamie 1253 *Summertime Angel* .... 50.00 - 75.00
Kent 455 *My Love She's Gone* .... 15.00 - 20.00
INTERIORS:
Worthy 1008 *Darling Little Angel* .... 8.00 - 12.00
INTERVALS:
Apt 25019 *I Still Love That Man* .... 5.00 - 8.00
Class 304 *Here's That Rainy Day* .... 5.00 - 8.00
INVICTAS:
Jack Bee 1003 *Gone So Long* .... 15.00 - 20.00
INVINCIBLES:
Chess 1727 *Mr. Moonglow* .... 7.00 - 10.00
JERRY IRBY:
Daffan 106 *Call For Me Darling* .... 8.00 - 12.00
108 *Clickety Clack* .... 15.00 - 20.00
111 *That's Too Bad* .... 10.00 - 15.00
Jer-Ray 222 *Chantilly Lace* .... 10.00 - 15.00
IRRIDESCENTS:
Hudson 8102 *Three Coins In The Fountain* ...... 10.00 - 15.00

ROBERT A. IRVINE:

Presto 525 *Fastest Short In Town* . . . .   -

JIMMY ISLE:

Roulette 4065 *Goin' Wild* . . . .   7.00 -   10.00

ISLEY BROTHERS:

Cindy 3009 *Don't Be Jealous* . . . .   15.00 -   20.00
Gone 5048 *My Love* . . . .   8.00 -   12.00
RCA Victor (LP) 2156 *Shout!* . . . .   20.00 -   30.00

IVAN:

Coral 62017 *Real Wild Child* . . . .   15.00 -   20.00
  62081 *Frankie Frankenstein* . . . .   20.00 -   30.00
  65607 *Real Wild Child* . . . .   10.00 -   15.00

JIMMY IVES:

Comet 2141 *My Fumbling Heart* . . . .   5.00 -   8.00

THE IVIES:

Brunswick 55112 *Sunshine* . . . .   8.00 -   12.00
Roulette 4183 *Voodoo* . . . .   8.00 -   12.00

THE IVORIES:

Jaguar 3019 *Alone* . . . .   30.00 -   40.00
Jaguar 3023 *Alone* . . . .   15.00 -   20.00
Mercury 71239 *Me And You* . . . .   8.00 -   12.00

SONNY JOE IVY:

Jewel 738 *Ruby And The Gambler* . . . .   5.00 -   8.00

IVY THREE:

Shell 302 *Nine Out Of Ten* . . . .   5.00 -   8.00
  306 *Bagoo* . . . .   5.00 -   8.00
  720 *Yogi* . . . . 5.00 -   8.00
  723 *Alone in the Chapel* . . . .   8.00 -   12.00

IVY TONES:

Red-Top 105 *Oo Wee Baby* (blue label) . . . .   8.00 -   12.00

J.B. & HIS BAYOU BOYS:

J.O.B. 1008 *The Mountain* . . . .   50.00 -   75.00

J.B. & HIS HAWKS:

Chance 1155 *Combination Boogie* . . . .   100.00 - 150.00
  1160 *Pet Cream Man* . . . .   150.00 - 200.00

JACK & JILL:

Caddy 110 *Party Time* . . . .   7.00 -   10.00
Imperial 5464 *Record Hop* . . . .   8.00 -   12.00

JACKIE & STARLITES:

Fury 1057 *I Found Out Too Late* . . . .   10.00 -   15.00
Mascot 128 *For All We Know* . . . .   15.00 -   20.00

JACKS:

Crown (LP) 372 *The Jacks* . . . .   15.00 -   20.00
  (LP) 5021 *Jumpin' With The Jacks* . . . .   20.00 -   25.00
RPM 428, 433, 444, 454, 458, 467 . . . .   5.00 -   10.00

JACKSON BROTHERS:

Atlantic 1034 *Love Me* . . . .   7.00 -   10.00
RCA Victor 5005 *We're Gonna Rock This Joint* . .   8.00 -   12.00
  5446 *Flat Foot Boogie* . . . .   8.00 -   12.00

BOBBY JACKSON:

Brunswick 55026 *Deep Elm Blues* . . . .   7.00 -   10.00

BULL MOOSE JACKSON:

Audio Lab (LP) 1524 *Bull Moose Jackson* . . . . .   30.00 -   50.00
Encino 1004 *Watch My Signals* . . . .   7.00 -   10.00
King (EP) 211 *Sings His All Time Hits* . . . .   50.00 -   75.00
  (EP) 261 . . . .   50.00 -   75.00
King 4181 *Sneaky Pete* . . . .   10.00 -   15.00
  4189 *I Want a Bowlegged Woman* . . . .   10.00 -   15.00
  4580 *Big Ten-Inch Record* . . . .   10.00 -   15.00

EDDIE JACKSON:

Fortune 186 *Rock 'N' Roll Baby* . . . .   10.00 -   15.00

HANDY JACKSON:

Sun 177 *Got My Application Baby* . . . .   100.00 - 150.00

LEE JACKSON:

Cobra 5007 *Fishin' In My Pond* . . . .   10.00 -   15.00
Keyhole 115 *Please Baby* . . . .   8.00 -   12.00

LIL/LITTLE SON JACKSON (& HIS ROCK & ROLLERS)

Imperial 5156 *Travelin' Woman* . . . .   30.00 -   40.00
  5165 *Upstairs Boogie* . . . .   30.00 -   40.00
  5175 *My Little Girl* . . . .   30.00 -   40.00
  5192 *Travelin' Alone* . . . .   30.00 -   40.00

  5204 *Journey Back Home* . . . .   30.00 -   40.00
  5218 *Black And Brown* . . . .   20.00 -   30.00
  5229 *Lonely Blues* . . . .   20.00 -   30.00
  5237 *Spending Money Blues* . . . .   30.00 -   40.00
  5248 *Confession* . . . .   20.00 -   30.00
  5259 *Dirty Work* . . . .   20.00 -   30.00
  5267 *Thrill Me Baby* . . . .   20.00 -   30.00
  5276 *Piggly Wiggly* . . . .   15.00 -   25.00
  5286 *Blues By The Hour* . . . .   15.00 -   25.00
  5300 *Let Me Down Easy* . . . .   10.00 -   15.00
  5312 *How Long* . . . .   10.00 -   15.00
  5319 *My Younger Days* . . . .   8.00 -   12.00
  5339 *Sugar Mama* . . . .   8.00 -   12.00
  5963 *Prison Bound* . . . .   5.00 -   8.00
Imperial (LP) 9142 *Rockin' & Rollin'* . . . .   100.00 - 150.00
Post 2014 *Lonely Blues* . . . .   20.00 -   30.00

WANDA JACKSON:

Capitol (LP) 1041 *Wanda Jackson* . . . .   40.00 -   60.00
  (LP) 1384 *Rockin' With Wanda* . . . .   75.00 - 100.00
  (LP) 1511 *There's A Party Goin' On* . . . .   75.00 - 100.00
  (LP) 1776 *Wonderful Wanda* . . . .   20.00 -   30.00
Capitol 3485 *I Gotta Know* . . . .   7.00 -   10.00
  3575 *Hot Dog That Made Him Mad* . . . .   7.00 -   10.00
  3637 *Baby Loves Him* . . . .   7.00 -   10.00
  3683 *Let Me Explain* . . . .   7.00 -   10.00
  3764 *Cool Love* . . . .   7.00 -   10.00
  3843 *Fujiyama Mama* . . . .   8.00 -   12.00
Capitol 3941 *Honey Bop* . . . .   7.00 -   10.00
  4026 *Mean Mean Mean* . . . .   10.00 -   15.00
  4081 *Rock Your Baby* . . . .   10.00 -   15.00
  4142 *Savin' My Love* . . . .   8.00 -   12.00
  4207 *You're The One For Me* . . . .   10.00 -   15.00
  4286 *I'd Rather Have You* . . . .   7.00 -   10.00
  4354 *My Destiny* . . . .   7.00 -   10.00
  4397 *Let's Have A Party* . . . .   10.00 -   15.00
  4469 *Mean Mean Man* . . . .   8.00 -   12.00
  4520 *Riot In Cell Block #9* . . . .   8.00 -   12.00
  4553 *Right Or Wrong* . . . .   5.00 -   8.00
  4635 *I'd Be Ashamed* . . . .   5.00 -   8.00
  4681 *I Don't Wanta Go* . . . .   5.00 -   8.00
Capitol most other issues . . . .   3.00 -   6.00
(Note: 78 rpm issues of above numbers are worth
  somewhat more.)
Decca 29253, 29514, 29627, 30153 . . . .   5.00 -   8.00

THE JAC-O-LACS:

Tampa 103 *Cindy Lou* . . . .   30.00 -   40.00

JIM JACONO & THE J'S:

Kay-Y 66783 *Take My Money* . . . .   -

JADES:

Ching (LP) 69 *So Tough!* . . . .   -
Nau-Voo 807 *Walking All Alone* . . . .   5.00 -   8.00
Time 1002 *So Blue* . . . .   5.00 -   8.00

JAGUARS:

Aardell 0003 *I Wanted You* . . . .   15.00 -   20.00
  0006 *You Don't Believe Me* . . . .   15.00 -   25.00
Ebb 129 *Hold Me Tonight* . . . .   7.00 -   10.00
Original Sound 06 *Thinking Of You* . . . .   5.00 -   8.00
R-Dell 11 *The Way You Look Tonight* (red plastic)   75.00 - 100.00
  11 same, but black plastic . . . .   20.00 -   30.00
Rendezvous 159 *It Finally Happened* . . . .   10.00 -   15.00

"JAMBOREE!":

(Complete score of musical, with Jimmy Bowen,
  Fats Domino, Buddy Knox, Jerry Lee Lewis,
  et al.) . . . . 100.00 -   up
(Note: The price of this rare album is
  conjectural; a copy was recently offered at
  auction with a minimum bid of several hundred
  dollars.)

BILL JAMES:

Mun Rab 104 *School's Out* . . . .   7.00 -   10.00

BOBBIE JAMES & 4 BUDDIES:

Club 51 104 *I Need You So* . . . .   75.00 - 100.00

DWIGHT JAMES:
Spindletop 111 *Walkin' Out* . . . . 10.00 - 15.00
ELMER JAMES:
Trumpet 186 *Gonna Find My Baby* . . . . 20.00 - 30.00
ELMORE JAMES (& HIS BROOMDUSTERS):
Ace 508 *Dust My Broom* . . . . 15.00 - 20.00
Checker 777 *Country Boogie* . . . . 100.00 - 150.00
Chess 1756 *I Can't Hold Out* . . . . 7.00 - 10.00
Chief 7001 *The Twelve Year Old Boy* . . . . . . 10.00 - 15.00
   7004 *It Hurts Me Too* . . . . 10.00 - 15.00
   7006 *Cry For Me Baby* . . . . 10.00 - 15.00
   7020 *Knocking At Your Door* . . . . 8.00 - 12.00
Crown (LP) 5168 *Blues After Hours* . . . . 35.00 - 50.00
Enjoy 2015, 2020 . . . . 5.00 - 8.00
Fire 504, 1011, 1016, 1023, 1031, 1503 . . . . 5.00 - 8.00
Flair 1011 *Early In The Morning* . . . . 50.00 - 75.00
   1014 *Make A Little Love* . . . . 50.00 - 75.00
   1022 *Please Find My Baby* . . . . 75.00 - 100.00
   1031 *Hand In Hand* . . . . 75.00 - 100.00
   1039 *1839 Blues* . . . . 60.00 - 80.00
   1048 *Dark And Dreary* . . . . 60.00 - 90.00
   1057 *Sunny Land* . . . . 40.00 - 60.00
   1062 *Late Hours At Midnight* . . . . 35.00 - 50.00
   1069 *Happy Home* . . . . 35.00 - 50.00
   1074 *Dust My Blues* . . . . 35.00 - 50.00
   1079 *Blues Before Sunrise* . . . . 35.00 - 50.00
Kent (LP) 5022 *Original Folk Blues* . . . . 35.00 - 50.00
Meteor 5000 *I Believe* . . . . 35.00 - 50.00
   5003 *Sinful Woman* . . . . 35.00 - 50.00
Sphere Sound (LP) 7002 *The Sky Is Crying* . . . . 30.00 - 40.00
   (LP) 7008 *I Need You* . . . . 30.00 - 40.00
Trumpet 146 *Dust My Broom* . . . . 15.00 - 20.00
Vee Jay 249, 259, 260 . . . . 7.00 - 10.00
ETTA JAMES (& THE PEACHES):
Argo (LP) 4003 *At Last* . . . . 30.00 - 40.00
Modern (M) 947 *Roll With Me Henry* . . . . 10.00 - 15.00
   957 *Hey Henry* . . . . 7.00 - 10.00
   962 *Good Rockin' Daddy* . . . . 7.00 - 10.00
   972 *W-O-M-A-N* . . . . 7.00 - 10.00
JESSIE JAMES:
Kent 314 *Red Hot Rockin' Blues* . . . . 15.00 - 20.00
McKINLEY JAMES:
Tomahawk 737 *Ain't Gonna Pick No Cotton* . . . . 15.00 - 20.00
SONNY JAMES:
Capitol (LP) 779 *Southern Gentleman* . . . . 10.00 - 15.00
   (LP) 867 *Sonny* . . . . 10.00 - 15.00
   (LP) 988 *Honey* . . . . 10.00 - 15.00
   (LP) 1178 *This Is Sonny James* . . . . 10.00 - 15.00
   3602 *Young Love* (78 rpm) . . . . 8.00 - 12.00
   3674 *First Date, First Kiss, First Love* (78 rpm) 7.00 - 10.00
   3840 *Uh-Huh-Mm* (78 rpm) . . . . 7.00 - 10.00
TOMMY JAMES (& THE SHONDELLS):
La Louisianne (LP) 109 *The Shondells At The
   Saturday Hop* . . . . 30.00 - 40.00
Philco (Hip Pocket) HP 1 *I Think We're Alone
   Now* . . . . — - —
(Hip Picket) HP 2 *Hanky Panky* . . . . — - —
(Above are 3-7/8 inches in diameter)
Red Fox 110 *Hanky Panky* . . . . — - —
Snap 102 *Hanky Panky* . . . . 15.00 - 20.00
JAN AND ARNIE:
Arwin 108 *Jennie Lee* (78 rpm) . . . . 15.00 - 20.00
Arwin 108, 111, 113 . . . . 5.00 - 10.00
Dore 522 *Baby Talk* (DJ) . . . . — - —
(Note: Most copies of Dore 522 are as by JAN &
   DEAN, which see)
Dot (EP) 1097 *Jan & Arnie* . . . . 75.00 - 100.00
JAN & DEAN:
Challenge 9111 *Those Words* . . . . 15.00 - 20.00
Dore (LP) 101 *Jan & Dean* . . . . 75.00 - 100.00
Dore 522 *Baby Talk* . . . . 8.00 - 12.00
531 *There's A Girl* . . . . 8.00 - 12.00

539 *Clementine* . . . . 8.00 - 12.00
548 *Cindy* . . . . 8.00 - 12.00
555 *We Go Together* . . . . 8.00 - 12.00
576 *Gee* . . . . 8.00 - 12.00
610 *Julie* . . . . 8.00 - 12.00
J & D 401 *California Lullaby* . . . . 15.00 - 20.00
   402 *Like A Summer Rain* . . . . 15.00 - 20.00
Jan & Dean 10 *Hawaii* . . . . 20.00 - 30.00
   11 *Fan Tan* . . . . 20.00 - 30.00
Liberty 55522 *She's Still Talking Baby Talk* . . . . 10.00 - 15.00
Liberty (most other issues) . . . . 4.00 - 8.00
Magic Lamp 401 *Summertime* . . . . 10.00 - 15.00
Warner Bros. 7219 *Laurel And Hardy* . . . . 10.00 - 15.00
JAN & THE RADIANTS:
Clock 1028 *Now Is The Hour* . . . . 8.00 - 12.00
Queen 24007 *Is It True* . . . . 10.00 - 15.00
JOHNNY JANIS:
ABC Paramount 9800 *I Played The Field* . . . . . . 5.00 - 8.00
   9840 *Later Baby* . . . . 5.00 - 8.00
Coral 61552 *Move It Or Lose It* . . . . 5.00 - 8.00
JOHNNY JANO:
Excello 2099 *Havin' A Whole Lot Of Fun* . . . . 10.00 - 15.00
Hollywood 1087 *Mabel's Gone* . . . . 10.00 - 15.00
THE JARMELS:
Laurie 3083, 3124 . . . . 5.00 - 8.00
FELTON JARVIS:
M-G-M 12982 *Goin' Down Town* . . . . 7.00 - 10.00
BOBBY JAY:
Imperial 5590 *Sweet Little Stranger* . . . . 10.00 - 15.00
DALE JAY:
Raven 001 *Shakin' All Over* . . . . 7.00 - 10.00
JOHNNY JAY:
Mercury 71232 *Sugar Doll* . . . . 5.00 - 8.00
   71232 *Sugar Doll* (78 rpm) . . . . 8.00 - 12.00
Play 1006 *That's What I Like About Love* . . . . 10.00 - 15.00
P. JAY & THE HAYSTACKERS:
Oak 1202/1203 *High School Rock 'N' Roll* . . . . 15.00 - 20.00
THE JAYES (Featuring BILL CURTISS):
Arc 4443 *Panic Stricken* . . . . 15.00 - 20.00
JAYHAWKS:
Aladdin 3379 *Johnny's House Party* . . . . 10.00 - 15.00
   3393 *Everyone Should Know* . . . . 15.00 - 20.00
Flash 105 *Counting My Teardrops* . . . . 35.00 - 50.00
   109 *Stranded In The Jungle* . . . . 7.00 - 10.00
   111 *Love Train* . . . . 8.00 - 12.00
JAYTONES:
Brunswick 55087 *Gasoline* . . . . 20.00 - 30.00
Cub 9057 *My Only Love* . . . . 8.00 - 12.00
JAZZBOMBERS:
Tattler 1001 *Bad Boy* . . . . —
ALICE JEAN (See: Mondellos)
CATHY JEAN & ROOMMATES:
Valmor (LP) 78 *Great Oldies* . . . . 75.00 - 100.00
JIMMY JEFFERS & THE JOKERS:
Da-Mor 9220 *Raining Teardrops* . . . . 8.00 - 12.00
Fraternity 837 *Teardrops From My Eyes* . . . . . . 5.00 - 8.00
EDDIE JEFFERSON:
Checker 855 *Billie's Bounce* . . . . 5.00 - 8.00
WALLY JEFFERY:
Do-Re-Mi 1402 *Oh Yeah* . . . . 30.00 - 50.00
BOBBY JENKINS:
Hamilton 50001 *White Shorts And A Red Tee
   Shirt* . . . . 7.00 - 10.00
BO BO JENKINS:
Boxer 202 *Tell Me Who* . . . . 10.00 - 15.00
Chess 1565 *Democrat Blues* . . . . 40.00 - 60.00
Duchess 101 *Tell Me Who* . . . . —
Fortune 838 *Ten Below Zero* . . . . 20.00 - 30.00
GUS JENKINS/JINKINS:
Flash 116, 123, 126, 128, 130, 131 . . . . 4.00 - 8.00
BABY BOY JENNINGS & THE SATELITES:
Savoy 1589 *Little Girl* . . . . 5.00 - 8.00

WAYLON JENNINGS:
Brunswick 55130 *Jole Blond* . . . . 50.00 - 75.00
Ramco 1989 *My Baby Walks All Over Me* . . . . . 7.00 - 10.00
Trend '63 106 *The Stage* . . . . 10.00 - 15.00

RALPH JEROME:
K.P. 1007 *Rockhouse* . . . . 12.00 - 18.00

JERRY & DEMAR:
Ford 501 *Cross-Eyed Alley Cat* . . . . 30.00 - 40.00

JESSE & BUZZY:
Savoy 1556 *Without Your Love* . . . . 4.00 - 7.00

JESSE & MARVIN:
Specialty 447 *Dream Girl* (red vinyl) . . . . 20.00 - 30.00

JESSIE & THE SEQUINS:
Profile 4008 *Hold My Hand* . . . . 10.00 - 15.00

THE JESTERS:
Winley 218 *So Strange* . . . . 15.00 - 20.00
221 *Please Let Me Love You* . . . . 7.00 - 10.00
225 *The Plea* . . . . 7.00 - 10.00
242 *The Wind* . . . . 7.00 - 10.00
248 *That's How It Goes* . . . . 8.00 - 12.00
252 *Come Let Me Show You* . . . . 8.00 - 12.00

THE JETS:
Aladdin 3247 *I'll Hide My Tears* . . . . 80.00 - 120.00
Gee 1020 *Heaven Above Me* . . . . 80.00 - 120.00
7-11 2102 *Volcano* . . . . 90.00 - 130.00

JEWELS:
Imperial 5351 *Hearts Can Be Broken* . . . . 8.00 - 12.00
5362 *Please Return* . . . . 8.00 - 12.00
5377 *How* . . . . 8.00 - 12.00
5387 *My Baby* . . . . 8.00 - 12.00
R & B 1301 *Hearts Of Stone* . . . . 15.00 - 20.00
1303 *A Fool In Paradise* . . . . 20.00 - 25.00
Rama 10 *Heartbreaker* . . . . 100.00 - Up
(Note: Above also issued as by THE CROWS)
RPM 474 *She's A Flirt* . . . . 10.00 - 15.00

THE JIANTS:
Claudra 112 *Tornado* . . . . 15.00 - 20.00

JILL & RAY:
Le Cam 929 *Hey Paula* . . . . 15.00 - 20.00

JIMMY & DUANE:
Preston 212 *Soda Fountain Girl* . . . . 50.00 - 75.00

JIMMY & JOHNNY (& THE JADES):
Chess 4863 *Love Me* . . . . 15.00 - 20.00
D1004 *I Can't Find The Door Knob* . . . . 10.00 - 15.00
D—*Don't Give Me That Look* . . . . -
Decca 29772 *Sweet Singing Daddy* . . . . 5.00 - 8.00
30061 *Sweet Love On My Mind* . . . . 15.00 - 20.00
TNT 184 *Don't Call Me, I'll Call You* . . . . 7.00 - 10.00

JIMMY & WALTER:
Sun 180 *Before Long* . . . . 100.00 - 150.00

GUS JINKINS (See GUS JENKINS)

THE JIVE-A-TONES:
Felsted 8506 *Flirty Gertie* . . . . 10.00 - 15.00
Fraternity 823 *The Wild Bird* . . . . 5.00 - 8.00

JIVE BOMBERS:
Savoy 1508 *Bad Boy* . . . . 5.00 - 8.00
1513, 1515, 1535 . . . . 3.00 - 5.00

THE JIVE FIVE:
Beltone 1006 *My True Story* . . . . 7.00 - 10.00
1014 *Never, Never* . . . . 7.00 - 10.00
Lana 105 *My True Story* . . . . 5.00 - 8.00

JIVERS:
Aladdin 3329 *Cherie* . . . . 25.00 - 35.00
3347 *Ray Pearl* . . . . 30.00 - 40.00

JIVETONES:
Apt 25020 *Geraldine* . . . . 10.00 - 15.00

JIVIN GENE:
Jin 109 *Going Out With The Tide* . . . . 10.00 - 15.00

JODIMARS:
Capitol 3285, 3360, 3436, 3512 . . . . 4.00 - 8.00

JOEY & THE LEXINGTONS:
Dunes 2029 *Bobbie* . . . . 10.00 - 15.00

JOHNNIE & JOE:
Chess 1654 *Over The Mountain Across The Sea* . 5.00 - 8.00
J & S 1630 *Warm Soft And Lovely* . . . . 7.00 - 10.00
1631 *False Love Has To Go* . . . . 7.00 - 10.00
1659 *There Goes My Heart* . . . . 7.00 - 10.00
1664 *Over The Mountain , Cross The Sea* . . . 15.00 - 20.00
1677 *I Was So Lonely* . . . . 7.00 - 10.00

JOHNNY & THE HURRICANES:
Big Top (LP) 1302 *The Big Sound Of* . . . . 30.00 - 40.00
Warwick (EP) 700 *Johnny & The Hurricanes* . . . 20.00 - 30.00
(LP) 2007 *Johnny & The Hurricanes* . . . . 20.00 - 30.00
(LP) 2010 *Stormsville* . . . . 20.00 - 30.00

JOHNNY & THE JAMMERS:
Dart 131 *School Day Blues* . . . . 30.00 - 50.00

JOHNNY & THE JOKERS:
Harvard 804 *Do-Re-Mi Rock* . . . . 8.00 - 12.00

JOHNNIE & JONIE:
Challenge 59001 *Kee-Ro-Ryin'* . . . . 5.00 - 8.00
59041 *Tijuana Jail* . . . . 5.00 - 8.00

JOHNSON BROTHERS:
Carrie 012 *Sleep With a Dream* . . . . 7.00 - 10.00

AL JOHNSON:
Ric 956 *You Done Me Wrong* . . . . 5.00 - 8.00

(BILL) BILL JOHNSON:
My Hot Rod Car . . . . -

BUDDY JOHNSON:
Mercury (LP) 20209 *Rock 'N' Roll* . . . . 20.00 - 30.00

CLIFF JOHNSON:
Columbia 40865 *Go 'Way Hound Dog* . . . . 15.00 - 20.00

CURTIS JOHNSON:
Event 426 *Baby, Baby* . . . . 10.00 - 15.00

DEE JOHNSON:
Dixie 2022 *Back To School* . . . . 10.00 - 15.00

GLENN JOHNSON:
Oak 0360 *I'm Gonna Leave You* . . . . 25.00 - 35.00

HOYT JOHNSON:
Erwin 555 *Eenie Meenie Miney Moe* . . . . 30.00 - 50.00
Satellite 110 *I Just Can't Learn* . . . . 10.00 - 15.00

JIMMY JOHNSON:
Class 237 *Cool Cool School* . . . . 8.00 - 12.00
Viv 3001 *Cat Daddy* . . . . 15.00 - 20.00

LONNIE JOHNSON:
King (EP) 267 *Tomorrow Night* . . . . 20.00 - 30.00
(LP) 520 *Lonesome Road* . . . . 50.00 - 75.00
King 4201 *Tomorrow Night* . . . . 10.00 - 15.00
4212 *Working Man's Blues* . . . . 10.00 - 15.00
4225 *I Want My Baby* . . . . 10.00 - 15.00
4245 *Pleasing You* . . . . 10.00 - 15.00
4261 *I Know It's Love* . . . . 10.00 - 15.00
4263 *So Tired* . . . . 10.00 - 15.00
4278 *You're Mine You* . . . . 10.00 - 15.00
4297 *I Found A Dream* . . . . 10.00 - 15.00
King 4317, 4336, 4346, 4388, 4411, 4423, 4450,
4459, 4473, 4492, 4510, 4553 . . . . 8.00 - 12.00
(Note: Some distinction may be made between
the original issues of the lower numbers, which
have -A and -AA suffixes to record numbers,
and subsequent pressings, which lack suffixes.
Also, any of foregoing, pressed of colored
vinyl, would being substantially higher prices.)
King (most other issues) . . . . 5.00 - 10.00
Rama 9 *My Woman Is Gone* . . . . 20.00 - 30.00
14 *Will You Remember* . . . . 12.00 - 16.00
19 *It's Been So Long* . . . . 15.00 - 20.00
20 *This Love Of Mine* . . . . 15.00 - 20.00

MARV JOHNSON:
Tamla 101 *Come To Me* . . . . 25.00 - 50.00
United Artists (EP) 100 . . . . 50.00 - 75.00
United Artist (LP) 3081 *Marvelous* . . . . 20.00 - 30.00

NEAL JOHNSON:
Specialty 688 *True To You Baby* . . . . 5.00 - 8.00

RAY JOHNSON:

Demon 1502 *A Yellow Mellow Hardtop*	7.00 -	10.00
RICK JOHNSON:		
Comet 104 *Me And My Baby*	5.00 -	10.00
STAN JOHNSON:		
Ruby 550 *Baby, Baby Doll*	15.00 -	20.00
THE JOKERS:		
Grace 510 *Little Mama*	15.00 -	20.00
Greco 610 *Red Headed Woman*	-	
Lin 5027 *Dogfight*	7.00 -	10.00
JOLLY JACKS:		
Dasher 501 *Ugly Face*	7.00 -	10.00
JONES BOYS: (See also JIMMY JONES)		
S-G 5007 *The Song Is Ended*	5.00 -	8.00
ALEX SNOOK JONES:		
Blue Boy 1001 *Mean Old Greyhound*	7.00 -	10.00
CORKY JONES:		
Pep 107 *Hot Dog*	40.00 -	60.00
DEAN JONES:		
MGM 12620 *Meet Me In The Study Hall*	8.00 -	12.00
DOTTIE JONES:		
TNT 139 *Honey Honey*	-	
EDDIE JONES (See: GUITAR SLIM)		
FLOYD JONES:		
Chess 1527 *Early Morning*	75.00 -	100.00
J.O.B. 1013 *On The Road Again*	75.00 -	100.00
Vee Jay 111 *Ain't Times Hard*	75.00 -	100.00
126 *Floyd's Blues*	40.00 -	60.00
GEORGE JONES:		
Mercury (LP) 20306 *Sings*	20.00 -	30.00
(LP) 20477 *Sings*	20.00 -	30.00
(LP) 20596 *Salutes Hank Williams*	20.00 -	30.00
Starday (LP) SLP-101 *Grand Ole Opry's New*		
Star	50.00 -	75.00
Starday 130 *No Money In This Deal*	10.00 -	15.00
202 *Why Baby Why*	8.00 -	12.00
216 *Still Hurtin'*	8.00 -	12.00
234, 247, 256, 264, 279	7.00 -	10.00
GRANDPA JONES:		
King (LP) 554 *Greatest Hits*	15.00 -	20.00
(LP) 625 *Strictly Country Tunes*	15.00 -	20.00
JIMMY JONES & THE JONES BOYS:		
Arrow 717 *Heaven In Your Eyes*	20.00 -	30.00
LITTLE JOHNNY JONES (With THE		
CHICAGO HOUND DOGS):		
Atlantic 1045 *Hoy Hoy*	15.00 -	20.00
Flair 1010 *I May Be Wrong*	20.00 -	30.00
RICKEY JONES:		
Herald 498 *Hate To Say Goodbye*	5.00 -	8.00
LITTLE SONNY JONES:		
Imperial 5275 *I Got Booted*	20.00 -	30.00
THUMPER JONES:		
Starday 240 *Rock It*	40.00 -	60.00
WILL JONES & THE CADETS (See THE		
CADETS)		
JONESY'S COMBO:		
Combo 79 *Ting, Ting Boom Scat*	8.00 -	12.00
JORDAN & THE FASCINATIONS:		
Carol 4116 *Once Upon A Time*	7.00 -	10.00
JORDAN BROS:		
Jamie 1112, 1125, 1133, 1169, 1205	7.00 -	10.00
JOHNNY JORDAN:		
Jolt 332 *Sweet Sweet Sweet*	8.00 -	12.00
LOUIS JORDAN:		
Aladdin 3223 *Whiskey Do Your Stuff*	8.00 -	12.00
3227 *Ooh Wee!*	8.00 -	12.00
3243 *A Dollar Down*	8.00 -	12.00
3246 *Messi Bessie*	8.00 -	12.00
3249 *Louis' Blues*	8.00 -	12.00
3264 *Yeah, Yeah, Baby*	8.00 -	12.00
3270 *The Dripper*	8.00 -	12.00
3279 *Time Is A-Passin'*	8.00 -	12.00
3295 *Gotta Go*	8.00 -	12.00
Decca (LP) 8551 *Let The Good Times Roll*	50.00 -	75.00
Decca (most issues)	4.00 -	8.00
Score (LP) 4007 *Go Blow Your Horn*	75.00 -	100.00
Wing (LP) 12126 *Somebody Up There Digs Me* ..	20.00 -	30.00
BENNIE JOY:		
Antler 4011 *Crash The Party*	20.00 -	30.00
Disc Jockey 41 *Crash The Party*	20.00 -	30.00
Dixie 2001 *Spin The Bottle*	75.00 -	100.00
Ram 1107 *Ittie Bittie Everything*	40.00 -	60.00
Tri-Dec *Spin The Bottle*	20.00 -	30.00
JOYLARKS:		
Snag 107 *Betty My Love*	20.00 -	30.00
JOYTONES:		
Rama 202 *Is This Really The End?*	8.00 -	12.00
JUBALAIRES:		
Capitol 821 *Blue Ribbon Gal*	20.00 -	30.00
845 *The Old Piano Roll Blues*	20.00 -	30.00
DON JULIAN & THE MEADOWLARKS:		
Dooto (EP) 203	50.00 -	80.00
Dootone 359 *Heaven And Paradise*	15.00 -	20.00
367 *Always And Always*	15.00 -	20.00
372 *This Must Be Paradise*	15.00 -	20.00
394 *Please Love A Fool*	20.00 -	30.00
405 *I'm A Believer*	15.00 -	20.00
Magnum 716 *Lie*	7.00 -	10.00
JOHNNY JUMPER:		
Vance *Walking Talking/Worried Over You*		
JUMPIN' JACKS:		
Bruce 115 *Embraceable You*	50.00 -	75.00
Lloyds 101 *Why Oh Why*	50.00 -	75.00
JUMPIN' JAGUARS:		
Decca 29938 *Shut The Door Baby*		
JUMPINTONES:		
Raven 8004 *I Wonder*	7.00 -	10.00
8005 *That Angel Is You*	7.00 -	10.00
BILL JUSTIS:		
Phillips 3519 *Raunchy* (78 rpm)	15.00 -	20.00
KADAKS (See: KODAKS)		
KALIN TWINS:		
Decca (LP) 8812 *The Kalin Twins*	20.00 -	30.00
30642 *When* (78 rpm)	8.00 -	12.00
KASANDREA With THE MIDNIGHT		
RIDERS:		
Sahara 101 *My Conscience Is Bothering Me*	10.00 -	15.00
ANNE KAYE:		
Gee 1015 *Every Fortune Teller Tells Me*	5.00 -	8.00
ERNIE K-DOE:		
Minit (LP) 00002 *Mother-In-Law*	20.00 -	30.00
RAMSEY KEARNEY:		
Jaxon 501 *Rock The Bop*	30.00 -	50.00
BILLY KEEN & THE TRADEWINDS:		
Lesley 1922 *Don't Call Me*	8.00 -	12.00
THE KELLY FOUR:		
Silver 1001 *Strollin' Guitar*	7.00 -	10.00
1006 *So, Fine, Be Mine!*	7.00 -	10.00
JIMMY KELLY:		
Cobra 5028 *Little Chickie*	15.00 -	20.00
PAT KELLY & THE SHAMROCKS:		
Chic 1009 *The Stranger Dressed In Black*	5.00 -	8.00
Jubilee 5315 *Hey Doll Baby/Cloud 13*	10.00 -	15.00
TINY KENNEDY:		
Capitol 840 *Sister Flat Top*	15.00 -	20.00
KENNEDY & THE CADETS:		
Randy 422 *Barbie* (pink label with blue type) ...100.00 -		Up
KENNY and DOOLITTLE:		
Sims 123 *Kitty Kat*	15.00 -	20.00
KENNY AND THE KASUALS:		
Mark (LP) 5000 *The Impact Sound Of Kenny*		
And The Kasuals	-	
(Note: High prices quoted for this album will		
undoubtedly be affected by a reissue.)		
KENNY & MOE (THE BLUE BOYS):		

De Luxe 6101, 6122, 6134, 6139, 6154	5.00 -	8.00

HERB KENNY & THE COMETS:

Federal 12083 *Only You*	30.00 -	50.00

BOBBY KENT & THE KENTONES:

Bay State 82159 *Don't Go 'Way*	8.00 -	12.00

THE KENTS:

Argo 5299 *With All My Heart And Soul*	8.00 -	12.00
Dome 501 *I Love You So*	10.00 -	15.00

KEYNOTES:

Apollo 478 *Suddenly*	20.00 -	30.00
484 *I Don't Know*	20.00 -	30.00
493 *Wish You Were Here*	20.00 -	30.00
498 *Now I Know*	20.00 -	30.00
503 *In The Evening*	20.00 -	30.00
513 *Now I Know*	15.00 -	20.00

KEYSTONES:

Epic 9187 *The Magic Kiss*	10.00 -	15.00
G&M *The Magic Kiss*	20.00 -	30.00

KEYTONES:

Old Town 1041 *Seven Wonders Of The World*	10.00 -	15.00

BILLY (THE) KIDD:

Jane 107 *Crazy Guitar*	7.00 -	10.00

KIDDS:

Imperial 5335 *Are You Forgetting Me*	125.00 -	175.00
Post 2003 *You Broke My Heart*	100.00 -	150.00

KIDS FROM TEXAS:

Blue Star 1613 *Shoot The Moon*	8.00 -	12.00
Hanover 4500 *Long Legged Linda*	10.00 -	15.00

MERLE KILGORE:

D 1042 *I Take A Trip To The Moon*	8.00 -	12.00
Imperial 5379 *Teenagers Holiday*	15.00 -	20.00
5409 *Ernie*	15.00 -	20.00
5555 *Hang Doll*	10.00 -	15.00
8300 *Funny Feelin'*	10.00 -	15.00
Starday 469, 497	5.00 -	8.00

BILLY J. KILLEN:

Meridian 1510 *Georgia Boy*	10.00 -	15.00

ALBERT KING:

Bobbin 114, 119, 126, 129, 135, 141, 143	4.00 -	7.00
Coun-Tree 1006 *C.O.D*	5.00 -	8.00
King (LP) 852 *The Big Blues*	20.00 -	30.00
5575, 5588, 5751	3.00 -	5.00
Parrot 798 *Bad Luck Blues*	50.00 -	75.00

B.B. (BLUES BOY) KING:

Crown (LP) 5020 *Singin' The Blues*	20.00 -	30.00
(LP) 5063 *The Blues*	20.00 -	30.00
(LP) 5115 *B.B King Wails*	30.00 -	40.00
(LP) 5119 *B.B. King Sings Spirituals*	15.00 -	20.00
(LP) 5143 *The Great B.B. King*	15.00 -	20.00
(LP) 5167 *King Of The Blues*	15.00 -	20.00
(LP) 5188 *My Kind Of Blues*	15.00 -	20.00
Kent 301, 307, 315, 317, 319, 321, 327, 329, 330,		
333, 346, 350, 351, 353, 358, 360, 362, 363 . . .	3.00 -	6.00
RPM 304 *Mistreated Woman*	20.00 -	30.00
311 *Other Night Blues*	20.00 -	30.00
318 *My Baby's Gone*	20.00 -	30.00
323 *She's Dynamite*	15.00 -	25.00
330 *Hard Working Woman*	10.00 -	15.00
339 *Three O'Clock Blues*	10.00 -	15.00
348 *Fine Lookin' Woman*	10.00 -	15.00
355 *Shake It Up And Go*	10.00 -	15.00
360 *Gotta Find My Baby*	10.00 -	15.00
363 *You Know I Love You*	7.00 -	10.00
374 *Boogie Woogie Woman*	7.00 -	10.00
380 *Woke Up This Morning*	7.00 -	10.00
386 *Highway Bound*	7.00 -	10.00
RPM 391, 395, 403, 408, 411, 412, 416, 421, 425,		
430, 435, 437, 451	5.00 -	8.00
RPM 457, 459, 468, 479, 486, 490, 492, 494,		
498, 501	4.00 -	7.00

CAROLE KING:

ABC Paramount 9921 *Goin' Wild*	15.00 -	20.00

9986 *Baby Sittin'*	15.00 -	20.00
Alpine 57 *Oh, Neil*	20.00 -	30.00
Companion 2000 *Nobody's Perfect*	10.00 -	15.00
Dimension 1009 *He's A Bad Boy*	5.00 -	10.00
RCA Victor 7560 *Queen Of The Beach*	15.00 -	20.00

EARL KING:

Ace 509 *Baby You Can Get Your Gun*	8.00 -	12.00
514 *My Love Is Strong*	7.00 -	10.00
Specialty 531 *No One But Me*	5.00 -	8.00

EDDIE KING:

J.O.B. 1122 *Shakin' Inside*	30.00 -	50.00

FREDDY KING:

El-Bee 157 *Country Boy*	20.00 -	30.00
Federal 12384, 12401, 12415, 12428, 12432, 12443,		
12450	3.00 -	5.00
King (LP) 762 *Freddy King Sings*	15.00 -	20.00
(LP) 773 *Let's Hide Away & Dance Away*	15.00 -	20.00
(LP) 821 *Bossa Nova & The Blues*	10.00 -	15.00

JACK KING:

4-Star 1725 *I Just Learned To Rock*	15.00 -	20.00

JIMMY KING:

Herald 535 *Knocking On Your Door*	10.00 -	15.00

KID KING'S COMBO:

Excello 2009, 2018, 2025, 2037, 2046, 2059,		
2070, 2109	5.00 -	10.00

PEE WEE KING & HIS BAND:

RCA Victor (LP) 1237 *Swing West*	20.00 -	30.00
(LP) 3028 (10")	20.00 -	30.00
(LP) 3071 (10") *Pee Wee King's Western Hits* . .	20.00 -	30.00
(LP) 3109 (10") *Waltzes*	20.00 -	30.00
(LP) 3280 (10") *Swing West*	20.00 -	30.00
6450 *Blue Suede Shoes*	8.00 -	12.00

RANDY KING:

TNT 9009 *Be Boppin' Baby/Whispering Wind* . . .	20.00 -	30.00

RAY KING:

Karl 222 *A Date At Eight*	75.00 -	100.00

SID KING (& HIS FIVE STRINGS): (See also FIVE STRINGS)

Columbia 21361 *I Like It*	7.00 -	10.00
21449 *Sag, Drag And Fall*	10.00 -	15.00
21489 *Purr, Kitty, Purr*	15.00 -	20.00
21505 *Blue Suede Shoes*	15.00 -	20.00
21564 *Good Rockin' Baby*	15.00 -	20.00
40680 *Oobie Doobie*	15.00 -	20.00
40833 *When My Baby Left Me*	10.00 -	15.00
41019 *I've Got The Blues*	10.00 -	15.00

SLEEPY KING:

Awake 852 *Rock Rock*	7.00 -	10.00

WILLIE KING with IKE TURNER'S BAND:

Vita 123 *Peg Leg Woman*	8.00 -	12.00

KING BEES with LLOYD PRICE'S ORCHESTRA:

Flip 323 *Puppy Love*	8.00 -	12.00
KRC 302 *Can't You Understand*	8.00 -	12.00

KING CROONERS:

Excello 2168 *Now That She's Gone*	15.00 -	20.00
2187 *School Daze*	15.00 -	20.00

KING TOPPERS:

Josie 811 *Walkin' And Talkin' The Blues*	20.00 -	30.00

KING VICTOR:

Madison 110 *Boppin' Bobbie Jean*	7.00 -	10.00

THE KINGLETS with LEROY THOMAS:

Bobbin 104 *Pretty Please*	5.00 -	8.00

THE KINGS: (See also BOBBY HALL):

Baton 245 *Long, Lonely Nights*	15.00 -	20.00
Epic 9370 *I Want To Know*	7.00 -	10.00
Gotham 316 *God Made You Mine*	20.00 -	25.00
Jalo 203 *Angel*	7.00 -	10.00
Jay Wing 5805 *Surrender*	7.00 -	10.00*
Specialty 497 *What Can I Do*	10.00 -	15.00

KINGS MEN:

Club-51 108 *Don't Say You're Sorry*	150.00 -	250.00

KINGSMEN:
Neil 102 *One Foolish Mistake* . . . . 15.00 - 20.00
KINKS:
Cameo 308 *Long Tall Sally* . . . . 30.00 - 40.00
    345 *Long Tall Sally* . . . . 15.00 - 20.00
    348 *You Still Want Me* . . . . 75.00 - 100.00
JIMMY KIRKLAND (With STAN GETZ & THE TOM CATS):
Fox 918/919 *Come On Baby* . . . . 15.00 - 20.00
Teen Life 918/919 *Come On Baby* . . . . 30.00 - 40.00
REX KLINGENSMITH:
Process 103 *Old Country Music* . . . . 8.00 - 12.00
KLIXS:
Music City 817 *This Is The End Of Love* . . . . . . 15.00 - 20.00
    823 *Elaine* . . . . 20.00 - 30.00
TOMMY KNACKIN:
Cascade *Worry Worry Worry* . . . . 8.00 - 12.00
KNICKERBOCKERS:
Natural 3000 *You Must Know* . . . . 150.00 - 200.00
BAKER KNIGHT (& THE KNIGHTMARES):
Coral 62132 *Takin' A Chance* . . . . 7.00 - 10.00
    62160 *Tag Along Blues* . . . . 7.00 - 10.00
Decca 30135 *Bring My Cadillac Back* . . . . 7.00 - 10.00
    30213 *Reelin' And Rockin'* . . . . 7.00 - 10.00
    30426 *Love-A Love-A Love-A* . . . . 7.00 - 10.00
Kit 900 *Bring My Cadillac Back* . . . . 15.00 - 20.00
GLADYS KNIGHT & THE PIPS:
Fury (LP) 1003 *Letter Full Of Tears* . . . . 50.00 - 75.00
JESSIE KNIGHT:
Checker 797 *Nothing But Money* . . . . 10.00 - 15.00
JOHNNY KNIGHT:
Morocco 1005 *Rock And Roll Guitar* . . . . 15.00 - 20.00
MARIE KNIGHT:
Mercury 70969 *Look At Me* . . . . 8.00 - 12.00
Wing 90069 *Tell Me Why* . . . . 5.00 - 8.00
SONNY KNIGHT:
Dot 15507 *Confidential* (78 rpm) . . . . 10.00 - 15.00
Eastman 787 *Lipstick Kisses* . . . . 4.00 - 7.00
    791 *Barbara* . . . . 4.00 - 7.00
    Go Go 711 *Teenage Party* . . . . -
Starla 10 *Once In A While* . . . . 7.00 - 10.00
Vita 137 *Confidential* . . . . 10.00 - 15.00
SUNNY KNIGHT:
Dot 15542 *Worthless And Lowdown* . . . . 7.00 - 10.00
KNOCKOUTS:
Shad 5013 *Darling Lorraine* . . . . 5.00 - 8.00
BUDDY KNOX (with THE (RHYTHM) ORCHIDS):
Blue Moon 402 *Party Doll* . . . . 50.00 - 75.00
Liberty (LP) 3251 *Golden Hits* . . . . 15.00 - 20.00
Roulette 4002, 4009, 4018, 4042, 4082 . . . . 3.00 - 5.00
    4002 *Party Doll* (78 rpm) . . . . 10.00 - 15.00
    4009 *Rock Your Little Baby To Sleep* (78 rpm) . 8.00 - 12.00
    4018 *Hula Love* (78 rpm) . . . . 8.00 - 12.00
    4042 *Swingin' Daddy* (78 rpm) . . . . 10.00 - 15.00
    4082 *C'mon Baby* (78 rpm) . . . . 10.00 - 15.00
    (LP) 25003 *Buddy Knox* . . . . 20.00 - 30.00
    (LP) 25048 *Buddy Knox And Jimmy Bowen* . . 30.00 - 40.00
Ruff 1001 *Jo Ann* . . . . 4.00 - 8.00
Triple-D 797 *Party Doll* . . . . 50.00 - 75.00
KODAKS:
Fury 1007 *Teenagers Dream* . . . . 15.00 - 20.00
    1015 *Make Believe World* . . . . 15.00 - 20.00
    1019 *My Baby And Me* . . . . 15.00 - 20.00
    1020 *Guardian Angel* . . . . 15.00 - 20.00
J & S 1683 *Don't Want No Teasing* . . . . 8.00 - 12.00
J & S 1684 *Look Up To The Sky* . . . . 8.00 - 12.00
Sphere Sound (LP) 7005 *The Kodaks vs. The Starlites* . . . . 20.00 - 30.00
FREDDY KOENIG:
Lori 9548 *Hey Clarice!* . . . . 15.00 - 20.00
Valerie 225 *Hey Clarice!* . . . . 10.00 - 15.00

THE KO KOS:
Combo 141 *The First Day Of School* . . . . 5.00 - 8.00
KOOL GENTS:
Bethlehem 3061 *Picture On The Wall* . . . . 8.00 - 12.00
Vee Jay 173 *This Is The Night* . . . . 25.00 - 35.00
    207 *I Just Can't Help Myself* . . . . 25.00 - 35.00
PAUL KOSTY:
Fleet—*Don't Rock, Let's Roll* . . . . -
KUF-LINX:
Challenge 1013 *So Tough* . . . . 5.00 - 10.00
    59004 *Eyeballin* . . . . 5.00 - 10.00
    59015 *All That's Good* . . . . 5.00 - 10.00
SLEEPY LA BEEF/LA BEFF:
Crescent 102 *Turn Me Loose* . . . . 30.00 - 50.00
Dixie (EP) 530 *Ballad Of A Teenage Queen* (other cuts on this EP are by other artists; issued without cardboard cover?) . . . . 25.00 - 40.00
Gulf 62760 *Can't Get You Off My Mind* . . . . . . 15.00 - 20.00
Mercury 71179 *All The Time* . . . . 15.00 - 20.00
Starday 292 *I'm Through* . . . . 40.00 - 60.00
TOMMY LA BEFF:
Wayside 1654 *Tore Up* . . . . 75.00 - 100.00
LABRADORS:
Chief 7009 *When Someone Loves You* . . . . 20.00 - 30.00
LENNY LACOUR:
Academy *Rockin' Rosalie* . . . . 15.00 - 20.00
LADDERS:
Holiday 2611 *Counting The Stars* . . . . 15.00 - 20.00
Vest 826 *My Love Is Gone* . . . . 10.00 - 15.00
THE LADDINS:
Angie 1003 *Push, Shake, Kick And Shout* . . . . . 5.00 - 8.00
Butane 779 *Dream Baby* . . . . 7.00 - 10.00
Central 2602 *Now You're Gone* . . . . 10.00 - 15.00
Grey Cliff 721 *Light A Candle* . . . . 10.00 - 15.00
Groove 64-5 *That's What You Do To Me* . . . . . . 5.00 - 8.00
Theatre 111 *There Once Was A Time* . . . . 8.00 - 12.00
LA DELL SISTERS:
Mercury 70888 *Rockin' Robert* . . . . 5.00 - 8.00
KENNY LAINE & HIS BULL DOGS:
Columbus Stockade Blues . . . . -
TOMMY LAM:
Nabor 103 *Speed Limit* . . . . 20.00 - 30.00
GENE LAMARR:
Flame 1102 *Just A Stranger* . . . . 10.00 - 15.00
Spry 113 *Moon Eyes* . . . . 20.00 - 30.00
JIMMY LAMBERTH:
Meteor 5044 *Latch On To Your Baby* . . . . 30.00 - 50.00
TONY & JACKIE LAMIE:
Sunset 706 *Wore To A Frazzell* . . . . 30.00 - 40.00
BILLY LAMONT:
Okeh 7125 *Country Boy* . . . . 15.00 - 20.00
    7131 *I'm Gonna Try* . . . . 5.00 - 8.00
TOMMY LAMPKIN:
Ebb 110 *Three Minus One* . . . . 5.00 - 8.00
Imperial 5361 *Eternal Love* . . . . 20.00 - 30.00
LAMPLIGHTERS:
Federal 12149 *Part Of Me* . . . . 35.00 - 50.00
    12152 *Give Me* . . . . 30.00 - 40.00
    12166 *I Cant Stand It* . . . . 25.00 - 35.00
    12176 *Tell Me You Care* . . . . 25.00 - 35.00
    12182 *Salty Dog* . . . . 20.00 - 30.00
    12192 *Five Minutes Longer* . . . . 15.00 - 20.00
    12197 *Yum Yum* . . . . 15.00 - 20.00
    12206 *Believe In Me* . . . . 15.00 - 20.00
    12212 *Love Rock And Thrill* . . . . 15.00 - 20.00
    12242 *Hug A Little, Kiss A Little* . . . . 15.00 - 20.00
    12255 *You Were Sent Down From Heaven* . . . . 15.00 - 20.00
    12261 *Everything's All Right* . . . . 15.00 - 20.00
MAJOR LANCE:
Okeh (LP) 12105 *Monkey Time* . . . . 15.00 - 20.00
JERRY LANDIS:
Amy 815 *The Lone Teen Ranger* . . . . 10.00 - 15.00
BUDDY LANDON:
Hollywood 1052 *Foxy* . . . . 8.00 - 12.00

Jaguar 3026 *Raunchy Little Baby*	10.00 -	15.00
3028 *A Bolt Of Lightning*	10.00 -	15.00

LANE BROTHERS:

Leader 804 *Two Dozen And A Half*	7.00 -	10.00
RCA Victor 6900 *Uh Huh Honey*	7.00 -	10.00
7107 *Don't Tempt Me Baby*	5.00 -	8.00
7220 *Boppin' in a Sack*	5.00 -	8.00

HARRY LANE:

RA-Q 602 *Gettin' Ready For Love*	7.00 -	10.00

JIMMY LANE & THE SUGARTONES:

Time 6602 *Let Your Conscience Be Your Guide*	7.00 -	10.00

RALPH LANE & THE WHITEY FOUR:

Cowtown 811 *You Gotta Show Me*	25.00 -	35.00

LANES:

Gee 1023 *Open Up Your Heart*	10.00 -	15.00

CURLEY LANGLEY:

Arcadia 110 *Rockin' & Rollin'*	30.00 -	50.00
Arcadia 111 *She Wasn't Always Your Girl*	15.00 -	20.00

DON LANIER:

Roulette 4021 *Pony Tail Girl*	7.00 -	10.00

PAUL LOUISE:

Eko 502 *Cock-A-Doodle*	20.00 -	30.00

LOUISIANA LANNIS:

Snowcap 1125 *Tongue Twister Boogie*	15.00 -	20.00

LARADOS:

Fox—*Now The Parting Begins*	20.00 -	30.00

LARGOS:

Dot 16292 *I Wonder Why*	7.00 -	10.00
Starmaker 1002 *Just A Picture*	-	
I Wonder Why	-	

LARKS:

Apollo 427 *Eyesight To The Blind*	150.00 -	250.00
429 *Hey Little Girl*	150.00 -	250.00
430 *I Don't Believe In Tomorrow*	150.00 -	250.00
435 *My Lost Love*	150.00 -	250.00
1184 *My Reverie*	300.00 -	500.00
1190 *In My Lonely Room*	200.00 -	300.00
1194 *I Live True To You*	200.00 -	300.00
(Note: Last three made of red-orange plastic)		
Jett 3001 *Love Me True*	8.00 -	12.00
Lloyds 110 *If It's A Crime*	40.00 -	60.00
111 *When You're Near*	40.00 -	60.00
112 *The World Is Waiting*	75.00 -	100.00
114 *Forget It*	50.00 -	75.00

THE LARKTONES:

ABC Paramount 9909 *The Letter*	10.00 -	15.00
Riki 140 *Why Are You Tearing Us Apart*	5.00 -	8.00

PAT LA ROCCA:

Bella 4284 *Rowena*	10.00 -	15.00

LARRY & THE STANDARDS:

Laurie 3119 *My Lucky Night*	7.00 -	10.00

ROC LA RUE & 3 PALS:

Rama 226 *Teenage Blues*	20.00 -	30.00

ROGER LARUE & HIS PALS:

Holland 7421 *I Don't Care If The Sun Don't Shine*	15.00 -	20.00

THE LATONS:

Port 70030 *So In Love*	8.00 -	12.00

LAURELS:

"X" 0143 *Truly, Truly*	75.00 -	100.00

ROD LAUREN:

RCA Victor (LP) 2176 *I'm Rod Lauren*	15.00 -	20.00

CHARLES LAVERNE:

Mark 117 *Hudson River Blues*	10.00 -	15.00

DALE LAVON:

Cavalier *The Rockin' Chair Roll*	8.00 -	12.00

ART LAW:

Gulfstream 1050 *Big Train*	15.00 -	20.00
1051 *Kitty Kat Rock*	20.00 -	30.00

MIKE LAWING & DISSONAIRES:

Altair 101 *One Love*	-	

BILL LAWRENCE:

B.I. 207 *Hey Baby*	30.00 -	40.00
Freedom 44004 *Hey Baby*	10.00 -	15.00

SYD LAWRENCE:

Cosmic 1001 *The Answer To Flyer Saucer*	5.00 -	8.00

BOBBY LAWSON:

Kyser 2122 *Burning Sensation*	10.00 -	15.00
M.R.C. 600 *Baby Don't Be That Way*	30.00 -	40.00

LAZY BILL & HIS BLUE RHYTHMS:

Chance 1148 *She Got Me Walkin'*	75.00 -	100.00

LAZY LESTER:

Excello 2095 *Lester's Stomp*	7.00 -	10.00
2107 *They Call Me Lazy*	5.00 -	8.00
2129 *Tell Me Pretty Baby*	5.00 -	8.00
Excello 2143, 2155, 2166, 2182, 2197	4.00 -	7.00
2206, 2219, 2230, 2235, 2243, 2274, 2277	3.00 -	6.00
(LP) 8006 *True Blues*	20.00 -	30.00

LILLIAN LEACH: (See: THE MELLOWS):

LEADBELLY:

Allegro (LP) 4027 (10") *Sinful Songs*	20.00 -	30.00
Capitol (LP) 369 (10") *Leadbelly*	30.00 -	50.00
Folkways (LP) 4, 14, 24, 43 (10")	8.00 -	12.00
(LP) 241, 242 *Last Sessions*	8.00 -	12.00
Stinson (LP) 17 (10") *Memorial*	10.00 -	15.00
(LP) 19 (10") *Memorial Vol.2*	10.00 -	15.00
(LP) 39 (10") *Plays Parties*	10.00 -	15.00
(LP) 41 (10") *Plays Parties, Vol. 2*	10.00 -	15.00
(LP) 48 (10") *Memorial, Vol. 3*	10.00 -	15.00
(LP) 51 (10") *Memorial, Vol. 4*	10.00 -	15.00

LEADERS:

Glory 235 *Stormy Weather*	8.00 -	12.00
239 *Dearest Beloved Darling*	15.00 -	20.00
243 *Can't Help Loving That Girl Of Mine*	15.00 -	20.00

LEE & THE LEOPARDS:

Gordy 7002 *Come Into My Palace*	10.00 -	15.00

"LITTLE" BRENDA LEE:

Decca 30050 *Bigelow 6-200*	7.00 -	10.00

BOB LEE:

Skyla 1117 *You Mostest Girl*	5.00 -	8.00

BOOKER LEE, JR.:

Federal 12321 *Rockin' Blues*	10.00 -	15.00

BUDDY LEE:

Brunswick 55228 *Ain't That Right*	5.00 -	8.00

DICKIE LEE (& THE COLLEGIATES):

Sun 280 *Good Lovin'*	7.00 -	10.00
297 *Fool Fool Fool*	10.00 -	15.00
Tampa 131 *Stay True Baby*	10.00 -	15.00

DON LEE:

Blue Chip 0013 *Echo, Echo, Echo*	-	

FLOYD LEE:

Enterprise 1233 *Go Boy*	10.00 -	15.00

HARRY LEE:

Igloo 101 *Rockin' On A Reindeer*	40.00 -	60.00
Raynard 2005 *Greedy Lips*		
Vin 1007 *You Don't Know*	8.00 -	12.00

JESSIE LEE With THE RHYTHMAIRES:

Mida 110 *Lonely Broken Heart*	7.00 -	10.00

JIMMY LEE:

Bandera 2506 *Chicago Jump*	10.00 -	15.00

JIMMY LEE AND JOHNNY MATHIS: (See also JIMMY & JOHNNY)

Chess 4865 *Love Me*	30.00 -	40.00

JOE LEE & HIS SEXTET With SCOTTY & BILL:

Fernwood 108 *Ethel Mae*	8.00 -	12.00

JOHN LEE:

Federal 12089 *Baby's Blues*	20.00 -	30.00

JOHNNY LEE:

De Luxe 6009 *I'm A Boogie Man*	15.00 -	20.00

JULIA LEE:

Capitol (LP) H-288 (10₀) *Party Time*	30.00 -	40.00
(LP) T-288 *Party Time*	30.00 -	40.00

LEONARD LEE:

LEE

Lamp 8001 *Tryin' To Fool Me* .... 7.00 - 10.00

LONESOME LEE:
Bandera 2501 *Lonely Travelin'* .... 15.00 - 20.00

MABEL LEE:
Hull 712 *He's My Guy* .... 5.00 - 8.00

MYRON LEE (& CADDIES):
Hep 2146 *Aw C'mon, Baby* .... 7.00 - 10.00
Jaro 77037 *From Now On* .... 5.00 - 8.00
Nor-Va-Jak 1326 *Blue, Lawdy Blues* ..... 10.00 - 15.00

NANCY LEE:
Acme 711 *So They Say* .... 7.00 - 10.00

ROOSEVELT LEE:
Excello 2022 *Lazy Pete* .... 30.00 - 40.00

TOMMY LEE:
Delta 403 *Highway 80 Blues* .... 50.00 - 75.00

WALLY LEE With THE STORMS:
Sundown 122 *I Never Felt This Way* .... 15.00 - 20.00

LEFT HAND CHARLIE:
Folk Star 1131 *But You Thrill Me* .... 15.00 - 20.00

HANK LE GAULT:
Stardale 703/704 *I Knew* .... 30.00 - 50.00

LEGENDS:
Capitol (LP) 1925 *Legends Let Loose* .... 20.00 - 30.00
Hull 727 *The Legend Of Love* .... 20.00 - 30.00
Melba 109 *The Eyes Of An Angel* .... 15.00 - 20.00
Peacock 1694 *Goodbye Jesse* .... 7.00 - 10.00

PRICE LEGGS:
Glen Dell 101 *Jailbird Blues* .... 8.00 - 12.00

GARY LEMEL:
Rev. 3520 *Rockin' In The Halls* .... 7.00 - 10.00

J.B. LENOIR/LENORE (& HIS COMBO):
Checker 844 *If I Give My Love To You* .... 5.00 - 8.00
856 *Don't Touch My Head* .... 5.00 - 8.00
874 *Five Years* .... 5.00 - 8.00
901 *She Don't Know* .... 5.00 - 8.00
J.O.B. 1008 *The Mountain* .... 20.00 - 30.00
1012 *The Mojo* .... 30.00 - 50.00
1016 *I Want My Baby* (red plastic) ...... 75.00 - 100.00
1102 *Play A Little While* .... 50.00 - 75.00
Parrot 802 *I'm In Korea/Eisenhower Blues* ..... 30.00 - 50.00
802 *I'm In Korea/Tax Paying Blues* .... 50.00 - 75.00
(Note: Parrot 802 was issued with two different couplings.)
Parrot 809 *Mama, Talk To Your Daughter* ...... 20.00 - 30.00
814 *What Have I Done* .... 20.00 - 30.00
821 *I Lost My Baby* .... 20.00 - 30.00
Shad 5012 *Lou Ella* .... 5.00 - 8.00
Vee Jay 352 *Do What I Say* .... 5.00 - 8.00

LESLIE BROTHERS:
Columbia 40651 *Ready Ruby Rock & Roll* ...... -

BOBBY LESTER & THE MOONGLOWS/ MOONLIGHTERS:
Checker 806 *Shoo Doo-Be Doo* .... 7.00 - 10.00
813 *Hug And A Kiss* .... 7.00 - 10.00
Checker 921 *Lonely Hearts* .... 10.00 - 15.00
Chess 1811 *Blue Velvet* .... 7.00 - 10.00
Chess (LP) 1471 *The Best Of Bobby Lester & The Moonglows* (black label) .... 30.00 - 40.00

JOHN LESTER & MELLOQUEENS:
C & M 500 *Getting Nearer* .... 7.00 - 10.00

BOBBY LEWIS:
Beltone (LP) *Tossin' And Turnin'* .... 20.00 - 30.00
Chess 1518 *Mumbles Blues* .... 30.00 - 50.00
Mercury 71245 *Mumbles Blues* .... 5.00 - 8.00
Spotlight 394 *Mumbles Blues* .... 8.00 - 12.00

GENE LEWIS:
Josie 819 *Too Young To Settle Down* ...... 5.00 - 8.00
R-Dell 103 *Crazy Legs* .... 10.00 - 15.00

JACK LEWIS:
Crest 1018 *Glendora* .... 7.00 - 10.00
1028 *Dilly Dally Sally Baby* .... 7.00 - 10.00
1033 *I.O.U.* .... 7.00 - 10.00

Imperial 5880 *Mop Top* .... 7.00 - 10.00

JERRY LEE LEWIS:
Sun (EP) 107, 108, 109, 110 .... 25.00 - 40.00
259 *Crazy Arms* .... 10.00 - 15.00
267 *Whole Lot Of Shakin' Going On* .... 5.00 - 8.00
(Note: 78 rpm issues of above command higher prices)
Sun 281 *Great Balls Of Fire* (78 rpm) .... 15.00 - 25.00
288 *Breathless* (78 rpm) .... 10.00 - 15.00
296 *High School Confidential* (78 rpm) ...... 15.00 - 20.00
(LP) 1230 *Jerry Lee Lewis* .... 35.00 - 50.00
(LP) 1265 *Jerry Lee's Greatest* .... 25.00 - 35.00
(Note: Promotional copies of Sun 45s, having white labels and Jerry Lee's picture stamped thereon, exist; their value is conjectural.)

JOHNNY LEWIS:
Rockin' 517 *She's Taking All My Money* .... 50.00 - 80.00

PETE (GUITAR) LEWIS:
Federal 12066 *Louisiana Hop* .... 30.00 - 40.00
12076 *Harmonica Boogie* .... 30.00 - 40.00
12103 *Scratchin' Boogie* .... 20.00 - 30.00
12112 *The Blast* .... 15.00 - 25.00
Peacock 1624 *Goin' Crazy* .... 15.00 - 25.00

SAMMY LEWIS & WILLIE JOHNSON:
Sun 218 *I Feel So Worried* .... 20.00 - 30.00

SIDNEY JO LEWIS:
Island 6 *Boppin' To Grandfather's Clock* .... 20.00 - 30.00

SMILEY LEWIS:
Imperial 5194 *Bells Are Ringing* .... 30.00 - 50.00
5208 *It's So Peaceful* .... 30.00 - 40.00
5234 *Play Girl* .... 20.00 - 30.00
5241 *Caldonia's Party* .... 20.00 - 30.00
5252 *It's Music* .... 20.00 - 30.00
5268 *Down The Road* .... 20.00 - 30.00
5279 *I Love You For Sentimental Reasons* .... 15.00 - 20.00
5296 *Can't Stop Loving You* .... 15.00 - 20.00
5316 *Too Many Drivers* .... 10.00 - 15.00
5325 *Jailbird* .... 10.00 - 15.00
5349 *Real Gone Lover* .... 10.00 - 15.00
5356 *I Hear You Knocking* .... 7.00 - 10.00
5372 *Queen Of Hearts* .... 7.00 - 10.00
5380, 5389, 5404, 5418, 5531, 5478, 5531 .... 5.00 - 10.00
(Note: Numbers lower than 5194 are usually found as 78 RPM records, with values of $5.00 to $10.00; 45 RPM issues of these lower numbers are valued at $25.00 to $50.00 and more, with even higher premiums for those pressed of colored vinyl.)
(LP) 9141 *I Hear You Knocking* .... 90.00 - 125.00
Okeh 7146 *Tore Up* .... 15.00 - 20.00

TOMMY LEWIS:
Cenco 115 *Angel* .... 4.00 - 6.00

WALLY LEWIS:
Dot 15763 *I'm With You* .... 5.00 - 8.00
Liberty 55211 *Lover Boy* .... 5.00 - 8.00
Tally 117 *Kathleen* .... 8.00 - 12.00

RAY LIBERTO:
Dot 15848 *Wicked Wicked Woman* .... 5.00 - 8.00
TNT 156 *Wicked Wicked Woman* .... 8.00 - 12.00
172 *I Want You To Love Me Tonight* .... 10.00 - 15.00

LICK, SLICK & SLIDE:
Savoy 1150 *I Got Drunk* .... 20.00 - 30.00

LIFEGUARDS:
ABC Paramount 10021 *Teenage Tango* .... 5.00 - 8.00
Casa Blanca 5535 *Everybody Outta The Pool* ... 10.00 - 15.00

JIMMY LIGGINS:
Specialty 427 *Low Down Blues* .... 10.00 - 15.00
434 *Dark Hour Blues* .... 10.00 - 15.00
470 *Drunk* .... 8.00 - 12.00
520 *I Can't Stop It* .... 7.00 - 10.00
521 *Cadillac Boogie* .... 10.00 - 15.00

(Note: 45 RPM records with numbers lower than 427 would command $15.00 to $20.00 or more; these are usually found as 78 RPM records, valued at $4.00 to $8.00. Any of above, or earlier issues, pressed of red vinyl, command substantial premiums over prices stated.)

JOE LIGGINS:

Specialty 338 *The Honeydripper*	15.00 -	20.00
430 *Dripper's Boogie*	10.00 -	15.00
465 *Farewell Blues*	8.00 -	12.00
484 *Come Back Home*	7.00 -	10.00
492 *A Bird In Hand*	7.00 -	10.00
529 *Whiskey, Women & Leaded Dice*	7.00 -	10.00

(Note: Numbers lower than 430 are usually found as 78 RPM records, valued at $4.00 to $8.00. Any of these earlier issues in 45 RPM form would bring $10.00 to $20.00; substantially more, if pressed of red vinyl.)

LIGHTCRUST DOUGHBOYS:

Audio Lab (LP) 1525	15.00 -	20.00

PAPA LIGHTFOOT:

Aladdin 3171 *P.L. Blues*	30.00 -	50.00
3304 *Jumpin' With Jarvis*	20.00 -	30.00
Imperial 5289 *Mean Old Train*	30.00 -	40.00
Savoy 1161 *Mean Old Train*	10.00 -	15.00

LIGHTNIN' JR. & THE EMPIRES:

Haralem 2334 *Ragged And Hungry*	50.00 -	75.00

LIGHTNIN' LEON:

Rita 106 *Repossession Blues*	7.00 -	10.00

LIGHTNIN' SLIM:

Ace 505 *Bad Feeling Blues*	10.00 -	15.00
Excello 2066 *Lightnin' Blues*	10.00 -	15.00
2075 *Sugar Plum*	10.00 -	15.00
2080 *Goin' Home*	10.00 -	15.00
2096 *Bad Luck And Trouble*	8.00 -	12.00
2106, 2116, 2131, 2142, 2150, 2160, 2169, 2173, 2179, 2186, 2195	5.00 -	10.00
(higher numbers)	3.00 -	5.00
(LP) 8000 *Rooster Blues*	20.00 -	30.00
(LP) 8004 *Bell Ringer*	20.00 -	30.00
Feature 3006 *Rock Me Mama*	40.00 -	60.00
3008 *New Orleans Bound*	15.00 -	20.00
3012 *Ethel Mae*	15.00 -	20.00

BOBBY LILE:

4 Star 1734 *All The Time*	5.00 -	8.00

LONNIE LILLIE:

Marathon 5003 *Truck Driver's Special*	50.00 -	75.00

LIMELIGHTERS:

Gilco 213 *This Lonely Boy*	20.00 -	30.00
Joz 794 *Cabin Hideaway*	50.00 -	75.00

X. LINCOLN:

Hermitage 779 *Take Me Home Naomi*	— -	—

LINCOLNS:

Atlas 1100 *Don't Let Me Shed Any More Tears*	15.00 -	20.00
Bud 113 *Sometime Somewhere*	5.00 -	8.00

KATHY LINDEN:

Felsted 8510 *Billy* (78 rpm)	10.00 -	15.00

THE LINTONS:

Erica 005 *Lost Love*	4.00 -	6.00

RICKY LISI:

Roulette 4511 *The River*	4.00 -	7.00

"LISTEN TO OUR STORY":

Brunswick (LP) 59001 (10") (various artists)	20.00 -	30.00

LITTLE AL:

Excello 2098 *Little Lean Woman*	7.00 -	10.00
2128 *Easy Ridin' Buggy*	8.00 -	12.00

LITTLE ANTHONY & THE IMPERIALS:

End 1027 *Tears On My Pillow*	3.00 -	5.00
1027 *Tears On My Pillow* (78 RPM)	15.00 -	20.00

LITTLE BEATS:

Mercury 71155 *Someone For Me*	15.00 -	20.00

LITTLE BOPPERS:

Glendale 1001 *Chattanooga Drummer Man*	10.00 -	15.00

LITTLE BUDDY:

N R C 010 *Let's Make Love*	5.00 -	8.00

LITTLE BUTCH & VELLS:

Angletone 535 *Over The Rainbow*	8.00 -	12.00

LITTLE CAESAR (& THE ROMANS):

Big Town 106 *Big Eyes*	7.00 -	10.00
110 *Wonder Why I'm Leaving*	7.00 -	10.00
Del-Fi (LP) 1218 *Memories Of These Oldies But Goodies*	40.00 -	60.00
Hollywood 234 *Long Time Baby*	8.00 -	12.00

LITTLE CLYDIE & THE TEENS:

RPM 462 *A Casual Look*	15.00 -	20.00

LITTLE COOL BREEZES:

Ebony 1014 *Pack Your Bags And Go*	30.00 -	50.00
1015 *Won't You Come In*	30.00 -	50.00

LITTLE DANNY:

Sharp 112 *Mind On Loving*	7.00 -	10.00

LITTLE DENNY & THE TORKEYS:

Perry 1 *Rock And Roll Blues*	30.00 -	50.00
2 *She's Everybody's Darling*	15.00 -	20.00

LITTLE DOUG: (See also DOUG SAHM)

Sarg 113 *Rollin', Rollin'*	20.00 -	30.00

LITTLE EDDIE & THE DON JUANS:

Fortune 836 *This Is A Miracle*	10.00 -	15.00

LITTLE ESTHER (& THE DOMINOES/With LITTLE WILLIE/With BOBBY NUNN/& THE ROBINS):

Federal 12016 *The Deacon Moves In*	75.00 -	100.00
12042 *Cryin' And Singing' The Blues*	30.00 -	40.00
12055 *Ring A Ding Doo*	30.00 -	40.00
12063 *The Storm*	30.00 -	40.00
12065 *Better Beware*	30.00 -	40.00
12090 *Ramblin' Blues*	30.00 -	40.00
12108 *Last Laugh Blues*	30.00 -	40.00
12115 *Hollerin' And Screamin'*	25.00 -	35.00
12122 *You Took My Love Too Fast*	25.00 -	35.00
12126 *Hound Dog*	25.00 -	40.00
12142 *Cherry Wine*	25.00 -	35.00
King (LP) 622 *"Melody Lane"*	200.00 -	300.00
Savoy 731 *Double Crossing Blues*	15.00 -	20.00

LITTLE HUDSON'S RED DEVIL TRIO:

J.O.B. 1015 *Rough Treatment*	100.00 -	150.00

LITTLE IKE With JIMMY BECK ORCH:

Champion 1011 *She Can Rock*	15.00 -	20.00

LITTLE JAN & THE RADIANTS:

Goldisc 15 *If You Love Me*	8.00 -	12.00

LITTLE JOE:

Epic (EP) 7198 *"The Thriller"*	35.00 -	50.00
House Of Sound 500 *Keep Your Arms Around Me*	30.00 -	40.00

LITTLE JOE BLUE:

Movin' 132 *Dirty Work Going On*	7.00 -	10.00

LITTLE JUNE & THE JANUARYS:

Profile 4009 *Oh What A Feeling*	10.00 -	15.00

LITTLE JUNIOR'S BLUE FLAMES:

Sun 187 *Feelin' Good*	30.00 -	40.00
192 *Mystery Train*	30.00 -	40.00

LITTLE LARRY:

Success 103 *Loretta*	5.00 -	8.00

LITTLE LINDA:

Coral 62279 *Hey Little Lover*	5.00 -	8.00

LITTLE LUTHER:

Apt 25060 *Ever Lovin' Baby*	5.00 -	8.00
Criss Cross 110 *Steppin' High*	5.00 -	8.00

LITTLE MAC/MACK:

Bea & Baby 109 *Don't Come Back*	7.00 -	10.00
118 *I'm Your Fool*	7.00 -	10.00
C.J. 606 *My Walking Blues* (blue label)	7.00 -	10.00
Checker 991 *I'm Happy Now*	5.00 -	8.00
Jay Bird 4001 *You Mistreated Me*	10.00 -	15.00

LITTLE MILTON:

Bobbin 101 *I'm A Lonely Man*	5.00 -	8.00

103 *Long Distance Operator*	5.00 -	8.00
112, 120, 125	4.00 -	6.00
Checker (LP) 2995 *We're Gonna Make It*	10.00 -	15.00
Delta 403 *Little Milton's Boogie*	— -	—
Meteor 5040 *Let's Boogie Baby* (black label) ...	30.00 -	40.00
Sun 194 *Beggin' My Baby*	50.00 -	75.00
200 *Alone And Blue*	50.00 -	75.00
220 *Looking For My Baby*	75.00 -	100.00

LITTLE MOJO:
Indigo 139 *Mojo Theme*	4.00 -	7.00
Norman 505 *You Ain't The One*	7.00 -	10.00

LITTLE NAT:
Pik 1 *Do This, Do That*	5.00 -	8.00

LITTLE NATE & THE CHRYSLERS:
Johnson 318 *Someone Up There*	15.00 -	20.00

LITTLE NORMAN:
Decca 30353 *Drag Strip Baby*	5.00 -	8.00

LITTLE PAPA JOE:
Blue Lake 116 *Easy Lovin'*	40.00 -	60.00

LITTLE RICHARD:
Camden (LP) 420 *Little Richard*	50.00 -	75.00
(EP) 446 *Little Richard Rocks*	50.00 -	75.00
Peacock 1658 *Little Richard's Boogie*	10.00 -	15.00
1673 *Maybe I'm Right*	15.00 -	20.00
RCA Victor 4392 *Taxi Blues*	50.00 -	75.00
4582 *Get Rich Quick*	50.00 -	75.00
4772 *Ain't Nothin' Happenin'*	50.00 -	75.00
5025 *Please Have Mercy On Me*	40.00 -	60.00
Specialty (EP) 100 *"Here's Little Richard"*	90.00 -	130.00
Specialty (EP) 400, 401, 402 *Here's Little Richard*	20.00 -	30.00
(EP) 403, 404, 405 *Little Richard*	20.00 -	30.00
561 *Tutti-Frutti*	5.00 -	8.00
561 *Tutti-Frutti* (78 rpm)	10.00 -	15.00
572 *Long Tall Sally*	4.00 -	7.00
572 *Long Tall Sally* (78 rpm)	10.00 -	15.00
584 *Heeby-Jeebies*	4.00 -	7.00
584 *Heeby-Jeebies* (78 rpm)	10.00 -	15.00
591 *All Around The World*	4.00 -	7.00
591 *All Around The World* (78 rpm) ...	10.00 -	15.00
598 *Lucille*	4.00 -	7.00
598 *Lucille* (78 rpm)	10.00 -	15.00
606 *Jenny, Jenny*	4.00 -	7.00
606 *Jenny, Jenny* (78 rpm)	10.00 -	15.00
611 *Keep A Knockin'*	4.00 -	6.00
611 *Keep A Knockin'* (78 rpm)	10.00 -	15.00
624 *Good Golly, Miss Molly*	4.00 -	6.00
624 *Good Golly, Miss Molly* (78 rpm)	15.00 -	20.00
633, 652, 660	3.00 -	5.00
633 *True, Fine Mama* (78 rpm)	8.00 -	12.00
652 *She Knows How To Rock* (78 rpm)	8.00 -	12.00
660 *Wonderin'* (78 rpm)	10.00 -	15.00
(LP) 2100 *Here's Little Richard*	30.00 -	50.00
(LP) 2103 *Little Richard*	30.00 -	50.00
(LP) 2114 *The Fabulous Little Richard*	20.00 -	30.00

LITTLE SAMMY:
Shade—*Can You Love Me*	15.00 -	20.00

LITTLE SHY GUY:
Calvert 107 *Let's Rock & Roll*	20.00 -	30.00

LITTLE SONNY:
Duke 186 *Hear My Woman Calling*	5.00 -	8.00
J.V.B. 5001 *I'll Love You Baby*	20.00 -	30.00

LITTLE STAN:
Decca 30638 *Block Party Rock*	— -	—

LITTLE TEMPLE & HIS "88":
Specialty 475 *I Ate The Wrong Part*	15.00 -	20.00

LITTLE VICTOR (& THE VISTAS):
Rendezvous 183 *No More*	8.00 -	12.00
Richland 2907 *Papa Lou and Gran*	15.00 -	20.00

LITTLE WALKING' WILLIE:
Jaguar 3012 *Clayhouse Blues*	10.00 -	15.00

LITTLE WALTER (& HIS JUKES/

NIGHT CAPS):
Checker 758 *Juke*	20.00 -	30.00
764 *Mean Old World*	10.00 -	15.00
767 *Tonight With A Fool*	10.00 -	15.00
770 *Off The Wall*	7.00 -	10.00
780 *Quarter To Twelve*	7.00 -	10.00
786 *Lights Out*	7.00 -	10.00
793 *Rocker*	7.00 -	10.00
799 *Blue Light*	7.00 -	10.00
805 *Mellow Down Easy*	7.00 -	10.00
811 *Thunder Bird*	7.00 -	10.00
817 *Roller Coaster*	7.00 -	10.00
(Note: Any of the foregoing, pressed of red vinyl, bring substantially more.)		
825, 833, 838, 845, 852, 859, 867	5.00 -	8.00
890, 904, 930, 939, 955, 968, 986, 1043, 1081, 1117	3.00 -	6.00
Chess (LP) 1428 *The Best Of Little Walter* (black label)	40.00 -	60.00

LITTLE WALTER, JR.:
Lapel 101 *Don't Know*	10.00 -	15.00

LEE ROY LITTLE:
Cee Jay 578 *Your Evil Thoughts*	4.00 -	6.00

LITTLE WILLIE JOHN:
King (LP) 564 *Fever*	15.00 -	20.00
(LP) 496 *Talk To Me*	10.00 -	15.00
(LP) 603 *Mister Little Willie John*	10.00 -	15.00

LITTLE WILLIE LITTLEFIELD:
Argyle 1013 *Ruby Ruby*	5.00 -	8.00
Bullseye 1005 *Ruby Ruby*	8.00 -	12.00
Federal 12101 *Sticking On You Baby*	10.00 -	15.00
12110 *K C. Loving*	10.00 -	15.00
12137 *My Best Wishes And Regards* ...	10.00 -	15.00
12148 *Miss K.C.'s Fine*	10.00 -	15.00
12163 *Don't Take My Heart Little Girl* ...	10.00 -	15.00
12174 *Goofy Dust Blues*	10.00 -	15.00
12221 *Jim Wilson's Boogie*	10.00 -	15.00
Rhythm 107 *Baby Shame*	15.00 -	20.00
108 *Ruby Ruby*	15.00 -	20.00
124 *Theresa*	10.00 -	15.00

BUBBA LITTRELL:
Manco 1037 *Ain't That Cool*	8.00 -	12.00

JIMMY LLOYD:
Roulette 4062 *I Got A Rocket In My Pocket*	10.00 -	15.00
7001 *Where The Rio De Rosa Flows*	10.00 -	15.00

ROBERT JR. LOCKWOOD:
J.O.B. 1107 *Sweet Woman From Maine* ...	75.00 -	100.00

WILLIE LOFTIN & THE DISCORDS:
Smoke 101 *Bad Habit*	10.00 -	15.00

LOGICS:
Everlast 5015 *One Love*	8.00 -	12.00

BOBBY LOLLAR:
Benton 101/102 *Bad Bad Boy*	75.00 -	100.00

LONESOME DRIFTER:
K 5812 *Eager Boy*	125.00 -	175.00
RAM 1738 *Honey Do You Love Me*	8.00 -	12.00

LONESOME LEE (See LEE)

LONESOME SUNDOWN:
Excello 2092 *Lost Without Love*	7.00 -	10.00
2102 *My Home Is A Prison*	5.00 -	8.00
2117, 2132, 2145, 2154, 2163, 2174	4.00 -	7.00
2202, 2213, 2236, 2242, 2249, 2254, 2259, 2264	3.00 -	5.00

BUDDY LONG:
Demon 1517 *It's Nothin' To Me*	5 .00 -	8.00

CURTIS LONG (& THE RHYTHM ROCKERS):
Linco 609 *Hootchy Cootchy*	30.00 -	40.00
Stardale 55800/55801 *Goin' Out Of Town*	15.00 -	20.00

LONG HAIRS:
Memphis 110 *Go- Go- Go*	15.00 -	20.00

LONG JOHN:

Duke 122 *Crazy Girl*	10.00	-	15.00

LONG TALL LESTER:

Duke 197 *Working Man*	5.00	-	8.00

LONNIE & CRISIS:

Universal 103 *Bells In The Chapel*	30.00	-	50.00

LORD LUTHER:

Imperial 5596 *A Thinkin' Man's Girl*	7.00	-	10.00

BOBBY LORD:

Columbia 21339 *No More. No More. No More.*	15.00	-	20.00
21498 *Pie Peachie Pie Pie*	10.00	-	15.00
21539 *Everybody's Rockin' But Me*	10.00	-	15.00
40666 *Beautiful Baby*	8.00	-	12.00
40819 *Your Sweet Love*	5.00	-	8.00
40927 *High Voltage*	7.00	-	10.00
41030 *Am I A Fool*	5.00	-	8.00
41155 *Fire Of Love*	5.00	-	8.00
41288 *When I've Learned*	5.00	-	8.00
41352 *Party Pooper*	8.00	-	12.00
Harmony (LP) 7322 *The Best Of*	40.00	-	60.00

DICK LORY:

Columbia 41224 *Wild Blooded Woman*	8.00	-	12.00
41276 *Crazy Little Daisy*	8.00	-	12.00
Dot 15496 *Cool It Baby*	10.00	-	15.00

LOU & GINNY:

Hep 2141 *Do I Do Right*	—	-	—

JOHN D. LOUDERMILK:

Columbia 41165 *Susie's House*	7.00	-	10.00
41209 *Yo Yo*	7.00	-	10.00
RCA Victor 8308 *Rhythm And Blues*	5.00	-	8.00

BOBBY LOUIS:

Capitol 4224 *Adult Western*	20.00	-	30.00
4272 *Call Of Love*	10.00	-	15.00

JOE HILL LOUIS:

Big Town 401 *Bad Woman Blues*	50.00	-	75.00
Checker 763 *Dorothy May*	100.00	-	150.00
Modern 839 *Big Legged Woman*	20.00	-	30.00
856 *Peace of Mind*	20.00	-	30.00

LESLIE LOUIS:

Rockin' 519 *Ridin' Home*	10.00	-	15.00

TOMMY LOUIS (& THE RHYTHM ROCKERS/With MARSHALL & THE VERSATILES):

Muriel 1001 *The Hurt Is On*	5.00	-	8.00
1002/1003 *Wail Baby Wail*	8.00	-	12.00

LOUISIANA RED:

Roulette (LP) 25200 *The Low Down Back Porch Blues*	15.00	-	20.00

THE LOUVIN BROTHERS:

Capitol (LP) 769 *Tragic Songs Of Life*	12.00	-	16.00
(LP) 825 *Nearer My God To Thee*	10.00	-	15.00
(LP) 910 *Ira & Charlie*	15.00	-	20.00

THE LOVE BROTHERS:

By Love 843 *Baby I'll Never Let You Go*	50.00	-	75.00

BILLY LOVE:

Chess 1508 *Drop Top*	20.00	-	30.00
1516 *My Teddy Bear Baby*	20.00	-	30.00

HOT SHOT LOVE:

Sun 196 *Wolf Call Boogie*	100.00	-	150.00

WILLIE LOVE & HIS THREE ACES:

Trumpet 172 *Fallin' Rain*	8.00	-	12.00
173 *Vanity Dresser Boogie*	8.00	-	12.00
174 *Shady Lane Blues*	8.00	-	12.00
175 *V-8 Ford*	8.00	-	12.00
209 *Way Back*	10.00	-	15.00

LOVE LARKS:

Mason's—*Diddle-Le-Bom*	20.00	-	30.00

LOVE LETTERS:

Acme 714 *Walking The Streets Alone*	30.00	-	40.00

LOVE NOTES:

Holiday 2605 *United*	15.00	-	20.00
2608 *If I Could Make You Mine*	15.00	-	20.00
Imperial 5254 *Surrender Your Heart*	100.00	-	150.00
Premium 611 *A Love Like Yours*	10.00	-	15.00

Rainbow 266 *I'm Sorry*	30.00	-	40.00
Riviera 970 *I'm Sorry*	100.00	-	150.00
975 *Since I Fell For You*	150.00	-	200.00
Wilshire 200 *Our Songs Of Love*	8.00	-	12.00

LOVERS:

Decca 29862 *Don't Touch Me*	7.00	-	10.00
Lamp 2005 *Darlin' It's Wonderful*	8.00	-	12.00
2013 *Let's Elope*	10.00	-	15.00

LOVETONES:

Plus 108 *Talk To An Angel*	35.00	-	50.00

BUDDY LOWE:

Crest 1049 *Ummmm-Kiss Me Goodnight*	8.00	-	12.00

JIM LOWE:

Dot (LP) 3051 *Songs They Sing Behind The Green Door*	20.00	-	30.00
(LP) 3114 *Wicked Women*	20.00	-	30.00
15456 *Blue Suede Shoes*	8.00	-	12.00

FRANKIE LOWERY:

Khoury's 716 *Kansas City Train*	8.00	-	12.00

JAY B. LOYD:

ABC Paramount 9922 *You're Just My Kind*	15.00	-	20.00
Hi 2017 *I'm So Lonely*	10.00	-	15.00

JIM LUCAS:

Republic 7123 *Tutti Frutti*	10.00	-	15.00

LUKE THE DRIFTER (See HANK WILLIAMS)

ROBIN LUKE:

Bertram International 206 *Susie Darlin'*	15.00	-	20.00
208 *My Girl*	8.00	-	12.00
210 *You Can't Stop Me From Dreamin'*	10.00	-	15.00
212 *Five Minutes More*	8.00	-	12.00
Dot (EP) 1092 *Susie Darlin'*	35.00	-	50.00
15781 *Susie Darlin'* (78 rpm)	15.00	-	20.00
15829 *Chica Chicka Honey*	5.00	-	8.00
15899 *Strollin' Blues*	5.00	-	8.00
15959 *Who's Gonna Hold Your Hand*	5.00	-	8.00

BOB LUMAN:

Capitol 2972 *I Know My Baby Cares*	5.00	-	7.00
Imperial 5705 *Red Cadillac And A Black Moustache*	10.00	-	15.00
8311 *Red Cadillac And A Black Moustache*	15.00	-	20.00
8315 *Make Up Your Mind*	10.00	-	15.00

(Note: Above two are maroon label; black label later pressings command smaller premiums.)

LUMBERJACKS:

Hollywood 1040 *Lonely Blues*	—	-	—

BOBBY LUMPKIN:

Felco 102 *One Way Ticket*	30.00	-	50.00

KENNY LUND & THE ROLLER COASTERS:

Holiday Inn 105 *Rip It Up Potatoe Chip*	7.00	-	10.00

NELLIE LUTCHER:

Capitol (LP) H-232 (10") *Real Gone*	20.00	-	30.00
(LP) T-232 *Real Gone*	20.00	-	30.00
Epic (LP) 1108 (10") *Whee! Nellie*	25.00	-	35.00
Liberty (LP) 3014 *Our New Nellie*	20.00	-	30.00

LY-DELLS:

Master 1 1 1 *Genie Of The Lamp*	15.00	-	20.00
251 *Wizard Love*	10.00	-	15.00

FRANKIE LYMON (& THE TEENAGERS):
(See also TEENAGERS)

Gee (EP) 601 *The Teenagers Go Rockin*	30.00	-	40.00
Gee (LP) 701 *The Teenagers featuring Frankie Lymon*	50.00	-	75.00
Gee 1018 *I Promise To Remember*	5.00	-	8.00
1018 *I Promise To Remember* (78 rpm)	8.00	-	12.00
1022 *The ABC's Of Love*	4.00	-	7.00
1022 *The ABC's Of Love* (78 rpm)	8.00	-	12.00
1026 *I'm Not A Juvenile Delinquent*	4.00	-	7.00
1026 *I'm Not A Juvenile Delinquent* (78 rpm)	8.00	-	12.00
1032, 1036, 1039	3.00	-	6.00
1032 *Paper Castles* (78 rpm)	7.00	-	10.00
1036 *Out In The Cold Again* (78 rpm)	7.00	-	10.00

1039 *Goody Goody* (78 rpm)	8.00 -	12.00
Roulette (EP) *At The London Palladium*	7.00 -	10.00
(LP) 25013 *Frankie Lymon At The London Palladium*	20.00 -	30.00
25036 *Rock And Roll*	20.00 -	30.00

LEWIS LYMON & THE TEENCHORDS:

End 1003 *Too Young*	10.00 -	15.00
1007 *I Found Out Why*	10.00 -	15.00
Fury 1000 *I'm So Happy*	8.00 -	12.00
1003 *Honey Honey*	8.00 -	12.00
1006 *I'm Not Too Young To Fall In Love*	8.00 -	12.00
Juanita 101 *Dance Girl*	8.00 -	12.00

DEBBIE LYNN:

Flight Seven 10001 *Fujiyama Mama*	7.00 -	10.00

JERRY LYNN:

D 1041 *Bugger Burns*	10.00 -	15.00

KATHY LYNN & HER PLAYBOYS:

Swan 4193 *I Got A Guy*	15.00 -	20.00

LORELEI LYNN:

Award 128 *Rock A Bop*	7.00 -	10.00

LORETTA LYNN:

Zero 107 *I'm A Honky Tonk Girl*	35.00 -	50.00
110 *Heartaches Meet Mr. Blues*	35.00 -	50.00
112 *The Darkest Day*	35.00 -	50.00

JOE LYONS & THE ARROWS:

Hollywood 1065 *Honey Chile*	15.00 -	20.00

LYRES:

J & G 101 *Ship Of Love*	50.00 -	75.00

LYRICS:

Coral 62322 *Oh, Please Love Me*	8.00 -	12.00
Goldwax 101 *Darling*	5.00 -	8.00
Harlem 101 *Oh, Please Love Me*	20.00 -	30.00
104 *The Beating Of My Heart*	15.00 -	20.00
Mid South 1500 *Crying Over You*	10.00 -	15.00
Rhythm 127 *Every Night*	50.00 -	75.00
Vee Jay 285 *Come On Home*	15.00 -	20.00
Wildcat 0028 *Oh, Please Love Me*	8.00 -	12.00

WILLIE MABON (& HIS COMBO):

Chess (LP) 1439 *Willie Mabon*	20.00 -	30.00
1531 *Worry Blues*	7.00 -	10.00
1538 *Night Latch*	7.00 -	10.00
1548 *Monday Woman*	7.00 -	10.00
1554, 1564, 1580, 1592, 1608, 1627	5.00 -	8.00
Federal 12306 *Light Up Your Lamp*	5.00 -	8.00

MAC & JAKE:

Meteor 5022 *Yakety Yak*	15.00 -	25.00

LOU MAC:

Blue Lake 119 *Move Me*	20.00 -	30.00

LEON MACH:

Lavender 1554 *You Hurt Me So*	15.00 -	20.00

BILL MACK:

Imperial 8177 *Play My Boogie*	20.00 -	30.00
8200 *I'm Not Free*	10.00 -	15.00
8212 *That's The Way I Like You*	10.00 -	15.00
8225 *That's How I Feel*	10.00 -	15.00
8242 *Crazed For Love*	10.00 -	15.00
8278 *Sue-Suzie Boogie*	15.00 -	20.00
8294 *A Fool For You*	8.00 -	12.00
Starday 231 *Kitty Kat*	35.00 -	50.00
252 *Cat Just Got In Town*	35.00 -	50.00
280 *It's Saturday Night*	35.00 -	50.00
313 *Cheatin' On Your Mind*	20.00 -	30.00
418 *Long, Long Train*	10.00 -	15.00

BILLY MACK:

Lewis Records 1001 *Tribute To Jerry Lee*	5.00 -	8.00

BOBBY MACK:

Tempus 1508 *She's My Little Baby*	5.00 -	8.00

JEANI MACK:

Class 230 *Dirty Dishes*	7.00 -	10.00
242 *Super Duper*	7.00 -	10.00

LONNIE MACK:

Fraternity (LP) 1014 *Wham Of The Memphis Man*	15.00 -	20.00

WARNER MACK:

Decca 30471, 30841	4.00 -	7.00

VINCENT MACREE & THE RHYTHM KINGS:

Gametime 103 *Teen-Age Talk*	8.00 -	12.00

JOHNNY MADARA:

Bamboo 503 *Good Golly Miss Mooly*	7.00 -	10.00
511 *A Story Untold*	5.00 -	8.00

JIMMIE MADDIN:

American International 525 *Bird Dog*	8.00 -	12.00
542 *Tongue Tied*	8.00 -	12.00
Dot 15641 *Tongue Tied*	8.00 -	12.00
Freedom 44007 *I'm Studyin' You*	8.00 -	12.00
Imperial 5494 *Jeanie, Jeanie, Jeanie*	5.00 -	8.00
5496 *Shirley Purley*	5.00 -	8.00
Tampa 102 *Let 'Em Roll*	5.00 -	8.00

MADDOX BROTHERS (& ROSE):

Columbia 21559 *The Death Of Rock And Roll* ...	10.00 -	15.00
40836 *Ugly And Slouchy*	7.00 -	10.00
41020 *Stop Whistlin' Wolf*	7.00 -	10.00

ROSE MADDOX:

Capitol (LP) 1312 *One Rose*	15.00 -	20.00
(LP) 1548 *A Big Bouquet Of Roses*	12.00 -	16.00
Columbia 21394 *Wild Wild Young Men*	5.00 -	8.00

MADDY BROTHERS:

Celestial 109 *Rockin' Party*	10.00 -	15.00

MADISON BROTHERS:

Cedargrove 314 *Trusting In You*	15.00 -	20.00
Sure-- *Give Me Your Heart*	8.00 -	12.00
V-Tone 231 *Did We Go Steady Too Soon?*	5.00 -	8.00

THE MAGICS:

Debra 1003 *Chapel Bells*	5.00 -	8.00

MAGIC SAM:

Chief 7013 *Mr. Charlie*	7.00 -	10.00
7017 *Square Dance Rock*	7.00 -	10.00
7026 *Do The Camel Walk*	7.00 -	10.00
7033 *Blue Light Boogie*	7.00 -	10.00
Cobra 5013 *All Your Love*	10.00 -	15.00
5021 *Look Watcha Done*	10.00 -	15.00
5025 *All Night Love*	8.00 -	12.00
5029 *Twenty One Days In Jail*	8.00 -	12.00

THE MAGNETS:

Groove 0058 *You Just Say The Word*	10.00 -	15.00

THE MAGNIFICENT FOUR:

Blast 210 *The Closer You Are*	10.00 -	15.00
Whale 506 *The Closer You Are*	15.00 -	20.00

MAGNIFICENTS:

Dee Gee 3008 *My Heart Is Calling*	7.00 -	10.00
Vee Jay 183 *Up On The Mountain*	10.00 -	15.00
208 *Caddy Bo*	7.00 -	10.00
235 *Off The Mountain*	12.00 -	16.00
281 *Don't Leave Me*	15.00 -	20.00

MAHARAJAHS:

Flip 332 *Why Don't You Answer?*	8.00 -	12.00

MOE MAHARREY:

Hi 2019 *I Cry For You*	5.00 -	8.00

SIDNEY MAIDEN:

Dig 138 *Hand Me Down Baby*	15.00 -	25.00
Flash 101 *Everything Is Wrong*	15.00 -	25.00
Imperial 5189 *Honey Bee Blues*	30.00 -	40.00

MAJESTICS:

Bim 1 *How Long Will It Last*	8.00 -	12.00
Chex 1000 *Give Me a Cigarette*	10.00 -	15.00
1004 *Unhappy And Blue*	10.00 -	15.00
1006 *Lonely Heart*	10.00 -	15.00
Knight 105 *Pennies For A Beggar*	10.00 -	15.00
Linda 111 *Strange World*	7.00 -	10.00
121 *Girl Of My Dreams*	7.00 -	10.00
Marlin 802 *Cave Man Rock*	—	—
NRC 502 *Please Don't Say No*	7.00 -	10.00
Pixie 6901 *Searching For A New Love*	10.00 -	15.00

VINCENT MALOY:

Angle Tone 520 *Flying Home* . . . . 10.00 - 15.00
End 1019 *Hubba Hubba Ding Bing* . . . . 10.00 - 15.00

GENE MALTAIS:
Decca 30387 *Crazy Baby* . . . . 30.00 - 50.00
Lilac 3159 *The Raging Sea* . . . . 50.00 - 75.00

MANDELLS:
Chess 1794 *Who, Me?* . . . . 8.00 - 12.00
Smart 323 *Darling I'm Home* . . . . 15.00 - 20.00
Smart— *Because I Love You* . . . . 15.00 - 20.00

MANHATTANS:
Carnival 506, 509, 512 . . . . 4.00 - 7.00
Ransom 787 *It Was A Night Like This* . . . . 50.00 - 75.00

GEORGE MANIS:
Eclaire— *Hep, Two, Three* . . . . — - —

BARRY MANN:
ABC Paramount (LP) 399 *Who Put The Bomp* . . 35.00 - 50.00

BILLY MANN:
Dig 120 *A Million Heartaches Ago* . . . . 8.00 - 12.00

CARL MANN (& THE KOOL KATS):
Jaxon 502 *Gonna Rock & Roll Tonight* . . . . 75.00 - 100.00
Phillips 3546 *Rockin' Love* . . . . 5.00 - 8.00
(LP) 1960 *Like, Mann* . . . . 100.00 - 150.00

CHUCK MANN:
Leona 3699 *Little Miss Muffet* . . . . 5.00 - 8.00

FRANKIE MANN & THE METEORS:
Apt 25024 *Toe To Toe* . . . . 5.00 - 8.00

GLORIA MANN & CARTER RAYS:
Jubilee 5142 *Goodnight, Sweetheart, Goodnight* . 15.00 - 20.00

SKIP MANNING:
Empire 508 *Ham 'N' Eggs* . . . . — - —

RED MANSEL & THE HILLBILLY BOYS:
Allstar 7160 *Johnny On The Spot* . . . . 10.00 - 15.00

JOE MAPHIS:
Columbia 21518 *Guitar Rock & Roll* . . . . 7.00 - 10.00
Republic 2006 *Water Baby Boogie* . . . . 7.00 - 10.00

MARATHONS:
Arvee (LP) 428 *Peanut Butter* . . . . 20.00 - 30.00
JC 101 *Don't Know Why* . . . . 5.00 - 8.00

MARBLES:
Lucky 002 *Golden Girl* . . . . — - —

MARCELS:
Colpix (LP) 416 *Blue Moon* . . . . 35.00 - 50.00

MARIGOLDS:
Excello 2057 *Rollin' Stone* . . . . 10.00 - 15.00
2061 *Two Strangers* . . . . 10.00 - 15.00
2081 *It's You, Darling, It's You* . . . . 15.00 - 20.00

MARKEES:
Gone 5028 *Along Came Love* . . . . 10.00 - 15.00

MORTY MARKER & THE IMPALAS:
Back Beat 521 *Tear Down The House* . . . . 7.00 - 10.00

MARKEYS:
20th Century 1210 *Eternal Love* . . . . — - —

MARK IV:
Cosmic 704 *45 RPM* (78 rpm) . . . . 10.00 - 15.00

ROOSEVELT MARKS ORCHESTRA With
CLAYTON LOVE:
Bobbin 102, 108 . . . . 4.00 - 7.00

MARQUEES:
Grand 141 *The Bells* . . . . 50.00 - 75.00
Okeh 7096 *Wyatt Earp* . . . . 10.00 - 15.00
Warner Bros. 5139 *Until I Die* . . . . 7.00 - 10.00

MARSHALL BROTHERS:
Savoy 825 *Who Will Be The Fool* . . . . 100.00 - 150.00
828 *Just Because* . . . . 100.00 - 150.00
833 *Why Make A Fool Out Of Me* . . . . 100.00 - 150.00

PERCY MARSHALL:
Marshall 16481 *Give Me My Guitar and My*
Traveling Shoes . . . . 8.00 - 12.00

MARTELLS:
Cessna 477 *Forgotten Spring* . . . . 15.00 - 20.00

MARTELS:
Nasco 6026 *Where Did My Woman Go* . . . . 8.00 - 12.00

BILLY MARTIN:
Lucky 0009 *If It's Lovin' That You Want* . . . . . . 15.00 - 20.00

BOBBY MARTIN:
Belkay 600 *Jo Jo Rock And Roll* . . . . 20.00 - 30.00

JANIS MARTIN:
Bella 1001 *Cracker Jack* . . . . 10.00 - 15.00
RCA Victor (EP) 4093 *Just Squeeze Me* . . . . 50.00 - 75.00
6491 *Drugstore Rock & Roll* . . . . 7.00 - 10.00
6560 *Ooby Dooby* . . . . 8.00 - 12.00
6652 *My Boy Elvis* . . . . 10.00 - 15.00
6744 *Let's Elope Baby* . . . . 7.00 - 10.00
6832 *Love Me To Pieces* . . . . 8.00 - 12.00
6983 *Love And Kisses* . . . . 8.00 - 12.00
7104 *All Right Baby* . . . . 10.00 - 15.00
7184 *Cracker Jack* . . . . 10.00 - 15.00
7318 *Bang Bang* . . . . 10.00 - 15.00

JERRY MARTIN:
Fredlo 5901 *Janet* . . . . 50.00 - 75.00
"R" 507 *Lover's Promise* . . . . — - —
"R" 510 *Deep In My Heart* . . . . — - —

JIMMY MARTIN:
Jaxon 501 *Rock The Bop* . . . . 30.00 - 40.00

RIC MARTIN:
Condor 101/102 *I Travel The Road* . . . . — - —
103/104 *Warm One* . . . . — - —

SONNY MARTIN:
Felsted 8507 *Rockabye Baby* . . . . 8.00 - 12.00

WINK MARTINDALE:
Dot (LP) 3245 *Deck Of Cards* . . . . 15.00 - 20.00
Dot 15728 *All Love Broke Loose* . . . . 7.00 - 10.00
OJ 1009 *Love's Got Me Thinkin'* . . . . 5.00 - 8.00

MARTINETS:
Success 110 *Baby Think It Over* . . . . 7.00 - 10.00

MARTINIQUES:
Dance Land 770 *Broken Hearted Me* . . . . 10.00 - 15.00
1002 *I Need Love* . . . . 10.00 - 15.00

MARTY:
Novelty 701 *Marty On Planet Mars* . . . . 7.00 - 10.00
(Note: 78 rpm pressing exists.)

MARVELIERS:
Cougar 1868 *Down* . . . . 15.00 - 20.00

MARVELLOS:
Exodus 6214 *She Told Me Lies* . . . . 8.00 - 12.00
Theron 117 *Calypso Mama* . . . . 75.00 - 125.00

MARVELLS:
Magnet—*Did She Leave You* . . . . 20.00 - 30.00

MARVELOWS:
ABC Paramount 10603 *A Friend* . . . . 10.00 - 15.00
10629 *I Do* . . . . 5.00 - 8.00
10708 *Shim Sham* . . . . 5.00 - 8.00
10756 *Do It* . . . . 5.00 - 8.00

MARVIN & THE CHIRPS:
Tip Top 202 *I'll Miss You This Christmas* . . . . . . 30.00 - 40.00

MARVIN & JOHNNY:
Crown (LP) 5381 *Marvin & Johnny* . . . . 15.00 - 25.00
Modern 968, 974 . . . . 7.00 - 10.00
Specialty 479 *Baby Doll* . . . . 5.00 - 8.00
530 *Flip* . . . . 4.00 - 7.00
Swingin' 645 *Second Helping Of Cherry Pie* . . . . 5.00 - 8.00

MARYLANDERS:
Jubilee 5079 *I'm A Sentimental Fool* . . . . 150.00 - 200.00
5091 *Make Me Thrill Again* . . . . 100.00 - 150.00
5114 *Good Old 99* (red plastic) . . . . 100.00 - 150.00

THE MASCOTS:
Blast 206 *Once Upon A Love* . . . . 10.00 - 15.00
King 5377 *The Story Of My Heart* . . . . 10.00 - 15.00
5435 *Lonely Rain* . . . . 10.00 - 15.00
MGM 11959 *Please Have Mercy* . . . . — - —

JAMES MASK:
Bandera 1306 *Save Your Love* . . . . 15.00 - 20.00

MASQUERADES:
Boyd 1027 *Fanessa* . . . . — - —

THE MASTERS:

Bingo 1008 *Lovely Way To Spend An Evening* ...	15.00 -	20.00
Le Sage 714 *Crying My Heart Out*	15.00 -	20.00

SAMMY MASTERS:

4 Star 1696 *Pink Cadillac*	10.00 -	15.00
1697 *Whop T Bop*	10.00 -	15.00
Galahad 526 *On Tour In Heaven*	4.00 -	7.00
Lode 108 *Rockin' Red Wing*	7.00 -	10.00

MASTER TONES:

Bruce 111 *Tell Me*	—	—

MATADORS:

Keith 6502 *If You Left Me Today*	7.00 -	10.00
Sue 700 *Vengeance*	20.00 -	30.00
701 *Be Good To Me*	15.00 -	20.00

BILLY MATCH & STARFIRES:

Starfire 664 *I Want My Baby*	7.00 -	10.00

LITTLE ARTHUR MATHEWS:

Federal 12232 *I'm Gonna Whale On You*	8.00 -	12.00

JOHNNY MATHIS:

Columbia 40851, 40993 (78 rpm)............	5.00 -	10.00

MIKE MATHIS:

Blue River 203 *I Can't Get Loose*	7.00 -	10.00

RAMON MAUPIN:

Fernwood 101 *Long Gone*	30.00 -	40.00
105 *Rockin' Rufus*	30.00 -	40.00

HOWARD MAYBERRY:

Dixie 908 *Proof Of Love*	50.00 -	75.00

ARTHUR LEE MAYE (& THE CROWNS):

Cash 1063 *Will You Be Mine*	20.00 -	30.00
1065 *All I Want Is Someone To Love*	20.00 -	30.00
Dig 124 *This Is The Night For Love*	20.00 -	30.00
133 *A Fool's Prayer*	20.00 -	30.00
RPM 424 *Truly*	30.00 -	40.00
429 *Love Me Always*	30.00 -	40.00
438 *Please Don't Leave Me*	30.00 -	40.00
Specialty 573 *Gloria*	15.00 -	20.00
Yvette 300 *Gloria*	10.00 -	15.00

NATHANIEL MAYER:

Fortune (LP) 8014 *Going Back To The Village Of Love*	30.00 -	40.00

PERCY MAYFIELD:

Chess 1599 *Double Dealing*	7.00 -	10.00
Specialty 416 *Cry Baby*	10.00 -	15.00
432 *Louisiana*	10.00 -	15.00
439 *Lonesome Highway*.................	8.00 -	12.00
451 *River's Invitation*	8.00 -	12.00
460 *Lost Mind*	7.00 -	10.00
473 *The Bachelor Blues*	7.00 -	10.00
485 *Loose Lips*	7.00 -	10.00
499 *You Don't Exist No More*	7.00 -	10.00

(Note: Earlier issues than those listed above are usually found as 78 RPM records, valued at $4-$7. 45 RPM counterparts of these lower numbers are valued at $15-20. Records pressed of colored vinyl are worth substantially more than prices quoted.)

MIKE McALISTER:

Hob Nob 441 *I Don't Dig It*	7.00 -	10.00

LEON McAULIFF:

ABC Paramount (LP) 394 *Cozy Inn*	15.00 -	20.00

DALE McBRIDE With GAYLON CHRISTIE & DOWNBEATS:

Fame 503 *It Might Have Been*	10.00 -	15.00
Kobb 1500 *If You See My Julie*	10.00 -	15.00

JERRY (BOOGIE) McCAIN (& HIS UPSTARTS):

Excello 2068 *Courtin' In A Cadillac*	8.00 -	12.00
2079 *If It Wasn't For My Baby*	4.00 -	7.00
2081, 2103, 2111	4.00 -	7.00
2127 *The Jig's Up*	5.00 -	10.00
Trumpet 217 *Wine O-Wine*	50.00 -	75.00
231 *Stay Out Of Automobiles*	50.00 -	75.00

MAC McCLANAHAN:

Tiger 104 *That Nonsense Stuff*	5.00 -	8.00

HAZEL McCOLLUM With THE EL DORADOS:

Vee Jay 118 *Annie's Answer*	30.00 -	50.00

JIMMY McCRACKLIN (& HIS BLUES BLASTERS):

Irma 102, 107, 109	7.00 -	10.00
Mercury 71516 *Georgia Slop*	5.00 -	8.00
Modern *Blues Blasters Boogie*	10.00 -	15.00
934 *Darling Share Your Love*	10.00 -	15.00
951 *Couldn't Be A Dream*	10.00 -	15.00
967 *That Ain't Right*	8.00 -	12.00
Peacock 1605 *She's Gone*	7.00 -	10.00
1615 *She Felt Too Good*	7.00 -	10.00
1634 *I Cried*	5.00 -	8.00
1639 *My Story*..................	5.00 -	8.00

JIM McCRORY:

Key 5803 *Parking Lot*	20.00 -	30.00
5805 *Rock Ya Baby*.................	20.00 -	30.00

GENE McDANIELS:

Liberty (LP) 3146 *In Times Like These*........	15.00 -	20.00

LUKE McDANIEL(S):

King 1247 *Drive On*	7.00 -	10.00
King 1338 *Automobile Song*	7.00 -	10.00
1380 *Money Bag Woman*	7.00 -	10.00
Trumpet 184 *No More*	15.00 -	20.00

JIM McDONALD:

KCM 3700 *Let's Have A Ball*	8.00 -	12.00

SKEETS McDONALD:

Capitol (LP) 1040 *Goin' Steady*	40.00 -	60.00
3461 *Heart Breakin' Mama*	15.00 -	20.00
Capitol (most other issues)	3.00 -	6.00

TOM McDONALD:

Go-Far 962 *One Woman Man*	—	—

BOB McFADDEN & DOR:

Brunswick (LP) 54056 *Songs Our Mummy Taught Us*..................................	40.00 -	60.00

RUTH McFADDEN & THE SUPREMES (See THE SUPREMES)

BROWNIE McGHEE (& HIS JOOK BLOCK BUSTERS):

Dot 1184 *Cheatin' And Lying*............	8.00 -	12.00
Encore 102 *High Price Blues*	10.00 -	15.00
Folkways (LP) 2030 (10″) *Blues*	—	—
(LP) 2421 *Blues Of America*	—	—
(LP) 3557 *Blues*	—	—
Harlem 2323 *Christina*	20.00 -	30.00
2329 *My Confession*	20.00 -	30.00
Jackson 2304 *Mean Old Frisco* (red vinyl) ..	50.00 -	75.00
Jax 304 *Key To The Highway*............	35.00 -	50.00
310 *Dissatisfed Woman*	35.00 -	50.00
312 *Cherry Red*..................	35.00 -	50.00
322 *Pawnshop Blues*	35.00 -	50.00
Old Town 1075 *She Loves So Easy*	4.00 -	7.00
Red Robin 111 *Don't Dog Your Woman* ...	75.00 -	100.00
Savoy 835 *Diamond Ring*	10.00 -	15.00
844 *Bottom Blues*	10.00 -	15.00
872 *Tell Me Baby*	10.00 -	15.00
1177 *Anna Mae*	7.00 -	10.00
1185 *When It's Love Time*.............	7.00 -	10.00
1564 *Be My Friend*	5.00 -	8.00
(LP) 14019 *Back Country Blues* (with Sonny Terry)	30.00 -	50.00
Sharp (LP) 2003 *Brownie McGhee*	50.00 -	75.00

STICK McGHEE:

Atlantic 991 *Meet You in the Morning*	10.00 -	15.00

(Note: Earlier numbers are usually found as 78 RPM records, which are listed in the Blues, etc., section of this book. 45 RPM records of these earlier issues would bring $15-$20, or more.)

Decca 48104 *Drinkin' Wine Spo-De-O-De* ...... 20.00 - 30.00
Essex 709 *My Little Rose* ...... 10.00 - 15.00
Herald 553 *Money Fever* ...... 7.00 - 10.00
King 4610 *Head Happy With Wine* ...... 8.00 - 12.00
    4628 *Whiskey, Women And Loaded Dice* ..... 8.00 - 12.00
    4672 *Jungle Juice* ...... 8.00 - 12.00
    4700 *I'm Doin' All The Time* ...... 7.00 - 10.00
    4783 *Double Crossin' Liquor* ...... 7.00 - 10.00
    4800 *Get Your Mind Out Of The Gutter* ..... 7.00 - 10.00
Savoy 1148 *Things Have Changed* ...... 5.00 - 8.00

BUTCH McGILLIS & THE ROCKATUNES:
Rock-A-Tune 1010 *Woman Fever* ...... 40.00 - 60.00

WAYNE McGINNIS:
Meteor 5035 *Rock And Roll Rhythm* ...... 20.00 - 30.00

MEL McGONNIGLE: .
Rocket 101 *Rattle Shakin' Mama* ...... 75.00 - 100.00

LOWELL McGUIRE:
Nasco 6007 *Leave My Girlie Alone* ...... 8.00 - 12.00

CHESTER McINTYRE:
Sarg 180 *I'm Gonna Rock With My Baby Tonight* . 7.00 - 10.00

GENE McKAY:
Clark 238 *What I Say* ...... 15.00 - 20.00

L.C. McKINLEY (& HIS ORCHESTRA):
Bea & Baby 102 *Nit Wit* ...... 8.00 - 12.00
States 135 *Weeping Willow Blues* ...... 40.00 - 60.00
Vee Jay 133 *She's Five Feet Three* ...... 15.00 - 20.00
    159 *I'm So Satisfied* ...... 10.00 - 15.00

GENE McKOWN:
Aggie 101 *Rock-A-Billy Rhythm* ...... 30.00 - 50.00

BUTCH McLAREY:
Kliff 103 *Rockin' Hall* ...... 40.00 - 60.00

OSCAR McLOLLIE (& THE HONEYJUMPERS):
Crown (LP) 5016 *Oscar McLollie & The*
    Honeyjumpers ...... 15.00 - 20.00
Modern 970 *Convicted* ...... 7.00 - 10.00

CECIL McNABB:
King 5116 *Clock Tickin' Rhythm* ...... 30.00 - 40.00

BIG JAY McNEELY:
King (LP) 530 *...In 3-D* ...... 15.00 - 20.00
Savoy (LP) 15045 *(10")* ...... 15.00 - 20.00

CLYDE McPHATTER (& THE DRIFTERS):
Atlantic (EP) 605 *Rock With Clyde McPhatter* ... 15.00 - 25.00
    (EP) 618 *Clyde McPhatter* ...... 15.00 - 25.00
    1185 *Come What May* (78 rpm) ...... 7.00 - 10.00
    1199 *A Lover's Question* (78 rpm) ...... 15.00 - 20.00
    2028 *Since You've Been Gone* (78 rpm) ...... 15.00 - 20.00
    2038 *There You Go* (78 rpm) ...... 15.00 - 20.00
    (LP) 8003 *Clyde McPhatter & The Drifters*
      (black label) ...... 30.00 - 40.00
    (LP) 8024 *Love Ballads* ...... 15.00 - 20.00
    (LP) 8031 *Clyde* ...... 15.00 - 20.00
King (LP) 559 *Clyde McPhatter With Billy Ward*
    & His Dominoes ...... 40.00 - 60.00
(Note: This album exists as Federal 559, which is
    considerably rarer than the King issue.)
MGM (LP) 3775 *Let's Start Over Again* ...... 15.00 - 25.00

CARL McVOY:
Hi 2001 *Tootsie* ...... 8.00 - 12.00
    2002 *Little John's Gone* ...... 7.00 - 10.00
Phillips 3526 *Tootsie* ...... 5.00 - 8.00

MEADOWLARKS: (See also DON JULIAN):
RPM 399 *Love Only You* ...... 20.00 - 30.00

MEDALLIONAIRES:
Mercury 71309 *Magic Moonlight* ...... 15.00 - 20.00

THE MEDALLIONS: (See also: VERNON GREEN)
Dooto (EP) 202 ...... 40.00 - 60.00
Dooto/Dootone 347 *Buick 59* ...... 10.00 - 15.00
    357 *The Telegram* ...... 10.00 - 15.00
    364 *Edna* ...... 10.00 - 15.00
    373 *My Pretty Baby* ...... 10.00 - 15.00

    379 *Dear Darling* ...... 10.00 - 15.00
    393 *I Want A Love* ...... 10.00 - 15.00
    400 *Shedding Tears For You* ...... 10.00 - 15.00
    419 *For Better Or For Worse* ...... 10.00 - 15.00
    454 *Behind The Door* ...... 8.00 - 12.00
Essex 901 *I Know* ...... 75.00 - 100.00
Sarg 191 *I Love You True* ...... 7.00 - 10.00
    194 *Lovin' Time* ...... 7.00 - 10.00
Singular 1002 *A Broken Heart* ...... 15.00 - 20.00

MELLO FELLOWS:
Lamp 8006 *My Friend Charlie* ...... 10.00 - 15.00

MELLO HARPS:
Do Re Mi 203 *Love Is A Vow* ...... 300.00 - Up
Tin Pan Alley 145 *I Love Only You* ...... 50.00 - 75.00
Tin Pan Alley 157 *What Good Are My Dreams* .. 50.00 - 75.00

MELLO-KINGS:
Herald (EP) 451 *The Fabulous* ...... 75.00 - 100.00
Herald 502 *Tonite, Tonite* ...... 10.00 - 15.00
    502 *Tonite, Tonite* (78 rpm) ...... 15.00 - 20.00
    507 *Chapel On The Hill* ...... 7.00 - 10.00
    518 *Valerie* ...... 8.00 - 12.00
    536 *Running To You* ...... 8.00 - 12.00
    536 *Chip Chip* (actually *Down In Cuba* by
      THE ROYAL HOLIDAYS) ...... 25.00 - 40.00
    548 *Our Love Is Beautiful* ...... 8.00 - 12.00
    554 *I Promise* ...... 8.00 - 12.00
    561 *Till There Was You* ...... 8.00 - 12.00
    (LP) 1013 *Tonight-Tonight* ...... 100.00 - 150.00

MELLO-MOODS/MELLO MOODS:
Hollywood 396 *Song Of Love* ...... 100.00 - 150.00
Prestige 799 *Call On Me* ...... 150.00 - 200.00
    856 *I'm Lost* ...... 150.00 - 200.00
Recorded in Hollywood--*Beautiful Love* ...... 15.00 - 20.00
Red Robin 104 *I Couldn't Sleep A Wink Last*
    Night ...... rare
    105 *How Could You* ...... — - —

MELLO-TONES/MELLOTONES:
Decca (EP) 2399 *Mellotones* ...... 20.00 - 30.00
    48318 *Man Loves Woman* ...... 75.00 - 100.00
Fascination 1001 *Rosie Lee* ...... 30.00 - 40.00
    —*Cassandra* ...... 10.00 - 15.00
Gee 1037 *Rosie Lee* ...... 7.00 - 10.00
    1037 *Rosie Lee* (78 rpm) ...... 10.00 - 15.00
Herald 502 *Tonite, Tonite* ...... 20.00 - 30.00
Lee Tone 700 *Prayer Of Love* (blue label) ...... 60.00 - 90.00

MELLOW KEYS:
Gee 1014 *I'm Not A Deceiver* ...... 15.00 - 20.00

MELLOWS:
Candelight 1011 *You're Gone* ...... 8.00 - 12.00
Jay Dee 793 *How Sentimental Can I Be* ...... 15.00 - 20.00
    797 *Smoke From Your Cigarette* ...... 7.00 - 10.00
    801 *I Still Care* ...... 15.00 - 20.00
    807 *Yesterday's Memories* ...... 15.00 - 20.00

MELO-AIRES:
Nasco 6019 *Indebted To You* ...... — - —

MELODAIRES:
Flyright 915 *Now You Know* ...... 7.00 - 10.00

THE MELODEERS:
Studio 9908 *Wishing Is For Fools* ...... 10.00 - 15.00

MEL-O-DOTS:
Apollo 1192 *Just How Long* ...... 150.00 - 250.00

MELO GENTS:
Warner Bros. 5056 *Baby Be Mine* ...... 10.00 - 15.00

MELOTONES (See MELLOTONES):

RAY MELTON:
Image 1005 *Boppin' Guitar* ...... 20.00 - 30.00

MEMORIES:
Way-Lin 101 *Love Bells* ...... 10.00 - 15.00

"MEMORY LANE HITS BY THE ORIGINAL GROUPS"
Fire (LP) 100 ...... 15.00 - 20.00

MEMPHIS MINNIE & HER COMBO/With

LITTLE JOE & HIS BAND:

Checker 771 *Me And My Chauffeur* (red plastic) .	75.00 -	100.00
J.O.B. 1101 *Kissing In The Dark* (red plastic)	75.00 -	100.00

MEMPHIS SLIM & HIS/THE HOUSE ROCKERS/ORCHESTRA:

Chess (LP) 1455 *Memphis Slim*	20.00 -	30.00
Folkways (LP) 3524 *The Real Boogie Woogie* ...	— -	—
Money 212 *My Country Gal*	7.00 -	10.00
United 138 *Back Alley*	8.00 -	12.00
156, 166, 176, 182, 186, 189, 201	5.00 -	8.00
Vee Jay 271, 294, 330, 343	4.00 -	6.00
(LP) 1012 *Memphis Slim At The Gate Of Horn*	20.00 -	30.00

MERCY BABY:

Ace 528 *Rock And Roll Blues*	7.00 -	10.00
535 *Mercy's Blues*	7.00 -	10.00
Mercy Baby 501 *You Ran Away*	10.00 -	15.00
502 *The Rock And Stomp*	10.00 -	15.00
Ric 995 *Don't Lie To Me*	5.00 -	8.00

MERCY DEE (See DEE):

MERRILL BROTHERS:

GM 102 *Mercy Blues*	8.00 -	12.00

BIG MACEO MERRIWEATHER:

Fortune (LP) 3002 *Big Maceo Merriweather & John Lee Hooker*	20.00 -	30.00

METALLICS:

Baronet 2 *Need Your Love*	10.00 -	15.00
14 *Get Lost*	10.00 -	15.00

METRONOMES:

Maureen 1000 *My Dearest Darling*	15.00 -	20.00
Specialty 472 *She's Gone*	15.00 -	20.00
Strand (LP) *The Metronomes Sing The Standard Hits*	20.00 -	30.00

THE METROPOLITANS:

Junior 395 *So Much In Love*	7.00 -	10.00

METROS:

Just 1502 *All Of My Life*	8.00 -	12.00

THE METROTONES:

Reserve 114 *More And More*	75.00 -	100.00
116 *Please Come Back*	75.00 -	100.00
(above black label)		

LOUIE MEYERS (& THE ACES):

Abco 104 *Blusey*	35.00 -	50.00

JOEY MICHAELS:

Arcade 150 *Sixteen Cats*	20.00 -	30.00

MICKEY & SYLVIA:

Groove (EP) 18 *Love Is Strange*	30.00 -	40.00
Rainbow 316 *Se Le Boom Run Dun*	10.00 -	15.00
Vik (LP) 1102 *New Sounds*	75.00 -	100.00

ELMON MICKLE (& HIS RHYTHM ACES):

Elko 003 *Flat Foot Sam*	30.00 -	40.00
E.M. 132 *Lonesome Highway*	20.00 -	30.00
EM & EP 133 *Short 'N' Fat*	15.00 -	20.00
J Gems 1908 *Short 'N' Fat*	8.00 -	12.00

GARY MIDDLETON:

Harlem 102 *Don't Be Shy*	15.00 -	20.00

MIDNIGHTERS: (See also HANK BALLARD)

Federal (LP) 295-90 (10") *The Midnighters*	100.00 -	150.00
Federal (EP) 333 *Midnighters Sing Their Greatest Hits*	30.00 -	50.00
(LP) 541 *Midnighters Sing Their Greatest Hits*	75.00 -	100.00
12169 *Work With Me Annie*	8.00 -	12.00
12185 *Sexy Ways*	7.00 -	10.00
12195 *Annie Had A Baby*	7.00 -	10.00
12202, 12205, 12210, 12220, 12224, 12227, 12230, 12240, 12243, 12251, 12260, 12270, 12285, 12293, 12299, 12305, 12317, 12339 ...	5.00 -	8.00
King (LP) 581...*Greatest Hits...Vol. 2*	15.00 -	25.00
Sarg 187 *Rockin' Romance*	7.00 -	10.00

MIDNIGHTS:

Music City 746 *Hear My Plea*	15.00 -	20.00
762 *Cheating On Me*	15.00 -	20.00

MIKE & THE UTOPIANS:

Gee Jay 574 *I Wish*	15.00 -	20.00

BOBBY MILANO:

Challenge 59005 *Double Talking Baby*	15.00 -	20.00

AMOS MILBURN (See also: PARTY AFTER HOURS):

Aladdin (LP) 704 (10") *Rockin' The Boogie* (red vinyl)	150.00 -	200.00
(LP) 810 *Rockin' The Boogie*	150.00 -	200.00
3105 *Boogie Woogie*	15.00 -	20.00
3124 *Trouble In Mind*	15.00 -	20.00
3125 *Flyin' Home*	15.00 -	20.00
3133 *Roll Mr. Jelly*	15.00 -	20.00
3146 *Button Your Lip*	15.00 -	20.00
3150 *Greyhound*	10.00 -	15.00
3159 *Rock Rock*	12.00 -	15.00
3164 *Let Me Go Home Whiskey*	10.00 -	15.00
3168, 3197, 3218, 3226, 3240, 3248, 3253, 3269, 3293, 3320, 3332, 3363, 3383, 3420	5.00 -	8.00
(Note: Numbers lower than those listed here are usually found as 78 RPM records; see Blues, etc. section. 45 RPM issues of such earlier numbers would bring $15-$30).		
Motown 1038 *I'll Make It Up To You Somehow* ..	— -	—
Score (LP) 4012 *Let's Have A Party*	50.00 -	75.00

MILLER SISTERS:

Ember 1004 *Guess Who*	7.00 -	10.00
Flip 504 *I Knew You Would*	25.00 -	35.00
Sun 230 *There's No Right Way To Do Me Wrong* .	30.00 -	40.00
255 *Ten Cats Down*	15.00 -	20.00
504 *I Knew You Would*	40.00 -	60.00

BOBBY MILLER:

Band Box 332 *Little Bo Beep*	5.00 -	8.00

BUDDY MILLER:

VEM 2226 *Teen Twist*	5.00 -	8.00

CARL MILLER:

Lu 503 *Rhythm Guitar*	25.00 -	40.00

CHUCK MILLER:

Mercury (LP) 20195 *After Hours*	20.00 -	30.00

CLINT MILLER:

ABC Paramount 9878 *Bertha Lou*	5.00 -	8.00
9938 *Teenage Dance*	5.00 -	8.00

DICK MILLER & SOUTHERN RAMBLERS:

M & M--*Humpty Dumpty Love*	— -	—

FRANKIE MILLER:

Audio Lab (LP) 1562 *Fine Country Singin'*	30.00 -	40.00
Columbia 21314 *It's No Big Thing To Me*	5.00 -	8.00
21378 *You Don't Show Me Much*	5.00 -	8.00
21420 *Paid In Full*	5.00 -	8.00
21472 *Paint, Powder And Perfume*	5.00 -	8.00
21519 *Day By Day*	5.00 -	8.00
Starday (LP) SLP-338 *Blackland Farmer* ..	20.00 -	30.00
Starday 457, 481, 496, 513, 525, 537, 550, 566, 655, 673, 691, 709	4.00 -	8.00

JODY MILLER:

Capitol (LP) 2349 *Queen Of The House*	10.00 -	15.00

ROGER MILLER:

Starday 356 *Can't Stop Lovin' You*	10.00 -	15.00

TAL MILLER:

Goldband 1059 *Life's Journey*	5.00 -	8.00
Hollywood 1094, 1097	5.00 -	8.00

WALTER MILLER With THE BARONS:

Meteor 5037 *My Last Mile*	20.00 -	30.00

WARREN MILLER:

United Artists 104 *Everybody's Got A Baby But Me*	15.00 -	20.00

LOU MILLET:

Republic 7130 *Slip Slip Slippin' In*	50.00 -	80.00

BUDDY MILTON & THE TWILIGHTERS:

RPM 419 *Oo Wah*	20.00 -	30.00

LITTLE MILTON (See LITTLE)

ROY MILTON:

Dooto (LP) 223 *Rock 'N' Roll Vs. Rhythm*

'N' Blues	35.00 -	50.00
Dootone 363, 369	7.00 -	10.00
Specialty 429, 438, 464, 480, 538, 545	5.00 -	10.00
(copies pressed of red vinyl command higher prices)		

SAL MINEO:

Epic (LP) 3404 *Dino*	15.00 -	20.00

ROSS MININI:

Gulfstream 7269 *Oh Janet*	20.00 -	30.00

JIIMMY MINOR:

Mercury 71623 *So Doggone Lonesome*	4.00 -	7.00

MINORBOPS:

Lamp 2012 *Need You Tonight*	15.00 -	25.00

THE MINOR CHORDS:

Lu Pine 112 *Many A Day*	— -	—

MINORS:

Celeste 3007 *Jerry*	100.00 -	Up

MINOR TONES:

Music City 816 *Forever Darling*	10.00 -	15.00

MINT JULEPS:

Herald 481 *Bells Of Love*	15.00 -	25.00

MINTS:

Lin 5001 *Busy Body Rock*	8.00 -	12.00
5007 *Night Air*	8.00 -	12.00

MIRACLES:

Baton 210 *A Lover's Chant*	8.00 -	12.00
Cash 1008 *You're An Angel*	20.00 -	30.00
End 1019 *Got A Job*	10.00 -	15.00
1029 *I Cry*	8.00 -	12.00
Fury 1002/1003 *Your Love*	50.00 -	75.00
Motown 1/2 *Bad Girl*	100.00 -	Up
Tamla (LP) 220 *Hi, We're The Miracles*	50.00 -	75.00
(LP) 223 *Cookin' With The Miracles*	50.00 -	75.00
(LP) 224 *Shop Around*	40.00 -	60.00
Tamla 54028 *The Feeling Is So Fine*	8.00 -	12.00
54034 *Shop Around*	5.00 -	8.00
54034 *Shop Around* (Master number on label and in wax reads: H-55518A2)	35.00 -	50.00
54044 *Mighty Good Lovin'*	8.00 -	12.00
(Note: Above 45s, if original issues, will have the "striped" label design.)		

BILLY MIRANDA:

Checker 957 *Run Rose*	5.00 -	8.00

MISS PEACHES:

Groove 0009 *Calling Moody Field*	7.00 -	10.00

BILLY MITCHELL:

Atlantic 974 *Bald Head Woman*	15.00 -	20.00

BOBBY MITCHELL (& THE TOPPERS):

Imperial 5250 *One Friday Morning*	40.00 -	60.00
5270 *Baby's Gone*	20.00 -	30.00
5295 *Wedding Bells Are Ringing*	35.00 -	50.00
5326 *I Wish I Knew*	20.00 -	30.00
5346 *I Cried*	15.00 -	20.00
5378, 5392	7.00 -	10.00

FREDDIE MITCHELL:

Rock & Roll 609 *Three Strikes You're Out*	7.00 -	10.00

LEE MITCHELL:

Sharp 0862 *Rootie Tootie Baby*	40.00 -	60.00

MARLON MITCHELL:

Vena 0100 *Ice Cold Baby*	25.00 -	40.00

STANLEY MITCHELL & THE TORNADOS:

Chess 1649 *Four O'Clock In The Morning*	20.00 -	30.00

TOMMIE MITCHELL:

Mercury 70930 *Little Mama*	10.00 -	15.00

WILLIE MITCHELL:

Stomper Time 1160 *Tell It To Me Baby*	10.00 -	15.00

MIXERS:

Bold 101 *You Said You're Leaving Me*	75.00 -	100.00

HANK MIZELL:

King 5236 *Jungle Rock*	25.00 -	35.00

BOBBY MIZZELL & LEE WAYNE:

20th Fox 160 *Same Thing*	10.00 -	15.00

RONNIE MOLLEEN:

King 5365 *Rockin' Up*	20.00 -	30.00

MONARCHS:

JAM 104 *This Old Heart*	15.00 -	20.00
Neil 101 *In My Younger Days*	10.00 -	15.00
103 *Always Be Faithful*	15.00 -	20.00
Sound Stage 2502 *This Old Heart*	7.00 -	10.00
Wing 90040 *Angels In The Sky*	30.00 -	40.00

MONDELLOS:

Rhythm 1003 *One Hundred Years From Today*	75.00 -	100.00

MONIQUES:

Centaur 105 *All The Way Now*	8.00 -	12.00

MONITORS:

Aladdin 3309 *Tonight's The Night*	15.00 -	25.00
Circus 219 *A Boy Friend's Prayer*	30.00 -	40.00
Specialty 595 *Our School Days*	10.00 -	15.00
622 *Closer To Heaven*	7.00 -	10.00
636 *Mama Linda*	5.00 -	8.00

MONOGRAMS:

Saga 1000 *My Baby Dearest Darling*	20.00 -	30.00

MONORAYS:

Nasco 6020 *It's Love Baby*	8.00 -	12.00
Red Rocket 476 *My Guardian Angel*	7.00 -	10.00
Tammy 1005 *My Guardian Angel*	7.00 -	10.00

MONOTONES:

Argo 5290 *Book Of Love*	5.00 -	8.00
5290 *Book Of Love* (78 rpm)	15.00 -	20.00
5301 *Tom Foolery*	7.00 -	10.00
5321 *The Legend Of Sleepy Hollow*	7.00 -	10.00
Hull 735 *Reading The Book Of Love*	20.00 -	30.00
Hull 743 *Tattle Tale*	10.00 -	15.00
Mascot 124 *Book Of Love*	50.00 -	75.00

MONTCLAIRS:

Audicon 111 *Good Night*	7.00 -	10.00
Hi-Q 5001 *Golden Angel*	10.00 -	15.00
Premium 404 *My Every Dream*	30.00 -	50.00
Rage 101 *Fool's Fall In Love*	25.00 -	35.00
Sonic 104 *All I Want Is Love*	10.00 -	15.00

MONTEREYS:

Arvin 130 *Goodbye My Love*	10.00 -	15.00
Dominion 1019 *First Kiss*	15.00 -	20.00
East West 121 *I'll Love You Again*	5.00 -	8.00
Impala 213 *Without A Girl*	15.00 -	20.00
Nestor 15 *Someone Like You*	40.00 -	60.00
Onyx 513 *Dearest One*	15.00 -	20.00
Planet 57 *Blast Off*	5.00 -	8.00
Rose 109 *You're The Girl For Me*	15.00 -	20.00
Teen Age 1001 *Someone Like You*	25.00 -	40.00

JOE MONTGOMERY:

Abbott 189 *Cool Cat*	— -	—

LITTLE BROTHER MONTGOMERY (& HIS BOGALUSA BOYS/VICKSBURGERS):

Ebony 1000 *Cow Cow Blues*	15.00 -	20.00
1002 *Fever*	15.00 -	20.00
1005 *Pinetops Boogie*	15.00 -	20.00
1030 *Gonna Raise A Ruckus Tonight*	15.00 -	20.00

THE MON-VALES:

Pen Joy 502 *Carol-Ann*	— -	—

MOODS:

Kool 1029 *Opp-Sy-Do*	5.00 -	8.00
1032 *Only The Young*	5.00 -	8.00
Sarg 162 *Little Alice*	10.00 -	15.00
176 *Easy Going*	7.00 -	10.00
179 *Let Me Have Your Love*	10.00 -	15.00
184 *Rockin' Santa Claus*	7.00 -	10.00
185 *On The Move*	7.00 -	10.00
TNT 189 *It's Goodbye And Not Goodnight*	10.00 -	15.00

MOONBEAMS:

Great 100 *A Lover's Plea*	5.00 -	8.00
Sapphire 1003 *Cryin' The Blues*	15.00 -	20.00

GLEN MOONEY:

Fraternity 898 *Go Steady With Me*	7.00 -	10.00

MOONGLOWS:

Champagne 7500 *I Just Can't Tell No Lie*	100.00 -	150.00
Chance 1147 *Baby, Please* (red plastic)	400.00 -	600.00
1150 *Just A Lonely Christmas*	200.00 -	300.00
1152 *Secret Love* (silver & blue label)	200.00 -	300.00
1152 *Secret Love* (yellow & black labe)	150.00 -	250.00
1156 *I Was Wrong* (black & white label)	100.00 -	150.00
1156 *I Was Wrong* (yellow & black label)	90.00 -	120.00
1161 *My Gal*	500.00 -	Up
Chess (LP) 1425 *Rock, Rock, Rock* (black label)	60.00 -	80.00
(LP) 1430 *Look, It's The Moonglows* (black label)	90.00 -	120.00
Chess 1581 *Sincerely*	10.00 -	15.00

(Note: This, and numbers through 1669, are of the Silver Top label)

1589 *Most Of All*	10.00 -	15.00
1598 *Foolish Me*	12.00 -	16.00
1605 *In Love*	12.00 -	16.00
1611 *In My Diary*	12.00 -	16.00
1619 *We Go Together*	10.00 -	15.00
1629 *When I'm With You*	8.00 -	12.00
1646 *I Knew From The Start*	8.00 -	12.00
1651 *I'm Afraid The Masquerade Is Over*	10.00 -	15.00
1661 *Please Send Me Someone To Love*	10.00 -	15.00
1669 *The Beating Of My Heart*	10.00 -	15.00
Chess 1681 *Too Late*	10.00 -	15.00

(Note: This, and subsequent issues, have all-blue label, Chess vertical)

1689 *In the Middle of the Night*	10.00 -	15.00
1701 *Sweeter Than Words*	10.00 -	15.00
1717 *I'll Never Stop Wanting You*	8.00 -	12.00
1770 *Junior*	10.00 -	15.00
Chess (EP) 5123 *Look, It's The Moonglows*	75.00 -	100.00
Vee Jay (LP) 1052 *The Moonglows Meet The Flamingos*	15.00 -	20.00

MOONLIGHTERS:

Josie 843 *Broken Heart*	5.00 -	8.00
Tara 100 *Glow Of Love*	20.00 -	30.00
Tara 102 *Rock-A-Bayou Baby*	30.00 -	40.00

CECIL MOORE:

Sarg 150 *Walkin' Fever*	8.00 -	12.00
165 *Kathy*	8.00 -	12.00
192 *My Money's Gone*	7.00 -	10.00
206 *Diamond Back*	4.00 -	6.00

DONNY LEE MOORE:

Shelley 1000 *I'm Buggin Out Little Baby*	20.00 -	30.00

GENE MOORE & THE METRONOMES (See: THE METRONOMES)

JIMMY MOORE & THE TABS:

Nobel 720 *Oops!*	10.00 -	15.00

JOHNNY MOORE; JOHNNY MOORE'S COMBO/THREE BLAZERS; JOHNNY MOORE with JIMMY HAGGETT BAND:

Aladdin 3106 *Cloudy Skies*	10.00 -	15.00
Blaze 101 *Every Time*	4.00 -	7.00
110 *Run Sinner Run*	4.00 -	7.00
Modern Hollywood 1001 *Strange Love*	7.00 -	10.00
1002 *Lonesome Train*	7.00 -	10.00
1012 *Diesel Drive*	7.00 -	10.00
1031 *Johnny Ace's Last Letter*	7.00 -	10.00
1045 *Christmas Eve Baby*	7.00 -	10.00
(Unnumbered) *Dragnet Blues*	7.00 -	10.00
Vaden 111 *Country Girl*	15.00 -	20.00

LATTIE MOORE:

ARC 8005 *Pretty Woman Blues*	15.00 -	25.00

MERRILL MOORE:

Capitol (EP) *Merrill Moore*	20.00 -	30.00
Capitol 2226 *Big Bug Boogie*	7.00 -	10.00
2386 *Bartender's Blues*	5.00 -	8.00
2574 *House Of Blue Lights*	7.00 -	10.00
2691 *Snatchin' And Grabbin'*	5.00 -	8.00
Capitol (most other issues)	4.00 -	7.00

RONNIE MOORE:

Teen's Choice 7 *Sweet Shop Doll*		-

RUDY MOORE:

Federal 12253 *I'm Mad With You*	8.00 -	12.00
12259 *Ring-A-Ling Dong*	8.00 -	12.00
12276 *Step It Up And Go*	10.00 -	15.00
12280 *Robbie Dobbie*	8.00 -	12.00

SCOTTY MOORE (TRIO):

Epic (LP) 24103 *The Guitar That Changed The World*	30.00 -	40.00
Fernwood 107 *Have Guitar Will Travel*	8.00 -	12.00

SPARKLE MOORE:

Fraternity 751 *Rock-A-Bop*	15.00 -	20.00
766 *Tiger*	15.00 -	20.00

MOOSE JOHN:

Ultra 102 *Wrong Doin' Woman*	15.00 -	20.00

PRENTICE MORELAND:

Dot 16173 *Sincerely*	8.00 -	12.00

RICHARD MORELAND:

Picture 6969 *Please Don't Ask Me*	10.00 -	15.00
7722 *Mailman Blues*	10.00 -	15.00

CHARLIE MORGAN:

Walmay 101 *South Of Chicago*	20.00 -	30.00

ROCKET MORGAN:

Zynn 502 *You're Humbuggin' Me*	15.00 -	20.00
507 *What Ya Gonna Do*	15.00 -	20.00
1003 *Walkin' Home*	15.00 -	20.00

JACKIE MORNINGSTAR:

Sandy 1018 *Rockin' To The Graveyard*	30.00 -	40.00

MOROCCANS:

Salem 1014 *Believe In Tomorrow*	50.00 -	75.00

MOROCCOS:

United 188 *Pardon My Tears*	75.00 -	100.00
193 *Somewhere Over The Rainbow*	50.00 -	75.00
204 *What Is A Teenager's Prayer*	75.00 -	100.00
207 *Sad Sad Hours*	100.00 -	150.00

TINY MORRIE:

Hurricane 6966 *Bernardine*	7.00 -	10.00

BOB MORRIS:

Cascade 5907 *Party Time*	7.00 -	10.00

ELMORE MORRIS:

Peacock 1660, 1668	5.00 -	8.00

GENE MORRIS:

Edmoral 1012 *Lovin' Honey*	30.00 -	40.00
Vik 0287 *Lovin' Honey*	15.00 -	20.00
Winston 1046 *If You Need My Love*	15.00 -	20.00

LEO MORRIS:

Ivory 41465 *I Don't Need You*	8.00 -	12.00

ROD MORRIS:

Capitol 1882, 1946, 2022, 2301, 2424, 2541	5.00 -	10.00
Ludwig 1002 *Ghost Of Casey Jones*	7.00 -	10.00

BILL MORRISON:

TNT 9029 *Set Me Free*	50.00 -	75.00
9031 *Baby Be Good*	50.00 -	75.00

JIM MORRISON:

Arctic 5001 *Ready To Rock*	50.00 -	75.00

ELLA MAE MORSE:

Capitol (LP) 513 *Barrelhouse, Boogie & Blues*	20.00 -	30.00

ROY MOSS:

Fascination 1002 *Wiggle Walking Baby*	15.00 -	20.00
Mercury 70770 *You Nearly Lose Your Mind*	20.00 -	30.00
70858 *You Don't Know My Mind*	15.00 -	25.00

DANNY MOTE:

Opal 001 *Done You Wrong*		-

"MOUNTAIN FROLIC":

Brunswick (LP) 5900 (10") (various artists)	20.00 -	30.00

JUNE MOY (& THE FEATHERS:)

Showtime 1103 *Castle Of Dreams*	75.00 -	100.00

MR. STRING BEAN:

Herald 418 *Pass The Juice Miss Lucy*	15.00 -	20.00

MR. X:

Vita 152 *Rock Dock*	— -	—

MUDDY WATERS:

Chess (LP) 1427 *The Best Of Muddy Waters*	50.00 -	75.00

(Note: Above LP has black label.)

Chess 1509 *Country Boy*	75.00 -	100.00
1514 *Please Have Mercy*	75.00 -	100.00
1526 *Gone To Main Street*	75.00 -	100.00
1537 *Sad, Sad Day*	75.00 -	100.00
1542 *Turn The Lamp Down Low*	40.00 -	60.00
1550 *Blow Wind Blow*	20.00 -	30.00
1560 *She's So Pretty*	15.00 -	20.00

(Note: Issues earlier than those above, i.e. lower numbers, are usually found as 78 RPM records, as listed in the Blues, etc., section, which see. 45 RPM issues of such lower numbers are valued at $75.00 to $100.00 and up, with premium prices for records pressed of colored vinyl.)

1571 *Oh Yeah*	10.00 -	15.00
1579 *I'm Ready*	10.00 -	15.00
1585 *Loving Man*	10.00 -	15.00
1596 *I Want To Be Loved*	10.00 -	15.00
1602 *Young Fashioned Ways*	10.00 -	15.00
1612 *Sugar Sweet*	10.00 -	15.00
1620 *All Aboard*	8.00 -	12.00
1630 *Diamonds At Your Feet*	8.00 -	12.00
1644, 1652, 1667, 1680, 1692, 1704, 1718, 1733, 1739, 1748, 1758, 1765, 1774, 1796, 1819, 1827, 1839, 1862	5.00 -	10.00

MOON MULLICAN:

Coral (LP) 57235 *Moon Over Mullican*	80.00 -	120.00
61994 *Jenny Lee*	30.00 -	50.00
62042 *Sweet Rockin' Music*	30.00 -	50.00
Dixie—*Good Times Gonna Roll Again*	-	
King (LP) 555 *Moon Mullican Sings His All Time Greatest Hits*	35.00 -	50.00
(LP) 628 *16 Favorite Tunes*	20.00 -	30.00
917 *I Was Sorta Wonderin'*	5.00 -	8.00
947 *Without A Port Of Love*	5.00 -	8.00
965 *Cherokee Boogie*	8.00 -	12.00
984 *Heartless Lover*	5.00 -	8.00
1043 *Shoot The Moon*	5.00 -	8.00
1060 *Triflin' Woman Blues*	7.00 -	10.00
1152 *A Thousand And One Sleepless Nights*	7.00 -	10.00
1164 *Oogle, Oogle, Olglie*	7.00 -	10.00
1198 *Rocket To The Moon*	7.00 -	10.00
1244 *Grandpa Stole My Baby*	7.00 -	10.00
1337 *Good Deal, Lucille*	7.00 -	10.00
1366 *No Stranger*	5.00 -	8.00
1408 *You Got The Best Of Me*	5.00 -	8.00
1467, 4894, 4915, 4979	4.00 -	8.00
Starday (LP) SLP-267 *Mister Piano Man*	35.00 -	50.00
Starday 527, 545, 556, 594, 596	5.00 -	8.00

DEE MULLIN:

D 1066 *I've Really Got A Right To Cry*	7.00 -	10.00

GENE MUMFORD & THE SERENADERS:

Whiz 1500 *Please Give Me One More Chance*	75.00 -	100.00

CHUCK MURPHY:

Columbia 21258 *Hocus Pocus*	-	
21305 *Rhythm Hall*	15.00 -	20.00

DON MURPHY:

Cosmopolitan 2264 *Mean Mama Blues*	30.00 -	40.00

JIMMY MURPHY:

Columbia 21486 *Here Kitty Kitty*	30.00 -	50.00
21534 *Sixteen Tons Rock & Roll*	30.00 -	50.00
21569 *Baboon Boogie*	35.00 -	50.00
Rev 3508 *I'm Gone Mama*	10.00 -	15.00

SAMMY MYERS:

Ace 536 *Sleeping In The Ground*	10.00 -	15.00
Fury 1035 *Sad, Sad Lonesome Day*	10.00 -	15.00

BIG BOY MYLES (& THE SHA-WEES):

Specialty 564 *That Girl I Married*	10.00 -	15.00
590 *Hickory Dickory Dock*	10.00 -	15.00

BILLY MYLES:

Ember 1026 *The Joker*	5.00 -	8.00
1026 *The Joker* (78 rpm)	15.00 -	20.00

THE MYSTICS:

Laune 3038, 3047, 3104	7.00 -	10.00

CLIFF/CLIFFIE NASH:

Do-Ra-Me 5028 *Jennie Lou*	15.00 -	20.00
Kim 1048 *This Little Boy's Gone Lookin'*	8.00 -	12.00

NATIVE BOYS:

Combo 113 *Strange Love*	10.00 -	15.00
115 *Tears*	15.00 -	20.00
119 *Laughing Love*	15.00 -	20.00
120 *Oh Let Me Dream*	15.00 -	20.00

JERRY NEAL:

Dot 15810 *I Hates Rabbits*	15.00 -	20.00

MEREDITH NEAL:

Blaze 101 *Gertrude*	20.00 -	30.00

TEX NEIGHBORS:

Emerald 2021 *Rockin' Beat*	20.00 -	30.00

FRED NEIL:

Look 1002 *Don't Put The Blame On Me*	8.00 -	12.00

FREDDY NEIL & FRIEND:

Brunswick 55177 *Listen Kitten*	8.00 -	12.00

BILLY NELSON & FIVE WINGS:

Savoy 1183 *Walk Along*	20.00 -	30.00

JIMMIE/JIMMY (T-99) NELSON:

RPM 325 *T-99 Blues*	30.00 -	50.00
329 *Baby Child*	30.00 -	50.00
353 *Bad Habit*	10.00 -	15.00
368 *Little Rich Girl*	10.00 -	15.00
377 *Little Miss Teasin' Brown*	10.00 -	15.00
385 *Married Men Like Sport*	7.00 -	10.00
389 *Big Mouth*	7.00 -	10.00
397 *Cry Hard Luck*	7.00 -	10.00

RICKY NELSON:

Imperial (EP) 153, 154, 155 *Ricky Nelson*	15.00 -	25.00
(EP) 156, 158, 159, 160, 161, 161, 162, 164	15.00 -	25.00
5463 *Be Bop Baby* (78 rpm)	15.00 -	20.00
5483 *Stood Up* (78 rpm)	15.00 -	20.00
5503 *Believe What You Say* (78 rpm)	15.00 -	25.00
5528 *Poor Little Fool* (78 rpm)	15.00 -	25.00
5545 *Lonesome Town* (78 rpm)	15.00 -	25.00
5565 *It's Late* (78 rpm)	15.00 -	25.00
(LP) 9048 *Ricky*	30.00 -	40.00
(LP) 9050 *Ricky Nelson*	30.00 -	40.00
(LP) 9059 *More Songs By Ricky*	30.00 -	40.00
(LP) 9061 *Ricky Sings Again*	30.00 -	40.00
(LP) 9082 *Songs By Ricky*	25.00 -	35.00
Verve (LP) 2083 *Teen Time*	75.00 -	100.00
Verve (EP) 5048 *Ricky*	40.00 -	50.00
10047 *Teenager's Romance* (78 rpm)	15.00 -	20.00
10070 *You're My One And Only Love* (78rpm)	15.00 -	20.00

TOMMY NELSON:

Dixie 2014 *Hobo Bop*	15.00 -	20.00

WILLIE NELSON:

Bellair 107 *Night Life* (red plastic)	15.00 -	20.00
Betty 5702 *Misery Mansion* (red plastic)	8.00 -	12.00
5703 *Man With The Blues*	5.00 -	8.00

NEONS:

Tetra 4449 *Road To Romance*	10.00 -	15.00
Angel Face	10.00 -	15.00

NERVOUS NORVUS:

Dot 15470 *Transfusion*	4.00 -	7.00
15485 *Ape Call*	5.00 -	8.00
15500 *The Fang*	7.00 -	10.00
Embee 177 *I Like Girls*	7.00 -	10.00

BILL NETTLES:

Starday 174 *Wine-O-Boogie*	10.00 -	15.00

JOE NETTLES & THE SATELLITES:

Circle 1174 *Oh Baby* .... 15.00 - 20.00
AARON NEVILLE:
Minit 618 *Show Me The Way* .... 7.00 - 10.00
CARL NEWMAN & HIS NIGHT HAWKS:
MAR-VEL 2350 *Rockin' And A-Boppin'* .... 20.00 - 30.00
Trio 849 *Rockin' And A-Boppin'* .... 50.00 - 80.00
JIMMY NEWMAN:
Dot 15766 *Carry On* .... 15.00 - 20.00
NEWPORT RHYTHMAIRES:
Newport 101 *Mornin' Blues* .... 7.00 - 10.00
THE NEWPORTS:
Kane 008 *If I Could Tonight* .... 5.00 - 8.00
Kent 380 *The Wonder Of Love* .... 5.00 - 8.00
NEW YORKERS (FIVE):
Danice 801 *Gloria My Darling* .... 50.00 - 80.00
Wall 547 *Dream A Little Dream* .... 8.00 - 12.00
BETTY NICKELL & THE ROCKETS:
Abbey 102 *Hot Dog* .... 15.00 - 20.00
NICKY & THE NOBLES:
Gone 5039 *School Bells* .... 7.00 - 10.00
ROCKY NIGHT WITH HIS NIGHT CATS:
Pearl 708 *Teen Age Bop* .... 30.00 - 40.00
NIGHT CAPS:
Vandan (LP) 8124 *Wine, Wine, Wine* .... 75.00 - 100.00
(Note: Original pressings of the above LP are
quite scarce, but a reissue has been extensively
distributed.)
**ROBERT NIGHTHAWK & THE
NIGHTHAWKS BAND:**
States 131 *Maggie Campbell* (red vinyl) .... 50.00 - 75.00
NIGHT OWLS:
Bethlehem 3087 *Bells Ring* .... 5.00 - 8.00
Cuca 1075 *Waitin' By The School* .... 15.00 - 20.00
NRC 015 *You Shouldn't Oughta Done It* .... 5.00 - 8.00
NIGHT RAIDERS (See MICKEY HAWKS)
NIPTONES:
Lorraine 1001 *Angie* .... 5.00 - 8.00
NITECAPS:
Groove 0134 *A Kiss And A Vow* .... 10.00 - 15.00
0147 *Sweet Thing* .... 15.00 - 20.00
0158 *You May Not Know* .... 15.00 - 20.00
0176 *In Each Corner Of My Heart* .... 15.00 - 20.00
NITE RIDERS:
Apollo 460 *Women And Cadillacs* .... 15.00 - 20.00
466 *Doctor Velvet* .... 15.00 - 20.00
MGM 12487 *Sittin' Sippin' Coffee* .... 5.00 - 8.00
FORD NIX & THE MOONSHINERS:
Clix 813 *Nine Times Out Of Ten* .... 30.00 - 40.00
HOYLE NIX:
Bo-Kay 110 *I Don't Lov-A Nobody* .... 8.00 - 12.00
WILLIE NIX:
Chance 1163 *Nervous Wreck* ....100.00 - 150.00
Checker 756 *Truckin' Little Woman* ....100.00 - 150.00
Sabre 104 *All By Myself* .... 75.00 - 100.00
Sun 179 *Baker Shop Boogie* ....150.00 - 200.00
ELMORE NIXON:
Imperial 5388 *You Left Me* .... 10.00 - 15.00
Post 2008 *Don't Do It* .... 10.00 - 15.00
EDDIE NOACK:
D 1019 *Have Blues—Will Travel* .... 10.00 - 15.00
1037 *Walk 'Em Off* .... 10.00 - 15.00
1060 *A Thinking Man's Woman* .... 10.00 - 15.00
TNT 110 *Too Hot To Handle* .... 10.00 - 15.00
NOBELLS:
Mar 101 *Crying Over You* .... 10.00 - 15.00
EDDIE NOBLE:
Suite 16 111 *Mean Old Blues* .... 10.00 - 15.00
EMMY NOBLE:
Liberty 55122 *I Done Done* .... 8.00 - 12.00
NOBLES:
Klik 305 *Poor Rock And Roll* .... 15.00 - 20.00
Sapphire 151 *Do You Love Me* .... 15.00 - 20.00

NOBLETONES:
C & M 182 *I Love You* .... 15.00 - 20.00
438 *I'm Crying* .... 15.00 - 20.00
SID NOEL:
Aladdin 3331 *Flying Saucer* .... 10.00 - 15.00
TERRY NOLAND:
Apt 25065 *Long Gone Baby* .... 10.00 - 15.00
Brunswick (LP) 54041 *Terry Noland* .... 50.00 - 75.00
55010 *Hypnotized* .... 4.00 - 7.00
55036 *Patty Baby* .... 5.00 - 8.00
55054 *Oh Baby Look At Me* .... 8.00 - 12.00
55069 *Crazy Dreams* .... 5.00 - 8.00
55092 *There Was A Fungus Among Us* .... 7.00 - 10.00
55122 *Guess I'm Gonna Fall* .... 7.00 - 10.00
JIMMY NOLEN:
Imperial 5363 *Let's Try Again* .... 7.00 - 10.00
LARRY NOLEN & HIS BANDITS:
Starday 668 *King Of The Ducktail Cats* .... 7.00 - 10.00
GENE NORMAN (& THE ROCKETS):
Snag 101 *Snaggle Tooth Ann* .... 75.00 - 100.00
Soma 1156 *No Help Wanted* .... 10.00 - 15.00
RAY NORMAN:
Nasco 6030 *Heartbreak Station* .... 8.00 - 12.00
BOBBY NORRIS:
Capitol 3945 *I Went Rockin'* .... 8.00 - 12.00
CHUCK NORRIS:
Atlantic 994 *Let Me Know* .... 10.00 - 15.00
NOTATIONS:
Wonder 100 *What A Night For Love* .... 50.00 - 75.00
NOTE MAKERS:
Sotoplay 007 *It Hurts To Wonder* .... 25.00 - 40.00
NOTES:
Capitol 3332 *Don't Leave Me Now* .... 25.00 - 40.00
MGM 12338 *Trust In Me* .... 50.00 - 75.00
Sarg 177 *Little Girl* .... 5.00 - 8.00
NOTE TORIALS:
Impala *My Valerie* .... .00 - .00
Sunbeam 119 *My Valerie* .... 30.00 - 40.00
ERNIE NOWLIN:
Missouri 640 *Tally Ho* .... 8.00 - 12.00
BOBBY NUNN & LITTLE ESTHER:
Federal 12100 *Mainliner* .... 30.00 - 40.00
NUTMEGS:
Herald 452 *Story Untold* .... 7.00 - 10.00
459 *Ship Of Love* .... 8.00 - 12.00
466 *Whispering Sorrows* .... 8.00 - 12.00
475 *Key To The Kingdom* .... 15.00 - 20.00
492 *A Love So True* .... 15.00 - 20.00
538 *My Story* .... 10.00 - 15.00
Tel 1014 *A Dream Of Love* .... 15.00 - 20.00
NU-TONES/NUTONES:
Baton 260 *Remember The Night* .... 15.00 - 20.00
Hollywood Star 798 *Believe* ....150.00 - 200.00
Goddess Of Love .... 80.00 - 120.00
NU-TRENDS:
Lawn 216 *Together* .... -
BOB OAKES & THE SULTANS:
Regent 7502 *You Gotta Rock And Roll* .... 8.00 - 12.00
OCAPELLOS:
General 107 *The Stars* .... 8.00 - 12.00
OCTAVES:
Val 1001 *Mambo Carolyn* .... 8.00 - 12.00
**DOYLE O'DELL & THE CASS
COUNTY BOYS:**
Era (LP) 20004 .... 20.00 - 30.00
LILLIAN OFFITT:
Chief 7012 *The Man Won't Work* .... 7.00 - 10.00
7015 *Oh Mama* .... 5.00 - 8.00
7029 *Shine On* .... 5.00 - 8.00
Excello 2104, 2124, 2139 .... 4.00 - 7.00
LOUIS OGLETREE:
Parrot 822 *Tell It Like It Is* .... 30.00 - 40.00

JOHNNY O'KEEFE:
Brunswick 55067 *Shake Baby Shake* . . . . 15.00 - 20.00
JOHNNY OLENN (& THE JOKERS):
Glenco 7001 *Sally Let Your Bangs Hang* . . . . 8.00 - 12.00
Liberty (LP) 3029 *Just Rollin' With Johnny*
Olenn . . . . 50.00 - 75.00
TNT 1016 *Sally Let Your Bangs Hang Down* . . . . 15.00 - 20.00
1018 *I Ain't Gonna Cry No More* . . . . 15.00 - 20.00
OLE SONNY BOY:
Excello 2086 *Blues And Misery* . . . . 20.00 - 30.00
BOBBY OLIVER:
Lucky Four 1004 *Where Do Dreams Go* . . . . 5.00 - 8.00
1006 *Lucille* . . . . 5.00 - 8.00
BIG DANNY OLIVER:
Trend 30-012 *Sapphire* . . . . 5.00 - 8.00
30-016 *Blues For The 49* . . . . 5.00 - 8.00
ROCKY OLSON:
Chess 1723 *Kansas City* . . . . 7.00 - 10.00
OLYMPICS:
Arvee (LP) 423 *Doin' The Hully Gully* . . . . 30.00 - 40.00
(LP) 424 *Dance By The Light Of The Moon* . . . 35.00 - 50.00
(LP) 429 *Party Time* . . . . 35.00 - 50.00
Demon 1508 *Western Movies* (78 rpm) . . . . 25.00 - 35.00
SLIM O'MARY:
Mar-Vel 20 *Row, Boy, Sink Or Swim* . . . . -
THE ONBEATS:
Granite 301 *Catastrophe* . . . . -
GRADY O'NEAL
Bella 2205 *Baby Oh Baby* . . . . 20.00 - 30.00
ONTARIOS:
Big Town 121 *Memories Of You* . . . . 50.00 - 80.00
OPALS:
Apollo 462 *My Heart's Desire* . . . . 25.00 - 40.00
"OPRY STARS—JAMBOREE":
Mercury (LP) 20350 (various artists) . . . . 10.00 - 15.00
GENE O'QUINN:
Captiol 1508 *Boogie Woogie Fever* . . . . 10.00 - 15.00
1708 *Triflin' Woman* . . . . 8.00 - 12.00
1821 *It's No Use* . . . . 8.00 - 12.00
Capitol 1943, 2050, 2075, 2210, 2344, 2490,
2655, 2715, 2843, 2935 . . . . 5.00 - 10.00
ROY ORBISON (& THE TEEN KINGS & THE
ROSES):
Monument (LP) 4002, 14002 *Lonely And Blue* . . 20.00 - 30.00
(LP) 4007, 14007 *Crying* . . . . 20.00 - 30.00
RCA Victor 7381 *Sweet And Innocent* . . . . 10.00 - 15.00
7447 *Almost Eighteen* . . . . 10.00 - 15.00
Sun 242 *Ooby Dooby* . . . . 10.00 - 15.00
251 *Rock House* . . . . 10.00 - 15.00
265 *Devil Doll* . . . . 10.00 - 15.00
284 *Chicken Hearted* . . . . 10.00 - 15.00
ORBITS:
Argo 5286 *Who Are You* . . . . 8.00 - 12.00
Flair-X 5000 *Message Of Love* . . . . 10.00 - 15.00
ORCHIDS:
King 4661 *Oh Why* . . . . 75.00 - 100.00
4663 *Beginning To Miss You* . . . . 75.00 - 100.00
Parrot 815 *You're Everything To Me* . . . . 50.00 - 75.00
819 *You Said You Loved Me* . . . . 50.00 - 75.00
ORIGINAL CASUALS:
Back Beat (EP) 40 *Three Kisses Past Midnight* . . 25.00 - 35.00
503 *So Tough* . . . . 5.00 - 8.00
510 *Don't Pass Me By* . . . . 7.00 - 10.00
514 *Three Kisses Past Midnight* . . . . 7.00 - 10.00
THE ORIGINAL DELL-VIKINGS (See
DELL-VIKINGS)
THE ORIGINALS (featuring TONY ALLEN):
Diamond 116 *You And I* . . . . 5.00 - 8.00
Original Sound 10 *Wishing Star* . . . . 7.00 - 10.00
ORIOLES:
Abner 1016 *Sugar Girl* . . . . 10.00 - 15.00
Jubilee (EP) 5000 *The Orioles Sing* . . . . 100.00 - 150.00

Jubilee 5008 *I Challenge Your Kiss* . . . . -
(Above may not exist as 45 RPM)
5016 *Forgive And Forget* . . . . 100.00 - 150.00
5017 *What Are You Doing New Years Eve* . . . . . 100.00 - 150.00
5025 *At Night* . . . . 150.00 - 200.00
5026 *Moonlight* . . . . 150.00 - 200.00
5031 *I'd Rather Have You Under The Moon* . . . 150.00 - 200.00
5040 *I Crossed My Fingers* . . . . 100.00 - 150.00
5045 *Oh Holy Night* . . . . 75.00 - 100.00
5051 *I Miss You So* . . . . 100.00 - 150.00
5061 *I'm Just A Fool In Love* . . . . 100.00 - 150.00
5065 *Baby Please Don't Go* . . . . 80.00 - 120.00
5071 *When You're Not Around* . . . . 80.00 - 120.00
5076 *Proud Of You* . . . . 100.00 - 150.00
5084 *Gettin' Tired Tired Tired* . . . . 80.00 - 120.00
5092 *Don't Cry Baby* . . . . 80.00 - 120.00
5102 *You Belong To Me* . . . . 80.00 - 120.00
(Note: Many of the above are pressed of colored
vinyl.)
5107 *Till Then* (red plastic) . . . . 80.00 - 120.00
5108 *Hold Me, Thrill Me, Kiss Me* (red plastic) 35.00 - 50.00
5115 *Bad Little Girl* (red plastic) . . . . 35.00 - 50.00
5120 *I Cover The Waterfront* (red plastic) . . . . . 50.00 - 75.00
5122 *Crying In The Chapel* . . . . 7.00 - 10.00
5127 *Write And Tell Me Why* . . . . 10.00 - 15.00
5134 *There' No One But You* . . . . 10.00 - 15.00
5137 *Secret Love* . . . . 10.00 - 15.00
5143 *Maybe You'll Be There* . . . . 10.00 - 15.00
5154 *In the Chapel In The Moonlight* . . . . 8.00 - 12.00
5161 *If You Believe* . . . . 10.00 - 15.00
5172 *Runaround* . . . . 10.00 - 15.00
5177 *I Love You Mostly* . . . . 10.00 - 15.00
5189 *I Need You Baby* . . . . 10.00 - 15.00
5221 *Moody Over You* . . . . 8.00 - 12.00
5363 *Tell Me So* . . . . 7.00 - 10.00
Vee Jay 196 *Happy Till The Letter* . . . . 10.00 - 15.00
228 *For All We Know* . . . . 12.00 - 16.00
244 *Sugar Girl* . . . . 15.00 - 20.00
ORLANDOS:
Cindy 3006 *Cloudburst* . . . . 30.00 - 40.00
TONY ORLANDO & THE MILOS:
Milo 101 *Ding Dong* . . . . 10.00 - 15.00
J.D. ORR & THE LONESOME VALLEY
BOYS:
Summit 105 *Hula Hoop Boogie* . . . . 75.00 - 100.00
DAVID ORRELL:
Felsted 8515 *You're The One* . . . . 10.00 - 15.00
BOBBY OSBORN:
Knickerbocker 1312 *Bound To Happen* . . . . -
THE OSBORNE BROTHERS & RED ALLEN:
MGM (LP) 3734 . . . . 15.00 - 20.00
MILT OSHINS:
Pelvis 169 *All About Elvis* . . . . 7.00 - 10.00
THE OSPREYS:
East West 110 *It's Good To Me* . . . . 10.00 - 15.00
JOHNNY OTIS:
Capitol (LP) 940 *The Johnny Otis Show* . . . . . . 40.00 - 60.00
(EP) 1134 *Johnny Otis* . . . . 30.00 - 50.00
Dig (LP) 104 *Rock & Roll Hit Parade* . . . . 100.00 - 150.00
Peacock 1625, 1636 . . . . 8.00 - 12.00
"OUR BEST TO YOU":
Everlast (LP) 201 (various artists) . . . . 25.00 - 35.00
DANNY OVERBEA:
Apex 7751 *Stop* . . . . 5.00 - 8.00
Checker 768 *Train, Train, Train* . . . . 10.00 - 15.00
774 *40 Cups Of Coffee* . . . . 10.00 - 15.00
784 *I Could—But I Won't* . . . . 7.00 - 10.00
796 *You're Mine* . . . . 10.00 - 15.00
808 *A Toast To Lovers* . . . . 7.00 - 10.00
816 *Do You Love Me* . . . . 7.00 - 10.00
Federal 12324 *Candy Bar* . . . . 7.00 - 10.00
KENNY OWEN:

Poplar 106 *I Got The Bug*	15.00 -	20.00

RUDY OWEN & THE RAVENS:

Startime 3287 *Pretty Linda*	10.00 -	15.00

BUCK OWENS: (See also CORKY JONES)

Nevstar 6418 *Hot Dog*	30.00 -	40.00
Pep 105, 106, 109	8.00 -	12.00

CLYDE OWENS:

Linco 1313 *Swing It Little Katy*	80.00 -	120.00

PACERS:

Calico 101 *I Found A Dream*	5.00 -	8.00
Guyden 1064 *How Sweet*	20.00 -	30.00

PACKARDS:

Paradise 105 *Dream Of Love*	20.00 -	30.00
Pla Bac 106 *Ladies*	100.00 -	150.00

ALLEN PAGE & THE DELTONES:

Moon 301 *Honeysuckle*	10.00 -	15.00
302 *Dateless Night*	10.00 -	15.00
303 *She's The One That Got It*	10.00 -	15.00

PAGEANTS:

Arlen 731 *Saturday Romance*	10.00 -	15.00
Du-Well 101 *Saturday Romance*	15.00 -	20.00
Goldisc 3013 *Happy Together*	8.00 -	12.00

HAL PAIGE (& THE WAILERS):

Atlantic 1032 *Big Foot Mae*	15.00 -	20.00
Fury 1024 *After Hours Blues*	8.00 -	12.00
J & S 1601 *Thunder Bird*	10.00 -	15.00

"PAJAMA PARTY":

Roulette (LP) 20521 (various artists)	15.00 -	25.00

THE PALISADES:

Calico 113 *Close Your Eyes*	8.00 -	12.00
Debra 1003 *Chapel Bells*	8.00 -	12.00

TOMMY PALM:

Bob 101 *Stroll With Me Baby*	10.00 -	15.00

CLARENCE PALMER & THE JIVE BOMBERS (See THE JIVE BOMBERS)

PALMS:

States 157 *Darling Patricia*	20.00 -	30.00

PALS:

Guyden 2019 *My Baby Likes To Rock*	5.00 -	8.00
Turf 1000 *Summer Is Here*	15.00 -	20.00

PAPA LIGHTFOOT (See LIGHTFOOT)

THE PARADONS:

Milestone 2003 *Diamonds and Pearls*	5.00 -	8.00
Warner Bros. 5186 *Take All Of Me*	5.00 -	8.00

PARAGONS:

Musictones 1141 *Wedding Bells*	8.00 -	12.00
Musicnotes (LP) 8001 *The Paragons Vs. The Harptones*	15.00 -	20.00
Tap 503 *In Midst Of Night*	15.00 -	20.00
Winley 215 *Florence*	10.00 -	15.00
220 *Let's Start All Over Again*	15.00 -	20.00
223 *Two Hearts Are Better Than One*	15.00 -	20.00
227 *Vows Of Love*	10.00 -	15.00
228 *Don't Cry Baby*	10.00 -	15.00
240 *So You Will Know*	10.00 -	15.00
250 *Kneel And Pray*	10.00 -	15.00

PARAKEETS:

Atlas 1071 *Teenage Rose*	30.00 -	40.00
Jubilee 5407 *Shangri-La*	8.00 -	12.00

KENNY PARCHMAN:

Jaxon *Don't You Know*	20.00 -	30.00
Lu *Get It Off Your Mind*	15.00 -	25.00

PARIS BROTHERS:

Brunswick 55132 *This Is It*	8.00 -	12.00
Coral 62220 *Funny Feeling*	5.00 -	8.00

(LITTLE) JUNIOR PARKER & HIS BAND/BLUE FLAMES/ORCHESTRA:

Duke (LP) 76 *Driving Wheel*	40.00 -	60.00
120 *Dirty Friend Blues*	8.00 -	12.00
127 *Please Baby Blues*	8.00 -	12.00
137, 147, 157, 164, 168, 177, 184, 193, 301, 324	4.00 -	7.00

(See also LITTLE JUNIOR'S BLUE FLAMES)

TIM PARKER:

Emmons 1005 *That' Alright Mama*	-	

RAY PARKS:

Capitol 3580 *You're Gonna Have To Bawl, That's All*	10.00 -	15.00

RAY PARKS & THE CANUCKS: (See THE CANUCKS with RAY PARKS)

FRED PARRIS & THE SATINS (See THE FIVE SATINS)

KENT PARRY & THE ROGUES:

Alton 600 *Stop Then Rock*	8.00 -	12.00

DEAN PARRISH:

Warner Bros. 5436 *Come On Down*	4.00 -	7.00

PARROTS:

Checker 772 *Please Don't Leave Me*	150.00 -	200.00

AL PARSONS:

Wait For Me Baby/Memories Of Yesterday	-	

BILL PARSONS:

Starday 526 *Hot Red Volkswagen*	8.00 -	12.00

"PARTY AFTER HOURS"

Aladdin (LP) 703 (10") (various artists) (red vinyl)	100.00 -	Up

PASSIONS:

Audicon 102, 105, 106, 108, 112	7.00 -	12.00
Capitol 3963 *My Aching Heart*	5.00 -	8.00
Diamond 146 *Sixteen Candles*	7.00 -	10.00
Octavia 8005 *I've Gotta Know*	15.00 -	20.00

PASTELS:

United 196 *Put Your Arms Around Me*	15.00 -	20.00

PAT AND DEE:

Dixie 2006 *Gee Whiz*	15.00 -	25.00

PRINCE PATRIDGE:

Big Moment 103/104 *Next Door Neighbors*	5.00 -	8.00
Crest 1006, 1022, 1009	4.00 -	7.00

FRANK PATT & ORCHESTRA:

Flash 117 *Gonna Hold On*	8.00 -	12.00

JIMMY PATTON (with ANN JONES):

Halligan 001 *Okie's In The Pokie*	80.00 -	120.00
Moon (LP) 101 *Make Room For The Blues*	25.00 -	35.00
Sage 241 *Yah—I'm Movin'*	30.00 -	50.00
Sims 103 *Guilty*	5.00 -	8.00
104 *Teen-Age Heart*	10.00 -	15.00
117 *Okie's In The Pokie*	35.00 -	50.00
(LP) 127 *Blue Darlin'*	20.00 -	30.00

PAT PATTON:

King 4942 *Flip Kitten*	7.00 -	10.00

JERRY PAUL:

Holiday 1001 *Step Out*	10.00 -	15.00

JOYCE PAUL:

Dot 15703 *Baby, You've Had It*	-	

DUSTY PAYNE (& HIS RHYTHM ROCKERS):

Bakersfield 119 *Long Time Gone*	8.00 -	12.00
Fire 111 *I Want You*	5.00 -	8.00

HAL PAYNE:

Starday—*Honky Tonk Stomp*	10.00 -	15.00

TOMMY PAYNE:

Felsted 8531 *I Go Ape*	7.00 -	10.00
XYZ 601 *Fire Engine Red Bandanna*	5.00 -	8.00
603 *Cruisin' Around*	5.00 -	8.00

PEACHEROOS:

Excello 2044 *Be-Bop Baby*	75.00 -	100.00

PEACOCKS:

Nobel 711 *I Want You To Know*	40.00 -	60.00

PEAR DEVINES:

Alco—*So Lonely*	20.00 -	30.00

PEARLS:

Atco 6057 *Shadow Of Love*	10.00 -	15.00
6066 *Bells Of Love*	15.00 -	20.00
On The Square 320 *Band Of Angels*	-	
Onyx 503 *Let's You And I Go Steady*	15.00 -	20.00
506 *Tree In The Meadow*	15.00 -	20.00

510 *Your Cheatin' Heart*	10.00 -	15.00
511 *Ice Cream Baby*	15.00 -	20.00
516 *The Wheel Of Love*	15.00 -	20.00

JIMMY PEARSON:
Dixie—*Nobody Cares/I'm Not Sure* .... -

RONNIE PEARSON:

500 *Hot Shot*	10.00 -	15.00
514 *She Bops A Lot*	10.00 -	15.00
516 *Flippin' Over You*	10.00 -	15.00

PAUL PEEK:

NRC 001 *The Rock Around*	5.00 -	8.00
NRC 002 *Sweet Skinny Jenny*	5.00 -	8.00
008 *Olds-Mo-William*	5.00 -	8.00

CARROLL (WILD RED) PEGUES:

GM Record Co. 109 *Rhythm Feet*	10.00 -	15.00

DANNY PEIL & THE APOLLOS:

Raynard 602 *Jungle Jump*	5.00 -	8.00

MORRIS PEJOE:

Abco 106 *Maybe Blues*	30.00 -	40.00
Atomic H410/411 *You Gone Away*	10.00 -	15.00
Checker 766 *Gonna Buy Me A Telephone*	75.00 -	100.00
781 *Can't Get Along*	30.00 -	50.00
Vee Jay 148 *You Gonna Need Me*	20.00 -	30.00

PELICANS:

Class 209 *I Bow To You*	80.00 -	100.00
Imperial 5307 *Chimes*	200.00 -	300.00
Parrot 793 *Aurelia* (red plastic)	300.00 -	Up

TRACY PENDARVIS:

Des Cant 1234 *First Love*	7.00 -	10.00
Scott 1202 *It Don't Pay*	10.00 -	15.00
1203 *All You Gotta Do*	10.00 -	15.00

PENGUINS:

Dooto (EP) 201 *The Penguins*	10.00 -	15.00
(EP) 241, 243, 244 *Cool Cool Penguins*	10.00 -	15.00
Dooto (LP) 242 *Cool Cool Penguins*	75.00 -	100.00
428 *That's How Much I Need You*	10.00 -	15.00
432 *Sweet Love*	10.00 -	15.00
435 *Do Not Pretend*	10.00 -	15.00
451 *To Keep Our Love*	10.00 -	15.00
Dootone 345 *When I Am Gone*	15.00 -	20.00
348 *Earth Angel*	7.00 -	10.00
353 *Ookey Oook*	8.00 -	12.00
362 *Kiss A Fool Goodbye*	15.00 -	20.00
Mercury 70610 *Be Mine Or Be A Fool*	8.00 -	12.00
70654 *It Only Happens With You*	8.00 -	12.00
70703 *Devil That I See*	8.00 -	12.00
70762 *A Christmas Prayer*	10.00 -	15.00
70799 *My Troubles Are Not At An End*	10.00 -	15.00
70943 *Earth Angel*	10.00 -	15.00
71033 *Will You Be Mine*	10.00 -	15.00
Wing 90076 *Peace of Mind*	8.00 -	12.00

WILLIAM PENIX:

Daffan 116 *Dig That Crazy Driver*	15.00 -	20.00

LITTLE LAMBSIE PENN:

Atco 6082 *I Wanna Spend Christmas With Elvis*	7.00 -	10.00

TONY PENN:

P.R.I. 101 *Shake Rattle And Roll*	10.00 -	15.00
P.R.I 7016 *I Don't Want To Stay Home*		-

DICK PENNER:

Sun 282 *Cindy Lou*	15.00 -	20.00

RAY PENNINGTON:

Lee 502 *Boogie Woogie Country Girl*	15.00 -	25.00

HANK PENNY:

Decca 29926 *Rock Of Gibraltar*	5.00 -	8.00

JOE PENNY:

Federal 12322 *Bip A Little, Bop A Lot*	15.00 -	20.00
Sims 173 *Hatty Fatty*	7.00 -	10.00

CURLEY PENROD:

QQ 703 *There's A Leak*	8.00 -	12.00

THE PENTAGONS:

Donna 1337 *To Be Loved*	7.00 -	10.00
Jamie 1210 *I'm In Love*	7.00 -	10.00

THE PEPPERS:

Chess 1577 *Rocking Chair Baby*	60.00 -	90.00

THE PEREZ BROTHERS:

Wolfie 103 *Dream A Little Dream*	8.00 -	12.00

THE PERFORMERS:

Tip Top 402 *Give Me Your Heart*	15.00 -	20.00

CARL PERKINS:

Columbia (LP) 1234 *Whole Lotta Shakin'*	50.00 -	75.00
(EP) 12341 *Whole Lotta Shakin'*	75.00 -	100.00
41131 *Pink Pedal Pushers*	8.00 -	12.00
41207 *Levi Jacket*	8.00 -	12.00
41379 *Pointed Toe Shoes*	8.00 -	12.00
Flip 501 *Movie Magg*	100.00 -	150.00
Sun (EP) 115 *Blue Suede Shoes*	50.00 -	75.00
224 *Gone, Gone, Gone*	15.00 -	20.00
234 *Blue Suede Shoes* (78 rpm)	10.00 -	15.00
235 *Tennessee/Sure To Fall*	Rare -	

(Note: This record may not have been issued.)

243 *Boppin' The Blues*	8.00 -	12.00
249, 261, 274, 287	7.00 -	12.00

(Note: 78 RPM issues of above four records command somewhat higher premiums.)

Sun (LP) 1225 *Teen Beat (The Best of Carl Perkins)*	15.00 -	30.00
(LP) 1225 *The Dance Album of Carl Perkins*	100.00 -	Up

JESSE PERKINS & THE BAD BOYS:

Savoy 1584 *Madly In Love*	5.00 -	8.00

JOE PERKINS & ROOKIES:

King 5005 *Time Alone Will Tell*	15.00 -	20.00

LAURA LEE PERKINS:

Imperial 5493 *Kiss Me Baby*	10.00 -	15.00
5507 *Don't Wait Up*	10.00 -	15.00

REGGIE PERKINS:

Gem 1201 *Saturday Night Party*	10.00 -	15.00
Ray Note 9 *Date Bait Baby*	10.00 -	15.00

ROY PERKINS:

Meladee 111 *You're On My Mind*	30.00 -	40.00
112 *You're Gone*	30.00 -	40.00
Mercury 71278 *Drop Top*	7.00 -	10.00
RAM 122 *That's What the Mailman Has To Say*	8.00 -	12.00

BOB PERRY:

Top Rank 2063 *Juke Box*	7.00 -	10.00

IKE PERRY & THE LYRICS:

Bridge 110 *Stairsteps to Heaven*		-
Courier 3614 *Don't Let It Get You Down*	15.00 -	20.00

PAUL PERRY:

Got A Gal Named Dee	20.00 -	30.00

THE PERSIANS:

Gold Eagle 1813 *Gee What A Girl*	5.00 -	8.00
Goldisc I *Vault Of Memories*	10.00 -	15.00
RSVP 111 *Tears Of Love*	10.00 -	15.00

PERSONALITIES:

Safari 1002 *Woe Woe Baby*	15.00 -	20.00

PETE & JIMMY & THE RHYTHM KNIGHTS:

Castle 504 *So Wild*	15.00 -	20.00

PETE PETERS:

Rockin' In My Sweet Baby's Arms	5.00 -	8.00

BOBBY PETERSON (QUINTET):

V-Tone 205, 214, 221	3.00 -	5.00

EARL PETERSON:

Columbia 21364 *Boogie Blues*	8.00 -	12.00
Sun 197 *Boone Blues*	30.00 -	50.00

MIKE PETTIT & THE STAGS:

Anthem 601227 *It's A Reamer*	10.00 -	15.00

DARYL PETTY:

Hornet 502 *The Day I Die*	8.00 -	12.00

VI PETTY:

Nor Va-Jak 1325 *True Love Ways*	15.00 -	20.00

PHANTOM:

Dot 16056 *Love Me*	30.00 -	40.00
16056 *Love Me* (with picture sleeve)	50.00 -	75.00

Phantom 100 *I'm The Phantom* . . . . 15.00 - 20.00
THE PHARAOS:
Donna 1327 *The Tender Touch* . . . . 7.00 - 10.00
THE PHAROAHS:
Class 202 *Teenagers Love Song* . . . . 10.00 - 15.00
Fascination 001 *Walking Sad* . . . . 40.00 - 60.00
JOHNNY PHELPS:
Ski 5505 *Tom Katt* . . . . 15.00 - 20.00
THE PHILADELPHIANS:
Guyden 2093 *My Love, My Love* . . . . 5.00 - 8.00
THE PHILHARMONICS:
Future 2200 *Why Don't You Write Me* . . . . 15.00 - 25.00
"PHILLIP MORRIS COUNTRY MUSIC SHOW"
Columbia (LP) 1048 (various artist) . . . . 10.00 - 15.00
BILL PHILLIPS:
Columbia 41218 *There's A Change In Me* . . . . 5.00 - 8.00
CARL PHILLIPS:
Bobbin 110 *Wigwam Willie* . . . . 50.00 - 75.00
CHARLIE PHILLIPS:
Coral 61970 *Be My Bride* . . . . 8.00 - 12.00
EARL PHILLIPS:
Vee Jay 158 *Nothing But Love* . . . . 8.00 - 12.00
MARVIN PHILLIPS:
Specialty 445 *Wine Woogie* . . . . 8.00 - 12.00
PHIL PHILLIPS with THE TWILIGHTS:
Clique 100 *Please Forgive Me* . . . . 5.00 - 8.00
Khoury's 711 *Sea Of Love* . . . . 35.00 - 50.00
LARRY PHILLIPSON:
Cinch 3858 *Bitter Feelings* . . . . 7.00 - 10.00
PIANO RED:
Checker 911 *So Worried* . . . . 5.00 - 8.00
Groove (EP) 3 *Jump Man Jump* . . . . 25.00 - 35.00
(EP) 6 *Piano Red In Concert* . . . . 25.00 - 35.00
(EP) 7 *Piano Red In Concert* . . . . 25.00 - 35.00
(EP) 8 *Piano Red In Concert* . . . . 25.00 - 35.00
0023 *Decatur Street Blues* . . . . 10.00 - 15.00
0101 *Pay It No Mind* . . . . 8.00 - 12.00
(LP) 0101 *Jump, Man, Jump* . . . . 80.00 - 120.00
0118 *Six O'Clock Boogie* . . . . 10.00 - 15.00
0126 *Red's Blues* . . . . 7.00 - 10.00
0136 *Jumpin' With Daddy* . . . . 8.00 - 12.00
0145 *That's My Desire* . . . . 8.00 - 12.00
0169 *Woo-Ee* . . . . 8.00 - 12.00
(LP) 1002 *Piano Red In Concert* . . . . 100.00 - 150.00
5000 *Red's Boogie* . . . . 5.00 - 8.00
Jax 1000 *This Old World* . . . . 7.00 - 10.00
RCA Victor (EP) 587 *Rockin' With Red* . . . . 30.00 - 40.00
4265 *Diggin' The Boogie* . . . . 15.00 - 20.00
4380 *Hey Good Lookin'* . . . . 15.00 - 20.00
4524 *Bouncin' With Red* . . . . 8.00 - 12.00
4766 *The Sales Tax Boogie* . . . . 8.00 - 12.00
4957 *Daybreak* . . . . 8.00 - 12.00
5101 *Everybody's Boogie* . . . . 8.00 - 12.00
5224 *She's Dynamite* . . . . 8.00 - 12.00
5337 *Decatur Street Boogie* . . . . 8.00 - 12.00
5544 *Right And Ready* . . . . 8.00 - 12.00
6856 *Wild Fire* . . . . 8.00 - 12.00
6953 *Please Don't Talk About Me* . . . . 8.00 - 12.00
7065 *South* . . . . 7.00 - 10.00
7217 *Comin' On* . . . . 7.00 - 10.00
50-0099 *Rockin' With Red* . . . . 7.00 - 10.00
50-0106 *My Gal Jo* . . . . 15.00 - 20.00
50-0118 *Jumpin' The Boogie* . . . . 10.00 - 15.00
50-0130 *Layin' The Boogie* . . . . 10.00 - 15.00
LITTLE "GUITAR" PICKETT:
Jack 101 *The Buzzard* . . . . 5.00 - 8.00
PICO PETE:
Jet 100 *Hot Dog* . . . . 8.00 - 12.00
WEBB PIERCE:
Decca 30045 *Teenage Boogie* . . . . 7.00 - 10.00
BILL PINKY & THE TURKS:

Phillips 3524 *After The Hop* . . . . 8.00 - 12.00
PIPES:
Dootone 388 *Be Fair* . . . . 30.00 - 40.00
401 *You Are An Angel* . . . . 20.00 - 30.00
Jacy 001 *Baby Please Don't Go* . . . . 15.00 - 20.00
PITCH PIKES:
Mercury 71099 *Zing Zing* . . . . 5.00 - 8.00
AL (DR. HORSE) PITTMAN:
Clown 3008 *Woman! You Talk Too Much* . . . . . . 7.00 - 10.00
GLORIA JEAN PITTS:
Imperial 5406 *I Don't Stand No Quittin'* . . . . . . 10.00 - 15.00
PLAIDS:
Nasco 6011 *My Pretty Baby* . . . . 5.00 - 8.00
THE PLANETS:
Era 1038 *Never Again* . . . . 7.00 - 10.00
1049 *Be Sure* . . . . 7.00 - 10.00
PLANTS: (See also BABY WASHINGTON)
J & S 248 *I Searched The Seven Seas* . . . . 10.00 - 15.00
1602 *Dear I Swear* . . . . 20.00 - 30.00
1617 *From Me* . . . . 20.00 - 30.00
THE PLATTERS (See also LINDA HAYES):
Federal (LP) 349-549 *The Platters* . . . . 150.00 - Up
(Note: This album is the same as King 549
below. Copies have been found on the Federal
label with King covers.)
12153 *Give Thanks* . . . . 50.00 - 75.00
12164 *I'll Cry When You're Gone* . . . . 50.00 - 75.00
12181 *Roses Of Picardy* . . . . 50.00 - 75.00
12188 *Tell The World* . . . . 20.00 - 30.00
12198 *Voo-Vee-Ah-Bee* . . . . 15.00 - 20.00
12204 *Take Me Back* . . . . 20.00 - 30.00
12244 *Only You* . . . . 30.00 - 50.00
12250 *Tell The World* . . . . 15.00 - 20.00
12271 *Give Thanks* . . . . 15.00 - 20.00
King (EP) 378 *The Platters* . . . . 20.00 - 30.00
(LP) 549 *The Platters* . . . . 150.00 - 200.00
(LP) 651 *The Platters* . . . . 35.00 - 50.00
Mercury (EP) 3336, 3341 . . . . 15.00 - 20.00
(LP) 20146 *The Platters* . . . . 15.00 - 20.00
(LP) 20216 *The Platters Vol. 2* . . . . 12.00 - 16.00
(LP) 20298 *The Flying Platters* . . . . 10.00 - 15.00
(LP) 20366 *Around The World* . . . . 10.00 - 15.00
(LP) 20410 *Remember When* . . . . 10.00 - 15.00
(LP) 20472 *Encore Of Golden Hits* . . . . 8.00 - 12.00
70633 *Only You* (maroon label) . . . . 7.00 - 10.00
70753 *The Great Pretender* (maroon label) . . . . 7.00 - 10.00
70819 *The Magic Touch* (maroon label) . . . . . 7.00 - 10.00
70893 *My Prayer* (maroon label) . . . . 7.00 - 10.00
70948 *You'll Never Never Know* (maroon label) 7.00 - 10.00
71011 *On My Word Of Honor* (maroon label) . . 7.00 - 10.00
(Note: 78 rpm issues of the last six titles usually
command somewhat higher prices.)
PLAYBOYS:
Cat 108 *Tell Me* . . . . 10.00 - 15.00
115 *Good Golly Miss Molly* . . . . 10.00 - 15.00
SRC 1221 *Rave On* . . . . 10.00 - 15.00
Tetra 4447 *One Question* . . . . 20.00 - 30.00
THE PLURALS:
Wanger 186 *Donna My Dear* . . . . 8.00 - 12.00
BOBBY POE:
White Rock 1112 *Rock & Roll Record Girl* . . . . . 60.00 - 80.00
POETS:
Flash 129 *Vowels Of Love* . . . . 10.00 - 15.00
Hade 1001 *I'll Never Let You Go* . . . . 15.00 - 20.00
Imperial 5664 *I'm In Love* . . . . 8.00 - 12.00
Pull 129 *Vowels Of Love* . . . . 12.00 - 16.00
Red Bird 10046 *Merry Christmas Baby* . . . . 7.00 - 10.00
BOBBY POORE:
Beta 1003 *Heartbreak Of Love* . . . . 8.00 - 12.00
(GROOVY) JOE POOVEY:
Dixie 733 *Careful Baby* . . . . 50.00 - 75.00
2018 *Ten Long Fingers* . . . . 75.00 - 100.00

POP CORN & THE MOHAWKS:
Motown 1002 *Shimmy Gully*	20.00 -	30.00
1019 *Real Good Lovin'*	30.00 -	40.00

POPPA/POPPY HOP:
Ivory 127 *My Woman Has A Black Cat Bone*	10.00 -	15.00
133 *I Met A Strange Woman*	10.00 -	15.00
134 *Merry Christmas Darling*	10.00 -	15.00
135 *Be Careful With The Blues*	10.00 -	15.00

WALTER POPULIST & THE TRUETONES:
Flame 10152 *Come Back To Me*	8.00 -	12.00

BRUCE PORTER:
Lee—*Rattlesnake*	15.00 -	20.00

ROCKY PORTER:
Stars 549(?) *First Sight*	15.00 -	20.00

ROYCE PORTER:
D 1026 *Lookin'*	30.00 -	40.00
Look 1001 *Yes I Do*	35.00 -	50.00
Mercury 71314 *Good Time*	10.00 -	15.00
Lookin'	8.00 -	12.00
Spade 1931 *A Woman Can Make You Blue*	50.00 -	75.00

SCHOOLBOY PORTER:
Chance 1114 *Rollin' Along*	30.00 -	40.00

THE POSSESSIONS:
Britton 1003/1004 *No More Love*	10.00 -	15.00

SCHOOLBOY PORTER:
Chance 1114 *Rollin' Along*	30.00 -	40.00

THE POSSESSIONS:
Britton 1003/1004 *No More Love*	10.00 -	15.00

CURTIS POTTER:
Fox 409 *I'm A Real Glad Daddy*	35.00 -	50.00

AUSTIN POWELL & THE JAMES QUINTET:
Atlantic 968 *What More Can I Ask?*	75.00 -	100.00

CHRIS POWELL & THE BLUE FLAMES:
Okeh 6875 *Darn That Dream*	15.00 -	25.00
6900 *Blue Boy*	30.00 -	50.00

DOUG POWELL:
Tip Top 713 *Jeannie With The Dark Blue Eyes*	15.00 -	25.00

JESSIE POWELL ORCHESTRA (See FLUFFY HUNTER)

JETT POWERS:
Design 811 *Go, Girl, Go*	30.00 -	50.00

JOHNNY POWERS (with STAN GETZ & THE TOM CATS/& HIS ROCKETS):
Fox 916/917 *Rock, Rock*	75.00 -	100.00
Fortune 199 *Honey, Let's Go*	30.00 -	50.00
HI-Q 5044 *Honey, Let's Go*	15.00 -	20.00
Sun 327 *Be Mine, All Mine*	8.00 -	12.00

P.Q. ROCK & ROLL (See MILT OSHINS)

BILLY PRAGER:
Crystal 106 *Do It Bop*	15.00 -	20.00

LYNN PRATT:
Hornet 1000 *Tom Cat Boogie*	20.00 -	30.00
1001 *I Don't Need*	20.00 -	30.00
1002 *Come Here Mama*	30.00 -	40.00

SCRAPPER PRATTS FALCONS:
Falcon 79492 *Guitar Man's Struggle*	15.00 -	20.00

HE PREACHERS:
Moonglow 5006 *Pain And Sorrow*	8.00 -	12.00

PRECISIONS:
Highland 300 *Eight Reasons Why I Love*	7.00 -	10.00

PRE-HISTORICS:
Edsel 779 *Alley-Oop-Cha-Cha-Cha*	7.00 -	10.00

PRELUDES:
Cub 9005 *Kingdom Of Love*	30.00 -	40.00
Empire 103 *Don't Fall In Love Too Soon*	15.00 -	20.00
Octavia 8000 *A Place For You*	15.00 -	20.00

PRELUDES FIVE:
Pik 230 *Straight*	10.00 -	15.00

PREMEERS:
Herald 577 *Diary Of Our Love*	8.00 -	12.00

PREMIERS:
Alert 706 *Jolene*	15.00 -	20.00

Cindy 3008 *China Doll*	10.00 -	15.00
Dig 113 *My Darling*	20.00 -	30.00
F-M—*Magic Of Love*	8.00 -	12.00
Ondex 1711 *Speaking Of You*	15.00 -	20.00

ELVIS PRESLEY:

(Note: The collecting of Elvis' records and other Elvis collectibles involves intricacies beyond the scope of this book. Seemingly insignificant variations in labels or record jackets can mean wide price differences. Record sleeves may have values higher than the records themselves; the sleeves of records not listed here due to the minimal value of the records may be worth several dollars or more. The same is true of promotional copies of common records not otherwise worthy of inclusion herein.

Also sought after are unofficial, "bootleg", and "fantasy" records—such as "Sun" records which were never originally produced by that company. Non-commercial issues, containing perhaps one track by Elvis, such as Armed Services radio transcriptions, are also in demand. Commercial issues which are often nothing more than repackagings of previously issued material, continue to proliferate with increasing emphasis on gimmickry such as colored vinyl and picture discs, and find a ready market, even at premium prices. Certain reissues, such as the higher-number maroon label EPs, command higher prices than their original issue counterparts. The listings below include only pre-1965 records issued commercially or promotionally; excluded are "bootleg" and spurious issues, foreign issues, recent reissues. etc.)

Those interested in pursing the intricacies of Elvis Presley records (and peripheral collectibles) should consult one of the books dealing with same, such as "The Official Price Guide to Memorabilia of Elvis Presley and The Beatles, by Osborne, Cox, and Lindsay.

Rainbow—*The Truth About Me* (78 rpm)	35.00 -	50.00

(Above is a magazine insert record, often found affixed to another 78 RPM record to facilitate playing)

RCA Victor (EP-2 records) SPD-22 *Elvis Presley*	100.00 -	Up
(EP 3 records) SPD-23 *Elvis Presley*	150.00 -	Up
(EP) 7-37 *Perfect For Parties*	25.00 -	35.00

(Above were issued for promotional purposes)

(EP) 747 *Elvis Presley*	20.00 -	30.00
(EP) 821 *Heartbreak Hotel*	20.00 -	30.00
(EP) 830 *Elvis Presley*	20.00 -	30.00
(EP) 940 *The Real Elvis*	20.00 -	30.00
(EP) 965 *Any Way You Want Me*	25.00 -	40.00
(EP) 992 *Elvis Vol. 1*	20.00 -	30.00
(EP) 993 *Elvis Vol. 2*	20.00 -	30.00
(EP) 994 *Strictly Elvis*	20.00 -	30.00
RCA Victor (LP) 1035 *Christmas Album* (Mono)	80.00 -	120.00
(EP-2 Records) 1254 *Elvis Presley* (4 songs on each record)	100.00 -	150.00
(EP-2 records) 1254 *Elvis Presley* (6 songs on each record)	200.00 -	Up
(EP) 1-1515 *Loving You*	15.00 -	20.00
(EP) 2-1515 *Loving You, Vol. 2*	15.00 -	20.00
(LP) 1254 *Elvis Presley*	25.00 -	50.00
(LP) 1382 *Elvis*	20.00 -	40.00

(Note: A number of variations in label and cover of LPM-1382 exist, some of which are valuable)

(LP) 1515 *Loving You*	15.00 -	30.00
(LP) 1707 *Elvis' Golden Records*	20.00 -	40.00
(LP) 1884 *King Creole*	20.00 -	50.00

(LP) 1951 *Elvis' Christmas Album* .... 20.00 - 50.00
(LP) 1990 *For LP Fans Only* .... 20.00 - 50.00
(LP) 2011 *A Date With Elvis* .... 30.00 - 50.00
(Note: Double-pocket version of this album, with
1960 calendar on back cover commands higher
premium.)
(LP) 2075 *50,000,000 Elvis Fans Can't Be
Wrong* .... 15.00 - 30.00
(LP) 2697 *It Happened At The Worlds Fair* .... 15.00 - 30.00
(LP) 3468 *Harum Scarum* .... 12.00 - 18.00
(LP) 3558 *Frankie And Johnny* .... 15.00 - 20.00
RCA Victor (LP) 3787 *Double Trouble* .... 20.00 - 30.00
(LP) 3893 *Clambake* .... 50.00 - 75.00
(LP) 3921 *Elvis' Gold Records, Vol. 4* ....200.00 - Up
(LP) 3989 *Speedway* ....300.00 - Up
(Note: Foregoing EPs and LPs are all original
MONO issues, with black labels having dog
logo at top. LPs have "LPM-" prefix to catalog
numbers. Subsequent pressings, including
Stereo issues with "LPS-" prefixes, are worth
substantially less.)
(EP) 4006 *Love Me Tender* .... 10.00 - 15.00
(EP) 4041 *Just For You* .... 10.00 - 15.00
(EP) 4054 *Peace In The Valley* .... 10.00 - 15.00
(EP) 4108 *Elvis Sings Christmas Songs* .... 10.00 - 15.00
(EP) 4114 *Jailhouse Rock* .... 10.00 - 15.00
(EP) 4319 *King Creole, Vol.1* .... 10.00 - 15.00
(EP) 4321 *King Creole, Vol. 2* .... 10.00 - 15.00
(EP) 4325 *Elvis Sails* .... 15.00 - 20.00
(EP) 4340 *Christmas With Elvis* .... 10.00 - 15.00
(EP) 4368 *Follow That Dream* .... 10.00 - 15.00
(EP) 4371 *Kid Galahad* .... 10.00 - 15.00
(Ep) 4382 *Viva Las Vegas* .... 10.00 - 15.00
(EP) 4283 *Tickle Me* .... 10.00 - 15.00
(Ep) 4387 *Easy Come, Easy Go* .... 10.00 - 15.00
(Ep) 5088 *A Touch Of Gold* ....100.00 - Up
(EP) 5101 *A Touch Of Gold, Vol 2* ....100.00 - Up
(EP) 5120 *The Real Elvis* ....100.00 - Up
(EP) 5121 *Peace In The Valley* ....100.00 - Up
(EP) 5122 *King Creole* ....100.00 - Up
(EP) 5141 *A Touch Of Gold, Vol. 3* ....100.00 - Up
(Note: Foregoing EPs are maroon label issues.
Subsequent issues, with black or orange labels
are worth only about $15.00 to $30.00 each.)
(EP) 5157 *Elvis Sails* .... 25.00 - 35.00
RCA Victor 6357 *Mystery Train* .... 15.00 - 20.00
6357 *Mystery Train* (78 RPM)............. 30.00 - 40.00
6380 *That's All Right* .... 15.00 - 20.00
6380 *That's All Right* (78 RPM) .... 30.00 - 40.00
6381 *Good Rockin' Tonight* .... 15.00 - 20.00
6381 *Good Rockin' Tonight* (78 RPM) ...... 30.00 - 40.00
6382 *Milkcow Blues Boogie* .... 15.00 - 20.00
6382 *Milkcow Blues Boogie* (78 RPM) ...... 30.00 - 40.00
6383 *Baby, Let's Play House* .... 15.00 - 20.00
6383 *Baby, Let's Play House* (78 RPM) ..... 30.00 - 40.00
6420, 6540, 6604 .... 5.00 - 10.00
6420 *Heartbreak Hotel* (78 RPM) .... 15.00 - 20.00
6540 *I Want You, I Need You* (78 RPM) ..... 15.00 - 20.00
6604 *Hound Dog* (78 RPM) .... 15.00 - 25.00
6636 *Blue Suede Shoes* .... 15.00 - 20.00
6636 *Blue Suede Shoes* (78 RPM).......... 35.00 - 50.00
6637 *I Got A Woman* .... 15.00 - 20.00
6637 *I Got A Woman* (78 RPM) .... 35.00 - 50.00
6638 *I'll Never Let You Go* .... 15.00 - 20.00
6638 *I'll Never Let You Go* (78 RPM)...... 35.00 - 50.00
6639 *Tryin' To Get To You* .... 15.00 - 20.00
6639 *Tryin' To Get To You* (78 RPM) ...... 35.00 - 50.00
6640 *Blue Moon*....................... 15.00 - 20.00
6640 *Blue Moon* (78 RPM) .... 35.00 - 50.00
6641 *Money Honey*..................... 15.00 - 20.00
6641 *Money Honey* (78 RPM) .... 35.00 - 50.00
6642 *Shake, Rattle And Roll* .... 15.00 - 20.00

6642 *Shake, Rattle And Roll* (78 RPM)....... 35.00 - 50.00
6643 *Love Me Tender*..................... 5.00 - 8.00
6643 *Love Me Tender* (78 RPM) .... 15.00 - 20.00
RCA Victor 6800, 6870, 7000, 7035, 7150, 7240,
7280, 7410......................... 4.00 - 8.00
6800 *Too Much* (78 RPM) .... 15.00 - 20.00
6870 *All Shook Up* (78 RPM) .... 15.00 - 20.00
7000 *Teddy Bear* (78 RPM) .... 15.00 - 25.00
7035 *Jailhouse Rock* (78 RPM) .... 20.00 - 30.00
7150 *I Beg Of You* (78 RPM) .... 20.00 - 30.00
7240 *Wear My Ring* (78 RPM) .... 20.00 - 30.00
7280 *Hard Headed Woman* (78 RPM) .... 30.00 - 50.00
7410 *I Got Stung* (78 RPM) ....100.00 - 150.00
(Note: The only copies seen of 7410 have come
from jukebox operators.)
RCA Victor 37-7850 *Surrender* (7" 33 1/3 RPM) 100.00 - Up
37-7880 *I Feel So Bad* (7" 33 1/3 RPM) ......100.00 - Up
37-7908 *Little Sister* (7" 33 1/3 RPM)........150.00 - Up
37-7968 *Can't Help Falling In Love* (7"
33 1/3 RPM)......................200.00 - Up
37-7992 *Good Luck Charm* (7" 33 1/3 RPM) ..300.00 - Up
37-8041 *She's Not You* (7" 33 1/3 RPM) ...... -
37-8100 *Return To Sender* (7" 33 1/3 RPM) ... -
(Note: Above issues should not be confused with
the usual 45 RPM issues, which have
corresponding catalog numbers; the 45s are of
nominal value only. Note the "37" prefix to
catalog numbers.)
The 33 1/3 RPM issues listed here command
widely varying prices, which have been quoted
as high as $1000.00 particularly for the later
issues. It is doubted that such high prices are
actually realized; these issues should be
regarded as highly speculative.)
RCA Victor 61-7740 *Stuck On You*
(STEREO 45 RPM).....................100.00 - Up
61-7777 *It's Now Or Never* (STEREO 45 RPM) 100.00 - Up
61-7850 *Surrender* (STEREO 45 RPM).......100.00 - Up
61-7880 *I Feel So Bad* (STEREO 45 RPM) ....100.00 - Up
(Note: Above three issues should not be confused
with the usual MONO 45 RPM issues, which
have corresponding catalog numbers. Note the
"61" prefix. The mono 45s have only nominal
value.)
RCA Victor 68-7850 *Surrender* (7" STEREO
33 1/3 RPM) ....200.00 - Up
68-7880 *I Feel So Bad* (7" STEREO
33 1/3 RPM)........................ -
(Note: Above should not be confused with the
usual 45 RPM records which have
corresponding catalog numbers. Note the "68"
prefix. Very high prices of hundreds of dollars
have been quoted for these records, but
whether such prices might actually be realized
is subject to doubt. These records should be
regarded as highly speculative.)
RCA Victor G8-MW-8705 *TV Guide Presents
Elvis Presley* .... Rare -
(Above is a special promotional record.
Extremely high prices have been quoted for it,
particularly where it is accompanied by the
original printed material.)
Sun 209 *That's All Right* ....150.00 - 200.00
210 *Good Rockin' Tonight* ....150.00 - 200.00
215 *Milkcow Blues Boogie* ....200.00 - 300.00
217 *Baby, Let's Play House* ....100.00 - 150.00
223 *Mystery Train* ....100.00 - 150.00

JOHNNY PRESTON:
Mercury (EP) 3397 *Johnny Preston* .... 15.00 - 25.00
(LP) 20592 *Running Bear* .... 25.00 - 40.00
(LP) 20609 *Come Rock With Me*............ 25.00 - 40.00

PRESTOS:

Mercury 70747 *Til We Meet Again* .... 15.00 - 25.00

PRETENDERS:
Bethlehem 3050 *Ding Dong Bells* .... 10.00 - 15.00
Central 2605 *Blue And Lonely* .... 20.00 - 30.00
Holiday 2610 *Tonight* .... 10.00 - 15.00
Power-Martin 1001 *Smile* .... 15.00 - 20.00
Rama 198 *Possessive Love* .... 10.00 - 15.00

PRETTY BOY:
Atlantic 1147 *Bip Bop Bip* .... 15.00 - 20.00
Big 617 *Rockin' The Mule* .... 15.00 - 20.00
Rhythm 1768 *Find My Baby* .... 30.00 - 50.00

LLOYD PRICE:
ABC Paramount (LP) 277 *The Exciting Lloyd*
   Price .... 15.00 - 25.00
   (LP) 297 *Mr. Personality* .... 15.00 - 25.00
   (LP) 315 *Sings The Blues* .... 15.00 - 20.00
   9792 *Just Because* (78 RPM) .... 10.00 - 15.00
   9972 *Stagger Lee* (78 RPM) .... 20.00 - 30.00
   9997 *Is It Really Love?* (78 RPM) .... 10.00 - 15.00
KRC 303 *Hello Little Girl* .... 5.00 - 8.00
Specialty 428 *Lawdy Miss Clawdy* .... 8.00 - 12.00
Specialty 440 *Restless Heart* .... 5.00 - 8.00
   452 *Ain't It A Shame?* .... 5.00 - 8.00
   457 *So Long* .... 5.00 - 8.00
   463 *Where You At?* .... 5.00 - 8.00
   483 *Too Late For Tears* .... 5.00 - 8.00
   494 *Walkin The Track* .... 5.00 - 8.00
(Above are found pressed of red plastic; these
   command higher prices)
   535, 571, 582, 602 .... 4.00 - 6.00
   (LP) 2105 *Lloyd Price* .... 20.00 - 30.00

MEL PRICE:
Dixie 2016 *Little Dog Blues/Until* .... 30.00 - 40.00

RAY PRICE:
Columbia (LP) 1015 *Ray Price Sings Heart Songs* 20.00 - 30.00
   (LP) 1148 *Talk To Your Heart* .... 20.00 - 30.00

RONNIE PRICE & VELVETS:
Carousel 1001 *White Bucks* .... 8.00 - 12.00

THE PRIMETTES:
LuPine 120 *Tears of Sorrow* .... 80.00 - 120.00

BOBBY PRINCE:
Chance 1128 *Tell Me Why, Why, Why* .... 15.00 - 20.00

PRISONAIRES:
Sun 186 *Just Walkin' In The Rain* .... 30.00 - 50.00
   189 *My God Is Real* .... 100.00 - 150.00
   191 *A Prisoner's Prayer* .... 100.00 - 150.00
   207 *There Is Love In You* .... 150.00 - 250.00

JIMMY PRITCHETT:
Crystal 503 *That's The Way I Feel* .... 20.00 - 30.00

PRODIGALS:
Abner 1015 *Won't You Believe* .... 15.00 - 20.00
Falcon 1011 *Marsha* .... 15.00 - 20.00

PROFESSOR LONGHAIR:
Atlantic 1020 *In The Night* .... 30.00 - 50.00
Ebb 101 *Cry Pretty Baby* .... 15.00 - 20.00
   106 *Look What You're Doin'* .... 15.00 - 20.00
   121 *Looka No Hair* .... 15.00 - 20.00
Ron 326 *Cuttin' Out* .... 7.00 - 10.00
   329 *Go To The Mardi Gras* .... 7.00 - 10.00

PROPHETS:
Atco 6078 *Stormy* .... 8.00 - 12.00

PROWLERS:
Aragon 302 *Rock Me Baby* .... 30.00 - 40.00

LEWIS PRUITT:
Peach 703 *Pretty Baby* .... 20.00 - 30.00
   710 *This Little Girl* .... 20.00 - 30.00

RALPH PRUITT with HIS RHYTHM BOYS:
Meridian 1506/1507 *Hey Mr. Porter* .... 20.00 - 30.00

SNOOKY PRYOR:
J.O.B. 1014 *Cryin' Shame* .... 100.00 - 150.00
   1126 *Boogie Twist* .... 40.00 - 60.00
Parrot 807 *Crosstown Blues* .... 50.00 - 75.00
Vee Jay 215 *Someone To Love Me* .... 10.00 - 15.00

RED PRYSOCK:
Mercury (LP) 20088 *Rock 'N' Roll* .... 20.00 - 30.00
   (LP) 20211 *Fruit Boots* .... 20.00 - 30.00
   (LP) 20307 *The Beat* .... 20.00 - 30.00
Red Robin 117 *Hard Rock* .... 15.00 - 20.00

DENNIS PUCKETT:
Emerald 2018 *Rockin' Teens* .... 35.00 - 50.00

WHITEY PULLEN:
Crown (LP) 332 *Country Music Star* .... 10.00 - 15.00
   (LP) 5332 *Country Music Star* .... 15.00 - 20.00
Sage 274 *Walk My Way Back Home* .... 15.00 - 25.00
   283 *You'll Get Yours Someday* .... 15.00 - 25.00
   294 *Let's Go Wild Tonight* .... 20.00 - 30.00
   313 *Tuscaloosa Lucy* .... 20.00 - 30.00

VERN PULLENS:
Spade 1927 *Bop Crazy Baby* .... 75.00 - 100.00
   Mama Don't Allow No Boppin' .... 75.00 - 100.00

PYRAMIDS:
C-Note 1206 *Someday* .... .00 - .00
Cub 9112 *Cryin'* .... 7.00 - 10.00
Davis 453 *At Any Cost* .... 5.00 - 8.00
   457 *Before It's Too Late* .... 5.00 - 8.00
Federal 12233 *Deep In My Heart For You* .... 75.00 - 100.00
Hollywood 1047 *Someday* .... 80.00 - 120.00
Shell 711 *Ankle Bracelet* .... 10.00 - 15.00

QUADRELLS:
Whirlin Disc 103 *Come To Me* .... 15.00 - 20.00

QUAILS:
DeLuxe 6085 *Things She Used To Do* .... 20.00 - 30.00
Harvey 114, 116, 120 .... 5.00 - 8.00

QUAILTONES:
Josie 779 *Tears Of Love* .... 25.00 - 40.00

THE QUARTER NOTES:
DeLuxe 6129 *My Fantasy* .... 5.00 - 8.00
Dot 15685 *Like You Bug Me* .... 8.00 - 12.00
Fox 2 *Teen Age Blues* .... 10.00 - 15.00

DOUG QUATTLEBAUM:
Gotham 7519 *Don't Be Funny Baby* .... 30.00 - 50.00

QUEENS: (See also SHIRLEY GUNTER)
Flair 1050 *Oop Shoop* .... 7.00 - 10.00

? (QUESTION MARK) & THE MYSTERIANS:
Pa-Go-Go 102 *96 Tears* .... 30.00 - 40.00

QUESTION MARKS:
Swingtime 346 *Another Soldier Gone* .... 200.00 - Up

ANDY QUINN:
Decca 30438 *Rock-A-Boogie* .... 10.00 - 15.00
   30521 *Sweet Treat* .... 10.00 - 15.00
   30843 *Sharon Lee* .... 10.00 - 15.00

QUINNS:
Cyclone 111 *Oh Starlight* .... 10.00 - 15.00

EDDIE QUINTEROS:
Brent 7009 *Come Dance With Me* .... 15.00 - 20.00
   7014 *Slow Down Sandy* .... 15.00 - 20.00

QUINTONES:
Chess 1685 *I Try So Hard* .... 15.00 - 20.00
Hunt 322 *There'll Be No Sorrow* .... 8.00 - 12.00
Park 57-112 *More Than A Notion* .... 30.00 - 40.00

THE QUOTATIONS:
Verve 10245 *Imagination* .... 10.00 - 15.00

DON RADAR:
Strate 8 1507 *Rock & Roll Granpa* .... 15.00 - 20.00

THE RADIANTS:
Dootone 451 *I'm Betting My Heart* .... 7.00 - 10.00

JANICE RADO & THE SEQUINS:
Edsel 782 *I'm Coming Home* .... 7.00 - 10.00

THE RAIDERS:
Van 00262 *Skipping Around* .... 10.00 - 15.00

RAINBOWS:
Dave 908 *I Know* .... 8.00 - 12.00
Pilgrim 703 *May Lee* .... 15.00 - 20.00
   711 *Shirley* .... 50.00 - 75.00
Rama 209 *They Say* .... 75.00 - 100.00

Red Robin 134 *Mary Lee*	50.00 -	75.00

RAINDROPS:

Apollo 494 *Inspirations*	20.00 -	30.00
Dore 561 *Love Is Like A Mountain*	5.00 -	8.00
Sotoplay 0028 *I Still Love You*	-	
Spin It 104 *I Found Heaven In Love*	15.00 -	25.00
Vega—*Dim Those Lights*	15.00 -	25.00

CHRIS RANIER & THE ELRODS:

Red Head 1005 *Eleven O'Clock*	8.00 -	12.00

JERRY RAINES:

Drew-Blan 1001 *Dangerous Redhead*	8.00 -	12.00

MARVIN RAINWATER:

Crown (LP) 307 *Marvin Rainwater*	10.00 -	15.00
MGM (EP) 1464 *Songs by Vol. 1*	20.00 -	30.00
(EP) 1465 *Songs by Vol. 2*	20.00 -	30.00
(EP) 1466 *Songs by Vol. 3*	20.00 -	30.00
MGM (LP) 3534 *Songs By Marvin Rainwater*	35.00 -	50.00
(LP) 4046 *Gonna Find Me A Bluebird*	35.00 -	50.00
(LP) 3721 *Marvin Rainwater Sings With A Heart/A Beat*	40.00 -	60.00
12152 *Dem Low Down Blues*	8.00 -	12.00
12240 *Hot And Cold*	20.00 -	30.00
12412 *Gonna Find Me A Bluebird* (78 RPM)	10.00 -	15.00
12511 *My Brand Of Blues*	7.00 -	10.00
12609 *Baby, Don't Go*	8.00 -	12.00
12653 *Moanin' The Blues*	5.00 -	8.00
12665 *I Dig You Baby*	7.00 -	10.00

RAJAHS:

Klik 7805 *I Fell In Love*	20.00 -	30.00

RAMBLERS:

Jax 319 *Search My Heart* (red plastic)	75.00 -	100.00
MGM 11850 *Vadunt-Un-Vada Song*	75.00 -	100.00

JOHNNY RAMISTELLA:

Suede 1401 *Two By Two*	.00 -	.00

THE RAMS:

Flair 1066 *Sweet Thing*	15.00 -	20.00

D.C. RAND & THE JOKERS:

Candy 003 *Shake It Up*	15.00 -	20.00

BILLY RANDALL:

Savoy 1570 *Rowena*	7.00 -	10.00

RANDY & THE RAINBOWS:

Rust 5059, 5073, 5080, 5091, 5101	8.00 -	12.00

WAYNE RANEY:

Decca 30212 *Shake Baby Shake*	7.00 -	10.00
Decca (most other issues)	4.00 -	7.00
King (LP) 588 *Songs From The Hills*	30.00 -	40.00
King (most issues)	4.00 -	8.00
(Note: earlier issues, pressed of red vinyl, bring somewhat more)		

RANNELS:

Boss 2122 *Boom Baby*	7.00 -	10.00

BOZO RATLIFF:

Space 100 *Rock Along Time*	25.00 -	40.00

RAVENS:

Argo 5255 *Kneel And Pray* (ship logo)	10.00 -	15.00
5261 *A Simple Prayer* (ship logo)	8.00 -	12.00
5276 *Dear One* (ship logo)	8.00 -	12.00
5284 *Here Is My Heart*	8.00 -	12.00
Columbia 6-903 *Time Takes Care Of Everything*	75.00 -	100.00
6-925 *I'm So Crazy For Love*	75.00 -	100.00
39112 *You Don't Have To Drop A Heart*	75.00 -	100.00
Jubilee 5184 *Happy Go Lucky Baby*	7.00 -	10.00
5203 *Green Eyes*	7.00 -	10.00
King (EP) 310 *The Ravens*	100.00 -	150.00
Mercury 5800 *Begin The Beguine*	15.00 -	20.00
5853 *Chloe*	15.00 -	20.00
8291 *Write Me One Sweet Letter*	15.00 -	20.00
70060 *Don't Mention My Name*	20.00 -	30.00
70119 *Come A Little Bit Closer*	10.00 -	15.00
70307 *September Song*	15.00 -	20.00
70413 *Love Is No Dream*	20.00 -	30.00
70505 *White Christmas*	15.00 -	25.00
70554 *Old Man River*	20.00 -	25.00
National 9111 *Count Every Star*	150.00 -	200.00
Okeh 6825 *The Wiffenpoof Song*	75.00 -	100.00
6843 *Everything But You*	75.00 -	100.00
6888 *Mam'selle*	75.00 -	100.00
Regent (LP) 6062 *Write Me A Letter* (green label)	15.00 -	25.00

THE RAVES:

Swade 104 *Tell Me One More Time*	15.00 -	20.00

DANNY RAY:

Vin 1025 *Love Me*	15.00 -	20.00

DAVID RAY:

Kliff 101 *Lonesome Baby Blues*	30.00 -	50.00
102 *Jitter Buggin' Baby*	30.00 -	50.00

DON RAY:

Rodeo 129 *Rock 'N' Roll Blues*	15.00 -	25.00
130 *Imogene*	15.00 -	25.00

GENE RAY:

Cowtown 802 *I'm Going To Hollywood*	50.00 -	75.00

RAY-O-VACS:

Atco 6085 *Crying All Alone*	7.00 -	10.00
Decca 48162 *Besame Mucho*	15.00 -	20.00
48197 *Goodnight My Love*	20.00 -	30.00
Josie 781 *I Still Love You*	10.00 -	15.00

RAYS:

Argo 1074 *How Long Must I Wait*	6.00 -	10.00
Cameo 117 *Silhouettes* (78 RPM)	15.00 -	20.00
Chess 1613 *Tippity Top*	15.00 -	20.00
1678 *How Long Must I Wait*	8.00 -	12.00
(EP) 5120 *Tippity Top*	75.00 -	100.00
Perri 1004 *Are You Happy Now*	10.00 -	15.00
XYZ 100 *My Steady Girl*	15.00 -	20.00
102 *Silhouettes*	20.00 -	30.00
600 *Why Do You Look The Other Way*	8.00 -	12.00
605 *Mediterranean Moon*	7.00 -	10.00
607 *Magic Moon*	7.00 -	10.00
608 *Silver Starlight*	7.00 -	10.00

"RCA CAMDEN ROCKERS"

Camden (LP) 435 (various artists)	15.00 -	25.00

R-DELLS:

Dade 1806 *You Know Baby*	30.00 -	50.00

OTIS READ:

Nanc 1118/1119 *Come On Baby*	8.00 -	12.00

BILL READER:

Voll-Para 100 *There Was A Time*	7.00 -	10.00
Remember You're Mine	-	

JIMMY REAGAN & THE RHYTHM ROCKERS:

G&G 128 *Lonely, Lonely Heart*	15.00 -	25.00

RICK REASON:

Mar-Vel 3300 *I Feel So Bad*	-	

PEARL REAVES & THE CONCORDS:

Harlem 2332 *I'm Not Ashamed*	75.00 -	100.00

JOHNNY REBB:

Bullseye 1027 *Rock On*	7.00 -	10.00
Flame 154 *My Body Can't Take It*	7.00 -	10.00

REBEL ROUSERS:

Memphis 107 *Thunder*	7.00 -	10.00
113 *Zombie Walks*	7.00 -	10.00

THE REBELS:

Marlee 009 *Wild Weekend*	10.00 -	15.00

JOHNNY REDD:

Corallen *Rockin' With Ruby*	20.00 -	30.00

TEDDY REDELL:

Atco 6162 *Judy*	8.00 -	12.00
Hi 2024 *Pipeliner*	8.00 -	12.00
Vaden 110 *Knockin' On The Backside*	20.00 -	30.00
115 *Gold Dust*	15.00 -	20.00
116 *Judy*	15.00 -	20.00
301 *I Want To Hold You*	10.00 -	15.00

RED JACKS:

Apt 25006 *Big Brown Eyes*	7.00 -	10.00

TERRY REDMAN:

MGM 12735 *Come On Back* . . . . 7.00 - 10.00

RED TOPPERS:

Dan 3214 *I Never Had A Girl Like You* . . . . . . 5.00 - 8.00

REED BROTHERS & THE STINGERS:

Award 122/123 *Swamp Rock* . . . . 15.00 - 20.00

A. C. REED:

Age 29101 *This Little Voice* . . . . 4.00 - 7.00

29103 *I Wanna Be Free* . . . . 5.00 - 8.00

29112 *Mean Cop* . . . . 5.00 - 8.00

29123 *Lotta Lovin'* . . . . 5.00 - 8.00

AL REED:

Dot—*I Love Her So* . . . . 7.00 - 10.00

TNT—*I Love Her So* . . . . 15.00 - 20.00

Winner 700 *Top Notch Grade A* . . . . 7.00 - 10.00

BOB REED & HIS BAND:

Melatone 1003 *I'm Leaving You* . . . . 5.00 - 8.00

CHUCK REED:

Hit 101 *Talkin' No Trash* . . . . 10.00 - 15.00

EARL REED:

Cherokee 779 *Flat Foot Sam* . . . . 7.00 - 10.00

JAMES REED (& HIS BAND):

Big Town 117 *You Better Hold Me* . . . . 30.00 - 40.00

Flair 1034 *This Is The End* . . . . 35.00 - 50.00

1042 *You Better Hold Me* . . . . 15.00 - 20.00

Money 201 *My Love Is Real* . . . . 20.00 - 30.00

Rhythm 1775 *I Wanna Know* . . . . 50.00 - 75.00

JERRI REED:

Bango 500 *While You're Gone* . . . . 5.00 - 8.00

JERRY REED:

Capitol 3882 *Bessie Baby* . . . . 7.00 - 10.00

JIMMY REED:

Chance 1142 *High And Lonesome* . . . . 100.00 - 150.00

Vee Jay 100 *High And Lonesome* (red plastic) . . . 100.00 - 150.00

105 *Jimmie's Boogie* (red plastic) . . . . . 50.00 - 75.00

119 *Boogie In The Dark* (red plastic) . . . . 50.00 - 75.00

132 *Pretty Thing* . . . . 8.00 - 12.00

153 *I Don't Go For That* . . . . 7.00 - 10.00

168 *Ain't That Lovin' You Baby* . . . . . 7.00 - 10.00

186, 203, 226, 237, 248, 253 . . . . 4.00 - 7.00

270, 275, 287, 298, 304, 314, 326, 333,

347, 357 . . . . 3.00 - 5.00

(LP) 1004 *I'm Jimmy Reed* (maroon label) . . . . 30.00 - 40.00

(LP) 1008 *Rockin' With Reed* (maroon label) . . 30.00 - 40.00

(LP) 1022 *Found Love* . . . . 20.00 - 30.00

(LP) 1025 *Now Appearing* . . . . 15.00 - 20.00

(LP) 1035 (2 records) *At Carnegie Hall* . . . . 15.00 - 20.00

(LP) 1039 *The Best Of Jimmy Reed* . . . . . . 10.00 - 15.00

(LP) 1050 *Just Jimmy Reed* . . . . 10.00 - 15.00

(LP) 1067, 1072, 1073 . . . . 8.00 - 12.00

LULU REED:

King (most issues) . . . . 4.00 - 8.00

King (LP) 604 *Moody And Blue* . . . . 80.00 - 120.00

DANNY REEVES:

D 1206 *Bell Hop Blues/I'm A Hobo* . . . . 50.00 - 75.00

GLENN REEVES (& HIS ROCK

BILLYS/TOWN & COUNTRY PLAYBOYS):

Atco 6080 *Drinkin' Wine Spo-Dee-O-Dee* . . . . . 10.00 - 15.00

Decca 30481 *My Tortured Heart* . . . . 8.00 - 12.00

Decca 30589 *Betty Bounce* . . . . 8.00 - 12.00

30780 *Tarzan* . . . . 8.00 - 12.00

Republic 7121 *That'll Be Love* . . . . 8.00 - 12.00

TNT 120 *I'm Johnny On The Spot* . . . . 20.00 - 30.00

129 *I Ain't Got Room To Rock* . . . . . . 20.00 - 30.00

JIM REEVES:

Abbott (LP) 5001 *Jim Reeves Sings* . . . . 100.00 - 150.00

RCA Victor (LP) 1256 *Singing Down The Lane* . . 20.00 - 30.00

(LP) 1410 *Bimbo* . . . . 15.00 - 20.00

(LP) 1576 *Jim Reeves* . . . . 10.00 - 15.00

(LP) 1685 *Girl's I Have Known* . . . . 10.00 - 15.00

REGALS:

Aladdin 3266 *Run Pretty Baby* . . . . 25.00 - 35.00

Atlantic 1062 *I'm So Lonely* . . . . 10.00 - 15.00

REGENTS:

Cousins 1002 *Barbara-Ann* . . . . 50.00 - 75.00

Gee (LP) 706 *Barbara-Ann* . . . . 50.00 - 75.00

Kayo 101 *No Hard Feelings* . . . . 8.00 - 12.00

BILLY REINSFORD:

Hermitage 803 *Magnolia* . . . . 20.00 - 30.00

THE RELATIONS:

Utopia 12 *Don't Let Me Down This Weekend* . . . . 8.00 - 12.00

BOBBY RELF (& THE LAURELS):

Cash 1019 *Our Love* . . . . 10.00 - 15.00

Dot 15510 *Little Fool* . . . . 10.00 - 15.00

Flair 1063 *Yours Alone* . . . . 50.00 - 75.00

REMINISCENTS:

Day 1000 *Oh Let Me Dream* . . . . 8.00 - 12.00

JOHNNY RENO:

Valley's Meadowlark 105-58 *Naughty Mama* . . . . 15.00 - 25.00

RENOWNS:

Everest 19396 *Wild One* . . . . 10.00 - 15.00

REVALONS:

Pet 802 *Dreams Are For Fools* . . . . 10.00 - 15.00

REVELERS:

G & C 1617 *What Was Once Was Once* . . . . 15.00 - 20.00

RE-VELS/REVELS:

Andie 5077 *Please* . . . . 5.00 - 8.00

Chess 1708 *False Alarm* . . . . 35.00 - 50.00

Norgolde 103 *Midnight Stroll* . . . . 7.00 - 10.00

104 *Foo Man Choo* . . . . 8.00 - 12.00

Sound 129 *You Lied To Me* . . . . 15.00 - 20.00

135 *Dream My Darling Dream* . . . . 10.00 - 15.00

Teen 122 *So In Love* . . . . 20.00 - 30.00

PAUL REVERE & THE RAIDERS:

Gardena 116 *Like Long Hair* . . . . 8.00 - 12.00

(LP) 1000 *Like Long Hair* . . . . 100.00 - 150.00

Sande (LP) 1001 *Paul Revere & The Raiders* . . . 100.00 - 150.00

THE REVERES:

Glory 272 *Leonore* . . . . 7.00 - 10.00

EDDIE REYNOLDS:

Dixie *What Was It* . . . . 15.00 - 25.00

BIG JACK REYNOLDS & HIS BLUE MEN:

Hi-Q 5036 *I Had A Little Dog* . . . . 7.00 - 10.00

JODY REYNOLDS:

Demon 1507 *Endless Sleep* (78 rpm) . . . . 10.00 - 15.00

1515 *Beulah Lee* . . . . 7.00 - 10.00

1524 *Stone Cold* . . . . 8.00 - 12.00

WESLEY REYNOLDS:

Rose 108 *Trip To The Moon* . . . . 15.00 - 20.00

117 *Rag Mop* . . . . 15.00 - 20.00

JIMMY RHODES & THE SHUFFLES:

Cupid 5005 *I Wanna Go* . . . . 7.00 - 10.00

SLIM RHODES:

Sun 216 *Uncertain Love* . . . . 20.00 - 30.00

225 *House Of Sin* . . . . 35.00 - 50.00

238 *Gonna Romp And Stomp* . . . . 15.00 - 20.00

256 *Do What I Do* . . . . 15.00 - 20.00

TEXAS RED RHODES:

Echo 1001 *Go Cats Go* . . . . 20.00 - 30.00

RHYTHM ACES:

Vee Jay 124 *I Wonder Why* . . . . 40.00 - 60.00

138 *Whisper To Me* . . . . 40.00 - 60.00

160 *That's My Sugar* . . . . 40.00 - 60.00

212 *Whisper To Me* . . . . 20.00 - 30.00

417 *Be Mine* . . . . 8.00 - 12.00

RHYTHM JESTERS:

Lectra 513 *Please Be Mine* . . . . 7.00 - 10.00

Rama 213 *Rock Music* . . . . 10.00 - 15.00

RHYTHM MASTERS:

Flip 314 *Baby We Two* . . . . 10.00 - 15.00

RHYTHM ROCKERS:

Cross Country 524 *Fiddle Bop* . . . . 20.00 - 30.00

Oasis 104 *Thinkin' About You* . . . . 20.00 - 30.00

Sun 248 *Fiddle Bop* . . . . 10.00 - 15.00

RHYTHM ROCKETS:

Gulfstream 6654 *My Shadow*	15.00	-	20.00

ELDON RICE:

El Rio 413 *Our Love Won't Die*	50.00	-	80.00

CHARLIE RICH:

Groove 58-0025 *Big Boss Man*	5.00	-	8.00
Phillips Int'l. (LP) 197 *Lonely Weekends*	75.00	-	100.00

DAVE RICH:

RCA Victor 7334 *Rosie Let's Get Cozy*	10.00	-	15.00

JAY RICHARDS & THE BLUES KINGS:

Goldband 1101 *Hear Love Knockin'*	7.00	-	10.00

JAPE RICHARDSON: (See also BIG BOPPER)

Mercury 71219 *Crazy Blues*	10.00	-	15.00
71312 *A Teen-Age Moon*	10.00	-	15.00

NOLAN RICHARDSON:

Jamaka 1005 *Money In The Bank*	20.00	-	30.00

RICHIE (& THE ROYALS):

Rello 1 *And When I'm Near You*	8.00	-	12.00
3 *Be My Girl*	8.00	-	12.00

RICKI & RIKATONES:

Manhattan 201 *T.N.T.*	8.00	-	12.00

JIMMY RICKS (& THE RAVENS):

Baton 236 *I'm A Fool To Want You*	7.00	-	10.00
Mercury 70213 *Who'll Be The Fool*	8.00	-	12.00

TOMMY RIDGELY:

Atlantic 1009 *Oh Lawdy*	15.00	-	20.00
Atlantic 1039 *Jam Up*	10.00	-	15.00

THE RIFFS:

Sunny 22 *Little Girl*	10.00	-	15.00

BILLY LEE RILEY:

Brunswick 55085 *Is That All To The Ball (Mr Hall)?*	25.00	-	35.00
Home Of The Blues 223 *Flip, Flop And Fly*	8.00	-	12.00
Sun 245 *Rock With Me Baby*	15.00	-	25.00
260 *Flying Saucer Rock & Roll*	15.00	-	25.00
277 *Red Hot*	10.00	-	15.00
289 *Baby Please Don't Go*	10.00	-	15.00
313 *Down By The Riverside*	5.00	-	8.00
322 *Got The Water Boiling*	15.00	-	25.00

BOB RILEY:

MGM 12612 *Wanda Jean*	15.00	-	20.00
York—*Big Dog*	15.00	-	20.00

OTIS RILEY:

Kappa 209 *Little Miss Bibbity Bobbity Boom*	5.00	-	8.00

RINKY DINKS:

Atco 6121 *Early In The Morning*	8.00	-	12.00
6121 *Early In The Morning* (78 RPM)	15.00	-	20.00
6128 *Mighty Mighty Man*	10.00	-	15.00
6128 *Mighty Mighty Man* (78 RPM)	15.00	-	20.00

CHUCK RIO:

Challenge 59019 *Denise*	5.00	-	8.00

RIP CHORDS:

Abco 105 *Let's Do The Razzle Dazzle*	75.00	-	100.00

GEORGE RITCHIE:

Smart 321 *But In A Million Years*	10.00	-	15.00

THE RIVALS:

Darryl 722 *I Must See You Again*	10.00	-	15.00
Lu Pine 118 *It's Gonna Work Out*	5.00	-	8.00

LITTLE BOBBY RIVERA (& THE HEMLOCKS):

Fury 1004 *Cora Lee* (maroon label)	15.00	-	20.00

CHUCK RIVERS:

Cenla 222 *All Alone At Night*	—	-	—

CLIFF RIVERS:

Thanks! - 1201 *True Lips*	15.00	-	20.00

RIVIERAS:

Algonquin 718 *A Night To Remember*	5.00	-	8.00
Coed 503 *Count Every Star*	8.00	-	12.00
508 *Moonlight Serenade*	8.00	-	12.00
513 *Our Love*	8.00	-	12.00
522 *Since I Made You Cry*	8.00	-	12.00
529 *Blessing Of Love*	8.00	-	12.00
538 *My Friend*	8.00	-	12.00

542 *Stay In My Heart*	8.00	-	12.00
551 *El Dorado*	8.00	-	12.00
592 *Moonlight Cocktails*	5.00	-	8.00
Riviera (LP) 701 *Campus Party*	40.00	-	60.00

RIVILEERS:

Baton 200 *A Thousand Stars*	15.00	-	20.00
201 *Forever*	20.00	-	30.00
205 *Eternal Love*	25.00	-	35.00
207 *For Sentimental Reasons*	15.00	-	20.00
209 *Don't Ever Leave Me*	20.00	-	30.00
241 *A Thousand Stars*	8.00	-	12.00

THE RIVINGTONS:

Liberty (LP) 3282 *Doin' The Bird*	30.00	-	40.00
55610 *Cherry*	10.00	-	15.00

ROAMERS:

Savoy 1147 *I'll Never Get Over You*	10.00	-	15.00
1149 *Women And Whiskey*	10.00	-	15.00
1156 *Chop Chop Ching-A-Ling*	10.00	-	15.00

EDDIE ROBBINS:

David 1001 *Janice*	8.00	-	12.00
Dot 15702 *A Girl Like You*	8.00	-	12.00
Power 214 *A Girl Like You*	15.00	-	20.00

MARTY ROBBINS:

Columbia (LP) 976 *The Song Of Robbins*	15.00	-	20.00
(LP) 1087 *Song Of The Islands*	15.00	-	20.00
(LP) 1189 *Marty Robbins*	15.00	-	20.00
Columbia (EP) B-2116 *Singing The Blues*	35.00	-	50.00
Columbia (EP) B-2134 *A White Sportcoat*	35.00	-	50.00
Columbia 2601 (LP) (10") *Rock'n Roll'n Robbins*	150.00	-	250.00
21351 *That's All Right*	10.00	-	15.00
21446 *Maybelline*	10.00	-	15.00
21461 *Pretty Mama*	8.00	-	12.00
21477 *Tennessee Toddy*	10.00	-	15.00
40679 *Long Tall Sally*	15.00	-	20.00
40706 *Respectfully Miss Brooks*	10.00	-	15.00
40864 *A White Sport Coat* (78 RPM)	10.00	-	15.00
41013 *The Story Of My Life* (78 RPM)	10.00	-	15.00

MEL ROBBINS:

Argo 5340 *Save It*	15.00	-	20.00

ROBERT & JOHNNY:

Old Town 1052 *I Believe In You* (78 RPM)	8.00	-	12.00

BOBBY ROBERTS with THE BAD HABITS:

Hut 881 *Hop Skip And Jump*	30.00	-	40.00
Sky 101 *Big Sandy*	50.00	-	75.00

DENNIS ROBERTS:

Sims 145 *Mule Skinner Blues*	7.00	-	10.00
Yucca 133 *Come On*	7.00	-	10.00

DON "RED" ROBERTS:

Chart 643 *Don't Say Maybe*		-	
Rama 230 *Don't Say Maybe*	10.00	-	15.00

LANCE ROBERTS:

Decca 30955 *Gonna Have Myself A Ball*	8.00	-	12.00

WALTER ROBERTSON:

Flair 1053 *Sputterin' Blues*	30.00	-	40.00

ROBINS:

Arvee 5001 *Just Like That*	5.00	-	8.00
Atco 6059 *Smokey Joe's Cafe*	7.00	-	10.00
Crown 106 *I Made A Vow*	50.00	-	75.00
120 *The Key To My Heart*	60.00	-	90.00
Knight 2008 *It's Never Too Late*	7.00	-	10.00
Lavender 001 *White Cliffs Of Dover*	10.00	-	15.00
RCA Victor 5175 *A Fool Such As I*	75.00	-	100.00
5271 *Oh Why*	60.00	-	90.00
5434 *How Would You Know*	60.00	-	80.00
5489 *Empty Bottles*	50.00	-	75.00
5564 *Get It Off You Mind*	50.00	-	75.00
Spark 103 *Riot In Cell Block Number Nine*	15.00	-	20.00
107 *Framed*	15.00	-	20.00
110 *If Tear Drops Were Kisses*	20.00	-	30.00
113 *One Kiss*	15.00	-	20.00
116 *I Must Be Dreaming*	15.00	-	20.00
122 *Smokey Joe's Cafe*	30.00	-	50.00

Whippet 100 *Cherry Lips*	8.00 -	12.00
101 *Hurt Me*	15.00 -	20.00
103 *That Old Black Magic*	15.00 -	20.00
(LP) 703 *Rock & Roll With The Robins*	90.00 -	120.00

BILL ROBINSON & THE QUAILS:

De Luxe 6030 *Lonely Star*	35.00 -	50.00
6047 *I Know She's Gone*	35.00 -	50.00
6057 *Somewhere Somebody Cares*	35.00 -	50.00
6059 *Heaven Is The Place*	35.00 -	50.00
6074 *Oh Sugar*	40.00 -	60.00

DICK ROBINSON:

MCI 1006 *Boppin' Martian*	15.00 -	25.00

FENTION/FENTON ROBINSON (& THE CASTLE ROCKERS/HIS DUKES):

Duke 190, 191, 312, 329	4.00 -	6.00
Meteor 5041 *Crying Out Loud* (black label)	35.00 -	50.00
U.S.A. 842 *From My Heart*	5.00 -	8.00

JIMMY LEE ROBINSON:

Bandera 2510 *Twist It Baby*	8.00 -	12.00

SUGAR CHILE ROBINSON:

MARK ROBINSON:

Tee Gee 104 *Pretty Jane*	10.00 -	15.00

SUGAR CHILE ROBINSON:

Capitol (LP) 589 *Boogie Woogie*	50.00 -	75.00

CARSON ROBINSON:

MGM 12266 *Rockin' And Rollin' With Granmaw*	20.00 -	30.00
MGM (most other issues)	3.00 -	7.00

TOMMY ROCCO:

Razorback 102 *I'll Cry Awhile*	5.00 -	8.00

"ROCK & ROLL FOREVER":

Atlantic (LP) 8010 (various artists) ...	15.00 -	20.00
(LP) 8021 Vol. 2 (various artists) ...	15.00 -	20.00

"ROCK & ROLL SOCK HOP":

Score 4018 (various artists)	30.00 -	40.00

"ROCK AND ROLL SPECTACULAR":

Dawn (LP) 119 (various artists)	15.00 -	20.00

ROCK-A-FELLAS:

Southern Sound 112 *Dear Someone*	15.00 -	20.00

ROCK A TEENS:

Doran 3515 *Woo-Hoo*	15.00 -	20.00
Roulette 4217 *Doggone It Baby*	8.00 -	12.00
Roulette (LP) 25109 *Woo-Hoo*	50.00 -	80.00

ROCK-A-TONES

Whammy 7450 *One More Chance*	-	

ROCKERS: (See also PAUL WINLEY):

Carter 3029 *Count Every Star*	100.00 -	150.00
Federal 12267 *What Am I To Do*	15.00 -	20.00
12273 *Down In The Bottom*	15.00 -	20.00
Premium 401 *Angel Child*	10.00 -	15.00

ROCKETONES:

Melba 113 *Mexico*	15.00 -	20.00

ROCKETS: (See also BILL BODAFORD):

Modern 992 *Be Lovey Dovey*	8.00 -	12.00
1021 *Johnny's House Party*	8.00 -	12.00
Tri-Dec 25725 *My Rockin' Baby*	20.00 -	30.00

ROCKETTES:

Parrot 789 *I Can't Forget*	150.00 -	200.00

ROCKIN' BRADLEY:

Fire 1007 *Look Out*	20.00 -	30.00

ROCKIN' CHAIRS:

Recorte 402 *Rockin' Chair Boogie* ...	10.00 -	15.00
404 *Come On Baby*	15.00 -	20.00

ROCKIN DUKES:

OJ 1007 *My Baby Left Me*	75.00 -	100.00

"ROCKIN '50s"

Atlantic (LP) 8037 (various artists) ...	10.00 -	15.00

ROCKING STOCKINGS:

Sun 1960 *Rockin-Lang-Syne*	8.00 -	12.00

ROCKIN' JESTERS:

Oklahoma *I Was Too Blind*	15.00 -	20.00

ROCKIN' KIDS:

Dot 15749 *Yea Yea (I'm In The Mood)*	8.00 -	12.00

ROCKIN' REBELS:

Swan (LP) 509 *Wild Weekend*	35.00 -	50.00

ROCKIN' RONALD:

End 1043 *Kansas City*	5.00 -	8.00

ROCKIN' R'S:

Tempus 7541 *Crazy Baby*	10.00 -	15.00

ROCKIN' SAINTS:

Decca 31144 *Cheat On Me Baby*	10.00 -	15.00

(COUNT) ROCKIN' SIDNEY/SYDNEY (& HIS ALL STARS/DUKES):

Goldband 1158, 1159, 1162, 1170	3.00 -	5.00
Jin 110 *My Little Girl*	10.00 -	15.00
156, 164, 168, 170, 174, 177	4.00 -	7.00

THE ROCK-ITS:

Spangle 2010 *It's L-O-V-E*	20.00 -	30.00

"ROCK, ROCK, ROCK"

Chess (LP) 1425 (black label) (From the motion picture; with Flamingos, Moonglows)	35.00 -	50.00

ROD & TERRY:

Cuca 1206 *That's All Right*	15.00 -	20.00

BUCK RODGERS:

Starday 245 *Little Rock Rock*	15.00 -	20.00

JIMMIE RODGERS:

Roulette 4015 *Honeycomb* (78 RPM)	15.00 -	20.00
4031 *Kisses Sweeter Than Wine* (78 RPM)	15.00 -	20.00
4045 *Oh-Oh, I'm Falling In Love Again* (78 RPM)	15.00 -	20.00
4070 *Secretly* (78 RPM)	10.00 -	15.00
4090 *Are You Really Mine* (78 RPM)	10.00 -	15.00
4116 *Bimbombey* (78 RPM)	20.00 -	30.00

TOMMY ROE & BOBBY LEE TRAMMELL:

Crown (LP) 5323 *Tommy Roe And Bobby Lee* ...	15.00 -	25.00
Judd 1022 *Sheila*	15.00 -	20.00

JESSE ROGERS:

Arcade 169 *Jump Cats Jump*	15.00 -	20.00

JIMMY ROGERS (& HIS ROCKING FOUR/TRIO):

Chess 1506 *Back Door Friend*	50.00 -	80.00
1519 *The Last Time*	50.00 -	80.00
1543 *Act Like You Love Me*	40.00 -	60.00
1574 *Sloppy Drunk*	35.00 -	50.00
1616, 1643, 1659	7.00 -	10.00
1687, 1721	5.00 -	10.00

KENNETH/KENNY ROGERS:

Carlton 454 *That Crazy Feeling*	15.00 -	20.00
Ken-Lee 102 *Jole Blon*	5.00 -	8.00
Spade—*That Crazy Feeling*	-	
We'll Always Have Each Other	-	

LELAN ROGERS:

Lynn 502 *Hold, Part 1/Part 2*	8.00 -	12.00

ROY ROGERS:

RCA Victor (LP) 1439 (& Dale Evans)	15.00 -	20.00
(LP) 3041 (10") *Souvenir Album*	15.00 -	20.00

WELDON (& WANDA) ROGERS:

Imperial 5451 *So Long, Good Luck, And Goodbye*	35.00 -	50.00
Je-Wel 103 *This Song Is Just For You*	75.00 -	100.00
104 *Women Drivers*	-	
105 *Heaven's Back Door*	-	
107 *If I Had One Day To Live*	-	
Peach 744 *If I Had One Day To Live*	-	
763 *I'm Hanging Up The Phone*	-	

ROLLING CREW:

Aladdin 3301 *Home On Alcatraz*	30.00 -	40.00

RICH ROMAN:

CG 5003 *T.T.B.*	10.00 -	15.00

ROMANCERS:

Bay-Tone 101 *You Don't Understand*	10.00 -	15.00
Celebrity 701 *No Greater Love*	8.00 -	12.00
Dootone 381 *I Still Remember*	30.00 -	40.00
404 *This Is Goodbye*	30.00 -	40.00

Linda 119 *My Heart Cries*	5.00 -	8.00
Marquee 711 *Take Me To Paradise*	5.00 -	8.00
Palette 5075 *It Only Happens With You*	7.00 -	10.00
ROMANS:		
M.M.I. 1238 *Wild Ideas*	5.00 -	8.00
ROMEOS:		
Apollo 461 *I Beg You Please*	50.00 -	75.00
Atco 6107 *Fine Fine Baby*	15.00 -	20.00
Fox 748/749 *Let's Be Partners*	30.00 -	40.00
845/846 *Moments To Remeber*	20.00 -	30.00
CHAN ROMERO:		
Del-Fi 4119 *If I Had My Way*	8.00 -	12.00
4126 *My Little Ruby*	8.00 -	12.00
RONETTES:		
Colpix (LP) 486 *The Ronettes*	40.00 -	60.00
Phillies (LP) 4006 *Presenting The Fabulous Ronettes*	50.00 -	80.00
(Note: Some copies read "Ronnettes")		
RONNIE & MARLENE:		
Westport 144 *Marlene*	10.00 -	15.00
THE ROOSTERS:		
Epic 9487 *Let's Try Again*	5.00 -	8.00
ANDY ROSE:		
Aamco 100 *Lov-A-Lov-A Love*	10.00 -	15.00
DANNY ROSS:		
Minor 107 *Look At You Go*	30.00 -	50.00
DOCTOR/DR. ROSS (& HIS JUMP & JIVE BOYS/ORBITS):		
Chess 1504 *Dr. Ross Boogie*	100.00 -	150.00
D.I.R. 101/102 *Industrial Boogie*	12.00 -	16.00
Fortune 538 *Sugar Mama*	8.00 -	12.00
857 *Cat Squirrel*	5.00 -	8.00
Hi-Q 5027 *Numbers Blues*	5.00 -	8.00
5033 *New York Breakdown*	5.00 -	8.00
Sun 193 *Come Back Baby*	100.00 -	150.00
212 *The Boogie Disease*	150.00 -	200.00
JERRY ROSS:		
Murco 1016 *Ever'body's Tryin'*	20.00 -	30.00
LEE ROSS:		
Liberty 55127 *Candy Lips*	5.00 -	8.00
PATTY ROSS:		
Aardell 107 *Rock It Davy, Rock It*	-	
BOB ROUBIAN:		
Prep 101 *Rocket To The Moon*	8.00 -	12.00
ROULETTES:		
Ebb 124 *The Way You Carry On*	15.00 -	20.00
ROVERS:		
Capitol 3078 *Why Oh-h*	15.00 -	25.00
Music City 750 *Why-Ohh* (red plastic)	35.00 -	50.00
780 *Salute To Johnny Ace*	35.00 -	50.00
792 *Whole Lot Of Love*	30.00 -	40.00
LYNN ROWE:		
Hitt 181 *Red Rover*	15.00 -	20.00
PECK ROWELL:		
Coin 101 *Take It Easy Greasy*	-	
ROXSTERS:		
Art 175 *So Long*	30.00 -	40.00
ROYALE MONARCHS:		
Dell 101 *Whole Lot Of Shakin' Goin' On*	-	
ROYAL HALOS:		
Aladdin 3460 *My Love Is True*	8.00 -	12.00
ROYAL HAWK:		
Flair 1013 *I Wonder Why*	15.00 -	20.00
ROYAL HOLIDAYS:		
Penthouse 9357 *Margaret*	15.00 -	20.00
ROYAL JESTERS:		
Cobra 2222 *Love Me*	7.00 -	10.00
ROYAL JOKERS:		
Atco 6052, 6077	8.00 -	12.00
Fortune 840 *Sweet Little Angel*	15.00 -	20.00
Hi-Q 5004 *September In The Rain*	15.00 -	20.00
ROYAL KINGS:		

Forlin 502 *Peter-Peter*	10.00 -	15.00
ROYAL KNIGHTS:		
Radio City 1001 *There's Going To Be A Wedding*	10.00 -	15.00
ROYAL LANCERS:		
Citation 5004 *Angel In My Eyes*	8.00 -	12.00
ROYAL NOTES:		
Athena 201 *Come Dance With Me*	10.00 -	15.00
Kellit 7032 *Three Speed Girl*	20.00 -	30.00
7034 *You Are My Love*	20.00 -	30.00
ROYALS:		
Federal 12064 *Every Beat Of My Heart*	150.00 -	200.00
12077 *Starting From Tonight*	200.00 -	300.00
12088 *Moonrise*	200.00 -	300.00
12098 *A Love In My Heart*	150.00 -	250.00
(Note: Any of above, pressed of colored vinyl, command even higher prices)		
12113 *Are You Forgetting*	80.00 -	100.00
12121 *The Shrine Of St. Cecilia*	40.00 -	60.00
12133 *Get It*	20.00 -	30.00
12150 *Hello Miss Fine*	15.00 -	20.00
12160 *Someone Like You*	15.00 -	20.00
12169 *Work With Me Annie*	8.00 -	12.00
ROYAL TEENS:		
ABC Paramount 9882 *Short Shorts* (78 RPM)	15.00 -	20.00
Capitol 4261 *Believe Me*	5.00 -	8.00
4335 *Was It A Dream*	8.00 -	12.00
4402 *It's The Talk Of The Town*	8.00 -	12.00
Mighty 109, 111, 112	5.00 -	8.00
Power 113 *Sittin' With My Baby*	15.00 -	20.00
215 *Short Shorts*	15.00 -	25.00
ROYALTONES:		
Old Town 1018 *Crazy Love*	20.00 -	30.00
RUBY & THE ROMANTICS:		
Kapp (most issues)	4.00 -	7.00
DON RUBY:		
Cub 9012 *Rockin' Piano, Outta Tune Guitar*	15.00 -	20.00
LAWSON RUDD:		
Harvest 709 *Shake This Town*	15.00 -	25.00
RAY RUFF:		
Bolo 741 *Pledge Of Love*	8.00 -	12.00
Lin 5034 *Beatle Maniacs*	7.00 -	10.00
5035 *I Took A Liking To You*	7.00 -	10.00
5036 *In Dreamland*	7.00 -	10.00
Norman 503 *Half-Pint Baby*	7.00 -	10.00
508 *Love Made a Fool Of You*	7.00 -	10.00
513 *Well Alright*	7.00 -	10.00
524 *My Gift To You*	7.00 -	10.00
528 *Lonely Hours*	7.00 -	10.00
539 *I'm Qualified*	7.00 -	10.00
MISTER RUFFIN:		
Spark 115 *Bring It On Back*	7.00 -	10.00
RIFF RUFFIN:		
Cash 1023 *If I Can't Have You*	5.00 -	8.00
"RUMBLE"		
Jubilee (LP) 1114 (various artists)	15.00 -	20.00
THE RUNAROUNDS/RUN-A-ROUNDS:		
Felsted 8710 *Send Her Back*	15.00 -	20.00
KC 116 *Unbelievable*	7.00 -	10.00
OTIS RUSH (& HIS BAND):		
Chess 1751, 1775	5.00 -	8.00
Cobra 5000, 5005, 5027, 5030, 5032	5.00 -	8.00
5010 *Groaning The Blues*	10.00 -	15.00
5015 *Jump Sister Bessie*	10.00 -	15.00
5023 *Three Times A Fool*	10.00 -	15.00
RUSS & THE STING-RAYS:		
Carol 102 *Do The Surf*	10.00 -	15.00
IRVIN RUSS:		
Felco 201 *Crazy Alligator*	40.00 -	60.00
BOBBY RUSSELL & THE IMPOLLOS:		
Felsted 8520 *She's Gonna Be Sorry*	5.00 -	8.00
TED RUSSELL:		
Terock 1000 *Bright Lights*	7.00 -	10.00

MIKE RUSSO:
Crosley 218 *I'm Gonna Knock On Your Door* ... 8.00 - 12.00
CATHY RYAN & THE ADMIRALS:
King 4792 *It's A Sad, Sad Feeling* .... 10.00 - 15.00
CHARLEY RYAN:
4-Star 1749 *Hot Rod Guitar* .... 8.00 - 12.00
Souvenir 101 *Hot Rod Lincoln* .... 20.00 - 30.00
BOBBY RYDELL:
Cameo 160, 164 .... 7.00 - 10.00
Cameo (LP) 1006 *We Got Love* .... 35.00 - 50.00
(LP) 1007 *Bobby Sings, Bobby Swings* .... 20.00 - 30.00
(LP) 1009 *Bobby's Biggest Hits* .... 20.00 - 30.00
JUNIOR RYDER AND THE PEACOCKS:
Duke 119 *Sad Story* .... 15.00 - 25.00
FORREST RYE:
Fortune 172 *Wild Cat Boogie* .... 10.00 - 15.00
RYTHM ROCKERS (See RHYTHM ROCKERS)
SABRES:
Cal-West 45847 *Always Forever* .... 40.00 - 70.00
Gala 114 *Hot Rod Kelly* .... 40.00 - 60.00
Kil-Mac 1412 *Take Up The Slack, Daddy-O* ..... 15.00 - 20.00
THE SAFARIS:
Eldo 101 *Image Of A Girl* .... 8.00 - 12.00
105 *Summer Nights* .... 10.00 - 15.00
110 *In The Still On The Night* .... 10.00 - 15.00
113 *Garden Of Love* .... 10.00 - 15.00
DOUG SAHM (& THE MARKAYS/ PHAROAHS/DELL-KINGS): (See also LITTLE DOUG)
Harlem 107 *Why, Why, Why* .... 10.00 - 15.00
108 *Baby Tell Me* .... 15.00 - 20.00
113 *Slow Down* .... 15.00 - 20.00
116 *Sapphire* (possibly unissued) ....
Renner 212 *Big Hat* .... 10.00 - 15.00
215 *Crazy Crazy Feeling* .... 15.00 - 20.00
226 *Two Hearts In Love* .... 10.00 - 15.00
232 *Little Angel* .... 10.00 - 15.00
240 *Lucky Me* .... 10.00 - 15.00
247 *Mister Kool* .... 15.00 - 20.00
Satin 100 *Crazy Daisy* .... 30.00 - 40.00
Warrior 507 *Crazy Daisy* .... 50.00 - 75.00
SAIGONS:
Dootone 375 *You're Heavenly* .... 50.00 - 75.00
SAILOR BOY:
Dig 116 *Country Home* .... 15.00 - 20.00
126 *What Have I Done Wrong* .... 15.00 - 20.00
NICKY ST. CLAIR (See THE FIVE TROJANS)
ST. LOUIS JIMMY:
Duke 110 *Drinkin' Woman* .... 50.00 - 75.00
Herald 407 *Hard Luck Boogie* .... 75.00 - 100.00
Parrot 823 *Murder In The First Degree* ..... 40.00 - 60.00
ST. LOUIS MAC:
Bea & Baby 113 *Broken Heart* .... 8.00 - 12.00
MAC SALES:
Meteor 5022 *A Gal Named Joe* (red label) ...... 20.00 - 30.00
SAMMY SALVO:
Imperial 5615 *Marble Heart* .... 5.00 - 8.00
SAM THE SHAM & THE PHAROAHS:
XL 906 *Wooly Bully* .... 15.00 - 20.00
SAMMY & THE DEL-LARKS:
En-Jay 100 *I Never Will Forget* .... 10.00 - 15.00
CLARENCE SAMUELS:
Apt 25028 *We're Going To The Hop* .... 8.00 - 12.00
Excello 2093 *Chicken Hearted Woman* .... 10.00 - 15.00
Lamp 8004 *Crazy With The Heart* .... 10.00 - 15.00
8005 *Lightnin' Struck Me* .... 10.00 - 15.00
CURLEY SANDERS (& THE SANTONES):
Concept *Walking Blues* .... 15.00 - 20.00
Jamboree 509 *Brand New Rock & Roll* .... 15.00 - 20.00
HANK SANDERS:
Crest 1039 *How Much How Much* .... 15.00 - 20.00

SLIM SANDERS:
V-M 612 *All My Love* .... 10.00 - 15.00
WILLIS SANDERS & THE EMBERS:
Juno 215 *I'll Be With You* .... -
Jupiter 213 *Taking A Chance On You* .... 15.00 - 20.00
SANDMEN: (See also CHUCK WILLIS)
Okeh 7052 *Somebody To Love* .... 15.00 - 20.00
TOMMY SANDS:
RCA Victor 5435 *Love Pains* .... 7.00 - 10.00
5800 *Don't Drop It* .... 5.00 - 8.00
FRANK SANDY & THE JACKALS:
MGM 12678 *Let's Go Rock 'N' Roll* .... 15.00 - 20.00
RALPH SANFORD:
King 1403 *Oo-Ee-Baby* .... 7.00 - 10.00
JOHNNY SARDO:
Chock Full Of Hits 104 *Romance In The Dark* .. 15.00 - 20.00
Hip Hop Take A Ride With Me .... -
Warner Bros. 5014 *I Wanna Rock* .... 8.00 - 12.00
SATELLITES:
Class 234 *Heavenly Angel* .... 8.00 - 12.00
Cupid 5004 *Linda Jean* .... 25.00 - 35.00
Malynn 234 *Heavenly Angel* .... 15.00 - 20.00
SATINTONES:
Motown 1000 *My Beloved* .... 30.00 - 40.00
1006 *A Love That Can Never Be* .... 30.00 - 50.00
1006 *Angel* .... -
(Note: #1006 occurs with different titles, of which "Angel" is scarcer)
1020 *Zing Went The Strings Of My Heart* ... 50.00 - 80.00
SATISFACTIONS:
Chesapeake *We Will Walk Together* .... 7.00 - 10.00
SAUCERS:
Felco 104 *Why Do I Dream* .... 15.00 - 20.00
Kick 100 *Hi-Oom* .... 20.00 - 30.00
Lynne 101 *Hello Darling* .... 15.00 - 20.00
LITTLE BUTCHIE SAUNDERS & HIS BUDDIES:
Herald 485, 491 .... 7.00 - 10.00
DUKE SAVAGE & ARRIBINS:
Argo 5346 *Your Love* .... 5.00 - 8.00
ASHTON SAVOY & HIS COMBO:
Hollywood 1081 *Juke Joint* .... 15.00 - 20.00
SAVOYS:
Combo 75 *Darling Stay With Me* .... 25.00 - 35.00
81 *Evil Ways* .... 20.00 - 30.00
Combo 90 *Chip Chop Boom* .... 15.00 - 25.00
Savoy 1188 *Say You're Mine* .... 8.00 - 12.00
Tip Top 1008 *Sweetheart Darling* .... 60.00 - 90.00
HENRY SAWYER & THE JUPITERS:
Planet-X 9621 *It Takes Two* .... -
RAY SAWYER:
Sandy 1030 *Rockin' Satellite* .... 10.00 - 15.00
SAXONS:
Contender 1313 *Is It True* .... 25.00 - 35.00
Tampa 139 *My Love Is True* .... 10.00 - 15.00
ALONZO SCALES:
Wing 90020 *My Baby Likes To Shuffle* .... 15.00 - 25.00
90049 *Hard Luck Child* .... 15.00 - 25.00
SCALE-TONES:
Jay-Dee 810 *Everlasting Love* .... 20.00 - 30.00
SCAMPS:
Peacock 1655 *Yes, My Baby* .... 15.00 - 20.00
SCARLETS:
Cine Vista 1001 *Joannie* .... 8.00 - 12.00
Fury 1036 *Truly Yours* .... 10.00 - 15.00
Klik 7905 *She's Gone* .... 10.00 - 15.00
Red Robin 128 *Dear One* .... 75.00 - 100.00
133 *Love Doll* .... 75.00 - 100.00
135 *True Love* .... 75.00 - 100.00
138 *Kiss Me* .... 75.00 - 100.00
MURRAY SCHAFF'S ARISTOCRATS:
Essex 366 *Believe Me* .... -

Sound 101 *Believe Me*	-	

STEVE SCHICKEL:

Mercury 70999 *Leave My Sideburns Be*	8.00 -	12.00

TYRONE SCHMIDLING:

Andex 4022 *Honey Don't*	35.00 -	50.00

THE SCHOLARS:

Imperial 5449 *Beloved*	5.00 -	8.00

SCHOOLBOY CLEVE:

Feature 3013 *Strange Letter Blues*	35.00 -	50.00

SCHOOLBOYS:

Juanita 103 *Angel Of Love*	8.00 -	12.00
Okeh 7076 *Shirley*	10.00 -	15.00
7085 *Mary*	10.00 -	15.00
7090 *Pearl*	10.00 -	15.00

DUANE SCHURB:

Enterprise 1226 *Rolly Polly*	15.00 -	20.00

STEVE SCHULTE:

Felsted 8502 *Too Blue To Cry*	7.00 -	10.00

SCOOTERS:

Dawn 224 *Someday We'll Meet Again*	15.00 -	25.00

SCOTT BROTHERS:

Fabor 117 *Yuggi Duggi*	5.00 -	8.00

JACK SCOTT:

ABC Paramount 9818 *Baby She's Gone*	30.00 -	50.00
9860 *Two Timin' Woman*	30.00 -	50.00
Capitol (LP) 2035 *Burning Bridges*	40.00 -	60.00
Carlton (LP) 107 *Jack Scott*	50.00 -	80.00
(LP) 122 *What Am I Living For*	50.00 -	80.00
462, 483, 504, 514, 519	4.00 -	8.00
(EP) 1070, 1071 *Presenting Jack Scott*	30.00 -	40.00
(EP) 1072 *Jack Scott Sings*	30.00 -	40.00
Groove 58-0031, 58-0037, 58-0042	5.00 -	10.00
Guaranteed 211 *Go Wild Little Sadie*	7.00 -	10.00
Jubilee 5606 *My Special Angel*	4.00 -	7.00
Sesac (LP) 4201/4202 *Soul Stirring*	-	
Top Rank (LP) 319, 619 *I Remember Hank*		
Williams	50.00 -	75.00
Top Rank (LP) 326, 626 *What In The World's*		
Come Over You	50.00 -	75.00
2055, 2075, 2093	3.00 -	6.00

MABEL SCOTT:

Parrot 780 *Mabel's Blues* (red plastic)	30.00 -	40.00

RAY SCOTT (& THE SHADES):

Erwin 700 *Boppin' Wigwam Willie*	75.00 -	100.00
Satellite 104 *You Drive Me Crazy*	80.00 -	120.00
Stomper Time *High Heel Sneakers*	-	
1161 *Boy Meets Girl*	30.00 -	50.00
Tri Ess 1001 *We Need Love*	7.00 -	10.00

RODNEY SCOTT:

Canon 225 *Granny Went Rockin'*	35.00 -	50.00
231 *You're So Square*	35.00 -	50.00

SANDY SCOTT:

Choice 5606 *Shake It Up*	15.00 -	20.00

SHEREE SCOTT:

Robbins 101 *Whole Lotta Shakin'*	20.00 -	30.00
Sherree Heart 1479 *Easy Payments*	20.00 -	30.00

TOMMY SCOTT:

Federal 10003 *Rockin' And Rollin'*	10.00 -	15.00
10011 *Tennessee*	10.00 -	15.00

LEVI SEABURY:

Blues Boy Kingdom 101 *Boogie Beat*	40.00 -	60.00

EDDIE SEACREST:

KRC 5001 *Shakin' With A Flavor*	15.00 -	20.00

THE SEARCHERS:

Class 223 *Wow Wow Baby*	7.00 -	10.00

KELLY SEARS:

Quintet 104 *Barnyard Rock*	5.00 -	8.00

DICK SEATON:

K-Ark *Juke Box Rock*	15.00 -	20.00

SEBASTIAN:

Take 30 2002 *Darling I Do*	7.00 -	10.00

SECRETS:

Decca 30350 *See You Next Year*	5.00 -	8.00

NEIL SEDAKA:

Decca 30520 *Laura Lee*	10.00 -	15.00
Guyden 2004 *Ring-A-Rockin'*	10.00 -	15.00
Legion 133 *Ring-A-Rockin'*	15.00 -	20.00
RCA Victor (EP) 433 *I Go Ape*	30.00 -	50.00
RCA Victor 7473 *I Go Ape*	8.00 -	12.00

THE SEDATES:

Port 70004 *I Found*	8.00 -	12.00

ALVIE SELF:

Don-Ray 5960 *Let' Go Wild*	15.00 -	20.00

JIMMY SELF:

Coral 62009 *Oh Babe*	8.00 -	12.00

RONNIE SELF:

ABC Paramount 9714 *Pretty Bad Blues*	35.00 -	50.00
9768 *Sweet Love*	35.00 -	50.00
Columbia (EP) 2149 *Ain't I'm A Dog*	80.00 -	120.00
40875 *Big Fool*	15.00 -	20.00
40989 *Ain't I'm A Dog*	10.00 -	15.00
41101 *Bop-A-Lena*	10.00 -	15.00
41166 *Date Bate*	15.00 -	20.00
41241 *Petrified*	20.00 -	30.00
Decca 30958, 31131	3.00 -	5.00

STEWART SELF:

Starrett 5709 *Mary Ellen*	8.00 -	12.00

JOHNNY SELLERS:

Chance 1120 *Rock Me In The Cradle*	40.00 -	60.00
1123 *Mighty Lonesome*	40.00 -	60.00
1138 *Mirror Blues*	40.00 -	60.00
King 4498 *Don't Knock At My Door*	15.00 -	20.00
4567 *Heavyweight Mama*	15.00 -	20.00

SENATORS:

Golden Crest 514 *Loretta*	7.00 -	10.00
Winn 1917 *Wedding Bells*	7.00 -	10.00

SENIORS:

Excello 2130 *Why Did You Leave Me*	20.00 -	30.00
Interlude 163 *It's Been A Long Time*	-	
Tetra 4446 *Evening Shadows Falling*	35.00 -	50.00

CHARLES SENNS:

OJ 1014 *Gee Whiz Liz*	20.00 -	30.00

SENSATIONS:

Argo (LP) 4022 *Let Me In*	20.00 -	30.00
Argo 5391 *A Part Of Me*	5.00 -	8.00
Atco 6056, 6067, 6090	7.00 -	10.00

SENTIMENTALS:

Checker 875 *I Want To Love You*	15.00 -	20.00
Mint 802 *Wedding Bells*	7.00 -	10.00
803 *I'm Your Fool Always*	7.00 -	10.00

SEQUINS:

Red Robin 140 *Don't Fall In Love*	35.00 -	50.00

SERENADERS:

Chock-Full-Of-Hits 102 *I Wrote A Letter*	50.00 -	75.00
De Luxe 6022 *Please, Please Forgive Me*	75.00 -	100.00
J V-B 2001 *Tomorrow Night*	75.00 -	100.00
M-G-M 12623 *Never Let Me Go*	30.00 -	40.00
12666 *Give Me A Girl*	30.00 -	40.00
Red Robin 115 *I Want To Love You Baby*	75.00 -	100.00
Riverside 4549 *Two Lovers Make One Fool*	10.00 -	15.00
Swing Time 347 *Ain't Gonna Cry No More*	75.00 -	100.00
Teen Life 9 *Gates Of Gold*	60.00 -	80.00
V.I.P. 25002 *I'll Cry Tomorrow*	15.00 -	20.00

SEVILLES:

Galaxy 721 *Charlena*	5.00 -	8.00
J-C 116 *Charlena*	7.00 -	10.00

SHADOWS:

Decca 48307 *Tell Her*	50.00 -	75.00
48322 *Better Than Gold*	40.00 -	60.00
Del-Fi 4109 *Under The Stars Of Love*	10.00 -	15.00
Delta 1509 *There Stands The Glass*	30.00 -	40.00

SHAKEY JAKE:

Artistic 1502 *Roll Your Money Maker*	10.00 -	15.00
The Blues 303 *Respect Me Baby*	7.00 -	10.00

DEL SHANNON:

Big Top (LP) 1303 *Runaway*	30.00 -	50.00
Big Top (LP) *Runaway* (STEREO)	100.00 -	Up
(LP) 1308 *Little Town Flirt*	30.00 -	50.00

SHANTONS:

Jay-Mar 164 *Lover's March*	15.00 -	20.00
241 *Lucille*	15.00 -	20.00
Pam 112 *Why Don't You Believe Me*	15.00 -	20.00

SHARPS:

Aladdin 3401 *What Will I Gain*	10.00 -	15.00
Chess 1690 *6 Months, Three Weeks*	10.00 -	15.00
Combo 146 *All My Love*	15.00 -	20.00
Dot 15806 *All My Love*	10.00 -	15.00
Jamie 1040 *Come On*	10.00 -	15.00
1108 *Look At Me*	10.00 -	15.00
1114 *Here's My Heart*	10.00 -	15.00
Lamp 2007 *Lock My Heart*	15.00 -	20.00
2 Mikes 101 *Heaven Only Knows*	80.00 -	120.00
Vik 0264 *Come On*	10.00 -	15.00

THE SHARP TONES:

Post 2009 *Since I Fell For You*	100.00 -	Up

LAWRENCE SHAUL:

Reed 1049 *Tutti Frutti*	20.00 -	30.00

SHA-WEEZ:

Aladdin 3170 *No One To Love Me*	150.00 -	250.00

THE SH-BOOMS:

Cat 117 *Could It Be*	8.00 -	12.00

JERRY SHEELY & THE VERSATILES:

Star 220 *Love Only Me*		

THE SHEIKS (See SHIEKS) JIM SHELBY:

Barton 409 *I'm A Long Gone Daddy*	10.00 -	15.00
LeGrand 1013 *Why Should I Dance*		

THE SHELLS:

Johnson 104 *Baby Oh Baby*	10.00 -	15.00
107 *Explain It To Me*	7.00 -	10.00
109 *Better Forget Him*	7.00 -	10.00
110 *In The Dim Light Of Dark*	7.00 -	10.00
119 *Deep In My Heart*	7.00 -	10.00

GARY SHELTON:

Mark 143 *Goodbye Little Darlin' Goodbye*	30.00 -	40.00
Mercury 71310 *Kissin' At The Drive-In*	8.00 -	12.00

ROSCOE SHELTON:

Excello 2146, 2167, 2170, 2176, 2181, 2192, 2198	3.00 -	5.00
(LP) 8002 *Roscoe Shelton*	15.00 -	20.00

SHEP & THE LIMELITES:

Hull (LP) 1001 *Our Anniversary*	75.00 -	100.00

BUDDY SHEPPARD:

Sabina 510 *That Background Sound*	8.00 -	12.00

THE SHEPPARDS:

Apex 7750 *Never Felt This Way Before*	8.00 -	12.00
7760 *Just Like You*	8.00 -	12.00
7762 *Tragic*	8.00 -	12.00
PAM 1001 *Never Let Me Go*	15.00 -	20.00
Theron 112 *Love*	100.00 -	150.00
United 198 *Sherry*	75.00 -	100.00
Wes 7750 *The Glitter In Your Eyes*	7.00 -	10.00

TONY SHERIDAN & THE BEAT BROTHERS:

Decca 31382 *My Bonnie/The Saints*	300.00 -	Up

(Note: Prices as high as $1000.00 have been quoted for this Beatle record! Promotional copies are commoner than regular commercial copies.)

SHERIFF & REVELS:

Vee Jay 306 *Shambalor*	10.00 -	15.00

SHERMAN & THE DARTS:

Fury 1014 *Remember (It's Only You And I)*	15.00 -	20.00

BILL(Y) SHERRELL/SHERRILL (& THE DELL TONES):

Mercury 71679 *Like Makin' Love*	5.00 -	8.00
See 1005 *Hear Her Rave On*	15.00 -	20.00
Tyme 102 *Cadillac Baby*	30.00 -	50.00
104 *Kool Kat*	40.00 -	60.00

106 *Rock On Baby*	30.00 -	50.00

SHERWOODS:

Johnson 121 *Sneakin' Around*	10.00 -	15.00
Magnifico 105 *Happy Holiday*	7.00 -	10.00

SHIEKS:

Cat 116 *Walk That Walk*	7.00 -	10.00
Ef-N-De 100 *Baby Please Don't Cry* (red label)	100.00 -	150.00
Federal 12237 *Sentimental Heart*	15.00 -	20.00
12355 *Sentimental Heart*	10.00 -	15.00

SHIELDS:

Dot 15856 *I'm Sorry Now*	10.00 -	15.00
Falcon 100 *You'll Be Coming Home Soon*		-
Tender 513 *You Cheated*	10.00 -	15.00
Tender 521 *Play The Game Fair*	10.00 -	15.00

THE SHINDIGS:

Mustang 3003 *Wolfman*	7.00 -	10.00

REESE SHIPLEY:

Valley 106 *Catfish Boogie*	8.00 -	12.00

SHIRELLES:

Decca 30669 *My Love Is A Charm*	8.00 -	12.00
30761 *I Got The Message*	8.00 -	12.00
Scepter (LP) 501 *Tonight's The Night*	50.00 -	75.00
(LP) 504 *Baby It's You*	30.00 -	50.00
Scepter (LP) 507 *Greatest Hits*	15.00 -	20.00
Scepter 1203 *Dedicated To The One I Love*	10.00 -	15.00
1205 *A Teardrop and a Lollipop*	10.00 -	15.00
1208 *Tonight's The Night* (pink & black label)	10.00 -	15.00
1211 *Will You Love Me Tomorrow*	10.00 -	15.00
(Note: Above are white label)		
1220 *A Thing of the Past*	8.00 -	12.00
Scepter (most other issues)	5.00 -	8.00
Tiara 6112 *I Met Him On on a Sunday*	35.00 -	50.00

SHIRLEY & LEE:

Aladdin (LP) 807 *Let The Good Times Roll*	125.00 -	200.00
Aladdin 3153 *I'm Gone*	15.00 -	20.00
3173 *Baby*	15.00 -	20.00
3192 *So In Love*	15.00 -	20.00
3205 *The Proposal*	10.00 -	15.00
3222 *Lee Goofed*	10.00 -	15.00
3244 *Confessin'*	10.00 -	15.00
3289 *Feel So Good*	8.00 -	12.00
3302 *Lee's Dream*	8.00 -	12.00
3318, 3325, 3338, 3362, 3369, 3380, 3390	5.00 -	10.00
Imperial (LP) 9179 *Let The Good Times Roll*	40.00 -	60.00
Score (LP) 4023 *Let The Good Times Roll*	60.00 -	90.00
Warwick (LP) 2028 *Let The Good Times Roll*	30.00 -	50.00

RUFUS SHOFFNER:

American Artist *Orbit Twist*	35.00 -	50.00

THE SHONDELLS (See TOMMY JAMES):

SHOWCASES:

Galaxy 732 *This Love Is Real*	— -	—

HAROLD SHUTTERS:

Golden Rod 204 *Rock 'N' Roll Mr. Moon*	75.00 -	100.00
300 *Bunny Honey*	75.00 -	100.00

SHYTANS:

Bruce 110 *Skokiann*	7.00 -	10.00

JERRY SIEFERT:

Note 10018 *Dirty White Bucks And The Tight Peg Pants*	15.00 -	20.00

SILHOUETTES:

Ace 552 *I Sold My Heart To The Junkman*	8.00 -	12.00
Ember 1029, 1032	5.00 -	10.00
1029 *Get A Job* (78 RPM)	15.00 -	25.00
1032 *Headin' For The Poorhouse* (78 RPM)	7.00 -	10.00
Ember 1037 *Bing Bong*	10.00 -	15.00
Junior 391 *Get A Job*	35.00 -	50.00
Junior 396 *I Sold My Heart To The Junkman*	15.00 -	20.00
400 *Evelyn*	15.00 -	20.00
593 *Get A Job*	30.00 -	40.00
(Note: Above should have brown label.)		
20th Fox 240 *Never*	10.00 -	15.00

BOB SILVA:

Monarch *Weepin' And Wailin'*	—	—

SID SILVER:
Bakersfield 510 *Bumble Rumble*	8.00 -	12.00

JOHNNIE SILVERS:
Sims 111 *Tuff Stuff* (blue label)	10.00 -	15.00

SILVERTONES:
Joey 302 *Canadian Sunset*	15.00 -	20.00

AL SIMMONS:
Dig 138 *Old Folks Boogie*	12.00 -	16.00
142 *You Ain't Too Old*	12.00 -	16.00

GENE SIMMONS:
Sun 299 *Dunkin' Wine*	30.00 -	50.00

MACK SIMMONS & HIS BOYS:
C.J. 607 *Jumping At The Cadillac*	5.00 -	8.00

FRANK SIMON:
4 Star 1647 *Sugar Plum Boogie*	8.00 -	12.00

JERRY SIMMS:
RCA Victor 7483 *Dancing With a Memory*	7.00 -	10.00

DONALD SIMPSON & THE ROCKENETTES:
Major 1002 *Save Me Your Love*	50.00 -	80.00

HOKE SIMPSON:
Colonial 530 *Number One*	8.00 -	12.00

CHUCK SIMS:
Trend 30-000 *Little Pigeon*	7.00 -	10.00

FRANKIE LEE SIMS:
Ace 524, 527, 539	7.00 -	10.00
Speciality 459 *Lucy Mae Blues*	10.00 -	15.00
478 *I'm Long Gone*	10.00 -	15.00
487 *I'll Get Along Somehow*	10.00 -	15.00
(LP) 2124 *Lucy Mae Blues*	10.00 -	15.00
Vin 1006 *Well Goodbye Baby*	5.00 -	8.00

MAC SIMS:
Pacer 1201 *Drivin' Wheel*	8.00 -	12.00

BEAD SINGLETON & THE NOTES:
Stentor 101 *Shrine Of Echoes*	15.00 -	20.00

CHARLIE SINGLETON:
Decca 48193 *Alligator Meat*	10.00 -	15.00

EDDIE SINGLETON & THE CHROMATICS:
Brunswick 55080 *Too Late*	15.00 -	25.00

BOBBY SISCO:
Chess 1650 *Go, Go, Go*	35.00 -	50.00
Mar-Vel 111 *Honky Tonkin Rhythm*	30.00 -	40.00

GENE SISCO:
Dess 7001 *Grandma Rock And Roll*	20.00 -	30.00

SIX TEENS:
Flip 315, 322, 326	7.00 -	10.00
315 *A Casual Look* (78 RPM)	10.00 -	15.00

SKEE BROTHERS:
Epic 9275 *Big Deal*	15.00 -	20.00
Okeh 7108 *That's All She Wrote*	15.00 -	20.00

EDDIE SKELTON:
Dixie 2011 *Keep It Swinging*	50.00 -	75.00
Starday 294 *My Heart Gets Lonely*	20.00 -	30.00
315 *That's Love*	20.00 -	30.00

BILL SKIDMORE III:
Crest 1040 *Date Bait*	10.00 -	15.00

MACY (SKIP) SKIPPER:
Light 2020 *Who Put The Squeeze*	15.00 -	25.00

NORM SKYLAR:
Crest 104 *Rock 'N' Roll Blues*	20.00 -	30.00

SKYLARKS:
Decca 48241 *You And I*	80.00 -	120.00

THE SKYLINERS:
Calico 103, 109, 117	7.00 -	10.00
(LP) 3000 *The Skyliners*	75.00 -	100.00
Colpix 188 *I'll Close My Eyes*	10.00 -	15.00

THE SKYSCRAPERS:
Mercury 70795 *I Thought You'd Care*	20.00 -	30.00

FREDDIE SLACK:
Wing (LP) 60003 *Boogie Woogie On The 88*	20.00 -	30.00

SLADES:
Domino 500 *You Cheated*	10.00 -	15.00

800 *You Gambled*	12.00 -	16.00
901 *Just You*	15.00 -	20.00
Liberty 55118 *Baby*	7.00 -	10.00

SLICK SLAVIN:
Imperial 5540 *Speed Crazy*	8.00 -	12.00

SLIM HARPO (See HARPO)

SLY FOX:
Spark 108 *Hoo-Doo Say*	20.00 -	30.00
112 *My Four Women*	20.00 -	30.00

SMART TONES:
Herald 529 *Bob-O-Link*	10.00 -	15.00

AL SMITH:
Goldband 1092 *If I Don't See You*	5.00 -	8.00

ARTHUR SMITH:
MGM (LP) 236 (10") *Foolish Questions*	40.00 -	60.00
(LP) 533 (10") *Fingers On Fire*	40.00 -	60.00
(LP) 3301 (10") *Specials*	40.00 -	60.00
(LP) 3525 *Fingers On Fire*	40.00 -	60.00
12544 *Teen-Aged Rebel*	10.00 -	15.00

BILLY SMITH:
Red Head *Tell Me Baby*	—	—

BOBBY SMITH (& SPINNERS):
Fox 104 *She's Gone From Me*	15.00 -	20.00
Tri-Phi 1018 *She Don't Love Me*	5.00 -	8.00

BUDDY SMITH:
Hanover 4533 *Tennessee*	8.00 -	12.00

CARL SMITH:
Columbia (LP) 959 *Sunday Down South*	12.00 -	18.00
(LP) 1022 *Smith's The Name*	12.00 -	18.00
(LP) 1172 *Let's Live A Little*	10.00 -	15.00
(LP) 2579 (10")	25.00 -	35.00
(LP) 9023 (10") *Soft And Tenderly*	25.00 -	35.00
(LP) 9025 (10") *Sentimental Songs*	25.00 -	35.00
(EP) 9591, 10222	8.00 -	12.00

CHESTER SMITH:
Decca 30603 *You Gotta Move*	8.00 -	12.00

DAPPA SMITH:
Peach 709 *China Doll*	—	—

DAYTON SMITH:
Warrior 501 *What Will The Answer Be*	10.00 -	15.00

FLOYD SMITH & THE MONTCLAIRS:
Fortune 540 *This Is A Miracle*	7.00 -	10.00

GENE SMITH:
Rem 458 *I'm Gone*	15.00 -	20.00

(LITTLE) GEORGE SMITH (& HIS HARMONICA):
Carolyn 1420 *Nobody Knows*	7.00 -	10.00
J&M 001 *Go Ahead On Women*	25.00 -	35.00
RPM 434 *Telephone Blues*	15.00 -	20.00
442 *Blues Stay Away*	15.00 -	20.00
456 *Love Life*	15.00 -	20.00
478 *You Don't Love Me*	10.00 -	15.00

HANK SMITH & ROCKATUNES:
Rock-A-Tune 1012 *Rock 'n' Roll Hep Cat*	40.00 -	60.00

HENRY SMITH:
Dot 1220 *Good Rocking Mama*	25.00 -	40.00

HUEY (PIANO) SMITH & HIS CLOWNS:
Ace (EP) 104 *Having Fun With Huey Smith*	10.00 -	15.00
530 *Rocking Pneumonia & The Boogie Woogie Flu* (78 RPM)	15.00 -	20.00
538 *Just A Lonely Clown* (78 RPM)	8.00 -	12.00
(LP) 1004 *Having A Good Time*	30.00 -	40.00
(LP) 1015 *For Dancing*	30.00 -	40.00
(LP) 1027 *'Twas The Night Before Christmas*	35.00 -	50.00
8008 *Quiet As It's Kept*	—	—

KENNY SMITH:
Rural Rhythm 507 *Walkin' By My Lonesome*	20.00 -	30.00

L.C. SMITH & THE SOUTHERN PLAYBOYS:
Wango (unnumbered) *Radio Boogie*	35.00 -	50.00

LENDON SMITH with THE JESTERS:
Meteor 5030 *Lost Love*	20.00 -	30.00

MACK ALLEN SMITH:

Statue 602 *Such A Night*	5.00 -	8.00
607 *Mean Old Frisco*	5.00 -	8.00

RAY SMITH: (See also PAT CUPP)

Infinity 007 *Let Yourself Go*	5.00 -	8.00
Judd (LP) 701 *Travelin' With Ray*	75.00 -	100.00
Sun 298 *Right Behind You Baby*	15.00 -	20.00
308 *Why Why Why*	7.00 -	10.00
319 *Rockin' Bandit*	7.00 -	10.00
372 *Travelin' Salesman*	5.00 -	8.00
375 *Candy Doll*	5.00 -	8.00
Tollie 9029 *Did We Have A Party*	8.00 -	12.00

ROBERT CURTIS SMITH:

Bluesville (LP) 1064 *Clarksville Blues*	15.00 -	25.00

RONNIE/RONNY SMITH:

Brunswick 55137 *Lookie, Lookie, Lookie*	8.00 -	12.00
Hamilton 50003 *My Babe*	7.00 -	10.00
Imperial 5667 *Long Time No Love*	7.00 -	10.00
5679 *I Hear You Knocking*	7.00 -	10.00

SAMMY SMITH:

Wee Rebel 102 *Alaska Rock*	30.00 -	40.00

SHELBY SMITH:

Rebel 728 *Rockin' Mama*	15.00 -	20.00
Smitty 55783 *What's On Your Mind*	100.00 -	150.00

WARREN SMITH:

Sun 239 *Rock 'N' Roll Ruby*	15.00 -	20.00
250 *Ubangi Stomp*	15.00 -	20.00
268 *Miss Froggie*	7.00 -	10.00
286 *I've Got Love If You Want It*	10.00 -	15.00
314 *Sweet Sweet Girl*	7.00 -	10.00

LONNIE SMITHSON:

Starday 330 *Me And The Blues*	15.00 -	25.00

SMOKEY JOE:

Flip 228 *Signifying Monkey*	30.00 -	40.00
Sun 228 *Signifying Monkey*	35.00 -	50.00

SMOOTHTONES:

Jem 412 *Bring Back Your Love To Me*	30.00 -	50.00

SMOKEY SMOTHERS:

Federal 12385, 12395, 12405, 12420, 12441, 12466, 12488, 12503	3.00 -	6.00
King (LP) 779	40.00 -	60.00

THE SNAPPERS:

20th Fox 148 *If There Were*	10.00 -	15.00

LESLIE SNEED:

Cascade 103 *Oh, Baby Doll*	10.00 -	15.00

EDDIE SNOW:

Sun 226 *Ain't That Right*	50.00 -	80.00

HANK SNOW:

RCA Victor (LP) 1113 *Just Keep A-Movin'*	15.00 -	25.00
(LP) 1156 *Old Doc Brown*	20.00 -	30.00
(LP) 1233 *Country Classics*	15.00 -	20.00
(LP) 1419 *Country & Western Jamboree*	15.00 -	20.00
(LP) 1435 *Country Guitar Vol. 2*	15.00 -	20.00
(LP) 3026 (10") *Hank Snow*	20.00 -	30.00
(LP) 3070 (10") *Hank Snow Sings*	15.00 -	25.00
(LP) 3131 (10") *Hank Snow Salutes Jimmy Rodgers*	20.00 -	30.00
(LP) 3267 (10") *Country Guitar*	15.00 -	25.00

THE SOLATAIRES/SOLITAIRES:

Argo 5316 *Please Kiss This Letter*	8.00 -	12.00
Old Town 1000 *Blue Valentine*	75.00 -	100.00
1003 *If I Loved You*	50.00 -	75.00
1006 *Please Remember My Heart*	75.00 -	100.00
1006/1007 *Please Remember My Heart*	75.00 -	100.00
(Note: Later issues have #1006 on both sides)		
Old Town 1008 *Lonely*	75.00 -	100.00
1010 *I Don't Stand A Ghost Of A Chance*	75.00 -	100.00
1012 *My Dear*	50.00 -	75.00
1014 *The Wedding*	35.00 -	50.00
1015 *Magic Rose*	35.00 -	50.00
1019 *The Honeymoon*	35.00 -	50.00
1026 *The Angels Sang*	25.00 -	35.00
1032 *Give Me, One More Chance*	25.00 -	35.00

1034 *Please Kiss This Letter*	20.00 -	30.00
1044 *I Really Love You So*	20.00 -	30.00
1049 *No More Sorrows*	15.00 -	20.00
1059 *Please Remember My Heart*	15.00 -	20.00
1066 *Embraceable You*	15.00 -	20.00
1071 *Light A Candle In The Chapel*	15.00 -	20.00
1096 *Lonesome Lover*	10.00 -	15.00
1139 *The Time Is Here*	10.00 -	15.00

KING SOLOMON:

Big Town 102 *Mean Train*	15.00 -	20.00

SOLOTONES:

Excello 2060 *Front Page Blues*	35.00 -	50.00

SONICS:

Checker 922 *You Made Me Cry*	7.00 -	10.00
Groove 0112 *As I Live On*	30.00 -	40.00
Harvard 801 *This Broken Heart*	15.00 -	20.00
X-Tra #107 *Once In A Lifetime*	40.00 -	60.00

SONNETS:

Herald 477 *Please Won't You Call Me*	15.00 -	20.00

SONNY GUITAR:

Yucca 136 *Betty Lou*	8.00 -	12.00

SONS OF THE PIONEERS:

Camden (LP) *413 Wagons West*	8.00 -	12.00
RCA Victor (LP) 1130 *Favorites*	10.00 -	15.00
(LP) 1431 *How Great Thou Art*	10.00 -	15.00
(LP) 1483 *One Man's Songs*	10.00 -	15.00
(LP) 3032 (10")	15.00 -	20.00
(LP) 3095 (10")	15.00 -	20.00
(LP) 3162 (10") *Western Classics*	15.00 -	20.00

SOOTHERS:

Part 70041 *I Believe In You*	7.00 -	10.00

THE SOPHOMORES:

Dawn 216 *Cool Cool Baby*	10.00 -	15.00
218 *I Get A Thrill*	10.00 -	15.00
Epic 9259 *Charade*	7.00 -	10.00

THE SOUL STIRRERS featuring SAM COOKE:

Specialty (LP) 2106	15.00 -	25.00

SOUNDS:

Modern 981 *Sweet Sixteen*	15.00 -	20.00
Sarg 172 *Life*	10.00 -	15.00
181 *My Pillow Of Dreams*	10.00 -	15.00

SOUVENIERS:

Inferno 2001 *I Could Have Danced All Night*	10.00 -	15.00

RED SOVINE:

Decca 30239 *Juke Joint Johnny*	8.00 -	12.00

BOB B. SOXX & THE BLUE JEANS:

Philles (LP) 1002 *Zip-A-Dee Doo Dah* (blue label)	35.00 -	50.00

SPADES:

Major 1007 *Close To You*	15.00 -	20.00

DICK SPAIN:

Oasis 1001 *Straw Broom Boogie*	30.00 -	40.00

SPANIELS:

Chance 1141 *Baby It's You* (red plastic)	150.00 -	200.00
Neptune 125 *For Sentimental Reasons*	7.00 -	10.00
Vee Jay 101 *Baby It's You* (red plastic)	250.00 -	Up
103 *The Bells Ring Out*	75.00 -	100.00
107 *Goodnite Sweetheart, Goodnite*	50.00 -	80.00
107 same, but red plastic	200.00 -	Up
116 *Let's Make Up* (red plastic)	200.00 -	Up
116 *Let's Make Up* (black plastic)	50.00 -	75.00
131 *Don'cha Go*	30.00 -	40.00
(Note: Other early *Vee Jay* issues, pressed of red vinyl, have brought more than double the values for black vinyl counterparts, according to reports.)		
154 *Painted Picture*	15.00 -	20.00
178 *False Love*	15.00 -	20.00
189 *Dear Heart*	15.00 -	20.00
202 *Since I Fell For You*	15.00 -	20.00

229 *You Gave Me Peace Of Mind*	15.00 -	20.00
246 *I. O. U*	10.00 -	15.00
257 *I Need Your Kisses*	10.00 -	15.00
264 *I Lost You*	10.00 -	15.00
278 *Tina*	10.00 -	15.00
290 *Stormy Weather*	10.00 -	15.00
301 *Heart And Soul*	10.00 -	15.00
310 *Trees*	8.00 -	12.00
328 *100 Years From Today*	8.00 -	12.00
342 *People Will Say We're In Love*	8.00 -	12.00
350 *Bus Fare Home*	8.00 -	12.00
(LP) 1002 *Goodnight, It's Time To Go* (maroon label)	100.00 -	150.00
(LP) 1002 (black label)	50.00 -	75.00
(LP) 1024 *The Spaniels*	100.00 -	150.00

OTIS SPANN:

Checker 807 *It Must Have Been The Devil*	75.00 -	100.00

SPARKS:

Hull 723 *Danny Boy*	50.00 -	80.00
724 *Adreann*	15.00 -	20.00
RPM 417 *Make A Little Love*	30.00 -	50.00

SPARKS OF RHYTHM:

Apollo 479 *Don't Love You Any More*	15.00 -	20.00
Stars Are In The Sky	10.00 -	15.00
541 *Everybody Rock And Go*	10.00 -	15.00

JERRY SPARKS:

Fidelity 4058 *My Tears*	5.00 -	8.00

SPARROWS:

Davis 456-45 *Love Me Tender*	30.00 -	40.00
Jay Dee 783 *Tell Me Baby*	30.00 -	40.00
790 *I'll Be Lovin' You*	30.00 -	40.00

MERLE SPEARS:

Whit 711 *Gonna Move*	7.00 -	10.00

SPECK & DOYLE:

Syrup Bucket 1000 *Big Noise, Bright Lights*	35.00 -	50.00

RONNIE SPEEKS & THE ELRODS:

King 5548 *What Is Your Technique*	8.00 -	12.00

SPELLBINDERS:

Date 1556 *Since I Don't Have You*	5.00 -	8.00

JIMMY SPELLMAN:

Dot 15607 *Doggonit*	10.00 -	15.00
Viv 1005 *Lover Man*	10.00 -	15.00

SPENCER & SPENCER:

Gone 5053 *Stagger Lawrence*	7.00 -	10.00

BOB SPENCER:

Epic 9139 *Roll, Hot Rod, Roll*	10.00 -	15.00

SONNY SPENCER:

Memo 17984 *Gilee*	5.00 -	8.00

SPIDERS:

Imperial 5265 *I Didn't Want To Do It*	15.00 -	25.00
5280 *I'll Stop Crying*	15.00 -	25.00
5291 *I'm Slippin' In*	15.00 -	20.00
(above are blue label with script letters)		
Imperial 5305 *The Real Thing*	15.00 -	20.00
5318 *She Keeps Me Wondering*	15.00 -	20.00
5331 *That's Enough*	15.00 -	20.00
5344 *Am I The One*	15.00 -	20.00
5354 *Bells In My Heart*	8.00 -	12.00
5366, 5376, 5393, 5405, 5423, 5714	5.00 -	10.00
(LP) 9140 *I Didn't Want To Do It*	75.00 -	100.00

SPIEDELS:

Crosley 201 *Dear Joan*	5.00 -	8.00

THE SPINNERS (See also: BOBBY SMITH):

Capitol 3955 *Lovers Prayer*	10.00 -	15.00
Rhythm 125 *My Love And Your Love*	50.00 -	75.00
Tri-Phi 1001 *That's What Girls Are Made For*	5.00 -	8.00
Tri-Phi 1004 *Love (I Am So Glad I Found You)*	5.00 -	8.00
1007 *What Did She Use?*	5.00 -	8.00
1013 *I've Been Hurt*	5.00 -	8.00

SPLENDORS:

Taurus 10 *The Golden Years*	7.00 -	10.00

SPOTLIGHTERS:

Aladdin 3436 *Whisper*	30.00 -	40.00
Imperial 5342 *It's Cold*	20.00 -	30.00

SPROUTS:

Spangle 2002 *Teen Billy Baby*	15.00 -	20.00

TOMMY SPURLIN:

Art 109 *One Eyed Sam*	50.00 -	80.00
Perfect 109 *Hang Loose*	50.00 -	80.00

THE SPUTNIKS:

Class 217 *My Love Is Gone*	8.00 -	12.00

SPY DELS/SPYDELS:

Addit 1220 *We're In Love*	5.00 -	8.00
Cracker Jack 4001 *We'll Be Together*	15.00 -	20.00
MZ 009 *No More Teasing*	15.00 -	20.00

SQUIRES:

Aladdin 3360 *Dreamy Eyes*	15.00 -	20.00
Boss 2120 *It's Time*	—	—
Combo 35 *Let's Give Love a Try*	40.00 -	60.00
42 *My Little Girl*	40.00 -	60.00
Congress 223 *Joyce*	8.00 -	12.00
Dice 478 *Every Word Of This Song*	8.00 -	12.00
Gee 1082 *So Many Tears Ago*	10.00 -	15.00
Herald 580 *Why Should I Suffer*	7.00 -	10.00
Kicks 1 *Lucy Lou*	—	—
Mambo 105 *Sindy*	40.00 -	60.00
Vita 113 *Me And My Deal*	30.00 -	40.00
116 *Heavenly Angel*	30.00 -	40.00
128 *Breath Of Air*	30.00 -	40.00

CLYDE STACY:

Bullseye 1004 *Baby Shame*	8.00 -	12.00
1008 *Honky Tonk Hardwood Floor*	15.00 -	20.00
1014 *You Want Love*	7.00 -	10.00
Candlelight 1015 *Hoy Hoy*	10.00 -	15.00
1018 *Dream Boy*	10.00 -	15.00
G & H 101 *Baby Shame*	10.00 -	15.00
Len 1015 *You're Satisfied*	8.00 -	12.00

SONNY STAFFORD:

Blue Moon 476 *Record Hop Blues*	35.00 -	50.00

JOHNNY STANDLEY:

Magnolia 1003 *Rock & Roll Must Go*	10.00 -	15.00

DOUG STANFORD:

D 1034 *Won't You Tell On Me*	7.00 -	10.00

RAY STANLEY:

Argo 5280 *Over A Coke* (ship logo label)	8.00 -	12.00
Zephyr 011 *Pushin'*	8.00 -	12.00
022 *My Lovin' Baby*	8.00 -	12.00

STAR COMBO:

Skippy 102 *Mr. Rock And Roll*	15.00 -	25.00

JOHNNY STARK:

Crystalette 709 *Roll Baby Roll*	15.00 -	20.00
713 *Cold Coffee*	15.00 -	20.00
715 *Rockin' Billy*	15.00 -	20.00

DOC STARKES:

Linda 109 *Rockin' To School*	15.00 -	25.00

STARLARKS:

Ember 1013 *Fountain Of Love*	20.00 -	30.00

STARLIGHTERS:

Hi-Q 5016 *Zoom*	8.00 -	12.00
Irma 101 *Love Cry*	75.00 -	100.00
Sun Coast 1001 *Until You Return*	50.00 -	75.00

STARLINGS:

Dawn 212 *I'm Just A Crying Fool*	50.00 -	75.00
Josie 760 *My Plea For Love*	75.00 -	100.00

STARLITES: (See also JACKIE & THE STARLITES)

Combo 73 *Arline*	30.00 -	40.00
Ember 1011 *They Call Me A Dreamer*	20.00 -	30.00
1021 *Tears Are Just For Fools*	15.00 -	25.00
Fury 1034 *Valarie*	8.00 -	12.00
1045 *Silver Lining*	8.00 -	12.00
Peak 5000 *Missing You*	20.00 -	30.00

ANDY STARR:

Arcade 115 *I Love My Baby*	35.00 -	50.00

MGM 12263 *Rockin' Rollin' Stone*	30.00	-	40.00
12315 *She's A-Goin' Jessie*	30.00	-	40.00
12364 *Round And Round*	30.00	-	40.00
12421 *No Room For Your Kind*	30.00	-	40.00

BILLY STARR:

Imperial 8186 *Hound Dog*	15.00	-	20.00

FRANK/FRANKIE STARR:

Holiday Inn 104 *Knees Shakin'*	10.00	-	15.00
Lin 5009 *Dig Them Squeaky Shoes*	35.00	-	50.00
5013 *Tell Me Why*	8.00	-	12.00
5033 *Me & The Fool*	8.00	-	12.00
Sims 212 *Elevator Baby*	8.00	-	12.00
Star-Win 7003 *Elevator Boogie*	15.00	-	20.00

JIMMY STARR:

Debbie 101 *Oooh Crazy*	4.00	-	7.00

JIMMY STAYTON:

Blue Hen 220 *Hot Hot Mama*	75.00	-	100.00

SONNY STEELE:

Republic 2020 *Mine Mine Mine*	8.00	-	12.00

PAUL STEFEN & THE ROYAL LANCERS:

Citation 5004 *Say Mama*	10.00	-	15.00

N.A. STEPHENSON:

Westwood 201 *Boogie Woogie Country Girl*	35.00	-	50.00

RAY STEVENS:

Capitol 4030 *Cat Pants*	7.00	-	10.00

SCOTT STEVENS:

APT 25031 *Why Why Why*	7.00	-	10.00

SONNY STEVENSON:

Onda 111 *Bessie Lou*	—	-	—

DON STEWART:

DAD 104 *More Than Words Can Tell*	—	-	—

FRANKLIN STEWART:

Lu 501 *That Long Black Train*	25.00	-	40.00

GENE STEWART:

King 5124 *Oh Baby, Lance With Me*	7.00	-	10.00

SANDY STEWART:

Atco 6137 *Playmates*	5.00	-	8.00

VERNON STEWART:

Peach 751 *Mean Mean Baby*	15.00	-	20.00

WYNN STEWART:

Jackpot 48005 *Come On*	8.00	-	12.00

ARBEE STIDHAM:

Abco 100 *Meet Me Halfway*	20.00	-	30.00
107 *When I Find My Baby*	20.00	-	30.00
Checker 778 *I Don't Play*	20.00	-	30.00
RCA Victor 47-4951 *I Found Out For Myself*	15.00	-	20.00
50-0003 *I Found Out For Myself*	20.00	-	30.00
50-0024 *Falling Blues*	20.00	-	30.00
50-0037 *Barbecue Lounge*	20.00	-	30.00
50-0083 *Any Time Ring My Bell*	20.00	-	30.00
50-0093 *Squeeze Me Baby*	20.00	-	30.00
50-0101 *You'll Be Sorry*	20.00	-	30.00

(Note: #50-0003 through 50-0101 are orange plastic.)

States 164 *I Stayed Away Too Long*	15.00	-	20.00

STINTON BROS.:

Arko — *Diggin' That Rock And Roll*	—	-	—

TINY STOKES:

Big T 235 *Blackfoot Boogie*	10.00	-	15.00

THE STOMPERS:

Gone 5120 *Forgive Me*	10.00	-	15.00
Landa 684 *Foolish One*	5.00	-	8.00
Souvenie 1003 *Blue Moon of Kentucky*	15.00	-	20.00

DOUG STONE:

Cee Dee 101 *Memphis Yodel Blues*	7.00	-	10.00

JEFF STONE:

Sarg 151 *Everybody Rock*	30.00	-	40.00

JERRY STONE with THE FOUR DOTS:

Freedom 44002 *My Baby (She Loves Me)*	15.00	-	20.00

LAWRENCE STONE:

Dig 130 *Everytime*	7.00	-	10.00

BILLY STORM: (See also THE VALIANTS)

Barbary Coast 1001 *The Way To My Heart*	7.00	-	10.00

WARREN STORM:

Nasco 6015 *Mama Mama Mama* (78 RPM)	10.00	-	15.00
6025 *Troubles, Troubles*	7.00	-	10.00
6028 *So Long, So Long*	7.00	-	10.00
6031 *Birmingham Jail*	7.00	-	10.00
Rocko 512 *Oh Oh Baby*	7.00	-	10.00
Zynn 1019 *Blues Stop Knocking*	—	-	—
1021 *This Should Go On Forever*	—	-	—
1024 *Let Me Know*	—	-	—

STORMY HERMAN & HIS MIDNIGHT RAMBLERS:

Dooto 358 *Bad Luck*	15.00	-	20.00

CARL STORY:

Columbia 21250 *Step It Up And Go*	8.00	-	12.00

JIMMY STRANGE & FLAHERTY'S CARAVAN:

Jenn 101 *Real Gone Daddy*	25.00	-	35.00

STRANGERS:

King 4697 *I've Got Eyes*	75.00	-	100.00
4709 *Blue Flowers*	75.00	-	125.00
4745 *Get It One More Time*	50.00	-	80.00
4821 *Without A Friend*	50.00	-	80.00
Titan 1702, 1702, 1704	7.00	-	10.00

RON STRAWN:

Eko 503 *Drivin'*	40.00	-	60.00

RICHARD STREET & THE DISTANTS:

Thelma TY 4 2282 *Answer Me*	20.00	-	30.00

JOHNNY STRICKLAND:

Roulette 4119 *She's Mine*	10.00	-	15.00
4147 *I've Heard That Line Before*	8.00	-	12.00
4221 *Sweet Talkin' Baby*	8.00	-	12.00
4335 *Fools' Hall Of Fame*	8.00	-	12.00

STRIDERS:

Apollo 480 *Hesitating Fool*	75.00	-	100.00

BOBBY STRIGO:

Renown 109 *The Pad*	8.00	-	12.00

STRIKES:

Imperial 5443 *If You Can't Rock Me*	8.00	-	12.00
5446 *Rockin'*	8.00	-	12.00
Lin 5006 *If You Can't Rock Me*	15.00	-	20.00

STROLLERS:

Club 9060 *Favors*	7.00	-	10.00
States 163 *In Your Dreams*	30.00	-	50.00

BARRETT STRONG:

Anna 1111 *Money* (78 RPM)	50.00	-	UP

(Note: The existence of this very late 78 RPM issue has been verified.)

NOLAN STRONG & THE DIABLOS:

Fortune 509, 510, 511, 514, 516, 519, 522	7.00	-	12.00
Fortune 525 *Can't We Talk This Over*	10.00	-	15.00
536 *Since You're Gone*	10.00	-	15.00
841 *Harriet*	10.00	-	15.00
(LP) 8012 *Fortune Of Hits*	20.00	-	30.00
(LP) 8015 *Mind Over Matter*	20.00	-	30.00

RAY STRONG:

Rocket 754 *You're Gonna Reap What You Sow*	—	-	—

STUDENTS:

Checker 902 *I'm So Young*	8.00	-	12.00
1004 *My Vow To You*	8.00	-	12.00
Note 10012 *I'm So Young*	75.00	-	100.00
10019 *My Vow To You*	75.00	-	100.00
Red Top 100 *My Heart Is An Open Door*	25.00	-	35.00

GENE STUMP & BILL SWAIN:

Clix 830 *Stream Of Love*	—	-	—

STYLERS:

Kicks 2 *Gentle As A Teardrop*	—	-	—
Gordy 7018 *Pushing Up Daisies*	8.00	-	12.00

THE SUADES:

Spinning 6011 *Wrong Yo-Yo*	10.00	-	15.00

SUBURBANS: (See also ANN COLE)

Baton 227 *TV Baby*	10.00	-	15.00

SUGAR BOY (& HIS CANE-CUTTERS):
Checker 783 *Overboard*	15.00 -	20.00
787 *Jock-O-Mo*	15.00 -	20.00
795 *I Bowed On My Knees*	10.00 -	15.00

SUGARCANE & HIS VIOLIN:
Eldo 103 *They Say You Never Can Miss*	7.00 -	10.00

SUGARTONES/SUGAR-TONES:
Cannon 391 *How Can I Pretend*	10.00 -	15.00
392 *How Can You Forget So Soon*	10.00 -	15.00
Okeh 6814 *Your Fool Again*	15.00 -	25.00
6877 *Wishin'*	15.00 -	20.00
6992 *I Just Want To Dream*	15.00 -	20.00

BRAD SUGGS:
Meteor 5034 *Bop, Baby, Bop* (black label)	30.00 -	50.00

JERRY SULLIVAN:
Vee 100 *Ella Mae*	15.00 -	20.00

SULTANS:
DeCade 101 *God Made An Angel*	7.00 -	10.00
Duke 125 *How Deep Is The The Ocean*	20.00 -	30.00
133 *I Cried My Heart Out*	20.00 -	30.00
135 *What Makes Me Feel This Way*	20.00 -	30.00
178 *If I Could Tell*	12.00 -	18.00
Jam 103 *Toss In My Sleep*	8.00 -	12.00
Jubilee 5054 *You Captured My Heart*	80.00 -	120.00
5077 *Don't Be Angry*	80.00 -	120.00
Tilt 782 *It'll Be Easy*	8.00 -	12.00

GENE SUMMERS:
Capri 507 *Alabama Shake*	8.00 -	12.00
Jan 100 *School Of Rock 'N' Roll*	20.00 -	30.00
102 *Gotta Lotta That*	15.00 -	20.00
106 *Twixteen*	15.00 -	20.00

SUNBEAMS:
Acme 109 *Please Say You'll Be Mine*	25.00 -	40.00
Herald 451 *Tell Me Why*	30.00 -	40.00

THE SUNDOWNERS featuring WILBUR MARTIN:
T R.C. 2839 *Live It Up*	15.00 -	20.00

SUNNYLAND SLIM (TRIO) (& HIS BOYS/PLAYBOYS):
Blue Lake 105 *Going Back To Memphis*	75.00 -	100.00
107 *Shake It Baby*	75.00 -	100.00
Club 51 106 *Be Mine Alone*	40.00 -	60.00
Cobra 5006 *Highway 61*	15.00 -	20.00
J.O.B. 1003 *Leaving Your Town*	— -	—
1105 *Shake It Baby*	50.00 -	75.00
1108 *Four Day Bounce*	50.00 -	75.00

SUNRAYS:
Sun 293 *Lonely Hours*	15.00 -	20.00

SUNSETS:
Petal 1040 *Lydia*	7.00 -	10.00

SUPERBS:
Heritage 103 *Rainbow Of Love*	5.00 -	8.00
Melmar—*My Love For You*	10.00 -	15.00

SUPERIORS:
Main Line 104 *Lost Love*	75.00 -	100.00
Verve 10370 *What Would I Do*	5.00 -	8.00

SUPREMES:
Ace 534 *Just For You And I*	15.00 -	20.00
Kitten 6969 *Could This Be You*	30.00 -	40.00
Motown (LP) 606 *Meet The Supremes* (cover shows girls sitting on stools)	75.00 -	100.00
Motown 1027, 1034	7.00 -	10.00
Motown 1040 *You Bring Back Memories*	10.00 -	15.00
1054 *Run, Run, Run*	10.00 -	15.00
Old Town 1017 *Darling Listen To The Words*	— -	—
1024 *Tonight*	— -	—
Tamla 54038 *I Want A Guy*	20.00 -	30.00
54045 *Who's Loving You*	15.00 -	20.00

(Note: Above are Tamla label with horizontal lines)

SURFARIS:
DFS 11/12 *Wipe-Out*	30.00 -	40.00

Princess 50 *Wipe-Out*	15.00 -	20.00

SURF RIDERS:
Nasco 6008 *Rocko Socko*	15.00 -	20.00

SURVIVORS:
Capitol 5102 *Pamela Jean*	50.00 -	75.00

RONNIE SUTTON:
Mar-Vel 5000 *Country Rock And Roll*	— -	—

DEL SWADE:
Production 65216 *Better Get Ready, Betty*	20.00 -	30.00

SWALLOWS:
After Hours 104 *My Baby*	150.00 -	200.00
Federal 12319 *Angel Baby*	10.00 -	15.00
12328 *We Want To Rock*	8.00 -	12.00
12329 *Beside You*	8.00 -	12.00
12333 *Itchy Twitchy Feeling*	8.00 -	12.00
King 4458 *Dearest*	150.00 -	200.00
4466 *Since You've Been Gone Away*	150.00 -	200.00
4501 *Eternally*	100.00 -	150.00
4515 *Roll Roll Pretty Baby*	100.00 -	150.00
4525 *Beside You*	75.00 -	100.00
4533 *I Only Have Eyes For You*	100.00 -	150.00
4579 *Please Baby Please*	100.00 -	150.00
4612 *Laugh (Though You Want To Cry)*	75.00 -	100.00
4632 *Nobodys Lovin' Me*	75.00 -	100.00
4656 *Trust Me*	75.00 -	100.00
4676 *I'll Be Waiting*	80.00 -	120.00

JIMMY SWAN:
MGM 12226 *Hey, Baby, Baby*	7.00 -	10.00
12348 *Country Cattin'*	7.00 -	10.00
Trumpet 176 *Juke Joint Mama*	15.00 -	20.00
177 *Triflin' On Me*	10.00 -	15.00
197 *Losers Weepers*	10.00 -	15.00
198 *Lonesome Daddy Blues*	10.00 -	15.00

SWANNEE & THE ROCKABILLIES:
Clix 825 *Thrill Happy*	— -	—

SWANS:
Ballad 1006 *Night Train*	— -	—
Fortune 822 *Mister Cool Breeze*	30.00 -	50.00
Rainbow 233 *My True Love*	150.00 -	250.00

BOBBY SWANSON & THE SONICS:
Igloo 1003 *Rockin' Little Eskimo*	50.00 -	75.00

HANK SWATLEY:
Aron 101 *Oakie Boogie*	35.00 -	50.00

AL SWEATT:
Keen 289 *Little Red Wagon*	20.00 -	30.00

JIM SWEENEY:
Date 1001 *The Midnight Hour*	5.00 -	8.00

SWINGING HEARTS:
Diamond 162 *Please Say It Isn't So*	8.00 -	12.00
Lucky Four 1011 *Please Say It Isn't So*	10.00 -	15.00
Magic Touch 2001 *You Speak Of Love*	10.00 -	15.00

HAWARD/HOWARD SWORDS WITH THE BLUE LIGHT BOYS:
Meteor 5019 *You Will Have To Pay*	20.00 -	30.00

THE SYCAMORES:
Groove 0121 *I'll Be Waiting*	50.00 -	75.00

BOBBY SYKES:
Decca 30573 *Touch Of Loving*	7.00 -	10.00

ROOSEVELT SYKES (& HIS HONEYDRIPPERS):
Crown (LP) 5287 *Roosevelt Sykes Sings The Blues*	15.00 -	20.00
House Of Sound 505 *She's Jail Bait*	15.00 -	20.00
Imperial 5347 *Sweet Old Chicago*	10.00 -	15.00
5367 *Crazy Fox*	10.00 -	15.00
Kent 384, 434	3.00 -	5.00
RCA Victor 50-0025 *Stop Her Papa*	30.00 -	50.00
50-0040 *My Baby Is Gone*	30.00 -	50.00

(Note: Above two are made of orange plastic.)

United 129 *Security Blues*	20.00 -	30.00
139 *Four O'Clock Blues*	15.00 -	20.00
152 *Tell Me True*	15.00 -	20.00

(Note: Above, if pressed of red vinyl, bring substantially more.)

SYLVIA & MICKEY:
Cat 102 *Speed Life* . . . . 5.00 - 8.00

BOBBY SYSOM:
Blue Moon 304 *Big Time Mama* . . . . 30.00 - 50.00

TABBYS:
Time 1008 *My Darling* . . . . 10.00 - 15.00

TABS:
Nasco 6016 *Will We Meet Again* . . . . 8.00 - 12.00
Noble 719 *Never Forget* . . . . 8.00 - 12.00
720 *Oops* . . . . 8.00 - 12.00

DICK TACKER:
Kingston--*Rock All Night With Me* . . . . 30.00 - 40.00

THE TADS:
Dot 15518 *You Reason* . . . . 10.00 - 15.00

TOM TALL:
Crest 1038 *Stack-A-Records* . . . . 20.00 - 30.00
1051 *High School Dance* . . . . 10.00 - 15.00
Fabor 132 *Hot Rod Is Her Name* . . . . 10.00 - 15.00

JOHNNY T. TALLEY:
Mercury 70902 *Lonesome Train* . . . . 15.00 - 20.00

TAMPA RED:
RCA Victor 4275 *Boogie Woogie Woman* . . . . . . 20.00 - 30.00
4898 *True Love* . . . . 20.00 - 30.00
5134 *Too Late, Too Long* . . . . 15.00 - 20.00
50-0019 *Come On, If You're Coming* . . . . 30.00 - 50.00
50-0027 *It's A Brand New Boogie* . . . . 30.00 - 50.00
50-0041 *That's Her Own Business* . . . . 30.00 - 50.00
50-0056 *It's Too Late Now* . . . . 30.00 - 50.00
50-0084 *1950 Blues* . . . . 30.00 - 50.00
(Note: Last five records are made of orange plastic.)

ROY TAN:
Dot 15551 *I Don't Like It* . . . . 4.00 - 7.00
15551 *I Don't Like It* (78 RPM) . . . . 10.00 - 15.00
15595 *Hot Rod Queen* . . . . 7.00 - 10.00

TANGENTS:
Fresh 1 *I Can't Live Alone* . . . . 5.00 - 8.00

TANGIERS:
A-J 905 *The Plea* . . . . 8.00 - 12.00
Class 224 *Don't Try* . . . . 10.00 - 15.00
Decca 29603 *Tabarin* . . . . 25.00 - 40.00
29971 *Oh, Baby!* . . . . 25.00 - 35.00
Strand 25039 *Don't Stop The Music* . . . . 10.00 - 15.00

ROY TANN (See ROY TAN) TANTONES:
Lamp 2002 *I Love You Really I Do* . . . . 15.00 - 20.00
2008 *So Afraid* . . . . 15.00 - 20.00

TARHEEL SLIM (& LITTLE ANN):
Fire 1000, 1009 . . . . 7.00 - 10.00
(Note: 78 RPM issues of above exist.)
Fury 1016 *Number 9 Train* . . . . 10.00 - 15.00

FRANKIE TARO:
G&G 111 *Susy Ann* . . . . 25.00 - 40.00

JOE TATE:
Roulette 4059 *Satellite Rock* . . . . 7.00 - 10.00

BILL TAYLOR (& THE CYCLONES/& SMOKEY JO):
Flip 502 *Split Personality* . . . . 100.00 - 150.00
Trophy 500 *Nelda Jane* . . . . 8.00 - 12.00
—*Wombie Zomie/I'm Young* . . . . — - —

WILD BILL TAYLOR:
Fame 502 *Little Jewel* . . . . 50.00 - 80.00

BOB TAYLOR:
Yucca 110 *Don't Be Unfair* . . . . 15.00 - 20.00

CARMEN TAYLOR (& THE BOLEROS):
Apollo 489 *Teen-Age Ball* . . . . 15.00 - 20.00
Atlantic 1002 *Lovin' Daddy* . . . . 15.00 - 20.00
Atlantic 1041 *Freddie* . . . . 40.00 - 60.00

EDDIE TAYLOR:
Vee Jay 149 *E.T Blues* . . . . 20.00 - 30.00
185 *Big Town Playboy* . . . . 10.00 - 15.00

206 *Don't Knock At My Door* . . . . 8.00 - 12.00
267 *Lookin' For Trouble* . . . . 8.00 - 12.00
Vivid 104 *I'm Sitting Here* . . . . 7.00 - 10.00

FAITH TAYLOR & THE SWEET TEENS:
Bea & Baby, 104, 105 . . . . 10.00 - 15.00

HOUND DOG TAYLOR:
Bea & Baby 112 *My Baby's Coming Home* . . . . . 10.00 - 15.00
Firma 626 *Alley Music* . . . . 7.00 - 10.00

KIRK TAYLOR & THE MAJESTICS:
Bandera 2507 *From Out Of This World* . . . . 7.00 - 10.00

KOKO TAYLOR:
Checker 1092 *I Got What It Takes* . . . . 5.00 - 8.00
1135, 1148 . . . . 3.00 - 6.00
U.S.A. 745 *Honkey Tonky* . . . . 4.00 - 7.00

MORRIS TAYLOR:
Key 5718 *Look-A-What* . . . . 15.00 - 20.00

R. DEAN TAYLOR:
Mala 444 *Long Way To St. Louis* . . . . 5.00 - 8.00

RAY TAYLOR with THE ALABAMA PALS:
Clix 801 *Clockin' My Card* . . . . 80.00 - 120.00
802 *Connie Lou* . . . . 80.00 - 120.00

TRUE TAYLOR:
Big 614 *True Or False* . . . . 10.00 - 15.00

VERNON TAYLOR:
Dot 15632 *I've Got The Blues* . . . . 10.00 - 15.00

WILLIAM TELL TAYLOR with JIMMY HEAP & THE MELODY MASTERS:
D 1051 *I Like It* . . . . 20.00 - 30.00

TEARDROPS:
Josie 766 *The Stars Are Out Tonight* . . . . 50.00 - 75.00
Josie 771 *My Heart* . . . . 50.00 - 75.00
Josie 856 *We Won't Tell* . . . . 8.00 - 12.00
862 *Cry No More* . . . . 8.00 - 12.00
873 *Daddy's Little Girl* . . . . 8.00 - 12.00
King 5004 *My Inspiration* . . . . 15.00 - 20.00
King 5037 *Don't Be Afraid To Love* . . . . 15.00 - 20.00
Port 70019 *The Stars Are Out Tonight* . . . . 8.00 - 12.00
Sampson 634 *Come Back To Me* . . . . 150.00 - 200.00
Saxony 1007 *That's Why I'll Get By* . . . . 7.00 - 10.00

THE TEARS:
Astronaut 5001 *She's Mine* . . . . 7.00 - 10.00
Dig 112 *Until The Day I Die* . . . . 10.00 - 15.00

TEASERS:
Checker 800 *How Could You Hurt Me So* . . . . . 100.00 - 150.00

TED AND JOHNNY:
Peach 0566 *Teenage Party* . . . . 10.00 - 15.00

TEDDY & THE CONTINENTALS:
Richie 445 *Do You* . . . . 40.00 - 60.00

THE TEDDY BEARS:
Imperial 5562 *I Don't Need You Anymore* . . . . . 7.00 - 10.00
5594 *Don't Go Away* . . . . 7.00 - 10.00
Imperial (LP) 9067 *The Teddy Bears Sing!* (Mono) . . . . 50.00 - 75.00
(LP) 12067 *The Teddy Bears Sing!* (Stereo) . . . 100.00 - 150.00

TEENAGE MOONLIGHTERS:
Mark 134 *I Want To Cry* . . . . 25.00 - 35.00

"TEENAGE PARTY"
Gee (LP) 702 (The Crows, Cleftones, et al.) . . . . 15.00 - 20.00

THE TEENAGERS (featuring FRANKIE LYMON):
Gee (EP) 601 *The Teenagers Go Rockin'* . . . . . . 15.00 - 20.00
(EP) 602 *The Teenagers Go Romantic* . . . . 10.00 - 15.00
(LP) 701 *The Teenagers featuring Frankie Lymon* (mono) (red label) . . . . 100.00 - 150.00
1002, 1012 . . . . 5.00 - 10.00
1002 *Why Do Fools Fall In Love* (78 RPM) . . . . 10.00 - 15.00
1012 *I Want You To Be My Girl* (78 RPM) . . . . 10.00 - 15.00

TEENANGELS:
Sun 388 (DJ) *Tell Me My Love* . . . . 15.00 - 20.00

TEENCHORDS (See LEWIS LYMON) TEEN KINGS; TEEN KINGS (Vocal, Roy Orbison):
Bee 1114 *Tell Me If You Know* . . . . 7.00 - 10.00

Je-Wel 101 *Ooby Dooby* . . . . .200.00 - UP
(Note: This record has supposedly been sold for
  as much as $500.00 at auction; no transaction
  at such a lofty figure or anything close to it has
  been verified.)

TEENOS:
Dub 2839 *Love Only One* . . . . 8.00 - 12.00

TEEN QUEENS:
Crown (LP) 373 *Teen Oueens* . . . . 15.00 - 25.00
  (LP) 5022 *Eddie My Love* . . . . 30.00 - 40.00
Kent 348 *Eddie My Love* . . . . 5.00 - 8.00
RPM 453 *Eddie My Love* . . . . 7.00 - 10.00
  453 *Eddie My Love* (78 RPM) . . . . 8.00 - 12.00
  460, 464, 470, 484 . . . . 5.00 - 8.00

TEEN TONES:
Decca 30895 *Don't Call Me Baby, I'll Call You* . 7.00 - 10.00

TELLERS:
Fire 1038 *Tears Fell From My Eyes* . . . . 15.00 - 20.00

BOB TEMPLE:
King 4958 *Come Back Come Back* . . . . 8.00 - 12.00

TEMPO MENTALS:
Ebb 112 *Dearest* . . . . 15.00 - 20.00

TEMPOS:
Kapp 213 *I Got A Job* . . . . 4.00 - 6.00

TEMPO TONES:
Acme 102 *Find Yourself Another Fool* . . . . 15.00 - 20.00
  103 *On Your Radio* . . . . 15.00 - 20.00
Acme 713 *Ride Along* . . . . 15.00 - 20.00
  715 *In My Dreams* . . . . 15.00 - 20.00
  718 *Come Into My Heart* . . . . 15.00 - 20.00

TEMPO TOPPERS: (See also DUCES OF
RHYTHM)
Peacock 1628 *Always* . . . . 15.00 - 20.00

THE TEMPTATIONS:
Goldisc 3007 *Letter Of Devotion* . . . . 7.00 - 10.00
Gordy 7001 *Dream Come True* . . . . 10.00 - 15.00
Gordy 7010, 7015, 7020 . . . . 7.00 - 10.00
King 5118 *Standing Alone* . . . . 30.00 - 50.00
Miracle 5 *On Mother Of Mine* . . . . — - —
  12 *Check Yourself* . . . . — - —
Pasrkway 803 *Birds 'n' Bees* . . . . 10.00 - 15.00
Savoy 1532 *Mister Juke Box* . . . . 7.00 - 10.00
  1550 *Don't You Know* . . . . 7.00 - 10.00

TENDERFOOTS:
Federal 12214 *Kissing Bug* . . . . 15.00 - 20.00
  12219 *My Confession* . . . . 15.00 - 20.00
  12225 *Those Golden Bells* . . . . 20.00 - 30.00
  12228 *Sindy* . . . . 20.00 - 30.00

TENDER SLIM:
Herald 571 *Don't Cut Out On Me* . . . . 7.00 - 10.00

TENNESSEE DRIFTER:
Maid 1000 *The Drifter* . . . . .100.00 - 150.00

TENNESSEE DRIFTERS:
Dot 1166 *Boogie Woogie Baby* . . . . 30.00 - 50.00
  1187 *Corrine Corrina* . . . . 30.00 - 50.00

TENNESSEE JIM:
Choise 852 *My Baby She's Rockin'* . . . . 15.00 - 20.00

TERMITES:
Bee— *Give My Your Heart* . . . . 20.00 - 30.00

TERRACE TONES:
Apt 25016 *Words Of Wisdom* . . . . 15.00 - 25.00

TERRANS:
Graham 801 *Moonrise* . . . . 7.00 - 10.00

CLYDE TERRELL:
Excello 2151 *Poor Folk* . . . . 5.00 - 8.00

SISTER O.M. TERRELL:
Columbia 21092 *The Gambling Man* . . . . 10.00 - 15.00

DON TERRY:
Lin 5018 *Knees Shakin'* . . . . 30.00 - 40.00

DOSSIE TERRY:
King 5072 *I Got a Watch Dog* . . . . 10.00 - 15.00

FLASH TERRY:

Indigo 135 *Cool It* . . . . 10.00 - 15.00
Kent 310 *On My Way Back Home* . . . . 15.00 - 20.00
Suncoast 1003 *She's My Baby* . . . . 15.00 - 20.00

GENE TERRY & HIS DOWN BEATS:
Savoy 1559 *Fine-Fine* . . . . 8.00 - 12.00

GORDON TERRY:
RCA Victor 7428 *It Ain't Right* . . . . 7.00 - 10.00
  7632 *A Lotta Lotta Woman* . . . . 10.00 - 15.00

LARRY TERRY:
Testa 0006 *Hep Cat* . . . . 50.00 - 80.00

MARK TERRY:
Kem 2746 *Nobody's Darling* . . . . — - —

SONNY TERRY (with BROWNIE McGHEE):
(See also BROWNIE McGHEE)
Elektra (LP) 14 (10″) *Folk Blues* . . . . 20.00 - 30.00
Everest (LP) 206 *Sonny Terry* . . . . 20.00 - 30.00
Fantasy (LP) 3254 *Sonny Terry* . . . . 20.00 - 30.00
Folkways (LP) 35 (10″) *Harmonica* . . . . — - —
  (LP) 2006 (10″) *Washboard Band* . . . . — - —
  (LP) 2035 (10″) *Harmonica* . . . . — - —
  (LP) 2327 (10″) *Blues & Folksongs* . . . . — - —
Gotham 517 *Four O'Clock Blues* . . . . 15.00 - 20.00
  518 *Lonesome Room* . . . . 15.00 - 20.00
Gramercy 1004 *Hootin' Blues* (red plastic) . . . . 25.00 - 40.00
Groove 0015 *Louise* . . . . 10.00 - 15.00
  0135 *Hootin' Blues No. 2* . . . . 10.00 - 15.00
Harlem 2327 *Dangerous Woman* . . . . 20.00 - 30.00
Jax 305 *I Don't Worry* (red vinyl) . . . . 30.00 - 40.00
Josie 828 *Fast Freight Blues* . . . . 8.00 - 12.00
Old Town 1023 *Uncle Bud* . . . . 8.00 - 12.00
RCA Victor 5492 *Hootin' And Jumpin'* . . . . 15.00 - 20.00
  5577 *I'm Gonna Rock My Wig* . . . . 15.00 - 20.00
Red Robin 110 *Harmonica Hop* . . . . 35.00 - 50.00
Riverside (LP) 12-644...*And His Mouth Harp* . . 20.00 - 30.00
Roulette (LP) 25074 *Folk Songs* . . . . 15.00 - 20.00
Stinson (LP) 55 (10″) *Blues* . . . . — - —

THE TEXANS:
Gothic 001 *Rockin' Johnny Home* . . . . 8.00 - 12.00
Infinity 001 *Green Grass Of Texas* . . . . 8.00 - 12.00

TEXAS MATADORS:
IMA—*Flower Blossom* . . . . 7.00 - 10.00

TEXAS RED (& JIMMY):
Bullseye 1009 *Coming Home* . . . . 10.00 - 15.00
Checker 879 *Black Snake Blues* . . . . 7.00 - 10.00

JOHN TEXIERA:
G & G 100 *Strike It Rich* . . . . 15.00 - 20.00

RUDY THACKER:
Lucky 0012 *Black Train* . . . . 15.00 - 20.00

CHUCK THARP & FIREBALLS:
Jaro 77029 *Long Long Ponytail* . . . . 20.00 - 30.00

SISTER ROSETTA THARPE:
Promenade (LP) 2234 *Spirituals In Rhythm* . . . . 35.00 - 50.00

FRANK THAYER:
Outlaw 1 *Evening Shadows* . . . . 15.00 - 20.00

THEMES (with JACK SNOW):
Excello 2152 *The Magic Of You* . . . . 8.00 - 12.00
Stork 001 *There's No Moon Out Tonight* . . . . . . 8.00 - 12.00

JOE THERRIEN, JR. (& THE
ROCKETS/SULLY TRIO):
Brunswick 55005 *Hey Babe, Let's Go Down*
Town . . . . 15.00 - 20.00
Brunswick 55017 *You're Long Gone* . . . . 15.00 - 20.00
Jat 101 *I Ain't Gonna Be Around* . . . . 20.00 - 30.00
Lido 505 *Hey Babe, Let's Go Down Town* . . . . . 20.00 - 30.00

FATSO THEUS & THE FLAIRS:
Aladdin 3324 *Be Cool My Heart* . . . . 40.00 - 50.00

THE 13TH FLOOR ELEVATORS:
International Artists (LP) 1 *The Psychedelic*
Sound Of . . . . 40.00 - 50.00
  (LP) 9 *Bull Of The Woods* . . . . 35.00 - 50.00
  111, 113, 126 . . . . 5.00 - 10.00

ALEXANDER "MUDCAT" THOMAS:

NRC 062 *Step It Up And Go*	5.00 -	8.00

B.J. THOMAS:

Pacemaker (LP) 3001 *So Lonesome I Could Cry*	35.00 -	50.00

CLIFF THOMAS:

Phillips Int. 3521 *Treat Me Right*	8.00 -	12.00

JERRY THOMAS:

Orchid 274 *Jungle Dan*	15.00 -	20.00

JESSE THOMAS:

Elko 107 *Another Fool Like Me*	50.00 -	75.00
Hollywood 1072 *Cool Kind Lover*	10.00 -	15.00

KID THOMAS:

Federal 12298 *The Wolf Pack*	20.00 -	30.00
T.R.C 1012 *Rockin' This Joint Tonight*	35.00 -	50.00

LAFAYETTE THOMAS:

Savoy 1574 *Lafayette's A-Comin'*	10.00 -	15.00

MULE THOMAS:

Hollywood 1091 *Blow My Baby Back Home*	30.00 -	40.00

PLAY BOY THOMAS:

Parrot 785 *No Doubt About It*	75.00 -	100.00
Swing Time 340 *Too Much Pride*	50.00 -	75.00

RUFUS THOMAS (JR.):

Chess 1517 *Juanita*	150.00 -	200.00
Sun 181 *Bear Cat*	50.00 -	80.00
188 *Tiger Man*	50.00 -	80.00

TAB(BY) THOMAS:

Delta 416 *Thinking Blues*	20.00 -	30.00
Excello 2212, 2222, 2281	3.00 -	5.00
Feature 3007 *Tomorrow*	10.00 -	15.00
Rocko 511 *Too Late Blues*	5.00 -	8.00
Zynn 1002 *My Baby's Got It*	5.00 -	8.00

BUDDY THOMPSON:

Atco 6095 *This Is The Night*	8.00 -	12.00

CHUCK THOMPSON:

Granite 13775 *Tired Of Fooling Around*	15.00 -	20.00

FRED THOMPSON:

Jim Dandy 4501 *Please Be Fair*	5.00 -	8.00

HANK THOMPSON:

Capitol (LP) 418 (10") *Brazos Valley Songs*	20.00 -	30.00
(LP) 418 *Brazos Valley Songs*	20.00 -	30.00
(LP) 618 *North Of The Rio Grande*	15.00 -	20.00
(LP) 729 *All Time Hits*	12.00 -	16.00
(LP) 826 *Hank*	12.00 -	16.00
(LP) 975 *Dance Ranch*	12.00 -	16.00
(LP) 1246 *Songs For Rounders*	10.00 -	15.00
3623 *Rockin' In The Congo*	3.00 -	6.00

HAYDEN THOMPSON:

Phillips 3517 *Love My Baby*	15.00 -	25.00
Profile 4015 *Whatcha Gonna Do*	20.00 -	30.00

JUNIOR THOMPSON:

Meteor 5029 *Mama's Litlle Baby* (red label)	50.00 -	80.00
Tune (unnumbered) *How Come You Do Me?*	75.00 -	100.00

KID GUITAR THOMPSON:

Dore 581 *My Baby Done Me Wrong*	7.00 -	10.00

LORETTA THOMPSON:

Skoop 1050	20.00 -	30.00
United 214 *Hi De Ho Rock And Roll*	15.00 -	20.00

WILLIE MAE ("BIG MAMA") THORNTON:

Bay Tone 107 *Big Mama's Blues*	7.00 -	10.00
Kent 424 *Before Day*	3.00 -	5.00
Peacock 1567 *All Fed Up*	15.00 -	20.00
1587 *Let Your Tears Fall Baby*	15.00 -	20.00
1603 *Michievous Boogie*	15.00 -	20.00
1612 *Hound Dog*	35.00 -	50.00
1621 *Cotton Picking Blues*	10.00 -	15.00
1626 *The Big Change*	10.00 -	15.00
1632 *I Smell A Rat*	10.00 -	15.00
1642 *Stop Hoppin' On Me*	10.00 -	15.00
1647 *Walking Blues*	10.00 -	15.00
(Note: Above are red or maroon labels.)		
Peacock 1650, 1654, 1681	5.00 -	8.00

"THOSE GOOD OLD MEMORIES"

Capitol (LP) 1414 (various artists)	15.00 -	20.00

THRASHERS:

Mason's 178 *Jeannie*	40.00 -	60.00
178 *Jeannie* (red plastic)	75.00 -	100.00

THREE CHUCKLES:

Boulevard 100 *Run Around*	20.00 -	30.00
Vik (LP) 1067	30.00 -	40.00

THREE D'S:

Paris 511 *Crazy Little Woman*	5.00 -	8.00
514 *Jumpin' Jack*	5.00 -	8.00
Square 502 *Squeeze*	10.00 -	15.00

3 DOTS AND A DASH:

Imperial 5115 *Don't Cry Baby*	150.00 -	200.00
5164 *Let's Do It*	100.00 -	150.00

THE THREE HONEYDROPS:

Music City 814 *Rockin' Satellite*	8.00 -	12.00

THREE RAMBLERS:

Ozark 716 *Walking Talking Baby Doll*	10.00 -	15.00

THRILLERS:

Big Town 109 *The Drunkard*	50.00 -	75.00
Herald 432 *Lizabeth*	50.00 -	75.00
Thriller 3530 *I'm Gonna Live My Life Alone*	100.00 -	150.00

THUNDERBIRDS:

De Luxe 6075 *Baby Let's Play House*	35.00 -	50.00
G.G. 103 *Love Is A Problem*	20.00 -	30.00

TIFANOS:

Tifco 822 *It's Raining*	20.00 -	30.00

SONNY TIL (See ORIOLES)

BIG SON TILLIS & D.C. BENDER:

Elko 821 *Rocks Is My Pillow*	75.00 -	100.00
822 *Ten Long Years*	75.00 -	100.00
823 *Dayton Stomp*	75.00 -	100.00

CLYDE TILLIS:

Cash 10541 *It Makes No Difference Now*	7.00 -	10.00

MEL TILLIS:

Columbia 40944 *Juke Box Man*	8.00 -	12.00
41026 *Hearts Of Stone*	8.00 -	12.00
41115 *Teen Age Wedding*	8.00 -	12.00

TIM TAM & THE TURN-ONS:

Palmer 5006 *Kimberly*	15.00 -	20.00

TINO & REVLONS:

Dearborn 525 *Rave On*	8.00 -	12.00

TITANS:

Specialty 614 *Sweet Peach*	7.00 -	10.00
625 *Don't You Just Know It*	7.00 -	10.00
632 *Arlene*	7.00 -	10.00
Vita 148 *So Hard To Laugh, So Easy To Cry*	15.00 -	20.00
158 *Look What You're Doing Baby*	15.00 -	20.00

TITONES:

Scepter 1206 *Symbol Of Love*	8.00 -	12.00

BUD TITUS:

Sage 244 *Hocus Pocus*	10.00 -	15.00

"TODAY'S HITS"

Philles (LP) 4004 (various artists)	30.00 -	50.00

JOHNNY TODD:

Modern 1003 *Pink Cadillac*	20.00 -	30.00

TOKENS:

Gary 1006 *Doom-Long*	15.00 -	25.00
Melba 104 *I Love My Baby*	15.00 -	20.00
RCA Victor (LP) 2514 *The Lion Sleeps Tonight*	20.00 -	30.00

TOMMIE TOLLESON:

Kool 1005 *A Girl Named Sue*	15.00 -	20.00

TOM & JERRY:

Big 613 *Hey, Schoolgirl*	8.00 -	12.00
616 *Our Song*	10.00 -	15.00
618 *That's My Story*	10.00 -	15.00
621 *Baby Talk*	15.00 -	20.00
Hunt 319 *That's My Story*	15.00 -	20.00

KENNY TOMERLIN:

Teen Ager 1001 *Crazy Little Teen*	5.00 -	8.00

TONY & THE MASQUINS:

Ruthie 1000 *My Angel Eyes*	20.00 -	30.00

TONY & THE RAINDROPS:

Chesapeake 609 *While Walking*	10.00	-	15.00
TONY & THE TECHNICS:			
Chex 1010 *Ha Ha He Told On You*	8.00	-	12.00
TONY & THE TWILIGHTERS:			
Jalynne 106 *Did You Make Up Your Mind*	20.00	-	30.00
JACKSON TOOMBS:			
Excello 2083 *Kiss-A-Me-Ouick*	15.00	-	20.00
TOPICS:			
Perri 1007 *The Girl In My Dreams*	15.00	-	20.00
THE TOP NOTES:			
Atlantic 2080 *Warm Your Heart*	10.00	-	15.00
TOPPERS: (See also BOBBY MITCHELL)			
Jubilee 5136 *Baby Let Me Bang Your Box*	30.00	-	40.00
TOPPS:			
Red Robin 126 *Tippin'*	30.00	-	40.00
THE TOPS:			
Singular 712 *An Innocent Kiss*	8.00	-	12.00
THE TOREADORS:			
Midas 1001 *Do You Remember?*	15.00	-	20.00
THE TORNADOS:			
Bumble Bee 503 *Love In Your Life*	8.00	-	12.00
TORQUAYS:			
Holly 4701 *Pineapple Moon*	10.00	-	15.00
JACKIE TORRELL:			
Dude *I'm Gonna Look*		-	
"TOWN HALL PARTY"			
Columbia (LP) CL-1072 (various artists)	20.00	-	30.00
TOWN THREE: (See also WES VOIGHT)			
De Luxe 6176 *Another Guy's Line*	10.00	-	15.00
6180 *I Want A Lover*	10.00	-	15.00
THE TOYS:			
Dyno Voice (LP) 9002 *Sing A Lover's Concerto*	20.00	-	30.00
BUCK TRAIL:			
Trail 100 *Knocked Out Joint On Mars*	30.00	-	50.00
TRAILBLAZERS:			
Watson 500 *Grandpa's Rock*	35.00	-	50.00
TRAITS: (See also ROY HEAD)			
Renner 221 *Little Mama*	15.00	-	20.00
229 *Got My Mojo Working*	15.00	-	20.00
TNT 164 *One More Time*	15.00	-	20.00
175 *Live It Up*	15.00	-	20.00
185 *Night Time Blues*	15.00	-	20.00
BOBBY LEE TRAMMELL:			
ABC Paramount 9890 *Shirley Lee*	15.00	-	20.00
Alley 1001 *It's All Your Fault*	7.00	-	10.00
Alley 1004 *Come On Baby*	8.00	-	12.00
Atlanta 1501 *Sally Twist*	5.00	-	8.00
1502 *Come On*	5.00	-	8.00
Atlanta (LP) 1503 *"Arkansas Twist"*	30.00	-	40.00
Fabor 127 *You Mostest Girl*	7.00	-	10.00
4038 *Shirley Lee*	15.00	-	20.00
Radio 102 *You Mostest Girl*	15.00	-	20.00
Sims 183 *New Dance In France*	5.00	-	8.00
Vaden 304 *Been A-Walking*	15.00	-	20.00
Warrior 1554 *Woe Is Me*	20.00	-	30.00
CARL TRANTHAM (& RHYTHM ALL STARS):			
Lincoln 643 *Where There's A Will*	30.00	-	40.00
Starday 361 *Our True Love*	15.00	-	25.00
TRAVELERS:			
Atlas 1086 *Lenora*	20.00	-	30.00
TRAVIS & BOB:			
Sandy 1017 *We're Too Young*	7.00	-	10.00
1019 *Little Bitty Johnny*	7.00	-	10.00
1024 *Oh Yeah*	7.00	-	10.00
1029 *That's How Long*	7.00	-	10.00
MERLE TRAVIS:			
Capitol (LP) 891 *Back Home*	25.00	-	35.00
TREBLE CHORDS:			
Decca 31015 *Teresa*	15.00	-	25.00
TREMAINES:			
Cash 100 *Jingle Jingle*	75.00	-	100.00
Old Town 1051 *Jingle Jingle*	20.00	-	30.00
Val 101 *Jingle Jingle*	30.00	-	40.00
V-Tone 507 *Heavenly*	8.00	-	12.00
TOMMY TREMBLE & THE SHADOWS:			
Sound Tex 641013 *She Said*	7.00	-	10.00
THE TREMONTS:			
Brunswick 55217 *Legend Of Love*	10.00	-	15.00
THE TRENIERS:			
Epic (EP) 7014 *"Go Go Go"*	15.00	-	20.00
(EP) 7114 *"Those Crazy Treniers"*	20.00	-	30.00
TREND TONES:			
Superb 100 *Never Again*	10.00	-	15.00
GRAY TREXLER:			
Rev 3507 *Teen Baby*	8.00	-	12.00
TREYS:			
Bella 16 *Come To Me*	10.00	-	15.00
TRIDELLS:			
San Dee 1009 *Land Of Love*	10.00	-	15.00
TRI-LADS:			
Bullseye 1003 *Cherry Pie*	7.00	-	10.00
FRANK TRIOLO:			
Flagship 106 *Ice Cream Baby*	50.00	-	80.00
TRITONES:			
Jamie 1035 *Blues In The Closet*		-	
DELBERT TROILINDER:			
Mist 1012 *So We Walked*	20.00	-	30.00
TROJANS:			
Tender 516 *Alone In This World*	12.00	-	16.00
TROOPERS:			
Lamp 2009 *My Resolution*	40.00	-	60.00
TROPHIES:			
Challenge 9133 *Desire*	10.00	-	15.00
TROUPERS:			
Red Top—*Peter, Pumpkin Eater*	8.00	-	12.00
TRUETONES:			
Felsted 8625 *Singing Waters*	10.00	-	15.00
Monument 4501 *Honey Honey*	40.00	-	60.00
THE TRUMPETEERS:			
Grand (LP) 7701 *The Last Supper*		-	
Score (LP) 4021 *Milky White Way*	80.00	-	120.00
TRU-TONES:			
Chart 634 *Tears In My Eyes*	50.00	-	80.00
ERNEST TUBB:			
Decca (LP) 5301 (10") *Favorites*	20.00	-	30.00
(LP) 5344 (10") *The Old Rugged Cross*	20.00	-	30.00
(LP) 5336 (10") *Sings Jimmy Rodgers Songs*	30.00	-	50.00
(LP) 8291 *Favorites*	15.00	-	20.00
(LP) 8553 *Daddy Of 'Em All*	15.00	-	20.00
JUSTIN TUBB:			
Decca 30606 *Rock It On Down To My House*	7.00	-	10.00
ANITA TUCKER:			
Capitol 3277 *Let's Make Love*	10.00	-	15.00
BILLY JOE TUCKER:			
Maha 103 *Boogie Woogie Bill*	30.00	-	40.00
ERNEST TUCKER:			
Jubilee 5340 *Mirror, Mirror On The Wall*	5.00	-	8.00
ORRIN TUCKER:			
White Rock 1115 *Been Lookin' For Love*	10.00	-	15.00
RICK TUCKER & THE TURKS:			
Veeda 4005 *I'll Be There*	8.00	-	12.00
LEE TULLY:			
Flair-X 3007 *Elwood Pretzel*	10.00	-	15.00
TUNE BLENDERS:			
Federal 12201 *Oh Yes I Know*	20.00	-	30.00
TUNEMASTERS:			
Mark 7002 *Sending This Letter*	15.00	-	25.00
TUNE ROCKERS:			
Pet—*No Stoppin' This Boppin'*		-	
United Artists 139 *The Green Mosquito* (78 RPM)			
(Note: The existence of this record in 78 RPM			
form has not been verified; foreign 78s do			
exist.)			

TUNE TONES:
Herald 539 *She's Right For Me* . . . . 8.00 - 12.00
THE TUNE WEAVERS:
Casa Grande 101 *Little Boy* . . . . 10.00 - 15.00
Casa Grande 4037 *"Happy, Happy Birthday*
Baby" . . . . 20.00 - 30.00
   4038 *This Can't Be Love* . . . . 10.00 - 15.00
   4040 *There Stands My Love* . . . . 10.00 - 15.00
Checker 872 *Happy, Happy Birthday Baby* . . . . . 5.00 - 8.00
  872 *Happy, Happy Birthday Baby* (78 RPM) . 10.00 - 15.00
(Checker 872 occurs with two different flip sides)
TURBANS:
Herald 458 *When You Dance* . . . . 7.00 - 10.00
  458 *When You Dance* (78 RPM) . . . . 10.00 - 15.00
  469 *Sister Sookey* . . . . 8.00 - 12.00
  478 *B-I-N-G-O* (Bingo) . . . . 8.00 - 12.00
  486 *All Of My Love* . . . . 8.00 - 12.00
  495 *Valley Of Love* . . . . 8.00 - 12.00
  510 *Congratulations* . . . . 8.00 - 12.00
Imperial 5807, 5828, 5847 . . . . 5.00 - 10.00
Money 209 *No No Cherry* . . . . 15.00 - 20.00
  211 *When I Return* . . . . 15.00 - 20.00
(Note: flip side of Money 211 is by THE
TURKS)
Roulette 4281, 4326 . . . . 4.00 - 8.00
THE TURKS:
(See also RICK TUCKER)
Ball 101 *Emily* . . . . 7.00 - 10.00
Bally 1017 *This Heart Of Mine* . . . . 10.00 - 15.00
Cash 1042 *It Can't Be True* . . . . 10.00 - 15.00
Class 256 *Rockville U.S.A.* . . . . 5.00 - 8.00
Imperial 5783 *I'm A Fool* . . . . 5.00 - 8.00
Knight 2005 *It Can't Be True* . . . . 10.00 - 15.00
Money 211 *Emily* . . . . 15.00 - 20.00
(Note: Flip side of Money 211 is by THE
TURBANS)
  215 *I've Been Accused* . . . . 15.00 - 20.00
RICHARD TURLEY:
Fraternity 845 *Makin' Love To My Baby* . . . . . 10.00 - 15.00
IKE TURNER & KINGS OF RHYTHM:
Cobra 5033 *Walking Down The Aisle* . . . . 8.00 - 12.00
JACK TURNER:
Hickory 1050 *Everybody's Rockin' But Me* . . . . 15.00 - 20.00
JESSIE LEE TURNER:
Carlton 509 *Baby Please Don't Tease* . . . . 5.00 - 8.00
Imperial 5649 *I'm The Little Space Girl's Father* 7.00 - 10.00
Sudden 105 *The Elopers* . . . . 4.00 - 7.00
(BIG) JOE TURNER:
Atlantic (EP) 536 *Joe Turner Sings* . . . . 30.00 - 40.00
  (EP) 565 *Joe Turner* . . . . 30.00 - 40.00
  (EP) 606 *Rock With Joe Turner* . . . . 35.00 - 50.00
  982 *Still In Love* . . . . 10.00 - 15.00
  1001 *Honey Hush* . . . . 8.00 - 12.00
  1016 *TV Mama* . . . . 7.00 - 10.00
  1026 *Shake, Rattle & Roll* . . . . 7.00 - 10.00
  1040 *Well All Right* . . . . 5.00 - 8.00
  1053 *Flip, Flop And Fly* . . . . 5.00 - 8.00
  1069 *Midnight Cannonball* . . . . 5.00 - 8.00
  1080 *The Chicken And The Hawk* . . . . 5.00 - 8.00
  (LP) 1234 *Boss Of The Blues* . . . . 30.00 - 40.00
  (LP) 1243 *Joe Turner Sings Kansas City Jazz*
   (black label) . . . . 30.00 - 40.00
  (LP) 1332 *Big Joe Rides Again* . . . . 30.00 - 40.00
  (LP) 8005 *Joe Turner* (black label) . . . . . . 30.00 - 40.00
  (LP) 8023 *Rockin' The Blues* . . . . 50.00 - 75.00
  (LP) 8033 *Big Joe Is Here* . . . . 40.00 - 60.00
Crown (LP) 5295 *Joe Turner With Red Nelson* . 15.00 - 20.00
Decca 29711 *Piney Brown Blues* . . . . 8.00 - 12.00
  29924 *Corrine, Corrina* . . . . 8.00 - 12.00
Savoy (LP) 14012 . . . *And The Blues* . . . . . . 15.00 - 20.00
  (LP) 14016 *Careless Love* . . . . 15.00 - 20.00
TU TONES:

Lin 5021 *Saccharin Sally* . . . . 10.00 - 15.00
BILL TUTT:
Gilt-Edge 5082 *Monkey On My Back* . . . . — - —
TV SLIM: (See also OSCAR WILLS)
Checker 870 *Flat Foot Sam* . . . . 7.00 - 10.00
  1029 *The Big Fight* . . . . 7.00 - 10.00
Clif 103 *Flat Foot Sam* . . . . 30.00 - 50.00
Speed 704 *Flat Foot Sam Meets Jim Dandy* . . . . 10.00 - 15.00
  705 *My Ship Is Sinking* . . . . 10.00 - 15.00
  706 *My Baby Is Gone* . . . . 10.00 - 15.00
  711 *Don't Reach 'Cross My Plate* . . . . 10.00 - 15.00
  714, 715, 803, 807, 808, 810 . . . . 7.00 - 10.00
  6865 *To Prove My Love* . . . . 7.00 - 10.00
"TWELVE FLIP HITS"
Flip (LP) 1001 (various artists) . . . . 20.00 - 30.00
TWILIGHTERS (& DONALD RICHARDS):
Bubble 1334 *My Silent Prayer* . . . . 10.00 - 15.00
Cholly 712 *Let There Be Love* . . . . 15.00 - 20.00
Ebb 117 *Live Like A King* . . . . 15.00 - 20.00
Groove 0154 *Sittin' In A Corner* . . . . 15.00 - 20.00
J-V-B 83 *How Many Times* . . . . 50.00 - 80.00
Marshall 702 *Please Tell Me You're Mine*
  (red plastic) . . . . 80.00 - 120.00
MGM 55011 *Little Did I Dream* . . . . 50.00 - 75.00
  55014 *Half Angel* . . . . 50.00 - 75.00
Paloma 100 *You Better Make It* . . . . — - —
Pico 2801 *Eternally* . . . . — - —
RPM 419 *Oo Wah* . . . . 10.00 - 15.00
Specialty 548 *It's True* . . . . 10.00 - 15.00
Spin 1 *Yes You Are* . . . . 7.00 - 10.00
Super— *Please Come Home* . . . . 10.00 - 15.00
TWILIGHTS:
Finesse 1717 *My Heart Belongs Only To You* . . . 15.00 - 20.00
Six Star 1002 *Little Richard* . . . . 8.00 - 12.00
TWILITERS (See TWILIGHTERS)
CONWAY TWITTY:
Mercury 71086 *I Need Your Lovin'* (maroon label) 10.00 - 15.00
  71148 *Shake It Up* . . . . 15.00 - 20.00
  71384 *Double Talk Baby* . . . . 10.00 - 15.00
Metro (LP) 512 *It's Only Make Believe* . . . . . 12.00 - 18.00
MGM (LP) 3744 *Conway Twitty Sings* . . . . . . 30.00 - 40.00
  (LP) 3786 *Saturday Night* . . . . 25.00 - 50.00
  (LP) 3818 *Lonely Blue Boy* . . . . 20.00 - 30.00
MGM (LP) 3907 *The Rock And Roll Story* . . . . 30.00 - 40.00
BIG "T" TYLER:
Aladdin 3384 *King Kong* . . . . 10.00 - 15.00
FRANKIE TYLER:
Okeh 7103 *I Go Ape* . . . . 15.00 - 20.00
JOHNNY TYLER:
Ekko 1000 *Devil's Hot Rod* (red plastic) . . . . . 35.00 - 50.00
Rural Rhythm 515 *Lie To Me Baby* (red plastic) . 40.00 - 60.00
Starday 263 *Lie To Me Baby* . . . . 30.00 - 40.00
KIP TYLER (& HIS FLIPS):
Challenge 1014 *She Got Eyes* . . . . 8.00 - 12.00
  59008 *Ooh Yeah Baby* . . . . 8.00 - 12.00
Ebb 154 *She's My Witch* . . . . 15.00 - 20.00
  156 *Oh Linda* . . . . 10.00 - 15.00
Starla 003 *Let's Monkey Around* . . . . 10.00 - 15.00
RUCKUS TYLER:
Fabor 135 *Rollin' And A-Rockin'* . . . . 15.00 - 25.00
TYMES:
Parkway (LP) 7032 *So Much In Love* . . . . . . 30.00 - 50.00
  (LP) 7038 *The Sound of the Wonderful Tymes* . — - —
UNIQUES:
End 1012 *Tell The Angels* . . . . 15.00 - 20.00
Lucky Four 1024 *Silver Moon* . . . . 10.00 - 15.00
Mr. Cee 100 *Look At Me* . . . . 8.00 - 12.00
Peacock 1695 *Picture Of My Baby* . . . . 8.00 - 12.00
Tee Kay 112 *A Miilion Miles Away* . . . . 15.00 - 20.00
UNIQUE TEENS:
Dynamic 110 *Whatcha Know Now* . . . . 7.00 - 10.00
UNIVERSALS:

Cora-Lee 101 *The Pictures*	15.00 -	20.00
Mark-X 7004 *Again*	30.00 -	40.00
Shepherd— *A Love Only You Can Give*	7.00 -	10.00
UPFRONTS:		
Lummtone 103 *It Took Time*	10.00 -	15.00
UPSETTERS:		
Little Star 123 *Every Night About This Time*	7.00 -	10.00
128 *Valley Of Tears*	7.00 -	10.00
UPSTARTS:		
Apollo 468 *Feed Me Baby*	15.00 -	20.00
THE UPTONES:		
Lute 6025 *I'll Be There*	10.00 -	15.00
6029 *Be Mine*	10.00 -	15.00
AL URBAN:		
Sarg 148 *Lookin' For Money*	15.00 -	20.00
158 *Won't Tell You Her Name*	15.00 -	20.00
UTAH CARL:		
Starday 301 *Lovin' You*	10.00 -	15.00
VAL-CHORDS:		
Gametime 104 *Candy Store Love*	15.00 -	20.00
BLACKIE VALE:		
Hurricane 100 *If I Had Me A Woman*	35.00 -	50.00
RITCHIE VALENS:		
Del-Fi (LP) PR-1 *Ritchie Valens*	20.00 -	30.00
(LP) 1201 *Ritchie Valens*	40.00 -	60.00
(LP) 1206 *Ritchie*	35.00 -	50.00
(LP) 1214—*In Concert At Pacoima Jr. High* ...	30.00 -	40.00
(LP) 1225 *His Greatest Hits*	15.00 -	25.00
(LP) 1247 *His Greatest Hits, VoL 2*	20.00 -	30.00
VALENTINES:		
Old Town 1009 *Tonight Kathleen*	100.00 -	150.00
Rama 171 *Liiy Maebelle* (blue label)	25.00 -	35.00
181 *I Love You Darling* (blue label)	25.00 -	35.00
186 *Christmas Prayer* (blue label)	80.00 -	120.00
196 *The Woo Woo Train*	10.00 -	15.00
201 *I'll Never Let You Go*	10.00 -	15.00
208 *Nature's Creation*	10.00 -	15.00
228 *Don't Say Goodnight*	10.00 -	15.00
THE VALETS:		
Jon 4219 *You And You Alone*	8.00 -	12.00
VALIANTS:		
Ensign 4035 *Walkin' Girl*	7.00 -	10.00
Keen 34004 *This Is The Night*	10.00 -	15.00
3-4007 *Walkin' Girl*	10.00 -	15.00
3-4026 *Please Wait My Love*	10.00 -	15.00
FRANKIE VALLE/VALLEY/VALLI/VALLY (&		
THE ROMANS THE TRAVELLERS):		
Cindy 3012 *Real*	30.00 -	40.00
Corona 1234 *My Mother's Eyes*	75.00 -	100.00
Decca 30994 *Please Take A Chance*	35.00 -	50.00
Mercury 70381 *Forgive And Forget* (maroon label)	35.00 -	50.00
VALQUINS:		
Gaity 161 *Falling Star*	15.00 -	25.00
VAL-TONES:		
DeLuxe 6084 *Tender Darling*	15.00 -	20.00
Gee 1004 *You Belong To My Heart*	— -	—
AL VANCE:		
Goldwax 116 *Every Woman I Know*	7.00 -	10.00
VAN DYKES:		
Decca 30654 *The Fixer*	15.00 -	20.00
De Luxe 6193 *The Bells Are Ringing*	5.00 -	8.00
8.00		
ARNOLD VAN WINKLE:		
Ruby 540 *A Rusty Old Dime*	15.00 -	20.00
VARIETEERS:		
Hickory 1025 *Call My Gal, Miss Jones*	50.00 -	75.00
VARNELLS:		
Arnold 1003 *Who Created Love*	15.00 -	20.00
1006 *All Because*	15.00 -	20.00
BOBBY VAUGHN:		
Whiz 503 *Good Good Lovin'*	8.00 -	12.00
DALE VAUGHN:		

Von 480 *High Steppin'*	80.00 -	120.00
DELL VAUGHN with THE FORTUNE AIRES:		
Fortune—*Rock The Universe*	15.00 -	20.00
Hi-Q 5044 *Rock The Universe*	8.00 -	12.00
VECTORS:		
Standard 700 *One Day*	— -	—
RUSS VEERS:		
Trend 30010 *Warm As Toast*	15.00 -	20.00
VELAIRES:		
Jamie 1198 *Roll Over Beethoven*	8.00 -	12.00
1203 *Sticks And Stones*	7.00 -	10.00
1211 *Ubangi Stomp*	7.00 -	10.00
GENE VELL:		
Whiz 9001 *I Done Got Over*	8.00 -	12.00
VELOURS:		
Cub 9001 *Remember*	10.00 -	15.00
9014 *Crazy Love*	10.00 -	15.00
9029 *Blue Velvet*	8.00 -	12.00
End 1090 *Lover Come Back*	8.00 -	12.00
Onyx 501 *My Love Come Back*	30.00 -	40.00
Onyx 508 *Romeo*	50.00 -	80.00
512 *Can I Come Over Tonight*	25.00 -	35.00
515 *This Could Be The Night*	20.00 -	30.00
Onyx 520 *Remember*	15.00 -	20.00
Orbit 9001 *Remember*	12.00 -	18.00
VELS:		
Trebco 16 *Please Be Mine*	20.00 -	30.00
VELVATONES:		
Meteor 5042 *Real Gone Baby*	20.00 -	30.00
VELVETEENS:		
Stark 102 *Teen Prayer*	8.00 -	12.00
VELVETEERS:		
Spitfire 15 *Tell Me You're Mine*	150.00 -	UP
VELVETONES:		
Aladdin 3372 *The Glory Of Love*	30.00 -	50.00
3391 *I Found My Love*	30.00 -	40.00
Ascot 2117 *I Want Him So Bad*	4.00 -	7.00
D 1049 *Penalty Of Love*	15.00 -	20.00
1072 *Worried Over You*	15.00 -	20.00
Deb 1008 *Stars Of Wonder*	8.00 -	12.00
Imperial 5878 *The Glory Of Love*	5.00 -	8.00
Milmart 113 *A Prayer At Gettysburg*	30.00 -	40.00
THE VELVETS:		
Fury 1012 *I-I-I (Love You So-So-So)*	10.00 -	15.00
Red Robin 120 *They Tried*	35.00 -	50.00
122 *I*	35.00 -	50.00
27 *I Cried*	35.00 -	50.00
20th Fox 165 *If I Could Be With You*	— -	—
THE VELVITONES (See VELVETONES)		
NICK VENET:		
Imperial 5522 *Love In Be Bop Time*	8.00 -	12.00
RCA Victor (EP) 4100 *Flippin'*	15.00 -	20.00
VENTURES:		
Blue Horizon 100 *Cookies And Cake*	8.00 -	12.00
VERNALLS:		
Ru Lu 6753 *Raindrops*	40.00 -	60.00
LARRY VERNE:		
Era (LP) 104 *Mister Larry Verne*	20.00 -	30.00
VERNON & CLIFF:		
Dootone 443 *You Came Along*	5.00 -	8.00
VERNON & THE JEWELS:		
Kayo 5104 *The Thought Of You*	7.00 -	10.00
RAY VERNON:		
Rumble 1349 *Evil Angel*	8.00 -	12.00
THE VERSATILES: (See also JERRY		
SHEELY):		
Atlantic 2004 *Passing By*	10.00 -	15.00
Coaster 800 *In The Garden Of Love*	8.00 -	12.00
Peacock 1910 *The White Cliffs Of Dover*	8.00 -	12.00
Rocal 1002 *Lundee Dundee*	15.00 -	20.00
VERSATONES:		
All Star 501 *Tight Skirt And Sweater*	15.00 -	20.00

THE VESTELLES:
Decca 30733 *Ditta Wa Do* . . . . 7.00 - 10.00
THE VETS:
Swami 551 *Wipe The Tears From Your Eyes* . . . . . 10.00 - 15.00
VIBES:
ABC Paramount 9810 *Darling* . . . . 10.00 - 15.00
Allied 10006 *What's Her Name* . . . . 10.00 - 15.00
Chariot 105 *Stop Torturing Me* . . . . .150.00 - 200.00
VIBRAHARPS:
Atco 6134 *It Must Be Magic* . . . . 8.00 - 12.00
Beech 713 *Walk Beside Me* . . . . 15.00 - 20.00
VIBRANAIRES:
After Hours 103 *Doll Face* (red plastic) . . . . . . .200.00 - 300.00
Chariot 103 *Doll Face* . . . . .150.00 - 200.00
VICEROYS:
Original Sound 15 *Dreamy Eyes* . . . . 8.00 - 12.00
MAC VICKERY:
Abco 502 *Bell Bottom Jeans* . . . . — - —
Gone 5075 *Meant To Be* . . . . 8.00 - 12.00
RAY VICT & THE BOP ROCKERS:
Goldband 1042 *Bop Stop Rock* . . . . 15.00 - 25.00
VICTORIANS:
Selma 1002 *Wedding Bells* . . . . 15.00 - 20.00
Specialty 411 *Don't Break My Heart Again* . . . . . 50.00 - 75.00
420 *Part Time Sweetheart* . . . . 50.00 - 75.00
VIDALTONES:
Josie 900 *Forever* . . . . 7.00 - 10.00
VIDELS:
JDS 5004 *Mister Lonely* . . . . 10.00 - 15.00
5005 *She's Not Coming Home* . . . . 10.00 - 15.00
Kapp 405 *A Letter From Ann* . . . . 15.00 - 20.00
Rhody 2000 *Be My Girl* . . . . 15.00 - 20.00
THE VIDEOS:
Casino 102 *Moonglow You Know* . . . . 10.00 - 15.00
105 *Love Or Infatuation* . . . . 15.00 - 25.00
VI-KINGS:
Del-Mann 544 *Rock A Little Bit* . . . . 8.00 - 12.00
DARRYL VINCENT:
Sandy 1016 *Daddy's Gone Batty* . . . . 15.00 - 20.00
1020 *Wild Wild Party* . . . . 15.00 - 25.00
GENE VINCENT & THE BLUE CAPS:
Capitol (EP) 764 *Bluejean Bop! each* . . . . 50.00 - 75.00
(Note: The EP is actually three, together
comprising the LP following. Although the EP
catalog numbers have prefixes 1-, 2-, and
3-designating parts 1, 2, and 3, these prefixes
are omitted here and in the case of other EPs
in series.)
Capitol (LP) 764 *Bluejean Bop!* . . . . .100.00 - 150.00
(EP) 811 *Gene Vincent And The Blue Caps*
(3 parts) (each) . . . . 50.00 - 75.00
(LP) 811 *Gene Vincent And The Blues Caps* . . .100.00 - 150.00
(EP) *Gene Vincent Rocks And The Blue Caps*
Roll (3 parts) (each) . . . . 50.00 - 75.00
(LP) 970 *Gene Vincent Rocks And The Blues*
Caps Roll . . . . 75.00 - 100.00
(EP) 985 *Hot Rod Gang* . . . . .100.00 - 150.00
(EP) 1059 *A Gene Vincent Record Date*
(3 parts) . . . . 50.00 - 75.00
(LP) 1059 *A Gene Vincent Record Date* . . . . . . 80.00 - 120.00
(LP) 1207 *Sounds Like Gene Vincent* . . . . 80.00 - 120.00
(LP) 1342 *Crazy Times* . . . . 80.00 - 120.00
Capitol 3450 *Be Bop A Lula* (78 RPM) . . . . 15.00 - 20.00
3450 *Be Bop A Lula* . . . . 7.00 - 10.00
3530 *Race With The Devil* . . . . 5.00 - 8.00
3558 *Bluejean Bop* . . . . 7.00 - 10.00
3558 *Bluejean Bop* (78 RPM) . . . . 15.00 - 20.00
3617 *Crazy Legs* . . . . 5.00 - 8.00
3678 *Five Days Five Days* . . . . 8.00 - 12.00
3763 *Lotta Lovin'* . . . . 7.00 - 10.00
3763 *Lotta Lovin'* (78 RPM) . . . . 15.00 - 20.00
3839 *Dance To The Bop* (78 RPM) . . . . 15.00 - 20.00

3839 *Dance To The Bop* . . . . 7.00 - 10.00
3874 *I Gotta Baby* . . . . 8.00 - 12.00
3959 *Baby Blue* . . . . 8.00 - 12.00
4010 *Rocky Road Blues* . . . . 8.00 - 12.00
4051 *Git It* . . . . 10.00 - 15.00
4105 *BE Bop Boogie Boy* . . . . 10.00 - 15.00
4153 *Who's Pushn' Your Swing* . . . . 10.00 - 15.00
4237 *Right Now* . . . . 10.00 - 15.00
4313 *Wild Cat* . . . . 15.00 - 20.00
4442 *Pistol Packin' Mama* . . . . 10.00 - 15.00
4525 *If You Want My Lovin'* . . . . 10.00 - 15.00
4665 *Lucky Star* . . . . 15.00 - 20.00
Challenge 59365 *Hurtin' For You Baby* . . . . 5.00 - 8.00
VINES:
Cee-Jay 582 *I Must See You Again* . . . . 7.00 - 10.00
DOT VINSON:
MGM 12734 *Livin' With The Blues* . . . . 7.00 - 10.00
EDDIE "CLEANHEAD" VINSON: (See also
Battle of The Blues)
Aamco (LP) 74 *Clean Heads Back In Town* . . . . . 20.00 - 30.00
King 4563 *I Need You Tonight* . . . . 8.00 - 12.00
4582 *Person To Person* . . . . 8.00 - 12.00
(Note: Earlier issues, usually found as 78 RPM
records valued at $4-$8, may be found as 45s,
valued at $10 to $15)
Mercury 70334 *Old Man Boogie* . . . . 8.00 - 12.00
70525 *Anxious Heart* . . . . 7.00 - 10.00
(Note: Earlier issues, in the Mercury 2000 and
8000 series, are 78 rpm records, valued
at $4-$8)
VIOLINAIRES:
Drummond 4000 *Another Soldier Gone* . . . . .150.00 - 200.00
VISCOUNTS:
Amy (LP) 8008 *Harlem Nocturne* . . . . 20.00 - 30.00
Madison (LP) 1001 *The Viscounts* . . . . 25.00 - 35.00
Mercury 71073 *My Girl* . . . . 5.00 - 8.00
Star-Fax 1002 *Wondering*
THE VISIONS:
Big Top 3092 *Tell Me You're Mine* . . . . 8.00 - 12.00
R & R 3002 *It's You I Love* . . . . .00 - .00
VISUALS:
Poplar 115 *Submarine Race* . . . . 7.00 - 10.00
117 *My Juanita* . . . . 7.00 - 10.00
121 *Please Don't Be Mad At Me* . . . . 10.00 - 15.00
VITO & SALUTATIONS:
Rayna 5009 *Gloria* . . . . 10.00 - 15.00
THE VOCALEERS:
Paradise 113 *I Need Your Love So Bad* . . . . 10.00 - 15.00
Red Robin 113 *Be True* . . . . 50.00 - 80.00
114 *Is It A Dream* . . . . 50.00 - 80.00
119 *I Walk Alone* . . . . 50.00 - 80.00
125 *Love You* . . . . 50.00 - 80.00
132 *Angel Face* . . . . 50.00 - 80.00
Twistime 45-T-II *A Golden Tear* . . . . 10.00 - 15.00
Vest 832 *Hear My Plea* . . . . 7.00 - 10.00
VOCALTONES:
Apollo 488 *My Girl* . . . . 35.00 - 50.00
492 *Darling* . . . . 35.00 - 50.00
497 *My Version Of Love* . . . . 35.00 - 50.00
Cindy 3004 *Walkin' By Baby* . . . . 20.00 - 30.00
VOICE MASTERS:
Anna 102 *Needed* . . . . 10.00 - 15.00
123 *Everytime* . . . . 10.00 - 15.00
VOICES:
Cash 1011 *Why* . . . . 15.00 - 25.00
1016 *Santa Claus Boogie* . . . . 15.00 - 25.00
VOICES FIVE:
Craft 116 *For Sentimental Reasons* . . . . 7.00 - 10.00
WES VOIGHT: (See aliso TOWN THREE)
King 5211 *I'm Movin' In* . . . . 15.00 - 20.00
VOLTONES:
Dynamic 107 *If She Should Call* . . . . 40.00 - 60.00

THE VOLUMES:

Chex 1002 *I Love You*	7.00 -	10.00
1005 *Come Back Into My Heart*	7.00 -	10.00
Ivy 104 *In My Heart*	8.00 -	12.00
Jaguar 3004 *I Won't Tell A Soul*	30.00 -	50.00
3006 *So Disappointed With Love*	30.00 -	50.00
Jubilee 5446 *Teenage Paradise*	4.00 -	7.00

VONDELLS:

Marvello *Valentino*	10.00 -	15.00

THE VOWS:

Tamara 760 *Dottie*	8.00 -	12.00

THE VOXPOPPERS:

Mercury 71315 *Ping Pong Baby*	5.00 -	8.00

LYNN VROOMAN:

Penguin 1010 *Let The Good Times Roll*	7.00 -	10.00

WADE & DICK:

Sun 269 *Bop Bop Baby*	8.00 -	12.00

DON WADE:

San 206 *Gone, Gone, Gone*	15.00 -	20.00

RONNIE WADE:

King 5061 *Gotta Make Her Mine*	10.00 -	15.00
5078 *I Know But I'll Never Tell*	10.00 -	15.00
5112 *All I Want*	10.00 -	15.00

CHARLIE WAGGONER:

Linco 503 *One Eyed Sam*	15.00 -	20.00

PORTER WAGONER:

RCA Victor (LP) 1358 *Satisfied Man*	15.00 -	20.00

THE WAILERS:

Golden Crest (LP) 3075 *The Fabulous Wailers*	20.00 -	30.00

HAPPY WAINWRIGHT:

Sandy 1004 *My Baby Don't Love Me No More*	30.00 -	50.00

LES WALDROOP:

Flop 1012 *Got It Made In The Shade*	-	

JACKIE WALKER:

Imperial 5473 *Peggy Sue*	10.00 -	15.00
Imperial 5490 *Only Teenagers Allowed*	8.00 -	12.00

LANIE WALKER

Blue Hen *Eenie Meenie Miney Mo/No Use Knocking*	30.00 -	50.00

T-BONE WALKER:

Atlantic 1065 *T-Bone Shuffle*	8.00 -	12.00
1074 *Play On Little Girl*	8.00 -	12.00
(LP) 8020 *T Bone Blues*	25.00 -	35.00
Capitol (LP) 370 *T-Bone Walker (10")*	50.00 -	80.00
(LP) 1958 *The Great Blues Vocals & Guitar Of T-Bone Walker*	30.00 -	40.00
Imperial 5171 *Cold Cold Boogie* (blue label)	30.00 -	40.00
5202 *Street Walking Woman*	30.00 -	40.00
5216 *Blue Mood*	20.00 -	30.00
5228 *Long Distance Blues*	20.00 -	30.00
5239 *Party Girl*	20.00 -	30.00
5284 *Wanderin' Heart*	15.00 -	25.00
5311 *High Society*	15.00 -	25.00
(LP) 9098 *T-Bone Walker Sings The Blues*	50.00 -	75.00
(LP) 9116 *Singing The Blues*	50.00 -	75.00
(LP) 9146 *I Get So Weary*	50.00 -	75.00

WAYNE WALKER:

Brunswick 55133 *You've Got Me*	8.00 -	12.00
Everest 19380 *Love, Love, Love*	7.00 -	10.00

SHADY WALL:

Decca 30539 *The New Raunchy*	5.00 -	8.00

BILLY WALLACE (& THE BAMA DRIFTERS):

Deb 1003 *Don't Flirt With My Baby*	10.00 -	15.00
Mercury 70876 *That's My Reward*	10.00 -	15.00
70957 *Burning Wind*	10.00 -	15.00

JOE WALLACE & THE OWLS:

Moon 304 *Leopard Man*	10.00 -	15.00

VANN WALLS & THE ROCKETS:

Atlantic 988 *Open The Door*	35.00 -	50.00

WALTON & SILVER LAKE BOYS:

Lael 1137 *Man What A Party*	75.00 -	100.00

JAMES WALTON & HIS BLUES KINGS:

Hi-Q 5029 *Miss Jessie James*	5.00 -	10.00

SQUARE WALTON:

RCA Victor 5493 *Gimme Your Bank Roll*	20.00 -	30.00
5584 *Bad Hangover*	20.00 -	30.00

WANDERERS:

Cub 9023, 9094	5.00 -	10.00
Kent 356 *Everybody's Somebody's Fool*	10.00 -	15.00
Onyx 518 *Thinking Of You*	15.00 -	25.00
Savoy 1109 *We Could Find Happiness*	50.00 -	75.00

BILLY WARD & HIS DOMINOES (See also: The Dominoes & Clyde McPhatter)

Decca (EP) 2549 *Billy Ward & The Dominoes*	50.00 -	75.00
(LP) 8621 *Billy Ward & The Dominoes*	50.00 -	80.00
29933, 30043, 30149	7.00 -	10.00
30420 *To Each His Own*	10.00 -	15.00
Federal (LP) 295-94 (10-inch)	150.00 -	200.00
(LP) 395-94 (12-inch)	150.00 -	200.00
Federal (LP) 548 *Billy Ward & His Dominoes*	50.00 -	80.00
12139 *You Can't Keep A Good Man Down*	15.00 -	20.00
12162 *Until The Real Thing Comes Along*	10.00 -	15.00
12178 *Tootsie Roll*	10.00 -	15.00
12184 *Handwriting On The Wall*	10.00 -	15.00
12193 *Above Jacob's Ladder*	15.00 -	20.00
12209 *Can't Do Sixty No More*	10.00 -	15.00
12218 *Cave Man*	10.00 -	15.00
12263 *Bobby Sox Baby*	8.00 -	12.00
12301 *One Moment With You*	8.00 -	12.00
12308 *Have Mercy Baby*	8.00 -	12.00
Jubilee 5163 *Come To Me Baby*	8.00 -	12.00
5213 *Take Me Back To Heaven*	8.00 -	12.00
King (LP) 548 *Billy Ward & His Dominoes with Clyde McPhatter*	40.00 -	60.00
(King 548 is a repackaging of Federal 548, above)		
(LP) 733 *Billy Ward And His Dominoes*	35.00 -	50.00
1280 *Rags To Riches*	8.00 -	12.00
1281 *Christmas In Heaven*	20.00 -	30.00
1342 *Tenderly*	10.00 -	15.00
1364 *Three Coins In The Fountain*	8.00 -	12.00
1365 *Little Things Mean A Lot*	10.00 -	15.00
1492 *Learnin' The Blues*	10.00 -	15.00
1502 *Give Me You*	10.00 -	15.00
5463 *Lay In On The Line*	7.00 -	10.00
Liberty (LP) 3056 *Sea Of Glass*	15.00 -	20.00

WILLIE WARD:

Fee-Bee 233 *I'm A Madman*	15.00 -	20.00

EDDIE WARE & HIS BAND:

States 130 *Lonely Broken Heart*	15.00 -	25.00

BABY BOY WARREN:

Blue Lake 106 *Santa Fe* (red plastic)	100.00 -	150.00
Drummond 3003 *Stop Breakin' Down*	100.00 -	150.00

DOUG WARREN & THE RAYS:

Image 1011 *Around Midnight*	8.00 -	12.00

JOEY WARREN:

Superior 3305 *Goatee*	4.00 -	7.00

WASHBOARD SAM:

Chess 1545 *Diggin' My Potatoes*	75.00 -	100.00
RCA Victor 50-0023 *I'm Just Tired*	30.00 -	40.00
50-0048 *Market Street Swing*	30.00 -	40.00
50-0090 *Motherless Child Blues*	30.00 -	40.00
(Note: Above RCA Victor records are made of orange plastic.)		

BABY WASHINGTON & THE PLANTS:

J & S 1632 *I Hate To See You Go*	7.00 -	10.00

LEROY WASHINGTON:

Excello 2144 *Wild Cherry*	8.00 -	12.00

CROWN PRINCE WATERFORD (See: Party After Hours, and Blues, etc. section)

BILL WATKINS:

Tip-Toe 14321 *I Got Troubles*	20.00 -	30.00

KATIE WATKINS:

Checker 879 *Snake Blues* .... 5.00 - 8.00

GENE WATSON & THE ROCKETS:
Tri-Dec 8357 *My Rockin' Baby* .... 30.00 - 40.00

JIMMY WATSON:
Brunswick 55079 *Daisy* .... 5.00 - 8.00

YOUNG JOHN WATSON:
Federal 12120 *Highway 60* .... 30.00 - 50.00
    12131 *Motor Head Baby* .... 30.00 - 50.00
    12143 *I Got Eyes* .... 20.00 - 30.00
    12157 *What's Going On* .... 20.00 - 30.00
    12175 *Space Guitar* .... 15.00 - 20.00

JOHNNY WATSON:
Cactus *I'm Not Crazy* .... 15.00 - 20.00

JOHNNY "GUITAR" WATSON:
Class 246 *One More Kiss* .... 3.00 - 5.00
Goth 101 *Rat Now* .... 4.00 - 7.00
Jowat 118 *Baby Don't Leave* .... 5.00 - 8.00
King (LP) 857 *Johnny "Guitar" Watson* .... 30.00 - 40.00
RPM 455 *Three Hours Past Midnight* .... 8.00 - 12.00

HUNTER WATTS:
Hammond 103 *Wild Man Rock* .... 15.00 - 20.00

NOBLE ("THIN MAN") WATTS:
Baton 246, 249, 251, 254, 257, 266, 273 .... 4.00 - 7.00

SLIM WATTS:
Starday 282 *Tu La Lou* .... 20.00 - 30.00

ALVIS WAYNE:
Westport 132 *Swing Bop Boogie* .... 30.00 - 50.00
    138 *Don't Mean Maybe, Baby* ...... 30.00 - 50.00
    140 *You Are The One* .... 8.00 - 12.00

BILLY WAYNE:
Hill Crest 778 *I Love My Baby* .... 25.00 - 40.00

BOBBY WAYNE (with THE WARRIORS):
LV 101 *Sally Ann* .... 15.00 - 20.00
Mercury 71070 *Gone* .... 7.00 - 10.00

GAYLON WAYNE:
Universal Artist 52071 *High School's On Fire* ... 10.00 - 15.00

LITTLE JACKIE WAYNE:
Rem 306 *White Felt Hat* .... — - —

JAMES WAYNE:
Aladdin 3234 *Crying In Vain* .... 15.00 - 20.00
Imperial 5258 *Sweet Little Woman* .... 20.00 - 30.00
Peacock 1672 *Please Be Mine* .... 7.00 - 10.00

ROY WAYNE:
Clif 101 *Honey Won't You Listen* ..... 30.00 - 50.00

SCOTTY WAYNE:
Talent Scout 1008 *Only One* .... 8.00 - 12.00
    1011 *Roobie Doobie* .... 8.00 - 12.00

THOMAS WAYNE:
Mercury 71287 *You're The One That Done It* .... 15.00 - 20.00
Boppin' The Blues .... —

WEE WILLIE WAYNE:
Imperial 5355 *Travelin' Mood* .... 10.00 - 15.00
    5368 *Good News* .... 10.00 - 15.00
    5737 *I Got To Be Careful* .... 7.00 - 10.00
    (LP) 9144 *Travelin' Mood* .... 50.00 - 75.00

ALFY WEATHERBEE:
Roulette 4005 *49 Jukeboxes* .... 7.00 - 10.00

JOE WEAVER & THE BLUENOTES/
DON JUANS:
Fortune 825 *Baby, I Love You So* ..... 10.00 - 15.00
Jaguar 3011 *Lazy Susan* .... 15.00 - 20.00

BOBBY WEBB (& THE JETS):
Jazzmar 1 *Feel The Same* .... 10.00 - 15.00
Webb 429 *Tears Over You* .... 10.00 - 15.00

BOOGIE BILL WEBB:
Imperial 5257 *Bad Dog* .... 35.00 - 50.00

DON WEBB:
Brunswick 55158 *I'll Be Back Home* .... 8.00 - 12.00

HOYT WEBB:
Ruby 320 *Baby Won't You Slow It Down* .... 15.00 - 20.00

WEBS:
Sotoplay 660 *Let Me Take You Home* .... 25.00 - 40.00

KATIE WEBSTER:
Action 1000 *Close To My Heart* ...... 5.00 - 8.00
Rocko 503, 513 .... 7.00 - 10.00
U.S.A. 736, 742 .... 3.00 - 5.00
Zynn 505 *Hoowee, Sweet Daddy* ..... 8.00 - 12.00

THE WEBTONES:
MGM 12724 *My Lost Love* .... 8.00 - 12.00

RUSTY WELLINGTON (& HIS BLUE RANGERS):
Arcade 124 *I Want A Little Lovin'* .... 10.00 - 15.00
MGM 12581 *Rocking Chair On The Moon* .... 15.00 - 20.00

ARDIS WELLS:
Azalea 132 *Baby Doll* .... 8.00 - 12.00

GLENN WELLS & THE BLENDS:
Jin 122 *Lesson In Love* .... 8.00 - 12.00

JUNIOR WELLS (& HIS EAGLE ROCKERS):
Chief 7005 *Two Headed Woman* ..... 7.00 - 10.00
Chief 7016, 7021, 7034, 7035, 7038, 7048 ..... 7.00 - 10.00
Profile 4005 *I Could Cry* .... 5.00 - 8.00
    4011 *Come On In This House* ...... 5.00 - 8.00
    4013 *You Don't Care* .... 5.00 - 8.00
Shad 5010 *So Tired* .... 5.00 - 8.00
States 122 *Cut That Out* (red plastic) .... 80.00 - 120.00
    134 *Junior's Wail* (red plastic) ...... 80.00 - 120.00
    139 *'Bout The Break Of Day* (red plastic) .... 80.00 - 120.00
    143 *So All Alone* (red plastic) ...... 75.00 - 100.00

COY WERLEY:
Sundown 122 *Black Jack* .... 15.00 - 20.00

JIMMY WERT:
Skyline 752 *Bingo Blues* .... 30.00 - 40.00

JOE WEST:
Bandbox 276 *Maybe You're The One* .... 7.00 - 10.00

PENNY WEST:
Ozark 102 *Needle In A Haystack* .... — - —

SONNEE WEST:
Nor Va Jak 1956 *Rock Ola Ruby* .... 150.00 - 200.00

SONNY WEST:
Atlantic 1174 *Rave On* .... 10.00 - 15.00

SPEEDY WEST:
Capitol (LP) 1341 *Steel Guitar* ...... 15.00 - 20.00

KENT WESTBERRY:
Art 172 *My Baby Don't Rock Me* .... — - —

WALT WESTBROOK:
Bobbin 106, 119 .... 7.00 - 10.00

GEORGE WESTON:
Jackpot 48013 *Hey Little Car Hop* ... 10.00 - 15.00
    48017 *Shelley Shelley* .... 6.00 - 10.00
Talley 118 *Hold Still Baby* .... 10.00 - 15.00

ONIE WHEELER:
Columbia 21371, 21418, 21454, 21500, 21523,
    40787, 40917 .... 5.00 - 10.00
K-Ark 671 *Too Hot To Handle* .... 10.00 - 15.00
Okeh 18022 *Run 'Em Off* .... 8.00 - 12.00
    18049 *Little Mama* .... 10.00 - 15.00

WHEELERS:
Cenco 107 *Once I Had A Girl* .... 25.00 - 40.00

WHEELS:
Premium 405 *My Hearts Desire* ...... 10.00 - 15.00
    408 *Teasin' Heart* .... 10.00 - 15.00
Time 1003 *So Young And So In Love* ..... 8.00 - 12.00

THE WHIPS:
Flair 1025 *Pleading Heart* .... 50.00 - 80.00

WHIRLERS:
Port 70025 *Magic Mirror* .... 5.00 - 8.00
Whirlin Disc 108 *Magic Mirror* ...... 15.00 - 25.00

THE WHIRLWINDS:
Guyden 2052 *Angel Love* .... 10.00 - 15.00

WHISPERS:
Gotham 7309 *Fool Heart* .... 30.00 - 40.00
    7312 *Are You Sorry* .... 50.00 - 75.00

DONNIE WHITE:
King 5122 *That's My Doll* .... 10.00 - 15.00

FLOYD WHITE & THE DEALERS:
Criterion 1 *Cinderella* . . . . 15.00 - 20.00
JOSH WHITE:
Decca (LP) 5082 (10″) *Ballads* . . . . 15.00 - 25.00
   (LP) 5247 (10″) *Ballads, Vol. 2* . . . . 15.00 - 25.00
   (LP) 8665 *Josh White* . . . . 15.00 - 25.00
Elektra (LP) 102 *Josh At Midnight* . . . . 20.00 - 30.00
   (LP) 114 *Josh* . . . . 20.00 - 30.00
   (LP) 123 *25th Anniversary Album* . . . . 20.00 - 30.00
   (LP) 158 *Chain Gang Songs* . . . . 15.00 - 25.00
London (LP) 338 (10″) . . . . 15.00 - 20.00
   (LP) 1341 *Josh White Program* . . . . 20.00 - 30.00
Mercury (LP) 25014 (10″) *Josh White Sings* . . . . . 15.00 - 20.00
   (LP) 20203 *Josh White's Blues* . . . . 20.00 - 30.00
Period (LP) 1209 *(And Big Bill Broonzy)* . . . . . . 20.00 - 30.00
Stinson (LP) 14 (10″) *Blues* . . . . — - —
   (LP) 15 (10″) *Folk Songs* . . . . — - —
WILBUR WHITFIELD & THE PLEASERS:
Aladdin 3381 *P. B. Baby* . . . . 8.00 - 12.00
RAY WHITLEY:
Vee Jay 433 *Yessirree-Yessirree* . . . . 7.00 - 10.00
SLIM WHITMAN:
Imperial (EP) 106, 131, 132, 133, 134, 135,
   136, 137 . . . . 20.00 - 30.00
   8134 *My Love Is Growing Stale* . . . . 10.00 - 15.00
   8144 *Bandera Waltz* . . . . 10.00 - 15.00
   8156 *China Doll* . . . . 10.00 - 15.00
   8163 *By The Waters Of The Minnetonka* . . . . . 8.00 - 12.00
   8169 *Keep It A Secret* . . . . 8.00 - 12.00
   8180 *How Can I Tell?* . . . . 10.00 - 15.00
   8189 *Restless Heart* . . . . 8.00 - 12.00
   8201 *Danny Boy* . . . . 7.00 - 10.00
   8208 *Darlin' Don't Cry* . . . . 7.00 - 10.00
   8220 *Stairway To Heaven* . . . . 7.00 - 10.00
   8223 *Secret Love* . . . . 7.00 - 10.00
   8236 *We Stood At The Altar* . . . . 7.00 - 10.00
(above are blue label with script lettering;
   following are red label with script lettering)
Imperial 8257 *Beautiful Dreamer* . . . . 7.00 - 10.00
   8267 *The Singing Hills* . . . . 7.00 - 10.00
   8281 *Cattle Call* . . . . 7.00 - 10.00
   8290 *Roll On, Silvery Moon* . . . . 7.00 - 10.00
   8298 *I'll Never Stop Loving You* . . . . 7.00 - 10.00
   8299 *You Have My Heart* . . . . 7.00 - 10.00
   8304, 8305, 8307, 8308, 8309, 9310, 8312,
     8316, 8317, 8318, 8319, 8320, 8321, 8322,
     8323, 8326, 8327, 8328, 8329 . . . . 5.00 - 10.00
   5731, 5746, 5766, 5778, 5791, 5821, 5859, 5871,
     5900, 5919, 5938, 5966 . . . . 4.00 - 7.00
   (LP) 9003 *Slim Whitman Favorites*
     (maroon label) . . . . 20.00 - 30.00
   (LP) 9026 *Slim Whitman Sings* . . . . 20.00 - 30.00
   (LP) 9056 *Slim Whitman* . . . . 15.00 - 25.00
   (LP) 9064 *Country Favorites* . . . . 15.00 - 25.00
RCA Victor (LP) 3217 (10″) *Sings & Yodels* . . . . . 100.00 - 150.00
   48-0145 *Birmingham Jail* . . . . 20.00 - 30.00
(Above is pressed of translucent green plastic)
WHOOPING CRANES:
El Ray 1000 *Heart And Soul* . . . . 5.00 - 8.00
"WHOOPERS":
Jubilee (LP) 1119 (The Dominoes, Orioles, et al.) . . 30.00 - 50.00
JOHNNY WICK:
United 116 *Jockey Jack Boogle* . . . . 50.00 - 80.00
WALLY WIGGINS:
Mercury 71645 *Maybe Someday* . . . . 10.00 - 15.00
COYE WILCOX:
Azalea 124 *Zippy, Hippy, Dippy* . . . . 7.00 - 10.00
THE WILD CHILDS:
Cascade 102 *I'm Leaving Town Baby* . . . . 8.00 - 12.00
RICHARD WILKINSON:
Tone 1126 *Wicked Woman* . . . . 7.00 - 10.00
CHUCK WILEY:

United Artists 113 *Tear It Up* . . . . 15.00 - 20.00
JESS WILLARD:
Ekko 1018 *Don't Hold Her So Close* . . . . 7.00 - 10.00
SLIM WILLETT:
Audio Lab (LP) 1542 . . . . — - —
4-Star 1614 *Hadacol Corners* . . . . 5.00 - 8.00
Winston 1036 *Toolpusher* . . . . 7.00 - 10.00
WALLY WILLETTE:
Flag 118 *Eenie Meenie* . . . . 75.00 - 100.00
AL WILLIAMS & THE BARDS:
Dawn 208 *I'm A Winedrinker* . . . . 10.00 - 15.00
ANDRE WILLIAMS (& THE DON JUANS):
Epic 9196 *Bacon Fat* . . . . 5.00 - 8.00
Fortune 824 *Pulling Time* . . . . 5.00 - 8.00
   834 *Mean Jean* . . . . 5.00 - 8.00
   837 *Jail Bait* . . . . 5.00 - 8.00
Ronald 1001 *Please Give Me A Chance* . . . . 8.00 - 12.00
BERNIE WILLIAMS:
Imperial 5360 *Don't Tease Me* . . . . 7.00 - 10.00
BILLY WILLIAMS:
Coral (LP) 57251 *Half Sweet, Half Beat* . . . . 20.00 - 30.00
   61363 *Smoke From Your Cigarette* . . . . 4.00 - 7.00
Mercury (LP) 20317 *Oh Yeah* . . . . 25.00 - 35.00
BOB WILLIAMS: (See also THE CYCLONES)
Debonair 161 *My Goose Is Cooked* . . . . 5.00 - 8.00
BUZZ WILLIAMS:
Worthmore (DP) 185 *Blue Suede Shoes;*
   Heartbreak Hotel other cuts by other artist of
   no interest) . . . . 7.00 - 10.00
CORA WILLIAMS with THE FOUR JACKS:
Federal 12079 *Sure Cure For The Blues* . . . . 40.00 - 60.00
EDDIE WILLIAMS:
Excello 2158 *You Broke Your Vows* . . . . 7.00 - 10.00
FLETCHER WILLIAMS:
Bullseye 1001 *Mary Lou* . . . . 5.00 - 8.00
HANK WILLIAMS:
MGM (LP) 107 (10″) *Hank William Sings* . . . . . . 40.00 - 60.00
   (LP) 168 (10″) *Moanin' The Blues* . . . . 50.00 - 75.00
   (LP) 202 (10″) *Memorial Album* . . . . 35.00 - 50.00
   (LP) 203 (10″) *Hank Williams As Luke The*
     Drifter . . . . 75.00 - 100.00
   (LP) 242 (10″) *Honky Tonkin'* . . . . 50.00 - 75.00
   (LP) 243 (10″) *I Saw The Light* . . . . 50.00 - 75.00
   (LP) 291 (10″) *Ramblin' Man* . . . . 15.00 - 20.00
   (EP) 1014 *Crazy Heart* . . . . 15.00 - 20.00
   (EP) 1076 *Move It On Over* . . . . 15.00 - 20.00
   (EP) 1082 *There'll Be No Teardrops Tonight* . . . 15.00 - 20.00
   (EP) 1101, 1102 *Hank Williams Sings* . . . . 15.00 - 20.00
   (EP) 1135, 1136 *Ramblin' Man* . . . . 35.00 - 50.00
   (EP) 1165 *Luke The Drifter* . . . . 15.00 - 20.00
   (EP) 1215, 1216, 1217 *Moanin' The Blues* . . . . 15.00 - 20.00
   (EP) 1218 *I Saw The Light* . . . . 15.00 - 20.00
   (EP) 1317, 1318, 1319 *Honky Tonkin'* . . . . . . 15.00 - 20.00
   (EP) 1491, 1492, 1493 *Sing Me A Blue Song* . . . 15.00 - 20.00
   (EP) 1554, 1555, 1556 *The Immortal Hank*
     Williams . . . . 10.00 - 15.00
   (LP) 3219 *Ramblin' Man* . . . . 40.00 - 70.00
   (LP) 3267 *Hank Williams As Luke The Drifter* . 50.00 - 80.00
   (LP) 3272 *Memorial Album* . . . . 35.00 - 60.00
   (LP) 3330 *Moanin' The Blues* . . . . 35.00 - 60.00
   (LP) 3331 *I Saw The Light* . . . . 40.00 - 70.00
   (LP) 3412 *Honky Tonkin'* . . . . 35.00 - 50.00
   (LP) 3560 *Sing Me A Blue Song* . . . . 35.00 - 50.00
   (LP) 3605 *The Immortal Hank Williams* . . . . . 35.00 - 50.00
   (LP) 3733 *The Unforgettable* . . . . 25.00 - 35.00
   (LP) 3803 *The Lonesome Sound Of* . . . . 20.00 - 30.00
(Note: Above must have original yellow and
   black labels.)
MGM 30751, 30752, 30753, 30754 together
   comprise 45 RPM album set –202, *Hank*
   Williams Memorial Album . . . . 30.00 - 40.00
   30755, 30756, 30757, 30758 together comprise

45 RPM album set –203, *Hank Williams As*
Luke The Drifter . . . . 30.00 - 50.00

JIM(MIE) WILLIAMS:
Dub 2842 *You're Always Late* . . . . 15.00 - 25.00
Sun 270 *That Depends On You* . . . . 10.00 - 15.00

JODY WILLIAMS:
Argo 5274 *Lucky Lou* . . . . 8.00 - 12.00

PO' JOE WILLIAMS:
Atomic H (unnumbered) *Rock 'N' Roll Boogie* . . 15.00 - 25.00

LARRY WILLIAMS:
Specialty 608 *Short Fat Fannie* . . . . 5.00 - 8.00
608 *Short Fat Fannie (78 RPM)* . . . . 10.00 - 15.00
615 *Bony Moronie* . . . . 5.00 - 8.00
615 *Bony Moronie (78 RPM)* . . . . 10.00 - 15.00
626 *Dizzy, Miss Lizzy* . . . . 5.00 - 8.00
626 *Dizzy, Miss Lizzy (78 RPM)* . . . . 10.00 - 15.00
634 *Hootchy-Koo* . . . . 5.00 - 8.00
634 *Hootchy-Koo (78 RPM)* . . . . 7.00 - 10.00
647 *I Was A Fool* . . . . 3.00 - 5.00
647 *I Was A Fool (78 RPM)* . . . . 8.00 - 12.00
(LP) 2109 *Here's Larry Williams* . . . . 20.00 - 30.00

LAWTON WILLIAMS:
Colony 101 *Get On The Ball, Paul* . . . . — - —

LESTER WILLIAMS:
Duke 123 *Let's Do It* . . . . 10.00 - 15.00
131 *Crazy 'Bout My Baby* . . . . 10.00 - 15.00
Imperial 5402 *McDonald's Daughter* . . . . 15.00 - 20.00

LEW WILLIAMS:
Imperial 5411 *Bop Bop Ba Doo Bop* . . . . 15.00 - 20.00
5429 *Centipede* . . . . 15.00 - 20.00
8306 *I'll Play Your Game* . . . . 15.00 - 20.00

MAURICE WILLIAMS & THE ZODIACS:
Herald (LP) 1014 *Stay* . . . . 50.00 - 80.00

MEL WILLIAMS (& THE MONTCLAIRS):
Decca 29370 *Lessons In Love* . . . . 7.00 - 10.00
Dig (LP) 103 *All Through The Night* . . . . 50.00 - 80.00
107 *Here At My Phone* . . . . 5.00 - 8.00
114 *Hold Me* . . . . 5.00 - 8.00
123 *Don't Cry Baby* . . . . 5.00 - 8.00
128 *All Through The Night* . . . . 5.00 - 8.00

MORRY WILLIAMS & THE KIDS:
Tee Vee 301 *Are You My Girl Friends* . . . . 8.00 - 12.00

OTIS WILLIAMS & HIS CHARMS/
NEW GROUP:
De Luxe 6088, 6090, 6091, 6095, 6097, 6098,
6105, 6115, 6130, 6137, 6138, 6149, 6158, 6165,
6174 . . . . 4.00 - 8.00
6093 *Ivory Tower (78 RPM)* . . . . 7.00 - 10.00
King (LP) 560 *Otis Williams & His Charms Sing*
All Time Hits . . . . 75.00 - 125.00
(LP) 614 *This is Otis Williams & The Charms* . 50.00 - 75.00

PO' JO WILLIAMS (See JOE WILLIAMS)

REBECCA WILLIAMS:
Lamp 2011 *Please Give Me A Match* . . . . 7.00 - 10.00

ROBERT WILLIAMS & THE GROOVERS:
Tip Top 730 *Cranberry Blues* . . . . 8.00 - 12.00

RON WILLIAMS (& THE CUSTOMS):
Imperial 5729 *On Top Of Old Smokey* . . . . 7.00 - 10.00
5800 *Don't Tell Me Maybe* . . . . 7.00 - 10.00
Pastel 404 *Hey Little Pearl* . . . . 7.00 - 10.00
Ty-Tex 100 *Sue Sue Baby* . . . . 20.00 - 30.00

SONNY BOY WILLIAMS:
Duplex 9005 *Alice Mae Blues* . . . . 10.00 - 15.00

SUGAR BOY WILLIAMS:
Herald 555 *Five Long Years* . . . . 8.00 - 12.00

TONY WILLIAMS (See PLATTERS)

WAYNE WILLIAMS & THE SURE SHOTS:
Sure 1001 *Red Hot Mama* . . . . 100.00 - 150.00

JAMES WILLIAMSON:
Chance 1131 *The Woman I Love* . . . . 150.00 - 200.00

SONNY BOY WILLIAMSON:
Ace 511 *Boppin' With Sonny* . . . . 7.00 - 10.00

Checker 824 *Don't Start Me To Talkin'* . . . . 8.00 - 12.00
834 *Let Me Explain* . . . . 7.00 - 10.00
847 *The Key To Your Door* . . . . 5.00 - 8.00
864 *Fattening Frogs For Snakes* . . . . 5.00 - 8.00
883, 894, 910, 927, 943, 956, 963, 975, 1003,
1036, 1065,1080,1134 . . . . 3.00 - 6.00
(LP) 1437 *Sonny Boy Williamson (black label)* . 35.00 - 50.00
RAM 2501 *Mailman, Mailman* . . . . 3.00 - 6.00
RCA Victor 50-0005 *Little Girl (orange plastic)* . 15.00 - 20.00
50-0030 *Southern Dream (orange plastic)* . . . 15.00 - 20.00
Trumpet 144 *West Memphis Blues* . . . . 30.00 - 50.00
Trumpet 145 *Pontiac Blues* . . . . 10.00 - 15.00
166 *Nine Below Zero* . . . . 15.00 - 20.00
168 *Stop Now Baby* . . . . 15.00 - 20.00
212 *Cat Hop* . . . . 15.00 - 20.00
215 *Gettin' Out Of Town* . . . . 15.00 - 20.00
216 *Red Hot Kisses* . . . . 10.00 - 15.00
228 *Empty Bedroom* . . . . 10.00 - 15.00

CHUCK WILLIS (with THE ROYALS/& THE
SANDMEN):
Atlantic (EP) 591 *It's Too Late* . . . . 25.00 - 35.00
(EP) 608, 609, *Rock With Chuck Willis* . . . . . . 25.00 - 35.00
(EP) 612 *What Am I Living For* . . . . 25.00 - 35.00
1130, 1168, 1179, 1192, 2029 . . . . 5.00 - 8.00
(Note: 78 RPM issues command somewhat
higher premiums.)
Atlantic (LP) 8018 *The King Of The Stroll*
(black label) . . . . 50.00 - 80.00
Epic (LP) 3425 *Chuck Willis Wails The Blues* . . 75.00 - 100.00
Okeh 6985 *I've Been Treated Wrong Too Long* . . 10.00 - 15.00
7015 *You're Still My Baby* . . . . 7.00 - 10.00
7041 *Change My Mind* . . . . 7.00 - 10.00
7051 *Lawdy Miss Mary* . . . . 7.00 - 10.00
7055 *I Can Tell* . . . . 8.00 - 12.00
7067 *It Were You* . . . . 7.00 - 10.00

DON WILLIS:
Satellite 101 *Boppin' High School Baby* . . . . 90.00 - 120.00

HAL WILLIS:
Athens 704 *Walkin' Dream* . . . . 15.00 - 20.00
Atlantic 1114 *My Pink Cadillac* . . . . 30.00 - 40.00

LITTLE SON WILLIS:
Swing Time 304 *Operator Blues* . . . . 75.00 - 100.00
305 *Harlem Blues* . . . . 75.00 - 100.00
306 *Nothing But The Blues* . . . . 75.00 - 100.00
341 *Roll Me Over Slow* . . . . 75.00 - 100.00

RAY WILLIS:
Jane 103 *Whatta You Do* . . . . 10.00 - 15.00

ROD WILLIS:
Chic 1010 *Somebody's Been Rocking My Baby* . . . 7.00 - 10.00

SLIM WILLIS:
C. J. 622, 627, 635 . . . . 5.00 - 10.00

WILLOWS:
Club 1014 *This Is The End* . . . . 15.00 - 20.00
Eldorado 508 *The First Taste Of Love* . . . . 8.00 - 12.00
Heidi 107 *Sit By The Fire* . . . . 7.00 - 10.00
Melba (LP) 102 *Church Bells May Ring* . . . . 75.00 - 100.00
102 *Church Bells Are Ringing* . . . . 30.00 - 40.00
102 *Church Bells May Ring* . . . . 8.00 - 12.00
106 *My Angel* . . . . 10.00 - 15.00

BILLY JACK WILLS:
MGM 11966 *There's Good Rocking Tonight* . . . . . 20.00 - 30.00

BOB WILLS (& HIS TEXAS PLAYBOYS)
Columbia (LP) 9003 *Round Up* . . . . 20.00 - 30.00
Harmony (LP) 7036 *Bob Wills Special* . . . . 12.00 - 16.00
MGM (LP) 91 (10") *Ranch House Favorites* . . . . 20.00 - 30.00

OSCAR WILLS: (See also TV SLIM)
Argo 5277 *Flatfoot Sam (ship logo label)* . . . . . 7.00 - 10.00

WILLY & RUTH:
Spark 105 *Love Me* . . . . 15.00 - 20.00

ANDY WILSON:
Athens 700 *Little Mama* . . . . 8.00 - 12.00
Back Beat 518 *Too Much Of Not Enough* . . . . . . 7.00 - 10.00

Bullseye 1012 *Teenage Martha*	7.00 -	10.00
1020 *Worry Worry*	7.00 -	10.00
1023 *Little Boy Blue*	7.00 -	10.00
Dot 1127 *Hillbilly Boogie*	10.00 -	15.00

DALLAS WILSON:
Rodeo 127 *High Steppin' Daddy*	10.00 -	15.00

DOYLE WILSON:
Lamp 2015 *Hey Hey*	15.00 -	20.00

EASY DEAL WILSON:
Sims 112 *Gotta Have You*	8.00 -	12.00

HENRY WILSON & THE BLUENOTES:
Dot 15692 *Mighty Low*	15.00 -	20.00

HOP WILSON (& HIS TWO BUDDIES):
Goldband 1071 *Chicken Stuff*	8.00 -	12.00
1078 *Broke And Hungry*	8.00 -	12.00

J. FRANK WILSON:
Josie (LP) 4006 *Last Kiss*	30.00 -	40.00
Le Cam 722 *Last Kiss*	10.00 -	15.00
Tamara 761 *Last Kiss*	7.00 -	10.00

JACKIE WILSON:
Brunswick (LP) 54042 *He's So Fine*	35.00 -	50.00
(LP) 54045 *Lonely Teardrops*	35.00 -	50.00
55105 *Lonely Teardrops (78 RPM)*	50.00 -	75.00

JIMMY WILSON (& THE BLUES BLASTERS):
Big Town 101 *Tin Pan Alley*	7.00 -	10.00
107 *Blues At Sundown*	5.00 -	8.00
113 *Mountain Climber*	10.00 -	15.00
115 *Trouble In My House*	10.00 -	15.00
123 *I've Found Out*	10.00 -	15.00
Chart 610 *Alley Blues*	10.00 -	15.00
629 *Send Me The Key*	10.00 -	15.00
Goldband 1074 *Big Wheel Rolling*	10.00 -	15.00
1091 *Could I Be Wrong*	8.00 -	12.00
1095 *That Is Why I'm Happy*	8.00 -	12.00
Imperial 5549 *Big Wheel Rolling*	7.00 -	10.00
Irma 108 *Blues In The Alley*	8.00 -	12.00
Rhythm 1765 *Strangest Blues*	40.00 -	60.00
7-11 2104 *Ethel Mae*	15.00 -	20.00
2105 *Crying Like A Baby Child*	15.00 -	20.00

JOHNNY WILSON:
Coronado 001 *Twi-Light-Zone*	15.00 -	20.00

PEANUTS WILSON:
Brunswick 55039 *Cast Iron Arm*	40.00 -	60.00

TOM WILSON:
Crest 1007 *Can You Bop?*	15.00 -	20.00

MAGGIE SUE SIMBERLEY:
Sun 229 *How Long*	20.00 -	30.00

DANNY WINCHELL:
Recorte 406, 410, 415	5.00 -	10.00

DON WINDLE:
Republic 7060 *Girl Down The Street*	— -	—

PAUL WINLEY & THE ROCKERS:
Premium 401 *Angel Child*	10.00 -	15.00

WINNERS:
Rainbow 331 *Can This Be Love*	8.00 -	12.00

JACK WINSTON:
Jay Bee *It's Rock 'N' Roll*	15.00 -	20.00

JOHNNY WINTER (& THE CRYSTALIERS):
Frolic 501 *That's What Love Does*	10.00 -	15.00
503 *Ease My Pain*	10.00 -	15.00
509 *Gangster Of Love*	10.00 -	15.00
512 *I Won't Believe It*	10.00 -	15.00
KRCO 106 *Creepy*	20.00 -	30.00
107 *One Night Of Love*	20.00 -	30.00
Sonobeat 107 *Rollin' And Tumblin'*	5.00 -	8.00

DON WINTERS:
Coin 102 *Pretty Moon*	15.00 -	20.00

MAC WISEMAN:
Dot 15544 *Step It Up And Go*	7.00 -	10.00

NORMAN WITCHER:
Poor Boy 102 *Somebody's Been Rocking My Boat*	50.00 -	75.00

JIMMY WITHERSPOON (See also: Battle of The Blues)
Checker 798 *Big Daddy*	10.00 -	15.00
810 *Waiting For Your Return*	8.00 -	12.00
826 *It Ain't No Sedan*	8.00 -	12.00
Crown (LP) 5156 *Jimmy Witherspoon*	15.00 -	20.00
(LP) 5192 *Jimmy Witherspoon Sings The Blues*	15.00 -	20.00
Federal 12095 *Foolish Prayer*	20.00 -	30.00
12099 *Lucille*	20.00 -	30.00
12107 *Corn Whiskey*	20.00 -	30.00
12118 *Jay's Blues*	15.00 -	20.00
12138 *East Mile*	15.00 -	20.00
12155 *Miss Mistreater*	15.00 -	20.00
12156 *Sad Life*	15.00 -	20.00
12173 *Just For You*	8.00 -	12.00
12188 *Highway To Happiness*	8.00 -	12.00
12189 *I Done Told You*	8.00 -	12.00
HI Firecord (LP) 421 *At Monterey*	10.00 -	15.00
King (LP) 634 *Jimmy Witherspoon*	40.00 -	60.00
Pacific Jazz (LP) 1267 *Singin' The Blues*	20.00 -	30.00
RCA Victor (LP) 1639 *Goin' To Kansas City Blues*	20.00 -	30.00
6977 *Who Baby Who*	4.00 -	7.00

DICK WOLF:
Dale 101 *Spine Tinglin' Love*	— -	—

DANNY WOLFE:
Dot 15571 *Pretty Blue Jean Baby*	8.00 -	12.00
15667 *Let's Flat Get It*	15.00 -	20.00
15715 *Pucker Point*	8.00 -	12.00

JIMMY WOLFORD:
Capitol 4606 *Goin' Steady With The Blues*	7.00 -	10.00
4 Star 1714 *My Name Is Jimmy*	30.00 -	40.00

BOBBY WOOD:
Pen 113 *Everybody's Searchin'*	10.00 -	15.00

NORMAN WOOD:
Tamm 2015 *Black Lake Boogie*	— -	—

TOMMY WOOD:
D 1000 *Can't Play Hookey*	20.00 -	30.00

JERRY WOODARD:
RCA Victor 7616 *Who's Gonna Rock My Baby* ...	8.00 -	12.00
Reed 1017 *Who's Gonna Rock My Baby*	15.00 -	20.00

BILL WOODS:
Bakersfield *Phone Me, Baby*	20.00 -	30.00
Fire 100 *Go Crazy Man*	20.00 -	30.00

BOB WOODS:
Kingsport 100 *Greasy Corner Boogie*	— -	—
110 *Sunshine Boogie*	— -	—

DONALD WOODS & THE VEL-AIRES:
Flip 306 *Death Of An Angel*	8.00 -	12.00

JOHNNY WOODS & FAMOUS RHYTHM ACES:
Bo-Kay 113 *Valley Of The Blues*	— -	—

SONNY WOODS (& THE DOWNBEATS/with THE TWIGS):
Hollywood 1015 *Chapel Of Memories*	15.00 -	20.00
Peacock 1679 *So Many Tears*	8.00 -	12.00
1689 *Someday She'll Come Along*	8.00 -	12.00

DON WOODY:
Arco 4623 *Not I*	15.00 -	20.00
Decca 30277 *Bird Dog*	15.00 -	20.00

SHEB WOOLEY:
MGM (EP) 1188, 1189, 1190 *Sheb Wooley*	10.00 -	15.00
(EP) 1607 *Purple People Eater Plays Earth Music*	15.00 -	20.00
(EP) 1607 *The Purple People Eater*	15.00 -	2].00
(LP) 3299 *Sheb Wooley*	15.00 -	20.00

JIMMY WORK:
All 502 *Tennessee Border*	— -	—

WAYNE WORLEY:
Brent 7024 *Red Headed Woman*	10.00 -	15.00
Elbridge 11016 *Red Headed Woman*	30.00 -	40.00

JOHN WORTHAN:

Peach 711 *Too Too Many* .... 15.00 - 20.00
   722 *I Wrote You A Letter* .... 15.00 - 20.00
DOUG WRAY:
Epic 9322 *Goose Bumps* .... 7.00 - 10.00
LINK WRAY (& HIS WRAYMEN):
Cadence 1347 *Rumble* (78 RPM) .... 10.00 - 15.00
Epic (LP) 3661 *Link Wray And His Wraymen* .... 25.00 - 35.00
Swan (LP) 510 *Jack The Ripper* .... 30.00 - 40.00
LUCKY WRAY:
Starday 552 *It's Music She Says* .... 20.00 - 30.00
   575 *Got Another Baby* .... 20.00 - 30.00
   608 *Teenage Cutie* .... 20.00 - 30.00
WRENS:
Rama 65 *Come Back My Love* .... 50.00 - 75.00
   174 *Serenade Of The Bells* .... 50.00 - 75.00
   175 *Betty Jean* .... 50.00 - 75.00
   184 *I Won't Come To Your Wedding* .... 70.00 - 100.00
   194 *C'est La Vie* .... 50.00 - 75.00
DALE WRIGHT (& THE WRIGHT GUYS):
Fraternity 804, 818, 831, 837............. 5.00 - 10.00
JOHNNY WRIGHT with IKE TURNER:
RPM 443 *Suffocate* (red label) .... 8.00 - 12.00
STEVE WRIGHT:
Lin 5022 *Wild Wild Woman* .... 15.00 - 20.00
GENE WYATT:
Ebb 123 *Love Fever* .... 10.00 - 15.00
Lucky Seven 101 *Music And Arithmetic* .... 10.00 - 15.00
JIMMY YANCEY:
Atlantic (LP) 103 (10") *Yancy Special* .... 50.00 - 75.00
   (LP) 130 *Jimmy & Mama Yancey* .... 50.00 - 75.00
   (LP) 134 *Jimmy & Mama Yancey* .... 50.00 - 75.00
   (Note: Above two are 10" LPs.)
   (LP) 1231 *Pure Blues Jimmy & Mama Yancey* . 30.00 - 40.00
LAFAYETTE YARBOROUGH:
Bart (?)— *Comic Book Crazy* .... 30.00 - 40.00
MALCOLM YELVINGTON:
Sun 211 *Drinkin' Wine Spodee-O-Dee* .... 30.00 - 40.00
   246 *Rocking With My Baby* .... 15.00 - 20.00
RUSTY YORK:
Chess 1730 *Sugaree*..................... 7.00 - 10.00
King 5103 *Shake 'Em Up Baby* .... 10.00 - 15.00
   5511, 5587........................ 4.00 - 7.00
Note 10021 *Sugaree* .... 20.00 - 30.00
P.J. 100 *Sugaree* .... 7.00 - 10.00
Sage— *Sadie Mae* .... 8.00 - 12.00
DONNIE YOUNG:
Decca 31077 *Shakin' The Blues*............. 10.00 - 15.00
FARON YOUNG:
Capitol (LP) 778 *Sweethearts Or Strangers* ..... 20.00 - 30.00
   (LP) 1004 *The Object Of My Affection* .... 20.00 - 30.00
   (LP) 1096 *This Is Faron Young* .... 15.00 - 20.00
   (LP) 1185 *My Garden Of Prayer* .... 15.00 - 20.00
   (LP) 1245 *Talk About Hits* .... 10.00 - 15.00
GEORGE YOUNG:
Mercury 71259 *Can't Stop Me* .... 15.00 - 20.00

MIGHTY JOE YOUNG:
Fire 1033 *Empty Arms* .... 7.00 - 10.00
LENNY YOUNG & THE JAY BIRDS:
Jackpot 48006 *Lovable* .... 4.00 - 7.00
NELSON YOUNG:
Lucky 0002 *Rock Old Sputnick*.............. 30.00 - 40.00
Starday 341 *So Easy To Fall In Love* .... 15.00 - 20.00
ROY YOUNG:
Can. Hall (?)—*Big Fat Mama/Just Keep It Up* ... — - —
YOUNGHEARTS:
Infinity 006 *Do Not Forsake Me* .... — - —
YOUNG LADS:
Felice 712 *Night After Night* .... 15.00 - 20.00
Neil 100 *Moonlight* .... 15.00 - 20.00
YOUNG LIONS:
Dot 16172 *Little Girl* .... 10.00 - 15.00
YOUNGSTERS:
Empire 104 *Shattered Dreams* .... 15.00 - 20.00
   109 *Dreamy Eyes* .... 10.00 - 15.00
Lesley 1925 *You Told Another Lie* .... 8.00 - 12.00
YOUNGTONES:
Brunswick 55089 *Oh Tell Me* .... 20.00 - 30.00
X-Tra 104 *You I Adore* .... 15.00 - 20.00
   110 *Patricia* .... 15.00 - 20.00
   120/121 *Can I Come Over* .... 10.00 - 15.00
"YOUR FAVORITE SINGING GROUPS":
Hull (LP) 1002 (various artists) .... 50.00 - 75.00
"YOUR OLD FAVORITES":
Old Town (LP) 101 (various artists) .... 30.00 - 50.00
EDDIE ZACK (& COUSIN RICHIE):
Columbia 21387 *Rocky Road Blues* .... 15.00 - 20.00
   21441 *I'm Gonna Roll And Rock* .... 15.00 - 20.00
FRANCIS ZAMBON:
Vamalco 503 *Our Love Will Last* .... 7.00 - 10.00
TEX ZARIO:
Arcade 163 *Jukebox Cannonball*............. 10.00 - 15.00
Skyrocket 1001 *Go Man Go, Get Gone* .... 15.00 - 20.00
ZEBULONS:
Cub 9069 *Falling Water*.................... 15.00 - 20.00
DANNY ZELLA (& THE LARADOS/HIS ZELL ROCKS):
Dial 100 *Sapphire* .... 10.00 - 15.00
Fox 10056/10057 *Wicked Ruby* .... 7.00 - 10.00
BEN JOE ZEPPA:
Award 124 *Shame On You Miss Lindy* .... 8.00 - 12.00
Era 1042 *Topsy Turvy* .... 8.00 - 12.00
Metrol 9001 *Shame On You Miss Lindy* .... 10.00 - 15.00
ZIRCONS:
Heigh Ho 607 *Where There's A Will*........... 10.00 - 15.00
   608/609 *I Couldn't Stop Crying* .... 10.00 - 15.00
MelloMood 1000 *Lonely Way* .... 15.00 - 20.00
Winston 1022 *Return My Love* .... 15.00 - 20.00

BIBLIOGRAPHY

Steven C. Barr, THE (ALMOST) COMPLETE 78RPM RECORD DATING GUIDE, Toronto, Canada, published by the author, 1979, 1980.

Brian Case & Stan Britt, THE ILLUSTRATED ENCYCLOPEDIA OF JAZZ, Harmony Books, New York, 1978. (Contains selective discography of albums, photos of album jackets, short biographies of over 400 jazz artists.)

Ken Clee, THE DIRECTORY OF AMERICAN 45 R.P.M. RECORDS, privately published by Stak-O-Wax, P.O. Box 11412, Philadelphia, Pennsylvania 19111. (Four volumes, loose-leaf format. Discography, or more properly, a collection of artist and label discographies. Records listed in order of release with titles of both sides. Volumes are available individually or as a set.)

Ron Dethlefson and Ray Wile, EDISON DISC ARTISTS AND RECORDS, 1910-1929, APM Press, 502 East 17th Street, Brooklyn, New York 11226, 1990. (Contains listings by title and artist for all Edison LP and 78 rpm records, photos of artists, all known label varieties, listings for many Edison Diamond Discs by title and artist, and photos of typical labels.)

Robert Dixon & John Godrich, RECORDING THE BLUES, Stein and Day, New York, 1970. (The story of recording companies; how and where they recorded the artists they recorded; many interesting reproductions and illustrations of record labels and record company promotional materials.)

Galen Gart, THE AMERICAN RECORD LABEL DIRECTORY & DATING GUIDE, 1940-1959, Big Nickel Publications, P.O. Box 157, Milford, New Hampshire 03055.

John Godrich & Robert Dixon, BLUES & GOSPEL RECORDS, 1902-1943, Third Edition, Storyville Publications & Co., Ltd., 66 Fairfax Drive, Chigwell, Essex IG7 6HS, England. (A massive discography, arranged alphabetically by artist, providing 78 rpm issue numbers, all songs recorded by each artist in chronological order, including unissued titles; recording dates, accompaniment personnels, recording locations, master numbers, "take" numbers. Prefatory material includes information about "race" labels and recording "field trips.")

Roger D. Kinkle, THE COMPLETE ENCYCLOPEDIA OF POPULAR MUSIC AND JAZZ, 1900-1950. Arlington House, New Rochelle, New York. 1974. (Four volumes, 2642 pages. Data on movie musicals; performers, with biographies; singers; composers; bandleaders; musicians; listings of 100 to 200 songs, most popular, for each year; representative recordings for each year; Broadway musicals; numerical listings of 9 major labels.)

Mike Leadbitter & Neil Slaven, BLUES RECORDS 1943-1966, Oak Publications, New York, 1968. (Discography, containing the recorded work of over 1,000 artists. Recording dates, records issued, personnels, recording locations.)

Dan Mahoney, THE COLUMBIA 13/14000-D SERIES—A Numerical Listing, Walter C. Allen, Stanhope, New Jersey, 1961. (Interesting, in-depth treatment of the Columbia "Race" series, Artists, Song titles, master numbers, dates, and even quantities of records ordered.)

Bill C. Malone, COUNTRY MUSIC U.S.A., University of Texas Press, Austin, Texas, 1968.

Robert R. Olson, BANNER, privately published by Robert R. Olson, 232 Beatty Street, Medford, Oregon 97501. (Numerical listing of 1920s-early 1930s Banner label.)

Oliver Read & Walter L. Welch, FROM TIN FOIL TO STEREO: Evolution of the Phonograph, Howard W. Sams, Inc., Indianapolis, Indiana, 1976. (In addition to detailed and scholarly treatment of its main subject, contains information about record companies and their corporate genealogy.)

Brian Rust, THE AMERICAN DANCE BAND DISCOGRAPHY, 1917-1942, Arlington House Publishers, New Rochelle, New York, 1975. (Two volumes, 2066 Pages. Discography, providing 78 rpm issues numbers, all songs recorded by each artist/band in chronological order, including unissued titles; recording dates; personnels; recording locations; master numbers; "takes.")

(Note: the above set is out-of-print, but is expected to be republished by Scarecrow Press, possibly in 1993.)

Brian Rust, THE AMERICAN RECORD LABEL BOOK. DaCapo Press, Inc., 233 Spring Street, New York, New York, 10013. (Information about, and in most cases, photographs of, many American and some British labels up to about 1942.)

Brian Rust, THE COMPLETE ENTERTAINMENT DISCOGRAPHY, FROM THE MID-1890s TO 1942, DaCapo Press, Inc., 233 Spring Street, New York, New York 10013. (Covers the recorded output of celebrities and personalities. Includes brief biographies of artists, details of their 78 rpm record issues: unissued recordings; recording dates, locations, accompanying personnels.)

Brian Rust, JAZZ RECORDS, 1897-1942, Fifth Edition, Storyville Publications & Co., Ltd., 66 Fairfax Drive, Chigwell, Essex IG7 6HS, England. (Two massive volumes covering virtually all known 78 rpm records of jazz interest. In addition to the usual thorough discographical data, this set includes a song index. This, and the other discographies by Rust, above, cannot be praised too highly!)

Claude Seary, COLUMBIA RECORDS "A SERIES, privately published by Claude Seary, 2863 Glen Lake Road, Victoria, British Columbia, Canada V9B 4A8. (Numerical listing of Columbia records from November, 1908 to December, 1923, with master numbers, issue dates. When complete, the series is expected to comprise five volumes, plus an artists' volume.)

Nick Toches, COUNTRY-THE BIGGEST MUSIC IN AMERICA, Stein and Day, New York, 1977 (Animated, knowledgeable treatment of the subject and more; rockabilly, blues, etc.)

Joel Whitburn, POP MEMORIES, 1890-1954, Record Research, P.O. Box 200, Menominee Falls, Wisconsin 53051. (Lists, by artist, "every recording to appear on America's popular music charts from 1890 through 1954." While this claim has been disputed, essentially because of a dearth of meaningful "charts" from the early years, the book is useful and fascinating.)

Joel Whitburn, TOP COUNTRY SINGLES, 1944-1988, Record Research, Inc., P.O. Box 200, Menominee Falls, Wisconsin 53051. (Compiled from Billboard's country music charts, lists 13,000 country singles.)

Joel Whitburn, TOP POP SINGLES, 1955-1990, Record Research, Inc., P.O. Box 200, Menominee Falls, Wisconsin 53051. (Lists, by artist, all 45 RPM records to appear on the national charts of Billboard Magazine, showing debut dates, peak positions on charts, biographical information for artists, etc.)

PUBLICATIONS

ANTIQUE PHONOGRAPH MONTHLY
Allen Koenigsberg, Editor, 502 East 17th Street, Brooklyn, New York 11226 (Early phonographs and recording processes; pioneer recording artists and their recordings. Advertising, mostly relating to phonographs, parts, repairs, and restoration; records, including cylinders.)

BLUES UNLIMITED
38A Sackville Road, Bexhill-On-Sea, Sussex, England (Blues, Rhythm & Blues)

DISCoveries
P.O. Box 255, Port Townsend, Washington 98368. Phone: 1-800-666-DISC (Large, monthly, with features, interviews, reviews, numerous ads offering records for direct sale and at auction, and a "Mailbox" section to encourage reader participation. Mainly rock 'n' roll, rhythm & blues of the 1950s and 1960s, with efforts toward wider scope.)

GOLDMINE
700 East State Street, Iola, Wisconsin 54990, Phone: (715) 445-2214. (Large bi-weekly, with features, discographies, reviews, and an extensive auction/for sale section offering mainly Rock 'n' Roll, Rhythm & Blues, and later forms of music, of the 1950s to the present, including CDs. Has incorporated its subsidiary publication, *Music Mart*, resulting in a large classified section of more diverse coverage than the main portion of the publication.)

THE GUNN REPORT
John & Carol Gunn, "Hollybank," Bramble Hall Lane, Daws Heath, Hadleigh, Essex, England SS7 2XG (Marketplace for 78 RPM dance bands, jazz, largely and not surprisingly of English origin; some articles and editorial content.)

I.A.J.R.C. JOURNAL
(Quarterly publication of the International Association of Jazz Record Collectors; sent to members. Yearly dues: $20.00. Write to: Gil Erskine, Registrar, P.O. Box 800, Grand Central Station, New York, New York 10163. (Articles, research, and an excellent source of information on available reissues of jazz; the club itself offers to members low-priced LP reissues of its own.)

JOSLIN'S JAZZ JOURNAL
Gene Joslin, Editor and Publisher, Box 213, Parsons, Kansas 67357 (Attractively produced quarterly tabloid, primarily of interest to collectors of jazz and dance band 78s and LPs. Contains articles, research, and reviews, in addition to advertisements and auctions.)

NEEDLE TIME
Brian Rust, Editor and Publisher, "The Moorings," 50 Ulwell Road, Swanage, Dorset, England BH19 1LN. (Quarterly, with some articles, research and discographical information on jazz and dance bands; 78 rpm records for sale at auction.)

NEW AMBEROLA GRAPHIC
Martin F. Bryan, Editor, 37 Caledonia Street, St. Johnsbury, Vermont 05819. (Quarterly, concerned largely with artists, recordings, and phonographs of the very early days of recording, with a penchant for exploring the odd and curious. Of late, consisting of two sections, to accomodate a growing auction section—which regularly contains cylinders, as well as disc records.)

RECORD FINDER
Walter Smith, Publisher, 8754 Landmark Road, Richmond, Virginia 23228 Telephone: (804) 266-1154 (Monthly, featuring sales of 78s, 45s, and LPs of all styles, from easy listening and pop, to rock 'n' roll. Some articles, but mostly a market place. Its "Collector Wants" section, in which record seekers can have their wants listed inexpensively, is organized by artist.)

RECORD RESEARCH
65 Grand Avenue, Brooklyn, New York 11205 (Largely discographical information, primarily of interest to collectors of 78 RPM records of various styles. Features are often presented serially. Newcomers may wish to take advantage of the availability of back issues to obtain earlier segments of long-running series. "Blues Research" is a subsidiary publication, appearing very irregularly, sometimes as part of the parent publication; it deals with post-war blues and rhythm & blues).

78 QUARTERLY
Pete Whelan, Editor, P.O. Box 283, Key West, Florida 33041 (Published infrequently, title notwithstanding, this 96-page magazine explores the byways of record collecting, with emphasis on the rare and obscure in blues, and, to a lesser extent, jazz and country. One feature is an ongoing survey of the "rarest" records, which, although hardly scientific, is most interesting. Features on rare labels, with lots of pictures; chronicles of an old-time collector; the history of a major "race" label; and a "jackpot" find: It's sort of like sitting in on a bull-session of some of the cognoscenti.)

STORYVILLE
Storyville Publications & Co., Ltd., 66 Fairview Drive, Chigwell, Essex, England IG7 6HS (Bi-monthly magazine covering vintage jazz and blues, with articles, interviews, research and reviews.)

VINTAGE JAZZ MART
Russ Shor, Editor, P.O. Box R184, Radnor, Pennsylvania 19087. (Primarily an international marketplace for collectors of jazz, dance band, blues, and country 78s, and jazz LPs, consisting mostly of offerings at auction. Quarterly.)

WHISKEY, WOMEN AND...The Rhythm and Blues Jubilee
Dan Kochakian, Editor, P.O. Box 1245, Haverhill, Massachusetts 01830 ("Dedicated to Blues & Rhythm Music from then to now")

SOURCES

Following are some sources of publications, references, supplies, equipment, and services of interest to record collectors. The sources mentioned are not the only ones; others' advertisements may be found in the various collector publications. The listing of any source is not intended to be a recommendation. It is intended merely to provide information in response to common inquiries, and to spare me the burden of answering these inquiries individually.

ANTIQUE PHONOGRAPH MONTHLY, 502 East 17th Street, Brooklyn, New York 11226 Telephone: (708) 941-6835

In addition to publishing the magazine (see "Publications"), APM is an excellent source of reference materials and memorabilia pertaining to vintage phonographs, records, and recording artists; books, catalogs, manuals, magazines, discographies, posters, etc. Included are facsimiles and reprints of original catalogs, manuals, and sales materials.

ANTIQUE PHONOGRAPH SUPPLY COMPANY, Route 23, Box 123, Davenport Center, New York 13751 Telephone: (607) 278-6218

Accessories, parts for the maintenance, repair, and restoration of vintage phonographs; literature; sleeves for 78 RPM records. Issues a catalog of its offerings and services.

ESOTERIC SOUND, 4813 Wallbank Avenue, Downers Grove, Illinois 60515

Specializes in high-performance audio equipment used for the reproduction of vintage recordings: turntables (with up to six speeds, including "78 RPM"), equalizers, styli, etc.

EXPERT STYLUS COMPANY, P.O. Box 3, Ashtead, Surrey, England KT21 2QD

Stylus replacement service for all types of cartridges, for acoustical and electrical playing of various types of vintage records, laterally and vertically recorded.

JELLYROLL PRODUCTIONS, INC., P.O. Box 29, Boyne Falls, Michigan 49713

Publishes and promotes books relating to music, record collecting, and memorabilia, primarily from the 1950s and later.

NATIONAL DIRECTORY OF COLLECTIBLE RECORD DEALERS, compiled by Walter Smith, Record Finder Publications, 8754

Landmark Road, Richmond, Virginia 23228

NOSTALGIA CORRUGATED RECORD CARE PRODUCTS P.O. Box 3996, El Paso, Texas 79923

Products and materials for the storage, display, and shipping of records.

ROBERT R. OLSON, 232 Beatty Street, Medford, Oregon 97501

Researcher and compiler of numericals of various 78 RPM records labels of the 1920s and 1930s, particularly country series. Has published listings of *Banner* (see Bibliography), *Decca* 5000 series, and *Grey Gull* 4000 series.

OWL AUDIO PRODUCTS, INC., P.O. Box 3122, Linden, New Jersey 07036

High-performance audio equipment for the reproduction of vintage recordings, including cylinders: Equalizers, styli, etc.

RECORD RESEARCH, INC., P.O. Box 200, Menominee Falls, Wisconsin 53051 Telephone: (414) 251-5408

Publisher of at least twenty books by Joel Whitburn on "charted" music (three of which are listed in the Bibliography, which see).

SHURE BROTHERS, INC., 222 Hartrey Avenue, Evanston, Illinois 60202-3696

Cartridges and styli; extensive selection of specialized types, including those for 78 RPM play.

Aaronson, Irving	59	All Star Band	60	Anderson & The Keynotes, Gene	304
Abbot, Larry	59	All Star Californians	60	Andrew Sisters, The	60
Abney, Peg Leg Ben	187	All Star Collegians	60	Andrews, Debbie	304
Abrams & His Orchestra, Irwin	59	All Star Orchestra	60	Andrews, Ed	183
Academics, The	303	All Star Rhythm Boys	60	Andrews, Gary	304
Accents, The	303	All Star Rock & Roll Revue (LP)	304	Andrews, Lee	304
Ace, Johnny	303	All Time Country & Hillbilly		Andrews, Mose	188
Ace, Sonny	303	Favorites	304	Andy Boy	188
Acey, Johnny	303	All Time Country & Western Hits	304	Andy & Live Wires	304
Acorns	303	Allard with String Band, Weldon	247	Angel, Johnny	304
Acuff, Roy	247, 303	Alleghenny Highlanders	247	Angelos, The	304
Acuff & His Crazy Tennesseans		Allen, Billy	304	Angels, The	304
/Smoky Mountain Boys, Roy	247	Allen, Charlie	304	Anglin Brothers, The	247
Adams, Art	303	Allen, Clay	247	Anka, Paul	304
Adams, Arthur K.	303	Allen, Connie	304	Ann, Pattie	305
Adams, Billy	303	Allen, Danny	304	Ann and Zeke with Pete, Judy	247
Adams, Charlie	247, 303	Allen, Harold	304	Annette & Cecil Null	305
Adams, Clarence	247	Allen, Henry,Jr.	60	Annuals, The	305
Adams, Faye	303	Allen, Ira	304	Answers, The	305
Adams, Jo Jo	303	Allen, Jules	247	Anthony, Paul	305
Adams, Woodrow	303	Allen, Lee	247, 304	Anthony, Vince	305
Adams & The Lone Star Playboys,		Allen, Milton	304	Antrim, Roosevelt	188
Charlie	247	Allen, Ray	304	Apollos, The	305
Addison, Bernard	59	Allen, Rex	304	Appalachian Vagabond	248
Adelphis	303	Allen, Ronnie	304	Appel, Dave	305
Adkins, Katherine	187	Allen, Tony	304	Appleblossom, Captain	248
Admiral Tones	303	Allen Brothers	247	Aquatones, The	305
Admirals, The	303	Alley, Shelley Lee	247	Aqua-Nites, The	305
Adrian's Orch.	59	Allison, George	187	Arabians, The	305
Adventurers, The	303	Allison, Joe	304	Arcadia Peacock Orch. of St. Louis	61
Agee, Ray	304	Allison's Sacred Harp Singers	247	Arcadian Serenaders	61
Aggie Dukes	304	Almond, Herschel	304	Archer & His Orch., Harry	61
Aiken Country String Band	247	Almond, Lucky Joe	304	Archibald	188, 305
Aiona's Novelty Four, Andrew	59	Alomo Garden Band/Jazzers	60	Arden-Ohman & Their Orch.	61
Akers, Garfield	187		59	Arist-O-Kats	305
Akins, Jim	304	Alston, Henry	304	Arkansas Barefoot Boys	248
Akin's Birmingham Boys	247	Alston & His Orch., Ovie	60	Arkansas Charlie	248
Alabama Creole Band	59	Altier, Danny	60	Arkansas Shorty	188
Alabama Four	187, 247	Alton and the Flames	304	Arkansas Travelers	61
Alabama Fuzzy Wuzzies	59	Alvans	304	Arkansas Trio	61
Alabama Harmony Boys	59	Ambassadors, The	60, 304	Arkansas Woodchopper	248
Alabama Jazz Pirates	59	Ambers, The	304	Armen, Smokey	305
Alabama Jim	187	Amelio, Johnny	304	Armstrong, Fred	61
Alabama Jug Band	59	American Beetles	304	Armstrong, Lil	61
Alabama Rascals	59	American Marimbaphone Band	60	Armstrong, Louis	61
Alabama Red Jackets	59	Amerson, Doug	304	Armstrong, May	188
Alabama Red Peppers	59	Ames, Tessie	187	Armstrong, Richard	188
Alabama Sam	187	Ammons & His Rhythm Kings, Albert	60	Armstrong, Shelly	188
Alabama Serenaders	59	Amos	187	Armstrong and Ashley	248
Alabama Shieks	187	Amos, Blind Joe	187	Armstrong and Jacobs	248
Alabama Slim	187	Amos, Ira	187	Armstrong's Players	248
Alabama Washboard Stompers	59	Amos 'n' Andy	60	Arndt, Felix	63
Aladdins, The	304	Amy, Curtis	187	Arnheim & His Orch., Gus	63
Alameda Wonder Players/Orchestra	59	Anderson, Andy	304	Arnold, Billy Boy	305
Alan, Dennie	304	Anderson, Bill	304	Arnold, Eddy	305
Albert, Don	59	Anderson, Eddie "Rochester"	60	Arnold, Gene	248
Albert, Mel	304	Anderson, Elton	304	Arnold, Kokomo	188
Alberts & His Orchestra, Al	59	Anderson, Jelly Roll	187	Arnold and the Chalecos, Jack	305
Albin, Jack	60	Anderson, Jimmie	187	Arp, James	305
Alexander, Hilda	187	Anderson, Jimmy	304	Arrogants, The	305
Alexander, Little David	187	Anderson, Leroy	247	Arrows, The	305
Alexander, Max	304	Anderson, Les 'Carrot Top'	247	Arthur & Rexroat	248
Alexander, Ora	187	Anderson, Louise	187	Arthur, Richie	305
Alexander, Texas	187	Anderson, Maybelle	187	Artistics, The	305
Alexander, Van	60	Anderson, Missouri	187	Artwood, Little Joe	305
Alexander and Miller	247	Anderson, Mozelle	187	Artz & His Orch., Billy	63
Alexander Brothers	187	Anderson, Pink	188	Ascots, The	305
Alford, Annie	304	Anderson, Walter	60	Ash, Paul	63
Algers, The	304	Anderson, 'Talking Billy'	187	Ashford Quartet	248
Alimo, Steve	304	Anderson and Her Boys from		Ashley, Clarence	248
Alix, May	187	Dixie, Ivie	60	Ashley, Clyde	248

Ashley, Foster	248	Baker, C.B.	188
Ashley, John	305	Baker, Donny	306
Ashley, Thomas C.	248	Baker, Dorothy	188
Ashley's Melody Makers/Men	248	Baker, Eldon	249
Asparagus Joe	248	Baker, Katherine	188
Astaire, Fred	63	Baker, Laverne	306
Astorites, The	63	Baker, Mr. & Mrs.	249
Astronauts	305	Baker, Viola	188
Atcher, Bob	248, 305	Baker, Willie	188, 306
Atha, Chuck	305	Baker and the Deltones, Ronnie	306
Atkins, Dave	305	Bakers Group, Frank	65
Atlanta Merrymakers	63	Baldwin, Luke	250
Atlanta Syncopators	63	Ball, Bentley	250
Atlantics	305	Ball, Earl	306
Auburn, Frank	63	Ballads, The	306
Audrey	305	Ballard, Frank	306
Augusta Trio	248	Ballard, Hank	306
Auld & His Orch., George	64	Ballard, Jerry	306
Austin, Don	305	Ballard, Wolfe	250
Austin, Gene	64	Ballew, Smith	65
Austin, Lovie	64	Baltimore Bellhops, The	65
Austin, Mildred	188	Baltimore Society Orch.	65
Austin and Lee Allen	248	Baltineers, The	306
Austin and the Chromatics,		Baltzell, John	250
Little Augie	305	Bang Boys	250
Austin and The Hearts, Billy	305	Banister, James	306
Austin & His Musical Ambassadors	64	Banjo Boys	250
Austin's Serenaders	64	Banjo Buddy	65
Autry, Gene	305	Banjo Ike (See Ivory Chittison)	65
Avalon, Frankie	305	Banjo Joe	188
Avalons, The	305	Banks, Billy	65
Avery, Charles	64	Banks, Dick	306
Avolonians, The	64	Banks, Mack	306
Ayers, Harvey	249	Banks, Otis	306
Ayre's, John Orch.	64	Bankston, Emmett	250
Babs & Her Brothers	64	Banners, The	65, 306
Baby Aristocrats	64	Banta, Frank	65
Baby Bonnie	188	Bar Harbor (Society) Orch.	65
Baby Boy	188	Barbary Coast Orch.	65
Baby Dee	305	Barbecue Bob	188
Baby Doo	188	Barbecue Joe	65
Baby Face Leroy	188	Barbecue Pete	65
Baby Rose Marie	64	Barbee, John Henry	189
Bachelors, The	305	Barber, Don	306
Back Porch Boys, The	188	Barber, Glen	250, 306
Bacon, Gar	306	Barclay & The Sliders, Phil	306
Bacon, Shorty	306	Bare, Bobby	306
Badgers, The	64	Barefield & His Quintette, Eddie	65
Baer & His Wardman Park		Barefoot Bill	189
Orch., Moe	64	Barfield, John	250
Bailey, Buster	65	Bargy, Roy	65
Bailey, DeFord	188	Barker, Delbert	306
Bailey, Jack	306	Barker, Tom	65
Bailey, Jene	65	Barker Bros.	306
Bailey, Kid	188	Barkle, Al	306
Bailey, Little Marie	306	Barlow, Dean	306
Bailey, Mildred	65	Barlow, Jerry	250
Bailey, Morris	306	Barlow & The Montereys, Dean	306
Bailey, Red Mike	188	Barner, Juke Boy	306
Bailey, William	65	Barner, Wiley	189
Bailey Swing Group	65	Barnes, Benny	306
Bailey's Dixie Dudes	64	Barnes, Billie	66
Bailey's Lucky Seven	64	Barnes, David	306
Baines, Houston	188	Barnes, Fae	189
Baird, Maynard	65	Barnes, Faye	66
Baker, Belle	65	Barnes, H.M.	250
Baker, Blind Bobby	188	Barnes, Jimmy	306
Baker, Bob	306	Barnes, Walter	66
Baker, Buddy	249	Barnes, Willie	189
Baker, Charles	249	Barnes, Yodeling Frankie	250
Baker, Charlie	306	Barnet, Charlie	66

Barnstormers, The	250
Barnyard Steve	250
Barons, The	306
Barr, Chuck	306
Barr, Martha	189
Barrel House Annie	189
Barrel House Buck	189
Barrel House Five	66
Barrelhouse Frankie	189
Barrelhouse Sammy	189
Barrett, Hugh	306
Barrett, Richard	306
Barrett Singers	306
Barrie & His Orch., Dick	66
Barrix, Billy	306
Barron, Lonnie	306
Barron & His Orch., Blue	66
Barrow, Raymond	66
Barry, Dave	306
Barry, Jay	306
Barry, Jeff	306
Barry, Joe	306
Bart, Teddy	306
Bartell, Ted	66
Bartha, Alex	66
Bartholomew, Dave	306
Bartlett, Slim	66
Bartlett, Viola	189
Bartlett's Boosters	250
Barton, Bart	306
Barton, Billy	306
Barton, Dick	307
Barton, John	250
Barton, Kenneth	250
Barton, Slim	189
Barton, Tippy	189
Bash, Otto	307
Basie, Count	66
Baskerville, Norven	307
Bassett, Tony	307
Bat The Humming Bird	189
Batchelors, The	307
Bates, Deacon L.J.	189
Battle of the Blues	307
Batts, Ray	250, 307
Batts, Will	189
Baucom, Dave	307
Baum, Allen	307
Baxter, Helen	189
Baxter Family Trio	250
Baxter, Phil	66
Baxter & A.J. Andrew, Jim	189
Bay Bops, The	307
Bayersdorffer, Johnny	66
Baylor's Berlyn Orch.	66
Beach, Bill	307
Beach Boys, The	307
Beachum, Rufus	307
Beale Street Five	66
Beale Street Rounders	189
Beale Street Seven	66
Beale St. Sheiks	189
Beale Street Washboard Band	66
Beaman, Lottie	189
Bean, Mumford	250
Beard, Dean	307
Beasley, Good Rockin' Sam	307
Beasley, Helen	189
Beasley, Irene	66
Beasley, Jimmy	307
Beasley, Walter	189

Beatles, The	307	Berry, Chuck	309	Bisbee, Jasper	251
Beatnicks	308	Berry, Dorothy	309	Bishop, Billy	251
Beatty, E.C.	308	Berry, Lou	309	Bivens, Lester Pete	251
Beatty, Josephine	66	Berry, Richard	309	Bix & His Rhythm Jugglers	68
Beau-Marks, The	308	Berry Cups	309	Black, Frankie	68, 191
Beaver, Stan	308	Berry Kids	309	Black, Jimmie	251
Beaver, The	308	Berry & The Bell Raves, Red	309	Black, Lewis	191
Bechet, Sidney	67	Berton, Vic	67	Black Ace	190
Beck, Johnny	189	Bertrand, Jimmy	67	Black Boy Shine	190
Becky, Charles-Elder Charlie	189	Bessemer Melody Boys	190	Black Brothers	251
Becky, Son	189	Best of Rhythm and Blues, The	309	Black Diamond	68, 191
Bee, Johnnie	250	Bestor & His Orch., Don	67	Black Diamond Serenaders	68
Bee, Willie	189	Beverly Hill Billies	250	Black Dominoes, The	68
Beery, Noah	67	Biagini & His Orch., Henry	68	Black Ivory King	191
Bees, The	308	Biddleville Quintette	190	Black Kids of Harmony	68
Beeson & His Orch., Dick	67	Biese & His Orch., Paul	68	Black Pirates, The	68
Behrens, Jerry	250	Big Aces, The	68	Black Spider Dumplin	191
Beiderbecke, Bix	67	Big Bill et al	190	Black Swan Dance Orch.	68
Belasco & His Orch., Leon	67	Big Bloke	190	Blackard, Dad	251
Belew, Carl	308	Big Bopper (See Jape Richardson)	309	Blackbirds of Paradise	68
Bell, Anna	67	Big Chief	190	Blackburn, Mamie	191
Bell, Bill	308	Big Connie	309	Blackwell, Otis	310
Bell, Brother	189	Big Daddy	309	Blackwell, Willie '61'	191
Bell, Carl	308	Big Ed	309	Blackwell Scrapper, Francis	191
Bell, Dick	250	Big Five	309	Blackwells, The	310
Bell, Dwain	308	Big Four	309	Blair, Sunny	191
Bell, Ed	189	Big Jeff and the Radio Playboys	250	Blake, Charley	251
Bell, Eddie/Eddy	308	Big Joe And His Rhythm Washboard		Blake, Curley	251
Bell, Freddie	308	Band	190	Blake, Eubie	68
Bell, Johnnie	308	Big John	190	Blake, Tommy	310
Bell, Tommy	308	Big Mac	309	Blakeley, Cliff	310
Bell Notes, The	308	Big Maceo	190, 310	Blakeley, Jimmy	310
Bell Record Boys	67	Big Maybelle	310	Blakeley, Wellington	310
Bells, The	308	Big Memphis Ma Rainey	190, 310	Blakely, Cornell	310
Belltones, The	308	Big Oscar	190	Blakeman, Guy	251
Bellus, Tony	308	Big Richard	190	Blakenship Brothers	310
Belmonts, The	308	Big Sister	190	Blankenship Family	251
Belshaw, George	67	Big Three Trio	190	Blake's Jazzone Orch.	68
Belvederes	308	Big Walter	310	Blalock and Yates	251
Belvideers	308	Big Willie	190	Blanchard, Dan	251
Belvin, Jessie	308	Bigard, Barney	68	Blanchard, Jackie	310
Bel-Airs, The	308	Bigeon, Ester	190	Bland, Billy	310
Bel-Larks, The	308	Bilbro, D.H.	190	Bland, Bobbie Blue	310
Ben's Bad Boys	67	Bill and Slim	190	Bland, Glenn	310
Benbow, Baby	189	Billings, Bud and Joe	250	Bland, Jack	68
Bennett, Arnold	309	Bills, Dick	310	Blasers	310
Bennett, Barbara	309	Billy and Jesse	190	Jules Blattner	310
Bennett, Boyd	309	Billy Bird	190	Blazer Boy	310
Bennett, Chuck	309	Billy Boy	310	Bledsoe, Blazer Boy Steve	310
Bennett, Cliff	309	Billy Guitar	310	Blendairs, The	310
Bennett, Eloise	189	Billy The Kid	310	Blenders, The	310
Bennett, Phil	67	Billy & Lillie	310	Blends, The	310
Bennett, Will	189	Binder, Long Man	310	Blendtones, The	310
Bennett's Swamplanders	67	Bine, Doug	250	Blevins, Frank	251
Benson, Joe	309	Bing Bones	310	Blevins, Rubye	251
Benson Orch. of Chicago	67	Binkley Brothers	250	Blihove, Marv	310
Benson's Orch, Benny	67	Binney, Jack	68	Blind Andy	251
Bentley, Gladys	189	Bip and Bop	310	Blind Arthur	191
Bentley Boys	250	Bird, Connie	250	Blind Blake	191
Benton, Brook	309	Bird, Happy/String Band, Elmer	250	Blind Gary	191
Benton, Buster	309	Bird, Louis	251	Blind Mack	191
Benton, Merve	309	Bird, Nat	251	Blind Norris	191
Benton, Walt	309	Birdhead, L.O.	251	Blind Percy	191
Bergeron, Shirley	309	Birdson, Larry	310	Blind Sammie	191
Berigan, Bunny	67	Bird's Kentucky Corn Crackers	250	Blind Willie	191
Bernard, Al	67	Birmingham, Sam	190	Blockbusters, The	310
Bernard, Glory	190	Birmingham Bluetette	68	Bloom, Rube	68
Bernard, Mike	67	Birmingham Five	68	Blue, Bob	69
Bernard, Rod	309	Birmingham Jug Band	68	Blue, Bud	69, 251
Bernie, Ben	67	Birmingham Quartet	190	Blue Angels, The	310
Berry, Chu	67	Birmingham Serenaders	68	Blue Belles, The	191, 310

Blue Bill	191	
Blue Boy	191	
Blue Boys	191, 251	
Blue Charlie	310	
Blue Chips	310	
Blue Diamonds, The	310	
Blue Dots	310	
Blue Flames (see Little Jr.)	310	
Blue Grass Footwarmers	68	
Blue Harmony Boys	191	
Blue Jacks, The	191	
Blue Jay Boys	68	
Blue Moon Melody Boys	68, 251	
Blue Notes, The	310	
Blue Rhythm Band/Boys	68	
Blue Rhythm Orchestra	68	
Blue Ribbon Boys/Band	68	
Blue Ribbon Syncopators	68	
Blue Ridge Cornshuckers	251	
Blue Ridge Duo	251	
Blue Ridge Highballers	251	
Blue Ridge Hillbillies	251	
Blue Ridge Mountain Entertainers	251	
Blue Ridge Mountain Girls	251	
Blue Ridge Mountain Singers	251	
Blue Ridge Mountaineer	251	
Blue Ridge Playboys	251	
Blue Room Orch.	69	
Blue Sky Boys Trio	251	
Blue Smitty	191	
Blue Tones, The	311	
Bluebirds, The	68	
Blues, The	311	
Blues Birdhead	191	
Blues Chasers, The	69	
Blues King, The	191	
Blues Man, The	191	
Blues Rockers, The	191, 311	
Blues Slim	311	
Blues Toppers, The	311	
Bluie, Louie	191	
Blumenberg's Orch.	69	
Blu-Disc Orchestra, The	68	
Blythe, Jimmy	69	
Blythe's Blue Boys	69	
Blythe's Sinful Five	69	
Blythe's Washboard Band	69	
Boatman, Tooter	311	
Boaz, Calvin	191	
Boazeman, Harmon	311	
Boa's Pine Cabin Boys	251	
Bob and Lucille	311	
Bob and Monte	251	
Bob and Ray	311	
Bob and Sherri	311	
Bob and the Rockabillies	311	
Bobbettes, The	311	
Bobby & Orbits	311	
Bobby's Revelers	69	
Bodaford, Bill	311	
Bodine (Loy)	251	
Bogan, Lucille	191	
Bogan's Birmingham Busters	69	
Boggs, 'Dock'	251	
Bohn, Tommy	69	
Boines, Houston	192	
Bolden, Lela	192	
Bollin, ZuZu	192	
Bolling, Pillie	192	
Bolognese & His Orch., Paul	69	
Bolten, Hattie	192	

Bolton & Cipriani's Westchester Biltmore Orch.	69	
Bond, Eddie	311	
Bond, Johnny	311	
Bond, Luther	311	
Bonds, Gary U.S.	311	
Bonds, Son	192	
Bonds, U.S.	311	
Boni, Johnny	311	
Bonner, Captain M.J.	251	
Bonner, Juke Boy	311	
Bonnevilles, The	311	
Bontsema & His Hotel Tuller Orch. of Detroit, Pete	69	
Bon-Aires, The	311	
Boogaloo	311	
Boogie Jake	311	
Boogie Kings	311	
Boogie Man, The	192	
Booker, Charley	192	
Booker, John Lee	192, 311	
Booker and Mack, Connie	192	
Booker Orch.	69	
Books, Connie	311	
Boone, Alonzo	192	
Boone, Claude	252	
Boone, Jimmy	252	
Boone, Pat	311	
Boone, Rev. Edward & (Mrs.) & (Miss Olive Boone)	252	
Boone County Entertainers	251	
Boots and His Buddies	69, 252	
Bop Chords, The	311	
Boppin' (LP)	311	
Borbee's Jass Orch.	69	
Borg, Benny	252	
Borton, Godfrey	252	
Borton, Kenneth	252	
Bosstones	311	
Bostick, Calvin	192	
Boston, Bobby	311	
Boston Society Orch.	69	
Bostonians, The	69	
Boswell, Connie	69	
Boswell, Leo	252	
Boswell Sisters	69	
Bouchillon, Chris	252	
Bowen, Bill & The Rockets	311	
Bowen, Jimmy	311	
Bowers, Chuck	252	
Bowers, Earl	252	
Bowers and Lewis	252	
Bowles, Doug	311	
Bowman, Cecil	311	
Bowman, Charlie	252	
Bowman Sisters	252	
Bowser, Donnie	311	
Bowshier, Little Donnie	252	
Box, David	311	
Boyd, Aaron	252	
Boyd, Bill	252	
Boyd, Eddie	192, 311	
Boyd, Ernie	192	
Boyd, Georgia	192	
Boyd, Jimmy	312	
Boyd, Raymond	192	
Boyd, Robert	312	
Boyd & His Southerners, John	252	
Boys from Wildcat Hollow	252	
Boze, Calvin	192	
Bozeman, Helen	312	

Bozman, Virgel	252	
Bracey, Ishman	192	
Bracey, Mississippi	192	
Bracken, Jimmy	69	
Braden, Tommy	312	
Bradford, Auntie Mary	192	
Bradford, Mary H.	192	
Bradford, Perry	69	
Bradford, Walter	192	
Bradix, Big Charlie	192	
Bradley, Marie	192	
Bradley, Rockin'	312	
Bradley, Tommy	192	
Bradley, Velma	192	
Bradley & His Orch., Will	70	
Bradshaw, Jack	312	
Bradshaw, Tiny	70, 312	
Brady, Jean	192	
Bragg, Ardelle	70	
Bragg, Dobby	192	
Bragg, Doug	312	
Bragg, Johnny	312	
Bragg & His Rhythm Five, J.H.	70	
Branch, Ernest	252	
Branch and Coleman	252	
Branham, Ronnie	312	
Brant, Bobby	312	
Brashear's California Orchestra	70	
Brasswell, Frank	192	
Bray (Accompanied by Sunny Clapp & His Band O'Sunshine), Lew	70	
Bray's Orch., Bruce	70	
Brazzell, Nicky	312	
Breedlove, Jimmy	312	
Breed's (Shepard Colonial) Orchestra, Perley	70	
Brenston, Jackie	192, 312	
Brent, Frankie	312	
Brent, Ronnie	312	
Brentwoods	312	
Brians, Robin Hood	312	
Briarhopper, Homer	252	
Brickey, Evelyn	192	
Brier Hopper (see also Red Headed Brier Hopper)	252	
Briggs, Billy	252	
Brigode & His Ten/Fourteen Virginians, Ace	70	
Brillhardt's Orchestra	70	
Brim, Grace	192	
Brim, John	192	
Brim, Mrs. John	192	
Brinkley, Jay	312	
Brinkley, Larry	312	
Bristol, Florence	192	
Britt, Darryl	312	
Britt, Elton	312	
Britt, Matt	70	
Britt Brothers	252	
Britton, Maynard	252	
Broadway Bell-Hops	70	
Broadway Broadcasters	70	
Broadway Dance Orchestra	71	
Broadway Melody Makers	71	
Broadway Pickers	71	
Broadway Players	71	
Broadway Rastus	71	
Broadway Seven	71	
Broadway Syncopators	71	
Brock and Dudley	252	
Brock Sisters	252	

Brodsky, Irving	71	Brown, Thomas	253	Bunn, Billy	314
Brookes, Bobby	312	Brown, Tommy	313	Bunn, Teddy	194
Brooklyn Boys	312	Brown, Walter	313	Burbank, Jack & Jim	253
Brooks, Billy	252	Brown, Willie	193, 313	Burden, Ray	314
Brooks, Bob	252	Brown, Yodeling Kid	193	Burdette, Jack	253
Brooks, Charlie (C.S.)	252	Brown, 'Elder' J.C.	193	Burgess, Dave	314
Brooks, Chuck	312	Brown, 'HI' Henry	193	Burgess, Sonny	314
Brooks, Dusty	193	Brown and Bunch	252	Burgett, Jim	314
Brooks, Emory	193	Brown and Her Boyfriends, Wini	313	Burke, (Fiddlin') Jim	253
Brooks, Harvey	71	Brown & Duke, Flossie	193	Burk & The Counts, Tommy	314
Brooks, Junior	193	Brown & Her Boys, Ida	71	Burke, Buddy	314
Brooks, Lillian	312	Brown & His Blue Band, Kid	71	Burke, Eddie	314
Brooks, Louis	312	Brown & His Brownies, Bill	71	Burke Brothers	253
Brooks, Richard	252	Brown & His Orch., Les	71	Burke, Sonny	72
Brooks, Sonny	312	Brown & Terry's Jazzola Boys	71	Burke Trio, Pete	253
Broomsley, Big Bill	193	Brownagle & His Orch., Ted	71	Burkhardt, Abner	253
Broonzy, Big Bill	312	Browne, Alta	193	Burks, Pinetop	194
Brother Bell	193	Browne, Doris	313	Burleson, Hattie	194
Brother Blues	193	Browne, Sam	71	Burley, Dan	194
Brother George	193	Browning, Bill	313	Burnette, Dorsey	314
Brothers, The	312	Brownlee's Orch.	71	Burnette, Johnny	314
Brown, Ada	193	Brown's Happy Four	252	Burnette, Linda	314
Brown, Alberta	193	Brown's Musical Brownies	252, 253	Burnette, Smiley	253
Brown, Bessie	193	Brown-Morris Orch.	71	Burnette and Miller	253
Brown, Bill	193	Brox Sisters	71	Burnette Brothers, The	253, 314
Brown, Billy	312	Bruce, Edwin	313	Burnette & Ruttledge	253
Brown, Bobby	312	Bruner, Bill	253	Burney, Mac	314
Brown, Buster	312	Brunies, Albert	71	Burns, Daphne	253
Brown, Charles	312	Brunies, Merritt	71	Burns, Eddie	194, 314
Brown, Charlie	312	Brunson, Frank	313	Burns, Jackie	314
Brown, Chocolate	193	Bryan, Billy	313	Burns, Ruben	252
Brown, Cleo	71	Bryan, Dave	313	Burns, Sonny	314
Brown, Daniel	193	Bryan, Wes	313	Burrage, Harold	314
Brown, Danny	312	Bryant, Elder Richard	194	Burris, Johnny	72
Brown, Dudley	193	Bryant, Gladys	193	Burris & His Night Owls, Sammy	72
Brown, Dusty	312	Bryant, Laura	71	Burse, Charlie (See Memphis	
Brown, Earl 'Good Rockin'	313	Bryant, Willie	71	Jug Band)	72, 194
Brown, Edward & The Browns, Jim	313	Bryant, (Hoyt) 'Slim'	253	Burston, Clara	194
Brown, Eliza	193	Bryant's Jubilee Quartet	193	Burton, Bob	314
Brown, Frank	71	Brymn & His Black Devil Orch.,		Burton, Buddy	195
Brown, Freddie	193	Tim	71	Burton, Dave	314
Brown, Gabriel	193	BUA, Gene	313	Burton, John	253
Brown, Gatemouth	193, 313	Bubbling-over Five	71	Burton, Russell & Louis	253
Brown, Gene	313	Buccaneers	313	Burton, W.H.	195
Brown, Gray and Dilly	252	Buchanan, Wes	313	Burton's Orch., Dick	72
Brown, Guy	313	Buchanan & Ancell	313	Busby, Frank	195
Brown, Henry	71	Buchanan & Goodman	313	Busby, Wayne	314
Brown, Hershall	253	Buchanan & Greenfield	313	Bush, Eddie	314
Brown, Hylo	313	Buchanon, Art	313	Busse's Buzzards; Henry Busse &	
Brown, James 'Widemouth'	193, 313	Buck, Gary	313	His Orch.	72
Brown, Jimmy	253, 313	Buck, Peter	313	Buster & Jack	253
Brown, Joe	193	Buck Mountain Band	253	Butanes	314
Brown, Judson	193	Buck & Bubbles	71	Butcher, Dwight	253
Brown, J.T.	313	Buckeye Boys	253	Butera, Sam	314
Brown, Kitty	193	Buckeyes	313	Butler, Cliff	314
Brown, Lee	193	Bucktown Five	71	Butler, Jerry	314
Brown, Lil	193	Bucky and Premiers	313	Butler, Mary	195
Brown, Lottie	193	Buffalodians, The	71	Butler, Sam	195
Brown, Lucille	193	Bull City Red	194	Butler, Trixie	195
Brown, Marcus	313	Bullard, John	314	Butterbeans & Susie	195
Brown, Milton	253, 313	Bullard Quartet, John	194	Buzzingtons Rube Band	72
Brown, Nappy	313	Bullock, Chuck	72	Byers & His Orch., Hale	72
Brown, Ora	193	Bullock, Norman	314	Byrd, John	195
Brown, Oscar	253	Bumble Bee Slim	194	Byrd, Josephine	195
Brown, Richard	193	Bunch, Alvin	253	Byrd, Robert	314
Brown, Roy	193, 313	Bunch, Billy	72	Byrd, Roland	195
Brown, Russell	71	Bunch, Carl	253	Byrd, Roy 'Baldhead'	195, 314
Brown, Ruth	313	Bunch, Frank	72	Byrd and the Birds, Bobby	314
Brown, Sammy	193	Bunch, Sam	253	Byrne, Jerry	314
Brown, Skeet	193	Bunch of Goodies	314	Byrhes, Ed	314
Brown, Texas Johnny	193	Bunn, Allen	194	Byron, Jimmie	314

Cauley & Lake Howard, Roland	257	
Causer, Bob	77	
Cavalier, Johnny	317	
Cavello, Jimmy	317	
Cavello & House Rockers, Jimmy	317	
Caves, John W.	317	
Cawley, Jack	257	
Cedar Creek Sheik	257	
Cedar Crest Singers	257	
Celestin's Original Tuxedo	77	
Cellar Boys, The	77	
Cellos, The	317	
Celtics, The	317	
Centuries, The	317	
Century's	317	
Chadwick & His Orch., Ron	77	
Chaffin, Ernie	317	
Chalets	317	
Challenge Dance Orch.	77	
Chalons	317	
Chamberlain Bros.	317	
Chamblee, Eddie	317	
Champion, Hollis	317	
Champion, Johnny	317	
Champion Rhythm Kings	77	
Champions, The	317	
Champs, The	317	
Chancellors	317	
Chanceteers, The	317	
Chandaliers, The	317	
Chandler, Elaine	317	
Chandler, Lee	317	
Chandler, Wayland	317	
Chanier, Cliston	317	
Channel, Bruce	317	
Channels, The	317	
Chantays	317	
Chantels, The	317	
Chanters, The	317	
Chanticleers, The	317	
Chantones, The	318	
Chants, The	318	
Chapel, Jean	318	
Chapell, Bill	318	
Chaperones	318	
Chaplain, Paul	318	
Chaplin Conducting Lyman's Orch., Charlie	77	
Chapman, Charlie	197	
Chapman, Gene	318	
Chapman & His (Drake Hotel) Orch., Jack	77	
Chappel, Leon	318	
Chappelear, Leon	257	
Chappelli Stinnette, Juanita	77	
Charioteers, The	318	
Chariots	318	
Charles, Andy	318	
Charles, Bobby	318	
Charles, Henry	197	
Charles, Ray	318	
Charleston Blues Trio, The	197	
Charleston Chasers, The	77	
Charleston Entertainers	257	
Charleston Melody Syncopators	77	
Charleston Seven, The	77	
Charlie Bop Trio	318	
Charmers, The	318	
Charms, The	318	
Charters, The	318	
Charts, The	318	
Chase, Chezz	257	
Chastain, Jody	318	
Chateaus, The	318	
Chatman, Andy	197	
Chatman, Bo	197	
Chatman, Christine	318	
Chatman, Earl	318	
Chatman, Peter	197	
Chatman Brothers	197	
Chatmon, Harry	197	
Chavelles, The	318	
Chavis Boozoo	318	
Chavis Brothers, The	318	
Checker Box Boys	77	
Checker, Chubby	318	
Checker, Dots	318	
Checkers, The	318	
Chelmors	318	
Chenier, Big	318	
Chenier, Clifton	318	
Chenoweth's Cornfield	257	
Cherokee Ramblers, The	257	
Cherokees, The	319	
Cherwin & His Orch., Dick	78	
Cher-Vali, Frankie	319	
Chesnut, Ted	257	
Chess & The Merry Makers, Fred	78	
Chesterfields	319	
Chesters, The	319	
Chestnuts, The	319	
Chevelles	319	
Chev-rons, The	319	
Chicago Black Swans	78	
Chicago Blues Dance Orch.	78	
Chicago De Lux Orch.	78	
Chicago Five	197	
Chicago Foot Warmers, The	78	
Chicago Hot Five	78	
Chicago Hottentots	78	
Chicago Loopers, The	78	
Chicago Rhythm Kings	78	
Chicago Sheiks, The	197	
Chicago Stompers	78	
Chicago Sunny Boy	197	
Chick and the Hotrods	319	
Chickasaw Syncopators, The	78	
Chief Shunatonk, Doug, McTague, Snookum	257	
Chiffons, The	319	
Childers, Bill	257	
Childers, Virgil	197	
Childers, W.C.	257	
Childers & White	257	
Childre, Lew	257	
Childress, Buddy	319	
Chiles, Buddy	197	
Chimes, The	319	
Chippendales	319	
Chips, The	319	
Chisholm, Anna Lee	197	
Chittison, Ivory	78	
Chitwood, Bill	257	
Choates, Harry	257	
Chocolate Dandies	78	
Chocolateers	319	
Choo Choo Jazzers	78	
Chorals, The	319	
Chordcats, The	319	
Chordells, The	319	
Chords, The	319	
Christian, Ben	257	
Christian, Buddy	78	
Christian, Lillie Delk	78	
Christian & His Orch., Tommy	78	
Christian (Four Cry Babies), Buddy	197	
Christmas Gift For You	319	
Christmon, John	319	
Christopher, Homer	257	
Chromatics	319	
Chubb-Steinberg Orchestra	78	
Chuck and Bill	319	
Chuck Wagon Gang	257, 319	
Chuckles	319	
Chumbler Family	257	
Chumblers Breakdown Gang	257	
Church, Blind Clyde	197	
Church, Eugene	319	
Cincinnati Jug Band	78	
Cincinnatians	319	
Cindy & Sandy	319	
Cineramas, The	319	
Ciolino, Pete	319	
Circle C Band	319	
Clanton, Jimmy	319	
Clapp, Sunny	78	
Clardy & Stan Clemens, Gene	257	
Claremonts, The	319	
Clarinet Joe	78	
Clark, Charles	319	
Clark, Dee	319	
Clark, Don	78	
Clark, Dot	197	
Clark, Ethel	197	
Clark, Frank	258	
Clark, Fred	319	
Clark, John	258	
Clark, Leonard	319	
Clark, Lonnie	197	
Clark, Luther B.	258	
Clark, Sanford	319	
Clark, Theo & Gus	258	
Clark Brothers	257	
Clark & The Demons, Ray	319	
Clarke, George	197	
Clarke, Jim	78	
Clarke & Howell	258	
Classics, The	319	
Classmates	319	
Clauser, Al	258	
Clay, Joe	319	
Clay & His Orch., Sonny	78	
Clayton, Doctor	197, 319	
Clayton, Doug	319	
Clayton, Jackson, & Durante	78	
Clayton, Jesse	197	
Clayton, Johnny	319	
Clayton, Peter J.	197	
Clayton & His Melody Mountaineers	258	
Clear Waters	319	
Cleary, Eddie	319	
Clefs, The	319	
Cleftones, The	319	
Cleighton, Peter	197	
Clem and Harry	258	
Clem & Prince Albert Hunt, Harmon	258	
Clemens, Albert	197	
Clement, Henry	320	
Clement, Jack	320	
Clements, Stanley	258	
Cleo & The Crystaliers	320	
Clesi's Aerolians, Johnny	78	
Cleveland, Big Boy	197	

Crabtree, Riley	259, 322	Cubs, The	324
Craddock, Bill(Y) ('Crash')	322	Cues, The	324
Craig, Jimmy	322	Cufflinks, The	324
Craig, Pee Wee	322	Cufflinx, The	324
Craig & His Orch., Frances	82	Culver, Bruce	324
Crain, Edward L.	259	Cumberland Ridge Runners	260
Crain, Jimmy	322	Cumberland String Band	260
Crammer Brothers	259	Cummins & His Orch., Bernie	83
Crane, Bob	198	Cupids, The	324
Cranford & Ernest Thompson, Bob	259	Cupp, Pat	324
Craver & Charlie Wells, Al	259	Curley, Jim	324
Crawford, Alvin	259	Curran & His Orchestra, Joe	83
Crawford, Blackie	322	Curry, Ben	198
Crawford, Fred	322	Curry, Earl	324
Crawford, Jack	82	Curry, Edler	198
Crawford, James	198	Curry, James	324
Crawford, Rosetta	198	Curtis, C.C.	324
Crawford, Sugar Boy	322	Curtis, Don	324
Crawley, Wilton	82	Curtis, Eddie	324
Crayton, Pee Wee	198, 322	Curtis, Eddie (Tex)	324
Crazy Hill Billies Band	259	Curtis, Max	324
Creager & His Orch/Entertainers/		Curtis, Sonny	324
Rhythm Aces, Willie	82	Cutrell, Dave	260
Creath's Jazzo-Maniacs, Charles	82	Cyclones, The	324
Creations, The	322	Cymbal, Johnny	324
Creators, The	323	Cymbals	324
Crescendos, The	323	Cypress, Buddy	324
Crescents, The	323	Czars of Rhythm	324
Crests, The	323	Da Costa Woltz	260
Crew Cuts, The	323	Dabney's Band/(Syncopated)	
Crickets (Dean Barlow), The	323	(Novelty) Orch., Ford	83
Crickets (with Buddy Holly), The	323	Daddy Cleanhead	324
Crippen, Katie	198	Daddy Stovepipe	198
Crocker and Cannon	259	D'Agostin, Dick	324
Crockett, Davy G.	323	Dailey, Dusky	198
Crockett, Howard	323	Dailey's Meadowbrooks/Orchestra/	
Crockett, Johnny And Albert	259	Meadowbrook Orch., Frank	84
Crockett Family Mountaineers	259	Dale, Dick & The Del-Tones	324
Cromwell, George	323	Dale, Flora	84
Cronin, Jerry	323	Dale, Jimmy	324
Croom and Croom Brothers, Dillard	323	Dale, Kenny	324
Crosby, Bing	82	Dale, Larry	324
Crosby, Bob	83	Dale, Sally	199
Crosby & The Pine Tree Boys, Harold	323	Dales	324
Cross, Ballard	259	Daley, Jimmy	324
Cross, Bob	259	Dalhart, Vernon	260
Cross, David	198	Dallis, Chuck	324
Cross, McCartt, Nichols, Puckett	259	Dallas, Chuck	324
Crosstown Ramblers	83	Dallas, Jackie	324
Crow, Hank	323	Dallas, Leroy	199
Crowder Brothers	259	Dallas Jamboree Jug Band	84
Crown, Bobby	323	Dallas Red	199
Crowns, The	323	Dallas String Band	199
Crows, The	323	Dalton, Big Lloyd	324
Crudup, Arthur 'Big Boy'	198, 323	Dalton, Jack	84
Crudup, Percy Lee	198	Daly, Durwood	324
Cruisers, The	323	Daly, Terry	324
Crum, Al	323	D'Ambra & The Embers, Joe	324
Crum, Simon	323	Dameron, Donna	324
Crum & His Orch., Frank	83	Dance The Rock And Roll	324
Crumpton, Dennis	198	Dance Tunes from the Vault	324
Cruse & Sounds Quartette, Manny	324	Dancing Champions	84
Crutchfield, Paul	260	Dancing Stevedores	84
Cruthers Brothers	260	Danderliers, The	324
Crysel Boys w/Allen Bullard	260	Dandevilles	324
Crystaliers	324	Dandies, The	324
Crystals, The	324	Dandridge, Putney	84
Crystals Spring Ramblers	260	Dandurand, Tommy	260
C-Tones	324	Danford & His Ben Franklin Hotel	
Cuban Dance Players	83	Orch., Jack	84
Cubans, The	324	Daniels, Eddie	325

Daniels, Jeff	325
Daniels, Julius & Torrence	199
Danleers, The	325
Danny Boy & His Blue Guitar	325
Danny & The Juniors	325
Danny & The Memories	325
Dant, Charles Bud	325
Dante & The Evergreens	325
Dappers	325
Daps, The	325
Darby, Blind Blues	199
Darby, Teddy	199
Darby & Jimmie Tarlton, Tom	260
Dare, Dot (See Annette Hanshaw	
Gay Ellis)	84
Dare, Mountain Dew	260
Darin & The Jaybirds, Bobby	325
Darling, Chuck	260
Darling, Denver	325
Darling, Johnny	325
Darnell, Don	325
Darnell and Dreams	325
Darnell and Oxfords	325
Darren, James	325
Darts, The	325
Darty, Chuck	325
Dash, Frankie	325
Daugherty & His Orch., Doc	84
Dave the Stereos	325
Dave & Howard	260
Davenport, Charles	84
Davenport, Emmett	260
Davenport, Jed	84
Davenport, (Cow Cow) and Smith	
(Iva/Ivy)	84
Davenport & His Beale Street Jug	
Band, Jed	84
Davenport & His Gang, Carl	260
Davenport & The Young Brothers,	
Homer	260
Davenport,(Cow Cow) and Sam Theard	84
Davey & Doo Rays	325
Dave's Harlem Highlights	84
Davie's Kentuckians, Jack	84
Davis, Al	325
Davis, Blind Willie	200
Davis, Bo	325
Davis, Bob	325
Davis, Carl	84
Davis, Charlie/C.W.	84, 260
Davis, Claude (Trio)	260
Davis, Eddie	325
Davis, Emmett/Emmit	325
Davis, Eunice	325
Davis, Eva	260
Davis, Gene	325
Davis, Genevieve	84, 199
Davis, George	199
Davis, Happy Jack	325
Davis, Harley	325
Davis, Henryette	199
Davis, Jasper	84
Davis, Jewell	260
Davis, Jimmie	261, 325
Davis, Johnnie	85
Davis, Judge	325
Davis, Julia	85
Davis, Ken	325
Davis, King	325
Davis, Larry	325
Davis, Larry & Dixie	325

Dixon, Perry	200	Dowlands	330	Dunn, Webster Jr.	331
Dixon, Webb	328	Down Home Boys	200	Dunn, Blind Willie (Gin Bottle Four)	89
Dixon, Willie	328	Down Home Serenaders	88	Dunroe, Barney	262
Dixon Brothers	262	Down Home Trio	200	Duponts, The	331
Dixon Trio	262	Down South Boys	200	Dupree, Champion Jack	201, 331
Dixon & Channey	87	Downbeats, The	330	Duprees, The	331
Dixon & His Pencils, Vance Hoppers	87	Downhomers, The	262	Dupree's Rome Boys	262
Dixon's Chicago Serenaders	87	Downing, Al ('Big')	330	Duprey, Nelda	331
Dixon's Clod Hoppers	262	Downing, Wayne	330	Durante, Jimmy	89
Dixon's Jazz Duo/Maniacs	87	Doyle Bros.	262	Durden, Tommy	331
Dobkins, Carl Jr.	328	Dozier Boys, The	330	Durham, Paul	331
Dobson, Leroy	328	Dranes, Arizona	200	Durst, L.	201
Dockery, Chuck	328	Draper, Rusty	330	Dusters, The	331
Doctor Clayton's Buddy	200			Duvall, Huelyn	331
Dodds, Johnny	87, 262	Dream Kings, The	330	Duvals, The	331
Dodds and Parham	88	Dreamers, The	330	Dwellers, The	331
Dodgers, The	328	Dreamlovers	330	Dycus, Connie	331
Doerr & His Orch., Clyde	88	Dreams, The	330	Dye's Sacred Heart Singers	262
Doggett, Bill	328	Dreamtones, The	330	Dyke, Jerry	331
Doggett, Ray	328	Drew, George	88	Dykes Magic City Trio	262
Dole, Little Buddy	200	Dreyer & His Orch., Leo	88	Dylan, Bob	331
Doll, Andy	329	Drifters, The	330	Dynamics, The	331
Dollahan & His Orch., Pat	88	Drifting Charles	330	Dyson & His Musical Texans, Dick	262
Dolphins	329	Driftin' Slim/Smith	200	Eager, Johnny	331
Domino, Fats	329	Drink Small & His Guitar	330	Eager & His Trio, Jimmy	201
Dominoes,	329	Drivers, The	330	Eagles, The	331
Don, Dick & Jimmy	329	Droesch & His Orch., Eddie	88	Eaglin, Ford	331
Don Clairs, The	329	Druck, George	88	Earl & Bill	262
Don Juans, The	329	Dr. Hepcat	200	Earle, Burt	89
Don & Dewey	329	Du Droppers, The	330	Earls, The	331
Don & His Roses	329	Du Mauriers, The	331	Earls & The Jimbos, Jack	331
Donald, Charlie	329	Duals	330	Earthquakes, The	331
Donaldson Quartet	262	Dubin's Dandies	88	East Texas Serenaders	262
Donaldson & Hoke Rice, Louis	262	Dubs, The	330	Easton & His Orch., Amos	201
Donaldson Trio	262	Duces of Rhythm & The Tempo	330	Eaton, Charlie	89
Donn, Johnny	329	Duchin & His Orch., Eddie	89	Eay, Eddie	332
Donn, Larry	329	Duckett & Pig Norwood	200	Ebb Tides	332
Donnell, Blind Joe	200	Dudads, The	330	Ebbtones	332
Donner, Ral	329	Dudgeon, Frank	262	Ebonaires, The	332
Donohue, Al	88	Dudley, Dave	330	Eboniers	332
Dooley, George	329	Dudley, Roberta	89	Ebony Moods	332
Dootones, The	329	Duerson, Herve	89	Ebony Three	201
Dornberger & His Orch., Charles	88	Duff, Arlie	330	Echo Valley Boys, The	332
D'Orsay Dance Orch.	88	Duffie, Sally	200	Echoes, The	332
Dorsey, Jimmy	88	Duffill, Tam	330	Echomores	332
Dorsey, Lee	329	Dugosh, Eddie	330	Echotones	332
Dorsey, Mattie	200	Duke, Bernice	201	Eckhardt & His (Cafe LaFayette)	
Dorsey Brothers Orchestra	88	Duke, Billy	331	Orch., George Jr.	89
Dorsey & Chuck Wayne, Mel	329	Duke, Roy	331	Eckler & Ronald Gaines, Garner	262
Dorsey & Novelty Orchestra, Tom	88	Duke Bayou & His Mystic Six	201	Eckstein, Willie	89
Dortch, Slim	329	Duke of Earl	331	Eddie & Oscar	201
Doss, Bob	329	Duke & Null (See Denver Duke &		Eddie & Sugar Lou's Hotel	
Doss, Buster	329	Jeffrey Null)	330, 331	Tyler Orch.	89
Doss & His Arkansas Playboys,		Dukes, The	331	Eddie's Hot Shots	89
Buster	262	Dukes, Willie	201	Eddy, Duane	332
Dots	329	Dumaine, Louis (Jazzola Eight)	89	Eddy, Teddy	201
Dotson, Big Bill	200	Dunaway, Shelton	331	Edgewater Crows	89
Dotson, Jimmy	329	Dunbar, Frank	262	Edgin's George	262
Doty & His Orch., Mike	88	Duncan, Bill	331	Edinborough, Eddie	89
Dougherty, Big Bob	329	Duncan, Don	331	Edison, Thomas A.(See also "Holiday	
Douglas, Daisy	200	Duncan, Herbie	331	Greetings From The Bunch	
Douglas, Davy	329	Duncan Boys	262	At Orange")	90
Douglas, Dick	329	Duncan Sisters	262	Edminister, Corky	332
Douglas, Glenn	329	Dunford, Uncle Eck	262	Edsels, The	332
Douglas, K.C.	200, 330	Dunham, Andrew	201	Edwards, Bernice	201
Douglas, Mel	330	Dunham & His Orch., Sonny	89	Edwards, Big Boy	201
Douglas, Sheri Lee	330	Duniven, Bill	331	Edwards, Big Boy Teddy	201
Douglas, Shy Guy	330	Dunlap, Gene	331	Edwards, Carrie	201
Douglas & Nate Smith, Evan	262	Dunn, Fred	201	Edwards, Chuck	332
Dove & His String Band, Jerry	330	Dunn, John	331	Edwards, Cliff	90
Dowd, Larry	330	Dunn, Johnny	89	Edwards, Dave	262

Edwards, David	90	Emotions, The	333	Excellents, The	334
Edwards, Eddie Alvis	332	Emperors, The	91, 333	Excels, The	334
Edwards, Frank	201	Empires, The	333	Excelsior Quartette	202
Edwards, Gwen	332	Enchanters, The	333	Exciters, The	334
Edwards, Harold	262	Enchantments, The	333	Exclusives, The	334
Edwards, Honeyboy	201	Enchords, The	333	Execs, The	334
Edwards, Jimmy	332	Encores, The	333	Extremes, The	334
Edwards, Joan	90	Endorsers	333	Ezba, Denny	334
Edwards, J.D.	201	Engel, Scott	333	Ezell, Will	92
Edwards, Piano Kid	201	England, Benny	333	Ezra & The Ivies	334
Edwards, Tenderfoot	201	England, Hank	333	Fabares, Shelley	334
Edwards, Tibby	332	English, Peggy	91	Fabian	334
Edwards, Tommy	332	English, Sharlie	91	Fabulaires, The	334
Edwards & His Orch., Gus C.	90	Ensenators	333	Fabulons, The	334
Edwards & The White Caps, Johnny	332	Epics	333	Fabulous Egyptians, The	334
Edwins, Charles	332	Epp, Al	333	Fabulous Enchanters, The	334
Effros, Bob	90	Epperson, Don	333	Fabulous Fabuliers	334
Egan, Willie	332	Epps, Earl	333	Fabulous Five Flames, The	334
Eggleston, Cozy	332	Equinox Orch.	91	Fabulous Flames, The	334
Ehret, Bob	332	Erby, Jack	201	Fabulous Four, The	334
El Capris, The	332	Erby, John	201	Fabulous Gardenias	334
El Darados, The	332	Erickson Coliseum Orch., Wally	91	Fabulous Pearls, The	334
El Domingos, The	332	Erik & The Vikings	333	Fabulous Playboys	334
El Dorados, The	332	Erlene & Her Girlfriends	333	Fabulous Three	334
El Pollos, The	332	Ermines, The	333	Fabulous Twilights	334
El Rayes, The	332	Ervin, Frankie	333	Fabulous Winds, The	334
El Reyes	332	Ervin, Leroy	201	Facenda, Tommy	334
El Tempos	333	Ervin, Odie	333	Fagan & The Scores, Dick	334
El Tones, The	333	Erwing Brothers' Orch	91	Fagan, Bob	263
El Torros, The	333	Escorts, The	333	Faile, Tommy	334
El Venos, The	333	Esquerita	333	Fain, Sammy	92
Elbert, Donnie	332	Esquire Boys, The	333	Fair, Jimmie	263
Elchords, The	332	Esquires, The	333	Fairburn, Werly	334
El Cota	90	Essex	333	Faire, Johnny	334
Eldridge, Billy	332	Essex Club Orch.	91	Fairlaines, The	334
Eldridge & His Orch., Roy	90	Ester, Sidney	333	Falcons, The	334
Electras	332	Estes, Sleepy John	201	Fallen Angels	335
Elegants, The	332	Eternals,	333	Fallin, Johnny	335
Elgart & His Orch., Les	332	Etta & Harvey	333	Fallon & His Californians, Owen	92
Elgar's Creole Orch.	90	Etting, Ruth	91	Famous Hokum Boys	202
Elgin, Johnny	332	Etzel, Roy	333	Fanning, Jay	335
Elgins, The	332	Europe's 369th Infantry (Hell Fighers)		Fantastics, The	335
Elites, The	332	Band, Lt. Jim	92	Fantasys, The	335
Elizalde's Orch.	90			Farley, J.D.	263
Elk Creek Trio	263	Eustis, Billy	333	Farm Hands	263
Elkins, Ray	263	Evans, Charlotte	201	Farmer, Wayne	335
Elkins & His Dextra Singers, W.C.	201	Evans, Edith	92	Farmer Boys, The	335
Elkins' Stringed Steppers	263	Evans, Jimmy	333	Farmer & His Orch., Willie	92
Ellington, Duke	90	Evans, Joe	201	Farr, Harvey	263
Elliot & Mitchell	263	Evans, John B.	263	Farr, Little Joey	335
Elliott, Fay	91	Evans, Mark	334	Farrell, Billy	335
Ellis, Rex	332	Evans, Marty	334	Farrell, Mickey	335
Ellis Brothers, The	332	Evans, Paul	334	Farrell & His (Greenwich Village Inn)	
Ellis & His Rhythm, Big Boy	201	Evans, Roy	92	Orch., Frank	92
Ellis & His (Choirs of Brass) Orch.,		Evans, Rusty	334	Fascinations, The	335
Seger	91	Evans Band, Clyde	263	Fascinators, The	335
Ellsworth, Ray	332	Evans Old Timers	263	Fat Man, The	202
Elm City Quartet	263	Evans & McClain	202	Fay, Johnny	335
Elman & His Orch., Ziggy	91	Eventuals, The	334	Fay & The Jaywalkers	263
Elmer & Jud	263	Everett, Bracey	334	Faye, Alice	92
Elmore, Johnny	332	Everett, Vince	334	Feathers, Charlie	335
Emanon Four	333	Everett & His Orch., Eliot	92	Feathers, The	335
Embers, The	333	Everett & The Daylighters, Betty	334	Feathers & Frogs	202
Embraceables, The	333	Everetts, Dorothy	202	Federals, The	335
Embry, Ted	333	Everett's Serenaders	92	Feger, Don	335
Emcees, The	333	Evergreens, The	334	Fell, Terry	335
Emeralds, The	333	Everheart and The North Carolina		Felts, Derrell	335
Emerson, Billy (The Kid)	201, 333	Cooper Boys, Clay	263	Felts, Narvel	335
Emerson Dance/Symphony Orch;		Everly Brothers, The	334	Fender, Freddy	335
Emerson Military Band	91	Everson, Lottie	202	Fenderman, The	335
Emersons	333	Everybody Digs the Boss Record Hop	334	Fenders	335

Four Harmony Kings	203	Frazier, Jake	95	Garia, Louis "King" & His Swing		
Four Haven Knights	339	Frazier, Lee	264	Band		96
Four Hawaiian Guitars (See Q.R.S.		Frazier, Ray	340	Garland, Hattie	96, 203	
Boys)	94	Frazier & His Plantation Orch., Eddie	95	Garland, Judy		96
Four Imperials	339	Freberg, Stan	340	Garlow, Clarence 'Bon Ton'		203
Four Jacks	339	Frederick, Dotty	340	Garner, Billy		341
Four Jokers	339	Frederick & Mason	264	Garner, Cora		203
Four Kings	339	Freed, Alan	340	Garner, Gabby		341
Four Knights	339	Freed & Moore	264	Garner, Johnny		341
Four Lovers	339	Freeman, Bobby	340	Garnett, Blind Leroy		96
Four Notes	340	Freeman, Ernie	340	Garnett, Jim		341
Four Pages	340	Freeman & Ashcraft	264	Garrett, Bobby		341
Four Pals	340	Freeman & His Orchestra, Bud	95	Garrett, Robert		341
Four Pearls	340	Freeman & His Orch., Jay/Jerry	95	Garrison, Glen		341
Four Pennies	340	Freeny's Barn Dance Band	264	Garry, Sid		96
Four Pharoahs	340	Freezone	203	Gartin, Jimmy		341
Four Pickled Peppers	264	Freidman's Ben Orch.	95	Gaspard, Blind Uncle		264
Four Plaid Throats	340	French, Don	340	Gass, Aubrey		264
Four Pods of Pepper	203	French's String Band	95	Gassers		341
Four Rockets	203	Friars Society Orch.	95	Gates, David		341
Four Seasons	340	Friedman & His Orch., Al	95	Gates, Johnnie		264
Four Sensations	340	Frisco Synacopators	95	Gates & His Orch./		
Four Sons	340	Frisco 'Jass' Band	95	Tom		96
Four Southern Singers	203	Fritz, Joe	203	Gatorvettes		341
Four Southerners	203	Fritz & His Playboys, Hal	340	Gatwood Square Dance Band		264
Four Spades, The	94	Frizzell, Lefty	340	Gaudet, Dee Dee		341
Four Speeds	340	Froeba & His Swing Band, Frank	95	Gavin, Tony		341
Four Teens	340	Frontiersmen	264	Gay Knights		341
Four Tops	340	Frost, Frank	340	Gay Larks		341
Four Troys	340	Fruit Jar Guzzlers	264	Gay Notes		341
Four Tunes	340	Frys Million Dollar Pier Orch.	95	Gay Poppers		341
Four Vagabonds	340	Fulcher & His Orch., Charles	95	Gay Tunes		342
Four Vanes	340	Fuller, Blind Boy	203	Gay & His Orch., Carl		96
Four Virginians	264	Fuller, Bob	95	Gay & Jack Wellman, Red		264
Four Voices	340	Fuller, Bobby	340	Gay & The Sparkeltones, Bobby		341
Four (4) Deep Tone	203	Fuller, Jep	264	Gaydon, Whit		264
Four (4) Epics	339	Fuller, Jerry	340	Gayle, Norman		264
Fournia & Rocking Rels, Ray	339	Fuller, Jesse	340	Gayles, The		341
Four/4 J's	339	Fuller, Johnnie	340	Gazelles		342
Fowler, Jimmy	340	Fuller, Johnny	340	G-Clefs		342
Fowler, Lemuel	94	Fuller, Rocky	203	Geddins & His Cavaliers, Bob		203
Fox, Curley	264	Fuller's Famous Jazz Band/Rector		Geer, Gloria		96
Fox, Eugene	340	Novelty Orch., Earl	95	Gems		342
Fox, John D.	203	Fulsom, Lowell	203, 341	Gendron & His Strand Roof Orch.,		
Fox, Orville	340	Fulton, Sonny	341	Henri		96
Fox, Oscar	264	Furness Bros.	341	Gene & Eunice		342
Fox, The	340	Gadabouts	341	Gene & His Glorians		96
Fox Chasers	264	Gaddy, Bob	341	Genies		342
Fox & Davis	264	Gaddy (& His Alley Cats/Keys), Bob	203	Geno, Sonny		342
Fox & His Yellow Jackets, Cody	264	Gail Tones	341	Gent, J.C.		342
Fox & Joe Wilson, Glen	264	Gaillard & His Flatfoot Foogie Boys,		Gentile & His Orch., Al		96
Fox & the Rob Roys, Norman	340	Slim	95	Gentlemen		342
Frady, Duel	264	Gaines, Eddie	341	Gentry, Bill		342
Framer, Eli	203	Gaines, Roy	341	George, Barbara		342
France, Steve	340	Gaither, Gene	341	George, Lloyd		342
Francis, William	94	Gaither, (Little) Bill	203	George & Earl		342
Francisco Orch.	94	Galaxys	341	Georgettes, The		342
Frank, Arnold	94	Gale & His Boys, Albert	95	George's Hot Shots		264
Frank & His (Rogers Cafe) Orch.,		Gale & The Larks, Barbara	341	Georgia, Bill		203
Arnold	94	Gales	341	Georgia Browns, The		203
Frankie and Johnny	340	Gallagher, James	341	Georgia Cotton Pickers	96, 204	
Frankie & Clara	203	Gallagher, Jay	341	Georgia Crackers		264
Frankie & Johnnie Orch.	95	Gallahads, The	341	Georgia Jumpers		96
Frankie & Her Jazz Devils	94	Gallion, Bob	341	Georgia Melodians		96
Franklin, Buck	203	Galveston Serenaders	95	Georgia Melody Boys		264
Franklin, Emery	203	Gant, Pvt. Cecil	203	Georgia Organ Grinders		264
Franklin, Joe	340	Ganus, Clarence	264, 341	Georgia Pine Boy		204
Franklin, Tiny	203	Garber, Jan & His Orch.	95	Georgia Pot Lickers		264
Franko & His Louisianians, Frankie	95	Gardner, Dave	264	Georgia Serenaders		264
Franks, Tillman	340	Gardner's, Fred	96	Georgia Slim		204
Frazier, Calvin	203, 340	Gardner, Jack	96	Georgia Strutters		96

Georgia Tom	204	Golden Rod	343	Graves & Tanner		265
Georgia Tom & Hannah May	204	Goldentones	343	Gray, Betty		205
Georgia Tom & Jane Lucas	204	Goldkette & His (Book-Cadillac)		Gray, Billy		343
Georgia Tom & Tampa Red	204	Orch., Jean	99	Gray, Christina		205
Georgia Washboard Stompers	96	Goldrush	205	Gray, Claude		343
Georgia Wildcats	264	Good Jelly Bess	343	Gray, Geneva		205
Georgia Yellow Hammers	264	Good Rockin Sammy T	343	Gray, Glen		101
Georgians, The	96	Good Rockin' Bob	343	Gray, Jane		101
Gerard & Evans, Dixon	265	Goodman, Benny	99	Gray, Kitty		101
Gerdsen, Ray	342	Goodman, Dickie	343	Gray, Mommie, Owen, Otto Cowboy		
Gershwin, George	97	Goodman & His Tenn. Valley Boys,		Band		265
Gerun/Gerunovitch & His (Roof		Herald	265	Gray, Phil		343
Garden) Orch., Tom	97	Goodner, Lillian	100	Gray, Rudy		343
Get Happy Band, The	97	Goodson, Hal	343	Gray Arvella		343
Gibbons, Irene	97	Goodson, Price	265	Gray & His Orch., Russell		101
Gibbs, Georgia	342	Goodwin, Bill	343	Gray & Nelson		265
Gibbs, Hugh	265	Goody's Good Timers	100	Gray & Seven Foot Dilly, A.A.		265
Gibbs Brothers & Claude Davis	265	Good's Box Whittlers	265	Grayson & Henry Whitter, G.B.		265
Gibbs & His Orch., Arthur	97	Goofers, The	343	Grayzell, Rudy		343
Gibson, Cleo	97	Goofus Five, The	100	Great Gap Entertainers		265
Gibson, Clifford	204	Goosby, Fannie Mae	205	Greatest Rock & Roll		343
Gibson, Daddyo	342	Goose Creek Jumpers	265	Greatest Western Hits		343
Gibson, Don	342	Gordon, Alex	265	Green, Bobby		343
Gibson, Granddaddy	342	Gordon, Curtis	343	Green, Boy		205
Gibson, Joe D.	342	Gordon, James/Jimmie	205	Green, George		343
Gibson & The Red Caps, Steve	342	Gordon, Roscoe/Rosco	205, 343	Green, Jerry		265
Gifford, Gene	97	Gordon, Slim	205	Green, Lil	205, 343
Giggers, Grinnell	265	Gordon, Stomp	343	Green, L.C.		205
Gill & His Orch., Emerson	97	Gordon & El Tempos, Mike	343	Green, L.M.		205
Gillespie, Darlene	342	Gordon & His Aces, Rex	100	Green, Pork Chop		205
Gilley, Mickey	342	Gordon & His Orch., Ralph	100	Green, Rosa		205
Gillham, Art	97	Gordon & His Tic-Toc Rhythm, Gray	100	Green, Rudy		343
Gilliam, Earl	342	Gordon & His Vip Vop Band, Jimmie	100	Green, Ruth		205
Gillum & His Jazz Boys, Bill/Jazz	204, 342	Gordon & His (Hotel Adelphia/Ten		Green, Sadie		205
Gilmore, Boyd	204	Eyck)(Whispring) Orch., Herb(ert)	100	Green, Slim	205, 343
Gilmore, Gene	204	Gordon & The Angels, Sonny	343	Green, Vernon		343
Gilmore & His Boys, Max	97	Gordon & The Corn Huskers, Tommy	265	Green and Russell		265
Giordano, Lou	342	Gordon's Eddie Band	100	Green Brothers' Novelty Band		101
Gipson, Wild Child	342	Gore, Charlie	343	Green Parrot Inn Orch.		101
Girl Friend, The	204	Gorham, Georgia	205	Green & His Boys, Uncle George		265
Girls of the Golden West	265	Gorman & His Orch., Ross	100	Green & His Orch., Johnny		101
Gish & His Orch., Joseph	97	Gospel Camp Meeting Singers	205	Green & Turner, R.		205
Gitfiddle, Jim	204	Gospel Minnie	205	Greene, Amos		265
Glad Rags	342	Gossett's Ted (Band)	265	Greene, Clarence		265
Gladiolas	342	Gotham Nightingales, The	100	Greene, Lem		266
Glascoe, Percy	97	Gotham Stompers, The	100	Greene & The Four Buddies, Rudy		343
Glasser, Billy	342	Gotroe, Jackie	343	Greenwich Village Orch.		101
Glasser, Dick	342	Gover, Emma	205	Greenwood & The Four Jacks, Lil		343
Glassner & His Colonial Inn Orch.,		Gowans, Sammy	343	Green's Dance Orch., Bob		101
Jack	97	Gowan's Rhapsody Makers	100	Green's String Band		265
Glaze & Hot Shot Willie, Ruby	204	Gowdlock, Jack	205	Greer, Professor & Mrs.		266
Glen, Emery	204	Gowdy, Ruby	205	Greer & His Memphis Men, Sonny		101
Glenn, Darrell	342	Go-Carts	342	Greer & His Rhythm Rockers, Big		
Glenn, Glen	342	Gracie, Charlie	343	John		343
Glenns	342	Grady Family	265	Gregory, Bobby		266
Glinn, Lillian	204	Graham, Henry	265	Gresh & His Orch., Earl		101
Glitters	342	Graham, Lou	343	Grey, Chuck		343
Glover, Mae	204	Graham Brothers	265	Grey, Wallace		266
The "G" Notes	342	Grainger, Porter	100	Grier & His Orch., Jimmy		101
Go, Johnny, Go	343	Grammer, Billy	343	Griffin, Buck		344
Go Boys	342	Granahan, Gerry	343	Griffin, Curley		344
Godwin, Shorty	265	Grand Central Red Cap Quartet	205	Griffin, Floyd		205
Goering's Collegians, Al	97	Grandview Inn Orch.	100	Griffin, Marie		206
Gold & His Orch., Lou	97	Grant Brothers & Their Music	265	Griffin, Rex		266
Golden, Dan	265	Grant Trio	265	Griffin, Tommy		206
Golden, Ernie	98	Grant & The Downbeats, O.S.	343	Griffin Bros.		344
Golden Gate Orch.	98	Grant & Wilson	205	Griffins		344
Golden Gate Quartet	343	Grapevine Coon Hunters	265	Griffith & His Teenage Rebels, Joe		344
Golden Gate Serenaders	99	Gravely, Junior	343	Griffith, Peggy		344
Golden Leaf Quartet	204	Graves, Lee	205	Griggs Melody Makers, Taylor		266
Golden Melody Boys	265	Graves & His Brothers, Roosevelt	205	Grimes, Gordon		102

Harris, Bob (Little Bobby Harris)	206
Harris, Clarence	206
Harris, Earl	267
Harris, Genee	346
Harris, George	267
Harris, Helen	106, 206
Harris, James	206
Harris, John	206
Harris, Johnny Ray	346
Harris, J.D.	267
Harris, Lillian	106
Harris, Magnolia	206
Harris, Marion	106
Harris, Mary	206
Harris, Maxine	206
Harris, Otis	206
Harris, Peppermint	206
Harris, Ray	346
Harris, Slim	267
Harris, Thurston	346
Harris, Willard	346
Harris, William	206
Harris, Willie	207
Harris, Wynonie	346
Harris Brothers Texans	106
Harris & Harris	206
Harris & His Sunset Royal Orch., Ace	106
Harris & His (Cocoanut Grove) Orch., Phil	106
Harrison, Danny & Audrey	346
Harrison, Happy Bud	267
Harrison, Johnny	346
Harrison, Lee	347
Harrison, Smokey	207
Harrison, Wilbert	347
Harry's Happy Four	106
Harry's Melody Men	106
Harry's Reckless Five	106
Hart, Billy	347
Hart, Casey	347
Hart, Freddie	347
Hart, Hattie	207
Hart, Larry	347
Hart and Ogle	267
Hart Brothers	267
Hart & Cates	267
Hartman & His Orch., Bob	106
Hartman's Heartbreakers	267
Hartsell, Bob	268
Harum Scarums	207
Harves with Lightning Guitar, Cleo	207
Harvey, Georgia	106
Harvey, Roy et. al	268
Harvey & The Moonglows	347
Hass, Wayne (See Haas)	347
Hatcher, Willie	207
Hatfield, Overton	268
Hatton, Bert (Snake Root)	207
Hauulea Entertainers	268
Haven & Four Jacks, Shirley	347
Having a Ball	347
Hawaiian Pals	268
Hawk	347
Hawk & His Buddies, Buddy	268
Hawkettes	347
Hawkins, Buddy Boy	207
Hawkins, Dale	347
Hawkins, Erskine	106
Hawkins, Hawkshaw	347

Hawkins, Roy	207, 347
Hawkins, Screamin' Jay	347
Hawkins, Uncle Ben	268
Hawkins, Uncle Billy	268
Hawkins, Uncle Jim	268
Hawkins, Walter	207
Hawkins & His Orch., Coleman	106
Hawkins & Puckett	268
Hawkins (& The Hawks), Ronnie	347
Hawkins' Mountaineers, Ted	268
Hawks	347
Hawks, Mickey	347
Hawley, Bill	106
Hayden, Rudy	347
Hayden, Willie	347
Haydock, Ron	347
Hayes, Blind Roger	207
Hayes, Ed	268
Hayes, Jimmy	347
Hayes, Selma & Dewey	268
Hayes Lsvl. Stompers, Clifford	106
Hayes & His Boys, Daddy Moon	207
Hayes & His Orch., Bill	207
Hayes & His Orch., Edgar	106
Hayes, Jenkins	268
Hayes, Linda & The Platters	347
Hayes, Nap	106
Hayes (Carolina Troubadour), Dewey	268
Haymes & His Orch., Joe	106
Haywood County Ramblers	268
Hazel & His Orch., Monk	106
Head, Don	347
Head, Eddie	207
Head, Johnnie	207
Head & The Traits, Roy	347
Heap, Jimmy	347
Heard & His Combo, Buddy	347
Heart Breakers	347
Heart Throbs	348
Heartbeats/Heart Beats	347
Hearts	347
Heartspinners	347
Hegamin, Lucille	106
Heidt & His Orch., Horace	107
Heller & His Orch., Sig	107
Helms, Bobby	348
Helms & His Band, Bud	107
Helms & His Upson County Band, Bill	268
Helms & Riley Puckett, Bill	268
Helton, Ernest	268
Henderson, Bertha	107
Henderson, Big Bertha	207, 348
Henderson, Catherine	107
Henderson, Edmonia	107
Henderson, Katherine	208
Henderson, Leroy	208
Henderson, Red	268
Henderson, Rosa	207
Henderson Brothers	268
Henderson, Jocko	348
Henderson & His Orch., Fletcher	107
Henderson & His Orch., Frank	108
Henderson & His Orch., Horace	108
Hendley, Fisher	268
Hendon, R.D.	348
Hendricks, Bobby	348
Hendrickson, Henny	108
Hendrix, Al	348
Henry, Clarence (Frogman)	348

Henry, Curtis	207
Henry, Hound Head	207
Henry, Lena	207
Henry, Robert	207, 348
Henry, Sloppy	207
Henry, Tal	108
Henry's (Chief) String Band	268
Henslee, Gene	348
Hensley, Taylor & Walker	268
Henton, Laura	288
Heralds	348
Herbeck, Ray	108
Herbuveaux, Jules	108
Herby Joe	348
Here Are The Hits	348
Herlihy & His Orch., Joe	108
Herman, Sticks	348
Herman Brothers	268
Herman & His Orch., Woody	108
Hernandez Brothers	268
Herrera, Little Julia	348
Herring, Clara	208
Herrelson Zeb	268
Herrold, Dennis	348
Herth Trio, Milt	108
Herwin Hot Shots	108
Hess, Bennie	268, 348
Hewitt, Ben	348
Heywood & His Jazz Six, Eddie	108
Hickey, Ersel	348
Hickory Nuts	268
Hicks, Bobby	348
Hicks, Edna	208
Hicks, Minnie	208
Hicks, Ramona	109
Hicks, Robert	208
Hicks, Robert & Charlie	208
Hicks & His Sizzlin Six, Billy	109
Hide-A-Ways	348
Hifidelity's	348
Higginbottham & His Six Hicks, J.C.	109
Higgins, Billy	208
Higgins, Chuck	348
Higgins, Len & Joe	268
Higgins & His Sodbusters, Si	109
High Hatters, The	109
High Neighbor Boys	268
High Steppers, The	109
Highlanders	268
Highnight & His Ozark Strutters, Luke	268
Hightower, Donna	348
Hightower, Willie	348
Hightower's Night Hawks	109
Highway of Blues	348
Hilites	348
Hill, Bertha 'Chippie'	208
Hill, Bob	268
Hill, Charlie	208
Hill, Frank	269
Hill, Harvey, Jr.	348
Hill, Henry	348
Hill, Jaycee	348
Hill, Joel	348
Hill, J.C.	348
Hill, King Solomon	208
Hill, Raymond	208, 348
Hill, Robert	208
Hill, Sam (from Louisville)	208
Hill, Sammy	208
Hill & Henry Johnson, Ezra	269

Impressions	351	Jackson, Smoke	112
Impressors	351	Jackson, Violet	211
Indiana Five	112	Jackson, Wanda	352
Indiana Hotel Broadcasters	112	Jackson, Willie	211
Indiana Syncopators	112	Jackson Blue Boys	210
Individuals	351	Jackson Brothers	352
Infatuators	351	Jackson County Barn Owls	271
Ingram, Benny	351	Jackson County Ramblers	271
Ink Spots	112, 351	Jackson & Bessie Jones, George	211
Inman, Autry	351	Jackson & His Southern Stompers	112
Inman & Impollos, Jimmy	351	Jackson (Plantation Orch.), Alex	112
Inspirations	351	Jackson (Trio), Slim	112
Inspirators	351	Jacksonville Harmony Trio	112
Intentions	351	Jackson Dewey (Peacock Orch.)	112
Interiors	351	Jackson : Serenaders, Duke	112
International Dance Orch.	112	Jack's Fast Steppin Bellhops	112
Interstate Blue Jackets	112	Jacobs, Walter	211
Intervals	351	Jacobson, Bud	113
Invictas	351	Jacoby Brothers	271
Invincibles	351	Jacono, Jim	352
Ipana Troubadours	112	Jac-O-Lacs	352
Irby, Jerry	270, 351	Jades	352
Irridescents	351	Jaffe's Collegians	113
Irvin, Kitty	112	Jaguars	352
Irvine, Robert A.	352	Jamaica Jazzers	113
Irwin, Harvey	270	Jamboree LP	352
Irwin & His Orch., Vic/Victor	112	James, Bill	113, 352
Isabell, Wallie & Tex	271	James, Bobbie	352
Isle, Jimmy	352	James, Corky	113
Isley Brothers	352	James, Dwight	353
Ivan	352	James, Elmer	211, 353
Ives, Jimmy	352	James, Elmo/Elmore	211, 353
Ivies, The	352	James, Etta	353
Ivories, The	352	James, Frank	211
Ivy, Sonny Joe	352	James, Harry	113
Ivy Three	352	James, Jeanette	113
Ivy Tones	352	James, Jelly	113
Jack Harmonica Players	271	James, Jesse	211, 353
Jack O'Diamonds	210	James, Madelyn	113
Jack & Bill	271	James, McKinley	353
Jack & Tony	271	James, Pauline	211
Jackie Boy & Little Walter	210	James, Sadie	211
Jack & Jill	352	James, Skip	211
Jackie & The Starlites	352	James, Sonny	353
Jacks	352	James, Springback	211
Jackson, Aunt Molly	271	James, Sunny	211
Jackson, Bessie	210	James, Tommy	353
Jackson, Bo Weavil	210	James, Ulysses	211
Jackson, Bobby	352	James, W. Lawrence	211
Jackson, Bull Moose	352	Jammin' Jim	211
Jackson, Charlie	210	Jan & Arnie	353
Jackson, Deacon	210	Jan & Dean	353
Jackson, Earl	112	Jan & The Radiants	353
Jackson, Eddie	352	Janis, Johnny	353
Jackson, Frankie	211	Jano, Johnny	353
Jackson, Frisky Foot	112	Jarmels	353
Jackson, Handy	211, 352	Jarrell, Ben	271
Jackson, Jack	271	Jarrett, Art	113
Jackson, Jim	211	Jarvis, Felton	353
Jackson, Lee	352	Jarvis & Justice	271
Jackson, Lil Son	211, 352	Jarvis (& Her Gang), Hotsy	113
Jackson, Lillian	211	Jaudas' Society Orch.	113
Jackson, Little Joe	112	Jaxon, Frankie 'Half Pint'	113
Jackson, Lulu	211	Jay, Bobby	353
Jackson, Mary	112	Jay, Dale	353
Jackson, Mike	112	Jay, Johnny	353
Jackson, Monroe 'Moe'	211	Jay & The Haystackers, P.	353
Jackson, Odis	211	Jayes, The	353
Jackson, Pork Chop	211	Jayhawks	353
Jackson, Preston	112	Jaytones	353
Jackson, Sadie	211	Jazz Harmonists/Harmonizers, The	113

Jazz Masters	113
Jazzbo, Tommy	211
Jazzbombers	353
Jazzopators, The	113
Jazz-Bo's Carolina Serenaders	113
Jazz-O-Harmonists, The	113
J. B. & His Bayou Boys	352
J.B. & His Hawks	352
Jean, Alice (See:Mondellos)	353
Jean & Roomates, Cathy	353
Jeffries, Speed	113
Jeffers, Jimmy	353
Jefferson, Blind Lemon	212
Jefferson, Eddie	353
Jefferson, George	212
Jeffery, Wally	353
Jelly Belly & Slim Seward	212
Jelly Whippers, The	113
Jenkins, Blind Andrew	271
Jenkins, Bo Bo	353
Jenkins, Bobby	353
Jenkins, Frank	271
Jenkins, Freddy	114
Jenkins, Gooby	271
Jenkins, Gus	353
Jenkins, Hazekia	212
Jenkins, Robert	212
Jenkins Mountaineers, Oscar	271
Jenkins & Jenkins	212
Jenney, Jack	114
Jennings, Baby Boy	353
Jennings, Herb	271
Jennings, Waylon	354
Jennings Brothers	271
Jerome, Ralph	354
Jerry & Demar	354
Jesse & Buzzy	354
Jesse & Marvin	354
Jesse's String Five	271
Jessie & the Sequins	354
Jesters	354
Jeter-Pillar Orch.	114
Jets, The	354
Jewels	354
Jiants, The	354
Jill & Ray	354
Jim Dandies, The	114
Jim Jam	212
Jimmies' Blue Melody Boys	114
Jimmie's Joys	114
Jimmy & Duane	354
Jimmy & Johnny & The Jades	354
Jimmy & Walter	212, 354
Jinkins, Gus	354
Jive Bombers	354
Jive Five, The	354
Jivers	354
Jivetones	354
Jivin Gene	354
Jiv-A-Tones	354
Jodimars	354
Joe Joe	212
Joe & His Rhythm Orch.	114
Joey & The Lexingtons	354
Joe's Hot Babies	114
Johnnie & Joe	354
Johnnie & Jonie	354
Johnny & Slim	271
Johnny & The Hurricanes	354
Johnny & The Jammers	354
Johnny & The Jokers	354

Kansas City Frank	116	Keyes & His Orch., Frank	119	Klingensmith, Rex	357
Kansas City Kitty	216	Keynotes	356	Klixs	357
Kansas City Stompers	116	Keystones	356	Knackin, Tommy	357
Kansas Joe	216	Keytones	356	Knickerbockers, The	119, 357
Kansas Katie	216	Kid and Coot	216	Knight, Baker	357
Kaplan & His Orch., Dave	116	Kid Coley	216	Knight, Jessie	216, 357
Kardos, Gene	116	Kid Stormy Weather	216	Knight, Johnny	357
Karl (Davis) & Harty (Taylor)	272	Kidd, Billy The	356	Knight, Marie	357
Karle & His Boys, Art	117	Kidds	356	Knight, Sonny	357
Karnes, Alfred G.	272	Kidoodlers	273	Knight, Sunny	357
Kasandrea W/Midnight Riders	355	Kids From Texas	356	Knight & The Pips, Gladys	357
Kashman, Betty	117	Kilgore, Merle	356	Knockouts	357
Kassel, Art	117	Killen, Billy J.	356	Knowles, Bert	273
Katz & His Kittens, Al	117	Kimbrough, Lena & Sylvester	216	Knowles, Vance & Red Bay	273
Kaufman, Irving	117	Kimbrough, Lottie & Holmes	216	Knox, Big Boy	216
Kaufman, Jack	117	Kimbrough, Sylvester	216	Knox, Buddy	357
Kaufman & His Orch., Whitey	117	Kincaid, Bradley	273	Kodaks	357
Kay, Dolly	117	Kincaid, B.F.	273	Koenig, Freddy	357
Kay Brothers	272	King, Albert	356	Ko Kos	357
Kaye, Anne	355	King, Carole	356	Kolster Dance Orch.	120
Kaye & His Orch., Sammy	117	King, Chickie	273	Kool Gents	357
Kayser & His Novelty Orch., Joe	117	King, Earl	356	Kopp, Howard	120
Kazee, Buell	272	King, Eddie	356	Kosty, Paul	357
K-Doe, Ernie	355	King, Frances	119	Krueger & His Orch., Art	120
Kearney, Ramsey	355	King, Freddy	356	Krueger & His Orch., Bennie	120
Keating & His Music, Lloyd	117	King, Jack	356	Kruger, Jerry	120
Keen & Tradewinds, Billy	355	King, Jimmy	356	Krupa & His Orch., Gene	120
Keene, Hank	272	King, Julius	216	Kuf-Linx	357
Keese & Loy Bodine, Howard	272	King, Martin	273	Kutter, Don	273
Keghouse	216	King, Randy	273, 356	KXYZ Novelty Band	120
Kelly Four	355	King, Ray	356	Kyle, Billy	120
Kelly, George (See:The Original Six)	118	King, Richard	216	Kyle, Charlie	216
Kelly, Jack	216	King, Sid	356	Kyser, Kay	120
Kelly, Jimmy	355	King, Sleepy	356	La Beef, Tommy/Sleepy/LaBeff	357
Kelly, Pat	355	King Bees	356	La Dell Sisters	357
Kelly, Rex	272	King Brady's Clarinet Band	119	La Dieu, Pierre	273
Kelly, Willie	216	King Crooners	356	La Palina Broadcasters	122
Kelly Brothers	272	King David's Jug Band	119	La Rue, Sophisticated Jimmy	216
Kelly & His Harmonica, Sam	216	King George (of England)	119	La Veeda Dance Orch.	123
Kelly & Julius Dunn, R.D.	272	King Mutt & Tennessee Thumpers	119	La Vizzo, Thelma	123
Kelly's (Washboard Band), Eddie	118	King Toppers	356	Labradors	357
Kelton & His Trio, Robert	216	King Tut	216	Lacour, Lenny	357
Kemp, Hal	118	King Victor	356	Lacy, Rube	216
Ken, Chuck & Jim	272	King & His Band, Pee Wee	356	Lada's Louisiana Lads Orch.	120
Kenin & His Ambassador/Multnomah		King & His Kentuckians, Chuck	119	Ladders	357
Hotel Orch., Herman	118	King & His Kings of Tempo, Tempo	119	Laddins, The	357
Kennedy (The Cadets)	355	King & His Orch., Henry	119	Ladd's Black Aces	120
Kennedy, Joe	118	King & His Orch., Roy	119	Ladnier, Tommy	120
Kennedy, Tiny	216, 355	King & His Orch., Wayne	119	Ladson & Three Shadows, Ruth	216
Kenny, Ken	118	King & His Sovereigns, Rex	119	Laine & His Bull Dogs, Kenny	357
Kenny & Doolittle	355	King & Ike Turner's Band, Willie	356	Lake, Slim	273
Kenny & Moe	355	King (Blue Boys), B.B.	216, 356	Lam, Tommy	357
Kenny & The Comets, Herb	356	Kinglets	356	Lam & His Green County Singers,	
Kenny & The Kasuals	355	Kings	356	Bella	273
Kent & The Ketones, Bobby	356	Kings Combo, Kid	356	Lamar, Justine	216
Kents	356	Kings Men	357	Lamar & His Southerners, Slim	120
Kentucky Blowers, The	118	King's Jesters (and Louise), The	119	Lamarr, Gene	357
Kentucky Colonels, The	118	Kinks	357	Lambert & Hillpot	273
Kentucky Girls	272	Kirby, Fred	273	Lamberth, Jimmy	357
Kentucky Grasshoppers	118	Kirby, John	119	Lamie, Tony & Jackie	357
Kentucky Hot Hoppers	118	Kirby & Phillips	273	Lamont, Billy	357
Kentucky Jazz Babies	118	Kirby (& Don White/Cliff Carlisle),		Lamour, Dorothy	120
Kentucky Jug Band	118	Fred	273	Lampe's Orch.	120
Kentucky Mountain Boys	272	Kirby's Kings of Jazz	119	Lampkin, Tommy	357
Kentucky Ramblers	272	Kirk, Andy	119	Lamplighters	357
Kentucky Serenaders	118, 272	Kirk, Wee Willie	216	Lancaster, G.E.	273
Kentucky String Ticklers	272	Kirkland, Jimmy	357	Lance, Major	357
Kentucky Thorobreds	272	Kirkland, Little Eddie	216	Land & Miles	274
Keppard's Jazz Cardinals, Freddie	119	Kirkland, Rocky	273	Landau, Mike	120
Kerr, Charlie	119	Kirkman, Lillie Mae	216	Landers, Lee	273
Kessinger Brothers	272	Klein & His Orch., Mannie	119	Landis, Jerry	357

Landon, Buddy	357	Lee, Bessie	217	Lewis, Archie	217, 274
Landress, Uncle Bud	273	Lee, Bob	358	Lewis, Bobby	359
Landry & His Orch., Art	120	Lee, Booker, Jr.	358	Lewis, Buddy	217
Lane, Duke	274	Lee, Buddy	358	Lewis, Ernest	217
Lane, Ernest	216	Lee, Caroline	217	Lewis, Furry	217
Lane, Willie	216	Lee, Chauncey C.	123	Lewis, Gene	359
Lane Brothers	358	Lee, Dickie	358	Lewis, Ida	217
Lane, Harry	358	Lee, Don	358	Lewis, Jack	359
Lane & Sugartones, Jimmy	358	Lee, Eliza Christmas	217	Lewis, Jerry Lee	359
Lane & Whitey Four, Ralph	358	Lee, Floyd	358	Lewis, Johnny	217, 359
Lanes	358	Lee, George E.	123	Lewis, Kate	217
Lang, Eddie	121	Lee, Harry	358	Lewis, Meade Lux	124
Lange & His Orch., Art/Arthur	121	Lee, Jerry	217	Lewis, Noah (Jug Band)	124
Lange & His (Baker Hotel) Orch.,		Lee, Jimmy	358	Lewis, Pete (Guitar)	217, 359
Henry	121	Lee, John	217, 358	Lewis, Ray	217
Lange-McKay Orch.	121	Lee, Johnny	217, 358	Lewis, Sammy	124, 217, 359
Langford, Frances	121	Lee, Julia	123, 358	Lewis, Sidney Jo	359
Langley, Curley	358	Lee, Leonard	358	Lewis, Smiley	359
Lanier, Don	358	Lee, Little Brenda	358	Lewis, Ted	124
Lanin's Red Heads	121	Lee, Lonesome	359	Lewis, Tommy	359
Lanin's Southern Serenaders	121	Lee, Mabel	359	Lewis, Wally	359
Lannis, Louisiana	358	Lee, Mae Belle	217	Lewis Bronzeville Five	217
Larados	358	Lee, Mandy	123	Lewis Brothers	274
Largos	358	Lee, Marquerite	123	Lewis & Lonestar Cowboys, Texas Jim	274
Larkan, Fiddlin Bob/Larkan	274	Lee, Nancy	274, 359	Liberto, Ray	359
Larks	358	Lee, Roosevelt	359	Lichters (Strand Symphonists), Joie	124
Larktones, The	358	Lee, Russell & Daisy Wright	217	Lick, Slick & Slide	359
Larry & The Standards	358	Lee, Ruth	123	Lietzke's Midnight/Midnite	
La Rocca, Pat	358	Lee, Tommy	217, 359	Serenaders, (Glen)	124
La Rue, Poc	358	Lee, Verdi	217	Lifeguards	359
LaRue, Sophisticated Jimmy	216	Lee, Wally	359	Liggins, Jimmy	359
Larue & His Pals, Roger	358	Lee, Winthrop	123	Liggins, Joe	360
Laska, Hal	122	Lee Brothers Trio	274	Light Crust Doughboys	274, 360
Lasky, Louis	216	Lee with the Rhythmaires, Jessie	358	Lightfoot Papa	217, 360
Latons	358	Lee & His Sextet, Joe	358	Lightnin Jr. & The Empires	360
Lattimore, Harlan	123	Lee & Johnny Mathis, Jimmy	358	Lightnin Leon	360
Laughing, Charley	216	Lee & The Leopards	358	Lightnin Slim	360
Laurels	358	Lee & Trio, Emma Dell	217	Lile, Bobby	360
Lauren, Rod	358	Lee (& Caddies), Myron	359	Lillard, Preston	217
Laverne, Charles	358	Leecan, Bobbie	123	Lillie, Lonnie	360
Lavon, Dale	358	Lee's Black Diamonds	123	Lillie Mae	217
Law, Art	358	Left Hand Charlie	359	Lillienfield, Louis	124
Lawing & Dissonaires, Mike	358	Leftwich & Roy Lilly, Woody	274	Lill's Hot Shots	125
Lawman, Charlie	274	Legends	359	Limelighters	360
Lawrence, Bill	358	Legette, Malcom	274	Lincoln, Charlie	217
Lawrence, Gertrude	123	Leggs, Price	359	Lincoln, X.	360
Lawrence, Sara	123	Leighton, Chester	123	Lincolns	360
Lawrence, Syd	358	Leithner & His Orch., Frank	123	Linden, Kathy	360
Lawson, Bobby	358	Lem, Harold	123	Lindley, Donald	125
Lawson, Dave	123	Lemel, Gary	359	Lindsay, Add	274
Lawson, Jimmie	274	Lenoir, J.B./Lenore	217, 359	Lindsey, Red	274
Lawson, Yank	123	Lenox Dance Orch.	123	Lindsey & Alvin Conder, W.A.	274
Layman, Zora	274	Lent, James I. with Arthur Pryor's		Linthecome, Joe	217
Layne, Bert	274	Band	123	Lintons	360
Lazy Bill & His Blue Rhythms	216, 358	Lentz & His (Dance) Orch., Al	123	Linx, Jack	125
Lazy Lester	358	Leonard, Harlan	123	List, Ricky	360
Lazy Levee Loungers	123	Leonard & His Red Jackets, Harold	123	Listen To our Story	360
Lazy Slim Jim	216	Leon's Lone Star Cowboys	274	Liston, Virginia	217
Le Gault, Hank	359	Leroy's Buddy	217	Little Aces, The	125
Leach, Lillian (See:The Mellows)	358	Leroy's Dallas Band	123	Little Al	360
Leadbelly (Huddie)	216, 358	Leslie, Nate	124	Little Anthony & Imperials	360
Leaders	358	Leslie Brothers	359	Little Beats	360
Leaders, Bennie	274	Leslie's Lew (Blackbirds)	123	Little Bill	217
Leake County Revelers	274	Lester, Bobby	359	Little Boppers	360
Leatherman Sisters	274	Lester, Joe	274	Little Brother	218
Ledbetter with the Golden Gate		Lester & Melloqueens, John	359	Little Buddy	360
Quartet, Huddie	217	Levee, Joe	217	Little Butch & Vells	360
Ledford, Steve	274	Levee Loungers	124	Little Caesar & The Romans	360
Lee, A. et.al.	274	Levee Serenaders	124	Little Chocolate Dandies, The	125
Lee, Barron	123	Levee Syncopators	124	Little Clyde and the Teens	360
Lee, Bertha	217	Lewis, Alfred	124	Little Cool Breezes	360

Little Danny	360	London, Johnny	218	Lucas, Jim	362	
Little David	218	Lone Star Cowboys	275	Lucas & Georgia Tom, Jane	218	
Little Denny & Torkeys	360	Lone Star Rangers	275	Lucky Ten Entertainers	126	
Little Doug	360	Lonesome Cowboy	274	Luke the Drifter (See Hank		
Little Eddie & Don Juans	360	Lonesome Cowgirl	274	Williams)	275, 362	
Little Esther, et.al.	360	Lonesome Drifter	361	Luke, Robin	362	
Little Hudson's Red Devil Trio	218, 360	Lonesome Luke	274	Lullaby Larkers	275	
Little Ike	360	Lonesome Pine Twins	275	Lulu Belle & Scotty	275	
Little Jack Little	125	Lonesome Sundowm	361	Luman, Bob	362	
Little Jan & The Radiants	360	Long, Beverly & Jimmy	275	Lumberjacks	126, 362	
Little Jimmie	274	Long, Buddy	361	Lumpkin, Bobby	362	
Little Jimmy	218	Long, Curtis	361	Lumpkin, Guy	127	
Little Joe	360	Long, Jimmie	275	Lunceford, Jimmy	127	
Little Joe Blue	360	Long, John	361	Lund, Kenny	362	
Little Johnny	218	Long Brothers	275	Lunsford, Bascom Lamar	275	
Little June & The Januarys	360	Long Hairs	361	Lunsford, Ted	275	
Little Junior's Blue Flames	218, 360	Long Tall Lester	362	Lunsford & His Clarinet, Hunk	127	
Little Larry	360	Long & His Long Horns, Clay	275	Lutcher, Nellie	362	
Little Leroy	361	Longshaw, Fred	125	Luther, Frank	275	
Little Linda	360	Lonnie & Crisis	362	Luverte & His Society Troubadours,		
Little Luther	360	Lookout Mountain Revelers	275	Jimmy	127	
Little Mac/Mack	360	Lookout Mt. Boys	275	Lyman, Abe	127	
Little Milton	218, 360	Loomis, Ernest	125	Lymon, Frankie	362	
Little Mojo	361	Lopez, Vincent	125	Lymon, Lewis	363	
Little Mr. Midnight	218	Lord, Bobby	362	Lynch & His Orch., Al	127	
Little Nat	361	Lord, Luther	362	Lynch's Rhythm Aces	127	
Little Nate & The Chryslers	361	Lory, Dick	362	Lynn, Debbie	363	
Little Norman	361	Los Angeles Biltmore Hotel Trio	125	Lynn, Jerry	363	
Little Papa Joe	218, 361	Lottie & Winston	218	Lynn, Kathy	363	
Little Ramblers	125	Lou & Ginny	362	Lynn, Lorelei	363	
Little Richard	361	Lou & His Ginger Snaps	125	Lynn, Loretta	363	
Little Sammy	361	Loudermilk, John D.	362	Lynn, Smiling Smokey	219	
Little Shy Guy	361	Louis, Bobby	362	Lyons, Joe	363	
Little Sister	218	Louis, Joe Hill	218, 362	Lyons, Lonnie	218	
Little Son Joe	218	Louis, Leslie	218, 362	Lyres	363	
Little Sonny	361	Louis & Rhythm Rockers, Tommy	362	Lyrics	363	
Little Stan	361	Louise, Paul	358	Lyte & His Orch., Glen	128	
Little Star	361	Louisiana Johnny	218	Lytell, Jimmy	128	
Little T-Bone	218	Louisiana Five Jazz Orch.	125	Ly-Dells	362	
Little Temple & His "88"	361	Louisiana Joe & Slim	126	Mabon, Willie	363	
Little, Victor	361	Louisiana Lou	275	Mac	275	
Little Walkin Willie	361	Louisiana Red	362	Mac, Lou	363	
Little, Walter	218, 361	Louisiana Rhythm Kings	126	Mac & Jake	363	
Little Walter, Jr.	361	Louisiana Rhythmmakers	126	MacBeth, W.W.	275	
Little Willie John	361	Louisiana Rounders	275	MacFarland, Buck	220	
Littlefield, Little Willie	218, 361	Louisiana Stompers	126	MacGimsey, Bob	275	
Little's Collegians	125	Louisiana Strollers	275	Mack, Alura	219	
Littrell, Bubba	361	Louisiana Sugar Babies	126	Mack, Baby	128	
Lloyd, Jimmy	361	Louisiana Washboard Band	126	Mack, Bill	275, 363	
Lloyd & His Orch., Ed	125	Louis' Harlem Stompers	125	Mack, Billy & Mary	219, 363	
Lloyd & Howard Maxy, Doctor	274	Louvin Brothers	362	Mack, Bobby	363	
Loch Orch., Paul	125	Love, Billy	362	Mack, Charles E.	128	
Locke, Rusty	274	Love, Hot Shot	218, 362	Mack, Ida Mae	219	
Locke Brothers Rhythm Orch.	125	Love, John	275	Mack, Jeani	363	
Lockett, Jesse	218	Love, Willie	362	Mack, Leon	363	
Locklin, Hank	274	Love Bros.	362	Mack, Lonnie	363	
Locks, James	218	Love Larks	362	Mack, Red	219	
Lockwood, Robert	218, 361	Love Letters	362	Mack, Warner	363	
Lockwood, Robert, Jr.	218	Love Notes	362	Mack Bros.	275	
Lofner-Harris St. Francis Hotel Orch.	125	Love & His Three Aces, Willie	218	Macon, Uncle Dave	276	
Loftin & The Discords, Willie	218, 361	Lovers	362	Macon Ed	219	
Lofton, Cripple Clarence	218	Lovetones	362	Macon Quartette	275	
Lofton, Poor Boy	218	Lovin Sam	218	Macree & Rhthm Kings, Vincent	363	
Log Cabin Boys	274	Lowe, Buddy	362	Madara, Johnny	363	
Logan, George E.	274	Lowe, Jim	362	Maddin, Jimmie	363	
Logan, Ray	218	Lowery, Florence	218	Maddox, Rose	363	
Logics	361	Lowery, Frankie	362	Maddox Brothers & Rose	277, 363	
Lollar, Bobby	361	Lowery, Ramblin' Red	275	Maddux Family	277	
Lombardo & His Royal Canadians,		Lown, Bert	126	Maddy Brothers	363	
Guy	125	Loyd, Jay B.	362	Madison Brothers	363	
London, Clarence	218	Loyd & His Orch., Ed	126	Madisonville String Band	277	

McFadden, Ruth	365	Mellow Keys	366	Mickey & Sylvia	367
McFarland & Bob Gardner, Lester	279	Mellows	366	Mickle, Elmon	367
McFarlane & Daughter, M.D.	279	Melo Gents	366	Middleton, Gary	367
McFayden, Alphus	279	Melodaires	366	Midnight Airedales, The	133
McGee, Dennis	279	Melodeers	366	Midnight Ramblers, The	133, 222
McGee, Sam & Kirk	279	Melody Four, The	131	Midnight Rounders, The	133
McGhee, Brownie	220, 365	Melody Kings Dance Orch.	131	Midnight Serenaders	133
McGhee, Howard	130	Melody Sheiks, The	131	Midnighters	367
McGhee, John	279	Melotones	366	Midnights	367
McGhee, Kirk	279	Melo-Aires	366	Midway Dance Orch., The	133
McGhee, Sticks	221, 365	Melton, James	131	Midway Garden Orch.	133
McGhee & Coger	279	Melton, Ray	366	Mike & the Utopians	367
McGillis, Butch	366	Melton & Minter	280	Milano, Bobby	367
McGinnis, Wayne	366	Memories	366	Milburn, Amos	222, 367
McGinty's Oklahoma (Cowboy Band)	279	Memory Lane Hits (LP)	366	Miles, Arthur	280
McGonnigle, Mel	366	Memphis, Eddie	221	Miles, Eddie	133
McGowan, Bob	130	Memphis, Jimmy	221	Miles, Josie	222
McGuire, Leon	279	Memphis Bell Hops	131	Miles, Lizzie	222
McGuire, Lowell	366	Memphis Bob	280, 131	Miles, Paul	280
McHugh's (Bostonians), Jimmy	130	Memphis Daddy & His Boys	131	Miley & His Mileage Makers, Bubber	133
McIntorsh, Elders & Edwards	221	Memphis Five	131	Miller, Al	223
McIntyre, Chester	366	Memphis Hot Shots	131	Miller, Bob	280
McKay, Arthur	221	Memphis Jazzers	131	Miller, Bobby	280
McKay, Gene	366	Memphis Joe	221	Miller, Buddy	367
McKay, Marion	130	Memphis Jug Band	132	Miller, Carl	367
McKenzie, Billy	221	Memphis Melody Boys	132	Miller, Chuck	367
McKenzie, Red	131	Memphis Melody Men	132	Miller, Clint	367
McKenzie, Willie Mae	221	Memphis Melody Players	132	Miller, David	280
McKenzie & Condons Chicagoans	131	Memphis Minnie	221, 366, 367	Miller, Dick	367
McKenzie & Crump	221	Memphis Mose	222	Miller, Eddie	223
McKinley, Bill	221	Memphis Night Hawks	132	Miller, Emmett	133, 280
McKinley, David Pete	221	Memphis Sam & John	222	Miller, Frankie	367
McKinley, L.C.	366	Memphis Sheiks	132	Miller, Glenn	133
McKinley (Jazz Band), Ray	131	Memphis Slim	222, 367	Miller, Jim	223
McKinney, Sadie	221	Memphis Stompers	132	Miller, Jody	367
McKinney Brothers	279	Memphis Strutters	132	Miller, John	280
McKinney's Cotton Pickers	131	Mendellos Dance Orch.	132	Miller, Johnnie	133
McKown, Gene	366	Mercer, Johnny	132	Miller, Lillian	223
McLain, Jimmy	221	Mercy Baby	367	Miller, Luella	223
McLarey, Butch	366	Mercy Dee	367	Miller, Mae Belle	223
McLaughlins Melody Makers	279	Meridian Hustlers	280	Miller, Ray	133
McLaughlin's Melodians	131	Meroff, Benny	132	Miller, Roger	367
McLean, Connie	131	Merrill Brothers	367	Miller, Sisters	367
McLollie, Oscar	366	Merritt, Roy	132	Miller, Sodarisa	223
McMann & Roberts	279	Merrivale, Cyril	132	Miller, Stanley	280
McMichen et.al, Clayton	279	Merriweather, Big Maceo	367	Miller, Tal	367
McMillan & His Fadeways, Cab	221	Mert's Hometown Serenaders	280	Miller, Walter	367
McMillon, Dennis	221	Messon, Sara	222	Miller, Warren	367
McMullen, Fred	221	Metallics	367	Miller & Burnett	280
McMurray's California Thumpers	131	Metomkin Inn Orch.	132	Miller & Rodgers	223
McNabb, Cecil	366	Metronomes	367	Miller's Bull Frog Entertainers	280
McNeely, Big Jay	366	Metropolitan Dance Players	132	Millet, Lou	367
McPartland's Squirels, Jimmy	131	Metropolitan Orch.	132	Mills Blue Rhythm Band	134
McPhail, Black Bottom	221	Metropolitans	367	Mills, Irving	134
McPhatter, Clyde	366	Metros	367	Mills, Josie	223
McPherson, Ozie	221	Metrotones	367	Mills, Maude	223
McPherson, Whitey	280	Metzgers Campus Night Owls	132	Mills, Owen	280
McShann, Jay	131	Meyers, Anna	222	Mills, Violet	223
McTell, Blind Willie	221	Meyers, Hazel	222	Mills Brothers, The	134
McVoy, Carl	366	Meyers, Ken	132	Mills Cavalcade Orch.	134
McWinders, Oddie	280	Meyers, Vic	132	Mills Merry Makers	134
Meadowlarks	366	Meyers (& The Aces), Louis	367	Mills Musical Clowns	134
Means, Grace	280	Mezzrow, Mezz	133	Mills Swinphonic Orch.	134
Medallionaires	366	Miami Garden Orch.	133	Mills Ten Black Berries	134
Medallions, The (See: Vernon Green)	366	Miami Lucky Seven	133	Mills Ten Blackberries	134
Meeks, Dick	280	Miami Royal Palm Orch.	133	Milner & Curtis	280
Mel O Dots	366	Michaels, Joey	367	Milton, Billy	280
Mello Fellows	366	Michall & His New Orleans Boys, Ernest	133	Milton, Buddy	367
Mello Harps	366			Milton, Little	367
Mello Kings	366	Mickey Mouse & The Turtle (See: Williams' Washboard Band)	133	Milton, Roy	367
Mello Moods	366			Mims, Irene	223

Mineo, Sal	368	Montgomery, 'E'	224	Morris, Elmore	369
Ming's Pep Steppers, Floyd	280	Montgomery Orch., J. Neal	135	Morris, Gene	369
Minini, Ross	368	Montrose & His Orch., Jack	135	Morris, Frank	281
Minor, Jimmy	368	Mon-Vales, The	368	Morris, Leo	369
Minor Tones	368	Moods	368	Morris, Rod	369
Minorbops	368	Moody, Julia	224	Morris, Thomas	136
Minorchords	368	Moon, Henry	135	Morris, Walter	281
Minors	368	Moonbeams	368	Morris, Zeke	282
Mint Juleps	368	Mooney, Art	135	Morrison, Bill	369
Mints	368	Mooney, Etta	224	Morrison, Jim	369
Miracles	368	Mooney, Glenn	368	Morrison Band, Bros.	282
Miranda, Billy	368	Mooney, Tommy	281	Morrison & Charles Nelsen of W.L.S.,	
Miss Frankie	223	Moonglows	369	Herb	136
Miss Peaches	368	Moonlight Revelers	135	Morse, Ella Mae	369
Mississippi Blacksnakes	223	Moonlight Serenaders	135	Morse and Frank	136
Mississippi Jook Band	223	Moonlighters	369	Morse (& Her Blue Grass Boys),	
Mississippi Matilda	223	Moonshine Dave	281	(Miss) Lee	136
Mississippi Maulers	134	Moonshine Harry	281	Morton, Bond & Williams	282
Mississippi Moaner, The	223	Moonshine Kate	281	Morton, Ferd 'Jelly Roll'	136
Mississippi Mud Mashers	223	Moonshiners	281	Morton Orch., Benny	136
Mississippi Mud Steppers	223	Moore, Alice	224	Morton & Crane	282
Mississippi Mudder	223	Moore, Arah 'Baby'	224	Morton's Orch., Tom/Tommy	137
Mississippi Music Makers	134	Moore, Bill	224	Mosby, Curtis	137
Mississippi Sara	223	Moore, Burnette & Rutherford	281	Mosby & Sykes	225
Mississippi Sheiks	223	Moore, Byrd	281	Moser, Jack	282
Mississippi Trio	134	Moore, Cecil	369	Mosiello's Radio Stars, Mike	137
Mississippi 'Possum Hunters'	280	Moore, Donny Lee	369	Moskowitz, Joseph	137
Missouri Dance Orch.	134	Moore, Grant	135	Mosley & His Band, Snub	137
Missourians, The	134	Moore, John	281	Moss, Buddy	225
Mitchell, Billy	368	Moore, Johnny	369	Moss, Roy	369
Mitchell, Bobby	368	Moore, Kid Prince	224	Moss, Teddy	225
Mitchell, Eddie	135	Moore, Lattie	281, 369	Moss & Long	282
Mitchell, Freddie	368	Moore, Merrill	369	Mote, Danny	369
Mitchell, Lee	368	Moore, Monette	224	Mote, Otis	282
Mitchell, Marlon	368	Moore, O.	281	Moten's Orch., Bennie	137
Mitchell, Tommie	368	Moore, Ronnie	369	Mounce, Bill	282
Mitchell, Walter	224	Moore, Rosie Mae	225	Mound City Blue Blowers	138
Mitchell, Willie	368	Moore, Rudy	369	Mountain Frolic	369
Mitchell Family Trio	280	Black Devils	136	Moy & The Feathers, June	369
Mitchell & Tornados, Stanley	368	Moore, Sam	136, 281	Moyer, Ken 'Goof'	138
Mixers	368	Moore, Sparkle	369	Mr. Freddie	225
Mizell, Hank	368	Moore, Whistlin Alex	224	Mr. Stringbean	369
Mizzell & Lee Wayne, Bobby	368	Moore, William	225	Mr. X	369
Moatsville String Ticklers	280	Moore Trio, Scotty	369	Muddy Waters	225, 369
Modern Mountaineers	280	Moore & Freed	281	Mullican, Moon	370
Modernists, The	135	Moore & Green	281	Mullin, Dee	370
Mole (Little Molers), Miff	135	Moore & High Hatters, Webster	136	Mumbles	225
Molleen, Ronnie	368	Moore & Horace Davis, Sam	281	Mumford & The Serenaders, Gene	370
Monarch Jazz Quartet	224	Moore & Smeck	281	Mundy, Jimmy	138
Monarchs	368	Moore & The Metonomes, Gene		Murphy, Chuck	370
Mondello & His Orch., Toots	135	(See:The Metronomes)	369	Murphy, Don	370
Mondellos	368	Moore & The Tabs, Jimmy	369	Murphy, Jimmy	370
Moniques	368	Morable's Fate (Society Syncopators)	136	Murphy Brothers	282
Monitors	368	Moran & Mack	136	Murphy & His Orch., Larry	138
Monkey Joe	224	Morehouse & Swing Six, Chauncy	136	Murphy & His Orch., Lyle 'Spud'	138
Monograms	368	Moreland, Peg	281	Murray, Billy	138
Monorays	368	Moreland, Prentice	369	Murray, Gladys	138, 225
Monotones	368	Moreland, Richard	369	Music Masters, The	138
Monroe, Alex	224	Morgan, Charlie	369	Musical Comedy Orch.	138
Monroe, Bill	281	Morgan, Eddie	225	Musical Comrades	138
Monroe Brothers	280	Morgan, Everett	281	Musical Maniacs, The	138
Monroe Country Bottle Tippers	281	Morgan, Rocket	369	Musical Stevedores	138
Monroe's Charlie Boys	281	Morgan, Russ	136	Musical Trio	138
Montana, Patsy	281	Morgan (Jazz Band), Sam	136	Musical Voyagers, The	138
Montana Slim	281	Morningstar, Jackie	369	Muskateers	370
Montclairs	368	Moroccans	369	Mustang Band of S.M.U.	138
Montereys	368	Moroccos	369	Myers, Sammy	370
Montgomery, Joe	368	Morrie, Tiny	369	Myers, Vick	138
Montgomery, Little Brother	224, 368	Morris, Bob	369	Myers' Melody Orch., Vic	138
Montgomery, Phil	281	Morris Brothers	281	Myles, Billy	370
Montgomery, Sam	224	Morris, Clara	225		

Rhinehart, Mack	229	Rivieras	381	Rockin' Rebels	382
Rhodes, Slim	380	Rivileers	381	Rockin' Ronald	382
Rhodes, Texas Red	380	Rivingtons	381	Rockin' Saints	382
Rhodes, Walter	229	Rizzo & His Hotel Sylvania		Rockin' Sidney	382
Rhodes & The Shufflers, Jimmy	380	Orch., Vincent	154	Rocking Stockings	382
Rhythm Aces	153, 380	Roamers	381	Rockin' 50's (LP)	382
Rhythm Jesters	380	Roane County Ramblers	289	Rockin' Kids	382
Rhythm Makers, The	380	Roane's Pennsylvanians	154	Rocky Mountain Rangers	290
Rhythm Masters	153	Roanoke Jug Band	289	Rocky Mountain Trio	155
Rhythm Rockers, The	380	Roark, George	289	Rock-A-Fellas	382
Rhythm Rockets	380	Roark & Family, Shortbuckle	289	Rock-A-Teens	382
Rhythm Willie & His Gang	229	Robbins, Eddie	381	Rock-A-Tones	382
Rhythm Wreckers	153	Robbins, Everett	154	Rock-Its	382
Rialto Dance Orch.	153	Robbins, Marty	381	Rod & Terry	382
Rice, Davis & Thomas	288	Robbins, Mel	381	Rodemich & His Orch., Gene	155
Rice, Edd	288	Robechaux, Joseph	154	Roden, Hugh	290
Rice, Eldon	381	Roberson, Hubert	229	Rodeo Trio	290
Rice, Glen	288	Roberson, Orlando	155	Rodgers, Buck	382
Rice, Hoke	289	Robert & Johnny	381	Rodgers, Ike	155
Rice Brothers' Gang	288	Roberts, Bobby	381	Rodgers, Jessie	290
Rich, Charlie	381	Roberts, Dennis	381	Rodgers, Jimmy	290
Rich, Dave	381	Roberts, Don (Red)	381	Rodgers, Mrs. Jimmie	382
Rich, Fred	153	Roberts, Gip	229	Rodin, Gil	155
Rich & Carl Bradshaw, Renus	289	Roberts, Helen	229	Roe Brothers	291
Richard, Robert	229	Roberts, James	289	Roe & Bobby Trammell, Tommy	382
Richard, Seth	229	Roberts, Lance	381	Rogers, Buddy	156
Richard Bros.	229	Roberts, Sally	229	Rogers, Ernest	291
Richards, Chuck	154	Roberts, Sister Minnie Pearl	229	Rogers, Ginger	156
Richards, Fred	289	Roberts, Snitcher	229	Rogers, Jesse	382
		Roberts (Dance) Orch., Cliff	155	Rogers, Jimmy	229, 291, 382
Richards, Pete	154	Robertson, A.C.	289	Rogers, Kenneth/Kenny	382
Richards, Uncle Charlie	229	Robertson, Dick	155	Rogers, Lelan	382
Richards & His Orch., Vincent	154	Robertson, Texas Jim	289	Rogers, Mack	156
Richards & The Blue Kings, Jay	381	Robertson, Walter	381	Rogers, Mae	229
Richardson, Dick	154	Robinette & Byrd Moore, Melvin	289	Rogers, May	229
Richardson, Inez	154	Robins	381	Rogers, Rodney	156
Richardson, Jape (See:Big Bopper)	381	Robinson, Alexander	229	Rogers, Roy	291, 382
Richardson, Mooch	229	Robinson, Bill	155, 382	Rogers, Weldon	382
Richardson, Nolan	381	Robinson, Bob	155	Rogers, Will	156
Richardson, Ralph	289	Robinson Bros.	229, 382	Roland, Walter	229
Richie & His Boys, Bud	154	Robison, Carson	155, 229	Rolfe, B.A.	156
Richie & The Royals	381	Robinson, Dick	382	Rollickers, The	156
Richman, Harry	154	Robinson, Elzadie	155	Rolling Crew	382
Richmond Starlight Jazz Quartet	229	Robinson, Fenton	382	Rolling Stones	291
Ricketts Band, Bob	154	Robinson, Hubert	229	Rollini, Adrian	156
Ricki & Rikatones	381	Robinson, Ikey	155	Rollins & His Orch., Todd	157
Ricks & The Ravens, Jimmy	381	Robinson, James (Bat)	229	Roman, Rich	382
Ridgel's Fountain Citians	289	Robinson, Jimmy Lee	382	Romance of Harmony Orch.	157
Ridley, Ethel	229	Robinson, Mable	229	Romancers	382
Ridley, Tommy	381	Robinson, Mark	382	Romano & His Orch., Phil	157
Riffers, The	154	Robinson, Mushmouth	229	Romans	383
Riffs, The	381	Robinson, Nettie	229	Romeos	383
Right, Willie	229	Robinson, Rob	155	Romer, Mamie	230
Riley, Billy Lee	381	Robinson, Sugar Chile	382	Romero, Chan	383
Riley, Bob	381	Robinson & Mack	229	Ronettes	383
Riley, George	289	Robinson's Knights of Rest	155	Ronnie & Marlene	383
Riley, Otis	381	Robison, Willard	155	Roosevelt, Theodore	157
Riley et.al., Mike	154	Rocco, Tommy	382	Roosters, The	383
Ring, Justin	154	Rock, Rock Rock (LP)	382	Rorer, Posey	291
Ringgold, Issie	229	Rock, Tom	155	Rose, Andy	383
Rinky Dinks	381	Rock & Roll Forever (LP)	382	Rose, Bayless	230
Rio, Chuck	381	Rock & Roll Sock Hop (LP)	382	Rose, David	157
Rip Cords	381	Rock & Roll Spectacular	382	Rose, Jack	291
Ritchie, George	381	Rockers	382	Rose, Lucy	230
Ritter, Tex	289	Rocketones	382	Rose, Vincent	157
Ritz, Sally	229	Rockets (See:Bill Bodaford)	382	Rose Family	291
Rivals	381	Rockettes	382	Rose Room Orch.	157
River, Little Bobby	381	Rockin' Bradley	382	Roseland Dance Orch.	157
Rivers, Chuck	381	Rockin' Chairs	382	Rosenkrantz, Timmie	157
Rivers, Cliff	381	Rockin' Dukes	382	Rosenthal, Harry	157
Riverside Ramblers	289	Rockin' Jesters	382	Ross, Arthur	157

Tobacco Tags	297	Trexler, Gary	395	Tuttle, Bill	297
Tobier, Ben	170	Treys	395	Tuttle, Frank	298
Tobins Midnight Serenaders	170	Triangle Harmony Boys	171	Tuxedo Syncopators	171
Today's Hits (LP)	394	Triangle Quartette	239	TV Slim	396
Todd, Johnny	394	Trice, Rich	239	Tweedy Bros.	298
Tokens	394	Trice, Welly	239	Twelve Flip Hits (LP)	396
Tolbert & His Gentlemen Of Swing, Skeets	170	Tridells	395	Twilighters (& Donald Richards)	396
Tolleson, Tommie	394	Trimble, Carl	297	Twilights	396
Tom and Chuck	297	Trimble & His Oklahomans, Barney	171	Twin Cities Dance Orch.	172
Tom & Jerry	170, 394	Troilinder, Delbert	395	Twin City Bell Hops	172
Tom & Roy	297	Triolo, Frank	395	Twitty, Conway	396
Tomerlin, Kenny	394	Tritones	395	Twitty, John D.	240
Tomlin, Kingfish Bill	239	Tri-Lads	395	Two Black Crows	172
Tomlin, Pinky	170	Trojans	395	Two Boys From Savannah	240
Tommie & Willie	297	Trombone Red	171	Two Charlies, The	240
Tommy and Jimmy	239	Troopers	395	Two Of Spades, The	240
Tompkins, Ted	297	Trophies	395	Two Poor Boys	240
Tompkins, Tommy Red	170	Troupers	395	Tyler, Big 'T'	396
Tony & Raindrops	394	Troutts (Melody Artists), Charlie	171	Tyler, Frankie	396
Tony & Technics	395	Trowbridge, Dorethea	239	Tyler, Johnny	396
Tony & The Masquins	394	Troy Harmonists, The	171	Tyler, Ruckus	396
Tony & Twilighters	395	Trumbauer, Frankie	171	Tyler & His Flips, Kip	396
Too Bad Boys, The	239	Trumpeteers	395	Tymes	396
Too Tight Henry	239	Trump's Ambassador Bell Hops Orch.	171	Tyus, Charles	240
Toombs, Jack	297	Tru-Tones	395	Tyus & Tyus	240
Toombs, Jackson	395	Truetones	395	T.C.I. Section Crews	238
Toomey, Welby	297	Tu Tones	396	Umbrian Glee Club	240
Toon, George	297	Tub Jug Washboard Band	239	Uncle Bud & His Plowboys	298
Top Notes	395	Tubb, Ernest	297, 395	Uncle Skipper	240
Topics	395	Tubb, Justin	395	Underwood, Chas.	298
Toppers	395	Tucker, Anita	395	Underwood, Marion	298
Topps	395	Tucker, Bessie	239	Underwood, Sugar	172
Tops	395	Tucker, Billy Joe	395	Unique Teens	396
Toreadors	395	Tucker, Ernest	395	Uniques	396
Torey, George	239	Tucker, George	171	United States Marine Band	172
Tornados	395	Tucker, Orrin	395	United States Naval Reserve Band	172
Torok, Mitchell	297	Tucker, Sophie	171	Universal Dance Orch.	172
Torquays	395	Tucker, Tommy Time	171	Universal Sextette	172
Torrell, Jackie	395	Tucker & His Californians/Orch., Tommy	171	Universals	396
Towel, Jim	239	Tucker & The Turks, Rick	395	University Boys	172
Town Hall Party	395	Tully, Lee	395	University Eight	172
Town Three	395	Tune Blenders	395	University Six	172
Townsend, Henry	239	Tune Rockers	395	Upfronts	397
Townsend, Jessie	239	Tune Tones	395, 396	Upsetters	397
Townsend, Sam	239	Tune Weavers	396	Upstarts	397
Toys	395	Tune Wranglers	297	Uptones, The	397
Tracy-Brown's Orch.	170	Tunemasters	395	Urban, Al	397
Trail, Buck	395	Turbans	396	Utah Carl	397
Trailblazers	395	Turks, The (See: Rick Tucker)	396	Vagabond Yodeler	298
Traits	395	Turk's Orch., Al	171	Vagabonds, The	172, 298
Tram, Bix & Eddie	170	Turley, Richard	396	Val Chords	397
Tram, Bix & Lang	170	Turner, Annie	239	Val & Pete	298
Trammell, Bobby Lee	395	Turner, Baby Face	239	Vale, Blackie	397
Trantham, Carl	395	Turner, Bee	239	Valens, Ritchie	397
Travelers	170, 297, 395	Turner, Big Joe	396	Valentine, Syd	173
Travers & His Orch., Vincent	170	Turner, Blind Squire	240	Valentines	397
Travis, Merle	395	Turner, Buck	297	Valentino, Rudolph	173
Travis & Bob	395	Turner, Cal	297	Valets	397
Travis-Carlton Orch.	171	Turner, Dave	297	Valiants	397
Traymore Orch., The	171	Turner, Hobo Jack	297	Vallee & His Connecticut Yankees, Rudy	173
Treble Chords	395	Turner, Ike	239, 396	Valley Inn Orch.	174
Tremaine, Paul	171	Turner, Jack	396	Valquins	397
Tremaines	395	Turner, Jessie Lee	396	Val-Tones	397
Tremble & Shadows, Tommy	395	Turner, Joe	171, 239	Van Dykes	397
Tremer, George H.	171	Turner, Lavinia	239	Van Eps Trio/Banjo Orch.	174
Tremonts	395	Turner, Lemuel	297	Van Eps-Banta Dance Orch.	174
Trend Tones	395	Turner, Smiley	240	Van Loan & His Orch., Paul	174
Treniers, The	395	Turner & His Orch., Lloyd	171	Van Winkle, Arnold	397
Trent, Aplhonse	171	Turner & Winston Holmes, Charlie	239	Vance, Al	397
Trent, Jo	171	Tutt, Bill	396	Vance's Tennessee Breakdowners	298